Lecture Notes in Computer Science 11778

More information about this series at http://www.springer.com/series/7409

Chiara Ghidini · Olaf Hartig ·
Maria Maleshkova · Vojtěch Svátek ·
Isabel Cruz · Aidan Hogan ·
Jie Song · Maxime Lefrançois ·
Fabien Gandon (Eds.)

The Semantic Web – ISWC 2019

18th International Semantic Web Conference
Auckland, New Zealand, October 26–30, 2019
Proceedings, Part I

Editors
Chiara Ghidini
Fondazione Bruno Kessler
Trento, Italy

Maria Maleshkova
University of Bonn
Bonn, Germany

Isabel Cruz
University of Illinois at Chicago
Chicago, IL, USA

Jie Song
Memect Technology
Beijing, China

Fabien Gandon
Inria Sophia Antipolis - Méditerranée
Sophia Antipolis, France

Olaf Hartig
Linköping University
Linköping, Sweden

Vojtěch Svátek
University of Economics Prague
Prague, Czech Republic

Aidan Hogan
University of Chile
Santiago, Chile

Maxime Lefrançois
Mines Saint-Etienne
Saint-Etienne, France

ISSN 0302-9743 ISSN 1611-3349 (electronic)
Lecture Notes in Computer Science
ISBN 978-3-030-30792-9 ISBN 978-3-030-30793-6 (eBook)
https://doi.org/10.1007/978-3-030-30793-6

LNCS Sublibrary: SL3 – Information Systems and Applications, incl. Internet/Web, and HCI

This Springer imprint is published by the registered company Springer Nature Switzerland AG
The registered company address is: Gewerbestrasse 11, 6330 Cham, Switzerland

Preface

Knowledge graphs, linked data, linked schemas and AI ... on the Web.

Now in its 18th edition, the ISWC conference is the most important international venue to discuss and present latest advances and applications of the Semantic Web, Linked Data, Knowledge Graphs, Knowledge Representation, and Intelligent Processing on the Web. At the beginning of the 2000s this research community was formed, starting with the first international Semantic Web Working Symposium (SWWS), a workshop held in Stanford, Palo Alto, held during July 30 to August 1, 2001. The following year the symposium became the International Semantic Web Conference (ISWC) series in Sardinia, Italy, and at that time the website was predicting that it would be a major international forum at which research on all aspects of the Semantic Web would be presented. And indeed, as in previous editions, ISWC 2019 brought together researchers and practitioners from all over the world to present fundamental research, new technologies, visionary ideas, new applications, and discuss experiences. It featured a balanced mix of fundamental research, innovations, scientific artefacts such as datasets, software, ontologies, or benchmarks, and applications that showcase the power and latest advances of semantics, data, and artificial intelligence on the Web.

In 2019 we celebrated the 30th anniversary of the Web [2]. Happy birthday to you, Web! But our community also remembers that 25 years ago, Tim Berners-Lee et al. were already proposing in an article of the Communications of the ACM August 1994, to provide on the Web "more machine-oriented semantic information, allowing more sophisticated processing" [1]. And since the beginning, the Semantic Web community in general, and ISWC participants in particular, have always been interested in providing intelligent processing of the linked data and linked schemata of the Web, starting with querying, reasoning, and learning [3, 4]. This remains a core challenge of our community, tackling problems in using open data of very different sources and quality, as well as ensuring the best results possible and scaling the methods so they can face the real World Wide Web. For these reasons, and to explore the links between the Semantic Web and the latest advances in AI and knowledge graphs, the motto for ISWC 2019 was "knowledge graphs, linked data, linked schemas and AI on the Web."

Several facets of this topic were addressed in three distinguished keynote talks and a panel. Dougal Watt's keynote is entitled "Semantics: the business technology disruptor of the future" and defends the role of semantics in bringing meaning to business data. The keynote of Jerôme Euzenat is entitled "For Knowledge" and defends the grand goal of formally expressing knowledge on the Web and supporting its evolution, distribution, and diversity. After this keynote, a panel entitled "How Much Semantics Goes How Long a Way?" continued the discussion on linked knowledge, schemas, and ontologies on the Web. Finally, in her keynote entitled "Extracting Knowledge from the Data Deluge to Reveal the Mysteries of the Universe," Melanie Johnston-Hollitt introduced us to one of the most data-intensive research fields (radio astronomy) that requires many innovations to achieve scalability and the "big data" regime.

The proceedings of ISWC 2019 are presented in two volumes: the first one containing the research track papers and the second one the resource track and in-use track papers. All these papers were peer reviewed. Combined, these tracks received a total of 283 submissions of which 443 reviewers accepted 74 papers: 42 in the research track, 11 in the in-use track, and 21 in the resource track. Beyond these three tracks and at the moment of writing this preface, this edition of the international conference ISWC already involved more than 1,300 authors of submitted papers, demos, posters, etc. and more than 660 reviewers for all the tracks, amounting to them being of 44 different nationalities. This year again, the number of papers in the resources category attests the commitment of the community to sharing and collaboration.

The excellent reputation of ISWC as a prime scientific conference was confirmed again this year. The research track received 194 valid full paper submissions, out of which 42 papers were selected, leading to an acceptance rate of 21.6%. This year, a double-blind approach was applied to the reviewing process; that is, the identity of the submission authors was not revealed to the reviewers and vice versa. The Program Committee (PC) comprised 26 Senior PC members and 270 regular PC members. In addition, 70 sub-reviewers were recruited to help with the review process. The PC chairs thank all these committee members for the time and energy they have put into the process. ISWC has very rigorous reviewing criteria. The papers were assessed for originality, novelty, relevance and impact of the research contributions, soundness, rigor and reproducibility, clarity and quality of presentation, and grounding in the literature. This year, the vast majority of papers were reviewed by a team comprising four reviewers and a senior PC member, who engaged in a discussion phase after the initial reviews were prepared and the authors responses were made available. Each paper was then discussed among the research track PC chairs and the senior PC members, so as to reach a consensus on the final list of accepted papers.

For the first time in the history of ISWC, we organized a specific initiative to evaluate the reproducibility of research papers. This innovative track was led by Alejandra Gonzalez-Beltran and Michael Cochez. Authors of accepted papers were invited to share their experimental setup and code for evaluation. We received 11 submissions which were assessed in their varying degrees of reproducibility by a member of the Reproducibility Committee. The 'reproducer', rather than reviewer, interacted with the authors and aimed to execute the code and obtain results similar to what was reported in the paper. If the results were reproducible, the paper received the reproducibility label.

The resources track promoted the sharing of high-quality information artifacts that have contributed to the generation of novel scientific work. Resources could be datasets, ontologies, vocabularies, ontology design patterns, benchmarks, crowdsourcing designs, software frameworks, workflows, protocols, or metrics, among others. This track demonstrates how important it is for our community to share reusable resources in order to allow other researchers to compare new results, reproduce experimental research, and explore new lines of research, in accordance with the FAIR principles for scientific data management. All published resources address a set of requirements: persistent URI, indicator for impact, support for reuse, license specification, to mention a few. This year the track chairs Maria Maleshkova and Vojtěch Svátek received 64 submissions, of which 21 were accepted (a 33% acceptance rate), covering a wide range of resource types such as benchmarks, ontologies, datasets, and software frameworks, in a variety of domains such as music, health, scholar, drama, and audio, and addressing multiple problems such as RDF querying, ontology alignment, linked data analytics, or recommending systems. The reviewing process involved 87 PC members and 7 sub-reviewers, supported by 8 senior PC members. The average number of reviews per paper was 3.1 (at least three per paper), plus a meta-review provided by a senior PC member. Papers were evaluated based on the availability of the resource, its design and technical quality, impact, and reusability; owing to the mandatory dereferenceability and community-visibility of the resources (precluding the author anonymity), the papers were reviewed in a single-blind mode. The review process also included a rebuttal phase and further discussions among reviewers and senior PC members, who provided recommendations. Final decisions were taken following a detailed analysis and discussion of each paper conducted by the program chairs and the senior PC.

The in-use track aimed to showcase and learn from the growing adoption of Semantic Web and related technologies in real-world settings, in particular to address questions such as: where are such technologies being used, what are their benefits, and how can they be improved with further research? The track chairs Isabel Cruz and Aidan Hogan received 25 paper submissions and 11 papers were accepted, giving an acceptance rate of 44%; this reflects a significant increase in papers accepted over previous years, indicative of a growing maturation and adoption of Semantic Web and related technologies. In the in-use track, 39 PC members contributed three reviews per paper and took part in an extensive discussion on each paper, to ensure a high-quality program. The accepted papers describe successful applications of technologies including ontologies, knowledge graphs, linked data, and RDB2RDF. The results described by these papers were developed in whole, or with collaboration from, both large companies (e.g., Pinterest, Springer Nature, IBM, and JOT Internet Media), start-ups (Capsenta), as well as public organizations (e.g., Norwegian Institute for Water Research and European Commission).

The industry track provided an opportunity for industry adopters to highlight and share the key learnings and challenges faced by real world implementations. This year, the track chairs Anna Lisa Gentile and Christophe Guéret received 24 submissions from a wide range of companies of different sizes and 16 submissions were accepted. The submissions were assessed in terms of: quantitative and/or qualitative value proposition provided; amount of discussion of innovative aspects, experiences, impact, lessons learned, and business value in the application domain; and degree to which semantic technologies are critical to the offering. Each paper received 3 assigned reviewers from a panel of academic and industry Semantic Web experts.

The main conference program was complemented by presentations from the journal, industry, and posters and demos tracks, as well as the Semantic Web Challenge and a panel on future trends in knowledge graphs.

The journal track was intended as a forum for presenting significant Semantic Web-related research results that have been recently published in well-known and well-established journals but that have not been presented at a Semantic Web-related conference. The goal was to highlight these results at ISWC and promote discussions potentially leading to meaningful multi-disciplinary collaborations. Traditionally only articles published in the *Journal of Web Semantics* (JWS) and the *Semantic Web Journal* (SWJ) were considered for the ISWC journal track. However, with the goal of enabling cross-fertilization with other related communities, this year our two chairs Claudia d'Amato and Lalana Kagal included additional journals such as: the *Journal of Network and Computer Applications*, *IEEE Transactions on Neural Networks and Learning Systems*, the *Journal of Machine Learning Research*, the *Data Mining and Knowledge Discovery Journal*, *ACM Transactions on the Web*, *ACM Computing Surveys*, *IEEE Transactions on Knowledge and Data Engineering*, *ACM Transactions on Computer-Human Interaction*, *Artificial Intelligence Journal*, *Proceedings of the Very Large Database Endowment*, and the *Journal of Information Science*. Papers that fell within the ISWC topics which had been published within the listed journals starting from January 1, 2017, were considered eligible for submission to the journal track. We received 24 extended abstract submissions, out of which 13 were accepted and collected as CEUR proceedings. Each submission was reviewed by at least two members of the PC in order to assess how interesting it was as well as its novelty, relevance, and attractiveness for the ISWC audience. Also taken into consideration was the quality of the extended abstracts and the diversity of the topics, spanning from scalable reasoning and triple storage, machine translation, fact predictions on (probabilistic) knowledge graphs, modeling linked open data for different domains, and semantic sensor networks.

The conference included several events appreciated by the community, which created more opportunities to present and discuss emerging ideas, network, learn, and mentor. Thanks to H. Sofia Pinto and 武田 英明 (Hideaki Takeda), the workshops and tutorials program included a mix of established topics such as ontology matching, ontology design patterns, and semantics-powered data mining, as well as analytics alongside newer ones that reflect the commitment of the community to innovate and help create systems and technologies that people want and deserve, including semantic explainability or blockchain enabled Semantic Web. Application-centric workshops ranged from solutions for large-scale biomedical data analytics to health data management. The tutorials covered topics such as scalable sustainable construction of knowledge bases, linked data querying, reasoning and benchmarking, GraphQL, solid and comunica, blockchain and Semantic Web, provenance for scientific reproducibility, and an historical perspective and context on the roots of knowledge graphs.

The conference also included a Doctoral Consortium (DC) track, which was chaired by 乔淼 (Miao Qiao) and Mauro Dragoni. The DC afforded PhD students from the Semantic Web community the opportunity to share their research ideas in a critical but supportive environment, where they received feedback from both the senior members of the community and the other students. Indeed, students participated also in the review process in order to have a first tangible experience of it. This year the PC accepted 13 papers for oral presentation out of the 16 submissions received. All student participants were paired with mentors from the PC who provided guidance on improving their research, producing slides and giving presentations.

This program was complemented by activities put together by our student coordinating chairs ඔෂානි සෙනෙවිරත්න (Oshani Seneviratne) and 岑超榮 (Bruce Sham), who secured funding for travel grants, managed the grants application process, and organized the mentoring lunch alongside other informal opportunities for students and other newcomers to get to know the community.

Posters and demos are one of the most vibrant part of every ISWC. This year, the track was chaired by Mari Carmen Suárez-Figueroa and 程龚 (Gong Cheng). For the first time, poster submissions were subject to double-blind review, whereas demo submissions were single-blind as in previous years due to the possible inclusion of online demos. We received 59 poster and 43 demo submissions. We had to remove four poster and one demo submissions, as they exceeded the page limit. The PC, consisting of 41 members for posters and 44 members for demos, accepted 39 posters and 37 demos. Decisions were mainly based on relevance, originality, and clarity. Additionally, we conditionally accepted one poster that was transferred from the industry track.

The Semantic Web Challenge has now been a part of ISWC for 16 years. The 2019 edition of the challenge followed a new direction started in 2017: all challenges define fixed datasets, objective measures, and provide their participants with a benchmarking platform. In contrast to 2017 and 2018, this year the challenges were open. This means that a call for challenge was issued and potential challenge organizers submitted proposals for challenges, which were reviewed by the organizers. Two challenges made the cut. The aim of the first challenge was to evaluate the performance of matching systems for tables. The participants were to devise means to link entries in tables to classes, resource, or relations from a predefined knowledge graph. The second challenge evaluated the performance of fact validation systems. For each fact in the benchmark data, the participants were to return a score which expressed how likely said fact was to be true. The best solutions were then presented and discussed at the conference in a dedicated challenge session and during the poster session.

Newly reintroduced last year after an initial showing in 2011, the outrages ideas track solicits visionary ideas, long term challenges, and opportunities for the Semantic Web. This track was chaired by Maria Keet and Abraham Bernstein and it featured a special award funded by the Computer Community Consortium's Blue Sky Ideas initiative. We received nine submissions of which two were accepted.

Finally, the Minute Madness is a tradition at the International Semantic Web Conference that started back in 2011. It usually provides conference participants with a quick and fun overview of the presented works at the conference, since each speaker is allowed to pitch his/her work with a 60 second speech. This year, the two chairs Irene Celino and Armin Haller split the Minute Madness into two separate sessions, both in plenary: the traditional slot for poster and demo authors, to generate interest and traction for the following dedicated event, and a stand-alone session, open to all conference participants, allowed to submit their contribution proposal through the dedicated Minute Madness call.

Organizing a conference is so much more than assembling a program. An international event of the scale and complexity of ISWC requires the commitment, support, resources, and time of hundreds of people, organizers of satellite events, reviewers, volunteers, and sponsors. We are very grateful to our local team at the University of Auckland, and in particular to the local chairs, 孙敬 (Jing Sun) and Gill Dobbie as well as their Conference Coordinator Alex Harvey. They expertly managed the conference logistics down to every detail and make it a splendid event that we want to attend every year. This year again, they helped us grow this exciting scientific community and connect with the local scientific community of the venue.

Our thanks also go to Valentina Ivanova and فؤاد زبليط (Fouad Zablith), our proactive publicity chairs, and นชา ชลดำรงค์กุล (Nacha Chondamrongkul) our hyper-responsive Web chair - they played a critical role in ensuring that all conference activities and updates were communicated and promoted on the Web and across mailing lists and on social media. Maribel Acosta and Andrea Giovanni Nuzzolese were the metadata chairs this year and their ensured that all relevant information about the conference was available in a format that could be used across all applications, continuing a tradition established at ISWC many years ago. Also, we are especially thankful to our proceedings chairs, 宋劼 (Jie Song) and Maxime Lefrançois, who oversaw the publication of these volumes.

Sponsorship is crucial to realize the conference in its current form. We had a highly committed trio of sponsorship chairs, 彭麗姬 (Lai Kei Pang), Cédric Pruski, and Oktie Hassanzadeh, who went above and beyond to find new ways to engage with sponsors and promote the conference to them. Thanks to them, the conference now features a social program that is almost as exciting as the scientific one.

Finally, our special thanks go to the Semantic Web Science Association (SWSA) for their continuing support and guidance and to the organizers of the conference from 2017 and 2018 who were a constant inspiration, role models, and source of knowledge, advice, and experience.

August 2019

Chiara Ghidini
Olaf Hartig
Maria Maleshkova
Vojtěch Svátek
Isabel Cruz
Aidan Hogan
宋劼 (Jie Song)
Maxime Lefrançois
Fabien Gandon

References

1. T. Berners-Lee, R. Cailliau, A. Luotonen, H. F. Nielsen, and A. Secret. The World-Wide Web. *Commun. ACM*, 37(8):76–82, Aug. 1994.
2. F. Gandon. For everything: Tim Berners-Lee, winner of the 2016 Turing award for having invented… the Web. *1024: Bulletin de la Société Informatique de France*, (11):21, Sept. 2017.
3. F. Gandon. A Survey of the First 20 Years of Research on Semantic Web and Linked Data. *Revue des Sciences et Technologies de l'Information - Série ISI: Ingénierie des Systèmes d'Information*, Dec. 2018.
4. F. Gandon, M. Sabou, and H. Sack. Weaving a Web of Linked Resources. Semantic Web Journal Sepcial Issue, 2017.

Organization

Organizing Committee

General Chair

Fabien Gandon — Inria, Université Côte d'Azur, CNRS, I3S Sophia Antipolis, France

Local Chairs

孙敬 (Jing Sun) — The University of Auckland, New Zealand
Gill Dobbie — The University of Auckland, New Zealand

Research Track Chairs

Chiara Ghidini — Fondazione Bruno Kessler (FBK), Italy
Olaf Hartig — Linköping University, Sweden

Resources Track Chairs

Maria Maleshkova — SDA, University of Bonn, Germany
Vojtěch Svátek — University of Economics in Prague, Czech Republic

In-Use Track Chairs

Isabel Cruz — University of Illinois at Chicago, USA
Aidan Hogan — DCC, Universidad de Chile, Chile

Reproducibility Track Chairs

Alejandra Gonzalez-Beltran — Science and Technology Facilities Council, UK
Michael Cochez — Fraunhofer Institute for Applied Information Technology, RWTH Aachen University, Germany, and University of Jyvaskyla, Finland

Industry Track Chairs

Anna Lisa Gentile — IBM Research, USA
Christophe Guéret — Accenture Labs Dublin, Ireland

Journal Track Chairs

Claudia d'Amato — University of Bari, Italy
Lalana Kagal — MIT, USA

Workshop and Tutorial Chairs

H. Sofia Pinto	INESC-ID, Instituto Superior Técnico, Universidade de Lisboa, Portugal
武田 英明 (Hideaki Takeda)	National Institute of Informatics, Japan

Semantic Web Challenges Track Chairs

Gianluca Demartini	The University of Queensland, Australia
Valentina Presutti	STLab-ISTC, National Research Council, Italy
Axel Ngonga	Paderborn University, Germany

Poster and Demo Track Chairs

Mari Carmen Suárez-Figueroa	Universidad Politécnica de Madrid (UPM), Ontology Engineering Group (OEG), Spain
程龚 (Gong Cheng)	Nanjing University, China

Doctoral Consortium Chairs

乔淼 (Miao Qiao)	The University of Auckland, New Zealand
Mauro Dragoni	Fondazione Bruno Kessler, Italy

Student Coordination Chairs

ඔෂානි සෙනෙවිරත්න (Oshani Seneviratne)	Oshani Rensselaer Polytechnic Institute, USA
岑超榮 (Bruce, Chiu-Wing Sham)	The University of Auckland, New Zealand

Minute Madness Chairs

Irene Celino	Cefriel, Italy
Armin Haller	Australian National University, Australia

Outrageous Ideas Track Chairs

Maria Keet	University of Cape Town, South Africa
Abraham Bernstein	University of Zurich, Switzerland

Proceedings Chairs

宋劼 (Jie Song)	Memect Technology, China
Maxime Lefrançois	MINES Saint-Étienne, France

Metadata Chairs

Maribel Acosta	Karlsruhe Institute of Technology, Germany
Andrea Giovanni Nuzzolese	STLab, ISTC-CNR, Italy

Publicity Chairs

Valentina Ivanova	RISE Research Institutes of Sweden, Sweden
فؤاد زبليط (Fouad Zablith)	American University of Beirut, Lebanon

Sponsorship Chairs

彭麗姬 (Lai Kei Pang)	University of Auckland Libraries and Learning Services, New Zealand
Cédric Pruski	Luxembourg Institute of Science and Technology, Luxembourg
Oktie Hassanzadeh	IBM Research, USA

Web Site Chair

นชา ชลดำรงค์กุล (Nacha Chondamrongkul)	The University of Auckland, New Zealand

Program Committee

Senior Program Committee – Research Track

Lora Aroyo	Google
Paul Buitelaar	Insight Centre for Data Analytics, National University of Ireland Galway
Emanuele Della Valle	Politecnico di Milano
Gianluca Demartini	The University of Queensland
Armin Haller	Australian National University
Annika Hinze	University of Waikato
Katja Hose	Aalborg University
Andreas Hotho	University of Wuerzburg
Wei Hu	Nanjing University
Mustafa Jarrar	Birzeit University
Sabrina Kirrane	Vienna University of Economics and Business
Markus Luczak-Roesch	Victoria University of Wellington
David Martin	Samsung Research America
Tommie Meyer	University of Cape Town, CAIR
Matteo Palmonari	University of Milano-Bicocca
Jorge Pérez	Universidad de Chile
Achim Rettinger	Trier University
Marco Rospocher	Università degli Studi di Verona
Hideaki Takeda	National Institute of Informatics
Valentina Tamma	University of Liverpool
Kerry Taylor	Australian National University and University of Surrey
Tania Tudorache	Stanford University
Axel Polleres	WU Wien
Maria Esther Vidal	Universidad Simon Bolivar
Paul Groth	University of Amsterdam
Luciano Serafini	Fondazione Bruno Kessler

Program Committee – Research Track

Maribel Acosta	Karlsruhe Institute of Technology
Harith Alani	The Open University
Jose Julio Alferes	Universidade NOVA de Lisboa
Muhammad Intizar Ali	Insight Centre for Data Analytics, National University of Ireland Galway
Marjan Alirezaie	Orebro University
Tahani Alsubait	Umm Al-Qura University
José Luis Ambite	University of Southern California
Renzo Angles	Universidad de Talca
Mihael Arcan	Insight @ NUI Galway
Manuel Atencia	Université Grenoble Alpes
Maurizio Atzori	University of Cagliari
Payam Barnaghi	University of Surrey
Pierpaolo Basile	University of Bari
Valerio Basile	University of Turin
Srikanta Bedathur	IIT Delhi
Zohra Bellahsene	LIRMM
Ladjel Bellatreche	LIAS/ENSMA
Maria Bermudez-Edo	University of Granada
Leopoldo Bertossi	Relational AI Inc., Carleton University
Eva Blomqvist	Linköping University
Fernando Bobillo	University of Zaragoza
Alex Borgida	Rutgers University
Stefano Borgo	Laboratory for Applied Ontology, ISTC-CNR (Trento)
Loris Bozzato	Fondazione Bruno Kessler
Alessandro Bozzon	Delft University of Technology
John Breslin	NUI Galway
Carlos Buil Aranda	Universidad Técnica Federico Santa Maria
Marut Buranarach	NECTEC
Aljoscha Burchardt	DFKI
Elena Cabrio	Université Côte d'Azur, CNRS, Inria, I3S
Jean-Paul Calbimonte	HES-SO University of Applied Sciences and Arts Western Switzerland
David Carral	TU Dresden
Vinay Chaudhri	Independent Consultant, San Francisco Bay Area
Huajun Chen	Zhejiang University
Huiyuan Chen	Case Western Reserve University
Gong Cheng	Nanjing University
Philipp Cimiano	Bielefeld University
Michael Cochez	Fraunhofer Institute for Applied Information Technology
Jack G. Conrad	Thomson Reuters

Olivier Corby	Inria
Oscar Corcho	Universidad Politécnica de Madrid
Francesco Corcoglioniti	Fondazione Bruno Kessler
Luca Costabello	Accenture Labs
Fabio Cozman	University of São Paulo
Isabel Cruz	University of Illinois at Chicago
Philippe Cudre-Mauroux	University of Fribourg
Olivier Curé	Université Paris-Est, LIGM
Claudia d'Amato	University of Bari
Mathieu D'Aquin	Insight Centre for Data Analytics, National University of Ireland Galway
Jérôme David	Inria
Jeremy Debattista	Trinity College Dublin
Thierry Declerck	DFKI GmbH and University of Saarland
Daniele Dell'Aglio	University of Zurich
Elena Demidova	L3S Research Center
Chiara Di Francescomarino	FBK-irst
Stefan Dietze	GESIS – Leibniz Institute for the Social Sciences
Mauro Dragoni	FBK-irst
Jianfeng Du	Guangdong University of Foreign Studies
Michel Dumontier	Maastricht University
Shady Elbassuoni	American University of Beirut
Lorena Etcheverry	Instituto de Computación, Universidad de la República
Jérôme Euzenat	Inria, Université Grenoble Alpes
Stefano Faralli	University of Rome Unitelma Sapienza
Alessandro Faraotti	IBM
Catherine Faron Zucker	University Nice Sophia Antipolis
Anna Fensel	Semantic Technology Institute (STI) Innsbruck, University of Innsbruck
Alba Fernandez	Universidad Politécnica de Madrid
Miriam Fernandez	Knowledge Media Institute
Javier D. Fernández	Vienna University of Economics and Business
Besnik Fetahu	L3S Research Center
Valeria Fionda	Università della Calabria
Antske Fokkens	Vrije Universiteit Amsterdam
Flavius Frasincar	Erasmus University Rotterdam
Fred Freitas	Universidade Federal de Pernambuco (UFPE)
Francesca Frontini	Université Paul-Valéry Montpellier 3, Praxiling UMR 5267 CNRS
Naoki Fukuta	Shizuoka University
Michael Färber	University of Freiburg
Luis Galárraga	Aalborg University
Raúl García-Castro	Universidad Politécnica de Madrid
Daniel Garijo	Information Sciences Institute
Anna Lisa Gentile	IBM
Aurona Gerber	CAIR, University of Pretoria

Jose Manuel Gomez-Perez	ExpertSystem
Rafael S. Gonçalves	Stanford University
Guido Governatori	CSIRO
Jorge Gracia	University of Zaragoza
Dagmar Gromann	TU Dresden
Tudor Groza	The Garvan Institute of Medical Research
Claudio Gutierrez	Universidad de Chile
Peter Haase	metaphacts
Andreas Harth	University of Erlangen-Nuremberg, Fraunhofer IIS-SCS
Bernhard Haslhofer	AIT Austrian Institute of Technology
Oktie Hassanzadeh	IBM
Pascal Hitzler	Wright State University
Rinke Hoekstra	University of Amsterdam
Aidan Hogan	DCC, Universidad de Chile
Geert-Jan Houben	Delft University of Technology
Wen Hua	The University of Queensland
Eero Hyvönen	Aalto University and University of Helsinki (HELDIG)
Luis Ibanez-Gonzalez	University of Southampton
Ryutaro Ichise	National Institute of Informatics
Nancy Ide	Vassar College
Oana Inel	Delft University of Technology
Prateek Jain	Nuance Communications Inc.
Krzysztof Janowicz	University of California
Caroline Jay	The University of Manchester
Ernesto Jimenez-Ruiz	The Alan Turing Institute
Lucie-Aimée Kaffee	University of Southampton
Evangelos Kalampokis	University of Macedonia
Maulik R. Kamdar	Stanford Center for Biomedical Informatics Research, Stanford University
Megan Katsumi	University of Toronto
Tomi Kauppinen	Aalto University School of Science
Takahiro Kawamura	Japan Science and Technology Agency
Maria Keet	University of Cape Town
Mayank Kejriwal	Information Sciences Institute
Thomas Kipf	University of Amsterdam
Matthias Klusch	DFKI
Stasinos Konstantopoulos	NCSR Demokritos
Roman Kontchakov	Birkbeck, University of London
Dimitris Kontokostas	University of Leipzig
Manolis Koubarakis	National and Kapodistrian University of Athens
Kouji Kozaki	Osaka University
Adila A. Krisnadhi	University of Indonesia
Tobias Kuhn	Vrije Universiteit Amsterdam
Tobias Käfer	Karlsruhe Institute of Technology
Jose Emilio Labra Gayo	Universidad de Oviedo

Giulio Petrucci	Google
Rafael Peñaloza	University of Milano-Bicocca
Patrick Philipp	Forschungszentrum Informatik (FZI)
Reinhard Pichler	TU Wien
Giuseppe Pirrò	Sapienza University of Rome
Alessandro Piscopo	BBC
Dimitris Plexousakis	FORTH
María Poveda-Villalón	Universidad Politécnica de Madrid
Guilin Qi	Southeast University
Yuzhong Qu	Nanjing University
Alexandre Rademaker	IBM Research Brazil, EMAp/FGV
Maya Ramanath	IIT Delhi
David Ratcliffe	Defence
Simon Razniewski	Max Planck Institute for Informatics
Blake Regalia	University of California
Georg Rehm	DFKI
Juan L. Reutter	Pontificia Universidad Católica
Martin Rezk	DMM.com
Giuseppe Rizzo	LINKS Foundation
Mariano Rodríguez Muro	Google
Dumitru Roman	SINTEF
Gaetano Rossiello	University of Bari
Ana Roxin	University of Burgundy, UMR CNRS 6306
Sebastian Rudolph	TU Dresden
Anisa Rula	University of Milano-Bicocca
Harald Sack	FIZ Karlsruhe – Leibniz Institute for Information Infrastructure, KIT Karlsruhe
Angelo Antonio Salatino	The Open University
Muhammad Saleem	AKSW, University of Leizpig
Kai-Uwe Sattler	TU Ilmenau
Simon Scerri	Fraunhofer
Ralph Schaefermeier	University of Leipzig
Bernhard Schandl	mySugr GmbH
Ralf Schenkel	University of Trier
Stefan Schlobach	Vrije Universiteit Amsterdam
Andreas Schmidt	University of Kassel
Giovanni Semeraro	University of Bari
Juan F. Sequeda	Capsenta Labs
Gilles Serasset	LIG, Université Grenoble Alpes
Yanfeng Shu	CSIRO
Gerardo Simari	Universidad Nacional del Sur, CONICET
Hala Skaf-Molli	University of Nantes, LS2N
Sebastian Skritek	TU Wien
Dezhao Song	Thomson Reuters

Steffen Staab	Institut WeST, University Koblenz-Landau and WAIS, University of Southampton
Armando Stellato	University of Rome
Simon Steyskal	Siemens AG Austria
Markus Stocker	German National Library of Science and Technology (TIB)
Audun Stolpe	Norwegian Defence Research Establishment (FFI)
Umberto Straccia	ISTI-CNR
Heiner Stuckenschmidt	University of Mannheim
York Sure-Vetter	Karlsruhe Institute of Technology
Pedro Szekely	USC – Information Sciences Institute
Mohsen Taheriyan	Google
Naoya Takeishi	RIKEN Center for Advanced Intelligence Project
Sergio Tessaris	Free University of Bozen-Bolzano
Andrea Tettamanzi	University Nice Sophia Antipolis
Kia Teymourian	Boston University
Harsh Thakkar	University of Bonn
Andreas Thalhammer	F. Hoffmann-La Roche AG
Ilaria Tiddi	Vrije University
David Toman	University of Waterloo
Yannick Toussaint	Loria
Sebastian Tramp	eccenca GmbH
Cassia Trojahn	UT2J, IRIT
Anni-Yasmin Turhan	TU Dresden
Takanori Ugai	Fujitsu Laboratories Ltd.
Jürgen Umbrich	Vienna University of Economy and Business
Joerg Unbehauen	University of Leipzig
Jacopo Urbani	Vrije Universiteit Amsterdam
Dmitry Ustalov	University of Mannheim
Alejandro A. Vaisman	Instituto Tecnológico de Buenos Aires
Marieke van Erp	KNAW Humanities Cluster
Jacco van Ossenbruggen	CWI, VU University Amsterdam
Miel Vander Sande	Ghent University
Ruben Verborgh	Ghent University – imec
Serena Villata	CNRS – Laboratoire d'Informatique, Signaux et Systèmes de Sophia-Antipolis
Boris Villazon-Terrazas	Majorel
Piek Vossen	Vrije Universiteit Amsterdam
Domagoj Vrgoc	Pontificia Universidad Católica de Chile
Simon Walk	Graz University of Technology
Kewen Wang	Griffith University
Xin Wang	Tianjin University
Zhichun Wang	Beijing Normal University
Grant Weddell	University of Waterloo
Gregory Todd Williams	Hulu

Frank Wolter	University of Liverpool
Josiane Xavier Parreira	Siemens AG Österreich
Guohui Xiao	KRDB Research Centre, Free University of Bozen-Bolzano
Fouad Zablith	American University of Beirut
Ondřej Zamazal	University of Economics in Prague
Veruska Zamborlini	University of Amsterdam
Amrapali Zaveri	Maastricht University
Sergej Zerr	L3S Research Center
Kalliopi Zervanou	Eindhoven University of Technology
Lei Zhang	FIZ Karlsruhe – Leibniz Institute for Information Infrastructure
Wei Emma Zhang	Macquarie University
Xiaowang Zhang	Tianjin University
Ziqi Zhang	Sheffield University
Jun Zhao	University of Oxford
Lihua Zhao	Accenture
Antoine Zimmermann	MINES Saint-Étienne
Amal Zouaq	University of Ottawa

Additional Reviewers – Research Track

Dimitris Alivanistos	Elsevier
Andrea Bellandi	Institute for Computational Linguistics
Mohamed Ben Ellefi	Aix-Marseille University, Lis-Lab
Nabila Berkani	ESI
Federico Bianchi	University of Milan-Bicocca
Zeyd Boukhers	University of Siegen
Marco Brambilla	Politecnico di Milano
Janez Brank	Jožef Stefan Institute
Angelos Charalambidis	University of Athens
Marco Cremaschi	Università di Milano-Bicocca
Ronald Denaux	ExpertSystem
Dimitar Dimitrov	GESIS
Monireh Ebrahimi	Wright State University
Cristina Feier	University of Bremen
Oliver Fernandez Gil	TU Dresden
Giorgos Flouris	FORTH-ICS
Jorge Galicia Auyon	ISAE-ENSMA
Andrés García-Silva	ExpertSystem
Genet Asefa Gesese	FIZ Karlsruhe
Pouya Ghiasnezhad Omran	Griffith University and Australian National University
Simon Gottschalk	L3S Research Center
Jonas Halvorsen	Norwegian Defence Research Establishment (FFI)
Dave Hendricksen	Thomson Reuters
Annika Hinze	University of Waikato

Yuncheng Hua	Southeast University
Gao Huan	Southeast University
John Hudzina	Thomson Reuters
Robert Isele	eccenca GmbH
Chen Jiaoyan	University of Oxford
Anas Fahad Khan	Istituto di Linguistica Computazionale Antonio Zampolli
Haris Kondylakis	FORTH
George Konstantinidis	University of Southampton
Cedric Kulbach	FZI - AIFB
Artem Lutov	University of Fribourg
Andrea Mauri	Delft University of Technology
Sepideh Mesbah	Delft University of Technology
Payal Mitra	.
Piero Molino	Università di Bari Aldo Moro
Anna Nguyen	Karlsruhe Institute of Technology
Kristian Noullet	University of Freiburg
Erik Novak	Jožef Stefan Institute
Inna Novalija	Jožef Stefan Institute
Wolfgang Otto	GESIS
Romana Pernischová	University of Zurich
Freddy Priyatna	Universidad Politécnica de Madrid
Joe Raad	Vrije Universiteit Amsterdam
Jan Rörden	AIT Austrian Institute of Technology
Leif Sabellek	University of Bremen
Filipe Santana Da Silva	Fundação Universidade Federal de Ciências da Saúde de Porto Alegre (UFCSPA)
Lukas Schmelzeisen	University of Koblenz-Landau
Miroslav Shaltev	L3S
Cogan Shimizu	Wright State University
Lucia Siciliani	University of Bari
Alisa Smirnova	University of Fribourg
Blerina Spahiu	Università degli Studi di Milano Bicocca
Nicolas Tempelmeier	L3S Research Center
Elodie Thieblin	IRIT
Riccardo Tommasini	Politecnico di Milano
Philip Turk	SINTEF
Rima Türker	FIZ Karlsruhe
Roman Vlasov	IDA GmbH, RSM Intelligence
Zhe Wang	Griffith University
Kemas Wiharja	University of Aberdeen
Bo Yan	University of California
Dingqi Yang	eXascale Infolab, University of Fribourg
Lingxi Yue	Shandong University
Rui Zhu	University of California
Thomas Zielund	Thomson Reuters

Sarah de Nigris	Institute WeST, Koblenz-Landau Universität
Remzi Çelebi	Ege University

Senior Program Committee – Research Track

Anna Lisa Gentile	IBM
Sebastian Rudolph	TU Dresden
Heiko Paulheim	University of Mannheim
Maria Esther Vidal	Universidad Simon Bolivar
Agnieszka Lawrynowicz	Poznan University of Technology
Stefan Dietze	GESIS – Leibniz Institute for the Social Sciences
Steffen Lohmann	Fraunhofer
Francesco Osborne	The Open University

Program Committee – Resources Track

Muhammad Intizar Ali	Insight Centre for Data Analytics, National University of Ireland
Ghislain Auguste Atemezing	Mondeca
Maurizio Atzori	University of Cagliari
Elena Cabrio	Université Côte d'Azur, CNRS, Inria, I3S
Irene Celino	CEFRIEL
Timothy Clark	University of Virginia
Francesco Corcoglioniti	Fondazione Bruno Kessler
Victor de Boer	Vrije Universiteit Amsterdam
Daniele Dell'Aglio	University of Zurich
Emanuele Della Valle	Politecnico di Milano
Anastasia Dimou	Ghent University
Ying Ding	Indiana University Bloomington
Mauro Dragoni	FBK-irst
Mohnish Dubey	University of Bonn
Marek Dudáš	University of Economics in Prague
Fajar J. Ekaputra	Vienna University of Technology
Ivan Ermilov	Universität Leipzig
Diego Esteves	Fraunhofer
Michael Färber	University of Freiburg
Michael Galkin	Fraunhofer IAIS University of Bonn and ITMO University
Aldo Gangemi	Università di Bologna, CNR-ISTC
Raúl Garcia-Castro	Universidad Politécnica de Madrid
Daniel Garijo	Information Sciences Institute
Jose Manuel Gomez-Perez	ExpertSystem
Alejandra Gonzalez-Beltran	University of Oxford
Rafael S. Gonçalves	Stanford University
Alasdair Gray	Heriot-Watt University
Tudor Groza	The Garvan Institute of Medical Research

Amelie Gyrard	Kno.e.sis – Ohio Center of Excellence in Knowledge-enabled Computing
Armin Haller	Australian National University
Karl Hammar	Jönköping University
Rinke Hoekstra	University of Amsterdam
Antoine Isaac	Europeana, VU University Amsterdam
Ernesto Jimenez-Ruiz	The Alan Turing Institute
Simon Jupp	European Bioinformatics Institute
Tomi Kauppinen	Aalto University School of Science
Elmar Kiesling	Vienna University of Technology
Tomáš Kliegr	University of Economics in Prague
Jakub Klímek	Charles University
Adila A. Krisnadhi	University of Indonesia
Markus Krötzsch	TU Dresden
Christoph Lange	University of Bonn, Fraunhofer IAIS
Maxime Lefrançois	MINES Saint-Étienne
Ioanna Lytra	Enterprise Information Systems, University of Bonn
Simon Mayer	University of St. Gallen and ETH Zurich
Jim McCusker	Rensselaer Polytechnic Institute
Fiona McNeill	Heriot Watt University
Nicole Merkle	FZI Forschungszentrum Informatik am KIT
Nandana Mihindukula-sooriya	Universidad Politécnica de Madrid
Raghava Mutharaju	IIIT Delhi
Lionel Médini	LIRIS, University of Lyon
Giulio Napolitano	Fraunhofer Institute, University of Bonn
Mojtaba Nayyeri	University of Bonn
Martin Nečaský	Charles University
Vinh Nguyen	National Library of Medicine, NIH
Andrea Giovanni Nuzzolese	University of Bologna
Alessandro Oltramari	Bosch Research and Technology Center
Bijan Parsia	The University of Manchester
Silvio Peroni	University of Bologna
Guilin Qi	Southeast University
Mariano Rico	Universidad Politécnica de Madrid
German Rigau	IXA Group, UPV/EHU
Giuseppe Rizzo	LINKS Foundation
Mariano Rodríguez Muro	Google
Edna Ruckhaus	Universidad Politécnica de Madrid
Anisa Rula	University of Milano-Bicocca
Michele Ruta	Politecnico di Bari
Satya Sahoo	Case Western Reserve University
Miel Vander Sande	Ghent University
Marco Luca Sbodio	IBM
Stefan Schlobach	Vrije Universiteit Amsterdam
Gezim Sejdiu	University of Bonn

Nicolas Seydoux	LAAS-CNRS, IRIT
Ruben Taelman	Ghent University – imec
Harsh Thakkar	University of Bonn
Allan Third	The Open University
Krishnaprasad Thirunarayan	Wright State University
Konstantin Todorov	LIRMM, University of Montpellier
Priyansh Trivedi	University of Bonn
Cassia Trojahn	UT2J, IRIT
Federico Ulliana	Université Montpellier
Natalia Villanueva-Rosales	University of Texas at El Paso
Tobias Weller	Karlsruhe Institute of Technology
Fouad Zablith	American University of Beirut
Ondřej Zamazal	University of Economics in Prague
Amrapali Zaveri	Maastricht University
Jun Zhao	University of Oxford

Additional Reviewers – Resources Track

Pierre-Antoine Champin	Universite Claude Bernard Lyon 1
Nathan Elazar	Australian National University
Kuldeep Singh	Fraunhofer IAIS
Blerina Spahiu	Bicocca University
Xander Wilcke	Vrije Universiteit Amsterdam
Tianxing Wu	Nanyang Technological University
Hong Yung Yip	Wright State University

Program Committee – In-Use Track

Renzo Angles	Universidad de Talca
Sonia Bergamaschi	University of Modena
Carlos Buil-Aranda	Universidad Técnica Federico Santa María
Irene Celino	Cefriel
Oscar Corcho	Universidad Politécnica de Madrid
Philippe Cudre-Mauroux	University of Fribourg
Brian Davis	National University of Ireland Maynooth
Mauro Dragoni	Fondazione Bruno Kessler
Achille Fokoue	IBM
Daniel Garijo	Information Sciences Institute, University of Southern California
Jose Manuel Gomez-Perez	ExpertSystem
Rafael Gonçalves	Stanford University
Paul Groth	University of Amsterdam
Tudor Groza	The Garvan Institute of Medical Research
Peter Haase	metaphacts
Armin Haller	Australian National University
Tomi Kauppinen	Aalto University
Sabrina Kirrane	Vienna University of Economics and Business

Craig Knoblock	USC Information Sciences Institute
Freddy Lecue	CortAIx, Canada, and Inria, Sophia Antipolis
Vanessa Lopez	IBM Research Ireland
Andriy Nikolov	metaphacts GmbH
Francesco Osborne	The Open University
Matteo Palmonari	University of Milan-Bicocca
Jeff Z. Pan	University of Aberdeen
Josiane Xavier Parreira	Siemens AG Österreich
Catia Pesquita	LASIGE, University of Lisbon
Artem Revenko	Semantic Web Company GmbH
Mariano Rico	Universidad Politécnica de Madrid
Dumitru Roman	SINTEF AS, University of Oslo
Anisa Rula	University of Milan-Bicocca
Juan F. Sequeda	Capsenta Labs
Dezhao Song	Thomson Reuters
Thomas Steiner	Google
Ilaria Tiddi	VU Amsterdam
Anna Tordai	Elsevier
Raphaël Troncy	EURECOM
Benjamin Zapilko	GESIS – Leibniz Institute for the Social Sciences
Matthäus Zloch	GESIS – Leibniz Institute for the Social Sciences

Additional Reviewers – In-Use Track

Akansha Bhardwaj	eXascale Infolab, University of Fribourg
Luca Gagliardelli	Università degli Studi di Modena e Reggio Emilia
Elena Montiel-Ponsoda	Universidad Politécnica de Madrid
Nikolay Nikolov	University of Oxford
Joe Raad	Vrije Universiteit Amsterdam
Giovanni Simonini	MIT
Ahmet Soylu	Norwegian University of Science and Technology

Sponsors

Gold Plus Sponsor

IBM **Research**

http://www.research.ibm.com

Gold Sponsor

https://metaphacts.com

Silver Sponsors

GE Global Research

https://www.ge.com/research

Google

https://www.google.com

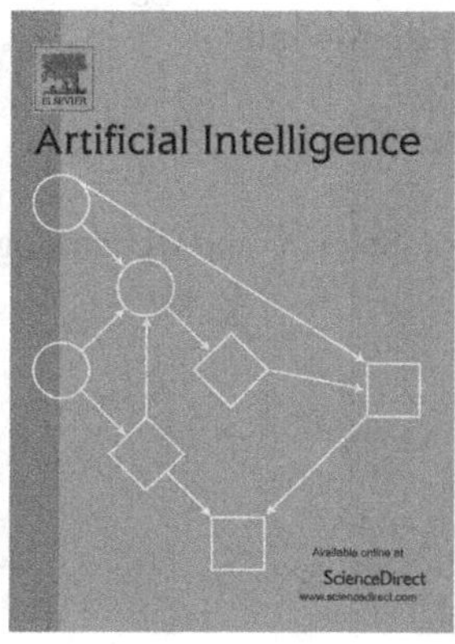

https://www.journals.elsevier.com/artificial-intelligence

100% PURE
NEW ZEALAND

https://www.tourismnewzealand.com

Bronze Sponsors

https://www.springer.com

https://www.auckland.ac.nz/en/science.html

http://aucklandconventions.co.nz

http://cs.auckland.ac.nz

Other Sponsors

https://franz.com

https://www.inria.fr/en

Student Travel Award Sponsors

http://swsa.semanticweb.org

https://www.nsf.gov

Abstracts of Keynotes

For Knowledge

Jérôme Euzenat

Inria, Grenoble, France

Abstract. A large range of animals are able to learn from their environment, but human beings are special among them because they can articulate knowledge and they can communicate it. Written expression and communication have allowed us to get rid of time and space in knowledge transmission. They allow learning directly from elaborated knowledge instead of by experience. These key features have led the creation of whole cultures, providing a selective advantage to the species. The World Wide Web facilitating cultural exchange is a culminating point in this story, so far.
Hence, the idea of a semantic web allowing machines to have a grasp on this knowledge is a tremendous idea. Alas, after twenty years, the semantic web field is mostly focused on data, even when it is made of so-called knowledge graphs. Of course, there are schemata and vocabularies, but they are only a simple kind of knowledge. Although data may be open, knowledge eventually learnt by machines is very often not disclosed nor prone to communication. This brings us down the knowledge evolution ladder.
The grand goal of formally expressing knowledge on the Web must be rehabilitated. We do not need knowledge cast in stone forever, but knowledge that can seamlessly evolve; we do not need to build one single knowledge source, but encourage diversity which is source of disputation and robustness; we do not need consistent knowledge at the Web scale, but local theories that can be combined. We will discuss in particular how knowledge can be made live and evolve by taking inspiration from cultural evolution and evolutionary epistemology.

Extracting Knowledge from the Data Deluge to Reveal the Mysteries of the Universe

Melanie Johnston-Hollitt

Curtin University, Perth, Australia

Abstract. Astrophysics is one of the most data intensive research fields of the modern world and, as such, provides a unique context to drive many of the required innovations in the "big data" regime. In particular, radio astronomy is foremost in the field in terms of big data generation, and thanks to sustained global investment in the discipline over the last decade, present telescopes generate tens of petabytes of data per annum. The pinnacle of this so-called on-going 'radio renaissance' will be the Square Kilometre Array (SKA)—a global observatory tasked with probing the deepest mysteries of the Universe. The SKA will create the highest resolution, fastest frame rate movie of the evolving Universe ever and in doing so will generate 160 terrabytes of raw data a day, or close to 5 zettabytes of data per annum. These data will be processed into order of 1 petabyte of image cubes per day which will be processed, curated, and ultimately distributed via a network of coordinated tiered compute facilities to the global astronomical community for scientific exploitation. However, this truly data-rich environment will require new automated and semantic processes to fully exploit the vast sea of results generated. In fact, to fully realize the enormous scientific potential of this endeavour, we will need not only better data tagging and coordination mechanisms, but also improved algorithms, artificial intelligence, semantics, and ontologies to track and extract knowledge in an automated way at a scale not yet attempted in science. In this keynote I will present an overview of the SKA project, outline the "big data" challenges the project faces and discuss some of the approaches we are taking to tame this astronomical data deluge.

Semantics: The Business Technology Disruptor of the Future

Dougal Watt

Meaningful Technology, Auckland, New Zealand

Abstract. Semantics has a vital role to play in bringing meaning to business data. In this talk I will show how semantic technology can help solve the modern data complexity, integration, and flexibility issues for business computing technologies, both from a technical and psychological perspective, and suggest some challenges and opportunities for further research and collaboration.

Contents – Part I

Research Track

Contents – Part II

Resources Track

In-Use Track

Research Track

Decentralized Indexing over a Network of RDF Peers

Christian Aebeloe(✉), Gabriela Montoya, and Katja Hose

Aalborg University, Aalborg, Denmark
{caebel,gmontoya,khose}@cs.aau.dk

Abstract. Despite the prospect of a vast Web of interlinked data, the Semantic Web today mostly fails to meet its potential. One of the main problems it faces is rooted in its current architecture, which totally relies on the availability of the servers providing access to the data. These servers are subject to failures, which often results in situations where some data is unavailable. Recent advances have proposed decentralized peer-to-peer based architectures to alleviate this problem. However, for query processing these approaches mostly rely on flooding, a standard technique for peer-to-peer systems, which can easily result in very high network traffic and hence cause high query response times. To still enable efficient query processing in such networks, this paper proposes two indexing schemes, which in a decentralized fashion aim at efficiently finding nodes with relevant data for a given query: Locational Indexes and Prefix-Partitioned Bloom Filters. Our experiments show that such indexing schemes are able to considerably speed up query processing times compared to existing approaches.

1 Introduction

While there is a huge potential of possible applications of Linked Data and although more and more information is being published in RDF, it is currently not possible to rely on the availability of these datasets. Data providers publish their data as downloadable data dumps, queryable SPARQL endpoints or TPF interfaces, or dereferenceable URIs.

As highlighted in several recent studies [1,3,10,22], it is a huge burden for data providers to keep the data available at all times, making many endpoints often unavailable. Multiple recent studies [1,4,8] therefore explored and evidenced the importance of avoiding a single point of failure, e.g. a central server, and maintain a decentralized architecture where data is available even if the original uploader fails through data replication. These approaches, however, either introduce a structured overlay over a peer-to-peer (P2P) network [4], use unstable nodes with limited storage capabilities [8], or make use of inefficient query processing algorithms, such as flooding [1]. Applying a structured overlay to a network of peers restricts peer autonomy as some kind of global knowledge is used to allocate the data at certain peers and to find relevant data for a given query. Apart from general problems, such as finding an optimal way to allocate

C. Ghidini et al. (Eds.): ISWC 2019, LNCS 11778, pp. 3–20, 2019.
https://doi.org/10.1007/978-3-030-30793-6_1

data at peers, structured overlays need to adjust the overlay when new peers leave or join the network, which may cause problems when a high number of nodes leaves or joins.

Unstructured P2P networks, on the other hand, retain the maximum degree of peer autonomy but with the lack of global knowledge about data placement efficient query processing is considerably more challenging. Hence, unstructured P2P systems typically rely on expensive algorithms, such as flooding, which creates a large overhead and involves exchanging a high number of messages between nodes until the relevant data is actually found and processed. Assuming that each node in the network has N neighbors, flooding results in $\sum_{i=1}^{ttl} N^i$ messages to reach all nodes within a hop distance of ttl (time-to-live value). For example, given a network with $N = 5$ and $ttl = 5$, flooding results in 3,905 messages. Query processing in an unstructured architecture has been addressed previously [8,9,16]. However, they either focus on reducing the load on servers by splitting the query processing tasks between multiple clients or rely on unstable nodes with limited storage capabilities. The lack of global knowledge impacts the answer completeness as evidenced in [9], where the average completeness remains under 45%.

In this paper, we do not aim to reduce the server loads or provide users with low-cost but incomplete answers. Instead, to overcome the lack of global knowledge in unstructured architectures and enable efficient query processing, this paper proposes the use of novel indexes, inspired by routing indexes [6], which are tailored for RDF datasets, and provide a node with information about which data its neighbors can provide access to within a distance of several hops. In summary, this paper makes the following contributions:

- Two indexing schemes to determine relevant data based on common subjects and objects: (i) a baseline approach: Locational Index and (ii) an advanced index based on bloom filters: Prefix-Partitioned Bloom Filters.
- Efficient query processing techniques for unstructured decentralized networks using the proposed indexing schemes, and
- An extensive evaluation of the proposed techniques.

This paper is structured as follows: while Sect. 2 discusses related work, Sect. 3 describes preliminaries and provides background information. Section 4 proposes the Locational Indexing scheme, followed by Prefix-Partitioned Bloom Filters in Sect. 5. Query processing is described in Sect. 6. The results of our experimental study are discussed in Sect. 7 and the paper concludes with a summary and an outlook to future work in Sect. 8.

2 Related Work

Although decentralization is not an entirely novel concept, it has gained more and more attention over the last couple of years, especially in the Semantic Web community. The Solid platform [15], for instance, proposes to store personal data in RDF format in a decentralized manner, in so-called Personal Online

Datastores (PODs). A POD can be stored on any server at any location, and applications can ask for access to some of its data. This means that data is scattered around the world and that, even if a server fails, most peoples' PODs will still be available. The current focus of Solid, however, is more on protection of private data, whereas we focus on indexing schemes and query processing in decentralized architectures.

To improve availability of data by reducing the load at the servers running SPARQL endpoints, Triple Pattern Fragments (TPF) [22] have been proposed. By processing only triple pattern requests at the servers, query processing load can be reduced and shifted to the clients that then have to process expensive operations, such as joins. Bindings-Restricted TPF (brTPF) [10] further reduces the server load, by bulking bindings from previously evaluated triple patterns, thereby reducing the amount of requests. Other approaches [9,16] have similarly sought to divide the query processing load among multiple clients, or multiple RDF interfaces [17], in order to speed up query processing. While the previously mentioned approaches greatly reduce the server load, they still have some limitations. Some of these approaches [10,17,22] rely on a single server, or a fixed set of servers, that are vulnerable to attacks and represent single points of failure; if the servers fail, all their data will become unavailable, while other approaches [9,16] rely on unstable nodes with limited storage capabilities. Instead, we focus on architectures in which data is stored, and possibly replicated, in a decentralized and more stable manner, and on reducing the amount of messages sent within such an architecture.

Several decentralized architectures for RDF data are based on structured overlays over a P2P network [4,13,14]. These overlays allow to easily identify the nodes that have relevant data to evaluate queries. However, while they have been shown to provide fast query processing, they are vulnerable to churn. This is the case, since each time a node leaves or joins the network, the overlay has to be adapted. This creates a frequent overhead, making such architectures inflexible in unstable environments. Moreover, such structured overlays often impose the placement of data within the network, which is not applicable to the scenario considered in this paper. Therefore, such overlays are not applicable for source selection in our case.

In unstructured networks where the placement of data to the nodes is not imposed, several strategies have been proposed to access the data scattered through the network. Accessing the data may rely on centralized indexes, where one single node is responsible to maintain a full overview of the whole data in the network, and distributed indexes, where nodes are only responsible to provide an overview of the data they store. Centralized indexes represent a single point of failure and it is a challenge to keep the information up-to-date. Diverse approaches, such as [6,7,23], represent improvements over the basic flooding algorithm, which distributes the requests to all the nodes in the network, by reducing the number of contacted nodes to answer a query. For instance, routing indexes [6] extend the information that each node includes in its distributed index to include an entry for each of its neighbors and some aggregated information about what data can be accessed by contacting that neighbor within a distance of several hops, locally or by routing the query to a neighbor that has access to such information.

Diverse RDF indexing approaches have been proposed in contexts such as query optimization and source selection [5,18,21]. These approaches are mainly based on the structure of the graphs, such as finding representative nodes within the graph, common patterns in the data, or statistical information, such as number of class instances. Our general approach can be combined with many of these approaches, however for our concrete implementation we have focused on summaries based statistical information, since they provide a good tradeoff between index creation time and precision of the indexes. In our case, each node computes its own statistical information, either a locational or PPBF index, and exchanges this information with its neighbors.

3 Preliminaries

Today's standard data format for semantic data is the Resource Description Framework (RDF)[1]. RDF structures data into triples, which can be visualized as edges in a knowledge graph.

Definition 1 (RDF Triple). *Given the infinite and disjoint sets U (the set of all URIs/IRIs), B (the set of all blank nodes), and L (the set of all literals), an RDF triple is a triple of the form $(s, p, o) \in (U \cup B) \times U \times (U \cup B \cup L)$ where s is called the subject, p the predicate, and o the object.*

An *RDF graph* g is a finite set of RDF triples. In order to query an RDF graph containing a set of RDF triples, SPARQL[2] is widely used. The building block of a SPARQL query is a *triple pattern*. Triple patterns, like RDF triples, have three elements: subject, predicate, and object, but unlike RDF triples any of these elements could be a variable.

Definition 2 (Triple Pattern). *Given the infinite and disjoint sets U, B, and L from Definition 1, and V (the set of all variables), a triple pattern is a straightforward extension of an RDF triple, i.e., a triple of the form $(s, p, o) \in (U \cup B \cup V) \times (U \cup V) \times (U \cup B \cup L \cup V)$.*

If there is a mapping from the variables in the triple pattern to elements in $U \cup B \cup L$, such that the resulting RDF triple is in an RDF graph, then we say that the triple pattern matches those RDF triples, and that the triple pattern has solutions within the RDF graph. Moreover, in a SPARQL query triple patterns are organized into Basic Graph Patterns (BGPs). A BGP matches only if all the triple patterns within the BGP match. Furthermore, BGP may be combined with other SPARQL operators, such as OPTIONAL or UNION. Even if our approach works well for SPARQL queries with any SPARQL operators, we use examples

[1] http://www.w3.org/TR/2004/REC-rdf-concepts-20040210/.
[2] http://www.w3.org/TR/rdf-sparql-query/.

and descriptions with a single BGP as it makes the explanations simpler and can be naturally extended to SPARQL queries with any number of BGPs.

In an unstructured P2P system, nodes function as both clients and servers. Each node maintains a limited local datastore and a partial view over the network. In the limited local datastore, the node may include one or more RDF graphs. To ease the management of replicated graphs on several nodes, each graph is identified by a URI g. Then, the set of graphs in the local repository of node n is denoted as $\mathcal{G}_n$. To keep the network structure stable and up-to-date, peers periodically update their neighbors following certain protocols, such as [23]. The specifics of the partial view over the network may vary from system to system. For example, some systems [1,7] rank neighbors based on various metrics, e.g., the issued queries or the degree to which the data can be joined.

In this paper, we provide a general approach to identify relevant RDF data within a network. Our approach is based on indexing techniques that are defined independently of specific data placement strategies or network infrastructure. Therefore, our approach can be used in combination with different systems, in particular unstructured P2P networks, which we provide specific details for in Sect. 6. Furthermore, our general approach to identify relevant RDF data may be used in combination with diverse RDF interfaces to efficiently process queries.

4 Locational Index

Let $P(g)$ be a function that returns the set of predicates within a graph g and $\mathcal{G}_n$ be the set of graphs in the local repository of node n. n's locational index $I_L^i(\text{n})$ then summarizes the graphs that can be reached within a distance of i hops.

Definition 3 (Locational Index). *Let $\mathcal{N}$ be the set of nodes, $\mathcal{P}$ the set of predicates, and $\mathcal{G}$ the set of graphs, a locational index is a tuple $I_L^i(n) = \langle \gamma, \eta \rangle$, with $\gamma : \mathcal{P} \rightarrow 2^{\mathcal{G}}$ and $\eta : \mathcal{G} \rightarrow 2^{\mathcal{N}}$. $\gamma(p)$ returns the set of graphs gs s.t. $\forall g \in gs : p \in P(g)$. $\eta(g)$ returns the set of nodes ns such that $g \in \mathcal{G}_{n_i}$ such that n_i is within i hops from n.*

More formally, given that a node n can be described as a triple $n = \langle \mathcal{G}_n, N, u \rangle$, with $\mathcal{G}_n$ being the set of graphs that n stores, N being the set of direct neighbors, and u being a URI that identifies n, a locational index of depth 0 (covering only local graphs) at node n is defined as $I_L^0(n) = \langle \gamma, \eta \rangle$, where:

$$\gamma(p) = \{g \mid g \in \mathcal{G}_n \wedge p \in P(g)\} \quad (1)$$

$$\eta(g) = \{n\}, \forall g \in \mathcal{G}_n \quad (2)$$

The locational index of depth i for a node n is defined as $I^i_L(n) = \langle \gamma, \eta \rangle$, where:

$$\gamma = I^0_L(n).\gamma \oplus \bigoplus_{n' \in n.N} I^{i-1}_L(n').\gamma \tag{3}$$

$$\eta = I^0_L(n).\eta \oplus \bigoplus_{n' \in n.N} I^{i-1}_L(n').\eta \tag{4}$$

With $(f \oplus g)(x) = f(x) \cup g(x)$ if f and g are defined at x and $f(x), g(x)$ are sets, $(f \oplus g)(x) = f(x)$ if only f is defined at x, and $(f \oplus g)(x) = g(x)$ if only g is defined at x.

Example 1 (Locational Index). Consider the graphs in Table 1a and the nodes and connections in Fig. 1b. Applying Eqs. 3–4 to create a locational index of depth 2 for node n_1 results in $I^2_L(n_1)$ as shown in Table 1c.

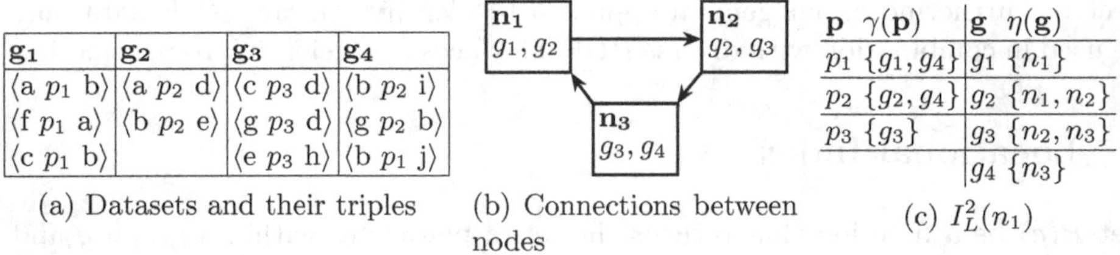

g_1	g_2	g_3	g_4
⟨a p_1 b⟩	⟨a p_2 d⟩	⟨c p_3 d⟩	⟨b p_2 i⟩
⟨f p_1 a⟩	⟨b p_2 e⟩	⟨g p_3 d⟩	⟨g p_2 b⟩
⟨c p_1 b⟩		⟨e p_3 h⟩	⟨b p_1 j⟩

(a) Datasets and their triples

(b) Connections between nodes

p	γ(p)	g	η(g)
p_1	$\{g_1, g_4\}$	g_1	$\{n_1\}$
p_2	$\{g_2, g_4\}$	g_2	$\{n_1, n_2\}$
p_3	$\{g_3\}$	g_3	$\{n_2, n_3\}$
		g_4	$\{n_3\}$

(c) $I^2_L(n_1)$

Fig. 1. Locational index obtained from a set of datasets and connections

In a real system, locational indexes are built by flooding the network for a specified amount of steps, where each reached node replies with its precomputed locational index.

The nodes that are relevant to evaluate a triple pattern tp, with predicate p_{tp}, are given by $\bigcup_{g \in \gamma(p_{tp})} takeOne(\eta(g))$, if p_{tp} is a URI, or $\bigcup_{g \in range(\gamma)} takeOne(\eta(g))$, if p_{tp} is a variable. *takeOne(s)* returns one element in the set s and it allows for evaluating the triple pattern only once against each graph. Thereby, flooding an entire network can be avoided by only sending triple patterns to relevant nodes. Even in the case of triple patterns with a variable as predicate, the number of requests can be significantly reduced, especially when replicas of graphs are stored at multiple nodes.

Example 2 (Node Selection with a Locational Index). Given node n_1 that issues the query, and the triple pattern $tp = \langle ?v_1, p_2, ?v_2 \rangle$, the set of selected nodes from $I^2_L(n_1)$ in Table 1c is $\{n_1, n_3\}$, since $\gamma(p_2) = \{g_2, g_4\}$, $n_1 \in \eta(g_2)$, and $n_3 \in \eta(g_4)$. The set of selected nodes could be $\{n_2, n_3\}$ because n_2 is also in $\eta(g_2)$, but n_1 may be preferable as it corresponds to using the local repository.

5 Prefix-Partitioned Bloom Filters

Building upon the baseline of locational indexes, this section presents Prefix-Partitioned Bloom Filters (PPBFs). The idea is to summarize entities and properties in a graph as a Bloom Filter [2] and rely on efficient bitwise operations on Bloom Filters to estimate if two graphs may have elements in common. We use Bloom Filters since they provide space-efficient bit vectors, and have previously been shown beneficial in reducing information processing for distributed systems [20]. Such knowledge can be used during query processing to reduce intermediate results by only evaluating triple patterns with a join variable over graphs that may have common elements. As such, PPBFs are not complementary to locational indexes, but encode similar information. As we shall see, this further narrows down the list of relevant nodes for a given query.

A Bloom Filter $\mathcal{B}$ for a set S of size n is a tuple $\mathcal{B} = (\hat{b}, H)$, where $\hat{b}$ is a bit vector of size m and H is a set of k hash functions. Each hash function maps the elements from S to a position in $\hat{b}$. To create the Bloom Filter of S, each hash function in H is applied to each element in S, and the resulting positions in $\hat{b}$ are set. o is estimated to be an element of S if all the positions given by applying the hash functions in H to o are set in $\hat{b}$. If at least one corresponding bit is not set, then it is certain that $o \notin S$. However, if all corresponding bits are set, it is still possible that $o \notin S$, meaning a Bloom filter answers the question *is o in S?* with either *no* or *maybe*, rather than *no* or *yes*. The probability of such false positives is given by formula $(1 - e^{-kn/m})^k$ [2]. Furthermore, the cardinality of a set that is represented by a Bloom Filter where t bits are set, can be approximated by the following formula [19]:

$$\hat{S}^{-1}(t) = \frac{ln(1 - t/m)}{k \cdot ln(1 - t/m)} \tag{5}$$

Given two sets s_1 and s_2 and their Bloom Filters $\mathcal{B}_1$ and $\mathcal{B}_2$, with bit vectors of the same size and with the same hash functions, $\mathcal{B}_1 \,\&\, \mathcal{B}_2$ approximates the Bloom Filter of $s1 \cap s2$, and $\mathcal{B}_1 | \mathcal{B}_2$ corresponds to the Bloom Filter of $s1 \cup s2$ [12]. Therefore, the number of URIs in two graphs can be approximated using Formula 5 on the Bloom Filter resulting of applying the bitwise **and** on the graphs' Bloom Filters.

5.1 Partitioning Bloom Filters

In order to have a relatively low false positive probability, the bit vectors should have multiple bits per each possible element. However, in large scale scenarios, e.g., with 500 million distinct URIs, so large bit vectors are not feasible to store for all graphs. If we instead use as few bits as the largest PPBF use, we would still have a high false-positive rate (just above 51% in our experiments). Therefore, instead of having a unique Bloom Filter per graph, we will have a prefix-based partitioning, with a Bloom Filter for each different URI prefix used in the graph.

This has the advantage that not only do most partitions have a low false-positive rate (less than 0.1% in our experiments in Sect. 7), but even for the partitions that have a high false-positive rate, this is more tolerable since if two URIs have the same prefix, they are more likely to be contained in the same graph, since a prefix typically encodes the domain/source. The prefix of a URI is the URI minus the name of the entity, e.g., the URI http://dbpedia.org/resource/Auckland has the prefix http://dbpedia.org/resource and the name `Auckland`.

Definition 4 (Prefix-Partitioned Bloom Filter). *A PPBF $\mathcal{B}^P$ is a 4-tuple $\mathcal{B}^P = \langle P, \hat{B}, \theta, H\rangle$ with the following elements:*

- *a set of prefixes P,*
- *a set of bit vectors $\hat{B}$,*
- *a prefix-mapping function $\theta : P \rightarrow \hat{B}$, and*
- *a set of hash functions H.*

All bit vectors in $\hat{B}$ have the same size. For each $p_i \in P$, $\mathcal{B}_i = (\theta(p_i), H)$, is the Bloom Filter that encodes the URIs' names with prefix p_i. $\mathcal{B}_i$ is called a partition of $\mathcal{B}^P$.

The false positive risk of $\mathcal{B}^P$, is given by its partition with the highest risk. A PPBF for a graph g is denoted $\mathcal{B}^P(g)$ and corresponds to the PPBF for the set of URIs in g. The cardinality of a PPBF is the sum its partitions' cardinalities.

Example 3 (Prefix-Partitioned Bloom Filter). Inserting a URI into an Unpartitioned Bloom Filter is visualized in Fig. 2a. Inserting the same URI into a PPBF is visualized in Fig. 2b. Only the name of the entity is hashed, and its hash values set bits only in the partition of its prefix.

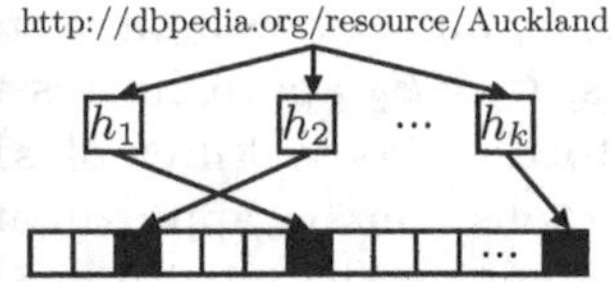

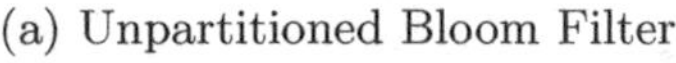

(a) Unpartitioned Bloom Filter

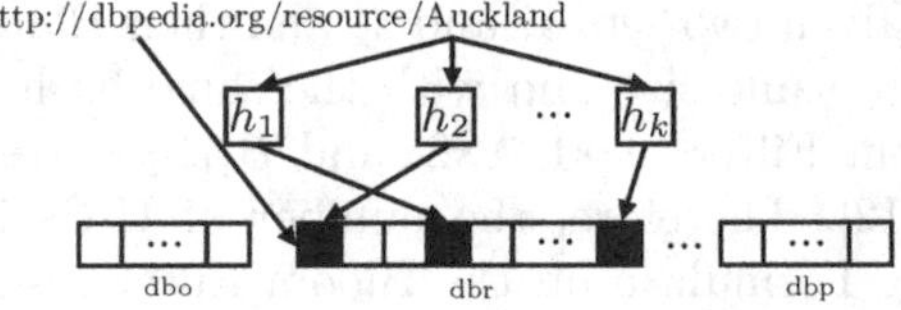

(b) Prefix-Partitioned Bloom Filter

Fig. 2. Insertion of a URI into an Unpartitioned Bloom Filter and a Prefix-Partitioned Bloom Filter. *dbo, dbr and dbp are short for prefixes from DBpedia,* `ontology`*,* `resource` *and* `property`*, respectively.*

For simplicity, we say that a URI u with prefix p may be in a PPBF $\mathcal{B}^P$, denoted $u \sqsubseteq \mathcal{B}^P$, iff all the positions given by the hash functions applied to u's name are set in the bit vector $\theta(p)$. Correspondingly, we say that a PPBF $\mathcal{B}^P$ is empty, denoted $\mathcal{B}^P = \emptyset$ iff no bit in any partition in $\mathcal{B}^P$ is set, or it has no partitions. Given that the intersection of two Bloom Filters is given by the bitwise and operation, the intersection of two PPBFs is given by:

Definition 5 (Prefix-Partitioned Bloom Filter Intersection). *The intersection of two PPBFs with the same set of hash functions H and bit vectors of the same size, denoted $\mathcal{B}_1^P \cap \mathcal{B}_2^P$, is $\mathcal{B}_1^P \cap \mathcal{B}_2^P = \langle P_\cap, \hat{B}_\cap, \theta_\cap, H\rangle$, where $P_\cap = \mathcal{B}_1^P.P \cap \mathcal{B}_2^P.P$, $\hat{B}_\cap = \{\mathcal{B}_1^P.\theta(p)$ **and** $\mathcal{B}_2^P.\theta(p) \mid p \in P_\cap\}$, and $\theta_\cap : P_\cap \rightarrow \hat{B}_\cap$.*

That is, partitions with the same prefix are intersected, while other partitions are not part of $\mathcal{B}_1^P \cap \mathcal{B}_2^P$. The intersection of two PPBFs thereby approximates the common URIs of the graphs that they represent, and Formula 5 can use used to approximate the number of common URIs.

Example 4 (Prefix-Partitioned Bloom Filter Intersection). The intersection of two Unpartitioned Bloom Filters is visualized in Fig. 3a. The intersection of two PPBFs is visualized in Fig. 3b.

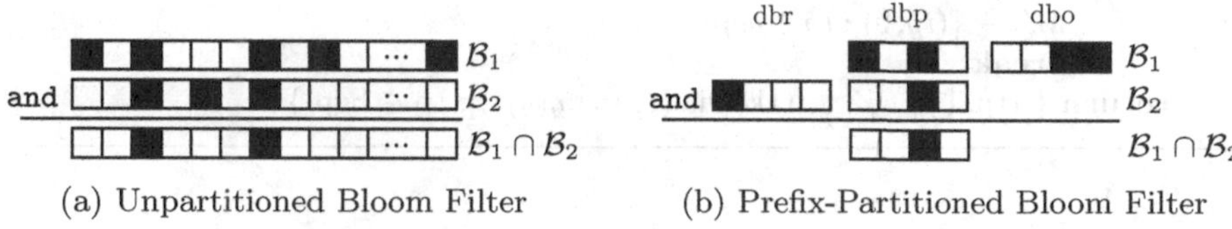

Fig. 3. Intersection of Unpartitioned Bloom Filters and Prefix-Partitioned Bloom Filters. *dbo, dbr and dbp are short for prefixes from DBpedia,* `ontology`, `resource` *and* `property`, *respectively.*

Building a PPBF for a graph is straightforward. For each URI in the graph, its prefix p identifies the relevant partition $\theta(p)$, and the application of hash functions H to its name determines the bits to set in $\theta(p)$. If θ is not defined for p, it is a bit vector with no bits set, before applying the hash functions.

The intersection of PPBFs can be used at query processing time to prune graphs if they do not have joinable entities for queries with a join variable, even if they contain corresponding URIs. Before execution time, each node can compute PPBFs for the graphs in its local datastore and download PPBFs from nodes in the neighborhood to compute the approximate number of URIs of the graphs in the local datastore in common with the reachable graphs. Any network maintenance strategy could be used to ensure regular updates in order to keep the approximations up-to-date, e.g. periodic shuffles [1].

Definition 6 (Prefix-Partitioned Bloom Filter Index). *Let $\mathcal{N}$ be the set of nodes, $\mathcal{U}$ the set of URIs, and $\mathcal{G}$ the set of graphs, a PPBF index is a tuple $I_P^i(n) = \langle \upsilon, \eta\rangle$ with $\upsilon : \mathcal{U} \rightarrow 2^{\mathcal{G}}$ and $\eta : \mathcal{G} \rightarrow 2^{\mathcal{N}}$. $\upsilon(u)$ returns the set of graphs gs such that $u \sqsubseteq \mathcal{B}^P(g)$, $\forall g \in gs$. $\eta(g)$ returns the set of nodes ns such that $g \in \mathcal{G}_{n_i}$ $\forall n_i \in ns$ and n_i is within i hops from n.*

Algorithm 1. Match BGP To PPBF Index

Input: BGP *bgp*; Node n; PPBF Index $I^i_P(n) = \langle \upsilon, \eta \rangle$
Output: Node Mapping M_n

1: **function** *matchBGPToPPBFIndex(bgp,n,I^i_P)*
2: $M_g \leftarrow \{$ (tp, range$(I^i_P(n).\upsilon) \cap \bigcap_{t \in uris(tp)} I^i_P(n).\upsilon(t))$: tp $\in$ bgp $\}$
3: $M'_g \leftarrow \{$ (tp, $\emptyset$) : tp $\in$ bgp $\}$
4: **for all** $tp_1, tp_2 \in$ bgp s.t. $vars(tp_1) \cap vars(tp_2) \neq \emptyset$ **do**
5: $G'_1, G'_2 \leftarrow \emptyset$
6: **for all** (g_1, g_2) s.t. $g_1 \in M_g(tp_1)$ and $g_2 \in M_g(tp_2)$ **do**
7: **if** $\mathcal{B}^P(g_1) \cap \mathcal{B}^P(g_2) \neq \emptyset$ **then**
8: $G'_1 \leftarrow G'_1 \cup \{g_1\}$
9: $G'_2 \leftarrow G'_2 \cup \{g_2\}$
10: **if** $G'_1 \neq \emptyset \wedge G'_2 \neq \emptyset$ **then**
11: $M'_g(tp_1) \leftarrow M'_g(tp_1) \cup \{G'_1\}$
12: $M'_g(tp_2) \leftarrow M'_g(tp_2) \cup \{G'_2\}$
13: **else**
14: $M'_g \leftarrow \{(tp, \emptyset) : tp \in bgp\}$
15: **break**
16: **return** $\{$ (tp, $\bigcup_{g \in M'_g(tp)}$ takeOne$(I^i_P(n).\eta(g)))$: tp $\in$ bgp $\}$

5.2 Matching Triple Patterns to Nodes

The relevant nodes for a triple pattern have graphs containing all URIs given in the triple pattern. PPBFs allow for efficiently checking if the graph has these URIs. Similarly to matching triple patterns using the locational index, first, we find the graphs with triples that match the triple patterns in the query. Then, for every pair of triple patterns that share a join variable, we prune graphs that, even if they are relevant for each triple pattern, do not have any common URI. Finally, the set of relevant nodes for each triple pattern is obtained, from these reduced set of relevant graphs, in the same way as when using the locational index.

Algorithm 1 shows how a PPBF index is used to identify the relevant nodes to evaluate the triple patterns in a BGP bgp. Given the PPBF index $I^i_P(n) = \langle \upsilon, \eta \rangle$, the graph mapping M_g, which associates triple patterns to set of graphs, is initialized (line 2) for every $tp \in bgp$ as the set of graphs gs such that $u \sqsubseteq \mathcal{B}^P(g)$ for all $g \in gs$ if the set of URIs in tp, $uris(tp)$, is not empty, or $range(I^i_P(n).\upsilon)$ otherwise. The function $uris(tp)$ returns the set of URIs in the triple pattern tp. Lines 4–15 select among all the relevant graphs for the triple patterns, computed in line 2, the ones that have some URIs in common for triple patterns with a common join variable. This is, the algorithm selects the graphs that may satisfy the join condition. The PPBFs of the relevant graphs, $\mathcal{B}^P(g_1)$ and $\mathcal{B}^P(g_2)$ are used to approximate if these graphs have any URI in common (line 7), and in such case, these graphs are selected as relevant for tp_1 and tp_2, respectively (lines 8–9). Once all the relevant graphs have been considered, if any of them have been selected, then the graph mapping M'_g is extended with values for the triple patterns tp_1 and tp_2 (lines 11–12). In other case, it is not possible to find answers for the given bgp and therefore the graph mapping M'_g is initialized again and the loop ends (lines 14–15). Finally, the node mapping M_n is computed in line 16 by using the selected graphs in M'_g and the function $I^i_P(n).\eta(g)$. The function *takeOne*(*ns*) returns one of the nodes in *ns*, if the number of hops between n and the nodes in ns is known, then *takeOne*(*ns*) could be implemented to take the node closest to n. In that case, if triple pattern tp is mapped to $\{g_1\}$, $I^i_P(n).\eta(g_1) = \{n_1, n_2\}$, and n_1 is closer to n than n_2, takeOne($\{n_1, n_2\}$)=n_1, and therefore $M_n(tp) = \{n_1\}$. The returned node mapping M_n specifies which nodes should be queried for each triple pattern.

Example 5 (Node Mapping). Consider the query Q in Listing 1.1 and the set of graphs in Fig. 1a and I^i_P in Table 1a. Applying Algorithm 1 to Q's bgp results in the set of mappings in Fig. 1b. Besides checking whether each URI in a triple pattern is contained within a PPBF, the algorithm prunes g_4 from the second triple pattern. This is the case, since $p_2, b \in \mathcal{B}^P(g_4)$, but $\mathcal{B}^P(g_4) \cap \mathcal{B}^P(g_3) = \emptyset$. Since g_3 is matched to the third triple pattern, and they join on ?v2, g_4 is pruned.

```
SELECT * WHERE {
   ?v1 p1 b    .
   b    p2 ?v2 .
   ?v2 p3 ?v3
}
```

Listing 1.1. Example query Q.

Table 1. PPBF index for a set of graphs and the resulting node mappings

(a) $I^i_P(n_1)$

u	v(u)	g	η(g)
p_1	$\{g_1, g_4\}$	g_1	$\{n_1\}$
p_2	$\{g_2, g_4\}$	g_2	$\{n_1, n_2\}$
p_3	$\{g_3\}$	g_3	$\{n_2, n_3\}$
b	$\{g_1, g_2, g_4\}$	g_4	$\{n_3\}$

(b) M_n

tp	$\mathbf{M_n(tp)}$
$(?v_1, p_1, b)$	$\{n_1\}$
$(b, p_2, ?v_2)$	$\{n_1\}$
$(?v_2, p_3, ?v_3)$	$\{n_2\}$

Using intersections of PPBFs allows for reducing the set of graphs to consider for a query. This is evident from our experiments (Sect. 7), where multiple intersections of PPBFs with common prefixes were indeed empty, and less data as a result was transferred between nodes.

6 Query Processing

For simplicity, and in-line with recent proposals on query processing [10,22], we assume that queries are evaluated triple pattern by triple pattern, and that expensive operations, such as joins, are executed locally at the issuer after executing relevant triple patterns over graphs on nodes identified by our indexes.

The evaluation of a triple pattern relies on evaluating the triple pattern against the graphs in the local repositories of a set of nodes. Therefore, we define operators to evaluate a triple pattern using either a locational or PPBF index.

Definitions 7 and 8 formally specify operators for retrieving a set of nodes given a triple pattern, using a locational index and PPBF index, respectively. Definition 9 then specifies an operator for evaluating a triple pattern given such a set of nodes.

Definition 7 (Locational Selection σ^L). *Let the function $\mathcal{I}(I_L^i(n), p)$ denote the set of nodes that is obtained by using $I_L^i(n)$ to find the relevant nodes to evaluate a triple pattern with predicate p, and $n_1 \in I_L^i(n)$ denote that $n_1 \in \eta(g)$ for some $g \in I_L^i(n).\gamma(p)$. Locational selection for a triple pattern tp on a locational index $I_L^i(n)$ of depth i, denoted $\sigma_{tp}^L(I_L^i(n))$, is the set $\{n_1 \mid n_1 \in I_L^i(n)\}$ if p_{tp} is a variable, or $\{n_1 \mid n_1 \in \mathcal{I}(I_L^i(n), p_{tp})\}$ otherwise.*

Definition 8 (PPBF Selection σ^P). *Let M_n be the node mapping obtained after applying Algorithm 1 to the BGP which includes tp in the query Q. Given a query Q, the PPBF selection for a triple pattern $tp \in bgp$ and bgp a BGP of Q, obtained using the PPBF index $I_P^i(n)$ of depth i, denoted $\sigma_{tp,Q}^P(I_P^i(n))$, is the selection of the nodes $M_n(tp)$.*

Definition 9 (Node Projection π^N). *Given a set of nodes $\mathcal{N}$, node projection on a triple pattern, denoted $\pi_{tp}^N(\mathcal{N})$, is the set of triples obtained by evaluating tp on the local datastore of the nodes in $\mathcal{N}$. Given the function $\mathcal{T}(n, tp)$, that evaluates tp on n's local datastore, node projection is formally defined as:* $\pi_{tp}^N(\mathcal{N}) = \bigcup_{n \in \mathcal{N}} \mathcal{T}(n, tp)$

Implementation Details. The proposed indexes can be used in a broad range of applications. However, motivated by recent efforts in the area of decentralization [1], we show their benefits in the context of an unstructured P2P system. Nodes in an unstructured P2P network often have a limited amount of space for datastores. As such, it does not make sense for a node to download entire graphs. Therefore, we adopt the basic setup outlined in PIQNIC [1]. That is, graphs are split into smaller subgraphs, called *fragments*, based on the predicate of the triples. Each fragment is replicated among multiple nodes. For our setup, we simply view a fragment as a graph and extend the original graph's name with the predicate in the subgraph. Hence, there is no need to encode predicates in PPBFs, which therefore only contain URIs that are either a subject or object in the fragment.

In PIQNIC, query processing is based on the brTPF [10] style of processing queries; triple patterns are flooded throughout the network individually, bound by previous mappings. Locational indexes and PPBFs are useful for avoiding flooding since the query processor can use them to identify precisely which nodes are to be queried. Specifically, a query Q at a node n is processed as follows:

1. Reorder triple patterns in Q based on selectivity. More selective triple patterns (estimated by variable counting) are evaluated first.

2. Evaluate each triple pattern $tp \in Q$ by the following steps:
   (a) Apply either locational selection (σ^L) or PPBF selection (σ^P) on n's local index in order to select the nodes N_{tp} that contain answers to tp.
   (b) For each node $n_i \in N_{tp}$, apply node projection (π^N) by evaluating tp on n_i's local datastore.
3. Compute the answer to the query by combining intermediate results from previous steps using the SPARQL operators specified in the query.

Since we use the brTPF style of query processing, the iterative process in step 2 is completed by sending bulks of bindings from previously evaluated triple patterns to the nodes selected by the indexes.

7 Evaluation

To evidence the gains in performance and potential benefits of using our proposed indexing schemes, we implemented locational indexes and PPBF indexes as a module in Java 8[3]. We modified Apache Jena[4] to use the indexes during query processing and extended PIQNIC [1] with support for our module in order to provide a fair comparison with an existing system.

7.1 Experimental Setup

Our experiments were run on a single server with 4xAMD Opteron 6373 processors, each with 16 cores (64 cores in total) running at 2.3 GHz, with 768 KB L1 cache and 16 MB L2 and L3 cache. The server has 516 GB RAM. We executed several experiments with variations of some parameters, such as *ttl*, replication factor, and number of neighbors. However, due to space restrictions, we only show the most relevant results in this section. Additional results can be found on our website[5]. The results presented in this section focus on experiments with the following parameters: 200 nodes, TTL: 5, number of neighbors per node: 5. The timeout was set to 1200 s (20 min). The replication factor was 5%, meaning that with 200 nodes, fragments were replicated on 10 nodes. While, in theory, these parameters should give nodes access to well over 200 nodes, in reality nodes within the same neighborhood often share some neighbors, giving them access to far less nodes. In our experiments, each node had, on average, access to 129.43 nodes. By increasing the TTL value to a sufficiently large number, our indexes could provide a global view, however as nodes are free to join and leave the network, keeping this global view up-to-date can easily become quite expensive. Each dataset was assigned to a random owner, which replicated the fragments across its neighborhood.

We use the queries and datasets in the extended LargeRDFBench [11]. LargeRDFBench comprises 13 different datasets, some of them interconnected, with

[3] The source code is available on our GitHub at https://github.com/Chraebe/PPBFs.
[4] https://jena.apache.org/.
[5] Additional results are available on our website at https://relweb.cs.aau.dk/ppbfs.

over 1 billion triples. It includes 40 SPARQL queries, divided into four sets: Simple (S), Complex (C), Large Data (L), and Complex and Large Data (CH). We measure the following metrics:

- *Execution Time (ET)*: The amount of time in milliseconds spent to process a given query.
- *Completeness (COM)*: The percentage of the query answers obtained by a system. To determine completeness, we computed the results in a centralized system and compared them to the results given by the decentralized setup.
- *Number of Transferred Bytes (NTB)*: The total number of transferred bytes between nodes in the network during query processing.
- *Number of Exchanged Messages (NEM)*: The total number of messages exchanged, in both directions, between nodes during query processing.

Queries were run sequentially on random nodes. At most 37 nodes were active at the same time during our experiments. We report averages over three runs.

Storage and Building Times. As we shall see, in most real cases PPBFs outperform locational indexes in terms of performance and data transfer. However, in our experiments, the index creation time was, on average 6,495 ms for locational indexes and 10,992 ms for PPBF indexes. PPBFs used 427 MB per node, while locational indexes used 685 KB per node. Furthermore, matching triple patterns to nodes is less complex for locational indexes. This means, that for cases where resources are limited, locational indexes might overall be the best choice, given that they still increase performance overall.

7.2 Experimental Results

During all experiments, we compared PIQNIC without modifications, PIQNIC with locational indexes, and PIQNIC with PPBF indexes. The objective is to verify that locational indexes and PPBF indexes can improve query processing, especially for the typically challenging queries.

Performance Gains Using Locational Indexes and PPBF Indexes. Figure 4 shows ET for query group S. The extended versions with locational indexes and PPBF indexes perform significantly better than the unmodified version for all the queries. Moreover, the version extended with PPBF indexes is more efficient than the version extended with locational indexes in all cases except queries S6 and S7. For queries S6 and S7, using the PPBF indexes does not allow for pruning any additional nodes than using the locational indexes, and so the slightly larger overhead of testing the graphs for common URIs leads to slightly larger query processing times. However, since all these times are below 100 ms, this is negligible compared to the improvements that PPBF indexes provide for other queries. Moreover, for query S9, a locational index does not help. This is due to a triple pattern where all constituents are variables. Because of this, the locational index returns all nodes within the neighborhood, the same set of nodes that PIQNIC uses. The version extended with the PPBF indexes is able to eliminate some of these nodes and thus improve performance.

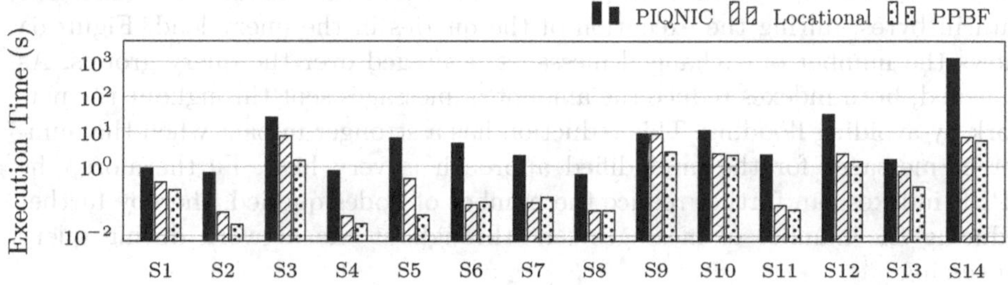

Fig. 4. ET for PIQNIC, PIQNIC with locational indexes, and PIQNIC with PPBF indexes over query group S. *Note that the y-axis is in log scale.*

Figure 5 shows ET for query groups L and CH. Generally, queries which were not computable before, are computable with PPBF indexes, alluding to a significantly improved performance. For some queries, such as S14, CH3 and CH6, the improvement was especially significant. Though, some especially large queries could not be processed within the time out. Given enough time, however, we were able to execute these with ET between 2K–10K s. The only exception was L5, which has proven to be particularly challenging for state of the art federated processors [11]. Even though we do not show the results for query group C, they showed the same pattern; an improvement in performance using locational indexes, and further improvement using PPBF indexes.

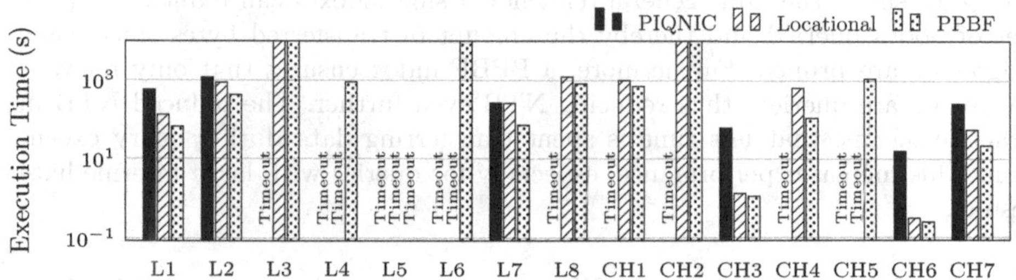

Fig. 5. ET for PIQNIC, PIQNIC with locational index, and PIQNIC with PPBF indexes over query groups L and CH. *Note that the y-axis is in log scale.*

In our experiments, all queries that finished had the same completeness for all approaches. Figure 6b shows the average COM over query groups. Since the indexes make query processing more efficient, we experienced fewer timeouts, which caused the higher completeness for some query groups.

Index Impact on Network Traffic. One of the major advantages of the indexes presented in this paper is the fact that flooding can be avoided, thus the number of messages exchanged between nodes is significantly reduced.

To evidence the improvement wrt. the network traffic, we measured the amount of messages exchanged between nodes, and the amount of transferred data in bytes, during the execution of the queries in the query load. Figure 6a shows the number of exchanged messages, averaged over the query groups. As expected, both indexes reduce the amount of messages sent throughout the network by avoiding flooding. This reduction has a stronger impact when the number of messages for the unmodified approach is very high. Furthermore, the PPBF indexes can further reduce the number of nodes queried, thereby further reducing the number of messages sent throughout the network during query processing.

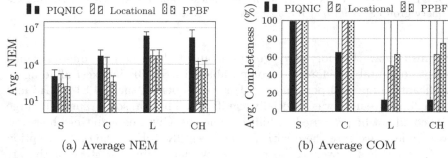

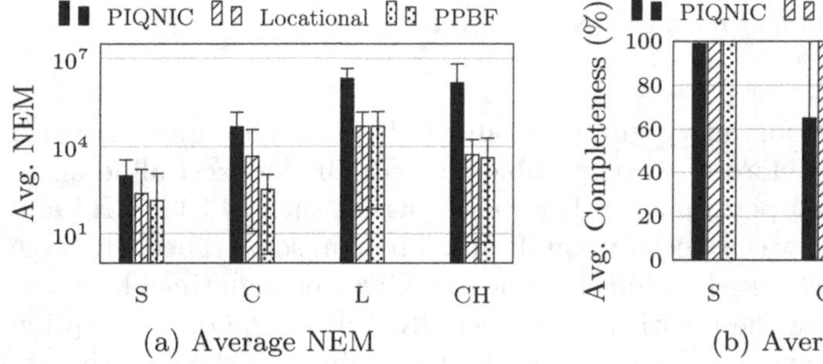

Fig. 6. Average NEM and COM for PIQNIC, locational index, and PPBFs over query groups. *Note that for (a), the y-axis is in log scale.*

The amount of transferred bytes during query execution (Fig. 7 for query group S), shows the same general tendency. Using indexes can reduce the number of nodes queried and thereby the amount of transferred bytes since some fragments are pruned. Furthermore, a PPBF index ensures that only relevant fragments are queried, thus reducing NTB even further. The reduced NTB in practice means, that less time is spent transferring data during query execution. This increases performance, especially for queries with large intermediate results.

Impact of Other Parameters. We ran experiments where we varied the time-to-live value, replication factor, and the number of neighbors for each node. For all these experiments, query execution times for the modified approaches were only negligibly affected by the varied network structure, since node matching still only require simple lookups. For the unmodified approach, query execution times were much more affected by the varied network structure. This means, that in terms of completeness, we saw a much greater improvement for the modified approaches than in Fig. 6b, since less queries were completed by the unmodified approach.

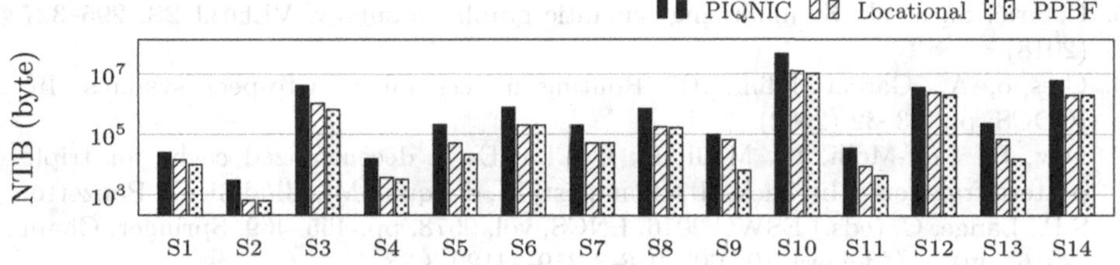

Fig. 7. NTB for PIQNIC, PIQNIC with locational index, and PIQNIC with PPBF indexes over query group S. *Note that the y-axis is in log scale.*

8 Conclusions

In this paper, we proposed two schemes for indexing RDF nodes in decentralized architectures: Locational Indexes and Prefix-Partitioned Bloom Filter (PPBF) indexes. Locational indexes establish a baseline, that PPBF indexes extend to provide much more precise indexes. PPBF indexes are based on Bloom Filters and provide summaries of the graph's constituents that are small enough to retrieve the indexes of the reachables nodes without using too much time or space. We implemented both indexing schemes in a module, that could be adapted for use in any decentralized architecture or federated query processing engine. Our experiments show, that both indexing schemes are able to reduce the amount of traffic within the network, and thereby improve query processing times. In the case of PPBF indexes, the improvement is more significant than for locational indexes. Using PPBFs during join processing to check if a fragment may contain matches given specific values to a join variable could further speed up query processing. This, and studying the impact of using filters with varying sizes, is part of our future work.

Acknowledgments. This research was partially funded by the Danish Council for Independent Research (DFF) under grant agreement no. DFF-8048-00051B & DFF-4093-00301B and Aalborg University's Talent Programme.

References

1. Aebeloe, C., Montoya, G., Hose, K.: A decentralized architecture for sharing and querying semantic data. In: Hitzler, P., et al. (eds.) ESWC 2019. LNCS, vol. 11503, pp. 3–18. Springer, Cham (2019). https://doi.org/10.1007/978-3-030-21348-0_1
2. Bloom, B.H.: Space/time trade-offs in hash coding with allowable errors. Commun. ACM **13**(7), 422–426 (1970)
3. Buil-Aranda, C., Hogan, A., Umbrich, J., Vandenbussche, P.-Y.: SPARQL web-querying infrastructure: ready for action? In: Alani, H., et al. (eds.) ISWC 2013. LNCS, vol. 8219, pp. 277–293. Springer, Heidelberg (2013). https://doi.org/10.1007/978-3-642-41338-4_18
4. Cai, M., Frank, M.R.: RDFPeers: a scalable distributed RDF repository based on a structured peer-to-peer network. In: WWW, pp. 650–657 (2004)

5. Čebirić, Š., et al.: Summarizing semantic graphs: a survey. VLDBJ **28**, 295–327 (2018)
6. Crespo, A., Garcia-Molina, H.: Routing indices for peer-to-peer systems. In: ICDCS, pp. 23–32 (2002)
7. Folz, P., Skaf-Molli, H., Molli, P.: CyCLaDEs: a decentralized cache for triple pattern fragments. In: Sack, H., Blomqvist, E., d'Aquin, M., Ghidini, C., Ponzetto, S.P., Lange, C. (eds.) ESWC 2016. LNCS, vol. 9678, pp. 455–469. Springer, Cham (2016). https://doi.org/10.1007/978-3-319-34129-3_28
8. Grall, A., et al.: Ladda: SPARQL queries in the fog of browsers. In: Blomqvist, E., Hose, K., Paulheim, H., Ławrynowicz, A., Ciravegna, F., Hartig, O. (eds.) ESWC 2017. LNCS, vol. 10577, pp. 126–131. Springer, Cham (2017). https://doi.org/10.1007/978-3-319-70407-4_24
9. Grall, A., Skaf-Molli, H., Molli, P.: SPARQL query execution in networks of web browsers. In: DeSemWeb@ISWC 2018 (2018)
10. Hartig, O., Aranda, C.B.: Bindings-restricted triple pattern fragments. In: Debruyne, C., et al. (eds.) OTM 2016. LNCS, vol. 10033, pp. 762–779. Springer, Cham (2016). https://doi.org/10.1007/978-3-319-48472-3_48
11. Hasnain, A., Saleem, M., Ngomo, A.N., Rebholz-Schuhmann, D.: Extending largeRDFBench for multi-source data at scale for SPARQL endpoint federation. In: SSWS@ISWC, pp. 203–218 (2018)
12. Jeffrey, M.C., Steffan, J.G.: Understanding bloom filter intersection for lazy address-set disambiguation. SPAA **2011**, 345–354 (2011)
13. Kaoudi, Z., Koubarakis, M., Kyzirakos, K., Miliaraki, I., Magiridou, M., Papadakis-Pesaresi, A.: Atlas: storing, updating and querying RDF(S) data on top of DHTs. J. Web Sem. **8**(4), 271–277 (2010)
14. Karnstedt, M., et al.: UniStore: querying a DHT-based universal storage. ICDE 2007, pp. 1503–1504 (2007)
15. Mansour, E., et al.: A demonstration of the solid platform for social web applications. In: WWW Companion, pp. 223–226 (2016)
16. Molli, P., Skaf-Molli, H.: Semantic web in the fog of browsers. In: DeSemWeb@ISWC 2017 (2017)
17. Montoya, G., Aebeloe, C., Hose, K.: Towards efficient query processing over heterogeneous RDF interfaces. In: ISWC 2018 Satellite Events, pp. 39–53 (2018)
18. Montoya, G., Skaf-Molli, H., Hose, K.: The odyssey approach for optimizing federated SPARQL queries. In: d'Amato, C., et al. (eds.) ISWC 2017. LNCS, vol. 10587, pp. 471–489. Springer, Cham (2017). https://doi.org/10.1007/978-3-319-68288-4_28
19. Papapetrou, O., Siberski, W., Nejdl, W.: Cardinality estimation and dynamic length adaptation for bloom filters. Distrib. Parallel Databases **28**(2–3), 119–156 (2010)
20. Tarkoma, S., Rothenberg, C.E., Lagerspetz, E.: Theory and practice of bloom filters for distributed systems. IEEE Commun. Surv. Tutor. **14**(1), 131–155 (2012)
21. Umbrich, J., Hose, K., Karnstedt, M., Harth, A., Polleres, A.: Comparing data summaries for processing live queries over linked data. WWW **14**(5–6), 495–544 (2011)
22. Verborgh, R., et al.: Triple pattern fragments: a low-cost knowledge graph interface for the web. J. Web Semant. **37–38**, 184–206 (2016)
23. Voulgaris, S., Gavidia, D., van Steen, M.: CYCLON: inexpensive membership management for unstructured P2P overlays. J. Netw. Syst. Manag. **13**(2), 197–217 (2005)

Datalog Materialisation in Distributed RDF Stores with Dynamic Data Exchange

Temitope Ajileye(✉), Boris Motik, and Ian Horrocks

Department of Computer Science, University of Oxford, Oxford, UK

Abstract. Several centralised RDF systems support datalog reasoning by precomputing and storing all logically implied triples using the well-known *seminaïve algorithm*. Large RDF datasets often exceed the capacity of centralised RDF systems, and a common solution is to distribute the datasets in a cluster of shared-nothing servers. While numerous distributed query answering techniques are known, distributed seminaïve evaluation of arbitrary datalog rules is less understood. In fact, most distributed RDF stores either support no reasoning or can handle only limited datalog fragments. In this paper, we extend the *dynamic data exchange* approach for distributed query answering by Potter et al. [13] to a reasoning algorithm that can handle arbitrary rules while preserving important properties such as nonrepetition of inferences. We also show empirically that our algorithm scales well to very large RDF datasets.

1 Introduction

Reasoning with datalog rules over RDF data plays a key role on the Semantic Web. Datalog can capture the structure of an application domain using if-then rules, and OWL 2 RL ontologies can be translated into datalog rules. Datalog reasoning is supported in several RDF management systems such as Oracle's database [8], GraphDB,[1] Amazon Neptune,[2] VLog [18], and RDFox [11].[3] All of these system use a *materialisation* approach to reasoning, where all facts implied by the dataset and the rules are precomputed and stored in a preprocessing step. This is usually done using the *seminaïve algorithm* [2], which ensures the *nonrepetition property*: no rule is applied to the same facts more than once.

Many RDF management systems are *centralised* in that they store and process all data on a single server. To scale to workloads that cannot fit into a single server, it is common to distribute the data in a cluster of interconnected, shared-nothing servers and use a distributed query answering strategy. Abdelaziz et al. [1] present a comprehensive survey of 22 approaches to distributed query answering, and Potter et al. [13] discuss several additional systems. There is considerable variation between these approaches: some use data replication, some

[1] http://graphdb.ontotext.com/.

[2] http://aws.amazon.com/neptune/.

[3] http://www.cs.ox.ac.uk/isg/tools/RDFox/.

C. Ghidini et al. (Eds.): ISWC 2019, LNCS 11778, pp. 21–37, 2019.
https://doi.org/10.1007/978-3-030-30793-6_2

compute joins on a dedicated server, others use distributed join algorithms, and many leverage big data frameworks such as Hadoop and Spark for data storage and query processing. In contrast, distributed datalog materialisation is less well understood, and it is more technically challenging. Newly derived facts must be stored so that they can be taken into account in future rule applications, but without repeating derivations. Moreover, synchronisation between rule applications should be reduced to allow parallel computation.

Several theoretical frameworks developed in the 90s aim to address these questions [5,14,16,20,22]. As we discuss in more detail in Sect. 3, they constrain the rules so that each server performs only certain rule applications, and they send the derived facts to all servers where these facts could participate in further rule applications. Thus, the same facts can be stored on more than one server, which can severely limit the scalability of such systems.

The Semantic Web community has recently developed several RDF-specific approaches. A number of them are hardwired to fixed datalog rules, such as RDFS [7,19] or the so-called *ter Horst fragment* [6,17]. Focusing on a fixed set of rules considerably simplifies the problem. PLogSPARK [21] and SPOWL [10] handle arbitrary rules, but they do not seem to use seminaïve evaluation. Finally, several probabilistic algorithms aim to handle large datasets [10,12], but these approaches are approximate and are thus unsuitable for many applications. Distributed SociaLite [15] is the only system we are aware of that provides seminaïve evaluation for arbitrary datalog rules. It uses a custom graph model, but the approach can readily be adapted to RDF. Moreover, its rules must explicitly encode the communication and storage strategy, which increases complexity.

In this paper we present a new technique for distributed materialisation of arbitrary datalog rules. Unlike SociaLite, we do not require any distributed processing hints in the rules. We also do not duplicate any data and thus remove an obstacle to scalability. Our approach is based on the earlier work by Potter et al. [13] on distributed query answering using *dynamic data exchange*, from which it inherits several important properties. First, inferences that can be made within a single server do not require any communication; coupled with careful data partitioning, this can very effectively minimise network communication. Second, rule evaluation is completely asynchronous, which promotes parallelism. This, however, introduces a complication: to ensure nonrepetition of inferences, we must be able to partially order rule derivations across the cluster, which we achieve using *Lamport timestamps* [9]. We discuss the motivation and the novelty in more detail in Sect. 3, and in Sect. 4 we present the approach formally.

We have implemented our approach in a new prototype system called DMAT, and in Sect. 5 we present the results of our empirical evaluation. We compared DMAT with WebPIE [17], investigated how it scales with increasing data loads, and compared it with RDFox to understand the impact of distribution on concurrency. Our results show that DMAT outperforms WebPIE by an order of magnitude (albeit with some differences in the setting), and that it can handle well increasing data loads; moreover, DMAT's performance is comparable to that of RDFox on a single server. Our algorithms are thus a welcome addition to the techniques for implementing truly scalable semantic systems.

2 Preliminaries

We now recapitulate the syntax and the semantics of RDF and datalog. A *constant* is an IRI, a blank node, or a literal. A *term* is a constant or a *variable*. An *atom* a has the form $a = \langle t_s, t_p, t_o \rangle$ over terms t_s (*subject*), t_p (*predicate*), and t_o (*object*). A *fact* is an variable-free atom. A *dataset* is a finite set of facts.

Since the focus of our work is on datalog reasoning, we chose to follow terminology commonly used in datalog literature. Constants are often called *RDF terms* in RDF literature, but we do not use this notion to avoid confusion with datalog terms, which include variables. For the sake of consistency, we then use the datalog notions of atoms, facts, and datasets, instead of the corresponding RDF notions of *triple patterns*, *triples*, and *RDF graphs*, respectively.

We define the set of *positions* as $\Pi = \{s, p, o\}$. Then, for $a = \langle t_s, t_p, t_o \rangle$ and $\pi \in \Pi$, we define $a|_\pi = t_\pi$—that is, $a|_\pi$ is the term that occurs in a at position π. A *substitution* σ is a partial function that maps finitely many variables to constants. For α a term or an atom, $\alpha\sigma$ is the result of replacing with $\sigma(x)$ each occurrence of a variable x in α on which σ is defined.

A *query* Q is a conjunction of atoms $a_1 \wedge \dots \wedge a_n$. Substitution σ is an *answer* to Q on a dataset I if $a_i\sigma \in I$ holds for each $1 \leq i \leq n$.

A datalog *rule* r is an implication of the form $h \leftarrow b_1 \wedge \dots \wedge b_n$, where h is the *head* atom, all b_i are *body* atoms, and each variable occurring in h also occurs in some b_i. A datalog *program* is a finite set of rules. Let I be a dataset. The result of applying r to I is $r(I) = I \cup \{h\sigma \mid \sigma \text{ is an answer to } b_1 \wedge \dots \wedge b_n \text{ on } I\}$. For P a program, let $P(I) = \bigcup_{r \in P} r(I)$; let $P^0(I) = I$; and let $P^{i+1}(I) = P(P^i(I))$ for $i \geq 0$. Then, $P^\infty(I) = \bigcup_{i \geq 0} P^i(I)$ is the *materialisation* of P on I. This paper deals with the problem of computing $P^\infty(I)$ where I is distributed across of a cluster of servers such that each fact is stored in precisely one server.

3 Motivation and Related Work

We can compute $P^\infty(I)$ using the definition in Sect. 2: we evaluate the body of each rule $r \in P$ as a query over I and instantiate the head of r for each query answer, we eliminate duplicate facts, and we repeat the process until no new facts can be derived. However, since $P^i(I) \subseteq P^{i+1}(I)$ holds for each $i \geq 0$, such a *naïve* approach repeats in each round of rule applications the work from all previous rounds. The *seminaive strategy* [2] avoids this problem: when matching a rule r in round $i + 1$, at least one body atom of r must be matched to a fact derived in round i. We next discuss now these ideas are implemented in the existing approaches to distributed materialisation, and then we present an overview of our approach and discuss its novelty.

3.1 Related Approaches to Distributed Materialisation

Several approaches to distributed reasoning partition rule applications across servers. For example, to evaluate rule $\langle x, R, z\rangle \leftarrow \langle x, R, y\rangle \wedge \langle y, R, z\rangle$ on ℓ servers, one can let each server i with $1 \leq i \leq \ell$ evaluate rule

$$\langle x, R, z\rangle \leftarrow \langle x, R, y\rangle \wedge \langle y, R, z\rangle \wedge h(y) = i, \tag{1}$$

where $h(y)$ is a *partition function* that maps values of y to integers between 1 and ℓ. If h is uniform, then each server receives roughly the same fraction of the workload, which benefits parallelisation. However, since a triple of the form $\langle s, R, o\rangle$ can match either atom in the body of (1), each such triple must be replicated to servers $h(s)$ and $h(o)$ so they can participate in rule applications. Based on this idea, Ganguly et al. [5] show how to handle general datalog; Zhang et al. [22] study different partition functions; Seib and Lausen [14] identify programs and partition functions where no replication of derived facts is needed; Shao et al. [16] further break rules in segments; and Wolfson and Ozeri [20] replicate all facts to all servers. The primary motivation behind these approaches seems to be parallelisation of computation, which explains why the high rates of data replication were not seen as a problem. However, high replication rates are not acceptable when data distribution is used to increase a system's capacity.

Materialisation can also be implemented without any data replication. First, one must select a triple partitioning strategy: a common approach is to assign each $\langle s, p, o\rangle$ to server $h(s)$ for a suitable hash function h, and another popular option is to use a distributed file system (e.g., HDFS) and thus leverage its partitioning mechanism. Then, one can evaluate the rules using a suitable distributed query algorithm and distribute the newly derived triples using the partitioning strategy. These principles were used to realise RDFS reasoning [7,19], and they are also implicitly present in approaches implemented on top of big data frameworks such as Hadoop [17] and Spark [6,10,21]. However, most of these can handle only fixed rule sets, which considerably simplifies algorithm design. For example, seminaïve evaluation is not needed in the RDFS fragment since these nonrepetition of inferences can be ensured by evaluating rules in a particular order [6]. PLogSPARK [21] and SPOWL [10] handle arbitrary rules using the naïve algorithm, which can be detrimental when programs are complex.

Distributed SociaLite [15] is the only system known to us that implements distributed seminaïve evaluation for general datalog. It requires users to explicitly specify the data distribution strategy and communication patterns. For example, by writing a fact $R(a, b)$ as $R[a](b)$, one can specify that the fact is to be stored on server $h(a)$ for some hash function h. Rule (1) can then be written in SociaLite as $R[x](z) \leftarrow R[x](y) \wedge R[y](z)$, specifying that the rule should be evaluated by sending each fact $R[a](b)$ to server $h(b)$, joining such facts with $R[b](c)$, and sending the resulting facts $R[a](c)$ to server $h(a)$. While the evaluation of some of these rules can be parallelised, all servers in a cluster must synchronise after each round of rule application.

3.2 Dynamic Data Exchange for Query Answering

Before describing our approach to distributed datalog materialisation, we next recapitulate the earlier work by Potter et al. [13] on distributed query answering using *dynamic data exchange*, which provides the foundation for our work.

This approach to query answering assumes that all triples are partitioned into ℓ mutually disjoint datasets $I_1, \ldots, I_\ell$, with ℓ being the number of servers. The main objectives of dynamic exchange are to reduce communication and eliminate synchronisation between servers. To achieve the former goal, each server k maintains three *occurrence mappings* $\mu_{k,s}$, $\mu_{k,p}$, and $\mu_{k,o}$. For each constant c occurring in I_k, set $\mu_{k,s}(c)$ contains all servers where c occurs in the subject position, and $\mu_{k,p}(c)$ and $\mu_{k,o}(c)$ provide analogous information for the predicate and object positions. To understand how occurrences are used, consider evaluating $Q = \langle x, R, y \rangle \wedge \langle y, R, z \rangle$ over datasets $I_1 = \{\langle a, R, b \rangle, \langle b, R, c \rangle\}$ and $I_2 = \{\langle b, R, d \rangle, \langle d, R, e \rangle\}$. Both servers evaluate Q using index nested loop joins. Thus, server 1 evaluates $\langle x, R, y \rangle$ over I_1, which produces a *partial* answer $\sigma_1 = \{x \mapsto a, y \mapsto b\}$. Server 1 then evaluates $\langle y, R, z \rangle \sigma_1 = \langle b, R, z \rangle$ over I_1 and thus obtains one full answer $\sigma_2 = \{x \mapsto a, y \mapsto b, z \mapsto c\}$. To see whether $\langle b, R, z \rangle$ can be matched on other servers, server 1 consults its occurrence mappings for all constants in the atom. Since $\mu_{1,s}(b) = \mu_{1,p}(R) = \{1, 2\}$, server 1 sends the partial answer σ_1 to server 2, telling it to continue matching the query. After receiving σ_1, server 2 matches atom $\langle b, R, z \rangle$ in I_2 to obtain another full answer $\sigma_3 = \{x \mapsto a, y \mapsto b, z \mapsto d\}$. However, server 2 also evaluates $\langle x, R, y \rangle$ over I_2, obtaining partial answer $\sigma_4 = \{x \mapsto b, y \mapsto d\}$, and it consults its occurrences to determine which servers can match $\langle y, R, z \rangle \sigma_4 = \langle d, R, z \rangle$. Since $\mu_{2,s}(d) = \{2\}$, server 2 knows it is the only one that can match this atom, so it proceeds without any communication and computes $\sigma_5 = \{x \mapsto b, y \mapsto d, z \mapsto e\}$.

This strategy has several important benefits. First, all answers that can be produced within a single server, such as σ_5 in our example, are produced without any communication. Second, the location of every constant is explicitly recorded, rather than computed using a fixed rule such as a hash function. We use this to partition a graph based on its structural properties and thus collocate highly interconnected constants. Combined with the first property, this can significantly reduce network communication. Third, the system is completely asynchronous: when server 1 sends σ_1 to server 2, server 1 does not need to wait for server 2 to finish, and server 2 can process σ_1 whenever it can. This eliminates the need for synchronisation between servers, which is beneficial for parallelisation.

3.3 Our Contribution

In this paper we extend the dynamic data exchange framework to datalog materialisation. We draw inspiration from the work by Motik et al. [11] on parallelising datalog materialisation in centralised, shared memory systems. Intuitively, their algorithm considers each triple in the dataset, identifies each rule and body atom that can be matched to the triple, and evaluates the rest of the rule as a query.

This approach is amenable to parallelisation since distinct processors can simultaneously process distinct triples; since the number of triples is generally very large, the likelihood of workload skew among processors is very low.

Our distributed materialisation algorithm is based on the same general principle: each server matches the rules to locally stored triples, but the resulting queries are evaluated using dynamic data exchange. This approach requires no synchronisation between servers, and it reduces communication in the same way as described in Sect. 3.2. We thus expect our approach to exhibit the same good properties as the approach to query answering by Potter et al. [13].

The lack of synchronisation between servers introduces a technical complication. Remember that, to avoid repeating derivations, at least one body atom in a rule must be matched to a fact derived in the previous round of rule application. However, due to asynchronous rule application, there is no global notion of a rule application round (unlike, say, in SociaLite). A naïve solution would be to associate each fact with a timestamp recording when the fact has derived in hope that the order of fact derivation could be recovered by comparing timestamps. However, this would require maintaining a high coherence of server clocks in the cluster, which is generally impractical. Instead, we use Lamport timestamps [9], which provide us with a simple way of determining a partial order of events across a cluster. We describe this technique in more detail in Sect. 4.

Another complication is due to the fact that the occurrence mappings stored in the servers may need to be updated due to the derivation of new triples. For completeness, it is critical that all servers are updated before such triples are used in rule applications. Our solution to this problem is fully asynchronous, which again benefits parallelisation.

Finally, since no central coordinator keeps track of the state of the computation of different servers, detecting when the system as a whole can terminate is not straightforward. We solve this problem using a well-known termination detection algorithm based on token passing [4].

4 Distributed Materialisation Algorithm

We now present our distributed materialisation algorithm and prove its correctness. We present the algorithm in steps. In Sect. 4.1 we discuss data structures that the servers use to store their triples and implement Lamport timestamps. In Sect. 4.2 we discuss the occurrence mappings. In Sect. 4.3 we discuss the communication infrastructure and the message types used. In Sect. 4.4 we present the algorithm's pseudocode. In Sect. 4.5 we discuss how to detect termination. Finally, in Sect. 4.6 we argue about the algorithm's correctness.

4.1 Adding Lamport Timestamps to Triples

As already mentioned, to avoid repeating derivations, our algorithm uses Lamport timestamps [9], which is a technique for establishing a causal order of events in a distributed system. If all servers in the system could share a global clock, we could trivially associate each event with a global timestamp, which would allow us to recover the 'happens-before' relationship between events by comparing timestamps. However, maintaining a precise global clock in a distributed system is technically very challenging, and Lamport timestamps provide a much simpler solution. In particular, each event is annotated an integer timestamp in a way that guarantees the following property $(*)$:

> if there is any way for an event A to possibly influence an event B, then the timestamp of A is strictly smaller then the timestamp of B.

To achieve this, each server maintains a local integer clock that is incremented each time an event of interest occurs, which clearly ensures $(*)$ if A and B occur within one server. Now assume that A occurs in server s_1 and B occurs in s_2; clearly, A can influence B only if s_1 sends a message to s_2, and s_2 processes this message before event B takes place. To ensure that property $(*)$ holds in such a case as well, server s_1 includes its current clock value into the message it sends to s_2; moreover, when processing this message, server s_2 updates its local clock to the maximum of the message clock and the local clock, and then increments the local clock. Thus, when B happens after receiving the message, it is guaranteed to have a timestamp that is larger than the timestamp of A.

To map this idea to datalog materialisation, a derivation of a fact corresponds to the notion of an event, and using a fact to derive another fact corresponds to the 'influences' notion. Thus, we associates facts with integer timestamps.

More precisely, each server k in the cluster maintains an integer C_k called the *local clock*, a set I_k of the derived triples, and a partial function $T_k : I_k \rightarrow \mathbb{N}$ that associates triples with natural numbers. Function T_k is partial because timestamps are not assigned to facts upon derivation, but during timestamp synchronisation. Before the algorithm is started, C_k must be initialised to zero, and all input facts (i.e., the facts given by the user) partitioned to server k should be loaded into I_k and assigned a timestamp of zero.

To capture formally how timestamps are used during query evaluation, we introduce the notion of an *annotated query* as a conjunction of the form

$$Q = a_1^{\bowtie_1} \wedge \cdots \wedge a_n^{\bowtie_n}, \tag{2}$$

where each $a_i^{\bowtie_i}$ is called an *annotated atom* and it consists of an atom a_i and a symbol $\bowtie_i$ which can be $<$ or $\leq$. An annotated query requires a timestamp to be evaluated. More precisely, a substitution σ is an answer to Q on I_k and T_k w.r.t. a timestamp τ if (i) σ is an answer to the 'ordinary' query $a_1 \wedge \cdots \wedge a_n$ on I_k, and (ii) for each $1 \leq i \leq n$, the value of T_k is defined for $a_i\sigma$ and it satisfies $T_k(a_i\sigma) \bowtie \tau$. For example, let Q, I, and T be as follows, and let $\tau = 2$.

$$Q = \langle x, R, y\rangle^{<} \wedge \langle y, S, z\rangle^{\leq} \qquad I = \{\langle a, R, b\rangle, \langle b, S, c\rangle, \langle b, S, d\rangle, \langle b, S, e\rangle\}$$
$$T = \{\langle a, R, b\rangle \mapsto 1,\ \langle b, S, c\rangle \mapsto 2,\ \langle b, S, d\rangle \mapsto 3\}$$

Then, $\sigma_1 = \{x \mapsto a, y \mapsto b, z \mapsto c\}$ is an answer to Q on I and T w.r.t. τ. In contrast, $\sigma_2 = \{x \mapsto a, y \mapsto b, z \mapsto d\}$ is not an answer to Q on I and T w.r.t. τ

due to $T(\langle b, S, d \rangle) \geq 2$, and $\sigma_3 = \{x \mapsto a, y \mapsto b, z \mapsto e\}$ is not an answer because the timestamp of $\langle b, S, e \rangle$ is undefined.

To incorporate this notion into our algorithm, we assume that each server can evaluate a single annotated atom. Specifically, given an annotated $a^{\bowtie}$, a timestamp τ, and a substitution σ, server k can call $\text{EVALUATE}(a^{\bowtie}, \tau, I_k, T_k, \sigma)$. The call returns each substitution ρ defined over the variables in a and σ such that $\sigma \subseteq \rho$ holds, $a\rho \in I_k$ holds, and T_k is defied on $a\rho$ and it satisfies $T(a\rho) \bowtie \tau$. In other words, EVALUATE matches $a^{\bowtie}$ in I_k and T_k w.r.t. τ and it returns each extension of σ that agrees with $a^{\bowtie}$ and τ. For efficiency, server k should index the facts in I_k; any RDF indexing scheme can be used, and one can modify index lookup to simply skip over facts whose timestamps do not match τ.

Finally, we describe how rule matching is mapped to answering annotated queries. Let P be a datalog program to be materialised. Given a fact f, function $\text{MATCHRULES}(f, P)$ considers each rule $h \leftarrow b_1 \wedge \cdots \wedge b_n \in P$ and each body atom b_p with $1 \leq p \leq n$, and, for each substitution σ over the variables of b_p where $f = b_p\sigma$, it returns (σ, b_p, Q, h) where Q is the annotated query

$$b_1^{<} \wedge \cdots \wedge b_{p-1}^{<} \wedge b_{p+1}^{\leq} \wedge \cdots \wedge b_n^{\leq}. \quad (3)$$

Intuitively, MATCHRULES identifies each rule and each *pivot* body atom b_p that can be matched to f via substitution σ. This σ will be extended to all body atoms of the rule by matching all remaining atoms in nested loops using function EVALUATE. The annotations in (3) specify how to match the remaining atoms without repetition: facts matched to atoms before (resp. after) the pivot must have timestamps strictly smaller (resp. smaller or equal) than the timestamp of f. As is usual in query evaluation, the atoms of (3) may need to be reordered to obtain an efficient query plan. This can be achieved using any known technique, and further discussion of this issue is out of scope of this paper.

4.2 Occurrence Mappings

To decide whether rule matching may need to proceed on other servers, each server k must store indexes $\mu_{k,s}$, $\mu_{k,p}$, and $\mu_{k,o}$, called *occurrence mappings*, that map constants to sets of server IDs. We say that a constant c is *local* to server k is c occurs in I_k at any position. To ensure scalability, $\mu_{k,s}$, $\mu_{k,p}$, and $\mu_{k,o}$ need only to be defined on local constants: if, say, $\mu_{k,s}$ is not defined on constant c, we will assume that c can occur on any server. However, these mappings will need to be correct during algorithm's execution: if a constant c is local to I_k, and if c occurs on some other server j in position π, then $\mu_{k,\pi}$ must be defined on c and it must contain j. Moreover, all servers will have to know the initial locations of all constants occurring in the heads of the rules in P.

Storing only partial occurrences at each server introduces a complication: when a server processes a partial match σ received from another server, its local occurrence mappings may not cover some of the constants in σ. Potter et al. [13] solve this by accompanying each partial match σ with a vector $\boldsymbol{\lambda} = \lambda_s, \lambda_p, \lambda_o$ of *partial occurrences*. Whenever a server extends σ by matching an atom, it also records in $\boldsymbol{\lambda}$ its local occurrences for each constant added to σ so that this information can be propagated to subsequent servers.

Occurrence mappings are initialised on each server k for each constant that initially occurs in I_k, but they may need to be updated as fresh triples are derived. To ensure that the occurrences correctly reflect the distribution of constants at all times, occurrence mappings of all servers must be updated *before* a triple can be added to the set of derived triples of the target server.

Our algorithm must decide where to store each freshly derived triple. It is common practice in distributed RDF systems to store all triples with the same subject on the same server. This is beneficial since it allows subject–subject joins—the most common type of join in practice—to be answered without any communication. We follow this well-established practice and ensure that the derived triples are grouped by subject. Consequently, we require that $\mu_{k,s}(c)$, whenever it is defined, contains exactly one server. Thus, to decide where to store a derived triple, the server from the subject's occurrences is used, and, if the subject occurrences are unavailable, then a predetermined server is used.

4.3 Communication Infrastructure and Message Types

We assume that the servers can communicate asynchronously by passing messages: each server can call $\textsc{Send}(m, d)$ to send a message m to a destination server d. This function can return immediately, and the receiver can processes the message later. Also, our core algorithm is correct as long as each sent message is processed eventually, regardless of whether the messages are processed in the order in which they are sent between servers. We next describe the two types of message used in our algorithm. The approach used to detect termination can introduce other message types and might place constraints on the order of message delivery; we discuss this in more detail in Sect. 4.5.

Message $\mathsf{PAR}[i, \sigma, Q, h, \tau, \boldsymbol{\lambda}]$ informs a server that σ is a partial match obtained by matching some fact with timestamp τ to the body of a rule with head atom h; moreover, the remaining atoms to be matched are given by an annotated query Q starting from the atom with index i. The partial occurrences for all constants mentioned in σ are recorded in $\boldsymbol{\lambda}$.

Message $\mathsf{FCT}[f, D, k_h, \tau, \boldsymbol{\lambda}]$ says that f is a freshly derived fact that should be stored at server k_h. Set D contains servers whose occurrences must be updated due to the addition of f. Timestamp τ corresponds to the time at which the message was sent. Finally, $\boldsymbol{\lambda}$ are the partial occurrences for the constants in f.

Potter et al. [13] already observed PAR messages correspond to partial join results so a large number of such messages can be produced during query evaluation. To facilitate asynchronous processing, the PAR messages may need to be buffered on the receiving server, which can easily require excessive space. They also presented a flow control mechanism that can be used to restrict memory consumption at each server without jeopardising completeness. This solution is directly applicable to our problem as well, so we do not discuss it any further.

4.4 The Algorithm

With these definitions in mind, Algorithms 1 and 2 comprise our approach to distributed datalog materialisation. Before starting, each server k loads its subset of the input RDF graph into I_k, sets the timestamp of each fact in I_k to zero, initialises C_k to zero, and receives the copy of the program P to be materialised. The server then starts an arbitrary number of server threads, each executing the SERVERTHREAD function. Each thread repeatedly processes either an unprocessed fact f in I_k or an unprocessed message m; if both are available, they can be processed in arbitrary order. Otherwise, the termination condition is processed as we discuss later in Sect. 4.5.

Function SYNCHRONISE updates the local clock C_k with a timestamp τ. This must be done in a critical section (i.e., two threads should not execute it simultaneously). The local clock is updated if $C_k \leq \tau$ holds; moreover, all facts in I_k without a timestamp are timestamped with C_k since they are derived before the event corresponding to τ. Assigning timestamps to facts in this way reduces the need for synchronising access to C_k between threads.

Function PROCESSFACT kickstarts the matching of the rules to fact f. After synchronising the clock with the timestamp of f, the function simply calls the MATCHRULES function to identify all rules where one atom matches to f, and then it calls the FINISHMATCH function to finish matching the pivot atom.

A PAR message is processed by matching atom $a_i^{\bowtie_i}$ of the annotated query in I_k and T_k w.r.t. τ, and forwarding each match to FINISHMATCH.

A FCT message informs server k that fact f will be added to the set I_{k_h} of facts derived at server k_h. Set D lists all remaining servers that need to be informed of the addition, and partial occurrences $\boldsymbol{\lambda}$ are guaranteed to correctly reflect the occurrences of each constant in f. Server k updates its $\mu_{k,\pi}(c)$ by appending $\lambda_\pi(c)$ (line 19). Since servers can simultaneously process FCT messages, server k adds to D all servers that might have been added to $\mu_{k,\pi}(c)$ since the point when $\lambda_\pi(c)$ had been constructed (line 18), and it also updates $\lambda_\pi(c)$ (line 19). Finally, the server adds f to I_k if k is the last server (line 20), and otherwise it forwards the message to another server d form D.

Function FINISHMATCH finishes matching atom a_{last} by (i) extending $\boldsymbol{\lambda}$ with the occurrences of all constants that might be relevant for the remaining body atoms or the rule head, and (ii) either matching the next body atom or deriving the rule head. For the former task, the algorithm identifies in line 30 each variable x in the matched atom that either occurs in the rule head or in a remaining atom, and for each π it adds the occurrences of $x\sigma$ to λ_π. Now if Q has been matched completely (line 31), the server also ensures that the partial occurrences are correctly defined for the constants occurring in the rule head (lines 32–33), it identifies the server k_h that should receive the derived fact as described in Sect. 4.2, it identifies the set D of the destination servers whose occurrences need to be updated, and it sends the FCT message to one server from D. Otherwise, atom $a_{i+i}\sigma$ must be matched next. To determine the set D of servers that could possibly match this atom, server k intersects the occurrences of each constant from $a_{i+i}\sigma$ (line 44) and sends a PAR message to all servers in D.

Algorithm 1. Distributed Materialisation Algorithm at Server k

function ServerThread
  while cannot terminate **do**
    if I_k contains an unprocessed fact f, or a message m is pending **then**
      ProcessFact(f) or ProcessMessage(m), as appropriate
    else if the termination token has been received **then**
      Process the termination token

function ProcessFact(f)
  Synchronise($T_k(f)$)
  for each $(\sigma, a, Q, h) \in$ MatchRules(f, P) **do**
    FinishMatch($0, \sigma, a, Q, h, T_k(f), \boldsymbol{\emptyset}$)

function ProcessMessage($\mathsf{PAR}[i, \sigma, Q, h, \tau, \boldsymbol{\lambda}]$) where $Q = a_1^{\bowtie_1} \wedge \cdots \wedge a_n^{\bowtie_n}$
  Synchronise(τ)
  for each substitution $\sigma' \in$ Evaluate($a_i^{\bowtie_i}, \tau, I_k, T_k, \sigma$) **do**
    FinishMatch($i, \sigma', a_i, Q, h, \tau, \boldsymbol{\lambda}$)

function ProcessMessage($\mathsf{FCT}[f, D, k_h, \tau, \boldsymbol{\lambda}]$)
  Synchronise(τ)
  for each constant c in f and each position $\pi \in \Pi$ **do**
    $D := D \cup [\mu_{k,\pi}(c) \setminus \lambda_\pi(c)]$
    $\lambda_\pi(c) := \mu_{k,\pi}(c) := \lambda_\pi(c) \cup \mu_{k,\pi}(c)$
  if $D = \emptyset$ **then** Add f to I_k
  else
    Remove an element d from D, preferring any element over k_h if possible
    Send($\mathsf{FCT}[f, D, k_h, C_k, \boldsymbol{\lambda}], d$)

function Synchronise(τ) (must be executed in a critical section)
  if $C_k \leq \tau$ **then**
    for each fact $f \in I_k$ such that T_k is undefined on f **do** $T_k(f) := C_k$
    $C_k := \tau + 1$

4.5 Termination Detection

Since no server has complete information about the progress of any other server, detecting termination is nontrivial; however, we can reuse an existing solution.

When messages between each pair of servers are guaranteed to be delivered in order in which they are sent (as is the case in our implementation), one can use Dijkstra's token ring algorithm [4], which we summarise next. All servers in the cluster are numbered from 1 to ℓ and are arranged in a ring (i.e., server 1 comes after server ℓ). Each server can be black or white, and the servers will pass between them a *token* that can also be black or white. Initially, all servers are white and server 1 has a white token. The algorithm proceeds as follows.

- When server 1 has the token and it becomes idle (i.e., it has no pending work or messages), it sends a white token to the next server in the ring.

Algorithm 2. Distributed Materialisation Algorithm at Server k (Continued)

28: **function** FINISHMATCH($i, \sigma, a_{last}, Q, h, \tau, \boldsymbol{\lambda}$) where $Q = a_1^{\bowtie_1} \wedge \cdots \wedge a_n^{\bowtie_n}$
29:     **for each** var. x occurring in a_{last} and in h or a_j with $j > i$, and each $\pi \in \Pi$ **do**
30:         Extend λ_π with the mapping $x\sigma \mapsto \mu_{k,\pi}(x\sigma)$
31:     **if** $i = n$ **then**
32:         **for each** constant c occurring in h and each $\pi \in \Pi$ **do**
33:             Extend λ_π with the mapping $c \mapsto \mu_{k,\pi}(c)$
34:         $k_h :=$ the owner server for the derived fact
35:         $D := \{k_h\}$
36:         **for each** position $\pi \in \Pi$ and $c = h\sigma|_\pi$ where $k_h \notin \lambda_\pi(c)$ **do**
37:             Add k_h to $\lambda_\pi(c)$
38:             **for each** $\pi' \in \Pi$ **do** Add $\lambda_{\pi'}(c)$ to D
39:         Remove an element d from D, preferring any element over k_h if possible
40:         **if** $d = k$ **then** PROCESSMESSAGE(FCT[$h\sigma, D, k_h, C_k, \boldsymbol{\lambda}$])
41:         **else** SEND(FCT[$h\sigma, D, k_h, C_k, \boldsymbol{\lambda}$], d)
42:     **else**
43:         $D :=$ the set of all servers
44:         **for each** position $\pi \in \Pi$ where $a_{i+1}\sigma|_\pi$ is a constant c **do** $D := D \cap \lambda_\pi(c)$
45:         **for each** $d \in D$ **do**
46:             **if** $d = k$ **then** PROCESSMESSAGE(PAR[$i+1, \sigma, Q, h, \tau, \boldsymbol{\lambda}$])
47:             **else** SEND(PAR[$i+1, \sigma, Q, h, \tau, \boldsymbol{\lambda}$], d)

- When a server other than 1 has the token and it becomes idle, the server changes the token's colour to black if the server is itself black (and it leaves the token's colour unchanged otherwise); the server forwards the token to the next server in the ring; and the server changes its colour to white.
- A server i turns black whenever it sends a message to a server $j < i$.
- All servers can terminate when server 1 receives a white token.

The Dijkstra–Scholten algorithm extends this approach to the case when the order of message delivery cannot be guaranteed.

4.6 Correctness

We next prove that our algorithm is correct and that it exhibits the nonrepetition property. We present here only an outline of the correctness argument, and give the full proof in an extended version of this paper [3].

Let us fix a run of Algorithms 1 and 2 on some input. First, we show that Lamport timestamps capture the causality of fact derivation in this run. To this end, we introduce four event types relating to an arbitrary fact f. Event $\mathsf{add}_k(f)$ occurs when f is assigned a timestamp on server k in line 26. Event $\mathsf{process}_k(f)$ occurs when server k starts processing a new fact in line 8. Event $\mathsf{PAR}_k(f, i)$ occurs when server k completes line 12 for a PAR message with index i originating from a call to MATCHRULES on fact f. Finally, event $\mathsf{FCT}_k(f)$ occurs when server k completes line 16 for a FCT message for fact f. We write $e_1 \rightsquigarrow e_2$ if event e_1 occurs chronologically before event e_2; this relation is clearly transitive and irreflexive. Since each fact is stored and assigned a timestamp on just one server, we define $T(f)$ as $T_k(f)$ for the unique server k that satisfies $f \in I_k$. Lemma 1 then essentially says that the 'happens-before' relationship between facts and events on facts agrees with the timestamps assigned to the facts.

Lemma 1. *In each run of the algorithm, for each server k, and all facts f_1 and f_2, we have $T(f_1) < T(f_2)$ whenever one of the following holds:*

- $\mathsf{PAR}_k(f_1, i) \rightsquigarrow \mathsf{add}_k(f_2)$ *for some i,*
- $\mathsf{process}_k(f_1) \rightsquigarrow \mathsf{FCT}_k(f_2)$, *or*
- $\mathsf{PAR}_k(f_1, i) \rightsquigarrow \mathsf{FCT}_k(f_2)$ *for some i.*

Next, we show that then the occurrence mappings $\mu_{k,\pi}$ on each relevant server k are updated whenever a triple is added to some I_j. This condition is formally captured in Lemma 2, and it ensures that partial answers are sent to all relevant servers that can possibly match an atom in a query. Note that the implication in Lemma 2 is the only relevant direction: if $\mu_{k,\pi}(c)$ contains irrelevant servers, we can have redundant PAR messages, but this does not affect correctness.

Lemma 2. *At any point in the algorithm's run, for all servers k and j, each position $\pi \in \Pi$, and each constant c that is local to server k and that occurs in I_j at position π, property $j \in \mu_{k,\pi}(c)$ holds at that point.*

Using Lemmas 1 and 2, we prove our main claim.

Theorem 1. *For $I_1, \ldots, I_\ell$ the sets obtained by applying Algorithms 1 and 2 to an input set of facts I and program P, we have $P^\infty(I) = I_1 \cup \cdots \cup I_\ell$. Moreover, the algorithm exhibits the nonrepetition property.*

5 Evaluation

To evaluate the practical applicability of our approach, we have implemented a prototype distributed datalog reasoned that we call DMAT. We have used RDFox—a state-of-the-art centralised RDF system—to store and index triples in RAM, on top of which we have implemented a mechanism for associating triples with timestamps. To implement the EVALUATE function, we use the interface of RDFox for answering individual atoms and then simply filter out the answers whose timestamp does not match the given one. For simplicity, DMAT currently uses only one thread per server, but this limitation will be removed in future.

We have evaluated our system's performance in three different ways, each aimed at analysing a specific aspect of the problem. First, to establish a baseline for the performance of DMAT, as well as to see whether distributing the data can speed up the computation, we compared DMAT with RDFox on a relatively small dataset. Second, to compare our approach with the state of the art, we compared DMAT with WebPIE [17]—a distributed RDF reasoner based on MapReduce.

Third, we studied the scalability of our approach by proportionally increasing the input data and the number of servers.

Few truly large RDF datasets are publicly available, so the evaluation of distributed reasoning is commonly based on the well-known LUBM[4] benchmark (e.g., [10,17,21]). Following this well-established practice, in our evaluation we used LUBM datasets of sizes ranging from 134 M to 6.5 G triples. We also used the *lower bound* program, which was obtained by extracting the OWL 2 RL portion of the LUBM ontology and translating it into datalog. The executable of DMAT and the datalog program we used are available online,[5] and the datasets can be reproduced using the LUBM generator.

We conducted all tests with DMAT on the Amazon Elastic Compute Cloud (EC2). We used the *r4.8xlarge* servers,[6] each equipped with a 2.3 GHz Intel Broadwell processors and 244 GB of RAM; such a large amount of RAM was needed since we use RDFox to store triples, and RDFox is RAM-based. An additional, identical server stored the dictionary (i.e., a data structure mapping constants to integers): this server did not participate in materialisation, but was used only to distribute the program and the data to the cluster. The servers were connected using 10 Gbps network. In all tests apart from the ones where we compared DMAT to WebPIE, we partitioned the dataset by using the graph partitioning approach by Potter et al. [13]: this approach aims to place strongly connected constants on the same server and thus reduce communication overhead. Unfortunately, our graph partitioning algorithm ran out of memory on the very large datasets we used to compare DMAT with WebPIE, so in these tests we partitioned the data using subject hashing. For each test, we loaded the input triples and the program into all servers, and computed the materialisation while recording the wall-clock time. Apart from reporting this time, we also report the *reasoning throughput* measured in thousands of triples derived per second and worker (ktps/w). We next discuss the results of our experiments.

Comparison with RDFox. First, we ran RDFox and DMAT on a fixed dataset while increasing the number of threads for RDFox and the numbers of servers for DMAT. Since RDFox requires the materialised dataset to fit into RAM of a single server, we used a small input dataset of just 134 M triples. The results, shown in Table 1, provide us with two insights. First, the comparison on one thread establishes a baseline for the DMAT's performance. In particular, DMAT is slower than RDFox, which is not surprising: RDFox is a mature and tuned system, whereas DMAT is just a prototype. However, DMAT is still competitive with RDFox, suggesting that our approach is free of any overheads that might make it uncompetitive. Second, the comparison on multiple threads shows how effective our approach is at achieving concurrency. RDFox was specifically designed with that goal in mind in a shared-memory setting. However, as one can see from our results, DMAT also parallelises computation well: in some cases the speedup is

[4] http://swat.cse.lehigh.edu/projects/lubm/.

[5] http://krr-nas.cs.ox.ac.uk/2019/distributed-materialisation/.

[6] http://aws.amazon.com/ec2/instance-types/.

Table 1. Comparison of centralised and distributed reasoning

	Threads/servers							
	1		2		4		8	
	RDFox	DMAT	RDFox	DMAT	RDFox	DMAT	RDFox	DMAT
Times (s)	86	256	56	140	35	82	16	53
Speed-up	1.0x	1.0x	1.5x	1.8x	2.5x	3.1x	5.4x	4.8x
Size	$134M \rightarrow 182M$							

Table 2. Comparison with WebPIE

Dataset	Sizes (G)		WebPIE (64 workers)		DMAT (12 servers)	
	Input	Output	Time (s)	ktps/w	Time (s)	ktps/w
4K	0.5	0.729	1920	4.1	224	85
8K	1	1.457	2100	7.5	461	81
36K	5	6.516	3120	24.9	2087	71

Table 3. Scalability experiments

Workers	Dataset	Input size (G)	Output size (G)	Time (s)	Rate (ktps/w)
2	4K	0.5	0.73	646	212
6	12K	1.6	2.19	769	173
10	20K	2.65	3.64	887	151

larger than in the case of RDFox. This seems to be the case mainly because data partitioning allows each server to handle an isolated portion of the graph, which can reduce the need for synchronisation.

Comparison with WebPIE. Next, we compared DMAT with WebPIE to see how our approach compares with the state of the art in distributed materialisation. To keep the experimentation effort manageable, we did not rerun WebPIE ourselves; rather, we considered the same input dataset sizes as Urbani et al. [17] and reused their published results. The setting of these experiments thus does not quite match our setting: (i) WebPIE handles only the ter Horst fragment of OWL and thus cannot handle all axioms in the OWL 2 RL subset of the LUBM ontology; (ii) experiments with WebPIE were run on physical (rather than virtualised) servers with only 24 GB of RAM each; and (iii) WebPie used 64 workers, while DMAT used just 12 servers. Nevertheless, as one can see from Table 2, despite using more than five times fewer servers, DMAT is faster by an order of magnitude. Hadoop is a disk-based system so lower performance is to be expected to some extent, but this may not be the only reason: triples in

DMAT are partitioned by subject so, unlike WebPIE, DMAT does not perform any communication on subject–subject joins.

Scalability Experiments. Finally, to investigate the scalability of DMAT, we measured how the system's performance changes when the input data and the number of servers increase proportionally. The results are shown in Table 3. As one can see, increasing the size of the input does introduce an overhead for each server. Our analysis suggests that this is mainly because handling a larger dataset requires sending more messages, and communication seems to be the main source of overhead in the system. This, in turn, leads to a moderate reduction in throughout. Nevertheless, the system still exhibits very high inferences rates and clearly scales to very large inputs.

6 Conclusion

In this paper, we have presented a novel approach to datalog reasoning in distributed RDF systems. Our work extends the distributed query answering algorithm by Potter et al. [13], from which it inherits several benefits. First, the servers in our system are asynchronous, which is beneficial for concurrency. Second, dynamic data exchange is effective at reducing network communication, particularly when input data is partitioned so that related triples are co-located. Third, we have shown empirically that our prototype system is an order of magnitude faster than WebPIE [18], and that it scales to increasing data loads.

We see several interesting avenues for our future work. First, we shall extend our evaluation to cover a broader range of systems, datasets, and rule sets. Second, better approaches to partitioning the input data are needed: hash partitioning does not guarantee that joins other than subject–subject ones are processed on one server, and graph partitioning cannot handle large input graphs. Third, supporting more advanced features of datalog, such as stratified negation and aggregation is also needed in many practical applications.

Acknowledgments. This work was supported by the SIRIUS Centre for Scalable Access in the Oil and Gas Domain, and the EPSRC projects AnaLOG and ED3.

References

1. Abdelaziz, I., Harbi, R., Khayyat, Z., Kalnis, P.: A survey and experimental comparison of distributed SPARQL engines for very large RDF data. PVLDB **10**(13), 2049–2060 (2017)
2. Abiteboul, S., Hull, R., Vianu, V.: Foundations of Databases. Addison-Wesley (1995)
3. Ajileye, T., Motik, B., Horrocks, I.: Datalog materialisation in distributed RDF stores with dynamic data exchange. CoRR abs/1906.10261 (2019)
4. Dijkstra, E., Feijen, W., van Gasteren, A.: Derivation of a termination detection algorithm for distributed computations. Inf. Process. Lett. **16**(5), 217–219 (1983)

5. Ganguly, S., Silberschatz, A., Tsur, S.: Parallel bottom-up processing of datalog queries. J. Log. Program. **14**(1–2), 101–126 (1992)
6. Gu, R., Wang, S., Wang, F., Yuan, C., Huang, Y.: Cichlid: efficient large scale RDFS/OWL reasoning with spark. In: IPDPS, pp. 700–709 (2015)
7. Kaoudi, Z., Miliaraki, I., Koubarakis, M.: RDFS reasoning and query answering on top of DHTs. In: Sheth, A., et al. (eds.) ISWC 2008. LNCS, vol. 5318, pp. 499–516. Springer, Heidelberg (2008)
8. Kolovski, V., Wu, Z., Eadon, G.: Optimizing enterprise-scale OWL 2 RL reasoning in a relational database system. In: Patel-Schneide, P.F., et al. (eds.) ISWC 2010. LNCS, vol. 6496, pp. 436–452. Springer, Heidelberg (2010)
9. Lamport, L.: Time, clocks, and the ordering of events in a distributed system. CACM **21**(7), 558–565 (1978)
10. Liu, Y., McBrien, P.: SPOWL: spark-based OWL 2 reasoning materialisation. In: BeyondMR@SIGMOD 2017, pp. 3:1–3:10 (2017)
11. Motik, B., Nenov, Y., Piro, R., Horrocks, I., Olteanu, D.: Parallel materialisation of datalog programs in centralised, main-memory RDF systems. In: AAAI, pp. 129–137 (2014)
12. Oren, E., Kotoulas, S., Anadiotis, G., Siebes, R., ten Teije, A., van Harmelen, F.: Marvin: distributed reasoning over large-scale semantic web data. JWS **7**(4), 305–316 (2009)
13. Potter, A., Motik, B., Nenov, Y., Horrocks, I.: Dynamic data exchange in distributed RDF stores. IEEE TKDE **30**(12), 2312–2325 (2018)
14. Seib, J., Lausen, G.: Parallelizing datalog programs by generalized pivoting. In: PODS, pp. 241–251 (1991)
15. Seo, J., Park, J., Shin, J., Lam, M.: Distributed SociaLite: a datalog-based language for large-scale graph analysis. PVLDB **6**(14), 1906–1917 (2013)
16. Shao, J., Bell, D., Hull, E.: Combining rule decomposition and data partitioning in parallel datalog processing. In: PDIS, pp. 106–115 (1991)
17. Urbani, J., Kotoulas, S., Maassen, J., van Harmelen, F., Bal, H.: WebPIE: a web-scale parallel inference engine using mapreduce. JWS 2010 (2012)
18. Urbani, J., Jacobs, C., Krötzsch, M.: Column-oriented datalog materialization for large knowledge graphs. In: AAAI, pp. 258–264 (2016)
19. Weaver, J., Hendler, J.A.: Parallel materialization of the finite RDFS closure for hundreds of millions of triples. In: ISWC, pp. 682–697 (2009)
20. Wolfson, O., Ozeri, A.: Parallel and distributed processing of rules by data-reduction. IEEE TKDE **5**(3), 523–530 (1993)
21. Wu, H., Liu, J., Wang, T., Ye, D., Wei, J., Zhong, H.: Parallel materialization of datalog programs with spark for scalable reasoning. In: Cellary, W., Mokbel, M.F., Wang, J., Wang, H., Zhou, R., Zhang, Y. (eds.) WISE 2016. LNCS, vol. 10041, pp. 363–379. Springer, Cham (2016)
22. Zhang, W., Wang, K., Chau, S.C.: Data partition and parallel evaluation of datalog programs. IEEE TKDE **7**(1), 163–176 (1995)

How to Make Latent Factors Interpretable by Feeding Factorization Machines with Knowledge Graphs

Vito Walter Anelli[1(✉)], Tommaso Di Noia[1], Eugenio Di Sciascio[1], Azzurra Ragone[2], and Joseph Trotta[1]

[1] Polytechnic University of Bari, Bari, Italy
{vitowalter.anelli,tommaso.dinoia,eugenio.disciascio, joseph.trotta}@poliba.it
[2] Milan, Italy
azzurraragone@gmail.com

Abstract. Model-based approaches to recommendation can recommend items with a very high level of accuracy. Unfortunately, even when the model embeds content-based information, if we move to a latent space we miss references to the actual semantics of recommended items. Consequently, this makes non-trivial the interpretation of a recommendation process. In this paper, we show how to initialize latent factors in Factorization Machines by using semantic features coming from a knowledge graph in order to train an interpretable model. With our model, semantic features are injected into the learning process to retain the original informativeness of the items available in the dataset. The accuracy and effectiveness of the trained model have been tested using two well-known recommender systems datasets. By relying on the information encoded in the original knowledge graph, we have also evaluated the semantic accuracy and robustness for the knowledge-aware interpretability of the final model.

1 Introduction

Transparency and interpretability of predictive models are gaining momentum since they been recognized as a key element in the next generation of recommendation algorithms. Interpretability may increase user awareness in the decision-making process and lead to fast (efficiency), conscious and right (effectiveness) decisions. When equipped with interpretability of recommendation results, a system ceases to be just a black-box [36,40,45] and users are more willing to extensively exploit the predictions [21,39]. Indeed, transparency increases their trust [17] (also exploiting specific semantic structures [16]), and satisfaction in using the system. Among interpretable models for Recommender Systems (RS), we may distinguish between those based on Content-based (CB) approaches

Authors are listed in alphabetical order.

C. Ghidini et al. (Eds.): ISWC 2019, LNCS 11778, pp. 38–56, 2019.
https://doi.org/10.1007/978-3-030-30793-6_3

and those based on Collaborative filtering (CF) ones. CB algorithms provide recommendations by exploiting the available content and matching it with a user profile [10, 26]. The use of content features makes the model interpretable even though attention has to be paid since a CB approach "*lacks serendipity and requires extensive manual efforts to match the user interests to content profiles*" [46]. On the other hand, the interpretation of CF results will inevitably reflect the approach adopted by the algorithm. For instance, an item-based and a user-based recommendation could be interpreted, respectively, as "*other users who have experienced A have experienced B*" or "*similar users have experienced B*". Unfortunately, things change when we adopt more powerful and accurate Deep Learning [8] or model-based algorithms and techniques for the computation of a recommendation list. Such approaches project items and users in a new vector space of latent features [24] thus making the final result not directly interpretable. In the last years, many approaches have been proposed that take advantage of side information to enhance the performance of latent factor models. Side information can refer to items as well as users [43] and can be either structured [38] or semi-structured [6, 9, 47]. Interestingly, in [46] the authors argue about a new generation of knowledge-aware recommendation engines able to exploit information encoded in knowledge graphs (KG) to produce meaningful recommendations: "*For example, with knowledge graph about movies, actors, and directors, the system can explain to the user a movie is recommended because he has watched many movies starred by an actor*".

In this work, we propose a *knowledge-aware Hybrid Factorization Machine* (`kaHFM`) to train interpretable models in recommendation scenarios taking advantage of semantics-aware information (Sect. 2.1). `kaHFM` relies on Factorization Machines [29] and it extends them in different key aspects by making use of the semantic information encoded in a knowledge graph. With `kaHFM` we address the following research questions:

RQ1 Can we develop a model-based recommendation engine whose results are very accurate and, at the same time, interpretable with respect to an explicitly stated semantics coming from a knowledge graph?

RQ2 Can we evaluate that the original semantics of items features is preserved after the model has been trained?

RQ3 How to measure with an offline evaluation that the proposed model is really able to identify meaningful features by exploiting their explicit semantics?

We show how `kaHFM` may exploit data coming from knowledge graphs as side information to build a recommender system whose final results are accurate and, at the same time, semantically interpretable. With `kaHFM`, we build a model in which the meaning of each latent factor is bound to an explicit content-based feature extracted from a knowledge graph. Doing this, after the model has been trained, we still have an explicit reference to the original semantics of the features describing the items, thus making possible the interpretation of the final results. To answer RQ2, and RQ3 we introduce two metrics, Semantic Accuracy (SA@K) (Sect. 3.1) and Robustness (n-Rob@K) (Sect. 3.2), to measure the interpretability of a knowledge-aware recommendation engine. The remainder of this paper is structured as follows: we evaluated `kaHFM` on two different publicly available datasets by getting content-based explicit features from data encoded in the `DBpedia` knowledge graph. We analyzed the performance of the approach in terms of accuracy of results (Sect. 4.1) by exploiting categorical, ontological and factual features (see Sect. 2.1). Finally, we tested the robustness of `kaHFM` with respect to its interpretability (Sects. 4.2 and 4.3) showing that it ranks meaningful features higher and is able to regenerate them in case they are removed from the original dataset.

2 Knowledge-Aware Hybrid Factorization Machines for Top-N Recommendation

In this section, we briefly recap the main technologies we adopted to develop `kaHFM`. We introduce Vector Space Models for recommender systems, and then we give a quick overview of Factorization Machines (FM).

Content-based recommender systems rely on the assumption that it is possible to predict the future behavior of users based on their personalized profile. Profiles for users can be built by exploiting the characteristics of the items they liked in the past or some other available side information. Several approaches have been proposed, that take advantage of side information in different ways: some of them consider tags [41], demographic data [49] or they extract information from collective knowledge bases [14] to mitigate the cold start problem [18]. Many of the most popular and adopted CB approaches make use of a Vector Space Model (VSM). In VSM users and items are represented by means of Boolean or weighted vectors. Their respective positions and the distance, or better the proximity, between them, provides a measure of how these two entities are related or similar. The choice of item features may substantially differ depending on their availability and application scenario: crowd-sourced tags, categorical, ontological, or textual knowledge are just some of the most exploited ones. All in all, in a CB approach we need (i) to get reliable items descriptions, (ii) a way to measure the strength of each feature for each item, (iii) to represent users and finally (iv) to measure similarities. Regarding the first point, nowadays we can easily get descriptions related to an item from the Web. In particular, thanks to the Linked Open Data initiative a lot of semantically structured knowledge is publicly available in the form of Linked Data datasets.

2.1 From Factorization Machines to Knowledge-Aware Hybrid Factorization Machines

Factorization models have proven to be very effective in a recommendation scenario [31]. High prediction accuracy and the subtle modeling of user-item interactions let these models operate efficiently even in very sparse settings. Among all the different factorization models, factorization machines propose a unified general model to represent most of them. Here we report the definition related to a factorization model of order 2 for a recommendation problem involving only implicit ratings. Nevertheless, the model can be easily extended to a more expressive representation by taking into account, e.g., demographic and social information [4], multi-criteria [3], and even relations between contexts [50].

For each user $u \in U$ and each item $i \in I$ we build a binary vector $\mathbf{x}^{\mathbf{ui}} \in \mathbb{R}^{1 \times n}$, with $n = |U| + |I|$, representing the interaction between u and i in the original user-item rating matrix. In this modeling, $\mathbf{x}^{\mathbf{ui}}$ contains only two 1 values corresponding to u and i while all the other values are set to 0 (see Fig. 1). We then denote with $\mathbf{X} \in \mathbb{R}^{n \times m}$ the matrix containing as rows all possible $\mathbf{x}^{\mathbf{ui}}$ we can build starting from the original user-item rating matrix as shown in Fig. 1.

	User					Item					
	U_1	U_2	U_3	U_4	...	I_1	I_2	I_3	I_4	I_5	...
x^1	1	0	0	0	...	1	0	0	0	0	...
x^2	1	0	0	0	...	0	1	0	0	0	...
x^3	1	0	0	0	...	0	0	1	0	0	...
x^4	0	1	0	0	...	0	0	1	0	0	...
x^5	0	1	0	0	...	0	0	0	1	0	...
x^6	0	0	1	0	...	1	0	0	0	0	...
x^7	0	0	1	0	...	0	0	1	0	0	...

Fig. 1. A visual representation of $\mathbf{X}$ for sparse real valued vectors $\mathbf{x}^{\mathbf{ui}}$.

The FM score for each vector $\mathbf{x}$ is defined as:

$$\hat{y}(\mathbf{x}^{\mathbf{ui}}) = w_0 + \sum_{j=1}^{n} w_j \cdot x_j + \sum_{j=1}^{n} \sum_{p=j+1}^{n} x_j \cdot x_p \cdot \sum_{f=1}^{k} v_{(j,f)} \cdot v_{(p,f)} \tag{1}$$

where the parameters to be learned are: w_0 representing the global bias; w_j giving the importance to every single x_j; the pair $v_{(j,f)}$ and $v_{(p,f)}$ in $\sum_{f=1}^{k} v_{(j,f)} \cdot v_{(p,f)}$ measuring the strength of the interaction between each pair of variables: x_j and x_p. The number of latent factors is represented by k. This value is usually selected at design time when implementing the FM.

In order to make the recommendation results computed by `kaHFM` as semantically interpretable, we inject the knowledge encoded within a knowledge graph in a Factorization Machine. In a knowledge graph, each triple represents the connection $\sigma \xrightarrow{\rho} \omega$ between two nodes, named *subject* (σ) and *object* (ω), through the *relation* (*predicate*) ρ. Given a set of features retrieved from a KG [13] we first bind them to the latent factors and then, since we address a Top-N recommendation problem, we train the model by using a Bayesian Personalized Ranking (BPR) criterion that takes into account entities within the original knowledge graph. In [15], the authors originally proposed to encode a Linked Data knowledge graph in a vector space model to develop a CB recommender system. Given a set of items $I = \{i_1, i_2, \dots, i_N\}$ in a catalog and their associated triples $\langle i, \rho, \omega \rangle$ in a knowledge graph $\mathcal{KG}$, we may build the set of all possible features as $F = \{\langle \rho, \omega \rangle \mid \langle i, \rho, \omega \rangle \in \mathcal{KG} \text{ with } i \in I\}$. Each item can be then represented as a vector of weights $\mathbf{i} = [v_{(i,1)}, \ldots, v_{(i,\langle \rho,\omega \rangle)}, \ldots, v_{(i,|F|)}]$, where $v_{(i,\langle \rho,\omega \rangle)}$ is computed as the normalized TF-IDF value for $\langle \rho, \omega \rangle$ as follows:

$$v_{(i,\langle \rho,\omega \rangle)} = \underbrace{\frac{|\{\langle \rho, \omega \rangle \mid \langle i, \rho, \omega \rangle \in \mathcal{KG}\}|}{\sqrt{\sum_{\langle \rho,\omega \rangle \in F} |\{\langle \rho, \omega \rangle \mid \langle i, \rho, \omega \rangle \in \mathcal{KG}\}|^2}}}_{TF^{\mathcal{KG}}} \cdot \log \underbrace{\frac{|I|}{|\{j \mid \langle j, \rho, \omega \rangle \in \mathcal{KG} \text{ and } j \in I\}|}}_{IDF^{\mathcal{KG}}} \tag{2}$$

Since the numerator of $TF^{\mathcal{KG}}$ can only take values 0 or 1 and, each feature under the root in the denominator has value 0 or 1, $v_{(i,\langle \rho,\omega \rangle)}$ is zero if $\langle \rho, \omega \rangle \notin \mathcal{KG}$, and otherwise:

$$v_{(i,\langle \rho,\omega \rangle)} = \frac{\log |I| - \log |\langle j, \rho, \omega \rangle \cap \mathcal{KG} | j \in I|}{\sqrt{\sum_{\langle \rho,\omega \rangle \in F} |\{\langle \rho, \omega \rangle \mid \langle i, \rho, \omega \rangle \in \mathcal{KG}\}|}} \tag{3}$$

Analogously, when we have a set U of users, we may represent them using the features describing the items they enjoyed in the past. In the following, when no confusion arises, we use f to denote a feature $\langle \rho, \omega \rangle \in F$. Given a user u, if we denote with I^u the set of the items enjoyed by u, we may introduce the vector $\mathbf{u} = [v_{(u,1)}, \ldots, v_{(u,f)} \ldots, v_{(u,|F|)}]$, where $v_{(u,f)}$ is:

$$v_{(u,f)} = \frac{\sum_{i \in I^u} v_{(i,f)}}{|\{i \mid i \in I^u \text{ and } v_{(i,f)} \neq 0\}|}$$

Given the vectors $\mathbf{u}_j$, with $j \in [1 \ldots |U|]$, and $\mathbf{i}_p$, with $p \in [1 \ldots |I|]$, we build the matrix $\mathbf{V} \in \mathbb{R}^{n \times |F|}$ (see Fig. 2) where the first $|U|$ rows have a one to one mapping with $\mathbf{u}_j$ while the last ones correspond to $\mathbf{i}_p$. If we go back to Eq. (1) we may see that, for each $\mathbf{x}$, the term $\sum_{j=1}^{n} \sum_{p=j+1}^{n} x_j \cdot x_{j'} \cdot \sum_{f=1}^{k} v_{(j,f)} \cdot v_{(p,f)}$

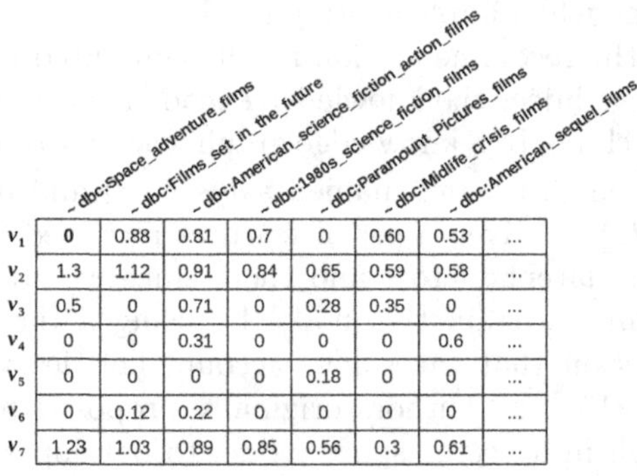

	dbc:Space_adventure_films	dbc:Films_set_in_the_future	dbc:American_science_fiction_action_films	dbc:1980s_science_fiction_films	dbc:Paramount_Pictures_films	dbc:Midlife_crisis_films	dbc:American_sequel_films	
v_1	0	0.88	0.81	0.7	0	0.60	0.53	...
v_2	1.3	1.12	0.91	0.84	0.65	0.59	0.58	...
v_3	0.5	0	0.71	0	0.28	0.35	0	...
v_4	0	0	0.31	0	0	0	0.6	...
v_5	0	0	0	0	0.18	0	0	...
v_6	0	0.12	0.22	0	0	0	0	...
v_7	1.23	1.03	0.89	0.85	0.56	0.3	0.61	...

Fig. 2. Example of real valued feature vectors for different items v_j. For lack of space we omitted the predicate *dcterms:subject*

is not zero only once, i.e., when both x_j and x_p are equal to 1. In the matrix depicted in Fig. 1, this happens when there is an interaction between a user and an item. Moreover, the summation $\sum_{f=1}^{k} v_{(j,f)} \cdot v_{(p,f)}$ represents the dot product between two vectors: $\mathbf{v}_j$ and $\mathbf{v}_p$ with a size equal to k. Hence, $\mathbf{v}_j$ represents a latent representation of a user, $\mathbf{v}_p$ that of an item within the same latent space, and their interaction is evaluated through their dot product.

In order to inject the knowledge coming from $\mathcal{KG}$ into `kaHFM`, we keep Eq. (1) and we set $k = |F|$. In other words, we impose a number of latent factors equal to the number of features describing all the items in our catalog. We want to stress here that our aim is not representing each feature through a latent vector, but to associate each factor to an explicit feature, obtaining latent vectors that are composed by explicit semantic features. Hence, we initialize the parameters $\mathbf{v}_j$ and $\mathbf{v}_p$ with their corresponding rows from $\mathbf{V}$ which in turn represent respectively $\mathbf{u}_j$ and $\mathbf{i}_p$. In this way, we try to identify each latent factor with a corresponding explicit feature. The intuition is that after the training phase, the resulting matrix $\hat{\mathbf{V}}$ still refers to the original features but contains better values for $v_{(j,f)}$ and $v_{(p,f)}$ that take into account also the latent interactions between users, items and features. It is noteworthy that after the training phase $\mathbf{u}_j$ and $\mathbf{i}_p$ (corresponding to $v_{(j,f)}$ and $v_{(p,f)}$ in $\mathbf{V}$) contain non-zero values also for features that are not originally in the description of the user u or of the item i. We extract the items vectors $\mathbf{v}_j$ from the matrix $\hat{\mathbf{V}}$, with the associated optimal values and we use them to implement an Item-kNN recommendation approach. We measure similarities between each pair of items i and j by evaluating the cosine similarity of their corresponding vectors in $\hat{\mathbf{V}}$:

$$cs(i,j) = \frac{\mathbf{v}_i \cdot \mathbf{v}_j}{\parallel \mathbf{v}_i \parallel \cdot \parallel \mathbf{v}_j \parallel}$$

Let us define N^i as the set of neighbors for the item i, composed by the items which are more similar to i according to the selected similarity measure. Denoted as N^i. It is possible to choose i such that $i \notin I^u$ and a user u, we predict the score assigned by u to i as

$$score(u,i) = \frac{\sum\limits_{j \in N^i \cap I^u} cs(i,j)}{\sum\limits_{j \in N^i} cs(i,j)} \tag{4}$$

Factorization machines can be easily trained to reduce the prediction error via gradient descent methods, alternating least-squares (ALS) and MCMC. Since we formulated our problem as a *top-N* recommendation task, `kaHFM` can be trained using a learning to rank approach like Bayesian Personalized Ranking Criterion (BPR) [32]. The BPR criterion is optimized using a stochastic gradient descent algorithm on a set D_S of triples (u, i, j), with $i \in I^u$ and $j \notin I^u$, selected through a random sampling from a uniform distribution. Once the training phase returns the optimal model parameters, the item recommendation step can take place.

In an RDF knowledge graph, we usually find different types of encoded information.

Table 1. Top-10 features computed by `kaHFM` for the movie `"Star Trek II - The Wrath of Khan"`.

`kaHFM`	TF-IDF	Predicate	Object
1.3669	0.2584	dct:subject	dbc:Space_adventure_films
1.1252	0.2730	dct:subject	dbc:Films_set_in_the_future
0.9133	0.2355	dct:subject	dbc:American_science_fiction_action_films
0.8485	0.3190	dct:subject	dbc:1980s_science_fiction_films
0.6529	0.1549	dct:subject	dbc:Paramount_Pictures_films
0.5989	0.3468	dct:subject	dbc:Midlife_crisis_films
0.5940	0.1797	dct:subject	dbc:American_sequel_films
0.5862	0.2661	dct:subject	dbc:Film_scores_by_James_Horner
0.5634	0.2502	dct:subject	dbc:Films_shot_in_San_Francisco
0.5583	0.1999	dct:subject	dbc:1980s_action_thriller_films

- **Factual.** This refers to statements such has *The Matrix was directed by the Wachowskis* or *Melbourne is located in Australia* when we describe attributes of an entity;
- **Categorical.** It is mainly used to state something about the subject of an entity. In this direction, the categories of Wikipedia pages are an excellent example. Categories can be used to cluster entities and are often organized hierarchically thus making possible to define them in a more generic or specific way;
- **Ontological.** This is a more restrictive and formal way to classify entities via a hierarchical structure of classes. Differently from categories, sub-classes and super-classes are connected through IS-A (transitive) relations.

In Table 1 we show an example for categorical values obtained after the training (in the column `kaHFM`) together with the original TF-IDF ones computed for a movie from the Yahoo! Movies[1] dataset.

3 Semantic Accuracy and Generative Robustness

The proposed approach let us keep the meaning of the "latent" factors computed via a factorization machine thus making possible an interpretation of the recommended results. To assess that `kaHFM` preserves the semantics of the features in $\mathbf{V}$ after the training phase, we propose an automated offline procedure to measure *Semantic Accuracy*. Moreover, we define as *Robustness* the ability to assign a higher value to important features after one or more feature removals.

[1] http://research.yahoo.com/Academic_Relations.

3.1 Semantic Accuracy

The main idea behind Semantic Accuracy is to evaluate, given an item i, how well kaHFM is able to return its original features available in the computed top-K list $\mathbf{v}_i$. In other words, given the set of features of i represented by $F^i = \{f_1^i, \ldots, f_m^i, \ldots f_M^i\}$, with $F^i \subseteq F$, we check if the values in $\mathbf{v}_i$, corresponding to $f_{m,i} \in F^i$, are higher than those corresponding to $f \notin F^i$. For the set of M features initially describing i we see how many of them appear in the set $top(\mathbf{v}_i, M)$ representing the top-M features in $\mathbf{v}_i$. We then normalize this number by the size of F^i and average on all the items within the catalog I.

$$\texttt{Semantic Accuracy (SA@}M\texttt{)} = \frac{\sum_{i \in I} \frac{|top(\mathbf{v}_i, M) \cap F^i|}{|F^i|}}{|I|}$$

In many practical scenarios we may have $|F| \gg M$. Hence, we might also be interested in measuring the accuracy for different sizes of the top list. Since items could be described with a different number of features, the size of the top list could be a function of the original size of the item description. Thus, we measured SA@nM with $n \in \{1, 2, 3, 4, 5, \ldots\}$ and evaluate the number of features in F^i available in the top-$n \cdot M$ elements of $\mathbf{v}_i$.

$$\texttt{SA@}nM = \frac{\sum_{i \in I} \frac{|top(\mathbf{v}_i, n \cdot M) \cap F^i|}{|F^i|}}{|I|}$$

3.2 Robustness

Although SA@nM may result very useful to understand if kaHFM assigns weights according to the original description of item i, we still do not know if a high value in $\mathbf{v}_i$ really means that the corresponding feature is important to define i. In other words, are we sure that kaHFM promotes important features for i?

In order to provide a way to measure such "meaningfulness" for a given feature, we suppose, for a moment, that a particular feature $\langle \rho, \omega \rangle$ is useful to describe an item i but the corresponding triple $\langle i, \rho, \omega \rangle$ is not represented in the knowledge graph. In case kaHFM was robust in generating weights for unknown features, it should discover the importance of that feature and modify its value to make it enter the Top-K features in $\mathbf{v}_i$. Starting from this observation, the idea to measure robustness is then to "forget" a triple involving i and check if kaHFM can generate it. In order to implement such process we proceed by following these steps:

- we train kaHFM thus obtaining optimal values v_i for all the features in F^i;
- the feature $f_{MAX}^i \in F^i$ with the highest value in v_i is identified;
- we retrain the model again initializing $f_{MAX}^i = 0$ and we compute v_i'.

After the above steps, if $f_{MAX}^i \in top(v_i', M)$ then we can say that kaHFM shows a high robustness in identifying important features. Given a catalog I, we may then define the *Robustness for 1 removed feature @M* (1-Rob@M) as the number of items for which $f^i_{MAX} \in top(v'_i, M)$ divided by the size of I.

$$\texttt{1-Rob@M} = \frac{\sum_{i \in I} |\{i \mid f^i_{MAX} \in top(v'_i, M)\}|}{|I|}$$

Similarly to SA@nM, we may define 1-Rob@nM.

4 Experimental Evaluation

In this section, we will detail three distinct experiments. We specifically designed them to answer the research questions posed in Sect. 1. In details, we want to assess if: (i) kaHFM's recommendations are accurate; (ii) kaHFM generally preserves the semantics of original features; (iii) kaHFM promotes significant features.

Datasets. To provide an answer to our research questions, we evaluated the performance of our method on two well-known datasets for recommender systems belonging to movies domain. Yahoo!Movies (Yahoo! Webscope dataset ydata-ymovies-user-movie-ratings-content-v1_0)[2] contains movies ratings generated on Yahoo! Movies up to November 2003. It provides content, demographic and ratings information on a [1..5] scale, and mappings to MovieLens and EachMovie datasets. Facebook Movies dataset has been released for the Linked Open Data challenge co-located with ESWC 2015[3]. Only implicit feedback is available for this dataset, but for each item a link to DBpedia is provided. To map items in Yahoo!Movies and other well-known datasets, we extracted all the updated items-features mappings and we made them publicly available[4]. Datasets statistics are shown in Table 2.

Experimental Setting. "All Unrated Items" [37] protocol has been adopted to compare different algorithms. We have split the dataset using Hold-Out 80-20 retaining for every user the 80% of their ratings in the training set and the remaining 20% in the test set. Moreover, a temporal split has been performed [19] whenever timestamps associated to every transaction is available.

Extraction. Thanks to the publicly available mappings, all the items from the datasets represented in Table 2 come with a DBpedia link. Exploiting this reference, we retrieved all the $\langle \rho, \omega \rangle$ pairs. Some noisy features (based on the following predicates) have been excluded: owl:sameAs, dbo:thumbnail, foaf:depiction, prov:wasDerivedFrom, foaf:isPrimaryTopicOf.

Selection. We performed our experiments with three different settings to analyze the impact of the different kind of features. The features have been chosen as they are present in all the different domains and because of their factual, categorical or ontological meaning:

[2] http://research.yahoo.com/Academic_Relations.

[3] https://2015.eswc-conferences.org/program/semwebeval.html.

[4] https://github.com/sisinflab/LinkedDatasets/.

Table 2. Datasets statistics.

Dataset	#Users	#Items	#Transactions	#Features	Sparsity
Yahoo! Movies	4000	2,626	69,846	988,734	99.34%
Facebook Movies	32143	3,901	689,561	180,573	99.45%

- **Categorical Setting (CS):** We selected only the features containing the property `dcterms:subject`.
- **Ontological Setting (OS):** In this case the only feature we considered is `rdf:type`.
- **Factual Setting (FS):** We considered all the features but those involving the properties selected in OS, and CS.

Filtering. This last step corresponds to the removal of irrelevant features, that bring little value to the recommendation task, but, at the same time, pose scalability issues. The pre-processing phase has been done following [13], and [25] with a unique threshold. Thresholds (corresponding to *tm* [13], and *p* [25] for missing values) and the considered features for each dataset are represented in Table 3.

Table 3. Considered features in the different settings

		Categorical setting		Ontological setting		Factual setting	
Datasets	Threshold	Total	Selected	Total	Selected	Total	Selected
`Yahoo!Movies`	99.62	26155	747	38699	1240	950035	3186
`Facebook Movies`	99.74	8843	1103	13828	1848	166745	5427

4.1 Accuracy Evaluation

The goal of this evaluation is to assess if the controlled injection of `Linked Data` positively affects the training of Factorization Machines. For this reason, `kaHFM` is not compared with other state-of-art interpretable models but with only the algorithms that are more related to our approach. We compared `kaHFM`[5] w.r.t. a canonical 2 degree Factorization Machine (users and items are intended as features of the original formulation) by optimizing the recommendation list ranking via BPR (BPR-FM). In order to preserve the expressiveness of the model, we used the same number of hidden factors (see the "Selected" column in Table 3). Since we use items similarity in the last step of our approach (see Eq. (4)), we compared `kaHFM` against an *Attribute Based Item-kNN* (ABItem-kNN) algorithm, where each item is represented as a vector of weights,

[5] https://github.com/sisinflab/HybridFactorizationMachines.

computed through a TF-IDF model. In this model, the attributes are computed via Eq. (2). We also compared `kaHFM` also against a pure Item-kNN, that is an item-based implementation of the k-nearest neighbors algorithm. It finds the k-nearest item neighbors based on Pearson Correlation. https://github.com/sisinflab/HybridFactorizationMachines Regarding BPR parameters, *learning rate*, *bias regularization*, *user regularization*, *positive item regularization*, and *negative item regularization* have been set respectively to 0.05, 0, 0.0025, 0.0025 and 0.00025 while a sampler "without replacement" has been adopted in order to sample the triples as suggested by authors [32]. We compared `kaHFM` also against the corresponding User-based nearest neighbor scheme, and Most-Popular, a simple baseline that shows high performance in specific scenarios [11]. In our context, we considered mandatory to also compare against a pure knowledge-graph content-based baseline based on Vector Space Model (VSM) [15]. In order to evaluate our approach, we measured accuracy through Precision@N ($Prec@N$) and Normalized Discounted Cumulative Gain ($nDCG@N$). The evaluation has been performed considering Top-10 [11] recommendations for all the datasets. When a rating score was available (`Yahoo!Movies`), a *Threshold-based relevant items* condition [5,7] was adopted with a relevance threshold of 4 over 5 stars in order to take into account only relevant items. Figure 3 shows the results of our experiments regarding accuracy. In all the tables we highlight in **bold** the best result while we underline the second one. Statistically significant results are denoted with a * mark considering Student's paired t-test with a 0.05 level. `Yahoo!Movies` experiments show that in Categorical and Ontological settings our method is the most accurate. In the `Yahoo!Movies` mapping, a strong popularity bias is present and it is interesting to notice that this affects only the Factual setting leading our approach to be less precise than ABItem-kNN. In `Facebook Movies` we see very a good improvement in terms of accuracy as it almost doubles up the ABItem-kNN algorithm values. We compared `kaHFM` against ABItem-kNN to check if the collaborative trained features may lead to better similarity values. This hypothesis seems to be confirmed since in former experiments `kaHFM` beats ABItem-kNN in almost all settings. This suggests that collaborative trained features achieve better accuracy results. Moreover, we want to check if a knowledge-graph-based initialization of latent factors may improve the performance of Factorization Machines. `kaHFM` always beats BPR-FM, and in our opinion, this happens since the random initialization takes a while to drive the Factorization machine to reach good performance. Finally, we want to check if collaborative trained features lead to better accuracy results than a purely informativeness-based Vector Space Model even though it is in its knowledge-graph-aware version. This seems to be confirmed in our experiments, since `kaHFM` beats VSM in almost all cases. In order to strengthen the results we got, we computed recommendations with $0, 1, 5, 10, 15, 30$ iterations. For the sake of brevity we report here[6] only the plots related to Categorical setting (Fig. 3) It is worth to notice that in every case we considered, we show the best performance in

[6] Results of the full experiments: https://github.com/sisinflab/papers-results/tree/master/kahfm-results/.

	Facebook	Yahoo!	
Categorical Setting (CS)	P@10	P@10	nDCG@10
ABItem-kNN	0.0173*	0.0421*	0.1174*
BPR-FM	0.0158*	0.0189*	0.0344*
MostPopular	0.0118*	0.0154*	0.0271*
ItemKnn	0.0262*	0.0203*	0.0427*
UserKnn	0.0168*	0.0231*	0.0474*
VSM	0.0185*	0.0385*	0.1129*
kaHFM	**0.0296**	**0.0524**	**0.1399**
Ontological Setting (OS)	P@10	P@10	nDCG@10
ABItem-kNN	0.0172	0.0427*	0.1223*
BPR-FM	0.0155*	0.0199*	0.0356*
MostPopular	0.0118*	0.0154*	0.0271*
ItemKnn	0.0263*	0.0203*	0.0427*
UserKnn	0.0168*	0.0232*	0.0474*
VSM	0.0181*	0.0349*	0.1083*
kaHFM	**0.0273**	**0.0521**	**0.1380**
Factual Setting (FS)	P@10	P@10	nDCG@10
ABItem-kNN	0.0234	0.0619	**0.1764**
BPR-FM	0.0157	0.0177	0.0305
MostPopular	0.0123	0.0154	0.0271
ItemKnn	**0.0273**	0.0203	0.0427
UserKnn	0.0176	0.0232	0.0474
VSM	0.0219	**0.0627**	0.1725
kaHFM	0.0240	0.0564	0.1434

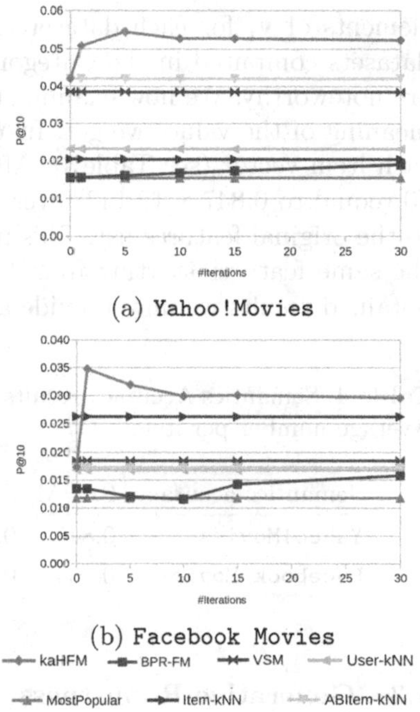

(a) Yahoo!Movies

(b) Facebook Movies

Fig. 3. Accuracy results for Facebook Movies, and Yahoo!Movies. In figures: Precision@10 varying # iterations 0, 1, 5, 10, 15, 30

one of these iterations. Moreover, the positive influence of the initialization of the feature vectors is particularly evident in all the datasets, with performances being very similar to the ones depicted in [32]. Given the obtained results we may say that the answer to RQ1 is positive when adopting kaHFM.

4.2 Semantic Accuracy

The previous experiments showed the effectiveness of our approach in terms of accuracy of recommendation. In practical terms, we proved that: (i) content initialization generally lead to better performance with our method, (ii) the obtained items vectors are fine-tuned better than the original ones for a *top-N* item recommendation task, (iii) results may depend on the features we extract from the Knowledge Graph. However, we still do not know if the original semantics of the features is preserved in the new space computed after the training of kaHFM (as we want to assess by posing RQ2). In Sect. 3.1 we introduced Semantics Accuracy ($SA@nM$) as a metric to automatically check if the importance computed by kaHFM and associated to each feature reflects the actual meaning of that feature. Thus, we measured SA@nM with $n \in \{1, 2, 3, 4, 5\}$ and $M = 10$, and evaluated the number of ground features available in the top-nM

elements of $\mathbf{v}_i$ for each dataset. Table 4 shows the results for all the different datasets computed in the Categorical setting. In general, the results we obtain are noteworthy. We now examine the worst one to better understand the actual meaning of the values we get. In `Yahoo!Movies`, 747 different features compose each item vector (see Table 3). After the training phase, on average, more than 10 (equal to 0.847×12.143) over 12 features (last column in Table 4) are equal to the original features list. This means that `kaHFM` was able to compute almost the same features starting from hundreds of them. Also in this case, given the obtained results we may provide a positive answer to RQ2.

Table 4. Semantics Accuracy results for different values of M. F.A. denotes the Feature Average number per item.

Semantics accuracy	SA@M	SA@2M	SA@3M	SA@4M	SA@5M	F.A.
`Yahoo!Movies`	0.847	0.863	0.865	0.868	0.873	12.143
`Facebook Movies`	0.864	0.883	0.889	0.894	0.899	12.856

4.3 Generative Robustness

The previous experiment showed that the features computed by `kaHFM` keep their original semantics if already present in the item description. In Sect. 3.2, we introduced a procedure to measure the capability of `kaHFM` to compute meaningful features. Here, we computed `1-Rob@nM` for the two adopted datasets. Results are represented in Table 5. In this case, we focus on the CS setting which provides the best results in terms of accuracy. For a better understanding of the obtained results, we start by focusing on `Yahoo!Movies` which apparently has bad behavior. Table 4 showed that `kaHFM` was able to guess 10 on 12 different features for `Yahoo!Movies`. In this experiment, we remove one of the ten features (thus, based on Table 4, `kaHFM` will guess an average of $10 - 1 = 9$ features). Since the number of features is 12 we have 3 remaining "slots". What we measure now is if `kaHFM` is able to guess the removed feature in these "slots". Results in Table 5 show that our method is able to put the removed feature in one of the three slots the 48.7% of the times starting from 747 overall features. This example should help the reader to appreciate even more `Facebook Movies` results. Hence, we

Table 5. 1-Robustness for different values of M. Column F.A. denotes the Feature Average number per item.

1-Robustness	`1-Rob@M`	`1-Rob@2M`	`1-Rob@3M`	`1-Rob@4M`	`1-Rob@5M`	F.A.
`Yahoo!Movies`	0.487	0.645	0.713	0.756	0.793	12.143
`Facebook Movies`	0.821	0.945	0.970	0.980	0.984	12.856

could confidently assess that `kaHFM` is able to propose meaningful features as we asked with RQ3.

5 Related Work

In recent years, several interpretable recommendation models that exploit matrix factorization have been proposed. It is well-known that one of the main issues of matrix factorization methods is that they are not easily interpretable (since latent factors meaning is basically unknown). One of the first attempts to overcome this problem was proposed in [47]. In this work, the authors propose Explicit Factor Model (EFM). Products' features and users' opinions are extracted with phrase-level sentiment analysis from users' reviews to feed a matrix factorization framework. After that, a few improvements to EFM have been proposed to deal with temporal dynamics [48] and to use tensor factorization [9]. In particular, in the latter the aim is to predict both user preferences on features (extracted from textual reviews) and items. This is achieved by exploiting the Bayesian Personalized Ranking (BPR) criterion [32]. Further advances in MF-based interpretable recommendation models have been proposed with Explainable Matrix Factorization (EMF) [1] in which the generated explanations are based on a neighborhood model. Similarly, in [2] an interpretable Restricted Boltzmann Machine model has been proposed. It learns a network model (with an additional visible layer) that takes into account a degree of explainability. Finally, an interesting work incorporates sentiments and ratings into a matrix factorization model, named Sentiment Utility Logistic Model (SULM) [6]. In [28] recommendations are computed by generating and ranking personalized explanations in the form of explanation chains. OCuLaR [42] provides interpretable recommendations from positive examples based on the detection of co-clusters between users (clients) and items (products). In [22] authors propose a Multi Level Attraction Model (MLAM) in which they build two attraction models, for cast and story. The interpretability of the model is then provided in terms of attractiveness of Sentence level, Word level, and Cast member. In [27] the authors train a matrix factorization model to compute a set of association rules that interprets the obtained recommendations. In [12] the authors prove that, given the conversion probabilities for all actions of customer features, it is possible to transform the original historical data to a new space in order to compute a set of interpretable recommendation rules. The core of our model is a general Factorization Machines (FM) model [30]. Nowadays FMs are the most widely used factorization models because they offer a number of advantages w.r.t. other latent factors models such as SVD++ [23], PITF [35], FPMC [33]. First of all, FMs are designed for a generic prediction task while the others can be exploited only for specific tasks. Moreover, it is a linear model and parameters can be estimated accurately even in high data sparsity scenarios. Nevertheless, several improvements have been proposed for FMs. For instance Neural Factorization

Machines [20] have been developed to fix the inability of classical FMs to capture non linear structure of real-world data. This goal is achieved by exploiting the non linearity of neural networks. Furthermore, Attentional Factorization Machines [44] have been proposed that use an attention network to learn the importance of feature interactions. Finally, FMs have been specialized to better work as Context-Aware recommender systems [34].

6 Conclusion and Future Work

In this work, we have proposed an interpretable method for recommendation scenario, `kaHFM`, in which we bind the meaning of latent factors for a Factorization machine to data coming from a knowledge graph. We evaluated `kaHFM` on two different publicly available datasets on different sets of semantics-aware features. In particular, in this paper we considered Ontological, Categorical and Factual information coming from `DBpedia` and we have shown that the generated recommendation lists are more precise and personalized. Summing up, performed experiments show that: (RQ1) the learned model shows very good performance in terms of accuracy and, at the same time, is effectively interpretable; (RQ2) the computed features are semantically meaningful; (RQ3) the model is robust regarding computed features. In the future we want to test the `kaHFM` performance in different scenarios, other than recommender systems. Moreover, the model can be improved in many different ways. Different relevance metrics could be beneficial in different scenarios, as the method itself is agnostic to the specific adopted measure. This work focused on the items' vector; however, an interesting key point would be analyzing the learned users' vectors to extract more accurate profiles. Furthermore, it would be useful to exploit `kaHFM` in order to provide suggestions to knowledge graphs maintainers while adding relevant missing features to the knowledge base. In this direction, we would like to evaluate our approach in knowledge graph completion task.

References

1. Abdollahi, B., Nasraoui, O.: Explainable matrix factorization for collaborative filtering. In: Proceedings of the 25th International Conference on World Wide Web, WWW 2016, Montreal, Canada, 11–15 April 2016, Companion Volume, pp. 5–6 (2016)
2. Abdollahi, B., Nasraoui, O.: Explainable restricted Boltzmann machines for collaborative filtering. CoRR abs/1606.07129 (2016)
3. Adomavicius, G., Kwon, Y.O.: Multi-criteria recommender systems. In: Ricci, F., Rokach, L., Shapira, B. (eds.) Recommender Systems Handbook, pp. 847–880. Springer, Boston, MA (2015). https://doi.org/10.1007/978-1-4899-7637-6_25
4. Adomavicius, G., Tuzhilin, A.: Context-aware recommender systems. In: Ricci, F., Rokach, L., Shapira, B., Kantor, P.B. (eds.) Recommender Systems Handbook, pp. 217–253. Springer, Boston, MA (2011). https://doi.org/10.1007/978-0-387-85820-3_7

5. Anelli, V.W., Bellini, V., Di Noia, T., Bruna, W.L., Tomeo, P., Di Sciascio, E.: An analysis on time- and session-aware diversification in recommender systems. In: Bieliková, M., Herder, E., Cena, F., Desmarais, M.C. (eds.) Proceedings of the 25th Conference on User Modeling, Adaptation and Personalization, UMAP 2017, Bratislava, Slovakia, 09–12 July 2017, pp. 270–274. ACM (2017)
6. Bauman, K., Liu, B., Tuzhilin, A.: Aspect based recommendations: recommending items with the most valuable aspects based on user reviews. In: Proceedings of the 23rd ACM SIGKDD International Conference on Knowledge Discovery and Data Mining, Halifax, NS, Canada, 13–17 August 2017, pp. 717–725 (2017)
7. Campos, P.G., Díez, F., Cantador, I.: Time-aware recommender systems: a comprehensive survey and analysis of existing evaluation protocols. User Model. User-Adapt. Interact. **24**(1–2), 67–119 (2014)
8. Chakraborty, S., et al.: Interpretability of deep learning models: a survey of results. In: 2017 IEEE SmartWorld/SCALCOM/UIC/ATC/CBDCom/IOP/SCI, pp. 1–6 (2017)
9. Chen, X., Qin, Z., Zhang, Y.,Xu, T.: Learning to rank features for recommendation over multiple categories. In: Proceedings of the 39th International ACM SIGIR Conference on Research and Development in Information Retrieval, SIGIR 2016, Pisa, Italy, 17–21 July 2016, pp. 305–314 (2016)
10. Cramer, H.S.M., et al.: The effects of transparency on trust in and acceptance of a content-based art recommender. User Model. User-Adapt. Interact. **18**(5), 455–496 (2008)
11. Cremonesi, P., Koren, Y., Turrin, R.: Performance of recommender algorithms on top-n recommendation tasks. In: Proceedings of the 2010 ACM Conference on Recommender Systems, RecSys 2010, Barcelona, Spain, 26–30 September 2010, pp. 39–46 (2010)
12. Dhurandhar, A., Oh, S., Petrik, M.: Building an interpretable recommender via loss-preserving transformation. CoRR abs/1606.05819 (2016)
13. Di Noia, T., Magarelli, C., Maurino, A., Palmonari, M., Rula, A.: Using ontology-based data summarization to develop semantics-aware recommender systems. In: Gangemi, A., et al. (eds.) ESWC 2018. LNCS, vol. 10843, pp. 128–144. Springer, Cham (2018). https://doi.org/10.1007/978-3-319-93417-4_9
14. Di Noia, T., Mirizzi, R., Ostuni, V.C., Romito, D.: Exploiting the web of data in model-based recommender systems. In: Sixth ACM Conference on Recommender Systems, RecSys 2012, Dublin, Ireland, 9–13 September 2012, pp. 253–256 (2012)
15. Di Noia, T., Mirizzi, R., Ostuni, V.C., Romito, D., Zanker, M.: Linked open data to support content-based recommender systems. In: I-SEMANTICS 2012–8th International Conference on Semantic Systems, I-SEMANTICS 2012, Graz, Austria, 5–7 September 2012, pp. 1–8 (2012)
16. Drawel, N., Qu, H., Bentahar, J., Shakshuki, E.: Specification and automatic verification of trust-based multi-agent systems. Future Gener. Comput. Syst. (2018). https://doi.org/10.1016/j.future.2018.01.040
17. Falcone, R., Sapienza, A., Castelfranchi, C.: The relevance of categories for trusting information sources. ACM Trans. Internet Technol. **15**(4), 13:1–13:21 (2015)
18. Fernández-Tobías, I., Cantador, I., Tomeo, P., Anelli, V.W., Noia, T.D.: Addressing the user cold start with cross-domain collaborative filtering: exploiting item metadata in matrix factorization. User Model. User-Adapt. Interact. **29**(2), 443–486 (2019)
19. Gunawardana, A., Shani, G.: Evaluating recommender systems. In: Recommender Systems Handbook, pp. 265–308 (2015)

20. He, X., Chua, T.: Neural factorization machines for sparse predictive analytics. In: Proceedings of the 40th International ACM SIGIR Conference on Research and Development in Information Retrieval, Shinjuku, Tokyo, 7–11 August 2017, pp. 355–364 (2017)
21. Herlocker, J.L., Konstan, J.A., Riedl, J.: Explaining collaborative filtering recommendations. In: CSCW 2000, Proceeding on the ACM 2000 Conference on Computer Supported Cooperative Work, Philadelphia, PA, USA, 2–6 December 2000, pp. 241–250 (2000)
22. Hu, L., Jian, S., Cao, L., Chen, Q.: Interpretable recommendation via attraction modeling: learning multilevel attractiveness over multimodal movie contents. In: Proceedings of the Twenty-Seventh International Joint Conference on Artificial Intelligence, IJCAI 2018, Stockholm, Sweden, 13–19 July 2018, pp. 3400–3406 (2018)
23. Koren, Y.: Factorization meets the neighborhood: a multifaceted collaborative filtering model. In: Proceedings of the 14th ACM SIGKDD International Conference on Knowledge Discovery and Data Mining, Las Vegas, Nevada, USA, 24–27 August 2008, pp. 426–434 (2008)
24. Koren, Y., Bell, R.M., Volinsky, C.: Matrix factorization techniques for recommender systems. IEEE Comput. **42**(8), 30–37 (2009)
25. Paulheim, H., Fürnkranz, J.: Unsupervised generation of data mining features from linked open data. In: 2nd International Conference on Web Intelligence, Mining and Semantics, WIMS 2012, Craiova, Romania, 6–8 June 2012, pp. 31:1–31:12 (2012)
26. Pazzani, M.J., Billsus, D.: Content-based recommendation systems. In: Brusilovsky, P., Kobsa, A., Nejdl, W. (eds.) The Adaptive Web. LNCS, vol. 4321, pp. 325–341. Springer, Heidelberg (2007). https://doi.org/10.1007/978-3-540-72079-9_10
27. Peake, G., Wang, J.: Explanation mining: post hoc interpretability of latent factor models for recommendation systems. In: Proceedings of the 24th ACM SIGKDD International Conference on Knowledge Discovery & Data Mining, KDD 2018, London, UK, 19–23 August 2018, pp. 2060–2069 (2018)
28. Rana, A., Bridge, D.: Explanation chains: recommendations by explanation. In: Proceedings of the Poster Track of the 11th ACM Conference on Recommender Systems (RecSys 2017), Como, Italy, 28 August 2017 (2017)
29. Rendle, S.: Factorization machines. In: 2010 IEEE 10th International Conference on Data Mining (ICDM), pp. 995–1000. IEEE (2010)
30. Rendle, S.: Factorization machines. In: ICDM 2010, The 10th IEEE International Conference on Data Mining, Sydney, Australia, 14–17 December 2010, pp. 995–1000 (2010)
31. Rendle, S.: Context-Aware Ranking with Factorization Models. Springer, Heidelberg (2011). https://doi.org/10.1007/978-3-642-16898-7
32. Rendle, S., Freudenthaler, C., Gantner, Z., Schmidt-Thieme, L.: BPR: Bayesian personalized ranking from implicit feedback. In: UAI 2009, Proceedings of the Twenty-Fifth Conference on Uncertainty in Artificial Intelligence, Montreal, QC, Canada, 18–21 June 2009, pp. 452–461 (2009)
33. Rendle, S., Freudenthaler, C., Schmidt-Thieme, L.: Factorizing personalized Markov chains for next-basket recommendation. In: Proceedings of the 19th International Conference on World Wide Web, WWW 2010, Raleigh, North Carolina, USA, 26–30 April 2010, pp. 811–820 (2010)
34. Rendle, S., Gantner, Z., Freudenthaler, C., Schmidt-Thieme, L.: Fast context-aware recommendations with factorization machines. In: Proceeding of the 34th Inter-

national ACM SIGIR Conference on Research and Development in Information Retrieval, SIGIR 2011, Beijing, China, 25–29 July 2011, pp. 635–644 (2011)
35. Rendle, S., Schmidt-Thieme, L.: Pairwise interaction tensor factorization for personalized tag recommendation. In: Proceedings of the Third International Conference on Web Search and Web Data Mining, WSDM 2010, 4–6 February 2010, pp. 81–90 (2010)
36. Sinha, R.R., Swearingen, K.: The role of transparency in recommender systems. In: Extended abstracts of the 2002 Conference on Human Factors in Computing Systems, CHI 2002, Minneapolis, Minnesota, USA, 20–25 April 2002, pp. 830–831 (2002)
37. Steck, H.: Evaluation of recommendations: rating-prediction and ranking. In: Proceedings of the 7th ACM Conference on Recommender Systems, pp. 213–220. ACM (2013)
38. Sun, Z., Yang, J., Zhang, J., Bozzon, A., Huang, L., Xu, C.: Recurrent knowledge graph embedding for effective recommendation. In: Proceedings of the 12th ACM Conference on Recommender Systems, RecSys 2018, Vancouver, BC, Canada, 2–7 October 2018, pp. 297–305 (2018)
39. Tintarev, N., Masthoff, J.: A survey of explanations in recommender systems. In: Proceedings of the 23rd International Conference on Data Engineering Workshops, ICDE 2007, 15–20 April 2007, Istanbul, Turkey, pp. 801–810 (2007)
40. Tintarev, N., Masthoff, J.: Designing and evaluating explanations for recommender systems. In: Ricci, F., Rokach, L., Shapira, B., Kantor, P.B. (eds.) Recommender Systems Handbook, pp. 479–510. Springer, Boston, MA (2011). https://doi.org/10.1007/978-0-387-85820-3_15
41. Vig, J., Sen, S., Riedl, J.: Tagsplanations: explaining recommendations using tags. In: Proceedings of the 14th International Conference on Intelligent User Interfaces, IUI 2009, Sanibel Island, Florida, USA, 8–11 February 2009, pp. 47–56 (2009)
42. Vlachos, M., Duenner, C., Heckel, R., Vassiliadis, V.G., Parnell, T., Atasu, K.: Addressing interpretability and cold-start in matrix factorization for recommender systems. IEEE Trans. Knowl. Data Eng. **31**, 1253–1266 (2018)
43. Wang, X., He, X., Feng, F., Nie, L., Chua, T.: TEM: tree-enhanced embedding model for explainable recommendation. In: Proceedings of the 2018 World Wide Web Conference on World Wide Web, WWW 2018, Lyon, France 23–27 April 2018, pp. 1543–1552 (2018)
44. Xiao, J., Ye, H., He, X., Zhang, H., Wu, F., Chua, T.: Attentional factorization machines: learning the weight of feature interactions via attention networks. In: Proceedings of the Twenty-Sixth International Joint Conference on Artificial Intelligence, IJCAI 2017, Melbourne, Australia, 19–25 August 2017, pp. 3119–3125 (2017)
45. Zanker, M.: The influence of knowledgeable explanations on users' perception of a recommender system. In: Sixth ACM Conference on Recommender Systems, RecSys 2012, Dublin, Ireland, 9–13 September 2012, pp. 269–272 (2012)
46. Zhang, Y., Chen, X.: Explainable recommendation: a survey and new perspectives. CoRR abs/1804.11192 (2018)
47. Zhang, Y., Lai, G., Zhang, M., Zhang, Y., Liu, Y., Ma, S.: Explicit factor models for explainable recommendation based on phrase-level sentiment analysis. In: The 37th International Conference on Research and Development in Information Retrieval, SIGIR 2014, Gold Coast, QLD, Australia, pp. 83–92 (2014)
48. Zhang, Y., et al.: Daily-aware personalized recommendation based on feature-level time series analysis. In: Proceedings of the 24th International Conference on World Wide Web, WWW 2015, Florence, Italy, 18–22 May 2015, pp. 1373–1383 (2015)

49. Zhao, W.X., Li, S., He, Y., Wang, L., Wen, J., Li, X.: Exploring demographic information in social media for product recommendation. Knowl. Inf. Syst. **49**(1), 61–89 (2016)
50. Zheng, Y., Mobasher, B., Burke, R.D.: Incorporating context correlation into context-aware matrix factorization. In: Proceedings of the IJCAI 2015 Joint Workshop on Constraints and Preferences for Configuration and Recommendation and Intelligent Techniques for Web Personalization co-located with the 24th International Joint Conference on Artificial Intelligence (IJCAI 2015), Buenos Aires, Argentina, 27 July 2015 (2015)

Observing LOD Using Equivalent Set Graphs: It Is Mostly Flat and Sparsely Linked

Luigi Asprino[1,2(✉)], Wouter Beek[3], Paolo Ciancarini[2], Frank van Harmelen[3], and Valentina Presutti[1]

[1] STLab, ISTC-CNR, Rome, Italy
luigi.asprino@istc.cnr.it, valentina.presutti@cnr.it
[2] University of Bologna, Bologna, Italy
paolo.ciancarini@unibo.it
[3] Department of Computer Science, VU University Amsterdam, Amsterdam, The Netherlands
{w.g.j.beek,frank.van.harmelen}@vu.nl

Abstract. This paper presents an empirical study aiming at understanding the modeling style and the overall semantic structure of Linked Open Data. We observe how classes, properties and individuals are used in practice. We also investigate how hierarchies of concepts are structured, and how much they are linked. In addition to discussing the results, this paper contributes *(i)* a conceptual framework, including a set of metrics, which generalises over the observable constructs; *(ii)* an open source implementation that facilitates its application to other Linked Data knowledge graphs.

Keywords: Semantic Web · Linked Open Data · Empirical semantics

1 Analysing the Modeling Structure and Style of LOD

The interlinked collection of Linked Open Data (LOD) datasets forms the largest publicly accessible Knowledge Graph (KG) that is available on the Web today.[1] LOD distinguishes itself from most other forms of open data in that it has a formal semantics. Various studies have analysed different aspects of the formal

[1] This paper uses the following RDF prefix declarations for brevity, and uses the empty prefix (:) to denote an arbitrary example namespace.

- `dbo`: http://dbpedia.org/ontology/.
- `dul`: http://www.ontologydesignpatterns.org/ont/dul/DUL.owl.
- `foaf`: http://xmlns.com/foaf/0.1/.
- `org`: http://www.w3.org/ns/org.
- `rdfs`: http://www.w3.org/2000/01/rdf-schema.
- `owl`: http://www.w3.org/2002/07/owl.

C. Ghidini et al. (Eds.): ISWC 2019, LNCS 11778, pp. 57–74, 2019.
https://doi.org/10.1007/978-3-030-30793-6_4

semantics of LOD. However, existing analyses have often been based on relatively small samples of the ever evolving LOD KG. Moreover, it is not always clear how representative the chosen samples are. This is especially the case when observations are based on one dataset (e.g., DBpedia), or on a small number of datasets that are drawn from the much larger LOD Cloud.

This paper presents observations that have been conducted across (a very large subset of) the LOD KG. As such, this paper is not about the design of individual ontologies, rather, it is about observing *the design of the globally shared Linked Open Data ontology*. Specifically, this paper focuses on the globally shared hierarchies of classes and properties, together with their usage in instance data. This paper provides new insights about *(i)* the number of concepts defined in the LOD KG, *(ii)* the shape of ontological hierarchies, *(iii)* the extent in which recommended practices for ontology alignment are followed, and *(iv)* whether classes and properties are instantiated in a homogeneous way.

In order to conduct large-scale semantic analyses, it is necessary to calculate the deductive closure of very large hierarchical structures. Unfortunately, contemporary reasoners cannot be applied at this scale, unless they rely on expensive hardware such as a multi-node in-memory cluster. In order to handle this type of large-scale semantic analysis on commodity hardware such as regular laptops, we introduce the formal notion of an *Equivalence Set Graph*. With this notion we are able to implement efficient algorithms to build the large hierarchical structures that we need for our study.

We use the formalization and implementation presented in this paper to compute two (very large) Equivalence Set Graphs: one for classes and one for properties. By querying them, we are able to quantify various aspects of formal semantics at the scale of the LOD KG. Our observations show that there is a lack of explicit links (alignment) between ontological entities and that there is a significant number of concepts with empty extension. Furthermore, property hierarchies are observed to be mainly flat, while class hierarchies have varying depth degree, although most of them are flat too.

This paper makes the following contributions:

1. A new formal concept (Equivalence Set Graph) that allows us to specify compressed views of a LOD KG (presented in Sect. 3.2).
2. An implementation of efficient algorithms that allow Equivalence Set Graphs to be calculated on commodity hardware (cf. Sect. 4).
3. A detailed analysis of how classes and properties are used at the level of the whole LOD KG, using the formalization and implementation of Equivalence Set Graphs.

The remaining of this paper is organized as follows: Sect. 2 summarizes related work. The approach is presented in Sect. 3. Section 4 describes the algorithm for computing an Equivalence Set Graph form a RDF dataset. Section 3.4 defines a set of metrics that are measured in Sect. 5. Section 6 discusses the observed values and concludes.

2 Related Work

Although large-scale analyses of LOD have been performed since the early years of the Semantic Web, we could not find previous work directly comparable with ours. The closest we found are not recent and performed on a much smaller scale. In 2004, Gil and García [8] showed that the Semantic Web (at that time consisting of 1.3 million triples distributed over 282 datasets) behaves as a Complex System: the average path length between nodes is short (small world property), there is a high probability that two neighbors of a node are also neighbors of one another (high clustering factor), and nodes follow a power-law degree distribution. In 2008, similar results were reported by [14] in an individual analysis of 250 schemas. These two studies focus on topological graph aspects exclusively, and do not take semantics into account.

In 2005, Ding et al. [6] analysed the use of the Friend-of-a-Friend (FOAF) vocabulary on the Semantic Web. They harvested 1.5 million RDF datasets, and computed a social network based on those data datasets. They observed that the number of instances per dataset follows the Zipf distribution.

In 2006, Ding et al. [4] analysed 1.7 million datasets, containing 300 million triples. They reported various statistics over this data collection, such as the number of datasets per namespace, the number of triples per dataset, and the number of class- and property-denoting terms. The semantic observation in this study is limited since no deduction was applied.

In 2006, a survey by Wang et al. [16] aimed at assessing the use of OWL and RDF schema vocabularies in 1,300 ontologies harvested from the Web. This study reported statistics such as the number of classes, properties, and instances of these ontologies. Our study provides both an updated view on these statistics, and a much larger scale of the observation (we analysed ontological entities defined in ∼650k datasets crawled by LOD-a-lot [7]).

Several studies [2,5,9] analysed common issues with the use of `owl:sameAs` in practice. Mallea et al. [11] showed that blank nodes, although discouraged by guidelines, are prevalent on the Semantic Web. Recent studies [13] experimented on analysing the coherence of large LOD datasets, such as DBpedia, by leveraging foundational ontologies. Observations on the presence of foundational distinctions in LOD has been studied in [1].

These studies have a similar goal as ours: to answer the question how knowledge representation is used in practice in the Semantic Web, although the focus may partially overlap. We generalise over all equivalence (or identity) constructs instead of focusing on one specific, we observe the overall design of LOD ontologies, analysing a very large subject of it, we take semantics into account by analysing the asserted as well as the inferred data.

3 Approach

3.1 Input Source

Ideally, our input is the whole LOD Cloud, which is (a common metonymy for identifying) a very large and distributed Knowledge Graph. The two largest available crawls of LOD available today are WebDataCommons and LOD-a-lot.

WebDataCommons[2] [12] consists of ~31B triples that have been extracted from the CommonCrawl datasets (November 2018 version). Since its focus is mostly on RDFa, microdata, and microformats, WebDataCommons contains a very large number of relatively small graph components that use the Schema.org[3] vocabulary.

LOD-a-lot[4] [7] contains ~28B unique triples that are the result of merging the graphs that have been crawled by LOD Laundromat [3] into one single graph. The LOD Laundromat crawl is based on data dumps that are published as part of the LOD Cloud, hence it contains relatively large graphs that are highly interlinked. The LOD-a-lot datadump is more likely to contain RDFS and OWL annotations than WebDataCommons. Since this study focuses on the *semantics* of Linked Open Data, it uses the LOD-a-lot datadump.

LOD-a-lot only contains explicit assertions, i.e., triples that have been literally published by some data owner. This means that the implicit assertions, i.e., triples that can be derived from explicit assertions and/or other implicit assertions, are not part of it and must be calculated by a reasoner. Unfortunately, contemporary reasoners are unable to compute the semantic closure over 28B triples. Advanced alternatives for large-scale reasoning, such as the use of clustering computing techniques (e.g., [15]) require expensive resources in terms of CPU/time and memory/space. Since we want to make running large-scale semantic analysis a frequent activity in Linked Data Science, we present a new way to perform such large-scale analyses against very low hardware cost.

This section outlines our approach for performing large-scale semantic analyses of the LOD KG. We start out by introducing the new notion of Equivalence Set Graph (ESG) (Sect. 3.2). Once Equivalence Set Graphs have been informally introduced, the corresponding formal definitions are given in Sect. 3.3. Finally, the metrics that will be measured using the ESGs are defined in Sect. 3.4.

3.2 Introducing Equivalence Set Graphs

An Equivalence Set Graph (ESG) is a tuple $\langle \mathcal{V}, \mathcal{E}, p_{eq}, p_{sub}, p_e, p_s \rangle$. The nodes $\mathcal{V}$ of an ESG are equivalence sets of terms from the universe of discourse. The directed edges $\mathcal{E}$ of an ESG are specialization relations between those equivalence sets. p_{eq} is an equivalence relation that determines which equivalence sets are formed from the terms in the universe of discourse. p_{sub} is a partial order relation that determines the specialization relation between the equivalence sets.

---

[2] See http://webdatacommons.org.

[3] See https://schema.org.

[4] See http://lod-a-lot.lod.labs.vu.nl.

In order to handle equivalences and specializations of p_{eq} and p_{sub} (see below for details and examples), we introduce p_e, an equivalence relation over properties (e.g., `owl:equivalentProperty`) that allows to retrieve all the properties that are equivalent to p_{eq} and p_{sub}, and p_s which is a specialization relation over properties (e.g., `rdfs:subPropertyOf`) that allows to retrieve all the properties that specialize p_{eq} and p_{sub}.

The inclusion of the parameters p_{eq}, p_{sub}, p_e, and p_s makes the Equivalence Set Graph a very generic concept. By changing the equivalence relation (p_{eq}), ESG can be applied to classes (`owl:equivalentClass`), properties (`owl:equivalentProperty`), or instances (`owl:sameAs`). By changing the specialization relation (p_{sub}), ESG can be applied to class hierarchies (`rdfs:subClassOf`), property hierarchies (`rdfs:subPropertyOf`), or concept hierarchies (`skos:broader`).

An Equivalence Set Graph is created starting from a given RDF Knowledge Graph. The triples in the RDF KG are referred to as its *explicit* statements. The *implicit* statements are those that can be inferred from the explicit statements. An ESG must be built taking into account both the explicit and the *implicit* statements. For example, if p_{eq} is `owl:equivalentClass`, then the following Triple Patterns (TP) retrieve the terms `?y` that are explicitly equivalent to a given ground term `:x`:

```
{ :x owl:equivalentClass ?y } union { ?y owl:equivalentClass :x }
```

In order to identify the terms that are *implicitly* equivalent to `:x`, we also have to take into account the following:

1. The closure of the equivalence predicate (reflexive, symmetric, transitive).
2. Equivalences (w.r.t. p_e) and/or specializations (w.r.t. p_s) of the equivalence predicate (p_{eq}). E.g., the equivalence between `:x` and `:y` is asserted with the `:sameClass` predicate, which is equivalent to `owl:equivalentClass`):

```
:sameClass owl:equivalentProperty owl:equivalentClass.
:x :sameClass :y.
```

3. Equivalences (w.r.t. p_e) and/or specializations (w.r.t. p_s) of predicates (i.e. p_e and p_s) for asserting equivalence or specialization relations among properties. E.g., the equivalence between `:x` and `:y` is asserted with the `:sameClass` predicate, which is a specialization of `owl:equivalentClass` according to `:sameProperty`, which it itself a specialization of `owl:equivalentProperty`:

```
:sameProperty rdfs:subPropertyOf owl:equivalentProperty.
:sameClass :sameProperty owl:equivalentClass.
:x :sameClass :y.
```

The same distinction between explicit and implicit statements can be made with respect to the specialization relation (p_{sub}). E.g., for an Equivalence Set Graph that uses `rdfs:subClassOf` as its specialization relation, the following TP retrieves the terms `?y` that explicitly specialize a given ground term `:x`:

```
?y rdfs:subClassOf :x.
```

In order to identify the entities that are *implicit* specializations of `:x`, we must also take the following into account:

1. The closure of the specialization predicate (reflexive, anti-symmetric, transitive).
2. Equivalences (w.r.t. p_e) and/or specializations (w.r.t. p_s) of the specialization predicate (p_{sub}). E.g, `:y` is a specialization of `:x` according to the `:subClass` property, which is itself a specialization of the `rdfs:subClassOf` predicate:

```
:subClass rdfs:subPropertyOf rdfs:subClassOf.
:y :subClass :x.
```

3. Equivalences (w.r.t. p_e) and/or specializations (w.r.t. p_s) of predicates (i.e. p_e and p_s) for asserting equivalence or specialization relations among properties:

```
:subProperty rdfs:subPropertyOf rdfs:subPropertyOf.
:subClass :subProperty rdfs:subClassOf.
:y :subClass :x.
```

Although there exist alternative ways for asserting an equivalence (specialization) relation between two entities e_1 and e_2 (e.g., $e_1 = e_2 \sqcap \exists p.\top$ implies $e_1 \sqsubseteq e_2$), we focused on the most explicit ones, namely, those in which e_1 and e_2 are connected by a path having as edges p_{eq} (p_{sub}) or properties that are equivalent or subsumed by p_{eq} (called *Closure Path* cf. Definition 2). We argue that for statistical observations explicit assertions provide acceptable approximations of the overall picture.

Figure 1 shows an example of an RDF Knowledge Graph (Fig. 1a). The equivalence predicate (p_{eq}) is `owl:equivalentClass`; the specialization predicate (p_{sub}) is `rdfs:subClassOf`, the property for asserting equivalences among predicates (p_e) is `owl:equivalentProperty`, the property for asserting specializations among predicates (p_s) is (`rdfs:subPropertyOf`). The corresponding Equivalence Set Graph (Fig. 1b) contains four equivalence sets. The top node represents the agent node, which encapsulates entities in DOLCE and W3C's Organization ontology. Three nodes inherit from the agent node. Two nodes contain classes that specialize `dul:Agent` in the DOLCE ontology (i.e. `dul:PhysicalAgent` and `dul:SocialAgent`). The third node represents the person concept, which encapsulates entities in DBpedia, DOLCE, and FOAF. The equivalence of these classes is asserted by `owl:equivalentClass` and `:myEquivalentClass`. Since `foaf:Person` specialises `org:Agent` (using `:mySubClassOf` which specialises `rdfs:subClassOf`) and `dul:Person` specialises `dul:Agent` the ESG contains an edge between the person and the agent concept.

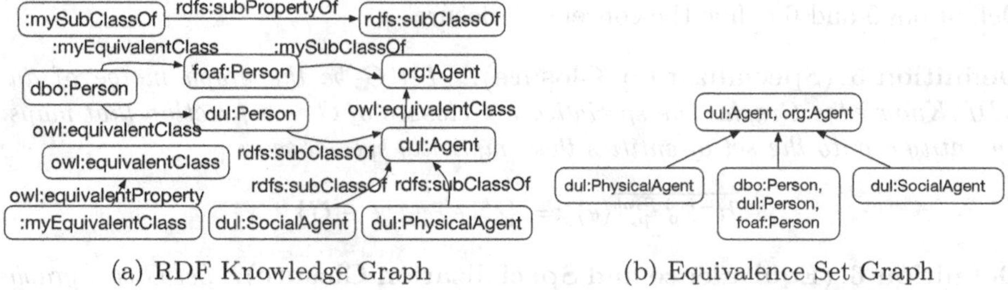

(a) RDF Knowledge Graph (b) Equivalence Set Graph

Fig. 1. An example of an RDF Knowledge Graph and its corresponding Equivalence Set Graph.

3.3 Formalizing Equivalence Set Graphs

This section contains the formalization of ESGs that were informally introduced above. An ESG must be configured with ground terms for the following parameters: *(i)* p_{eq}: the equivalence property for the observed entities; *(ii)* p_{sub}: the specialization property for the observed entities; *(iii)* p_e the equivalence property for properties; *(iv)* p_s the specialization property for properties.

Definition 1 specifies the deductive closure over an arbitrary property p with respect to p_e and p_s. This is the set of properties that are implicitly equivalent to or subsumed by p. It is worth noticing that, in the general case, a deductive closure for a class of (observed) entities depends on all the four parameters: p_{eq} and p_{sub} are needed for retrieving equivalences and specializations among entities, and p_e and p_s are need for retrieving equivalences and specializations of p_{eq} and p_{sub}. It is easy to see that when the subject of observation are properties p_{eq} and p_{sub} coincide with p_e and p_s respectively.

Definition 1 (Deductive Closure of Properties). $\overline{\mathcal{C}^{p_e,p_s}_{p_e,p_s}}(p)$ *is the deductive closure of property* p *with respect to* p_e *and* p_s.

Definition 2 (Closure Path). $\overset{p+}{\Longleftrightarrow}$ *denotes any path, consisting of one or more occurrences of predicates from* $\overline{\mathcal{C}^{p_e,p_s}_{p_e,p_s}}(p)$.

Once the four custom parameters have been specified, a specific Equivalence Set Graph is determined by Definitions 3 and 4.

Definition 3 (ESG Nodes). *Let G be the graph merge [10] of an RDF Knowledge Graph. The set of nodes of the corresponding Equivalence Set Graph is:*

$$\mathcal{V}^{p_{eq},p_{sub}}_{p_e,p_s} := \{v = \{e_1, \ldots, e_n\} \mid (\forall e_i, e_j \in v)(e_i \overset{p_{eq}+}{\Longleftrightarrow} e_j \in G)\}$$

Definition 4 (ESG Edges). *Let G be the graph merge of an RDF Knowledge Graph. The set of edges of the corresponding Equivalence Set Graph is:*

$$\mathcal{E}^{p_{eq},p_{sub}}_{p_e,p_s} := \{(v = \{v_1, \ldots, v_n\}, z = \{z_1, \ldots, z_n\}) \mid (\exists v_i \in v)(\exists z_j \in z)(\exists p \in \overline{\mathcal{C}^{p_e,p_s}_{p_e,p_s}}(p_{sub}))(\langle v_i, p, z_j \rangle \in G)\}$$

Definitions 5 and 6 define the concept of closure.

Definition 5 (Specialization Closure). *Let G be the graph merge of an RDF Knowledge Graph. The specialization closure of G is a function that maps an entity e onto the set of entities that implicitly specialise e:*

$$\overline{\mathcal{H}+^{p_{eq},p_{sub}}_{p_e,p_s}}(e) := \{e' \mid e' \overset{p_{sub}}{\Longrightarrow}{+} e \in G\}$$

Definition 6 (Equivalence and Specialization Closure). *Let G be a graph merge of an RDF Knowledge Graph, the equivalence and specialization closure of G is a function that given an entity e returns all the entities that are either implicitly equivalent to e, or implicitly specialize e. I.e.:*

$$\overline{\mathcal{C}^{p_{eq},p_{sub}}_{p_e,p_s}}(e) := \{e' \mid (\exists v \in \mathcal{V}^{p_{eq},p_{sub}}_{p_e,p_s})(e \in v \wedge e' \in v)\} \cup \overline{\mathcal{H}+^{p_{eq},p_{sub}}_{p_e,p_s}}(e)$$

3.4 Metrics

In this section we define a set of metrics that can be computed by querying Equivalence Set Graphs.

Number of Equivalence Sets (ES), Number of Observed Entities (OE), and Ratio (R). The number of equivalence sets (ES) is the number of nodes in an Equivalence Set Graph, i.e., $|\mathcal{V}^{p_{eq},p_{sub}}_{p_e,p_s}|$. Equivalence sets contain equivalent entities (classes, properties or individuals). The number of observed entities (OE) is the size of the universe of discourse: i.e. $|\{e \in v \mid v \in \mathcal{V}^{p_{eq},p_{sub}}_{p_e,p_s}\}|$. The ratio $\frac{ES}{OE}$ (R) between the number of equivalence sets and the number of entities indicates to what extent equivalence is used among the observed entities. If equivalence is rarely used, R approaches 1.0.

Number of Edges (E). The total number of edges is $|\mathcal{E}^{p_{eq},p_{sub}}_{p_e,p_s}|$.

Height of Nodes. The height $h(v)$ of a node v is defined as the length of the longest path from a leaf node until v. The maximum height of an ESG is defined as $H_{max} = \text{argmax}_{v \in V}\, h(v)$. *Distribution of the height*: for n ranging from 0 to H_{max} we compute the percentage of nodes having that height (i.e. H(n)).

Number of Isolated Equivalent Sets (IN), Number of Top Level Equivalence Sets (TL). In order to observe the shape and structure of hierarchies in LOD, we compute the number Isolated Equivalent Sets (IN) in the graph, and the number of Top Level Equivalence Sets (TL). An IES is a node without incoming or outgoing edges. A TL is a node without outgoing edges.

Extensional Size of Observed Entities. Let c be a class in LOD, and t a property in the deductive closure of `rdf:type`. We define the extensional size of c (i.e. $S(c)$) as the number of triples having c as object and t as predicate (i.e. $S(c) = \sum_{t \in \overline{\mathcal{C}}} |\{\langle e,t,c\rangle | \exists e. \langle e,t,c\rangle \in G\}|$ where $\overline{\mathcal{C}}$ is $\overline{\mathcal{C}^{p_e,p_s}_{p_e,p_s}}$). We define the extensional size of a property p (i.e. $S(p)$) as the number of triples having p as predicate (i.e. $S(p) = |\{\langle s,p,o\rangle | \exists p,o. \langle s,p,o\rangle \in G\}|$).

Extensional Size of Equivalence Sets. We define two measures: *direct extensional size* (i.e. DES) and *indirect extensional size* (i.e. IES). DES is defined as the sum of the extensional size of the entities belonging to the set. The IES is its DES summed with the DES of all equivalence sets in its closure.

Number of Blank Nodes. Blank nodes are anonymous RDF resource used (for example) within ontologies to define class restrictions. We compute the number of blank nodes in LOD and we compute the above metrics both including and excluding blank nodes.

Number of Connected Components. Given a directed graph G, a strongly connected component (SCC) is a sub-graph of G where any two nodes are connected to each other by at least one path; a weakly connected component (WCC) is the undirected version of a sub-graph of G where any two nodes are connected by any path. We compute the number and the size of SCC and WCC of an ESG, to observe its distribution. Observing these values (especially on WCC) provides insights on the shape of hierarchical structures formed by the observed entities, at LOD scale.

4 Computing Equivalence Set Graphs

In this Section we describe the algorithm for computing an equivalence set graph from a RDF dataset. An implementation of the algorithm is available online[5].

Selecting Entities to Observe. The first step of the procedure for computing an ESG is to select the entities to observe, from the input KG. To this end, a set of criteria for selecting these entities can be defined. In our study we want to observe the behaviour of classes and properties, hence our criteria are the followings: *(i)* A class is an entity that belongs to `rdfs:Class`. We assume that the property for declaring that an entity belongs to a class is `rdf:type`. *(ii)* A class is the subject (object) of a triple where the property has `rdfs:Class` as domain (range). We assume that the property for declaring the domain (range) of a property is `rdfs:domain` (`rdfs:range`). *(iii)* A property is the predicate of a triple. *(iv)* A property is an entity that belongs to `rdf:Property`. *(v)* A property is the subject (object) of a triple where the property has `rdf:Property` as domain (range). We defined these criteria since the object of our observation are classes and properties, but the framework can be also configured for observing other kinds of entities (e.g. individuals).

As discussed in Sect. 3.2 we have to take into account possible equivalences and/or specializations of the ground terms, i.e. `rdf:type`, `rdfs:range`, `rdfs:domain` and the classes `rdfs:Class` and `rdf:Property`.

Computing Equivalence Set Graph. As we saw in the previous section, for computing an ESG a preliminary step is needed in order to compute the deductive closure of properties (which is an ESG itself). We can distinguish two cases depending if condition $p_{eq} = p_e$ and $p_{sub} = p_s$ holds or not. If this condition

[5] https://w3id.org/edwin/repository.

holds (e.g. when the procedure is set for computing the ESG of properties), then for retrieving equivalences and specializations of p_{eq} and p_{sub} the procedure has to use the ESG is building (cf. UPDATEPSETS). Otherwise, the procedure has to compute an ESG (i.e. $\overline{\mathcal{C}^{p_e,p_s}_{p_e,p_s}}$) using p_e as p_{eq} and p_s as p_{sub}. We describe how the algorithm works in the first case (in the second case, the algorithm acts in a similar way, unless that P_e and P_s are filled with $\overline{\mathcal{C}^{p_e,p_s}_{p_e,p_s}}(p_{eq})$ and $\overline{\mathcal{C}^{p_e,p_s}_{p_e,p_s}}(p_{sub})$ respectively and UPDATEPSETS is not used).

The input of the main procedure (i.e. Algorithm 1) includes: *(i)* a set P_e of equivalence relations. In our case P_e will contain `owl:equivalentProperty` for the ESG of properties, and (the deductive closure of) `owl:equivalentClass` for the ESG of classes; *(ii)* a set P_s of specialisation relations. In our case P_s will contain `rdfs:subPropertyOf` for the ESG of properties, and (the deductive closure of) `rdfs:subClassOf` for the ESG of classes. The output of the algorithm is a set of maps and multi-maps which store nodes and edges of the computed ESG:

ID a map that, given an IRI of an entity, returns the identifier of the ES it belongs to;

IS a multi-map that, given an identifier of an ES, returns the set of entities it contains;

H (H^-) a multi-map that, given an identifier of an ES, returns the identifiers of the explicit super (sub) ESs.

The algorithm also uses two additional data structures: *(i)* P'_e is a set that stores the equivalence relations already processed (which are removed from P_e as soon as they are processed); *(ii)* P'_s is a set that stores the specialisations relations already processed (which are removed from P_s as soon as they are processed).

The algorithm repeats three sub-procedures until P_e and P_s become empty: *(i)* Compute Equivalence Sets (Algorithm 2), *(ii)* Compute the Specialisation Relation among the Equivalence Sets (Algorithm 4), *(iii)* Update P_e and P_s (i.e. UPDATEPSETS).

Algorithm 2 iterates over P_e, and at each iteration moves a property p from P_e to P'_e, until P_e is empty. For each triple $\langle r_1, p, r_2\rangle \in G$, it tests the following conditions and behaves accordingly:

1. r_1 and r_2 do not belong to any ES, then: a new ES containing $\{r_1, r_2\}$ is created and assigned an identifier i. (r_1,i) and (r_2,i) are added to ID, and (i, $\{r_1, r_2\}$) to IS;
2. r_1 (r_2) belongs to the ES with identifier i_1 (i_2) and r_2 (r_1) does not belong to any ES. Then ID and IS are updated to include r_2 (r_1) in i_1 (i_2);
3. r_1 belongs to an ES with identifier i_1 and r_2 belongs to an ES with identifier i_2 (with $i_1 \neq i_2$). Then i_1 and i_2 are merged into a new ES with identifier i_3 and the hierarchy is updated by Algorithm 3. This algorithm ensures both the followings: *(i)* the super (sub) set of i_3 is the union of the super (sub) sets of i_1 and i_2; *(ii)* the super (sub) sets that are pointed by (points to) (through H or H^-) i_1 or i_2, are pointed by (points to) i_3 and no longer by/to i_1 or i_2.

The procedure for computing the specialization (i.e. Algorithm 4) moves p from P_s to P_s' until P_s becomes empty. For each triple $\langle r_1, p, r_2 \rangle \in G$ the algorithm ensures that r_1 is in an equivalence set with identifier i_1 and r_2 is in an equivalence set with identifier i_2:

1. If r_1 and r_2 do not belong to any ES, then IS and ID are updated to include two new ESs $\{r_1\}$ with identifier i_1 and $\{r_2\}$ with identifier i_2;
2. if r_1 (r_2) belongs to an ES with identifier i_1 (i_2) and r_2 (r_1) does not belong to any ES, then IS and ID are updated to include a new ES $\{r_2\}$ ($\{r_1\}$) with identifier i_2 (i_1).

At this point r_1 is in i_1 and r_2 is in i_2 (i_1 and i_2 may be equal) and then i_2 is added to $H(i_1)$ and i_1 is added to $H^-(i_2)$.

The procedure UPDATEPSETS (the last called by Algorithm 1) adds to P_e (P_s) the properties in the deductive closure of properties in P_e' (P_s'). For each property p in P_e' (P_s'), UPDATEPSETS uses ID to retrieve the identifier of the ES of p, then it uses H^- to traverse the graph in order retrieve all the ESs that are subsumed by ID(p). If a property p' belongs to ID(p) or to any of the traversed ESs is not in P_e' (P_s), then p' is added to P_e (P_s).

Algorithm Time Complexity. Assuming that retrieving all triples having a certain predicate and inserting/retrieving values from maps costs O(1). The algorithm steps once per each equivalence or subsumption triple. FIXHIEARCHY costs in the worst case $O(n_{eq})$ where n_{eq} is the number of equivalence triples in the input dataset. n_{sub} is the number of specialization triples in the input dataset. Hence, time complexity of the algorithm is $O(n_{eq}^2 + n_{sub})$.

Algorithm Space Complexity. In the worst case the algorithm needs to create an equivalence set for each equivalence triple and a specialization relation for each specialization triple. Storing ID and IS maps costs ~2n (where n is the number of observed entities from the input dataset), whereas storing H and H^- costs $\sim 4n^2$. Hence, the space complexity of the algorithm is $O(n^2)$.

5 Results

In order to analyse the modeling structure and style of LOD we compute two ESGs from LOD-a-lot: one for classes and one for properties. Both graphs are available for download[6]. We used a laptop (3 Ghz Intel Core i7, 16 GB of RAM). Building the two ESGs took ~11 h, computing their extension took ~15 h. Once the ESG are built, we can query them to compute the metrics defined in Sect. 3.4 and make observations at LOD scale within the order of a handful of seconds/minutes. Queries to compute indirect extensional dimension may take longer, in our experience up to 40 min.

The choice of analysing classes and properties separately reflects the distinctions made by RDF(S) and OWL models. However, this distinction is sometimes overlooked in LOD ontologies. We observed the presence of the following triples:

[6] https://w3id.org/edwin/iswc2019_esgs.

Algorithm 1. Main Procedure

procedure MAIN(P_e, P_s)
  $P_e^{'} = P_s^{'} = \emptyset$
  Init ID: $IRI \rightarrow ID_{IS}$
  Init IS: $ID_{IS} \rightarrow IS$
  Init H: $ID_{IS} \rightarrow 2^{ID_{IS}}$
  Init H^{-}: $ID_{IS} \rightarrow 2^{ID_{IS}}$
  Init C: $ID_{IS} \rightarrow 2^{ID_{IS}}$
  Init C^{-}: $ID_{IS} \rightarrow 2^{ID_{IS}}$
  while $P_e \neq \emptyset || P_s \neq \emptyset$ **do**
    COMPUTEESS( )
    COMPUTEHIERARCHY( )
    UPDATEPSETS( )
  end while
end procedure
procedure UPDATEPSETS( )
  for $p_e' \in P_e' || p_s' \in P_s'$ **do**
    for p_e s.t. $\overline{C^{p_e,p_s}_{p_e,p_s}}(p_e')$ **do**
      Add p_e to P_e if $p_e \notin P_e'$
    end for
    for p_s s.t. $\overline{C^{p_e,p_s}_{p_e,p_s}}(p_s')$ **do**
      Add p_s to P_s if $p_s \notin P_s'$
    end for
  end for
end procedure

Algorithm 2. Compute Equivalence Sets

procedure COMPUTEESS( )
  for $p_e \in P_e$ **do**
    Remove p from P_e and Put p in $P_e^{'}$
    for $\langle r_1, p_e, r_2 \rangle \in G$ **do**
      if $ID(r_1) = \emptyset \wedge ID(r_2) = \emptyset$ **then**
        Let i be a new identifier
        Put (r_1, i) and (r_2, i) in ID
        Put $(i, \{r_1, r_2\})$ in IS
      else if $ID(r_1) = i_1 \wedge ID(r_2) = \emptyset$ **then**
        Put (r_2, i_1) in ID and Put r_2 in $IS(i_1)$
      else if $ID(r_1) = \emptyset \wedge ID(r_2) = i_2$ **then**
        Put (r_1, i_2) in ID and Put r_1 in $IS(i_2)$
      else if $ID(r_1)=i_1 \wedge ID(r_2)=i_2 \wedge i_1 \neq i_2$ **then**
        Let $IS_3 \leftarrow IS(i_1) \cup IS(i_1)$
        Let i_3 be a new identifier
        Put (i_3, IS_3) in IS
        Put (r_3, i_3) in ID for all $r_3 \in IS_3$
        Remove $(i_1, IS(i_1))$ from IS
        Remove $(i_2, IS(i_2))$ from IS
        FIXHIERARCHY(i_1,i_2,i_3)
      end if
    end for
  end for
end procedure

```
rdfs:subPropertyOf rdfs:domain rdf:Property .  # From W3C
rdfs:subClassOf rdfs:domain rdfs:Class .       # From W3C
rdfs:subClassOf rdfs:subPropertyOf rdfs:subPropertyOf . # From BTC
```

The first two triples come from RDFS vocabulary defined by W3C, and the third can be found in the Billion Triple Challenge datasets[7]. These triples imply that if a property p_1 is subsumed by a property p_2, then p_1 and p_2 become classes. Since our objective is to observe classes and property separately we can not accept the third statement. For similar reasons, we can not accept the following triple:

```
rdf:type rdfs:subPropertyOf rdfs:subClassOf . # From BTC
```

which implies that whatever has a type becomes a class. It is worth noticing that these statements does not violate RDF(S) semantics, but they do have far-reaching consequences for the entire Semantic Web, most of which are unwanted.

Equivalence Set Graph for Properties. We implemented the algorithm presented in Sect. 4 to compute the ESG for properties contained in LOD-a-lot [7]. Our input parameters to the algorithm are: *(i)* $P_{eq} = \{$`owl:equivalentProperty`$\}$; *(ii)*

[7] https://github.com/timrdf/DataFAQs/wiki/Billion-Triples-Challenge.

Algorithm 3

procedure FIXHIERARCHY(i_1, i_2, i_3)
  $H(i_3) = H(i_1) \cup H(i_2)$
  $H^-(i_3) = H^-(i_1) \cup H^-(i_2)$
  for $i_{11} \in H(i_1)$ **do**
    Remove i_1 from $H^-(i_{11})$
    Add i_3 to $H^-(i_{11})$
  end for
  for $i_{11} \in H^-(i_1)$ **do**
    Remove i_1 from $H(i_{11})$
    Add i_3 to $H(i_{11})$
  end for
  for $i_{21} \in H(i_2)$ **do**
    Remove i_2 from $H^-(i_{21})$
    Add i_3 to $H^-(i_{21})$
  end for
  for $i_{21} \in H^-(i_2)$ **do**
    Remove i_2 from $H(i_{21})$
    Add i_3 to $H(i_{21})$
  end for
end procedure

Algorithm 4

procedure COMPUTEHIERARCHY( )
  for $p_s \in P_s$ **do**
    Remove p from P_s and put p in $P_s^{'}$
    for $\langle r_1, p_s, r_2 \rangle$ **do**
      if $ID(r_1) = \emptyset \wedge ID(r_2) = \emptyset$ **then**
        Let i_1 and i_2 be new identifiers
        Put (r_1, i_1) and (r_2, i_2) in ID
        Put $(i_1, \{r_1\})$ and $(i_2, \{r_2\})$ in IS
      else if $ID(r_1) = i_1 \wedge ID(r_2) = \emptyset$ **then**
        Let i_2 be a new identifier
        Put (r_2, i_2) in ID and $(i_2, \{r_2\})$ in IS
      else if $ID(r_1) = \emptyset \wedge ID(r_2) = i_2$ **then**
        Let i_1 be a new identifier
        Put (r_1, i_1) in ID
        Put $(i_1, \{r_1\})$ in IS
      end if
      Put $(i_1, H(i_1) \cup \{i_2\})$ in H
      Put $(i_2, H^-(i_2) \cup \{i_1\})$ in H^-
    end for
  end for
end procedure

$P_s = \{$`rdfs:subPropertyOf`$\}$. Since `owl:equivalentProperty` is neither equivalent to nor subsumed by any other property in LOD-a-lot, the algorithm used only this property for retrieving equivalence relations. Instead, for computing the hierarchy of equivalence sets the algorithm used 451 properties which have been found implicitly equivalent to or subsumed by `rdfs:subPropertyOf`.

Table 1 presents the metrics (cf. Sect. 3.4) computed from the equivalence set graph for properties. It is quite evident that the properties are poorly linked. *(i)* The ratio (R) tends to 1, indicating that few properties are declared equivalent to other properties; *(ii)* the ratio between the number of equivalence sets (ES) and the number of isolated sets (IN) is 0.88, indicating that most of properties are defined outside of a hierarchy; *(iii)* the height distribution of ESG nodes (cf. Fig. 2a) shows that all the nodes have height less than 1; *(iv)* the high number of Weakly Connected Components (WCC) is close to the total number of ES. Figure 2c shows that the dimension of ESs follows the Zipf's law (a trend also observed in [6]): many ESs with few instances and few ESs with many instances. Most properties (~90%) have at least one instance. This result is in contrast with one of the findings of Ding and Finin in 2006 [4] who observed that most properties have never been instantiated. We note that blank nodes are present in property hierarchies, although they cannot be instantiated. This is probably due to some erroneous statement.

Equivalence Set Graph for Classes. From the ESG for properties we extract all the properties implicitly equivalent to or subsumed by `owl:equivalentClass`

Table 1. Statistics computed on the equivalent set graph for properties and classes, from LOD-a-lot. They include the metrics defined in Sect. 3.4. IES(n) indicates the Number of Equivalent Sets having indirect size n or greater. The term *entity* is here used to refer to classes and properties.

Metrics		Property	Class
# of Observed Entities	OE	1,308,946	4,857,653
# of Observed Entities without BNs	OE_{bn}	1,301,756	3,719,371
# of Blank Nodes (BNs)	BN	7,190	1,013,224
# of Equivalence Sets (ESs)	ES	1,305,364	4,038,722
# of Equivalence Sets (ESs) without BNs	ES_{bn}	1,298,174	3,092,523
Ratio between ES and OE	R	.997	.831
Ratio between ES and OE without BNs	R_{bn}	.997	.831
# of Edges	E	147,606	5,090,482
Maximum Height	H_{max}	14	77
# Isolated ESs	IN	1,157,825	288,614
# of Top Level ESs	TL	1,181,583	1,281,758
# of Top Level ESs without BNs	TL_{bn}	1,174,717	341,792
# of OE in Top Level ESs	$OE\text{-}TL$	1,185,591	1,334,631
# of OE in Top Level ESs without BNs	$OE\text{-}TL_{bn}$	1,178,725	348,599
Ratio between TL and OE-TL	RTL	.996	.960
Ratio between TL and OE-TL without BNs	RTL_{bn}	.996	.980
# of Weakly Connected Components	WCC	1,174,152	449,332
# of Strongly Connected Components	SCC	1,305,364	4,038,011
# of OE with Empty Extension	OE_0	140,014	4,024,374
# of OE with Empty Extension without BNs	OE_{0bn}	132,824	2,912,700
# of ES with Empty Extension	ES_0	131,854	3,060,467
# of ES with Empty Extension without BNs	ES_{0bn}	124,717	2,251,626
# of ES with extensional size greater than 1	$IES(1)$	1,173,510	978,255
# of ES with extensional size greater than 10	$IES(10)$	558,864	478,746
# of ES with extensional size greater than 100	$IES(100)$	246,719	138,803
# of ES with extensional size greater than 1K	$IES(1K)$	79,473	30,623
# of ES with extensional size greater than 1M	$IES(1M)$	1,762	3,869
# of ES with extensional size greater than 1B	$IES(1B)$	34	1,833
# of OE-TL with Empty Extension	$OE\text{-}TL_0$	26,640	1,043,099
# of OE-TL with Empty Extension w/o BNs	$OE\text{-}TL_{0bn}$	19,774	83,674
# of TL with Empty Extension	TL_0	18,884	869,443
# of TL with Empty Extension w/o BNs	TL_{0bn}	12,071	66,805

(2 properties) and put them in P_{eq}, the input parameter of the algorithm. P_s includes 381 properties that are implicitly equivalent to or subsumed by `rdfs:subClassOf`.

Table 1 reports the metrics (cf. Sect. 3.4) computed from the ESG for classes. Although class equivalence is more common than property equivalence, the value of R is still very high (0.83), suggesting that equivalence relations among classes are poorly used. Differently from properties, classes form deeper hierarchies: the maximum height of a node is 77 (compared to 14 for properties), only 7% of nodes are isolated and only 31% are top level nodes, we observe from Fig. 2a that the height distribution has a smoother trend than for properties but still it quickly reaches values slightly higher than 0. We observe that (unlike properties) most of class ES are not instantiated: only 31.7% of ES have at least one instance. A similar result emerges from the analysis carried out in 2006 by Ding and Finin [4] who reported that 95% of semantic web terms (properties and classes) have no instances (note that in [4] no RDFS and OWL inferencing was done). It is worth noticing that part (800K) of these empty sets contain only black node that cannot be directly instantiated. As for properties, the dimension of ES follows the Zipf's distribution (cf. Fig. 2d), a trend already observed in the early stages of the Semantic Web [4]. We also note that blank nodes are more frequent in class hierarchies than in property hierarchies (25% of ES of classes contain at least one blank node).

6 Discussion

We have presented an empirical study aiming at understanding the modeling style and the overall semantic structure of the Linked Open Data cloud. We observed how classes, properties and individuals are used in practice, and we also investigated how hierarchies of concepts are structured, and how much they are linked.

Even if our conclusions on the issues with LOD data are not revolutionarily (the community is in general aware of the stated problems for Linked Data), we have presented a framework and concrete metrics to obtain concrete results that underpin these shared informal intuitions. We now briefly revisit our main findings:

LOD Ontologies are Sparsely Interlinked. The values computed for metric R (ratio between ES and OE) tell us that LOD classes and properties are sparsely linked with equivalence relations. We can only speculate as to whether ontology linking is considered less important or more difficult than linking individuals, or whether the unlinked classes belong to very diverse domains. However, we find a high value for metric TL (top level ES) with an average of ~1.1 classes per ES. Considering that the number of top level classes (without counting BN) is ~348k, it is reasonable to suspect a high number of conceptual duplicates. The situation for properties is even worse: the average number of properties per TL ES is 1 and the number of top level properties approximates their total number.

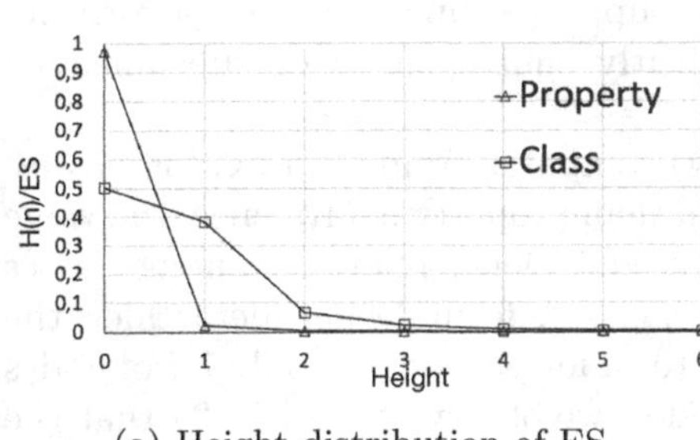

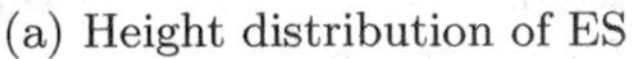
(a) Height distribution of ES

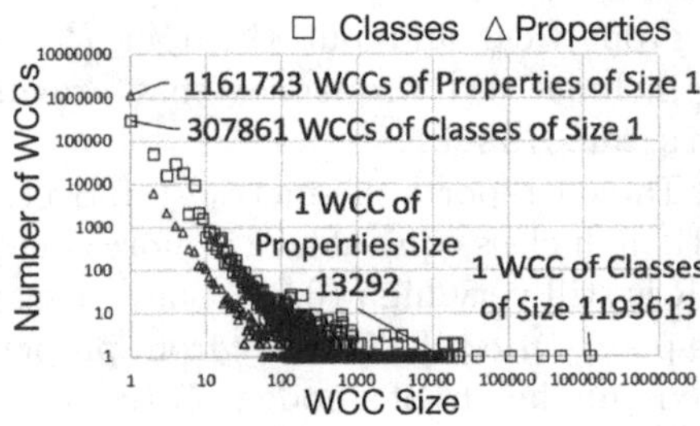

(b) Distribution of the size of Weakly Connected Components. The function shows how many WCC have a certain size.

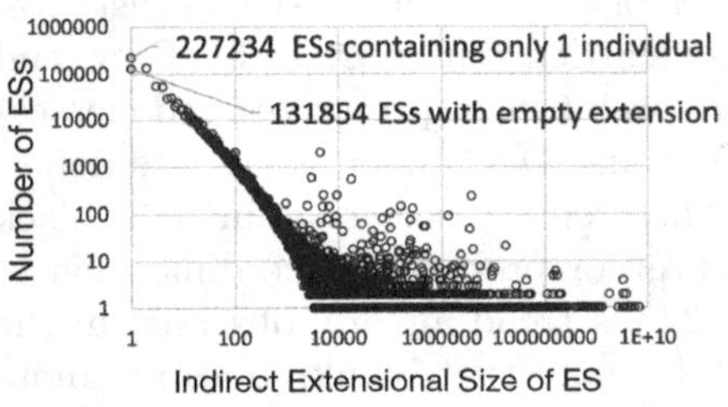

(c) Distribution of IES for properties: the extension size of property ES. The function indicates how many ES have a certain extension size.

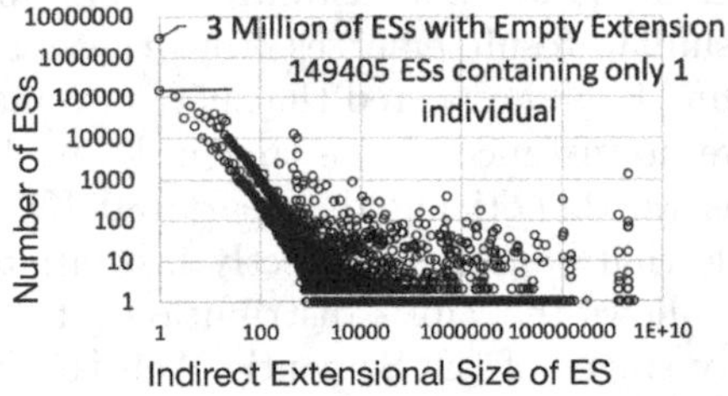

(d) Distribution of IES for classes: the extension size of class ES. The function indicates how many ES have a certain extension size.

Fig. 2. (a) shows the normalised number of nodes per height, (b) shows the number of weakly connected component per component size, (c) and (d) show the number of ESs per indirect extensional size. (b), (c) and (d) are in logarithmic scale.

LOD ontologies are also linked by means of specialisation relations (`rdfs:subClassOf` and `rdfs:subPropertyOf`). Although the situation is less dramatic here, it confirms the previous finding. As for properties, ~88.7% of ES are isolated (cf. IN). Classes exhibit *better* behaviour in this regard, with only 7% of isolated classes. This confirms that classes are more linked than properties, although mostly by means of specialisation relations.

LOD Ontologies are Mostly Flat. The maximum height of ESG nodes is 14 for properties and 77 for classes. Their height's distribution (Fig. 2a) shows that almost all ES (~100%) belong to flat hierarchies. This observation, combined with the values previously observed (cf. IN and R), reinforces the claim that LOD must contain a large number of duplicate concepts.

As for classes, ~50% of ES have no specialising concepts, i.e., height = 0 (Fig. 2a). However, a bit less than the remaining ES have at least one specialising ES. Only a handful of ES reach up to 3 hierarchical levels. The WCC distribution (Fig. 2b) confirms that classes in non-flat hierarchies are mostly organised as siblings in short-depth trees. We speculate that ontology engineers put more care into designing their classes than they put in designing their properties.

LOD Ontologies Contain Many Uninstantiated Concepts. We find that properties are mostly instantiated (~90%), which suggests that they are defined in response to actual need. However, most classes – even not counting blank nodes – have no instances: ~67% of TL ES have no instances. A possible interpretation is that ontology designers tend to over-engineer ontologies beyond their actual requirements, with overly general concepts.

6.1 Future Work

We are working on additional metrics that can be computed on ESGs, and on extending the framework to analyse other kinds of relations (e.g. disjointness). We are also making a step towards assessing possible relations between the domain of knowledge addressed by LOD ontologies and the observations made.

References

1. Asprino, L., Basile, V., Ciancarini, P., Presutti, V.: Empirical analysis of foundational distinctions in linked open data. In: Proceedings of IJCAI-ECAI 2018, pp. 3962–3969 (2018)
2. Beek, W., Raad, J., Wielemaker, J., van Harmelen, F.: sameAs.cc: the closure of 500M `owl:sameAs` statements. In: Gangemi, A., et al. (eds.) ESWC 2018. LNCS, vol. 10843, pp. 65–80. Springer, Cham (2018). https://doi.org/10.1007/978-3-319-93417-4_5
3. Beek, W., Rietveld, L., Bazoobandi, H.R., Wielemaker, J., Schlobach, S.: LOD laundromat: a uniform way of publishing other people's dirty data. In: Mika, P., et al. (eds.) ISWC 2014. LNCS, vol. 8796, pp. 213–228. Springer, Cham (2014). https://doi.org/10.1007/978-3-319-11964-9_14
4. Ding, L., Finin, T.: Characterizing the semantic web on the web. In: Cruz, I., et al. (eds.) ISWC 2006. LNCS, vol. 4273, pp. 242–257. Springer, Heidelberg (2006). https://doi.org/10.1007/11926078_18
5. Ding, L., Shinavier, J., Shangguan, Z., McGuinness, D.L.: SameAs networks and beyond: analyzing deployment status and implications of owl:sameAs in linked data. In: Patel-Schneider, P.F., et al. (eds.) ISWC 2010. LNCS, vol. 6496, pp. 145–160. Springer, Heidelberg (2010). https://doi.org/10.1007/978-3-642-17746-0_10
6. Ding, L., Zhou, L., Finin, T., Joshi, A.: How the semantic web is being used: an analysis of FOAF documents. In: Proceedings of HICSS-38 (2005)
7. Fernández, J., Beek, W., Martínez-Prieto, M., Arias, M.: LOD-a-lot - a queryable dump of the LOD cloud. In: Proceedings of ISWC 2017, pp. 75–83 (2017)
8. Gil, R., García, R., Delgado, J.: Measuring the semantic web. AISSIGSEMIS Bull. **1**(2), 69–72 (2004)
9. Halpin, H., Hayes, P.J., McCusker, J.P., McGuinness, D.L., Thompson, H.S.: When owl:sameAs isn't the same: an analysis of identity in linked data. In: Patel-Schneider, P.F., et al. (eds.) ISWC 2010. LNCS, vol. 6496, pp. 305–320. Springer, Heidelberg (2010). https://doi.org/10.1007/978-3-642-17746-0_20

10. Hayes, P., Patel-Schneider, P.F.: RDF 1.1 Semantics, February 2014
11. Mallea, A., Arenas, M., Hogan, A., Polleres, A.: On blank nodes. In: Aroyo, L., et al. (eds.) ISWC 2011. LNCS, vol. 7031, pp. 421–437. Springer, Heidelberg (2011). https://doi.org/10.1007/978-3-642-25073-6_27
12. Meusel, R., Petrovski, P., Bizer, C.: The WebDataCommons microdata, RDFa and microformat dataset series. In: Mika, P., et al. (eds.) ISWC 2014. LNCS, vol. 8796, pp. 277–292. Springer, Cham (2014). https://doi.org/10.1007/978-3-319-11964-9_18
13. Paulheim, H., Gangemi, A.: Serving DBpedia with DOLCE – more than just adding a cherry on top. In: Arenas, M., et al. (eds.) ISWC 2015. LNCS, vol. 9366, pp. 180–196. Springer, Cham (2015). https://doi.org/10.1007/978-3-319-25007-6_11
14. Theoharis, Y., Tzitzikas, Y., Kotzinos, D., Christophides, V.: On graph features of SemanticWeb schemas. IEEE Trans. Knowl. Data Eng. **20**(5), 692–702 (2008)
15. Urbani, J., Kotoulas, S., Maassen, J., van Harmelen, F., Bal, H.: OWL reasoning with WebPIE: calculating the closure of 100 billion triples. In: Aroyo, L., et al. (eds.) ESWC 2010. LNCS, vol. 6088, pp. 213–227. Springer, Heidelberg (2010). https://doi.org/10.1007/978-3-642-13486-9_15
16. Wang, T.D., Parsia, B., Hendler, J.: A survey of the web ontology landscape. In: Cruz, I., et al. (eds.) ISWC 2006. LNCS, vol. 4273, pp. 682–694. Springer, Heidelberg (2006). https://doi.org/10.1007/11926078_49

Optimizing Horn-$\mathcal{SHIQ}$ Reasoning for OBDA

Labinot Bajraktari[1(✉)], Magdalena Ortiz[1], and Guohui Xiao[2]

[1] Faculty of Informatics, Vienna University of Technology, Vienna, Austria
{bajraktari,ortiz}@kr.tuwien.ac.at

[2] Faculty of Computer Science, Free University of Bozen-Bolzano, Bolzano, Italy
xiao@inf.unibz.it

Abstract. The ontology-based data access (OBDA) paradigm can ease access to heterogeneous and incomplete data sources in many application domains. However, state-of-the-art tools are still based on the DL-Lite family of description logics (DLs) that underlies OWL 2 QL, which despite its usefulness is not sufficiently expressive for many domains. Accommodating more expressive ontology languages remains an open challenge, and the consensus is that Horn DLs like Horn-$\mathcal{SHIQ}$ are particularly promising. Query answering in Horn-$\mathcal{SHIQ}$, a prerequisite for OBDA, is supported in existing reasoners, but many ontologies cannot be handled. This is largely because algorithms build on an ABox-independent approach to ontological reasoning that easily incurs in an exponential behaviour. As an alternative to full ABox-independence, in this paper we advocate taking into account general information about the structure of the ABoxes of interest. This is especially natural in the setting of OBDA, where ABoxes are generated via mappings, and thus have a predictable structure. We present a simple yet effective approach that guides ontological reasoning using the possible combinations of concepts that may occur in the ABox, which can be obtained from the mappings of an OBDA specification. We implemented and tested our optimization in the Clipper reasoner with encouraging results.

1 Introduction

The *ontology-based data access (OBDA)* paradigm [22] eases access to possibly heterogeneous and incomplete data sources using an *ontology*, a formal representation of the conceptualization of the domain that is written in a shareable, machine-readable language. The user queries can be expressed over the familiar ontology vocabulary, and the knowledge in the ontology can be leveraged to infer implicit facts and obtain more query answers. Different sources can be linked to the same ontology, making OBDA a very effective alternative to the costly integration of data sources [23]. Let us consider a scenario where, to facilitate compliance, a regulatory body shares with financial institutions an ontology that

This work was supported by the Austrian Science Fund (FWF) projects P30360, P30873, W1255 and by the Free University of Bozen-Bolzano projects STyLoLa, OBATS and QUADRO.

C. Ghidini et al. (Eds.): ISWC 2019, LNCS 11778, pp. 75–92, 2019.
https://doi.org/10.1007/978-3-030-30793-6_5

includes, among others, the axiom $\mathsf{Account} \sqcap \exists \mathsf{hasOwner.PEP} \sqsubseteq \mathsf{MonitoredAcc}$ which states that accounts of politically exposed persons (PEP) must be monitored. Queries of interest for the regulatory body could be similar to this one, which returns the owners of accounts that interact with a monitored account:

$$\mathsf{q}(y) \leftarrow \mathsf{Account}(x), \mathsf{hasOwner}(x, y), \mathsf{interactsWith}(x, z), \mathsf{MonitoredAcc}(z)$$

When evaluating the query we can infer which accounts are monitored, without this flag being explicitly stored in the data. Moreover, the actual storage of the accounts, owners and interactions may be rather complex, spanning different tables and databases, and is likely to differ between different (sub)organizations and financial institutions. In OBDA this is overcome by using *mappings* such as

$$\begin{aligned} \mathsf{sql}_1(x, y) &\rightsquigarrow \mathsf{interactedWith}(x, y), \mathsf{Account}(x), \mathsf{Account}(y) \\ \mathsf{sql}_2(x, y) &\rightsquigarrow \mathsf{hasOwner}(x, y) \\ \mathsf{sql}_3(x) &\rightsquigarrow \mathsf{PEP}(x) \end{aligned}$$

where $\mathsf{sql}_1 - \mathsf{sql}_3$ are (possibly complex) SQL queries that specify how the data in one specific organization's database is mapped to the vocabulary of the ontology.

The ontology of an OBDA specification is usually in the so-called *DL-Lite* family of description logics (DLs), which underlies OWL 2 QL [7]. DL-Lite is tailored so that queries over the ontology can be transformed, using reasoning, into standard SQL queries that already incorporate the relevant ontological knowledge and can be evaluated with existing database query engines. This central property is key to OBDA being efficiently implementable on top of current database management systems. However, many domains call for expressive features not supported in DL-Lite. For example, the axiom above uses conjunction $\sqcap$ and a *qualified existential restriction* $\exists r.B$ on the left-hand-side. Both constructs are not expressible in the DL-Lite family, but they are found in many ontologies [4], and they are in fact the basis of the OWL 2 EL profile popular for life science ontologies,[1] e.g. SNOMED CT, NCI, and GENE ontologies.

Considerable research efforts have been devoted to more expressive DLs. The so-called *Horn* DLs are particularly appealing: they can support the features above while remaining computationally manageable. In contrast to their non-Horn counterparts, the data complexity of reasoning in Horn DLs is in PTIME [3]. Some advanced reasoning problems, like query emptiness and query inseparability, are more manageable for Horn DLs [1,5,6], and they have proved much more amenable to implementation [9,11,13]. Horn-$\mathcal{SHIQ}$, which can be seen as the Horn fragment of OWL Lite, is a very popular Horn DL that, additionally to the features above, supports *transitive roles* and some *number restrictions*. In our example, we could make interactedWith transitive to detect interactions through a chain of accounts, or we could use an axiom such as $\mathsf{Account} \sqsubseteq\ \leqslant 1\, \mathsf{hasOwner.Person}$ to say that an account can have only one owner.

Horn-$\mathcal{SHIQ}$ is relatively well understood, and there are existing reasoners for traditional reasoning problems like satisfiability and classification [13] as well as for *ontology mediated querying (OMQ)* which, in a nutshell, is the simplification of OBDA (and a prerequisite thereof) that omits the mapping layer: one

[1] https://www.w3.org/TR/owl2-profiles/#OWL_2_EL.

assumes that the data is already an *ABox*, that is, a set of facts over the ontology vocabulary. Unlike DL-Lite, it is in general not possible to reduce query answering in the presence of a Horn-$\mathcal{SHIQ}$ ontology to plain SQL query evaluation. Some alternative approaches have been proposed in order to make OBDA with Horn-$\mathcal{SHIQ}$ feasible on top of existing database technologies. For example, to rewrite (exactly or approximately) an ontology into a weaker DL [17,19], or to compile some of the extra expressivity into the mappings [4]. Another possibility is to compile the query and the ontology into a more expressive query language than SQL, like Datalog, as done in the CLIPPER system [11].

CLIPPER is a query rewriting engine that takes as input an ontology and possibly a set of queries. After a so-called 'saturation' step that uses a *consequence-driven* calculus to add axioms implied by the ontology, it generates a Datalog rewriting of the given queries. CLIPPER can handle realistic ontologies and queries, despite being a relatively simple prototype. It is among the richest query answering engines for Horn DLs, and has inspired recent adaptations [8,16]. However, CLIPPER has stark limitations and there are many ontologies that it cannot process in reasonable time [9]. This is largely due to the ABox independence of the saturation step: some axioms that could be omitted for simpler tasks like *classification* [13], must be inferred by CLIPPER since they may be made relevant by the assertions in some input ABox.

To overcome this obstacle, we propose to mildly compromise ABox independence, by allowing the saturation step to depend on the structure of the possible ABoxes, but not on concrete assertions. Specifically, we propose a version (described in Sect. 3) of the CLIPPER saturation that is parametrized by a set of sets of concept names, which are used to guide the inference of new axioms. Intuitively, these concept names are the concept combinations that may occur in the relevant ABoxes. A nice feature of our approach is that if new ABoxes become relevant, new sets of concepts can be added and the saturation re-executed on top of the previous output, and all previous derivations remain valid. Our approach is particularly meaningful for OBDA, where the virtual ABoxes arising from the mappings have a restricted and predictable structure. In Sect. 4 we show that, meaningful sets of concept sets for guiding the algorithm can be easily extracted from the mappings of an OBDA specification. Our approach is simple yet effective: as we show with an implemented proof of concept, it significantly improves the efficiency of CLIPPER on existing ontologies; these results are reported in Sect. 5.

2 Preliminaries

We recall the definition of Horn-$\mathcal{SHIQ}$ and the basics of OBDA.

The Description Logic Horn-$\mathcal{SHIQ}$. We consider countably infinite pairwise disjoint sets $\mathsf{N_C} \supset \{\top, \bot\}$ of *atomic concepts*, $\mathsf{N_R}$ of *role names*, and $\mathsf{N_I}$ of *individual names*. The set of *roles* is $\mathsf{N}_\mathsf{R}^\pm = \mathsf{N_R} \cup \{r^- \mid r \in \mathsf{N_R}\}$. If $r \in \mathsf{N_R}$, then $\mathsf{inv}(r) = r^-$ and $\mathsf{inv}(r^-) = r$. *Concepts* are inductively defined as follows: (a) each $A \in \mathsf{N_C}$ is a concept, and (b) if C, D are concepts and r is a role, then

$C \sqcap D$, $C \sqcup D$, $\neg C$, $\forall r.C$, $\exists r.C$, $\geqslant n\, r.C$ and $\leqslant n\, r.C$, for $n \geq 1$, are concepts. An expression $C \sqsubseteq D$, where C, D are concepts, is a *general concept inclusion axiom (GCI)*. An expression $r \sqsubseteq s$, where r, s are roles, is a *role inclusion (RI)*. A *transitivity axiom* is an expression *trans*(r), where r is a role. A TBox $\mathcal{T}$ is a finite set of GCIs, RIs and transitivity axioms. We let $\sqsubseteq_{\mathcal{T}}^*$ denote the reflexive transitive closure of $\{(r, s) \mid r \sqsubseteq s \in \mathcal{T} \text{ or } \mathsf{inv}(r) \sqsubseteq \mathsf{inv}(s) \in \mathcal{T}\}$. We assume w.l.o.g. that there are no $r \neq s$ in $\mathsf{N}_\mathsf{R}^\pm$ such that $r \sqsubseteq_{\mathcal{T}}^* s$ and $s \sqsubseteq_{\mathcal{T}}^* r$. A role s is *transitive* in $\mathcal{T}$ if *trans*$(s) \in \mathcal{T}$ or *trans*$(s^-) \in \mathcal{T}$. A role s is *simple* in $\mathcal{T}$ if there is no transitive r in $\mathcal{T}$ s.t. $r \sqsubseteq_{\mathcal{T}}^* s$.

A TBox $\mathcal{T}$ is a Horn-$\mathcal{SHIQ}$ TBox (in normalized form), if each GCI in $\mathcal{T}$ takes one the following forms:

$$\text{(F1) } A_1 \sqcap \ldots \sqcap A_n \sqsubseteq B \qquad \text{(F3) } A_1 \sqsubseteq \forall r.B$$
$$\text{(F2) } A_1 \sqsubseteq \exists r.B \qquad \text{(F4) } A_1 \sqsubseteq \leqslant 1\, r.B$$

where $A_1, \ldots, A_n, B$ are concept names and r is a role, and all roles in concepts of the form $\leqslant 1\, r.B$ are simple. Axioms (F2) are called *existential*. W.l.o.g. we treat here only Horn-$\mathcal{SHIQ}$ TBoxes in normalized form; our results generalize to full Horn-$\mathcal{SHIQ}$ by means of TBox *normalization*; see e.g. [13,14] for a definition and normalization procedures. A Horn-$\mathcal{ALCHIQ}$ TBox is a Horn-$\mathcal{SHIQ}$ TBox with no transitivity axioms, and Horn-$\mathcal{ALCHIQ}^\sqcap$ TBoxes are obtained by additionally allowing *role conjunction* $r_1 \sqcap r_2$, where r_1, r_2 are roles. We let $\mathsf{inv}(r_1 \sqcap r_2) = \mathsf{inv}(r_1) \sqcap \mathsf{inv}(r_2)$ and assume w.l.o.g. that for each role inclusion $r \sqsubseteq s$ of an Horn-$\mathcal{ALCHIQ}^\sqcap$ TBox $\mathcal{T}$, $s \in \mathsf{N}_\mathsf{R}^\pm$ and $\mathsf{inv}(r) \sqsubseteq \mathsf{inv}(s) \in \mathcal{T}$.

An assertion is $A(a)$ or $r(a, b)$, where $A \in \mathsf{N_C}$, $r \in \mathsf{N_R}$, and a, $b \in \mathsf{N_I}$. An ABox $\mathcal{A}$ is a finite set of assertions. Abusing notation, we may write $r(a, b) \in \mathcal{A}$ for $r \in \mathsf{N}_\mathsf{R}^\pm$, meaning $r(a, b) \in \mathcal{A}$ if $r \in \mathsf{N_R}$, and $\mathsf{inv}(r)(b, a) \in \mathcal{A}$ otherwise.

The semantics for TBoxes and ABoxes is given by *interpretations* $\mathcal{I} = \langle \Delta^\mathcal{I}, \cdot^\mathcal{I} \rangle$ which map each $a \in \mathsf{N_I}$ to some $a^\mathcal{I} \in \mathcal{I}$, each $A \in \mathsf{N_C}$ to some $A^\mathcal{I} \subseteq \Delta^\mathcal{I}$, and each $r \in \mathsf{N_R}$ to some $r^\mathcal{I} \subseteq \Delta^\mathcal{I} \times \Delta^\mathcal{I}$, such that $\top^\mathcal{I} = \Delta^\mathcal{I}$, $\bot^\mathcal{I} = \emptyset$. The map $\cdot^\mathcal{I}$ is extended to all concepts and remaining roles as usual, and modelhood is defined in the usual way, see [2] for details. As common in OBDA, we make the unique name assumption (UNA), i.e., we require $a^\mathcal{I} \neq b^\mathcal{I}$ for all $a, b \in \mathsf{N_I}$ and every interpretation. We remark that our theoretical results also hold in the absence of the UNA, however, the proposed optimization trivializes in that case.

Databases and Ontology Based Data Access. A database schema $\mathcal{S}$ consists of a set of relations R and a set of functional dependencies (FD) $\mathcal{F}$. The columns of a relation R are identified by their positions $1, \ldots, n$. For a set $\boldsymbol{i}$ of columns of R, and a tuple t of R, $t[\boldsymbol{i}]$ denotes the projection of t over $\boldsymbol{i}$. An FD F over R has the form $R : \boldsymbol{i} \rightarrow \boldsymbol{j}$, where $\boldsymbol{i}$ and $\boldsymbol{j}$ are tuples of columns in R; we call each $j \in \boldsymbol{j}$ a functional attribute in F. This FD holds in an instance $\mathcal{D}$ if the values of $\boldsymbol{i}$ determine the values of $\boldsymbol{j}$, i.e. $\boldsymbol{t_1}[\boldsymbol{i}] = \boldsymbol{t_2}[\boldsymbol{i}]$ implies $\boldsymbol{t_1}[\boldsymbol{j}] = \boldsymbol{t_2}[\boldsymbol{j}]$ for every pair of tuples $\boldsymbol{t_1}$ and $\boldsymbol{t_2}$ such that $\{R(\boldsymbol{t_1}), R(\boldsymbol{t_2})\} \subseteq \mathcal{D}$.

An *OBDA specification* is a triple $\mathcal{P} = (\mathcal{T}, \mathcal{M}, \mathcal{S})$, where $\mathcal{T}$ is a TBox (in e.g, DL-Lite or Horn-$\mathcal{SHIQ}$), $\mathcal{S}$ is a database schema, $\mathcal{M}$ is a mapping consisting of mapping assertions that link predicates in $\mathcal{T}$ to queries over $\mathcal{S}$. The standard

W3C language for mappings is R2RML [10], however here we use a more concise syntax that is common in the OBDA literature. Formally, a *mapping* $\mathcal{M}$ is a set of *mapping assertions* m that take the form

$$\text{conj}(\boldsymbol{y}) \rightsquigarrow X(\boldsymbol{f}, \boldsymbol{x})$$

consisting of a *source* part $\text{conj}(\boldsymbol{y})$, which is a conjunction of database atoms whose variables are $\boldsymbol{y}$, and a *target* part $X(\boldsymbol{f}, \boldsymbol{x})$, which is an atom whose predicate is X over terms built using function symbols $\boldsymbol{f}$ and variables $\boldsymbol{x} \subseteq \boldsymbol{y}$. In this paper $X(\boldsymbol{f}, \boldsymbol{x})$ takes either the form $C(f(\boldsymbol{x_1}))$ for a concept name C, or the form $r(f(\boldsymbol{x_1}), g(\boldsymbol{x_2}))$ for a role name r. We say that such mapping assertion m *defines the predicate* X. We use $body(m)$ to refer to the source part $\text{conj}(\boldsymbol{y})$ of a mapping m as above, and $head(m)$ to refer to its head $X(\boldsymbol{f}, \boldsymbol{x})$.

We make the following assumptions: *(i)* $\boldsymbol{a} \neq \boldsymbol{b}$ implies $f(\boldsymbol{a}) \neq f(\boldsymbol{b})$, for any f, and *(ii)* $f_1 \neq f_2$ implies $f_1(\boldsymbol{a}) \neq f_2(\boldsymbol{b})$, for any $\boldsymbol{a}, \boldsymbol{b}$. Both assumptions are in-line with the use of function symbols in OBDA systems [18], where they act as *templates* for producing a unique identifier for each input value. Assumption *(i)* is ensured in the R2RML standard using "safe separators", and although *(ii)* is not built into R2RML, it is assumed in existing OBDA tools like Ontop version 1 (implicitly in [20]).

For a database instance $\mathcal{D}$ and mapping $\mathcal{M}$, the ABox $\mathcal{M}(\mathcal{D})$ is the set of atoms $X(\boldsymbol{f}, \boldsymbol{a})$, for all $\text{conj}(\boldsymbol{y}) \rightsquigarrow X(\boldsymbol{f}, \boldsymbol{x}) \in \mathcal{M}$ and all tuples $\mathbf{a}$ of constants in $\mathcal{D}$ such that $\text{conj}(\mathbf{a})$ holds in $\mathcal{D}$. An *OBDA instance* is a pair $(\mathcal{P}, \mathcal{D})$, where $\mathcal{P}$ is an OBDA specification and $\mathcal{D}$ is a database instance that satisfies the dependencies in $\mathcal{S}$ from $\mathcal{P}$. The semantics of $(\mathcal{P}, \mathcal{D})$ is given by the models of $\mathcal{T}$ and $\mathcal{M}(\mathcal{D})$).

3 Restricting Horn-$\mathcal{SHIQ}$ Saturation

The query rewriting algorithm for Horn-$\mathcal{SHIQ}$ described in [11] first saturates a given TBox $\mathcal{T}$ by adding axioms, and then uses the saturated TBox to rewrite a given input query. The saturation step is critical and can be costly. Before describing how we can improve it using information about the ABox structure, we discuss in more detail how ABox-independence impacts scalability.

3.1 Bottleneck of ABox-Independent Saturation

The calculus of [11] is as shown in Table 1, but without the side conditions after ":" and rules Λ^*, Λ^+, Λ^-, which represent the core of our optimization discussed below. This algorithm is sound and complete for every possible ABox, and it can be implemented in a relatively simple way. However, it is computationally expensive. It is well-known that the algorithm is (unavoidably) worst-case exponential, but the problem is that this is not just a hypothetical worst-case: an unmanageable combinatorial explosion of inferred axioms may occur for realistic ontologies as well. Roughly, this is because there may be many axioms that are relevant for building the universal model of some ABox, but which are not relevant for the ABoxes we are interested in. We illustrate this through the example below:

Table 1. Optimized inference calculus. Possibly primed M, N are conjunctions of concept names, and S of roles; Λ is a set of activators and α, α' are activators in Λ. The calculus in [11] omits the side conditions and the rules Λ^*, Λ^+, Λ^-.

Rule	Inference	Side condition
$(\mathbf{R}^c_{\sqsubseteq})$	$\dfrac{M \sqsubseteq \exists S.(N \sqcap N') \quad N \sqsubseteq A}{M \sqsubseteq \exists S.(N \sqcap N' \sqcap A)}$	$: \mathcal{M} \subseteq \alpha, \alpha \in \Lambda$
$(\mathbf{R}^r_{\sqsubseteq})$	$\dfrac{M \sqsubseteq \exists (S \sqcap S').N \quad S \sqsubseteq r}{M \sqsubseteq \exists (S \sqcap S' \sqcap r).N}$	$: M \subseteq \alpha, \alpha \in \Lambda$
$(\mathbf{R}_{\bot})$	$\dfrac{M \sqsubseteq \exists S.(N \sqcap \bot)}{M \sqsubseteq \bot}$	$: M \subseteq \alpha, \alpha \in \Lambda$
$(\mathbf{R}_{\forall})$	$\dfrac{M \sqsubseteq \exists (S \sqcap r).N \quad A \sqsubseteq \forall r.B}{M \sqcap A \sqsubseteq \exists (S \sqcap r).(N \sqcap B)}$	$: M \cup A \subseteq \alpha, \alpha \in \Lambda$
$(\mathbf{R}^-_{\forall})$	$\dfrac{M \sqsubseteq \exists (S \sqcap \mathsf{inv}(r)).(N \sqcap A) \quad A \sqsubseteq \forall r.B}{M \sqsubseteq B}$	$: M \subseteq \alpha, \alpha \in \Lambda$
$(\mathbf{R}_{\leq})$	$\dfrac{M \sqsubseteq \exists (S \sqcap r).(N \sqcap B) \quad A \sqsubseteq \leqslant 1\, r.B \qquad M' \sqsubseteq \exists (S' \sqcap r).(N' \sqcap B)}{M \sqcap M' \sqcap A \sqsubseteq \exists (S \sqcap S' \sqcap r).(N \sqcap N' \sqcap B)}$	$: M \cup M' \cup A \subseteq \alpha, \alpha \in \Lambda$
$(\mathbf{R}^-_{\leq})$	$\dfrac{M \sqsubseteq \exists (S \sqcap \mathsf{inv}(r)).(N_1 \sqcap N_2 \sqcap A) \quad A \sqsubseteq \leqslant 1\, r.B \qquad N_1 \sqsubseteq \exists (S' \sqcap r).(N' \sqcap B \sqcap C)}{M \sqcap B \sqsubseteq C \quad M \sqcap B \sqsubseteq \exists (S \sqcap \mathsf{inv}(S' \sqcap r)).(N_1 \sqcap N_2 \sqcap A)}$	$: M \cup B \subseteq \alpha, \alpha \in \Lambda$

$(\Lambda^*)\ \dfrac{M \sqsubseteq B \quad M \subseteq \alpha}{\Lambda = \Lambda \cup \{\alpha \cup \{B\}\}} \qquad (\Lambda^+)\ \dfrac{M \sqsubseteq \exists R.N}{\Lambda = \Lambda \cup \{N\}} \qquad (\Lambda^-)\ \dfrac{\alpha' \subseteq \alpha}{\Lambda = \Lambda \setminus \alpha'}$

Example 1. The following axioms stipulate different flags for monitored accounts:

$$\mathsf{MonitoredAccount} \sqsubseteq \exists \mathsf{hasFlag}.\top \qquad \mathsf{IndividualAcc} \sqsubseteq \forall \mathsf{hasFlag}.\mathsf{YellowFlag}$$
$$\mathsf{SmallBusinessAcc} \sqsubseteq \forall \mathsf{hasFlag}.\mathsf{RedFlag} \qquad \mathsf{BigBusinessAcc} \sqsubseteq \forall \mathsf{hasFlag}.\mathsf{YellowFlag}$$

When running the calculus on this ontology we obtain several axioms of the form $\mathsf{MonitoredAccount} \sqcap C \sqsubseteq \exists \mathsf{hasFlag}.D$, where C is some conjunction of account types such as $\mathsf{IndividualAcc} \sqcap \mathsf{SmallBusinessAcc}$, $\mathsf{IndividualAcc} \sqcap \mathsf{BigBusinessAcc}$, etc., and D is some conjunction of flag colors. However, if we know that an account will only have one account type, we do not need all these axioms. If the ontology includes axioms stating the disjointness of account and flag types, the algorithm would discard some of the axioms after inferring them. Our approach, in contrast, is effective even when such axioms are not given, and allows us to save the computation of this axioms in advance if we know that an account is never declared to have two types in the data. Note also that the same role $\mathsf{hasFlag}$ could be used to flag something other than accounts, such as transactions, and then the calculus would also derive axioms for all combinations of types of transactions and types of accounts. Our observations suggest that such patterns are not uncommon, and obvious "common sense" disjointness assertions (such as saying that transactions are not accounts, or that accounts are not persons) are often omitted. This may not affect other reasoning techniques (such as tableau for consistency testing), but can have a major impact on this kind of ABox independent saturation.

3.2 Constraining the Derivation

We propose to use knowledge about the structure of relevant ABoxes to guide the calculus and avoid inferring irrelevant axioms as illustrated above.

Definition 1 (Propagating concepts and activators). *Concept names in* $\mathsf{N_C}$ *and expressions of the form* $\exists r$ *with* r *a role are called* basic concepts.

Let a *be an individual and* $\mathcal{A}$ *an ABox. The* ABox type of a in $\mathcal{A}$ *is the following set of basic concepts:*

$$atyp_{\mathcal{A}}(a) = \{A \mid A(a) \in \mathcal{A}\} \cup \{\exists r \mid r(a,b) \in \mathcal{A}\}$$

For a TBox $\mathcal{T}$ *and a set* τ *of basic concepts, the* $\mathcal{T}$-propagating concepts of τ *are:*

$$prop(\tau, \mathcal{T}) = \{B | A \sqsubseteq \forall s.B \in \mathcal{T}, r \sqsubseteq^*_{\mathcal{T}} s, \exists \mathsf{inv}(r) \in \tau\}$$

An activator α *is just a set of concept names. We say that a set* Λ *of activators* covers *an ABox* $\mathcal{A}$ *w.r.t. a TBox* $\mathcal{T}$ *if for each individual* a *occurring in* $\mathcal{A}$*, there is some activator* $\alpha \in \Lambda$ *such that*

$$\tau_a|_{\mathsf{N_C}} \cup prop(\tau_a, \mathcal{T}) \subseteq \alpha$$

where $\tau_a = atyp_{\mathcal{A}}(a)$ *and* $\tau_a|_{\mathsf{N_C}}$ *denotes its restriction to concept names only.*

Note that in covering sets of activators, we require that for each individual there is an activator that contains not only its type, but also its propagating concepts. In a way, this over-approximates its actual type in the universal model. Given a TBox $\mathcal{T}$, the singleton set that contains exactly the set of all concept names occurring in $\mathcal{T}$ is a set of activators that covers any ABox over the signature of $\mathcal{T}$. However, such a large activator would not prevent the derivation of irrelevant axioms in our calculus. For a concrete ABox we can be more accurate, and take as set of activators precisely the set of all $\alpha_a = \tau_a|_{\mathsf{N_C}} \cup prop(\tau_a, \mathcal{T})$ where a is an individual in $\mathcal{A}$ with $\tau_a = atyp_{\mathcal{A}}(a)$. In fact, we use such activators sets in our experiments in Sect. 5.

In Table 1 we present the optimized version of the calculus, which takes as input and maintains a set of activators. Each rule has a side condition that checks if the left hand side of the axiom we want to derive is contained in an existing activator. There are three additional rules Λ^*, Λ^+ and Λ^- not present in [11]. The rule Λ^* is used to close the maintained activators under axioms of the form ($F1$), while Λ^+ is used to create fresh activators for inferred axioms of the form ($F2$), and Λ^- drops redundant activators.

Before saturation, we drop transitivity axioms from the input TBox, and instead add axioms of the form (F3) that ensure the effect of transitivity is accounted for during saturation. The saturation starts from the resulting Horn-$\mathcal{ALCHIQ}$ TBox, but since it may introduce role conjunctions, it keeps a set of Horn-$\mathcal{ALCHIQ}^{\sqcap}$ axioms.

Definition 2. *Given an Horn-$\mathcal{SHIQ}$ ontology, let $\mathcal{T}^*$ be the result of dropping all transitivity axioms trans(r) from $\mathcal{T}$, and adding, for every $A \sqsubseteq \forall s.B \in \mathcal{T}$ and every transitive role r with $r \sqsubseteq^*_{\mathcal{T}} s$, the axioms $A \sqsubseteq \forall r.B^r$, $B^r \sqsubseteq \forall r.B^r$ and $B^r \sqsubseteq B$, where B^r is a fresh concept name.*

We denote by $\nabla(\mathcal{T}, \Lambda)$ the result of saturating $\mathcal{T}^*$ with the rules in Table 1 and set of initial activators Λ.

Formally $\nabla(\mathcal{T}, \Lambda)$ is a pair of an Horn-$\mathcal{ALCHIQ}^{\sqcap}$ TBox and a set of activators, but we may abuse notation and use $\nabla(\mathcal{T}, \Lambda)$ to denote the TBox alone.

Similarly as in [11], the saturated set of axioms contains all inferences from the ontology that are relevant for reasoning about any covered ABox; not only for checking consistency, but also for other problems like query rewriting.

Definition 3. *For an ABox $\mathcal{A}$, we denote by $\mathcal{A}^{\nabla(\mathcal{T},\Lambda)}$ the result of closing $\mathcal{A}$ under the following rules:*

- *$A_1 \sqcap \ldots \sqcap A_n \sqsubseteq B \in \nabla(\mathcal{T}, \Lambda)$ and $\{A_1(a), \ldots A_n(a)\} \in \mathcal{A}$, then $B(a) \in \mathcal{A}$;*
- *$A \sqsubseteq \forall r.B \in \nabla(\mathcal{T}, \Lambda)$ and $r(a, b) \in \mathcal{A}, A(a) \in \mathcal{A}$, then $B(b) \in \mathcal{A}$;*
- *$r \sqsubseteq s \in \mathcal{T}$ and $r(a, b) \in \mathcal{A}$, then $s(a, b) \in \mathcal{A}$;*
- *$A \sqsubseteq\ \leqslant 1\, r B \in \mathcal{T}$ and $A(a), r(a, b), r(a, c), B(b), B(c)$, then $\bot(a) \in \mathcal{A}$*
- *$A_1 \sqcap \ldots \sqcap A_n \sqsubseteq \exists(r_1 \sqcap \ldots \sqcap r_m).(B_1 \sqcap \ldots \sqcap B_k)$, $A \sqsubseteq\ \leqslant 1\, r.B \in \nabla(\mathcal{T}, \Lambda)$ such that for some i, j we have $r = r_i, B = B_j$ and $A(a), r(a, b) \in \mathcal{A}$, then $\{B_1(b), \ldots, B_k(b), r_1(a, b), \ldots, r_k(a, b)\} \subseteq \mathcal{A}$.*

We call $\mathcal{A}^{\nabla(\mathcal{T},\Lambda)}$ contradiction-free *if there are no assertions of the form $\bot(a)$.*

To test if a given ABox covered by Λ is consistent with $\mathcal{T}$, it is enough to check $\mathcal{A}^{\nabla(\mathcal{T},\Lambda)}$ for contradiction-freeness.

Proposition 1. *Let $\mathcal{A}$ be an ABox covered by Λ. Then $(\mathcal{T}, \mathcal{A})$ is consistent iff $\mathcal{A}^{\nabla(\mathcal{T},\Lambda)}$ is contradiction-free.*

However, we do not want to only test consistency. Our motivation is OBDA, and we want support for instance and conjunctive queries for different ABoxes. We thus provide the standard guarantee one would expect in this setting: from the computed axioms and a consistent ABox, we can build a *universal model.* As usual, the Horn-$\mathcal{ALCHIQ}^{\sqcap}$ TBox that results from saturation is used to build so-called *pre-models* with standard chase techniques, which become models once the extensions of non-simple roles are updated to satisfy transitivity axioms.

Definition 4. ($\mathcal{T}$-chase, universal model). *Let $\mathcal{T}$ be a Horn-$\mathcal{ALCHIQ}^{\sqcap}$ TBox and $\mathcal{I}$ an interpretation. We say that an axiom of the form $M \sqsubseteq \exists S.N$ is* applicable at $e \in \Delta^{\mathcal{I}}$ *if*

(a) $e \in M^{\mathcal{I}}$,

(b) *there is no* $e' \in \Delta^{\mathcal{I}}$ *with* $(e, e') \in S^{\mathcal{I}}$ *and* $e' \in N^{\mathcal{I}}$,
(c) *there is no axiom* $M' \sqsubseteq \exists S'.N' \in \mathcal{T}$ *such that* $e \in (M')^{\mathcal{I}}$, $S \subseteq S'$, $N \subseteq N'$, *and* $S \subset S'$ *or* $N \subset N'$.

If $M \sqsubseteq \exists S.N$ *is applicable at* $e \in \Delta^{\mathcal{I}}$, *then we obtain an interpretation* $\mathcal{I}'$ *by applying* $M \sqsubseteq \exists S.N$ *in* $\mathcal{I}$ *as follows:*

- $\Delta^{\mathcal{I}'} = \Delta^{\mathcal{I}} \cup \{e'\}$ *with* e' *a new element not present in* $\Delta^{\mathcal{I}}$,
- *for each* $A \in \mathsf{N_C}$, *we have* $A^{\mathcal{I}'} = A^{\mathcal{I}} \cup \{e'\}$ *if* $A \in N$, *and* $A^{\mathcal{I}'} = A^{\mathcal{I}}$ *otherwise,*
- *for each* $r \in \mathsf{N_R}$, *we have* $r^{\mathcal{I}'} = r^{\mathcal{I}} \cup \{(e, e')\}$ *if* $r \in S$, $r^{\mathcal{I}'} = r^{\mathcal{I}} \cup \{(e', e)\}$ *if* $r^- \in S$, $r^{\mathcal{I}'} = r^{\mathcal{I}}$ *otherwise.*

For a contradiction-free ABox $\mathcal{A}$, *we let* $\mathcal{I}^{\mathcal{A}}$ *denote the interpretation whose domain are the individuals in* $\mathcal{A}$, *and that has* $A^{\mathcal{I}^{\mathcal{A}}} = \{a \mid A(a) \in \mathcal{A}\}$ *for all* $A \in \mathsf{N_C}$, *and* $r^{\mathcal{I}^{\mathcal{A}}} = \{(a, b) \mid r(a, b) \in \mathcal{A}\}$ *for all* $r \in \mathsf{N_R}$.

The $\mathcal{T}$*-chase of a contradiction-free ABox* $\mathcal{A}$ *is the possibly infinite interpretation obtained from* $\mathcal{I}^{\mathcal{A}}$ *by fairly applying the existential axioms in* $\mathcal{T}$ *(that is, every applicable axiom is eventually applied).*

Let $\mathcal{J}$ *denote the* $\mathcal{T}$*-chase of* $\mathcal{A}^{\nabla(\mathcal{T},\Lambda)}$. *Then* $\mathcal{I}^{(\mathcal{T},\Lambda,\mathcal{A})}$ *is the interpretation with* $\Delta^{(\mathcal{T},\Lambda,\mathcal{A})} = \Delta^{\mathcal{J}}$, $A^{\mathcal{I}^{(\mathcal{T},\Lambda,\mathcal{A})}} = A^{\mathcal{J}}$ *for every* $A \in \mathsf{N_C}$, *and*

$$r^{\mathcal{I}^{(\mathcal{T},\Lambda,\mathcal{A})}} = \bigcup_{s \sqsubseteq^*_{\mathcal{T}} r} s^{\mathcal{J}}_{+} \qquad \text{for every } r \in \mathsf{N}^{\pm}_{\mathsf{R}}$$

where $s^{\mathcal{J}}_{+}$ *is the transitive closure of* $s^{\mathcal{J}}$ *if* $trans(s) \in \mathcal{T}$, *and* $s^{\mathcal{J}}_{+} = s^{\mathcal{J}}$ *otherwise.*

It is standard to show that $\mathcal{I}^{(\mathcal{T},\Lambda,\mathcal{A})}$ is indeed a universal model:

Proposition 2. *Let* $(\mathcal{T}, \mathcal{A})$ *be a consistent Horn-*$\mathcal{SHIQ}$ *KB, and* Λ *a set of activators, such that* Λ *covers* $\mathcal{A}$ *w.r.t.* $\mathcal{T}$. *The following hold:*

(a) *if* $(\mathcal{T}, \mathcal{A})$ *is consistent then* $\mathcal{I}^{(\mathcal{T},\Lambda,\mathcal{A})} \models (\mathcal{T}, \mathcal{A})$, *and*
(b) $\mathcal{I}^{(\mathcal{T},\Lambda,\mathcal{A})}$ *can be homomorphically embedded into any model of* $\mathcal{K}$.

This proposition is analogous to Proposition 2 in [11]. By guaranteeing that we can build a universal model of any ABox that is consistent with $\mathcal{T}$, we can use $\nabla(\mathcal{T}, \Lambda)$ as a representation of models that is sufficient for query answering. As in the work of Eiter et al., the finite $\nabla(\mathcal{T}, \Lambda)$ allows us to rewrite the query in such a way that it can be evaluated over a small and easy to compute part of the possibly infinite represented universal model, we refer to [11] for details.

Note that the output of the original algorithm in [11] coincides with $\nabla(\mathcal{T}, \Lambda)$ if Λ contains only the set of all the concept names appearing in $\mathcal{T}$. In terms of computational complexity, the same upper bounds apply for the size of the saturated sets obtained with either version of the calculus: it may be single exponential in $\mathcal{T}$, and this exponential blow-up is in general unavoidable. But as we discuss in Sect. 5.1, in practice the version with activators is faster, builds smaller sets, and can handle more ontologies.

Incremental Computation. Assume that we have computed $\nabla(\mathcal{T}, \Lambda)$, and let $\mathcal{T}_1$ and Λ_1 be the obtained TBox and set of activators. Now, suppose that we want to query an ABox $\mathcal{A}$ that is not covered by Λ (this could be, for example, because the underlying OBDA specification changed). Then we can simply take a set Λ' of activators that covers the new ABox profiles. To compute $\mathcal{T}_2 = \nabla(\mathcal{T}, \Lambda \cup \Lambda')$, we can reuse the previous output and simply compute $\mathcal{T}_2 = \nabla(\mathcal{T}_1, \Lambda_1 \cup \Lambda')$. All axioms in $\mathcal{T}_1$ are preserved, and new ones may be derived.

4 Activators from Mappings

In this section we show how one can obtain initial activators for our optimized calculus directly from an OBDA specification $\mathcal{P} = (\mathcal{T}, \mathcal{M}, \mathcal{S})$, so that the extracted activators cover the ABox $\mathcal{M}(\mathcal{D})$ for any database $\mathcal{D}$. In this section, we will rely on our assumptions about the function symbols in OBDA specifications, namely, that $\boldsymbol{a} \neq \boldsymbol{b}$ implies $f(\boldsymbol{a}) \neq f(\boldsymbol{b})$ for every f, and that $f_1 \neq f_2$ implies $f_1(\boldsymbol{a}) \neq f_2(\boldsymbol{b})$, for any $\boldsymbol{a}, \boldsymbol{b}$.

One simple way to obtain the activators would be take as an ABox type all the head predicates of mappings that share the same functional symbol, roughly treating each function symbol as the same constant in the ABox. After all, if all the mappings that share some $f(x)$ in the head would fire for some x, they can all yield assertions for the same individual. Such an approach would be complete, but could potentially generate quite large ABox types. As we report in Sect. 5.2, we observed that real-world specifications do contain mappings that share the same function symbol in the head, but frequently they cannot fire for the same value of x due to the functional dependencies. To leverage this and obtain a more fine-grained set of activators, we first define conflicting mappings.

Definition 5 (Conflicting mapping assertions). *Let $F = R : \boldsymbol{i} \to \boldsymbol{j}$ a functional dependency and let $j \in \boldsymbol{j}$ be one of its functional attributes. We call a pair m, m' of mapping assertions* (F, j)-conflicting *if the following hold:*

- *there are terms $f(\boldsymbol{x})$ in head(m) and $f(\boldsymbol{y})$ in head(m'), for some function symbol f, and*
- *there are atoms $R(\mathbf{t}) \in$ body(m) and $R(\mathbf{t'}) \in$ body(m') such that, for each $i \in \boldsymbol{i}$ we have $\mathbf{t}[i] = x_i$, $\mathbf{t'}[i] = y_i$, where $x_i \in \boldsymbol{x}$, $y_i \in \boldsymbol{y}$, and there exists a $j \in \boldsymbol{j}$, such that $\mathbf{t}[j]$, $\mathbf{t'}[j]$ are two different constants.*

Example 2. Consider the following $\mathcal{M}$ for the ontology from Example 1.

$$
\begin{aligned}
m_1 : \mathsf{transfers}(x, y) &\rightsquigarrow \mathsf{interactedWith}(f_1(x), f_1(y)),\\
&\quad\ \mathsf{Account}(f_1(x)), \mathsf{Account}(f_1(y))\\
m_2 : \mathsf{account\_owners}(x, y, \text{‘}politician\text{'}) &\rightsquigarrow \mathsf{PEP}(f_2(x))\\
m_3 : \mathsf{account\_owners}(x, y, z) &\rightsquigarrow \mathsf{hasOwner}(f_1(x), f_2(y))\\
m_4 : \mathsf{account\_details}(x, \text{‘}business\text{'}, \text{‘}big\text{'}) &\rightsquigarrow \mathsf{BigBusinessAcc}(f_1(x))\\
m_5 : \mathsf{account\_details}(x, \text{‘}business\text{'}, \text{‘}small\text{'}) &\rightsquigarrow \mathsf{SmallBusinessAcc}(f_1(x))\\
m_6 : \mathsf{account\_details}(x, \text{‘}private\text{'}, y) &\rightsquigarrow \mathsf{IndividualAcc}(f_1(x))
\end{aligned}
$$

Now consider a functional dependency $F_1 : id \rightarrow type, size$ over the relation account_details($id, type, size$). Then, according to Definition 5, pairs m_4,m_6 and m_5,m_6 are $(F_1, type)$-conflicting, while the pair m_4,m_5 is $(F_1, size)$-conflicting.

Note that we define conflicts in a way that they are easy to identify, and that we can guarantee that conflicting mapping assertions cannot fire to create assertions about the same constant. There may be other reasons why two mappings do not fire together that we disregard, but this does not compromise the correctness of our approach, it may simply result in larger activators, which may lead to more irrelevant inferences.

For a functional symbol f, we denote by $\mathcal{M}(f)$ the set of all mapping assertions in $\mathcal{M}$ such that f occurs in the head. A subset $\mathcal{M}'$ of $\mathcal{M}(f)$ is conflict-free if there are no mapping assertions m and m' in $\mathcal{M}'$ that are (F, j)-conflicting for some F and j. With $\mathbb{M}_f$ we denote the set of maximal conflict-free subsets of $\mathcal{M}(f)$. Then we can guarantee the coverage of $\mathcal{M}(\mathcal{D})$ by creating an ABox type and an activator for each function symbol f and each $M_i \in \mathbb{M}_f$.

The problem of computing maximal conflict-free subsets can be solved by using the notions of maximal cliques from graph theory and the hitting set problem. Recall that a clique in an undirected graph is a subset of the vertices such that every two distinct vertices are adjacent; a maximal clique is a clique that cannot be extended by adding one more vertex. For a set of sets Ω, H is a hitting set of Ω if for all $S \in \Omega, H \cap S \neq \emptyset$; a hitting set H is minimal if there exists no other hitting set H', such that $H' \subseteq H$. To compute $\mathbb{M}_f$, we first create a graph G_f where the node set is $\mathcal{M}(f)$ and the edge set is $\{(m, m') \mid m, m' \text{ are } (F, j)\text{-conflicting for some } (F, j)\}$. Next let Ω_f be the set of maximal cliques of G_f. Note that each set in Ω_f also includes the set of conflict free mapping assertions. Then every minimal hitting set of Ω_f is a maximal conflict-free subset of $\mathcal{M}(f)$. One can use any hitting set algorithm, e.g. [21], for this task. We note that despite the lack of tractability, there are efficient algorithms available for the maximal clique and minimal hitting set problems, and in the sizes of the generated instances in this case are relatively small. Moreover, the minimality of the hitting sets is not so critical, an efficient approximation algorithm can also be employed.

Definition 6 (Activators from an OBDA specification). *Given an OBDA specification $\mathcal{P} = (\mathcal{T}, \mathcal{M}, \mathcal{S})$, let f be a function symbol occurring in $\mathcal{M}$, and let $\mathbb{M}_f$ be the set of maximal conflict-free subsets of $\mathcal{M}(f)$. Then we define, for each $M_i \in \mathbb{M}_f$:*

$$\begin{aligned} atyp_{\mathcal{M}}(f, M_i) = &\{A \mid \text{some } m \in M_i \text{ has } head(m) \text{ of the form } A(f(x))\} \cup \\ &\{\exists r \mid \text{some } m \in M_i \text{ has } head(m) \text{ of the form } r(f(x), t)\} \cup \\ &\{\exists r^- \mid \text{some } m \in M_i \text{ has } head(m) \text{ of the form } r(t, f(x))\} \end{aligned}$$

Finally, we denote by $\Lambda(\mathcal{P})$ the set of activators whose elements are, for each function symbols f occurring in $\mathcal{M}$ and each $M_i \in \mathbb{M}_f$:

$$atyp_{\mathcal{M}}(f, M_i)|_{\mathsf{N_C}} \cup prop(atyp_{\mathcal{M}}(f, M_i), \mathcal{T})$$

where $atyp_{\mathcal{M}}(f, M_i)|_{\mathsf{N_C}}$ denotes the restriction of $atyp_{\mathcal{M}}(f, M_i)$ to $\mathsf{N_C}$ only.

Using the fact that, for all $\mathcal{D}$, each assertion in $\mathcal{M}(\mathcal{D})$ comes from some mapping in $\mathcal{M}$, and that by our assumptions only non-conflicting mappings that share a function symbol can produce assertions about a common individual, the following is not hard to show.

Proposition 3. *For every OBDA instance* $(\mathcal{P}, \mathcal{D})$*,* $\Lambda(\mathcal{P})$ *covers the ABox* $\mathcal{M}(\mathcal{D})$*.*

Example 3. Let's consider our running example. For the functional symbol f_1, the graph $G_{f_1} = (E_{f_1}, V_{f_1})$, where $E_{f_1} = \{m_1, m_3, m_4, m_5, m_6\}$, and $V_{f_1} = \{(m_4, m_5), (m_4, m_6), (m_5, m_6)\}$. The maximal cliques are $\Omega_{f_1} = \{\{m_1\}, \{m_3\}, \{m_4, m_5, m_6\}\}$. Thus, the maximal conflict-free sets $\mathbb{M}_{f_1}$ are the minimal hitting sets of Ω_{f_1}, i.e. $\mathbb{M}_{f_1} = \{M_1, M_2, M_3\}$, where $M_1 = \{m_1, m_3, m_4\}$, $M_2 = \{m_1, m_3, m_5\}$, $M_3 = \{m_1, m_3, m_6\}$. Similarly, the maximal conflict-free sets for f_2 is $\mathbb{M}_{f_2} = \{M_4\}$ where $M_4 = \{m_2, m_3\}$. Then by Definition 6 we get:

$$\begin{aligned}
\mathsf{atyp}_{\mathsf{f}_1}(M_1) &= \{\exists\mathsf{interactedWith}, \exists\mathsf{interactedWith}^-, \mathsf{Account}, \mathsf{hasOwner}, \mathsf{BigBusinessAcc}\}\\
\mathsf{atyp}_{\mathsf{f}_1}(M_2) &= \{\exists\mathsf{interactedWith}, \exists\mathsf{interactedWith}^-, \mathsf{Account}, \mathsf{hasOwner}, \mathsf{BigBusinessAcc}\}\\
\mathsf{atyp}_{\mathsf{f}_1}(M_3) &= \{\exists\mathsf{interactedWith}, \exists\mathsf{interactedWith}^-, \mathsf{Account}, \mathsf{hasOwner}, \mathsf{IndividualAcc}\}\\
\mathsf{atyp}_{\mathsf{f}_2}(M_4) &= \{\exists\mathsf{hasOwner}^-, \mathsf{Politician}\}
\end{aligned}$$

and, the following set of activators:

$$\begin{aligned}
\Lambda = \{&\{\mathsf{Account}, \mathsf{BigBusinessAcc}\}, \{\mathsf{Account}, \mathsf{SmallBusinessAcc}\},\\
&\{\mathsf{Account}, \mathsf{IndividualAcc}\}, \{\mathsf{Politician}\}\}
\end{aligned}$$

Note that with this Λ, the $\mathbf{R}_\forall$ rule of the optimized calculus will not derive the irrelevant axioms discussed in Example 1.

5 Evaluation

We implemented the optimized calculus in Table 1 in the Clipper reasoner. From here on we refer to Clipper with C-orig and to our implementation with C-opt. We tested the feasibility of our approach in two directions:

Optimized TBox saturation. We tested C-opt on a large test set of ontologies from the Oxford Ontology Repository,[2] and compared its performance to C-orig. The activators that were given as input to C-opt were obtained from the respective ABoxes that these ontologies include.

Activator extraction from mappings. We extracted activators from three large OBDA specifications, and analysed the resulting activators.

We remark that, on the one hand, the OBDA specifications that we used in the second part come with *DL-Lite* ontologies, for which the combinatorial behaviour of Horn-$\mathcal{SHIQ}$ does not arise and C-opt brings no improvement. The expressive ontologies of the Oxford repository, on the other hand, have no accompanying mapping specifications. The lack of test cases with both an

[2] http://www.cs.ox.ac.uk/isg/ontologies/UID/.

expressive ontology and realistic mappings, while unfortunate, is not surprising, as existing OBDA engines only support *DL-Lite*.

The test ontologies, the compiled C-OPT, and files with the mapping analysis can be found in https://github.com/ghxiao/clipper-materials/tree/master/iswc-2019.

5.1 Optimized TBox Saturation

The instances for these tests came from Oxford Ontology Repository, which contains 797 ontologies. From those, only 370 had ABoxes, and out of them 18 yielded exceptions while loading on C-ORIG. From the remaining ontologies, 131 were uninteresting since their normalized TBoxes did not contain existential axioms (F2) in which case the saturation step trivializes. From the resulting 221 ontologies we dropped all axioms not expressible in Horn-$\mathcal{SHIQ}$. Table 2 shows the distribution of our 221 ontologies with respect to TBox and ABox size. We categorized them into (S)mall, (M)edium, (L)arge and (V)ery (L)arge, with boundaries of up to 100, up to 1000, up to 10000, and above 10000 axioms/assertions. There is a fair mix of sizes, and around half of the ontologies have both ABox and TBox that are large or very large.

Table 2. Distribution of ontologies by their respective ABox and TBox sizes.

		TBox sizes				Total
		S	M	L	VL	
ABox sizes	S	5.12%	6.51%	4.65%	0.47%	16.75%
	M	0%	9.3%	3.72%	0.93%	13.95%
	L	0%	5.12%	12.09%	0.47%	17.68%
	VL	0.47%	11.63%	14.88%	24.64%	51.62%
	Total	5.59%	32.56%	35.34%	26.51%	

All experiments were run on a PC with an Intel i7 2.4 GHz CPU with 4 cores running 64 bit LinuxMint 17, and a Java heap of 4 GB. A time-out limit of 2 min was set. This was the total time allowed for loading and normalizing the TBox, saturating it, and in the case of C-OPT, also the time used to obtain activators from the ABox.

Additionally to successfully saturating all ontologies that C-ORIG succeeded on, C-OPT showed a 37.96% increase in the success rate: C-OPT succeeded in 149 out of 221 (67.71%), while C-ORIG in 108 out of 221 (49.33%). Our of the 221 ontologies, 52 are in the *DL-Lite* or $\mathcal{EL}$ profiles. For them, C-OPT succeeded in 49 vs 48 for C-ORIG. If we take into account only ontologies in more expressive fragments, beyond *DL-Lite* and $\mathcal{EL}$, the performance improvement is even more pronounced: our C-OPT succeeded in 100 cases our of 169 ontologies (59.17%), while C-ORIG succeeds only in 60 cases (35.5%), resulting in an increase of 66.67% in the success rate.

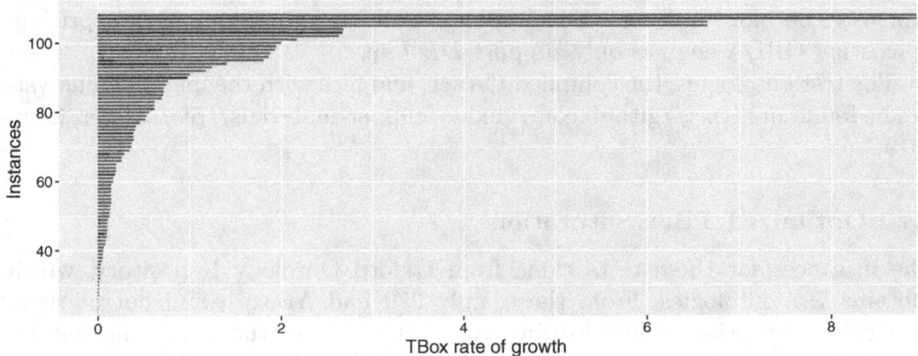

Fig. 1. TBox rate of growth for both versions (C-ORIG = red, C-OPT = blue). (Color figure online)

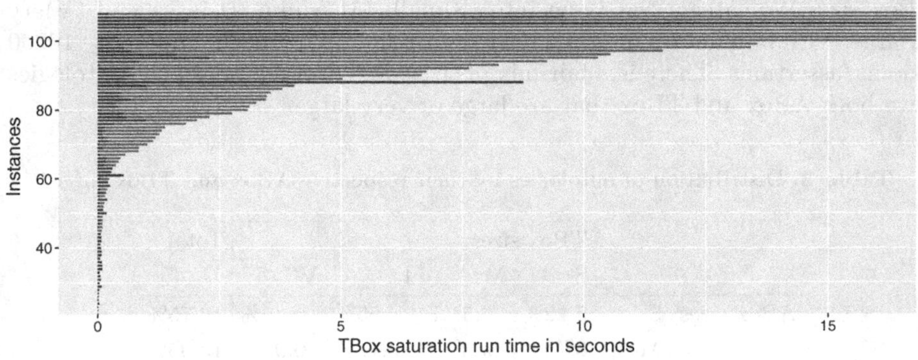

Fig. 2. TBox saturation run time for both versions (C-ORIG = red, C-OPT = blue). (Color figure online)

In what follows, we zoom in into three aspects of these tests. First we make a more fine grained comparison of C-ORIG and C-OPT, by comparing their behavior on the 108 ontologies that both succeeded on **(P1)**. Then we look at the performance of C-OPT on the 41 ontologies that it succeeded on while C-ORIG did not **(P2)**. Finally, to shed some light on the limits of our optimization, we look more closely at the ontologies that C-OPT could not saturate **(P3)**.

(P1). We compare the sizes of the saturated sets and the run times of both versions, on the 108 ontologies that both succeeded on. To understand how much smaller the saturated set is in the optimized version, independently of the size of the original TBox, we show the *TBox rate of growth* given by the number of axioms of (F1)-(F2) in the saturated TBox, divided by their total in the initial (normalized) TBox. Figure 1 depicts the TBox rate of growth for all ontologies; blue bars for C-OPT are plotted over red bars for C-ORIG. Note that the y-axis is simply the 108 ontologies, ordered by the rate of growth of C-ORIG for better

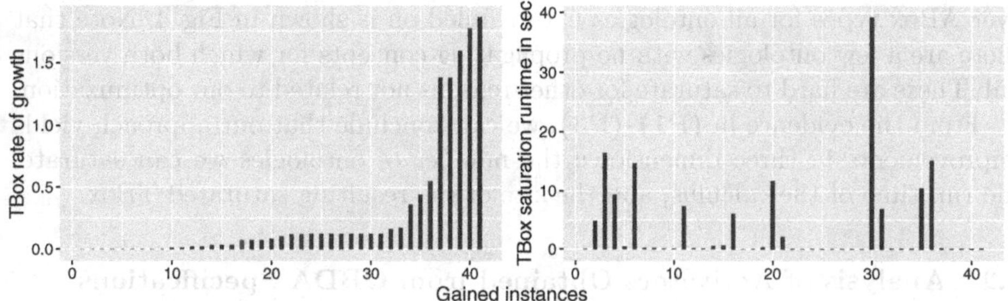

Fig. 3. Gained instances with C-OPT.

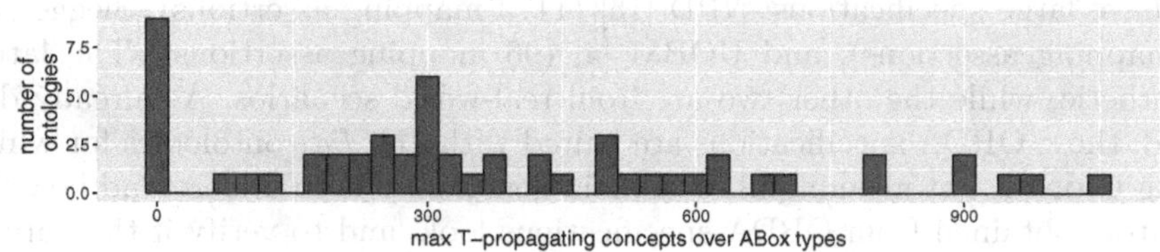

Fig. 4. Failed instances with both versions.

visualization. The x-axis is cut-off; the rate of growth of C-ORIG in fact reached a 20-fold growth. The rate of growth of the optimized version was nearly always smaller, often just a small fraction of the original, in the worst case they are equal. For 88 ontologies instances the rate of growth for C-OPT was 0, i.e. no new axioms were derived (see the bars without blue color). This means that all the axioms derived by C-ORIG were irrelevant for the ABox in the ontology, and for any ABox covered by the same profiles.

Figure 2 shows the run time of the TBox saturation (x-axis) over all ontologies (y-axis, ordered by runtime of C-ORIG). Similarly as in Fig. 1, the run time of C-OPT (blue) is plotted on top of C-ORIG (red). C-OPT outperformed C-ORIG in most of the cases. With one exception, these were ontologies where C-OPT was so fast (typically under 100 ms), that the overhead of handling the activators did not pay off.

(P2). The growth rate and saturation run times of the 41 ontologies gained with C-OPT are shown in the Fig. 3. In both graphs, the ontologies are ordered by the TBox rate of growth. The left graph shows that the rate of growth for these ontologies is in line with the growth reported in **(P1)**, remaining below double the original size even in the worst-case. On the right we see that the run time for most ontologies was under 10 s, also in line with the run times in **(P1)**.

(P3). We analysed the ontologies that we could not saturate, and observed that the maximal size of $\mathcal{T}$-propagating concepts over ABox types plays a key role, for both C-ORIG and C-OPT. C-ORIG always failed when this number was above 20. C-OPT could handle some ontologies with up to almost a hundred, but failed in all ontologies with more than that. The maximal size of $\mathcal{T}$-propagating concepts over ABox types for all ontologies C-opt failed on is shown in Fig. 4. Note that there are a few ontologies with no propagating concepts for which both versions fail. These are hard to saturate for other reasons not related to our optimization.

From the evidence in **(P1)**–**(P3)**, we can conclude that our approach yields improvements in three dimensions: the number of ontologies we can saturate, the run time of the calculus, and the size of the resulting saturated TBox.

5.2 Analysis of Activators Obtained from OBDA Specifications

With the purpose of understanding the feasibility of our approach when ABoxes come from real OBDA specifications, we analysed three existing benchmarks that have large specifications: NPD [15] (1173 mapping assertions), Slegge [12] (62 mapping assertions), and UOBM [4] (96 mapping assertions). The latter is synthetic, while the other two are from real-world scenarios. As already discussed, these OBDA specifications are paired with *DL-Lite* ontologies for which testing C-opt is not meaningful. Our main goal here was to understand how the activators obtained from OBDA specifications look, and to verify if they are in line with the activators from ABoxes that we used for testing C-opt.

Using the approach in Sect. 4, that exploits functional dependencies, we obtained a set of activators where the largest set has size 9 for NPD, 3 for Slegge and 11 for UOBM. We expect these activator sizes to be quite manageable for C-opt, since its average runtime was under 2 s over all ontologies from the Oxford repository with similar ABoxes (namely, 5 or more assertions in the ABox type of some individual). We remark than in all these cases, since the ontologies are simple there are no propagating concepts, so the activators coincide with the actual ABox types that the mappings induce.

The size of the obtained activator sets was over 600 for NPD, but only 4 for Slegge and 12 for UOBM. We note that the number of mappings sharing the same function symbol f in the head was up to 30 for NPD, 4 for Slegge, and 15 for UOBM, hence taking only one activator per function symbol would probably result in a rather poor performance of C-opt.

6 Conclusion

In this paper we proposed an optimization of Horn-$\mathcal{SHIQ}$ reasoning that can be useful for OBDA. We illustrated the problems of current ABox-independent approaches to TBox saturation, which often manifests exponential behaviour, and proposed a way to overcome this. In a nutshell, we avoid the derivation of axioms that are useless since they consider combinations of concepts that can not occur in the real data. We achieve this by constraining the axiom derivation with *activators* that reflect the possible structure of the data. We implemented our approach as an optimization of the Clipper reasoner [11], which scales well in general, and can handle considerably more ontologies than the original Clipper. Crucially, the ABox structure information that is needed in our approach can be obtained directly from the mapping assertions of an OBDA specification; we corroborated this on existing OBDA specifications. We hope this work brings closer the goal of realizing OBDA with ontologies beyond DL-Lite.

In future work, we plan to explore more fine-grained algorithms for extracting activators from mappings, and more generally, to further develop approaches to optimize reasoning techniques that are almost data-independent, but that allow to leverage some general features of the data to improve performance.

References

1. Baader, F., Bienvenu, M., Lutz, C., Wolter, F.: Query and predicate emptiness in ontology-based data access. J. Artif. Intell. Res. **56**, 1–59 (2016)
2. Baader, F., Calvanese, D., McGuinness, D., Nardi, D., Patel-Schneider, P. (eds.): The Description Logic Handbook: Theory, Implementation, and Applications, 2nd edn. Cambridge University Press, Cambridge (2007)
3. Bienvenu, M., Ortiz, M.: Ontology-mediated query answering with data-tractable description logics. In: Faber, W., Paschke, A. (eds.) Reasoning Web 2015. LNCS, vol. 9203, pp. 218–307. Springer, Cham (2015). https://doi.org/10.1007/978-3-319-21768-0_9
4. Botoeva, E., Calvanese, D., Santarelli, V., Savo, D.F., Solimando, A., Xiao, G.: Beyond OWL 2 QL in OBDA: rewritings and approximations. In: Proceedings of of AAAI, pp. 921–928. AAAI Press (2016)
5. Botoeva, E., Kontchakov, R., Ryzhikov, V., Wolter, F., Zakharyaschev, M.: Games for query inseparability of description logic knowledge bases. Artif. Intell. **234**, 78–119 (2016)
6. Botoeva, E., Lutz, C., Ryzhikov, V., Wolter, F., Zakharyaschev, M.: Query inseparability for ALC ontologies. CoRR abs/1902.00014 (2019)
7. Calvanese, D., De Giacomo, G., Lembo, D., Lenzerini, M., Rosati, R.: Tractable reasoning and efficient query answering in description logics: the DL-Lite family. J. Autom. Reas. **39**(3), 385–429 (2007)
8. Carral, D., Dragoste, I., Krötzsch, M.: The combined approach to query answering in Horn-ALCHOIQ. In: Proceedings of KR, pp. 339–348. AAAI Press (2018)
9. Carral, D., González, L., Koopmann, P.: From Horn-SRIQ to datalog: a data-independent transformation that preserves assertion entailment. In: Proceedings of AAAI. AAAI Press (2019)
10. Das, S., Sundara, S., Cyganiak, R.: R2RML: RDB to RDF mapping language. In: W3C Recommendation, W3C (2012)
11. Eiter, T., Ortiz, M., Simkus, M., Tran, T., Xiao, G.: Query rewriting for Horn-SHIQ plus rules. In: Proceedings of AAAI, pp. 726–733. AAAI Press (2012)
12. Hovland, D., Kontchakov, R., Skjæveland, M.G., Waaler, A., Zakharyaschev, M.: Ontology-based data access to Slegge. In: d'Amato, C., et al. (eds.) ISWC 2017. LNCS, vol. 10588, pp. 120–129. Springer, Cham (2017). https://doi.org/10.1007/978-3-319-68204-4_12
13. Kazakov, Y.: Consequence-driven reasoning for Horn SHIQ ontologies. In: Proceedings of IJCAI, pp. 2040–2045 (2009)
14. Krötzsch, M., Rudolph, S., Hitzler, P.: Complexity boundaries for Horn description logics. In: Proceedings of AAAI, pp. 452–457. AAAI Press (2007)
15. Lanti, D., Rezk, M., Xiao, G., Calvanese, D.: The NPD benchmark: reality check for OBDA systems. In: Proceedings of EDBT. ACM Press (2015)

16. Leone, N., Manna, M., Terracina, G., Veltri, P.: Fast query answering over existential rules. ACM Trans. Comput. Log. **20**(2), 1–48 (2019). https://doi.org/10.1145/3308448
17. Lutz, C., Walther, D., Wolter, F.: Conservative extensions in expressive description logics. In: Proceedings of IJCAI, pp. 453–458 (2007)
18. Poggi, A., Lembo, D., Calvanese, D., De Giacomo, G., Lenzerini, M., Rosati, R.: Linking data to ontologies. J. Data Semant. **10**, 133–173 (2008)
19. Ren, Y., Pan, J.Z., Zhao, Y.: Soundness preserving approximation for TBox reasoning. In: Proceedings of AAAI, pp. 351–356. AAAI Press (2010)
20. Rodriguez-Muro, M., Rezk, M.: Efficient SPARQL-to-SQL with R2RML mappings. J. Web Semant. **33**, 141–169 (2015)
21. Shi, L., Cai, X.: An exact fast algorithm for minimum hitting set. In: Third International Joint Conference on Computational Science and Optimization, vol. 1, pp. 64–67 (2010)
22. Xiao, G., et al.: Ontology-based data access: a survey. In: Proceedings of IJCAI, pp. 5511–5519 (2018)
23. Xiao, G., Ding, L., Cogrel, B., Calvanese, D.: Virtual knowledge graphs: an overview of systems and use cases. Data Intell. **1**, 201–223 (2019)

Using a KG-Copy Network for Non-goal Oriented Dialogues

Debanjan Chaudhuri[1,2(✉)], Md. Rashad Al Hasan Rony[1,2], Simon Jordan[3], and Jens Lehmann[1,2]

[1] Enterprise Information Systems Department, Fraunhofer IAIS, Dresden and St. Augustin, Germany
{debanjan.chaudhuri,md.rashad.al.hasan.rony, jens.lehmann}@iais.fraunhofer.de

[2] Smart Data Analytics Group, University of Bonn, Bonn, Germany
{chaudhur,jens.lehmann}@cs.uni-bonn.de, s6mdrony@uni-bonn.de

[3] Volkswagen Group Research, Wolfsburg, Germany
simon.jordan@volkswagen.de

http://iais.fraunhofer.de, http://sda.tech

Abstract. Non-goal oriented, generative dialogue systems lack the ability to generate answers with grounded facts. A knowledge graph can be considered an abstraction of the real world consisting of well-grounded facts. This paper addresses the problem of generating well-grounded responses by integrating knowledge graphs into the dialogue system's response generation process, in an end-to-end manner. A dataset for non-goal oriented dialogues is proposed in this paper in the domain of soccer, conversing on different clubs and national teams along with a knowledge graph for each of these teams. A novel neural network architecture is also proposed as a baseline on this dataset, which can integrate knowledge graphs into the response generation process, producing well articulated, knowledge grounded responses. Empirical evidence suggests that the proposed model performs better than other state-of-the-art models for knowledge graph integrated dialogue systems.

Keywords: Non-goal oriented dialogues · Knowledge grounded dialogues · Knowledge graphs

1 Introduction

With the recent advancements in neural network based techniques for language understanding and generation, there is an upheaved interest in having systems which are able to have articulate conversations with humans. Dialogue systems can generally be classified into goal and non-goal oriented systems, based on the nature of the conversation. The former category includes systems which are able to solve specific set of tasks for users within a particular domain, e.g. restaurant

C. Ghidini et al. (Eds.): ISWC 2019, LNCS 11778, pp. 93–109, 2019.
https://doi.org/10.1007/978-3-030-30793-6_6

or flight booking. Non-goal oriented dialogue systems, on the other hand, are a first step towards chit-chat scenarios where humans engage in conversations with bots over non-trivial topics. Both types of dialogue systems can benefit from added additional world knowledge [9,11,38].

For the case of non-goal oriented dialogues, the systems should be able to handle factoid as well as non-factoid queries like chit-chats or opinions on different subjects/domains. Generally, such systems are realized by using an extrinsic dialogue managers using intent detection subsequently followed by response generation (for the predicted intent) [1,2]. Furthermore, in case of factoid queries posed to such systems, it is very important that they generate well articulated responses which are knowledge grounded. The systems must be able to generate a grammatically correct as well as factually grounded responses to such queries, while preserving co-references across the dialogue contexts. For better understanding, let us consider an example dialogue and the involved knowledge graph snippet in Fig. 1. The conversation consists of chit-chat as well as factoid queries. For the factoid question "do you know what is the home ground of Arsenal?", the system must be able to answer with the correct entity (Emirates Stadium) along with a grammatically correct sentence; as well as handle co-references("its" in the third user utterance meaning the stadium). Ideally, for an end-to-end system for non-goal oriented dialogues, the system should be able to handle all these kind of queries using a single, end-to-end architecture.

There are existing conversation datasets supported by knowledge graphs for well-grounded response generation. [11] introduced an in-car dialogue dataset for multi-domain, task-oriented dialogues along with a knowledge graph which can be used to answer questions about the task the user wants to be assisted with. The dataset consists of dialogues from the following domains: calendar scheduling, weather information retrieval, and point-of interest navigation. For non-goal oriented dialogues, [10] proposed a dataset in the movie domain. The proposed dataset contains short dialogues for factoid question answering over movies or for recommendations. They also provide a knowledge graph consisting of triples as (s, r, o). Where s is the subject, r stands for relations and o being the object. An example of a triple from the dataset is: (Flags of Our Fathers, directed_by, Clint Eastwood). The movie dialogues can utilize this provided knowledge graph for recommendation and question answering purposes. However, this dataset only tackles the problem of factual response generation in dialogues, and not well articulated ones.

To cater to the problem of generating well articulated, knowledge grounded responses for non-goal oriented dialogue systems, we propose a new dataset in the domain of soccer. We also propose the KG-Copy network which is able to copy facts from the KGs in case of factoid questions while generating well-articulated sentences as well as implicitly handling chit-chats, opinions by generating responses like a traditional sequence-to-sequence model.

The contributions of the paper can be summarized as follows:

- A new dataset of 2,990 conversations for non-goal oriented dialogues in the domain of soccer, over various club and national teams.

USER:	Hey what's up?
SYSTEM:	Nothing much, how are you? Do you want to talk soccer?
USER:	I am fine, thanks. Yeah, do you know what is the home ground of Arsenal ?
SYSTEM:	Arsenal's home ground is *Emirates Stadium*.
USER:	Oh ok, what's its capacity?
SYSTEM:	It has a capacity of *60,338*.

Subject	Predicate	Object
Arsenal	Home venue	Emirates Stadium
Emirates Stadium	capacity	60,338
Arsenal	chairman	Chips Keswick
Arsenal	Head coach	Unai Emery

Arsenal Knowledge Graph snippet.

Fig. 1. A conversation about the football club Arsenal and the Knowledge Graph involved.

- A soccer knowledge graph which consists of facts, as triples, curated from wikipedia.
- An end-to-end based, novel neural network architecture as a baseline approach on this dataset. The network is empirically evaluated against other state-of-the-art architectures for knowledge grounded dialogue systems. The evaluation is done based on both knowledge groundedness using entity-F1 score and also standard, automated metrics (BLEU) for evaluating dialogue systems.

The rest of the paper is organized as follows: we first introduce related work in Sect. 2. Then we cover the soccer dataset, which serves as background knowledge for our model in Sect. 3. The proposed model is explained in Sect. 4 and the training procedure is detailed in Sect. 5. In Sect. 6, we compare our model with other state-of-the-art models. We do a qualitative analysis of the model in Sect. 7, followed by an error analysis. In Sect. 8, finally we conclude.

2 Related Work

Systems that are able to converse with humans have been one of the main focus of research from the early days of artificial intelligence. Such conversational systems can be designed as generative or retrieval based. A system produces automatic responses from the training vocabulary for the former, while selecting a best response from a set of possible responses for the latter. Automatic response generation was previously devised by [24] using a phrased-based generative method. Later onwards, sequence-to-sequence based neural network models has been mainly used for dialogue generation [19,27,29]. These models are further improved using hierarchical RNN based architectures for incorporating more contextual information in the response generation process [26]. Reinforcement learning-based end-to-end generative system were also proposed by [37] for jointly learning dialogue state-tracking [32] and policy learning [5].

[17] introduced the first multi-turn, retrieval based dataset which motivated a lot of further research on such systems. A lot of models are proposed on this dataset using both CNN [3,36] and RNN [31,34] based architectures. Both generative and retrieval based models can benefit from additional world knowledge as mentioned previously. However, the task of incorporating such additional knowledge (both structured and unstructured) into dialogue systems is challenging and is also a widely researched topic. [9,16,35] proposed architectures for incorporating unstructured knowledge into retrieval based systems. More recently, [12] incorporated unstructured knowledge as facts into generative dialogue systems as well.

Integration of structured knowledge comes in the form of incorporating knowledge graphs into the response generation process. [11] proposed a Key-Value retrieval network along with the in-car dataset (consisting of goal-oriented dialogues) for KG integration into sequence-to-sequence model. [20] proposed a generative model namely Mem2Seq for a task-oriented dialog system which combines multi-hop attention over memories with pointer networks. The model learns to generate dynamic queries to control the memory access. Mem2Seq is the current state-of-the-art on the in-car dataset. Further improvements on the task are proposed by [14] using joint embeddings and entity loss based regularization techniques. However, they learn the KG embeddings globally instead of per dialogue, so we evaluate our proposed system (KG-Copy network) against Mem2Seq.

Alongside the previously mentioned datasets for knowledge grounded dialogues, there is also a challenging dataset for complex sequential question answering which was introduced by [25]. It contains around 200 K sequential queries that require a large KG to answer. The dataset contains questions that require inference and logical reasoning over the KG to answer. Although the dataset is the first non-goal oriented dataset which aims at knolwedge graph integration, but it lacks proper conversational turns between utterances.

3 Soccer Dialogues Dataset

3.1 Wizard-of-Oz Style Data Collection

The proposed dataset for conversations over soccer is collected using AMT (Amazon Mechanical Turk) [8]. The dialogues are collected in an wizard-of-oz style [23] setup. In such a setup, humans believe they are interacting with machines, while the interaction is completely done by humans. The turkers, acting as users, were instructed to initiate a conversation about the given team with any query or opinion or just have some small-talks. This initial utterance is again posted as another AMT task for replying, this time a different turker is acting as a system. Turkers assigned to the system role were asked to use Wikipedia to answer questions posed by the user. We encouraged the turkers to ask factual questions as well as posing opinions over the given teams, or have chit chat conversations. After a sequence of 7–8 utterances, the turkers were instructed to eventually end the conversation. A screenshot from the experimental setup is shown in Fig. 2. We restricted the knowledge graph to a limited set of teams. The teams are picked based on popularity, the national teams chosen are: Sweden, Spain, Senegal, Portugal, Nigeria, Mexico, Italy, Iceland, Germany, France, Croatia, Colombia, Brazil, Belgium, Argentina, Uruguay and Switzerland. The club teams provided for conversing are: F.C. Barcelona, Real Madrid, Juventus F.C., Manchester United, Paris Saint Germain F.C., Liverpool F.C., Chelsea F.C., Atletico Madrid, F.C. Bayern Munich, F.C. Porto and Borussia Dortmund. We also encouraged people to converse about soccer without any particular team. The number of conversations are equally distributed across all teams. The statistics of the total number of conversations are given in Table 1.

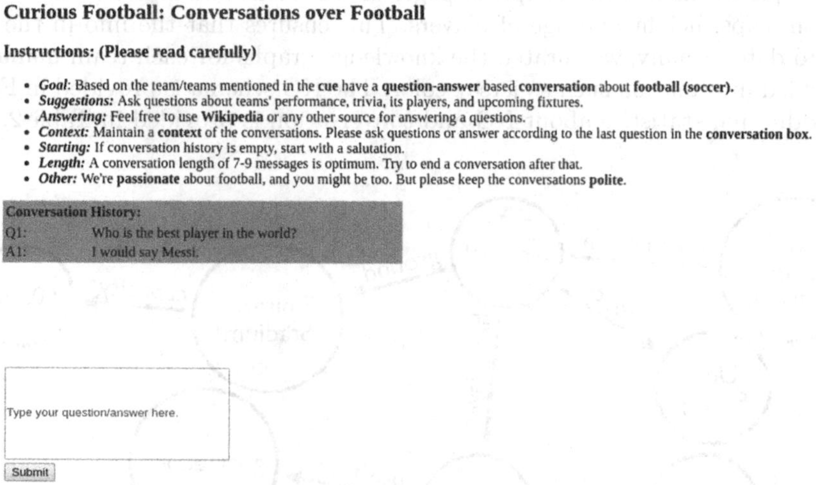

Curious Football: Conversations over Football
Instructions: (Please read carefully)
• Goal: Based on the team/teams mentioned in the cue have a question-answer based conversation about football (soccer).
• Suggestions: Ask questions about teams' performance, trivia, its players, and upcoming fixtures.
• Answering: Feel free to use Wikipedia or any other source for answering a questions.
• Context: Maintain a context of the conversations. Please ask questions or answer according to the last question in the conversation box.
• Starting: If conversation history is empty, start with a salutation.
• Length: A conversation length of 7-9 messages is optimum. Try to end a conversation after that.
• Other: We're passionate about football, and you might be too. But please keep the conversations polite.
Conversation History:
Q1: Who is the best player in the world?
A1: I would say Messi.
Type your question/answer here.
Submit

Fig. 2. AMT setup for getting conversations over soccer.

3.2 Ensuring Coherence

In order to ensure coherent dialogues between turkers, an additional task is created for each dialogue, where turkers were asked to annotate if the give dialogue is coherent or incoherent. Dialogues which are tagged incoherent by turkers are discarded.

Table 1. Statistics of soccer dataset.

Dataset	# of dialogues	# of utterances
Train	2,493	12,243
Validation	149	737
Test	348	1,727

3.3 Soccer Knowledge Graph

A KG in the context of this paper is a directed, multi-relational graph that represents entities as nodes, and their relations as edges, which can be used as an abstraction of the real world. KGs consists of triples of the form (s,r,o) $\in KG$, where s and o denote the subject and object entities, respectively, and r denotes their relation.

Following [6], we created a soccer knowledge graph from WikiData [30] which consists of information such as a team's coach, captain and also information such as home ground and its capacity for soccer clubs. For information about players, we have parsed individual wikipedia pages of the teams and mined goals scored, position, caps, height and age of players. This ensures that the info in the KG is up to date. Finally, we curated the knowledge graphs for each team manually and added information such as jersey color. The KG schema is provided in Fig. 3 and additional statistics about KG and conversation is provided in Table 2.

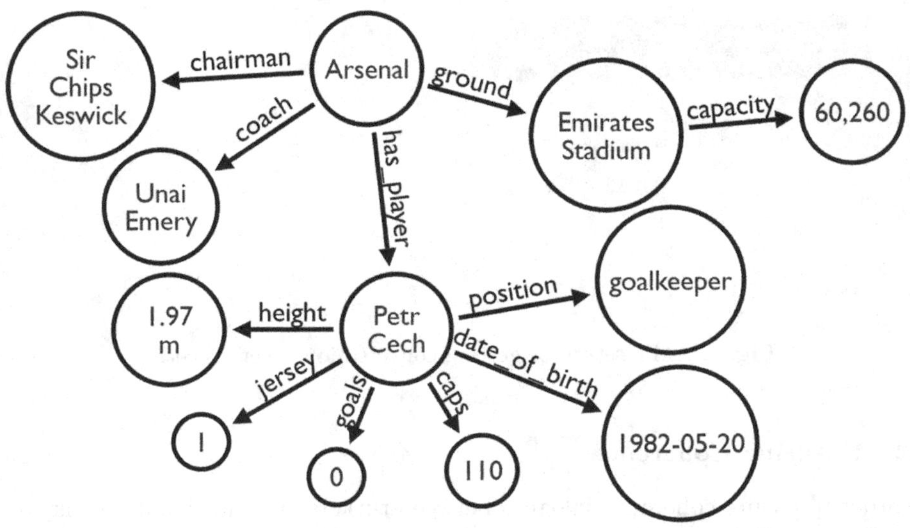

Fig. 3. Schema of the proposed Knowledge Graph for Arsenal.

Table 2. KG statistics.

Statistics	Count
Total vocabulary words (v)	4782
Avg. number of conversations/team	83
Avg. number of triples/team	148
Avg. number of entities/ team	108
Avg. number of relations/team	13

4 KG-Copy Model

The problem we are tackling in this paper is: given a knowledge graph (KG), and an input context in a dialogue, the model should be able to generate factual as well as well articulated response. During the dialogue generation process, at every time-step t, the model could either use the KG or generate a word from the vocabulary. We propose the KG Copy model which tackles this particular problem of producing well-grounded response generation.

KG-Copy is essentially a sequence-to-sequence encoder-decoder based neural network model, where the decoder can generate words either from the vocabulary or from the knowledge graph. The model is mainly influenced by the copynets approach [13]. However, unlike copynets, KG-Copy copies tokens from the local knowledge graph using a special gating mechanism. Here, local KG depicts the KG for the team the dialogue is about. We introduce the KG-Copy's encoder, decoder and the gating mechanism below.

4.1 KG-Copy Encoder

The encoder is based on a recurrent neural network (RNN), more specifically a long-short term memory network (LSTM). It encodes the given input word sequence $X = [x_1, x_2..., x_T]$ to a fixed length vector c. The hidden states are defined by

$$h_t = f_{enc}(x_t, h_{t-1}) \tag{1}$$

where f_{enc} is the encoder recurrent function and the context vector c is given by

$$c = \phi(h_1, h_2...h_T) \tag{2}$$

Here in, ϕ is the summarization function given the hidden states h_t. It can be computed by taking the last hidden state h_T or applying attention over the hidden states [4,18] and getting a weighted value of the hidden states (attention).

4.2 KG-Copy Decoder

The decoder is an attention based RNN (LSTM) model. The input to the decoder is the context c from the encoder along with h_T. At time-step t, the hidden-state of the decoder is given by

$$h_t^d = f_{dec}(x_t, h_{t-1}) \tag{3}$$

where f_{dec} is the recurrent function of the decoder. The decoder hidden-states are initialized using h_T and the first token is <sos>. The attention mechanism [18]. The attention weights are calculated by concatenating the hidden states h_t^d along with h_t .

$$\alpha_t = softmax(W_s(tanh(W_c[h_t; h_t^d]))) \tag{4}$$

Here in, W_c and W_s are the weights of the attention model. The final weighted context representation is given by

$$\tilde{h_t} = \sum_t \alpha_t h_t \tag{5}$$

This representation is concatenated (represented by ;) with the hidden states of the decoder to generate an output from the vocabulary with size v.

The output is then given by

$$o_t = W_o([h_t; \tilde{h_t^d}]) \tag{6}$$

In the above equation, W_o are the output weights with dimension $\mathbf{R}^{h_{dim} X v}$. h_{dim} is the dimension of the hidden layer of the decoder RNN.

4.3 Sentient Gating

The sentient gating, as mentioned previously, is inspired mainly by [13,21]. This gate acts as a sentinel mechanism which decides whether to copy from the local KG or to generate a word from training vocabulary (v). The final objective function can be written as the probability of predicting the next word during decoding based on the encoder hidden-states and the knowledge graph (KG).

$$p(y_t|h_t..h_1, KG) \tag{7}$$

The proposed gating is an embedding based model. At every time-step t, the input query and the input to the decoder are fed into the sentient gate. Firstly, a simple averaging of the input query embedding is done generating emb_q, which can be treated as an vector representation of the input context.

$$emb_q = \frac{1}{N} \sum (emb_{w1}....emb_{wt}) \tag{8}$$

emb_{wt} is the embedding of the tth word in the context. N.B. we only consider noun and verb phrases in the context to calculate emb_q. For the KG representation, an embedding average of the local KG's subject entity and relation labels for each triple is performed yielding a KG embedding emb_{kg}. We consider a total of k triples in the local KG.

Finally, the query embedding is matched with these KG embeddings using a similarity function (cosine similarity in this case).

$$kg_{sim} = tanh(cos(emb_q, emb_{kg}^1), cos(emb_q, emb_{kg}^2)...cos(emb_q, emb_{kg}^k)) \tag{9}$$

The input to the decoder at t is fed into the embedding too as mentioned previously yielding emb_d.

The final sentient value at t is given by :

$$s_t = sigmoid(W_{sent}[emb_q + emb_d; kg_{sim}; s_{t-1}]) \tag{10}$$

W_{sent} is another trainable parameter of the model and ";" is the concatenation operation. The final prediction is given by:

$$out_t = s_t * kg_{sim} + (1 - s_t) * o_t \tag{11}$$

The model is visualized in Fig. 4.

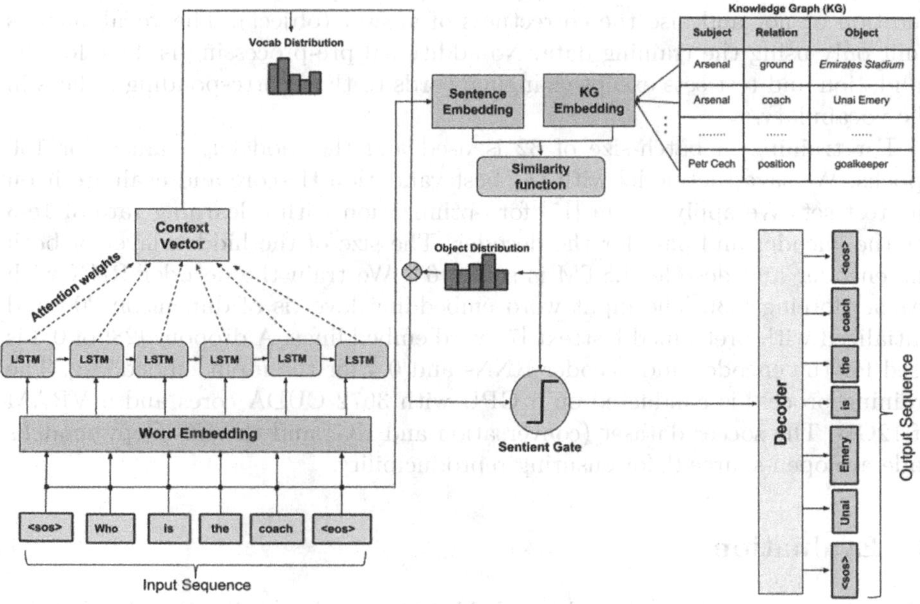

Fig. 4. KG-Copy model encoder-decoder architecture for Knowledge Grounded response generation.

5 Training and Model Hyper-parameters

5.1 Training Objective

The model is trained based on a multi-task objective, where the final objective is to optimize the cross-entropy based vocabulary loss (l_{vocab}) and also the binary cross-entropy loss ($L_{sentient}$) for the sentient gate (s_g). This value is 1 if the generated token at that step comes from the KG, otherwise 0. For example, in the example provided in Fig. 1, for the 2nd system utterance, this value would be 1 for $t = 5$ (Emirates Stadium), but 0 for the previous time-steps. The total loss is given by:

$$L_{tot} = L_{vocab} + L_{sentient} \tag{12}$$

5.2 Training Details

To train the model, we perform a string similarity over KG for each of the questions in training data set to find which questions are answerable from the KG. Then we replace those answers with the position number of the triples where the answer (object) belongs in the KG, during pre-processing. This is followed by a manual step where we verify whether the input query is simple, factoid question or not and also the correctness of answer (object). The vocabulary is built only using the training data. No additional pre-processing is done for the validation and test sets except changing words to their corresponding indices in the vocabulary.

For training, a batch-size of 32 is used and the model is trained for 100 epochs. We save the model with the best validation f1-score and evaluate it on the test set. We apply Adam [15] for optimization with a learning rate of 1e-3 for the encoder and 5e-3 for the decoder. The size of the hidden layer of both the encoder and decoder LSTM is set to 64. We train the decoder RNN with teacher-forcing [33]. The input word embedding layer is of dimension 300 and initialized with pretrained fasttext [7] word embeddings. A dropout [28] of 0.3 is used for the encoder and decoder RNNs and 0.4 for the input embedding. The training process is conducted on a GPU with 3072 CUDA cores and a VRAM of 12GB. The soccer dataset (conversation and KG) and the KG-Copy model's code are open-sourced[1] for ensuring reproducibility.

6 Evaluation

We compare our proposed model with Mem2Seq and a vanilla encoder-decoder with attention. We report the BLEU scores [22] and also the entity-F1 scores on both the proposed soccer dataset and the In-car dialogue dataset. The results show that our proposed model performs better than both the vanilla attention sequence-to-sequence models and Mem2Seq model across both metrics. Our model outperforms Mem2Seq by 1.51 in BLEU score and 15 % on entity-F1 score. It performs better than the vanilla sequence-to-sequence model by 1.21 on the BLEU metric on the soccer dataset. Interestingly, Mem2Seq performs better than the vanilla model on validation, but it fails to generalize on test set. The proposed model although has lower BLEU on the in-car dialogue dataset, but has a better entity f1 scores (by 19.4 %), implying stronger reasoning capabilities over entities and relations [20] (Tables 3 and 4).

[1] https://github.com/SmartDataAnalytics/KG-Copy_Network.

Table 3. Results on soccer dataset.

Model	BLEU		Entity-F1	
	Valid	Test	Valid	Test
Vanilla encoder-decoder with attention	1.04	0.82	–	–
Mem2Seq [20]	1.30	0.52	6.78	7.03
KG Copy (proposed model)	**2.56**	**2.05**	24.98	23.58

Table 4. Results on the in-car dialogue dataset.

Model	BLEU	Entity-F1
Vanilla encoder-decoder with attention	8.4	10.3
Mem2Seq [20]	**12.6**	33.4
KG Copy (proposed model)	9.6	**52.8**

7 Discussion

7.1 Qualitative Analysis

In this section, we will qualitatively analyze the response generation of our model along with the background knowledge integration (grounding) and compare it with both Mem2Seq and vanilla sequence-to-sequence models.

Some example response from test are given in Table 6. As seen, the KG-copy model is able to have more articulate responses compare to sequence-to-sequence and Mem2Seq models. The model is also able to form well articulate opinions compared to other models (2nd column)[2].

Some more examples along with the response from our model are given in Table 7. As observed, all those responses are well grounded. The first response is factually correct and also a well-articulate one; interestingly, even the true human response on the other hand is not. The last response is knowledge ground but not well articulate. The model is also able to perform co-reference resolution implicitly while generating responses. To verify, let us consider another conversation between an user with the deployed KG-copy model.

User utterance: i like the team pretty much
Response: i don't think they're a lot of winning.
User utterance: who is the captain of argentina ?
Response: lionel messi is the captain
User utterance: do you know the name of their coach ?
Response: lionel scaloni is the coach
In the last response, the model is able to identify that the pronoun "their" refers to the team and is able to maintain a knowledge grounded, as well as articulate responses even for relatively long dialogue turns. For time-step $t = 0$, the

[2] Seq2Seq model has generated a more articulated response based on the given context but it is factually wrong: Senegal is nicknamed the Lions of Teranga and not Nigeria.

visualization of the sentient gating mechanism is provided in Fig. 5. The vocabulary distribution is over v, and the object distribution here is over the local KG for the team.

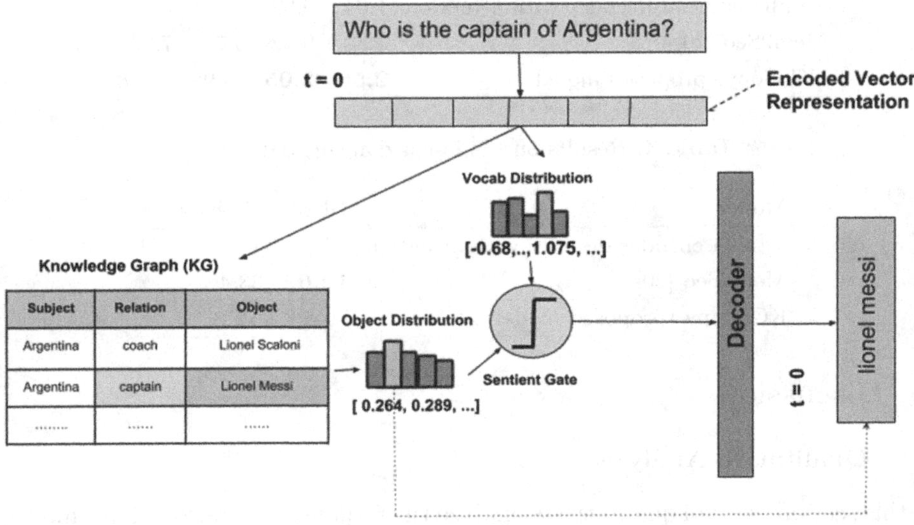

Fig. 5. Response generation during decoding for KG-Copy model.

Furthermore, following [11], we did an internal survey regarding the responses generated by KG-Copy network, judging the quality of responses based on the context on a scale of 1–5 on correctness and human-like sentence formation. The former measures how correct the generated response is with respect to the true response from the turker, and the latter how grammatically correct the produced response is. We randomly pick 50 conversation utterances from the test set and report this human evaluation both on Mem2Seq and KG-copy in Table 5.

7.2 Error Analysis

Although the model is able to generate some well articulated, knowledge grounded responses for factual queries as seen in Tables 6 and 7, the model often fails in producing factually correct responses as also evident from Table 5. More of those cases are analyzed below.

Table 5. Human evaluation of generated responses.

Model	Correctness	Human-like
Mem2Seq	1.30	2.44
KG-Copy	2.26	3.88

Table 6. KG-copy response for factoid and non-factoid queries.

Context type	Factoid	Opinions
Input contexts	What is the name of the captain of mexico?	I like this team
True response	Andres guardado (captain)	Nigeria is a very well performing team and i like them a lot as well
Seq2Seq	The is is	They are nicknamed the Lions of Teranga
Mem2Seq	Mexico is the	They are a
KG-Copy	Andres guardado	They are a good team

Table 7. KG Copy model's knowledge grounded responses.

Input contexts	Turker response	KG copy response
Who is the captain of iceland?	Aron gunnarsson	Aron gunnarsson is the captain
Who is the captain of italy?	Chiellini	Giorgio chiellini is the captain
Who is the coach for italy?	I think roberto mancini	Roberto mancini is the coach
Who is the coach of bayern munich?	Niko kovac is the current manager	Niko kovac

The model produces too generic and non-factual responses to queries about opinions about favorite players as shown in Table 8. This is mostly because the vocabulary size is relatively large compare to the size of training dialogues. This can be improved with more training data, especially with more knowledge grounded conversations. For the first response, the model is not able to interpret the question and generates a generic response. For the second case, the generated response is not factual because the question is about Argentina, but Eden Hazard is from a different team (Belgium).

The KG-copy model also often suffers when more complex quantitative and other reasoning skills are required to respond to the context. For example, for the first context in Table 9, the model needs to perform a count operation over the KG to answer it, which is currently unsupported. Similarly, for the second case the model would require better language inferencing to respond. The model also suffers from the problem of unknown words in the test set.

Table 8. Incorrect opinionated responses from KG-Copy model.

Input contexts	True response	KG copy response
Who is senegal's best current player not including mane?	Keita balde diao	I think it is the best player in the world cup
Who's your favorite player?	Messi	I think eden hazard is the best player

Table 9. Incorrect factual responses from KG Copy model.

Input contexts	How many world cups has the brazil team won?	Who was the top scorer in the world cup for belgium?
True response	Brazil has won the fifa world cup five times	Eden hazard
Predicted	They won the world cup	I think it was the top scorer for the world cup

8 Conclusion and Future Work

In this paper, we introduce a new dataset for non-goal oriented, factual conversations over soccer (football). We also provide a knowledge graph for different club and national football teams which are the topic of these conversations.

Furthermore, we propose a relatively simple, novel, neural network architecture called KG-copy Network, as a baseline model, which can produce knowledge grounded responses as well as articulate responses via copying objects from the team KG based on the presented context of the question. Although the dataset is relatively small, the model can still learn the objective of producing grounded response as evident from the BLEU and entity-F1 scores compare to other models, and also from the examples provided in the paper. The proposed model also produces more knowledge grounded response (better entity f1 scores) on the in-car dialogue dataset [11] compared to other approaches. However, it should be noted that the BLEU scores in case of the non-goal oriented soccer dataset is lower compare to the goal oriented dataset (in-car). This can be attributed to the fact that the vocabulary size in case of the former is much larger (3 times), hence proving it to be a much harder problem. We also outlined weaknesses and limitations, e.g. for building factually correct responses, which can spur future research in this direction.

As a future work, we would like to consider a bigger study for gathering more knowledge-grounded, non-goal oriented conversations extending to more domains other than soccer. One of the problem with the dataset is that some responses from the turkers themselves are not articulate enough as evident from Table 7. To counter this, we would like to include more conversation verification steps and filter out conversations based on inter annotator agreements (IAA) between the turkers. Also, the proposed model can only respond to simple factoid questions based on word embedding based similarities between the context and the KG. We would like to extend the model to do better entity and relation linking between the query contexts and the knowledge graph in an end-to-end manner. The handling of out-of-vocabulary words also provides room for further research. Moreover, we would also like to investigate recently proposed transformer or BERT based sequence-to-sequence models for the task of knowledge grounded response generation.

Acknowledgement. This work has been supported by the Fraunhofer-Cluster of Excellence "Cognitive Internet Technologies" (CCIT).

References

1. Agrawal, P., Suri, A., Menon, T.: A trustworthy, responsible and interpretable system to handle chit-chat in conversational bots. In: The Second AAAI Workshop on Reasoning and Learning for Human-Machine Dialogues, November 2018
2. Akasaki, S., Kaji, N.: Chat detection in an intelligent assistant: combining task-oriented and non-task-oriented spoken dialogue systems. In: Proceedings of the 55th Annual Meeting of the Association for Computational Linguistics (Volume 1: Long Papers), pp. 1308–1319. Association for Computational Linguistics, Vancouver, July 2017. https://doi.org/10.18653/v1/P17-1120
3. An, G., Shafiee, M., Shamsi, D.: Improving retrieval modeling using cross convolution networks and multi frequency word embedding. arXiv preprint arXiv:1802.05373 (2018)
4. Bahdanau, D., Cho, K., Bengio, Y.: Neural machine translation by jointly learning to align and translate. arXiv preprint arXiv:1409.0473 (2014)
5. Baird, L.: Residual algorithms: reinforcement learning with function approximation. In: Machine Learning Proceedings 1995, pp. 30–37. Elsevier (1995)
6. Bergmann, T., et al.: In: Sabou, M., Blomqvist, E., Noia, T.D., Sack, H., Pellegrini, T. (eds.): I-SEMANTICS, pp. 146–149. ACM (2013)
7. Bojanowski, P., Grave, E., Joulin, A., Mikolov, T.: Enriching word vectors with subword information. Trans. Assoc. Comput. Linguist. **5**, 135–146 (2017)
8. Buhrmester, M., Kwang, T., Gosling, S.D.: Amazon's mechanical turk: a new source of inexpensive, yet high-quality, data? Perspect. Psychol. Sci. **6**(1), 3–5 (2011). https://doi.org/10.1177/1745691610393980. pMID: 26162106
9. Chaudhuri, D., Kristiadi, A., Lehmann, J., Fischer, A.: Improving response selection in multi-turn dialogue systems by incorporating domain knowledge. In: Proceedings of the 22nd Conference on Computational Natural Language Learning, pp. 497–507. Association for Computational Linguistics, Brussels, October 2018
10. Dodge, J., et al.: Evaluating prerequisite qualities for learning end-to-end dialog systems. In: ICLR (2016)
11. Eric, M., Krishnan, L., Charette, F., Manning, C.D.: Key-value retrieval networks for task-oriented dialogue. In: Proceedings of the 18th Annual SIGdial Meeting on Discourse and Dialogue, pp. 37–49. Association for Computational Linguistics (2017). https://doi.org/10.18653/v1/W17-5506
12. Ghazvininejad, M., et al.: A knowledge-grounded neural conversation model. In: Thirty-Second AAAI Conference on Artificial Intelligence (2018)

13. Gu, J., Lu, Z., Li, H., Li, V.O.: Incorporating copying mechanism in sequence-to-sequence learning. In: Proceedings of the 54th Annual Meeting of the Association for Computational Linguistics (Volume 1: Long Papers), pp. 1631–1640. Association for Computational Linguistics (2016). https://doi.org/10.18653/v1/P16-1154
14. Kassawat, F., Chaudhuri, D., Lehmann, J.: Incorporating joint embeddings into goal-oriented dialogues with multi-task learning. In: ESWC (2019)
15. Kingma, D.P., Ba, J.: Adam: a method for stochastic optimization. arXiv preprint arXiv:1412.6980 (2014)
16. Lowe, R., Pow, N., Serban, I., Charlin, L., Pineau, J.: Incorporating unstructured textual knowledge sources into neural dialogue systems. In: Neural Information Processing Systems Workshop on Machine Learning for Spoken Language Understanding (2015)
17. Lowe, R., Pow, N., Serban, I., Pineau, J.: The ubuntu dialogue corpus: a large dataset for research in unstructured multi-turn dialogue systems. arXiv preprint arXiv:1506.08909 (2015)
18. Luong, M.T., Pham, H., Manning, C.D.: Effective approaches to attention-based neural machine translation. arXiv preprint arXiv:1508.04025 (2015)
19. Luong, T., Sutskever, I., Le, Q., Vinyals, O., Zaremba, W.: Addressing the rare word problem in neural machine translation. In: Proceedings of the 53rd Annual Meeting of the Association for Computational Linguistics and the 7th International Joint Conference on Natural Language Processing (Volume 1: Long Papers), pp. 11–19. Association for Computational Linguistics, Beijing July 2015. https://doi.org/10.3115/v1/P15-1002
20. Madotto, A., Wu, C.S., Fung, P.: Mem2Seq: effectively incorporating knowledge bases into end-to-end task-oriented dialog systems. In: Proceedings of the 56th Annual Meeting of the Association for Computational Linguistics (Volume 1: Long Papers), pp. 1468–1478. Association for Computational Linguistics, Melbourne, July 2018
21. Merity, S., Xiong, C., Bradbury, J., Socher, R.: Pointer sentinel mixture models. arXiv preprint arXiv:1609.07843 (2016)
22. Papineni, K., Roukos, S., Ward, T., Zhu, W.J.: BLEU: a method for automatic evaluation of machine translation. In: Proceedings of the 40th Annual Meeting on Association for Computational Linguistics, pp. 311–318. Association for Computational Linguistics (2002)
23. Rieser, V., Lemon, O.: Learning effective multimodal dialogue strategies from Wizard-of-Oz data: Bootstrapping and evaluation. In: Proceedings of ACL-08: HLT, pp. 638–646 (2008)
24. Ritter, A., Cherry, C., Dolan, W.B.: Data-driven response generation in social media. In: Proceedings of the Conference on Empirical Methods in Natural Language Processing, pp. 583–593. Association for Computational Linguistics (2011)
25. Saha, A., Pahuja, V., Khapra, M.M., Sankaranarayanan, K., Chandar, S.: Complex sequential question answering: towards learning to converse over linked question answer pairs with a knowledge graph. In: Thirty-Second AAAI Conference on Artificial Intelligence (2018)
26. Serban, I.V., Sordoni, A., Bengio, Y., Courville, A., Pineau, J.: Building end-to-end dialogue systems using generative hierarchical neural network models. In: Thirtieth AAAI Conference on Artificial Intelligence (2016)

27. Shang, L., Lu, Z., Li, H.: Neural responding machine for short-text conversation. In: Proceedings of the 53rd Annual Meeting of the Association for Computational Linguistics and the 7th International Joint Conference on Natural Language Processing (Volume 1: Long Papers), pp. 1577–1586. Association for Computational Linguistics, Beijing, July 2015. https://doi.org/10.3115/v1/P15-1152
28. Srivastava, N., Hinton, G., Krizhevsky, A., Sutskever, I., Salakhutdinov, R.: Dropout: a simple way to prevent neural networks from overfitting. J. Mach. Learn. Res. **15**(1), 1929–1958 (2014)
29. Vinyals, O., Le, Q.V.: A neural conversational model. ArXiv abs/1506.05869 (2015)
30. Vrandečić, D., Krötzsch, M.: Wikidata: a free collaborative knowledgebase. Commun. ACM **57**(10), 78–85 (2014). https://doi.org/10.1145/2629489
31. Wang, S., Jiang, J.: Learning natural language inference with LSTM. In: Proceedings of NAACL-HLT 2016 (2016)
32. Williams, J., Raux, A., Ramachandran, D., Black, A.: The dialog state tracking challenge. In: Proceedings of the SIGDIAL 2013 Conference, pp. 404–413 (2013)
33. Williams, R.J., Zipser, D.: A learning algorithm for continually running fully recurrent neural networks. Neural Comput. **1**(2), 270–280 (1989)
34. Wu, Y., Wu, W., Xing, C., Zhou, M., Li, Z.: Sequential matching network: a new architecture for multi-turn response selection in retrieval-based chatbots. In: Proceedings of the 55th Annual Meeting of the Association for Computational Linguistics (Volume 1: Long Papers), vol. 1, pp. 496–505 (2017)
35. Xu, Z., Liu, B., Wang, B., Sun, C., Wang, X.: Incorporating loose-structured knowledge into LSTM with recall gate for conversation modeling. arXiv preprint arXiv:1605.05110 3 (2016)
36. Yan, R., Song, Y., Wu, H.: Learning to respond with deep neural networks for retrieval-based human-computer conversation system. In: Proceedings of the 39th International ACM SIGIR Conference on Research and Development in Information Retrieval, pp. 55–64. ACM (2016)
37. Zhao, T., Eskenazi, M.: Towards end-to-end learning for dialog state tracking and management using deep reinforcement learning. arXiv preprint arXiv:1606.02560 (2016)
38. Zhu, W., Mo, K., Zhang, Y., Zhu, Z., Peng, X., Yang, Q.: Flexible end-to-end dialogue system for knowledge grounded conversation. arXiv preprint arXiv:1709.04264 (2017)

Canonicalizing Knowledge Base Literals

Jiaoyan Chen[1(✉)], Ernesto Jiménez-Ruiz[2,3], and Ian Horrocks[1,2]

[1] Department of Computer Science, University of Oxford, Oxford, UK
jiaoyan.chen@cs.ox.ac.uk

[2] The Alan Turing Institute, London, UK

[3] Department of Informatics, University of Oslo, Oslo, Norway

Abstract. Ontology-based knowledge bases (KBs) like DBpedia are very valuable resources, but their usefulness and usability are limited by various quality issues. One such issue is the use of string literals instead of semantically typed entities. In this paper we study the automated *canonicalization* of such literals, i.e., replacing the literal with an existing entity from the KB or with a new entity that is typed using classes from the KB. We propose a framework that combines both reasoning and machine learning in order to predict the relevant entities and types, and we evaluate this framework against state-of-the-art baselines for both semantic typing and entity matching.

Keywords: Knowledge base correction · Literal canonicalization · Knowledge-based learning · Recurrent Neural Network

1 Introduction

Ontology-based knowledge bases (KBs) like DBpedia [2] are playing an increasingly important role in domains such knowledge management, data analysis and natural language understanding. Although they are very valuable resources, the usefulness and usability of such KBs is limited by various quality issues [10,22,31]. One such issue is the use of string literals (both explicitly typed and plain literals) instead of semantically typed entities; for example in the triple ⟨*River_Thames*, *passesArea*, *"Port Meadow, Oxford"*⟩. This weakens the KB as it does not capture the semantics of such literals. If, in contrast, the object of the triple were an entity, then this entity could, e.g., be typed as *Wetland* and *Park*, and its location given as *Oxford*. This problem is pervasive and hence results in a significant loss of information: according to statistics from Gunaratna et al. [14], in 2016, the DBpedia property *dbp:location* has over 105,000 unique string literals that could be matched with entities. Besides DBpedia, such literals can also be found in some other KBs from encyclopedias (e.g., zhishi.me [21]), in RDF graphs transformed from tabular data (e.g., LinkedGeoData [3]), in aligned or evolving KBs, etc.

C. Ghidini et al. (Eds.): ISWC 2019, LNCS 11778, pp. 110–127, 2019.
https://doi.org/10.1007/978-3-030-30793-6_7

One possible remedy for this problem is to apply automated semantic typing and entity matching (AKA *canonicalization*[1]) to such literals. To the best of our knowledge, semantic typing of KB literals has rarely been studied. Gunaratna et al. [14] used semantic typing in their entity summarization method, first identifying the so called focus term of a phrase via grammatical structure analysis, and then matching the focus term with both KB types and entities. Their method is, however, rather simplistic: it neither utilizes the literal's context, such as the associated property and subject, nor captures the contextual meaning of the relevant words. What has been widely studied is the semantic annotation of KB entities [13,23,28] and of noun phrases outside the KB (e.g., from web tables) [4,9,18]; in such cases, however, the context is very different, and entity typing can, for example, exploit structured information such as the entity's linked Wikipedia page [13] and the domain and range of properties that the entity is associated with [23].

With the development of deep learning, semantic embedding and feature learning have been widely adopted for exploring different kinds of contextual semantics in prediction, with Recurrent Neural Network (RNN) being a state-of-the-art method for dealing with structured data and text. One well known example is *word2vec*—an RNN language model which can represent words in a vector space that retains their meaning [20]. Another example is a recent study by Kartsaklis et al. [15], which maps text to KB entities with a Long-short Term Memory RNN for textual feature learning. These methods offer the potential for developing accurate prediction-based methods for KB literal typing and entity matching where the contextual semantics is fully exploited.

In this study, we investigate KB literal canonicalization using a combination of RNN-based learning and semantic technologies. We first predict the semantic types of a literal by: *(i)* identifying candidate classes via lexical entity matching and KB queries; *(ii)* automatically generating positive and negative examples via KB sampling, with external semantics (e.g., from other KBs) injected for improved quality; *(iii)* training classifiers using relevant subject-predicate-literal triples embedded in an attentive bidirectional RNN (AttBiRNN); and *(iv)* using the trained classifiers and KB class hierarchy to predict candidate types. The novelty of our framework lies in its knowledge-based learning; this includes automatic candidate class extraction and sampling from the KB, triple embedding with different importance degrees suggesting different semantics, and using the predicted types to identify a potential canonical entity from the KB. We have evaluated our framework using a synthetic literal set (S-Lite) and a real literal set (R-Lite) from DBpedia [2]. The results are very promising, with significant improvements over several baselines, including the existing state-of-the-art.

[1] Note this is different from canonical mapping of literal values in the RDF standard by W3C.

2 Method

2.1 Problem Statement

In this study we consider a knowledge base (KB) that includes both ontological axioms that induce (at least) a hierarchy of semantic types (i.e., classes), and assertions that describe concrete entities (individuals). Each such assertion is assumed to be in the form of an RDF triple $\langle s, p, o \rangle$, where s is an entity, p is a property and o can be either an entity or a literal (i.e., a typed or untyped data value such as a string or integer).

We focus on triples of the form $\langle s, p, l \rangle$, where l is a string literal; such literals can be identified by regular expressions, as in [14], or by data type inference as in [8]. Our aim is to cononicalize l by first identifying the *type* of l, i.e., a set of classes $\mathcal{C}_l$ that an entity corresponding to l should be an instance of, and then determining if such an entity already exists in the KB. The first subtask is modeled as a machine learning classification problem where a real value score in $[0, 1]$ is assigned to each class c occurring in the KB, and $\mathcal{C}_l$ is the set of classes determined by the assigned score with strategies e.g., adopting a class if its score exceeds some threshold. The second subtask is modeled as an entity lookup problem constrained by $\mathcal{C}_l$. It is important to note that:

(i) When we talk about a literal l we mean the occurrence of l in a triple $\langle s, p, l \rangle$. Lexically equivalent literals might be treated very differently depending on their triple contexts.
(ii) If the KB is an OWL DL ontology, then the set of *object properties* (which connect two entities) and *data properties* (which connect an entity to a literal) should be disjoint. In practice, however, KBs such as DBpedia often do not respect this constraint. In any case, we avoid the issue by simply computing the relevant typing and canonicalization information, and leaving it up to applications as to how they want to exploit it.
(iii) We assume that no manual annotations or external labels are given—the classifier is automatically trained using the KB.

2.2 Technical Framework

The technical framework for the classification problem is shown in Fig. 1. It involves three main steps: *(i)* candidate class extraction; *(ii)* model training and prediction; and *(iii)* literal typing and canonicalization.

Candidate Class Extraction. Popular KBs like DBpedia often contain a large number of classes. For efficiency reasons, and to reduce noise in the learning process, we first identify a subset of candidate classes. This selection should be rather inclusive so as to maximize potential recall. In order to achieve this, we pool the candidate classes for all literals occurring in triples with a given property; i.e., to compute the candidate classes for a literal l occurring in a triple $\langle s, p, l \rangle$, we consider all triples that use property p. Note that, as discussed

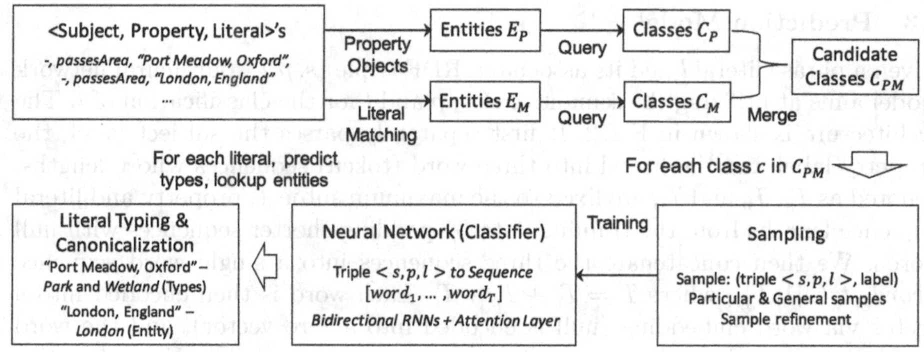

Fig. 1. The technical framework for KB literal canonicalization.

above, in practice such triples may include both literals and entities as their objects. We thus use two techniques for identifying candidate classes from the given set of triples. In the case where the object of the triple is an entity, the candidates are just the set of classes that this entity is an instance of. In practice we identify the candidates for the set of all such entities, which we denote E_P, via a SPARQL query to the KB, with the resulting set of classes being denoted C_P. In the case where the object of the triple is a literal, we first match the literal to entities using a lexical index which is built based on the entity's name, labels and anchor text (description). To maximize recall, the literal as well as its sub-phrases are used to retrieve entities by lexical matching; this technique is particularly effective when the literal is a long phrase. As in the first case, we identify all relevant entities, which we denote E_M, and then retrieve the relevant classes C_M using a SPARQL query. The candidate class set is simply the union of C_P and C_M, denoted as C_{PM}.

Model Training and Prediction. We adopt the strategy of training one binary classifier for each candidate class, instead of multi-class classification, so as to facilitate dealing with the class hierarchy [27]. The classifier architecture includes an input layer with word embedding, an encoding layer with bidirectional RNNs, an attention layer and a fully connected (FC) layer for modeling the contextual semantics of the literal. To train a classifier, both positive and negative entities (samples), including those from E_M (particular samples) and those outside E_M (general samples) are extracted from the KB, with external KBs and logical constraints being used to improve sample quality. The trained classifiers are used to compute a score for each candidate class.

Literal Typing and Canonicalization. The final stage is to semantically type and, where possible, canonicalize literals. For a given literal, two strategies, independent and hierarchical, are used to determine its types (classes), with a score for each type. We then use these types and scores to try to identify an entity in the KB that could reasonably be substituted for the literal.

2.3 Prediction Model

Given a phrase literal l and its associated RDF triple $\langle s, p, l \rangle$, our neural network model aims at utilizing the semantics of s, p and l for the classification of l. The architecture is shown in Fig. 2. It first separately parses the subject label, the property label and the literal into three word (token) sequences whose lengths, denoted as T_s, T_p and T_l, are fixed to the maximum subject, property and literal sequence lengths from the training data by padding shorter sequences with null words. We then concatenate the three sequences into a single word sequence $(word_t, t \in [1, T])$, where $T = T_s + T_p + T_l$. Each word is then encoded into a vector via word embedding (null is encoded into a zero vector), and the word sequence is transformed into a vector sequence $(x_t, t \in [1, T])$. Note that this preserves information about the position of words in s, p and l.

The semantics of forward and backward surrounding words is effective in predicting a word's semantics. For example, "Port" and "Meadow" are more likely to indicate a place as they appear after "Area" and before "Oxford". To embed such contextual semantics into a feature vector, we stack a layer composed of bidirectional Recurrent Neural Networks (BiRNNs) with Gated Recurrent Unit (GRU) [5]. Within each RNN, a reset gate r_t is used to control the contribution of the past word, and an update gate z_t is used to balance the contributions of the past words and the new words. The hidden state (embedding) at position t is computed as

$$\begin{cases} h_t = (1 - z_t) \odot h_{t-1} + z_t \odot \tilde{h}_t, \\ \tilde{h}_t = \tau(W_h x_t + r_t \odot (U_h h_{t-1}) + b_h), \\ z_t = \sigma(W_z x_t + U_z h_{t-1} + b_z), \\ r_t = \sigma(W_r x_t + U_r h_{t-1} + b_r), \end{cases} \tag{1}$$

where $\odot$ denotes the Hadamard product, σ and τ denote the activation function of *sigmod* and *tanh* respectively, and W_h, U_h, b_h, W_z, U_z, b_z, W_r, U_r and b_r are parameters to learn. With the two bidirectional RNNs, one forward hidden state and one backward hidden state are calculated for the sequence, denoted as $(\overrightarrow{h_t}, t \in [1, T])$ and $(\overleftarrow{h_t}, t \in [T, 1])$ respectively. They are concatenated as the output of the RNN layer: $h_t = \left[\overrightarrow{h_t}, \overleftarrow{h_t}\right], t \in [1, T]$.

We assume different words are differently informative towards the type of the literal. For example, the word "port" is more important than the other words in distinguishing the type *Wetland* from other concrete types of *Place*. To this end, an attention layer is further stacked. Given the input from the RNN layer $(h_t, t \in [1, T])$, the attention layer outputs $h_a = [\alpha_t h_t], t \in [1, T]$, where α_t is the normalized weight of the word at position t and is calculated as

$$\begin{cases} \alpha_t = \frac{exp(u_t^T u_w)}{\sum_{t \in [1,T]} exp(u_t^T u_w)} \\ u_t = \tau(W_w h_t + b_w), \end{cases} \tag{2}$$

where u_w, W_w and b_w are parameters to learn. Specifically, u_w denotes the general informative degrees of all the words, while α_t denotes the attention

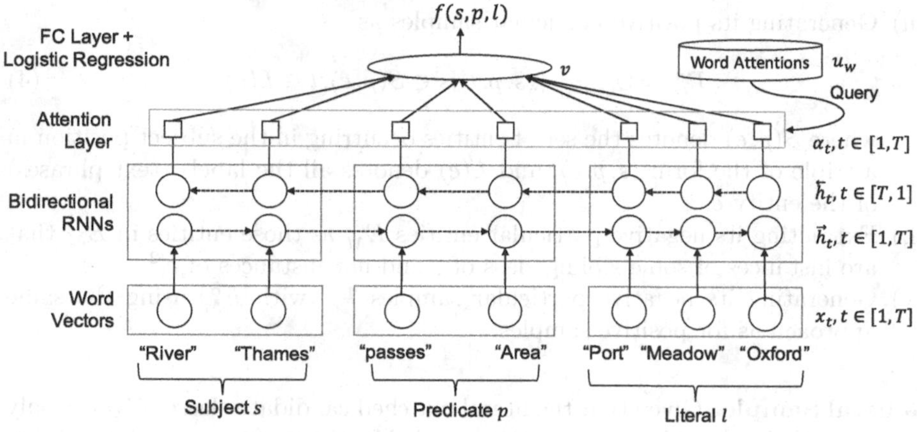

Fig. 2. The architecture of the neural network.

of the word at position t w.r.t. other words in the sequence. Note that the attention weights can also be utilized to justify a prediction. In order to exploit information about the location of a word in the subject, property or literal, we do not calculate the weighted sum of the BiRNN output but concatenate the weighted vectors. The dimension of each RNN hidden state (i.e., $\overleftarrow{h_t}$ and $\overrightarrow{h_t}$), denoted as d_r, and the dimension of each attention layer output (i.e., $\alpha_t h_t$), denoted as d_a, are two hyper parameters of the network architecture.

A fully connected (FC) layer and a logistic regression layer are finally stacked for modeling the nonlinear relationship and calculating the output score respectively:

$$f(s, p, l) = \sigma(W_f h_a + b_f), \tag{3}$$

where W_f and b_f are the parameters to learn, σ denotes the *sigmod* function, and f denotes the function of the whole network.

2.4 Sampling and Training

We first extract both particular samples and general samples from the KB using SPARQL queries and reasoning; we then improve sample quality by detecting and repairing wrong and missing entity classifications with the help of external KBs; and finally we train the classifiers.

Particular Sample. Particular samples are based on the entities E_M that are lexically matched by the literals. For each literal candidate class c in C_M, its particular samples are generated by:

(i) Extracting its positive particular entities: $E_M^c = \{e|e \in E_M, e \text{ is an instance of } c\}$;

(ii) Generating its positive particular samples as

$$\mathcal{P}_c^+ = \cup_{e \in E_M^c} \{\langle s, p, l \rangle | s \in S(p, e), l \in L(e)\}, \quad (4)$$

where $S(p, e)$ denotes the set of entities occurring in the subject position in a triple of the form $\langle s, p, e \rangle$, and $L(e)$ denotes all the labels (text phrases) of the entity e;

(iii) Extracting its negative particular entities $E_M^{\tilde{c}}$ as those entities in E_M that are instances of some sibling class of c and not instances of c;[2]

(iv) Generating its negative particular samples $\mathcal{P}_c^-$ with $E_M^{\tilde{c}}$ using the same approach as for positive samples.

General Sample. Given that the literal matched candidate classes C_M are only a part of all the candidate classes C_{PM}, and that the size of particular samples may be too small to train the neural network, we additionally generate general samples based on common KB entities. For each candidate class c in C_{PM}, all its entities in the KB, denoted as E^c, are extracted and then its positive general samples, denoted as $\mathcal{G}_c^+$, are generated from E^c using the same approach as for particular samples. Similarly, entities of the sibling classes of c, denoted as $E^{\tilde{c}}$, are extracted, and general negative samples, denoted as $\mathcal{G}_c^-$, are generated from $E^{\tilde{c}}$. As for negative particular entities, we check each entity in $E^{\tilde{c}}$ and remove those that are instances of c.

Unlike the particular samples, the positive and negative general samples are balanced. This means that we reduce the size of $\mathcal{G}_c^+$ and $\mathcal{G}_c^-$ to the minimum of $\#(\mathcal{G}_c^+)$, $\#(\mathcal{G}_c^-)$ and N_0, where $\#()$ denotes set cardinality, and N_0 is a hyper parameter for sampling. Size reduction is implemented via random sampling.

Sample Refinement. Many KBs are quite noisy, with wrong or missing entity classifications. For example, when using the SPARQL endpoint of DBpedia, *dbr:Scotland* is classified as *dbo:MusicalArtist* instead of as *dbo:Country*, while *dbr:Afghan* appears without a type. We have corrected and complemented the sample generation by combining the outputs of more than one KB. For example, the DBpedia endpoint suggestions are compared against Wikidata and the DBpedia lookup service. Most DBpedia entities are mapped to Wikidata entities whose types are used to validate and complement the suggested types from the DBpedia endpoint. In addition, the lookup service, although incomplete, typically provides very precise types that can also confirm the validity of the DBpedia endpoint types. The validation is performed by identifying if the types suggested by one KB are compatible with those returned by other KBs, that is, if the relevant types belong to the same branch of the hierarchy (e.g., the DBpedia taxonomy). With the new entity classifications, the samples are revised accordingly.

---

[2] We use sibling classes to generate negative examples as, in practice, sibling classes are often disjoint.

Training. We train a binary classifier f^c for each class c in C_{PM}. It is first pre-trained with general samples $\mathcal{G}_c^+ \cup \mathcal{G}_c^-$, and then fine-tuned with particular samples $\mathcal{P}_c^+ \cup \mathcal{P}_c^-$. Pre-training deals with the shortage of particular samples, while fine-tuning bridges the gap between common KB entities and the entities associated with the literals, which is also known as *domain adaptation*. Given that pre-training is the most time consuming step, but is task agnostic, classifiers for all the classes in a KB could be pre-trained in advance to accelerate a specific literal canonicalization task.

2.5 Independent and Hierarchical Typing

In prediction, the binary classifier for class c, denoted as f^c, outputs a score y_l^c indicating the probability that a literal l belongs to class c: $y_l^c = f^c(l)$, $y_l^c \in [0,1]$. With the predicted scores, we adopt two strategies – *independent* and *hierarchical* to determine the types. In the independent strategy, the relationship between classes is not considered. A class c is selected as a type of l if its score $y_l^c \geq \theta$, where θ is a threshold hyper parameter in $[0,1]$.

The hierarchical strategy considers the class hierarchy and the disjointness between sibling classes. We first calculate a *hierarchical score* for each class with the predicted scores of itself and its descendants:

$$s_l^c = max\left\{y_l^{c'} | c' \sqsubseteq c,\ c' \in C_{PM}\right\}, \tag{5}$$

where $\sqsubseteq$ denotes the subclass relationship between two classes, C_{PM} is the set of candidate classes for l, and max denotes the maximum value of a set. For a candidate class c' in C_{PM}, we denote all disjoint candidate classes as $\mathcal{D}(C_{PM}, c')$. They can be defined as sibling classes of both c' and its ancestors, or via logical constraints in the KB. A class c is selected as a type of l if *(i)* its hierarchical score $s_l^c \geq \theta$, and *(ii)* it satisfies the following soft exclusion condition:

$$s_l^c - max\left\{s_l^{c'} | c' \in \mathcal{D}(C_{PM}, c)\right\} \geq \kappa, \tag{6}$$

where κ is a relaxation hyper parameter. The exclusion of disjoint classes is hard if κ is set to 0, and relaxed if κ is set to a negative float with a small absolute value e.g., -0.1.

Finally, for a given literal l, we return the set of all selected classes as its types $\mathcal{C}_l$.

2.6 Canonicalization

Given a literal l, we use $\mathcal{C}_l$ to try to identify an associated entity. A set of candidate entities are first retrieved using the lexical index that is built on the entity's name, label, anchor text, etc. Unlike candidate class extraction, here we use the whole text phrase of the literal, and rank the candidate entities according to their lexical similarities. Those entities that are not instances of any classes in $\mathcal{C}_l$ are then filtered out, and the most similar entity among the remainder is selected as the associated entity for l. If no entities are retrieved, or all the retrieved entities are filtered out, then the literal could be associated with a new entity whose types are those most specific classes in $\mathcal{C}_l$. In either case we can improve the quality of our results by checking that the resulting entities would be consistent if added to the KB, and discarding any entity associations that would lead to inconsistency.

3 Evaluation

3.1 Experiment Setting

Data Sets. In the experiments, we adopt a real literal set (R-Lite) and a synthetic literal set (S-Lite)[3] , both of which are extracted from DBpedia. R-Lite is based on the property and literal pairs published by Gunaratna et al. in 2016 [14]. We refine the data by *(i)* removing literals that no longer exist in the current version of DBpedia; *(ii)* extracting new literals from DBpedia for properties whose existing literals were all removed in step *(i)*; *(iii)* extending each property and literal pair with an associated subject; and *(iv)* manually adding ground truth types selected from classes defined in the DBpedia Ontology (DBO).[4] To fully evaluate the study with more data, we additionally constructed S-Lite from DBpedia by repeatedly: *(i)* selecting a DBpedia triple of the form $\langle s, p, e \rangle$, where e is an entity; *(ii)* replacing e with it's label l to give a triple $\langle s, p, l \rangle$; *(iii)* eliminating the entity e from DBpedia; and *(iv)* adding as ground truth types the DBpedia classes of which e is (implicitly) an instance. More data details are shown in Table 1.

Table 1. Statistics of S-Lite and R-Lite.

	Properties #	Literals #	Ground truth types # (per literal)	Characters (Tokens) # per literal
S-Lite	41	1746	256 (2.94)	16.66 (2.40)
R-Lite	142	820	123 (3.11)	19.44 (3.25)

Metrics. In evaluating the typing performance, Precision, Recall and F1 Score are used. For a literal l, the computed types $\mathcal{C}_l$ are compared with the ground truths $\mathcal{C}_l^{gt}$, and the following micro metrics are calculated: $P_l = \#(\mathcal{C}_l \cap \mathcal{C}_l^{gt}) / \#(\mathcal{C}_l)$, $R_l = \#(\mathcal{C}_l \cap \mathcal{C}_l^{gt}) / \#(\mathcal{C}_l^{gt})$, and $F1_l = (2 \times P_l \times R_l) / (P_l + R_l)$. They are then averaged over all the literals as the final Precision, Recall and F1 Score of a literal set. Although F1 Score measures the overall performance with both Precision and

[3] Data and codes: https://github.com/ChenJiaoyan/KG_Curation.

[4] Classes with the prefix http://dbpedia.org/ontology/.

Recall considered, it depends on the threshold hyper parameter θ as with Precision and Recall. Thus we let θ range from 0 to 1 with a step of 0.01, and calculate the average of all the F1 Scores (AvgF1@all) and top 5 highest F1 Scores (AvgF1@top5). AvgF1@all measures the overall pattern recognition capability, while AvgF1@top5 is relevant in real applications where we often use a validation data set to find a θ setting that is close to the optimum. We also use the highest (top) Precision in evaluating the sample refinement.

In evaluating entity matching performance, Precision is measured by manually checking whether the identified entity is correct or not. S-Lite is not used for entity matching evaluation as the corresponding entities for all its literals are assumed to be excluded from the KB. We are not able to measure recall for entity matching as we do not have the ground truths; instead, we have evaluated entity matching with different confidence thresholds and compared the number of correct results.

Baselines and Settings. The evaluation includes three aspects. We first compare different settings of the typing framework, analyzing the impacts of sample refinement, fine tuning by particular samples, BiRNN and the attention mechanism. We also compare the independent and hierarchical typing strategies. We then compare the overall typing performance of our framework with *(i)* Gunaratna et al. [14], which matches the literal to both classes and entities; *(ii)* an entity lookup based method; and *(iii)* a probabilistic property range estimation method. Finally, we analyze the performance of entity matching with and without the predicted types.

The DBpedia lookup service, which is based on the Spotlight index [19], is used for entity lookup (retrieval). The DBpedia SPARQL endpoint is used for query answering and reasoning. The reported results are based on the following settings: the Adam optimizer together with cross-entropy loss are used for network training; d_r and d_a are set to 200 and 50 respectively; N_0 is set to $1,200$; *word2vec* trained with the latest Wikipedia article dump is adopted for word embedding; and (T_s, T_p, T_l) are set to (12, 4, 12) for S-Lite and (12, 4, 15) for R-Lite. The experiments are run on a workstation with Intel(R) Xeon(R) CPU E5-2670 @2.60GHz, with programs implemented by Tensorflow.

3.2 Results on Framework Settings

We first evaluate the impact of the neural network architecture, fine tuning and different typing strategies, with their typing results on S-Lite shown in Table 2 and Fig. 3. Our findings are supported by comparable results on R-Lite. We further evaluate sample refinement, with some statistics of the refinement operations as well as performance improvements shown in Fig. 4.

Network Architecture and Fine Tuning. According to Table 2, we find BiRNN significantly outperforms Multiple Layer Perceptron (MLP), a basic but widely used neural network model, while stacking an attention layer (AttBiRNN) further improves AvgF1@all and AvgF1@top5, for example by 3.7% and 3.1% respectively with hierarchical typing ($\kappa = -0.1$). The result is consistent for both pre-trained models and fine tuned models, using both independent and hierarchical typing strategies. This indicates the effectiveness of our neural network architecture. Meanwhile, the performance of all the models is significantly improved after they are fine tuned by the particular samples, as expected. For example, when the independent typing strategy is used, AvgF1@all and AvgF1@top5 of AttBiRNN are improved by 54.1% and 35.2% respectively.

Table 2. Typing performance of our framework on S-Lite under different settings.

Framework settings		Independent		Hierarchical ($\kappa = -0.1$)		Hierarchical ($\kappa = 0$)	
		AvgF1@all	AvgF1@top5	AvgF1@all	AvgF1@top5	AvgF1@all	AvgF1@top5
Pre-training	MLP	0.4102	0.4832	0.5060	0.5458	0.5916	0.5923
	BiRNN	0.4686	0.5566	0.5295	0.5649	0.5977	0.5985
	AttBiRNN	0.4728	0.5590	0.5420	0.5912	0.6049	0.6052
Fine tuning	MLP	0.6506	0.6948	0.6859	0.6989	0.6429	0.6626
	BiRNN	0.7008	0.7434	0.7167	0.7372	0.6697	0.6850
	AttBiRNN	0.7286	0.7557	0.7429	0.7601	0.6918	0.7070

Independent and Hierarchical Typing. The impact of independent and hierarchical typing strategies is more complex. As shown in Table 2, when the classifier is weak (e.g., pre-trained BiRNN), hierarchical typing with both hard exclusion ($\kappa = 0$) and relaxed exclusion ($\kappa = -0.1$) has higher AvgF1@all and AvgF1@top5 than independent typing. However, when a strong classifier (e.g., fine tuned AttBiRNN) is used, AvgF1@all and AvgF1@top5 of hierarchical typing with relaxed exclusion are close to independent typing, while hierarchical typing with hard exclusion has worse performance. We further analyze Precision, Recall and F1 Score of both typing strategies under varying threshold (θ) values, as shown in Fig. 3. In comparison with independent typing, hierarchical typing achieves *(i)* more stable Precision, Recall and F1 Score curves; and *(ii)* significantly higher Precision, especially when θ is small. Meanwhile, as with the results in Table 2, relaxed exclusion outperforms hard exclusion in hierarchical typing except for Precision when θ is between 0 and 0.05.

Sample Refinement. Figure 4 [Right] shows the ratio of positive and negative particular samples that are deleted and added during sample refinement. The AttBiRNN classifiers fine-tuned by the refined particular samples are compared with those fine-tuned by the original particular samples. The improvements on AvgF1@all, AvgF1@top5 and top Precision, which are based on the average of the three above typing settings, are shown in Fig. 4 [Left]. On the one hand, we find sample refinement benefits both S-Lite and R-Lite, as expected. On the other hand, we find the improvement on S-Lite is limited, while the improvement on R-Lite is quite significant: F1@all and top Precision, e.g., are improved by around 0.8% and 1.8% respectively on S-Lite, but 4.3% and 7.4% respectively on R-Lite. This may be due to two factors: *(i)* the ground truths of S-Lite are the entities'

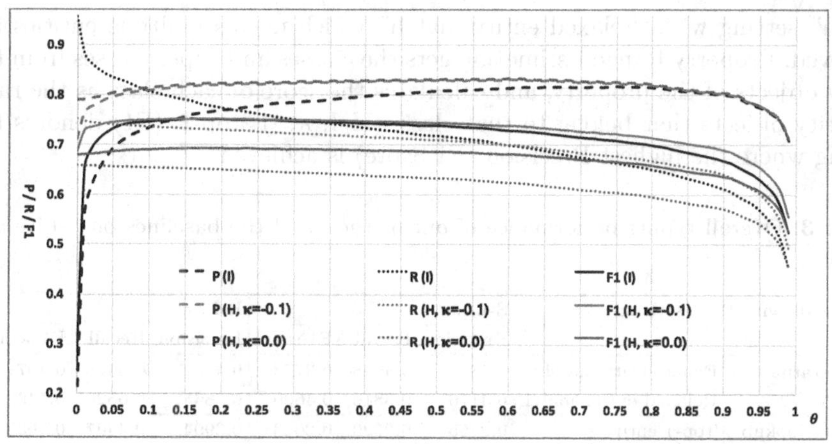

Fig. 3. (P)recision, (R)ecall and (F1) Score of independent (I) and hierarchical (H) typing for S-Lite, with the scores predicted by the fine-tuned AttBiRNN.

class and super classes inferred from the KB itself, while the ground truths of R-Lite are manually labeled; *(ii)* sample refinement deletes many more noisy positive and negative samples (which are caused by wrong entity classifications of the KB) on R-Lite than on S-Lite, as shown in Fig. 4 [Right].

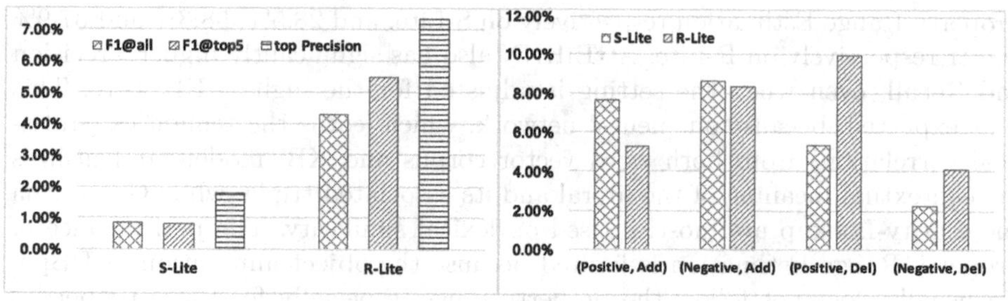

Fig. 4. [Left] Performance improvement (%) by sample refinement; [Right] Ratio (%) of added (deleted) positive (negative) particular sample per classifier during sample refinement.

3.3 Results on Semantic Typing

Table 3 displays the overall semantic typing performance of our method and the baselines. Results for two optimum settings are reported for each method. The baseline Entity-Lookup retrieves one or several entities using the whole phrase of the literal, and uses their classes and super classes as the types. Gunaratna [14] matches the literal's focus term (head word) to an exact class, then an exact entity, and then a class with the highest similarity score. It stops as soon as some classes or entities are matched. We extend its original "exact entity match" setting with "relaxed entity match" which means multiple entities are retrieved. Property Range Estimation gets the classes and super classes from the entity objects of the property, and calculates the score of each class as the ratio of entity objects that belong to that class. (H/I, κ, $\cdot$)@top-P (F1) denotes the setting where the highest Precision (F1 Score) is achieved.

Table 3. Overall typing performance of our method and the baselines on S-Lite and R-Lite.

Methods with their settings		S-Lite			R-Lite		
		Precision	Recall	F1 score	Precision	Recall	F1 score
Gunaratna	Exact entity match	0.3825	0.4038	0.3773	0.4761	0.5528	0.4971
	Relaxed entity match	0.4176	0.5816	0.4600	0.3865	0.6526	0.4469
Entity-lookup	Top-1 entity	0.2765	0.2620	0.2623	0.3994	0.4407	0.4035
	Top-3 entities	0.2728	0.3615	0.2962	0.3168	0.5201	0.3655
Property range	(H/I, κ, θ)@top-P	0.7563	0.5583	0.6210	0.5266	0.4015	0.4364
Estimation	(H/I, κ, θ)@top-F1	0.6874	0.7166	0.6773	0.4520	0.5069	0.4632
AttBiRNN	(H/I, κ, θ)@top-P	**0.8320**	0.7325	0.7641	**0.7466**	0.5819	0.6340
	(H/I, κ, θ)@top-F1	0.8179	**0.7546**	**0.7708**	0.6759	**0.6451**	**0.6386**

As we can see, AttBiRNN achieves much higher performance than all three baselines on both S-Lite and R-Lite. For example, the F1 Score of AttBiRNN is 67.6%, 160.2% and 13.8% higher than those of Gunaratna, Entity-Lookup and Property Range Estimation respectively on S-Lite, and 28.5%, 58.3% and 37.9% higher respectively on R-Lite. AttBiRNN also has significantly higher Precision and Recall, even when the setting is adjusted for the highest F1 Score. This is as expected, because our neural network, which learns the semantics (statistical correlation) from both word vector corpus and KB, models and utilizes the contextual meaning of the literal and its associated triple, while Gunaratna and Entity-Lookup are mostly based on lexical similarity. The performance of Property Range Estimation is limited because the object annotation in DBpedia usually does not follow the property range, especially for those properties in R-Lite. For example, objects of the property *dbp:office* have 35 DBO classes, ranging from *dbo:City* and *dbo:Country* to *dbo:Company*.

It is also notable that AttBiRNN and Property Range Estimation perform better on S-Lite than on R-Lite. The top F1 Score is 20.7% and 46.2% higher respectively, while the top Precision is 11.4% and 43.6% higher respectively. This is because R-Lite is more noisy, with longer literals, and has more ground truth types on average (cf. Table 1), while S-Lite has fewer properties, and each property has a large number of entity objects, which significantly benefits Property Range Estimation. In contrast, the two entity matching based methods, Gunaratna and Entity-Lookup, perform worse on S-Lite than on R-Lite; this is because the construction of S-Lite removes those KB entities from which literals were derived. Gunaratna outperforms Entity-Lookup as it extracts the head word and matches it to both entities and classes. Note that the head word is also included in our candidate class extraction with lookup.

3.4 Results on Entity Matching

Table 4 displays the number of correct matched entities and the Precision of entity matching on R-Lite. The types are predicted by the fine-tuned AttBiRNN with independent typing and two threshold settings. We can see that Precision is improved when the retrieved entities that do not belong to any of the predicted types are filtered out. The improvement is 6.1% and 5.8% when θ is set to 0.15 and 0.01 respectively. Meanwhile, although the total number of matches may decrease because of the filtering, the number of correct matches still increases from 396 to 404 ($\theta = 0.01$). This means that Recall is also improved.

Table 4. Overall performance of entity matching on R-Lite with and without type constraint.

Metrics	Pure Lookup	Lookup-Type ($\theta = 0.15$)	Lookup-Type ($\theta = 0.01$)
Correct Matches #	396	400	**404**
Precision	0.6781	**0.7194**	0.7176

4 Related Work

Work on KB quality issues can can be divided into KB quality assessment [10,31], and KB quality improvement/refinement [22]. The former includes error and anomaly detection methods, such as test-driven and query template based approaches [11,16], with statistical methods [6] and consistency reasoning [24] also being applied to assess KB quality with different kinds of metric. The latter includes *(i)* KB completion, such as entity classification [13,23,28], relation prediction [17] and data typing [8]; and *(ii)* KB diagnosis and repair, such as abnormal value detection [11], erroneous identity link detection [26] and data mapping (e.g., links to Wikipedia pages) correction [7].

KB canonicalization refers to those refinement works that deal with redundant and ambiguous KB components as well as poorly expressed knowledge with limited reasoning potential. Some works in open information extraction (IE) [12,29,30] aim to identify synonymous noun phrases and relation phrases of open KBs which are composed of triple assertions extracted from text without any ontologies. For example, the recently proposed CESI method [29] utilizes both learned KB embeddings and side information like WordNet to find synonyms via clustering. Other works analyze synonyms for ontological KBs. Abedjan et al. [1] discovered synonymously used predicates for query expansion on DBpedia. Pujara et al. [25] identified coreferent entities of NELL with ontological constraints considered. These clustering, embedding, or entity linking based methods in open IE, however, can not be directly applied or do not work well for our KB literal canonicalization. The utilization of these techniques will be in our future work.

String literals in ontological KBs such as DBpedia often represent poorly expressed knowledge, with semantic types and coreferent entities missed. As far as we known, canonicalization of such literals has been little studied. Gunaratna et al. [14] typed the literal by matching its head term to ontology classes and KB entities, but the literal context (e.g., the associated subject and property) and semantic meaning of the composition words were not utilized. Some ideas of entity classification can be borrowed for literal typing but will become ineffective as the context differs. For example, the baseline Property Range Estimation in our experiments uses the idea of *SDType* [23]—utilizing the statistical distribution of types in the subject position and object position of properties to estimate an entity's type probabilities. As a literal is associated with only one property, such probabilistic estimation becomes inaccurate (cf. results in Table 3).

Our literal classification model is in some degree inspired by those natural language understanding and web table annotation works that match external noun phrases to KB types and entities [4,15,18] using neural networks and semantic embeddings for modeling the contextual semantics. For example, Luo et al. [18] learned features from the surrounding cells of a target cell to predict its entity association. However the context in those works is very different, i.e., a simple regular structure of rows/columns with limited (table) metadata. In contrast, KBs have a complex irregular structure and rich metadata (the knowledge captured in the KB). Differently from these works, we developed different methods, e.g., candidate class extraction and high quality sampling, to learn the network from the KB with its assertions, terminologies and reasoning capability.

5 Discussion and Outlook

In this paper we present our study on KB literal canonicalization—an important problem on KB quality that has been little studied. A new technical framework is proposed with neural network and knowledge-based learning. It *(i)* extracts candidate classes as well as their positive and negative samples from the KB by lookup and query answering, with their quality improved using an external KB; *(ii)* trains classifiers that can effectively learn a literal's contextual features with BiRNNs and an attention mechanism; *(iii)* identifies types and matches entity for canonicalization. We use a real data set and a synthetic data set, both extracted from DBpedia, for evaluation. It achieves much higher performance than the baselines that include the state-of-the-art. We discuss below some more subjective observations and possible directions for future work.

Neural Network and Prediction Justification. The network architecture aims to learn features from a literal's context. In our AttBiRNN, a triple is modeled as a word sequence with three size-fixed segments allocated for the subject, object and literal respectively. The cooccurrence of words and the importance of each word are learned by BiRNNs and the attention mechanism respectively, where word position (including whether it is in the subject, property or literal) is significant. The effectiveness of such a design has been validated in Sect. 3.2.

However, the current design does not exploit further semantics of the subject, such as its relation to other entities. We believe that this will provide limited indication of the literal's semantic type, but this could be explored using graph embedding methods such as random walks and Graph Convolutional Networks.

We believe that it would be interesting to explore the possible use of the learned attention weights (α_t) in justifying the predictions. For example, considering the literal in triple ⟨*dbr:Byron_White, dbp:battles, "World War II"*⟩ and the classifier of type *dbo:MilitaryConflict*, *"War"* gets a dominant attention weight of 0.919, *"battles"* and *"II"* get attention weights 0.051 and 0.025 respectively, while the attention weights of other words and the padded empty tokens are all less than 0.0015. Similarly, in the triple ⟨*dbr:Larry_Bird, dbp:statsLeague, "NBA"* ⟩, the total attention weights of the subject, property and literal are 0.008, 0.801 and 0.191 respectively w.r.t. the classifier of *dbo:Organisation*, but become 0.077, 0.152 and 0.771 w.r.t. the classifier of *dbo:BasketballLeague*, where the signal of basketball is focused.

Knowledge-Based Learning. We developed some strategies to fully train our neural networks with the supervision of the KB itself. One strategy is the separated extraction of general samples and particular samples. It *(i)* eliminates the time consuming pre-training step from a specific task, reducing for example the total typing time per literal of S-Lite from 10.5 s to 2.5 s (training and prediction are run with at most 10 parallel threads), and *(ii)* adapts the domain of the classifier toward the target literals through fine tuning, which significantly improves the accuracy as shown in Table 2. Another strategy that has been evaluated in Sect. 3.2 is sample refinement by validating entity classifications with external knowledge from Wikidata. However, we believe that this could be further extended with more external KBs, as well as with logical constraints and rules.

Entity Matching. We currently search for the corresponding entity of a literal by lexical lookup, and filter out those that are not instances of any of the predicted types. The extension with prediction does improve the performance in comparison with pure lookup (cf. Section 3.4), but not as significantly as semantic typing, especially on the metric of the number of correct matches. One reason is that entity matching itself has relatively few ground truths as many literals in R-Lite have no corresponding entities in the KB. Another reason is that we post-process the entities from lookup instead of directly predicting the correspondence. This means that those missed by pure lookup are still missed. In the future we plan to explore direct prediction of the matching entity using semantic embedding and graph feature learning.

Acknowledgments. The work is supported by the AIDA project, The Alan Turing Institute under the EPSRC grant EP/N510129/1, the SIRIUS Centre for Scalable Data Access (Research Council of Norway, project 237889), the Royal Society, EPSRC projects DBOnto, MaSI^3 and ED^3.

References

1. Abedjan, Z., Naumann, F.: Synonym analysis for predicate expansion. In: Cimiano, P., Corcho, O., Presutti, V., Hollink, L., Rudolph, S. (eds.) ESWC 2013. LNCS, vol. 7882, pp. 140–154. Springer, Heidelberg (2013). https://doi.org/10.1007/978-3-642-38288-8_10
2. Auer, S., Bizer, C., Kobilarov, G., Lehmann, J., Cyganiak, R., Ives, Z.: DBpedia: a nucleus for a web of open data. In: Aberer, A., et al. (eds.) ASWC/ISWC -2007. LNCS, vol. 4825, pp. 722–735. Springer, Heidelberg (2007). https://doi.org/10.1007/978-3-540-76298-0_52
3. Auer, S., Lehmann, J., Hellmann, S.: LinkedGeoData: adding a spatial dimension to the web of data. In: Bernstein, A., et al. (eds.) ISWC 2009. LNCS, vol. 5823, pp. 731–746. Springer, Heidelberg (2009). https://doi.org/10.1007/978-3-642-04930-9_46
4. Chen, J., Jimenez-Ruiz, E., Horrocks, I., Sutton, C.: ColNet: embedding the semantics of web tables for column type prediction. In: AAAI (2019)
5. Cho, K., et al.: Learning phrase representations using RNN encoder-decoder for statistical machine translation. In: Proceedings of the 2014 Conference on Empirical Methods in Natural Language Processing, pp. 1724–1734 (2014)
6. Debattista, J., Londoño, S., Lange, C., Auer, S.: Quality assessment of linked datasets using probabilistic approximation. In: Gandon, F., Sabou, M., Sack, H., d'Amato, C., Cudré-Mauroux, P., Zimmermann, A. (eds.) ESWC 2015. LNCS, vol. 9088, pp. 221–236. Springer, Cham (2015). https://doi.org/10.1007/978-3-319-18818-8_14
7. Dimou, A., et al.: Assessing and refining mappingsto RDF to improve dataset quality. In: Arenas, M., et al. (eds.) ISWC 2015. LNCS, vol. 9367, pp. 133–149. Springer, Cham (2015). https://doi.org/10.1007/978-3-319-25010-6_8
8. Dongo, I., Cardinale, Y., Al-Khalil, F., Chbeir, R.: Semantic web datatype inference: towards better RDF matching. In: Bouguettaya, A., et al. (eds.) WISE 2017. LNCS, vol. 10570, pp. 57–74. Springer, Cham (2017). https://doi.org/10.1007/978-3-319-68786-5_5
9. Efthymiou, V., Hassanzadeh, O., Rodriguez-Muro, M., Christophides, V.: Matching web tables with knowledge base entities: from entity lookups to entity embeddings. In: d'Amato, C., et al. (eds.) ISWC 2017. LNCS, vol. 10587, pp. 260–277. Springer, Cham (2017). https://doi.org/10.1007/978-3-319-68288-4_16
10. Färber, M., Bartscherer, F., Menne, C., Rettinger, A.: Linked data quality of DBpedia, Freebase, OpenCyc, Wikidata, and YAGO. Semant. Web **9**(1), 77–129 (2018)
11. Fleischhacker, D., Paulheim, H., Bryl, V., Völker, J., Bizer, C.: Detecting errors in numerical linked data using cross-checked outlier detection. In: Mika, P., et al. (eds.) ISWC 2014. LNCS, vol. 8796, pp. 357–372. Springer, Cham (2014). https://doi.org/10.1007/978-3-319-11964-9_23
12. Galárraga, L., Heitz, G., Murphy, K., Suchanek, F.M.: Canonicalizing open knowledge bases. In: Proceedings of the 23rd ACM International Conference on Conference on Information and Knowledge Management, pp. 1679–1688 (2014)
13. Gangemi, A., Nuzzolese, A.G., Presutti, V., Draicchio, F., Musetti, A., Ciancarini, P.: Automatic typing of DBpedia entities. In: Cudré-Mauroux, P., et al. (eds.) ISWC 2012. LNCS, vol. 7649, pp. 65–81. Springer, Heidelberg (2012). https://doi.org/10.1007/978-3-642-35176-1_5

14. Gunaratna, K., Thirunarayan, K., Sheth, A., Cheng, G.: Gleaning types for literals in RDF triples with application to entity summarization. In: Sack, H., Blomqvist, E., d'Aquin, M., Ghidini, C., Ponzetto, S.P., Lange, C. (eds.) ESWC 2016. LNCS, vol. 9678, pp. 85–100. Springer, Cham (2016). https://doi.org/10.1007/978-3-319-34129-3_6
15. Kartsaklis, D., Pilehvar, M.T., Collier, N.: Mapping text to knowledge graph entities using multi-sense LSTMS. In: Proceedings of the 2018 Conference on Empirical Methods in Natural Language Processing, pp. 1959–1970 (2018)
16. Kontokostas, D., et al.: Test-driven evaluation of linked data quality. In: Proceedings of the 23rd International Conference on World Wide Web, pp. 747–758. ACM (2014)
17. Krompaß, D., Baier, S., Tresp, V.: Type-constrained representation learning in knowledge graphs. In: Arenas, M., et al. (eds.) ISWC 2015. LNCS, vol. 9366, pp. 640–655. Springer, Cham (2015). https://doi.org/10.1007/978-3-319-25007-6_37
18. Luo, X., Luo, K., Chen, X., Zhu, K.Q.: Cross-lingual entity linking for web tables. In: AAAI, pp. 362–369 (2018)
19. Mendes, P.N., Jakob, M., García-Silva, A., Bizer, C.: DBpedia spotlight: shedding light on the web of documents. In: Proceedings of the 7th International Conference on Semantic Systems, pp. 1–8. ACM (2011)
20. Mikolov, T., Chen, K., Corrado, G., Dean, J.: Efficient estimation of word representations in vector space. arXiv preprint arXiv:1301.3781 (2013)
21. Niu, X., Sun, X., Wang, H., Rong, S., Qi, G., Yu, Y.: Zhishi.me - weaving chinese linking open data. In: Aroyo, L., et al. (eds.) ISWC 2011. LNCS, vol. 7032, pp. 205–220. Springer, Heidelberg (2011). https://doi.org/10.1007/978-3-642-25093-4_14
22. Paulheim, H.: Knowledge graph refinement: a survey of approaches and evaluation methods. Seman. Web **8**(3), 489–508 (2017)
23. Paulheim, H., Bizer, C.: Type inference on noisy RDF data. In: Alani, H., et al. (eds.) ISWC 2013. LNCS, vol. 8218, pp. 510–525. Springer, Heidelberg (2013). https://doi.org/10.1007/978-3-642-41335-3_32
24. Paulheim, H., Gangemi, A.: Serving DBpedia with DOLCE – more than just adding a cherry on top. In: Arenas, M., et al. (eds.) ISWC 2015. LNCS, vol. 9366, pp. 180–196. Springer, Cham (2015). https://doi.org/10.1007/978-3-319-25007-6_11
25. Pujara, J., Miao, H., Getoor, L., Cohen, W.: Knowledge graph identification. In: Alani, H., et al. (eds.) ISWC 2013. LNCS, vol. 8218, pp. 542–557. Springer, Heidelberg (2013). https://doi.org/10.1007/978-3-642-41335-3_34
26. Raad, J., Beek, W., van Harmelen, F., Pernelle, N., Saïs, F.: Detecting erroneous identity links on the web using network metrics. In: Vrandečić, D., et al. (eds.) ISWC 2018. LNCS, vol. 11136, pp. 391–407. Springer, Cham (2018). https://doi.org/10.1007/978-3-030-00671-6_23
27. Silla, C.N., Freitas, A.A.: A survey of hierarchical classification across different application domains. Data Min. Knowl. Disc. **22**(1–2), 31–72 (2011)
28. Sleeman, J., Finin, T., Joshi, A.: Entity type recognition for heterogeneous semantic graphs. AI Mag. **36**(1), 75–86 (2015)
29. Vashishth, S., Jain, P., Talukdar, P.: CESI: canonicalizing open knowledge bases using embeddings and side information. In: Proceedings of the 2018 World Wide Web Conference on World Wide Web, pp. 1317–1327 (2018)
30. Wu, T.H., Wu, Z., Kao, B., Yin, P.: Towards practical open knowledge base canonicalization. In: Proceedings of the 27th ACM International Conference on Information and Knowledge Management, pp. 883–892 (2018)
31. Zaveri, A., Rula, A., Maurino, A., Pietrobon, R., Lehmann, J., Auer, S.: Quality assessment for linked data: a survey. Semant. Web **7**(1), 63–93 (2016)

Bag Semantics of DL-Lite with Functionality Axioms

Gianluca Cima[1(✉)], Charalampos Nikolaou[2,3(✉)], Egor V. Kostylev[2(✉)], Mark Kaminski[2(✉)], Bernardo Cuenca Grau[2(✉)], and Ian Horrocks[2(✉)]

[1] Sapienza Università di Roma, Rome, Italy
cima@diag.uniroma1.it

[2] Department of Computer Science, University of Oxford, Oxford, UK
{egor.kostylev,mark.kaminski,bernardo.cuenca.grau,ian.horrocks}@cs.ox.ac.uk

[3] Infor, Farnborough, UK
charalampos.nikolaou@infor.com

Abstract. Ontology-based data access (OBDA) is a popular approach for integrating and querying multiple data sources by means of an ontology, which is usually expressed in a description logic (DL) of DL-Lite family. The conventional semantics of OBDA and DLs is set-based—that is, duplicates are disregarded. This disagrees with the standard database bag (multiset) semantics, which is especially important for the correct evaluation of aggregate queries. In this article, we study two variants of bag semantics for query answering over *DL-Lite*$_\mathcal{F}$, extending basic *DL-Lite*$_{\text{core}}$ with functional roles. For our first semantics, which follows the semantics of primary keys in SQL, conjunctive query (CQ) answering is coNP-hard in data complexity in general, but it is in TC^0 for the restricted class of rooted CQs; such CQs are also rewritable to the bag relational algebra. For our second semantics, the results are the same except that TC^0 membership and rewritability hold only for the restricted class of ontologies identified by a new notion of functional weak acyclicity.

1 Introduction

Ontology-based data access (OBDA) is an increasingly popular approach for integrating multiple relational data sources under a global schema [7,24,32]. In OBDA, an ontology provides a unifying conceptual model for the data sources, which is linked to each source by mappings assigning views over the data to ontology predicates. Users access the data by means of queries formulated using the vocabulary of the ontology; query answering amounts to computing the certain answers to the query over the union of ontology and the materialisation of the views defined by the mappings. The formalism of choice for representing ontologies in OBDA is usually the lightweight description logic *DL-Lite*$_\mathcal{R}$ [8], which underpins OWL 2 QL [28]. *DL-Lite*$_\mathcal{R}$ was designed to ensure that conjunctive queries (CQs) against the ontology are *first-order rewritable*—that is, they can be reformulated as relational database queries over the sources [8].

C. Ghidini et al. (Eds.): ISWC 2019, LNCS 11778, pp. 128–144, 2019.
https://doi.org/10.1007/978-3-030-30793-6_8

There is, however, an important semantic mismatch between standard database query languages, such as SQL, and OBDA: the former commit to a bag (multiset) semantics, where tuples are allowed to occur multiple times in query answers, whereas the latter is usually set-based, where multiplicities are disregarded. This semantic difference becomes apparent when evaluating queries with aggregation, where the multiplicities of tuples are important [1]. Motivated by the need to support database-style aggregate queries in OBDA systems and inspired by the work of Kostylev and Reutter [23] on the support of aggregates queries in $\mathit{DL\text{-}Lite}_{\mathcal{R}}$, Nikolaou et al. [30,31] proposed a bag semantics for $\mathit{DL\text{-}Lite}_{\mathcal{R}}$ and OBDA, where duplicates in the views defined by the mappings are retained. The most common reasoning tasks of ontology satisfiability and query answering in this new language, called $\mathit{DL\text{-}Lite}^{\mathsf{b}}_{\mathcal{R}}$, generalise the counterpart problems defined under the traditional set semantics. This generalisation does not come for free though as it raises the data complexity of query answering from AC^0 to coNP-hard, and this holds already for the core fragment $\mathit{DL\text{-}Lite}^{\mathsf{b}}_{core}$ of $\mathit{DL\text{-}Lite}^{\mathsf{b}}_{\mathcal{R}}$. To regain tractability, Nikolaou et al. [30,31] studied restrictions on CQs and showed that query answering for the class of so-called *rooted CQs* [6] becomes again tractable in data complexity. This result was obtained by showing that rooted CQs are rewritable to BCALC, a logical counterpart of the relational algebra BALG[1] for bags [15,26] whose evaluation problem is known to be in TC^0 in data complexity [25].

In this paper, building on the work of Nikolaou et al. [30,31], we consider the logic $\mathit{DL\text{-}Lite}^{\mathsf{b}}_{\mathcal{F}}$—that is, the extension of $\mathit{DL\text{-}Lite}^{\mathsf{b}}_{core}$ with functionality axioms. Such axioms comprise a desirable feature in description logics and OBDA since they are able to deliver various modelling scenarios encountered in information systems [9,10,27,33], such as key and identification constraints. We propose two alternative semantics for $\mathit{DL\text{-}Lite}^{\mathsf{b}}_{\mathcal{F}}$, both of which generalise the standard set-based semantics, and which differ from each other in the way they handle functionality axioms. Our first semantics, called *SQL semantics*, interprets functionality axioms following the semantics of primary keys in SQL—that is, the interpretation of a functional role is required to be a set satisfying the key constraint in the sense that for each first component in the interpretation of a functional role there exists exactly one second component, and, moreover, the multiplicity of this relation between the components is exactly one. By contrast, our second semantics, called *multiplicity-respectful (MR) semantics*, retains the key constraint requirement but allows for several copies of the same pair in the interpretation.

Our results are summarised below. First, we study how the two semantics relate to the set-based semantics of $\mathit{DL\text{-}Lite}_{\mathcal{F}}$ and to each other in terms of the standard reasoning tasks of satisfiability checking and query answering. On the one hand, we show that under the MR semantics both problems generalise the corresponding ones under set semantics. On the other hand, under the SQL semantics the notion of satisfiability becomes stronger than under set semantics, while query answering for satisfiable ontologies again generalises set semantics. Second, we investigate whether the class of rooted CQs is rewritable to BCALC under each of the semantics. For the SQL semantics, we obtain a positive answer, which implies that query answering is feasible in TC^0 in data complexity. For the MR semantics, however, we obtain LogSpace-hardness of query answering even for the simple class of instance queries, which prevents rewritability to BCALC (under the usual complexity-theoretic assumptions). To address this, we identify a class of TBoxes, called *functionally weakly acyclic*, for which rooted CQs become rewritable to BCALC, thus regaining feasibility of query answering.

The rest of the paper is organised as follows. Section 2 introduces the relevant background. Section 3 defines the SQL and MR semantics as extensions of the bag semantics proposed in [30,31] accounting for functionality axioms, and relates the new semantics to the set semantics and to each other. Section 4 studies the query answering problem, establishing the rewritability and complexity results. Last, Sect. 5 discusses related work and Sect. 6 concludes the paper.

2 Preliminaries

We start by defining *DL-Lite*$_{\mathcal{F}}$ ontologies as well as the notions of query answering and rewriting over such ontologies, all over the usual set semantics [4,8], after which we summarise the bag semantics of queries in databases [15,26,31].

Syntax of *DL-Lite*$_{\mathcal{F}}$. We fix a vocabulary consisting of countably infinite and pairwise disjoint sets of *individuals* $\mathbf{I}$ (i.e., constants), *atomic concepts* $\mathbf{C}$ (i.e., unary predicates) and *atomic roles* $\mathbf{R}$ (i.e., binary predicates). A *role* is an atomic role $P \in \mathbf{R}$ or its *inverse* P^-. A *concept* is an atomic concept in $\mathbf{C}$ or an expression $\exists R$ with R a role. Expressions $C_1 \sqsubseteq C_2$ and $\mathsf{Disj}(C_1, C_2)$ with C_1, C_2 concepts are *inclusion* and *disjointness axioms*, respectively. An expression $(\mathsf{funct}\ R)$ with R a role is a *functionality axiom*. A *DL-Lite*$_{\mathcal{F}}$ *TBox* is a finite set of inclusion, disjointness, and functionality axioms. A *concept assertion* is $A(a)$ with $a \in \mathbf{I}$ and $A \in \mathbf{C}$, and a *role assertion* is $P(a, b)$ with $a, b \in \mathbf{I}$ and $P \in \mathbf{R}$. A (*set*) *ABox* is a finite set of concept and role assertions. A *DL-Lite*$_{\mathcal{F}}$ *ontology* is a pair $(\mathcal{T}, \mathcal{A})$ with $\mathcal{T}$ a *DL-Lite*$_{\mathcal{F}}$ TBox and $\mathcal{A}$ an ABox. A *DL-Lite*$_{\mathsf{core}}$ *ontology* is the same except that functionality axioms are disallowed.

Semantics of *DL-Lite*$_{\mathcal{F}}$. A (*set*) *interpretation* $\mathcal{I}$ is a pair $(\Delta^{\mathcal{I}}, \cdot^{\mathcal{I}})$, where the *domain* $\Delta^{\mathcal{I}}$ is a non-empty set, and the *interpretation function* $\cdot^{\mathcal{I}}$ maps each $a \in \mathbf{I}$ to an element $a^{\mathcal{I}} \in \Delta^{\mathcal{I}}$ such that $a^{\mathcal{I}} \neq b^{\mathcal{I}}$ for all distinct $a, b \in \mathbf{I}$ (i.e., as usual for *DL-Lite* we adopt the UNA—that is, the unique name assumption), each $A \in \mathbf{C}$ to $A^{\mathcal{I}} \subseteq \Delta^{\mathcal{I}}$, and each $P \in \mathbf{R}$ to $P^{\mathcal{I}} \subseteq \Delta^{\mathcal{I}} \times \Delta^{\mathcal{I}}$. Interpretation function $\cdot^{\mathcal{I}}$ extends to non-atomic concepts and roles as follows, for each $P \in \mathbf{R}$ and each role R:

$$(P^-)^{\mathcal{I}} = \{(u, u') \mid (u', u) \in P^{\mathcal{I}}\},\ (\exists R)^{\mathcal{I}} = \{u \in \Delta^{\mathcal{I}} \mid \exists u' \in \Delta^{\mathcal{I}} :\ (u, u') \in R^{\mathcal{I}}\}.$$

An interpretation $\mathcal{I}$ *satisfies* a *DL-Lite*$_{\mathcal{F}}$ TBox $\mathcal{T}$ if $C_1^{\mathcal{I}} \subseteq C_2^{\mathcal{I}}$ for each inclusion axiom $C_1 \sqsubseteq C_2$ in $\mathcal{T}$, $C_1^{\mathcal{I}} \cap C_2^{\mathcal{I}} = \emptyset$ for each disjointness axiom $\mathsf{Disj}(C_1, C_2)$ in $\mathcal{T}$, and $v_1 = v_2$ for each $(u, v_1), (u, v_2)$ in $R^{\mathcal{I}}$ with functionality axiom $(\mathsf{funct}\ R)$ in $\mathcal{T}$. Interpretation $\mathcal{I}$ *satisfies* an ABox $\mathcal{A}$ if $a^{\mathcal{I}} \in A^{\mathcal{I}}$ for all $A(a) \in \mathcal{A}$ and $(a^{\mathcal{I}}, b^{\mathcal{I}}) \in P^{\mathcal{I}}$

for all $P(a, b) \in \mathcal{A}$. An interpretation $\mathcal{I}$ is a *model* of an ontology $(\mathcal{T}, \mathcal{A})$ if it satisfies both $\mathcal{T}$ and $\mathcal{A}$. An ontology is *satisfiable* if it has a model. Checking satisfiability of a *DL-Lite*$_\mathcal{F}$ ontology is NLOGSPACE-complete in general and in AC^0 if the TBox is fixed [4,8] (note however that the latter problem becomes P-complete if the UNA is dropped).

Queries over *DL-Lite*$_\mathcal{F}$. A *conjunctive query* (*CQ*) $q(\mathbf{x})$ with *answer* variables $\mathbf{x}$ is a formula $\exists \mathbf{y}.\, \phi(\mathbf{x}, \mathbf{y})$, where $\mathbf{x}$, $\mathbf{y}$ are (possibly empty) repetition-free disjoint tuples of variables from a set $\mathbf{X}$ disjoint from $\mathbf{I}$, $\mathbf{C}$ and $\mathbf{R}$, and $\phi(\mathbf{x}, \mathbf{y})$ is a conjunction of atoms of the form $A(t)$, $P(t_1, t_2)$ or $(z = t)$, where $A \in \mathbf{C}$, $P \in \mathbf{R}$, $z \in \mathbf{x} \cup \mathbf{y}$, and $t, t_1, t_2 \in \mathbf{x} \cup \mathbf{y} \cup \mathbf{I}$. If $\mathbf{x}$ is inessential, then we write q instead of $q(\mathbf{x})$. The equality atoms $(z = t)$ in $\phi(\mathbf{x}, \mathbf{y})$ yield an equivalence relation $\sim$ on terms $\mathbf{x} \cup \mathbf{y} \cup \mathbf{I}$, and we write $\tilde{t}$ for the equivalence class of a term t. The *Gaifman graph* of $q(\mathbf{x})$ has a node $\tilde{t}$ for each $t \in \mathbf{x} \cup \mathbf{y} \cup \mathbf{I}$ in ϕ, and an edge $\{\tilde{t}_1, \tilde{t}_2\}$ for each atom in ϕ over t_1 and t_2. We assume that all CQs are *safe*—that is, for each $z \in \mathbf{x} \cup \mathbf{y}$, $\tilde{z}$ contains a term mentioned in an atom of $\phi(\mathbf{x}, \mathbf{y})$ that is not equality. A CQ $q(\mathbf{x})$ is *rooted* if each connected component of its Gaifman graph has a node with a term in $\mathbf{x} \cup \mathbf{I}$ [6]. A *union* of CQs (*UCQ*) is a disjunction of CQs with the same answer variables. The *certain answers* $q^\mathcal{K}$ to a (U)CQ $q(\mathbf{x})$ over a *DL-Lite*$_\mathcal{F}$ ontology $\mathcal{K}$ are the set of all tuples $\mathbf{a}$ of individuals such that $q(\mathbf{a})$ holds in every model of $\mathcal{K}$. Checking whether a tuple of individuals is in the certain answers to a (U)CQ over a *DL-Lite*$_\mathcal{F}$ ontology is an NP-complete problem with AC^0 data complexity (i.e., when the query and TBox are fixed) [4,8]. The latter follows from the *rewritability* of the class of UCQs to itself over *DL-Lite*$_\mathcal{F}$—that is, from the fact that for each UCQ q and *DL-Lite*$_\mathcal{F}$ TBox $\mathcal{T}$ there is a UCQ q_1 such that $q^{(\mathcal{T},\mathcal{A})} = q_1^{(\emptyset,\mathcal{A})}$ for each ABox $\mathcal{A}$ [8].

Bags. A *bag* over a set M is a function $\Omega : M \to \mathbb{N}_0^\infty$, where $\mathbb{N}_0^\infty$ is the set $\mathbb{N}_0$ of non-negative integers extended with the (positive) infinity ∞. The value $\Omega(c)$ is the *multiplicity* of element c in Ω. A bag Ω is *finite* if there are finitely many $c \in M$ with $\Omega(c) > 0$ and there is no c with $\Omega(c) = \infty$. The *empty bag* $\emptyset$ over M is the bag such that $\emptyset(c) = 0$ for each $c \in M$. A bag Ω_1 over M is a *subbag* of a bag Ω_2 over M, in symbols $\Omega_1 \subseteq \Omega_2$, if $\Omega_1(c) \leq \Omega_2(c)$ for each $c \in M$. Often we will use an alternative syntax for bags: for instance, we will write $\{\!| c : 5, d : 3 |\!\}$ for the bag that assigns 5 to c, 3 to d, and 0 to all other elements. We use the following common operators on bags [15,26]: the *intersection* $\cap$, *maximal union* $\cup$, *arithmetic union* $\uplus$, and *difference* $-$ are the binary operators defined, for bags Ω_1 and Ω_2 over a set M, and for every $c \in M$, as follows:

$$(\Omega_1 \cap \Omega_2)(c) = \min\{\Omega_1(c), \Omega_2(c)\}, \quad (\Omega_1 \cup \Omega_2)(c) = \max\{\Omega_1(c), \Omega_2(c)\},$$
$$(\Omega_1 \uplus \Omega_2)(c) = \Omega_1(c) + \Omega_2(c), \quad (\Omega_1 - \Omega_2)(c) = \max\{0, \Omega_1(c) - \Omega_2(c)\}.$$

Note that bag difference is well-defined only if $\Omega_2(c)$ is a finite number for each $c \in M$. The unary *duplicate elimination* operator ε is defined for a bag Ω over M and for each $c \in M$ as $(\varepsilon(\Omega))(c) = 1$ if $\Omega(c) > 0$ and $(\varepsilon(\Omega))(c) = 0$ otherwise.

Queries over Bags. Following [31], a BCALC *query* $\Phi(\mathbf{x})$ with (a tuple of) *answer* variables $\mathbf{x}$ is any of the following, for Ψ, Ψ_1, and Ψ_2 BCALC queries:

- $S(\mathbf{t})$, where $S \in \mathbf{C} \cup \mathbf{R}$ and $\mathbf{t}$ is a tuple over $\mathbf{x} \cup \mathbf{I}$ mentioning all $\mathbf{x}$;
- $\Psi_1(\mathbf{x}_1) \wedge \Psi_2(\mathbf{x}_2)$, where $\mathbf{x} = \mathbf{x}_1 \cup \mathbf{x}_2$;
- $\Psi(\mathbf{x}_0) \wedge (x = t)$, where $x \in \mathbf{x}_0$, $t \in \mathbf{X} \cup \mathbf{I}$, and $\mathbf{x} = \mathbf{x}_0 \cup (\{t\} \setminus \mathbf{I})$;
- $\exists \mathbf{y}.\, \Psi(\mathbf{x}, \mathbf{y})$, where $\mathbf{y}$ is a tuple of distinct variables from $\mathbf{X}$ that are not in $\mathbf{x}$;
- $\Psi_1(\mathbf{x}) \,\mathsf{op}\, \Psi_2(\mathbf{x})$, where $\mathsf{op} \in \{\vee, \veebar, \setminus\}$; or
- $\delta\, \Psi(\mathbf{x})$.

In particular, all UCQs are syntactically BCALC queries. BCALC queries are evaluated over bag database instances, which are, in the context of this paper, *bag ABoxes*—that is, finite bags over the set of concept and role assertions. The *bag answers* $\Phi^{\mathcal{A}}$ to a BCALC query $\Phi(\mathbf{x})$ over a bag ABox $\mathcal{A}$ is the finite bag over $\mathbf{I}^{|\mathbf{x}|}$ defined inductively as follows, for every tuple $\mathbf{a}$ over $\mathbf{I}$ with $|\mathbf{a}| = |\mathbf{x}|$, where $\nu : \mathbf{x} \cup \mathbf{I} \to \mathbf{I}$ is the function such that $\nu(\mathbf{x}) = \mathbf{a}$ and $\nu(a) = a$ for all $a \in \mathbf{I}$:

- $\Phi^{\mathcal{A}}(\mathbf{a}) = \mathcal{A}(S(\nu(\mathbf{t})))$, if $\Phi(\mathbf{x}) = S(\mathbf{t})$;
- $\Phi^{\mathcal{A}}(\mathbf{a}) = \Psi_1^{\mathcal{A}}(\nu(\mathbf{x}_1)) \times \Psi_2^{\mathcal{A}}(\nu(\mathbf{x}_2))$, if $\Phi(\mathbf{x}) = \Psi_1(\mathbf{x}_1) \wedge \Psi_2(\mathbf{x}_2)$;
- $\Phi^{\mathcal{A}}(\mathbf{a}) = \Psi^{\mathcal{A}}(\nu(\mathbf{x}_0))$, if $\Phi(\mathbf{x}) = \Psi(\mathbf{x}_0) \wedge (x = t)$ and $\nu(x) = \nu(t)$;
- $\Phi^{\mathcal{A}}(\mathbf{a}) = 0$, if $\Phi(\mathbf{x}) = \Psi(\mathbf{x}_0) \wedge (x = t)$ and $\nu(x) \neq \nu(t)$;
- $\Phi^{\mathcal{A}}(\mathbf{a}) = \sum_{\nu' : \mathbf{y} \to \mathbf{I}} \Psi^{\mathcal{A}}(\mathbf{a}, \nu'(\mathbf{y}))$, if $\Phi(\mathbf{x}) = \exists \mathbf{y}.\, \Psi(\mathbf{x}, \mathbf{y})$;
- $\Phi^{\mathcal{A}}(\mathbf{a}) = (\Psi_1^{\mathcal{A}} \,\mathsf{op}\, \Psi_2^{\mathcal{A}})(\mathbf{a})$, if $\Phi(\mathbf{x}) = \Psi_1(\mathbf{x}) \,\mathsf{op}'\, \Psi_2(\mathbf{x})$, where op is $\cup$, $\uplus$, or $-$, and op' is $\vee$, $\veebar$, or $\setminus$, respectively;
- $\Phi^{\mathcal{A}}(\mathbf{a}) = \big(\varepsilon(\Psi^{\mathcal{A}})\big)(\mathbf{a})$, if $\Phi(\mathbf{x}) = \delta\, \Psi(\mathbf{x})$.

As shown in [31], BCALC is a logical counterpart of the bag relational algebra BALG[1] [15], with the same expressive power. Evaluation of a fixed BALG[1] (and hence BCALC) query is in TC^0 [25] (i.e., between AC^0 and LOGSPACE).

3 *DL-Lite*$_{\mathcal{F}}$ Under Bag Semantics

In this section we introduce the bag version *DL-Lite*$_{\mathcal{F}}^{\mathsf{b}}$ of the ontology language *DL-Lite*$_{\mathcal{F}}$ by proposing two semantics and then study their properties and relationships. Both semantics extend the bag semantics of *DL-Lite*$_{core}$ proposed by Nikolaou et al. [30,31] but differ in their interpretation of functionality axioms.

3.1 Syntax and Semantics of *DL-Lite*$_{\mathcal{F}}^{\mathsf{b}}$

Syntactically, *DL-Lite*$_{\mathcal{F}}^{\mathsf{b}}$ is the same as *DL-Lite*$_{\mathcal{F}}$ except that assertions in ABoxes may have arbitrary finite multiplicities—that is, bag ABoxes are considered instead of set ABoxes. Thus, at the syntax level *DL-Lite*$_{\mathcal{F}}^{\mathsf{b}}$ is a conservative extension of *DL-Lite*$_{\mathcal{F}}$ since each set ABox can be seen as a bag ABox with assertion multiplicities 0 and 1.

Definition 1. *A* *DL-Lite*$_{\mathcal{F}}^{\mathsf{b}}$ ontology *is a pair* $(\mathcal{T}, \mathcal{A})$ *of a* *DL-Lite*$_{\mathcal{F}}$ *TBox* $\mathcal{T}$ *and a bag ABox* $\mathcal{A}$. *A* *DL-Lite*$_{core}^{\mathsf{b}}$ ontology *is the same except that* $\mathcal{T}$ *is* *DL-Lite*$_{core}$.

The semantics of $DL\text{-}Lite^{\mathsf{b}}_{\mathcal{F}}$ ontologies is based on bag interpretations, which are the same as set interpretations except that concepts and roles are interpreted as bags rather than sets. The extension of the interpretation function to non-atomic concepts and roles is defined in a way that respects the multiplicities: for example, the concept $\exists P$ for an atomic role P is interpreted by a bag interpretation $\mathcal{I}$ as the bag projection of $P^{\mathcal{I}}$ to its first component, where each occurrence of a pair (u, v) in $P^{\mathcal{I}}$ contributes separately to the multiplicity of u in $(\exists P)^{\mathcal{I}}$.

Definition 2. *A* bag interpretation $\mathcal{I}$ *is a pair* $(\Delta^{\mathcal{I}}, \cdot^{\mathcal{I}})$ *where the* domain $\Delta^{\mathcal{I}}$ *is a non-empty set, and the* interpretation function $\cdot^{\mathcal{I}}$ *maps each individual* $a \in \mathbf{I}$ *to an element* $a^{\mathcal{I}} \in \Delta^{\mathcal{I}}$ *such that* $a^{\mathcal{I}} \neq b^{\mathcal{I}}$ *for all distinct* $a, b \in \mathbf{I}$*, each atomic concept* $A \in \mathbf{C}$ *to a bag* $A^{\mathcal{I}}$ *over* $\Delta^{\mathcal{I}}$*, and each atomic role* $P \in \mathbf{R}$ *to a bag* $P^{\mathcal{I}}$ *over* $\Delta^{\mathcal{I}} \times \Delta^{\mathcal{I}}$*. Interpretation function* $\cdot^{\mathcal{I}}$ *extends to non-atomic concepts and roles as follows, for all* $P \in \mathbf{R}$*,* R *a role, and* $u, u' \in \Delta^{\mathcal{I}}$*:*

$$(P^{-})^{\mathcal{I}}(u, u') = P^{\mathcal{I}}(u', u) \quad \text{and} \quad (\exists R)^{\mathcal{I}}(u) = \sum\nolimits_{u' \in \Delta^{\mathcal{I}}} R^{\mathcal{I}}(u, u').$$

Note that, same as in the set case, we adopt the UNA by requiring different individuals be interpreted by different domain elements.

We are now ready to present our two semantics of $DL\text{-}Lite^{\mathsf{b}}_{\mathcal{F}}$. Both semantics extend the semantics of $DL\text{-}Lite^{\mathsf{b}}_{core}$ considered in [31], but handle the functional axioms differently. Our first semantics, called SQL, follows the semantics of primary keys in SQL: if R is a functional role then for every domain element u of a model there exists at most one element u' related to u by R; moreover, the multiplicity of the tuple (u, u') in R cannot be more than one. Our second semantics, called MR (i.e., multiplicity-respectful), allows more freedom for functional roles: same as before, only one u' may be related to u by a functional role R, but the multiplicity of (u, u') may be arbitrary.

Definition 3. *A bag interpretation* $\mathcal{I}$ satisfies *an inclusion axiom* $C_1 \sqsubseteq C_2$ *if* $C_1^{\mathcal{I}} \subseteq C_2^{\mathcal{I}}$*. It* satisfies *a disjointness axiom* $\mathsf{Disj}(C_1, C_2)$ *if* $C_1^{\mathcal{I}} \cap C_2^{\mathcal{I}} = \emptyset$*. It* satisfies *a functionality axiom* $(\mathsf{funct}\ R)$ under SQL semantics *(or* SQL-satisfies, *for short) if* $u' = u''$ *and* $R^{\mathcal{I}}(u, u') = R^{\mathcal{I}}(u, u'') = 1$ *for every* u*,* u'*, and* u'' *in* $\Delta^{\mathcal{I}}$ *such that* $R^{\mathcal{I}}(u, u') > 0$ *and* $R^{\mathcal{I}}(u, u'') > 0$*; it satisfies* $(\mathsf{funct}\ R)$ under MR semantics *(or* MR-satisfies*) if the same holds except that the requirement* $R^{\mathcal{I}}(u, u') = R^{\mathcal{I}}(u, u'') = 1$ *is not imposed.*

For X *being* SQL *or* MR*, a bag interpretation* $\mathcal{I}$ X-satisfies *a* $DL\text{-}Lite_{\mathcal{F}}$ *TBox* $\mathcal{T}$*, written* $\mathcal{I} \models_X \mathcal{T}$*, if it satisfies every inclusion and disjointness axiom in* $\mathcal{T}$ *and* X*-satisfies every functionality axiom in* $\mathcal{T}$*. A bag interpretation* $\mathcal{I}$ satisfies *a bag ABox* $\mathcal{A}$*, written* $\mathcal{I} \models \mathcal{A}$*, if* $\mathcal{A}(A(a)) \leq A^{\mathcal{I}}(a^{\mathcal{I}})$ *and* $\mathcal{A}(P(a, b)) \leq P^{\mathcal{I}}(a^{\mathcal{I}}, b^{\mathcal{I}})$ *for each concept assertion* $A(a)$ *and role assertion* $P(a, b)$*, respectively. A bag interpretation* $\mathcal{I}$ *is an* X-model *of a* $DL\text{-}Lite^{\mathsf{b}}_{\mathcal{F}}$ *ontology* $(\mathcal{T}, \mathcal{A})$*, written* $\mathcal{I} \models_X (\mathcal{T}, \mathcal{A})$*, if* $\mathcal{I} \models_X \mathcal{T}$ *and* $\mathcal{I} \models \mathcal{A}$*. A* $DL\text{-}Lite^{\mathsf{b}}_{\mathcal{F}}$ *ontology is* X-satisfiable *if it has an* X*-model.*

Since MR-satisfaction is a relaxation of SQL-satisfaction, every SQL-model of a $DL\text{-}Lite^{\mathsf{b}}_{\mathcal{F}}$ ontology is also an MR-model of this ontology. However, as illustrated by the following example, the opposite does not hold.

Example 1. Consider an online store that employs atomic concept $\mathsf{Customer}$ and atomic roles $\mathsf{hasItem}$, $\mathsf{placedBy}$ for recording the items ordered by customers in a purchase. A sample $\mathit{DL\text{-}Lite}^{\mathsf{b}}_{\mathcal{F}}$ ontology recording customers' orders is $\mathcal{K}_{\text{ex}} = (\mathcal{T}_{ex}, \mathcal{A}_{ex})$ with

$$\mathcal{T}_{ex} = \{\exists \mathsf{hasItem} \sqsubseteq \exists \mathsf{placedBy},\ \exists \mathsf{placedBy}^{-} \sqsubseteq \mathsf{Customer},\ (\mathsf{funct\ placedBy})\} \text{ and}$$
$$\mathcal{A}_{ex} = \{\!| \mathsf{hasItem}(o, i_1) : 1,\ \mathsf{hasItem}(o, i_2) : 1,\ \mathsf{placedBy}(o, c) : 1,\ \mathsf{Customer}(c) : 1 |\!\}.$$

Let $\mathcal{I}_{ex}$ be the bag interpretation that interprets all individuals by themselves, and the atomic roles and concepts as follows: $\mathsf{Customer}^{\mathcal{I}_{ex}} = \{\!| c : 2 |\!\}$, $\mathsf{hasItem}^{\mathcal{I}_{ex}} = \{\!| (o, i_1) : 1, (o, i_2) : 1 |\!\}$, and $\mathsf{placedBy}^{\mathcal{I}_{ex}} = \{\!| (o, c) : 2 |\!\}$. It is immediate that $\mathcal{I}_{ex}$ is an MR-model of $\mathcal{K}_{\text{ex}}$ but not a SQL-model. ◁

To conclude this section, we note that each semantics has its advantages and drawbacks. Indeed, on the one hand, SQL semantics is compatible with primary keys in SQL, so a large fragment of $\mathit{DL\text{-}Lite}^{\mathsf{b}}_{\mathcal{F}}$ under this semantics can be easily simulated by a SQL engine. On the other hand, one can show that entailment of axioms under set and bag semantics coincides only for the case of MR models; this means that the adoption of MR semantics does not affect the standard TBox reasoning services implemented in ontology development tools. So neither of the two semantics is clearly preferable to the other.

3.2 Queries over $\mathit{DL\text{-}Lite}^{\mathsf{b}}_{\mathcal{F}}$

We next define the answers $q^{\mathcal{I}}$ to a CQ $q(\mathbf{x})$ over a bag interpretation $\mathcal{I}$ as the bag of tuples of individuals such that each valid embedding λ of the atoms in q into $\mathcal{I}$ contributes separately to the multiplicity of the tuple $\lambda(\mathbf{x})$ in $q^{\mathcal{I}}$, and where the contribution of each specific λ is the product of the multiplicities of the images of the query atoms under λ in $\mathcal{I}$. This may be seen as usual CQ answering under bag semantics over relational databases when the interpretation is seen as a bag database instance [12]. In fact, when q is evaluated over this bag database instance as a BCALC query (see Sect. 2), it produces exactly $q^{\mathcal{I}}$.

Definition 4. *Let $q(\mathbf{x}) = \exists \mathbf{y}.\, \phi(\mathbf{x}, \mathbf{y})$ be a CQ and $\mathcal{I} = (\Delta^{\mathcal{I}}, \cdot^{\mathcal{I}})$ be a bag interpretation. The* bag answers *$q^{\mathcal{I}}$ to q over $\mathcal{I}$ are the bag over tuples of individuals from $\mathbf{I}$ of size $|\mathbf{x}|$ such that, for every such tuple $\mathbf{a}$,*

$$q^{\mathcal{I}}(\mathbf{a}) \quad = \quad \sum\nolimits_{\lambda \in \Lambda} \prod\nolimits_{S(\mathbf{t}) \text{ in } \phi(\mathbf{x}, \mathbf{y})} S^{\mathcal{I}}(\lambda(\mathbf{t})),$$

where Λ is the set of all valuations *$\lambda : \mathbf{x} \cup \mathbf{y} \cup \mathbf{I} \to \Delta^{\mathcal{I}}$ such that $\lambda(\mathbf{x}) = \mathbf{a}^{\mathcal{I}}$, $\lambda(a) = a^{\mathcal{I}}$ for each $a \in \mathbf{I}$, and $\lambda(z) = \lambda(t)$ for each $z = t$ in $\phi(\mathbf{x}, \mathbf{y})$.*

Note that conjunction $\phi(\mathbf{x}, \mathbf{y})$ in a CQ may contain repeated atoms, and hence can be seen as a bag of atoms; while repeated atoms are redundant in the set case, they are essential in the bag setting [12,18], and thus in the definition of $q^{\mathcal{I}}(\mathbf{a})$ each occurrence of a query atom $S(\mathbf{t})$ is treated separately in the product.

The following definition of certain answers, which captures open-world query answering, is a natural extension of certain answers for $\mathit{DL\text{-}Lite}_{\mathcal{F}}$ to bags. For $\mathit{DL\text{-}Lite}^{\mathsf{b}}_{core}$, this definition coincides with the one in [31] for both semantics.

Definition 5. *For X being* SQL *or* MR, *the X*-bag certain answers $q_X^{\mathcal{K}}$ *to a CQ q over a DL-Lite$^{\mathsf{b}}_{\mathcal{F}}$ ontology $\mathcal{K}$ are the bag $\bigcap_{\mathcal{I} \models_X \mathcal{K}} q^{\mathcal{I}}$.*

Note that in this definition the intersection is the bag intersection, and we assume that the intersection of zero bags (which is relevant when $\mathcal{K}$ is not X-satisfiable) assigns ∞ to all tuples over $\mathbf{I}$.

The (data complexity version of the) decision problem corresponding to computing the X-bag certain answers to a CQ q over an ontology with a *DL-Lite$_{\mathcal{F}}$* TBox $\mathcal{T}$, for X begin SQL or MR, is defined as follows, assuming that all numbers in the input are represented in unary.

BAGCERT$_X[q, \mathcal{T}]$

Input:	ABox $\mathcal{A}$, tuple $\mathbf{a}$ of individuals from $\mathbf{I}$, and $k \in \mathbb{N}_0^{\infty}$.
Question:	Is $q_X^{(\mathcal{T},\mathcal{A})}(\mathbf{a}) \geq k$?

The idea of bag certain answers is illustrated by the following example.

Example 2. Recall ontology $(\mathcal{T}_{ex}, \mathcal{A}_{ex})$ and interpretation $\mathcal{I}_{ex}$ specified in Example 1, and let $q(x) = \exists y.\, \mathsf{placedBy}(x, y) \wedge \mathsf{Customer}(y)$ be the rooted CQ requesting orders placed by customers. The bag answers $q^{\mathcal{I}_{ex}}$ to q over interpretation $\mathcal{I}_{ex}$ is the bag $\{\!| o : 4 |\!\}$. Moreover, it is not hard to see that the MR-bag certain answers to q over $(\mathcal{T}_{ex}, \mathcal{A}_{ex})$ coincide with bag $q^{\mathcal{I}_{ex}}$, and that $q_{\mathrm{SQL}}^{(\mathcal{T}_{ex},\mathcal{A}_{ex})}(a) = \infty$ for every $a \in \mathbf{I}$ since $(\mathcal{T}_{ex}, \mathcal{A}_{ex})$ does not have any SQL-model. ◁

Besides the complexity of query answering, an important related property of any description logic is query rewritability: since TBoxes are much more stable than ABoxes in practice, it is desirable to be able to rewrite a query and a TBox into another query so that the answers to the original query over each satisfiable ontology with this TBox are the same as the answers to the rewriting over the ABox alone. The rewriting may be in a richer query language than the language of the original query, provided we have an efficient query engine for the target language; it is important, however, that the rewriting does not depend on the ABox. As mentioned above, rewritings of (U)CQs to UCQs are usually considered in the set setting. In our bag setting, the source language is CQs and the target language is BCALC, which can be easily translated to SQL.

Definition 6. *For X being* SQL *or* MR, *a* BCALC *query Φ is an X*-rewriting *of a CQ q with respect to a DL-Lite$_{\mathcal{F}}$ TBox $\mathcal{T}$ if $q_X^{(\mathcal{T},\mathcal{A})} = \Phi^{\mathcal{A}}$ for every bag ABox $\mathcal{A}$ with $(\mathcal{T}, \mathcal{A})$ X-satisfiable. A class $\mathcal{Q}$ of CQs is X*-rewritable *to a class $\mathcal{Q}'$ of* BCALC *queries over a sublanguage $\mathcal{L}$ of DL-Lite$_{\mathcal{F}}$ if, for every CQ in $\mathcal{Q}$ and TBox in $\mathcal{L}$, there is an X-rewriting of the CQ with respect to the TBox in $\mathcal{Q}'$.*

Since evaluation of fixed BCALC queries is in TC^0 [25], rewritability to BCALC implies TC^0 data complexity of query answering provided rewritings are effectively constructible. BAGCERT$_X[q, \mathcal{T}]$ is coNP-hard even for *DL-Lite$^{\mathsf{b}}_{\mathrm{core}}$* ontologies (for both X) [31], which precludes efficient query answering and (constructive) BCALC rewritability (under the usual complexity-theoretic assumptions). However, rewritability and TC^0 complexity of query answering are regained for rooted CQs, which are common in practice. The main goal of this paper is to understand to what extent these results transfer to $\mathit{DL\text{-}Lite}^{\mathsf{b}}_{\mathcal{F}}$.

We next establish some basic properties of the proposed bag semantics and relate them to the standard set semantics. The following theorem states that satisfiability and query answering under the set semantics and MR semantics are essentially equivalent when multiplicities are ignored, while SQL semantics is in a sense stronger as only one direction of the statements holds.

Theorem 1. *The following statements hold for every* $\mathit{DL\text{-}Lite}_{\mathcal{F}}$ *TBox* $\mathcal{T}$ *and every bag ABox* $\mathcal{A}$ *(recall that* ε *is the duplicate elimination operator):*

1. *if* $(\mathcal{T}, \mathcal{A})$ *is* SQL*-satisfiable then* $(\mathcal{T}, \varepsilon(\mathcal{A}))$ *is satisfiable; and*
2. *for every tuple* $\mathbf{a}$ *over* $\mathbf{I}$*, if* $\mathbf{a} \in q^{(\mathcal{T}, \varepsilon(\mathcal{A}))}$ *then* $q_{\mathrm{SQL}}^{(\mathcal{T}, \mathcal{A})}(\mathbf{a}) \geq 1$*, and the converse holds whenever* $(\mathcal{T}, \mathcal{A})$ *is* SQL*-satisfiable.*

The same holds when MR *semantics is considered instead of* SQL*; moreover, in this case the converses of both statements hold unconditionally.*

In fact, the converse direction of statement 1 does not hold for SQL semantics; indeed, the $\mathit{DL\text{-}Lite}^{\mathsf{b}}_{\mathcal{F}}$ ontology $\mathcal{K}_{\mathrm{ex}}$ of Example 1 is not SQL-satisfiable but ontology $(\mathcal{T}_{\mathrm{ex}}, \varepsilon(\mathcal{A}_{\mathrm{ex}}))$ is satisfiable.

Statement 1 for MR semantics implies that we can check MR-satisfiability of $\mathit{DL\text{-}Lite}^{\mathsf{b}}_{\mathcal{F}}$ ontologies using standard techniques for $\mathit{DL\text{-}Lite}_{\mathcal{F}}$ under the set semantics; in particular, we can do it in AC^0 for fixed TBoxes. The following proposition says that for SQL semantics the problem is not much more difficult.

Proposition 1. *The problem of checking whether a* $\mathit{DL\text{-}Lite}^{\mathsf{b}}_{\mathcal{F}}$ *ontology is SQL-satisfiable is in* TC^0 *when the TBox is fixed.*

Finally, note that, since every SQL-model of a $\mathit{DL\text{-}Lite}^{\mathsf{b}}_{\mathcal{F}}$ ontology is also an MR-model, $q_{\mathrm{MR}}^{\mathcal{K}} \subseteq q_{\mathrm{SQL}}^{\mathcal{K}}$ for every CQ q and $\mathit{DL\text{-}Lite}^{\mathsf{b}}_{\mathcal{F}}$ ontology $\mathcal{K}$; it is not difficult to see that the inclusion may be strict even if $\mathcal{K}$ is SQL-satisfiable.

4 Rewriting and Query Answering in $\mathit{DL\text{-}Lite}^{\mathsf{b}}_{\mathcal{F}}$

We next study rewritability of rooted CQs to BCALC over $\mathit{DL\text{-}Lite}^{\mathsf{b}}_{\mathcal{F}}$ under our two semantics (recall that the class of all CQs are not rewritable even over $\mathit{DL\text{-}Lite}^{\mathsf{b}}_{\mathit{core}}$ [31]). We first show that for SQL semantics and satisfiable ontologies we can apply the same rewriting as for $\mathit{DL\text{-}Lite}^{\mathsf{b}}_{\mathit{core}}$ [31], which implies TC^0 data complexity of query answering. However, MR semantics is more complex, because, as we show, even simple rooted CQs (in particular, instance queries) have LogSpace-hard query answering, which precludes rewritability (assuming $\mathrm{TC}^0 \subsetneq$ LogSpace). To address this limitation, we introduce a new acyclicity condition on TBoxes, for which we show that the rewritability is regained.

4.1 SQL Semantics

The key ingredient for rewritability and tractability of CQ answering in many description logics is the existence of a universal model.

Definition 7. *For X being* SQL *or* MR*, an X-model $\mathcal{I}$ of a DL-Lite$^{\mathsf{b}}_{\mathcal{F}}$ ontology $\mathcal{K}$ is X-*universal *for a class of CQs $\mathcal{Q}$ if $q_X^{\mathcal{K}} = q^{\mathcal{I}}$ for every $q \in \mathcal{Q}$.*

In the set case, it is well-known that if the ontology is satisfiable, then the so-called canonical interpretation, which can be constructed by the chase procedure, is always a universal model for all CQs [4,8]. Nikolaou et al. generalised this idea to *DL-Lite*$^{\mathsf{b}}_{core}$ [31] and rooted CQs, and it turns out that their canonical interpretation is a universal model for rooted CQs also for *DL-Lite*$^{\mathsf{b}}_{\mathcal{F}}$ under SQL semantics. Before we give the main construction, we introduce the relevant notions from [31].

The *concept closure* $\mathsf{ccl}_{\mathcal{T}}[u, \mathcal{I}]$ of an element $u \in \Delta^{\mathcal{I}}$ in a bag interpretation $\mathcal{I} = (\Delta^{\mathcal{I}}, \cdot^{\mathcal{I}})$ over a TBox $\mathcal{T}$ is the bag of concepts such that, for any concept C,

$$\mathsf{ccl}_{\mathcal{T}}[u, \mathcal{I}](C) = \max\{C_0^{\mathcal{I}}(u) \mid \mathcal{T} \models C_0 \sqsubseteq C\}.$$

In other words, $\mathsf{ccl}_{\mathcal{T}}[u, \mathcal{I}](C)$ is the minimal multiplicity of $C^{\mathcal{J}}(u)$ required for an extension $\mathcal{J}$ of $\mathcal{I}$ to satisfy TBox $\mathcal{T}$ locally in u.

The *union* $\mathcal{I} \cup \mathcal{J}$ of bag interpretations $\mathcal{I} = (\Delta^{\mathcal{I}}, \cdot^{\mathcal{I}})$ and $\mathcal{J} = (\Delta^{\mathcal{J}}, \cdot^{\mathcal{J}})$ interpreting all the individuals in the same way—that is, such that $a^{\mathcal{I}} = a^{\mathcal{J}}$ for each $a \in \mathbf{I}$—is the bag interpretation $(\Delta^{\mathcal{I}} \cup \Delta^{\mathcal{J}}, \cdot^{\mathcal{I} \cup \mathcal{J}})$ with $a^{\mathcal{I} \cup \mathcal{J}} = a^{\mathcal{I}}$ for all $a \in \mathbf{I}$ and $S^{\mathcal{I} \cup \mathcal{J}} = S^{\mathcal{I}} \cup S^{\mathcal{J}}$ for all atomic concepts and roles $S \in \mathbf{C} \cup \mathbf{R}$.

Finally, given a bag ABox $\mathcal{A}$ we denote with $\mathcal{I}_{\mathcal{A}} = (\Delta^{\mathcal{I}_{\mathcal{A}}}, \cdot^{\mathcal{I}_{\mathcal{A}}})$ the *standard interpretation* of $\mathcal{A}$ that is defined as follows: $\Delta^{\mathcal{I}_{\mathcal{A}}} = \mathbf{I}$, $a^{\mathcal{I}_{\mathcal{A}}} = a$ for each $a \in \mathbf{I}$, and $S^{\mathcal{I}_{\mathcal{A}}}(\mathbf{a}) = \mathcal{A}(S(\mathbf{a}))$ for each $S \in \mathbf{C} \cup \mathbf{R}$ and tuple of individuals $\mathbf{a}$.

Definition 8 (Nikolaou et al. [31]**).** *The* SQL-canonical bag interpretation *$\mathcal{C}_{\mathrm{SQL}}(\mathcal{K})$ of a DL-Lite$^{\mathsf{b}}_{\mathcal{F}}$ ontology $\mathcal{K} = (\mathcal{T}, \mathcal{A})$ is the bag interpretation that is the union $\bigcup_{i \geq 0} \mathcal{C}^i_{\mathrm{SQL}}(\mathcal{K})$ of the bag interpretations $\mathcal{C}^i_{\mathrm{SQL}}(\mathcal{K}) = (\Delta^{\mathcal{C}^i_{\mathrm{SQL}}(\mathcal{K})}, \cdot^{\mathcal{C}^i_{\mathrm{SQL}}(\mathcal{K})})$ such that $\mathcal{C}^0_{\mathrm{SQL}}(\mathcal{K}) = \mathcal{I}_{\mathcal{A}}$ and, for each $i > 0$, $\mathcal{C}^i_{\mathrm{SQL}}(\mathcal{K})$ is constructed from $\mathcal{C}^{i-1}_{\mathrm{SQL}}(\mathcal{K})$ as follows:*

- *$\Delta^{\mathcal{C}^i_{\mathrm{SQL}}(\mathcal{K})}$ extends $\Delta^{\mathcal{C}^{i-1}_{\mathrm{SQL}}(\mathcal{K})}$ by fresh* anonymous *elements $w^1_{u,R}, \ldots, w^{\delta}_{u,R}$ for each $u \in \Delta^{\mathcal{C}^{i-1}_{\mathrm{SQL}}(\mathcal{K})}$ and role R with*

$$\delta = \mathsf{ccl}_{\mathcal{T}}[u, \mathcal{C}^{i-1}_{\mathrm{SQL}}(\mathcal{K})](\exists R) - (\exists R)^{\mathcal{C}^{i-1}_{\mathrm{SQL}}(\mathcal{K})}(u);$$

- *$a^{\mathcal{C}^i_{\mathrm{SQL}}(\mathcal{K})} = a$ for all $a \in \mathbf{I}$, and, for all $A \in \mathbf{C}$, $P \in \mathbf{R}$ and u, v in $\Delta^{\mathcal{C}^i_{\mathrm{SQL}}(\mathcal{K})}$,*

$$A^{\mathcal{C}^i_{\mathrm{SQL}}(\mathcal{K})}(u) = \begin{cases} \mathsf{ccl}_{\mathcal{T}}[u, \mathcal{C}^{i-1}_{\mathrm{SQL}}(\mathcal{K})](A), & \textit{if } u \in \Delta^{\mathcal{C}^{i-1}_{\mathrm{SQL}}(\mathcal{K})}, \\ 0, & \textit{otherwise}, \end{cases}$$

$$P^{\mathcal{C}^i_{\mathrm{SQL}}(\mathcal{K})}(u, v) = \begin{cases} P^{\mathcal{C}^{i-1}_{\mathrm{SQL}}(\mathcal{K})}(u, v), & \textit{if } u, v \in \Delta^{\mathcal{C}^{i-1}_{\mathrm{SQL}}(\mathcal{K})}, \\ 1, & \textit{if } u = w^j_{v,P} \textit{ or } v = w^j_{u,P^-}, \\ 0, & \textit{otherwise}. \end{cases}$$

The following example illustrates the construction of SQL-canonical models.

Example 3. Consider the *DL-Lite*$^{\mathsf{b}}_{\mathcal{F}}$ ontology $\mathcal{K}'_{ex} = (\mathcal{T}'_{ex}, \mathcal{A}'_{ex})$ with

$$\mathcal{T}'_{ex} = \{\mathsf{Order} \sqsubseteq \exists\mathsf{placedBy},\ \mathsf{Customer} \sqsubseteq \exists\mathsf{placedBy}^-,\ (\mathsf{funct}\ \mathsf{placedBy})\} \text{ and}$$
$$\mathcal{A}'_{ex} = \{\!|\ \mathsf{Order}(o) : 1,\ \mathsf{placedBy}(o, c) : 1,\ \mathsf{Customer}(c) : 4\ |\!\}.$$

To compute the SQL-canonical interpretation $\mathcal{C}_{\mathrm{SQL}}(\mathcal{K}'_{ex})$ of $\mathcal{K}'_{ex}$, we first set $\mathcal{C}^0_{\mathrm{SQL}}(\mathcal{K}'_{ex}) = \mathcal{I}_{\mathcal{A}'_{ex}}$. For the second step we take $\mathsf{Order}^{\mathcal{C}^1_{\mathrm{SQL}}(\mathcal{K}'_{ex})} = \mathsf{Order}^{\mathcal{C}^0_{\mathrm{SQL}}(\mathcal{K}'_{ex})}$ and $\mathsf{Customer}^{\mathcal{C}^1_{\mathrm{SQL}}(\mathcal{K}'_{ex})} = \mathsf{Customer}^{\mathcal{C}^0_{\mathrm{SQL}}(\mathcal{K}'_{ex})}$ as neither of the concepts subsumes another concept in $\mathcal{T}'_{ex}$. The interpretation of $\mathsf{placedBy}$ by $\mathcal{C}^1_{\mathrm{SQL}}(\mathcal{K}'_{ex})$ is then determined by the concept closures of o and c for the concepts $\exists\mathsf{placedBy}$ and $\exists\mathsf{placedBy}^-$ over $\mathcal{T}'_{ex}$, respectively. Since the former is equal to the multiplicity that o has in $(\exists\mathsf{placedBy})^{\mathcal{C}^0_{\mathrm{SQL}}(\mathcal{K}'_{ex})}$, no new $\exists\mathsf{placedBy}$-successor is added for o. However, the latter is larger than the multiplicity of c in $(\exists\mathsf{placedBy}^-)^{\mathcal{C}^0_{\mathrm{SQL}}(\mathcal{K}'_{ex})}$ by three, and hence c must be associated with new anonymous $\exists\mathsf{placedBy}^-$-successors $w^1_{c,\exists\mathsf{placedBy}^-}, \dots, w^3_{c,\exists\mathsf{placedBy}^-}$. Therefore, $\mathcal{C}^1_{\mathrm{SQL}}(\mathcal{K}'_{ex})$ has domain $\mathbf{I} \cup \{w^1_{c,\exists\mathsf{placedBy}^-}, \dots, w^3_{c,\exists\mathsf{placedBy}^-}\}$, and interprets concepts and roles as follows:

$$\mathsf{Order}^{\mathcal{C}^1_{\mathrm{SQL}}(\mathcal{K}'_{ex})} = \{\!|\ o : 1\ |\!\},\quad \mathsf{Customer}^{\mathcal{C}^1_{\mathrm{SQL}}(\mathcal{K}'_{ex})} = \{\!|\ c : 4\ |\!\}, \text{ and}$$
$$\mathsf{placedBy}^{\mathcal{C}^1_{\mathrm{SQL}}(\mathcal{K}'_{ex})} = \{\!|\ (o, c) : 1, (w^1_{c,\exists\mathsf{placedBy}^-}, c) : 1, \dots, (w^3_{c,\exists\mathsf{placedBy}^-}, c) : 1\ |\!\}.$$

Since there is no violation of axioms in $\mathcal{C}^1_{\mathrm{SQL}}(\mathcal{K}'_{ex})$, the process terminates at the following step, and we take $\mathcal{C}_{\mathrm{SQL}}(\mathcal{K}'_{ex}) = \mathcal{C}^2_{\mathrm{SQL}}(\mathcal{K}'_{ex}) = \mathcal{C}^1_{\mathrm{SQL}}(\mathcal{K}'_{ex})$. ◁

We are ready to show that the SQL-canonical bag interpretation is indeed SQL-universal for rooted CQs.

Theorem 2. *The* SQL*-canonical bag interpretation of an* SQL*-satisfiable DL-Lite*$^{\mathsf{b}}_{\mathcal{F}}$ *ontology* $\mathcal{K}$ *is an* SQL*-universal model for the class of rooted CQs.*

Having this result at hand, we can reuse the rewriting of rooted CQs over *DL-Lite*$^{\mathsf{b}}_{\mathit{core}}$ introduced in [31] for the SQL semantics of *DL-Lite*$^{\mathsf{b}}_{\mathcal{F}}$.

Corollary 1. *Rooted CQs are* SQL*-rewritable to BCALC over DL-Lite*$^{\mathsf{b}}_{\mathcal{F}}$.

Since the proof of rewritability in [31] is constructive, SQL-satisfiability is in TC^0, and BCALC evaluation is in TC^0, rooted CQ answering is also in TC^0.

Corollary 2. *Problem* $\textsc{BagCert}_{\mathrm{SQL}}[q, \mathcal{T}]$ *is in* TC^0 *for every rooted CQ* q *and DL-Lite*$_{\mathcal{F}}$ *TBox* $\mathcal{T}$.

4.2 MR Semantics

We begin the study of MR semantics by proving LogSpace-hardness for answering even very simple rooted CQs (in particular, instance queries), which emphasises the difference with SQL semantics. Since answering BCALC queries is in TC^0, this result says that such queries are unlikely to be MR-rewritable to BCALC.

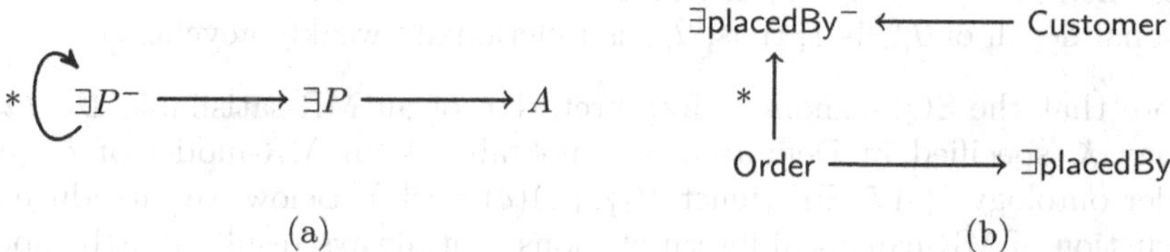

Fig. 1. The functional dependency graphs of TBoxes $\mathcal{T}$ and $\mathcal{T}'_{ex}$ from Example 4

Theorem 3. *There exist a rooted CQ of the form $A(a)$ with $A \in \mathbf{C}$ and $a \in \mathbf{I}$, and a DL-Lite$_\mathcal{F}$ TBox $\mathcal{T}$ such that* BagCert$_{\mathrm{MR}}[A(a), \mathcal{T}]$ *is* LogSpace*-hard.*

Proof (Sketch). The proof is by an AC^0 reduction from the 1GAP decision problem which is a prototypical complete problem for LogSpace (under AC^0 reductions) [17,20]. The input of 1GAP consists of a directed acyclic graph $H = (V, E)$ with nodes V and edges E such that each node has at most one outgoing edge, and two nodes s, t in V, and the question is whether t is reachable from s in H. For the reduction, we define a *DL-Lite*$^{\mathsf{b}}_\mathcal{F}$ ontology $(\mathcal{T}, \mathcal{A}_H)$ over atomic concept A and role P, where the *DL-Lite*$_\mathcal{F}$ TBox $\mathcal{T}$ comprises axioms $\exists P^- \sqsubseteq \exists P$, $(\mathsf{funct}\ P)$, and $\exists P^- \sqsubseteq A$, and $\mathcal{A}_H$ is the bag ABox defined as follows, for individuals a_v, for each $v \in V$, and $a_\star$:

$$\mathcal{A}_H(P(a_1, a_2)) = \begin{cases} 1, & \text{if } a_1 = a_v \text{ and } a_2 = a_u \text{ for } (v, u) \in E, \\ |V|, & \text{if } a_1 = a_\star \text{ and } a_2 = a_s, \\ 0, & \text{otherwise.} \end{cases}$$

Now t is reachable from s in H if and only if $q_{\mathrm{MR}}^{(\mathcal{T}, \mathcal{A}_H)}() \geq |V|$ for $q = A(a_t)$. □

Recalling that evaluation of BCALC queries is in TC^0, the previous theorem implies that even very simple rooted CQs are unlikely to be MR-rewritable to BCALC. Next we introduce a restriction on TBoxes which, as we will see, guarantees MR-rewritability. The restriction is based on the notions of *functional dependency graphs* and *functional weakly acyclic* TBoxes that respectively specialise the notions of dependency graphs and weak acyclicity defined for sets of tuple-generating dependencies in the context of data exchange [14].

Definition 9. *The* functional dependency graph $G_\mathcal{T}$ *of a DL-Lite$_\mathcal{F}$ $\mathcal{T}$ is the directed graph that has all the concepts appearing in $\mathcal{T}$ as nodes, a usual edge*

(C_1, C_2) for each $C_1 \sqsubseteq C_2$ in $\mathcal{T}$, and a special edge $(C_1, \exists R^-)^*$ for each $C_1 \sqsubseteq \exists R$ with (funct R) *in $\mathcal{T}$, where, for $P \in \mathbf{R}$, R^- is P if R is P^-. TBox $\mathcal{T}$ is* functionally weakly acyclic *if $G_\mathcal{T}$ has no cycle through a special edge. The* f-depth *of such a TBox $\mathcal{T}$ is the maximum number of special edges along a path in $G_\mathcal{T}$.*

Example 4. The functional dependency graphs of TBoxes $\mathcal{T}$ and $\mathcal{T}'_{ex}$ specified respectively in the proof of Theorem 3 and in Example 3 are depicted in Fig. 1. From the graph of Fig. 1a, we have that the functional depth of $\mathcal{T}$ is ∞; thus, $\mathcal{T}$ is not functionally weakly acyclic. From the graph of Fig. 1b, we have that the functional depth of $\mathcal{T}'_{ex}$ is 1; thus, $\mathcal{T}'_{ex}$ is functionally weakly acyclic. ◁

Note that the SQL-canonical interpretation of an MR-satisfiable *DL-Lite*$^\mathsf{b}_\mathcal{F}$ ontology $\mathcal{K}$ specified in Definition 8 is not always an MR-model of $\mathcal{K}$ (e.g., consider ontology $(\{A \sqsubseteq \exists P, (\mathsf{funct}\ P)\}, \{\!| A(e) : 2 |\!\})$). Below we introduce the construction of MR-canonical interpretations that always results in MR-models for MR-satisfiable ontologies, and start with the auxiliary notion of *closure*.

The *closure* $\mathcal{L}(\mathcal{K})$ of a *DL-Lite*$^\mathsf{b}_\mathcal{F}$ ontology $\mathcal{K} = (\mathcal{T}, \mathcal{A})$ is the union $\bigcup_{i \geq 0} \mathcal{L}^i(\mathcal{K})$ of bag interpretations $\mathcal{L}^i(\mathcal{K}) = (\Delta^{\mathcal{L}^i(\mathcal{K})}, \cdot^{\mathcal{L}^i(\mathcal{K})})$ with $\Delta^{\mathcal{L}^i(\mathcal{K})} = \mathbf{I}$ such that $\mathcal{L}^0(\mathcal{K}) = \mathcal{I}_\mathcal{A}$ and, for each $i \geq 1$, $\mathcal{L}^i(\mathcal{K})$ extends $\mathcal{L}^{i-1}(\mathcal{K})$ so that $a^{\mathcal{L}^i(\mathcal{K})} = a$ for all $a \in \mathbf{I}$, and, for all $A \in \mathbf{C}$, $P \in \mathbf{R}$, and $a, b, c, c' \in \mathbf{I}$,

$$A^{\mathcal{L}^i(\mathcal{K})}(a) = \mathsf{ccl}_\mathcal{T}[a, \mathcal{L}^{i-1}(\mathcal{K})](A),$$

$$P^{\mathcal{L}^i(\mathcal{K})}(a,b) = \begin{cases} 0, & \text{if } P^{\mathcal{L}^{i-1}(\mathcal{K})}(a,b) = 0, \\ \max\{\ell_P(a,b), \ell_{P^-}(b,a)\}, & \text{otherwise, where} \end{cases}$$

$$\ell_R(c,c') = \begin{cases} \mathsf{ccl}_\mathcal{T}[c, \mathcal{L}^{i-1}(\mathcal{K})](\exists R), & \text{if } (\mathsf{funct}\ R) \text{ is in } \mathcal{T}, \\ R^{\mathcal{L}^{i-1}(\mathcal{K})}(c,c'), & \text{otherwise.} \end{cases}$$

In fact, if the TBox of $\mathcal{K}$ is functionally weakly acyclic then the closure can be computed in a finite number of steps that does not depend on the ABox.

Proposition 2. *For every DL-Lite$^\mathsf{b}_\mathcal{F}$ ontology $\mathcal{K} = (\mathcal{T}, \mathcal{A})$ with a functionally weakly acyclic TBox $\mathcal{T}$ we have $\mathcal{L}(\mathcal{K}) = \bigcup_{i=0}^{d_\mathcal{T}+1} \mathcal{L}^i(\mathcal{K})$.*

The example below demonstrates the notion of closure.

Example 5. Consider the *DL-Lite*$^\mathsf{b}_\mathcal{F}$ ontology $\mathcal{K}'_{ex} = (\mathcal{T}'_{ex}, \mathcal{A}'_{ex})$ with $\mathcal{T}'_{ex}$ as in Example 3 and $\mathcal{A}'_{ex} = \{\!| \mathsf{Order}(o) : 3,\ \mathsf{placedBy}(o,c) : 1,\ \mathsf{Customer}(c) : 4 |\!\}$. Following the definition of closure on $\mathcal{K}'_{ex}$, we initialise $\mathcal{L}^0(\mathcal{K}'_{ex})$ to $\mathcal{I}_{\mathcal{A}'_{ex}}$ and then, for the next step we trivially have that $\mathsf{Order}^{\mathcal{L}^1(\mathcal{K}'_{ex})} = \mathsf{Order}^{\mathcal{I}_{\mathcal{A}'_{ex}}} = \{\!| o : 3 |\!\}$ and $\mathsf{Customer}^{\mathcal{L}^1(\mathcal{K}'_{ex})} = \mathsf{Customer}^{\mathcal{I}_{\mathcal{A}'_{ex}}} = \{\!| c : 4 |\!\}$ since both Order and Customer do not subsume any concept in $\mathcal{T}'_{ex}$. Then, it can be easily seen that $\mathsf{placedBy}^{\mathcal{L}^1(\mathcal{K}'_{ex})}$ includes only tuple (o, c) with a non-zero multiplicity expressed as the maximum of $\mathsf{ccl}_{\mathcal{T}'_{ex}}[o, \mathcal{L}^0(\mathcal{K}'_{ex})](\exists \mathsf{placedBy}) = 3$ and $\mathsf{placedBy}^{\mathcal{L}^0(\mathcal{K}'_{ex})}(o,c) = 1$; thus $\mathsf{placedBy}^{\mathcal{L}^1(\mathcal{K}'_{ex})} = \{\!| (o,c) : 3 |\!\}$. Since all axioms in $\mathcal{K}'_{ex}$ are now satisfied, we obtain that $\mathcal{L}^2(\mathcal{K}'_{ex}) = \mathcal{L}^1(\mathcal{K}'_{ex})$; thus $\mathcal{L}(\mathcal{K}'_{ex}) = \bigcup_{i=0}^{d_{\mathcal{T}'_{ex}}+1} \mathcal{L}^i(\mathcal{K}'_{ex}) = \mathcal{L}^2(\mathcal{K}'_{ex})$. ◁

We use the closure in the following definition of MR-canonical interpretations. Note the difference in handling functional and non-functional roles when creating anonymous elements, which always produces a most general possible interpretation in each case.

Definition 10. *The* MR-canonical bag interpretation $\mathcal{C}_{\mathrm{MR}}(\mathcal{K})$ *of a DL-Lite*$^{\mathsf{b}}_{\mathcal{F}}$ *ontology* $\mathcal{K} = (\mathcal{T}, \mathcal{A})$ *is the union* $\bigcup_{i\geq 0} \mathcal{C}^i_{\mathrm{MR}}(\mathcal{K})$ *such that* $\mathcal{C}^0_{\mathrm{MR}}(\mathcal{K}) = \mathcal{L}(\mathcal{K})$ *and, for each* $i \geq 1$, $\mathcal{C}^i_{\mathrm{MR}}(\mathcal{K})$ *is obtained from* $\mathcal{C}^{i-1}_{\mathrm{MR}}(\mathcal{K})$ *as follows:*

- $\Delta^{\mathcal{C}^i_{\mathrm{MR}}(\mathcal{K})}$ *extends* $\Delta^{\mathcal{C}^{i-1}_{\mathrm{MR}}(\mathcal{K})}$ *by*
  - *a* fresh anonymous *element* $w_{u,R}$ *for each* $u \in \Delta^{\mathcal{C}^{i-1}_{\mathrm{MR}}(\mathcal{K})}$ *and each role* R *with* $(\mathsf{funct}\ R) \in \mathcal{T}$, $\mathsf{ccl}_{\mathcal{T}}[u, \mathcal{C}^{i-1}_{\mathrm{MR}}(\mathcal{K})](\exists R) > 0$, *and* $(\exists R)^{\mathcal{C}^{i-1}_{\mathrm{MR}}(\mathcal{K})}(u) = 0$,
  - *fresh* anonymous *elements* $w^1_{u,R}, \ldots, w^\delta_{u,R}$ *for each* $u \in \Delta^{\mathcal{C}^{i-1}_{\mathrm{MR}}(\mathcal{K})}$ *and each role* R *with* $(\mathsf{funct}\ R) \notin \mathcal{T}$ *and* $\delta = \mathsf{ccl}_{\mathcal{T}}[u, \mathcal{C}^{i-1}_{\mathrm{MR}}(\mathcal{K})](\exists R) - (\exists R)^{\mathcal{C}^{i-1}_{\mathrm{MR}}(\mathcal{K})}(u)$;
- $a^{\mathcal{C}^i_{\mathrm{MR}}(\mathcal{K})} = a$ *for all* $a \in \mathbf{I}$, *and, for all* $A \in \mathbf{C}$, $P \in \mathbf{R}$, *and* u, v *in* $\Delta^{\mathcal{C}^i_{\mathrm{MR}}(\mathcal{K})}$,

$$A^{\mathcal{C}^i_{\mathrm{MR}}(\mathcal{K})}(u) = \begin{cases} \mathsf{ccl}_{\mathcal{T}}[u, \mathcal{C}^{i-1}_{\mathrm{MR}}(\mathcal{K})](A), & \text{if } u \in \Delta^{\mathcal{C}^{i-1}_{\mathrm{MR}}(\mathcal{K})}, \\ 0, & \text{otherwise}, \end{cases}$$

$$P^{\mathcal{C}^i_{\mathrm{MR}}(\mathcal{K})}(u,v) = \begin{cases} P^{\mathcal{C}^{i-1}_{\mathrm{MR}}(\mathcal{K})}(u,v), & \text{if } u, v \in \Delta^{\mathcal{C}^{i-1}_{\mathrm{MR}}(\mathcal{K})}, \\ \mathsf{ccl}_{\mathcal{T}}[u, \mathcal{C}^{i-1}_{\mathrm{MR}}(\mathcal{K})](\exists P), & \text{if } u \in \Delta^{\mathcal{C}^{i-1}_{\mathrm{MR}}(\mathcal{K})} \text{ and } v = w_{u,P}, \\ \mathsf{ccl}_{\mathcal{T}}[v, \mathcal{C}^{i-1}_{\mathrm{MR}}(\mathcal{K})](\exists P^-), & \text{if } v \in \Delta^{\mathcal{C}^{i-1}_{\mathrm{MR}}(\mathcal{K})} \text{ and } u = w_{v,P^-}, \\ 1, & \text{if } v = w^j_{u,P} \text{ or } u = w^j_{v,P^-}, \\ 0, & \text{otherwise}. \end{cases}$$

MR-canonical bag interpretations are illustrated in the following example.

Example 6. Consider the functionally weakly acyclic ontology $\mathcal{K}'_{ex} = (\mathcal{T}'_{ex}, \mathcal{A}'_{ex})$ and its closure $\mathcal{L}(\mathcal{K}'_{ex})$ specified in Example 5. Following Definition 10, the MR-canonical interpretation $\mathcal{C}_{\mathrm{MR}}(\mathcal{K}'_{ex})$ is constructed on the basis of $\mathcal{L}(\mathcal{K}'_{ex})$ by first setting $\mathcal{C}^0_{\mathrm{MR}}(\mathcal{K}'_{ex}) = \mathcal{L}(\mathcal{K}'_{ex})$. Then, for the next step we set

$$\mathsf{Order}^{\mathcal{C}^1_{\mathrm{MR}}(\mathcal{K}'_{ex})} = \mathsf{Order}^{\mathcal{C}^0_{\mathrm{MR}}(\mathcal{K}'_{ex})} \text{ and } \mathsf{Customer}^{\mathcal{C}^1_{\mathrm{MR}}(\mathcal{K}'_{ex})} = \mathsf{Customer}^{\mathcal{C}^0_{\mathrm{MR}}(\mathcal{K}'_{ex})}$$

as neither Order nor $\mathsf{Customer}$ subsumes any concept in $\mathcal{T}'_{ex}$, and set $\mathsf{placedBy}^{\mathcal{C}^1_{\mathrm{MR}}(\mathcal{K}'_{ex})} = \{\!|\, (o,c) : 3, (w^1_{c,\exists\mathsf{placedBy}^-}, c) : 1 \,|\!\}$. The latter follows by the fact that o has already a $\mathsf{placedBy}$-successor in $\mathcal{C}^0_{\mathrm{MR}}(\mathcal{K})$ while at the same time the multiplicity of c in the extension of $\exists\mathsf{placedBy}^-$ under $\mathcal{C}^1_{\mathrm{MR}}(\mathcal{K})$ must be increased by 1 so that inclusion $\mathsf{Customer} \sqsubseteq \exists\mathsf{placedBy}^-$ is satisfied; since $(\mathsf{funct}\ \mathsf{placedBy}^-)$ is not in $\mathcal{T}_{ex}$, this must be done by introducing a fresh anonymous element $w^1_{c,\exists\mathsf{placedBy}^-}$ to the domain of $\mathcal{C}^1_{\mathrm{MR}}(\mathcal{K})$ and making it a $\exists\mathsf{placedBy}^-$-successor of c. All axioms are satisfied in $\mathcal{C}^1_{\mathrm{MR}}(\mathcal{K}'_{ex})$, and hence $\mathcal{C}_{\mathrm{MR}}(\mathcal{K}'_{ex}) = \mathcal{C}^1_{\mathrm{MR}}(\mathcal{K}'_{ex})$. ◁

As the following theorem says, the MR-canonical bag interpretation is an MR-universal model, as desired.

Theorem 4. *The* MR*-canonical bag interpretation* $\mathcal{C}_{\text{MR}}(\mathcal{K})$ *of an* MR*-satisfiable DL-Lite*$^{\mathsf{b}}_{\mathcal{F}}$ *ontology* $\mathcal{K} = (\mathcal{T}, \mathcal{A})$ *with* $\mathcal{T}$ *functionally weakly acyclic is an* MR*-universal model for the class of rooted CQs.*

Example 7. Consider ontology $\mathcal{K}'_{ex}$ and its MR-canonical interpretation $\mathcal{C}_{\text{MR}}(\mathcal{K}'_{ex})$ as in Example 6. Consider also rooted CQs $q_1(x) = \exists y.\, \mathsf{placedBy}(x, y)$ and $q_2(x) = \exists y.\, \mathsf{placedBy}(y, x)$. It is straightforward to verify that the MR-bag certain answers to q_1 and q_2 over $\mathcal{K}'_{ex}$ are respectively given by bags $q_1{}^{\mathcal{K}'_{ex}}_{\text{MR}} = \{\!| o : 3 |\!\}$ and $q_2{}^{\mathcal{K}'_{ex}}_{\text{MR}} = \{\!| c : 4 |\!\}$, and that these bags coincide with the bag answers to q_1 and q_2 over $\mathcal{C}_{\text{MR}}(\mathcal{K}'_{ex})$, respectively. This supports our expectation that $\mathcal{C}_{\text{MR}}(\mathcal{K}'_{ex})$ is an MR-universal model of $\mathcal{K}'_{ex}$ for the class of rooted CQs. $\triangleleft$

By adapting and extending the techniques in [31], we establish that rooted CQs are MR-rewritable to BCALC over the restricted ontology language.

Theorem 5. *Rooted CQs are* MR*-rewritable to BCALC over DL-Lite*$^{\mathsf{b}}_{\mathcal{F}}$ *with functionally weakly acyclic TBoxes.*

Hence, under the restrictions, query answering is indeed feasible in TC^0.

Corollary 3. *Problem* $\text{BagCert}_{\text{MR}}[q, \mathcal{T}]$ *is in* TC^0 *for every rooted CQ* q *and functionally weakly acyclic DL-Lite*$_{\mathcal{F}}$ *TBox* $\mathcal{T}$.

5 Related Work

Jiang [19] was the first to propose a bag semantics for the DL $\mathcal{ALC}$, which is however incompatible with SQL and incomparable to the semantics developed in this work. Motivated by the semantic differences arising between the set-based theory and bag-based practice of OBDA and data exchange settings, Nikolaou et al. [30,31] as well as Hernich and Kolaitis [16] studied respectively the foundations of OBDA and data exchange settings under a bag semantics compatible with SQL. To the best of our knowledge, our work, which builds on [30,31], is the first one to study the interaction of functionality and inclusion axioms under a bag semantics. A bag semantics for functional dependencies, which generalises our SQL semantics, has been studied before by Köhler and Link [22] who, however, studied only schema design issues. Owing to the aforementioned works and the work by Console et al. [13], there is now a better understanding of CQ answering under bag semantics for frameworks managing incomplete information. This latter problem is closely related to answering queries using aggregate functions the semantics of which has been studied before in the context of inconsistent databases [3], data exchange [2], and *DL-Lite* [11,23], where the resulting frameworks do not treat bags as first-class citizens. Handling bags through sets was also the approach followed in the 90's by Mumick et al. [29] for supporting bags in Datalog and recently by Bertossi et al. [5] for Datalog$^{\pm}$.

6 Conclusions and Future Work

In this paper, we studied two bag semantics for functionality axioms: our first SQL semantics follows the bag semantics of SQL for primary keys, while the second MR semantics is more general and gives more modelling freedom. Combining the semantics with the bag semantics of *DL-Lite*$_{core}$ of [30,31], we studied the problems of satisfiability, query answering, and rewritability for the resulting logical language *DL-Lite*$^{b}_{\mathcal{F}}$. It is interesting to see how our work generalises to the case of n-ary predicates. This case has been studied only recently in the context of data exchange settings [16] and Datalog$^{\pm}$ [5], which, however, do not consider functional dependencies. We also anticipate our work will be useful for laying the foundations of aggregate queries in SPARQL under entailment regimes [21].

Acknowledgements. This research was supported by the SIRIUS Centre for Scalable Data Access and the EPSRC projects DBOnto, MaSI[3], and ED[3].

References

1. Abiteboul, S., Hull, R., Vianu, V.: Foundations of Databases. Addison-Wesley (1995)
2. Afrati, F.N., Kolaitis, P.G.: Answering aggregate queries in data exchange. In: Proceedings of PODS, pp. 129–138 (2008)
3. Arenas, M., Bertossi, L.E., Chomicki, J., He, X., Raghavan, V., Spinrad, J.P.: Scalar aggregation in inconsistent databases. Theor. Comput. Sci. **296**(3), 405–434 (2003)
4. Artale, A., Calvanese, D., Kontchakov, R., Zakharyaschev, M.: The DL-Lite family and relations. J. Artif. Intell. Res. **36**, 1–69 (2009)
5. Bertossi, L.E., Gottlob, G., Pichler, R.: Datalog: bag semantics via set semantics. In: Proceedings of ICDT, pp. 16:1–16:19 (2019)
6. Bienvenu, M., Lutz, C., Wolter, F.: Query containment in description logics reconsidered. In: Proceedings of KR, pp. 221–231 (2012)
7. Calvanese, D., et al.: Ontop: answering SPARQL queries over relational databases. Semant. Web **8**(3), 471–487 (2017)
8. Calvanese, D., De Giacomo, G., Lembo, D., Lenzerini, M., Rosati, R.: Tractable reasoning and efficient query answering in description logics: the DL-Lite family. J. Autom. Reason. **39**(3), 385–429 (2007)
9. Calvanese, D., De Giacomo, G., Lembo, D., Lenzerini, M., Rosati, R.: Path-based identification constraints in description logics. In: Proceedings of KR, pp. 231–241 (2008)
10. Calvanese, D., De Giacomo, G., Lenzerini, M.: Identification constraints and functional dependencies in description logics. In: Proceedings of IJCAI, pp. 155–160 (2001)
11. Calvanese, D., Kharlamov, E., Nutt, W., Thorne, C.: Aggregate queries over ontologies. In: Proceedings of ONISW, pp. 97–104 (2008)
12. Chaudhuri, S., Vardi, M.Y.: Optimization of real conjunctive queries. In: Proceedings of PODS, pp. 59–70 (1993)
13. Console, M., Guagliardo, P., Libkin, L.: On querying incomplete information in databases under bag semantics. In: Proceedings of IJCAI, pp. 993–999 (2017)

14. Fagin, R., Kolaitis, P.G., Miller, R.J., Popa, L.: Data exchange: semantics and query answering. Theor. Comput. Sci. **336**(1), 89–124 (2005)
15. Grumbach, S., Milo, T.: Towards tractable algebras for bags. J. Comput. Syst. Sci. **52**(3), 570–588 (1996)
16. Hernich, A., Kolaitis, P.G.: Foundations of information integration under bag semantics. In: Proceedings of LICS, pp. 1–12 (2017)
17. Immerman, N.: Languages that capture complexity classes. SIAM J. Comput. **16**(4), 760–778 (1987)
18. Ioannidis, Y.E., Ramakrishnan, R.: Containment of conjunctive queries: beyond relations as sets. ACM Trans. Database Syst. **20**(3), 288–324 (1995)
19. Jiang, Y.: Description logics over multisets. In: Proceedings of the 6th International Workshop on Uncertainty Reasoning for the Semantic Web, pp. 1–12 (2010)
20. Jones, N.D.: Space-bounded reducibility among combinatorial problems. J. Comput. Syst. Sci. **11**(1), 68–85 (1975)
21. Kaminski, M., Kostylev, E.V., Cuenca Grau, B.: Query nesting, assignment, and aggregation in SPARQL 1.1. ACM Trans. Database Syst. **42**(3), 17:1–17:46 (2017)
22. Köhler, H., Link, S.: Armstrong axioms and Boyce-Codd-Heath normal form under bag semantics. Inf. Process. Lett. **110**(16), 717–724 (2010)
23. Kostylev, E.V., Reutter, J.L.: Complexity of answering counting aggregate queries over DL-Lite. Web Semant. **33**, 94–111 (2015)
24. Lenzerini, M.: Data integration: a theoretical perspective. In: Proceedings of PODS, pp. 233–246 (2002)
25. Libkin, L.: Expressive power of SQL. Theor. Comput. Sci. **296**(3), 379–404 (2003)
26. Libkin, L., Wong, L.: Query languages for bags and aggregate functions. J. Comput. Syst. Sci. **55**(2), 241–272 (1997)
27. Lutz, C., Areces, C., Horrocks, I., Sattler, U.: Keys, nominals, and concrete domains. J. Artif. Intell. Res. **23**, 667–726 (2005)
28. Motik, B., Cuenca Grau, B., Horrocks, I., Wu, Z., Fokoue, A., Lutz, C.: OWL 2 Web Ontology Language Profiles (Second Edition). W3C recommendation, W3C (2012). http://www.w3.org/TR/owl2-profiles/
29. Mumick, I.S., Pirahesh, H., Ramakrishnan, R.: The magic of duplicates and aggregates. In: Proceedings of VLDB, pp. 264–277 (1990)
30. Nikolaou, C., Kostylev, E.V., Konstantinidis, G., Kaminski, M., Cuenca Grau, B., Horrocks, I.: The bag semantics of ontology-based data access. In: Proceedings of IJCAI, pp. 1224–1230 (2017)
31. Nikolaou, C., Kostylev, E.V., Konstantinidis, G., Kaminski, M., Cuenca Grau, B., Horrocks, I.: Foundations of ontology-based data access under bag semantics. Artif. Intell. **274**, 91–132 (2019)
32. Poggi, A., Lembo, D., Calvanese, D., De Giacomo, G., Lenzerini, M., Rosati, R.: Linking data to ontologies. J. Data Semant. **10**, 133–173 (2008)
33. Toman, D., Weddell, G.E.: On keys and functional dependencies as first-class citizens in description logics. J. Autom. Reason. **40**(2–3), 117–132 (2008)

Validating SHACL Constraints over a SPARQL Endpoint

Julien Corman[1(✉)], Fernando Florenzano[2], Juan L. Reutter[2], and Ognjen Savković[1]

[1] Free University of Bozen-Bolzano, Bolzano, Italy
corman@inf.unibz.it

[2] PUC Chile and IMFD, Santiago, Chile

Abstract. SHACL (Shapes Constraint Language) is a specification for describing and validating RDF graphs that has recently become a W3C recommendation. While the language is gaining traction in the industry, algorithms for SHACL constraint validation are still at an early stage. A first challenge comes from the fact that RDF graphs are often exposed as SPARQL endpoints, and therefore only accessible via queries. Another difficulty is the absence of guidelines about the way recursive constraints should be handled. In this paper, we provide algorithms for validating a graph against a SHACL schema, which can be executed over a SPARQL endpoint. We first investigate the possibility of validating a graph through a single query for non-recursive constraints. Then for the recursive case, since the problem has been shown to be NP-hard, we propose a strategy that consists in evaluating a small number of SPARQL queries over the endpoint, and using the answers to build a set of propositional formulas that are passed to a SAT solver. Finally, we show that the process can be optimized when dealing with recursive but tractable fragments of SHACL, without the need for an external solver. We also present a proof-of-concept evaluation of this last approach.

1 Introduction

SHACL (for SHApes Constraint Language),[1] is an expressive constraint language for RDF graph, which has become a W3C recommendation in 2017. A SHACL *schema* is a set of so-called *shapes*, to which some nodes in the graph must conform. Figure 1 presents two simple SHACL shapes. The left one, called `:MovieShape`, is meant to define movies in DBPedia. The triple `:MovieShape sh:targetClass dbo:Film` is the *target definition* of this shape, and specifies that all instances of the class `dbo:Film` must conform to this shape. These are called the *target nodes* of a shape. The next triples specify the constraints that must be satisfied by such nodes, namely that they must have an Imdb identifier, and that their directors (i.e. their `dbo:director`-successors in the graph), if any, must conform to the shape `:DirectorShape`. The rightmost shape, called `:DirectorShape`,

[1] https://www.w3.org/TR/shacl/.

C. Ghidini et al. (Eds.): ISWC 2019, LNCS 11778, pp. 145–163, 2019.
https://doi.org/10.1007/978-3-030-30793-6_9

```
:MovieShape                              :DirectorShape
  a sh:NodeShape ;                         a sh:NodeShape ;
  sh:targetClass dbo:Film ;                sh:property [
  sh:property [                              sh:path dbo:birthDate;
    sh:path dbo:imdbId ;                     sh:minCount 1 ;
    sh:minCount 1 ] ;                        sh:maxCount 1 ];
  sh:property [                            sh:property [
    sh:path dbo:director ;                   sh:inversePath dbo:director ;
    sh:node :DirectorShape ] .               sh:node :MovieShape ] .
```

Fig. 1. Two SHACL shapes, about movies and directors

```
:PulpFiction a dbo:Film .
:PulpFiction dbo:imdbId 24451 .
:PulpFiction dbo:director :QuentinTarantino .
:QuentinTarantino dbo:birthDate "1963-03-27" .
-----------------------------------------------
:Brazil a dbo:Film .
:Brazil dbo:imdbId 15047 .
:Brazil dbo:director :TerryGilliam .
-----------------------------------------------
:CitizenKane dbo:director :OrsonWelles .
```

Fig. 2. Three RDF graphs, respectively valid, invalid and valid against the shapes of Fig. 1

is meant to define movie directors in DBPedia. It does not have a target definition (therefore no target node either), and states that a director must have exactly one birth date, and can only direct movies that conform to the shape `:MovieShape`.

The possibility for a shape to refer to another (like `MovieShape` refers to `:DirectorShape` for instance), or to itself, is a key feature of SHACL. This allows designing schemas in a modular fashion, but also reusing existing shapes in a new schema, thus favoring semantic interoperability.

The SHACL specification provides a semantics for *graph validation*, i.e. what it means for a graph to conform to a set of shapes: a graph is *valid* against a set of shapes if each target node of each shape satisfies the constraints associated to it. If these constraints contain shape references, then the propagated constraints (to neighbors, neighbors of neighbors, etc.) must be satisfied as well.

Unfortunately, the SHACL specification leaves explicitly undefined the semantics of validation for schemas with circular references (called *recursive* below), such as the one of Fig. 1, where `:MovieShape` and `:DirectorShape` refer to each other. Such schemas can be expected to appear in practice though, either by design (e.g. to characterize relations between events, or a structure of unbounded size, such as a tree), or as a simple side-effect of the growth of the number of shapes (like an object-oriented program may have cyclic references as its number of classes grows). A semantics for graph validation against possibly recursive shapes was later proposed in [10] (for the so-called "core constraint components" of the SHACL specification). It complies with the specification in the non-recursive case. Based on to this semantics, the first graph in Fig. 2 is valid against the shapes of Fig. 1. The second graph is not, because the director misses a birth date. The third graph is trivially valid, since there is no target node to initiate validation.

Negation is another important feature of the SHACL specification (allowing for instance to state that a node cannot conform to two given shapes at the same time, or to express functionality, like "exactly one birth date" in Fig. 1). But as shown in [10], the interplay between recursion and negation makes the graph validation problem significantly more complex (NP-hard in the size of the graph, for stratified constraints already).

As SHACL is gaining traction, more validation engines become available.[2] However, guidance about the way graph validation may be implemented is still lacking. In particular, to our knowledge, existing implementations deal with recursive schemas in their own terms, without a principled approach to handle the interplay between recursion and negation.

Another key aspect of graph validation is the way the data can be accessed. RDF graphs are generally exposed as SPARQL endpoints, i.e. primarily (and sometimes exclusively) accessible via SPARQL queries. This is often the case for large graphs that may not fit into memory, exposed via triple stores. Therefore an important feature of a SHACL validation engine is the possibility to check conformance of a graph by issuing SPARQL queries over it. This may also be needed when integrating several data sources not meant to be materialized together, or simply to test conformance of data that one does not own.

Several engines can already perform validation via SPARQL queries for fragments of SHACL but, to our knowledge, not in the presence of recursive constraints.[3] This should not come as a surprise: as will be shown in this article, recursive shapes go beyond the expressive power of SPARQL, making validation via SPARQL queries significantly more involved: if the schema is recursive, it is not possible in general to retrieve target nodes violating a given shape by issuing a single SPARQL query. This means that some extra computation (in addition to SPARQL query evaluation) needs to be performed, in memory.

This article provides a theoretical and empirical investigation of graph validation against (possibly recursive) SHACL schemas, when the graph is only accessible via SPARQL queries, and based on the semantics defined in [10]. First, we show that validation can be performed via SPARQL queries only (without extra computation) if the schema is non-recursive, and that some recursive fragments can (in theory) be handled this way if one extends SPARQL with fixed-point iteration. We also show that this strategy cannot be applied for arbitrary SHACL schemas.

Therefore we investigate a second strategy, allowing some in-memory computation, while still accessing the endpoint via queries only. Because the validation problem is NP-hard (in the size of the graph) for the full language, we first define

---

[2] https://w3c.github.io/data-shapes/data-shapes-test-suite/.

[3] with the exception of *Shaclex* [4], which can handle recursion, but not recursion and negation together in a principled way.

a robust validation approach, that evaluates a limited number of queries over the endpoint, and reduces validation to satisfiability of a propositional formula, potentially leveraging the mature optimization techniques of SAT solvers. We then focus on recursive but tractable fragments of SHACL. For these, we devise an efficient algorithm that relies on the same queries as previously, but performs all the necessary inference on the fly. Finally, we describe a proof-of-concept evaluation of this last approach, performed by validating DBPedia against different schemas, and, for the non-recursive ones, comparing its performance with full delegation to the endpoint.

Organization. Section 2 introduces preliminary notions and Sect. 3 presents the graph validation problem. Section 4 studies the usage of a single query, whereas Sects. 5 and 6 focus on the strategy with in-memory computation, first for the full language, and then for recursive but tractable fragments. Section 7 provides empirical results for this algorithm and full delegation, while Sects. 8 and 9 discuss related work and perspectives. Due to space limitations, proofs of propositions are provided in the extended version of this paper, available at [2].

2 Preliminaries

We assume familiarity with RDF and SPARQL. We abstract away from the concrete RDF syntax though, representing an RDF graph $\mathcal{G}$ as a labeled oriented graph $\mathcal{G} = \langle V_\mathcal{G}, E_\mathcal{G} \rangle$, where $V_\mathcal{G}$ is the set of nodes of $\mathcal{G}$, and $E_\mathcal{G}$ is a set of triples of the from (v_1, p, v_2), meaning that there is an edge in $\mathcal{G}$ from v_1 to v_2 labeled with property p. We make this simplification for readability, since distinctions such as RDF term types are irrelevant for the content of this paper.

We use $[\![Q]\!]^\mathcal{G}$ to denote the evaluation of a SPARQL query Q over an RDF graph $\mathcal{G}$. As usual, this evaluation is given as a set of *solution mappings*, each of which maps variables of Q to nodes of $\mathcal{G}$. All solution mappings considered in this article are *total* functions over the variables projected by Q. We use $\{?x_1 \mapsto v_1, \dots, ?x_n \mapsto v_n\}$ to denote the solution mapping that maps $?x_i$ to v_i for $i \in [1..n]$. However, if Q is a *unary* query (i.e. if it projects only one variable), we may also represent $[\![Q]\!]^\mathcal{G} = \{\{?x \mapsto v_1\}, .., \{?x \mapsto v_m\}\}$ as the set of nodes $\{v_1, .., v_m\}$.

SHACL. This article follows the abstract syntax for SHACL core constraint components introduced in [10]. In the following, we review this syntax and the associated semantics for graph validation.

A *shape schema* $\mathcal{S}$ is represented as a triple $\langle S, \text{targ}, \text{def} \rangle$, where S is a set of *shape names*, targ is a function that assigns a *target query* to each $s \in S$, and def is a function that assigns a *constraint* to each $s \in S$.

For each $s \in S$, $\text{targ}(s)$ is a unary query, which can be evaluated over the graph under validation in order to retrieve the *target nodes* of s. The SHACL specification only allows target queries with a limited expressivity, but for the purpose of this article, $\text{targ}(s)$ can be assumed to be an arbitrary unary SPARQL query. If a shape has no target definition (like the shape `:DirectorShape` in

Table 1. Evaluation of constraint ϕ at node v in graph $\mathcal{G}$ given total assignment σ. We use $(v, v') \in [\![r]\!]^{\mathcal{G}}$ to say that v and v' are connected via SHACL path r.

$$
\begin{aligned}
[\top]^{\mathcal{G},v,\sigma} &= 1\\
[\neg\phi]^{\mathcal{G},v,\sigma} &= 1 - [\phi]^{\mathcal{G},v,\sigma}\\
[\phi_1 \wedge \phi_2]^{\mathcal{G},v,\sigma} &= \min\{[\phi_1]^{\mathcal{G},v,\sigma}, [\phi_2]^{\mathcal{G},v,\sigma}\}\\
[\mathrm{EQ}(r_1, r_2)]^{\mathcal{G},v,\sigma} &= 1 \text{ iff } \{v' \mid (v,v') \in [\![r_1]\!]^{\mathcal{G}}\} = \{v' \mid (v,v') \in [\![r_2]\!]^{\mathcal{G}}\}\\
[I]^{\mathcal{G},v,\sigma} &= 1 \text{ iff } v \text{ is the IRI I}\\
[s]^{\mathcal{G},v,\sigma} &= 1 \text{ iff } s(v) \in \sigma\\
[\geq_n r.\phi]^{\mathcal{G},v,\sigma} &= 1 \text{ iff } |\{v' \mid (v,v') \in [\![r]\!]^{\mathcal{G}} \text{ and } [\phi]^{\mathcal{G},v',\sigma} = 1\}| \geq n
\end{aligned}
$$

Fig. 1), we use an arbitrary empty SPARQL query (i.e. with no answer, in any graph), denoted with $\bot$.

The constraint def(s) for shape s is represented as a formula ϕ verifying the following grammar:

$$\phi \quad ::= \quad \top \mid s \mid I \mid \phi \wedge \phi \mid \neg\phi \mid \ \geq_n r.\phi \mid \mathrm{EQ}(r_1, r_2)$$

where s is a shape name, I is an IRI,[4] r is a SHACL path[5], and $n \in \mathbb{N}^+$. As syntactic sugar, we use $\phi_1 \vee \phi_2$ for $\neg(\neg\phi_1 \wedge \neg\phi_2)$, $\leq_n r.\phi$ for $\neg(\geq_{n+1} r.\phi)$, and $=_n r.\phi$ for $(\geq_n r.\phi) \wedge (\leq_n r.\phi)$. A translation from SHACL core constraint components to this grammar and conversely can be found in [11].

Example 1. The shapes of Fig. 1 are abstractly represented as follows:

targ(`:MovieShape`) = `SELECT ?x WHERE {?x a dbo:Film}`
targ(`:DirectorShape`) $= \bot$
def(`:MovieShape`) = $(\geq_1$ `dbo:imdbId.`$\top) \wedge (\leq_0$ `dbo:director.`$\neg$`:DirectorShape`)
def(`:DirectorShape`) = $(=_1$ `dbo:birthDate.`$\top) \wedge (\leq_0$ `dbo:director.`$\neg$`:MovieShape`)

The *dependency graph* of a schema $\mathcal{S} = \langle S, \text{targ}, \text{def}\rangle$ is a graph whose nodes are S, and such that there is an edge from s_1 to s_2 iff s_2 appears in def(s_1). This edge is called negative if such reference is in the scope of at least one negation, and positive otherwise. A schema is *recursive* if its dependency graph contains a cycle, and *stratified* if the dependency graph does not contain a cycle with at least one negative edge. In Example 1, we see that shapes are recursive, since `:MovieShape` references `:DirectorShape` and vice-versa. Since this reference is in the scope of a negation, the schema is not stratified.

Semantics. Since the semantics for recursive schemas is left undefined in the SHACL specification, we use the framework proposed in [10]. The evaluation of a

4 More exactly, I is an abstraction, standing for any syntactic constraint over an RDF term: exact value, datatype, regex, etc.

5 SHACL paths are built like SPARQL property paths, but without the *NegatedPropertySet* operator.

formula is defined with respect to a given assignment, i.e. intuitively a labeling of the nodes of the graph with sets of shape names.

Formally, an *assignment* σ for a graph $\mathcal{G}$ and a schema $\mathcal{S} = \langle S, \text{targ}, \text{def}\rangle$ can be represented as a set of atoms of the form $s(v)$ or $\neg s(v)$, with $s \in S$ and $v \in V_{\mathcal{G}}$, that does not contain both $s(v)$ and $\neg s(v)$ for any $s \in S$ or $v \in V_{\mathcal{G}}$. An assignment σ is *total* if for every $s \in S$ and $v \in V_{\mathcal{G}}$, one of $s(v)$ or $\neg s(v)$ belongs to σ. Otherwise (if there are s, v such that neither $s(v)$ not $\neg s(v)$ belong to σ), the assignment is *partial*.

The semantics of a constraint ϕ is given in terms of a function $[\phi]^{\mathcal{G},v,\sigma}$, for a graph $\mathcal{G}$, node v and assignment σ. This function evaluates whether v satisfies ϕ given σ. This semantics depends on which type of assignments is considered. If we only consider *total* assignments, then $[\phi]^{\mathcal{G},v,\sigma}$ is always true or false, and its semantics is defined in Table 1.

We remark that [10] provides a semantics in terms of *partial* assignments. In this case, the inductive evaluation of $[\phi]^{\mathcal{G},v,\sigma}$ is based on Kleene's 3-valued logic. We omit this definition for simplicity, since it is not required in this article, and refer to [10] instead.

3 Validation and Tractable Fragments of SHACL

In this section, we define what it means for a graph to be valid against a schema. Then we identify tractable fragments of SHACL (including some recursive ones) for which we will introduce either a full SPARQL rewriting (in Sect. 4) or a validation algorithm (in Sect. 6).

Validation Problem. A graph $\mathcal{G}$ satisfies a schema $\mathcal{S}$ if there is a way to assign shapes names to nodes of $\mathcal{G}$ such that all targets and constraints in $\mathcal{S}$ are satisfied. For instance, in Fig. 2 (first graph), one may assign shape `:MovieShape` to node `:PulpFiction`, and shape `:DirectorShape` to node `:QuentinTarantino` while satisfying all targets and constraints. Since we consider two kinds of assignments (total and partial), we also define two types of validation.

Definition 1. *A graph $\mathcal{G}$ is* valid *against a shape schema $\mathcal{S} = \langle S, \text{targ}, \text{def}\rangle$ with respect to total (resp. partial) assignments iff there is a total (resp. partial) assignment σ for $\mathcal{G}$ and $\mathcal{S}$ that verifies the following, for each shape name $s \in S$:*

- *$s(v) \in \sigma$ for each node v in $[\![\text{targ}(s)]\!]^{\mathcal{G}}$, and*
- *if $s(v) \in \sigma$, then $[\text{def}(s)]^{\mathcal{G},v,\sigma} = 1$, and if $\neg s(v) \in \sigma$, then $[\text{def}(s)]^{\mathcal{G},v,\sigma} = 0$.*

The first condition ensures that all targets of a shape are assigned this shape, and the second condition that the assignment is consistent w.r.t. shape constraints.

We note that a total assignment is a specific case of partial assignment. So if $\mathcal{G}$ is valid against $\mathcal{S}$ with respect to total assignments, it is also valid with respect to partial assignments. The converse does not necessarily hold though. But as we see below, it holds for all the tractable fragments considered in this paper. We use this property several times in the following sections.

Table 2. Data complexity of the validation problem.

	$\mathcal{L}^{\text{non-rec}}$	$\mathcal{L}_{\vee}^{+}$	$\mathcal{L}^{s}$	full SHACL
Complexity of VALIDATION	NL-c	PTIME-c	PTIME-c	NP-c

Tractable Fragments of SHACL. As is usual in the database literature, we measure complexity in the size of the graph only (*data complexity*), and not of the schema, given that the size of the graph is likely to grow much faster. The Validation problem then asks, given a graph $\mathcal{G}$ and a fixed schema $\mathcal{S}$, whether $\mathcal{G}$ is valid against $\mathcal{S}$ with respect to total assignments. We also define the Partial-Validation problem, by focusing instead on partial assignments. Unfortunately, both problems have been shown to be NP-complete in [10] for full SHACL.

Two tractable recursive fragments of SHACL were identified in [10] and [12] though. The first fragment simply disallows negated constraints, and allows disjunction ($\vee$) as a native operator. We call this fragment $\mathcal{L}_{\vee}^{+}$ below. The second fragment allows all operators, but restricts interplay between recursion and negation. Due to the lack of space, we refer to [12] for a formal definition. We call this fragment $\mathcal{L}^{s}$ below. Finally, we also consider non-recursive shapes, the only fragment whose semantics is fully described by the SHACL specification. We call this fragment $\mathcal{L}^{\text{non-rec}}$ below. All these fragments share a property that is key for the correctness of our validation algorithms:

Proposition 1. *The Validation and Partial-Validation problems coincide for* $\mathcal{L}_{\vee}^{+}$, $\mathcal{L}^{s}$ *and* $\mathcal{L}^{\text{non-rec}}$ *schemas.*

Complexity. Table 2 summarizes data complexity for full SHACL and all three fragments. All results are new (to our knowledge), aside from the one for full SHACL, borrowed from [10]. Proofs are provided in the online appendix.

Such complexity results do not guarantee that efficient algorithms for the tractable fragments can be found though. Moreover, none of the results considers validation over an endpoint. One can nonetheless use these bounds as a guideline, to devise validation procedures for each fragment. In particular, the NP upper bound for the general case suggests that one can take advantage of existing tools optimized for NP-complete problems. And it can indeed be shown that each of the algorithms below is worst-case optimal for the fragments that it addresses.

4 Validation via a Single Query for Non-recursive SHACL

In this section, we address the question of whether validation can be performed by evaluating a single SPARQL query. To state our results, we say that a schema $\mathcal{S}$ can be *expressed* in SPARQL if there is a SPARQL query $q_{\mathcal{S}}$ such that, for every graph $\mathcal{G}$, it holds that $[\![q_{\mathcal{S}}]\!]^{\mathcal{G}} = \emptyset$ iff $\mathcal{G}$ is valid against $\mathcal{S}$.

We start with negative results. As shown above, validation for full SHACL is NP-hard in data complexity, whereas SPARQL query evaluation is tractable, which immediately suggests that the former cannot be reduced to the latter. We provide a stronger claim, namely that inexpressibility still holds for much milder classes of schemas, and without complexity assumptions.

Proposition 2. *There is a schema that is in both $L^+_\vee$ and $\mathcal{L}^s$, and cannot be expressed in* SPARQL

On the positive side, one can express non-recursive SHACL schemas in SPARQL:

Proposition 3. *Every schema in $\mathcal{L}^{non\text{-}rec}$ can be expressed in* SPARQL

We provide the main intuition behind this observation (the full construction can be found in appendix). Given a non-recursive shape schema $\mathcal{S} = \langle S, \text{targ}, \text{def}\rangle$, it is possible to associate to each shape $s \in S$ a SPARQL query that retrieves the target nodes of s violating the constraints for s. The query is of the form:

SELECT ?x WHERE { $\mathcal{T}(\text{targ}(s), ?\text{x})$ FILTER NOT EXISTS { $\mathcal{C}(\text{def}(s), ?\text{x})$ } }

where $\mathcal{T}(\text{targ}(s), ?\text{x})$ is a BGP identical to targ(s) (with target nodes bound to variable ?x), and $\mathcal{C}(\text{def}(s), ?\text{x})$ is a BGP retrieving all nodes verifying def(s) (again bound to variable ?x), defined by induction on the structure of def(s). Then the query $q_\mathcal{S}$ above is defined as the union of all such queries (one for each $s \in S$) so that $[\![q_\mathcal{S}]\!]^\mathcal{G} = \emptyset$ iff $\mathcal{G}$ is valid.

Example 2. As a simple example, consider the schema from Fig. 1, To make it non-recursive, the triples `sh:property [ sh:inversePath dbo:director ; sh:Node :MovieShape ]` can be dropped from shape `:DirectorShape`. Then we get:

$\mathcal{T}$(targ(`:MovieShape`), ?x) = `{?x a dbo:Film}`

$\mathcal{C}$(def(`:MovieShape`), ?x) = `{?x dbo:imdbId ?y0 .?x dbo:director ?y1 .`

`?y1 dbo:birthDate ?y2 .FILTER NOT EXISTS{`

`?y1 dbo:birthDate ?y3 .FILTER(?y2 != ?y3)}}`

Interestingly, if one uses the recursive SPARQL extension introduced in [15], then both $L^+_\vee$ and $\mathcal{L}^s$ can be expressed:

Proposition 4. *Every schema in $\mathcal{L}^+_\vee$ or $\mathcal{L}^s$ can be expressed in recursive* SPARQL.

5 Validation via Multiple Queries for Full SHACL

This section provides an algorithm for validating arbitrary SHACL shapes over a SPARQL endpoint. The approach reduces validation to satisfiability of a propositional formula, possibly leveraging the optimization techniques of a SAT solver.

Given a graph $\mathcal{G}$ to validate against a shape schema $\mathcal{S}$, the roadmap of this solution is as follows. First, we define a *normal form* for shape schemas. This will allow us to simplify the exposition. Next, we associate one SPARQL query to each

If $\phi = \neg\text{EQ}(r_1, r_2)$, then:
$q_\phi =$ `SELECT ?x WHERE {?x` r_1 w_1 `. ?x` r_2 w_2 `. FILTER (`w_1 `!=` w_2 `)}`

otherwise:
$q_\phi =$ `SELECT` vars(ϕ) `WHERE {`triples(ϕ) `FILTER` (filters(ϕ))`}`

with:

$$\begin{array}{llllll} \text{vars}(\top) & = \{?x\} & \text{triples}(\top) & = V & \text{filters}(\top) & = \{?x = ?x\} \\ \text{vars}(I) & = \{?x\} & \text{triples}(I) & = V & \text{filters}(I) & = \{?x = I\} \\ \text{vars}(s) & = \{?x\} & \text{triples}(s) & = V & \text{filters}(s) & = \{?x = ?x\} \\ \text{vars}(\neg\beta) & = \{?x\} & \text{triples}(\neg\beta) & = V & \text{filters}(\neg\beta) & = \{!f \mid f \in \text{filters}(\beta)\} \end{array}$$

If ϕ is of the form $\phi_1 \wedge \phi_2$, then:

$$\begin{array}{lll} \text{vars}(\phi) & = & \text{vars}(\phi_1) \cup \text{vars}(\phi_2) \\ \text{triples}(\phi) & = & \text{triples}(\phi_1) \cup \text{triples}(\phi_2) \\ \text{filters}(\phi) & = & \text{filters}(\phi_1) \cup \text{filters}(\phi_2) \end{array}$$

If ϕ is of the form $\geq_n r.\phi'$, then:

$$\begin{array}{lll} \text{vars}(\phi) & = & \text{vars}(\phi') \cup \{w_1, \ldots, w_n\} \\ \text{triples}(\phi) & = & \{(?x\ r\ w_i) \mid 1 \leq i \leq n\} \\ \text{filters}(\phi) & = & \{f[?x/w_i] \mid f \in \text{filters}(\phi'), 1 \leq i \leq n\} \cup \{w_i != w_j \mid i \neq j\} \end{array}$$

Fig. 3. Inductive definition of the SPARQL query $q_{\text{def}(s)}$, for each shape s in a normalized schema, where V is a SPARQL subquery that retrieves all nodes in the graph and $f[w/w']$ designates filter expression f, where each occurrence of variable w is replaced by variable w'. SPARQL connectors ("." for triples and `AND` for filters) are omitted for readability. All w_i are fresh variables for each occurrence.

shape in a normalized schema. From the evaluation of these queries we construct a set of rules of the form $l_0 \wedge .. \wedge l_n \rightarrow s(v)$, where each l_i is either $s_i(v_i)$ or $\neg s_i(v_i)$, for some $s_i \in S$ and $v_i \in V_\mathcal{G}$. Intuitively, a rule such as $s_1(v_1) \wedge \neg s_2(v_2) \rightarrow s(v)$ means that, if node v_1 conforms to shape s_1 and node v_2 does not conform to shape s_2, then node v conforms to shape s. These rules alone are not sufficient for a sound validation algorithm, so we complement them with additional rules (encoding in particular the targets, and the fact that a node cannot be inferred to conform to a given shape). Finally, we show that $\mathcal{G}$ satisfies $\mathcal{S}$ if and only if the set of constructed formulas is satisfiable.

The approach can handle validations with respect to either total or partial assignments. For validation with respect to partial assignments the set of rules must be satisfiable under 3-valued (Kleene's) logic. For validation with respect to total assignments the set of rules must be satisfiable under standard (2-valued) propositional logic. And as shown in [10], if the schema is stratified, then both notions of validation coincide.

Interestingly, the machinery presented in this section can also be use to design a more efficient algorithm, for the three tractable fragments of SHACL identified in Sect. 3. This algorithm will be presented in Sect. 6.

Normal Form. A shape schema $\langle S, \text{targ}, \text{def}\rangle$ is *in normal form* if the set S of shape names can be partitioned into two sets S^+ and S^{NEQ}, such that for each $s \in S^+$ (resp. $s \in S^{\text{NEQ}}$), def(s) verifies ϕ_{s^+} (resp. $\phi_{s^{\text{NEQ}}}$) in the following grammar:

$$p_{\text{def}(s)} = \left(\bigwedge \text{body}(\text{def}(s))\right) \rightarrow s(\texttt{?x}), \text{ with:}$$

$$\begin{array}{lcllcl}
\text{body}(\neg\text{EQ}(r_1, r_2)) & = & \{\top\} & & & \\
\text{body}(\top) & = & \{\top\} & \text{body}(\neg\top) & = & \{\top\} \\
\text{body}(I) & = & \{\top\} & \text{body}(\neg I) & = & \{\top\} \\
\text{body}(s') & = & \{s'(\texttt{?x})\} & \text{body}(\neg s') & = & \{\neg s'(\texttt{?x})\}
\end{array}$$

$$\begin{array}{lcl}
\text{body}(\phi_1 \wedge \phi_2) & = & \text{body}(\phi_1) \cup \text{body}(\phi_2) \\
\text{body}(\geq_n r.\phi) & = & \left\{\ell[\texttt{?x}/w] \mid \ell \in \text{body}(\phi) \text{ and } w \in \text{vars}(\phi)\right\}
\end{array}$$

Fig. 4. Inductive definition of the rule pattern $p_{\text{def}(s)}$. $l[w_1/w_2]$ designates literal l, where each occurrence of variable w_1 is replaced by variable w_2. vars(ϕ) is defined in Fig. 3

$$\begin{array}{rcl}
\phi_{s^+} & ::= & \alpha \mid \geq_n r.\alpha \mid \phi_{s^+} \wedge \phi_{s^+} \\
\phi_{s^{\text{NEQ}}} & ::= & \neg\text{EQ}(r_1, r_2) \\
\alpha & ::= & \beta \mid \neg\beta \\
\beta & ::= & \top \mid I \mid s
\end{array}$$

It is easy to verify that a shape schema can be transformed in linear time into an equivalent normalized one, by introducing fresh shape names (without target). "Equivalent" here means that both schemas validate exactly the same graphs, with exactly the same target violations.

SPARQL Queries. Such normalization allows us to associate a SPARQL query $q_{\text{def}(s)}$ to each shape name in the normalized schema. Intuitively, the query $q_{\text{def}(s)}$ retrieves nodes that may validate def(s), and also the neighboring nodes to which constraints may be propagated in order to satisfy def(s). For instance, let def$(s_0) = (\geq_1 p_1.s_1) \wedge (\geq_1 p_2.s_2)$. Then:[6]

$$q_{\text{def}(s_0)} = \texttt{SELECT ?x ?y1 ?y2 WHERE } \{\texttt{?x } p_1 \texttt{ ?y1 . ?x } p_2 \texttt{ ?y2 }\}$$

Figure 3 provides the definition of $q_{\text{def}(s)}$, by induction on the structure of def(s) (over each occurrence of a formula), based on the normal form.

Rule Patterns. Let $\mathcal{S} = \langle S, \text{targ}, \text{def}\rangle$ be a normalized schema. The next step consists in generating a set of propositional rules, based on the evaluation of the queries that have just been defined. To generate such formulas, we associate a *rule pattern* $p_{\text{def}(s)}$ to each shape $s \in S$. This rule pattern is of the form $l_1 \wedge .. \wedge l_n \rightarrow s(\texttt{?x})$, where each l_i is either $\top$, $s_i(w_i)$ or $\neg s_i(w_i)$, for some shape $s_i \in S$ and variable w. Figure 4 provides the definition of $p_{\text{def}(s)}$, by induction on the structure of def(s).

Continuing the example above, if def$(s_0) = (\geq_1 p_1.s_1) \wedge (\geq_1 p_2.s_2)$, then:

$$q_{\text{def}(s_0)} = \texttt{SELECT ?x ?y1 ?y2 WHERE } \{\texttt{?x } p_1 \texttt{ ?y1 . ?x } p_2 \texttt{ ?y2 }\}$$
$$p_{\text{def}(s_0)} = s_1(\texttt{?y1}) \wedge s_2(\texttt{?y2}) \rightarrow s_0(\texttt{?x})$$

[6] We omit the trivial `FILTER (?y1 = ?y1 AND ?y2 = ?y2)` for readability.

Each rule pattern $p_{\text{def}(s)}$ is then instantiated with the answers to $q_{\text{def}(s)}$ over the SPARQL endpoint, which yields a set $[\![p_{\text{def}(s)}]\!]^{\mathcal{G}}$ of propositional rules. For instance, assume that the endpoint returns the following mappings for $q_{\text{def}(s_0)}$:

$$\begin{aligned}[\![q_{\text{def}(s_0)}]\!]^{\mathcal{G}} = \{&\{\texttt{?x} \mapsto v_0, \texttt{?y1} \mapsto v_1, \texttt{?y2} \mapsto v_2\},\\ &\{\texttt{?x} \mapsto v_0, \texttt{?y1} \mapsto v_3, \texttt{?y2} \mapsto v_4\}\}\end{aligned}$$

Then the set $[\![p_{\text{def}(s_0)}]\!]^{\mathcal{G}}$ of propositional rules is:

$$[\![p_{\text{def}(s_0)}]\!]^{\mathcal{G}} = \{s_1(v_1) \land s_2(v_2) \to s_0(v_0), s_1(v_3) \land s_2(v_4) \to s_0(v_0)\}$$

Formally, $[\![p_{\text{def}(s)}]\!]^{\mathcal{G}}$ is the set of propositional formulas obtained by replacing, for each solution mapping $\gamma \in [\![q_{\text{def}(s)}]\!]^{\mathcal{G}}$, every occurrence of a variable w in $p_{\text{def}(s)}$ by $\gamma(w)$.[7] Then we use $[\![p_S]\!]^{\mathcal{G}}$ to designate the set of all generated rules, i.e.:

$$[\![p_S]\!]^{\mathcal{G}} = \bigcup_{s \in S} [\![p_{\text{def}(s)}]\!]^{\mathcal{G}}$$

We need more terminology. For each rule $r = l_1, .., l_n \to s(v)$, we call $s(v)$ the *head* of r, and $\{l_1, .., l_n\}$ the *body* of r. Finally, if l is a literal, we use $\neg l$ to designate its negation, i.e. $\neg l = \neg s(v)$ if $l = s(v)$, and $\neg l = s(v)$ if $l = \neg s(v)$.

Additional Formulas. So far, with a rule $s_1(v_1) \land s_2(v_2) \to s_0(v_0)$, we are capturing the idea that v_0 must be assigned shape s_0 whenever v_1 is assigned s_1 and v_2 is assigned s_2. But we also need to encode that the only way for v_0 to be assigned shape s_0 is to satisfy one of these rules. If there is just one rule with $s_0(v_0)$ as its head, we only need to extend our set of rules with $s_0(v_0) \to s_1(v_1) \land s_2(v_2)$. But for more generality, we construct a second set $[\![p_S^{\leftarrow}]\!]^{\mathcal{G}}$ of propositional formulas, as follows. For every literal $s(v)$ that appears as the head of a rule $\psi \to s(v)$ in $[\![p_S]\!]^{\mathcal{G}}$, let $\psi_1 \to s(v), .., \psi_\ell \to s(v)$ be all the rules that have $s(v)$ as head. Then we extend $[\![p_S^{\leftarrow}]\!]^{\mathcal{G}}$ with the formula $s(v) \to (\psi_1 \lor .. \lor \psi_\ell)$.

Next, we add the information about all target nodes, with the set $[\![t_S]\!]^{\mathcal{G}}$ of (atomic) formulas, defined by $[\![t_S]\!]^{\mathcal{G}} = \{s(v) \mid s \in S, s(v) \in \text{targ}(s)\}$.

Finally, we use a last set of formulas to ensure that the algorithm is sound and complete. Intuitively, the query $q_{\text{def}(s)}$ retrieves all nodes that may verify shape s (bound to variable ?x). But evaluating $q_{\text{def}(s)}$ also provides information about the nodes that are *not* retrieved: namely that they *cannot* verify shape s. A first naive idea is to extend our set of propositional formulas with every literal $\neg s(v)$ for which $[\![q_{\text{def}(s)}]\!]^{\mathcal{G}}$ does not contain any mapping where v is bound to ?x. But this may require retrieving all nodes in $\mathcal{G}$ beforehand, which is inefficient. One can do better, by considering only combinations of shapes and nodes that

7 For some normalized schemas, it could happen that $[\![q_{\text{def}(s)}]\!]^{\mathcal{G}}$ always retrieves all nodes from $\mathcal{G}$. This would be the case for example if $\text{def}(s) = s_1 \land s_2$. A simple optimization technique here consists in not executing such queries, and instantiate instead the rule pattern $p_{\text{def}(s)}$ with all nodes retrieved by all other queries (and bound to variable ?x).

are already in our rules. We thus construct another set $[\![a_{\mathcal{S}}]\!]^{\mathcal{G}}$ of facts. It contains all literals of the form $\neg s(v)$ such that: $\neg s(v)$ or $s(v)$ appears in some formula in $[\![p_{\mathcal{S}}]\!]^{\mathcal{G}} \cup [\![t_{\mathcal{S}}]\!]^{\mathcal{G}}$, and $s(v)$ is not the head of any formula in $[\![p_{\mathcal{S}}]\!]^{\mathcal{G}}$ (i.e. there is no rule of the form $\psi \rightarrow s(v)$ in $[\![p_{\mathcal{S}}]\!]^{\mathcal{G}}$).

Analysis. Let $\Gamma_{\mathcal{G},\mathcal{S}} = [\![p_{\mathcal{S}}]\!]^{\mathcal{G}} \cup [\![p_{\mathcal{S}}^{\leftarrow}]\!]^{\mathcal{G}} \cup [\![t_{\mathcal{S}}]\!]^{\mathcal{G}} \cup [\![a_{\mathcal{S}}]\!]^{\mathcal{G}}$ be the union of all the sets of formulas constructed so far. We treat $\Gamma_{\mathcal{G},\mathcal{S}}$ as a set of propositional formulas over the set $\{s(v) \mid s \in S, v \in V_{\mathcal{G}}\}$ of propositions. A first observation is that this set of formulas is polynomial in the size of $\mathcal{G}$. Perhaps more interestingly, one can show that the set $\Gamma_{\mathcal{G},\mathcal{S}}$ is also polynomial in the size of the evaluation of all queries $\text{def}(s)$ and $\text{targ}(s)$. For a finer-grained analysis, let us measure the size of a rule as the number of propositions it contains. From the construction, we get the following upper bounds.

Proposition 5.

- *The sizes of* $[\![p_{\mathcal{S}}]\!]^{\mathcal{G}}$, $[\![p_{\mathcal{S}}^{\leftarrow}]\!]^{\mathcal{G}}$ *and* $[\![a_{\mathcal{S}}]\!]^{\mathcal{G}}$ *are in* $O(\bigcup_{s \in \mathcal{S}} [\![q_{\text{def}(s)}]\!]^{\mathcal{G}})$.
- *The size of* $[\![t_{\mathcal{S}}]\!]^{\mathcal{G}}$ *is in* $O(|\bigcup_{s \in \mathcal{S}} [\![\text{targ}(s)]\!]^{\mathcal{G}}|)$.

Hence, the size of the rules we need for inference is not directly dependent on the size of the graph, but rather on the amount of targets and tuples that the SHACL schema selects to be validated.

The next result shows that validation can be reduced to checking whether $\Gamma_{\mathcal{G},\mathcal{S}}$ is satisfiable. "3-valued semantics" here refers to the semantics of Kleene's 3-valued logic (for $\wedge, \vee$ and $\neg$) and where $\psi_1 \rightarrow \psi_2$ is interpreted as $\neg\psi_1 \vee \psi_2$. Then a boolean formula ψ is *satisfiable* under boolean (resp. 3-valued) semantics iff there is a boolean (resp. 3-valued) valuation of the atoms in ψ such that the resulting formula evaluates to *true* under boolean (resp. 3-valued) semantics.

Proposition 6. *For every graph* $\mathcal{G}$ *and schema* $\mathcal{S}$ *we have that:*

- $\mathcal{G}$ *is valid against* $\mathcal{S}$ *with respect to total assignments iff* $\Gamma_{\mathcal{G},\mathcal{S}}$ *is satisfiable under boolean semantics.*
- $\mathcal{G}$ *is valid against* $\mathcal{S}$ *with respect to partial assignments iff* $\Gamma_{\mathcal{G},\mathcal{S}}$ *is satisfiable under 3-valued semantics.*

Hence, we can check for validity of schemas over graphs by constructing $\Gamma_{\mathcal{G},\mathcal{S}}$ and checking satisfiability with a SAT solver. This algorithm matches the NP upper bound in data complexity mentioned earlier, since each of $[\![q_{\text{def}(s)}]\!]^{\mathcal{G}}$ and $[\![\text{targ}(s)]\!]^{\mathcal{G}}$ can be computed in polynomial time, when $\mathcal{S}$ is considered to be fixed, and thus the set $\Gamma_{\mathcal{G},\mathcal{S}}$ of rules can be computed in polynomial time in data complexity.

6 Optimized Algorithm for Tractable Fragments

The propositional framework described in the previous section applies to arbitrary shape schemas. But it also allows us to devise a more efficient validation algorithm for the tractable fragments $\mathcal{L}^{\text{non-rec}}$, $\mathcal{L}_{\vee}^{+}$ and $\mathcal{L}^{s}$. One could, in theory,

Algorithm 1. TRACTABLE ALGORITHM FOR VALIDATION

Input: Graph $\mathcal{G}$, normalized schema $\mathcal{S} = \langle S, \text{def}, \text{targ} \rangle$, set $[\![t_\mathcal{S}]\!]^\mathcal{G}$ of targets.
1: $\sigma, R, S' \leftarrow \emptyset$
2: **repeat**
3: $\quad s \leftarrow$ SELECTSHAPE(S, S')
4: $\quad S' \leftarrow S' \cup \{s\}$
5: $\quad R \leftarrow R \cup [\![p_{\text{def}(s)}]\!]^\mathcal{G}$
6: $\quad$ SATURATE(σ, R, S')
7: **until** $S' = S$
8: SATURATE(σ, R, S)

feed the same formulas as above to a SAT solver for these fragments. Instead, the algorithm below performs this inference on-the-fly, without the need for a solver. In addition, the validity of the graph may in some cases be decided before evaluating all SPARQL queries (one per shape) against the endpoint.

The key property that enables this algorithm pertains to the notion of *minimal fixed-point assignment* for SHACL, defined in [10]. Due to space limitations, we only rephrase the results relevant for this algorithm in our own terms.

Lemma 1. *For every graph $\mathcal{G}$ and schema $\mathcal{S}$ in $\mathcal{L}^{non\text{-}rec}$, $\mathcal{L}^+_\vee$ or $\mathcal{L}^s$, there is a partial assignment $\sigma^{\mathcal{G},\mathcal{S}}_{\text{minFix}}$ such that:*

1. *$\sigma^{\mathcal{G},\mathcal{S}}_{\text{minFix}}$ can be computed in polynomial time from $\Gamma^{\mathcal{G},\mathcal{S}}$, and*
2. *$\mathcal{G}$ is valid against $\mathcal{S}$ iff $\neg s(v) \notin \sigma^{\mathcal{G},\mathcal{S}}_{\text{minFix}}$ holds for every $s(v) \in [\![t_\mathcal{S}]\!]^\mathcal{G}$*

Algorithm. The algorithm shares similarities with the one of Sect. 5. It proceeds shape by shape, materializing the rules $[\![p_{\text{def}(s)}]\!]^\mathcal{G}$ defined in Sect. 5. We will see that these rules are sufficient to compute the assignment $\sigma^{\mathcal{G},\mathcal{S}}_{\text{minFix}}$.

The whole procedure is given by Algorithm 1. Variable S' keeps track of the shapes already processed, variable R stores all rules that are known to hold, and σ is the assignment under construction. All arguments are passed by reference. We use procedure SELECTSHAPE (Line 3) to select from S the next shape s to be processed. This selection can be non-deterministic, but as we will see, this choice also opens room for optimization. All the necessary inference is performed by procedure SATURATE, explained below. In the worst case, the loop terminates when all shapes have been processed (i.e. when $S' = S$, Line 7).

We now describe the inference carried out by procedure SATURATE, whose detailed execution is given by Fig. 5. heads(R) (Line 3 in procedure NEGATE) designates the sets of all heads appearing in R, whereas $\bigcup$bodies(R) (Line 2 in procedure NEGATE) designates the union of all rule bodies in R. The inference is performed exhaustively by procedures NEGATE and INFER. Procedure NEGATE derives negative information. For any (possibly negated) atom $s(v)$ that is either a target or appears in some rule, we may be able to infer that $s(v)$ cannot hold. This is the case if $s(v)$ has not been inferred already (i.e. $s(v) \notin \sigma$), if the query $q_{\text{def}(s)}$ has already been evaluated, and if there is no rule in R with $s(v)$ as its head. In such case, $\neg s(v)$ is added to σ.

Procedure INFER performs two types of inference. First, the obvious one: if R contains a rule $l_1 \wedge \cdots \wedge l_n \rightarrow s(v)$ and each of $l_1, .., l_n$ has already been inferred, then $s(v)$ is inferred, and the rule is dropped. The second inference is negative: if the negation of any l_i has already been inferred, then this rule cannot be applied (to infer $s(v)$), so the entire rule is dropped.

```
procedure SATURATE(σ, R, S′)
    repeat
        σ′ ← σ
        NEGATE(σ, R, S′)
        INFER(σ, R)
    until σ = σ′
end procedure
```

```
procedure INFER(σ, R)
    R′ ← ∅
    for all l₁ ∧ .. ∧ lₙ → s(v) ∈ R do
        if {l₁, .., lₙ} ⊆ σ then
            σ ← σ ∪ {s(v)}
        else if {¬l₁, .., ¬lₙ} ∩ σ = ∅ then
            R′ ← R′ ∪ {l₁ ∧ .. ∧ lₙ → s(v)}
    end for
    R ← R′
end procedure
```

```
procedure NEGATE(σ, R, S′)
    for all l ∈ ⟦t_S⟧^G ∪ ⋃ bodies(R) do
        if (l = s(v) or l = ¬s(v)) and s ∈ S′ and s(v) ∉ σ ∪ heads(R) then
            σ ← σ ∪ {¬s(v)}
    end for
end procedure
```

Fig. 5. Components of in-memory saturation in Algorithm 1

Let $\sigma^{\mathcal{G},\mathcal{S}}_{\text{final}}$ be the state of variable σ after termination. We show:

Proposition 7. $\sigma^{\mathcal{G},\mathcal{S}}_{\text{final}} = \sigma^{\mathcal{G},\mathcal{S}}_{\text{minFix}}$

Interestingly, one can use this result to validate each target $s(v)$ individually: if $\neg s(v) \in \sigma^{\mathcal{G},\mathcal{S}}_{\text{final}}$, then v does not conform to shape s. Otherwise it conforms to it.

Optimization. An earlier termination condition may apply for Algorithm 1. Indeed, we observe that during the execution, the assignment σ under construction can only be extended. Therefore the algorithm may already terminate if all targets have been inferred to be valid or invalid, i.e. if $s(v) \in \sigma$ or $\neg s(v) \in \sigma$ for every target $s(v) \in [\![t_S]\!]^{\mathcal{G}}$. This means that one should also try to process the shapes in the best order possible. For instance, in the experiments reported below, function SELECTSHAPE (Line 3) first prioritizes the shapes that have a target definition, then the shapes referenced by these, and so on, in a depth-first fashion. Such an ordering offers another advantage, which pertains to traceability: when signaling to the user the reason why a given target is violated, it is arguably more informative to return an explanation at depth n than at depth $n + q$. Therefore this breadth-first strategy guarantees that one of the "most immediate" explanations for a constraint violation is always found.

Table 3. Validation using $\text{VALID}_{\text{rule}}$ for all 6 schemas, and $\text{VALID}_{\text{single}}$ for non-recursive schemas, on DBP_{full}. Here # **Queries** is the number of executed queries, **Query exec. max** (resp. **total**) is the maximum execution time for a query (resp. total time for all queries) in milliseconds, **#Query answ. max** (resp. **total**) is the max. number of solution mappings for a query (resp. total for all queries) **#Rules max** is the max. number of rules in memory during the execution, and **Total exec.** is the overall execution time in milliseconds

		#Queries	Query exec. (ms)		#Query answ.		#Rules	Total exec. (ms)
			max	total	max	total	max	
$\text{VALID}_{\text{single}}$	$\mathcal{S}^2_{\text{non-rec}}$	1	3596	3596	111113	111113	0	**3596**
	$\mathcal{S}^3_{\text{non-rec}}$	1	3976	3976	111629	111629	0	**3976**
	$\mathcal{S}^4_{\text{non-rec}}$	1	5269	5269	111906	111906	0	**5269**
$\text{VALID}_{\text{rule}}$	$\mathcal{S}^2_{\text{non-rec}}$	3	858	956	37040	38439	49278	**5305**
	$\mathcal{S}^3_{\text{non-rec}}$	4	827	1149	37040	52122	50774	**5553**
	$\mathcal{S}^4_{\text{non-rec}}$	7	1308	1944	39719	65175	64060	**6857**
	$\mathcal{S}^2_{\text{rec}}$	5	912	1278	37040	59382	59852	**5651**
	$\mathcal{S}^3_{\text{rec}}$	6	1489	3436	61355	146382	146104	**8318**
	$\mathcal{S}^4_{\text{rec}}$	8	1530	4955	61355	186593	159597	**11503**

7 Evaluation

We implemented a slightly optimized version of Algorithm 1, A prototype is available online [6], together with source code and execution and build instructions.

Shape Schemas. We designed two sets of simple shapes, called $M_{\text{non-rec}}$ and M_{rec} below. These shapes pertain to the domain of cinema (movies, actors, etc.), based on patterns observed in DBPedia [1], similarly to the shapes of Fig. 1. They were designed to cover several cases discussed in this article (shape reference, recursion, etc.). All shapes are available online [6]. The first set $M_{\text{non-rec}}$ contains shape references, but is non-recursive, whereas the second set M_{rec} is recursive. Out of $M_{\text{non-rec}}$, we created 3 shape schemas $\mathcal{S}^2_{\text{non-rec}}$, $\mathcal{S}^3_{\text{non-rec}}$ and $\mathcal{S}^4_{\text{non-rec}}$, containing 2, 3 and 4 shapes respectively. Similarly for M_2, we created 3 shape schemas $\mathcal{S}^2_{\text{rec}}$, $\mathcal{S}^3_{\text{rec}}$ and $\mathcal{S}^4_{\text{rec}}$.

Data. We used the latest version of DBPedia (2016-10), specifically the datasets "Person Data", "Instance Types", "Labels", "Mappingbased Literals" and "Mappingbased Objects" (in English), downloadable from [1], with around 61 million triples (7.7 GB in .ttl format). We denote this dataset as DBP_{full}. The number of targets to be validated in DBP_{full} is 111938. To test the scalability of the approach, we also produced four samples by randomly selecting 10%, 20% and 50% of triples in DBP_{full}. We denote these datasets as DBP_{10}, DBP_{20} and DBP_{50}.

Setting. We use $\text{VALID}_{\text{rule}}$ to designate our implementation of the rule-based procedure described by Algorithm 1. The implementation is essentially identical, but with a relaxed normal form for the input schema, and improvements geared towards increasing the selectivity of some queries. The ordering of query evaluation (Function SELECTSHAPE in Algorithm 1, Line 3) was based on the dependency graph, in a breadth-first fashion, starting with the only shape with non-empty target definition, then followed by the shapes it references (if not evaluated yet), etc. $\text{VALID}_{\text{single}}$ designates validation performed by executing a single query, as described in Sect. 4. This approach is only applicable to the non-recursive shape schemas $\mathcal{S}^2_{\text{non-rec}}$, $\mathcal{S}^3_{\text{non-rec}}$ and $\mathcal{S}^4_{\text{non-rec}}$.

We used Virtuoso v7.2.4 as triplestore. Queries were run on a 24 cores Intel Xeon CPU at 3.47 GHz, with a 5.4 TB 15k RPM RAID-5 hard-drive cluster and 108 GB of RAM. Only 1 GB of RAM was dedicated to the triplestore for caching and intermediate operations. In addition, the OS page cache was flushed every 5 s, to ensure that the endpoint could only exploit these 1 GB for caching. These precautions ensure that most of the dataset cannot be cached, which would artificially speed up query execution times.

Results. Table 3 provides statistics for the validation of DBP_{full} against all schemas. A first observation is that execution times remained very reasonable (less that 12 s) for a complete validation, given the high number of targets (111938) and the size of the dataset. Another immediate observation is that for the non-recursive schemas, $\text{VALID}_{\text{single}}$ consistently outperformed $\text{VALID}_{\text{rule}}$. However, execution times for both approaches remain in the same order of magnitude. Based on these results, the rule-based approach appears as a relatively small price to pay for an algorithm that is not only more robust (i.e. can handle recursion), but also guarantees traceability of each shape violation (whereas the single-query approach essentially uses the endpoint as a black-box). Figure 6(a) illustrates scalability of $\text{VALID}_{\text{single}}$ and $\text{VALID}_{\text{rule}}$. The focus is on scalability w.r.t to the size of the graph (data complexity) rather than in the size of the schema. The execution times are given for the different samples of DBPedia (DBP_{10}, DBP_{20}, DBP_{50} and DBP_{full}) against the largest shapes schemas ($\mathcal{S}^4_{\text{non-rec}}$ and $\mathcal{S}^4_{\text{rec}}$). The main observation is that for $\text{VALID}_{\text{rule}}$, execution time increased significantly faster for the recursive schema than for the non-recursive one. Finally, Fig. 6b describes how execution time was split between query answering, saturation and other tasks (mostly grounding rules with solution mappings), for $\text{VALID}_{\text{rule}}$, for each $\mathcal{S}^i_{\text{rec}}$ and for each sample of DBPedia. An important observation here is that the proportion of execution time dedicated to query answering increased with the data and number of shapes, even when the number of rules in memory was arguably large ($\geq$100000 for $\mathcal{S}^3_{\text{rec}}$ and $\mathcal{S}^4_{\text{rec}}$ with). This suggests that the extra cost induced by in-memory inference during the execution of Algorithm 1 may not be a bottleneck.

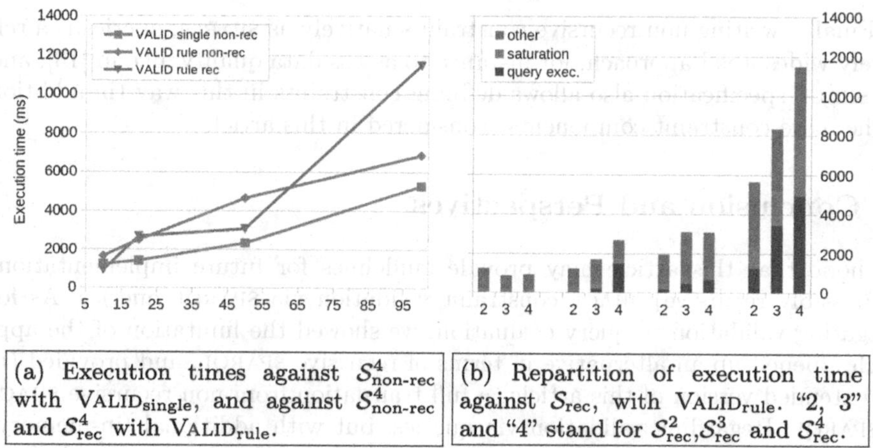

(a) Execution times against $\mathcal{S}^4_{\text{non-rec}}$ with VALID$_{\text{single}}$, and against $\mathcal{S}^4_{\text{non-rec}}$ and $\mathcal{S}^4_{\text{rec}}$ with VALID$_{\text{rule}}$.

(b) Repartition of execution time against $\mathcal{S}_{\text{rec}}$, with VALID$_{\text{rule}}$. "2, 3" and "4" stand for $\mathcal{S}^2_{\text{rec}}$,$\mathcal{S}^3_{\text{rec}}$ and $\mathcal{S}^4_{\text{rec}}$.

Fig. 6. Scalability over DBP_{10}, DBP_{20}, DBP_{50} and DBP_{full}

8 Related Work

TopBraid Composer [8] allows validating an RDF graph against a non-recursive SHACL schema via SPARQL queries, similarly to the approach described in Sect. 4). The tool was initially developed for the language SPIN, which largely influenced the design of the SHACL specification. A list of other implementations of SHACL validation can be found at [3] (together with unit tests for non-recursive shapes). To our knowledge, none of these can validate recursive constraints via SPARQL queries, with the exception of *Shaclex* [4], already mentioned (See footnote 3).

ShEx [9,16] is another popular constraint language for RDF, which shares many similarities with SHACL, but is inspired by XML schema languages. A semantics for (stratified) recursive ShEx schemas was proposed in [9], which differs from the one followed in this article for SHACL. ShEx validation is supported by several open-source implementations (like *shex.js* [5] or *Shaclex* [4]), either in memory or over a triple-store. To our knowledge, no procedure for validating recursive ShEx via SPARQL queries has been defined or implemented yet.

Prior to ShEx or SHACL, a common approach to define expressive constraints over RDF graphs was to use OWL axioms with (some form of) closed-world assumption (CWA) [14,17] However, OWL is originally designed to model incomplete knowledge (with the open-world assumption), therefore not well-suited to express constraints. In terms of implementation, [14] proposed an encoding of such constraints into complex logical programs, but the usage made of OWL does not allow for recursive constraints. Similarly, *Stardog* [7] offers the possibility to write constraints as OWL axioms under CWA, which are then converted to SPARQL queries. In contrast to SHACL though, these constraints are "local", i.e cannot refer to other constraints. Stardog also has a limited support for SHACL validation, currently in beta phase.

Finally, writing non-recursive constraints natively as SPARQL queries is a relatively widespread approach, for instance to assess data quality, like in [13], and the SHACL specification also allows defining constraints in this way (in addition to the "core constraint components" considered in this article).

9 Conclusion and Perspectives

We hope that this article may provide guidelines for future implementations of (possibly recursive) SHACL constraint validation via SPARQL queries. As for delegating validation to query evaluation, we showed the limitation of the approach, opened up an alternative in terms of recursive SPARQL, and provided (in the extended version of this article) a full translation from non-recursive SHACL to SPARQL. Regarding validation via queries, but with additional (in-memory) computation, we devised and evaluated and algorithm for three tractable fragments of SHACL, with encouraging performances. This strategy can also still be largely optimized, generating more selective queries and/or reducing the cost of in-memory inference. A natural extension of this work is the application to ShEx schemas, even though the semantics for recursive ShEx proposed in [9] differs from the one followed in this paper. Finally, a key feature of a constraint validation engine is the ability to provide explanations for target violations. Their number is potentially exponential though, so a natural continuation of this work is to define some preference over explanations, and devise algorithms that return an optimal one, without sacrificing performance.

References

1. DBpedia. wiki.dbpedia.org/downloads-2016-10
2. Extended version. https://www.inf.unibz.it/krdb/tech-reports/
3. SHACL Test Suite. w3c.github.io/data-shapes/data-shapes-test-suite/
4. Shaclex. http://github.com/labra/shaclex/
5. Shex.js. http://github.com/shexSpec/shex.js/
6. Source code and experiment's material. http://github.com/rdfshapes/shacl-sparql
7. Stardog ICV. https://www.stardog.com/blog/data-quality-with-icv/
8. TopBraid Composer. http://www.topquadrant.com/products/topbraid-composer/
9. Boneva, I., Labra Gayo, J.E., Prud'hommeaux, E.G.: Semantics and validation of shapes schemas for RDF. In: ISWC 2017
10. Corman, J., Reutter, J.L., Savković, O.: Semantics and validation of recursive SHACL. In: Vrandečić, D., Bontcheva, K., Suárez-Figueroa, M.C., Presutti, V., Celino, I., Sabou, M., Kaffee, L.-A., Simperl, E. (eds.) ISWC 2018. LNCS, vol. 11136, pp. 318–336. Springer, Cham (2018). https://doi.org/10.1007/978-3-030-00671-6_19
11. Corman, J., Reutter, J.L., Savković, O.: Semantics and validation of recursive SHACL (extended version). Technical report KRDB18-1, Free University Bozen-Bolzano (2018). https://www.inf.unibz.it/krdb/tech-reports/
12. Corman, J., Reutter, J.L., Savković, O.: A tractable notion of stratification for SHACL. In: ISWC 2018

13. Kontokostas, D., et al.: Test-driven evaluation of linked data quality. In: WWW (2014)
14. Motik, B., Horrocks, I., Sattler, U.: Bridging the gap between OWL and relational databases. Web Semant.: Sci. Serv. Agents World Wide Web **7**(2), 74–89 (2009)
15. Reutter, J.L., Soto, A., Vrgoč, D.: Recursion in SPARQL. In: Arenas, M., et al. (eds.) ISWC 2015. LNCS, vol. 9366, pp. 19–35. Springer, Cham (2015). https://doi.org/10.1007/978-3-319-25007-6_2
16. Staworko, S., Boneva, I., Labra Gayo, J.E., Hym, S., Prud'hommeaux, E.G., Solbrig, H.: Complexity and expressiveness of ShEx for RDF. In: ICDT (2015)
17. Tao, J., Sirin, E., Bao, J., McGuinness, D.L.: Integrity constraints in owl. In: AAAI (2010)

Mapping Factoid Adjective Constraints to Existential Restrictions over Knowledge Bases

Jiwei Ding, Wei Hu(✉), Qixin Xu, and Yuzhong Qu(✉)

State Key Laboratory for Novel Software Technology, Nanjing University, Nanjing, China
jwdingnju@outlook.com, qxxunju@outlook.com, {whu,yzqu}@nju.edu.cn

Abstract. The rapid progress of question answering (QA) systems over knowledge bases (KBs) enables end users to acquire knowledge with natural language questions. While mapping proper nouns and relational phrases to semantic constructs in KBs has been extensively studied, little attention has been devoted to adjectives, most of which play the role of factoid constraints on the modified nouns. In this paper, we study the problem of finding appropriate representations for adjectives over KBs. We propose a novel approach, called Adj2ER, to automatically map an adjective to several existential restrictions or their negation forms. Specifically, we leverage statistic measures for generating candidate existential restrictions and supervised learning for filtering the candidates, which largely reduce the search space and overcome the lexical gap. We create two question sets with adjectives from QALD and Yahoo! Answers, and conduct experiments over DBpedia. Our experimental results show that Adj2ER can generate high-quality mappings for most adjectives and significantly outperform several alternative approaches. Furthermore, current QA systems can gain a promising improvement when integrating our adjective mapping approach.

Keywords: Factoid adjective constraint · Question answering · KBQA

1 Introduction

With the rapid development of question answering (QA) systems over structured data [1,4,8,11], end users are able to query knowledge bases (KBs) with natural language questions, a.k.a. KBQA. Semantic parsing [5,24] is a key technique widely-used in these systems, which transforms natural language questions to structural queries like SPARQL queries. Entity linking [7,9] and relation mapping [16] are two major steps in most of the semantic parsing approaches, which map proper nouns and relational phrases to entities and relations (or relation chains) in given KBs, respectively. However, current approaches pay little attention to understanding adjectives over KBs. An example question with adjectives and its corresponding SPARQL query are shown in Table 1.

C. Ghidini et al. (Eds.): ISWC 2019, LNCS 11778, pp. 164–181, 2019.
https://doi.org/10.1007/978-3-030-30793-6_10

Table 1. An example for understanding adjectives by using a KB

Natural language question	List all American actors who are alive.
Existential restriction or its negation	$\exists$ *dbo:nationality.*{*dbr:United_States*} $\neg\exists$ *dbo:deathDate.*$\top$
SPARQL query over DBpedia	select distinct ?s where { ?s *rdf:type dbo:Actor* . ?s *dbo:nationality dbr:United_States* . filter not exists { ?s *dbo:deathDate* ?o } }

In linguistics, an adjective is a descriptive word, the main syntactic role of which is to qualify a noun or noun phrase, giving more information about the object signified. Except for the adjectives which appear in proper nouns or "how + adjective" questions, the majority of adjectives in questions takes the meanings of factoid constraints. In KBs, such adjectives can be captured by the existence of certain properties or facts. Inspired by this, we consider understanding adjectives by mapping them to existential restrictions or their negation forms in description logics [2], where concepts, roles and individuals used in the existential restrictions come from classes, properties and entities of a given KB, respectively. An example for understanding adjectives in question by using DBpedia is shown in the second row of Table 1. We map "American" to an existential restriction $\exists$*dbo:nationality.*{*dbr:United_States*}, giving the meaning that an "American actor" may have a fact about his *nationality* with value *dbr:United_States*. Similarly, "alive" is mapped to an existential restriction in negation form $\neg\exists$ *dbo:deathDate.*$\top$, meaning that "actors who are alive" should not have the facts about their death dates in DBpedia. Compared with current QA systems [1,26] which map adjectives to specific classes or entities, mapping adjectives to existential restrictions can cover a higher portion of adjectives and capture the meanings of natural language questions more precisely. We believe that, in addition to entity linking and relation mapping, adjective mapping should be another important step in semantic parsing.

According to our observations, there are two main challenges in generating appropriate mappings for adjectives. Firstly, the lexical gap between the input adjectives and vocabulary elements used in the target existential restrictions may be huge. For example, for adjective "alive", the appropriate mapping $\neg\exists$ *dbo:deathDate.*$\top$ cannot be found by a similarity-based searching approach (which is commonly used in mapping proper nouns or relational phrases), since the similarity between "alive" and "death date" is not obvious. Although some neural network based approaches [4,12] enhance the ability of semantic similarity calculation, they suffer from the lack of training data on this task. Secondly, the search space of this task is quite large, since many facts in the KB may express the meaning of an input adjective. Some adjectives require the representations in negation forms, making the search space even larger.

In order to cope with the above challenges, we propose a new adjective mapping approach, called Adj2ER, based on the following observation: entities that embody the meaning of an input adjective should have a different fact distribution compared to entities that do not. For example, most dead actors have a fact about their death date, while actors who are alive do not. Thus, the facts about *dbo:deathDate* are considered as discriminative for "alive", and $\neg\exists$ *dbo:deathDate*.$\top$ can be generated as a candidate existential restriction. Generating existential restrictions from such discriminative facts can reduce the search space and overcome the lexical gap at the same time. In our approach, the set of entities that embodies the meaning of an input adjective is collected by retrieving Wikipedia, and candidate existential restrictions are generated from related facts by using statistic measures, followed by a supervised filtering step to improve the accuracy. We created two question sets with adjectives from QALD and Yahoo! Answers, and conducted experiments over DBpedia. Our experimental results turn out to be promising.

The rest of this paper is structured as follows. In Sect. 2, we define the adjective mapping problem. Our approach to solving the adjective mapping problem is proposed in Sect. 3. In Sect. 4, we report the experimental results on adjective mapping and QA tasks. In Sect. 5, we discuss several findings in our experiments. Related work is presented in Sect. 6. Finally, Sect. 7 concludes this paper with future work.

2 Problem Definition

To see the usage of adjectives in natural language questions, we investigated the adjective occurrences in the 5th challenge on question answering over linked data (QALD-5) [21] dataset. Among all the 349 non-hybrid questions, 117 adjective occurrences are contained in 107 questions. We classified the 117 adjective occurrences into four categories (see Table 2).

In this paper, we mainly focus on the adjectives which take the meanings of factoid constraints (33.3%). For example, "American actor" means a subclass of "Actor" whose nationality is United States. In KBs, these constraints can be described as the existence of certain facts, so the primary target of our work is to map adjectives to existential restrictions in description logics. As for the adjectives used as the names of entities/relations, they should not be

Table 2. Classification of adjectives appeared in QALD-5

Categories	Percentage	Examples
Factoid constraint	33.3%	Give me all Swedish holidays
Name of entity/relation	32.5%	Himalayan mountain system
How + adjective	27.4%	How many companies [...]
Structural constraint	6.8%	Which other weapons [...]

Table 3. Forms of existential restrictions and examples

Logic form	Examples	
$\exists r.\top$	(Married people):	*dbo:Person* $\sqcap$ $\exists$*dbo:spouse.*$\top$
$\exists r.\{a\}$	(Chinese cities):	*dbo:City* $\sqcap$ $\exists$*dbo:country.*{*dbr:China*}
$\neg\exists r.\top$	(People who are alive):	*dbo:Person* $\sqcap$ $\neg\exists$*dbo:deathDate.*$\top$
$\neg\exists r.\{a\}$	(Hot food):	*dbo:Food* $\sqcap$ $\neg\exists$*dbo:servingTemperature.*{"*Cold*"}

interpreted alone and have already been considered in the entity linking and relation mapping tasks. Also, "how + adjectives" questions can be interpreted using template-based or rule-based parsing approaches [8,20]. For the remaining 6.8% of adjectives such as "same" and "other", they do not express the meanings of certain facts, but may influence the structures of target query graphs. We will consider these structural adjective constraints in the future.

The work in [10] showed that the meanings of adjectives vary when modifying nouns from different classes, e.g., "American actors" means actors who have nationality United States, while "American cities" means cities that are located in the United States. In this sense, we consider the *class* for the noun that an adjective modifies as an important factor for the adjective mapping problem. Since many studies [1,12] have been done to map natural language phrases to classes in KBs, we skip the class mapping part and mainly focus on the problem of mapping adjectives to existential restrictions. We define the adjective mapping problem as follow:

Definition 1 (Adjective Mapping Problem). *Given an adjective adj and a class C (which stands for the class of the modified noun) in a KB, the adjective mapping problem is to map (adj, C) to existential restrictions or negation forms in description logics, such as* $\exists r.\top$, $\exists r.\{a\}$, $\neg\exists r.\top$ *or* $\neg\exists r.\{a\}$, *where* r, a *are a specific role and an individual in the KB, respectively. The resulted restrictions should reflect the meaning of the given adjective on the class.*

Due to the diversity of knowledge representations, there may exist more than one candidate mapping, e.g., both $\exists$*dbo:nationality.*{*dbr:United_States*} and $\exists$*dbp:nationality.*{*"American"*} are appropriate for "American" on *dbo:Actor*. Our study aims to find all suitable mappings for an input adjective.

To simplify the adjective mapping problem, we only consider the existential restrictions (or their negation forms) that can be determined by the existence of one certain fact. The considered forms of existential restrictions are shown in Table 3, which cover 92.3% of the factoid adjective constraints in QALD-5. For the adjectives that can be mapped to more complex structures, such as $\exists r_1.\exists r_2.\top$, we discuss them in Sect. 5.

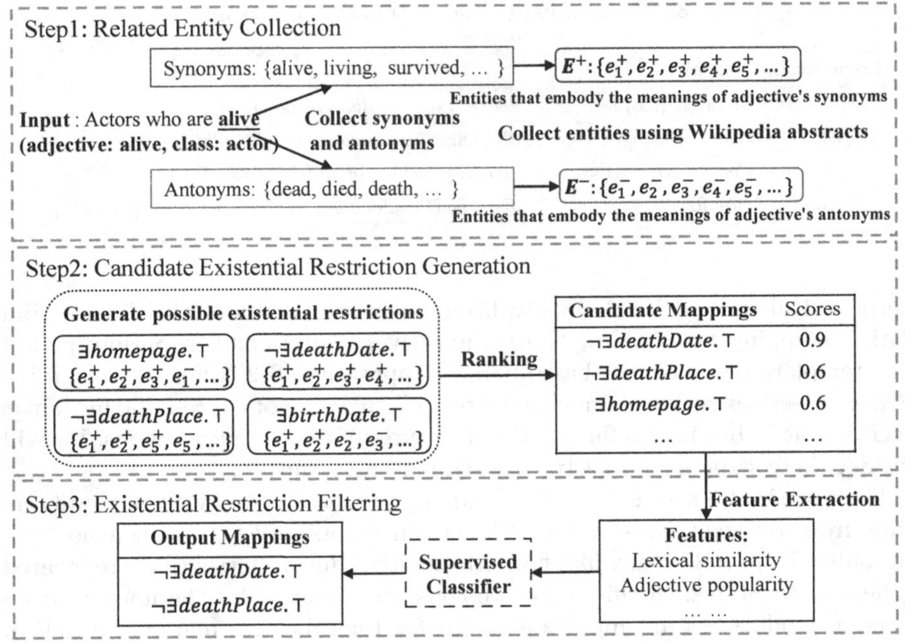

Fig. 1. Framework of the proposed approach

3 The Proposed Approach

In this section, we propose an approach, Adj2ER, to automatically map adjectives to several existential restrictions or their negation forms. The framework of the approach is shown in Fig. 1, which contains the following three steps:

1. **Related entity collection.** Two sets of entities (denoted by E^+ and E^-) are automatically collected by retrieving an adjective (or its synonyms and antonyms) in Web corpora such as Wikipedia abstracts, where E^+ denotes entities that embody the meanings of the input adjective's synonyms, and E^- denotes entities that embody the meanings of the adjective's antonyms.
2. **Candidate existential restriction generation.** Several candidate existential restrictions are generated from the facts about these entities in a given KB. Each candidate should cover most entities in E^+, and its negation should cover most entities in E^-.
3. **Existential restriction filtering.** A supervised learning method is designed to refine the candidate existential restrictions. The remaining restrictions are returned as the output of our approach.

Details for each step are described in the following three subsections.

3.1 Related Entity Collection

In this step, entity sets E^+ and E^- can be automatically collected by retrieving the co-occurrence of each entity and the adjective in Web corpora. In our approach, we choose Wikipedia abstracts, due to their high quality and good coverage, and they can be directly linked to entities in KBs through relations like *dbo:wikiPageID*.

For each entity e_i of class C in KB, we consider e_i as an element of E^+ if the input adjective appears in a sentence of its Wikipedia abstract. The following constraints are employed to ensure the accuracy:

- If the input adjective co-occurs with a negative word such as "never" or "not" in a sentence of e_i's Wikipedia abstract, this sentence is ignored.
- Sentences which begin with other entities may not describe e_i directly, thus they should not be considered during retrieving. These sentences can be detected and filtered out using page link information.
- Due to the incompleteness of KB, some unpopular entities may not have proper facts to embody the meaning of the adjective. Considering this, entities with less than 10 facts are not collected.

For some adjectives, e.g., "alive" and "dead", they rarely appear in Wikipedia abstracts, we automatically generate some alternative words for retrieving by using the following lexicons:

PPDB [17] is an automatically-extracted paraphrase database, which provides some equivalence and entailment relations between natural language words and phrases. For example, it provides both "died" and "death" for adjective "dead". We consider all the words that have a high-confidence equivalence or entailment relation[1] with the input adjective as alternative words.

WordNet [14] is a lexical database of English, where nouns, verbs, adjectives and adverbs are grouped into synsets, each expressing a different meaning. Each adjective participates in several synsets in WordNet, and it can be considered as an alternative word if it shares the same synset with the input adjective. However, some synsets contain rarely-used word senses of the input adjective, e.g., "dead" and "stagnant" share the same synset "not circulating or flowing", which is a rarely-used word sense for "dead". It may lower the precision if we consider "stagnant" as an alternative word for "dead". In this sense, we only consider top-2 synsets of each adjective when generating alternatives.

The method for collecting entities in E^- is very similar to E^+ after we fetch the antonyms of the input adjective in WordNet. For adjectives without any antonyms, we randomly sample some entities in class C which are not covered by E^+ to build E^-. The entities appearing in both E^+ and E^- should be removed from both sets, since it is hard to determine whether they embody the meaning of the adjective or not. Finally, a uniform random sampling method is used to make E^+ and E^- approximately the same in size.

[1] We used the S size PPDB downloaded from http://paraphrase.org/#/download.

3.2 Candidate Existential Restriction Generation

In this step, our approach generates some candidate existential restrictions using a statistical learning method. As shown in the middle of Fig. 1, our approach firstly generates all possible existential restrictions (or existential restrictions in negation forms) from the facts that are related to entities in E^+ and E^-, and then ranks them by a combined measurement based on the supporting degrees of E^+ and E^-.

For each fact about entity $e_i \in E^+$ in KB, this fact may describe the embodiment of the input adjective. Considering this, our approach generates two possible existential restrictions, $\exists r.\top$ and $\exists r.\{a\}$, for each fact about e_i in form of $(e_i, a) : r$. As for the facts in form of $(a, e_i) : r$, the approach also generates two possible existential restrictions, $\exists \bar{r}.\top$ and $\exists \bar{r}.\{a\}$, where $\bar{r}$ denotes the inverse of relation r. This step repeats for all $e_i \in E^+$. Particularly, we regard type as a role to make our approach unified, e.g., the fact "*Al_Pacino* : *Actor*" is regarded as "(*Al_Pacino*, *Actor*) : *type*".

If the input adjective has an antonym, each fact about entity $e_j \in E^-$ in KB may describe the embodiment of the antonym. Two possible existential restrictions in negation forms, $\neg\exists r.\top$ and $\neg\exists r.\{a\}$, are generated for each fact about e_j in form of $(e_j, a) : r$, which indicates that the entities embodying the meaning of the input adjective should not have such a fact in KB. Similarly, $\neg\exists \bar{r}.\top$ and $\neg\exists \bar{r}.\{a\}$ are generated for each fact about e_j in form of $(a, e_j) : r$.

After generating all the possible existential restrictions, our approach ranks them by a combined measurement. Let R_i be an existential restriction or a negation of existential restriction, we define the supporting degree on entity set E (E can be E^+ or E^-) as:

$$Sup(R_i, E) = \begin{cases} \dfrac{|\{e_i | e_i \in E \wedge e_i : R_i\}|}{|E|}, & \text{if } R_i \text{ contains no negation} \\ 1 - \dfrac{|\{e_i | e_i \in E \wedge e_i : \neg R_i\}|}{|E|}, & \text{otherwise} \end{cases} . \quad (1)$$

To calculate the supporting degrees, we also consider the facts inferred from sub-class and sub-property axioms, which are conducted in advance. Thus, the procedure of calculating the supporting degrees for R_i only needs to judge whether there is a certain fact for each $e_i \in E$. Since each fact is only related to two restrictions, it only needs to go through all the facts about entities in E^+ and E^- once the supporting degrees for all existential restrictions are calculated. Let F denote all the facts about entities in E^+ and E^-, the time complexity of calculating the supporting degrees is $O(2 \times |F|) = O(|F|)$, due to there are at most $2 \times |F|$ restrictions.

We adopt some measurements frequently used in information retrieval to rank all possible existential restrictions. First, a candidate existential restriction R_i should be supported by most of entities in E^+, while its negation $\neg R_i$ should be supported by most of entities in E^-. This assumption meets the goal of

Table 4. Features used in filtering for restriction R_i

Categories	#	Descriptions
Statistic	1, 2	Supporting degrees of R_i on E^+ and E^-, calculated by Eq. (1)
	3	Accuracy of R_i on E^+ and E^-, calculated by Eq. (2)
	4	Precision of R_i on E^+ and E^-, calculated by Eq. (3)
	5	Combined score of R_i on E^+ and E^-, calculated by Eq. (4)
Adjective popularity	6	Popularity of adjective in class C
	7	Popularity of adjective's antonym in class C (= 0 if no antonym)
Similarity	8	Lexical similarity between adjective (or its antonym) and R_i
	9	Semantic similarity between adjective (or its antonym) and R_i
Restriction form	10	Indicator: whether R_i contains negation
	11	Indicator: whether R_i contains an individual
	12	Indicator: whether R_i uses a reverse relation as role
	13	Indicator: whether R_i uses relation *type* as role

accuracy, which can be calculated as follow:

$$Acc(R_i, E^+, E^-) = \frac{Sup(R_i, E^+) + Sup(\neg R_i, E^-)}{2}. \tag{2}$$

Second, for any entity e_i in E^+ or E^-, if $e_i : R_i$ holds, the probability for $e_i \in E^+$ should be high. This assumption meets the goal of *precision*, which can be calculated as follow:

$$Prec(R_i, E^+, E^-) = \frac{Sup(R_i, E^+)}{Sup(R_i, E^+) + Sup(R_i, E^-)}. \tag{3}$$

The overall score for R_i is a combination of the above two measurements:

$$Score(R_i, E^+, E^-) = Acc(R_i, E^+, E^-) \times Prec(R_i, E^+, E^-). \tag{4}$$

We consider the top-M existential restrictions with *Score* larger than β as candidates. The whole time complexity is $O(|F|) + O(k \times 2 \times |F|) = O(|F|)$.

3.3 Existential Restriction Filtering

Although the existential restriction generation step generates several meaningful mappings, it only considers measurements on the supporting degrees of E^+ and E^-, which means that the precision of the candidates may highly associate with the quality of these two entity sets. Also, the meaning of the adjective itself is not considered. For example, we observed that our candidates contain $\exists$*foaf:homepage*.$\top$ for adjective "alive" on class *dbo:Person*, which means "people who are alive should have a homepage". This mapping is not precise but reasonable, since it captures a distribution characteristic for the facts on E^+ and E^-, which implies that most living people have a homepage (because people in the

KB are usually famous, and famous people usually have homepages), while most dead people do not (because there is even no computer when they were alive).

In this step, we design a supervised learning method to filter out inaccurate candidate mappings. We use a linear kernel SVM classifier, and consider four types of features for each existential restriction R_i, as shown in Table 4. *Statistic* features contain measurements considered in the candidate generation, such as the supporting degrees, accuracy and precision for R_i on E^+ and E^-. *Adjective popularity* features capture the frequency of the input adjective (or its antonym) in Wikipedia abstracts for entity with type C. Adjectives with low popularity may not have a proper mapping in a given KB. *Similarity* features consider the similarity between the adjective and the vocabulary elements used in R_i:

$$Similarity(adj, R_i) = \max_{w \in W(adj), l \in L(R_i)} Similarity(w, l), \tag{5}$$

where $W(adj)$ denotes all synonyms and antonyms of adj collected in the first step, and $L(R_i)$ denotes all labels for the role and individual appeared in R_i. We use the Levenshtein distance to calculate lexical similarity, and a pre-trained word embedding [18] to calculate semantic similarity (cosine similarity of word vectors). *Restriction form* features indicate which form of existential restriction R_i belongs to, which is defined in Table 3. Additionally, we add a feature to indicate whether R_i uses relation *type* as role, since some KBs usually use a subclass to capture the meaning of an adjective-modified class.

We manually label some existential restrictions for each input as training data. In the training procedure, we firstly execute Steps 1 and 2 to generate some candidates, and then calculate features mentioned above. To balance the number of positive and negative examples, we treat all candidates that appear in the answer set as positive examples, and select a part of remaining candidates according to the descending order of $Score$ as negative examples. During testing, all the existential restrictions that are labeled positive are treated as the output.

4 Experiments

We evaluated Adj2ER over DBpedia, with adjectives used in questions over structural data and community QA questions. Our experiments want to verify two hypotheses: (i) our approach can generate accurate mappings for most of adjectives in natural language questions, and (ii) current QA systems can benefit from integrating our adjective mapping approach. The question sets, source code, and experimental results are available at http://ws.nju.edu.cn/Adj2ER/.

4.1 Experiments on Adjective Mapping

Question Sets. Before building the question sets for evaluation, we implemented a simple method to identify questions with factoid adjective constraints. We first found all the questions that contain adjectives using the Stanford CoreNLP POS tagging module [13], and filtered out the questions in which adjectives only appear after "how". Also, we removed the questions in which adjectives only appear in proper nouns or relational phrases using EARL [9], a joint entity and relation linking system. Finally, we removed the questions with adjectives which represent structural constraints, such as "same", "other" and "different", using a manually-collected word list. This approach achieved an overall accuracy of 87% when we built the question sets for the following experiments, and the errors are mainly caused by relational phrase recognition failure.

QALDadj65 contains 65 (adj, C) pairs appearing in the questions from QALD-1 to QALD-9 [22]. We first extracted all the questions that contain factoid adjective constraints, and leveraged a type linking method [12] based on word embedding similarity to find a class in DBpedia for the noun that each adjective modifies. In some cases, the adjective modifies an entity, we took a minimal type of the entity as its class. Finally, 65 distinct (adj, C) pairs were generated. Furthermore, five Semantic Web majored graduate students were asked to build existential restrictions for each input. An existential restriction was considered as a reference answer only if more than three assessors had mentioned it in their answer sets. The agreement score between the assessors is good (Fleiss' $\kappa = 0.76$), and the average size of reference answers for each input is 3.72.

YAadj396 contains 396 frequently-used (adj, C) pairs in Yahoo! Answers Comprehensive Questions[2]. We firstly extracted the top-1,000 frequently-used (adj, C) pairs in questions. However, 412 of them contain adjectives like "good" and "favourite", whose meanings are related to personal preferences. Also, the assessors failed to achieve consistency answers for another 192 (adj, C) pairs, such as "new book" and "small city", and the meanings of most of these adjectives are not captured by DBpedia. For the remaining 396 input pairs, the average size of reference answers is 2.93. Considering the difficulty of this task, the agreement score between different assessors is acceptable (Fleiss' $\kappa = 0.62$) .

Metrics and Settings. For each input, we adopted precision (P), recall (R) and F1-score (F1) as the metrics. Especially, when the approach provided no answer for the input, we set P = R = F1 = 0. For each question set, we reported the average P, R and F1 values for all inputs. We performed 5-fold cross-validation on each question set. The following settings of Ajd2ER were evaluated:

Adj2ER-w/o filtering. We selected the top-K candidates according to the descending order of *Score* in Eq. (4), where K is a hyperparameter.

Adj2ER-full. We set parameter M to 20, and threshold β to 0.1 in the candidate generation step.

Comparative Approaches. We compared Adj2ER with the following two alternative approaches, which are commonly used in current QA systems:

Linking-based. Some existing QA systems [1,8,26] directly link adjectives or "adjective + noun" phrases to entities, classes or literals in the given KB. For

[2] https://webscope.sandbox.yahoo.com/.

Table 5. Evaluation results for adjective mapping

	QALDadj65			YAadj396			Time
	P	R	F1	P	R	F1	
Linking-based	31.90%	43.88%	32.66%	40.40%	34.18%	33.49%	**2.53s**
Network-based	40.26%	43.92%	36.48%	40.50%	40.54%	37.27%	89.15s
Adj2ER-w/o filtering	52.30%	36.89%	38.36%	39.98%	39.73%	36.54%	7.12s
Adj2ER-full	**71.30%**	**58.44%**	**59.65%**	**56.79%**	**46.29%**	**47.97%**	8.41s

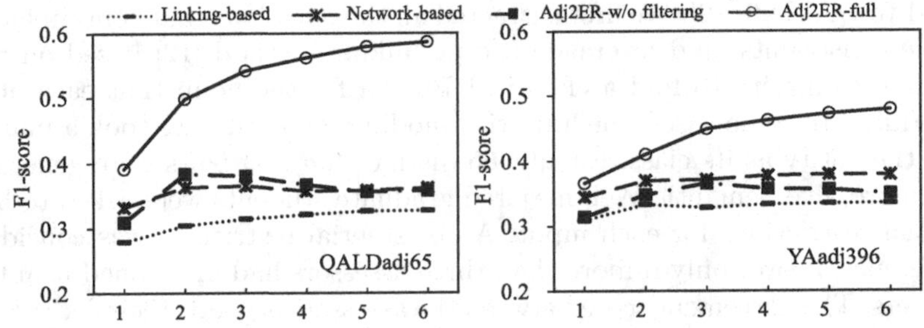

Fig. 2. F1-scores for top-K results of different approaches

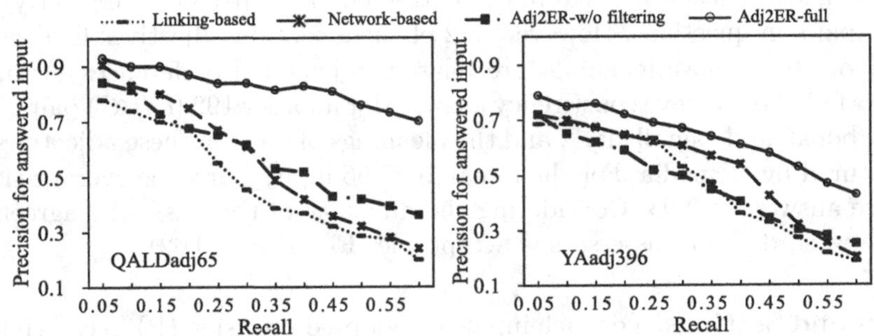

Fig. 3. Precision-recall curves for different approaches

each input (adj, C) pair, the linking-based approach links adj to some entities and classes using EARL [9], as well as some literals using Lucene search. Let a be the linking result from the above process. An existential restriction $\exists r.\{a\}$ is considered as a candidate if there is at least one entity $e : C$ which holds $(e, a) : r$ in KB. Then, a similarity score is calculated using cosine similarity between the averaged word embedding of each existential restriction and the "adjective + class" phrase. Finally, this approach considers the top-K existential restrictions satisfying similarity score larger than θ as the final output.

Network-based. Some recent QA systems [4,12] utilize neural networks to learn the semantic similarity between a natural language constraint expression and a target query component. For each input (adj, C) pair, the network-based approach randomly samples at most 1,000 entities of class C, and generates a large amount of candidate existential restrictions from all the facts about these entities. Then, all the candidates are ranked according to the semantic similarity with the input "adjective + noun" phrase, calculated by an encode-and-compare model [4]. The model consists of two convolutional neural networks which map the phrase and the existential restriction to 200-dimensional vectors, and the semantic similarity is calculated by the cosine similarity of the vectors. Finally, the top-K existential restrictions with similarity score larger than θ were considered as output.

Results. Table 5 shows the results for each adjective mapping approach, and Fig. 2 shows the F1-scores for top-K answers. The results on both question sets are quite similar, and our Adj2ER-full approach achieved the best performance. Compared with Adj2ER-w/o filtering, Adj2ER-full gained an improvement of more than 15% in precision, which indicated that the supervised filtering step successfully filtered out some inaccurate mappings. The average time cost by Adj2ER-full was 8.41 seconds, and approximately 80% of time was spent on getting data from the local DBpedia endpoint. We considered the time cost acceptable since we can prepare a lexicon for all adjectives before we integrate this approach into QA systems.

The results of the linking-based approach are not good (F1-scores are lower than 35% on both question sets), which indicated that the lexical gap between the adjectives and the target existential restrictions is huge. The network-based approach achieved similar results compared with Adj2ER-w/o filtering. However, it required labeled training data to train the semantic similarity model, while the latter only took weak supervisions from text. Also, the average time cost by the network-based approach was 10 times longer, since it took every fact about entities in class C as a possible representation for the adjective. By contrast, our approach leveraged statistic measures for generating candidates, which largely reduced the search space.

Also, we tested the performance change of each approach by setting varied thresholds for parameters. Figure 3 shows the precision-recall curves for the four approaches. The precision for Adj2ER-full kept larger than 60% when recall varied from 5% to 40%, which indicated that our approach can generate mappings of high quality for a considerable part of adjectives in natural language questions.

4.2 Experiments on Question Answering

Question Set. We built **AdjQuestions**, a question set containing 120 questions over structured data to verify if existing QA systems can benefit from our adjective mapping approach. We extracted all 70 questions that contain factoid adjective constraints from QALD-1 to QALD-9, and manually sampled 50 questions from Yahoo! Answers. For each question, a standard SPARQL query and its execution result over DBpedia-201510 were also provided.

Algorithm 1. Integrating Adj2ER into existing QA systems

Input: A natural language question Q
Output: A SPARQL query for the input question Q

```
procedure GENERATESPARQL(Q)
    S := ExistingQASystem.GENERATESPARQL(Q);
    for all (adj, C) pair in Q do
        Restrictions := Adj2ER(adj, C);
        if S contains a restriction ∈ Restrictions then continue;
        S' := S;
        Remove all restrictions in S' which have semantic similarity ≥ 0.6 with adj;
        for all restriction ∈ Restrictions do
            S* := Resulting SPARQL for adding restriction to S';
            if S* is a non-empty query then S := S*; break;
    return S;
```

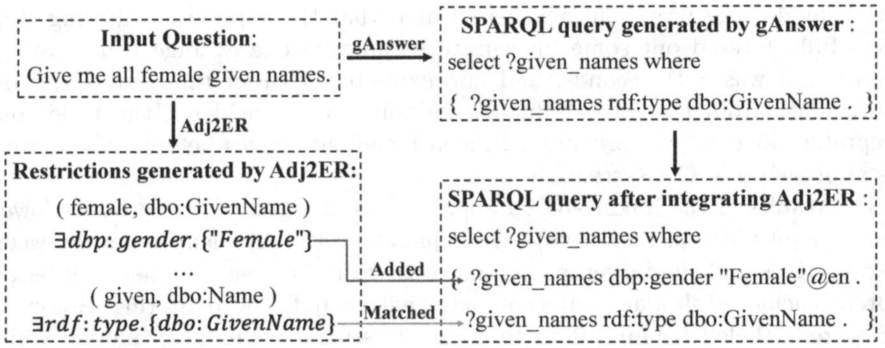

Fig. 4. Example for integrating Adj2ER into existing QA system

Table 6. QA results on AdjQuestions

	70 QALD questions			50 YA questions			Overall
	P	R	F1	P	R	F1	F1
gAnswer	30.49%	55.30%	29.75%	16.56%	36.26%	13.97%	23.18%
gAnswer + Adj2ER	**44.03%**	**62.25%**	**43.02%**	37.32%	**56.59%**	38.59%	**41.18%**
WDAqua	21.10%	26.64%	17.79%	23.53%	28.10%	22.04%	19.56%
WDAqua + Adj2ER	33.28%	43.86%	32.05%	**42.70%**	44.88%	**40.99%**	35.77%

Integrating Strategy. We integrated our adjective mapping approach into two state-of-the-art QA systems, namely gAnswer [11,26] and WDAqua [8], which ranked first and second in the QALD-9 challenge, respectively. The procedure for integrating Adj2ER into them is shown in Algorithm 1. An example to illustrate the procedure is shown in Fig. 4.

QA Results. Table 6 shows that, by integrating Adj2ER, gAnswer and WDAqua gained an improvement of 18.00% and 16.21% in macro F1-scores, respectively. Moreover, our integrating strategy modified 48.33% (58.33%) of SPARQL queries originally generated by gAnswer (WDAqua), and 33.33% (29.17%) questions gained an improvement in final F1-scores. Only 4.17% (5%) of questions had their F1-score decreased after integrating Adj2ER. It should be noticed that, sometimes even if the system understood the question correctly, it still cannot obtain the same result as the gold standard due to the difference in knowledge representations. For example, the final SPARQL query shown in Fig. 4 precisely expresses the meaning of the input question, and can be successfully executed over DBpedia with 728 answers returned. However, the SPRQAL query in gold standard expresses "female" in another way ($\exists$*dbo:gender.*{*dbr:Female*}), and its answer set is greatly different from ours. In order to test the real impact of our adjective understanding approach, we manually assessed whether each adjective is correctly interpreted. As a result, after integrating Adj2ER, the accuracy for interpreting adjectives improved from 32.50% (35.83%) to 61.66% (58.33%), which indicated that Adj2ER can greatly improve the performance of adjective understanding module in current QA systems.

5 Discussions

Limitations of Adj2ER. For the majority of adjectives used in the questions, our approach can generate the existential restrictions of high quality. However, there are still some adjectives that cannot be resolved by our approach, due to the following reasons: (i) a portion (3.04%) of compound adjectives rarely appear in Web corpora, such as "Chinese-speaking" and "non-extinct". They are also not covered by lexicons like WordNet and PPDB. Thus, Adj2ER did not collect enough related entities; (ii) a few adjectives should be mapped to more complex logic forms. For example, "widowed people" may be mapped to *dbo:Person*$\sqcap\exists$*dbo:spouse.*$\exists$*dbo:deathDate.*$\top$. Currently, our approach cannot generate such complex structures, due to the much larger search space and the difficulty in collecting related entities. We would like to consider dealing with these adjectives in the future.

It should also be noticed that, in this paper, we mainly focus on understanding adjectives for the KBQA task. From the perspective of adjective semantics [19], Adj2ER can handle most of intersective and subsective adjectives, but currently cannot handle scalar adjectives (e.g., "big cities") and intentional adjectives (e.g., "alleged criminal"), since these adjectives' meanings are not expressed in KBs, or the meanings are related to personal preferences. For example, when we say "big cities", we know that it represents a numerical constraint on cities' area or population, but there is no standard interpretation for "big". Such a question is considered inappropriate as a KBQA question, since even experts cannot provide consistent reference answers.

Error Analysis. There are several reasons causing the unsatisfactory result in QA. Firstly, 65% of error cases occurred in entity linking, relation mapping or query type detection, which are beyond the scope of this work. Particularly, several relational phrases, such as "official language", which should be mapped to simple relations, were detected as (adj, C) pairs by mistake. Secondly, in 23% of error cases Adj2ER generated inappropriate mappings for adjectives. Most of these adjectives are about time (e.g., past, current), and perhaps their meanings cannot be captured by existential restrictions. Finally, 12% of error cases were caused by our integrating strategy. The restrictions generated by Adj2ER were correct but added to wrong variables when there are multiple variables in the queries generated by the existing QA systems.

Other Findings. An interesting finding is that our approach can provide existential restrictions for different word senses of an adjective. For example, it provided both ∃*dbo:servingTemperature.*{*"Hot"*} and ∃*dbo:ingredient.*{*dbr:Chili_pepper*} for "hot" on class *dbo:Food*. The former existential restriction captures the meaning of "high temperature", while the latter one means "spicy". A word sense disambiguation method may be useful for better integration of Adj2ER in QA systems. Another interesting finding is that some existential restrictions, which were generated as candidates (before filtering), were not exact interpretation but entailed facts for most of the embodied entities, such as ∃*dbo:utcOffset.*{*"+8"*} for (Chinese, dbo:City). We would like to study how to exploit these candidates for information extraction in the future.

6 Related Work

This work is closely related to KBQA. Some existing systems [1,8,26] directly link adjectives or "adjective + noun" phrases to entities, classes or literals in the given KB, by using a similarity-based searching method or a pre-built lexicon. Although this solution can interpret "American actors" as "actors who are related to *dbr:United_States*", it cannot determine whether the phrase means "actors who have nationality *dbr:United_States*" or "actors who have death place *dbr:United_States*". Some recent systems [4,12] leverage the encode-and-compare networks to learn the semantic similarity between the natural language constraint expression and the target query component (in this work, the existential restriction). Our experiments showed that such solution may suffer from a huge search space and limited performance due to the lack of training data. Current QA systems cannot process adjectives in natural language questions precisely.

Semantic parsing is an important step in most QA systems, which translates natural language questions to structural queries, such as SPARQL, λ-DCS [5], CCG [6] and description logics [2]. Hu et al. [11] exploited semantic query graphs for question analysis based on the dependency structures of questions. Abujabal et al. [1] mapped questions to SPARQL templates automatically generated from question-answer pairs. However, all these approaches mainly focus on understanding proper nouns and relation phrases in questions, and do not have a specific step to recognize and interpret adjective constraints. Zhang et al. [25] studied the semantic interpretation of superlative expressions, by mapping each superlative adjective to a single relation in the KB with a neural network. However, this work cannot be applied to factoid adjective constraints, due to the diversity of knowledge representations and the lack of training data.

Entity linking and relation mapping are two essential steps in most of the semantic parsing approaches. Common entity linking approaches, e.g., [7,9], firstly generate candidates for possible entity mentions by running an exact string matching or lexical similarity based method over pre-built lexicons, and then focus on the problem of entity disambiguation. These approaches cannot be easily applied to adjective mapping, since the lexical gap between adjectives and structural knowledge is huge. The distant supervision method [15], which is frequently used to find mappings between relational phrases and KB relations, cannot handle the adjective mapping problem directly, as it is difficult to determine which facts in the KB express the meaning of the adjective.

In natural language processing area, there have been much work on clustering or identifying the meanings of adjectives [10,14]. Bakhshandeh and Allen [3] studied the problem of finding the aspect that an adjective describes through the WordNet glosses, such as "price" for "expensive". However, to the best of our knowledge, there is little work in studying the representations of adjectives over KBs. Walter et al. [23] proposed an approach for extracting adjective lexicalizations by analyzing the labels of objects occurring in DBpedia. However, this work only considers representations in form of $\exists r.\{a\}$, and requires a to be a meaningful string containing words related to the adjective. Our approach considers four forms of existential restrictions and is universal for all facts.

7 Conclusion

In this paper, we studied the problem of mapping factoid adjective constraints to existential restrictions over KBs. Our main contributions are listed below:

- We proposed a novel approach Adj2ER, which maps adjectives to existential restrictions or their negation forms in description logics.
- We leveraged statistic measures for generating candidate existential restrictions and supervised learning for filtering the candidates, which can largely reduce the search space and overcome the lexical gap.
- We created two question sets with adjectives used in QALD and Yahoo! Answers, and conducted experiments over DBpedia. Our experiments showed that Adj2ER generated mappings of high quality for most adjectives and significantly outperformed several alternative approaches. Furthermore, current QA systems gained an improvement of over 16% in F1-score by integrating our approach.

Understanding adjectives with KBs is still a difficult problem and deserves more attention. In future work, we plan to study other complex logic forms for adjective mapping. Also, we want to apply our approach to other tasks such as information extraction and question generation.

Acknowledgments. This work was supported by the National Key R&D Program of China (No. 2018YFB1004300), the National Natural Science Foundation of China (No. 61772264), and the Collaborative Innovation Center of Novel Software Technology and Industrialization. We would like to thank Xinqi Qian, Yuan Wang and Xin Yu for their helps in preparing evaluation.

References

1. Abujabal, A., Yahya, M., Riedewald, M., Weikum, G.: Automated template generation for question answering over knowledge graphs. In: WWW, pp. 1191–1200 (2017)
2. Baader, F., Calvanese, D., McGuinness, D.L., Nardi, D., Patel-Schneider, P.F.(eds.): The Description Logic Handbook: Theory, Implementation, and Applications. Cambridge University Press (2003)
3. Bakhshandeh, O., Allen, J.: From adjective glosses to attribute concepts: learning different aspects that an adjective can describe. In: IWCS, pp. 23–33 (2015)
4. Bao, J., Duan, N., Yan, Z., Zhou, M., Zhao, T.: Constraint-based question answering with knowledge graph. In: COLING, pp. 2503–2514 (2016)
5. Berant, J., Chou, A., Frostig, R., Liang, P.: Semantic parsing on freebase from question-answer pairs. In: EMNLP, pp. 1533–1544 (2013)
6. Bernardi, R.: The syntactic process: language, speech, and communication, mark steedman. J. Logic Lang. Inform. **13**(4), 526–530 (2004)
7. Deng, D., Li, G., Feng, J., Duan, Y., Gong, Z.: A unified framework for approximate dictionary-based entity extraction. VLDB J. **24**(1), 143–167 (2015)
8. Diefenbach, D., Singh, K., Maret, P.: WDAqua-core0: a question answering component for the research community. In: Dragoni, M., Solanki, M., Blomqvist, E. (eds.) SemWebEval 2017. CCIS, vol. 769, pp. 84–89. Springer, Cham (2017). https://doi.org/10.1007/978-3-319-69146-6_8
9. Dubey, M., Banerjee, D., Chaudhuri, D., Lehmann, J.: EARL: joint entity and relation linking for question answering over knowledge graphs. In: Vrandečić, D., et al. (eds.) ISWC 2018. LNCS, vol. 11136, pp. 108–126. Springer, Cham (2018). https://doi.org/10.1007/978-3-030-00671-6_7
10. Hartung, M., Frank, A.: Exploring supervised LDA models for assigning attributes to adjective-noun phrases. In: EMNLP, pp. 540–551 (2011)
11. Hu, S., Zou, L., Yu, J.X., Wang, H., Zhao, D.: Answering natural language questions by subgraph matching over knowledge graphs. IEEE Trans. Knowl. Data Eng. **30**(5), 824–837 (2018)
12. Luo, K., Lin, F., Luo, X., Zhu, K.Q.: Knowledge base question answering via encoding of complex query graphs. In: EMNLP, pp. 2185–2194 (2018)
13. Manning, C.D., Surdeanu, M., Bauer, J., Finkel, J.R., Bethard, S., McClosky, D.: The Stanford CoreNLP natural language processing toolkit. In: ACL, pp. 55–60 (2014)
14. Miller, G.A.: WordNet: a lexical database for English. Commun. ACM **38**(11), 39–41 (1995)
15. Mintz, M., Bills, S., Snow, R., Jurafsky, D.: Distant supervision for relation extraction without labeled data. In: ACL-IJCNLP, pp. 1003–1011 (2009)
16. Nakashole, N., Weikum, G., Suchanek, F.M.: PATTY: a taxonomy of relational patterns with semantic types. In: EMNLP-CoNLL, pp. 1135–1145 (2012)

17. Pavlick, E., Rastogi, P., Ganitkevitch, J., Durme, B.V., Callison-Burch, C.: PPDB 2.0: better paraphrase ranking, fine-grained entailment relations, word embeddings, and style classification. In: ACL, pp. 425–430 (2015)
18. Pennington, J., Socher, R., Manning, C.D.: GloVe: global vectors for word representation. In: EMNLP, pp. 1532–1543 (2014)
19. Pustejovsky, J.: Inference patterns with intensional adjectives. In: Joint ISO-ACL SIGSEM Workshop on Interoperable Semantic Annotation, pp. 85–89 (2013)
20. Unger, C., Bühmann, L., Lehmann, J., Ngomo, A.C.N., Gerber, D., Cimiano, P.: Template-based question answering over RDF data. In: WWW, pp. 639–648 (2012)
21. Unger, C., et al.: Question answering over linked data (QALD-5). In: CLEF (2015)
22. Usbeck, R., Gusmita, R.H., Ngomo, A.N., Saleem, M.: 9th challenge on question answering over linked data (QALD-9) (invited paper). In: ISWC Workshop on SemDeep-4/NLIWOD-4, pp. 58–64 (2018)
23. Walter, S., Unger, C., Cimiano, P.: Automatic acquisition of adjective lexicalizations of restriction classes: a machine learning approach. J. Data Semant. **6**(3), 113–123 (2017)
24. Yih, W., Chang, M., He, X., Gao, J.: Semantic parsing via staged query graph generation: question answering with knowledge base. In: ACL-IJCNLP, pp. 1321–1331 (2015)
25. Zhang, S., Feng, Y., Huang, S., Xu, K., Han, Z., Zhao, D.: Semantic interpretation of superlative expressions via structured knowledge bases. In: ACL-IJCNLP, pp. 225–230 (2015)
26. Zou, L., Huang, R., Wang, H., Yu, J.X., He, W., Zhao, D.: Natural language question answering over RDF: a graph data driven approach. In: SIGMOD, pp. 313–324 (2014)

Mining Significant Maximum Cardinalities in Knowledge Bases

Arnaud Giacometti, Béatrice Markhoff, and Arnaud Soulet(✉)

Université de Tours, LIFAT, Blois, France
{arnaud.giacometti,beatrice.markhoff,arnaud.soulet}@univ-tours.fr

Abstract. Semantic Web connects huge knowledge bases whose content has been generated from collaborative platforms and by integration of heterogeneous databases. Naturally, these knowledge bases are incomplete and contain erroneous data. Knowing their data quality is an essential long-term goal to guarantee that querying them returns reliable results. Having cardinality constraints for roles would be an important advance to distinguish correctly and completely described individuals from those having data either incorrect or insufficiently informed. In this paper, we propose a method for automatically discovering from the knowledge base's content the maximum cardinality of roles for each concept, when it exists. This method is robust thanks to the use of Hoeffding's inequality. We also design an algorithm, named C3M, for an exhaustive search of such constraints in a knowledge base benefiting from pruning properties that drastically reduce the search space. Experiments conducted on DBpedia demonstrate the scaling up of C3M, and also highlight the robustness of our method, with a precision higher than 95%.

Keywords: Cardinality mining · Contextual constraint · Knowledge base

1 Introduction

With the rise of the Semantic Web, knowledge bases (that we will denote KB) are growing and multiplying. At the worldwide level knowledge hubs are built from collaborative platforms, either by extraction from Wikipedia as DBpedia [1] or collaboratively collecting knowledge as for Wikidata [6], or integrating various sources using information retrieval algorithms as for YAGO [21]. These very large KBs represent a wealth of information for applications, as this is the case with Wikipedia for human beings. On a smaller scale, more and more knowledge bases are published on the Web, built from diverse data sources following Extract-Transform-Load integration processes that are based on a shared ontology (ontology-based data integration).

Due to the way they are generated, all of these KBs need to be enriched with more information to evaluate their quality with respect to the represented reality,

C. Ghidini et al. (Eds.): ISWC 2019, LNCS 11778, pp. 182–199, 2019.
https://doi.org/10.1007/978-3-030-30793-6_11

and reverse engineering techniques have already been considered to automatically obtain useful declarations such as keys [16,19]. In this paper we propose to automatically discover another kind of useful declaration about the represented data in a given KB: *role maximum cardinalities.* In knowledge representation, numerical restrictions which specify the number of occurrences of a role are particularly useful [2]. For example, a numerical restriction can be used to describe a concept[1] C as the set of individuals who have at most 3 children. Moreover, a numerical restriction can be used to declare a *maximum cardinality constraint on the role R in the context C*, for instance on the role `parent` in the context `Person`, for declaring that individuals of concept `Person` have at most twice the role `parent`. Such a declaration allows reasoners to infer whether all the assertions on role R exist in the KB for any individual belonging to C. This can be used to supplement the answers to queries with precise information on their quality in terms of *recall* with respect to reality [20].

Table 1. Cardinality distributions for some contexts/roles in DBpedia (with the role cardinality i, the number of individuals n_i having i times this role, the likelihood τ_i and the pessimistic likelihood $\widetilde{\tau}_i$ that are defined in Sect. 4.1)

Person / birthYear				Person / parent			
i	n_i	τ_i	$\widetilde{\tau}_i$	i	n_i	τ_i	$\widetilde{\tau}_i$
1	**159,841**	**0.999**	**0.996**	1	10,643	0.529	0.518
2	91	0.928	0.775	**2**	**9,392**	**0.991**	**0.975**
3	4	0.571	0.000	3	75	0.882	0.718
4	2	0.667	0.000	4	9	0.900	0.420
5	1	1.000	0.000	6	1	1.000	0.000

⊤ / team				FootballMatch / team			
i	n_i	τ_i	$\widetilde{\tau}_i$	i	n_i	τ_i	$\widetilde{\tau}_i$
1	1,221,202	0.901	0.900	1	26	0.008	0.000
2	20,505	0.153	0.148	**2**	**3,092**	**0.998**	**0.971**
3	16,876	0.148	0.144	3	3	0.500	0.000
...	...	...	...	4	2	0.667	0.000
20	2	1.000	0.000	5	1	1.000	0.000

To the best of our knowledge there is only one work dedicated to the extraction of cardinality constraint from a KB [15], maybe because compared to the traditional database framework, extracting *significant* cardinality constraints from a KB is a far more challenging task. Indeed, we are facing three important challenges. A *first challenge* is that a KB generally contains *inconsistent* data, either because of errors or because of duplicate descriptions. Due to these inconsistencies, the *observed* maximum cardinality for a role in a KB cannot be considered

[1] We use the Description Logics (DL) [2] terminology, as DL are the theoretical foundations of OWL, so we use the terms *concept* (i.e. class), *role* (i.e. property), *individual* and *fact* (i.e. instances).

to be its true maximum cardinality. For example, it is expected that a person will have at most one birth year and two parents. However, considering the roles `birthYear` and `parent` in DBpedia (see Table 1), some persons have 5 birth years or 6 parents. These few inconsistent assertions should not influence the maximum cardinality discovery. Then, a *second challenge* is that a KB is often *incomplete* for a given role. For this reason, the *most frequently observed* cardinality for a role in a KB cannot be considered to be its true maximum cardinality. Typically, most people described in DBpedia have only one informed parent. Nonetheless, we have to take into account that many people have two informed parents for not underestimating the maximum cardinality of the role `parent`. Finally, a *third challenge* is that the expected constraints depend on a *context*. For instance in DBpedia the role `team` is used to inform the teams to which a person has belonged and the teams of a football match. Thus, it is not possible to determine the maximum cardinality of the role `team` in DBpedia (context $\top$), but its maximum cardinality is expected to be 2 in the context of `FootballMatch`. Consequently, instead of exploring each role of a knowledge base, we have to explore each role for each concept. This leads to a huge search space and therefore it is necessary to prune it without missing relevant constraints. But, conversely, we have to avoid extracting redundant constraints. If we identify that a person has at most one birth year, it would be a shame to overwhelm the end user with the cardinality of `birthYear` for artists, scientists and so on.

Taking into account these challenges, we present in this paper two main contributions. Our first contribution is to propose *a method for computing a significant maximum cardinality.* The significance is guaranteed by the use of Hoeffding's inequality for computing corrected likelihood estimates of maximum cardinality. We show with experiments using DBpedia that we extract only reliable maximum cardinalities. More precisely, contrary to [15] it is important to note that we output a maximum cardinality if and only if it is actually significant. Our second contribution is C3M[2], *an algorithm for enumerating the set of all contextual maximum cardinalities* that are minimal (Definition 2) and significant (Definition 4). We use two sound pruning criteria that drastically reduce the exploration space, and ensure the scalability of C3M for large KBs. It is also interesting to notice that we implemented C3M in such a way that it explores Web KBs via their public SPARQL endpoints without centralizing data.

This paper is structured as follows. Section 2 reviews some related works. In Sect. 3, we first introduce some basic notions and formalize the problem. Then, in Sect. 4, we show how to detect a significant maximum cardinality of a role. Next, in Sect. 5, we present our algorithm C3M. Section 6 provides experimental results on DBpedia that shows its efficiency and its scalability, together with the meaningfulness of discovered constraints. We conclude in Sect. 7.

[2] The prototype and the results are available at https://github.com/asoulet/c3m, both in CSV and in RDF (Turtle); we provide also the schema of our constraints expressed in RDF.

2 Related Work

To increase knowledge about the quality of data contained in KB, some proposals calculate quality indicators like completeness [17] or representativeness [18], while others are interested in the enrichment of individuals or concepts with fine-grained assertions or constraints. Our proposal is in the line of these works, which we detail in what follows.

Works on Mining Role Cardinality for Individuals. Several works consist in enriching the set of assertions on individuals (ABox), and we can distinguish the *endogenous* approaches [9] relying on the assertions already present in the ABox, from the *exogenous* approaches [13] relying on external sources. [9] shows that it is important to determine when a particular role (such as `parent`) is missing for a particular individual (such as *Obama*). Their proposal of Partial Completeness Assumption states that when at least one assertion about a role R is informed for an individual s, then all assertions for this role R are informed for this individual s. In [13], the authors benefit from text mining applied on Wikipedia for improving the completeness of individuals described in Wikidata. This exogenous approach relies on syntactical patterns to identify cardinalities on individuals. More generally, in [8], the authors propose various kinds of endogenous and exogenous heuristics for characterizing the completeness of individuals, called Completeness Oracles, as for instance taking into account the popularity of individuals (i.e., a famous individual is more likely to have complete information). Our proposal is endogenous as it processes the facts already contained in the KB that we want to enrich. Nevertheless, it does not characterize the role cardinality for a specific *individual* but for a *concept*. It is therefore more general as the constraints for concept C apply for all the individuals of C.

Works on Mining Role Cardinality for Concepts. Other proposals have focused on the enrichment of the schema part (TBox) with new assertions or axioms allowing to partially or completely specify the cardinality of a role. In particular, several works [16,19] address the automated discovery of contextual keys in RDF datasets as it was done in relational databases. They find axioms stating that individuals of a concept C must have only one tuple of values for a given tuple of roles. The same kind of cardinality information is induced by [12]. Indeed, the authors propose to discover roles that are mandatory for individuals of a concept C. For this purpose, they compare the density of the role R for individuals of the concept C with the densities of R for other concepts in the concept hierarchy. Our proposal focuses on mining the maximum cardinality for a role R in a context C (if it exists). But, contrary to the previous work, we can get information about cardinalities greater than 1 (e.g., 2 parents for a child). To the best of our knowledge, [15] is the only work explicitly dedicated to the detection of minimum/maximum cardinalities. This approach proceeds in two stages: removal of outliers and calculation of bounds. Unfortunately, KBs are so incomplete that the filtering of outliers is ineffective (e.g., there are more children with only one parent than children with 2 parents). Moreover, their filtering method implicitly assumes that the cardinalities follow a normal distribution, or a distribution that is moderately asymmetric, which is not always the case (see the examples of Table 1). Consequently, for DBpedia their approach finds that a person has at most 2 years of birth (instead of 1) and 3 parents (instead of 2); and a football match has 3 teams (instead of 2). It is also important to note that the method extracts a cardinality constraint for every concept and role of the KB, whatever the number of observations and the distribution (e.g., a constraint for team is found in the context $\top$). Thus, many of these constraints are not significant. On the contrary, our approach benefits from Hoeffding's inequality for ensuring statisical significance. Finally, contrary to our approach, the authors do not envisage an algorithm to systematically explore the roles and concepts of the KB. An exploration strategy is yet crucial and not trivial in practice due to the huge search space.

Interest of Role Cardinality. Whatever the approach, all information extracted about role cardinalities is useful for improving many methods, as they reduce the uncertainty imposed by the open-world assumption. [9,20] show the necessity of reducing this uncertainty for data mining applied to KB. In particular, [8,9] propose to benefit from the previously mentioned Partial Completeness Assumption for improving the confidence estimation of association rules. More recently, [20] has further improved the confidence estimation of a rule by exploiting the bounds on the cardinality for an individual. Data mining is not the only field where insights about cardinalities are useful. [3,4,17] and more recently [10] propose to characterize query answers benefiting from the completeness degree of the queried data. Most of these methods can therefore directly benefit from the constraints that we investigate in this paper.

3 Preliminaries and Problem Formulation

3.1 Basic Notations

For talking about KB components, we use Description Logics (DL) [2] terminology. For instance DBpedia is a KB $\mathcal{K} = (\mathcal{T}, \mathcal{A})$, where $\mathcal{T}$ denotes its TBox and $\mathcal{A}$ denotes its ABox. One example of assertion in $\mathcal{T}$ is $\texttt{Artist} \sqsubseteq \texttt{Person}$, meaning that the concept `Artist` is subsumed by the concept `Person`, i.e. all artists are persons. $\mathcal{T}$ also includes assertions like $\exists\texttt{birthYear} \sqsubseteq \texttt{Person}$, meaning that the role `birthYear` is defined for persons. Note that the only part of the TBox used by our approach is the named hierarchies of concepts. Besides, $\texttt{Person}(Obama)$ and $\texttt{birthYear}(Obama, 1961)$ are assertions of DBpedia's ABox $\mathcal{A}$. The former indicates that *Obama* is a person, while the latter states that *Obama* was born in 1961. In this paper, we assume that a KB $\mathcal{K}$ contains only one hierarchy of concepts and we use the general top concept $\top$ which subsumes every concept in $\mathcal{K}$. In DL, a maximum cardinality M on the role R may be represented using the numerical restriction constructor $\leq M\ R$. $\mathcal{K} = (\mathcal{T}, \mathcal{A})$ implies[3] the constraint $\top \sqsubseteq (\leq M\ R)$, if for all subjects s, the number of objects o such that $R(s, o)$

[3] DL formal semantics are given in terms of interpretations, see [2].

belongs to $\mathcal{K}$ (i.e., $R(s, o) \in \mathcal{A}$ or $R(s, o)$ can be inferred from $\mathcal{T}$ and $\mathcal{A}$) is equal to or fewer than M.

We focus on cardinality constraints that are *contextual*, as stated in Definition 1. Intuitively, these constraints are not necessarily satisfied for all subjects of a role R, but for all the subjects of R that belong to a concept C.

Definition 1 (Contextual Constraint). *Given an integer $M \geq 1$, a role R and a concept C of a KB $\mathcal{K}$, a contextual maximum cardinality constraint defined on R for C is an expression of the form: $C \sqsubseteq (\leq M\ R)$.*

The concept C is called the context of the constraint $C \sqsubseteq (\leq M\ R)$. For example, the contextual constraint $\texttt{Person} \sqsubseteq (\leq 1\ \texttt{birthYear})$ means that each person has at most 1 birth year, while $\texttt{FootballMatch} \sqsubseteq (\leq 2\ \texttt{team})$ means that a football match has at most 2 teams. Note that asserting that an artist has at most one year of birth (i.e., $\texttt{Artist} \sqsubseteq (\leq 1\ \texttt{birthYear})$) is true, but less general than $\texttt{Person} \sqsubseteq (\leq 1\ \texttt{birthYear})$ because $\texttt{Artist} \sqsubset \texttt{Person}$. Similarly, asserting that 1,000 is a maximum cardinality for the parent role (i.e., $\texttt{Person} \sqsubseteq (\leq 1,000\ \texttt{parent})$) is true, but less specific than $\texttt{Person} \sqsubseteq (\leq 2\ \texttt{parent})$. We want to discover contextual maximum cardinality constraints that have a context as general as possible and a cardinality as small as possible. For this purpose, we introduce the notion of minimal contextual constraint:

Definition 2 (Minimal Contextual Constraint). *The contextual constraint $\gamma_1 : C_1 \sqsubseteq (\leq M_1\ R)$ is more general than the contextual constraint $\gamma_2 : C_2 \sqsubseteq (\leq M_2\ R)$, denoted by $\gamma_2 \sqsubset \gamma_1$, iff $C_2 \sqsubset C_1$[4] and $M_1 \leq M_2$, or $C_2 \equiv C_1$ and $M_1 < M_2$. For a given set of contextual constraints Γ, constraint $\gamma_1 \in \Gamma$ is minimal in Γ if there is no constraint $\gamma_2 \in \Gamma$ more general than γ_1: $(\nexists \gamma_2 \in \Gamma)(\gamma_1 \sqsubset \gamma_2)$.*

The notion of minimality restricts the mining to a set of constraints that is not redundant, meaning that we do not want to extract a maximum cardinality constraint γ_2 if it is logically implied by another maximum cardinality constraint γ_1. More precisely, it is easy to see that if a maximum cardinality constraint $\gamma_1 : C_1 \sqsubseteq (\leq M_1\ R)$ is more general than a maximum cardinality constraint $\gamma_2 : C_2 \sqsubseteq (\leq M_2\ R)$, then for all interpretation $\mathcal{I}$ of a KB $\mathcal{K}$, if $\mathcal{I}$ is a model of γ_1, then $\mathcal{I}$ is also a model of γ_2. Indeed, if $\mathcal{I}$ is a model of γ_1, we have $C_1^{\mathcal{I}} \subseteq \{o : \#\{o' : (o, o') \in R^{\mathcal{I}}\} \leq M_1\}$. Moreover, since γ_1 is more general than γ_2, we have $C_2^{\mathcal{I}} \subseteq C_1^{\mathcal{I}}$ and $M_1 \leq M_2$. Thus, we have $C_2^{\mathcal{I}} \subseteq C_1^{\mathcal{I}} \subseteq \{o : \#\{o' : (o, o') \in R^{\mathcal{I}}\} \leq M_1\} \subseteq \{o : \#\{o' : (o, o') \in R^{\mathcal{I}}\} \leq M_2\}$, which shows that $\mathcal{I}$ is a model of γ_2.

Note that our method relies on a named concept hierarchy for exploring possible contexts and using their subsumption relations. However, it is possible to generate such a hierarchy to explore more complex contexts in a pre-processing step. Such an approach is useful to analyze data by expressing the background knowledge of an expert through an analytical hierarchy.

[4] We denote $C \sqsubset C'$ when $C \sqsubseteq C'$ and $C' \not\sqsubseteq C$.

3.2 Problem Statement

Considering the statistics in DBpedia provided by Table 1, we do not want to discover the contextual constraints `Person` $\sqsubseteq$ ($\leq$6 `birthYear`) or `Person` $\sqsubseteq$ ($\leq$5 `parent`) even if these constraints are satisfied and minimal in $\mathcal{K}$. We would intend to extract the contextual constraints `Person` $\sqsubseteq$ ($\leq$1 `birthYear`) or `Person` $\sqsubseteq$ ($\leq$2 `parent`). Therefore, as defined in [14], we assume an ideal description of the world or ideal KB, denoted $\mathcal{K}^*$, in the sense that $\mathcal{K}^*$ is *correct* (it does not contain any inconsistancies) and *complete*. Note that in general, we have neither $\mathcal{K} \subseteq \mathcal{K}^*$, nor $\mathcal{K}^* \subseteq \mathcal{K}$, because $\mathcal{K}$ is inconsistent or incomplete. In this context, our problem can be formalized as follows:

Problem 1. Given a knowledge base $\mathcal{K}$, we aim at discovering the set of all contextual maximum cardinality constraints $C \sqsubseteq (\leq M\ R)$ where C and R are concept and role of $\mathcal{K}$, that are *satisfied* in $\mathcal{K}^*$ and *minimal* with respect to the concept hierarchy of $\mathcal{K}$.

In order to solve Problem 1 we have to deal with the two following challenges: (i) discover constraints that would be satisfied in $\mathcal{K}^*$ whereas this knowledge base is hypothetical and unknown (see Sect. 4), and (ii) efficiently explore the search space knowing that the number of possible contextual maximum cardinality constraints is huge (see Sect. 5).

4 Detecting Significant Maximum Cardinalities

This section use a probability framework relying on the hypothesis that the degree of completeness of a role is in general higher than its level of inconsistencies. For instance, this assumption is reasonable for DBpedia. Indeed, even if it is difficult to evaluate the completeness and the semantic accuracy of a knowledge base because it requires a gold standard [5], several results of the literature tend to show that the semantic accuracy of DBpedia is better than its completeness [7].

More formally, let us assume that M is the *true* maximum cardinality of the role R in the context C, meaning that the maximum cardinality constraint $\gamma : C \sqsubseteq (\leq M\ R)$ is satisfied in $\mathcal{K}^*$. In practice, the ideal KB $\mathcal{K}^*$ is unknown and we only have a sample $\mathcal{K}$ of the reality. Let X be the random variable that denotes for a subject s the number of assertions $R(s, o)$ observed in $\mathcal{K}$. We assume that:

- The level of inconsistencies in $\mathcal{K}$ is not significant, i.e. the probability $\mathbf{P}(X > M)$ to observe a cardinality greater than M for role R is low. For example, in Table 1, we can see that 85 individuals of context `Person` have more than 2 parents, but they represent less than 0.43% of the observed individuals.
- The degree of completeness (present roles) is significantly higher, i.e. the probability $\mathbf{P}(X = M)$ to observe the maximum cardinality M is significantly higher than $\mathbf{P}(X > M)$. For example, in Table 1, we can see that 9,342 individuals of context `Person` have 2 parents, which represents more than 46.7% of the observed individuals.

Under these hypotheses, the following property states that if M is the true maximum cardinality of the role R in the context C, then M is the integer i that maximizes the conditional probability $\mathbf{P}(X = i|X \geq i)$:

Property 1. Let M be the *true* maximum cardinality of the role R in the context C. If $\mathbf{P}(X = M) \geq \lambda$ and $\mathbf{P}(X > M) \leq \epsilon$, then we have $\mathbf{P}(X = M|X \geq M) \geq \frac{\lambda}{\lambda+\epsilon}$ and $\mathbf{P}(X = i|X \geq i) \leq (1-\lambda)$ for $i \in [1..M[$. Moreover, if $\lambda > 1/2(\sqrt{\epsilon^2+4\epsilon}-\epsilon)$, we have: $M = \arg\max_{i\in\mathbb{N}^+}\{\mathbf{P}(X = i|X \geq i) : \mathbf{P}(X = i) > \epsilon\}$.

Due to lack of space, we omit the proofs. Assuming an inconsistency level ϵ equal to 0.1% (resp. 1%), Property 1 states that it is possible to detect a true maximum cardinality if the degree of completeness λ is greater than $1/2(\sqrt{0.001^2+4\cdot 0.001}-0.001) = 3.2\%$ (resp. 9.5%). Moreover, a true maximum cardinality constraint M will be detected if $\mathbf{P}(X = M|X \geq M) \geq \frac{\lambda}{\lambda+\epsilon} \geq 97\%$ (resp. 90%). Finally, note that when there is no inconsistency (i.e., $\mathbf{P}(X > M) = 0$ and $\epsilon = 0$), if M is a true maximum cardinality, then $\mathbf{P}(X = M|X \geq M) = 1$.

Now, based on this assumption, we define in Sect. 4.1 the measure of *likelihood* to detect maximum cardinality constraints, and show how to use Hoeffding's inequality to obtain more accurate decisions. Besides, we introduce in Sect. 4.2 the notion of *significant constraint.*

4.1 Likelihood Measure

We now introduce the notion of likelihood to measure a frequency estimation of the conditional probability $\mathbf{P}(X = i|X \geq i)$ involved in Property 1 (for deciding whether a cardinality i for the role R in the context C is likely to be maximum):

Definition 3 (Likelihood). *Given a knowledge base $\mathcal{K}$, the likelihood of the maximum cardinality i of the role R for the context C is the ratio defined as follows: $\tau_i^{C,R}(\mathcal{K}) = \frac{n_i^{C,R}}{n_{\geq i}^{C,R}}$ if $n_{\geq i}^{C,R} > 0$ (0 otherwise) where $n_i^{C,R}$ (resp. $n_{\geq i}^{C,R}$) is the number of individuals s of the context C such that i facts $R(s,o)$ (resp. i facts or more) are stated in $\mathcal{K}$.*

When the context and the role are clear, we omit them in notations. In that case, n_i, $n_{\geq i}$ and $\tau_i(\mathcal{K})$ respectively denote $n_i^{C,R}$, $n_{\geq i}^{C,R}$ and $\tau_i^{C,R}(\mathcal{K})$.

For example, let us consider the context `Person` and the role `parent`. Using Table 1, it is easy to see that $n_{\geq 2}^{\texttt{Person,parent}} = 9,477$ $(9,477 = 9,392+75+9+1)$. Thereby, the likelihood $\tau_2^{\texttt{Person,parent}}(\mathcal{K})$ is 0.991 (i.e., 9,392/9,477). Note that this measure ignores the 10,643 persons that have only one informed parent (to evaluate if 2 is the true maximum cardinality for parents). Then, it is also easy to see that we have $\tau_6^{\texttt{Person,parent}}(\mathcal{K}) = 1$, whereas 6 is not the true maximum cardinality for the role `parent`. Intuitively, if the likelihood $\tau_6^{\texttt{Person,parent}}(\mathcal{K}) = 1$ does not make sense, it is due to an insufficient number of individuals for reinforcing this hypothesis (here, only 1 individual has 6 parents). In general, the estimation of $\mathbf{P}(X = i|X \geq i)$ by $\tau_i(\mathcal{K})$ must be corrected to be statistically valid. For this purpose, we benefit from the Hoeffding's inequality [11] which has the advantage of being true for any distribution. It provides an upper bound on the probability that an empirical mean (in our case, a likelihood $\tau_i(\mathcal{K})$) deviates from its expected value (the conditional probability $\mathbf{P}(X = i|X \geq i)$) by more than a given amount. More formally, we have the following property:

Property 2 (Lower bound). Given a knowledge base $\mathcal{K}$ and a confidence level $1 - \delta$, assuming that all the observations are independently and identically distributed, the conditional probability $\theta_i = \mathbf{P}(X = i|X \geq i)$ is greater than the pessimistic likelihood $\widetilde{\tau}_i(\mathcal{K})$ defined by (if $n_{\geq i} > 0$):

$$\widetilde{\tau}_i(\mathcal{K}) = \max\left\{\frac{n_i}{n_{\geq i}} - \sqrt{\frac{\log(1/\delta)}{2n_{\geq i}}}, 0\right\}$$

with a probability greater than $(1 - \delta)$, i.e. $\mathbf{P}(\theta_i \geq \widetilde{\tau}_i(\mathcal{K})) \geq (1 - \delta)$.

This property provides us an efficient tool to make confident decisions. For instance, for the role `parent` in Table 1, we observe that the correction strongly reduces the likelihood $\tau_i(\mathcal{K})$ for cardinalities 3, 4 and 6 (e.g., $\widetilde{\tau}_6^{\texttt{Person,parent}}(\mathcal{K}) = 0$). Conversely, we have $\widetilde{\tau}_2^{\texttt{Person,parent}}(\mathcal{K}) = 0.975$, a strong indicator to consider that 2 is the true maximum cardinality for the role `parent` in the context `Person`.

4.2 Significant Maximum Cardinality

Using Properties 1 and 2, we finally propose to detect a maximum cardinality M for a confidence level $1 - \delta$ if (i) the pessimistic likelihood $\widetilde{\tau}_M(\mathcal{K})$ is maximum, i.e. $\widetilde{\tau}_M(\mathcal{K}) = \max_{i>0} \widetilde{\tau}_M(\mathcal{K})$, and (ii) the pessimistic likelihood $\widetilde{\tau}_M(\mathcal{K})$ is greater than a minimum likelihood threshold min_τ. Based on this heuristic, we introduce the notion of *significant* maximum cardinality constraint:

Definition 4 (Significant Constraint). *Given a minimum likelihood threshold min_τ, a confidence level $1-\delta$ and a knowledge base $\mathcal{K}$, a contextual maximum cardinality constraint $C \sqsubseteq (\leq M\ R)$ is significant w.r.t. $\mathcal{K}$ iff $\widetilde{\tau}_M(\mathcal{K}) \geq min_\tau$ and $\widetilde{\tau}_M(\mathcal{K}) = max_{i\geq 1}\widetilde{\tau}_i(\mathcal{K})$.*

Compared to Property 1, note that in our heuristic, we do not test whether $\widetilde{\tau}_M$ is greater than ϵ, or not. However, it is easy to see that if $\widetilde{\tau}_M = \tau_M - \sqrt{\frac{\log(1/\delta)}{2n_{\geq M}}} \geq min_\tau$, then we necessarily have $n_{\geq M} \geq \frac{\log(1/\delta)}{2(1-min_\tau)^2}$, which guarantees that we will not make a decision if the number of observations $n_{\geq M}$ is too low. For example, with $1 - \delta = 99\%$ and $min_\tau = 0.97$, we will consider that M is a true maximum cardinality only if $n_{\geq M} \geq 2,558$.

In DBpedia for a confidence level $1 - \delta = 99\%$ and a threshold $min_\tau = 0.97$, we observe that the detected maximum cardinalities of the roles `birthYear` and `parent` in the context `Person` are 1 and 2 respectively (bold values in Table 1). Interestingly, with these same thresholds, no maximum cardinality is detected for the role `team` when no context is considered. This is because this role is used both to inform the teams to which a player has belonged and the teams present in a sport event. Thence, our method manages to detect the cardinality of 2 in the context of football matches.

By Definition 4, if a constraint is *significant* w.r.t. $\mathcal{K}$, it means that its pessimistic likelihood is greater than min_τ and that it is probably satisfied in $\mathcal{K}^*$ (using Properties 1 and 2). Now, our problem is expressed as follows:

Problem 2. Given a knowledge base $\mathcal{K}$ satisfying the assumptions expressed in Sect. 4 about its consistency and its completeness, a confidence level $1-\delta$ and a minimum likelihood threshold min_τ, we aim at discovering the set of all contextual maximum cardinality constraints $C \sqsubseteq (\leq M\ R)$ where C and R are concept and role of $\mathcal{K}$, that are *significant* w.r.t. $\mathcal{K}$ and *minimal* w.r.t. the concept hierarchy defined in the TBox of $\mathcal{K}$.

5 Extracting Maximum Cardinality Constraints

5.1 Pruning Criteria

For discovering all the contextual constraints of a knowledge base $\mathcal{K}$, a naive approach would consist in testing each role for each concept with our detection method. If N_C is the number of concepts and N_R the number of roles, this naive approach would require $N_C \times N_R$ tests. This is unfeasible for large knowledge bases such as DBpedia, containing more than 483k concepts and 60k roles. We design two pruning criteria (Properties 3 and 4) taking advantage of the two conditions that a constraint γ must satisfy to be mined: (i) the constraint γ has to be *significant* i.e., its pessimistic likelihood has to be greater than the minimum likelihood threshold min_τ, and (ii) the constraint γ has to be *minimal* with respect to the hierarchy of concepts defined in the TBox of $\mathcal{K}$.

First, we show that a constraint $C \sqsubseteq (\leq M\ R)$ cannot be significant if the number of individuals of the context C in $\mathcal{K}$ is too small. Indeed, if $|C|$ is too small, the confidence interval computed with Hoeffding's inequality is very large and consequently, the pessimistic likelihood is lower than the minimum threshold min_τ. This intuition is formally presented in this property:

Property 3 (Significance pruning). Given a confidence level $1-\delta$ and a minimum likelihood threshold min_τ, if one has $|C \sqcap (\exists R.\top)| < \frac{\log(1/\delta)}{2(1-min_\tau)^2}$ for the context C and the role R, then no contextual constraint $C' \sqsubseteq (\leq M\ R)$ with $C' \sqsubseteq C$ can be significant w.r.t. the knowledge base $\mathcal{K}$.

This property is very important to reduce the search space because if the number of individuals in $\mathcal{A}$ that belong to $C \sqcap (\exists R.\top)$, for a context C and a role R, is not large enough (if it is lower than $\log(1/\delta)/2(1-min_\tau)^2$), then it is impossible to find a significant constraint $C' \sqsubseteq (\leq M\ R)$ where C' is a concept more specific than C in the hierarchy of $\mathcal{K}$. For example, we use a minimum likelihood threshold min_τ of 97% and a confidence $1-\delta$ of 99% to extract constraints in DBpedia (see experimental sections), which means that at least

2,558 observations are needed for a role R in a context C. For this reason, since there are only 896 facts for the role `beatifiedDate` describing the context `Person`, we are sure that it is not necessary to explore this role for the sub-concepts like `Artist` or `Scientist`.

Assume now that we have extracted the constraint $C \sqsubseteq (\leq 1\ R)$ from the knowledge base $\mathcal{K}$. It is not possible to find another *minimal* constraint $C' \sqsubseteq (\leq M'\ R)$ with a context C' more specific than C because the cardinality M' cannot be smaller than 1. This property, which is a direct consequence of minimality (see Definition 2), is formalized as follows:

Property 4 (Minimality pruning). Let Γ be a set of contextual maximum cardinality constraints. If Γ contains a contextual constraint $C \sqsubseteq (\leq 1\ R)$, then no contextual constraint $C' \sqsubseteq (\leq M'\ R)$ with $C' \sqsubset C$ can be minimal in Γ.

Property 4 is also useful to reduce the search space because if a constraint $C \sqsubseteq (\leq 1\ R)$ has been detected as significant, then it is useless to explore all the constraints $C' \sqsubseteq (\leq M'\ R)$ where $C' \sqsubset C$. As soon as the constraint `Person` $\sqsubseteq$ ($\leq$1 `birthYear`) has been detected (meaning than a person has at most one birth year), it is no longer necessary to explore the constraint `Artist` $\sqsubseteq$ ($\leq M$ `birthYear`) which is more specific.

5.2 C3M: Contextual Cardinality Constraint Mining

Properties 3 and 4 are implemented in our algorithm called C3M (*C3M* for *Contextual Cardinality Constraint Mining*). Its main function, called *C3M-Main*, takes as input a knowledge base $\mathcal{K}$, a confidence level $1 - \delta$ and a minimum likelihood threshold min_τ. The exploration of the search space is performed independently for each role R of the knowledge base $\mathcal{K}$ (see the main loop of Algorithm 1 at line 2). In a first phase, given a role R of $\mathcal{K}$, Algorithm 1 carries out a depth-first exploration of cardinality constraints for R (line 4). This exploration starts from the top concept of $\mathcal{K}$, denoted by $\top$, by calling the recursive function *C3M-Explore*. Because the concepts of $\mathcal{K}$ may have multiple more general concepts, the set Γ_R of maximum cardinality constraints returned by function *C3M-Explore* may contain constraints that are not minimal. Therefore, in a second phase (line 6), the function *C3M-Main* checks for each constraint $\gamma \in \Gamma_R$ if Γ_R contains a constraint γ' that is more general than γ. When it is not the case constraint γ is added to the set of maximum cardinality constraints Γ_m that are minimal. Γ_m is finally returned by function *C3M-Main* (line 8).

The recursive function *C3M-Explore* benefits from the pruning criteria presented in Properties 3 and 4 during a depth-first exploration of the search space. First, it evaluates if the number of observations in $C \sqcap (\exists R.\top)$ is sufficiently important. If it is not the case, we know that there is no maximum cardinality constraint $C' \sqsubseteq (\leq M\ R)$ with $C' \sqsubseteq C$ that can be significant w.r.t. $\mathcal{K}$ (see Property 3) and the depth-first exploration is stopped (line 2 of Algorithm 2). Otherwise, the pessimistic likelihood $\widetilde{\tau}_i$ is computed for each cardinality value i

Algorithm 1. C3M-Main

Input: A knowledge base $\mathcal{K}$, a confidence level $1-\delta$ and a minimum likelihood threshold min_τ

Output: The set Γ_m of all maximum cardinality constraints that are significant and minimal w.r.t. $\mathcal{K}$

```
Γm := ∅
for all role in K do
    {Depth-first exploration of maximum cardinality constraints}
    ΓR := C3M-Explore(K, R, ⊤, ∞, δ, minτ)
    {Computation of maximum cardinality constraints that are minimal}
    Γm := {γ ∈ ΓR : (∄γ' ∈ ΓR)(γ ⊏ γ')} ∪ Γm
end for
return Γm
```

(lines 4–6) and the most likely cardinality i_M is selected (line 7). If the corresponding pessimistic likelihood $\widetilde{\tau}_{i_M}$ is lower than min_τ, it means that no maximum cardinality constraint is detected (for this level of the hierarchy of $\mathcal{K}$) and i_M is set to ∞ (line 8). Otherwise, if i_M is strictly lower than M (the maximum cardinality detected at a previous level of the hierarchy), it means that we detect a maximum constraint cardinality $\gamma : C \sqsubseteq (\leq i_M\ R)$ that is *potentially* minimal. As already mentioned, as a concept of the knowledge base $\mathcal{K}$ may have multiple super-concepts, we will have to check whether γ is really minimal in the second phase of function *C3M-Main*. Finally, using Property 4, we know that if $i_M = 1$, it is not necessary to explore the descendants $C' \sqsubset C$ to detect other constraints $C' \sqsubseteq (\leq M'\ R)$. Otherwise, *C3M-Explore* is recursively called (line 12) to explore all the direct sub-concepts of C (identified using the hierarchy in the TBox of $\mathcal{K}$).

Theorem 1. *Given a knowledge base $\mathcal{K}$, a confidence level $1-\delta$ and a minimum likelihood min_τ, our algorithm C3M-Main returns the set of all contextual cardinality constraints $C \sqsubseteq (\leq M\ R)$ that are significant w.r.t. $\mathcal{K}$ and minimal w.r.t. the hierarchy of concepts defined in the TBox of $\mathcal{K}$.*

Theorem 1 straightforwardly stems from Properties 3 and 4. Although these pruning criteria are not heuristic, we will see in the experimental section that algorithm *C3M-Main* is efficient enough to handle knowledge bases as large as DBpedia. Note that we have implemented the functions *C3M-Main* and *C3M-Explore* (client side) such that they consume a SPARQL endpoint (server side) to query the knowledge base $\mathcal{K}$. More precisely, given a context C and a role R, a SPARQL query is built and executed to compute the cardinality distribution $n_i^{C,R}$ ($i \in \mathbb{N}$), which is useful for calculating pessimistic likelihoods (see line 5 of Algorithm 2). Therefore, for each role R in $\mathcal{K}$, the server side executes N_C queries where N_C represents the number of concepts in the hierarchy of concepts of $\mathcal{K}$. It means that the complexity of our approach in number of queries is in $\mathcal{O}(N_C)$. On the other hand, on the client side (where the functions *C3M-Main* and *C3M-Explore* are executed), given a role R of $\mathcal{K}$, the complexity of our approach (in

Algorithm 2. C3M-Explore

Input: A knowledge base $\mathcal{K}$, a role R, a context C, a cardinality M, a confidence level $1-\delta$ and a minimum likelihood threshold min_τ

Output: A set Γ of constraints

$\alpha := \frac{log(1/\delta)}{2(1-min_\tau)^2}$ and $n_{\geq 0}^{C,R} := |C \sqcap (\exists R.\top)|$

if $(n_{\geq 0}^{C,R} < \alpha)$ **then return** $\emptyset$

$\Gamma := \emptyset$ and $i_{max} := \arg\max_{i \in \mathbb{N}}\{n_i^{C,R} > 0\}$

for all $i \in [1..min\{M, i_{max}\}]$ **do**

  $\widetilde{\tau}_i := \max\left\{ \frac{n_i^{C,R}}{n_{\geq i}^{C,R}} - \sqrt{\frac{\log(1/\delta)}{2n_{\geq i}^{C,R}}}; 0 \right\}$

end for

$i_M := \arg\max_{i \in [1..min\{M, i_{max}\}]}\{\widetilde{\tau}_i\}$

if $(\widetilde{\tau}_{i_M} < min_\tau)$ **then** $i_M := \infty$

if $(i_M < M)$ **then** $\Gamma := \{C \sqsubseteq (\leq i_M\ R)\}$

if $(i_M > 1)$ **then**

  for all direct sub-concept $C' \sqsubset C$ not yet explored **do**

    $\Gamma := \Gamma \cup$ *C3M-Explore*$(\mathcal{K}, R, C', i_M, \delta, min_\tau)$

  end for

end if

return Γ

number of operations) is in $\mathcal{O}(N_C \times i_{max})$ where $i_{max} = \arg\max_{i \in \mathbb{N}}\{n_i^{\top,R} > 0\}$. Intuitively, i_{max} represents the maximum integer for which there is at least one subject s such that i_{max} facts $R(s, o)$ belong to $\mathcal{K}$.

6 Experiments

The goal of this experimental study is mainly to evaluate the scaling of the C3M algorithm with a large knowledge base, the interest of minimality and the precision of the mined constraints. In this paper, we present and analyze experimental results using DBpedia, which contains more than 500 million triples with more than 480k distinct concepts and 60k distinct roles. The Github repository of C3M (see footnotes) also provides results obtained from 3 other SPARQL endpoints: YAGO, BNF and EUROPEANA.

Our algorithm is implemented in Java with the Apache Jena Library, and directly queries the KB via its SPARQL endpoint[5]. Note that we virtually add an element $\top$ that subsumes all concepts without parents including `owl:Thing`, and the confidence level is $1 - \delta = 99\%$ for all experiments[6]. Figure 1 varies the minimum likelihood threshold min_τ from 0.90 to 0.99 to observe the evolution of the collection of contextual maximum cardinality constraints.

[5] http://jena.apache.org and https://dbpedia.org.

[6] The results for $min_\tau = 0.97$ and the ground truth used to evaluate the precision are available at https://github.com/asoulet/c3m.

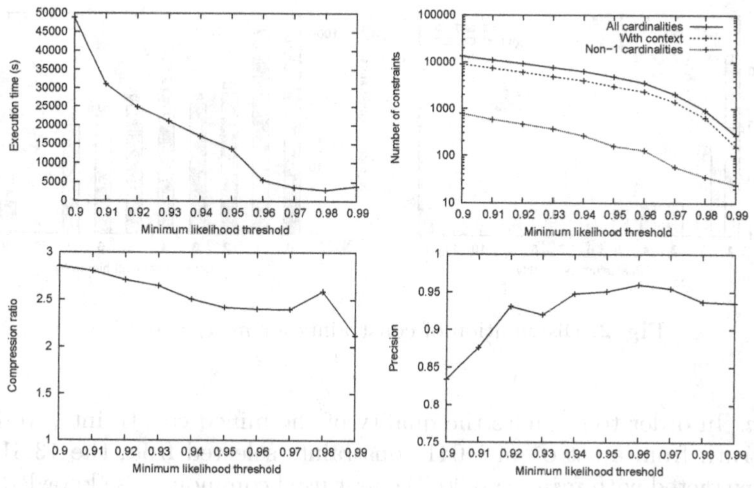

Fig. 1. Impact of the minimum likelihood threshold

Scalability. Figure 1 (left top) reports the execution time, which increases very rapidly when the likelihood threshold decreases. This is due to a very rapid increase of the size of the search space because the pruning properties are less selective. As a result, the number of extracted contextual constraints also increases with the decrease of the threshold min_{τ} as shown in Fig. 1 (right top). More precisely, it reports the total number of mined constraints, the number of constraints with a non-$\top$ context (i.e., with context different from $\top$), and the number of non-1 constraints (i.e., with maximum cardinality greater than 1). First, it is clear that a majority of constraints have 1 as cardinality. For a minimum likelihood threshold equal to 0.97, there are 1,979 constraints with 1 as maximum cardinality (see Fig. 2 (left) that details the distribution of constraints with cardinality). Second, we also observe that most of constraints have a non-$\top$ context that shows the usefulness of our approach based on contexts. For $min_{\tau} = 0.97$, Fig. 2 (right) plots the distribution of the constraints with the level of their context in the DBpedia hierarchy.

Minimality. Figure 1 (left bottom) plots the compression ratio due to minimality (i.e., number of minimal and non-minimal constraints divided by the number of minimal constraints) by varying the likelihood threshold. Interestingly, the reduction of the number of constraints thanks to minimality is important regardless of the threshold (between 2 and 3 times smaller). It is slightly less effective when the likelihood threshold is high, but much fewer constraints are identified. As a reminder, the non-minimal pruned constraints are not informative because redundant with more general ones. In other words, they are not useful for an inference system and in addition, they reduce the readability of the extraction for end users.

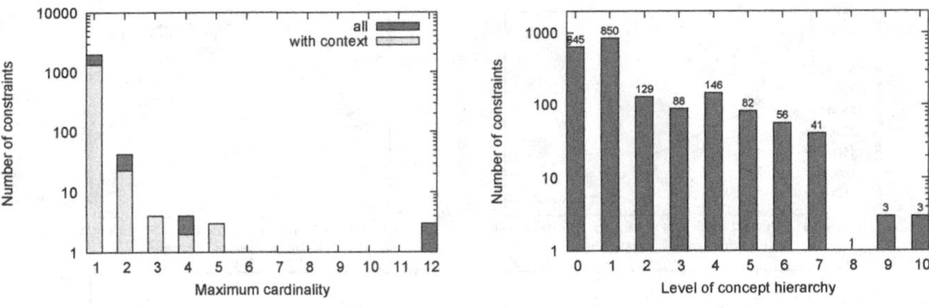

Fig. 2. Distribution of constraints for $min_\tau = 0.97$

Precision. In order to evaluate the quality of the mined constraints, we built a ground truth from a set $\mathcal{C}^*$ of 5,041 constraints selected from the 13,313 constraints extracted with $min_\tau = 0.90$. We first used common sense knowledge and information from the DBpedia pages to determine the maximum cardinalities of certain relations. For instance, since we have a single birth, the maximum cardinality for all birth dates and places has been set to 1. For some relations like `rdfs:label` or `rdfs:abstract`, the maximum cardinality has been set to 12 according to the documentation[7]. In a second step, we automatically extended the maximum cardinality constraints to the different contexts. The set $\mathcal{C}^*$ covers 667 distinct roles and 2,150 distinct concepts. Thereby, the precision of a set of constraints $\mathcal{C}$ corresponds to the proportion of correct constraints out of the number of constraints that are annotated (i.e., $\mathcal{C} \cap \mathcal{C}^*$). Figure 1 (right bottom) plots the precision of the set of constraints returned by C3M according to the minimum likelihood threshold min_τ[8]. We observe that precision increases with this threshold, but drops off for thresholds greater than 0.96. This is due to correct cardinality constraints which are not recognized as the needed number of individuals is too high. However, it is important to note that this decrease is not very significant because the number of mined constraints becomes very small for thresholds greater than 0.96. Interestingly, for a threshold greater than or equal to 0.94, the precision of our approach is excellent since about 95% of the constraints are correct.

We also qualitatively analyzed the maximum cardinality constraints for a minimum likelihood threshold equal to 0.97. We observe that the erroneous constraints often result from construction or representation biases. For instance, the method found the constraint `http://schema.org/School` $\sqsubseteq$ ($\leq$2 `country`) that is wrong because a school is located in a single country. But we observe in DBpedia that many English schools are attached to both England and the United Kingdom. It is clear that a single affiliation to England (part of the United Kingdom) would have been sufficient. Besides, at physical level, while each individual has

[7] https://wiki.dbpedia.org/services-resources/datasets/dbpedia-datasets.

[8] We do not compare our method with [15] because in the case of DBpedia, this method systematically returns a *wrong maximum* cardinality for all constraints.

a unique date of birth, we identify a cardinality of 2 because many dates are represented with two distinct encoding formats.

To summarize, our approach scales well on DBpedia with about 500 million triples thanks to the advanced pruning techniques used by C3M. The majority of the extracted constraints have a context demonstrating the interest of benefiting from the concept hierarchy of the knowledge base. Importantly, the precision of the mined constraints is about 95% for $min_\tau \geq 0.94$.

7 Conclusion

This paper provides the first proposal for a complete exploration of significant constraints of maximum cardinality in a knowledge base. We show how to find, from a knowledge base $\mathcal{K}$ that satisfies assumptions about its completeness and consistence degrees, a minimal set of contextual constraints $C \sqsubseteq (\leq M\ R)$ that are *significant*, i.e. that can be expected to occur in reality. Our experiments demonstrate the feasibility of a systematic exploration of large knowledge bases such as DBpedia (about 500 million triples) for the discovery of minimal contextual constraints of maximum cardinality thanks to the C3M algorithm. With a high minimum likelihood threshold, the precision of the mined constraints is about 95%, which is excellent. Additionally, the minimality exploited by our algorithm drastically reduce the number of obtained constraints, so that they can be manually analyzed by end users. In future work, we would intend to extend our approach to minimum cardinality constraints. This task is not completely symmetrical because under the open-world assumption, it is difficult to know if facts are missing or if the minimum cardinality is reached. For instance, a majority of people have only one informed parent in DBpedia but, of course, the true minimum cardinality is 2. Another future work is to improve C3M by benefiting more from reasoning capabilities. For the moment, we take into account the hierarchy of concepts to reduce the set of constraints, but we could improve our approach by fully exploiting OWL (e.g., with equivalent classes or properties).

Acknowledgements. This work was partially supported by the grant ANR-18-CE38-0009 ("SESAME").

References

1. Auer, S., Bizer, C., Kobilarov, G., Lehmann, J., Cyganiak, R., Ives, Z.: DBpedia: a nucleus for a web of open data. In: Aberer, K., et al. (eds.) ASWC/ISWC -2007. LNCS, vol. 4825, pp. 722–735. Springer, Heidelberg (2007). https://doi.org/10.1007/978-3-540-76298-0_52
2. Baader, F., Calvanese, D., McGuinness, D.L., Nardi, D., Patel-Schneider, P.F. (eds.): The Description Logic Handbook: Theory, Implementation, and Applications. Cambridge University Press, New York (2003)

3. Darari, F., Nutt, W., Pirrò, G., Razniewski, S.: Completeness statements about RDF data sources and their use for query answering. In: Alani, H., et al. (eds.) ISWC 2013. LNCS, vol. 8218, pp. 66–83. Springer, Heidelberg (2013). https://doi.org/10.1007/978-3-642-41335-3_5
4. Darari, F., Razniewski, S., Prasojo, R.E., Nutt, W.: Enabling fine-grained RDF data completeness assessment. In: Bozzon, A., Cudre-Maroux, P., Pautasso, C. (eds.) ICWE 2016. LNCS, vol. 9671, pp. 170–187. Springer, Cham (2016). https://doi.org/10.1007/978-3-319-38791-8_10
5. Debattista, J., Lange, C., Auer, S., Cortis, D.: Evaluating the quality of the LOD cloud: an empirical investigation. Semant. Web **9**(6), 859–901 (2018)
6. Erxleben, F., Günther, M., Krötzsch, M., Mendez, J., Vrandečić, D.: Introducing wikidata to the linked data web. In: Mika, P., et al. (eds.) ISWC 2014. LNCS, vol. 8796, pp. 50–65. Springer, Cham (2014). https://doi.org/10.1007/978-3-319-11964-9_4
7. Färber, M., Bartscherer, F., Menne, C., Rettinger, A.: Linked data quality of DBpedia, Freebase, OpenCyc, Wikidata, and YAGO. Semant. Web **9**(1), 77–129 (2018)
8. Galárraga, L., Razniewski, S., Amarilli, A., Suchanek, F.M.: Predicting completeness in knowledge bases. In: Proceedings of the 10th ACM International Conference on Web Search and Data Mining, pp. 375–383. ACM (2017)
9. Galárraga, L.A., Teflioudi, C., Hose, K., Suchanek, F.: AMIE: association rule mining under incomplete evidence in ontological knowledge bases. In: Proceedings of World Wide Web Conference, pp. 413–422. ACM (2013)
10. Galárraga, L., Hose, K., Razniewski, S.: Enabling completeness-aware querying in SPARQL. In: Proceedings of the 21st Workshop on the Web and Databases, pp. 19–22. ACM (2017)
11. Hoeffding, W.: Probability inequalities for sums of bounded random variables. J. Am. Stat. Assoc. **58**(310), 13–20 (1963)
12. Lajus, J., Suchanek, F.M.: Are all people married? Determining obligatory attributes in knowledge bases. In: Proceedings of World Wide Web Conference, pp. 1115–1124 (2018)
13. Mirza, P., Razniewski, S., Darari, F., Weikum, G.: Enriching knowledge bases with counting quantifiers. In: Vrandečić, D., et al. (eds.) ISWC 2018. LNCS, vol. 11136, pp. 179–197. Springer, Cham (2018). https://doi.org/10.1007/978-3-030-00671-6_11
14. Motro, A.: Integrity = validity + completeness. ACM Trans. Database Syst. **14**(4), 480–502 (1989)
15. Muñoz, E., Nickles, M.: Mining cardinalities from knowledge bases. In: Benslimane, D., Damiani, E., Grosky, W.I., Hameurlain, A., Sheth, A., Wagner, R.R. (eds.) DEXA 2017. LNCS, vol. 10438, pp. 447–462. Springer, Cham (2017). https://doi.org/10.1007/978-3-319-64468-4_34
16. Pernelle, N., Saïs, F., Symeonidou, D.: An automatic key discovery approach for data linking. Web Semant.: Sci. Serv. Agents World Wide Web **23**, 16–30 (2013)
17. Razniewski, S., Korn, F., Nutt, W., Srivastava, D.: Identifying the extent of completeness of query answers over partially complete databases. In: Proceedings of the ACM SIGMOD, pp. 561–576. ACM (2015)
18. Soulet, A., Giacometti, A., Markhoff, B., Suchanek, F.M.: Representativeness of knowledge bases with the generalized Benford's law. In: Vrandečić, D., et al. (eds.) ISWC 2018. LNCS, vol. 11136, pp. 374–390. Springer, Cham (2018). https://doi.org/10.1007/978-3-030-00671-6_22

19. Symeonidou, D., Galárraga, L., Pernelle, N., Saïs, F., Suchanek, F.: VICKEY: mining conditional keys on knowledge bases. In: d'Amato, C., et al. (eds.) ISWC 2017. LNCS, vol. 10587, pp. 661–677. Springer, Cham (2017). https://doi.org/10.1007/978-3-319-68288-4_39
20. Pellissier Tanon, T., Stepanova, D., Razniewski, S., Mirza, P., Weikum, G.: Completeness-aware rule learning from knowledge graphs. In: d'Amato, C., et al. (eds.) ISWC 2017. LNCS, vol. 10587, pp. 507–525. Springer, Cham (2017). https://doi.org/10.1007/978-3-319-68288-4_30
21. Weikum, G., Hoffart, J., Suchanek, F.M.: Ten years of knowledge harvesting: lessons and challenges. IEEE Data Eng. Bull. **39**(3), 41–50 (2016)

HapPenIng: Happen, Predict, Infer—Event Series Completion in a Knowledge Graph

Simon Gottschalk(✉) and Elena Demidova

L3S Research Center, Leibniz Universität Hannover, Hannover, Germany
{gottschalk,demidova}@L3S.de

Abstract. Event series, such as the Wimbledon Championships and the US presidential elections, represent important happenings in key societal areas including sports, culture and politics. However, semantic reference sources, such as Wikidata, DBpedia and EventKG knowledge graphs, provide only an incomplete event series representation. In this paper we target the problem of event series completion in a knowledge graph. We address two tasks: (1) prediction of sub-event relations, and (2) inference of real-world events that happened as a part of event series and are missing in the knowledge graph. To address these problems, our proposed supervised `HapPenIng` approach leverages structural features of event series. `HapPenIng` does not require any external knowledge - the characteristics making it unique in the context of event inference. Our experimental evaluation demonstrates that `HapPenIng` outperforms the baselines by 44 and 52% points in terms of precision for the sub-event prediction and the inference tasks, correspondingly.

1 Introduction

Event series, such as sports tournaments, music festivals and political elections are sequences of recurring events. Prominent examples include the Wimbledon Championships, the Summer Olympic Games, the United States presidential elections and the International Semantic Web Conference. The provision of reliable reference sources for event series is of crucial importance for many real-world applications, for example in the context of Digital Humanities and Web Science research [7,9,25], as well as media analytics and digital journalism [15,23].

Popular knowledge graphs (KGs) such as Wikidata [29], DBpedia [14] and EventKG [8,10] cover event series only to a limited extent. This is due to multiple reasons: First, entity-centric knowledge graphs such as Wikidata and DBpedia do not sufficiently cover events and their spatio-temporal relations [6]. Second, reference sources for knowledge graphs such as Wikipedia often focus on recent and current events to the detriment of past events [11]. This leads to the deficiency in supporting event-centric applications that rely on knowledge graphs.

In this work we tackle a novel problem of event series completion in a knowledge graph. In particular, we address two tasks: (1) We predict missing sub-event

C. Ghidini et al. (Eds.): ISWC 2019, LNCS 11778, pp. 200–218, 2019.
https://doi.org/10.1007/978-3-030-30793-6_12

relations between events existing in a knowledge graph; and (2) We infer real-world events that happened within a particular event series but are missing in the knowledge graph. We also infer specific properties of such inferred events such as a label, a time interval and locations, where possible. Both addressed tasks are interdependent. The prediction of sub-event relations leads to a more complete event series structure, facilitating inference of further missing events. In turn, event inference can also lead to the discovery of new sub-event relations.

The proposed `HapPenIng` approach exclusively utilizes information obtained from the knowledge graph, without referring to any external sources. This characteristic makes `HapPenIng` approach unique with respect to the event inference task. In contrast, related approaches that focus on the knowledge graphs population depend on external sources (e.g. on news [12,31]).
The contributions of this paper include:

- A novel supervised method for sub-event relation prediction in event series.
- An event inference approach to infer real-world events missing in an event series in the knowledge graph and properties of these events.
- A dataset containing new events and relations inferred by `HapPenIng`:
  - over 5,000 events and nearly 90,000 sub-event relations for Wikidata, and
  - over 1,000 events and more than 6,000 sub-event relations for DBpedia.

Our evaluation demonstrates that the proposed `HapPenIng` approach achieves a precision of 61% for the sub-event prediction task (outperforming the state-of-the-art embedding-based baseline by 52% points) and 70% for the event inference task (outperforming a naive baseline by 44% points). Our dataset with new sub-event relations and inferred events is available online[1].

1.1 Example: Wimbledon Championships

The Wimbledon Championships (WC), a famous tennis tournament, are an *event series* that takes place in London annually since 1877. Wikidata currently includes 132 WC editions and 915 related sub-events, for example Women's and Men's Singles and Wheelchair competitions. However, according to our analysis, this event series is incomplete. In particular, the `HapPenIng` approach proposed in this paper was able to generate 125 sub-event relations and 15 event instances related to this event series that are currently missing in Wikidata.

Figure 1 illustrates a small fraction of the *Event Graph* that contains event nodes and their relations as available in Wikidata as of Sep. 18th, 2018. For each year, Wikidata includes an event edition, such as the *2008 WC*. The individual competitions such as the *Men's Singles* are provided as sub-events of the corresponding edition.

In this example we can illustrate two tasks of the event series completion tackled in this paper: (i) Sub-event prediction: The missing sub-event relation between the Men's Singles final of 2008 and the Men's Singles competition in

[1] http://eventkg.l3s.uni-hannover.de/happening.

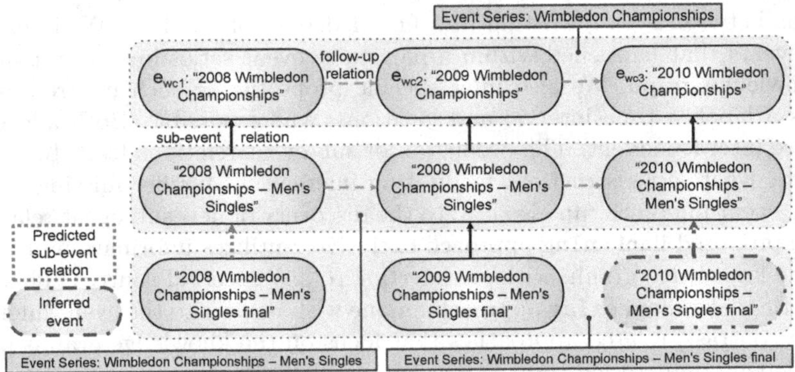

Fig. 1. A fraction of the *Event Graph* containing the Wimbledon Championships (WC) events. Nodes represent events. Solid arrows represent sub-event relations. Dashed arrows represent follow-up event relations. The three upper events are the *WC* editions.

2008 can be established; and (ii) Event inference: The missing event instance labeled *2010 WC—Men's Singles final* can be inferred as a sub-event of the Men's Singles 2010.

2 Problem Statement

We consider a typical *Knowledge Graph* that contains nodes representing real-world entities and events. The edges of a *Knowledge Graph* represent relations between entities and events. More formally:

Definition 1. ***Knowledge Graph:*** *A Knowledge Graph* $KG : \langle V, U \rangle$ *is a directed multi-graph. The nodes in* V *represent real-world entities and events. The directed edges in* U *represent relations of the entities and events in* V.

The *Event Graph* G is a sub-graph of the *Knowledge Graph*. The nodes of G represent real-world events. The edges represent their relations relevant in the context of event series (sub-event and follow-up relations). More formally:

Definition 2. ***Event Graph:*** *Given a Knowledge Graph* $KG : \langle V, U \rangle$, *an Event Graph* $G : \langle E, R \cup F \rangle$ *is a directed graph. The nodes of the Event Graph* $E \subseteq V$ *represent real-world events. The edges* R *represent sub-event relations:* $R \subseteq E \times E, R \subseteq U$. *The edges* F *represent follow-up event relations:* $F \subseteq E \times E, F \subseteq U$.

Events in G represent real-world happenings; the key properties of an event in the context of event series include an event identifier, an event label, a happening time interval and relevant locations.

Definition 3. ***Event:*** *Given an Event Graph* $G : \langle E, R \cup F \rangle$, *an event* $e \in E$ *is something that happened in the real world.* e *is represented as a tuple* $e =$

$\langle uri, l, t, L\rangle$, *where* uri *is an event identifier,* l *is an event label,* $t = \langle t_s, t_e\rangle$ *is the happening time interval with* t_s, t_e *being its start and end time.* L *is the set of event locations.*

An event can have multiple sub-events. For example, the *WC Men's single final 2009* is a sub-event of *2009 WC*.

Definition 4. ***Sub-event:*** *An event* $e_s \in E$ *is a sub-event of the event* $e_p \in E$, *i.e.* $(e_s, e_p) \in R$, *if* e_s *and* e_p *are topically related and* e_s *is narrower in scope.*

We refer to e_p as a parent event of e_s. Typically, e_s happens in a temporal and a geographical proximity of e_p.

An event can be a part of an event series. An example of an event series is the *WC* that has the *2008 WC* as one of its editions.

Definition 5. ***Event series and editions:*** *An event series* $s = \langle e_1, e_2, \ldots, e_n\rangle$, $\forall e_i \in s : e_i \in E$, *is a sequence of topically related events that occur repeatedly in a similar form. The sequence elements are ordered by the event start time and are called editions. We refer to the set of event series as* S.

The follow-up relations F connect event editions within an event series. For example, the *2009 WC* is the follow-up event of the *2008 WC*.

Definition 6. ***Follow-up relation:*** *Given an event series* $s = \langle e_1, e_2, \ldots, e_n\rangle$, e_j *is a follow-up event of* e_i, *i.e.* $(e_i, e_j) \in F$, *if* $e_i \in s$ *and* $e_j \in s$ *are the neighbor editions in* s *and* e_i *precedes* e_j.

The sub-event relations in an *Event Graph* are often incomplete. In particular, we denote the set of real-world sub-event relations not included in the *Event Graph* as R^+. Then the task of sub-event prediction can be defined as follows:

Definition 7. ***Sub-event prediction:*** *Given an Event Graph* $G : \langle E, R \cup F\rangle$ *and events* $e_s \in E$, $e_p \in E$, *the task of sub-event prediction is to decide if* e_s *is a sub-event of* e_p, *i.e. to determine if* $(e_s, e_p) \in R \cup R^+$, *where* R^+ *is a set of real-world sub-event relations not included in the Event Graph.*

The set of real-world event representations included in an *Event Graph* is often incomplete (open world assumption). The context of event series can help to infer real-world events missing in particular editions.

Definition 8. ***Event inference:*** *Given and Event Graph* $G : \langle E, R \cup F\rangle$ *and an event series* $s = \langle e_1, e_2, \ldots, e_n\rangle$, *with* $e_1, e_2, ..., e_n \in E$, *the task of event inference is to identify a real-world event* $e_f \in E \cup E^+$ *that belongs to the series* s. *Here,* E^+ *is a set of real-world events that are not included in the Event Graph. In particular,* e_f *is a sub-event of the edition* $e_i \in s$, *i.e.* $(e_f, e_i) \in R \cup R^+$.

3 Event Series Completion

We address event series completion in two steps: First, we adopt a classification method to predict sub-event relations among event pairs. Second, we develop a graph-based approach to infer events missing in particular editions through event series analysis. A pipeline of the overall approach is shown in Fig. 2.

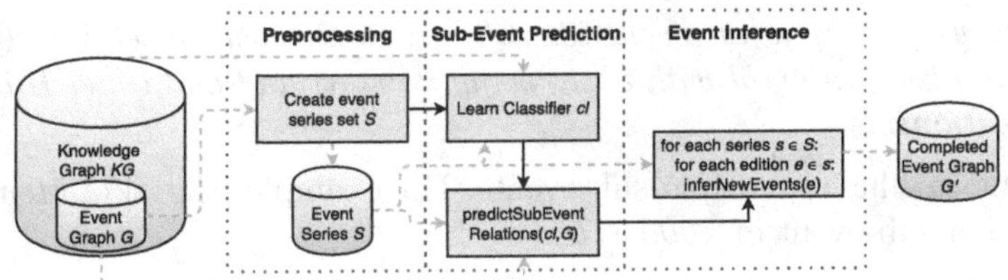

Fig. 2. The `HapPenIng` pipeline. Solid arrows represent the processing order. Dashed arrows represent the data flow.

3.1 Sub-event Prediction

We model the problem of sub-event prediction as a classification problem. Given an event pair (e_s, e_p), we aim to predict whether e_s is a sub-event of e_p:

$$sub - event(e_s, e_p) = \begin{cases} true, & \text{if}(e_s, e_p) \in R \cup R^+; \\ false, & \text{otherwise.} \end{cases} \tag{1}$$

Features. We adopt textual, spatio-temporal and embeddings features.

Textual Features (`TEX`): Events connected through a sub-event relation can have similar or overlapping labels whose similarity is measured using textual features. Such features are also applied on the *template labels*. Template labels are series labels obtained from the original event labels after removal of any digits. The textual features we consider include:

- Label Containment: 1, if $e_p.l$ is a sub-string of $e_s.l$, 0 otherwise.
- LCS Fraction: The length of the Longest Common Sub-string (LCS) of $e_s.l$ and $e_p.l$, compared to the shorter label: $f_{\text{LCS Fraction}}(e_s, e_p) = \frac{LCS(e_s.l, e_p.l)}{min(|e_s.l|, |e_p.l|)}$.
- Unigram Similarity: The labels of both events are split into word unigrams. The feature value is the Jaccard similarity between the unigram sets: $f_{\text{Unigram Similarity}}(e_s, e_p) = \frac{\text{unigrams}(e_s.l) \cap \text{unigrams}(e_p.l)}{\text{unigrams}(e_s.l) \cup \text{unigrams}(e_p.l)}$.
- Template Containment, Template LCS Fraction, Template Unigram Similarity: These features are computed equivalent to the label features, but are based on the template labels.
- Label Cosine Similarity: The cosine similarity between event labels based on tf-idf vectors to take frequency and selectivity of terms into account.
- Parent Event Label Length: $f_{\text{Parent Event Label Length}}(e_s, e_p) = |e_p.l|$.
- Sub-Event Label Length: $f_{\text{Sub-Event Label Length}}(e_s, e_p) = |e_s.l|$.

Spatio-Temporal Features (`STP`): We assume that sub-events happen in the temporal proximity of their parent events. We consider the temporal proximity through temporal overlap, containment and equality.

– Time Overlap: 1 if $e_s.t \cap e_p.t \neq \varnothing$, 0 otherwise.
– Time Containment: 1 if $e_s.t \subseteq e_p.t$, 0 otherwise.
– Time Equality: 1 if $e_s.t = e_p.t$, 0 otherwise.

Sub-events typically happen in the geographical proximity of their parent events. Therefore, we introduce Location Overlap - a spatial feature that assigns a higher score to the event pairs that share locations:

– Location Overlap: 1 if $e_s.L \cap e_p.L \neq \emptyset$, 0 otherwise.

Embedding Features (EMB): The link structure of the *Knowledge Graph* can be expected to provide important insights into possible event relations. First, we can expect that this structure provides useful hints towards predicting sub-event relations, e.g. follow-up events can be expected to have a common parent event. Second, events related to different topical domains (e.g. politics vs. sports) are unlikely to be related through a sub-event relation. To make use of this intuition, we train an embedding on the *Knowledge Graph* using any relations connecting two events in E. For this feature, we pre-train the embeddings following the STransE embedding model [18] which provides two relation-specific matrices $\boldsymbol{W_1}$ and $\boldsymbol{W_2}$, a relation vector $\boldsymbol{r}$ and entity vectors (here, $\boldsymbol{e_s}$ and $\boldsymbol{e_p}$). Intuitively, given that model, we can compare the embedding of an event with the embedding of the assumed parent event plus the embedding of the sub-event relation (sE):

– Embedding Score: $f_{\text{Embedding}}(e_s, e_p) = \|\boldsymbol{W}_{r_{\text{sE}},1}\boldsymbol{e}_p + \boldsymbol{r}_{\text{sE}} - \boldsymbol{W}_{r_{\text{sE}},2}\boldsymbol{e}_s\|_{\ell_1}$

Training the Sub-event Classifier. To train a classifier given the features presented above, a set of labeled event pairs is required. The set of positive examples contains all event pairs with known sub-event relations in the *Event Graph* G. Formally, given the set E of events, this is the set $C_+ = \{(e_s, e_p) | (e_s, e_p) \in R\}$.

In addition, a set of negative examples, i.e. event pairs without sub-event relation is required. When composing event pairs randomly, most of the paired events would be highly different (e.g. having highly dissimilar labels and no spatio-temporal overlap). Consequently, the model would only learn to distinguish the most simple cases. To address this problem, we collect a set of negative examples C_- that has as many event pairs as C_+, and consists of four equally-sized subsets with the following condition for each contained event pair (e_s, e_p):

– Both events are from the same event series, but $(e_s, e_p) \notin R$. Example: (*1997 WC—Women's Doubles, 2009 WC—Men's Singles final*).
– Both events have the same parent event. Example: (*2009 WC—Men's Singles, 2009 WC—Women's Singles*).
– The parent of e_s's parent is the same as e_p's parent. Example: (*2009 WC—Men's Singles final, 2009 WC—Women's Singles*).
– e_s is a transitive, but not a direct sub-event of e_p. Example: (*2009 WC—Men's Singles final, 2009 WC*).

Algorithm 1. Event Inference

```
procedure INFERSUBEVENTS(e)
    M ← getSubSeries(e.series)
    for each e_s ∈ {e_s|(e_s, e) ∈ R} do M = M \ e_s.series
    for each m ∈ M do
        if constraintsNotSatisfied(m, e) then continue
        newEvent ← inferEvent(e, m)
        if oldEvent ← findEvent(E, newEvent.l) ≠ ∅ then
            R = R ∪ (e, oldEvent)
        else
            E = E ∪ newEvent; R = R ∪ (e, newEvent)
    for each e_s ∈ {e_s|(e_s, e_p) ∈ R} do inferSubEvents(e_s)
```

Note that we only consider direct sub-event relations to be valid positive examples. In particular, we aim to learn to distinguish the directly connected sub-events from transitive relations, as well as to distinguish similar events that belong to different editions. Due to the inherent incompleteness of the *Event Graph*, a missing sub-event relation does not necessarily imply that this relation does not hold in the real world. However, we expect that false negative examples would occur only rarely in the training set, such that the resulting model will not be substantially affected by such cases.

Overall, the set of training and test instances C contains all positive sub-event examples C_+ found in the *Event Graph*, and an equally sized set of negative examples C_- that consists of the four event pair sets described above.

Predicting Sub-event Relations Using the Classifier. The trained classifier is adopted to predict missing sub-event relations within event series. We apply an iterative algorithm, given a classifier *cl* and the *Event Graph G*. As it is not feasible to conduct a pairwise comparison of all events in G, we limit the number of events compared with their potential parent event: For each potential parent event e_p that is part of an event series, a set of candidate sub-events is selected as the set of events with the largest term overlap with the potential parent event label. For each candidate event, the classifier *cl* predicts whether this event is a sub-event of e_p. To facilitate prediction of sub-event relations in cases where the parent event is not a part of the series initially, the procedure is run iteratively until no new sub-event relations are found.

3.2 Event Inference

The task of event inference is to infer real-world events not initially contained in the *Event Graph* (i.e. events in the set E^+). We infer such missing events and automatically generate their key properties such as label, time frame and location, where possible. The intuition behind event inference is that the *Event Graph* indicates certain patterns repeated across editions. Thus, we approach this task via comparison of different editions of the same event series to recognize such patterns. Consider the WC example in Fig. 1. Although there is no event

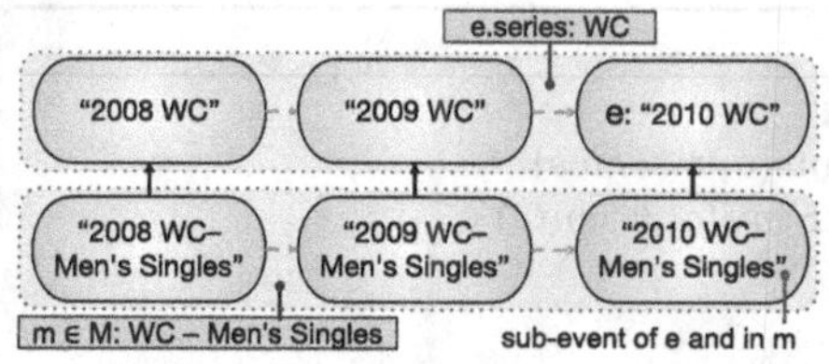

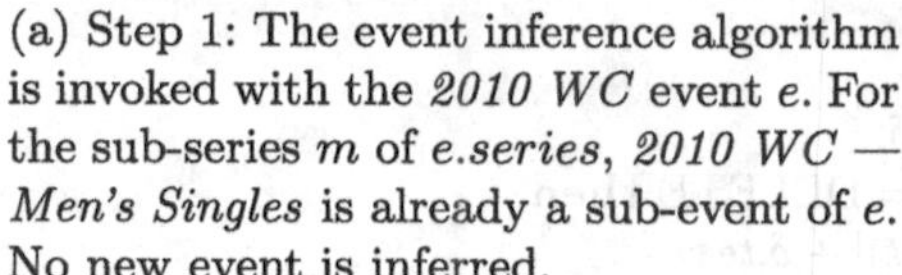

(a) Step 1: The event inference algorithm is invoked with the *2010 WC* event *e*. For the sub-series *m* of *e.series*, *2010 WC — Men's Singles* is already a sub-event of *e*. No new event is inferred.

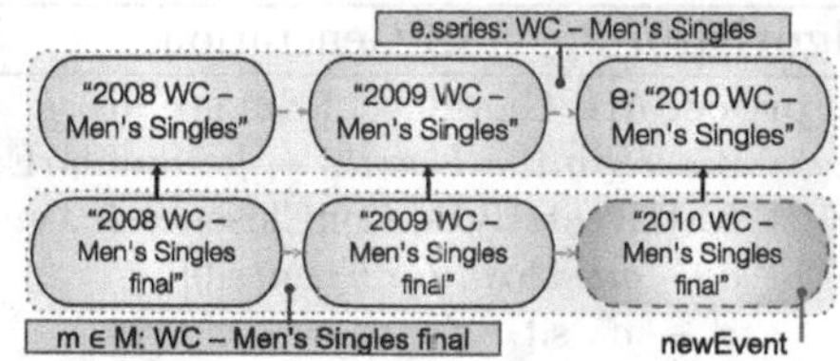

(b) Step 2: The algorithm is now invoked with the *WC 2010 — Men's Singles* event *e*. For the sub-series *m* of *e.series*, there is no sub-event of *e*. A new event is inferred.

Fig. 3. Event inference example for the Wimbledon Championships.

instance for the *2010 Men's Singles final*, we can infer such instance from the previous edition *2009 Men's Singles final*.

Event Series Pre-processing. We pre-process the set S of event series to avoid cycles or undesired dependencies within the single series. Each event series is transformed into a sequence of acyclic rooted trees where each root represents one particular edition of the series. Events or relations violating that structure are removed from the series. If removal is not possible, we exclude such series from S.

An important concept of the event inference is the concept of a sub-series: A series s_p has a sub-series s_s if the sub-series contains sub-events of s_p. For example, the *WC—Men's Singles final* series is a sub-series of the *WC—Men's Singles*, because the event *2009 WC—Men's Singles final* is a sub-event of *2009 WC—Men's Singles*. We determine sub-series relation as:

Definition 9. ***Sub-series:*** *An event series $s_s \in S$ is a sub-series of $s_p \in S$, if for an event $e_p \in s_p$ there is a sub-event in s_s: $\exists(e_s, e_p) \in R : e_p \in s_p \wedge e_s \in s_s$.*

Inferring New Events. The intuition behind event inference is to identify similar patterns in the different editions of an event series. According to Definition 5, the editions of an event series occur repeatedly in a similar form. This way, events repeated in most of the editions of the series, but missing in a particular edition can be inferred. To do so, we process all editions in the *Event Graph* and inspect whether its neighbored editions have a sub-event not covered in the particular edition.

Algorithm 1 illustrates our event inference approach. As shown in our pipeline (Fig. 2), this algorithm is invoked for each edition e of the event series in S. First, a set M is constructed that contains all sub-series of the current edition's series, i.e. *e.series* (line 2). Then, the algorithm removes all series from M for which the current edition contains events already (line 3). That way, M is reduced to a set of event series not covered by the sub-events of the current edition e.

For each remaining sub-series $m \in M$, a new event is inferred that is a sub-event of the current edition e and a part of m. Within the respective method

Algorithm 2. Label Generation

procedure GENERATELABEL(e, m)
  $mostSimilarEvents \leftarrow$ getSimilarEvents(e, $e.series$)
  sortEventsByEditionCloseness(e, $mostSimilarEvents$)
  $c \leftarrow mostSimilarEvents[0]$
  $c' \leftarrow c'$, s.t. $(c', c) \in R \wedge c' \in m$
  $l \leftarrow$ ""; $r \leftarrow c'.l$; $\delta_{prev} \leftarrow \emptyset$
  for each $\delta \in$ getEdits($c.l$, $e.l$) **do**
    if $\delta.op =$ DELETE **then** $\delta_{prev} \leftarrow \delta$
    else if $\delta.op =$ INSERT $\wedge$ $\delta_{prev}.op =$ DELETE **then**
      $l \leftarrow l + r[: r.indexOf(\delta_{prev}.text)] + \delta.text$
      $r \leftarrow l + r[r.indexOf(\delta_{prev}.text) + len(\delta_{prev}.text) :]$
    else if not ($\delta.op =$ EQUAL $\wedge$ $\delta_{prev} = \emptyset$) **then return** $\emptyset$
  return $l + r$

Table 1. Generating the label *2010 WC - Men's Singles*. The edit operations δ are the result of Myers' algorithm to detect the edit operations between *2009 WC - Men's Singles* and *2010 WC - Men's Singles*. The final label is the concatenation of l and r.

Step	δ.op	δ_{prev}.op	δ.text	l	r
init					2009 WC - Men's Singles final
1	DELETE		2009		2009 WC - Men's Singles final
2	INSERT	DELETE	2010	2010	WC - Men's Singles final
3	EQUAL		WC - Men's Singles	2010	WC - Men's Singles final

`inferEvent(e, M)`, a new label, time span and set of locations is generated as described later. The algorithm is invoked recursively with all known (also newly identified) sub-events. To increase precision, a sub-series m is only retained in M if a set of constraints is satisfied (line 5). These constraints are described later in this section.

The event inference algorithm can infer an event for which an equivalent event already exists in the *Event Graph*. To avoid the generation of such duplicate events, we check if an event with the same label as the newly inferred event exists in the *Event Graph*. In this case, the algorithm adds a new sub-event relation across the existing events to the *Event Graph* and discards the inferred event (line 8).

Wimbledon Championships Example: Consider the example in Fig. 1, with the goal to infer new events within the edition e_{wc_3}: *2010 WC*. Figure 3a depicts the first step when invoking the algorithm `InferSubEvents(`e_{wc_3}`)` (without constraints). The edition becomes the input event e and its series $e.series$ is *WC*. The event series *WC—Men's Singles* (m) is identified as one of its immediate sub-series in M. However, as there is already an event *2010 WC—Men's Singles* that is a sub-event of e and part of that sub-series m, it is removed from M. Therefore, M is empty and no new events are inferred at this point.

Subsequently, Algorithm 1 is executed with the sub-event *2010 WC—Men's Singles* as input edition e, as shown in Fig. 3b. Here, the sub-series is *WC—Men's Singles final* which is inserted in M. Consequently, a new event is created that is a sub-event of e and part of the event series *WC—Men's Singles final.*

Label Generation. Each newly generated event requires a label. This label is generated by exploiting the labels within its event series, as shown in Algorithm 2. The input is its future parent event e and its event series m. First, the events in the parent series *e.series* whose labels are most similar to the label of e are collected (line 2). Then, within this set of events, the one from the closest event edition and its sub-event in m is selected (lines 3–5). Finally, the label of that event is transformed into the new label by applying the same edit operations δ (i.e. equality, delete or insert) as if we transformed the parent event labels (lines 6–12). To identify the edits, we adopt the difference algorithm by Myers [16].

Example: Consider the newly added event in Fig. 3b. As an input to the algorithm, there is e which is the event *2010 WC—Men's Singles* and the series m consisting of the Men's Singles finals of 2008 and 2009. First, the event *2009 WC—Men's Singles* within *e.series* is identified as the most similar event c. c' is the sub-event of c that is also in m: *2009 WC—Men's Singles final.* Given $c'.l$ and the edit operations δ between the labels of e and c, Table 1 shows how they are used to generate the correct label *2010 WC—Men's Singles final.*

Location and Time Generation. Each event can be assigned a happening time and a set of locations. In both cases, we use a rule-based approach.

Locations: Some events such as the Olympic Games change their location with every edition. Currently we reconstruct event locations only if they remain unchanged across editions: If there is a location assigned to every event $s \in m$, this location is also assigned to e. In future work we intend to utilize sub-location relations, that facilitate the generation of correct locations at a lower level of geographical granularity.

Happening Times: Three rules are applied in the following order until a happening time is identified: (a) If the happening time of each event $s \in m$ equals its parent event's happening time, also e adopts its happening time directly from its parent event; (b) If the happening time of each event $s \in m$ is modelled as a whole year, the happening time of e is also modelled as the same year as any of its (transitive) parent events; (c) If the event label contains a year expression, that part is transformed into its happening time.

Constraints. We propose several configurations of constraints to decide whether an event should be created:

- Baseline (BSL): No constraints.
- Time Evolution (EVO): The constraints are only satisfied if there was at least one event in the series that happened before e. For example, the *Wimbledon*

Women's Doubles were held for the first time in 1913, so it would be wrong to generate an event for the *Women's Doubles* series in 1912 and before.
- Interval (`INT`): The constraints are only satisfied if there was at least one event in the series that happened before and at least one event in the series that happened after e. Under this constraint, events that re-occurred only until a specific edition are not generated for each edition. An example is the tug of war which was part of only six Olympic Summer Games.
- Window (`WIN`): Given a start and an end thresholds a and b, this constraint is satisfied if there is at least one event within the last a editions of the series that happened before e and at least one event in the following b editions that happened after e. For example, Tennis competitions in the Olympic Summer Games were held between 1896 and 1924, and then only since 1984. The Window constraint helps to identify such gaps.
- Coverage (`COV`): Event series are only valid if they are part of a sufficient fraction of the editions: $|m|/|S| \geq \alpha$, given a threshold α.
- Coverage Window (`CWI`): A combination of `WIN` and `COV`: The coverage is only computed after restricting both event series to the dynamic time window.
- Evolution Coverage Window (`ECW`): A combination of `EVO`, `WIN` and `COV`: The coverage is only computed after restricting both event series to the dynamic time window, and if at least one event in the series happened before e.

4 Evaluation

The goal of the evaluation is to assess the performance of the `HapPenIng` approach with respect to the sub-event prediction and event inference tasks.

4.1 Data Collection and Event Graph Construction

We run our experiments on *Event Graphs* extracted from two sources: (i) Wikidata [29] as of October 25, 2018 (*Wikidata Event Graph*), and (ii) DBpedia [14] from the October 2016 dump (*DBpedia Event Graph*). Both datasets are enriched with additional information regarding events obtained from the EventKG knowledge graph [8]. Compared to other knowledge graphs, EventKG contains more detailed information regarding spatio-temporal characteristics of events. More concretely, events in the *Event Graph* are enriched with location and time information using the properties *sem:hasPlace*, *sem:hasBeginTimeStamp* and *sem:hasEndTimeStamp* of EventKG.

One *Event Graph* containing events, sub-event relations and follow-up relations, as well as a set S of event series is constructed for each dataset. For the *Wikidata Event Graph*, we collect as events all data items that are (transitive) instances of the "event" class[2]. Event series are extracted using the "instance of"[3] and the "series"[4] properties in Wikidata. For the *DBpedia Event Graph*,

[2] https://www.wikidata.org/wiki/Q1656682.
[3] https://www.wikidata.org/wiki/Property:P31.
[4] https://www.wikidata.org/wiki/Property:P179.

we extract events using the "dbo:Event" class and series assignments using the provided Wikipedia categories. In both cases, we apply two heuristics to ensure that only event series compatible with Definition 5 are extracted: (i) We only consider series with mostly homogeneous editions. To this end, we make use of the Gini index [21], a standard measure for measuring impurity. In our context it is used to assess the diversity of the template labels of editions in an event series. We reject the (rare) cases of event series with high Gini impurity, where the edition labels do not follow any common pattern.[5] An event is kept in S, if the set of template labels of its editions shows a Gini impurity less than 0.9. Besides, we ignore editions whose removal decreases that impurity. (ii) We ignore events typed as military conflicts and natural disasters, because such events typically do not follow any regularity. If we can find connected sub-graphs of events in the *Event Graph* through sub-event and follow-up relations, but the data item representing that series is missing in the dataset, we add a new unlabeled event series to S. To train the embeddings, we collect all relations connected to events.

The extraction process results in a *Wikidata Event Graph* G containing $|E| = 352,235$ events (*DBpedia Event Graph*: 92,523) and $|S| = 9,007$ event series (*DBpedia Event Graph*: 1,871). As input to train the embeddings, there are 279,004,908 relations in Wikidata and 18,328,678 relations in DBpedia. Both *Event Graphs*, as well as embeddings, annotated samples and other evaluation datasets described in the remainder of this section are available online.[6]

4.2 Sub-event Prediction

Training and Test Set Generation. Before running the experiments, a set of positive and negative sub-event relations is created from the *Event Graphs* as described in Sect. 3.1. In total, this collection of relations consists of 55,217 event pairs within S that were extracted as correct sub-event pairs from Wikidata (DBpedia: 16,763) and the same number of negative event pairs.[7] This collection is split into ten folds to allow 10-fold cross-validation. We learn the STransE embeddings as described in Sect. 3.1 for each fold, with its parameters set as follows: SGD learning rate $\lambda = 0.0001$, the margin hyper-parameter $\gamma = 1$, vector size $k = 100$ and 1,000 epochs. While learning the embeddings on the folds, we exclude the sub-event relations from the respective test set.

Baseline. As a baseline for sub-event prediction, we utilize an embedding-based link prediction model based on the STransE embeddings [18]. Given an input

[5] For example, the event series "TED talk", whose set of edition template labels (e.g. "Avi Reichental: What's next in 3D printing" and "Amanda Palmer: The art of asking") has a high Gini impurity, is not included in the set of event series.

[6] http://eventkg.l3s.uni-hannover.de/happening.

[7] Existing benchmark datasets do not contain a sufficient amount of sub-event relations. For example, FB15K [3] only contains 224 triples containing one of the Freebase predicates */time/event/includes_event*, */time/event/included_in_event* or */time/event/instance_of_recurring_event*.

Table 2. 10-fold cross-validation of the sub-event prediction using different classifiers and all the introduced features. STransE is the baseline we compare to.

Method		Wikidata					DBpedia
		TP	TN	FP	FN	Accuracy	Accuracy
Baseline	STransE	46,479	43,143	6,949	13,859	0.81	0.50
HapPenIng configurations	LOG	54,345	46,605	3,487	5,993	0.91	0.87
	SVM	55,958	48,825	1,267	4,380	0.95	0.92
	RF	**58,649**	**49,497**	**595**	**1,689**	**0.98**	**0.97**

event, this model retrieves a ranked list of candidate sub-events with the corresponding scores. We use these scores to build a logistic regression classifier. STransE is a state-of-the-art approach that had been shown to outperform previous embedding models for the link prediction task on the FB15K benchmark [3].

Classifier Evaluation. Table 2 shows the results of the 10-fold cross-validation for the sub-event prediction task, with three different classifiers: LOG (Logistic Regression), RF (Random Forest) and SVM (Support Vector Machine with linear kernel and normalization) in terms of classification accuracy ($\frac{TP+TN}{TP+TN+FP+FN}$, where TP are true positives, TN true negatives, FP false positives and FN false negatives). Among our classifiers, the RF classifier performs best, with an accuracy of nearly 0.98 in the case of the *Wikidata Event Graph* and 0.97 for the *DBpedia Event Graph*. The results show a clear improvement over the STransE baseline, outperforming the baseline by more than 16% points in case of the RF classifier for Wikidata. For DBpedia, the STransE baseline is outperformed by a larger margin using our proposed features. This can be explained by the insufficient number of relations for training the embeddings in DBpedia.

Table 3 shows the performance of the RF classifier under cross-validation with different feature groups. The combination of all features leads to the best performance in terms of accuracy. Although the use of textual features already leads to a high accuracy (0.97), embedding features and spatio-temporal features help to further increase accuracy in the case of Wikidata (0.98). Again, while DBpedia does profit from the spatio-temporal features, there is no improvement when using embeddings, due to the insufficient data size.

Wikidata Statistics and Examples. While the classifiers demonstrate very accurate results on the test sets, the performance on predicting sub-event relations not yet contained in G requires a separate evaluation. As explained in Sect. 3.1, a large number of predictions is needed that could potentially also lead to a large number of false positives, even given a highly accurate classifier. The actual label distribution is skewed towards unrelated events and we are now only classifying event pairs not yet contained in R. In fact, running the sub-event prediction algorithm using the best-performing RF classifier with all features leads to

Table 3. 10-fold cross-validation of the sub-event prediction using the RF classifier for Wikidata and DBpedia with different feature sets.

Feature group	Wikidata accuracy	DBpedia accuracy
All features: TEX, STP, EMB	**0.98**	0.97
No spatio-temp. features: TEX, EMB	0.97	0.96
No textual features: STP, EMB	0.82	0.73
No embedding: TEX, STP	0.98	**0.97**

Table 4. Complementing corrupted event series. For each corruption factor (i.e. % of removed events), we report the percentage of events that could be reconstructed.

Constraints		Wikidata			DBpedia		
		Corruption factor					
		5%	10%	15%	5%	10%	15%
Baseline	BSL	61.81	63.13	61.83	39.58	38.40	38.17
HapPenIng configurations	EVO	53,63	54.70	53.12	31.04	31.32	30.12
	INT	46.68	47.89	46.39	24.58	24.04	23.46
	WIN	46.06	47.45	45.94	22.71	22.27	21.93
	COV	45.49	45.65	43.64	11.46	11.03	9.30
	CWI	53.36	53.93	51.32	23.96	21.96	19.43
	ECW	48.89	49.17	47.03	21.67	20.71	18.18

the prediction of 85, 805 new sub-event relations not yet contained in Wikidata and 5, 651 new sub-event relations in DBpedia.

To assess the quality of the predicted sub-event relations that are not initially contained in R, we extracted a random sample of 100 sub-event relations consisting of an event and its predicted sub-event and manually annotated each pair as correct or incorrect sub-event relation. According to this manual annotation, 61% of the sub-event relations predicted with our HapPenIng approach that are not yet contained in the *Event Graph* correctly represent real-world sub-event relations in Wikidata (DBpedia: 42%). In comparison, the STransE baseline predicted only 46, 807 new sub-event relations, and only 9% of them are correct based on a manual annotation of a random 100 relations sample (DBpedia: 2%). The difference in performance on the test set and on the predicted sub-event relations not contained in R can be explained by the large class disbalance in the set of relations collected in the sub-event prediction procedure, such that the majority of the candidate relations are negative examples.

4.3 Event Inference Performance

We evaluate the event inference performance in two steps: First, we conduct an automated evaluation of recall by reconstruction of corrupted event series. Second, we assess precision by annotating random samples of new events.

Table 5. Manual evaluation of the correctness of inferred events. For the baseline, each HapPenIng constraint and *Event Graph*, 100 inferred events were randomly sampled and judged as correct or not. The number of additional sub-event relations found during the event inference process is reported as well (P: Precision).

Constraints		Wikidata			DBpedia		
		Inferred events		Relations	Inferred events		Relations
		Number	P		Number	P	
Baseline	BSL	**114,077**	0.26	**16,877**	**31,410**	0.24	**3,420**
HapPenIng configurations	EVO	28,846	0.47	10,045	11,295	0.35	1,170
	INT	5,256	0.57	5,376	2,115	0.67	3,419
	WIN	3,363	0.56	4,547	936	**0.71**	783
	COV	7,297	0.54	2,712	1,313	0.45	417
	CWI	7,965	0.59	4,442	1,965	0.61	718
	ECW	5,010	**0.70**	3,687	1,364	0.70	655

Complementing Corrupted Event Series (Recall). To evaluate the recall of the event series completion, we remove events from the event series and investigate to which extent our *Event Graph* completion constraints are able to reconstruct them (we consider the naive unconstrained approach BSL as our baseline). To this end, we randomly remove leaf nodes (events without sub-events) from the whole set of event series S until a specific percentage (determined by the *corruption factor*) of leaf nodes is removed. For the *Wikidata Event Graph*, there are 45,203 such leaf events in total before corruption, for DBpedia 9,600. Table 4 shows the results for three corruption factors (5%, 10% and 15%) and the constraints introduced in Sect. 3.2 (we set the parameters to $a = b = 5$ and $\alpha = 0.5$). As expected, the unconstrained naive approach BSL results in the highest percentage of correctly reconstructed events: More than 60% of the Wikidata and nearly 40% of the DBpedia events can be recovered including their correct labels. If applying constraints, less events are reconstructed. In particular, the WIN constraint results in the lowest recall, as it demands to cover the event before and after the series edition within 5 editions.

Overall, we observe that HapPenIng is able to reconstruct more than 60% of missing events from a knowledge graph and correctly infer event labels.

Manual Assessment (Precision). To access precision, we created random samples of 100 newly inferred events for each of the constraints proposed in Sect. 3.2 and both *Event Graphs*, and manually annotated their correctness. Table 5 provides an overview of the results. While the naive unconstrained approach results in a precision of less than 0.30 for both *Event Graphs*, the inclusion of constraints leads to clear improvement, with a precision of up to 0.70 for the ECW constraint for Wikidata and 0.71 for the WIN constraint for DBpedia. Table 5 also reports the number of additional sub-event relations created during the event inference procedure when checking for duplicate events.

Discussion and Additional Statistics. The manual assessment shows that HapPenIng with the ECW constraints is able to infer 5, 010 new events with a precision of 70% in Wikidata and 1, 364 new DBpedia events with similar precision. Events are inferred wrongly in cases where sub-events are happening in an irregular manner. This includes e.g. the wrongly inferred event "1985 Australian Open – Mixed Doubles" that was extracted although there were no Mixed Doubles in that event series between 1970 and 1985 or competitions like the men's single scull in the World Rowing Championships that used to follow a highly unsteady schedule. In future, external knowledge can be used to verify the inferred events. Differences between the Wikidata and the DBpedia results can be explained by the less complete event type assignments and the lack of a proper sub-event relation in DBpedia, where we use category assignments instead.

As the ECW constraint is most precise for the *Wikidata Event Graph*, we provide more insights for this constraint and *Event Graph* in the following:

- Impact of the sub-event prediction on the event inference: If the sub-event prediction step is skipped, only 3, 558 new events are inferred, compared to 5, 010 events otherwise.
- Additional relations: 3, 687 new sub-event relations were created during the event inference step in addition to the 85, 805 sub-event relations from the sub-event prediction step (in total: 89, 492 new sub-event relations).
- Happening times: 99.36% of the inferred events are assigned a happening time. 0.38% of them were inferred by the first, 81.52% by the second and 18.10% by the third rule from Sect. 3.2.
- Locations: Only 79 of the 5, 010 inferred events were assigned a location under the strict conditions proposed in Sect. 3.2.

Overall, the two steps sub-event prediction and event inference enable HapPenIng to generate ten thousands of new sub-event relations and events. These relations and new instances can be given as a suggestion to be inserted in the respective dataset using human confirmation with external tools, such as the Primary Sources Tool for Wikidata [26].

5 Related Work

Knowledge Graph Completeness. Completeness is an important dataset quality dimension [5]. Due to the *open-world assumption* knowledge graphs are notoriously incomplete. The facts not present in the knowledge graph are unknown, and may or may not be true [22,27]. There has been research on several exemplary aspects of knowledge graph completeness, for example on the incompleteness of Wikidata [1,2] and the relation between obligatory attributes and missing attribute values [13]. In our previous work, we considered the problem of integration and fusion of event-centric information spread across different knowledge graphs and created the EventKG knowledge graph that integrates such information [8,10]. [28] addressed the inference of missing categorical information in event descriptions in Web markup. These works emphasize the need for knowledge graph completion, in particular regarding event-centric information.

Knowledge Graph Completion. None of the knowledge graph completion and refinement tasks has yet considered the inference of new nodes given only the knowledge graph itself [19,30]. Paulheim [19] identifies three different knowledge graph completion approaches: (i) *Type Assertions Completion.* Type assertions completion is the task of predicting a type or a class of an entity [19]. A common approach to this task is to probabilistically exploit type information that is inherent in the statement properties [20]. (ii) *Link Prediction.* With link prediction, a ranked lists of candidates for the missing item of an incomplete triple is generated, typically based on embeddings as performed in the TransE [3], STransE [18] and other graph embedding models [24,30]. In `HapPenIng` we generate new events not originally present in the knowledge graph and profit from the inclusion of textual and tempo-spatial features on top of embeddings. (iii) *External Methods.* Information extraction approaches and graph algorithms can be used to detect new relations [22] or entity/event nodes [12] from external textual data. Instead, `HapPenIng` solely relies on the information inherent to the knowledge graph and does not depend on the availability of the text corpora.

Knowledge Graph Completion Tools: A recent survey of link discovery frameworks is provided in [17]. As human-curated knowledge graphs such as Wikidata demand a high quality of inserted data, there have been several tools developed that help integrating automatically generated information with the respective knowledge graph. This includes the Primary Sources Tool [26], where suggestions for new relations are confirmed by humans and [4] that provides an overview of potentially missing information. Such tools can help to integrate inferred event series data into existing knowledge graphs.

6 Conclusion

In this paper we addressed a novel problem of event series completion in a knowledge graph. The proposed `HapPenIng` approach predicts sub-event relations and real-world events missing in the knowledge graph and does not require any external sources. Our evaluation on Wikidata and DBpedia datasets shows that `HapPenIng` predicts nearly 90, 000 sub-event relations missing in Wikidata (in DBpedia: over 6, 000), clearly outperforming the embedding-based baseline by more than 50% points, and infers over 5, 000 new events (in DBpedia: over 1, 300) with a precision of 70%. These events and relations can be used as valuable suggestions for insertion in Wikidata and DBpedia after manual verification. We make our dataset publicly available to encourage further research.

Acknowledgements. This work was partially funded by the EU Horizon 2020 under MSCA-ITN-2018 "Cleopatra" (812997), and the Federal Ministry of Education and Research, Germany (BMBF) under "Simple-ML" (01IS18054).

References

1. Ahmeti, A., Razniewski, S., Polleres, A.: Assessing the completeness of entities in knowledge bases. In: Blomqvist, E., Hose, K., Paulheim, H., Ławrynowicz, A., Ciravegna, F., Hartig, O. (eds.) ESWC 2017. LNCS, vol. 10577, pp. 7–11. Springer, Cham (2017)
2. Balaraman, V., Razniewski, S., Nutt, W.: Recoin: relative completeness in Wikidata. In: WWW Companion (2018)
3. Bordes, A., Usunier, N., Garcia-Duran, A., Weston, J., Yakhnenko, O.: Translating embeddings for modeling multi-relational data. In: NIPS, pp. 2787–2795 (2013)
4. Darari, F., et al.: COOL-WD: a completeness tool for Wikidata. In: ISWC (2017)
5. Ellefi, M.B., Bellahsene, Z., et al.: RDF dataset profiling - a survey of features, methods, vocabularies and applications. Semant. Web **9**(5), 677–705 (2018)
6. Färber, M., Ell, B., Menne, C., Rettinger, A.: A comparative survey of DBpedia, Freebase, OpenCyc, Wikidata, and YAGO. Semant. Web J. **1**, 1–5 (2015)
7. Gottschalk, S., Bernacchi, V., Rogers, R., Demidova, E.: Towards better understanding researcher strategies in cross-lingual event analytics. In: TPDL (2018)
8. Gottschalk, S., Demidova, E.: EventKG: a multilingual event-centric temporal knowledge graph. In: Gangemi, A., et al. (eds.) ESWC 2018. LNCS, vol. 10843, pp. 272–287. Springer, Cham (2018)
9. Gottschalk, S., Demidova, E.: EventKG+TL: creating cross-lingual timelines from an event-centric knowledge graph. In: ESWC Satellite Events (2018)
10. Gottschalk, S., Demidova, E.: EventKG - the hub of event knowledge on the web- and biographical timeline generation. Semant. Web (2019)
11. Kaltenbrunner, A., Laniado, D.: There is no deadline - time evolution of wikipedia discussions. In: WikiSym. ACM (2012)
12. Kuzey, E., Vreeken, J., Weikum, G.: A fresh look on knowledge bases: distilling named events from news. In: CIKM, pp. 1689–1698. ACM (2014)
13. Lajus, J., Suchanek, F.M.: Are all people married? Determining obligatory attributes in knowledge bases. In: WWW, pp. 1115–1124 (2018)
14. Lehmann, J., Isele, R., Jakob, M., et al.: DBpedia - a large-scale, multilingual knowledge base extracted from Wikipedia. Semant. Web **6**(2), 167–195 (2015)
15. Mishra, A., Berberich, K.: Leveraging semantic annotations to link Wikipedia and news archives. In: Ferro, N., et al. (eds.) ECIR 2016. LNCS, vol. 9626, pp. 30–42. Springer, Cham (2016)
16. Myers, E.W.: An O(ND) difference algorithm and its variations. Algorithmica **1**(1–4), 251–266 (1986)
17. Nentwig, M., Hartung, M., Ngomo, A.N., Rahm, E.: A survey of current link discovery frameworks. Semant. Web **8**(3), 419–436 (2017)
18. Nguyen, D.Q., Sirts, K., Qu, L., Johnson, M.: STransE: a novel embedding model of entities and relationships in knowledge bases. In: NAACL HLT (2016)
19. Paulheim, H.: Knowledge graph refinement: a survey of approaches and evaluation methods. Semant. Web **8**(3), 489–508 (2017)
20. Paulheim, H., Bizer, C.: Type inference on noisy RDF data. In: ISWC (2013)
21. Raileanu, L.E., Stoffel, K.: Theoretical comparison between the gini index and information gain criteria. Ann. Math. Artif. Intell. **41**(1), 77–93 (2004)
22. Razniewski, S., et al.: But what do we actually know? In: AKBC (2016)
23. Setty, V., Anand, A., Mishra, A., Anand, A.: Modeling event importance for ranking daily news events. In: WSDM. ACM (2017)

24. Shi, B., Weninger, T.: ProjE: embedding projection for knowledge graph completion. In: AAAI 2017, pp. 1236–1242 (2017)
25. Swan, R., Allan, J.: Automatic generation of overview timelines. In: SIGIR (2000)
26. Tanon Pellissier, T., et al.: From freebase to Wikidata: the great migration. In: WWW (2016)
27. Pellissier Tanon, T., Stepanova, D., Razniewski, S., Mirza, P., Weikum, G.: Completeness-aware rule learning from knowledge graphs. In: d'Amato, C., et al. (eds.) ISWC 2017. LNCS, vol. 10587, pp. 507–525. Springer, Cham (2017)
28. Tempelmeier, N., Demidova, E., Dietze, S.: Inferring missing categorical information in noisy and sparse web markup. In: The Web Conference (2018)
29. Vrandečić, D.: Wikidata: a new platform for collaborative data collection. In: WWW Companion. pp. 1063–1064. ACM (2012)
30. Wang, Q., Mao, Z., Wang, B., Guo, L.: Knowledge graph embedding: a survey of approaches and applications. IEEE TKDE **29**(12), 2724–2743 (2017)
31. Yuan, Q., et al.: Open-schema event profiling for massive news corpora. In: CIKM (2018)

Uncovering the Semantics of Wikipedia Categories

Nicolas Heist(✉) and Heiko Paulheim

Data and Web Science Group, University of Mannheim, Mannheim, Germany
{nico,heiko}@informatik.uni-mannheim.de

Abstract. The Wikipedia category graph serves as the taxonomic backbone for large-scale knowledge graphs like YAGO or Probase, and has been used extensively for tasks like entity disambiguation or semantic similarity estimation. Wikipedia's categories are a rich source of taxonomic as well as non-taxonomic information. The category *German science fiction writers*, for example, encodes the type of its resources (*Writer*), as well as their nationality (*German*) and genre (*Science Fiction*). Several approaches in the literature make use of fractions of this encoded information without exploiting its full potential. In this paper, we introduce an approach for the discovery of category axioms that uses information from the category network, category instances, and their lexicalisations. With DBpedia as background knowledge, we discover 703k axioms covering 502k of Wikipedia's categories and populate the DBpedia knowledge graph with additional 4.4M relation assertions and 3.3M type assertions at more than 87% and 90% precision, respectively.

Keywords: Knowledge graph completion · Wikipedia category graph · Ontology learning · DBpedia

1 Introduction

Two of the most prominent public knowledge graphs, DBpedia [16] and YAGO [18], build rich taxonomies using Wikipedia's infoboxes and category graph, respectively. They describe more than five million entities and contain multiple hundred millions of triples [27]. When it comes to relation assertions (RAs), however, we observe – even for basic properties – a rather low coverage: More than 50% of the 1.35 million persons in DBpedia have no birthplace assigned; even more than 80% of birthplaces are missing in YAGO. At the same time, type assertions (TAs) are not present as well for many instances – for example, there are about half a million persons in DBpedia not explicitly typed as such [23].

Missing knowledge in Wikipedia-based knowledge graphs can be attributed to absent information in Wikipedia, but also to the extraction procedures of knowledge graphs. DBpedia uses infobox mappings to extract RAs for individual instances, but it does not explicate any information implicitly encoded in categories. YAGO uses manually defined patterns to assign RAs to entities

C. Ghidini et al. (Eds.): ISWC 2019, LNCS 11778, pp. 219–236, 2019.
https://doi.org/10.1007/978-3-030-30793-6_13

of matching categories. For example, they extract a person's year of birth by exploiting categories ending with *births*. Consequently, all persons contained in the category *1879 births* are attributed with *1879* as *year of birth* [29]. Likewise, most existing works, such as [17] and [32] leverage textual patterns in the category names.

There are some limitations to such approaches, since, in many cases, very specific patterns are necessary (e.g. `county, Chester County` for the category `Townships in Chester County, Pennsylvania`), or the information is only indirectly encoded in the category (e.g. `timeZone, Eastern_Time_Zone` for the same category). In order to capture as much knowledge as possible from categories, we propose an approach that does not learn patterns only from the category names, but exploits the underlying knowledge graph as well.

While category names are plain strings, we aim at uncovering the semantics in those category names. To that end, we want to extract both type as well as relation information from categories. In the example in Fig. 1, we would, e.g., learn type (1) as well as relation (2–3) axioms, such as:

$$\exists category.\{Reggae\_albums\} \sqsubseteq Album \tag{1}$$

$$\exists category.\{Nine\_Inch\_Nails\_albums\} \sqsubseteq \exists artist.\{Nine\_Inch\_Nails\} \tag{2}$$

$$\exists category.\{Reggae\_albums\} \sqsubseteq \exists genre.\{Reggae\} \tag{3}$$

Once those axioms are defined, they can be used to fill in missing type and relation assertions for all instances for which those categories have been assigned.

In this paper, we propose the *Cat2Ax* approach to enrich Wikipedia-based knowledge graphs by explicating the semantics in category names. We combine the category graph structure, lexical patterns in category names, and instance information from the knowledge graph to learn patterns in category names (e.g., categories ending in *albums*), and map these patterns to type and relation axioms. The contributions of this paper are the following:

- We introduce an approach that extracts axioms for Wikipedia categories using features derived from the instances in a category and their lexicalisations.
- We extract more than 700k axioms for explicating the semantics of category names at a precision of more than 95%.
- Using those axioms, we generate more than 7.7M new assertions in DBpedia at a precision of more than 87%.

The rest of this paper is structured as follows. Section 2 frames the approach described in this paper in related works. Section 3 lays out the preliminaries of our work, followed by an introduction of our approach in Sect. 4. In Sect. 5, we discuss an empirical evaluation of our approach. We close with a summary and an outlook on future developments.

2 Related Work

With the wider adoption of general purpose knowledge graphs such as DBpedia [16], YAGO [18], or Wikidata [31], their quality has come into the focus of

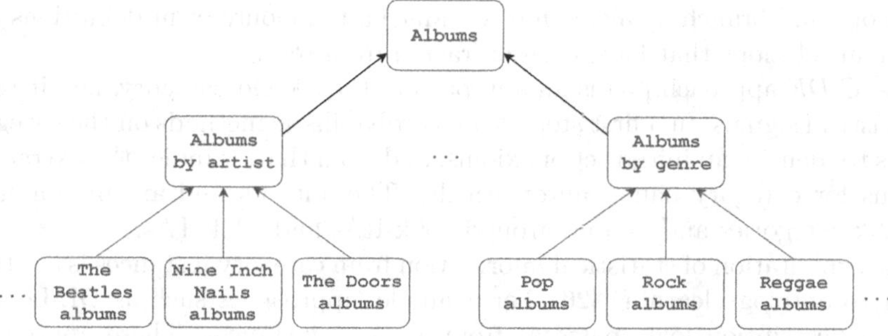

Fig. 1. Excerpt of the Wikipedia category graph showing the category **Albums** together with some of its subcategories.

recent research [3,33]. The systematic analysis of knowledge graph quality has inspired a lot of research around an automatic or semi-automatic improvement or refinement [22].

Generally, knowledge graph refinements can be distinguished along various dimensions: the goal (filling missing knowledge or identifying erroneous axioms), the target (e.g., schema or instance level, type or relation assertions, etc.), and the knowledge used (using only the knowledge graph as such or also external sources of knowledge). The approach discussed in this paper extracts axioms on schema level and assertions on instance level using Wikipedia categories as external source of knowledge.

There are quite a few refinement strategies using additional sources in Wikipedia especially for the extraction of new RAs. Most of them use the text of Wikipedia pages [1,7,9,19], but also Wikipedia-specific structures, such as tables [20,28] or list pages [13,24].

For extracting information from categories, there are two signals that can be exploited: (1) lexical information from the category's name, and (2) statistical information of the instances belonging to the category. YAGO, as discussed above, uses the first signal. A similar approach is *Catriple* [17], which exploits manually defined textual patterns (such as *X by Y*) to identify parent categories which organize instances by objects of a given relation: for example, the category *Albums by genre* has child categories whose instances share the same object for the relation *genre*, and can thus be used to generate axioms such as the one in Eq. 3 above. The Catriple approach does not explicitly extract category axioms, but finds 1.27M RAs. A similar approach is taken in [21], utilizing POS tagging to extract patterns from category names, but not deriving any knowledge graph axioms from them.

In the area of taxonomy induction, many approaches make use of lexical information when extracting hierarchies of terms. Using Hearst patterns [8] is one of the most well known method to extract hypernymy relations from text. It has been extended multiple times, e.g., by [12] who enhance their precision by starting with a set of pre-defined terms and post-filtering the final results. [30]

use an optimal branching algorithm to induce a taxonomy from definitions and hypernym relations that have been extracted from text.

The *C-DF* approach [32] is an approach of the second category, i.e., it relies on statistical signals. In a first step, it uses probabilistic methods on the category entities to identify an initial set of axioms, and from that, it mines the extraction patterns for category names automatically. The authors find axioms for more than 60k categories and extract around 700k RAs and 200k TAs.

The exploitation of statistical information from category instances is a setting similar to ontology learning [26]. For example, approaches such as DL-Learner [15] find description logic patterns from a set of instances. These approaches are very productive when there is enough training data and they provide exact results especially when both positive and negative examples are given. Both conditions are not trivially fulfilled for the problem setting in this paper: many categories are rather small (75% of categories have fewer than 10 members) and, due to the open world assumption, negative examples for category membership are not given. Therefore, we postulate that both, statistical and lexical information, have to be combined for deriving high-quality axioms from categories.

With Catriple and C-DF, we compare against the two closest approaches in the literature. While Catriple relies solely on lexical information in the category names, and C-DF relies solely on statistical information from the instances assigned to categories, we propose a *hybrid* approach which combines the lexical and statistical signals. Moreover, despite exploiting category names, we do not use any language-specific techniques, so that our approach is in principle language-agnostic.

There are other studies using Wikipedia categories for various tasks. Most prominently, taxonomic knowledge graphs such as WiBi [4] and DBTax [6] are created by cleaning the Wikipedia category graph (which is not an acyclic graph and therefore cannot directly be used as a taxonomy). Implicitly, they also learn type axioms and assertions, but no relation axioms and assertions.

3 Preliminaries

The Cat2Ax approach uses three kinds of sources: The Wikipedia category graph, background knowledge from a knowledge graph, and lexicalisations of resources and types in the knowledge graph. In this section, we provide relevant definitions and give background information about the respective sources.

Wikipedia Categories. In the version of October 2016,[1] the Wikipedia category graph contains 1,475,015 categories that are arranged in a directed, but not acyclic graph, although often referred to as a *category hierarchy*. This graph does not only contain categories used for the categorisation of content pages, but

[1] We use this version in order to be compatible with the most recent release of DBpedia from October 2016: https://wiki.dbpedia.org/develop/datasets.

also ones that are used for administrative purposes. We follow an approach similar to [25] and use only categories below `Main topic classifications` while also getting rid of categories having one of the following words in their name: *wikipedia, lists, template, stub*. This leaves us with 1,299,665 categories.

Background Knowledge. As background knowledge, our approach requires a knowledge graph KG that is based on Wikipedia. The knowledge graph is comprised of a set of *resources* which are connected by *relations*, and an *ontology* which defines their classes, interrelations, and restrictions of usage. A resource in the knowledge graph describes exactly one article in Wikipedia. When we are referring to DBpedia in our examples and experiments, we use the prefix *dbr:* for resources and *dbo:* for properties and types.

With *resources(c)* we refer to the set of resources with a corresponding article assigned to the category c. To get an estimate of how likely a combination of a property p and a value v occurs within the resources of a category c, we calculate their frequencies using background knowledge from the knowledge graph KG:

$$freq(c, p, v) = \frac{|\{r|r \in resources(c) \wedge (r, p, v) \in KG\}|}{|resources(c)|} \tag{4}$$

For $p =$ `rdf:type`, we compute type frequencies of c.

Example 1. The category `The Beatles albums` has 24 resources, 22 of which have the type `dbo:Album`. This results in a type frequency $freq$(`The Beatles albums, rdf:type, dbo:Album`) of 0.92.

For p being any other property of KG, we compute relation frequencies of c.

Example 2. Out of the 24 resources of `The Beatles albums`, 11 resources have `dbr:Rock_and_roll` as `dbo:genre`, resulting in a relation frequency $freq$(`The Beatles albums, dbo:genre, dbr:Rock_and_roll`) of 0.46.

Resource/Type Lexicalisations. A lexicalisation is a word or phrase used in natural language text that refers to a resource or type in the knowledge graph. For an entity e, *lex(e)* contains all its lexicalisations, and *lexCount(e, l)* is the count of how often a lexicalisation l has been found for e. When the count of a lexicalisation l is divided by the sum of all counts of lexicalisations for an entity e, we have an estimate of how likely e will be expressed by l.

We are, however, interested in the inverse problem: Given a lexicalisation l, we want the probability of it expressing an entity e. We define $lex^{-1}(l)$ as the set of entities having l as lexicalisation. The lexicalisation score – the probability of an entity e being expressed by the lexicalisation l – is then computed by the fraction of how often l expresses e compared to all other entities:

$$lexScore(e, l) = \frac{lexCount(e, l)}{\sum_{e' \in lex^{-1}(l)} lexCount(e', l)} \tag{5}$$

Example 3. We encounter the word `lennon` in Wikipedia and want to find out how likely it is that the word refers to the resource `dbr:John_Lennon`, i.e. we compute $lexScore$(`dbr:John_Lennon, lennon`). In total, we have 357 occurrences of the word for which we know the resource it refers to. 137 of them actually refer to `dbr:John_Lennon`, while others refer, e.g., to the soccer player `dbr:Aaron_Lennon` (54 times) or `dbr:Lennon,_Michigan` (14 times). We use the occurrence counts to compute a $lexScore$(`dbr:John_Lennon, lennon`) of 0.42.

We compute lexicalisation scores for both resources and types in our experiments with DBpedia. The lexicalisations of resources are already provided by DBpedia [2]. They are gathered by using the anchor texts of links between Wikipedia articles. For types, however, there is no such data set provided.

To gather type lexicalisations from Wikipedia, we apply the following methodology: For every type t in the DBpedia ontology, we crawl the articles of all resources having type t and extract hypernymy relationships using Hearst patterns [8]. To ensure that we are only extracting relationships for the correct type, we use exclusively the ones having a lexicalisation of the page's resource as their subject. To increase the coverage of type lexicalisations, we intentionally do not count complete phrases, but individual words of the extracted lexicalisation. For the calculation of the lexicalisation scores of a phrase, we simply sum up the counts of the phrase's words.

Example 4. We extract lexicalisations for the type `dbo:Band`. The resource `dbr:Nine_Inch_Nails` has the appropriate type, hence we extract hypernymy relationships in its article text. In the sentence *"Nine Inch Nails is an American industrial rock band [..]"* we find the subject *Nine Inch Nails* and the object *American industrial rock band.* As the subject is in lex(`dbr:Nine_Inch_Nails`), we accept the object as lexicalisation of `dbo:Band`. Consequently, the lexicalisation count of the words *American, industrial, rock, band* is increased by one, and, for each of those words encountered, the lexicalisation score for the class `dbo:Band` increases.

4 Approach

The overall approach of Cat2Ax is shown in Fig. 2. The external inputs have already been introduced in Sect. 3. The outputs of the approach (marked in bold font) are twofold: A set of axioms which define restrictions for resources in a category and thus can be used to enhance an ontology of a knowledge graph, and a set of assertions which are novel facts about resources in the graph.

The approach has four major steps: The *Candidate Selection* uses hierarchical relationships in the Wikipedia category graph to form sets of categories that are likely to share a property that can be described by a textual pattern.

In the *Pattern Mining* step, we identify such patterns in the names of categories that are characteristic for a property or type. To achieve that, we use

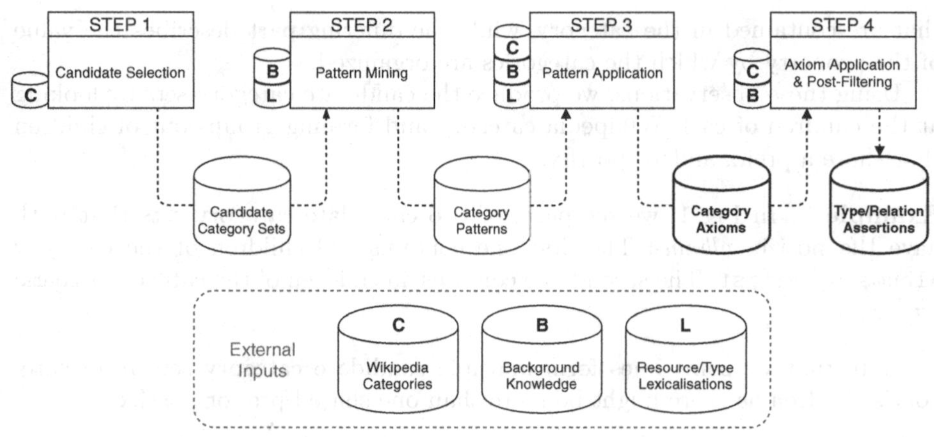

Fig. 2. Overview of the Cat2Ax approach.

background knowledge about resources in the respective categories as well as lexicalisations. Furthermore, we promote a pattern only if it applies to a majority of the categories in a candidate set.

In the *Pattern Application* step, we apply the extracted patterns to all categories in order to find category axioms. Here, we again rely on background knowledge and lexicalisations for the decision of whether a pattern is applicable to the category.

Finally, we generate assertions by applying the axioms of a category to its resources and subsequently use post-filtering to remove assertions that would create contradictions in the knowledge graph.

4.1 Candidate Selection

In this first step, we want to extract sets of categories with names that indicate a shared relation or type. We base the extraction of such candidate category sets on two observations:

The first one is inspired by the Catriple approach [17]. They observed that in a parent-child relationship of categories, the parent often organizes its children according to a certain property. Contrary to Catriple, we do not use the parent category to identify this property, but we rather use the complete set of children to find their similarities and differences.

As we now know from the first observation, the children of a category can have certain similarities (which are the reason that they have the same parent category) and differences (which are the reason that the parent was split up into child categories). As a second observation, we discovered that, when the children of a category are organized by a certain property, their names have a shared part (i.e. a common prefix and/or postfix) and a part that differs for each category. We found that the shared part is often an indicator for the type of resources that are contained in the category, while the differing part describes the value of the property by which the categories are organized.

Using these observations, we produce the candidate category sets by looking at the children of each Wikipedia category and forming groups out of children that share a prefix and/or postfix.

Example 5. In Fig. 1, we see parts of two candidate category sets that both have the postfix *albums*. The first one contains 143 children of the category `Albums by artist`. The second one contains 45 children of the category `Albums by genre`.

Note that we sometimes form multiple candidate category sets from category's children as there might be more than one shared pre- or postfix.

Example 6. The children of the category `Reality TV participants` yield three candidate sets ending on *participants*, *contestants*, and *members*.

4.2 Pattern Mining

For each of the candidate category sets, we want to discover a characteristic property and type. Therefore, we identify patterns that will be used in the subsequent steps to extract category axioms. Each of the patterns consists of a textual pattern (i.e. the shared part in the names of categories) and the implication (i.e. the shared property or type).

To determine the characteristic property, we inspect every individual category in the candidate set and compute a score for every possible relation in the category. As mentioned in Sect. 4.1, the value of a relation differs for the categories in a set. We thus focus on finding the property with the highest score and disregard relation values. To that end, we aggregate the scores from all categories and choose the property that performs best over the complete category set. For this property, we learn a pattern that covers the complete candidate category set.

The score of a relation *(p, v)* for a category *c* consists of two parts with one being based on background knowledge and the other on lexical information. The latter uses the part c_{var} of a category's name that differs between categories in the set to compute an estimate of how likely c_{var} expresses the value of the relation. The score is computed as follows:

$$score_{rel}(c, p, v) = freq(c, p, v) * lexScore(v, c_{var}) \tag{6}$$

Note that *freq(c,p,v)* is only greater than zero for relations of the resources in *resources(c)* which drastically reduces the amount of scores that have to be computed.

Example 7. For the category `The Beatles albums`, we compute an individual relation score for each property-value pair in KG having a resource in $resources($`The Beatles albums`$)$ as their subject. To compute, e.g.,

$score_{rel}$(`The Beatles albums, dbo:artist, dbr:The_Beatles`), we multiply the frequency $freq$(`The Beatles albums, dbo:artist, dbr:The_Beatles`) with the lexicalisation score $lexScore$(`dbr:The_Beatles, The Beatles`).

As an aggregation function for the scores we use the median. Heuristically, we found that the property with the highest median of scores is suited to be the characteristic property for a category set. To avoid learning incorrect patterns, we discard the property if it cannot be found in at least half of the categories in the set, i.e., if the median of scores is zero.

Example 8. After computing all the relation scores for all categories in the category set formed by the 143 children of `Albums by artist`, we aggregate the computed scores by their property and find `dbo:artist` to have the highest median score.

The support of a pattern is the count of how often a pattern has been learned for a category. If we discover a valid property for a category set, the support of the respective property pattern is increased by the number of categories in the set. We assume hereby that, if this property is characteristic for the majority of categories, then it is characteristic for all categories in the set.

For the extraction of characteristic types we apply the exact same methodology, except for the calculation of the score of a type. We compute the score of a type t in the category c using its frequency in c and a lexicalisation score derived from the shared part c_{fix} in a category's name:

$$score_{type}(c, t) = freq(c, \texttt{rdf:type}, t) * lexScore(t, c_{fix}) \tag{7}$$

Example 9. For the category sets formed by the children of `Albums by artist` and `Album by genre` in Fig. 1, we find the following property patterns to have the highest median scores:

- PP_1 = "<lex(*dbr:res*)> albums" $\sqsubseteq \exists$`dbo:artist`.{*dbr:res*}
- PP_2 = "<lex(*dbr:res*)> albums" $\sqsubseteq \exists$`dbo:genre`.{*dbr:res*}

We increase the support of PP_1 by 143 and PP_2 by 45. For both sets, we extract the type pattern TP_1 = "<lex(*dbr:res*)> albums" $\sqsubseteq$ `dbo:Album` and increase its support by 188 (respectively using the counts from Example 5).

4.3 Pattern Application

Before we can apply the patterns to the categories in Wikipedia to identify axioms, we need to define a measure for the confidence of a pattern. This is especially necessary because, as shown in Example 9, we can find multiple implications for the same textual pattern. We define the confidence $conf(P)$ of a pattern P as the quotient of the support of P and the sum of supports of all the patterns matching the same textual pattern as P.

Example 10. Assuming PP_1 and PP_2 of Example 9 are the only property patterns that we found, we have a pattern confidence of 0.76 for PP_1 and 0.24 for PP_2.

Next, we apply all our patterns to the categories of Wikipedia and compute an axiom confidence by calculating the fit between the category and the pattern. Therefore, we can reuse the scores from Eqs. 6–7 and combine them with the confidence of the pattern. As a relation pattern only specifies the property of the axiom, we compute the axiom confidence for every possible value of the axiom's property in order to have a ranking criterion. For a category c, a property pattern PP with property p_{PP} and a possible value v, we compute the confidence as follows:

$$conf(c, PP, v) = conf(PP) * score_{rel}(c, p_{PP}, v) \tag{8}$$

And similarly, for a type pattern TP with type t_{TP}:

$$conf(c, TP) = conf(TP) * score_{type}(c, t_{TP}) \tag{9}$$

Using the confidence scores, we can control the quality of extracted axioms by only accepting those with a confidence greater than a threshold τ. To find a reasonable threshold, we will inspect and evaluate the generated axioms during our experiments.

Example 11. Both patterns, PP_1 and PP_2, from Example 9 match the category `Reggae albums`. Using PP_1, we can not find an axiom for the category as there is no evidence in DBpedia for the property `dbo:artist` together with any resources that have the lexicalisation *Reggae* (i.e. $score_{rel}$ is equal to 0). For PP_2, however, we find the axiom (`Reggae albums, dbo:genre, dbr:Reggae`) with a confidence of 0.18.

For a single category, multiple property or type patterns can have a confidence greater than τ. The safest variant for property and type patterns is to accept only the pattern with the highest confidence and discard all the others. But we found that multiple patterns can imply valid axioms for a category and thus follow a more differentiated selection strategy.

For relation axioms, we accept multiple axioms as long as they have different properties. When the properties are equal, we accept only the axiom with higher confidence.

Example 12. For the category `Manufacturing companies established in 1912` (short: c_1), we find the axioms (c_1, `dbo:foundingYear`, 1912) and (c_1, `dbo:industry`, `dbr:Manufacturing`). As they have different properties, we accept both.

Example 13. For the category `People from Nynäshamn Municipality` (short: c_2), we find the axioms (c_2, `dbo:birthPlace`, `dbr:Nynäshamn_Municipality`) and (c_2, `dbo:birthPlace`, `dbr:Nynäshamn`). As they have the same property, we only accept the former as its confidence is higher.

For type axioms, we accept the axioms with the highest confidence and any axioms with a lower confidence that imply sub-types of the already accepted types.

Example 14. For the category `Missouri State Bears baseball coaches` (short: c_3), we find the axioms (c_3, `rdf:type`, `dbo:Person`) and (c_3, `rdf:type`, `dbo:CollegeCoach`). Despite the latter having a lower confidence than the former, we accept both because `dbo:CollegeCoach` is a sub-type of `dbo:Person`.

4.4 Axiom Application and Post-filtering

With the category axioms from the previous step, we generate new assertions by applying the axiom to every resource of the category.

Example 15. We apply the axiom (`Reggae albums`, `dbo:genre`, `dbr:Reggae`) to all resources of `Reggae albums` and generate 50 relation assertions, 13 of which are not yet present in DBpedia.

Categories can contain special resources that do not actually belong to the category itself but, for example, describe the topic of the category. The category `Landforms of India`, for example, contains several actual landforms but also the resource `Landforms of India`. To avoid generating wrong assertions for such special resources, we filter all generated assertions using the existing knowledge in the knowledge base.

For relation assertions, we use the functionality of its property to filter invalid assertions. Accordingly, we remove a relation assertion *(s, p, o)* if the property p is functional[2] and there is an assertion *(s, p, o')* with $o \neq o'$ already in the knowledge base.

Example 16. Out of the 13 new `dbo:genre` axioms generated for the category `Reggae albums` in the previous example, nine refer to resources which do not have a `dbo:genre` at all, and four add a genre to a resource which already has one or more values for `dbo:genre`. The latter is possible since `dbo:genre` is not functional.

Example 17. The relation assertion (`dbr:Bryan_Fisher`, `dbo:birthYear`, 1982) is removed because DBpedia contains the triple (`dbr:Bryan_Fisher`, `dbo:birthYear`, 1980) already, and `dbo:birthYear` is functional.

To identify invalid type assertions, we use the disjointness axioms of the ontology of the knowledge base, and remove any type assertion that, if added to the knowledge base, would lead to a conflict of disjointness.

Example 18. The assertion (`dbr:Air_de_Paris`, `rdf:type`, `dbo:Person`) is removed because the subject has already the type `dbo:Place`, which is disjoint with `dbo:Person`.

[2] Since the DBpedia ontology does not define any functional object properties, we use a heuristic approach and treat all properties which are used with multiple objects on the same subject in less than 5% of the subjects as functional. This heuristic marks 710 out of 1,355 object properties as functional.

5 Experiments

In this section, we first provide details about the application of the Cat2Ax approach with DBpedia as background knowledge. Subsequently, we discuss the evaluation of Cat2Ax and compare it to the related approaches. For the implementation of the approaches we used the Python libraries spaCy[3] and nltk[4]. The code of Cat2Ax[5] and all data[6] of the experiments are freely available.

5.1 Axiom Extraction Using DBpedia

The following results are extracted using the most recent release of DBpedia.[7]

Candidate Selection. We find 176,785 candidate category sets with an average size of eight categories per set. From those sets, 60,092 have a shared prefix, 76,791 a shared postfix, and 39,902 both a shared prefix and postfix.

Pattern Mining. We generate patterns matching 54,465 different textual patterns. For 24,079 of them we imply properties, for 54,096 we imply types. On average, a property pattern implies 1.22 different properties while a type pattern implies 1.08 different types. Table 1 lists exemplary patterns that match a prefix (rows 1–2), a postfix (rows 3–4), and both a prefix and a postfix (rows 5–6).

Pattern Application. We have to determine a threshold τ for the minimum confidence of an accepted axiom. Therefore, we have sampled 50 generated axioms for 10 confidence intervals each ($[0.01, 0.02)$, $[0.02, 0, 03)$, ..., $[0.09, 0.10)$ and $[0.10, 1.00]$), and manually evaluated their precision. The results are shown in Fig. 3. We can observe that the precision considerably drops for a threshold lower than $\tau = 0.05$, i.e., for those axioms which have a confidence score less than 5%. Hence, we choose $\tau = 0.05$ for a reasonable balance of axiom precision and category coverage.

With a confidence threshold τ of 0.05, we extract 272,707 relation axioms and 430,405 type axioms. In total, they cover 501,951 distinct Wikipedia categories.

Axiom Application and Post-filtering. Applying the extracted axioms to all Wikipedia categories results in 4,424,785 relation assertions and 1,444,210 type assertions which are not yet contained in DBpedia. For the type assertions, we also compute the transitive closure using the `rdfs:subclassOf` statements in the ontology (e.g., also asserting `dbo:MusicalWork` and `dbo:Work` for a type axiom learned for type `dbo:Album`), and thereby end up with 3,342,057 new type assertions (excluding the trivial type `owl:Thing`).

Finally, we remove 72,485 relation assertions and 15,564 type assertions with our post-filtering strategy. An inspection of a small sample of the removed assertions shows that approximately half of the removed assertions are actually incorrect.

[3] https://spacy.io/.
[4] https://www.nltk.org/.
[5] https://github.com/nheist/Cat2Ax.
[6] http://data.dws.informatik.uni-mannheim.de/Cat2Ax.
[7] Release of October 2016: https://wiki.dbpedia.org/develop/datasets.

Table 1. Examples of discovered textual patterns and possible implications.

	Textual pattern	Implication	Sup.	Conf.
1	Films directed by <lex(*dbr:res*)>	$\sqsubseteq \exists$dbo:director.{*dbr:res*}	7661	1.00
2	Films directed by <lex(*dbr:res*)>	$\sqsubseteq$ dbo:Film	7683	1.00
3	<lex(*dbr:res*)> albums	$\sqsubseteq \exists$dbo:artist.{*dbr:res*} $\sqsubseteq \exists$dbo:genre.{*dbr:res*} $\sqsubseteq \exists$dbo:recordLabel.{*dbr:res*}	31426 552 411	0.97 0.02 0.01
4	<lex(*dbr:res*)> albums	$\sqsubseteq$ dbo:Album	33542	1.00
5	Populated places in <lex(*dbr:res*)> district	$\sqsubseteq \exists$dbo:isPartOf.{*dbr:res*} $\sqsubseteq \exists$dbo:district.{*dbr:res*}	269 51	0.84 0.16
6	Populated places in <lex(*dbr:res*)> district	$\sqsubseteq$ dbo:Settlement	362	1.0

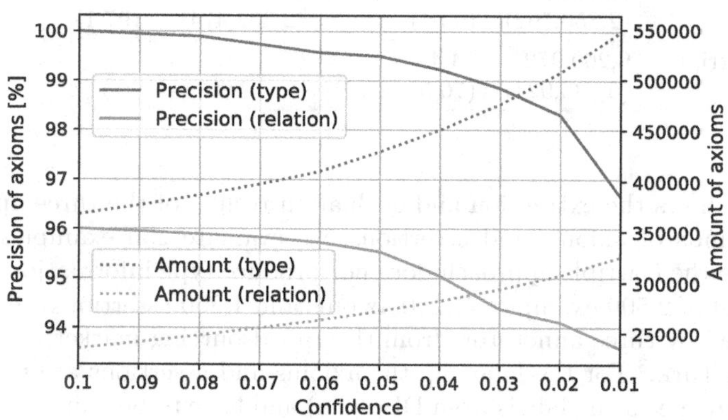

Fig. 3. Performance of the pattern application for varying confidence intervals. The precision values have been determined by the authors by manual evaluation of 50 examples per interval.

5.2 Comparison with Related Approaches

We compare Cat2Ax with the two approaches that also use Wikipedia categories to learn axioms and/or assertions for DBpedia: Catriple [17] and C-DF [32]. As both of them use earlier versions of DBpedia and there is no code available, we re-implemented both approaches and run them with the current version in order to have a fair comparison. For the implementation, we followed the algorithm descriptions in their papers and used the variant with the highest reported precision (i.e., for Catriple, we do not materialize the category hierarchy, and for C-DF, we do not apply patterns iteratively). Running Cat2Ax, Catriple, and C-DF with DBpedia takes 7, 8, and 12 h, respectively.

Table 2. Total number of axioms/assertions and precision scores, based on the crowd-sourced evaluation. Numbers in parentheses denote the *total* number of assertions generated (including those already existing in DBpedia), as well as the precision estimation of those total numbers. The latter were derived as a weighted average from the human annotations and the overall correctness of existing assertions in DBpedia according to [3].

Approach	Count	Precision [%]	Count	Precision [%]
	Relation axioms		Type axioms	
Cat2Ax	272,707	95.6	430,405	96.8
C-DF	143,850	83.6	28,247	92.0
Catriple	306,177	87.2	–	–
	Relation assertions		Type assertions	
Cat2Ax	4,424,785 (7,554,980)	87.2 (92.1)	3,342,057 (12,111,194)	90.8 (95.7)
C-DF	766,921 (2,856,592)	78.4 (93.4)	198,485 (2,352,474)	76.8 (97.1)
Catriple	6,260,972 (6,836,924)	74.4 (76.5)	–	–

Table 2 shows the extraction and evaluation results of the three approaches. For both kinds of axioms and assertions, we evaluate 250 examples per approach. Since the Catriple approach does not produce type information, this adds up to a total of 2,500 examples (1,250 axioms and 1,250 assertions). Each example is labeled by three annotators from the crowdsourcing marketplace Amazon Mechanical Turk.[8] For the labeling, the axioms and assertions are presented in natural language (using labels from DBpedia) and have to be annotated as being either correct or incorrect. The annotators evaluate batches of 50 examples which are selected from the complete example pool and displayed in a random order. The inter-annotator agreement according to Fleiss' kappa [5] is 0.54 for axioms and 0.53 for assertions which indicates moderate agreement according to [14].

In comparison with existing approaches, Cat2Ax outperforms C-DF both in quality and quantity of the created axioms. Catriple produces about 40% more relation assertions, but at a considerably lower precision, and is not able to generate type axioms and assertions.

Despite our efforts of post-filtering generated assertions, a large gap between the precision of axioms and assertions can be observed. This is more evident when looking at *new* assertions, while the overall precision considering both kinds of assertions, which are in DBpedia and which are not, is typically higher. Moreover, there is a small number of axioms which are incorrect and at the same time very productive, i.e., they contribute a lot of new incorrect assertions. To

[8] https://www.mturk.com/.

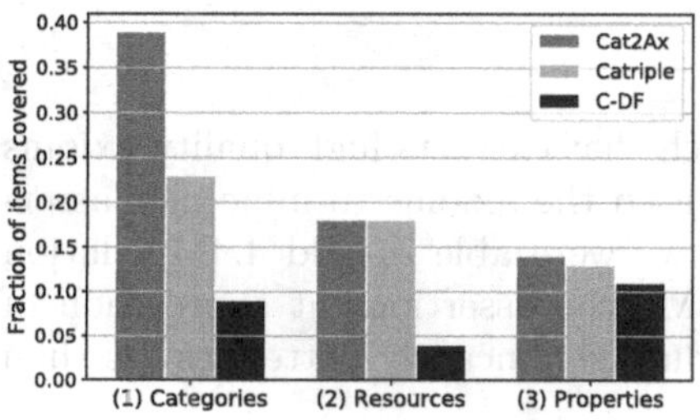

(a) Fraction of (1) categories with at least one axiom, (2) resources with at least one assertion, (3) properties with at least 100 assertions.

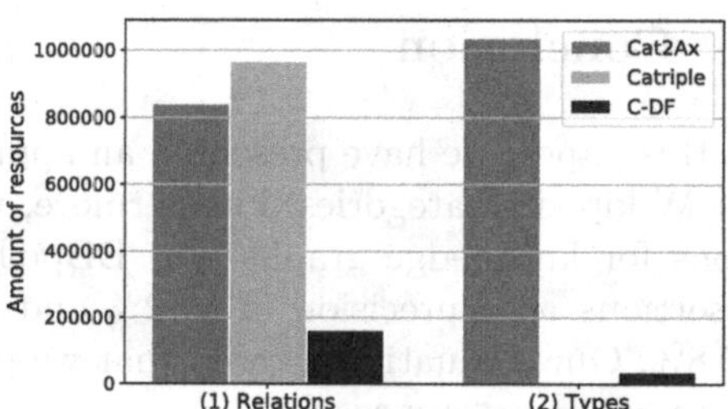

(b) Number of resources without assertions in DBpedia for which (1) a relation assertion or (2) type assertion has been found.

Fig. 4. Comparison of the extracted results.

further look into these issues, we manually inspected some of those axioms and identified three major causes of errors:

Incorrect Data in DBpedia. We extract the axiom (`Roads on the National Register of Historic Places in Arizona`, `rdf:type`, `dbo:Building`) because many roads in DBpedia are typed as buildings.

Correlation Instead of Causation. We extract the axiom (`University of Tabriz alumni`, `dbo:birthPlace`, `dbr:Tabriz`) because people often study in the vicinity of their birthplace.

Incorrect Generalisation. We extract the axiom (`Education in Nashik district`, `rdf:type`, `dbo:University`), which holds for many instances in the category, but not for all of them. This kind of error is most often observed for mixed categories – as in the example, the category contains both universities and schools.

In Fig. 4 we compare the results of the three approaches regarding their coverage of DBpedia. Figure 4a shows the number of covered (1) categories, (2) resources, and (3) properties. At (1) we see that Cat2Ax finds an axiom for almost 40% of Wikipedia's categories. The difference between Cat2Ax and Catriple is, however, not visible in (2) anymore. This can be traced back to Catriple not using any background knowledge during their creation of results and thus producing axioms that are more productive in terms of generated assertions. Furthermore, (3) shows that all approaches find assertions for a comparable number of properties.

Figure 4b shows statistics for resources that are currently not described by any relation or type in DBpedia. While Cat2Ax and Catriple both find relations for almost one million resources, Cat2Ax additionally finds types for more than one million untyped resources.

6 Conclusion

In this paper, we have presented an approach that extracts high-quality axioms for Wikipedia categories. Furthermore, we used the axioms to mine new assertions for knowledge graphs. For DBpedia, we were able to add 4.4M relation assertions at a precision of 87.2% and 3.3M type assertions at a precision of 90.8%. Our evaluation showed that we produce significantly better results than state-of-the-art approaches.

So far, we have only considered direct assignments to categories. Exploiting the containment relations between categories and materialising the category assignments would help the approach in two respects – the extraction of axioms is supported by more precise relation and type frequencies, and the extracted axioms can be applied to a larger number of resources, leading to a higher number of generated assertions. However, this materialisation is not straightforward as the Wikipedia category graph is not acyclic. Currently, we are working on extracting a proper hierarchy from the Wikipedia category graph, which can then be used as a basis for a refined approach.

Moreover, we currently consider all the generated patterns in isolation. But we plan to combine patterns on two dimensions. Firstly, we want to investigate methods to form more generalised patterns out of the currently extracted ones. We expect this to improve the quality of pattern confidence values and the patterns are applicable to more categories. Secondly, property and type patterns and their generated axioms can be combined to provide a better post-filtering of assertions. Given that we know that a relation axiom and a type axiom belong together, and we encounter a single inconsistency in their set of generated axioms, we can discard the complete set.

In previous works, the exploitation of list pages has been discussed for learning new type and relation assertions for instances [13,24]. We plan to extend the approach in this paper to list pages as well. To that end, we need to robustly extract entities from a list page (which is not straightforward since not all links on a list page necessarily link to entities of the corresponding set), and we need to allocate a list page to a position in the category graph.

It is important to note that, although we carried out experiments with DBpedia, the approach is not limited to only this knowledge graph. Any knowledge graph linked to Wikipedia (or DBpedia) can be extended with the approach discussed in this paper. This holds, e.g., for YAGO and Wikidata. Moreover, the approach could also be applied to knowledge graphs created from other Wikis, such as DBkWik [11], or used with different hierarchies, such as the Wikipedia Bitaxonomy [4] or WebIsALOD [10]. Hence, Cat2Ax has general potential which goes beyond DBpedia and Wikipedia.

References

1. Aprosio, A.P., Giuliano, C., Lavelli, A.: Extending the coverage of DBpedia properties using distant supervision over Wikipedia. In: NLP-DBpedia@ ISWC (2013)
2. Bryl, V., Bizer, C., Paulheim, H.: Gathering alternative surface forms for DBpedia entities. In: Workshop on NLP&DBpedia, pp. 13–24 (2015)
3. Färber, M., Bartscherer, F., Menne, C., Rettinger, A.: Linked data quality of DBpedia, Freebase, OpenCyc, Wikidata, and YAGO. Semant. Web **9**, 1–53 (2016)
4. Flati, T., et al.: Two is bigger (and better) than one: the Wikipedia bitaxonomy project. In: 52nd Annual Meeting of the ACL, vol. 1, pp. 945–955 (2014)
5. Fleiss, J.L.: Measuring nominal scale agreement among many raters. Psychol. Bull. **76**(5), 378 (1971)
6. Fossati, M., Kontokostas, D., Lehmann, J.: Unsupervised learning of an extensive and usable taxonomy for DBpedia. In: 11th International Conference on Semantic Systems, pp. 177–184. ACM (2015)
7. Gerber, D., Ngomo, A.C.N.: Bootstrapping the linked data web. In: 1st Workshop on Web Scale Knowledge Extraction@ ISWC, vol. 2011 (2011)
8. Hearst, M.A.: Automatic acquisition of hyponyms from large text corpora. In: 14th Conference on Computational Linguistics, vol. 2, pp. 539–545 (1992)
9. Heist, N., Hertling, S., Paulheim, H.: Language-agnostic relation extraction from abstracts in Wikis. Information **9**(4), 75 (2018)
10. Hertling, S., Paulheim, H.: WebIsALOD: providing hypernymy relations extracted from the Web as linked open data. In: d'Amato, C., Fernandez, M., Tamma, V., Lecue, F., Cudré-Mauroux, P., Sequeda, J., Lange, C., Heflin, J. (eds.) ISWC 2017. LNCS, vol. 10588, pp. 111–119. Springer, Cham (2017). https://doi.org/10.1007/978-3-319-68204-4_11
11. Hertling, S., Paulheim, H.: DBkWik: a consolidated knowledge graph from thousands of Wikis. In: IEEE International Conference on Big Knowledge, ICBK (2018)
12. Kozareva, Z., Hovy, E.: Learning arguments and supertypes of semantic relations using recursive patterns. In: 48th Annual Meeting of the ACL, pp. 1482–1491. ACL (2010)
13. Kuhn, P., Mischkewitz, S., et al.: Type inference on Wikipedia list pages. Informatik **46**, 2101–2111 (2016)
14. Landis, J.R., Koch, G.G.: The measurement of observer agreement for categorical data. Biometrics **33**, 159–174 (1977)
15. Lehmann, J.: DL-learner: learning concepts in description logics. J. Mach. Learn. Res. **10**(Nov), 2639–2642 (2009)
16. Lehmann, J., Isele, R., Jakob, M., et al.: Dbpedia-a large-scale, multilingual knowledge base extracted from Wikipedia. Semant. Web **6**(2), 167–195 (2015)
17. Liu, Q., Xu, K., Zhang, L., Wang, H., Yu, Y., Pan, Y.: Catriple: extracting triples from wikipedia categories. In: Domingue, J., Anutariya, C. (eds.) ASWC 2008. LNCS, vol. 5367, pp. 330–344. Springer, Heidelberg (2008). https://doi.org/10.1007/978-3-540-89704-0_23
18. Mahdisoltani, F., Biega, J., Suchanek, F.M.: YAGO3: a knowledge base from multilingual Wikipedias. In: CIDR (2013)
19. Mintz, M., Bills, S., et al.: Distant supervision for relation extraction without labeled data. ACL-AFNLP **2**, 1003–1011 (2009)
20. Muñoz, E., Hogan, A., Mileo, A.: Triplifying Wikipedia's tables. In: LD4IE@ ISWC, vol. 1057 (2013)

21. Nastase, V., Strube, M.: Decoding Wikipedia categories for knowledge acquisition. AAAI **8**, 1219–1224 (2008)
22. Paulheim, H.: Knowledge graph refinement: a survey of approaches and evaluation methods. Semant. Web **8**(3), 489–508 (2017)
23. Paulheim, H., Bizer, C.: Type inference on noisy RDF data. In: Alani, H., et al. (eds.) ISWC 2013. LNCS, vol. 8218, pp. 510–525. Springer, Heidelberg (2013). https://doi.org/10.1007/978-3-642-41335-3_32
24. Paulheim, H., Ponzetto, S.P.: Extending DBpedia with Wikipedia list pages. NLP-DBpedia ISWC **13**, 1–6 (2013)
25. Ponzetto, S.P., Strube, M.: Deriving a large scale taxonomy from Wikipedia. AAAI **7**, 1440–1445 (2007)
26. Rettinger, A., Lösch, U., Tresp, V., d'Amato, C., Fanizzi, N.: Mining the semantic web. Data Min. Knowl. Discov. **24**(3), 613–662 (2012)
27. Ringler, D., Paulheim, H.: One knowledge graph to rule them all? Analyzing the differences between DBpedia, YAGO, Wikidata & co. In: Kern-Isberner, G., Fürnkranz, J., Thimm, M. (eds.) KI 2017. LNCS, vol. 10505. Springer, Heidelberg (2017). https://doi.org/10.1007/978-3-319-67190-1_33
28. Ritze, D., Lehmberg, O., Bizer, C.: Matching HTML tables to DBpedia. In: 5th International Conference on Web Intelligence, Mining and Semantics, p. 10. ACM, New York (2015)
29. Suchanek, F.M., Kasneci, G., Weikum, G.: YAGO: a core of semantic knowledge. In: 16th International Conference on World Wide Web, pp. 697–706. ACM (2007)
30. Velardi, P., Faralli, S., Navigli, R.: OntoLearn reloaded: a graph-based algorithm for taxonomy induction. Comput. Linguist. **39**(3), 665–707 (2013)
31. Vrandečić, D., Krötzsch, M.: Wikidata: a free collaborative knowledgebase. Commun. ACM **57**(10), 78–85 (2014)
32. Xu, B., Xie, C., et al.: Learning defining features for categories. In: IJCAI, pp. 3924–3930 (2016)
33. Zaveri, A., Rula, A., Maurino, A., et al.: Quality assessment for linked data: a survey. Semant. Web **7**(1), 63–93 (2016)

Qsearch: Answering Quantity Queries from Text

Vinh Thinh Ho[1(✉)], Yusra Ibrahim[1], Koninika Pal[1], Klaus Berberich[1,2], and Gerhard Weikum[1]

[1] Max Planck Institute for Informatics, Saarbrücken, Germany
hvthinh@mpi-inf.mpg.de

[2] Saarland University of Applied Sciences, Saarbrücken, Germany

Abstract. Quantities appear in search queries in numerous forms: companies with annual revenue of at least 50 Mio USD, athletes who ran 200 m faster than 19.5 s, electric cars with range above 400 miles, and so on. Processing such queries requires the understanding of numbers present in the query to capture the contextual information about the queried entities. Modern search engines and QA systems can handle queries that involve entities and types, but they often fail on properly interpreting quantities in queries and candidate answers when the specifics of the search condition (less than, above, etc.), the units of interest (seconds, miles, meters, etc.) and the context of the quantity matter (annual or quarterly revenue, etc.). In this paper, we present a search and QA system, called Qsearch, that can effectively answer advanced queries with quantity conditions. Our solution is based on a deep neural network for extracting quantity-centric tuples from text sources, and a novel matching model to retrieve and rank answers from news articles and other web pages. Experiments demonstrate the effectiveness of Qsearch on benchmark queries collected by crowdsourcing.

Keywords: Semantic search · Question answering · Information extraction · Quantities

1 Introduction

Motivation. Quantities, such as $2B, 40 mpg or 19.19 s, are more than mere numbers; they express measures like revenue, fuel consumption or time in a race with a numeric value and a corresponding unit. The occurrence of a quantity in the text or a table of a web page is associated with an entity and interpretable only with the surrounding context. For example, in the sentence *"BMW i8 costs about 138k Euros in Germany and has a battery range between 50 and 60 km."*, the quantity €138.000 (after normalization) refers to the price of the car model BMW i8, and the quantity interval [50,60] km denotes the range for that car (note that this is in electric mode only as this is a hybrid car).

C. Ghidini et al. (Eds.): ISWC 2019, LNCS 11778, pp. 237–257, 2019.
https://doi.org/10.1007/978-3-030-30793-6_14

Table 1. Statistics on exemplary quantitative properties from Wikidata and DBpedia. #*E*: number of entities; #*P*: with property present; #*Q*: with explicit data type for the property.

Entity type/property	Wikidata			DBpedia		
	#*E*	#*P*	#*Q*	#*E*	#*P*	#*Q*
Car model/range	3195	4	4	6705	0	0
Car model/engine power	3195	0	0	6705	0	0
Mobile phone/display size	291	0	0	1358	1309	0
Marathon runner/best time	1629	18	18	3426	1346	601

Quantities are common in search queries, for example to find a product within a specific price range, cars or mobile phones with desired technical or environmental properties, or athletes who ran a race in a certain time. When a user issues a quantity search query, such as *"Hybrid cars with price under 35,000 Euros and battery range above 100* km", she expects the search engine to understand the quantities and to return relevant answers as a list of entities. However, Internet search engines treat quantities largely as strings ignoring their values and unit of measurements. As a result, they cannot handle numeric comparisons, they miss out on units or scale factors (such as "k" in "138k"), do not know about necessary conversions between units, and ultimately fail. The exceptional cases where search engines (incl. vertical product search) provide support for coping with quantities are money and date, but this is achieved by specialized techniques and fairly limited.

One would hope that semantic search over knowledge graphs (KG) like DBpedia or Wikidata goes further, but their coverage of quantitative facts is very limited and most literals, apart from dates, are merely represented as strings; e.g., battery capacity of the BMW i3 is shown as the string *"i3 94 Ah: 33 kWh lithium-ion battery"* in DBpedia. Important properties for cars, like fuel consumption, CO2 emission, etc. are not covered at all. Table 1 gives exemplary numbers for the quantity coverage in Wikidata and DBpedia.

This paper sets out to provide support for answering quantity queries from text, over a wide variety of expressive measures, to overcome this severe limitation of today's search engines and knowledge graphs. Our method extracts quantity-centric structure from Web contents, uncovering the hidden semantics of linking quantities with entities.

Problem Statement. We define our problem as follows. Given a quantity query and a corpus of text pages, find a ranked list of entities that match the given query. A quantity query is a triple (t^*, q^*, X^*), where t^* is the semantic type of the expected answers, q^* is a quantity-centric search condition, and X^* is the context that connects the entity type t^* with quantity condition q^*. For example, for the query *"Cars with price less than €35,000 in Germany"*, the triple (t^*, q^*, X^*) is: (*cars;<€35.000;{price, Germany}*). Our problem has two dimensions. The first is to understand the content of the text snippets and extract the relevant quantity facts. The second is to match such extracted assertions (inevitably with noise and errors) against a query and compute a ranked list of relevant entity answers.

Approach. This paper presents Qsearch, an end-to-end system for answering quantity queries. Qsearch employs a deep neural network to extract quantity facts from text, this way lifting textual information into semantic structures. Then, it utilizes a statistical matching model to retrieve and rank answers.

We model the first component, quantity fact extraction, as a Semantic Role Labeling (SRL) task [13] and devise a deep learning method to label words in the sentences with relevant roles. We label each word as entity, quantity or context (or other). Then we use these tags to extract quantity fact triples in form of *(entity, quantity, context)*. For the second component, query matching, we devise a novel matching method to retrieve a ranked list of relevant entities that answer the user's quantity query.

Contribution. The salient contributions of this work are as follows:

- We present Qsearch, a system for answering quantity queries from text.
- We propose a deep neural network for quantity fact extraction, and a matching model for answering quantity queries.
- We present extensive experiments on benchmark queries collected by crowdsourcing.

2 Computational Model and System Overview

In this section, we introduce the computational model for our approach and give an overview of the Qsearch system and its components.

2.1 Model for Facts, Queries and Answers

Extraction Model. The *input* of this model is a corpus of text documents $\mathcal{T}$ with text snippets (e.g., sentences or paragraphs) that contain entity and quantity mentions.

The *output* of this model is a set of *quantity facts* extracted from the text corpus, $\mathbb{F} = \{\mathcal{F}_1, \mathcal{F}_2, ...\}$, where a quantity fact is defined as follows.

Definition 1 (Quantity fact). *A quantity fact (Qfact) is a triple* $\mathcal{F} = (e, q, X)$, *where:*

- *e is an entity;*
- *$q = (v, u, r)$ is a quantity consisting of a numerical value v, a canonicalized unit u (e.g., km, \$) and a value resolution r (exact, approximate, upper/lower bound, interval);*

– $X = \{x_1, x_2, ...\}$ *is a context, which is a bag of words describing the relation between* e *and* q.

Example 1. Given the text snippet *"BMW i8 costs about 138k Euros in Germany and has a battery range between 50 and 60*km.*"*, we can extract the following Qfacts:

– $\mathcal{F}_1 : e =$ *BMW i8*; $q =$ *(138.000, €, approximate)*; $X = \{$*costs, Germany*$\}$

– $\mathcal{F}_2 : e =$ *BMW i8*; $q =$ *(50–60, km, interval)*; $X = \{$*range, battery*$\}$ □

The Qfact representation is similar to the RDF model [20], which represents each fact as a *(subject, predicate, object)* triple. In the Qfact model, the entity e and the quantity q correspond to the *subject* and the *object*, respectively. The context X in Qfacts is a proxy for the *predicate* in the RDF model. However, it differs in two essential points: first, the context X can capture more than one relation between e and q; second, the context X consists of a set of non-canonicalized tokens, instead of a unique canonicalized predicate in a knowledge graph.

This relaxed representation is a judicious design choice and essential for the flexibility of our approach: first, we can represent complex n-ary facts using a simple Qfact triple; second, our model can generalize to unseen relations; third, our model can cope with the inevitable diversity and uncertainty in the language expressions of the underlying text snippets. In theory, it is conceivable that all arguments that appear in the context X are also individually extracted and canonicalized to fill the slots of a frame-like structured record. However, approaches along these lines do not work robustly and suffer from heavy propagation of noise and errors.

The Qfact model allows different representations of the same fact, and the underlying text corpus may express the same knowledge by different paraphrases. Hence, Qfacts are more expressive towards answering queries via approximate matches and related phrases.

Matching Model. The *input* of this model is a set of Qfacts $\mathbb{F} = \{\mathcal{F}_1, \mathcal{F}_2, ...\}$ extracted from the text corpus, and a *quantity query* $\mathcal{Y}$ defined as:

Definition 2 (Quantity query). *A quantity query (Qquery) is a triple* $\mathcal{Y} = (t^*, q^*, X^*)$ *where:*

– t^* *is the semantic type of the target answers;*
– $q^* = (v, u, o)$ *is a quantity condition consisting of a numerical value* v*, a canonicalized unit* u *(e.g., km, \$) , and a comparison operator* o *(exact, approximate, upper/lower bound, interval);*
– $X^* = \{x_1, x_2, ...\}$ *is a context condition, expressed by a bag of words that describes the relation between* t^* *and* q^*.

Example 2. Given the query *"Cars with price less than 100k Euros in Germany"*, its corresponding Qquery is as follows:
- $\mathcal{Y} : t^* =$ *car*; $q^* =$ *(100.000, €, upper bound)*; $X^* = \{$*price, Germany*$\}$ □

Each part of a Qquery imposes a constraint on its counterpart in a Qfact considered as a candidate answer.

Definition 3 (Query answer). *A Qfact $\mathcal{F} = (e, q, X)$ is an answer for a Qquery $\mathcal{Y} = (t^*, q^*, X^*)$ iff (1) e is an entity of type t^*, (2) the quantity q satisfies the quantity condition q^* and (3) the context X (approximately) matches the context condition X^*.*

Example 3. Consider the Qquery in Example 2 and the two text segments *"German dealers sell the BMW X3 at a price as low as 55,000 Euros"* and *"Car dealers in Munich sell the BMW X3 starting at 55,000 Euros"*. The Qfact extracted from the first snippet with e = *BMW X3*, q = *(55.000, €, lower bound)*, and X = {*German, dealers, sell, price*} is a strong match for the query; whereas the Qfact extracted from the second snippet with e = *BMW X3*, q = *(55.000, €, lower bound)*, and X = {*car, dealers, Munich, sell*} is an approximate match (by embedding-based relatedness). □

The *output* of this model is a ranked list of entities $\mathcal{E}^* = \{e_1, e_2, e_3, ...\}$ from matching Qfacts with the Qquery, which will be discussed in Sect. 4.

2.2 Qsearch System

Figure 1 gives an overview of the architecture of Qsearch. The arrows in the figure depict information flow between the different system components. Qsearch consists of two main stages: *Extract* and *Answer*.

Extract. We preprocess the text corpus (Block 1) to recognize and disambiguate named entities and link them to an external knowledge base (KB). We also identify mentions of quantities in the text and normalize them into standard units. Subsequently, we run a deep neural network to extract Qfacts from the preprocessed text (Block 2). We learn and employ a specifically designed Long Short Term Memory (LSTM) network, which will be described in Sect. 3.

Extracted Qfacts are organized and grouped by their named entities, such that each individual entity e_i is mapped to a list of quantities and related contexts $L_{e_i} = \{(q_{i1}, X_{i1}), (q_{i2}, X_{i2}), ...\}$ (Block 3). All extracted Qfacts are stored in a data repository (Block 4, based on Elasticsearch in our implementation), where entities are linked to their semantic types from the KB.

Answer. We answer incoming Qqueries by matching them against the Qfacts from the *Extract* stage. For a Qquery (t^*, q^*, X^*) (Block 5), we first apply an entity-type filter, eliminating entities with the wrong type. This results in a set of candidate entities $\mathcal{C} = \{c_1, c_2, ...\}$ (Block 6) satisfying the type constraint t^*, along with their quantity-context pairs $\{L_{c_1}, L_{c_2}, ...\}$. In Block 7, we discard all candidate answers that do not satisfy the quantity condition q^*. Finally, we compute a matching score for each candidate entity $c \in \mathcal{C}$ based on the contexts X in the quantity-context pairs L_c, using a statistical language model or a text

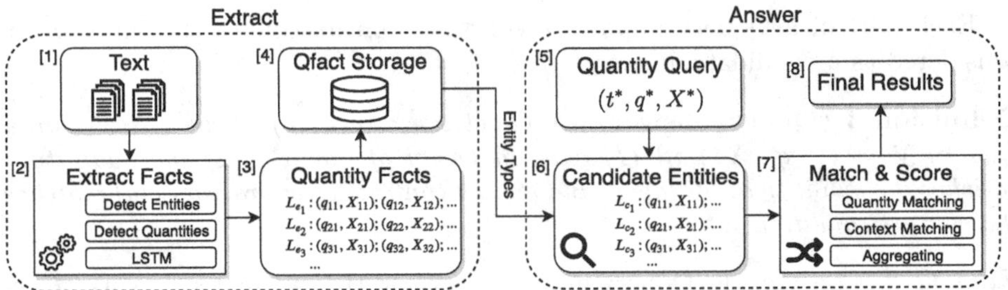

Fig. 1. Overview of Qsearch.

embedding method, which will be described in Sect. 4. The candidate entities are ranked by their scores and returned to the user (Block 8).

In the following Sects. 3 and 4, we discuss in detail the Qfact extraction model and the matching and answering model, respectively.

3 Quantity Fact Extraction from Text

In this section, we describe our method for extracting Qfacts from natural language text. At the core of our solution is a deep-learning neural network for sequence tagging, running on individual sentences.

Input Preprocessing. In the first step, we preprocess the input text corpus by detecting entities and quantities appearing in each individual input sentence. We perform Named Entity Disambiguation (NED) using the AIDA [16] system, which links named entities to the YAGO knowledge base [34]. To achieve a better detection quality, we run NED on a per-document instead of per-sentence basis. For detecting quantities, we make use of the Illinois Quantifier [28], a state-of-the-art tool for recognizing numeric quantities in text, along with some hand-crafted rules (e.g., regular expressions). Subsequently, each identified quantity is replaced by a placeholder *"_QT_"*.

Example 4. Input and output of this preprocessing step look as follows:

sentence | *BMW i8 has price of 138k Euros in Germany and range from 50 to 60 km on battery.*

preprocessed | *BMW i8* [e_1=<KB:BMW_i8>] *has price of* *_QT_* [q_1=(138.000,€,appr.)] *in* *Germany* [e_2=<KB:Germany>] *and range* *_QT_* [q_2=(50–60, km, interval)] *on battery .* □

Sequence Tagging Model. In the second step, we aim to extract complete Qfacts from the preprocessed sentences. For each quantity detected in the previous step, we want to identify the entity to which it refers and the relevant context tokens that express the entity-quantity relation.

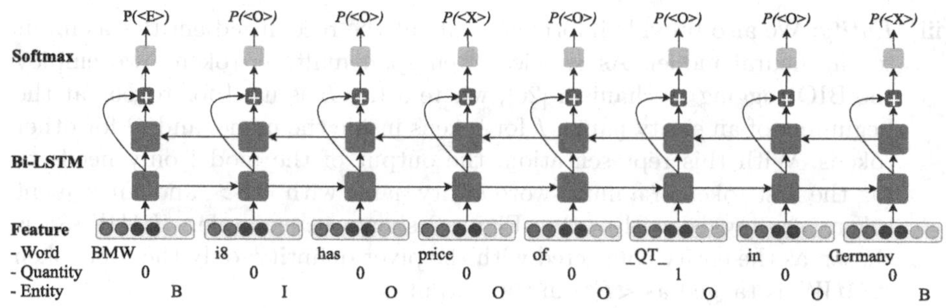

Fig. 2. The Qfact extraction model used by Qsearch.

Example 5. Consider the preprocessed sentence in Example 4. If we use the first quantity $q_1 =$ *(138.000, €, approximate)* as the input's pivot, we want to obtain the output $e(q_1) = e_1 = <KB : BMW\_i8>$ and $X(q_1) = \{price,\ Germany\}$. Analogously, with $q_2 =$ *(50–60, km, interval)* as pivot, the desired output is $e(q_2) = e_1 = <KB : BMW\_i8>$ and $X(q_2) = \{range,\ battery\}$. □

We formalize this task as a sequence labeling problem as follows.

Task 1 (Quantity Fact Extraction). *Given a preprocessed sentence S with the set of detected entities $\mathcal{E} = \{e_1, e_2, ...\}$, the set of detected quantities $\mathcal{Q} = \{q_1, q_2, ...\}$ and a selected pivot quantity of interest $q_i \in \mathcal{Q}$, the task of quantity fact extraction is to label each token of the sentence with one of the following tags: (i) <E>, for denoting the entity that q_i refers to; (ii) <X>, for denoting the context tokens that relate q_i and its entity; and (iii) <O>, for all other tokens.*

Our problem resembles the Semantic Role Labeling task [13], which is typically addressed by Conditional Random Fields (CRFs) or Long Short Term Memory (LSTM) models. Figure 2 depicts the bi-directional LSTM model that we devised for this task, inspired by prior work [14]. Other models for sequence labeling (e.g., [12,44]) could be easily incorporated as well. Our labeling network consists of three layers: Input Features, Bi-LSTM, and Softmax. While this general architecture is close to any other LSTM model, the most unique point here is the input representation, as described next.

Input Features. Each token of the preprocessed input sequence is represented as the concatenation of three input feature vectors:

(i) *Word*: We include word embeddings as an input feature, which enables the neural model to generalize to different words having similar meanings. In our implementation, we use Glove [24] precomputed embeddings.
(ii) *Quantity*: We provide the position of the pivot quantity to the model as input. When sentences contain multiple quantities (which is a relatively frequent case), our model operates one quantity at a time and we re-run the model for different quantities.

(iii) *Entity*: We also provide information about the recognized entities as input to the neural model. As entities often span multiple tokens, we employ the BIO tagging mechanism [26], where a tag *B* is used for tokens at the beginning of an entity name, *I* for tokens inside the name, and *O* for other tokens. With this representation, the output of the model only needs to tag the first token of a multi-word entity name with <*E*>, and subsequent tokens are tagged with <*O*>. Figure 2 shows an example: *"BMW i8"* is chosen as the entity connected with the pivot quantity; only the first token *"BMW"* is tagged as <*E*> in the output.

Output Constrained Decoding. The output of the model are the probabilities of each token word in the input belonging to each of the three tags <*E*>, <*X*> and <*O*>, produced by the Softmax layer. In neural models, usually the tag with the highest score will be assigned to each token word. However, this standard technique would not take into account the dependencies between output tags, and hence might give us an invalid tag sequence. To solve this issue, we impose the following two constraints on the output of the model at decoding time, and find the most probable tag sequence satisfying them: *(i)* only one tag <*E*> can appear in the output (namely, for the one entity to which the pivot quantity refers); and *(ii)* that tag <*E*> has to be at the start token of an entity name.

To find the most probable tag sequence, we use Dynamic Programming to decode from left to right. Specifically, we compute subsequences of tags $Seq_{i,j,k}$ for every $i \in \{1..n\}$ (n is the sentence length); $j \in \{<E>, <X>, <O>\}$; and $k \in \{0, 1\}$. Here, $Seq_{i,j,k}$ denotes tag subsequence with the highest probability for tokens from position 1 to position i, where the tag of token at position i is j, and the subsequence contains k <*E*> tags. Note that the probability of a tag subsequence is computed as the product of the probabilities of its constituent tags. The final tag sequence can be derived at $i = n$.

Distant Supervision Training. As training data is an important factor but difficult to obtain, and manual labeling at scale is too expensive, we employ distant supervision to generate training data for the Qfact extraction model. We use unsupervised, pattern-based Open Information Extraction (Open IE) to overlay an n-tuple structure (with triples or higher-arity tuples) on the input text. We employ the OpenIE4 tool [22] to this end, and then use its output tuples to generate training data. This process consists of two steps:

Step 1: Capture Information Areas: We define an *information area* as a subset of tokens from a sentence, which presents complete information about a fact. We run Open IE on the *unprocessed* sentence to detect all possible tuples expressed by the text. Each of these tuples has a confidence score; to ensure the quality of the generated training samples, we only keep tuples having a confidence score of at least 0.9. Each of the selected tuples corresponds to an information area.

Example 6. Consider the unprocessed sentence in Example 4, suppose the following tuples are extracted by Open IE: (1): *(BMW i8; has; price of 138k Euros; in Germany)*$^{0.95}$, (2): *(BMW i8; has; range from 50 to 60*km *on battery)*$^{0.9}$, (3): *(BMW i8; has; price of 138k Euros)*$^{0.8}$, (4): *(BMW i8; has; range from 50 to 60*km*)*$^{0.5}$, and (5): *(BMW i8; has; price)*$^{0.1}$. We only keep high-confidence tuples (1) and (2), which contain complete information. Then the following information areas are chosen for training:

(1): *BMW i8 has price of 138k Euros in Germany*

BMW i8 has price of 138k Euros in Germany and range from 50 to 60km on battery.

(2): *BMW i8 has* … *range from 50 to 60km on battery*

□

- *Step 2: Transform infomation areas into training samples:* We map the information areas obtained in Step 1 with entities and quantities detected from the preprocessing phase:

(1): *<KB:BMW_i8>has price of* $\_QT\__{(1)}$ *in<KB:Germany>*

<KB:BMW_i8>has price of $\_QT\__{(1)}$ *in<KB:Germany> and range* $\_QT\__{(2)}$ *on battery.*

(2): *<KB:BMW_i8>has* … *range* $\_QT\__{(2)}$ *on battery*

□

With this mapping, information areas yield training samples for the neural network. We apply conservative filters so that this self-training process minimizes spurious samples. First, we keep only information areas that contain exactly one quantity $\_QT\_$, the pivot quantity. Second, since English sentences tend to express quantity information in active voice, the entity connected to the pivot quantity should appear in the first argument (subject) of the Open IE tuple. For instance, information area (1) has two entities *<KB : BMW_i8>* and *<KB : Germany>*; we choose the former as the one to which quantity $\_QT\__{(1)}$ refers. Finally, we discard all information areas where the subject of the Open IE tuple contains more than one entity.

At this point, for each information area, we have a quantity and a unique entity to which it refers. The context between them is determined from the remaining tokens in the information area based on their Part-of-speech (POS) tags. We allow only the following POS patterns to form the context: noun (NN*), verb (VB*), adjective (JJ*), adverb (RB*), and foreign word (FW, to capture out-of-vocabulary names). We also use pre-defined stopwords to remove uninformative tokens from the context. The resulting Qfact, along with the *<E>*, *<X>*, *<O>* tags for its token sequence, becomes a positive training sample. As negative training samples, we collect all information areas where no entity could be identified to relate with the pivot quantity, i.e., all tokens are tagged as *<O>*.

4 Candidate Fact Matching Model

This section describes our method to answer Qqueries from the extracted Qfacts. To this end, each Qfact is assigned a score denoting its relevance to the given Qquery.

Query Parsing. Input questions are mapped into Qqueries by a rule-based parser for recognizing answer type and quantity condition; all other tokens (except stopwords) are included in the query context. The parser uses a dictionary of YAGO types and a dictionary of quantity units. An alternative to this rule-based technique would be to apply the same neural extraction method to questions that we have used to extract Qfacts from text. However, the questions are easier to handle, and the rule-based parser works well.

Task 2. (Quantity Fact Scoring). *Given Qquery* $\mathcal{Y} = (t^*, q^*, X^*)$ *and Qfact* $\mathcal{F} = (e, q, X)$*, compute a distance score* $d(\mathcal{F}, \mathcal{Y})$ *reflecting the relevance of* $\mathcal{F}$ *regarding* $\mathcal{Y}$*.*

Without loss of generality, we assume that a lower score denotes a better fact. $\mathcal{F}$ should be a high-ranked answer for $\mathcal{Y}$ iff the following three conditions hold: (1) e is an entity of type t^*, (2) q satisfies q^*, and (3) X is a good (approximate) match for X^*.

Entity - Type Matching. We only consider the Qfact $\mathcal{F}$ if the entity e has type t^*. Since the entities from text are linked to an external knowledge base, we make use of the type information from the KB to filter out unsuitable facts for $\mathcal{Y}$.

Quantity Matching. We also discard $\mathcal{F}$ if q does not satisfy q^*. This is the case when either (1) the units of q and q^* relate to different concepts (e.g. *km* (length) vs. €(money)) and are thus incomparable; or (2) their values (after conversion to the same unit) do not match the comparison operator of q^*. Since quantity matching is not the focus of our paper, we apply a simple matching method as follows. First, we use hand-crafted rules for unit conversions, re-scaling if needed (e.g., for kilo, mega, etc.), and value normalization. Second, we turn the quantity value into an interval based on its resolution. For example, when the query is about approximate matches, a quantity value v is smoothed into the interval $[v - \delta, v + \delta]$ with a configuration parameter δ. In experiments, we set δ to 5% of v. A comparison is considered a match when the two intervals overlap, and their units (after conversion and re-scaling) match.

Context Matching. If the Qfact $\mathcal{F}$ satisfies the above two constraints, we will consider the similarity between the query context X^* and the fact context X. We propose to use the following two approaches for measuring the context relevance: a *probabilistic* and an *embedding-based* approach.

Probabilistic Ranking Model. We adopt the Kullback-Leibler (KL) divergence between the query context X^* and the fact context X, which is typically used in statistical language models [42]. The scoring function is defined as follows:

$$d(\mathcal{F}, \mathcal{Y}) = KL(X^*, X) = H(X^*, X) - H(X^*)$$
$$\equiv H(X^*, X) = - \sum_{w \in \mathcal{V}} P(w|X^*) \log P(w|X)$$

where $\mathcal{V}$ is the word vocabulary, $H(X^*)$ is the entropy of X^*; $H(X^*, X)$ is the cross entropy between X^* and X; and $\equiv$ indicates rank equivalence (i.e., preserving order). Since we are only interested in ranking fact contexts in response to a query context, we can omit $H(X^*)$. The word probability $P(w|X^*)$ for the query context is estimated using Maximum Likelihood Estimation (MLE) on an expanded version X_E^* of X^* as:

$$P(w|X^*) = count(w \in X_E^*)/|X_E^*|$$

To expand a query context, we resort to WordNet [23] and add all synonyms of the context words to it. For the fact context, we estimate the word probability $P(w|X)$ using Jelinek-Mercer smoothing as:

$$P(w|X) = (1 - \lambda) \times count(w \in X)/|X| + \lambda \times P(w|B)$$

This linearly combines the MLE from the fact context X with the MLE obtained from a background corpus B. The smoothing parameter λ (set to $\lambda = 0.1$ in our system) controls the influence of the background corpus on the probability estimate. We construct the background corpus B from all sentences of the entire text corpus that contain at least one quantity (total 39 M sentences in our data).

Embedding-Based Ranking Model: We observed on our data that the query context X^* is often shorter than the fact context X, since sentences are often more verbose than the typically short queries. Hence, to measure the distance score of X with regard to X^*, we can match tokens between X^* and X using word embedding similarity as follows:

$$d(\mathcal{F}, \mathcal{Y}) = \left(\sum_{u \in X^*} \min_{v \in X}(dist(u, v)) \right) / |X^*|$$

where $dist(u, v) \geq 0$ is the semantic distance between two words u and v estimated from their pre-computed word embedding vectors [24]. We use cosine distance in the Qsearch implementation, re-scaled for normalization to [0,1]. In the above equation, we map each word of query context X^* to its closest word in the fact context X in the embedding space. This scoring formula gives the same weight to every token in the query context X^*, which might be misleading, since they could have a different degree of importance. This issue is overcome by giving higher weight to important words and lower weight to uninformative words, using the following distance function:

$$d(\mathcal{F}, \mathcal{Y}) = \frac{\sum_{u \in X^*} W(u) \min_{v \in X}(dist(u, v))}{\sum_{u \in X^*} W(u)} + 1$$

where $W(u) \geq 0$ is the importance weight of word u. There are several weighting functions that can be used for W (e.g., *inverse document frequency (idf)*, *term strength*, etc.); we use Robertson's *idf* [27]. We call the above formula the *directed embedding distance*, $ded(X^* \rightarrow X)$, between query and fact contexts.

$ded(X^* \rightarrow X)$ describes how well each word in X^* matches with some other word in X, but in many cases it fails to reflect the match between their meaning. The presence of a single word in the fact context X can totally change its meaning. Consider, as a concrete example, the two contexts $X^* = \{net, worth\}$ vs. $X = \{negative, net, worth\}$. Hence, our idea is to penalize the relevance score with an amount proportional to the directed embedding distance between X and X^*. Specifically, we define the *context embedding distance (ced)* that implements this idea:

$$d(\mathcal{F}, \mathcal{Y}) = ced(X^*, X) = ded(X^* \rightarrow X) \times ded(X \rightarrow X^*)^\alpha$$
$$= \left(\frac{\sum_{u \in X^*} W(u) \min_{v \in X}(dist(u,v))}{\sum_{u \in X^*} W(u)} + 1 \right) \times \left(\frac{\sum_{u \in X} W(u) \min_{v \in X^*}(dist(u,v))}{\sum_{u \in X} W(u)} + 1 \right)^\alpha$$

Intuitively, our *ced* measure is the product of two components: (1) $ded(X^* \rightarrow X)$ captures how well query context tokens match with fact context, and (2) $ded(X \rightarrow X^*)$ reflects how much additional terms in X shift its meaning, and hence, should be penalized. Parameter $\alpha \in [0, +\infty)$ controls how much the penalty scaling affects the total score.

Example 7. Consider the Qquery context $X^* = \{gross, domestic, product\}$ and two Qfact contexts $X_1 = \{gross, national, product\}$, $X_2 = \{gross, domestic, product, capita\}$. While we are more inclined to X_1 than X_2, the directed embedding distance $ded(X^* \rightarrow X_2)$ has a slightly better score than $ded(X^* \rightarrow X_1)$, as it does not penalize the word *"capita"* (which indicates that the GDP is per capita, not the total GDP). In contrast, $ded(X_1 \rightarrow X^*)$ is lower than $ded(X_2 \rightarrow X^*)$ (since *"national"* is close to *"domestic"*), preferring X_1 over X_2 with regard to X^*, which results in the desired ranking based on the context embedding distance *ced*. □

Entity Scoring. The output of Qsearch is a ranked list of entities from matching Qfacts with the Qquery. We assign a score for each candidate entity based on one of the above context distance models and aggregating over the entity's quantity-context pairs as follows:

$$score(c \in \mathcal{C}, \mathcal{Y}) = \min_{(q,X) \in L_c} d(\mathcal{F} = (c, q, X), \mathcal{Y})$$

where $d(\mathcal{F}, \mathcal{Y})$ is either the Kullback-Leibler divergence $KL(X^*, X)$ or the context embedding distance $ced(X^*, X)$. So when the same candidate entity appears in multiple Qfacts, we pick the best-scoring Qfact context distance.

5 Evaluation

We run experiments on a Linux machine with 80 CPU cores, 500 GB RAM, and 2 GPUs. To evaluate Qsearch, we perform an intrinsic evaluation of our *Qfact extraction model* and an extrinsic evaluation of the *end-to-end Qsearch system.*

Dataset. All experiments use a large collection of news articles, compiled from two real world datasets: the *STICS* project [15] with news from 2014 to 2018, and the *New York Times* archive [30] with news from 1986 to 2008. In total, our corpus consists of 7.6M documents.

5.1 Intrinsic Evaluation of the Quantity Fact Extraction Model

Training Setup. We implemented the LSTM network using Theano library, largely following [14] for the training configuration: using Adadelta with $\epsilon = 1e^6$ and $\rho = 0.95$; *lstm_hidden_unit* = *300*; *rnn_dropout_prob* = *0.1*; *batch_size* = *100*.

We extracted training samples from the corpus using the distant-supervision technique as described in Sect. 3 and conducted the training process with different settings. In the *General* setting, we use all available training data of 3.2M training samples, where we maintain the ratio 3:1 between the number of positive and negative samples. We also train our model for three other *measure-specific* settings, where only a subset of the training samples is used. In particular, we classify training samples into different categories based on the quantity unit. For example, training samples containing quantities with unit *Kilometer* or *Meter* are chosen to train the model in the *Length* setting, while the ones with unit *US dollar*, *Euro*, etc. are picked for the *Money* setting. Among many such categories, we selected the three most prevalent measures *Money*, *Percentage* and *Length*, containing 307K, 235K and 41 K training samples, respectively (also with ratio 3:1 between positive and negative samples). The trained models are then applied to the entire corpus to extract more Qfacts.

Performance of Extraction Model. As the test data does not have any ground-truth labels, we randomly selected 100 samples that contain at least two entities from the output tag sequences, for each training model, and manually assessed their validity. We evaluate the quality of the three output labels <*E*>, <*X*> and <*O*> by three measures: *Precision*, *Recall*, and *F1 score*. The results are shown in Table 2. We observe that all training models perform very well on entity tagging with more than 85% *F1 score*. We also see that the measure-specific training variants for Length and Money have slight advantages.

Table 2. Evaluation of Qfact extraction model of Qsearch on different settings.

Tag	Length			Money			Percentage			General		
	Prec.	Rec.	F1	Prec.	Rec.	F1	Prec.	Rec.	F1	Prec.	Rec.	F1
E	0.860	0.860	0.860	0.850	0.850	0.850	0.794	0.770	0.782	0.882	0.820	0.850
X	0.650	0.849	0.736	0.717	0.844	0.776	0.659	0.827	0.734	0.728	0.713	0.721
O	0.958	0.886	0.920	0.942	0.886	0.913	0.947	0.888	0.917	0.895	0.906	0.900
Macro-avg.	0.823	0.865	0.839	0.836	0.860	0.846	0.800	0.828	0.811	0.835	0.813	0.824

Table 3. Statistics of benchmark queries from each domain.

Domain	Distribution of queries based on unit of quantity				
	Money	Length	Percentage	Others	Examples for others
Finance	76%	-	12%	12%	No. of sales, albums, etc.
Transport	4%	32%	-	64%	MPG, mph, horsepower, etc.
Sports	8%	32%	-	60%	Sec, years, kg, no. of medals, etc.
Technology	20%	20%	8%	52%	Megapixels, Watt, mAh, etc

5.2 Extrinsic Evaluation of the End-to-End Qsearch System

We performed the extrinsic evaluation of Qsearch on a benchmark of 100 quantity queries, collected by crowdsourcing and covering four domains: *Finance*, *Transport*, *Sports* and *Technology*. These queries capture a wide diversity of measures and units as well as variety in query formulations (e.g., phrases for the comparison operators); see Table 3. Anecdotal examples of user queries and their answers produced by Qsearch are shown in Table 4. We also considered queries from the QALD-6-task-3 statistical QA benchmark [37], but out of total 150 training and test queries, we found only 6 with quantity conditions (as opposed to simpler property lookups).

In this evaluation, we use the Qfact extraction model trained under the *General* setting, as it generalizes to different measures and units.

Setup. For each Qquery, we consider top-10 results returned by Qsearch and evaluate their relevance and validity by judgements from crowd-workers (using Figure-Eight platform, formerly known as CrowdFlower). The judges were shown the query, the top-10 entity answers, and the corresponding 10 sentences from which the answers were extracted. Each result was annotated as *relevant* or *irrelevant* to the query based on the cue given in its corresponding sentence. For each query, we collected three judgements and used the majority label as gold standard. Overall, we obtained a high inter-annotator agreement with Fleiss' Kappa value of 0.54.

Baselines. Although our Qsearch system produces entities as main result, we still want to compare it with standard search systems, which produce snippets. As there is no other system that can handle quantity queries with crisp

Table 4. Anecdotal examples of quantity queries and results from Qsearch.

Domain	Query
Finance	**Q1:** Coal companies with more than 200 Million dollar annual profit
Transport	**Q2:** Sport utility vehicles with engine power at least 150 horsepower
Sports	**Q3:** Sprinters who ran 100 meter in less than 10 seconds
Technology	**Q4:** Digital cameras with focal length of lens more than 18 mm

Query	Result	Corresponding Sentence
Q1	Duke Energy	Duke Energy had revenue of $ 23.9 billion and profit of $ 1.9 billion last year.
Q2	Ford Escape	Its V-6 engine (the Escape is a four-cylinder) has 270 horsepower, 20 percent more than the Lexus RX330.
Q3	Andre Grasse	Andre De Grasse, a 20-year-old from Markham, Ont., has run the 100 metre in under 10 seconds three times this year.
Q4	Nikon D7100	For example, the D7100 can be found in a kit with 18-140 mm and 55-300 mm lenses , so you'll want to use the 55-300 mm and zoom in to 300 mm.

entity answers, we use search systems as baselines that produce text snippets as answers. Specifically, we ran all benchmark queries on Elasticsearch, locally indexing all sentences of our news corpus, and on Google web search retrieving the top-10 result snippets. Elasticsearch uses a text-oriented state-of-the-art ranking model based on BM25.

The baselines were given certain advantages, to avoid that Qsearch could be viewed as an unfair competitor. For Elasticsearch, we consider only sentences that contain an entity and a quantity. For the evaluation, we asked crowd-workers to annotate top-10 results, retrieved from Elasticsearch, as relevant or irrelevant based on whether they spotted a reasonable result for the quantity query. To evaluate result snippets from Google search, we instructed annotators to be generous, as the result snippets are not well-formed sentences (but could be synthesized from non-contiguous text segments with ellipses). For example, a text snippet that contains a correct entity and its quantity is considered relevant even if it also contains other entities or quantities. Such instructions to annotators give Google results an advantage because Qsearch results are considered relevant only if both entity and quantity are correctly extracted.

We also explored several state-of-the-art QA systems over linked open data: Frankenstein [32], QAnswer [9], Platypus [35], AskNow [10], Quint [1], SPARKLIS [11]. None of these systems is geared for handling quantity questions, except SPARKLIS, however it can only process quantities without associated unit. Moreover, their underlying KBs have poor coverage of quantities. They failed on almost all of our benchmark queries; so we excluded these systems from our comparative evaluation.

Performance of Qsearch. Table 5 shows the performance of Qsearch for the four domains and for all 100 queries together, using the two variants of our ranking models: KL divergence and context embedding distance (*ced*). For *ced*

Table 5. End-to-end evaluation of Qsearch.

Metric	Finance		Transport		Sports		Technology		All	
	KL-div.	Emb.	KL-div.	Emb.	KL-div.	Emb.	KL-div.	Emb.	KL-div.	Emb.
Pr.@1	0.720	0.800	0.480	0.600	0.560	0.680	0.640	0.680	0.600	0.690
Pr.@3	0.667	0.747	0.480	0.480	0.507	0.587	0.627	0.653	0.570	0.617
Pr.@5	0.632	0.672	0.412	0.412	0.480	0.528	0.550	0.624	0.519	0.559
Pr.@10	0.604	0.608	0.333	0.379	0.412	0.432	0.500	0.547	0.462	0.492
Hit@3	0.880	0.920	0.760	0.760	0.760	0.800	0.840	0.880	0.810	0.840
Hit@5	0.880	0.960	0.760	0.760	0.920	0.840	0.840	0.920	0.850	0.870
MRR	0.792	0.870	0.621	0.678	0.685	0.746	0.747	0.783	0.711	0.769

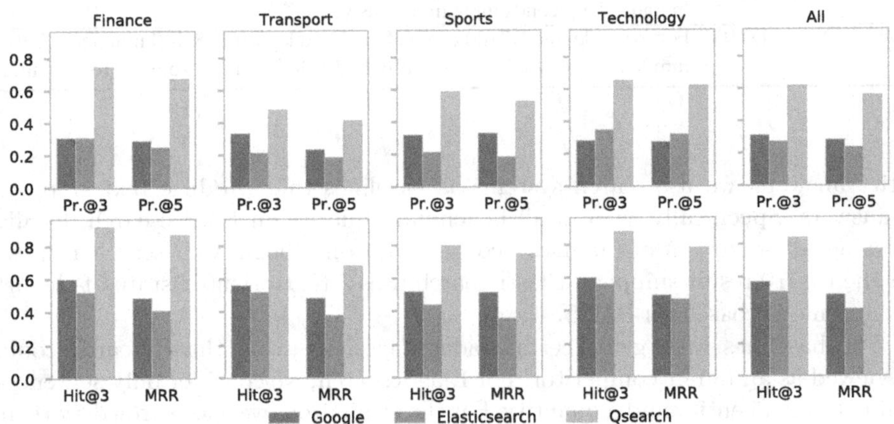

Fig. 3. Comparison of Qsearch against baselines.

we empirically tune the parameter $\alpha = 3$ based on results from 10 validation queries disjoint from the 100 test queries. We report three metrics: *Precision@k*, *Hit@k* and *Mean-Reciprocal-Rank (MRR)*, macro-averaged over queries. We do not discuss metrics like Recall or MAP, as these would require exhaustively annotating a huge pool of candidate answers.

Overall, Qsearch performs amazingly well, typically with MRR around 0.7 or better. The best results are for the Finance domain, which has the highest share in the corpus and is most represented in the Qfact extraction training. *Precision@1* is pretty good, but precision drops substantially when going deeper in the rankings. The embedding-based ranking model clearly outperformed the KL-divergence method by a significant margin.

Figure 3 presents the comparison of Qsearch with the *ced* ranking model against Elasticsearch and Google, showing the metrics *Prec.@3*, *Prec.@5*, *Hit@3* and *MRR*. The results clearly indicate that Qsearch outperforms both baselines by a large margin.

6 Related Work

Question Answering. QA over knowledge graphs and other linked data sources has received great attention over the last years; see [8,36] for surveys. State-of-the-art methods (e.g., [2,5,39,41,43]) translate questions into SPARQL queries, bridging the gap between question vocabulary and the terminology of the underlying data by means of templates and/or learning from training collections of question-answer pairs. Benchmarks like the long-standing QALD series and other competitions have shown great advances along these lines [38]. However, these benchmark tasks hardly contain any quantity queries of the kind addressed here (even in QALD-6-task-3, only 6 out of 150 questions are of this kind, others are mostly about quantity lookup). Note that look-ups of quantity attributes of qualifying entities (e.g., Jeff Bezos's net worth, 10 richest people, or fastest sprinter over 100m) are of a different nature, as they do not contain quantity comparisons between query and data (e.g., worth more than 50 million USD, running faster than 9.9 s). Moreover, the scope and diversity of the benchmark queries is necessarily restricted to relatively few numeric properties, as knowledge graphs hardly capture quantities in their full extent (with value and unit properly separated and normalized). This is our motivation to tap into text sources with more extensive coverage.

QA over text has considered a wide range of question types (e.g., [6,7,40]), but there is again hardly any awareness of quantity queries. Keyword search, including telegraphic queries, with quantity conditions have been considered by [18], and have been applied to web tables [25,31].

[4] and its follow-up work [31] focused on a specific kind of quantity query, namely, retrieving and aggregating numerical values associated with an attribute of a given entity (e.g., Bezos's net worth or GDP of India). To this end, learning-to-rank techniques over value distributions were developed to counter the uncertainty in the retrieved values, where web pages often contain crude estimates and lack exact values. In contrast to our setting, that work did not consider quantities in search conditions.

Information Extraction. Recognizing and extracting numeric expressions from text has been addressed using techniques like CRFs and LSTMs (e.g., [3,21,29]). However, this alone does not turn numbers into interpretable quantities, with units and proper reference to the entity with that quantity. Only few works attempted to canonicalize quantities by mappings to hand-crafted knowledge bases of measures [17], but these efforts are very limited in scope. The special case of temporal expressions has received substantial attention (e.g., [33]), but this solely covers dates as measures.

Most related to our approach are the works of [31] and [28]. The former used probabilistic context-free grammars to infer units of quantities, but focused specifically on web tables as inputs. The latter extended semantic role labeling (see below) to extract quantities and their units from natural language sentences. Neither of these can be readily applied to extracting quantities and their reference entities from arbitrary textual inputs.

Semantic Role Labeling. Semantic role labeling (SRL) has been intensively researched as a building block for many NLP tasks [13]. Given a verb phrase of a sentence viewed as a central predicate, SRL identifies phrases that are assigned to pre-defined roles to form a frame-like predicate-arguments structure. Modern SRL methods make use of pre-computed word embeddings and employ deep neural networks for role filling (e.g., [12,14,44]). Our approach differs from this state-of-the-art SRL, as we are not primarily focused on the verb-phrase predicate, but consider the numeric quantity in a sentence as the pivot and aim to capture quantity-specific roles.

To support exploration of quantitative facts in financial reports, [19] proposed a semantic representation for quantity-specific roles. [28] devised a quantity representation as an additional component of an SRL method, which is part of the Illinois Curator software suite. Our approach makes use of this technique, as a preprocessing step. However, we go further by learning how to connect quantities with their respective entities and to collect relevant context cues that enable our matching and ranking stage for query answering.

7 Conclusion

Awareness of entities and types has greatly advanced semantic search both for querying the web of linked data and for Internet search engines. In contrast, coping with quantities in text content and in query constraints has hardly received any attention, yet is an important case. This paper has presented the Qsearch system for full-fledged support of quantity queries, through new ways of information extraction and answer matching and ranking. We capture quantities in their full extent, including units of measures, reference entities and the relevant contexts. The model for Qfacts and Qqueries is relatively simple but highly versatile and effective. A key asset of Qsearch is its high quality in extracting Qfacts, recognizing the right entity-quantity pairs even in complex sentences.

Future work includes devising additional ways of aggregating Qfacts with the same candidate answer, so as to obtain strong signals from many noisy cues (i.e., when the same entity-quantity pair occurs in many pages, but mostly in the form of crude estimates or vague hints). Also, we plan to extend the Qquery model to incorporate queries that contain multiple quantity conditions (e.g., hybrid SUVs with range above 500 miles and energy consumption above 40 MPGe).

References

1. Abujabal, A., Roy, R.S., Yahya, M., Weikum, G.: QUINT: interpretable question answering over knowledge bases. In: Proceedings of the 2017 Conference on Empirical Methods in Natural Language Processing, EMNLP 2017, Copenhagen, Denmark, 9–11 September 2017 - System Demonstrations, pp. 61–66 (2017)
2. Abujabal, A., Roy, R.S., Yahya, M., Weikum, G.: Never-ending learning for open-domain question answering over knowledge bases. In: Proceedings of the 2018 World Wide Web Conference on World Wide Web, WWW 2018, Lyon, France, 23–27 April 2018, pp. 1053–1062 (2018)

3. Alonso, O., Sellam, T.: Quantitative information extraction from social data. In: The 41st International ACM SIGIR Conference on Research & Development in Information Retrieval, SIGIR 2018, Ann Arbor, MI, USA, 08–12 July 2018, pp. 1005–1008 (2018)
4. Banerjee, S., Chakrabarti, S., Ramakrishnan, G.: Learning to rank for quantity consensus queries. In: Proceedings of the 32nd Annual International ACM SIGIR Conference on Research and Development in Information Retrieval, SIGIR 2009, Boston, MA, USA, 19–23 July 2009, pp. 243–250 (2009)
5. Bast, H., Haussmann E.: More accurate question answering on freebase. In: Proceedings of the 24th ACM International Conference on Information and Knowledge Management, CIKM 2015, Melbourne, VIC, Australia, 19–23 October 2015, pp. 1431–1440 (2015)
6. Chen, D., Fisch, A., Weston, J., Bordes, A.: Reading Wikipedia to answer open-domain questions. In: Proceedings of the 55th Annual Meeting of the Association for Computational Linguistics, ACL 2017, Vancouver, Canada, 30 July–4 August, Volume 1: Long Papers, pp. 1870–1879 (2017)
7. Clark, C., Gardner, M.: Simple and effective multi-paragraph reading comprehension. In: Proceedings of the 56th Annual Meeting of the Association for Computational Linguistics, ACL 2018, Melbourne, Australia, 15–20 July 2018, Volume 1: Long Papers, pp. 845–855 (2018)
8. Diefenbach, D., López, V., Singh, K.D., Maret, P.: Core techniques of question answering systems over knowledge bases: a survey. Knowl. Inf. Syst. **55**(3), 529–569 (2018)
9. Diefenbach, D., Migliatti, P.H., Qawasmeh, O., Lully, V., Singh, K., Maret, P.: Qanswer: a question answering prototype bridging the gap between a considerable part of the LOD cloud and end-users. In: The World Wide Web Conference, WWW 2019, San Francisco, CA, USA, 13–17 May 2019, pp. 3507–3510 (2019)
10. Dubey, M., Dasgupta, S., Sharma, A., Höffner, K., Lehmann, J.: AskNow: a framework for natural language query formalization in SPARQL. In: Sack, H., Blomqvist, E., d'Aquin, M., Ghidini, C., Ponzetto, S.P., Lange, C. (eds.) ESWC 2016. LNCS, vol. 9678, pp. 300–316. Springer, Cham (2016). https://doi.org/10.1007/978-3-319-34129-3_19
11. Ferré, S.: SPARKLIS: an expressive query builder for SPARQL endpoints with guidance in natural language. Semant. Web **8**(3), 405–418 (2017)
12. FitzGerald, N., Täckström, O., Ganchev, K., Das, D.: Semantic role labeling with neural network factors. In: Proceedings of the 2015 Conference on Empirical Methods in Natural Language Processing, EMNLP 2015, Lisbon, Portugal, 17–21 September 2015, pp. 960–970 (2015)
13. Gildea, D., Jurafsky, D.: Automatic labeling of semantic roles. Comput. Linguist. **28**(3), 245–288 (2002)
14. He, L., Lee, K., Lewis, M., Zettlemoyer, L.: Deep semantic role labeling: what works and what's next. In: Proceedings of the 55th Annual Meeting of the Association for Computational Linguistics, ACL 2017, Vancouver, Canada, 30 July–4 August, Volume 1: Long Papers, pp. 473–483 (2017)
15. Hoffart, J., Milchevski, D., Weikum, G.: STICS: searching with strings, things, and cats. In: The 37th International ACM SIGIR Conference on Research and Development in Information Retrieval, SIGIR 2014, Gold Coast, QLD, Australia - 06–11 July 2014, pp. 1247–1248 (2014)

16. Hoffart, J., et al.: Robust disambiguation of named entities in text. In: Proceedings of the 2011 Conference on Empirical Methods in Natural Language Processing, EMNLP 2011, 27–31 July 2011, John McIntyre Conference Centre, Edinburgh, UK, A meeting of SIGDAT, a Special Interest Group of the ACL, pp. 782–792 (2011)
17. Ibrahim, Y., Riedewald, M., Weikum, G.: Making sense of entities and quantities in web tables. In: Proceedings of the 25th ACM International Conference on Information and Knowledge Management, CIKM 2016, Indianapolis, IN, USA, 24–28 October 2016, pp. 1703–1712 (2016)
18. Joshi, M., Sawant, U., Chakrabarti, S.: Knowledge graph and corpus driven segmentation and answer inference for telegraphic entity-seeking queries. In: Proceedings of the 2014 Conference on Empirical Methods in Natural Language Processing, EMNLP 2014, 25–29 October 2014, Doha, Qatar, a meeting of SIGDAT, a Special Interest Group of the ACL, pp. 1104–1114 (2014)
19. Lamm, M., Chaganty, A.T., Jurafsky, D., Manning, C.D., Liang, P.S.: QSRL: a semantic role-labeling schema for quantitative facts (2018)
20. Lassila, O., Swick, R.R.: Resource description framework (RDF) model and syntax specification (1999)
21. Madaan, A., Mittal, A., Mausam, M., Ramakrishnan, G., Sarawagi, S.: Numerical relation extraction with minimal supervision. In: Proceedings of the Thirtieth AAAI Conference on Artificial Intelligence, 12–17 February 2016, Phoenix, Arizona, USA, pp. 2764–2771 (2016)
22. Mausam, M.: Open information extraction systems and downstream applications. In: Proceedings of the Twenty-Fifth International Joint Conference on Artificial Intelligence, IJCAI 2016, New York, NY, USA, 9–15 July 2016, pp. 4074–4077 (2016)
23. Miller, G.A.: WordNet: a lexical database for English. Commun. ACM **38**(11), 39–41 (1995)
24. Pennington, J., Socher, R., Manning, C.D.: Glove: global vectors for word representation. In: Proceedings of the 2014 Conference on Empirical Methods in Natural Language Processing, EMNLP 2014, 25–29 October 2014, Doha, Qatar, A meeting of SIGDAT, a Special Interest Group of the ACL, pp. 1532–1543 (2014)
25. Pimplikar, R., Sarawagi, S.: Answering table queries on the web using column keywords. PVLDB **5**(10), 908–919 (2012)
26. Ramshaw, L.A., Marcus, M.: Text chunking using transformation-based learning. In: Third Workshop on Very Large Corpora, VLC@ACL 1995, Cambridge, Massachusetts, USA, 30 June 1995 (1995)
27. Robertson, S.: Understanding inverse document frequency: on theoretical arguments for IDF. J. Doc. **60**(5), 503–520 (2004)
28. Roy, S., Vieira, T., Roth, D.: Reasoning about quantities in natural language. TACL **3**, 1–13 (2015)
29. Saha, S., Pal, H.: Bootstrapping for numerical open IE. In: Proceedings of the 55th Annual Meeting of the Association for Computational Linguistics, ACL 2017, Vancouver, Canada, 30 July–4 August, Volume 2: Short Papers, pp. 317–323 (2017)
30. Sandhaus, E.: The New York times annotated corpus. Linguist. Data Consort. Phila. **6**, e26752 (2008)
31. Sarawagi, S., Chakrabarti, S.: Open-domain quantity queries on web tables: annotation, response, and consensus models. In: The 20th ACM SIGKDD International Conference on Knowledge Discovery and Data Mining, KDD 2014, New York, NY, USA - 24–27 August 2014, pp. 711–720 (2014)

32. Singh, K., et al.: Why reinvent the wheel: let's build question answering systems together. In: Proceedings of the 2018 World Wide Web Conference on World Wide Web, WWW 2018, Lyon, France, 23–27 April 2018, pp. 1247–1256 (2018)
33. Strötgen, J., Gertz, M.: Domain-Sensitive Temporal Tagging. Synthesis Lectures on Human Language Technologies. Morgan & Claypool Publishers, San Rafael (2016)
34. Suchanek, F.M., Kasneci, G., Weikum, G.: YAGO: a core of semantic knowledge. In: Proceedings of the 16th International Conference on World Wide Web, WWW 2007, Banff, Alberta, Canada, 8–12 May 2007, pp. 697–706 (2007)
35. Tanon, T.P., de Assunção, M.D., Caron, E., Suchanek, F.M.: Demoing platypus - a multilingual question answering platform for wikidata. In: The Semantic Web: ESWC 2018 Satellite Events - ESWC 2018 Satellite Events, Heraklion, Crete, Greece, 3–7 June 2018, Revised Selected Papers, pp. 111–116 (2018)
36. Unger, C., Freitas, A., Cimiano, P.: An introduction to question answering over linked data. In: Reasoning Web. Reasoning on the Web in the Big Data Era - 10th International Summer School 2014, Athens, Greece, 8–13 September 2014. Proceedings, pp. 100–140 (2014)
37. Unger, C., Ngomo, A.N., Cabrio, E.: 6th open challenge on question answering over linked data (QALD-6). In: Semantic Web Challenges - Third SemWebEval Challenge at ESWC 2016, Heraklion, Crete, Greece, 29 May–2 June 2016, Revised Selected Papers, pp. 171–177 (2016)
38. Usbeck, R., et al.: Benchmarking question answering systems. Semant. Web **10**(2), 293–304 (2019)
39. Xu, K., Reddy, S., Feng, Y., Huang, S., Zhao, D.: Question answering on freebase via relation extraction and textual evidence. In: Proceedings of the 54th Annual Meeting of the Association for Computational Linguistics, ACL 2016, 7–12 August 2016, Berlin, Germany, Volume 1: Long Papers (2016)
40. Yang, Z., et al.: HotpotQA: a dataset for diverse, explainable multi-hop question answering. In: Proceedings of the 2018 Conference on Empirical Methods in Natural Language Processing, Brussels, Belgium, 31 October–4 November 2018, pp. 2369–2380 (2018)
41. Yih, W., Chang, M., He, X., Gao, J. Semantic parsing via staged query graph generation: Question answering with knowledge base. In: Proceedings of the 53rd Annual Meeting of the Association for Computational Linguistics and the 7th International Joint Conference on Natural Language Processing of the Asian Federation of Natural Language Processing, ACL 2015, 26–31 July 2015, Beijing, China, Volume 1: Long Papers, pp. 1321–1331 (2015)
42. Zhai, C.: Statistical language models for information retrieval: a critical review. Found. Trends Inf. Retr. **2**(3), 137–213 (2008)
43. Zheng, W., Yu, J.X., Zou, L., Cheng, H.: Question answering over knowledge graphs: question understanding via template decomposition. PVLDB **11**(11), 1373–1386 (2018)
44. Zhou, J., Xu, W.: End-to-end learning of semantic role labeling using recurrent neural networks. In: Proceedings of the 53rd Annual Meeting of the Association for Computational Linguistics and the 7th International Joint Conference on Natural Language Processing of the Asian Federation of Natural Language Processing, ACL 2015, 26–31 July 2015, Beijing, China, Volume 1: Long Papers, pp. 1127–1137 (2015)

A Worst-Case Optimal Join Algorithm for SPARQL

Aidan Hogan[2,3(✉)], Cristian Riveros[1,3], Carlos Rojas[1,3], and Adrián Soto[1,3]

[1] Pontificia Universidad Católica de Chile, Santiago, Chile
[2] DCC, Universidad de Chile, Santiago, Chile
aidhog@gmail.com
[3] Millennium Institute for Foundational Research on Data, Santiago, Chile

Abstract. Worst-case optimal multiway join algorithms have recently gained a lot of attention in the database literature. These algorithms not only offer strong theoretical guarantees of efficiency, but have also been empirically demonstrated to significantly improve query runtimes for relational and graph databases. Despite these promising theoretical and practical results, however, the Semantic Web community has yet to adopt such techniques; to the best of our knowledge, no native RDF database currently supports such join algorithms, where in this paper we demonstrate that this should change. We propose a novel procedure for evaluating SPARQL queries based on an existing worst-case join algorithm called Leapfrog Triejoin. We propose an adaptation of this algorithm for evaluating SPARQL queries, and implement it in Apache Jena. We then present experiments over the Berlin and WatDiv SPARQL benchmarks, and a novel benchmark that we propose based on Wikidata that is designed to provide insights into join performance for a more diverse set of basic graph patterns. Our results show that with this new join algorithm, Apache Jena often runs orders of magnitude faster than the base version and two other SPARQL engines: Virtuoso and Blazegraph.

1 Introduction

Since its initial standardisation over a decade ago, the SPARQL query language has enjoyed broad adoption, having been implemented in a wide variety of engines (e.g., [1,16,23,30]) and supported by hundreds of public endpoints on the Web [8], the most prominent of which receive thousands or even millions of queries per day [14,22]. Despite these successes, however, there remains room for improvement. Though current SPARQL implementations now work well for processing large workloads of relatively simple queries [22], as we show in later experiments, they still struggle when evaluating queries with more complex joins; we argue that this is due, in part, to the fact that prominent SPARQL engines rely on traditional join algorithms that have not changed for over a decade.

On the other hand, a new family of join algorithms has received much attention in the recent database literature: the state-of-the-art for join evaluation has

C. Ghidini et al. (Eds.): ISWC 2019, LNCS 11778, pp. 258–275, 2019.
https://doi.org/10.1007/978-3-030-30793-6_15

moved away from pairwise join evaluation [29], towards multiway join evaluation where an arbitrary number of joins can be evaluated at once. One of the main benefits of the multiway approach is to minimise the number of intermediate results generated. In fact, a variety of modern multiway join algorithms – including, for example, Leapfrog Triejoin [31], Minesweeper [25], Tetris [21], CacheTrieJoin [19], etc. – have been proven to be *worst-case optimal* [26,27], meaning that the runtime of the algorithm is bounded by the worst-case cardinality of the query result (i.e. the AGM bound [11]); this theoretical guarantee implies that no other join algorithm can exist that is asymptotically faster for all database instances. Several systems (e.g. Logicblox [9] and Emptyheaded [4]) have further implemented these worst-case optimal strategies and demonstrated their superior performance in practice for evaluating queries with complex joins.

A natural idea, then, is to leverage worst-case optimal join algorithms for evaluating basic graph patterns, which form the core of SPARQL queries. However, though work has been done on adopting such algorithms for graph queries and analytics [4,20,28], to the best of our knowledge, no such work has addressed the evaluation of SPARQL basic graph patterns.

In this paper, we aim to fill this gap by investigating the benefits of worst-case optimal join algorithms for evaluating basic graph patterns. Given our goal that worst-case optimal join algorithms be widely adopted on the Semantic Web in the near future, we select Leapfrog Triejoin (LFTJ) [31] as our base algorithm since it is relatively straightforward to adapt to the case of SPARQL while still providing worst-case optimal guarantees. We propose some adaptations of the LTFJ algorithm for the SPARQL setting, proving that these adaptations do not affect the theoretical guarantees of the algorithm. We discuss how the resulting algorithm can be integrated and optimised within a native RDF store that supports multiple index orders and cardinality-based join ordering, reducing the cost of adoption. Analogously, we create a fork of Apache Jena (TDB) [1] that supports worst-case join evaluation, and proceed to evaluate its performance against the unmodified version of the engine, as well as two other prominent SPARQL engines: Virtuoso [16] and Blazegraph [30]. We run experiments on the Berlin [13] and WatDiv [6] SPARQL benchmarks, and thereafter on a novel benchmark based on Wikidata [32] from which we generate a large set of SPARQL basic graph patterns exhibiting a variety of increasingly complex join patterns. Our results show that our fork of Apache Jena can reduce the runtimes of queries with non-trivial joins by orders of magnitude versus the baseline systems.

2 Preliminaries

We introduce some brief preliminaries for RDF and SPARQL used throughout and thereafter discuss the central notion of worst-case optimal joins.

RDF: RDF is the graph-based data model at the heart of the Semantic Web. RDF terms can be IRIs ($\mathbf{I}$), literals ($\mathbf{L}$) or blank nodes ($\mathbf{B}$). A triple $(s, p, o) \in \mathbf{IB} \times \mathbf{I} \times \mathbf{IBL}$ is called an RDF triple, where s is called the subject, p the predicate, and o the object.[1] An RDF graph is a set of RDF triples.

[1] We use $\mathbf{IB}$ as a shortcut for $\mathbf{I} \cup \mathbf{B}$, etc.

SPARQL: SPARQL is the standard query language for RDF [3]. Let $\mathbf{V}$ be a set of variables. A tuple $t \in \mathbf{ILV} \times \mathbf{IV} \times \mathbf{ILV}$ is called a triple pattern. Blank nodes in triple patterns can be considered as query variables for our purposes. A set of triple patterns is called a basic graph pattern. We denote by $\text{var}(t)$ and $\text{var}(P)$ the set of variables found in a triple pattern t and basic graph pattern P, respectively. We call a variable $?\mathbf{x} \in \text{var}(P)$ a *join variable* if it appears in two or more triple patterns of P, and a *lonely variable* otherwise.

The semantics of SPARQL queries is defined in terms of mappings. A mapping μ is a partial function $\mu : \mathbf{V} \to \mathbf{IBL}$. The domain of μ, denoted $\text{dom}(\mu)$, is the set of variables on which μ is defined. Given a triple pattern t, we denote by $\mu(t)$ the image of the triple pattern t under μ: the triple obtained by replacing the variables in t according to μ. We say that two mappings μ_1 and μ_2 are compatible, denoted $\mu_1 \sim \mu_2$, iff $\mu_1(?\mathbf{x}) = \mu_2(?\mathbf{x})$ for every $?\mathbf{x} \in \text{dom}(\mu_1) \cap \text{dom}(\mu_2)$. Given sets of mappings Ω_1 and Ω_2, we then define their join as $\Omega_1 \bowtie \Omega_2 = \{\mu_1 \cup \mu_2 \mid \mu_1 \in \Omega_1, \mu_2 \in \Omega_2, \text{ and } \mu_1 \sim \mu_2\}$.

We can now define the evaluation of a triple pattern and a basic graph pattern over an RDF graph G (the latter being defined as a join over its triple patterns):

$$\llbracket t \rrbracket_G = \{\mu \mid \text{var}(t) = \text{dom}(\mu) \text{ and } \mu(t) \in G\}$$
$$\llbracket \{t_1, \ldots, t_n\} \rrbracket_G = \llbracket t_1 \rrbracket_G \bowtie \ldots \bowtie \llbracket t_n \rrbracket_G$$

Letting $\mu(P)$ denote the image of P under μ, with respect to the latter definition, we can equivalently say that $\llbracket P \rrbracket_G = \{\mu \mid \text{dom}(\mu) = \text{var}(P) \text{ and } \mu(P) \subseteq G\}$.

SPARQL further offers a wide range of query operators that can be used to combine or modify the results of basic graph patterns, such as union, optional, filters, aggregates, property paths, etc. In this paper, we focus on optimising the evaluation of basic graph patterns, which form the core of SPARQL queries; other SPARQL operators can be supported by applying standard techniques over the mappings generated from the query's basic graph patterns.[2] However, there is the possibility for bespoke methods that merge the evaluation of some of these operators – in particular optional, property paths, named graphs, etc. – with the evaluation of basic graph patterns by the proposed worst-case join algorithm. We leave the exploration of such embedded optimisations for future work. Furthermore, SPARQL assumes a default bag semantics, which preserves duplicates [7]; though we evaluate sets of solutions for basic graph patterns, such patterns alone never generate duplicate mappings, and thus our proposal is compatible with bag semantics being applied in higher-level query operators.

Worst Case Optimality: A join algorithm is called worst-case optimal if it satisfies the AGM bound [11], namely, if the running time over an instance G is bounded by the worst-case output size over all instances of the same size as G. Specifically, let P be a BGP and G an RDF graph. Consider the following linear program [11] adapted for the case of RDF and basic graph patterns:

[2] Other features like `BIND`, `VALUES`, `SERVICE`, etc., that generate or extend mappings can be evaluated in the standard way.

$$\begin{array}{lll} \text{minimize} & \sum_{t \in P} x_t \cdot \log(|[\![t]\!]_G|) & \\ \text{subject to} & \sum_{t:?\mathrm{x} \in \mathrm{var}(t)} x_t \geq 1 & \text{for each } ?\mathrm{x} \in \mathrm{var}(P) \\ & x_t \geq 0 & \text{for each } t \in P \end{array}$$

where x_t is a variable for each $t \in P$. If $\mathrm{MIN}(P, G)$ is the minimum for the above optimization problem, then the AGM bound states that $|[\![P]\!]_G| \leq 2^{\mathrm{MIN}(P,G)}$ and this bound is tight: there exists an RDF graph G' of the same size as G where $|[\![P]\!]_{G'}|$ is equal to $2^{\mathrm{MIN}(P,G)}$ up to a logarithmic factor. We call an evaluation algorithm for a basic graph pattern *worst case optimal* if its running time is at most $2^{\mathrm{MIN}(P,G)}$ up to a logarithmic factor. All of our algorithmic analysis is done in data complexity where the size of the query is considered as fixed.

3 Related Work

Our goal is to optimise the evaluation of basic graph patterns in SPARQL. Here we first discuss the standard evaluation methods used in popular SPARQL engines, proposals of multiway joins for SPARQL, works on worst-case optimal join algorithms, and a summary of the novelty of our present work.

Indexing: In order to efficiently evaluate triple patterns, SPARQL engines employ indexes that offer optimised access to the underlying data; such engines will often build a complete index that can efficiently evaluate a triple pattern with any combination of constants and variables [18]. A complete index is comprised of multiple index orders, where a single index order with prefix lookups can be used to evaluate multiple forms of triple pattern;[3] for example, the index order **pos** allows for directly evaluating triples patterns of the form $(?, ?, ?)$, $(?, p, ?)$, $(?, p, o)$ and (s, p, o) without filtering, but not $(s, ?, ?)$, which would require reading all triples from the **pos** index and filtering those whose subject does not match the triple pattern (a better choice would be an index order like **spo** or **sop**). Some SPARQL engines build complete indexes for triples [10,23,33], while others directly support named graphs by indexing quads [16,18]. In terms of indexing implementations, one option is to apply standard data structures known from relational databases, such as B+Tree indexes [16,18,23]; another option is to develop RDF-specific techniques, such as nested data structures [33], bit matrices [10], etc., that take advantage of the fixed arity of triples.

Pairwise Joins: While a complete index allows individual triple patterns to be evaluated efficiently, the evaluation of basic graph patterns requires applying join algorithms over the mappings generated from triple patterns. The most popular strategy for evaluating basic graph patterns is to use pairwise evaluation joining two sets of mappings at a time. In left-deep plans, the results of a triple pattern are joined with the current results of all joins thus far; for example, taking a basic graph pattern with four triple patterns, an example left-deep

[3] Following [18], we use the notation $(s|?, p|?, o|?)$ to denote eight forms of triple patterns where, for example, $(?, p, o)$ refers to the set of triple patterns with variable subject, constant predicate and constant object: $\mathbf{V} \times \mathbf{I} \times \mathbf{IL}$.

evaluation would be $(((t_1 \bowtie t_2) \bowtie t_3) \bowtie t_4)$ [18]. In bushy plans, two sets of join results can also be joined, leading to more balanced query plans; for example, $((t_1 \bowtie t_2) \bowtie (t_3 \bowtie t_n))$ is an instance of a bushy plan [23]. To implement such joins, SPARQL engines often use variants of well-known algorithms for join evaluation in relational databases, such as nested-loop joins [18,23], hash joins [23], and sort-merge joins [23]. An important aspect of optimising SPARQL query plans is then to exploit the commutativity and associativity of joins to find a query plan that minimises the number of intermediate results generated; a common strategy is to rely on cardinality estimates [16,18,23].

Multiway Joins: Multiway join algorithms perform joins over two or more sets of mappings at once; a common strategy is to group, evaluate and join triple patterns sharing a given variable as a single operation. Multiway join evaluation can thus reduce the number of intermediate results that are generated. To the best of our knowledge, few works have investigated multiway joins in the context of SPARQL. One exception is the recent work of Galkin et al. [17], who propose a join algorithm for SPARQL queries called SMJoin that groups blocks of star-shaped joins (where a common join variable is present in the subject position) and applies multiway joins over each block. Experimental results show that the multiway join performs well for selective query patterns, but is outperformed by a pairwise-join baseline for other types of queries (due to the latter applying selectivity-based join reordering not available to SMJoin).

Worst-Case Optimal Joins: Various works in the database literature have focused on worst-case optimal join algorithms [19,21,25,28,31], which have also been implemented as part of commercial databases [4,9]. A subset of such works have looked at the benefits of such algorithms for answering queries over graphs, incorporating experiments for evaluating queries based on graph patterns including cliques, trees, paths, etc. [4,19,28]; Aberger et al. [4] further provide experiments for analytical queries on graphs, such as Pagerank and shortest paths. While these works have provided evidence as to the value of worst-case optimal join algorithms for graphs, they do not address the SPARQL setting.

Novelty: We propose a multiway join algorithm for evaluating basic graph patterns in SPARQL based on Leapfrog Triejoin [31], modifying how it accesses indexes to ensure better compatibility with current SPARQL implementations. We prove that the adapted algorithm remains worst-case optimal, discuss its implementation in Jena, and provide experimental results analysing its runtime performance. Unlike the work of Galkin et al. [17], our multiway join algorithm is agnostic to the position of a join variable in a triple pattern. More generally, and to the best of our knowledge, this is the first work to explore the application of a worst-case join algorithm for evaluating SPARQL basic graph patterns.

4 Leapfrog Join for Basic Graph Patterns

Our goal is to investigate the potential benefits of using a worst-case optimal join algorithm on SPARQL query performance. Surveying the state-of-the-art algorithms in the database literature [19,21,24,25,28,31], we opted to base our algorithm on Leapfrog Triejoin algorithm (LFTJ) [31], mainly because it is the most concise among all such algorithms [24], and thus a good starting point for implementation within a SPARQL engine. We first present here a logical version of LFTJ that we call *Leapfrog Join* (LFJ), which includes only the core evaluation strategy on which LFTJ is based. LFJ can be divided into two main phases: *Leapfrog* and *variable elimination.* We begin by discussing both phases and give a running example of the algorithm. Later we propose a physical version of Leapfrog Join, designed to be easily integrated with existing SPARQL engines, mostly requiring adaptations at the index layer (see the discussion in Sect. 5).

Leapfrog: Unlike traditional join algorithms that evaluate triple pattern by triple pattern, Leapfrog Join rather proceeds by evaluating variable by variable. An important procedure in Leapfrog Join is to compute all *non-trivial outputs of a single variable*; more formally, given an RDF graph G, a basic graph pattern P and a variable ?x in var(P) we want to compute the following set:

$$\mathrm{LF}_G(P, ?\mathrm{x}) \;=\; \{\mu \mid \mathrm{dom}(\mu) = \{?\mathrm{x}\} \text{ and } [\![\mu(t)]\!]_G \neq \varnothing \text{ for all } t \in P\}\,.$$

In other words, we want to identify all single variable mappings μ such that, for every $t \in P$, the output of $\mu(t)$ over G is non-empty when ?x is replaced by $\mu(?\mathrm{x})$. Intuitively, if $\mu \in \mathrm{LF}_G(P, ?\mathrm{x})$, then μ is a good candidate for a partial mapping that can be extended to form an output mapping in $[\![P]\!]_G$. Note also that if ?x is the only variable used in P (i.e., $\mathrm{var}(P) = \{?\mathrm{x}\}$), then the set $\mathrm{LF}_G(P, ?\mathrm{x})$ is the same as computing the intersection of all sets $[\![t]\!]_G$. In Sect. 5, we will show how to implement this function for one or more variables by exploiting standard B+tree indexes while maintaining worst-case optimality.

Variable Elimination: While the Leapfrog phase evaluates a single variable, the variable elimination phase evaluates multiple variables. Given a basic graph pattern P with $\mathrm{var}(P) = \{x_1, \dots, x_n\}$, an RDF graph G, and a variable order $O_{\mathrm{var}} = ?\mathrm{x}_1, \dots, ?\mathrm{x}_m$, Algorithm 1 shows the nested structure of the variable elimination procedure, which constitutes the overall Leapfrog Join process. The procedure iterates over each variable $?\mathrm{x}_i$ in order, extending the mapping μ_i with a mapping $\mu \in \mathrm{LF}_G(\mu_i(P), ?\mathrm{x}_{i+1})$. Variable $?\mathrm{x}_i$ is fixed by extending μ with μ_i (i.e. $\mu_{i+1} = \mu_i \cup \mu$; note that $\mu_i \sim \mu$, so μ_{i+1} is also a mapping); in this way, variable $?\mathrm{x}_i$ is "eliminated" from P. The procedure moves on to eliminate the next variable $?\mathrm{x}_{i+1}$ analogously. After all variables $?\mathrm{x}_1, \dots, ?\mathrm{x}_m$ are eliminated, the mapping $\mu_{m-1} \cup \mu$ is output, and the search for the next output is continued.

Figure 1 provides an example of variable elimination for a basic graph pattern over an RDF graph. We assume the order $?\mathrm{x}_1 \dots ?\mathrm{x}_4$; how such an order is decided will be discussed later in Sect. 5.[4] Pairwise evaluation with this triple-

[4] Such an order would be produced by SPARQL engines in practice if we had a graph with many `:father` and `:mother` relations, outnumbering `:winner` relations.

Algorithm 1. Variable elimination for basic graph patterns

```
input : RDF graph G, BGP P, variable order O_var = ?x1 ... ?xn
output: All mappings [[P]]_G.
Function LFTJ-Eval (G, P, O_var)
    μ0 ← ∅
    foreach μ ∈ LF_G(μ0(P), ?x1) do
        μ1 ← μ0 ∪ μ
        foreach μ ∈ LF_G(μ1(P), ?x2) do
            μ2 ← μ1 ∪ μ
                ⋱
                foreach μ ∈ LF_G(μ_{n-1}(P), ?xn) do
                    Output μ_{n-1} ∪ μ // write to output and continue
```

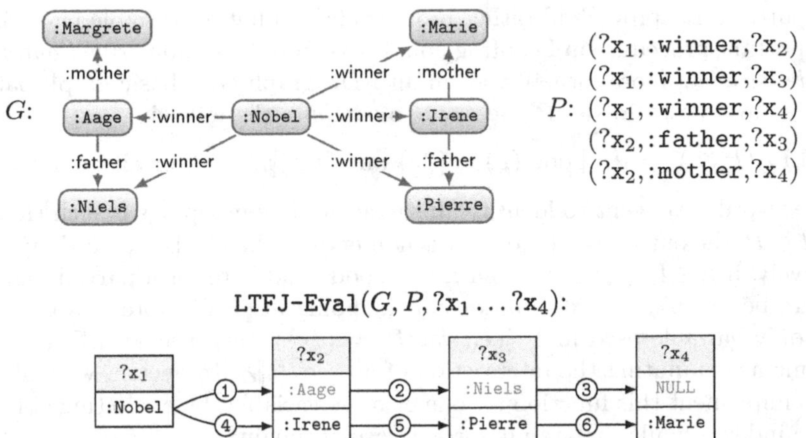

Fig. 1. Example of Leapfrog join for evaluating a SPARQL basic graph pattern

pattern order would naively produce $5^3 = 125$ intermediary results containing the Cartesian product of all five winners of the Nobel prize (as would the multi-way star-shaped join algorithm of Galkin et al. [17]). On the other hand, under Leapfrog Join, variable elimination ensures that when, e.g., $?x_2$ is evaluated, only those winners that have some father and some mother are considered. The lower graph then shows the recursion order producing the final result(s).

5 A Physical Operator for Leapfrog Join

We implement Leapfrog Join (LFJ) in Apache Jena TDB version 3.9.0, which implements nested-loop joins on top of B+tree indexes. We choose Jena as it is one of the most widely-deployed (fully) open source SPARQL engines; however the methods described can be generalised to other SPARQL engines. We now explain the main modifications required to support LFJ in Jena.

Indexes for LFJ: The first modification needed to run LFJ was to extend the index layer in Jena. Recall that a major phase in LFJ is to compute the set $\mathrm{LF}_G(P, ?\mathrm{x})$ given an RDF graph G, a basic graph pattern P and a variable ?x. The next result shows that Leapfrog Join is a worst-case optimal join algorithm whenever the computation of $\mathrm{LF}_G(P, ?\mathrm{x})$ is done in a reasonable time.

Theorem 1. *An implementation of Leapfrog Join is worst-case optimal if, for every RDF graph G, basic graph pattern P, and variable* ?x*, the computation of* $\mathrm{LF}_G(P, ?\mathrm{x})$ *is done in time at most:*

$$O\big(\max(\min_{t \in P : ?\mathtt{x} \in \mathrm{var}(t)} |\pi_{?\mathtt{x}}([\![t]\!]_G)|, 1) \cdot \log(|G|)\big)$$

where $\pi_{?\mathtt{x}}([\![t]\!]_G)$ *is the projection of* $[\![t]\!]_G$ *over* ?x.

The proof of Theorem 1 is given in Appendix A.

Calculating $\mathrm{LF}_G(P, ?\mathrm{x})$ is the same as computing the intersection of all sets $[\![t]\!]_G$; hence, one can use any adaptive intersection algorithm over n sets [12,15], which satisfies the time restriction of Theorem 1. In particular, our implementation of LFJ uses the intersection algorithm proposed by Veldhuizen [31].

The algorithm of adaptive intersection assumes that each set $\pi_{?\mathtt{x}}([\![t]\!]_G)$ can be navigated in increasing order. For this, we need an index I_G such that for every triple pattern t and every variable ?x in t, it provides a seek method $\mathrm{I}_G[t, ?\mathtt{x}]$.`seek(:a)` that outputs the least :b such that $:\mathrm{b} \geq :\mathrm{a}$ and $[\![\mu(t)]\!]_G \neq \emptyset$ for $\mu = \{?\mathtt{x} \to :\mathrm{b}\}$, or `NULL` if no such :b exists; in other words, the seek method jumps to the next non-trivial output for ?x in the order. To satisfy the bound of Theorem 1, the seek method is required to take time logarithmic in the size of G. Although the original LFTJ algorithm proposes to use tries for I_G, such a seek method can be supported using B+Trees adding all six orders over s, p and o. Hence to Jena's three default orders **spo**, **pos**, and **osp**, our implementation adds three more orders: **sop**, **pso**, and **ops**. This roughly doubles the size of the on-disk index and the number of update operations required to add/remove triples, but (as shown later) offers gains in query performance with LFJ.[5]

Each index order is assigned a B+tree, where the seek method could then be implemented by traversing the B+tree top-down from root to leaf in the standard

[5] We currently consider querying over a single RDF graph; if we were to consider a complete index on quads in order to support named graphs, the number of required indexes would jump to 24. In such a case, however, practical steps can be taken to reduce the number of indexes where, for example, some such orders will be rarely accessed by real-world queries and can thus be removed.

way. However, given that the seek method requests values in sequential order, we use a stack to store the current node in the iteration, its leaf, and its parents; when the next value is requested, we can read the next value in the order from the leaf or, starting from there, search the B+tree upwards and then back down in case that the next value is in another leaf. This bottom-up seek method offers constant amortized time when only one variable is unbound [31], logarithmic time when two variables are unbound, and is more efficient in practice.

LFJ Operator: We add a new LFJ join operator to Jena that takes a basic graph pattern and evaluates it using our implementation of LFJ (per Algorithm 1). Note that the original LFTJ algorithm applies some restrictions: (1) each relation symbol must appear only once, (2) the order of attributes of the relations (triple patterns in our case) must follow the global attribute order, (3) constants cannot appear within the join query and (4) each attribute can appear at most once in each relation (triple pattern in our case). The first restriction does not apply for our implementation. Restrictions (2) and (3) are not required to maintain worst-case optimality and are addressed by our indexes. The case of variables occurring twice in a triple pattern requires some extra care, but can be addressed with special indexes for triples repeating the same term in the given positions (which are typically uncommon in RDF data), or using a fresh variable and applying a low-level filter/intersection; we omit these details for brevity.

Variable Order: The performance of LFJ is dependent on the chosen variable order [5]; referring back to Fig. 1, for example, a more efficient order would be to swap $?x_2$ and $?x_4$, which would allow for more quickly rejecting the incomplete mapping involving `:Aage` in G. In principle, the goal of finding a variable ordering is similar to that for ordering triple patterns: in both cases, we wish to evaluate highly-selective triple patterns/variables that help to filter mappings early on. Along these lines, while specialised variable orderings have been proposed for worst-case optimal join algorithms [5], we propose a solution based on Jena's existing triple ordering; this has the additional advantage of making experiments between the baseline version of Jena and Jena with LFJ more comparable.

Given a triple-pattern order O_{trip} returned by Jena, we first choose join variables in order of appearance, and then select lonely variables in order of appearance; for example, if Jena gives $O_{\text{trip}} = (\texttt{?z}, \texttt{:p3}, \texttt{?u}), (\texttt{?x}, \texttt{:p2}, \texttt{?z}), (\texttt{?x}, \texttt{:p1}, \texttt{?y})$, we will choose the variable order $O_{\text{var}} = \texttt{?z}, \texttt{?x}, \texttt{?u}, \texttt{?y}$ since `?z` is the first join variable that appears in O_{trip}, and `?x` is the second join variable that appears in O_{trip}; given that `?u` and `?y` are lonely variables (appearing in one triple pattern), they come after the join variables, again based on order of appearance. In fact, as we now discuss, the order of lonely variables will not affect performance.

Enumerating Mappings: Early experiments comparing Jena with and without LFJ found that the performance of the former was sometimes orders of magnitude *worse* than the latter. We identified the issue as relating to how lonely variables are handled. To illustrate this issue, consider a graph pattern P' containing only the first three triple patterns of P in Fig. 1 such that $?x_2$, $?x_3$ and $?x_4$ are lonely variables. Applying the procedure of Algorithm 1, after assigning $?\mathtt{x}_1 \rightarrow$ `:Nobel`, we still require $5 \times 5 \times 5$ steps through the recursion, repetitively evaluating the same partially-bound triple patterns. This final recursion is unnecessary: since lonely variables are evaluated last, we know that the final mappings must be extended by the Cartesian product of the non-trivial outputs of the remaining lonely variables. To address this, assume a variable order $O_{\text{var}} = ?\mathtt{x}_1, \ldots, ?\mathtt{x}_m, ?\mathtt{x}_{m+1}, \ldots ?\mathtt{x}_n$ where $?\mathtt{x}_1, \ldots, ?\mathtt{x}_m$ are join variables and $?\mathtt{x}_{m+1}, \ldots, ?\mathtt{x}_n$ are lonely variables. Assume also that $t_1, \ldots, t_k$ are the triple patterns where $?\mathtt{x}_{m+1}, \ldots, ?\mathtt{x}_n$ are mentioned (each such triple pattern may mention one or more lonely variables). We eliminate $?\mathtt{x}_1, \ldots, ?\mathtt{x}_m$ per Algorithm 1, and for each partial solution μ_m generated, we compute the Cartesian product $\mu_m \times [\![\mu_m(t_1)]\!]_G \times \ldots \times [\![\mu_m(t_k)]\!]_G$, requiring k (note that $k < n - m$) additional calls to $[\![\mu_m(\cdot)]\!]_G$ for each μ_m (rather than having to call LF a total of $1 + \sum_{i=m}^{n-2} \prod_{j=m}^{i} |\,\mathrm{LF}_G(\mu_m(P), ?\mathtt{x}_{j+1})|$ times for each μ_m).

6 Experiments and Results

We now compare the performance of query evaluation for Apache Jena (TDB) v.3.9.0 with LFJ, Apache Jena v.3.9.0 without LFJ, Virtuoso v.OS-7.2.7 [16] (one of the most deployed engines in practice [8]), and Blazegraph v.2.1.4 [30] (used by the Wikidata Query Service [22]). We run three sets of experiments using the Berlin SPARQL Benchmark [13], the WatDiv Benchmark [6], and a novel Wikidata Benchmark with complex graph patterns that we propose. We run all experiments on a single machine with Ubuntu 16.04.5, Intel Xeon CPU E5-2609 v4@1.70 GHz, Seagate 1TB Enterprise Capacity 2.5-Inch HDD, and 32 GB RAM. Code and configurations can be found online for reproducibility purposes [2].

6.1 Experiments on the Berlin SPARQL Benchmark

We first ran experiments over the Berlin SPARQL Benchmark (BSBM) [13], comparing query runtimes for Jena with (denoted Jena-LFJ) and without (denoted Jena) the LFJ modifications. We run the Explore Use-Case of BSBM, consisting of 12 queries using a mix of SPARQL 1.0 features, including optional, union, filter, graph, etc. In Fig. 2 we show the average time of each query in logarithmic scale. These experiments were done by running 10,500 queries; we found that on average each query took 49.3 ms for Jena-LFJ and 41.6 ms for Jena. We conclude that the BSBM results show no clear trend to suggest that one implementation outperforms the other. BSBM queries do not contain large intermediary results and, thus, Jena-LFJ offers no improvement. Furthermore, given that BSBM queries contain other features of SPARQL, the baseline of Jena can use optimisations for other operators not currently available for Jena-LFJ (in particular, pushing range filters, which appear in many BSBM queries).

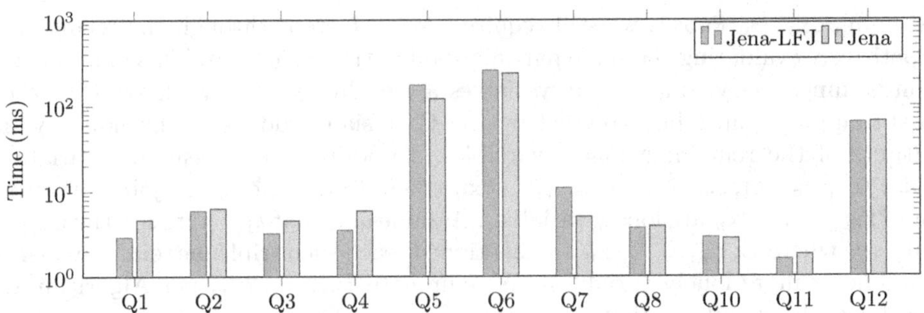

Fig. 2. Plot of runtimes for queries of the Berlin Benchmark with log y-axis.

6.2 Experiments on the WatDiv Benchmark

After reviewing the BSBM results, we still foresaw the need to run experiments on queries with more complex and diverse basic graph patterns. We chose the WatDiv benchmark [6] which is designed for this purpose. We generate 50 queries for each of the 20 abstract patterns proposed in the benchmark. Executing the $50 \times 20 = 1000$ query instances and taking the average over all of them, Virtuoso takes 64 s, Jena-LFJ takes 77 s, Blazegraph takes 99 s, and Jena takes 198 s. Box-plots of runtimes for each specific query pattern are shown in Figs. 3 and 4. Unlike in the BSBM experiments, here Jena-LFJ is at least twice as fast as Jena in terms of the overall query runtime and it also outperforms Blazegraph. Indeed, these plots suggest that the running time of Jena-LFJ is much more stable than other implementations; the interquartile difference is at most 40 ms. Since this benchmark is oriented towards testing basic graph patterns, we can see here that our implementation is competitive with respect to the other engines, being slightly outperformed by Virtuoso. Despite this analysis, the runtimes of these queries are still in the order of less than 100 ms, making it difficult to claim that Jena-LFJ or Virtuoso is the best approach.

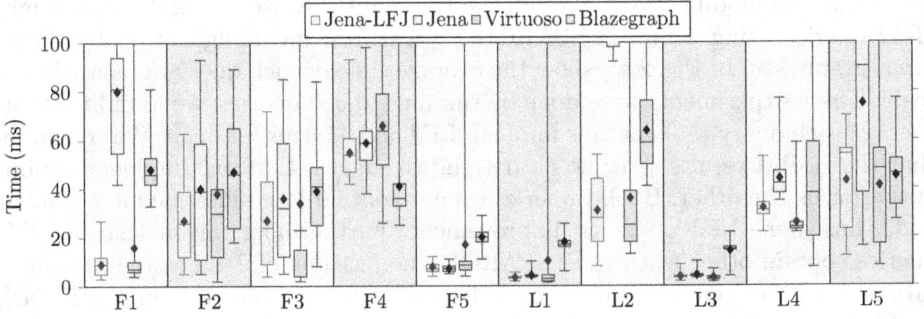

Fig. 3. Box plots of runtimes for queries L and F of the WatDiv Benchmark.

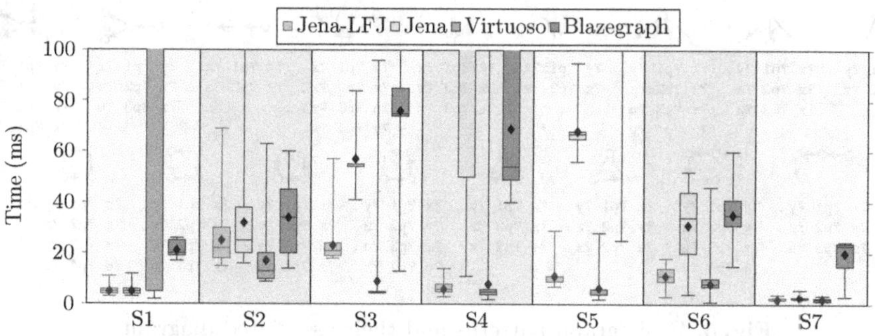

Fig. 4. Box plots of runtimes for queries S of the WatDiv Benchmark

6.3 Experiments on the Wikidata Graph Pattern Benchmark

Though WatDiv contains more complex graph patterns than Berlin, it does not contain (for example) graph patterns with cycles; furthermore, both benchmarks are based on synthetic data with relatively simple schemata (e.g., BSBM and WatDiv have 30 and 85 distinct predicates, respectively). In order to compare the four engines for real data and a more diverse set of both acyclical and cyclical graph patterns, we thus developed a new benchmark that we call the Wikidata Graph Pattern Benchmark (WGPB).

Dataset: To generate the WGPB dataset, we take the Wikidata "truthy" dump from 2018/11/15. This dump contains 3,303,288,386 triples. Given that our goal is to develop queries on the graph structure of Wikidata, we remove labels, aliases, and descriptions, leaving 969,496,651 triples with 5,419 unique predicates. Given that we will later apply random sampling, we removed triples whose predicate appeared fewer than 1,000 times to ensure that we avoid generating trivial query instances. Finally, we also remove triples whose predicates appear in more than 1,000,000 triples. The result, which we call the Wikidata Core Graph (WCG), contains 82,923,234 triples with 2,101 distinct predicates.

Queries: To achieve a set of queries with diverse graph patterns, we create instances of the 17 abstract basic graph patterns shown in Fig. 5; we focus on joins between subjects and objects as common in real-world queries [14]. For each abstract pattern we instantiate 50 queries using random walks in WCG per the given pattern; each instance replaces the predicate variables by the IRIs found on the walk; for example, the first pattern `?x ?p1 ?y . ?x ?p2 ?z` may be instantiated as `SELECT * WHERE{ ?x wdt:P57 ?y . ?x wdt:P166 ?z }`.

Results with Single Join Variable: We first present results for queries with a single join variable (the top row of Fig. 5), analysing the performance of the Leapfrog procedure of LFJ. Executing the $50 \times 9 = 450$ query instances, in terms of overall query runtime across all patterns, Jena-LFJ takes 4.0 s, Jena takes 14.0 s, Blazegraph takes 27.9 s, and Virtuoso takes 64.8 s. Figure 6 then shows the detailed results per query pattern, where we focus the y-axis in on the

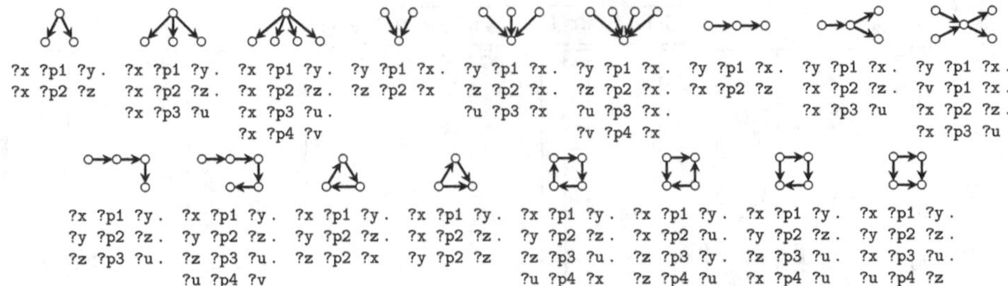

Fig. 5. Basic graph patterns and their associated diagram

range of 0–300 ms for clarity. Here we see that Jena-LFJ is at least twice as fast as Jena in terms of median or mean times, and can be 10–20 times faster than the slowest engine for some queries. The most notable speedup occurs when join variables appear in the object position, which may lead to many intermediate results when a node with high in-degree (e.g., a country) is involved; in such cases, LFJ performs better than other engines. One might consider that this speedup may be attributable to the lack of the three additional orders of **s**, **p** and **o** in the other engines. However, in the case of the best gains – i.e., joins in the object position – Jena-LFJ is using the **pos** index, which is already included in Jena; more generally, Jena uses index nested loop joins, which cannot benefit from further index orders when evaluating BGPs/equijoins.

We further observe that the runtimes for Jena-LFJ are more stable, with the maximum runtime never exceeding 55 ms; furthermore, within the 50 queries of each abstract pattern, the standard deviation in runtimes for Jena-LFJ is consistently around 9 ms, while Jena's standard deviation is always over 20 ms, and that of Virtuoso and Blazegraph is even higher, sometimes over 100 ms.

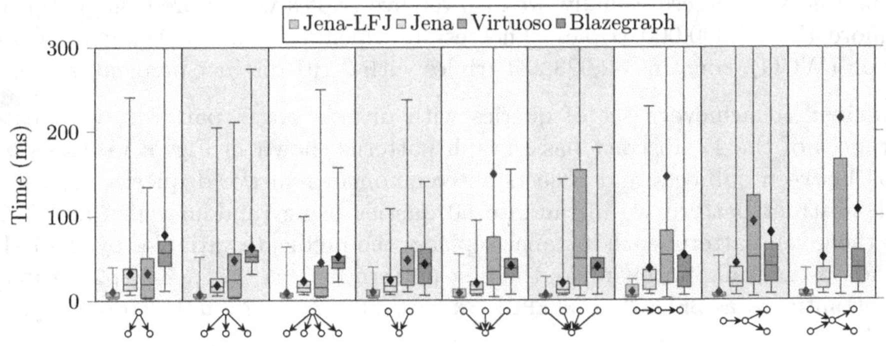

Fig. 6. Box plots of runtimes for queries with a single join variable

Results with Multiple Join Variables: We now present results for queries with multiple join variables (the bottom row of Fig. 5). Given that the previous

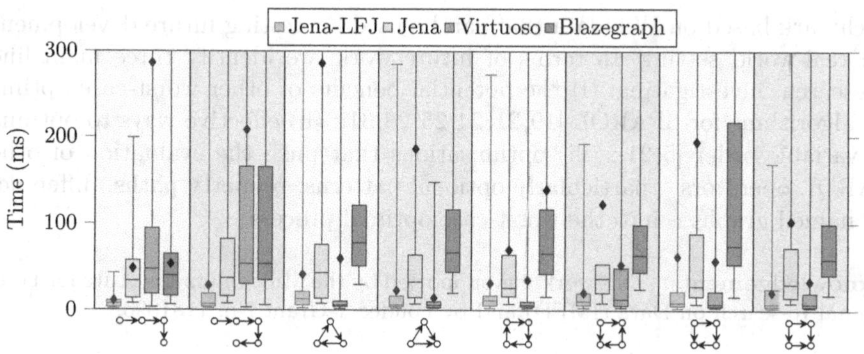

Fig. 7. Box plots of runtimes for queries with multiple join variables

experiments test the performance of Leapfrog for intersecting results for join variables in up to four patterns, our focus now is on the performance of variable elimination. We thus select abstract graph patterns where each variable appears in at most two triple patterns; such queries put as much emphasis as possible on the performance of the variable elimination phase versus the Leapfrog phase tested previously. Executing the $50 \times 8 = 400$ query instances, in terms of the overall query runtime across all patterns, Jena-LFJ takes 12 s, Virtuoso takes 37 s, Jena takes 112 s, and Blazegraph takes 35 s. Figure 7 again shows the detailed results focusing on the same y-axis range for clarity. We again see that Jena-LFJ generally exhibits the most stable runtimes, clearly outperforming Jena and Blazegraph for all patterns and Virtuoso for the first two patterns. Comparing Jena-LFJ and Virtuoso for the latter six patterns (those with cycles), Virtuoso is competitive with and sometimes even outperforms Jena-LFJ; analysing further, we found that Virtuoso often chooses a better execution order than Jena(-LFJ), where manually optimising the variable order in Jena-LFJ for such cases results in much better performance than Virtuoso; this suggests that the variable ordering of Jena-LFJ could be improved. Even with the current variable ordering of Jena-LFJ, however, the clear gains in the first two patterns vs. Virtuoso outweigh slight gains by Virtuoso in some of the latter six patterns, as evidenced by the total runtimes mentioned previously (12 s vs. 37 s).

7 Conclusions

To the best of our knowledge, this is the first work to look at the benefits of worst-case optimal join algorithms in a SPARQL setting. Based on our results, we believe that worst-case optimal joins should become widely adopted by SPARQL engines in the near future; we also firmly believe that our results are only a starting point in this line of research, and that there is still much room left for maximising the potential benefits of such algorithms in a SPARQL setting. Along these lines, we have released an open source fork of Apache Jena implementing LFJ that can serve as a baseline for future experiments, and a novel benchmark based on Wikidata that can be used for testing future developments in a real-world setting. In terms of future work, we identify three main lines of research, investigating: (i) the potential benefits of other worst-case optimal join algorithms for SPARQL [19,21,24,25,28,31]; (ii) effective ways to optimise the variable order [5,21]; (iii) optimisations that push the evaluation of other SPARQL operators – particularly optional patterns, property paths, difference, and named graphs – into the worst-case optimal process.

Acknowledgements. This work was supported by the Millennium Institute for Foundational Research on Data (IMFD) and by Fondecyt Grant No. 1181896.

A Proof of Theorem 1

Fix a basic graph pattern P, an RDF graph G, and $?\mathtt{x}_1, \ldots, ?\mathtt{x}_n$ the chosen variable order. Further assume that the computation of $\mathrm{LF}_G(P', ?\mathtt{x})$ takes time at most $\min_{t \in P' : ?\mathtt{x} \in \mathrm{var}(t)} |\pi_{?\mathtt{x}}([\![t]\!]_G)| \cdot \log(|G|)$ for every basic graph pattern P' (for simplicity, we will omit the trivial empty case where there exists $t \in P'$ such that $?\mathtt{x} \in \mathrm{var}(t)$ and $|\pi_{?\mathtt{x}}([\![t]\!]_G)| = 0$ since the time taken will be simply $\log(|G|)$). Finally, for every RDF graph G' we will say that G' is of size less than G whenever $|[\![t]\!]_{G_i}| \leq |[\![t]\!]_G|$ for all $t \in P$ (recall that P is fixed).

The proof of Theorem 1 goes in two steps. First, we will bound the time of Leapfrog Join by bounding the time T_i of each for-loop $?\mathtt{x}_i$ of Algorithm 1. Then for each level $?\mathtt{x}_i$ we define a new RDF graph G_i of size less than G such that $T_i = |[\![P]\!]_{G_i}| \leq 2^{\mathrm{MIN}(P,G)}$. The proof will follow by taking the sum over all T_i.

Fix a variable $?\mathtt{x}_i$ and denote by $\bar{x}_{i-1} = ?\mathtt{x}_1, \ldots, ?\mathtt{x}_{i-1}$ the order of variables before $?\mathtt{x}_i$ (for the sake of simplification, in the sequel we consider $\bar{x}_i$ also as a set). We start by bounding the time of the for-loop in Algorithm 1 corresponding to $?\mathtt{x}_i$. For this, consider the following extension of LF_G over $\bar{x}_{i-1}$:

$$\mathrm{LF}_G(P, \bar{x}_{i-1}) \;=\; \{\mu \mid \mathrm{dom}(\mu) = \bar{x}_{i-1} \text{ and } [\![\mu(t)]\!]_G \neq \varnothing \text{ for all } t \in P\}$$

Clearly, the number of times that the for-loop of $?\mathtt{x}_i$ will be called is given by $|\,\mathrm{LF}_G(P, \bar{x}_{i-1})|$. Then for each $\mu \in \mathrm{LF}_G(P, \bar{x}_{i-1})$ the Leapfrog procedure $\mathrm{LF}_G(\mu(P), ?\mathtt{x}_i)$ is called taking time at most $\min_{t \in \mu(P) : ?\mathtt{x}_i \in \mathrm{var}(t)} |\pi_{?\mathtt{x}_i}([\![t]\!]_G)|$ (omitting the $\log(|G|)$ factor for the moment). If we call T_i the number of steps that Algorithm 1 spends in the for-loop of $?\mathtt{x}_i$, we have that:

$$T_i \;=\; \sum_{\mu \in \mathrm{LF}_G(P, \bar{x}_{i-1})} \; \min_{t \in \mu(P) : ?\mathtt{x}_i \in \mathrm{var}(t)} |\pi_{?\mathtt{x}_i}([\![t]\!]_G)|$$

One can easily check that the total time of Algorithm 1 is given by $(\sum_{i=1}^{n} T_i) \cdot \log(G)$. Therefore, if we bound T_i by the AGM bound of P and G, then the worst case optimality of Leapfrog Join will be proven (recall that our analysis is in data complexity, omitting factors that depend on the size of P).

To bound the size of T_i, we build an RDF graph G_i such that $T_i = |[\![P]\!]_{G_i}|$ and the size of G_i is less that the size of G. Let $\bot$ be a dummy value. To build G_i define the set of mappings U_i such that $\mu \in U_i$ if and only if there exists $\mu' \in \mathrm{LF}_G(P, \bar{x}_{i-1})$ such that:

1. $\mu(?\mathrm{x}) = \mu'(?\mathrm{x})$ for every $?\mathrm{x} \in \bar{x}_{i-1}$,
2. $1 \leq \mu(?\mathrm{x}_i) \leq \min_{t \in \mu'(P):?\mathrm{x}_i \in \mathrm{var}(t)} |\pi_{?\mathrm{x}_i}([\![t]\!]_G)|$, and
3. $\mu(?\mathrm{x}) = \bot$ for every $?\mathrm{x} \in \{?\mathrm{x}_{i+1}, \ldots, ?\mathrm{x}_n\}$.

In other words, U_i contains all mappings built from mappings of $\mathrm{LF}_G(P, \bar{x}_{i-1})$ and extended by assigning to $?\mathrm{x}_i$ any value less than the time for computing $\mathrm{LF}_G(\mu'(P), ?\mathrm{x}_i)$. From U_i we can build the RDF graph G_i as follows:

$$G_i = \bigcup_{\mu \in U_i} \mu(P).$$

By construction, note that the size of G_i is less than the size of G. Furthermore, we have that $T_i = |[\![P]\!]_{G_i}|$. Indeed, for each $\mu' \in \mathrm{LF}_G(P, \bar{x}_{i-1})$ we will have $\left(\min_{t \in \mu'(P):?\mathrm{x}_i \in \mathrm{var}(t)} |\pi_{?\mathrm{x}_i}([\![t]\!]_G)|\right)$ different mappings in $[\![P]\!]_{G_i}$ and vice versa.

To finish the proof, recall the linear program associated to P and G, and its minimum value $\mathrm{MIN}(P, G)$. Consider also the same linear program but now for P and G_i. Given that G_i is of size less than G, then the minimization function associated to the linear program of P and G_i always satisfies:

$$\sum_{t \in P} x_t \cdot \log(|[\![t]\!]_{G_i}|) \leq \sum_{t \in P} x_t \cdot \log(|[\![t]\!]_G|).$$

Therefore, we can conclude that $\mathrm{MIN}(P, G_i) \leq \mathrm{MIN}(P, G)$ and thus:

$$T_i = |[\![P]\!]_{G_i}| \leq 2^{\mathrm{MIN}(P, G_i)} \leq 2^{\mathrm{MIN}(P, G)}$$

where the second inequality follows by the AGM bound. Given that each T_i is bounded by $2^{\mathrm{MIN}(P,G)}$ we conclude that the overall time is bounded by $n \cdot 2^{\mathrm{MIN}(P,G)} \cdot \log(G)$ and that Leapfrog Join is worst-case optimal.

References

1. Apache Jena. https://jena.apache.org/. Accessed 30 Dec 2018
2. Github project. https://gqgh5wfgzt.github.io/benchmark-leapfrog/
3. SPARQL 1.1 Query Language. https://www.w3.org/TR/sparql11-query/. Accessed 30 Dec 2018
4. Aberger, C.R., Lamb, A., Tu, S., Nötzli, A., Olukotun, K., Ré, C.: EmptyHeaded: a relational engine for graph processing. ACM Trans. Database Syst. (TODS) **42**(4), 20 (2017)
5. Abo Khamis, M., Ngo, H.Q., Rudra, A.: FAQ: questions asked frequently. In: Principles of Database Systems (PODS), pp. 13–28. ACM (2016)
6. Aluç, G., Hartig, O., Özsu, M.T., Daudjee, K.: Diversified stress testing of RDF data management systems. In: Mika, P., et al. (eds.) ISWC 2014. LNCS, vol. 8796, pp. 197–212. Springer, Cham (2014). https://doi.org/10.1007/978-3-319-11964-9_13
7. Angles, R., Gutierrez, C.: The multiset semantics of SPARQL patterns. In: Groth, P., et al. (eds.) ISWC 2016. LNCS, vol. 9981, pp. 20–36. Springer, Cham (2016). https://doi.org/10.1007/978-3-319-46523-4_2

8. Buil-Aranda, C., Hogan, A., Umbrich, J., Vandenbussche, P.-Y.: SPARQL web-querying infrastructure: ready for action? ISWC 2013. LNCS, vol. 8219, pp. 277–293. Springer, Heidelberg (2013). https://doi.org/10.1007/978-3-642-41338-4_18
9. Aref, M.: Design and implementation of the LogicBlox system. In: SIGMOD International Conference on Management of Data, pp. 1371–1382. ACM (2015)
10. Atre, M., Chaoji, V., Zaki, M.J., Hendler, J.A.: Matrix "Bit" loaded: a scalable lightweight join query processor for RDF data. In: World Wide Web (WWW), pp. 41–50 (2010)
11. Atserias, A., Grohe, M., Marx, D.: Size bounds and query plans for relational joins. In: Foundations of Computer Science (FOCS), pp. 739–748. IEEE (2008)
12. Barbay, J., Kenyon, C.: Adaptive intersection and t-threshold problems. In: Symposium on Discrete Algorithms (SODA), pp. 390–399. Society for Industrial and Applied Mathematics (2002)
13. Bizer, C., Schultz, A.: The Berlin SPARQL benchmark. Int. J. Semant. Web Inf. Syst. (IJSWIS) **5**(2), 1–24 (2009)
14. Bonifati, A., Martens, W., Timm, T.: An analytical study of large SPARQL query logs. PVLDB **11**(2), 149–161 (2017)
15. Demaine, E.D., López-Ortiz, A., Munro, J.I.: Adaptive set intersections, unions, and differences. In: Symposium on Discrete Algorithms (SODA). Citeseer (2000)
16. Erling, O., Mikhailov, I.: RDF support in the virtuoso DBMS. In: Pellegrini, T., Auer, S., Tochtermann, K., Schaffert, S. (eds.) Networked Knowledge - Networked Media. Studies in Computational Intelligence, vol. 221, pp. 7–24. Springer, Heidelberg (2009). https://doi.org/10.1007/978-3-642-02184-8_2
17. Galkin, M., Endris, K.M., Acosta, M., Collarana, D., Vidal, M., Auer, S.: SMJoin: a multi-way join operator for SPARQL queries. In: International Conference on Semantic Systems (SEMANTICS), pp. 104–111 (2017)
18. Harth, A., Decker, S.: Optimized index structures for querying RDF from the Web. In: Latin American Web Congress (LA-Web 2005), pp. 71–80 (2005)
19. Kalinsky, O., Etsion, Y., Kimelfeld B.: Flexible caching in Trie joins. In: International Conference on Extending Database Technology (EDBT), pp. 282–293. Springer (2017). https://doi.org/10.5441/002/edbt.2017.26
20. Kalinsky, O., Mishali, O., Hogan, A., Etsion, Y., Kimelfeld, B.: Efficiently charting RDF. CoRR, abs/1811.10955 (2018)
21. Khamis, M.A., Ngo, H.Q., Ré, C., Rudra, A.: Joins via geometric resolutions: worst case and beyond. ACM Trans. Database Syst. (TODS) **41**(4), 22 (2016)
22. Malyshev, S., Krötzsch, M., González, L., Gonsior, J., Bielefeldt, A.: Getting the most out of Wikidata: semantic technology usage in Wikipedia's knowledge graph. In: Vrandečić, D., et al. (eds.) ISWC 2018. LNCS, vol. 11137, pp. 376–394. Springer, Cham (2018). https://doi.org/10.1007/978-3-030-00668-6_23
23. Neumann, T., Weikum, G.: RDF-3X: a RISC-style engine for RDF. PVLDB **1**(1), 647–659 (2008)
24. Ngo, H.Q.: Worst-case optimal join algorithms: techniques, results, and open problems. In: Principles of Database Systems (PODS), pp. 111–124. ACM (2018)
25. Ngo, H.Q., Nguyen, D.T., Re, C., Rudra, A.: Beyond worst-case analysis for joins with minesweeper. In: Principles of Database Systems (PODS), pp. 234–245. ACM (2014)
26. Ngo, H.Q., Porat, E., Ré, C., Rudra, A.: Worst-case optimal join algorithms. In: Principles of Database Systems (PODS), pp. 37–48. ACM (2012)
27. Ngo, H.Q., Ré, C., Rudra, A.: Skew strikes back: new developments in the theory of join algorithms. arXiv preprint arXiv:1310.3314 (2013)

28. Nguyen, D., et al.: Join processing for graph patterns: an old dog with new tricks. In: GRADES, p. 2. ACM (2015)
29. Ramakrishnan, R., Gehrke, J.: Database Management Systems. McGraw Hill, New York (2000)
30. Thompson, B.B., Personick, M., Cutcher, M.: The Bigdata®RDF graph database. In: Linked Data Management, pp. 193–237 (2014)
31. Veldhuizen, T.L.: Leapfrog Triejoin: a simple, worst-case optimal join algorithm. In: ICDT, pp. 96–106 (2014)
32. Vrandečić, D., Krötzsch, M.: Wikidata: a free collaborative knowledgebase. Commun. ACM **57**, 78–85 (2014)
33. Weiss, C., Karras, P., Bernstein, A.: Hexastore: sextuple indexing for semantic web data management. PVLDB **1**(1), 1008–1019 (2008)

Knowledge Graph Consolidation by Unifying Synonymous Relationships

Jan-Christoph Kalo(✉), Philipp Ehler, and Wolf-Tilo Balke

Institut für Informationssysteme, Technische Universität Braunschweig, Mühlenpfordtstraße 23, 38106 Brunswick, Germany
{kalo,balke}@ifis.cs.tu-bs.de, p.ehler@tu-bs.de

Abstract. Entity-centric information resources in the form of huge RDF knowledge graphs have become an important part of today's information systems. But while the integration of independent sources promises rich information, their inherent heterogeneity also poses threats to the overall usefulness. To some degree challenges of heterogeneity have been addressed by creating underlying ontological structures. Yet, our analysis shows that synonymous relationships are still prevalent in current knowledge graphs. In this paper we compare state-of-the-art relational learning techniques to analyze the semantics of relationships for unifying synonymous relationships. By embedding relationships into latent feature models, we are able to identify relationships showing the same semantics in a data-driven fashion. The resulting relationship synonyms can be used for knowledge graph consolidation. We evaluate our technique on Wikidata, Freebase and DBpedia: we identify hundreds of existing relationship duplicates with very high precision, outperforming the current state-of-the-art method.

Keywords: Data quality · Synonym detection · Knowledge embedding

1 Introduction

Knowledge graphs (KG) efficiently collect entity-centric data in triple format and serve an increasing number of applications. Beginning with the Semantic Web standard RDF for knowledge representation, projects like Wikidata [27], DBpedia [4], Freebase [5], YAGO [25] and the Google Knowledge Vault [7] over the last years have grown significantly to support for instance Web search, question answering, and recommender systems.

But from the beginning, highly heterogeneous data items have caused severe problems in RDF databases, because a huge number of independent data sources needs to be integrated in a world-wide Semantic Web. During integration, heterogeneity issues are mostly manifested by having different RDF identifiers for the same real-world objects or relationships. However, while ontology alignment is extensively investigated for example at the Ontology Alignment Evaluation

C. Ghidini et al. (Eds.): ISWC 2019, LNCS 11778, pp. 276–292, 2019.
https://doi.org/10.1007/978-3-030-30793-6_16

Initiative[1] at ISWC, research has mainly focused on ontology and class alignments for two ontologies, often even requiring a complete OWL ontology. A detailed analysis of the DBpedia KG reveals that we are indeed facing another big problem: duplicates within the same KG. For instance, more than 26 different identifiers represent the birthplace relationship. For the entity Albert Einstein `dbo:birthPlace` is used, birthplaces of other persons use `dbp:birthCity` or even an identifier inspired by the French language `dbp:lieuDeNaissance`. Thus, queries asking for birthplaces using the `dbo:birthPlace` URI will be incomplete: persons whose birthplace is stated in some synonymous relationship will not be returned.

The problem of finding these *synonymous relationships* has hardly gotten any attention. Existing work [2] on this topic has only been evaluated on a small dataset, not reflecting the heterogeneities of today's large KGs. Traditional ontology alignment techniques often require two distinct ontologies as an input and are also pushed to their limits due to the lack of OWL statements in common KGs. Also natural language processing-based techniques like DOME from the OAEI 2018 [9] are often pushed to their limits here, because several KGs like Wikidata or Freebase use complex identifiers for naming relationships so that natural language techniques cannot be used.

In this paper, we detect synonymous relationships in a data-driven fashion only relying on the KG itself, thus not making any assumptions on the data: We are independent of a formal ontology in OWL and work with arbitrary identifiers for relationships. Our technique transfers ideas from synonym detection with word embeddings in natural language processing [17,22,30] into the field of KGs. Recently, relational learning techniques, also known as *knowledge embeddings*, have already been proposed to predict new triples in KGs [18,21,28]. In a nutshell, they are machine learning models trained on large sets of triples, learning latent vector representations of entities and relationships, which may be used to predict the correctness of known and unknown triples. We are the first work that makes use of the relationship representation in knowledge embeddings by showing that it may be used to reliably measure semantic similarity of knowledge graph's relationships. The main contributions of our work are:

- We develop a new method for identifying synonymous relationships in knowledge graphs by employing knowledge embeddings.
- Our method is purely data-driven not making any assumptions on the data and therefore is generalizable to all kinds of KGs.
- In an extensive evaluation with state-of-the-art knowledge embeddings (RESCAL [20], TransE [6], TransH [29], TransD [12], ComlEx [26], DistMult [31], HolE [19] and ANALOGY [16]) on Freebase, Wikidata and DBpedia, we demonstrate that we are able to identify synonyms with very high precision, outperforming a current state-of-the-art method.
- For reproducibility, we provide all our source code, datasets, and results in a publicly available Github repository.[2]

[1] http://oaei.ontologymatching.org/.

[2] https://github.com/JanKalo/RelAlign.

2 Related Work

Synonym Detection for relationships is about finding relationships with identical semantics within a single KG. To the best of our knowledge, only a single work on synonymous relationships [2] exists. Abedjan et al. [2] have noticed that particularly in DBpedia several synonymous predicates exist. To overcome problems in querying, they propose a query expansion process that builds on top of *synonymously used* relationships. They argue that for example the relationships `artist` and `starring`, even though they are not directly synonymous, in context of movies are synonymously used, making them good candidates for query expansion. Our manual analysis shows that the definition of synonymously used predicates is rather vague and differ from one application to another. Synonymous relationships as used in this paper are a subclass of synonymously used relationships, so the technique can serve as a baseline for this work.

The method of Abedjan et al. works with frequent item set mining. First, relationships that often co-occur for the same object entities are gathered in frequent item sets. Frequent item sets that exceed a certain minimum support threshold are further analyzed. The minimum support is an input parameter defined by the user, highly influencing precision and recall. All predicates within the same frequent item set are evaluated pairwise with the Reversed Correlation Coefficient together with their co-occurrence with the same subject entities. This is based on the assumption in mind that synonymous relationships should not co-occur for the same subject entities. In contrast, knowledge embedding based methods as proposed by us do not make any assumptions on the data. The authors evaluate their approach on a small manually built synonym dataset from DBpedia 3.7, Magnatune and Govwild. They show that their approach often achieves a precision value above 50%.

Ontology Alignment in contrast to synonym detection, is concerned with matching schemas of more than a single knowledge graph or RDF dataset. It has been a hot topic since the early days of the Semantic Web. Every year the Ontology Alignment Evaluation Initiative (OAEI) organizes a workshop for benchmarking different alignment systems. Its goal is to overcome problems like duplicate entities, classes and also relationships to integrate two or more ontologies [3,11,13,24]. Typically three different matching problems are addressed in the field of ontology alignment: Instance matching, class matching and sometimes also relationship matching. Instance matching or entity matching which is about finding synonymous entities between two or more knowledge bases [10,14]. These techniques rely on matching entities with similar relationships and properties. Class matching is about finding classes with equivalent semantics, relationship alignment about finding equivalent relationships.

DOME by Hertling et al. [9] is the only system that creates a relationship alignment in the knowledge graph track of OAEI 2018. However, its matching component relies on string similarity techniques, being very restrictive. Knowledge graphs often have complex identifiers as relationship URIs, making it impossible for such natural language based techniques to work at all.

Other ontology alignment tools (e.g. PARIS [24]) usually rely on two distinct ontologies and are not able to identify synonyms within a single knowledge graph, because their matching mechanism works on the relationships extensions, i.e. the entities taking part in the relations. In case of synonyms within a single knowledge graph this is usually not applicable, since synonymous relationships might have no overlap in their extension.

Furthermore, several ontology alignment systems that have been presented at OAEI over the last years are relying on a manually built ontology in OWL. They are not working on knowledge graphs that do not provide OWL information, as for example Wikidata and Freebase.

Knowledge Embeddings are usually used for predicting new triples in KGs, but can also be used for instance matching or entity resolution [18,28], which has some similarity to finding synonymous relationships. To the best of our knowledge there is only very few works that have looked concretely at the problem of finding instances of the same real-world entity with the help of knowledge embeddings. It has been proposed to formulate entity resolution as a link prediction task by predicting triples of the form (x, `owl:sameAs`, y) [20]. For RESCAL, Nickel et al. describe how to directly compare the entity representations to find identical entities, but they evaluate this idea only on a small dataset with about 2500 entities and only 7 relationships [20]. The idea of using relationship representations of knowledge embeddings has not been tested and evaluated before.

3 Preliminaries

In the Semantic Web, knowledge graphs are represented by the Resource Description Framework (RDF), a standard for knowledge representation by the W3C [1]. Knowledge in RDF has the form of subject, predicate, object *triples*: $(s, p, o) \in E \times R \times (E \cup L)$. Subjects stem from a set of resources E, representing entities or concepts (often from the real-world). Predicates stem from a set of relationships R. And objects are either resources like subjects or literals from the set L. They may be strings, numbers or dates. Resources and relationships are represented by Uniform Resource Identifiers (URIs). Due to better readability, in all our examples, we use textual labels instead of URIs for the identification of resources and relationships. Note that we focus on RDF without blank nodes and reification, since they cannot be processed by any of the knowledge embedding techniques we employ in this paper. A *knowledge graph* is a finite set of triples $KG \subseteq E \times R \times (E \cup L)$.

Since large KGs are usually created by crowd workers or automatic extraction, it may contain synonymous relationships or entities. With *synonymous* we refer to two (or more) distinct URIs either in E or R that refer to the same real-world entity, concept or relationship. As an example from DBpedia, the relationships `birthPlace` $\in R$ and `placeOfBirth` $\in R$ both refer to the relationship connecting a living being to its place of birth, which usually is a city. Similar to the work in [2], we are interested in finding *synonymous relationships* within a single knowledge base.

Given some knowledge graph *Knowledge Graph Consolidation* is the problem of finding all possible synonymous relationships so that they may be integrated. In the Semantic Web, these relationships are either collapsed into a single relationship or marked as identical by introducing a new triple with the `owl:sameAs` predicate.

4 Detecting Synonymous Relationships with Knowledge Embeddings

In this section, we present a new classification method for finding synonymous relationships in large KGs based on knowledge embedding techniques. Our idea is inspired by synonym search from natural language processing, which is often based on latent vector representations of words [17,22]. High-dimensional vector representations of RDF-based KGs (*knowledge embeddings*) are based on statistical relational learning techniques. For a detailed overview of existing knowledge embedding models is provided in the survey by Nickel et al. [18]. The latent vector representations of a knowledge embedding are learned from a KG by computing an optimization function on the set of correct triples from a KG and a set of automatically generated incorrect triples. During this optimization process, knowledge from the KG is encoded into an entity and a relationship representations which usually is combined to predict new triples. Empirical evaluations have shown that known triples from KG, but also unknown triples that have not been present in the KG are predicted by these models with high precision, at least when evaluated on small datasets like FB15K from Freebase and WN18 from Wordnet [6]. For entities it has been shown that their embeddings may be used to measure semantic similarity by applying distance metrics on the vectors [20,21].

Our approach uses a property of knowledge embeddings that has not been exploited before. We show that not only the entity representation can be used to measure semantic similarity, but also the latent representation of relationships can be used to measure its semantic similarity. Our work investigates the advantages and limits of this property for detecting synonymous relationships with knowledge embeddings, so relationships that have a very high semantic similarity. In this paper, we employ the knowledge embeddings RESCAL [20], TransE [6], TransH [29], TransD [12], ComplEx [26] DistMult [31], HolE [19] and ANALOGY [16]. From all models, we can obtain a relationship representation either in form of a vector, as a matrix, or as a concatenation of several matrices that can be used to measure the semantic similarity of the relationships in a vector space using classical vector metrics. Since knowledge embeddings are currently not able to embed literal values or relationships that are in triples with literal values, our method is restricted to relationships between resources.

4.1 Representing Relationships in a Knowledge Embedding

As already mentioned, knowledge embeddings have been created to predict new triples, usually by applying vector operations on subject, predicate, object vector representations. To give an intuition of why the techniques are suitable for finding synonymous relationships, we provide a small example: Given two true triples, (`Albert_Einstein`, `birthplace`, `Ulm`) and its synonymous counterpart (`Albert_Einstein`, `bornIn`, `Ulm`). `Albert_Einstein` and `Ulm` having unique vector representations in the knowledge embedding. The vector representation `Albert_Einstein` and the vector for `birthplace` can be combined in such a way that the vector of `Ulm` is predicted, using the prediction capabilities of the embedding. Since the same mechanism also works when combining the vector of `Albert_Einstein` and `bornIn`, usually the relationship vectors for `birthplace` and `bornIn` are identical. But also for the triple (`Max_Planck`, `placeOfBirth`, `Kiel`), the vector representations of `Max_Planck` would be similar Albert Einstein's, `Kiel`'s representation similar to Ulm. Thus `placeOfBirth` may also be detected as a synonym of the other relationships.

Our synonymous relationship detection technique makes use of this property by employing vector similarity as a measure for semantic similarity of relationships, whereas very similar vectors with a similarity larger than a certain threshold are likely to be semantically synonymous relationships. For measuring the semantic similarity between the relationship embeddings of vectors and matrices, we use standard vector norms. We have evaluated our method on the cosine similarity measure and on the L1-norm which is a distance measure. Note that a vector similarity of 1 means that two vectors are highly similar. Analogously, the vector distance of 0 implies high similarity. Cosine similarity is defined as $sim(r_i, r_j) = \frac{r_i \cdot r_j}{||r_i||||r_j||}$. It ranges from -1 to 1. The L1-norm is defined as $dist(r, r') = \sum_{i=1}^{d} |r_i - r'_i|$, d being the number of dimensions of the embedding. In contrast to cosine similarity, this norm is not restricted to a fixed interval, but is at least 0. If relationships are represented as a matrix, the entry-wise measures are computed. Computing the entry-wise measures of a matrix boils down to concatenate the columns of a matrix resulting in one large column vector. We use these similarity metrics for classifying relationship pairs as synonymous in the next step.

4.2 Classification of Synonymous Relationships

Finding synonymous relationships may be seen as a binary classification problem for some pair of relationships, where we have to separate synonyms from non-synonyms, based on their similarity. In the ideal case where knowledge embeddings can perfectly represent the semantics of a KG, very similar relationship representations imply that the relationships are synonym. For KG consolidation we need to classify all possible combinations of relationship pairs. Classification in our scenario is about determining a similarity or distance/similarity threshold for each relationships such that it separates synonymous from non-synonymous relationships.

As the first step, we compute a similarity histogram for every single relationship measuring its similarity/distance to all other relationships in the respective KG. Subsequently, we describe our method only based on distance metrics. However, the method is analogously used for similarity metrics.

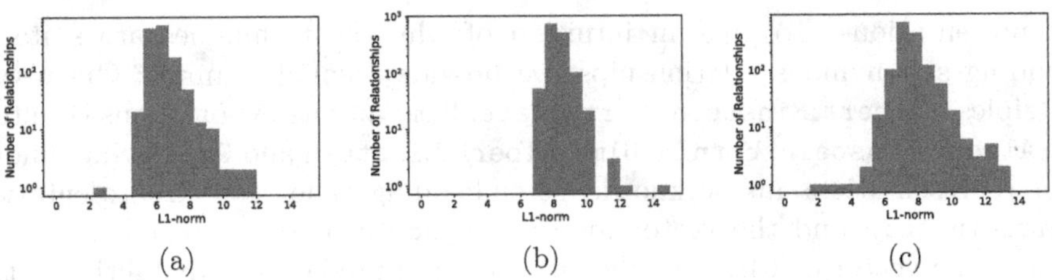

Fig. 1. (a) A histogram with clear outlier for the relation `award ceremony`, (b) without any outlier `friend` and (c) with very similar relationships, but without an explicit outliers `title`.

In Fig. 1, we provide three exemplar histograms that we have built from a TransE model on the FB15K dataset from Freebase. The more left a relationship is located in the histogram, the smaller its distance to the respective relationship and the higher its semantic similarity. In Fig. 1(a), the majority of the relationships have an L1 distance of 6, whereas a single relationship has a distance of only 2. This relationship is seen as a clear outlier on the left side of the mass of the distribution. Hence, its vector distance is drastically smaller and its semantic similarity should be much higher. Indeed, this outlier is a synonym.

In contrast, we cannot find such an outlier in Fig. 1(b). Here, the histogram's mass has an average distance of 8. Outliers in this histogram may only be found on the right side of the distribution, being extremely dissimilar. The minimum distance of any relationship is at least 7. And indeed the respective relationship does not have any synonyms within our dataset.

For some relationships, outliers are not that easy to identify. In Fig. 1(c) for example, the most similar relationship has a distance of 2. Due to this variety in similarity histograms, a static and global threshold valid for all relationships of a KG is not suitable for this classification task. Instead, we aim at computing a dynamic threshold individually for each relationship based on outlier detection. Actually the relationship from Fig. 1(c) has several synonyms, but they can hardly be separated from the remaining relationships. It turns out that outliers usually are synonymous relationships, but not all synonymous relationships can be clearly identified as outliers.

In the second step, we perform the actual classification on these relationship-specific histograms. Since the similarity distribution usually are hardly skewed, we rely on an outlier detection based on the Z-score [23]. Given a similarity histogram for relationship r_i, we compute a Z-score for all (r_i, r_j), where r_j is another relationship from the KG. The Z-score is defined as: $z_{ij} = \frac{dist(r_i,r_j)-\mu_{r_i}}{\sigma_{r_i}}$, μ_{r_i} being the arithmetic mean and σ_{r_i} the standard deviation. Since the Z-score detects outliers based on their distance in terms of standard deviations from the arithmetic mean of the distribution, a fixed Z-score is used for classification of very diverse similarity histograms. With varying thresholds for the Z-score we can either achieve very precise results with low thresholds, or recall-oriented results with high thresholds.

In practice, similarity histograms for relationships have several outliers which sometimes can hardly be distinguished from the rest of the distribution, which makes a classification only based on the histogram very difficult. In these cases however, even a manual binary classification is extremely difficult and cannot be performed without detailed background knowledge. Further details are discussed in the evaluation section.

5 Evaluation

In the experiments, 8 different knowledge embeddings on several real-world KGs are trained and compared to the method from Abedjan et al. from [2], which is used as a baseline. We employ the knowledge embeddings RESCAL, TransE, TransH, TransD, ComplEx, DistMult, HolE and ANALOGY on Wikidata, Freebase and DBpedia. Additional results for other parameters, diagrams, datasets and scripts for reproducing the results may all be found in our Github repository[3]. Our implementation of the knowledge embeddings is based on the framework OpenKE [8] which comprises 9 knowledge embedding models. TransR [15] is excluded from the evaluation, since it was not able to return any synonymous relationships at all. The implementation of our classification, the evaluation scripts and the baseline systems are in Python.

In this section, we wanted to evaluate synonym detection in a two-fold manner: (1) Experiments where we could evaluate precision and recall with synthetic synonyms, (2) but also a real-world scenario where we are not making any assumptions when generating synthetic synonyms.

Overall this resulted in three experiments:

1. We first experimented on a subset of Freebase (FB15K [6]) that is known to perform very well for training knowledge embedding models. To measure recall and precision, synthetic synonymous relationships are introduced into Freebase.
2. The second experiment is performed on synthetic synonyms in Wikidata. A KG that has due to its size and sparseness rarely been tested for knowledge embeddings. Since Wikidata's size is not suited for knowledge embeddings to be trained on, a special sampling techniques that still allows to find all synonymous relationships is used.
3. The third experiment on DBpedia, a manual evaluation of the *Precision@k* for a large sample of DBpedia, instead of introducing synthetic synonymous is performed. In contrast to Wikidata, DBpedia is much more heterogeneous because it comprises a larger number of relationships. A measurement of the recall is not suitable here, because no gold standard of synonymous relationships is available. Building a gold standard would require manually checking millions of possible synonym pairs.

---

[3] https://github.com/JanKalo/RelAlign.

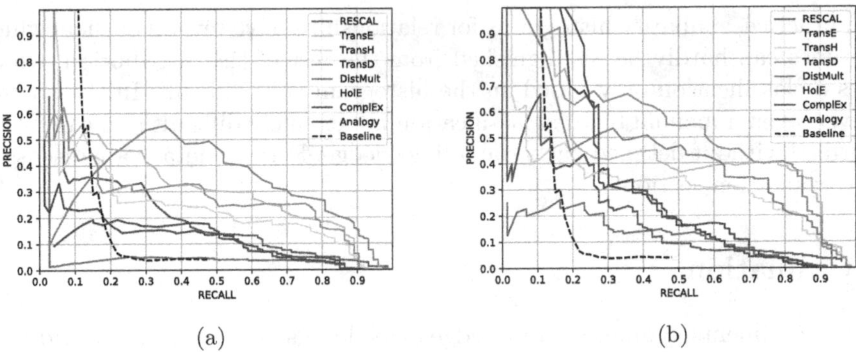

Fig. 2. Precision-recall-curves for synthetic synonyms on freebase. (a) Results with cosine similarity (b) Results with L1-Metric

In a final discussion, a comparison of the different experiments is made and cases where our technique could not identify synonymous relationships are further discussed. The discussion will also present the advantages and disadvantages of the different models and provide guidelines for choosing the right model for synonym detection.

Baseline Based on Frequent Itemsets. In all experiments, the 8 embedding models are compared to the baseline technique from [2]. Since no implementation is available for the baseline system for synonym detection from [2], we re-implemented the *Range Content Filtering* and *Reversed Correlation Coefficient* as described in the paper. Further details on our Python implementation are available in our Github repository. However, the technique has a *minimum support* as an input parameter for the range content filtering step, which highly influences precision and recall. We performed a grid search on the minimum support to tune this parameter to achieve highest F1 measure.

Synthetic Synonyms Generation. Synthetic synonyms are created by replacing relationship URIs with new (synthetic) URIs in existing triples of the dataset. As an example, we replace the triple (Albert Einstein, award, Nobel_Prize) with the triple (Albert Einstein, award_synonym, Nobel_Prize). `award` and `award_synonym` now have the identical meaning and are treated as synonymous relationships. To perform a proper relationship alignment task, the method has to re-identify these synthetic synonyms from the KG. For the synthetic synonym generation, an assumption from [2] is used so that the baseline can perform synonym detection. Abedjan et al. assume that synonymous relationships do not co-occur for the same subject entity. In case of our Einstein example, all triples about his awards would either use `award` or `award_synonym`, but should not mix the two for the same entity. This assumption stems from the idea that entities and their triples are often inserted at once by the same person or from the same data source. In such cases, synonymous relationships for the same entity are usually rare. For the experiments with synthetic synonyms, we introduced exactly one synthetic relationship for each relationship that occurs in at least 2000 triples and replaced it in 50% of the triples resulting in a 50-50 distribution of synonyms to non-synonyms. The F1-measure for all methods, including the baseline method, decreases the more skewed the distribution is, since it leads to some relationships being extremely rare, which negatively influences the embedding representation of a relationship. Results for the skewed distributions may also be found in our Github repository.

Sampling Method for Large Knowledge Graphs. Knowledge embedding training involves a lot of computational effort, which is why it should be performed on a fast GPU. Typical GPUs are very restricted in their memory size, making it impossible to train models for complete KGs. Training embeddings for example on the complete Wikidata dataset on a CPU is technically possible, but is around 10–100 times slower (i.e., several weeks) and thus prohibitive. To overcome this issue, we came up with a sampling technique that covers all relationships of a KG, but only a fraction of all triples. We randomly selected entities with all their triples in such a way that we have similarly many triples per relationship in our random sample. This sampling method guarantees for the knowledge embeddings still to work, while having enough information about each relationship so that its semantics is correctly be mapped to the latent vector space.

5.1 Evaluation of Synthetic Synonyms in Freebase

In this experiment, we compared knowledge embedding-based synonym detection with the baseline system on a subset from Freebase (FB15K) that is usually used to evaluate knowledge embeddings on link prediction [6]. FB15K comprises 592,213 triples about 15k entities, using 1,345 different relationship types. The dataset does not contain any literals, hence only triples where subject and object are resources. Originally, FB15K is a small part of Freebase that was chosen for link prediction, because it comprises a lot of triples per entity and lots of entities per relationship. It has been shown that this dataset is particularly well suited for training knowledge embeddings, also leading to good results in other tasks like link prediction. Since no gold standard for the existing synonymous relationships in FB15K is available, we have introduced synthetic synonyms. Overall 74 synonymous relationships have been added to FB15K.

The results of 8 knowledge embeddings and the baseline are presented in Fig. 2. The baseline achieves it highest precision of 1.0 at a recall of 0.11, but then drops to a precision of 0.05. For the minimum support of 0.02 leading to the best F1 measure, the recall never exceeds 0.5. This implies that 60% of the synonyms are never found. A lower minimum support also negatively influences the precision. Our knowledge embedding based approach on the other hand is evaluated with cosine and L1 metric. For the cosine similarity in Fig. 2(a), the baseline performs best for low recall values, but for a recall above 0.2 all models but DistMult perform better than the baseline approach. The results quality is even better for most models with L1 metric in (b). TransD is best in synonym

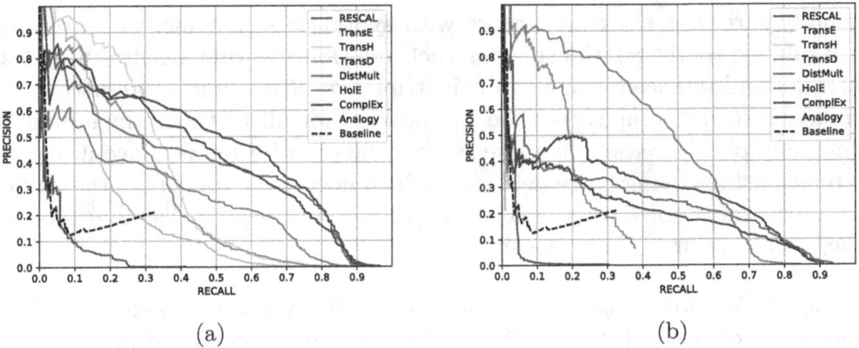

Fig. 3. Precision-recall-curves for synthetic synonyms on Wikidata. (a) Results with cosine similarity (b) Results with L1-metric

detection, achieving 1.0 precision at a recall of 0.1 and still 0.4 precision at a recall of 0.8.

Knowledge embeddings in this dataset achieve a high precision, for low recall values, but also find a lot of false positive synonymous relationships. These false positives are due to Freebase' fine granular modelling of relationships, leading to a high number of semantically very similar relationships that are not synonymous. Relationships in Freebase are defined for each entity type separately, implying that each relationship type is only used for a certain entity type. As an example several `genre` relationships are defined, depending on the class of the entities it is connected to. Differentiating `music_genre` from `film_genre` is quite difficult, but still possible with most embedding models. However, it gets even more difficult: FB15K contains 33 different `currency` relationships, all having a slightly different semantics, but very similar extensions. Hence being a problem for data-driven synonym detection techniques, when no background knowledge is given.

5.2 Synthetic Synonyms in Wikidata

The KG Wikidata is one of the fastest growing KGs that is openly available today. Our Wikidata version is from 9-19-2018. In contrast to other KGs, the Wikidata community is investing a lot of work into controlling its vocabulary. Therefore, it is supposed to be synonym free, which makes it a great candidate for evaluating our method with synthetic synonyms. Due to its size, we did not train knowledge embeddings on the complete Wikidata KG, but on a sample that comprises 15,663,641 million triples, with 341 synthetic synonymous relationships out of 1,797 relationships.

The precision and recall curves for all 8 models and the baseline are presented in Fig. 3. The knowledge embedding model-based approaches show a higher precision than the baseline for cosine similarity and L1-metric. Only RESCAL cannot hold up with any other system. The baselines starts with a high precision,

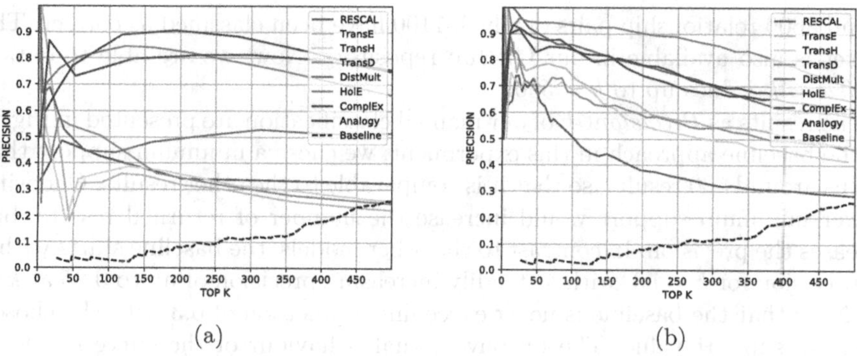

Fig. 4. Manually evaluated Precision@k for synonyms in DBPedia. (a) Results with cosine similarity (b) Results with L1-metric

but sharply decreases and ends at a precision of 0.2 at a recall of 0.3. For the optimally chosen minimum support, the baseline only returns one third of all synonymous relationships. ComplEx and HolE achieve best classification results, outperforming the baseline by far. HolE has a precision of 0.75 at a recall of 0.3 and then is decreasing (cf. Fig. 3(a)). ComplEx in contrast is starting with a lower precision, but still has a precision of over 0.5 at a recall of 0.5 (cf. Fig. 3(b)).

Training good knowledge embeddings on a knowledge graph that is as sparse as Wikidata leads to lower quality models in contrast to FB15K, impairing the knowledge embedding quality. This also impairs the quality of synonym classification. However, Wikidata in contrast to FB15K does not contain highly similar relationships that could be misjudged as false positives by the classification technique. These two factors even out each other leading to a comparable quality to FB15K from the previous experiment.

5.3 Finding Synonyms in DBpedia with Manual Evaluation

As a last experiment, we also want to show that our method identifies existing synonyms in a large scale and very heterogeneous KG. Therefore, we evaluate our method with all embedding models and the baseline on a sample of DBpedia-16-2010. Due to its size, again a random sample similar to the procedure before is taken, resulting in a dataset with 12,664,192 triples and 15,654 distinct relationships.

For the manual evaluation on DBpedia, the annotator were supposed to evaluate relationship pairs into *synonyms* and *non-synonyms*. To measure the difficulty of the task, we first measured the inter-annotator agreement on a small sample of our dataset. We achieved an annotator agreement of over 0.90 for two independent raters, implying that the raters came to very similar results. Due to this experiment and due to the size of the dataset, we decided for only a single annotator for the manual evaluation. This manually build dataset stems from the top 500 results for each embedding model and the baseline summing up to around 3600 relationship pairs of which 1100 have been classified as correct. The dataset is also available in our GitHub repository. Now, we are able to obtain *Precision@k* values up to $k = 500$.

The results as *Precision@k* of our manual classification are presented in Fig. 4. For the baseline approach in this experiment, we chose a minimum support that returns around 500 results, so that it is comparable to the other results. Choosing a lower minimum support would increase the number of returned results, but decreases the precision. In contrast to the other models, the baseline starts with a low precision for $k = 50$, with a steadily increasing precision of up to 0.25 at $k = 500$. Note that the baseline is never exceeding a precision of 0.3 with the chosen minimum support value. The unconventional behaviour of the curve is due to Abedjan et al. making an assumption on the data that is not valid for DBpedia: They penalize synonymous relationships that co-occur for the same subject. The precision of our classification method on top of knowledge embeddings is showing higher precision for almost all models. HolE, ComplEx and ANALOGY all show comparably high precision values, also for high k values, whereas the translation embedding models TransE, TransD and TransH are quite weak in contrast to the earlier experiments. HolE with L1-metric in Fig. 4 show the best results with a precision of 0.94 at $k = 50$ and still a precision of 0.7 at $k = 500$.

During the extensive manual evaluation of the models, we got a detailed insight into the advantages and disadvantages of the models on DBpedia. Very frequent synonymous relationships that can clearly be distinguished from others manually are also clearly identified as synonyms by the embedding models. These are for example relationships for `genre`, `almaMater`, `deathPlace`, `birthPlace` and `award`. Problematic, at least in DBpedia, are rarely used relationships (`fuelSystem`, `drums`), relationships with spelling errors in their label (`amaMater`, `birthPace`) and relationships that are very similar to others other existing relationships (`club`, `youthteam`). Several other false positives stem from DBpedia containing relationships that are automatically extracted from external data sources that should be integrated and reformulated. As an example, DBpedia imports an external baseball database by creating two relationships for every row of a table with two columns: e.g. `stat1label`, `stat1value` for the first row and `stat2label`, `stat2value`. These false positives are not synonymous relationships, but obviously problematic relationships that should be reformulated.

5.4 Discussion of the Results

In all three experiments, we have shown the advantages of our embedding-based classification method on a variety of knowledge graphs. The baseline has been outperformed with almost all embedding techniques, because it heavily relies on synonym relationships to share object entities. In contrast, knowledge embedding based approaches are able to detect synonyms even though they do not share any subject nor object entities. As an additional drawback, the baseline needed parameter tuning for the minimum support value which was a difficult trade-off between precision and recall.

We have seen that a large part of synonymous relationships are detected in knowledge graphs, if they are frequently used. The semantics of very rare relationships can hardly be mapped to the knowledge embedding, hindering data-driven synonym detection mechanism. All embedding models show varying qualities across the different datasets, with HolE showing consistently good if not the best results, when choosing L1-metric. For most other models also L1-metric is also showing better results. Still no model was able to identify all synonymous relationships with high quality only based on the KG itself.

The fine-grained modelling of relationships (as in Freebase and DBpedia) is often problematic, since these relationships may hardly be distinguished from real synonyms, even in our extensive manual evaluation. We observed that relationship pairs that have been counted as false positives often are pairs of relationships that are extremely similar.

For example `/education/university/local_tuition./.../currency` and `/education/university/domestic_tuition./.../currency` both are highly similar in their extension, however are, semantically speaking, slightly different. One is used for the currency of the tuition at universities for local students and one for domestic students. We believe that these relationships could be integrated and the information about local and domestic students could be modelled differently. Such a difference cannot be observed by a purely data-driven approach.

6 Conclusion

In this paper, the suitability of the relationship representation in knowledge embeddings to measure semantic similarity between relationships is analyzed for the first time. We develop a new classification technique for identifying synonymous relationships for knowledge graph consolidation. In several large-scale experiments on Freebase, Wikidata and DBpedia we demonstrate how our classification method, employing a variety of existing knowledge embeddings, identifies synonyms with high precision and recall. Our approach does not make any assumptions on the data or labels of relationships. Thus, as our experiments have shown, our approach is generalizable to arbitrary knowledge graphs and is not depending on any additional domain-specific knowledge.

We showed that a traditional technique based on frequent item set mining [2] is not capable of competing with the presented classification method using relation embeddings from state-of-the-art relational learning techniques. The baseline approach was outperformed by almost all models on all datasets, since it returns several false positives. This has shown that identifying synonymous relationships indeed is a very difficult problem. Our manual evaluation has revealed that sometimes the semantics of relationships is even difficult to grasp for humans, so that the difference between synonymous relationships and highly similar relationships is hardly noticeable if detailed background or domain knowledge is missing. To overcome such difficulties, in previous experiments, we have also experimented with employing additional ontological information like `range` and `domain` predicates, to improve the results for synonym detection. However, it was hardly possible to use this information for finding synonyms, because KGs often lack domain and range information, and even in the few cases where this information was present, it was not enough to improve synonym detection.

Moreover, in our experimental results almost all positively classified synonymous relationships already have compatible ranges and domains, thus the added value would be negligible. We believe that even though current relational learning models are far from achieving perfect results for synonymous relationship detection, it will be difficult to perform much better using a purely data-driven approach without any external domain knowledge. Overall, our knowledge embedding-based knowledge graph consolidation techniques have shown good performance on a variety of different knowledge graphs. If the precision of our approach is not sufficient it still may be used in a semi-automatic fashion making the task much simpler.

For future work, we plan to combine our work with our previous work on transitivity of synonyms in instance matching problems [10,14]. Furthermore, our manual evaluation has shown that the results are very promising for correcting badly chosen relationships, or for identifying misused relationships in triples. We would like to investigate this application more thoroughly. It would also be interesting to further follow the idea of using relationship embeddings for query expansion.

References

1. RDF documentation from W3C. https://www.w3.org/RDF/
2. Abedjan, Z., Naumann, F.: Synonym analysis for predicate expansion. In: Cimiano, P., Corcho, O., Presutti, V., Hollink, L., Rudolph, S. (eds.) ESWC 2013. LNCS, vol. 7882, pp. 140–154. Springer, Heidelberg (2013). https://doi.org/10.1007/978-3-642-38288-8_10
3. Algergawy, A., et al.: Results of the ontology alignment evaluation initiative 2018. In: CEUR-WS: Workshop Proceedings (2018)
4. Auer, S., Bizer, C., Kobilarov, G., Lehmann, J., Cyganiak, R., Ives, Z.: DBpedia: a nucleus for a web of open data. In: Aberer, K., et al. (eds.) ASWC/ISWC - 2007. LNCS, vol. 4825, pp. 722–735. Springer, Heidelberg (2007). https://doi.org/10.1007/978-3-540-76298-0_52
5. Bollacker, K., Evans, C., Paritosh, P., Sturge, T., Taylor, J.: Freebase: a collaboratively created graph database for structuring human knowledge. In: Proceedings of the 2008 ACM SIGMOD International Conference on Management of Data, SIGMOD 2008, pp. 1247–1250 (2008)
6. Bordes, A., Usunier, N., Garcia-Duran, A., Weston, J., Yakhnenko, O.: Translating embeddings for modeling multi-relational data. In: Advances in Neural Information Processing Systems, NIPS 2013, vol. 26, pp. 2787–2795 (2013)
7. Dong, X., et al.: Knowledge vault: a web-scale approach to probabilistic knowledge fusion. In: Proceedings of the 20th International Conference on Knowledge Discovery and Data Mining, SIGKDD 2014, pp. 601–610 (2014)
8. Han, X., et al.: Openke: an open toolkit for knowledge embedding. In: Proceedings of the 2018 Conference on Empirical Methods in Natural Language Processing: System Demonstrations, EMNLP 2018, pp. 139–144 (2018)

9. Hertling, S., Paulheim, H.: DOME results for OAEI 2018. In: OM 2018: Proceedings of the 13th International Workshop on Ontology Matching Co-located with the 17th International Semantic Web Conference (ISWC 2018), Monterey, CA, USA, 8 October 2018, vol. 2288, pp. 144–151 (2018)
10. Homoceanu, S., Kalo, J.-C., Balke, W.-T.: Putting instance matching to the test: is instance matching ready for reliable data linking? In: Andreasen, T., Christiansen, H., Cubero, J.-C., Raś, Z.W. (eds.) ISMIS 2014. LNCS (LNAI), vol. 8502, pp. 274–284. Springer, Cham (2014). https://doi.org/10.1007/978-3-319-08326-1_28
11. Jain, P., Hitzler, P., Sheth, A.P., Verma, K., Yeh, P.Z.: Ontology alignment for linked open data. In: Patel-Schneider, P.F., et al. (eds.) ISWC 2010. LNCS, vol. 6496, pp. 402–417. Springer, Heidelberg (2010). https://doi.org/10.1007/978-3-642-17746-0_26
12. Ji, G., He, S., Xu, L., Liu, K., Zhao, J.: Knowledge graph embedding via dynamic mapping matrix. In: Proceedings of the 53rd Annual Meeting of the Association for Computational Linguistics and the 7th International Joint Conference on Natural Language Processing, ACL 2015, pp. 687–696 (2015)
13. Li, J., Tang, J., Li, Y., Luo, Q.: RiMOM: a dynamic multistrategy ontology alignment framework. IEEE Trans. Knowl. Data Eng. **21**(8), 1218–1232 (2009)
14. Kalo, J.C., Homoceanu, S., Rose, J., Balke, W.T.: Avoiding Chinese whispers: controlling end-to-end join quality in linked open data stores. In: Proceedings of the ACM Web Science Conference, WebSci 2015, pp. 5:1–5:10 (2015)
15. Lin, Y., Liu, Z., Sun, M., Liu, Y., Zhu, X.: Learning entity and relation embeddings for knowledge graph completion. In: Proceedings of the Twenty-Ninth AAAI Conference on Artificial Intelligence, AAAI 2015, pp. 2181–2187 (2015)
16. Liu, H., Wu, Y., Yang, Y.: Analogical inference for multi-relational embeddings. In: Proceedings of the 34th International Conference on Machine Learning, ICML 2017, pp. 2168–2178 (2017)
17. Mikolov, T., Sutskever, I., Chen, K., Corrado, G., Dean, J.: Distributed representations of words and phrases and their compositionality. In: Proceedings of the 26th International Conference on Neural Information Processing Systems, NIPS 2013, vol. 2, pp. 3111–3119 (2013)
18. Nickel, M., Murphy, K., Tresp, V., Gabrilovich, E.: A review of relational machine learning for knowledge graphs. Proc. IEEE **104**(1), 11–33 (2016)
19. Nickel, M., Rosasco, L., Poggio, T.: Holographic embeddings of knowledge graphs. In: Proceedings of the 30th AAAI Conference on Artificial Intelligence, AAAI 2016, pp. 1955–1961. AAAI Press (2016)
20. Nickel, M., Tresp, V., Kriegel, H.P.: A three-way model for collective learning on multi-relational data. In: Proceedings of the 28th International Conference on Machine Learning, ICML 2011, pp. 809–816 (2011)
21. Nickel, M., Tresp, V., Kriegel, H.P.: Factorizing YAGO. In: Proceedings of the 21st International Conference on World Wide Web, WWW 2017, p. 271 (2012)
22. Pennington, J., Socher, R., Manning, C.D.: GloVe: global vectors for word representation. In: Proceedings of the 2014 Conference on Empirical Methods in Natural Language Processing, EMNLP 2014, pp. 1532–1543 (2014)
23. Rousseeuw, P.J., Hubert, M.: Robust statistics for outlier detection. Wiley Interdisc. Rev. Data Min. Knowl. Discov. **1**(1), 73–79 (2011)
24. Suchanek, F.M., Abiteboul, S., Senellart, P.: Paris: probabilistic alignment of relations, instances, and schema. Proc. VLDB Endow. **5**(3), 157–168 (2011)
25. Suchanek, F.M., Kasneci, G., Weikum, G.: YAGO: a core of semantic knowledge. In: Proceedings of the 16th International Conference on World Wide Web, WWW 2007, p. 697 (2007)

26. Trouillon, T., Welbl, J., Riedel, S., Gaussier, E., Bouchard, G.: Complex embeddings for simple link prediction. In: Proceedings of the 33rd International Conference on Machine Learning, ICML 2016, vol. 48, pp. 2071–2080 (2016)
27. Vrandečić, D.: Wikidata: a new platform for collaborative data collection. In: Proceedings of the 21st International Conference on companion on World Wide Web, WWW 2012 Companion, p. 1063 (2012)
28. Wang, Q., Mao, Z., Wang, B., Guo, L.: Knowledge graph embedding: a survey of approaches and applications. IEEE Trans. Knowl. Data Eng. **29**(12), 2724–2743 (2017)
29. Wang, Z., Zhang, J., Feng, J., Chen, Z.: Knowledge graph embedding by translating on hyperplanes. In: Proceedings of the Twenty-Eighth AAAI Conference on Artificial Intelligence, AAAI 2014, pp. 1112–1119 (2014)
30. Weeds, J., Clarke, D., Reffin, J., Weir, D., Keller, B.: Learning to distinguish hypernyms and co-hyponyms. In: Proceedings of the 25th International Conference on Computational Linguistics: Technical Papers, COLING 2014, pp. 2249–2259 (2014)
31. Yang, Q., Wooldridge, M.J., Codocedo, V., Napoli, A.: Twenty-Fourth International Joint Conference on Artificial Intelligence, IJCAI 2015, Buenos Aires, Argentina, 25–31 July 2015 (2015)

Skyline Queries over Knowledge Graphs

Ilkcan Keles(✉) and Katja Hose

Aalborg University, Aalborg, Denmark
{ilkcan,khose}@cs.aau.dk

Abstract. With the continuously growing amount of data offered in the form of knowledge graphs, users are often overwhelmed by the amount of potentially relevant information and entities. Hence, helping users find relevant data is a problem that becomes more and more important. Skyline queries are typically used in multi-criteria decision making applications to find a set of objects that are of interest to a user. This type of queries has been extensively studied over relational data in the database community. But only little attention has yet been paid to investigating if and how the skyline principle can help identifying sets of interesting entities in knowledge graphs. In this paper, we therefore show how the skyline principle can be applied to RDF knowledge graphs and help the user find interesting entities. In particular, we present algorithms using commonly used standard interfaces for accessing RDF data and a lightweight extension of existing interfaces (SkyTPF) to process skyline queries. Our experiments show that the proposed algorithms enable efficient and scalable skyline query processing over knowledge graphs.

1 Introduction

More and more knowledge graphs are becoming available in different fields. Whereas some knowledge graphs, such as DBpedia [15] and YAGO [9], offer factual information about real-world entities, others are used by private companies. For querying publicly accessible knowledge graphs, there are two widely accepted interfaces: SPARQL endpoints and Triple Pattern Fragments (TPF) [24]. SPARQL endpoints typically use indexes and advanced query planning techniques to enable efficient query processing. On the other hand, the drawback is that the server running the SPARQL endpoint handles all the query processing load whereas the client that sends the query simply waits for the result. Hence, when many clients access an endpoint concurrently, it is likely to have problems regarding performance and throughput. TPF [24] has been proposed to reduce the server load by assigning more tasks to the client. To achieve this, a TPF server is only capable of processing queries consisting of a single triple pattern instead of complex SPARQL queries. In order to process SPARQL queries, the client has to take care of the remaining query processing tasks, such as query planning, filtering, and joins.

Even though these interfaces provide means of querying knowledge graphs, it is often very difficult for users to find the entities that they are interested in.

C. Ghidini et al. (Eds.): ISWC 2019, LNCS 11778, pp. 293–310, 2019.
https://doi.org/10.1007/978-3-030-30793-6_17

For instance, assume that a user is doing research on planets, consults DBpedia, and wants to know about planets that have high densities (?d) and high average speeds (?as). The user is unable to provide a precise scoring function, such as $0.5 * ?d + 0.5 * ?as$, that could be used to rank the planets because he/she has neither any information about the attributes' domains and ranges nor a clear understanding of whether one criterion is more important than the other.

In such use cases, skyline queries [3] can help users find interesting entities without the need to provide a specific weight for each criterion. In other words, a skyline query allows users to simply provide a set of preferences on the attributes of interest and returns a set of "interesting" entities with respect to these preferences. More formally, a skyline set consists of all entities that are not dominated by any other entity; entity e_i dominates entity e_j if e_i is at least as good in all attributes and better in at least one attribute.

Assuming the above mentioned skyline query for planets with preferences on high density and high average speed is evaluated on the dataset illustrated in Fig. 1 (subset of planets in DBpedia), the skyline set consists of Earth and Venus (highlighted in red). Figure 1 also illustrates the dominance region of the planets in the skyline. Intuitively, with the given preferences a skyline point is clearly "preferable" over any planet contained in the dominance region – we therefore refer to the latter as being dominated.

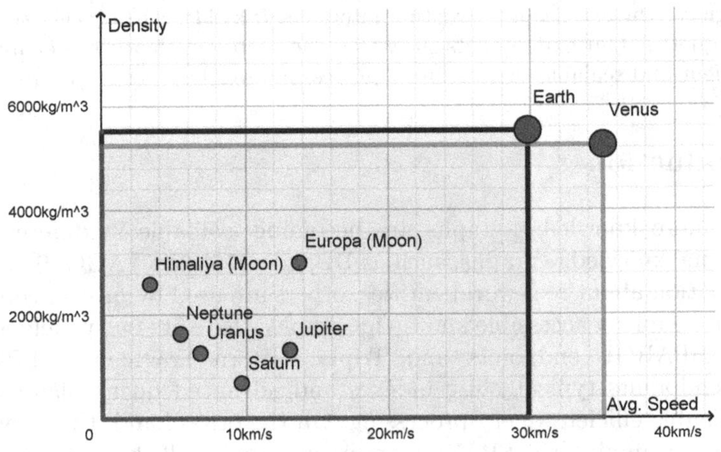

Fig. 1. Skyline of planets (Color figure online)

Efficient processing of skyline queries over relational databases [1–3,6,13,18,19,22,27] has been extensively studied. However, there is only very little related work [5,29] on processing skyline queries over knowledge graphs. These works assume direct control over the data source and how the data is stored. We, on the other hand, aim at supporting skyline computation over standard and lightweight interfaces that we do not control and that are not restricted to skyline queries only.

In this paper, we propose methods for skyline query computation over standard interfaces, such as SPARQL endpoints and TPF. In addition, we propose the SkyTPF interface, which extends TPF and aims at making skyline query processing more efficient. Finally, we provide an extensive experimental evaluation of the proposed methods. The experiments show that the proposed methods enable efficient skyline query processing over knowledge graphs. In summary, our main contributions are: (i) methods to enable skyline query processing over standard RDF interfaces (SPARQL endpoints and TPF), (ii) SkyTPF; a TPF-like interface on the server-side and a client-side algorithm to optimize and process skyline queries, (iii) an extensive experimental evaluation of these methods.

The remainder of this paper is organized as follows. Section 2 discusses related work, and Sect. 3 introduces background and definitions. While Sect. 4 presents how to process skylines over standard interfaces (SPARQL endpoints and TPF), Sect. 5 presents the SkyTPF interface as well as a client-side algorithm for skyline computation. Finally, Sect. 6 presents our evaluation, and Sect. 7 concludes the paper.

2 Related Work

The general problem of computing skyline queries was first introduced by Kung et al. [14] as the maximum vector problem in the field of computational geometry. The term skyline was first introduced by Börzsönyi et al. for relational databases [3]. Since then skyline queries have attracted significant interest in the database community as they enable finding interesting data objects in consideration of multiple preference criteria. To compute skyline queries over relational databases, Börzsönyi et al. [3] propose the Block Nested Loops (BNL) and Divide and Conquer (D&C) algorithms. BNL scans the database in several rounds and compares each data object with the current set of candidate skyline objects. If a data object p is not dominated by any of the current skyline candidates, p is added to that set and, if necessary, all data objects dominated by p are removed. The D&C algorithm is based on the divide and conquer principle. So, it first partitions a dataset into several subsets, computes the skyline in each of the subsets, and then combines the partial results by checking them for mutual dominance. The SFS algorithm [6] improves BNL by presorting the data objects with respect to a monotone function. Bartolini et al. [2] propose the SaLSa algorithm to eliminate the need to scan all the data objects in the database. All these algorithms target skyline computation over relational data, where all attributes of a data item are combined in a single relational tuple. In knowledge graphs, however, joins are required to obtain the attribute values. Whereas the BNL principle of comparing all data items against each other is of course applicable in arbitrary setups, the proposed optimizations are tailored towards relational data that is available locally and cannot be applied to our problem scenario.

The literature proposes a variety of algorithms [1,13,18,19,22,27] that focus on skyline computation over vertically partitioned data and for multi-relational settings where joins are required. Balke et al. [1] propose algorithms (BDS and

IDS) to compute skylines over vertically partitioned data where each server hosts a single skyline attribute. The BDS algorithm uses sorted access until a pivot data object is reached at all servers. Then, other attributes of the data objects that are better than the pivot object in at least one attribute are obtained by random access from the servers. The IDS algorithm improves BDS by using a combination of sorted and random access to reach the pivot object. Jin et al. [13] introduce the multi-relation skyline operator. Vlachou et al. [27] propose the sort-first skyline join (SFSJ) algorithm that provides an early termination condition and makes it possible to compute skyline objects progressively. Trimponias et al. [22] address the skyline computation problem in a setting where each server has a disjoint set of attributes together with a record ID. Their algorithm is able to support any decomposition of the attributes among the servers. Nagendra et al. [18,19] improve the state-of-the-art algorithms by applying region based pruning before skyline computation. In our case, we assume that we access the knowledge graph via standard interfaces – potentially on remote servers. Unfortunately, these interfaces do not provide sorted access and random access at the same time, which renders the above mentioned techniques inapplicable. There are also numerous approaches on horizontally partitioned data in P2P systems [10–12,26,28]. These systems differ substantially from our setup as the data is typically located on remote peers in a distance of several hops without knowing which peers exactly provide relevant data for a given query. In this paper, however, we assume a direct connection to the relevant server.

There are a couple of studies [5,20,21,23,29] on incorporating preference-based querying over knowledge graphs. Some studies [20,21,23] propose ways of extending SPARQL for expressing preferences. Siberski et al. [21] provide a proof-of-concept implementation based on BNL. We also use the BNL algorithm as a straightforward solution for skyline computation over existing interfaces. Troumpoukis et al. [23] compare the performance of NL, BNL, and query rewriting. Patel-Schneider et al. [20] claim the extension for preferences can be efficiently integrated into SPARQL endpoints by using union-find algorithms. We do not focus on extending SPARQL in this paper. Chen et al. [5] focus on skyline computation on knowledge graphs that are stored as vertically partitioned relations. They use a header point (pivot object) to prune non-skyline entities. However, as our goal is to enable skyline query processing using existing interfaces, we cannot make assumptions on how the data is stored. For this reason, the algorithms proposed in [5] are not applicable to our case. Zheng et al. [29] propose subgraph skyline analysis over knowledge graphs. However, their methods require precomputing additional bit-string encodings for each vertex and edge. Again, as we do not assume that we have control over how the knowledge graph is stored, this approach is not applicable to our problem scenario. In addition, we do not want to increase the load on the server too much by pushing more work to the server for skyline computation since that would reduce throughput and therefore counteract the idea of TPF.

In addition to skyline querying over knowledge graphs, Lukasiewicz et al. [16] extend Datalog+/- with preferences and propose algorithms to execute preference queries over ontologies [16]. These queries are defined using first order logic formulas that allow including more general preferences than skyline queries. However, preference queries on ontologies are out of scope of this paper.

3 Preliminaries

RDF [4] is a standard data format that is widely used to represent information on the Web; its basic building block is a triple. A triple is defined as a 3-tuple $t = \langle s, p, o \rangle$, where s, p, and o correspond to *subject, predicate* and *object*, respectively. The subject of a triple identifies an entity and is either an IRI or a blank node. The predicate is an IRI representing the relation between subject and object. And the object can be an IRI, a literal, or a blank node. A knowledge graph is then defined as a set of triples. In this paper, we assume that the knowledge graph does not contain blank nodes because blank nodes do not represent any entities.

Definition 1 (Triple Pattern and Basic Graph Pattern). *Let I, L, and V be the pairwise disjoint sets of IRIs, literals, and variables. A triple pattern then is an element of $(I \cup L \cup V) \times (I \cup V) \times (I \cup L \cup V)$. We say that a triple $t = \langle s, p, o \rangle$ is a matching triple for a triple pattern $tp = \langle s_{tp}, p_{tp}, o_{tp} \rangle$ or t satisfies tp if $(s_{tp} = s \vee s_{tp} \in V) \wedge (p_{tp} = p \vee p_{tp} \in V) \wedge (o_{tp} = o \vee o_{tp} \in V)$. The solution to a triple pattern is a mapping μ from V to $I \cup L$, i.e., the possible mappings for each variable in the triple pattern. A basic graph pattern (BGP) is a set of triple patterns. The solution to a BGP is the mappings obtained by joining the solution mappings of each triple pattern included in the BGP.*

After defining the basics of knowledge graphs, let us now define skyline sets and skyline queries.

Definition 2 (Skyline Set and Dominance). *Given a dataset D of n-dimensional data objects, $o_i \in D$ dominates $o_j \in D$ $(o_i \succ o_j)$ if o_i is better than or equal to o_j in all n dimensions and is strictly better than o_j in at least one dimension with respect to user-defined preference functions. The skyline set $S = \{o \mid o \in D \wedge \nexists e (e \in D \wedge e \succ o)\}$ consists of the objects that are not dominated by any other object. If two objects o_i and o_j do not have a dominance relation between them, we say that o_i and o_j are not comparable.*

In knowledge graphs, data objects correspond to real-life entities, such as people, cities, and countries. A skyline query over a knowledge graph is then defined as follows.

Definition 3 (Skyline Query over Knowledge Graphs). *Given a knowledge graph K, a skyline query is defined as a pair $q = \langle BGP, SV \rangle$, where BGP is a basic graph pattern and SV is a set of pairs, each of which is a skyline variable with its corresponding preference function (`MIN`, `MAX`). Skyline variables are a subset of variables included in the basic graph pattern. The result of a skyline query is the skyline set of the solutions to BGP computed with respect to the skyline variables and the preference functions. The variables of the skyline query* *that the preferences are defined on are called dimension variables. A query with two dimension variables is then called a 2-dimensional skyline query.*

For instance, $SV = \{\langle ?v_1, \texttt{MIN}\rangle, \langle ?v_2, \texttt{MAX}\rangle\}$ means that the user is interested in a skyline over $?v_1$ and $?v_2$, and MIN and MAX will be used to determine dominance between the solution mappings.

In line with [5], we use an extended version of SPARQL to express a skyline query. The extension contains a **SKYLINE** keyword together with **MIN** and **MAX** keywords to be able to express preference functions. The query for the motivational example is illustrated in Listing 1.1.

```
SELECT ?planet ?as ?d
WHERE
{ ?planet rdf:type dbpedia:Planet .                    #11826 triples
  ?planet dbpedia:averageSpeed ?as .                   #739 triples
  ?planet dbpedia:density ?d .                         #146 triples
}
SKYLINE OF ?as MAX, ?d MAX
```

Listing 1.1. Example Skyline Query

4 Skylines over Standard Interfaces

In this section, we propose client-side algorithms for processing skyline queries over knowledge graphs using standard interfaces (SPARQL endpoints and Triple Pattern Fragments) that are commonly used to provide access to knowledge graphs on the Web.

4.1 SPARQL Endpoint

SPARQL endpoints are widely used to query knowledge graphs on the Web using the SPARQL query language [7]. As SPARQL does not cover skyline queries, such servers do not directly support them. Hence, we propose a client-side algorithm that computes skylines while only sending standard SPARQL queries to the server (SPARQL endpoint).

The client-side algorithm first retrieves the solution mappings μ for the basic graph pattern of the query ($q.BGP$) from the SPARQL endpoint. Then, we compute the skyline over μ in a block-nested-loop fashion, i.e., we maintain a skyline set S and scan μ sequentially. When a mapping m is read from μ, the algorithm checks whether m is dominated by any mapping currently in S. If so, the algorithm continues with the next mapping. Otherwise, the mappings that are dominated by m are removed from S, and m is added to S. After iterating over all mappings in μ, S corresponds to the skyline set and it represents the output.

Example. Let us assume that Table 1 corresponds to the output mappings for the BGP of the example query from Listing 1.1. Saturn is read first and added to

Table 1. Output mappings for our example query

?planet	?as (km/s)	?d (kg/m^3)
Saturn	9.69	687
Europa (Moon)	13.74	3010
Neptune	5.43	1638
Jupiter	13.07	1326
Uranus	6.81	1270
Earth	29.78	5515
Venus	35.02	5243
Himalia (Moon)	3.312	2600

the skyline set S. Europa (Moon) is considered next. Since it dominates Saturn, it is added to S and Saturn is removed from S. Neptune, Jupiter, and Uranus are considered next consecutively but they are not added to S since they are dominated by Europa (Moon). Next, Earth is added to S since it dominates Europa (Moon) and the latter is removed from S. Venus is also added to S since it is incomparable with Earth: Venus has a higher average speed but Earth has a higher density. When Himalia (Moon) is read, it is not added to S since it is dominated by Earth. The final skyline set is then $S = \{\texttt{Earth}, \texttt{Venus}\}$.

4.2 Triple Pattern Fragments (TPF)

The TPF interface [25] was proposed to increase availability and throughput of the servers by reducing their computational load. A server hosting a SPARQL endpoint has to perform all the tasks that are related to query processing such as query planning, executing joins, and filtering operations included in the query. However, a TPF server is designed only to process triple pattern requests in a paged manner. A TPF request contains a single triple pattern and a page number. The response to a TPF request is a page containing a set of matching triples together with metadata containing an estimation of the total number of matching triples. Hence, a TPF server only returns the matching triples for an input triple pattern without having to invest extensive resources on query processing. For this reason, the workload of TPF servers is much lower than of SPARQL endpoints. On the other hand, the workload at the client is considerably higher.

Our client-side algorithm builds upon the query processing algorithm proposed by Verborgh et al. [25] to retrieve the solution mappings for the basic graph pattern of a skyline query ($q.BGP$). The algorithm first iterates over the triple patterns of $q.BGP$. At each iteration, the algorithm chooses the most selective triple pattern as the next triple pattern to process. In order to find the most selective triple pattern, the algorithm retrieves the first pages of each triple pattern in $q.BGP$ to obtain the number of matching triples for each triple pattern.

The algorithm then retrieves all matching triples for the most selective triple pattern. The remaining triple patterns are updated with respect to the obtained bindings.

For instance, to process the basic graph pattern of the query given in Listing 1.1, the algorithm first processes the third triple pattern since it has the least number of matching triples (146). If the number of triples per page is 100[1], we need to send two requests for this triple pattern with page numbers set to 1 and 2. After retrieving the triples and initializing the mappings for `?planet`, the algorithm instantiates 146 triple patterns for each remaining triple pattern by replacing `?planet` with these mappings. So, for processing the remaining two triple patterns, we have 292 instantiated triple patterns (requests). Once all requests have been successfully processed, the skyline is computed over the output mappings as described in Sect. 4.1.

4.3 Bindings-Restricted Triple Pattern Fragments

As explained in the previous section, the TPF interface was designed to reduce the workload of servers when querying knowledge graphs. However, it leads to a higher client-side workload since clients are responsible for processing joins. Moreover, it also creates a higher network load since a TPF client has to send a high number of requests to process a query. In order to address these drawbacks, Hartig et al. [8] proposed the Bindings-restricted Triple Pattern Fragments (brTPF) interface. The key consideration is that the request sent to the server does not only contain a triple pattern but also a set of mappings originating from intermediate results computed at the client, which are used to prune the matches of the triple pattern. The number of mappings sent together is determined by a parameter ($maxMpR$). In the original paper, this parameter is set to values between 5 to 50 since more than 50 bindings result in "414 (URI too long)" response due to being included in HTTP GET requests [8]. In this paper we set $maxMpR$ to 30[2].

Processing skyline queries over standard brTPF interfaces in principle works the same as with TPF interfaces. The only difference is that instead of sending separate requests for each mapping obtained from the first triple pattern, the algorithm sends mappings in groups of 30 in a single request to the brTPF server. This reduces the number of requests to 10 (5 for each remaining triple pattern) instead of 292 for the example query given in Listing 1.1. Once all requests have been successfully processed, the skyline is computed over the retrieved mappings as described in Sect. 4.1.

5 Skylines over SkyTPF Interface

In this section, we propose an extension of the brTPF interface for skyline query processing and a client-server hybrid algorithm to compute skylines efficiently.

[1] Recommended page size according to [25].

[2] Recommended value according to [8].

5.1 SkyTPF Interface

The client-side algorithms presented in Sect. 4 do not take the skyline properties into account while processing the skyline query and therefore return all matching triples regardless of whether the corresponding entities can be part of the skyline or not. However, by taking skyline properties into account, the server can prune the search space and increase efficiency.

The main idea behind SkyTPF is to use a pivot entity to prune the set of skyline candidates. It is a mapping for the variables in triple patterns processed so far. We add (i) a pivot entity, (ii) a skyline flag, (iii) a skyline variable, and (iv) a skyline preference function to the request sent to the server. If the skyline flag is not set, it is identical to brTPF. Otherwise, the server returns the triples whose corresponding entities are better than or equal to the pivot entity with respect to the given skyline variable and preference function. Since the same pivot entity is used for all the skyline triple patterns, i.e., the triple patterns containing skyline variables, any entity that is not returned from the server cannot be part of the skyline since it is guaranteed that any such entity is dominated by the pivot entity. We therefore propose a minimal extension to the brTPF interface to retain the characteristics of TPF (shifting load to the clients) while still improving skyline query performance.

In line with the definitions of bindings-restricted triple pattern selector and bindings restricted triple pattern fragment collection (Definitions 1 and 2, [8]), we define skyline binding-restricted triple pattern selector and skyline triple pattern fragment as follows:

Definition 4 (Skyline Binding-Restricted Triple Pattern Selector). *A selector is a function that selects triples from a knowledge graph according to the provided input. Given a triple pattern tp, a finite sequence of mappings Ω, a skyline flag sf that is either* 0 *or* 1*, a skyline preference function sp that is either* `MIN` *or* `MAX`*, a pivot entity pe that satisfies tp, a skyline triple pattern selector for tp, Ω, sf, sp and pe, denoted by $s_G(tp, \Omega, sf, sp, pe)$ for a knowledge graph G is defined by Eq. 1. In this equation, $m(tp, G, \Omega)$ denotes the matching triples for tp that are compatible with the mappings included in Ω. If $\Omega = \emptyset$, then $m(tp, G, \Omega)$ is simply the set of matching triples.*

$$s_G(tp,\Omega,sf,sp,pe) = \begin{cases} m(tp, G, \Omega) & \text{if } sf = 0 \\ \{t \mid t \in m(tp, G, \Omega) \wedge (t \succeq_{sp} pe)\} & \text{if } sf = 1 \wedge pe \text{ is set} \end{cases} \quad (1)$$

In Eq. 1, $t \succeq_{sp} pe$ denotes that corresponding entity of t either dominates or is equal to pe according to the skyline preference function sp and the skyline variable in tp. As shown in Eq. 1, when the skyline flag sf is 0*, the selector function is just a bindings-restricted triple pattern selector.*

Definition 5 (Skyline Triple Pattern Fragment). *A Linked Data Fragment (LDF) is defined as a 5-tuple $f = \langle u, s, \Gamma, M, C \rangle$, where u is a URI that hosts the fragment f, s is a selector function, Γ is the set of triples that are selected with respect to s, M is a finite set of RDF triples that contains metadata regarding f,* *and C is a finite set of hypermedia controls (Definition 2, [25]). A skyline triple pattern fragment (SkyTPF) collection is defined for a given hypermedia control c, and a maxMpR value. A specific LDF collection F is called a SkyTPF collection if there exists one LDF $\langle u, s, \Gamma, M, C \rangle \in F$ for any possible triple pattern tp, any finite sequence of solution mappings Ω with at most maxMpR mappings, any possible skyline flag sf, any possible skyline preference function sp, and any possible pivot entity pe with the following conditions: (i) The selector function s is a skyline bindings-restricted triple pattern selector for tp, Ω, sf, sp, pe, (ii) there is a triple $\langle \mathtt{u}, \mathtt{void{:}triples}, \mathtt{cnt} \rangle \in M$, where* `cnt` *represents a cardinality estimate for Γ (if $\Gamma = \emptyset$, then $\mathtt{cnt} = 0$), and (iii) $c \in C$.*

Implementation. The SkyTPF server is implemented using Java and extends the brTPF server implementation provided by Hartig et al. [8]. The implementation is available online[3] and uses RDF-HDT data sources [17].

A SkyTPF server is able to serve multiple data sources as TPF and brTPF. For each data source, the server creates an HDT index file, together with a dictionary-based index that holds the rank of each subject (i.e. entity) for each skyline preference function and for each predicate with a numeric value. To put differently, given a subject URI of an entity, it is possible to get the rank of the entity for a specific predicate and for a specific skyline preference function using the index. When a request is received, the server iterates over the mappings provided in the request to construct the set of triple patterns that will be used to query the data source. For each mapping, the server updates the variables of the input triple pattern according to the mapping and adds the triple pattern to this set. Then, the HDT backend is queried using these triple patterns. The resulting triples are added to the output set if their corresponding entity has a rank at least equal to the pivot entity according to the skyline preference function.

Client-Side Query Processing Algorithm. The complete algorithm to process skyline queries over SkyTPF interfaces is sketched in Algorithm 1.

The client first decomposes the skyline query into skyline and non-skyline subqueries (lines 1 and 2); the skyline subquery consists of the triple patterns containing skyline attributes and the remaining triple patterns constitute the non-skyline subquery. Then, the non-skyline subquery is processed using the SkyTPF endpoint (line 3); the skyline flag is set to 0 to process this subquery in a brTPF fashion.

Next, the algorithm determines the pivot using the skyline subquery (line 4) – we explain how to choose the pivot entity later. The set of candidate skyline results is populated by sending SkyTPF requests for each triple pattern in the skyline subquery (lines 6–15). Afterwards, the missing mappings for the skyline variables are retrieved for the incomplete mappings included in the candidate set. Finally, the algorithm computes the skyline in a block-nested-loop fashion and returns the output (lines 16 and 17).

[3] https://github.com/ilkcan/skyTPF-server.

Algorithm 1. Skyline query processing over SkyTPF interface

Input: $q = \langle BGP, SV \rangle$ - a skyline query, *url* - a SkyTPF endpoint URL
Output: S - the set of skyline entities

$sTPs \leftarrow$ triple patterns that contain a skyline attribute
$nsTPs \leftarrow q.BGP \setminus sTPs$
Process the non-skyline subquery and initialize the set of mappings μ by sending brTPF requests to *url*
$pe =$ **DeterminePivot**$(url, \mu, sTPs)$
$candSkylines = \emptyset$
for all tp in $sTPs$ **do**
  Retrieve the matching triples by sending a skyTPF request for tp with pe and the corresponding skyline preference function and initialize the mappings μ_{tp} wrt the triples
  for all m in μ_{tp} **do**
    if A mapping m_s contains the subject mapping of m exists in *candSkylines* **then**
      Extend m_s with m
    else
      Add m to *candSkylines*
    end if
  end for
end for
Retrieve missing skyline variables of *candSkylines* by sending brTPF requests
Compute the set of skyline entities S by applying BNL algorithm
return S

We extend our SkyTPF server to return triples in a paged manner when the skyline flag is set and no pivot mapping is provided. The output triples match with the input triple pattern and their corresponding entities are better than remaining entities that have a matching triple according to a skyline attribute and a skyline preference function. The motivation behind this extension is twofold. First, we need to guarantee that the pivot entity has a matching triple for each skyline triple pattern. Second, if a pivot entity is better than most of the entities that have matching triples for all skyline triple patterns, it provides a higher pruning power.

To determine the pivot, we first retrieve the first pages of all skyline triple patterns using this extension. If there is an entity that is present in the outputs of all skyline triple patterns and if this entity is included in the output of the non-skyline subquery, this entity is chosen as the pivot entity. Otherwise, the algorithm continues with the next page.

Example. The complete example for processing a 2-dimensional skyline query using the SkyTPF interface is given in Fig. 2. The query is defined as $q.BGP = \{\langle ?id, a_1, ?A_1 \rangle, \langle ?id, a_2, ?A_2 \rangle\}$ and $q.SV = \{\langle ?A_1, \texttt{MAX} \rangle \langle ?A_2, \texttt{MAX} \rangle\}$. For ease of presentation, we leave the non-skyline triple patterns out and assume that the non-skyline output is $O = \{A, B, C, D, E, F, G\}$. In order to determine the pivot

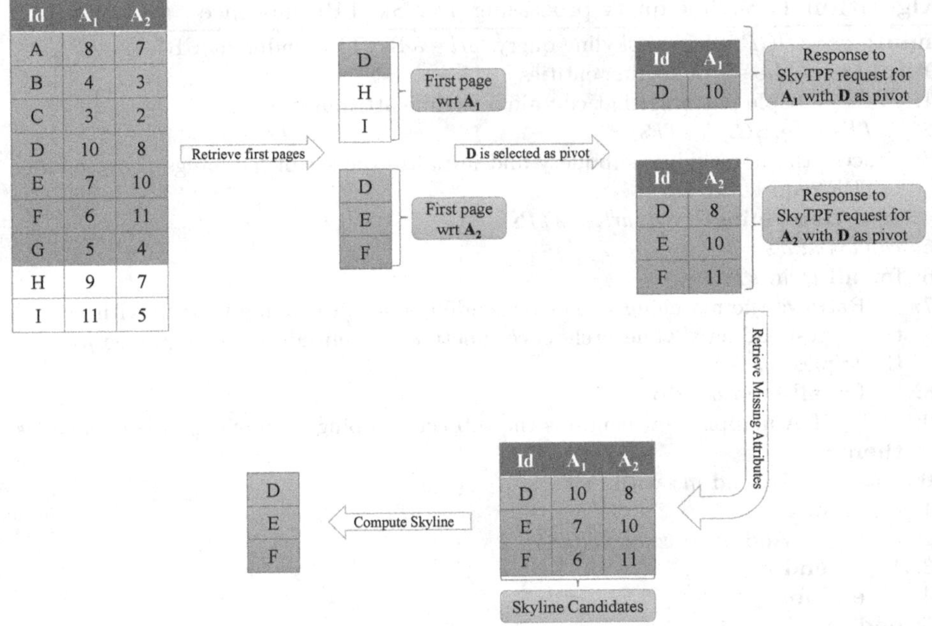

Fig. 2. Example skyline computation

entity, the algorithm requests first pages of the triple patterns that include the skyline attributes A_1 and A_2. Since D is part of both pages and is also included in the non-skyline output, it is selected as the pivot entity. Then, the algorithm determines the set of candidates $S_c = \{D, E, F\}$ by sending a SkyTPF request for each attribute and combine the responses. The algorithm then obtains the A_1 values for E and F by sending a brTPF request. Finally, we compute the skyline in a block-nested-loop fashion as described in Sect. 4 and obtain $\{D, E, F\}$ as the output.

5.2 Extensions

The proposed algorithms can be extended to cases where data is horizontally or vertically partitioned. Horizontal partitioning occurs when each server stores all triples of a set of entities and vertical partitioning occurs when each server stores a set of predicates. In the case of horizontal partitioning, the algorithm can be applied on each server to compute the skylines for the server and then a second iteration is needed to compute the global skylines. In the case of vertical partitioning, the client needs to send the requests to the server that contains the predicate included in the triple pattern.

6 Experimental Evaluation

This section discusses the results of our evaluation. We first explain the experimental setup in Sect. 6.1 and we discuss the evaluation results in Sect. 6.2.

6.1 Experimental Setup

For the experimental evaluation, we have implemented both single-threaded and multi-threaded versions of the proposed algorithms for TPF, brTPF, and SkyTPF. The multi-threaded versions send HTTP requests in parallel and the number of threads is set to the number of CPUs in the machine. We did not include the SPARQL endpoint based algorithm since it is shown to increase the load on the server significantly compared to TPF and brTPF [8,25].

We considered comparing our work against a client-side skyline query processing algorithm based on SPARQL query rewriting [23]. However, it has already been shown that BNL outperforms such an algorithm because of expensive not exists and filter clauses [23]; query re-writing performs better in only 1 out of 7 queries. Since we use the BNL algorithm in our client-side query processing algorithms, we do not include a comparison in our evaluation.

Datasets and Queries. We evaluate the proposed methods on synthetic datasets in line with the literature [2,3,5,6] due to a number of reasons. First, when we evaluate the methods on synthetic data, we know the underlying distribution and we are able to see the effect of the underlying distribution on the performance of the methods. Second, we might introduce a bias in favor of one algorithm due to the query selection procedure and due to missing information when we use real datasets. We generated synthetic datasets with independent, correlated, and anti-correlated distributions using the data generator provided by Börzsönyi et al. [3]. In the correlated distribution, if an entity is good in one dimension, it is highly likely that it is good in other dimensions as well. In the anti-correlated distribution, the opposite holds; good in one dimension, bad in another. In the independent distribution, the dimensions follow uniform distribution, so that the probability that an entity is better than another entity with respect to a skyline dimension is independent from their relationship with respect to another skyline dimension. The anti-correlated distribution is the worst scenario for any skyline algorithm since it means that almost every entity is part of the skyline and it is therefore quite difficult to prune the search space. The number of entities in the generated datasets is between 10,000 and 50,000, and the number of skyline dimensions is between 2 and 6. A skyline query in our setup contains all the skyline dimensions included in the dataset. If not explicitly mentioned otherwise, the default number of entities is 10,000 and the default number of skyline variables (dimensions) is 4.

Metrics. To evaluate and compare these approaches, we have measured the number of HTTP requests sent to the server, the number of candidates that the client computes the skylines on, and the query processing time. The number of HTTP requests provides a measure to assess the network load introduced by an algorithm. We present a single value for each method for this metric since multi-threading does not have an effect on it. We decided to include the number of skyline candidates metric in our experimental evaluation to assess the effect of pruning for the SkyTPF-based method.

Configuration. The server is hosted on a virtual machine with 4 2.29 GHZ CPUs and 8 GB of main memory and the client is hosted on a virtual machine with 2 2.29 GHZ CPUs and 2 GB of main memory.

6.2 Evaluation Results

Figure 3 shows the pruning power of SkyTPF's client algorithm for different dataset distributions. As expected, SkyTPF's pivot based pruning is quite effective for the correlated dataset. The number of skyline candidates for the independent dataset is below 50% of the number of entities even for 6 dimensions. Moreover, the number of skyline candidates for the dataset including 50K entities is less than 10K which means that our algorithm manages to prune 80% of the entities. As expected, the figure also shows that the algorithm based on SkyTPF has very low pruning power when the dataset is anti-correlated.

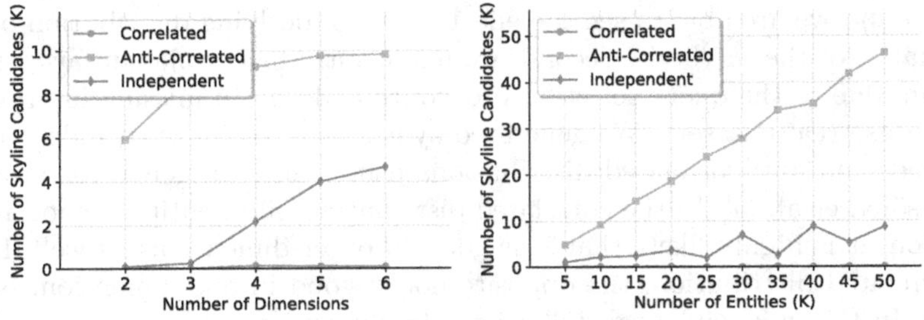

Fig. 3. Pruning power of SkyTPF's client algorithm

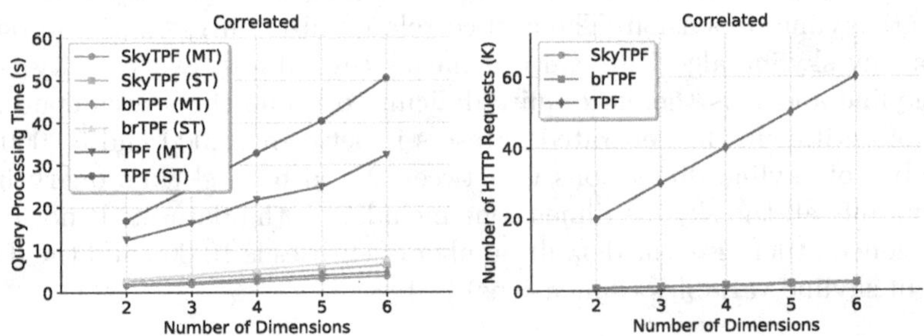

Fig. 4. Effect of the number of dimensions (correlated dataset)

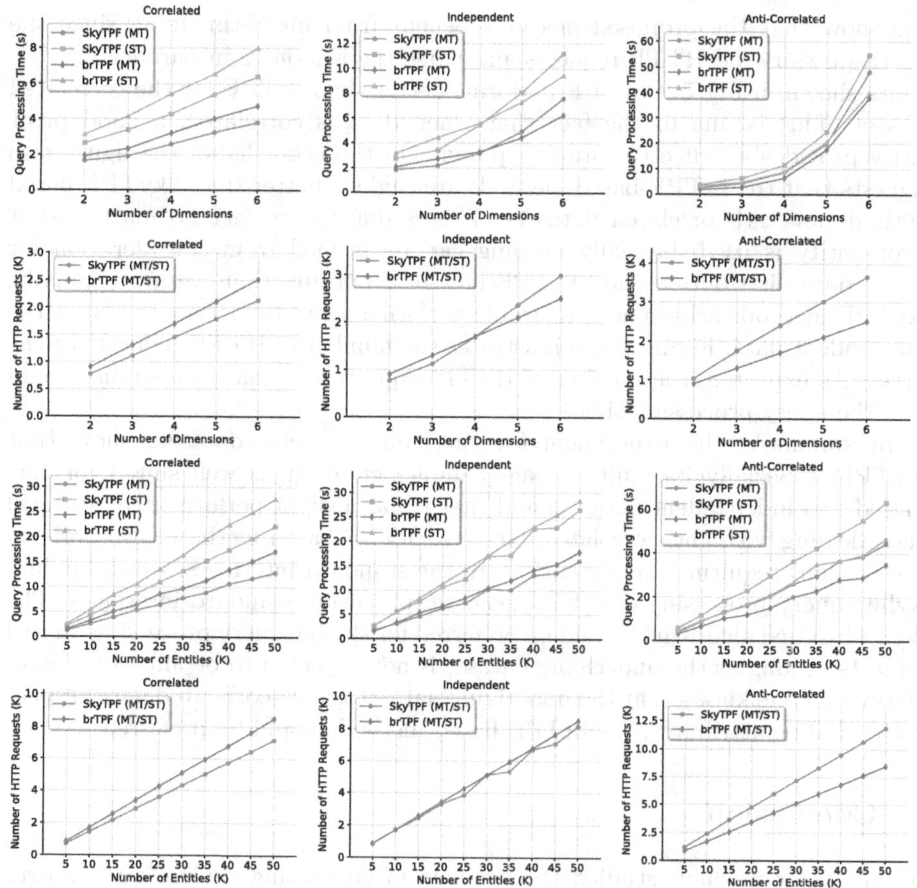

Fig. 5. Effect of the number of dimensions and the number of entities on brTPF-based and SkyTPF-based methods

Figure 4 illustrates the effect of the number of dimensions on the proposed algorithms for the correlated dataset. The TPF-based client-side algorithm performs significantly worse than the brTPF-based and SkyTPF-based algorithms. The TPF-based algorithm is between 6–8 times slower and needs at least an order of magnitude more HTTP requests to process skyline queries. To present the performance difference between algorithms more clearly and to demonstrate the results in a finer granularity, we omit our results for TPF.

Figure 5 shows the effect of the number of entities and the number of skyline dimensions on the proposed methods for different data distributions. The performance of the proposed methods becomes worse as the number of entities and the number of skyline variables increase for all distributions. This is expected since the number of dominance checks and the number of variables that the dominance will be checked on increases, respectively. The experimental results also show that the proposed methods benefit from multi-threading since the algorithm can send HTTP requests and parse the responses in parallel.

As shown in Fig. 5, SkyTPF performs better than brTPF for the correlated dataset. This is due to the fact that when data is correlated, a good pivot entity provides an effective pruning power. On the other hand, the figure also suggests that the brTPF-based methods are slightly better than SkyTPF-based methods for anti-correlated datasets. This is due to the fact no matter what pivot entity is used, basically nothing can be pruned from consideration for such a data distribution and SkyTPF has some optimization overhead. Finally, SkyTPF-methods achieve a comparable performance to brTPF-methods for the independent data. Figure 5 also illustrates the number of HTTP requests to the server. As expected, the number of HTTP requests also follows a similar trend with the query processing time.

In summary, the experimental results on synthetic datasets show that SkyTPF, especially its multi-threaded implementation, is well suited for correlated and independent datasets and that it has a slight performance overhead when dealing with anti-correlated datasets. brTPF-based methods also perform well without requiring any extensions to the standard interfaces, which enables skyline query processing over knowledge graphs using standard interfaces. The SkyTPF-based algorithm should be preferred for skyline query processing on real datasets as long as the underlying dataset is not expected to be anti-correlated. However, if one knows that the underlying dataset is anti-correlated with respect to the skyline attributes, the brTPF-based method should be preferred.

7 Conclusion

In this paper we have studied the problem of computing skyline queries over knowledge graphs and proposed solutions that exploit standard interfaces to help the user find interesting entities. Furthermore, we propose, SkyTPF, a lightweight extension of standard interfaces to process skyline queries more efficiently by pruning the search space. The experimental evaluation shows that the proposed methods are capable of computing skylines with reasonable response times. The evaluation also suggests that one should use SkyTPF-based method for skyline query processing unless the distribution of the data is expected to be anti-correlated. In our future work, we plan to increase efficiency of skyline computation by using index structures and support skyline query processing over federations of endpoints/knowledge graphs.

Acknowledgments. This research was partially funded by the Danish Council for Independent Research (DFF) under grant agreement no. DFF-4093-00301B and Aalborg University's Talent Programme.

References

1. Balke, W.-T., Güntzer, U., Zheng, J.X.: Efficient distributed skylining for web information systems. In: Bertino, E., et al. (eds.) EDBT 2004. LNCS, vol. 2992, pp. 256–273. Springer, Heidelberg (2004). https://doi.org/10.1007/978-3-540-24741-8_16
2. Bartolini, I., Ciaccia, P., Patella, M.: SaLSa: computing the skyline without scanning the whole sky. In: CIKM 2006, pp. 405–414 (2006)
3. Börzsönyi, S., Kossmann, D., Stocker, K.: The skyline operator. In: ICDE 2001, pp. 421–430 (2001)
4. Candan, K.S., Liu, H., Suvarna, R.: Resource description framework: metadata and its applications. SIGKDD Explor. Newsl. **3**(1), 6–19 (2001)
5. Chen, L., Gao, S., Anyanwu, K.: Efficiently evaluating skyline queries on RDF databases. In: Antoniou, G., et al. (eds.) ESWC 2011. LNCS, vol. 6644, pp. 123–138. Springer, Heidelberg (2011). https://doi.org/10.1007/978-3-642-21064-8_9
6. Chomicki, J., Godfrey, P., Gryz, J., Liang, D.: Skyline with presorting. In: ICDE 2003, pp. 717–719 (2003)
7. Clark, K., Feigenbaum, L., Williams, G., Torres, E.: SPARQL 1.1 protocol. W3C recommendation, W3C, March 2013. http://www.w3.org/TR/2013/REC-sparql11-protocol-20130321/
8. Hartig, O., Buil-Aranda, C.: Bindings-restricted triple pattern fragments. In: Debruyne, C., et al. (eds.) OTM 2016. LNCS, vol. 10033, pp. 762–779. Springer, Cham (2016). https://doi.org/10.1007/978-3-319-48472-3_48
9. Hoffart, J., Suchanek, F.M., Berberich, K., Weikum, G.: YAGO2: a spatially and temporally enhanced knowledge base from Wikipedia. Artif. Intell. **194**, 28–61 (2013)
10. Hose, K., Lemke, C., Sattler, K.-U.: Processing relaxed skylines in PDMS using distributed data summaries. In: CIKM 2006, pp. 425–434 (2006)
11. Hose, K., Lemke, C., Sattler, K.-U., Zinn, D.: A relaxed but not necessarily constrained way from the top to the sky. In: Meersman, R., Tari, Z. (eds.) OTM 2007. LNCS, vol. 4803, pp. 399–407. Springer, Heidelberg (2007). https://doi.org/10.1007/978-3-540-76848-7_27
12. Hose, K., Vlachou, A.: A survey of skyline processing in highly distributed environments. VLDB J. **21**(3), 359–384 (2012)
13. Jin, W., Ester, M., Hu, Z., Han, J.: The multi-relational skyline operator. In: ICDE 2007, pp. 1276–1280 (2007)
14. Kung, H.T., Luccio, F., Preparata, F.P.: On finding the maxima of a set of vectors. J. ACM **22**(4), 469–476 (1975)
15. Lehmann, J., et al.: Dbpedia - a large-scale, multilingual knowledge base extracted from Wikipedia. Semant. Web **6**(2), 167–195 (2015)
16. Lukasiewicz, T., Martinez, M.V., Simari, G.I.: Preference-based query answering in datalog+/- ontologies. In: IJCAI 2013, pp. 1017–1023 (2013)
17. Martínez-Prieto, M.A., Arias Gallego, M., Fernández, J.D.: Exchange and consumption of huge RDF data. In: Simperl, E., Cimiano, P., Polleres, A., Corcho, O., Presutti, V. (eds.) ESWC 2012. LNCS, vol. 7295, pp. 437–452. Springer, Heidelberg (2012). https://doi.org/10.1007/978-3-642-30284-8_36
18. Nagendra, M., Candan, K.S.: Skyline-sensitive joins with LR-pruning. In: EDBT 2012, pp. 252–263 (2012)
19. Nagendra, M., Candan, K.S.: Efficient processing of skyline-join queries over multiple data sources. ACM TODS **40**(2), 10:1–10:46 (2015)

20. Patel-Schneider, P.F., Polleres, A., Martin, D.: Comparative preferences in SPARQL. In: Faron Zucker, C., Ghidini, C., Napoli, A., Toussaint, Y. (eds.) EKAW 2018. LNCS (LNAI), vol. 11313, pp. 289–305. Springer, Cham (2018). https://doi.org/10.1007/978-3-030-03667-6_19
21. Siberski, W., Pan, J.Z., Thaden, U.: Querying the semantic web with preferences. In: Cruz, I., et al. (eds.) ISWC 2006. LNCS, vol. 4273, pp. 612–624. Springer, Heidelberg (2006). https://doi.org/10.1007/11926078_44
22. Trimponias, G., Bartolini, I., Papadias, D., Yang, Y.: Skyline processing on distributed vertical decompositions. IEEE TKDE **25**(4), 850–862 (2013)
23. Troumpoukis, A., Konstantopoulos, S., Charalambidis, A.: An extension of SPARQL for expressing qualitative preferences. In: d'Amato, C., et al. (eds.) ISWC 2017. LNCS, vol. 10587, pp. 711–727. Springer, Cham (2017). https://doi.org/10.1007/978-3-319-68288-4_42
24. Verborgh, R., et al.: Querying datasets on the web with high availability. In: Mika, P., et al. (eds.) ISWC 2014. LNCS, vol. 8796, pp. 180–196. Springer, Cham (2014). https://doi.org/10.1007/978-3-319-11964-9_12
25. Verborgh, R., et al.: Triple pattern fragments: a low-cost knowledge graph interface for the web. J. Web Semant. **37–38**, 184–206 (2016)
26. Vlachou, A., Doulkeridis, C., Kotidis, Y., Vazirgiannis, M.: SKYPEER: efficient subspace skyline computation over distributed data. In: ICDE, pp. 416–425 (2007)
27. Vlachou, A., Doulkeridis, C., Polyzotis, N.: Skyline query processing over joins. In: SIGMOD 2011, pp. 73–84 (2011)
28. Wang, S., Ooi, B.C., Tung, A.K.H., Xu, L.: Efficient skyline query processing on peer-to-peer networks. In: ICDE, pp. 1126–1135. IEEE Computer Society (2007)
29. Zheng, W., Lian, X., Zou, L., Hong, L., Zhao, D.: Online subgraph skyline analysis over knowledge graphs. IEEE TKDE **28**(7), 1805–1819 (2016)

Detecting Influences of Ontology Design Patterns in Biomedical Ontologies

Christian Kindermann(✉), Bijan Parsia, and Uli Sattler

University of Manchester, Manchester, UK
{christian.kindermann,bijan.parsia,uli.sattler}@manchester.ac.uk

Abstract. Ontology Design Patterns (ODP) have been proposed to facilitate ontology engineering. Despite numerous conceptual contributions for over more than a decade, there is little empirical work to support the often claimed benefits provided by ODPs. Determining ODP use from ontologies alone (without interviews or other supporting documentation) is challenging as there is no standard (or required) mechanism for stipulating the intended use of an ODP. Instead, we must rely on modelling features which are suggestive of a given ODP's influence. For the purpose of determining the prevalence of ODPs in ontologies, we developed a variety of techniques to detect these features with varying degrees of liberality. Using these techniques, we survey BioPortal with respect to well-known and publicly available repositories for ODPs. Our findings are predominantly negative. For the vast majority of ODPs we cannot find empirical evidence for their use in biomedical ontologies.

1 Introduction

The idea of Ontology Design Patterns (ODP) has been introduced as a means to facilitate ontology engineering [3,6]. Generally thought of as best practices and well-proven modelling solutions, a variety of different kinds of ODPs exist [1,3,7,26]. Despite conceptual contributions for more than a decade, there is very little empirical work to provide support for these claims. Ways of determining the prevalence of ODPs in practice is a first step into this direction. However, recognising ODP use from ontologies alone (without interviews or other supporting documentation) is challenging as there is no standard (or required) mechanism for stipulating the intended use of an ODP. In this paper, we take on this challenge and develop algorithmic techniques to automate the identification of a given ODP's influence.

The contributions are as follows: (i) we develop a variety of techniques to detect modelling features that are suggestive for a given ODP's influence, (ii) we characterise these techniques and discuss their informative value, (iii) and we perform an empirical study using these techniques to investigate the prevalence of ODPs in biomedical ontologies.

C. Ghidini et al. (Eds.): ISWC 2019, LNCS 11778, pp. 311–328, 2019.
https://doi.org/10.1007/978-3-030-30793-6_18

2 Background on Ontology Design Patterns

Different frameworks for working with patterns in Ontology Engineering have been proposed [3,4,6,12,20,22,25,28,29]. Each framework is based on a different approach for capturing the benefits of patterns and introduces its own terminology as well as its own notation. While these different approaches bear similarities to each other in some respects, there have been no efforts towards a standardisation process. Neither is there a generally accepted de facto standard for working with patterns in practice.

A unifying concept for a majority of frameworks for ODPs is a practical notion *pattern reuse*. Such notions often involve prefabricated components expressed in some representation formalism on the one hand, and operations to manipulate these components on the other.

Consider the following examples in which a pattern has been proposed to be reused as

- "[...] a first-order theory whose axioms are not part of the target knowledge base, but can be incorporated via renaming of their non-logical symbols [4]."
- "[*a*] distinguished ontolog[y]." The basic mechanism for its application is OWL ontology import in which pattern elements cannot be modified. Otherwise, common operations for patterns are "clone, specialisation, generalisation, composition, expansion" [20].
- "[...] an ontology fragment, including directly reusable elements (classes, properties, etc.) as well as demo-elements that would be replaced by the user's own. The directly reusable elements should typically be borrowed from upper level ontologies [28]."

Clearly, these ideas of pattern reuse are based on a set of predefined axioms that may or may not be modified. In the scope of this work, we will restrict our attention to ODPs of this kind, i.e., ODPs that are captured by a set of axioms or an OWL ontology. Such ODPs have been the focus of the academic literature for over a decade and are commonly classified into two types. One type addresses domain specific modelling problems, whereas the other is concerned with language specific modelling techniques. The former are generally discussed under the name of *Content Ontology Design Patterns* (CODP) and latter under the name of *Logical Ontology Design Patterns* (LODP).

CODPs are motivated as conceptual modelling solutions featuring a domain dependent signature, possibly extracted from Upper Level Ontologies to be applicable across different domains [20]. LODPs on the other hand are motivated as structural components that are domain-independent [6,21]. As a consequence, the former are characterised by a fixed set of unmodifiable axioms whereas the latter are characterised by a set of axioms containing variables.[1]

[1] These characterisations are not as clear-cut as they might appear. The discussion on the submission for the ODP `ContextSlices` http://ontologydesignpatterns.org/wiki/Submissions:Context_Slices exemplifies differences of opinion on the matter in the research community.

3 Pattern Detection

The lack of a generally agreed upon notion for ODP reuse poses a challenge for determining whether an ODP has in fact informed the design of a given ontology. Different approaches for ODP reuse result in different modelling features suggestive for a given ODP's influence. Therefore, we must design a detection mechanism that accounts for this uncertainty.

In the scope of this work, we limit our investigation to approaches that are based on ODPs documented with reusable components (cf. Sect. 2). Furthermore, we assume these components to be given in the form of ontologies or more generally sets of axioms. Given such a component $\mathcal{P}$, the problem of detecting modelling features which are suggestive of the ODP's influence in a given ontology $\mathcal{O}$ can be reduced to detecting features of $\mathcal{P}$ shared with $\mathcal{O}$. In the following, we formulate a list of non-exhaustive criteria that may be used to determine shared features between $\mathcal{P}$ and $\mathcal{O}$.

3.1 Detection Techniques

One of the earliest approaches for reusing an ODP's $\mathcal{P}$ proposed ontology import as the basic mechanism for reuse [20]. This approach has been adopted by the NeOn project[2] [21] and the large amount of work carried out in the context of this project has promulgated into the academic literature.

Import Containment. Detecting whether a given $\mathcal{P}$ of some ODP has been imported in an ontology $\mathcal{O}$ comes down to a straightforward analysis of $\mathcal{O}$'s import declaration. Given our primary concern of detecting an ODP's influence without any further qualification, we will generally equate an ontology with its import closure unless stated otherwise.

The analysis of $\mathcal{O}$'s import declarations is based on the two ways an ontology may be imported. Namely, *import by name* and *import by location*. Import by name is performed by interpreting the object of an import declaration as the name of an ontology in a predefined list of ontology repositories. If the object of an import declaration can be matched with the name of an ontology in said repositories, then the ontology is imported. Contrary, import by location is performed by interpreting the object of an import declaration as a physical location of an ontology. This location may be a location in the local file system.

Import by name allows for an unambiguous way to determine whether a given $\mathcal{P}$ has been imported, if its name in some ontology repository is known. Import by location on the other hand, poses a challenge due to the possibility of arbitrary renaming of local files. Nevertheless, it is reasonable to assume that the name of a local file is suggestive of its contents and to consider lexically similar import declarations as candidates for $\mathcal{P}$ reuse.

These consideration motivate a twofold detection procedure. First, check whether $\mathcal{P}$ is imported by using its known URL from a pattern repository as a

[2] http://neon-project.org/nw/Welcome_to_the_NeOn_Project.html.

name. If $\mathcal{P}$ is not found, test the import declarations in an ontology for lexically similar names to the one of $\mathcal{P}$. We refer to the former as the ImportByURLCheck and the latter as the ImportByLocation check.

Signature Overlap. It has been proposed to reuse a given $\mathcal{P}$ by copying its contents into a target $\mathcal{O}$ [24]. Copying any logical entities in $\mathcal{P}$ verbatim will result in syntactic traces, i.e, $\widetilde{\mathcal{P}} \cap \widetilde{\mathcal{O}} \neq \emptyset$, where $\widetilde{\mathcal{O}}$ denotes the signature of an ontology, i.e., its class, property, and individual names. Hence, we specify an IRICheck that tests for all logical axioms $\alpha \in \mathcal{P}$ whether the IRI of any entity name $e \in \widetilde{\alpha}$ occurs in $\mathcal{O}$. This occurrence test in $\mathcal{O}$ encompasses all of $\mathcal{O}$'s logical axioms as well as its non-logical components such as annotations and entity declarations.

In addition, we specify a NamespaceCheck that tests whether the object of a namespace declaration[3] in $\mathcal{P}$ can be matched within some IRI of entities in $\mathcal{O}$.

Lexical Variation. In addition to approaches preserving the IRIs of elements in $\mathcal{P}$ under reuse in $\mathcal{O}$, there are proposals allowing for the possibility of a renaming for copied elements [10]. In this case, the reuse of axioms $\alpha \in \mathcal{P}$ can be identified by some substitution[4] $\sigma : \widetilde{\mathcal{P}} \rightarrow \widetilde{\mathcal{O}}$ such that $\sigma(\alpha) \in \mathcal{O}$. However, with no information expressly declaring that $\mathcal{P}$ has been reused via some σ in $\mathcal{O}$, determining whether $\mathcal{P}$ has in fact been reused under some elusive substitution is a challenging task.

Based on the assumption that entities $p \in \widetilde{\alpha}$ ($\alpha \in \mathcal{P}$ being a logical axiom) exhibit lexical similarities to entities $\sigma(p) \in \widetilde{\mathcal{O}}$, we can attempt to generate candidate substitutions. Comparing an entity $p \in \widetilde{\mathcal{P}}$ with all entities $o \in \widetilde{\mathcal{O}}$ in terms of their lexical similarity, we can associate p with a set of possible renamings $R_p = \{r_1, \ldots, r_n\} \subseteq \widetilde{\mathcal{O}}$. Doing so for all entities $p_1, \ldots, p_n$ in $\mathcal{P}$'s signature results in a corresponding number of sets $R_{p_1}, \ldots, R_{p_n}$. Candidate substitutions σ are then generated by

$$\{\sigma \mid \sigma(p_i) \mapsto \pi_i(\boldsymbol{e}), \quad \boldsymbol{e} \in R_{p_1} \times \ldots \times R_{p_n}\},$$

where π_i is a projection map such that $\pi_i(\boldsymbol{e}) = e_i$ for $\boldsymbol{e} = (e_1, \ldots, e_n)$.

If $R_{p_1} \times \ldots \times R_{p_n}$ is non-empty, then there exists a candidate substitution σ. In that case, we specify a SubstitutionContainmentCheck that tests whether $\sigma(\alpha) \in \mathcal{O}$ holds for all $\alpha \in \mathcal{P}$ under some σ.

Logical Variation. Besides changing the signature of an ODP's $\mathcal{P}$, there have been proposals for ODP reuse based on reimplementing aspects of $\mathcal{P}$ by analogy [5]. In this case, both the logical structure as well as the signature

---

[3] https://www.w3.org/TR/2004/REC-owl-guide-20040210/#Namespaces.

[4] Substitutions are assumed to respect types, i.e., classes, properties, and individuals are only mapped to other classes, properties, and individuals respectively.

of axioms $\alpha \in \mathcal{P}$ may be subject to change. Based on motivations for logical rewritings of $\mathcal{P}$ [11], we specify a `SubstitutionEntailmentCheck` that tests whether there exists some substitution σ (generated as previously for the `SubstitutionContainmentCheck`) such that for all $\alpha \in \mathcal{P}$ it holds that $\mathcal{O} \models \sigma(\alpha)$.

Structural Axiom Agreement. In addition to detection techniques searching for positive evidence that is suggestive of a given ODP's $\mathcal{P}$, it is possible to test an ontology $\mathcal{O}$ for necessary structural conditions imposed by some notion of $\mathcal{P}$'s reuse. For example, positive evidence for $\mathcal{P}$ under the `SubstitutionContainmentCheck` requires an ontology $\mathcal{O}$ to contain structurally identical axioms to $\mathcal{P}$ since a simple renaming of entities in $\mathcal{P}$ does not affect the logical structure of axioms in $\mathcal{P}$. Therefore, if an ontology does not contain at least as many axioms of a given type as $\mathcal{P}$, then certain ways of $\mathcal{P}$'s reuse can be ruled out. Namely, any notion of ODP reuse that requires the explicit reuse of all axioms in $\mathcal{P}$.

Hence, we specify a structural `AxiomTypeCheck`, that tests whether $\mathcal{O}$ contains at least as many axioms of a given type[5] as $\mathcal{P}$.

Structural Expression Agreement. Orthogonal to a structural agreement in terms of axioms, we can specify structural expression checks that test whether some logical constructs or combination of logical constructs proposed by a given ODP's $\mathcal{P}$ occur in an ontology. For example, suppose a logical constructor, e.g. class union, occurs in some expression used in $\mathcal{P}$. If there is no such expression in a target ontology (as is often the case for biomedical ontologies conforming to the EL profile), then certain ways of reusing $\mathcal{P}$ can be ruled out.

In the context of this work, we specify expression checks for two logical structures that seem to be crucial for a fair number of ODPs. These structures are described by two LODPs, namely "Partition"[6] and "Nary-Relation"[7]. The former is characterised by a disjoint union of classes, whereas the latter is characterised by a class that is subsumed by at least two OWL restrictions. Accordingly, we define a `DisjointUnionCheck` that searches for the presence of disjoint unions as specified by the OWL Language Specification.[8] And furthermore, we define a `NaryRelationCheck` that searches for the presence of any class that is subsumed by at least two OWL restrictions.[9]

---

[5] The types of axioms we consider in this study are all subclasses of the OWLAxiom interface http://owlcs.github.io/owlapi/apidocs_5/org/semanticweb/owlapi/model/OWLAxiom.html of the well-known OWL API.

[6] http://odps.sourceforge.net/odp/html/Value_Partition.html.

[7] http://odps.sourceforge.net/odp/html/Nary_Relationship.html.

[8] https://www.w3.org/TR/owl2-syntax/#Disjoint_Union_of_Class_Expressions.

[9] http://owlcs.github.io/owlapi/apidocs_5/org/semanticweb/owlapi/model/OWLRestriction.

3.2 Characterisation of Detection Techniques

The detection techniques presented above all target some features of a given ODP's $\mathcal{P}$ which are deemed to be suggestive for an ODP's influence. The characteristics of these features allow us to qualify what kind of ODP reuse the respective detection technique is capable of identifying. For example, the `IRICheck` selects $\mathcal{P}$'s signature as a target feature of $\mathcal{P}$ for its detection. By doing so, the `IRICheck` is capable of detecting any notion of ODP reuse that preserves some element of $\mathcal{P}$'s signature. In the table below, we associate each detection technique (that searches for positive evidence of a given ODP's influence) with a corresponding notion of ODP reuse.[10] In the second column, we describe the potential kind of influence $\mathcal{I}$ of an ODP's $\mathcal{P}$ in a given ontology $\mathcal{O}$ and in the third column, we describe the relationship between $\mathcal{I}$ (occurring in $\mathcal{O}$) and $\mathcal{P}$. The influence $\mathcal{I}$ can manifest in several different forms, e.g. axioms, entities, annotations, etc. (Table 1).

Table 1. Association between detection techniques and notions of ODP reuse

Detection technique	Influence $\mathcal{I}$ in $\mathcal{O}$	Relation between $\mathcal{I}$ and $\mathcal{P}$	Notion of reuse
`ImportByURL`	$\mathcal{O}$ imports $\mathcal{I}$	$\mathcal{I} = \mathcal{P}$	Import
`ImportByLocation`	$\mathcal{O}$ imports $\mathcal{I}$	$\mathcal{I} = \mathcal{P}$	Import
`IRICheck`	$\widetilde{\mathcal{I}} \subseteq \widetilde{\mathcal{O}}$	$\widetilde{\mathcal{I}} \cap \widetilde{\mathcal{P}} \neq \emptyset$	Signature
`NamespaceCheck`	$\mathcal{I}$ occurs in $\mathcal{O}$	$\mathcal{I}$ points to $\mathcal{P}$	Reference
`SContainmentCheck`	$\mathcal{I} \subseteq \mathcal{O}$	$\sigma(\mathcal{I}) = \mathcal{P}$	Renaming
`EContainmentCheck`	$\mathcal{O} \models \mathcal{I}$	$\sigma(\mathcal{I}) = \mathcal{P}$	Rewriting

Furthermore, we can qualify the detectable notions of ODP reuse according to a number of characteristics. For example, the `SubstitutionContainmentCheck` targets notions of ODP reuse that allow for some form of *lexical* variation. However, it cannot detect influences of notions of ODP reuse that allow for *logical* variations, e.g, logically equivalent rewritings. Neither can it detect any notion of *partial* reuse that possibly omits some semantically relevant aspect of a given ODP. This is due to the requirement of *all* axioms $\alpha \in \mathcal{P}$ to be explicitly contained in $\mathcal{O}$ under some substitution (renaming) σ of entities $e \in \widetilde{\alpha}$ (cf. Sect. 3.1). Contrary, the `IRICheck` is able to detect influences of notions of partial ODP reuse that allow for logical variation. It only requires the preservation of some element of a given ODP's signature $\widetilde{\mathcal{P}}$.

In Table 2, we summarise characteristics of notions for ODP reuse that our detection techniques capture. We indicate for each notion of reuse whether variations of lexical or logical features are taken into account and whether a partial or complete reuse of a given ODP is assumed.

[10] The `SubstitutionContainmentCheck` has been abbreviated by `SContainmentCheck` for presentation purposes.

Table 2. Characterisation of detectable notions of ODP reuse

Detection technique	Notion of reuse	Feature variation	Reuse format
`ImportByURL`	Import	-	Complete
`ImportByLocation`	Import	-	Complete
`IRICheck`	Signature	Logical	Partial
`NamespaceCheck`	Reference	Lexical & Logical	Partial
`SContainmentCheck`	Renaming	Lexical	Complete
`EContainmentCheck`	Rewriting	Lexical & Logical	Complete

In addition to the detection techniques that aim to identify concrete positive evidence of a given ODP's influence, we have motivated detection techniques that can provide negative evidence for an ODP's reuse. Such negative evidence is established by the *absence* of distinguished features of a given ODP's $\mathcal{P}$. Accordingly, we can associate such detection techniques with features of $\mathcal{P}$ that are necessarily preserved under certain notions of reuse. On the one hand, there is the `AxiomTypeCheck` that is generally applicable for any ODP under any notion of reuse that preserves the logical structure of the pattern's corresponding $\mathcal{P}$. On the other hand, there are more specialised detection techniques that are tailored towards ODPs containing distinguished structural components, i.e. the `DisjointUnionCheck` and the `NAryRelationCheck`.

3.3 Algorithm

Most techniques introduced in the previous section involve some form of string comparison between entities of $\mathcal{O}$ and $\mathcal{P}$. In order to maximise the recall of lexical detection techniques, we employ a threefold string matching procedure – each step increasing the degree of liberality in terms of lexical similarity between two strings s_1 and s_2.

The first part is a strict equality that requires all symbols occurring in s_1 to coincide with symbols in s_2 at their respective positions. The second part is an approximate string match between s_1 and s_2. Here, all symbols not in the Latin alphabet are removed from both s_1 and s_2 and the remaining characters are converted to lower case. Then, a test for string containment of s_1 in s_2 is performed. The third part consists of calculating a string similarity greater that 0.8 based on the Levensthein distance.[11]

A lexical association between two elements $e_1 \in \widetilde{\mathcal{P}}$ and $e_2 \in \widetilde{\mathcal{O}}$ is established by applying the above string comparison procedure to

(1) both IRI's of e_1 and e_2,
(2) both ShortFormIRI's of e_1 and e_2,

[11] The distance is implemented via https://rosettacode.org/wiki/Levenshtein_distance#Java. The similarity score between $[0, 1]$ of two strings s_1, s_2 is calculated by $\frac{M - LevenstheinDistance(s_1,s_2)}{M}$ where M is $\max(s_1.length, s_2.length)$.

(3) the IRI of e_1 and the annotations of e_2,
(4) the ShortFormIRI of e_1 and the annotations of e_2.[12]

Using this string comparison procedure in lexical techniques as characterised in the previous section, we specify Algorithm 1 (see below) to detect influences of a given ODP exhibiting lexical modelling features.

For ODPs that only a structural reusable component $\mathcal{P}$ without a domain specific signature we cannot sensibly apply Algorithm 1. Instead, we only run the structural detection techniques, i.e. `AxiomTypeCheck`, `DisjointUnionCheck`, and `NAryRelationCheck`.

4 Methods

In Sect. 2, we have characterised the status quo of academic research around ODPs by a diversity of ideas regarding both the notion of ODPs itself and ODP reuse. This motivates an investigation of the research question as to how prevalent ODPs influences in biomedical ontologies are. In the following, we describe our procedure for answering this question.

Algorithm 1. Pattern Detection

Input : Ontology $\mathcal{O}$, Pattern $\mathcal{P}$
Output: Suggestive evidence for influence of $\mathcal{P}$ in $\mathcal{O}$

if *ImportByURL*($\mathcal{O}, \mathcal{P}$) **then**
  return *Import declarations in $\mathcal{O}$ containing $\mathcal{P}$*
if *ImportByLocation*($\mathcal{O}, \mathcal{P}$) **then**
  return *Import declarations in $\mathcal{O}$ containing $\mathcal{P}$*
if *IRICheck*($\mathcal{O}, \mathcal{P}$) **then**
  return *all $e \in \mathcal{O}$ that account for evidence of the check*
if *NamespaceCheck*($\mathcal{O}, \mathcal{P}$) **then**
  return *all $e \in \mathcal{O}$ that account for evidence of the check*
if *AxiomTypeCheck*($\mathcal{O}, \mathcal{P}$) **then**
  if *SubstitutionContainmentCheck*($\mathcal{O}, \mathcal{P}$) **then**
    return *All σ such that $\sigma(\mathcal{P}) \in \mathcal{O}$*
  end
if *SubstitutionEntailmentCheck*($\mathcal{O}, \mathcal{P}$) **then**
  return *All σ such that $\mathcal{O} \models \sigma(\mathcal{P})$*
end

4.1 Pattern Corpus

The most well-known catalogues for ODPs are (1) the ODP Semantic Web Portal,[13] and (2) the ODPs Public Catalog.[14] Both of these catalogues reflect the

[12] We also considered using the label of entities e_1 from $\mathcal{P}$. However, these either coincide with the ShortFormIRI of e_1 or are slight variations thereof. Such variations are captured by our string comparison procedure.
[13] http://ontologydesignpatterns.org.
[14] http://odps.sourceforge.net/odp/html/index.html.

focus of the academic literature on CODPs and LODPs and contain mostly submissions for these two types. We build our corpus of ODPs according to the following criteria.

(i) The pattern was categorised as either an LODP or CODP in catalogue (1).
(ii) The pattern was published together with an ontology as its reusable component or the pattern was published with an example ontology to demonstrate its reuse.
(iii) The reusable component or example ontology can be loaded and initialised with a reasoner by the OWL API.
(iv) A CODP is documented to belong to some biomedical related domain.

This selection procedure resulted in the selection of 47 out of 155 CODPs from (1), 4 out of 18 LODPs from (1), and all 16 ODPs from (2). Selected patterns according to criteria (iv) belong to at least one of the following domains: Agriculture, Biology, Cartography, Chemistry, Decision-making, Document Management, Earth Science or Geoscience, Ecology, Event Processing, Explanation, Fishery, General, Geology, Health-care, Management, Manufacturing, Materials Science, Organisation, Participation, Parts and Collections, Physics, Planning, Product Development, Scheduling, Software, Software Engineering, Social Science, Time, Work-flow.

4.2 Ontology Corpus

We used a publicly available snapshot of BioPortal from 2017.[15] Choosing the data set that contained all ontologies in their original state, we extracted all ontologies from the archive into one folder. Any ontology that could not be loaded or handled with a reasoner in the OWL API was excluded form the study. This procedure resulted in the exclusion of 78 out of 438 ontologies resulting in a study corpus of 360 ontologies.

4.3 Experimental Design

Our empirical investigation consists of four distinct experiments.

The first experiment is designed to provide positive indications for the prevalence of ODPs exhibiting lexical features in terms of class, property, and individual names. Algorithm 1 is run over all input combinations of ontologies from the ontology corpus and the 47 CODPs from catalogue (1).

The second experiment is designed to provide negative indications for ODPs exhibiting lexical features. Here, we run the `AxiomTypeCheck` over all input combinations of ontologies from the ontology corpus and the 47 CODPs from catalogue (1). The `AxiomTypeCheck` is performed under two conditions: (a) not including the imports closure of a given ODP's $\mathcal{P}$ and (b) including the imports closure of a given ODP's $\mathcal{P}$.

[15] https://zenodo.org/record/439510#.XKK-Nt-YVhE.

The third experiment is designed to provide positive indications for ODPs that do not exhibit lexical features by definition but focus on structural modelling aspects. The `DisjointUnionCheck` and the `NAryRelationCheck` are run over all ontologies from the ontology corpus to determine the prevalence of design structures often used in LODPs.

The fourth experiment is designed to provide negative indications for ODPs that do not exhibit lexical features by definition. Analogously to experiment two, the `AxiomTypeCheck`, is run over all input combinations of ontologies from the ontology corpus and LODPs from catalogue (1) as well as ODPs from catalogue (2).

We use OWL API version 5[16] to perform our experiments.

5 Results

5.1 Experiment 1: Positive Indications for CODPs

The results of experiment 1 for positive indications of ODPs exhibiting lexical design features are summarised in Table 3.[17] Each row reports on the data generated by each subcomponent of Algorithm 1. The reported numbers in each column encode the following information: "Overall $\mathcal{P}$" is a count for the total number of ODPs for which a detection technique has produced some evidence. "Overall $\mathcal{O}$" is a count for the total number of ontologies based on which a detection technique produced some evidence. "Max $\mathcal{P}$'s in $\mathcal{O}$" is a count for the maximum number of distinct ODPs for which some evidence could be produced in a given ontology. "Max $\mathcal{O}$'s for $\mathcal{P}$" is a count for the maximum count of distinct ontologies in which evidence for a given ODP could be produced.

Note, that evidence generated by `ImportByURL` is not counted again in subsequent detection techniques. In the following, we will provide further details on these results.

Table 3. Summary of generated evidence for CODPs

Detection technique	Overall $\mathcal{P}$	Overall $\mathcal{O}$	Max $\mathcal{P}$'s in $\mathcal{O}$	Max $\mathcal{O}$'s for $\mathcal{P}$
(1) `ImportByURL`	3	1	3	1
(2) `ImportByLocation`	5	6	1	2
(3) `IRICheck`	0	0	0	0
(4) `NamespaceCheck`	4	5	2	2
(5) `SContainmentCheck`	9	46	3	20
(6) `SEntailmentCheck`	0	0	0	0

[16] http://owlcs.github.io/owlapi/apidocs_5/.

[17] `SubstitutionContainmentCheck` has been abbreviated by `SContainmentCheck` for presentation purposes. Likewise for `SubstitutionEntailmentCheck`.

(1) The `ImportByURL` check detected three ODPs that were undisputedly reused by import, namely the AgentRole, ObjectRole, and Classification. Interestingly, this reuse by import was only detected due to AgentRole's occurrence in the corpus of ontologies. Since each ontology is contained in its own import closure, the detection of `AgentRole` is as expected. Likewise, the detection of ObjectRole and Classification is unsurprising since AgentRole imports both ObjecRole and Classification. Otherwise, the `ImportByURL` check did not produce any evidence for these or other ODPs in the corpus of ontologies.

(2) The `ImportByLocation` detected five import declarations as candidates for ODP reuse via import by location. For example, the pattern `Region` was generated as candidate in the "Ontology of Geographical Region" since it contained the ontology "http://www.owl-ontologies.com/GeographicalRegion.owl" in its import closure. However, in all cases, an inspection of the imported ontologies and the candidate ODPs did not reveal an obvious relationship.

(3) Except IRIs pertaining to AgentRole (which are not counted again), no other IRIs pertaining to some ODP could be detected in the corpus of ontologies.

(4) The `NamespaceCheck` performed with "http://ontologydesignpatterns.org" resulted in the detection of 5 entities in 3 different ontologies. In all cases, a "seeAlso" annotation referenced web pages related to ODPs. For example, the object property "part of" in the "human interaction network ontology" has been annotated with "rdfs:SeeAlso <http://ontologydesignpatterns.org/wiki/Submissions:PartOf>".

(5) The `SubstitutionContainmentCheck` generated candidate substitutions for 9 ODPs in 46 distinct ontologies. Two out of the ODPs account for 26 of the 46 ontologies in which substitutions could be generated. These two ODPS are TypesOfEntities and GOTop. The latter is also the pattern that has generated candidate substitutions in 20 distinct ontologies. Excluding both these ODPs would have resulted in an "Overall $\mathcal{O}$" count of 18 and a "Max $\mathcal{O}$'s for $\mathcal{P}$" of 10.

(6) The `SubstitutionEntailmentCheck` did not result in the generation of additional candidate substitutions.

5.2 Experiment 2: Negative Indications for CODPs

The results of experiment 2 for negative indications of ODPs exhibiting lexical design features are summarised in Table 4. The table is split in the middle by a double line. Each side contains the same information content only formulated differently.

For the left hand side, the percentage in the column "Ontologies" describes a lower bound for ontologies in the ontology corpus that exhibit at least as many axioms of a given type as the number of ODPs shown in columns "Patterns (a)" and "Patterns (b)", where (a) and (b) indicates the experimental condition as described in Sect. 4.3. For example, the first row expresses that at least 5% of all ontologies in the corpus have at least as many axioms of a given type as 42 out of the 47 tested ODPs.

The right hand side of the table, formulates the complementary implication of the left hand side. Continuing the example with the first row, we can infer that for $47 - 45 = 5$ ODPs, there exists only fewer than 5% of all ontologies containing at least as many axioms of a given type as the ODP. Consequently, it can be inferred that these patterns have not influenced 95% of ontologies by ODP reuse under import, complete copying, or copying with renaming.

Table 4. Result of `AxiomTypeCheck`

Ontologies	Patterns (a)	Patterns (b)	Patterns (a)'	Patterns (b)'	Ontologies'
at least 5%	42	32	5	15	less than 5%
at least 10%	38	26	9	21	less than 10%
at least 20%	16	11	31	36	less than 20%
at least 30%	4	2	43	45	less than 30%
at least 40%	3	1	44	46	less than 40%
at least 50%	2	1	45	46	less than 50%
at least 80%	2	1	45	46	less than 80%

5.3 Experiment 3: Positive Indications for LODPs

The `DisjointUnionCheck` found evidence in 24 ontologies. None of these instances made use of the syntactic shortcut "DisjointUnion" in OWL. The `NAryRelationCheck` revealed that nearly half of all ontologies (168 out of 360) contain at least one n-ary relation.

5.4 Experiment 4: Negative Indications for LODPs

The results of experiment 4 are reported in the same fashion as the results for experiment 2 (cf. Sect. 5.2) (Table 5).[18]

6 Discussion

The results of our investigation provide only scant evidence for influences of ODPs in biomedical ontologies. The negative results of the `ImportByURL` check show that a given ODP's component $\mathcal{P}$ is not reused in practice as originally envisioned by the NeOn project. Furthermore, the negative results of our `IRICheck` indicate that even parts of reusable components $\mathcal{P}$ do not directly influence the ontology engineering tasks in practice.

[18] Experiment 4 is not designed with two conditions for including or not including a given $\mathcal{P}$'s import closure as in Experiment 2. This is owed to the fact that ODPs focusing on logical modelling structures do not import other ontologies.

Table 5. Result of `AxiomTypeCheck`

Ontologies	Patterns	Patterns'	Ontologies'
at least 5%	13	7	less than 5%
at least 10%	11	9	less than 10%
at least 20%	6	14	less than 20%
at least 30%	1	19	less than 30%
at least 40%	1	19	less than 40%
at least 50%	1	19	less than 50%
at least 80%	1	19	less than 80%

Even though we could not find explicit evidence for any ODP being reused by import, we did find evidence by the mere presence of the AgentRole pattern in the corpus of ontologies. Through manual inspection of the original 438 ontologies in the BioPortal snapshot, we noticed that the AgentRole pattern was located in an archive file for the ontology ICPS. This archive also contained another pattern, namely Person. However, the ontology ICPS has been excluded during the process of the ontology corpus construction for the study. This observation raises the question whether our results are skewed by our ontology exclusion criteria for constructing the experimental ontology corpus. We can invalidate this concern due to the following. First, we downloaded a version of the BioPortal snapshot in which each ontology has been merged with its import closure. Then, we treated all ontologies as simple text files and reran the `NamespaceCheck`. Still, there is no positive hit to be reported.

Inspecting the positive evidence found by the `IRICheck`, it is quite clear that practitioners create their own entities instead of reusing IRIs from ODPs directly. Nevertheless, it remains unclear whether this is owed to a conscious modelling decision, mere personal preference, lack of know-how, or lack of tool support for ODPs.

Yet, there is a caveat with respect to reusing IRIs from ODPs that needs to be pointed out. Some ODPs published on http://ontologydesignpatterns.org are said to be "extracted from upper level ontologies". However, interestingly, their respective reusable components $\mathcal{P}$ are often self-contained ontologies not bearing any relation to upper level ontologies. This suggests that $\mathcal{P}$ is a somehow reimplemented fragment of the upper level ontology. This gets practitioners into the predicament of choosing between aligning their ontologies to an upper level ontology or an ODP (if they are so inclined in the first place). Hence, it is possible that practitioners prefer to work with the original upper level ontology rather than the extracted ODPs thereof.

Irrespective of any matter of renaming, the findings of our `AxiomTypeCheck` suggest that modelling features exhibited by most reusable components of ODPs are not highly prevalent in ontologies of the biomedical domain (the vast majority of ODPs contain axiom types that are not present in more than 70% of ontologies). It has been noted before that an ODP's required language expressivity is outside of the popular EL profile many biomedical ontologies conform to [11]. Moreover, it seems that a fair amount of published ODPs seem to propose property centric modelling approaches whereas ontologies in the biomedical domain tend to follow a class centric design.

Since a high percentage of ontologies do not contain at least the same number of axioms or axioms types as a given ODP, it is unsurprising to find a limited number of candidates under the `SubstitutinoContainmentCheck`. Likewise, it is equally unsurprising to find a limited number of candidates under the `SubstitutionEntailmentCheck`, given the observation that a fair number of ODPs make use of modelling techniques that are not expressible in the EL profile to which a lot of ontologies conform.

Given the above observation with respect to axiom types and differences in language requirements, we considered to relax the conditions of our substitution checks. Instead of requiring a substitution for *all* axioms $\alpha \in \mathcal{P}$, we only require a substitution for some subset $S \subseteq \mathcal{P}$ such that $\sigma(\alpha) \in \mathcal{O}$ holds for all $\alpha \in S$. Essentially, this corresponds to some notion of a *partial* reuse of $\mathcal{P}$. Allowing for arbitrary subsets $S \subseteq \mathcal{P}$ resulted in the generation of a large amount of spurious data due to our liberal lexical association procedure. Imposing some lower bound on the size of S is not straightforward as an ODP's $\mathcal{P}$ is often quite small to begin with. Limiting the search space for lexical associations in the target ontology $\mathcal{O}$ by some heuristics seems to be the most promising approach. For example, given a match between some $e \in \widetilde{\mathcal{P}}$ and $e' \in \widetilde{\mathcal{O}}$, limit the search for further lexical associations of elements in $\widetilde{\mathcal{P}}$ to the set $\{\alpha \in \mathcal{O} \mid e' \in \widetilde{\alpha}\}$ and proceed recursively. However, slight variations in heuristic search strategies result in drastic effects for the number of generated lexical associations. Overall, generating meaningful data for partial reuse of a given ODP's $\mathcal{P}$ turns out to be a challenging research endeavour in and of itself.

6.1 Limitations

Despite our intention to maximise the recall of our detection mechanism, there are a few limitations. Some patterns in our corpus are not intended to be directly reused via some reusable component $\mathcal{P}$. The ODP UpperLevelOntology[19] is such an example. This pattern motivates to align a given ontology to a chosen upper level ontology. Since all our detection techniques are agnostic to influences of upper level ontologies and only target lexical as well as structural modelling features, the prevalence of ontologies aligned to upper level ontologies is not determined and our negative results are inconclusive.

Another limitation is the manner in which we try to establish lexical associations between entities of ODPs and entities of domain ontologies. Entities of ODPs are arguably of general nature and might not easily be associated via with domain specific entities on a purely lexical basis. Instead, one might need to consider lexical relationships based on hyponyms and hypernyms. However, doing

[19] http://odps.sourceforge.net/odp/html/Upper_Level_Ontology.html.

so would require an more overall more sophisticated lexical matching procedure to prevent spurious associations.

The choice of both the ontology corpus as well as the ODP corpus limit the generalisability of our findings. Despite BioPortal's popularity for empirical research, based on a large variety of ontologies differing in size and complexity that are authored by a number of independent groups for diverse intents and purposes [16], there is still a possibility that the used BioPortal snapshot in our study is not representative for biomedical ontologies in general. Likewise, it is possible that the constructed corpus of ODPs is not representative of patterns that are relevant for the biomedical domain. However, if we (hypothetically) assume that the design of many biomedical ontologies is indeed informed by a pattern-based approach, then this would raise several questions such as why these patterns would not be readily available in well-known public repositories, or why would an ontology not document and advertise its pattern-based design explicitly.

6.2 Related Work

Empirical work on ODP reuse often falls into one of two categories. On the one hand, there are user studies that investigate how a given set of ODPs affects the completion of an ontology engineering tasks in an experimental setting. On the other hand, there are field studies that investigate qualities of ODP reuse outside an artificially created experimental setting.

Existing user studies reveal mixed user perceptions. ODPs are sometimes deemed useful [2] but are also often met with scepticism [8,10] and experiences from ontology engineers reveal tangible limitations of ODP reuse in practice [14,23].

Existing field studies on ODP reuse either aim to detect the reuse of known ODPs, or aim for the discovery of regularities in ontologies that may be interpreted as the reuse of (potentially unknown) ODPs.

Ontology enrichment has motivated one of the first attempts to automatically identify the reuse of ODPs in ontologies [19]. It is argued that the identification of partial ODP reuse may allow for ontology refinement by completing the missing parts of a pattern. The proposed mechanism to identify the partial reuse of known ODPs heavily depends on a lexical association procedure that is based on a number of heuristics. However, a large scale evaluation of the proposed mechanism is not performed.

The idea of using lexical associations between entities occurring in ontologies and entities occurring in ODPs has motivated the proposal of a detection mechanism that uses WordNet[20] to provide background knowledge for establishing such lexical associations [13]. However, a first empirical evaluation suggests that the results are "probably not reliable" because the background knowledge provided by WordNet is used in a way that skews the data towards patterns including a certain signature and produces spurious results.

[20] https://wordnet.princeton.edu/.

Acknowledging the limitations of lexical associations for the purpose of detecting ODP reuse, it has been proposed to combine lexical and structural aspects of an ODP's design into detection procedures [27]. The idea is to use query languages, e.g. SPARQL, to probe an ontology for axioms that satisfy structural constraints imposed by an ODP's design. Only if such axioms are found, a lexical association procedure is applied to identify a potential ODP's reuse. A preliminary evaluation suggests that the precision of the proposed approach needs to be improved by using query engines that are tailored towards OWL ontologies, e.g. SPARQL-DL.

Another study combining both lexical and structural aspects of an ODP for its detection aims disregards ODP reuse under lexical variation of its entities as this is considered an ill-defined task [18]. Here, a lexical search is performed to determine whether all entities of a given ODP occur in a target ontology. Only if instances for all entities of an ODP are found, then a structural comparison between both the ontology's and the ODP's axioms is performed under some notion of normalisation. A large scale study using this approach reveals the reuse of a small number of structurally simple ODP in biomedical ontologies.

Contrary to the negative results of studies searching for evidence of the reuse of published ODP, studies on regularities in ontologies report recurring pattern of axioms both within as well as across a large number of biomedical ontologies in BioPortal [15,17].

7 Conclusion

The results of our empirical evaluation corroborate the findings of previous studies to some degree [18]. Our pattern detection mechanism could not provide much concrete evidence for ODPs influence in biomedical ontologies. Even liberal notions for ODP reuse which can only be considered suggestive of a given ODP's influence do not allow for a different conclusion. While this negative finding appears unconstructive, we will qualify its implications in light of the nature of our chosen detection techniques.

The structural detection techniques, `AxiomTypeCheck` and `DisjointUnionCheck`, indicate that modelling solutions proposed by ODPs differ significantly compared with ontologies authored by practitioners. The data collected by the `AxiomTypeCheck` shows that the design of most biomedical ontologies are class centric while the design of ODPs published in catalogue (1) (cf. Sect. 4.1) places an emphasise on roles. As for disjoint unions, six out of 16 ODPs published in catalogue (2) (cf. Sect. 4.1) feature a disjoint union. Yet, only 7% of ontologies in our study make use of such an expression. Overall, it seems that currently, ODPs do not provide solutions to *common* ontology design tasks for ontology engineers in the biomedical domain. In particular, the scarce positive evidence for ODPs suggest that practitioners in the biomedical domain seem to limit the reuse of ODPs to the realm of annotations (cf. results of the `NamespaceCheck`).

Overall, there seems to be a discrepancy between the lack of reuse of publicly available ODPs on the one hand and ontology engineering techniques that give rise to regular logical structures in biomedical ontologies on the other hand, as shown in [15,17]. However, this discrepancy may be reconciled by motivating a data driven approach that automatically generates or at least informs the development of practically relevant ODPs. In such a scenario, detection techniques, such as the ones presented in this paper, can serve as some kind of quality measure for newly discovered pattern. After a pattern is discovered, one can either gauge its practical relevance by determining its prevalence in other ontologies or by monitoring the uptake of the discovered pattern by practitioners over time. The desire for such work has already been expressed [9].

References

1. Blomqvist, E.: Ontology patterns: typology and experiences from design pattern development. In: The Swedish AI Society Workshop, Uppsala University, 20–21 May 2010, no. 048, pp. 55–64. Linköping University Electronic Press (2010)
2. Blomqvist, E., Gangemi, A., Presutti, V.: Experiments on pattern-based ontology design. In: K-CAP, pp. 41–48. ACM (2009)
3. Blomqvist, E., Sandkuhl, K.: Patterns in ontology engineering-classification of ontology patterns. In: ICEIS 2005: Proceedings of the Seventh International Conference on Enterprise Information Systems, Miami, USA, 25–28 May 2005 (2005)
4. Clark, P.: Knowledge patterns. In: Gangemi, A., Euzenat, J. (eds.) EKAW 2008. LNCS (LNAI), vol. 5268, pp. 1–3. Springer, Heidelberg (2008). https://doi.org/10.1007/978-3-540-87696-0_1
5. de Almeida Falbo, R., Guizzardi, G., Gangemi, A., Presutti, V.: Ontology patterns: clarifying concepts and terminology. In: WOP, CEUR Workshop Proceedings, vol. 1188. CEUR-WS.org (2013)
6. Gangemi, A.: Ontology design patterns for semantic web content. In: Gil, Y., Motta, E., Benjamins, V.R., Musen, M.A. (eds.) ISWC 2005. LNCS, vol. 3729, pp. 262–276. Springer, Heidelberg (2005). https://doi.org/10.1007/11574620_21
7. Guizzardi, G.: Theoretical foundations and engineering tools for building ontologies as reference conceptual models. Semant. Web **1**(1–2), 3–10 (2010)
8. Hammar, K.: Ontology design patterns in use: lessons learnt from an ontology engineering case. In: Proceedings of the 3rd International Conference on Ontology Patterns, vol. 929, pp. 13–24. CEUR-WS.org (2012)
9. Hammar, K., et al.: Collected research questions concerning ontology design patterns. In: Ontology Engineering with Ontology Design Patterns. Studies on the Semantic Web, vol. 25, pp. 189–198. IOS Press (2016)
10. Hammar, K., Presutti, V.: Template-based content ODP instantiation. In; The 7th Workshop on Ontology and Semantic Web Patterns. IOS Press (2017)
11. Horridge, M., Aranguren, M.E., Mortensen, J., Musen, M.A., Noy, N.F.: Ontology design pattern language expressivity requirements. In: WOP, CEUR Workshop Proceedings, vol. 929. CEUR-WS.org (2012)
12. Hou, C.-S.J., Noy, N.F., Musen, M.A.: A template-based approach toward acquisition of logical sentences. In: Musen, M.A., Neumann, B., Studer, R. (eds.) IIP 2002. ITIFIP, vol. 93, pp. 77–89. Springer, Boston, MA (2002). https://doi.org/10.1007/978-0-387-35602-0_8
13. Khan, M.T., Blomqvist, E.: Ontology design pattern detection-initial method and usage scenarios. In: SEMAPRO 2010, The Fourth International Conference on Advances in Semantic Processing, pp. 19–24 (2010)

14. Lantow, B., Sandkuhl, K., Tarasov, V.: Ontology reuse. In: KEOD, pp. 163–170. SciTePress (2015)
15. Lawrynowicz, A., Potoniec, J., Robaczyk, M., Tudorache, T.: Discovery of emerging design patterns in ontologies using tree mining. Semant. Web **9**(4), 517–544 (2018)
16. Matentzoglu, N., Bail, S., Parsia, B.: A corpus of OWL DL ontologies. In: Description Logics, CEUR Workshop Proceedings, vol. 1014, pp. 829–841. CEUR-WS.org (2013)
17. Mikroyannidi, E., Manaf, N.A.A., Iannone, L., Stevens, R.: Analysing syntactic regularities in ontologies. In: OWLED, CEUR Workshop Proceedings, vol. 849. CEUR-WS.org (2012)
18. Mortensen, J., Horridge, M., Musen, M.A., Noy, N.F.: Modest use of ontology design patterns in a repository of biomedical ontologies. In: WOP, CEUR Workshop Proceedings, vol. 929. CEUR-WS.org (2012)
19. Nikitina, N., Rudolph, S., Blohm, S.: Refining ontologies by pattern-based completion. In: WOP, CEUR Workshop Proceedings, vol. 516. CEUR-WS.org (2009)
20. Presutti, V., Gangemi, A.: Content ontology design patterns as practical building blocks for web ontologies. In: Li, Q., Spaccapietra, S., Yu, E., Olivé, A. (eds.) ER 2008. LNCS, vol. 5231, pp. 128–141. Springer, Heidelberg (2008). https://doi.org/10.1007/978-3-540-87877-3_11
21. Presutti, V., et al.: D2.5.1: a library of ontology design patterns: reusable solutions for collaborative design of networked ontologies (2008). http://www.neon-project.org/
22. Renée Reich, J.: Onthological design patterns for the integration of molecular biological information. In: German Conference on Bioinformatics, pp. 156–166 (1999)
23. Rodriguez-Castro, B., Ge, M., Hepp, M.: Alignment of ontology design patterns: class as property value, value partition and normalisation. In: Meersman, R., et al. (eds.) OTM 2012. LNCS, vol. 7566, pp. 682–699. Springer, Heidelberg (2012). https://doi.org/10.1007/978-3-642-33615-7_16
24. Ruy, F.B., Reginato, C.C., Santos, V.A., Falbo, R.A., Guizzardi, G.: Ontology engineering by combining ontology patterns. In: Johannesson, P., Lee, M.L., Liddle, S.W., Opdahl, A.L., López, Ó.P. (eds.) ER 2015. LNCS, vol. 9381, pp. 173–186. Springer, Cham (2015). https://doi.org/10.1007/978-3-319-25264-3_13
25. Staab, S., Erdmann, M., Maedche, A.: Engineering ontologies using semantic patterns. In: OIS@IJCAI, CEUR Workshop Proceedings, vol. 47. CEUR-WS.org (2001)
26. Suárez-Figueroa, M.C., et al.: D5.1.1 NeOn modelling components, March 2007. http://www.neon-project.org
27. Sváb-Zamazal, O., Scharffe, F., Svátek, V.: Preliminary results of logical ontology pattern detection using SPARQL and lexical heuristics. In: WOP, CEUR Workshop Proceedings, vol. 516. CEUR-WS.org (2009)
28. Svátek, V.: Design patterns for semantic web ontologies: motivation and discussion. In: 7th Conference on Business Information Systems (BIS-2004) (2004)
29. Vrandecic, D.: Explicit knowledge engineering patterns with macros. In: Proceedings of the Ontology Patterns for the Semantic Web Workshop a the ISWC 2005, Galway, Ireland (2005)

Popularity-Driven Ontology Ranking Using Qualitative Features

Niklas Kolbe[1(✉)], Sylvain Kubler[2], and Yves Le Traon[1]

[1] University of Luxembourg, Luxembourg, Luxembourg
{niklas.kolbe,yves.letraon}@uni.lu
[2] Université de Lorraine and CRAN, Vandœuvre-lès-Nancy, France
s.kubler@univ-lorraine.fr

Abstract. Efficient ontology reuse is a key factor in the Semantic Web to enable and enhance the interoperability of computing systems. One important aspect of ontology reuse is concerned with ranking most relevant ontologies based on a keyword query. Apart from the semantic match of query and ontology, the state-of-the-art often relies on ontologies' occurrences in the Linked Open Data (LOD) cloud to determine relevance. We observe that ontologies of some application domains, in particular those related to Web of Things (WoT), often do not appear in the underlying LOD datasets used to define ontologies' popularity, resulting in ineffective ranking scores. This motivated us to investigate – based on the problematic WoT case – whether the scope of ranking models can be extended by relying on qualitative attributes instead of an explicit popularity feature. We propose a novel approach to ontology ranking by (i) selecting a range of relevant qualitative features, (ii) proposing a popularity measure for ontologies based on scholarly data, (iii) training a ranking model that uses ontologies' popularity as prediction target for the relevance degree, and (iv) confirming its validity by testing it on independent datasets derived from the state-of-the-art. We find that qualitative features help to improve the prediction of the relevance degree in terms of popularity. We further discuss the influence of these features on the ranking model.

Keywords: Learning to rank · Ontology reuse · Web of Things · Linked vocabularies · Semantic interoperability

1 Introduction

In the Semantic Web, efficient ontology reuse is a key factor to enable and enhance the interoperability of computing systems [29]. Approaches to ontology ranking are a key component in finding and selecting the most relevant ontologies based on a query [25]. The importance of ontology reuse is also increasing in Internet of Things (IoT) environments, in which the adoption of Semantic Web technologies has received great interest [2,4]. Emerging open innovation IoT ecosystems [15] aim for the seamless discovery, access and integration of

C. Ghidini et al. (Eds.): ISWC 2019, LNCS 11778, pp. 329–346, 2019.
https://doi.org/10.1007/978-3-030-30793-6_19

heterogeneous, sensor-originated data through the Web, also referred to as the Web of Things (WoT). Efficient ontology reuse for the semantic annotation of data streams based on existing ontologies is thus a prerequisite to overcome this semantic interoperability challenge in the WoT [15]. Moreover, it enables reasoning over data and establishing linkage to existing knowledge on the Web.

Motivation. This work is motivated by the need of researchers and practitioners to discover and select the most relevant ontologies for their needs. The large number of available ontologies and the fast-paced developments in domains often make it difficult to find and select the most appropriate ontologies. For the WoT case, this is evidenced through extensive surveys in the literature [1,10,13,16]. This does not only concern ontologies with regard to sensors and sensor network setups, but further to sensor observations [13] (e.g., in the context of smart city use cases with regard to the environment, transportation, health, homes, and factories). At the core of many state-of-the-art tools that facilitate ontology reuse – such as repositories, search engines and recommender systems – lies the ranking of ontologies for a user query in the form of keywords.

Importance of Popularity. Fundamental ontology reuse strategies rely on ontologies' *popularity*, which is typically understood as the measure of how often an ontology is used to model data in the Linked Open Data (LOD) cloud [27]. While rankings foremost take into account the semantic match of query and ontologies in the collection, current state-of-the-art tools such as Linked Open Vocabularies (LOV) [32], TermPicker [28], and vocab.cc [30] further incorporate such a popularity measure in their ranking model. This is crucial because it reflects the community's consensus on ontologies' relevance, instead of solely relying on how well ontologies semantically match the query. Thus, the approach of computing the popularity measure has an important influence on the performance of the ranking model.

Problem Statement. We find that the approach to derive popularity from LOD datasets, as computed in many state-of-the-art tools, can be problematic for ontologies of some domains. We illustrate this problem in Fig. 1, which shows the number of ontologies contained in the well-known LOV platform that have never been reused in LOD datasets[1]. In total, only ∼35% of the ontologies in the repository have been reused. We identify particular critical domains with no reuse in any LOD dataset for any ontology in the collection, namely: Services, Industry, IoT, Transport, and Health. We consider all these domains highly relevant to WoT application domains (e.g., smart mobility, smart health care, industry 4.0), which thus forms our motivating case to investigate qualitative ontology ranking from this perspective. From a more general viewpoint, this case highlights the problem that the likeliness of missing relevant information to

[1] Extracted from the LOV SPARQL endpoint: https://lov.linkeddata.es/dataset/lov/sparql – accessed 03/2019.

explicitly determine popularity for all ontologies in a collection is high, leading to the computation of ineffective popularity scores in the ranking model.

Contributions. This research contributes to the extension of scope and effectiveness of popularity-driven ontology ranking models, aiming to make these models less dependent on the underlying popularity measure, such as the selection of LOD datasets (and the way these datasets are assembled). In this respect, we investigate whether the relevance degree in terms of popularity can be predicted with qualitative properties of the ontology instead of relying on an explicit popularity feature as it is common in the state-of-the-art. We perform this study (based on the problematic WoT case) by learning a ranking model that uses the popularity as relevance degree for the prediction target. This approach to ontology ranking results in fairer scores for ontologies that were developed for use cases other than LOD publication, such as semantic sensor data annotation and the development of context-aware applications. In general, obtaining relevance labels for learning to rank is perceived as a major challenge and a costly

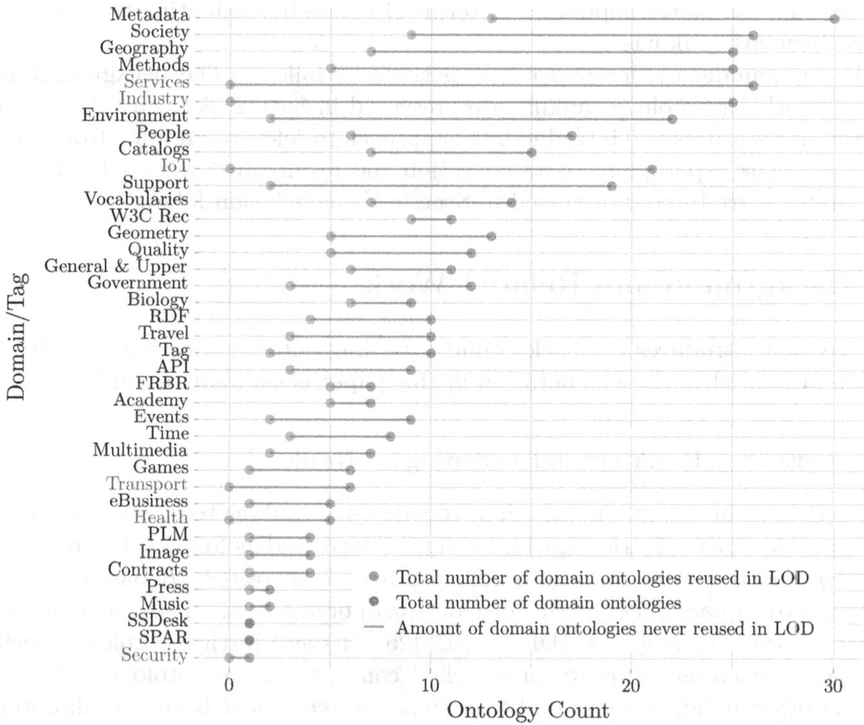

Fig. 1. Count of ontologies per category in the LOV repository that were never reused in LOD datasets, which is often used as underlying popularity measure in state-of-the-art rankings. It shows that this score is inefficient for many domains related to WoT applications, for which none of the ontologies appear in any LOD dataset.

Table 1. Notation.

Var.	Meaning	Function	Meaning
q	Keyword query	$\Phi(q, o, R)$	Relevance feature extractor
q_i	i^{th} term of query q	$\Phi(o, R)$	Importance feature extractor
o	Ontology	$\mathrm{TF}(q_i, o, R)$	Term frequency
R	Ontology repository	$\mathrm{IDF}(q_i, R)$	Inverse document frequency
M_{w2v}	Word2Vec vector space	$\mathrm{coord}(q, o)$	Scoring for number of q_i matches
D_{WN}	WordNet dictionary	$\mathrm{queryNorm}(q)$	Normalization factor
w_i	i^{th} word in collection w	$\mathrm{propertyBoost}(q_i, R)$	Boost based on matched property
Φ_i	i^{th} feature	$\mathrm{cosineDistance}(q, w_i, M_{w2v})$	Similarity of query and word
l	Relevance judgment	$\mathrm{sense}(q, D_{WN})$	Senses of query (WordNet)
π_l	Total order	$\mathrm{synonym}(q, D_{WN})$	Synonyms of query (WordNet)

process [17]. We propose a popularity measure for ontologies of WoT domains that relies on scholarly data (i.e., the citation history of ontologies' associated scientific publication) to determine relevance degrees in terms of popularity. This approach overcomes limitations of existing approaches, and we ensure that this measure approximates popularity in terms of reuses by evaluating the model on state-of-the-art rankings.

The remainder of this paper is structured as follows. The background and related work for ontology ranking are presented in Sect. 2. Section 3 defines the key ranking features and introduces the approach to relevance mining from scholarly data. The experiments, data collection and results are presented in Sect. 4. The findings are further discussed in Sect. 5; the conclusion follows.

2 Background and Related Work

This section introduces the background regarding ontology ranking, learning to rank and related work. The notation in this paper is summarized in Table 1.

2.1 Ontology Ranking and Learning to Rank

Approaches to ontology ranking adopt conventional ranking techniques and models from information retrieval, which can be categorized as follows [17]: *relevance ranking models* aim to rank an ontology o from a repository R based on their relevance to a query q, i.e., in the form of $\Phi(q, o)$ or $\Phi(q, o, R)$. These include well-known approaches (e.g., TF-IDF [26], BM25 [24]) and further ontology-specific approaches such as centrality of matched concepts in the ontology graph [8]. On the other hand, one can find *importance ranking models* that rank ontologies independently from the query, i.e., in the form of $\Phi(o)$ or $\Phi(o, R)$. Models that compute scores based on the quality of ontologies in a collection belong to this category. Well known approaches include PageRank [22]; ontology-specific approaches consider qualitative metrics such as ontologies' popularity, availability, interlinkage to other ontologies, etc. [15]. Some ontology ranking models have been studied in [7].

In most practical settings various of the previous introduced scoring functions Φ are combined to form a better performing ranking model $h(q, o, R)$. Learning-to-rank approaches allow to automatically tune the parameters when combining different ranking models by employing supervised machine learning algorithms [17]. The parameters are derived based on the correlations of features (i.e., relevance and importance scores) and a corresponding label that determines how relevant an ontology for a query is. Therefore, in order to obtain a training set for learning to rank of ontologies, one requires a ground truth that provides information about which ontologies o in a collection R are more relevant than others for a certain query q. Such a ground truth is obtained by (i) selecting a set of queries with a set of relevant ontologies per query, and by (ii) assigning relevance judgments l to each query-ontology pair. Obtaining a ground truth is a difficult task and annotating data with human assessors is costly [17]. Thus, several approaches are employed to automatically mine a ground truth by deriving labels from sources such as user click logs of existing search engines and exploiting usage patterns in LOD datasets. However, such approaches also have their limitations, e.g., using user click logs requires access to back-ends of existing search engines with a large user base, which are usually closed systems.

2.2 Related Work

Learning-to-rank techniques have been previously applied to build ontology ranking models. The CBRBench ground truth [6] was gathered through human labeling based on how well ontology terms meet their definition in a dictionary, comprising ten queries with a total of 819 relevance judgments. CBRBench was used to learn a ranking model in DWRank [8]. Termpicker [28] proposes a ground truth derived from LOD datasets and a ranking model that relies on popularity features, offering ontology term recommendations upon a query in form of triple patterns. In CARRank [33], a ground truth was obtained through human labeling for evaluation purposes, resulting in ∼400 query-term relevance judgments. Our work differs from these efforts, as we aim to rank ontologies instead of terms. Further, we aim to propose a ranking that uses popularity as a target instead of a feature, which is not captured in existing ground truths.

Ontology ranking models have been integrated in tools that help users to find and select relevant ontologies according to their need, such as the previously mentioned LOV platform [32], TermPicker [28], and vocab.cc [30]. Such tools have been previously surveyed in the literature, as in [15]. Ontology reuse has been studied from more holistic viewpoints, such as methodological guidelines [11] and choosing ontologies from a set of candidates [14]. This study contributes to ontology ranking with the overall aim to support the ontology reuse task and to improve related tools.

Ontology catalogs exist that aim at the collection and curation of ontologies related to WoT applications. The respective tools provide extensive lists of

Table 2. Overview of selected ranking features.

Category	Feature		Description
Relevance	Φ_1	Lucene	A Lucene match with property boost
	Φ_2	Word2Vec	Score based on closely related words of the query
	Φ_3	WordNet	Score based on senses and synonyms of the query
Importance	Φ_4	Availability	Whether the ontology is accessible at its URI
	Φ_5	Believability	Whether provenance information is provided
	Φ_6	Understandability	To which degree terms are labelled and commented
	Φ_7	Interlinking	To which degree the ontology refers to external terms
	Φ_8	PageRank	The importance derived through *owl:imports* statements
	Φ_9	Consistency	Whether a reasoner does not detect inconsistencies
	Φ_{10}	Richness (Width)	The size of the ontology in terms of width
	Φ_{11}	Richness (Depth)	The size of the ontology in terms of depth

ontologies and respective metadata, such as classifications, characteristics (e.g., ontology language), and background information. We are aware of three related projects: LOV4IoT[2] [12], the Smart City Ontology Catalogue[3] [23], and the Smart City Artifacts Web Portal[4] [3], which maintain an expert selection of respectively 499, 70, and 124 ontologies[5]. Whereas these projects provide valuable ontology collections for WoT application domains, to the best of our knowledge, no ranking mechanism that effectively considers these ontologies' popularity exists. We base our experiments on the collection of the LOV4IoT catalog as it contains the largest number of ontologies and more extensive metadata about the collection.

3 Ranking Features and Relevance Mining

This section presents the selected ranking features that are considered to constitute our proposed model as well as our approach to derive relevance labels for ontologies of WoT application domains. The selection of ranking features is based on comprehensive studies in the literature on ontology ranking and quality [15,34]. We include all attributes identified in survey [15] except for subjective features and those that only concern term ranking, not ontology ranking. Table 2 provides an overview of the selected features. Our interpretation of these features, as presented in the following, is guided by the review presented in [34].

3.1 Relevance Features

Relevance features aim to determine most suitable matches for a query and an ontology corpus, for which the following features are selected:

[2] http://lov4iot.appspot.com/.
[3] http://smartcity.linkeddata.es/.
[4] http://opensensingcity.emse.fr/scans/ontologies.
[5] Accessed 03/2019.

Lucene Match (Φ_1). Our fundamental feature to find relevant ontologies based on keywords is a Lucene match [19]. As argued in [32], ontologies are structured documents and more meaningful matches should be given a higher score. We adopt the approach of [32] and apply a property boost to the lucene match that aims at rewarding more important matches, such as local names, primary labels (e.g., *rdfs:label*), and secondary labels (e.g., *rdfs:comment*). The definition of the Lucene score is given in Eq. 1.

$$\begin{aligned}\text{Lucene}(q, o, R) = {} & \text{coord}(q, o) \cdot \text{queryNorm}(q) \cdot \\ & \sum_{i=1}^{n} \left(\text{TF}(q_i, o, R) \cdot \text{IDF}(q_i, R)^2 \cdot \text{propertyBoost}(q_i, R)\right)\end{aligned} \tag{1}$$

Word2Vec (Φ_2). Word2Vec [20] trains a neural network to predict the surroundings of a word. We employ this approach to find closely related words of the input search terms and compute a score based on the cosine distance and the lucene match. The respective matching score is given in Eq. 2.

$$\text{Word2VecMatch}(q, o, R) = \sum_{w_i \in \text{cosineDistance}(q, M_{w2v})} \text{cosineDistance}(q, w_i, M_{w2v}) \cdot \text{Lucene}(w_i, o, R) \tag{2}$$

WordNet (Φ_3). WordNet [21] is a lexical database in English. We use this source to find senses and synonyms of the keyword input and compute a score for these words based on the Lucene search, as given in Eq. 3.

$$\text{WordNetMatch}(q, o, R) = \sum_{\substack{w_i \in \text{sense}(q, D_{\text{WordNet}}) \,\cup \\ w_i \in \text{synonym}(q, D_{\text{WordNet}})}} \text{Lucene}(w_i, o, R) \tag{3}$$

3.2 Importance Features

Importance features aim to assign a score to an ontology within a collection independently from the query. The selected features that represent the ontologies' quality are defined as follows:

Availability (Φ_4). The availability indicates whether ontology o can be accessed at its indicated URI. We derive this feature as given in Eq. 4.

$$\text{Availability}(o) = \begin{cases} 1, & \text{if httpResponseCode(URI}(o)) = 200 \\ 0, & \text{otherwise} \end{cases} \tag{4}$$

Believability (Φ_5). The believability of a published ontology increases with the presence of provenance data (e.g., specification of authors and descriptions), and is computed based on DCMI metadata terms[6], as given in Eq. 5.

$$\text{Believability}(o) = \begin{cases} 1, & \text{if } \{\text{URI(o) } dc: creator \ ?c\} \cup \\ & \quad \{\text{URI(o) } dc: description \ ?d\} \neq \varnothing \\ 0, & \text{otherwise} \end{cases} \tag{5}$$

[6] http://purl.org/dc/terms/.

Understandability (Φ_6). The better a ontology is documented, the easier it is to reuse it. We measure the understandability of an ontology by computing how many of all defined terms in ontology o are labelled and commented.

$$\text{Understandability}(o) = \frac{|\,\text{labelledTerms}(o)|}{|\,\text{definedTerms}(o)|} + \frac{|\,\text{commentedTerms}(o)|}{|\,\text{definedTerms}(o)|} \quad (6)$$

Interlinking (Φ_7). Ontologies foster interoperability by establishing links to previously defined terms. Thus, we count the outlinks found in an ontology as formalized in Eq. 7.

$$\text{Interlinking}(o) = |\,\text{outlinks}(o)| \quad (7)$$

PageRank (Φ_8). PageRank [22] is an algorithm that helps to compute the importance of ontologies based on how often they have been referred to by others (i.e., inlinks). We compute the PageRank score based on *owl:imports* statements, as given in Eq. 8.

$$\text{PageRank}(o_i, R) = \frac{1-d}{|R|} + \sum_{o_j \in \text{importedBy}(o_i)} \frac{\text{PageRank}(o_j, R)}{|\,\text{imports}(o_j)|} \quad (8)$$

Consistency (Φ_9). Ontologies are expected to be logically consistent, which can be derived through OWL reasoners. We compute the consistency feature as given in Eq. 9.

$$\text{Consistency}(o) = \begin{cases} 1, & \text{if } \{\text{inconsistencies}(o)\} = \varnothing \\ 0, & \text{otherwise} \end{cases} \quad (9)$$

Richness (Φ_{10} & Φ_{11}). We further consider the size of the ontology in the form of its width (see Eq. 10) and depth (see Eq. 11).

$$\text{Width}(o) = |\,\text{typeStatements}(o)| \quad (10)$$

$$\text{Depth}(o) = |\,\text{subClassOfStatements}(o)| + |\,\text{subPropertyOfStatements}(o)| \quad (11)$$

3.3 Relevance Mining Approach

Learning to rank is a supervised machine learning approach that requires relevance labels for query-ontology pairs. We propose to derive a popularity measure based on corresponding scientific publications associated with an ontology. We are inspired to follow this approach as a large number of ontologies for WoT application domains emerge from research projects, as evidenced in [1,10,13,16]. Furthermore, it overcomes several limitations of other approaches: (i) as previously discussed, LOD does not provide a reliable source for ontology reuse in WoT application domains; (ii) deriving relevance through user click logs requires access to closed back-ends of existing ontology search engines with a large user base; (iii) human labeling is costly and, unlike mining relevance from scholarly data, does not come with the benefit of being reproducible.

Our popularity score is based on two measures; (i) *citationsPerYear*(o): citations per year are counted and divided by the number of ontologies described in the same publication to represent the overall impact of the ontology; and (ii) the $linearTrend(o)$: a linear regression of the citation history to reward positively trending ontologies combining the intercept and the slope of the linear model. The final relevance score, as given in Eq. 12, is the mean of both min-max normalized measures and used to derive the total order π_l for the set of ontologies associated with a query, for which an ontology with a higher popularity score is more relevant than another, i.e., $l_a \succ l_b$ if $popularity(o_a) > popularity(o_b)$.

$$\text{popularity}(o) = \frac{\text{citationsPerYear}(o) + \text{linearTrend}(o)}{2} \tag{12}$$

A ground truth mining process is always assumed to contain bias and noise: for relevance mining from scholarly data, all self-citations are subtracted from the citation history, and incomplete years are not considered (i.e., citations of the current year and of the year of publication). Although the citation history is often used to measure a study's impact, the associated reason for the citation remains unknown, which is a potential threat to the validity of our popularity scores. We assume that the proposed measure reflects the overall ontologies' relevance for the scientific community (e.g., we assume that for outdated ontologies the citation count will decline and the score is penalized accordingly through the linear trend). In the following experiments, the proposed ranking model is tested on completely independent datasets to evaluate whether our training data is accurate and the assumptions hold.

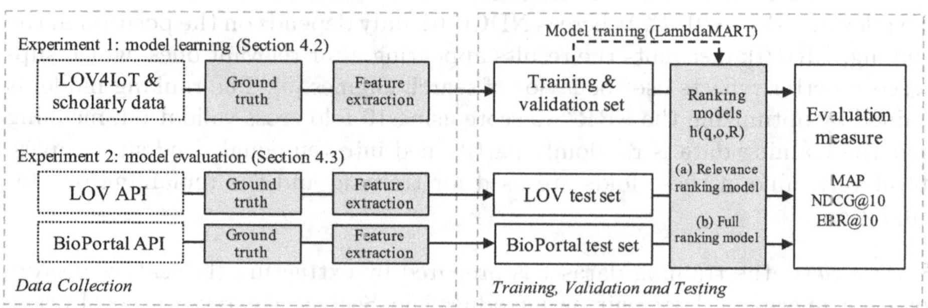

Fig. 2. Experiment overview.

4 Experiments

This section presents the experiments following the learning-to-rank approach to build a ranking model with qualitative properties of the ontologies to predict the relevance degree. An overview of the following experiments is illustrated in Fig. 2, whose aims are twofold; (i) to investigate whether qualitative features in the ranking model help to improve the ranking performance with regard to the relevance degree, and (ii) to confirm the validity of the results by testing the model on data sets derived from state-of-the-art ontology rankings.

4.1 Experiment Design

The design choices to learn and evaluate the ranking model are as follows:

Learning Algorithm: various learning-to-rank algorithms were proposed by the machine learning community. The ranking model is trained using the list-wise LambdaMART algorithm which has successfully been applied for real-world ranking problems [5] and has also been previously selected in related work for ontology ranking [8]. We rely on the LambdaMART implementation of the RankLib[7] library.

Evaluation Metrics: the performance of the ranking model is validated and tested based on the Mean Average Precision (MAP) [17], Normalized Discounted Cumulative Gain (NDCG@k) [17] and the Expected Reciprocal Rank (ERR@k) [9], considering the first ten elements (k = 10). A unified point-wise scale for relevance labels is required for some evaluation metrics, so popularity scores of query-ontology pairs are mapped to a scale of 0–4 for the experiments. While MAP is only a binary measure (i.e., 0: considered not relevant, 1–4: considered equally relevant), the NDCG@k and ERR@k scores do consider the multi-valued relevance labels (i.e., these metrics consider how well the ranking model matches the relevance degree 0–4). Whereas NDCG@k only depends on the position in the ranking, ERR@k discounts the results appearing after relevant ones, which supposedly better reflects user behavior of search engines [9]. The ranking model is trained by optimizing the ERR@10 score using 10-fold cross validation, meaning that the training data is randomly partitioned into ten equal sized subsamples. Iteratively, nine of these folds are used for training and the remaining one for validation.

Feature Sets: the training dataset is prepared by extracting the feature vectors for each query-ontology pair as introduced in Sect. 3. We rely on the Lucene search engine of the Stardog[8] triple store, the openllet[9] OWL reasoner to infer consistency and the GloVe word vector model[10] to compute the Word2Vec feature.

[7] https://sourceforge.net/p/lemur/wiki/RankLib/.
[8] https://www.stardog.com/.
[9] https://github.com/Galigator/openllet.
[10] https://github.com/stanfordnlp/GloVe.

4.2 Ranking Model Training and Validation

In the first experiment we train and validate the ranking model, as presented in the following.

Data Collection: the data for training and validation is collected from the LOV4IoT catalog[11]. 455 ontology files related to WoT applications could be downloaded through the catalog (each file being treated as a separate ontology). Only 433 files were syntactically correct and stored as named graphs in a local triple store. We derive training examples by using the available classification labels from the LOV4IoT catalog as queries (i.e., ontologies' domain[12] and described sensor devices[13]), and consider the correspondingly tagged ontologies as relevant. As previously motivated, we rely on scholarly data to derive degrees of relevance. From the initial collection, 395 ontologies could be assigned to 125 different scientific publications based on the LOV4IoT metadata. This collection resulted in $1.1M$ triples with $133K$ distinct terms and forms the ontology repository for the experiments. The citation history from Google Scholar of the assigned publications is used to derive a relevance score for the ontologies based on the approach presented in Sect. 3. The resulting scores are mapped to relevance labels 1–4 by dividing the range of the highest and lowest popularity score for each query into four equal-sized intervals, and a random set of irrelevant ontologies is added with the relevance label 0. The resulting ground truth contains 1028 query-ontology relevance judgments with 25 different queries, for which the previously introduced ranking features are extracted to finalize the training set.

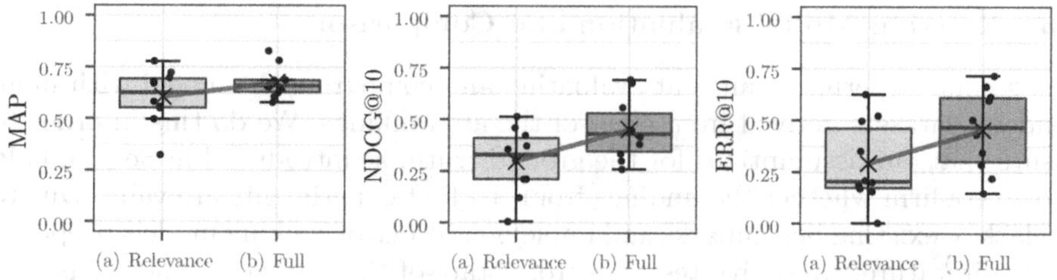

Fig. 3. Comparison of trained models with regard to MAP, NDCG@10 and ERR@10 on the validation set, for model (a) using only relevance features (Φ_1–Φ_3) and model (b) using further the importance features (Φ_1–Φ_{11}). The red lines indicate the difference of the respective metric's mean between the two models.

---

[11] http://lov4iot.appspot.com/.

[12] Denoted by <http://sensormeasurement.appspot.com/m3#hasContext>.

[13] Denoted by <http://sensormeasurement.appspot.com/m3#hasM2MDevice>.

Experiment and Results: the first experiment aims at investigating whether the selected qualitative importance features improve the ranking performance with regard to the relevance degree. Thus, we first train and validate a model only based on relevance features, and use this as a baseline to evaluate the performance of a model that further considers the importance features. The results are summarized in Fig. 3, showing the performance of two ranking models: the relevance model (a) is only trained with the relevance features (Φ_1–Φ_3), whereas the full model (b) also includes the importance features (Φ_1–Φ_{11}).

The results show that the trained ranking models appear to appropriately rank ontologies with regard to their relevance. We observe that the addition of qualitative features only has a small impact on the MAP score, but significantly improves the NDCG@10 and ERR@10 scores. This behavior is expected, as MAP effectively only measures the semantic match of query and relevant ontologies, whereas the qualitative features aim at ranking relevant ontologies according to their relevance degree. NDCG@10 and ERR@10 both reflect this degree, as they take into account multi-valued relevance labels. We thus conclude that qualitative features helped to improve the ranking with regard to the popularity-based relevance degree captured in the ground truth. Subsequently, this implies that the proposed approach can extend the scope of state-of-the-art rankings, by improving the performance for domains in which ontologies were never reused in LOD datasets. In such cases, the explicit popularity feature always results in the same score for all ontologies (i.e., zero) and effective ranking is only based on relevance (i.e., corresponding to model (a)). The presented approach in contrast predicts the popularity based on the qualitative features (i.e., corresponding to model (b)), even when no explicit information of popularity or reuse is present.

4.3 Ranking Model Evaluation and Comparison

The second experiment aims at evaluating and comparing the model with independent datasets derived from state-of-the-art rankings. We do this in order to ensure that our assumptions for the ground truth, as introduced in Sect. 3, hold and to confirm whether the findings from the first experiments are valid. Due to the lack of existing benchmarks and implementations of ranking models proposed in the literature, we derive test sets from state-of-the-art tools which must: (i) provide an open API that returns the computed ranking score of the top-ranked ontologies for a query; (ii) make the underlying ontology collection available for download; and (iii) incorporate a popularity measure in their ranking model. We choose to compare the proposed ranking model to approaches from two different domains that fulfill these requirements: the LOV repository [32], which measures popularity based on LOD occurrences (by excluding the problematic domains without any reuse in LOD for the test sets); and the NCBO recommender 2.0 of the BioPortal [18], which ranks biomedical ontologies and covers ontology's popularity in its notion of acceptance, derived by the number of other curated repositories that also keep an ontology in its collection.

Data Collection: we create the test sets based on the LOV REST API[14] and the BioPortal REST API[15]. For each platform, we (i) derive a set of test queries by extracting nouns and verbs from names and descriptions of all ontologies in the respective repository, (ii) use each test query to retrieve the ranking from the respective API that forms the ground truth, (iii) use the same strategy as for the training data to map the ranking scores to a scale of 1–4 and add a random set of irrelevant ontologies with a relevance of 0, and, lastly, (iv) complete the test set by extracting the features for all query-ontology pairs from a local triple store that contains the respective ontology collection. For the LOV test set we only consider domains with at least five ontologies that have been reused in LOD datasets, in order to ensure that the derived ground truth sufficiently reflects the ontologies' popularity (see Fig. 1). This process resulted in test datasets with 2998 (LOV) and 4313 (BioPortal) query-ontology relevance scores.

Experiment and Results: in the second experiment we test both, the validated relevance model (a) and the full model (b), from the first experiment on the newly derived datasets. The results are illustrated in Fig. 4, showing the comparison of the performance for the LOV and BioPortal test set, as well as the mean performance of the full ranking model from the first experiment (indicated by the dashed lines).

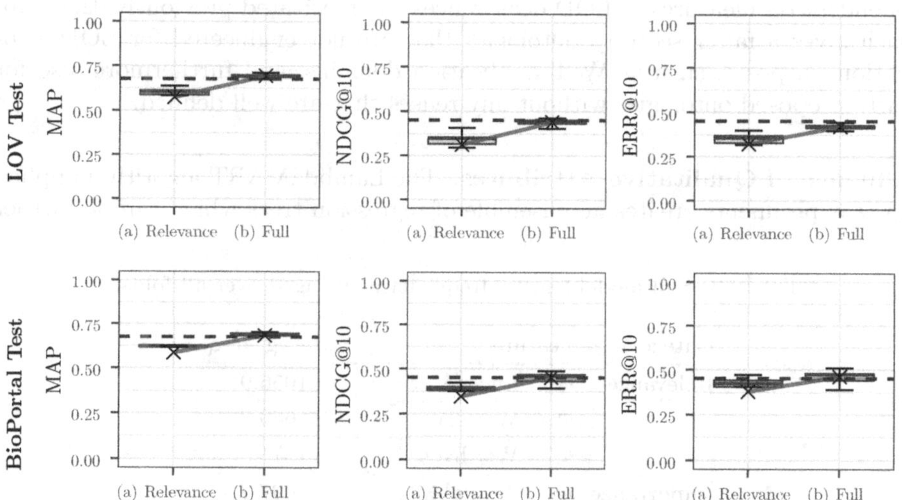

Fig. 4. Comparison of the validated ranking models from the first experiment with the LOV and BioPortal rankings. The dashed lines indicate the mean performance of the full model on the 10 fold validation sets, showing that the model performs similarly well on the test datasets. The red lines indicate the difference of the respective metric's mean between the two models. (Color figure online)

[14] https://lov.linkeddata.es/dataset/lov/api.
[15] http://data.bioontology.org/documentation.

The experiment results lead to two important conclusions. First, it shows that the learned models behave reasonably well on these completely independent datasets, evidenced by the similar performance compared to the first experiment. This confirms that the underlying ground truth to train our model is valid and, subsequently, implies that the citation history of ontologies in WoT domains is a fair approximation of their popularity. Secondly, we observe a similar behavior of the relevance and the full ranking model as in the first experiment, for which the full model improves the ranking in terms of relevance degree. Albeit the improvement on test sets is lower as in the previous experiment, it shows the same trend and thus validates our previous conclusion that the selected qualitative features help to predict the popularity-driven relevance degree of ontologies. The experimental results are further analyzed and discussed in the following.

5 Discussion

Experiment Summary. This study reveals that the prediction of ontologies' relevance for a query in terms of popularity can be improved with qualitative features. This confirms the hypothesis of a correlation between ontologies' popularity and its quality, based on the intuition that ontologies with better quality are more likely to be reused than others of the same domain. The presented approach extends the scope and applicability of the ranking model, as it is not dependent on measures of LOD occurrences. As motivated previously, this approach gives a fairer score to ontologies that are not engineered for LOD publication purposes, such as WoT application domains, and furthermore also for newly proposed ontologies without any reuses that are well-defined.

Influence of Qualitative Attributes. The LambdaMART algorithm applied in the experiments creates an ensemble of regression trees which can be further

Table 3. Full model feature frequencies averaged over all folds.

Category	Feature		Avg. freq.
Relevance	Φ_1	Lucene	1056.9
	Φ_2	Word2Vec	680.0
	Φ_3	WordNet	1375.5
Importance	Φ_4	Availability	697.7
	Φ_5	Believability	55.8
	Φ_6	Understandability	1237.9
	Φ_7	Interlinking	634.8
	Φ_8	PageRank	1302.1
	Φ_9	Consistency	777.7
	Φ_{10}	Richness (Width)	535.1
	Φ_{11}	Richness (Depth)	646.5

analyzed to better understand the model and its consequences. One way to infer the importance of each feature on the ranking model is the frequency it was used for classification of the training examples. We use these counts to discuss the model's implications and directions for future research. Table 3 reports the results for feature frequency. We derive the following insights based on the feature statistics, albeit detailed experimentation would be required to confirm them. One interesting observation is that the feature believability (Φ_5) barely contributes to the model and would be the first candidate to be replaced with another feature. This is surprising, as other approaches fundamentally rely on provenance information such as ontologies' authorship to compute the ranking [31]. Other observations include that an ontology's incoming links (Φ_8) appear to have much more significance than outgoing links (Φ_7). This is intuitive, as being imported by another ontology often requires the ontology to be considered relevant by ontology engineers other than the original authors. In addition, it can be observed that features that solely reflect the internal graph structure (Φ_{10} and Φ_{11}) are less often used by the model than more expressive qualitative scores such as understandability (Φ_6), consistency (Φ_9) and availability (Φ_4).

Implications of Proposed Ranking Approach. The experimental results of this study show that the proposed approach is promising to extend the scope of ontology ranking models. As evidenced through the experiments, this approach can also be adopted for other domains and we expect a model trained on domain-specific ontologies to perform better. This encourages further experimentation with more quality attributes, new interpretations of them, and with training sets from other domains in order to confirm the findings and achieve the development of better performing ranking models. The quality of learning-to-rank approaches also highly depends on the size of the training data. We expect future research to provide larger benchmarks that allow for the study of more complex models and better comparisons of ranking approaches, such as ground truths derived from user click logs of existing search engines. In a broader context, this approach to ranking could also encourage ontology engineers to put even more emphasis on qualitative traits of proposed ontologies in order to increase exposure and reuse in applications. Albeit the extraction of qualitative features can be computationally very expensive, these scores are independent from the user query and can be pre-computed. Thus, the lookup of these scores and re-ranking of relevant ontologies only has a minor impact on the run-time performance compared to the complexity of the semantic similarity search in the entire ontology corpus.

Novel Ontology Ranking Model for the WoT. To the best of our knowledge, the proposed full ranking model is the first that effectively considers popularity for ontologies in WoT application domains. We thus conclude that the proposed full ranking model contributes to ontology selection for these domains in the scope of open IoT ecosystems, e.g., for ontology collections such as the LOV4IoT catalog. The ranking model can be integrated in more complex user interfaces and combined with various other selection criteria in IoT domains, that, e.g., further consider important standardization efforts.

Limitations. A potential threat to validity of this study's experimental findings is the ground truth derived through popularity measures from scholarly data. While it is a common approach to use implicit user feedback as relevance score (such as user clicks), using citations arguably is a more ambiguous measure. Yet, as previously mentioned, this approach overcomes limitations of alternatives and our evaluation showed a reasonable performance. We conclude that further experimentation is required in order to confirm whether similar observations can be made for other domains than WoT, by using training examples with a relevance score derived from other popularity measures. From an ontology reuse perspective, this study is limited as it only considers ranking of single ontologies. However, practitioners often search for terms (e.g., as offered by LOV [32]) or combinations of ontologies (e.g., as offered by NCBO 2.0 [18]).

Resource Availability. The derived datasets, source files to replicate the experiments, as well as more detailed results of the ranking models are available online[16], and may be used for future experiments and comparison studies.

6 Conclusion

In this paper, we show that the prediction of ontologies' relevance in terms of popularity can be improved with qualitative features in the ranking model, making the model independent from explicit computed popularity metrics such as LOD occurrences. Moreover, we present a ranking model that effectively ranks ontologies of WoT domains with respect to their popularity. We show that the proposed model performs similarly well on test set derived from rankings of state-of-the-art tools, which is encouraging to adopt the presented approach also in other domains. Lastly, we discuss the importance of the qualitative features on the overall performance of the ranking model. The proposed model can be integrated in ontology selection mechanisms for practitioners and researchers in WoT use cases and thus contributes to establish semantic interoperability in emerging large-scale IoT ecosystems.

Acknowledgements. The research leading to this publication is supported by the EU's H2020 Research and Innovation program under grant agreement № 688203 – bIoTope.

References

1. Andročec, D., Novak, M., Oreški, D.: Using semantic web for internet of things interoperability: a systematic review. Int. J. Semant. Web Inf. Syst. (IJSWIS) **14**(4), 147–171 (2018). https://doi.org/10.4018/IJSWIS.2018100108
2. Atzori, L., Iera, A., Morabito, G.: The internet of things: a survey. Comput. Netw. **54**(15), 2787–2805 (2010). https://doi.org/10.1016/j.comnet.2010.05.010

[16] Supplemental material: https://tinyurl.com/y64sa6le.

3. Bakerally, N., Boissier, O., Zimmermann, A.: Smart city artifacts web portal. In: Sack, H., Rizzo, G., Steinmetz, N., Mladenić, D., Auer, S., Lange, C. (eds.) ESWC 2016. LNCS, vol. 9989, pp. 172–177. Springer, Cham (2016). https://doi.org/10.1007/978-3-319-47602-5_34
4. Barnaghi, P., Wang, W., Henson, C., Taylor, K.: Semantics for the internet of things: early progress and back to the future. Int. J. Semant. Web Inf. Syst. (IJSWIS) **8**(1), 1–21 (2012). https://doi.org/10.4018/jswis.2012010101
5. Burges, C.J.: From ranknet to lambdarank to lambdamart: an overview. Learning **11**(23–581), 81 (2010)
6. Butt, A.S.: Ontology search: finding the right ontologies on the web. In: Proceedings of the 24th International Conference on World Wide Web, pp. 487–491. ACM (2015). https://doi.org/10.1145/2740908.2741753
7. Butt, A.S., Haller, A., Xie, L.: Ontology search: an empirical evaluation. In: Mika, P., et al. (eds.) ISWC 2014. LNCS, vol. 8797, pp. 130–147. Springer, Cham (2014). https://doi.org/10.1007/978-3-319-11915-1_9
8. Butt, A.S., Haller, A., Xie, L.: DWRank: learning concept ranking for ontology search. Semant. Web **7**(4), 447–461 (2016). https://doi.org/10.3233/SW-150185
9. Chapelle, O., Metlzer, D., Zhang, Y., Grinspan, P.: Expected reciprocal rank for graded relevance. In: Proceedings of the 18th ACM Conference on Information and Knowledge Management, pp. 621–630. ACM (2009). https://doi.org/10.1145/1645953.1646033
10. Espinoza-Arias, P., Poveda-Villalón, M., García-Castro, R., Corcho, O.: Ontological representation of smart city data: from devices to cities. Appl. Sci. **9**(1), 32 (2019). https://doi.org/10.3390/app9010032
11. Fernández-López, M., Suárez-Figueroa, M.C., Gómez-Pérez, A.: Ontology development by reuse. In: Suárez-Figueroa, M.C., Gómez-Pérez, A., Motta, E., Gangemi, A. (eds.) Ontology Engineering in a Networked World, pp. 147–170. Springer, Heidelberg (2012). https://doi.org/10.1007/978-3-642-24794-1_7
12. Gyrard, A., Bonnet, C., Boudaoud, K., Serrano, M.: Lov4iot: a second life for ontology-based domain knowledge to build semantic web of things applications. In: IEEE 4th International Conference on Future Internet of Things and Cloud (FiCloud), pp. 254–261. IEEE (2016). https://doi.org/10.1109/FiCloud.2016.44
13. Gyrard, A., Zimmermann, A., Sheth, A.: Building IoT-based applications for smart cities: how can ontology catalogs help? IEEE Internet Things J. **5**(5), 3978–3990 (2018). https://doi.org/10.1109/JIOT.2018.2854278
14. Katsumi, M., Grüninger, M.: Choosing ontologies for reuse. Appl. Ontol. **12**(3–4), 195–221 (2017). https://doi.org/10.3233/AO-160171
15. Kolbe, N., Kubler, S., Robert, J., Le Traon, Y., Zaslavsky, A.: Linked vocabulary recommendation tools for internet of things: a survey. ACM Comput. Surv. (CSUR) **51**(6), 127 (2019). https://doi.org/10.1145/3284316
16. Kolchin, M., et al.: Ontologies for web of things: a pragmatic review. In: Klinov, P., Mouromtsev, D. (eds.) KESW 2015. CCIS, vol. 518, pp. 102–116. Springer, Cham (2015). https://doi.org/10.1007/978-3-319-24543-0_8
17. Liu, T.Y.: Learning to rank for information retrieval. Found. Trends Inf. Retrieval **3**(3), 225–331 (2009). https://doi.org/10.1007/978-3-642-14267-3
18. Martínez-Romero, M., Jonquet, C., O'Connor, M.J., Graybeal, J., Pazos, A., Musen, M.A.: NCBO ontology recommender 2.0: an enhanced approach for biomedical ontology recommendation. J. Biomed. Semant. **8**(1), 21 (2017). https://doi.org/10.1186/s13326-017-0128-y
19. McCandless, M., Hatcher, E., Gospodnetic, O.: Lucene in Action: Covers Apache Lucene 3.0. Manning Publications Co., Shelter Island (2010). ISBN 1933988177

20. Mikolov, T., Sutskever, I., Chen, K., Corrado, G.S., Dean, J.: Distributed representations of words and phrases and their compositionality. In: Advances in Neural Information Processing Systems, pp. 3111–3119 (2013)
21. Miller, G.A.: WordNet: a lexical database for English. Commun. ACM **38**(11), 39–41 (1995). https://doi.org/10.1145/219717.219748
22. Page, L., Brin, S., Motwani, R., Winograd, T.: The PageRank citation ranking: bringing order to the web. Technical report 1999-66, Stanford InfoLab (1999)
23. Poveda Villalón, M., García Castro, R., Gómez-Pérez, A.: Building an ontology catalogue for smart cities, pp. 829–839. CRC Press (2014)
24. Robertson, S.E.: Overview of the Okapi projects. J. Doc. **53**(1), 3–7 (1997). https://doi.org/10.1108/EUM0000000007186
25. Sabou, M., Lopez, V., Motta, E., Uren, V.: Ontology selection: ontology evaluation on the real semantic web. In: 4th International Workshop on Evaluation of Ontologies for the Web (2006)
26. Salton, G., Buckley, C.: Term-weighting approaches in automatic text retrieval. Inf. Process. Manag. **24**(5), 513–523 (1988). https://doi.org/10.1016/0306-4573(88)90021-0
27. Schaible, J., Gottron, T., Scherp, A.: Survey on common strategies of vocabulary reuse in linked open data modeling. In: Presutti, V., et al. (eds.) ESWC 2014. LNCS, vol. 8465, pp. 457–472. Springer, Cham (2014). https://doi.org/10.1007/978-3-319-07443-6_31
28. Schaible, J., Gottron, T., Scherp, A.: *TermPicker*: enabling the reuse of vocabulary terms by exploiting data from the linked open data cloud. In: Sack, H., Blomqvist, E., d'Aquin, M., Ghidini, C., Ponzetto, S.P., Lange, C. (eds.) ESWC 2016. LNCS, vol. 9678, pp. 101–117. Springer, Cham (2016). https://doi.org/10.1007/978-3-319-34129-3_7
29. Simperl, E.: Reusing ontologies on the semantic web: a feasibility study. Data Knowl. Eng. **68**(10), 905–925 (2009). https://doi.org/10.1016/j.datak.2009.02.002
30. Stadtmüller, S., Harth, A., Grobelnik, M.: Accessing information about linked data vocabularies with vocab.cc. In: Li, J., Qi, G., Zhao, D., Nejdl, W., Zheng, H.T. (eds.) Semantic Web and Web Science. Springer, New York (2013). https://doi.org/10.1007/978-1-4614-6880-6_34
31. Stavrakantonakis, I., Fensel, A., Fensel, D.: Linked open vocabulary ranking and terms discovery. In: Proceedings of the 12th International Conference on Semantic Systems, pp. 1–8. ACM (2016). https://doi.org/10.1145/2993318.2993338
32. Vandenbussche, P.Y., Atemezing, G.A., Poveda-Villalón, M., Vatant, B.: Linked open vocabularies (LOV): a gateway to reusable semantic vocabularies on the web. Semant. Web **8**(3), 437–452 (2017). https://doi.org/10.3233/SW-160213
33. Wu, G., Li, J., Feng, L., Wang, K.: Identifying potentially important concepts and relations in an ontology. In: Sheth, A., et al. (eds.) ISWC 2008. LNCS, vol. 5318, pp. 33–49. Springer, Heidelberg (2008). https://doi.org/10.1007/978-3-540-88564-1_3
34. Zaveri, A., Rula, A., Maurino, A., Pietrobon, R., Lehmann, J., Auer, S.: Quality assessment for linked data: a survey. Semant. Web **7**(1), 63–93 (2016). https://doi.org/10.3233/SW-150175

Incorporating Literals into Knowledge Graph Embeddings

Agustinus Kristiadi[3(✉)], Mohammad Asif Khan[1], Denis Lukovnikov[1], Jens Lehmann[1,2], and Asja Fischer[4]

[1] University of Bonn, Bonn, Germany
s6mokhan@uni-bonn.de, {lukovnik,jens.lehmann}@cs.uni-bonn.de
[2] Frauhofer IAIS, Sankt Augustin, Germany
[3] University of Tübingen, Tübingen, Germany
agustinus.kristiadi@uni-tuebingen.de
[4] Ruhr-University Bochum, Bochum, Germany
asja.fischer@rub.de

Abstract. Knowledge graphs are composed of different elements: entity nodes, relation edges, and literal nodes. Each literal node contains an entity's attribute value (e.g. the *height* of an entity of type *person*) and thereby encodes information which in general cannot be represented by relations between entities alone. However, most of the existing embedding- or latent-feature-based methods for knowledge graph analysis only consider entity nodes and relation edges, and thus do not take the information provided by literals into account. In this paper, we extend existing latent feature methods for link prediction by a simple portable module for incorporating literals, which we name LiteralE. Unlike in concurrent methods where literals are incorporated by adding a literal-dependent term to the output of the scoring function and thus only indirectly affect the entity embeddings, LiteralE directly enriches these embeddings with information from literals via a learnable parametrized function. This function can be easily integrated into the scoring function of existing methods and learned along with the entity embeddings in an end-to-end manner. In an extensive empirical study over three datasets, we evaluate LiteralE-extended versions of various state-of-the-art latent feature methods for link prediction and demonstrate that LiteralE presents an effective way to improve their performance. For these experiments, we augmented standard datasets with their literals, which we publicly provide as testbeds for further research. Moreover, we show that LiteralE leads to an qualitative improvement of the embeddings and that it can be easily extended to handle literals from different modalities.

Keywords: Knowledge graph · Relational learning

A. Kristiadi, M. A. Khan—Equal contribution.

C. Ghidini et al. (Eds.): ISWC 2019, LNCS 11778, pp. 347–363, 2019.
https://doi.org/10.1007/978-3-030-30793-6_20

1 Introduction

Knowledge graphs (KGs) form the backbone of a range of applications, for instance in the areas of search, question answering and data integration. Some well known KGs are DBpedia [9], Freebase [1], YAGO3 [10], and the Google Knowledge Graph [5]. There are different knowledge representation paradigms for modeling KGs such as the Resource Description Framework (RDF) and (labeled) property graphs. Within this paper, we consider a KG to be a set of triples, where each triple connects an entity (shown as circle in Fig. 1) to another entity or a literal (the latter shown as rectangle in Fig. 1) via relationships. Such KGs can be represented by the RDF and property graph paradigms, i.e. the methods presented in this paper are applicable to both. To give a concrete example, the KG depicted in Fig. 1 includes the triples (`John`, `Doe High School`, `studiesAt`) and (`Jane`, `2000`, `birthYear`). The first triple expresses the relationship between an entity and another entity. The second triple expresses a relationship between an entity and a literal[1].

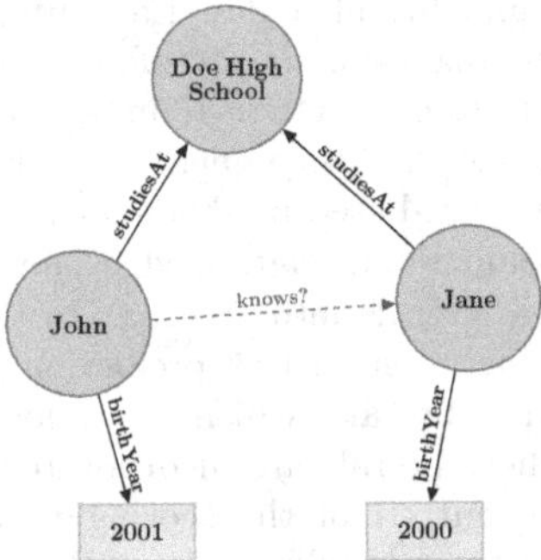

Fig. 1. Literals (box) encode information that cannot be represented by relations alone, and are useful for link prediction task. For instance, by considering both `birthYear` literals and the fact that `John` and `Jane` both study at `Doe High School`, we can be more confident that the relation `knows` between `John` and `Jane` exists.

Knowledge graphs aim to capture factual knowledge within a particular domain. However, they are often incomplete since, e.g., more information is provided for popular than for unknown entities or because the KG is partially or fully generated via an automatic extraction process. As a result, KGs rely heavily on methods predicting unknown triples given all known triples. This problem is usually referred to as link prediction. The closely related problem of detecting incorrect triples in KGs is referred to as link correction and is relevant for improving the quality of a KG.

---

[1] For more information about the RDF concepts see https://www.w3.org/TR/rdf11-concepts.

Due to the importance of the problem, many methods for link prediction and correction in KGs have been developed. The two main classes of these methods are graph feature and latent feature methods [11]. Graph feature methods predict the existence of triples based on features directly observed in the KG, such as the neighborhood of an entity and paths to other entities. They are well suited for modeling local graph patterns. In latent feature models, low-dimensional, latent representations (also called embeddings) of entities and relations are learned. These embeddings incorporate the KG structure, can capture global patterns, and allow to compute the likeliness of a given triple in terms of a probability or score function. However, most of the recent work on latent feature models only takes entities and their relations to other entities into account. Therefore, they are missing the additional information encoded in literals. For example, Fig. 1 shows two entities with both structural (visiting the same school) as well as literal (birth years) information. To maximize the accuracy of predicting a `knows` relation between these entities, structural and literal information should be combined as people visiting the same school and having similar age tend to have a higher probability of knowing each other.

In this paper, we investigate the advantage obtained by incorporating the additional information provided by literals into latent feature methods. We introduce LiteralE, a method to enrich entity embeddings with their literal information. Given an entity embedding, we incorporate its corresponding literals using a learnable parametric function, which gets the vanilla embedding and the entity's literals as input, and outputs a literal-enriched embedding. This embedding can then replace the vanilla embedding in any latent feature model, without changing its original scoring function and the resulting system can be jointly trained with stochastic gradient descent, or any other gradient based algorithm of choice, in an end-to-end manner. Therefore, LiteralE can be seen as an extension module that can be universally combined with any existing latent feature method. Within this paper, we mainly focus on numerical literals. However, we demonstrate that the principle can be directly generalized to other literal types, such as textual and image information, e.g. by providing low-dimensional vector representation of image or text [22,23] as an additional input to LiteralE.

Our contributions in this paper are threefold:

- We introduce LiteralE, a universal approach to enrich latent feature methods with literal information via a learnable parametric function. In contrast to other latent feature models including literals, our approach does not require specific prior knowledge, does not rely on a fixed function to combine entity embeddings and literals, can model interactions between an embedding of an entity and all its literal values and can be trained end-to-end.
- We evaluate LiteralE on standard link prediction datasets: FB15k, FB15k-237 and YAGO3-10. We extended FB15k and FB15k-237 with literals, in order to allow for direct comparison against other methods on these standard datasets. We provide these literal-extended versions (augmented with numerical and

textual literals) and hope they can serve as a testbed for future research on the inclusion of literals in KG modeling.[2]
- Based on experimental results on the extended datasets, we show that exploiting the information provided by literals significantly increases the link prediction performance of existing latent feature methods as well as the quality of their embeddings.

This paper is organized as follows. In Sect. 2 we review several latent feature methods for link prediction in KGs. In Sect. 3 we present LiteralE, our approach for incorporating literals into existing latent feature methods. We give a brief review of the related literatures and contrast LiteralE with other methods incorporating literals in Sect. 4. Our experiment methodology is described in Sect. 5, and in Sect. 6 we present our experiment results. Finally, we conclude our paper in Sect. 7.

Our implementation of the proposed methods and all datasets are publicly available at: https://github.com/SmartDataAnalytics/LiteralE.

2 Preliminaries

In the following we will describe the link prediction problem more formally and give a brief overview over well-known latent feature methods.

2.1 Problem Description

Link prediction is defined as the task of deciding whether a fact (represented by a triple) is true or false given a KG. More formally, let $\mathcal{E} = \{e_1, \cdots, e_{N_e}\}$ be the set of entities, $\mathcal{R} = \{r_1, \cdots, r_{N_r}\}$ be the set of relations connecting two entities, $\mathcal{D} = \{d_1, \cdots, d_{N_d}\}$ be the set of relations connecting an entity and a literal, i.e., the data relations, and $\mathcal{L}$ be the set of all literal values. A knowledge graph $\mathcal{G}$ is a subset of $(\mathcal{E} \times \mathcal{E} \times \mathcal{R}) \cup (\mathcal{E} \times \mathcal{L} \times \mathcal{D})$ representing the facts that are assumed to hold. Link prediction can be formulated by a function $\psi : \mathcal{E} \times \mathcal{E} \times \mathcal{R} \rightarrow \mathbb{R}$ mapping each possible fact represented by the corresponding triple $(e_i, e_j, r_k) \in \mathcal{E} \times \mathcal{E} \times \mathcal{R}$ to a score value, where a higher value implies the triple is more likely to be true.

2.2 Latent Feature Methods

In general, latent feature methods are a class of methods in which low dimensional vector representations of entities and relations, called *embeddings* or *latent features*, are learned. Let H be the embedding dimension. We define a score function $f : \mathbb{R}^H \times \mathbb{R}^H \times \mathbb{R}^H \rightarrow \mathbb{R}$ that maps a triple of embeddings $(\mathbf{e}_i, \mathbf{e}_j, \mathbf{r}_k)$ to a score $f(\mathbf{e}_i, \mathbf{e}_j, \mathbf{r}_k)$ that correlates with the truth value of the triple. In latent feature methods, the score of any triple $(e_i, e_j, r_k) \in \mathcal{E} \times \mathcal{E} \times \mathcal{R}$ is then defined as $\psi(e_i, e_j, r_k) \stackrel{\text{def}}{=} f(\mathbf{e}_i, \mathbf{e}_j, \mathbf{r}_k)$.

[2] A literal-extended version of YAGO3-10 is provided by Pezeshkpou *et al.* [12].

Latent feature methods for link predictions are well studied. These methods follow a score-based approach as described above but make use of different kind of scoring functions f. In this paper we study the potential benefit of incorporating numerical literals in three state of the art methods: DistMult [5], ComplEx [19], and ConvE [4], which are described in the following. Note however, that these are just an exemplary choice of methods and our approach for incorporating literals can easily be adopted to other latent feature methods.

The **DistMult** scoring function is defined as diagonal bilinear interaction between the two entity embeddings and the relation embedding corresponding to a given triple, as follows

$$f_{\text{DistMult}}(\mathbf{e}_i, \mathbf{e}_j, \mathbf{r}_k) = \langle \mathbf{e}_i, \mathbf{e}_j, \mathbf{r}_k \rangle = \mathbf{e}_i^{\mathsf{T}} \operatorname{diag}(\mathbf{r_k})\, \mathbf{e}_j. \tag{1}$$

Observe that DistMult is cheap to implement, both in terms of computational and space complexity.

ComplEx can be seen as DistMult analogue in the complex space. The embedding vectors have two parts: the real part $\text{Re}(\mathbf{e})$ and $\text{Re}(\mathbf{r})$, and the imaginary part $\text{Im}(\mathbf{e})$ and $\text{Im}(\mathbf{r})$, respectively. The scoring function is defined as

$$\begin{aligned} f_{\text{ComplEx}}(\mathbf{e}_i, \mathbf{e}_j, \mathbf{r}_k) &= \text{Re}(\langle \mathbf{e}_i, \bar{\mathbf{e}}_j, \mathbf{r}_k \rangle) \\ &= \langle \text{Re}(\mathbf{e}_i), \text{Re}(\mathbf{e}_j), \text{Re}(\mathbf{r}_k) \rangle \\ &+ \langle \text{Im}(\mathbf{e}_i), \text{Im}(\mathbf{e}_j), \text{Re}(\mathbf{r}_k) \rangle \\ &+ \langle \text{Re}(\mathbf{e}_i), \text{Im}(\mathbf{e}_j), \text{Im}(\mathbf{r}_k) \rangle \\ &- \langle \text{Im}(\mathbf{e}_i), \text{Re}(\mathbf{e}_j), \text{Im}(\mathbf{r}_k) \rangle. \end{aligned} \tag{2}$$

ComplEx thus has twice the number of parameters compared to DistMult but provides the benefit of modeling asymmetric relationships better, as discussed by Trouillon *et al.* [19].

ConvE employs a convolutional neural network to extract features from entity and relation embeddings. Let h be a nonlinear function, $\omega \in \mathcal{R}^{k \times m \times n}$ be convolution filters, and $\mathbf{W} \in \mathcal{R}^{kmn \times H}$ be a weight matrix. The ConvE score function is then defined by

$$f_{\text{ConvE}}(\mathbf{e}_i, \mathbf{e}_j, \mathbf{r}_k) = h(\mathbf{vec}(h([\mathbf{e}_i, \mathbf{r}_k] * \omega))\mathbf{W})\, \mathbf{e}_j, \tag{3}$$

where $\mathbf{vec}(\cdot)$ is the vectorization of output of convolutional filters. By employing deep feature extractors in the form of nonlinear convolutional layers, ConvE is able to encode more expressive features while remaining highly parameter efficient.

3 LiteralE

Our method of incorporating literals into existing latent feature methods, which we call LiteralE, is a simple, modular, and universal extension which can potentially enhance the performance of arbitrary latent feature methods.

Let $\mathbf{L} \in \mathbb{R}^{N_e \times N_d}$ be a matrix, where each entry $\mathbf{L}_{ik}$ contains the k-th literal value of the i-th entity if a triple with the i-th entity and the k-th data relation exists in the KGs, and zero otherwise. We will refer to the i-th row $\mathbf{l}_i$ of $\mathbf{L}$ as the literal vector of the i-th entity. As an illustration, consider the KG part depicted in Fig. 1 and imagine that there only exist three data relations in this specific KG: `heightCm`, `birthYear`, and `countryArea`. For the entity `John` we will then have the literal vector $(0, 2001, 0)$ in the particular row corresponding to `John` in matrix $\mathbf{L}$, as `John` only has literal information for `birthYear`.[3]

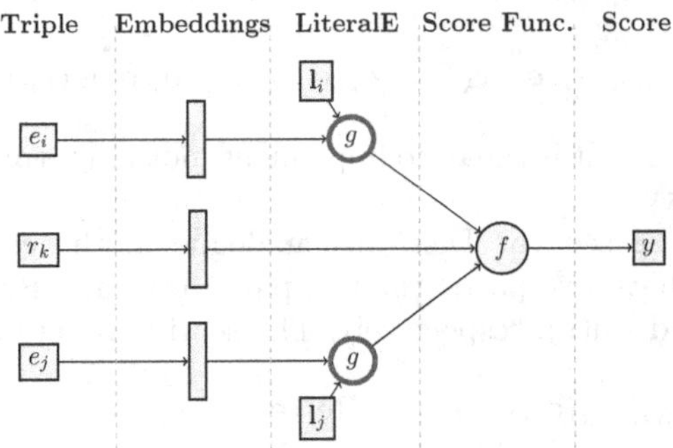

Fig. 2. Overview on how LiteralE is applied to the base scoring function f. LiteralE takes the embedding and the corresponding literals as input, and combines them via a learnable function g. The output is a joint embedding which is further used in the score function f.

At the core of LiteralE is a function $g : \mathbb{R}^H \times \mathbb{R}^{N_d} \rightarrow \mathbb{R}^H$ that takes an entity's embedding and a literal vector as inputs and maps them to a vector of the same dimension as the entity embedding. This vector forms an literal-enriched embedding vector that can replace the original embedding vector in the scoring function of any latent feature model. For example, in our experiments, we replace every entity embedding $\mathbf{e}_i$ with $\mathbf{e}_i^{\text{lit}} = g(\mathbf{e}_i, \mathbf{l}_i)$ in the scoring functions of DistMult and ConvE. For ComplEx, where the embeddings have a real and an imaginary part, we use two separate functions to map $\text{Re}(\mathbf{e}_i)$ and $\text{Im}(\mathbf{e}_i)$ to their literal-extended counterparts. Aside of these changes regarding the entity embeddings, the score functions are the same as described before in Eqs. (1), (2), and (3). For instance, the LiteralE-extended version of DistMult is given by $f_{\text{DistMult}}(\mathbf{e}_i^{\text{lit}}, \mathbf{e}_j^{\text{lit}}, \mathbf{r}_k)$.

We will now describe the function g in detail. First, since we would like g to be flexible, we need it to be learnable. Second, we would like g to be able to decide whether the additional literal information is useful or not, and adapt accordingly, e.g. by incorporating or ignoring that information. We therefore take cue from the gating mechanism present in RNNs, such as the gated recurrent

[3] Note that in practice, we normalize the literal values.

unit (GRU) [3], and let g be defined by

$$\begin{aligned} g : \mathbb{R}^H \times \mathbb{R}^{N_d} &\to \mathbb{R}^H \\ \mathbf{e}, \mathbf{l} &\mapsto \mathbf{z} \odot \mathbf{h} + (1 - \mathbf{z}) \odot \mathbf{e}\,, \end{aligned} \tag{4}$$

where $\odot$ is the pointwise multiplication and

$$\begin{aligned} \mathbf{z} &= \sigma(\mathbf{W}_{ze}^{\mathrm{T}} \mathbf{e} + \mathbf{W}_{zl}^{\mathrm{T}} \mathbf{l} + \mathbf{b}) \\ \mathbf{h} &= h(\mathbf{W}_h^{\mathrm{T}} [\mathbf{e}, \mathbf{l}])\,. \end{aligned} \tag{5}$$

Note that $\mathbf{W}_h \in \mathbb{R}^{H+N_d \times H}$, $\mathbf{W}_{ze} \in \mathbb{R}^{H \times H}$, $\mathbf{W}_{zl} \in \mathbb{R}^{N_d \times H}$, and $\mathbf{b} \in \mathbb{R}^H$ are the parameters of g, σ is the sigmoid function, and h is a component-wise nonlinearity (e.g. the hyperbolic tangent).

LiteralE introduces some overhead in the number of parameters compared to the base method. This overhead is equal to the number of parameters of the function g and is compared to that of other approaches for the incorporation of literals in Table 1. Specifically, there are $2H^2 + 2N_d H + H$ additional parameters corresponding to the dimensionality of $\mathbf{W}_h$, $\mathbf{W}_{ze}$, $\mathbf{W}_{zl}$, and $\mathbf{b}$ in Eq. (5). Thus, with this choice of g and given H, the number of additional parameters of LiteralE grows in $O(N_d)$, that is, linear to the number of data relations in the KG. Furthermore, the additional space complexity of LiteralE is in $O(N_e N_d)$ as one needs to store the matrix $\mathbf{L}$. Lastly, the additional computational complexity of LiteralE is only attributed to the cost of three matrix multiplication and one vector addition.

In summary, with our method LiteralE, we propose to replace the score function $f_X(\mathbf{e}_i, \mathbf{e}_j, \mathbf{r}_k)$ from the host method X with the function composition

$$f_X(g(\mathbf{e}_i, \mathbf{l}_i), g(\mathbf{e}_j, \mathbf{l}_j), \mathbf{r}_k)$$

as illustrated in Fig. 2. This new scoring function can be trained by gradient descent based optimization using the same training procedure as before.

4 Related Work

In the last years, several efforts to incorporate literals into KG embedding methods have been made. Toutantova *et al.* [18] and Tu *et al.* [20] make use of textual literals of entities in addition to relational embeddings. More specifically they learn additional entity embeddings from their textual description and use them in an additive term in the score function of latent distant methods. Xie *et al.* [22] and Xu *et al.* [23] also proposed methods to incorporate textual literals into latent distance methods such as TransE by encoding textual literals with recurrent or convolutional neural networks. Xie *et al.* [13] use image literals in their model by projecting entities' image features into an entity embeddings space. However, all of those approaches do not consider numerical literals. MultiModal [12] extends DistMult to also predict the likeliness of (subject, relation, literal)-triples, by replacing the object embedding in standard DistMult by its literal embedding (where literals of different modalities are taken into account). By doing so literals are incorporated into entity embeddings in an implicit manner. Sun *et al.* [14], proposes to employ literals to refine the joint embeddings in entity alignment tasks: They use literals to cluster together entities which have high literal correlations, thus only indirectly use the literal information in the entity embeddings. In contrast to all the aforementioned works, LiteralE combines the literals into the entity embedding directly and explicitly by the function g defined above.

KBLRN [6] handles literals in a separate function added to the vanilla scoring function and thus does not incorporate literals in to the entity embeddings themselves. The construction of features from the numerical literals is based on a prior knowledge: the difference between the numerical literals of the subject and object entity is a good predictor for a given relation. These features then serve as input to a fixed radial basis function (RBF), which is added to the score function of the base method (DistMult). In contrast, LiteralE incorporates literal information directly into the entity embeddings[4], and does not use any prior knowledge about the meaning of numerical literals.

Table 1. Model complexity in terms of number of parameters of methods for incorporating literals. We denote the number of parameters of base models (e.g. DistMult) with Γ. Furthermore, Z is the number of hidden units in a neural network (e.g. in LiteralE-MLP and MTKGNN's Attribute Networks). We leave out bias parameters for clarity.

Model	Number of parameters
KBLN	$\Gamma + N_r N_d$
MTKGNN	$\Gamma + N_d H + 2(2HZ + Z)$
LiteralE	$\Gamma + 2H^2 + 2N_d H + H$

MTKGNN [15] extends ERMLP [5] and incorporates numerical literals by introducing an additional learning task, more precisely, the task of predicting the literal value for a given entity. This multi-task learning approach of MTKGNN requires an additional *attribute-specific* training procedure. Therefore, adding another type or modality of literals is not straightforward and costly as another learning task needs to be devised. Similar to MTKGNN, TransEA [21] extends TransE by adding a numerical attribute prediction loss to the relational loss.

Lastly, the model recently proposed by Thoma *et al.* [16] can be seen as a special case of LiteralE where the function used instead of the function g defined above to combine literals of entities with their entity embeddings is a concatenation followed by singular value decomposition. Thus, they use a fixed function to combine the representations, whereas LiteralE employs an adaptable function and is therefore more flexible. Furthermore, they only consider image and text literals but no numerical literals.

[4] Note, that incorporating the literal information into the embeddings also seems advantageous for entity disambiguation or clustering.

5 Experiments

In the following we will describe the training approach, the datasets, the experimental setup, and the evaluation metrics applied in our experiments.

5.1 Training

We use the same training approach as Dettmers *et al.* [4] for all the tested methods. That is, for every given triple (e_i, e_j, r_k) in the KG, we compute the score for $(e_i, e'_j, r_k), \forall e'_j \in \mathcal{E}$ using the (original or LiteralE-extended) scoring function f, and apply the sigmoid function to the resulting score (i.e. $p = \sigma \circ f$), such that it can be interpreted as probability of existence of a given triple.

Table 2. Number of entities, relations, literals, and triples, for all datasets used in this paper.

Dataset	FB15k	FB15k-237	YAGO3-10
# Entities (N_e)	14,951	14,541	123,182
# Relations (N_r)	1,345	237	37
# Data rel. (N_d)	121	121	5
# Literals ($\lvert\mathcal{L}\rvert$)	18,741	18,741	111,406
# Relational triples	592,213	310,116	1,089,040
# Literal triples	70,257	70,257	111,406

Let $\mathbf{p} \in [0,1]^{N_e}$ be the probability vector, collecting the resulting probabilities with respect to all $e'_j \in \mathcal{E}$. The model is then trained by minimizing the binary cross-entropy loss between the probability vector $\mathbf{p}$ and the vector of ground truth labels $\mathbf{y} \in \{0,1\}^{N_e}$ indicating the existence of triples $(e_i, e'_j, r_k), \forall e'_j \in \mathcal{E}$ in the KG. That is, we minimize

$$L(\mathbf{p}, \mathbf{y}) = -\frac{1}{N_e} \sum_{x=1}^{N_e} (y_x \log(p_x) + (1 - y_x) \log(1 - p_x)), \tag{6}$$

where p_x and y_x are the predicted probability and the given truth value for the x-th element of our candidate set $\{(e_i, e'_j, r_k), e'_j \in \mathcal{E}\}$. We use Adam [7] to optimize this loss function.

Note, the above procedure of considering all triples (e_i, e'_j, r_k), $\forall e'_j \in \mathcal{E}$ if there is any triple (e_i, e_j, r_k) with head e_i and relation r_k in the training set is referred to as 1-N scoring [4] as for each triple, we compute scores of $N := N_e = |\mathcal{E}|$ triples. This is in contrast with 1-1 scoring, where one primarily considers the training example (e_i, e_j, r_k) and applies some other strategy for negative sampling (i.e. for the generation of non-existing triples). We refer the reader to [4] for a further discussion regarding this.

5.2 Datasets

We use three widely used datasets for evaluating link prediction performance: FB15k, FB15k-237, and YAGO3-10. FB15k [2] is a subset of Freebase where most triples are related to movies and sports. As discussed by Dettmers *et al.* [4], FB15k has a large number of test triples which can simply be obtained by inverting training triples. This results in a biased test set, for which a simple model which is symmetric with respect to object and subject entity is capable of achieving excellent results. To address this problem, FB15k-237 [17] was created by removing inverse relations from FB15k. YAGO3-10 [10] is a subset of the YAGO3 knowledge graph which mostly consists of triples related to people.

In this work, we only consider numerical literals, e.g. longitude, latitude, population, age, date of birth (in UNIX time format), etc. To enrich FB15k and FB15k-237 with these literals, we created a SPARQL endpoint for Freebase and extracted literals of all entities contained in FB15k. We further filtered the extracted literals based on their frequency, i.e we only consider data relations $d \in \mathcal{D}$ that occur at least in 5 triples in FB15k. We also remove all key and ID relations since their values are not meaningful as quantities. For YAGO3-10, we use numerical literals provided by YAGO3-10-plus [12], which is publicly available.[5] In case an entity has multiple literal values for a particular data relation, we arbitrarily select one of them. Some statistics of the datasets are provided in Table 2.

5.3 Experimental Setup

We implemented LieralE on top of ConvE's codebase, which is publicly available[6]. The hyperparameters used in all of our experiments across all datasets are: learning rate 0.001, batch size 128, embedding size 200, embedding dropout probability 0.2, and label smoothing 0.1. Additionally for ConvE, we used feature map dropout with probability 0.2 and projection layer dropout with probability 0.3. Note, that these hyperparameter values are the same as in the experiments of Dettmers *et al.* [4].

Except for experiments with ConvE, we run all of our experiments for a maximum of 100 epochs as we observed that this is sufficient for convergence. For ConvE, we used at most 1000 epochs, as described in the original paper [4]. We apply early stopping in all of the experiments by monitoring the Mean Reciprocal Rank (MRR) metric on the validation set every three epochs.

To validate our approach and to eliminate the effect of different environment setups, we re-implemented the related models, KBLN [6], and MTKGNN [15] as baselines. Note that we did not re-implement KBLRN [6] since the sub-model KBLN (i.e. the KBLRN model without making use of the relational information provided by graph feature methods) is directly comparable to LiteralE.[7] As

[5] https://github.com/pouyapez/multim-kb-embeddings.

[6] https://github.com/TimDettmers/ConvE.

[7] Note, that LiteralE could also be extended to incorporate graph features as an additional input to g.

Table 3. Link prediction results on FB15k, FB15k-237, and YAGO3-10. The best values comparing our implementation of base models, KBLN, MTKGNN and LiteralE are highlighted in bold text. Only numerical literals are used in the experiments.

Models	MR	MRR	Hits@1	Hits@3	Hits@10
FB15k					
DistMult	108	0.671	0.589	0.723	0.818
ComplEx	127	0.695	0.618	0.744	0.833
ConvE	49	0.692	0.596	0.760	0.853
KBLN [6]	129	0.739	0.668	**0.788**	0.859
MTKGNN [15]	87	0.669	0.586	0.722	0.82
DistMult-LiteralE	68	0.676	0.589	0.733	0.825
ComplEx-LiteralE	80	**0.746**	**0.686**	0.782	0.853
ConvE-LiteralE	**43**	0.733	0.656	0.785	**0.863**
FB15k-237					
DistMult	633	0.282	0.203	0.309	0.438
ComplEx	652	0.290	0.212	0.317	0.445
ConvE	297	0.313	0.228	0.344	0.479
KBLN [6]	358	0.301	0.215	0.333	0.468
MTKGNN [15]	532	0.285	0.204	0.312	0.445
DistMult-LiteralE	280	**0.317**	**0.232**	**0.348**	**0.483**
ComplEx-LiteralE	357	0.305	0.222	0.336	0.466
ConvE-LiteralE	**255**	0.303	0.219	0.33	0.471
YAGO3-10					
DistMult	2943	0.466	0.377	0.514	0.653
ComplEx	3768	0.493	0.411	0.536	0.649
ConvE	2141	0.505	0.422	0.554	0.660
KBLN	2666	0.487	0.405	0.531	0.642
MTKGNN [15]	2970	0.481	0.398	0.527	0.634
DistMult-LiteralE	1642	0.479	0.4	0.525	0.627
ComplEx-LiteralE	2508	0.485	0.412	0.527	0.618
ConvE-LiteralE	**1037**	**0.525**	**0.448**	**0.572**	**0.659**

in [4], we use a 1-N training approach, while KBLN and MTKGNN uses a 1-1 approach. Therefore, the RelNet in MTKGNN which is a neural network is infeasible to be implemented in our environment. Thus, as opposed to neural network, we use DistMult as base model in our re-implementation of an MTKGNN-like method. While this change does not allow to evaluate the performance of the original MTKGNN model, it makes our MTKGNN-like method directly comparable to the other methods that we consider in our experiments, since it uses the same base score function. All in all, due to these differences in the loss function and the overall framework which are necessary to make KBLN and MTKGNN comparable to LiteralE, the results we report for them might differ from those reported in the respective original papers. In addition, we obtain slightly different results compared to [4] for DistMult, ComplEx and ConvE for all three datasets (our results are mostly comparable or slightly better and in some case worse). This could be attributed to the hyperparameter tuning performed in [4].

5.4 Evaluation

For the evaluation of the performance of the different methods on the link prediction task, we follow the standard setup used in other studies. For each triple (e_i, e_j, r_k) in the test set, we generate a set of corrupted triples by either replacing the subject entity e_i or the object entity e_j with any other entity $e' \in \mathcal{E}$. We further compute the scores of these corrupted triples along with the score of the true triple. To evaluate the model, we rank all triples with respect to their scores and use the following standard evaluation metrics: Mean Rank (MR), Mean Reciprocal Rank (MRR), Hits@1, Hits@3, and Hits@10.

6 Results

6.1 Link Prediction

The results of our experiments for link prediction are summarized in Table 3. In general, LiteralE improves the base models (DistMult, ComplEx, and ConvE) significantly. For instance, we found that implementing LiteralE on top of DistMult improves the MRR score by 0.74%, 12.41%, and 2.7% for the FB15k, FB15k-237, and YAGO3-10 dataset, respectively. We also observed that the improvements brought by LiteralE when combined with ComplEx and ConvE are not as impressive as for DistMult, which might be attributed to the fact that these base models already achieve higher performance than DistMult. Compared to other methods that incorporate literals, namely KBLN and MTKGNN, LiteralE achieves a competitive or even better performance in our experiments. Moreover, note that, LiteralE directly and explicitly modifies the embedding vectors, whereas KBLN and MTKGNN do not. Thus, LiteralE embeddings could be more useful for tasks other than link prediction. This will be discussed further in Sect. 6.4.

6.2 Comparison to a Simple LiteralE Baseline

To validate our choice of the function g, we compare the performance of LiteralE with the g proposed in Sect. 3 to its variant based on a simple (but still learnable) linear transformation, dubbed g_{lin}. That is, $g_{\text{lin}} : \mathbb{R}^H \times \mathbb{R}^{N_d} \to \mathbb{R}^H$ is defined by $\mathbf{e}, \mathbf{l} \mapsto \mathbf{W}^{\mathrm{T}}[\mathbf{e}, \mathbf{l}]$, where $\mathbf{W} \in \mathbb{R}^{H+N_d \times H}$ is a learnable weight matrix. The results are presented in Table 4 (cf. Table 3).

The proposed g leads to better results than g_{lin} in 5 out of 9 experiments. While LiteralE with g provides a consistent performance improvement for all

Table 4. The link prediction performance of LiteralE employing a simple linear transformation g_{lin}.

Datasets	Functions	MRR	Hits@1	Hits@10
FB15k	DistMult-g_{lin}	0.583	0.476	0.771
	ComplEx-g_{lin}	**0.765**	**0.705**	**0.871**
	ConvE-g_{lin}	0.66	0.556	0.836
FB15k-237	DistMult-g_{lin}	**0.314**	**0.228**	**0.483**
	ComplEx-g_{lin}	0.299	0.214	0.467
	ConvE-g_{lin}	**0.314**	**0.228**	**0.483**
YAGO3-10	DistMult-g_{lin}	0.504	0.422	0.653
	ComplEx-g_{lin}	**0.509**	**0.433**	0.653
	ConvE-g_{lin}	0.506	0.422	**0.664**

Table 5. Link prediction results for DistMult-LiteralE on FB15k-237, with both numerical and text literals. "N" and "T" denotes the usage of numerical and text literals, respectively.

Models	MRR	Hits@1	Hits@10	MRR Improv.
DistMult	0.241	0.155	0.419	-
DistMult-LiteralE (N)	0.317	0.232	0.483	+31.54%
DistMult-LiteralE (N+T)	**0.32**	**0.234**	**0.488**	**+32.78%**

base models, DistMult-g_{lin} shows a decreased performance compared to DistMult on FB15k. This might be explained by the fact that – as [17] already reported – FB15k contains triples in the test set that have an inverse analog (i.e. the triple resulting from changing the position of subject and object entity) in the training set. The prediction for such triples can get difficult if the inverse has a different label. Since the vanilla DistMult already has difficulties in modeling asymmetric relations on FB15k, adding literals using a naive g_{lin} might only introduce noise, resulting in even lower performance. On the other hand, g_{lin} leads to better results than g in combination with ComplEx on FB15k.

In general, the results show that for performance-maximization purpose, it makes sense to investigate the performance of LiteralE in combination with different transformation functions. Given the right choice of transformation function for incorporating literals, LiteralE always improves the performance of the base model.

6.3 Experiment with Text Literals

LiteralE, as described in Sect. 3 can easily be extended to other types of literals, e.g. text and images. In this section this is briefly demonstrated for text literals. First, let us assume that text literals are represented by vectors in $\mathbb{R}^{N_t}$, i.e. as resulting from document embedding techniques [8].[8] Subsequently, let us redefine g to be a function mapping $\mathbb{R}^H \times \mathbb{R}^{N_d} \times \mathbb{R}^{N_t}$ to $\mathbb{R}^H$. Specifically, we redefine $\mathbf{W}_h$ (Eq. (5)) to be in $\mathbb{R}^{H+N_d+N_t \times H}$ and employ an additional gating weight matrix $\mathbf{W}_{zt} \in \mathbb{R}^{N_t \times H}$ to handle the additional text literal. Note, that this simple extension scheme can be used to extend LiteralE to incorporate literals of any other type (e.g. image literals) as long as those literals are encoded as vectors in $\mathbb{R}^N$, for some N.

The results for extending DistMult-LiteralE with the entities' text literals (i.e. the entity description) are presented in Table 5. We found that incorporating text literals results in a further increase of the link prediction performance of DistMult on FB15k-237.

6.4 Nearest Neighbor Analysis

For a further qualitative investigation, we present the nearest neighbors of some entities in the space of literals, the latent space learned by (i) DistMult, (ii) KBLN, (iii) MTKGNN, and (iv) DisMult-LiteralE in Table 6.[9]

In the embedding space of DistMult, geographical entities such as `North America` and `Philippines` are close to other entities of the same type. However, these neighboring entities are not intuitive, e.g. `North America` is close to `Pyrenees`, whereas `Philippines` is close to `Peru` and `Kuwait`. When we inspected the embedding space of DistMult-LiteralE that also takes literals information into account, these nearest neighbors (shown in bold font in Table 6) become more intuitive, i.e they consist of entities geographically close to each others. Furthermore, we found that DistMult-LiteralE's embeddings show clear qualitative advantage compared to that of vanilla DistMult also for entities from other types, e.g. comparing the nearest neighbors of `Roman Republic` which is of type 'empire'. In contrast, KBLN's embeddings tend to be close to the embeddings of unrelated entities: both `North America` and `Philippines` are close to the entities `House of Romanov`, `House of Hanover`, and `House of Stuart`, while `Roman Republic` is close to `Retinol`. Similarly, the embeddings of MTKGNN are also close to the embedding of unrelated entities, e.g., `North America` is close to `Pyrenees` and `Roman Repulic` is close to `North Island`. This findings demonstrates the advantage of incorporating literals on the embedding level (as done by LiterelE) over incorporating them at the score or loss function (as done by KBLN and MTKGNN, respectively).

When inspecting the nearest neighborhood of the same entities when represented only by their literal vectors, it becomes clear that these vectors themselves are already containing useful information indicating the closeness of similar entities. For example, geographical entities have `longitude` and `latitude` literals, while city, nation, and empire entities have `date_founded` and `date_dissolved` literals, which can explain the closeness of two entities given only their literal vectors. Note however, that the nearest neighbours in the literal space do not

[8] We use spaCy's pretrained GloVe embedding model. Available at https://spacy.io.

[9] The base model for all of these methods is DistMult.

Table 6. Comparison of nearest neighbors of selected entities from FB15k-237 embedded in (i) DistMult's latent space, (ii) KBLN's latent space, (iii) MTKGNN's latent space, (iv) the literal space, where each entity is represented only by its literals, and (v) the DisMult-LiteralE's latent space.

Entity	Methods	Nearest neighbors
North America	DistMult	Latin America, Pyrenees, Americas
	KBLN	House of Hanover, House of Stuart, House of Romanov
	MTKGNN	Latin America, Panama City, Pyrenees
	Num. lits. only	Soviet Union, Latin America, Africa
	LiteralE	**Americas, Latin America, Asia**
Philippines	DistMult	Peru, Thailand, Kuwait
	KBLN	House of Romanov, House of Hanover, House of Stuart
	MTKGNN	Thailand, Kuwait, Peru
	Num. lits. only	Peru, Poland, Pakistan
	LiteralE	**Thailand, Taiwan, Greece**
Roman Republic	DistMult	Republic of Venice, Israel Defense Force, Byzantine Empire
	KBLN	Republic of Venice, Carthage, Retinol
	MTKGNN	Republic of Venice, Carthage, North Island
	Num. lits. only	Alexandria, Yerevan, Cologne
	LiteralE	**Roman Empire, Kingdom of Greece, Byzantine Empire**

coincide with and are less informative than the nearest neighbours in the LiteralE embedding space.

All in all, our observations suggest that integrating the literal information into entity embeddings indeed improves their quality, which makes LiteralE embeddings promising for entity resolution and clustering tasks.

7 Conclusion and Future Work

In this paper, we introduced LiteralE: a simple method to incorporate literals into latent feature methods for knowledge graph analysis. It corresponds to a learnable function that merges entity embeddings with their literal information available in the knowledge graph. The resulting literal-enriched latent features can replace the vanilla entity embedding in any latent feature method, without any further modification. Therefore, LiteralE can be seen as an universal extension module. We showed that augmenting various state-of-the-art models (DistMult, ComplEx, and ConvE) with LiteralE significantly improves their link prediction performance. Moreover, as exemplarily demonstrated for text literals,

LiteralE can be easily extended other types of literals. In future work, LiteralE shall be further be extended to accommodate literals from the image domain. This can be achieved by extracting latent representations from images (for example with convolutional neural networks), and providing them as additional inputs to LiteralE for merging them with the vanilla entit y embeddings. Furthermore, our finding that LiteralE improves the quality of the entity embeddings makes it a promising candidate for improving other tasks in the field of knowledge graph analysis, such as entity resolution and knowledge graph clustering.

References

1. Bollacker, K., Evans, C., Paritosh, P., Sturge, T., Taylor, J.: Freebase: a collaboratively created graph database for structuring human knowledge. In: Proceedings of the 2008 ACM SIGMOD International Conference on Management of Data, pp. 1247–1250. ACM (2008)
2. Bordes, A., Usunier, N., Garcia-Duran, A., Weston, J., Yakhnenko, O.: Translating embeddings for modeling multi-relational data. In: Advances in Neural Information Processing Systems, pp. 2787–2795 (2013)
3. Cho, K., et al.: Learning phrase representations using RNN encoder-decoder for statistical machine translation. In: Proceedings of the 2014 Conference on Empirical Methods in Natural Language Processing (EMNLP), pp. 1724–1734. Association for Computational Linguistics, Doha, October 2014. http://www.aclweb.org/anthology/D14-1179
4. Dettmers, T., Pasquale, M., Pontus, S., Riedel, S.: Convolutional 2D knowledge graph embeddings. In: Proceedings of the 32nd AAAI Conference on Artificial Intelligence, February 2018. https://arxiv.org/abs/1707.01476
5. Dong, X., et al.: Knowledge vault: a web-scale approach to probabilistic knowledge fusion. In: Proceedings of the 20th ACM SIGKDD International Conference on Knowledge Discovery and Data Mining, pp. 601–610. ACM (2014)
6. Garcia-Duran, A., Niepert, M.: KBLRN: end-to-end learning of knowledge base representations with latent, relational, and numerical features. arXiv preprint arXiv:1709.04676 (2017)
7. Kingma, D.P., Ba, J.: Adam: a method for stochastic optimization. In: 3rd International Conference for Learning Representations. ICLR (2015)
8. Le, Q., Mikolov, T.: Distributed representations of sentences and documents. In: International Conference on Machine Learning, pp. 1188–1196 (2014)
9. Lehmann, J., et al.: DBpedia - a large-scale, multilingual knowledge base extracted from Wikipedia. Semant. Web **6**(2), 167–195 (2015)
10. Mahdisoltani, F., Biega, J., Suchanek, F.: YAGO3: a knowledge base from multilingual Wikipedias. In: 7th Biennial Conference on Innovative Data Systems Research, CIDR Conference (2014)
11. Nickel, M., Murphy, K., Tresp, V., Gabrilovich, E.: A review of relational machine learning for knowledge graphs. Proc. IEEE **104**(1), 11–33 (2016)
12. Pezeshkpour, P., Irvine, C., Chen, L., Singh, S.: Embedding multimodal relational data (2017)
13. Xie, R., Liu, Z., Luan, H., Sun, M.: Image-embodied knowledge representation learning. In: Proceedings of the Twenty-Sixth International Joint Conference on Artificial Intelligence, IJCAI-2017, pp. 3140–3146 (2017). https://doi.org/10.24963/ijcai.2017/438

14. Sun, Z., Hu, W., Li, C.: Cross-lingual entity alignment via joint attribute-preserving embedding. In: d'Amato, C., et al. (eds.) ISWC 2017. LNCS, vol. 10587, pp. 628–644. Springer, Cham (2017). https://doi.org/10.1007/978-3-319-68288-4_37
15. Tay, Y., Tuan, L.A., Phan, M.C., Hui, S.C.: Multi-task neural network for non-discrete attribute prediction in knowledge graphs. In: Proceedings of the 2017 ACM on Conference on Information and Knowledge Management, pp. 1029–1038. ACM (2017)
16. Thoma, S., Rettinger, A., Both, F.: Towards holistic concept representations: embedding relational knowledge, visual attributes, and distributional word semantics. In: d'Amato, C., et al. (eds.) ISWC 2017. LNCS, vol. 10587, pp. 694–710. Springer, Cham (2017). https://doi.org/10.1007/978-3-319-68288-4_41
17. Toutanova, K., Chen, D.: Observed versus latent features for knowledge base and text inference. In: Proceedings of the 3rd Workshop on Continuous Vector Space Models and their Compositionality, pp. 57–66 (2015)
18. Toutanova, K., Chen, D., Pantel, P., Poon, H., Choudhury, P., Gamon, M.: Representing text for joint embedding of text and knowledge bases. In: EMNLP, vol. 15, pp. 1499–1509 (2015)
19. Trouillon, T., Welbl, J., Riedel, S., Gaussier, É., Bouchard, G.: Complex embeddings for simple link prediction. In: International Conference on Machine Learning, pp. 2071–2080 (2016)
20. Tu, C., Liu, H., Liu, Z., Sun, M.: CANE: context-aware network embedding for relation modeling. In: Proceedings of the 55th Annual Meeting of the Association for Computational Linguistics: Long Papers, vol. 1, pp. 1722–1731 (2017)
21. Wu, Y., Wang, Z.: Knowledge graph embedding with numeric attributes of entities. In: Proceedings of the Third Workshop on Representation Learning for NLP, pp. 132–136 (2018)
22. Xie, R., Liu, Z., Jia, J., Luan, H., Sun, M.: Representation learning of knowledge graphs with entity descriptions. In: AAAI, pp. 2659–2665 (2016)
23. Xu, J., Chen, K., Qiu, X., Huang, X.: Knowledge graph representation with jointly structural and textual encoding. In: IJCAI (2016)

Extracting Novel Facts from Tables for Knowledge Graph Completion

Benno Kruit[1,2(✉)], Peter Boncz[1], and Jacopo Urbani[2]

[1] Centrum Wiskunde & Informatica, Amsterdam, The Netherlands
{kruit,p.boncz}@cwi.nl

[2] Department of Computer Science, Vrije Universiteit Amsterdam, Amsterdam, The Netherlands
jacopo@cs.vu.nl

Abstract. We propose a new end-to-end method for extending a Knowledge Graph (KG) from tables. Existing techniques tend to interpret tables by focusing on information that is already in the KG, and therefore tend to extract many redundant facts. Our method aims to find more novel facts. We introduce a new technique for table interpretation based on a scalable graphical model using entity similarities. Our method further disambiguates cell values using KG embeddings as additional ranking method. Other distinctive features are the lack of assumptions about the underlying KG and the enabling of a fine-grained tuning of the precision/recall trade-off of extracted facts. Our experiments show that our approach has a higher recall during the interpretation process than the state-of-the-art, and is more resistant against the bias observed in extracting mostly redundant facts since it produces more novel extractions.

1 Introduction

Motivation. Much of the world's information exists as tabular data. These are available as HTML tables on web pages, as spreadsheets, or as publicly available datasets in many different formats. There has been more than a decade of research in recognizing, cleaning and capturing these so-called *web tables* [4]. Because of their relational nature, such large collections of web tables are suitable for supporting table search [31] or for answering specific factual queries [28]. In certain web tables, the rows describe attributes or relationships of entities. This makes them suitable sources for extending the coverage of Knowledge Graphs (KGs), which is a task known as *KG completion*.

Problem. In order to perform KG completion from web tables, we must first align their structure and content with the KG, a problem broadly referred to as *table interpretation*. Table interpretation has been the subject of several prior works [9,12,16–18,26,27,32]. Similar to our research, these works primarily focus on the interpretation of entity tables, i.e., tables where each row describes one entity and columns represent attributes. In this case, the interpretation process

C. Ghidini et al. (Eds.): ISWC 2019, LNCS 11778, pp. 364–381, 2019.
https://doi.org/10.1007/978-3-030-30793-6_21

consists of two operations. First, each row is linked with an entity in the KG, and optionally the entire table is linked to a class. Then, each column is associated to a KG relation.

After the table is correctly interpreted, we can extract novel triples from the table and add them to the KG. This last operation is also known as *slot-filling*, as the empty 'slots' in the KG are filled with new facts [26]. Table interpretation strongly affects the quality of slot-filling, since errors in the former can no longer be corrected. Because of this, state-of-the-art table interpretation techniques (an overview is given in Sect. 6) aim for high precision by pruning out many potential assignments already at early stages. While high precision is desirable in some contexts (e.g., table search), it has been observed [14] that this strategy leads to a high number of redundant extractions during slot-filling, since only the assignments to entities that are well-covered in the KG are retained.

Contribution. With the goal of maximizing the number of novel extractions without sacrificing precision, we present a new method for KG completion from web tables. In contrast to existing approaches, our method does not prune out row-entity assignments, but performs the interpretation by performing inference over all possible assignments using a Probabilistic Graphical Model (PGM). The PGM uses label similarities as priors, and then updates its likelihood scoring to maximise the *coherence* of entity assignments across the rows using Loopy Belief Propagation (LBP). Coherence is not computed using a predefined metric (such as class membership) but is automatically selected as a combination of properties that are shared by the entities in the table. This is a novel feature of our method which makes it capable of working with KGs with different topologies and/or relations. Since we use both label similarities and coherence based on salient common attributes, our method is able to maintain a high accuracy for the row-entity assignments. At the same time, it is also able to return many more novel extractions since we did not prune out any assignments.

We also propose an approach to perform slot-filling by disambiguating attribute cells in a novel link-prediction framework. Our approach makes use of embeddings of KG entities and relations to improve the quality of the disambiguation whenever label matching is not sufficient. This furthers our aim to find novel facts for KG completion.

We compared our method to several state-of-the-art systems. Additionally, we evaluated the performance of these systems with regard to the redundancy of the facts that they extract from the tables. Our experiments on popular benchmark datasets show that our approach yields slightly lower precision, but significantly higher recall on entity predictions. This leads to many more novel extractions than what is possible with existing methods. Finally, to test the scalability of our method we perform a large-scale evaluation on 786K tables from Wikipedia. An extended version of this paper is available at [15].

2 Background

KGs. A KG $\mathcal{K}$ is a repository of factual knowledge that can be seen as a directed labeled graph where the nodes are entities and the edges represent semantic relations. We define $\mathcal{K}$ as a tuple $(\mathcal{E}, \mathcal{R}, \mathcal{F})$ where $\mathcal{E}$ is the set of entities (nodes), $\mathcal{R}$ is the set of relations, and $\mathcal{F}$ is the set of facts (edges) in the graph. Each entity is associated to a finite set of labels $\mathsf{Labels}(e)$. We use the notation $\langle s, r, o\rangle$ to denote a fact in $\mathcal{F}$ where $s, o \in \mathcal{E}$ and $r \in \mathcal{R}$. Realistic KGs contain facts of various types: For instance, they either indicate type memberships (e.g., ⟨`Netherlands`, `type`, `Country`⟩), or encode more generic binary relations (e.g., ⟨`Amsterdam`, `capitalOf`, `Netherlands`⟩), and are normally encoded in RDF [11].

Table Interpretation. Tables represent an important source of knowledge that is not yet in the KG. A class of tables that is particularly useful for enriching KGs is the one that contains *entity tables*, i.e., tables where one column contains the name of entities (the *key-column*) and all others contain the entity attributes. While these tables ostensibly contain structured data, the textual content of cells and identifiers is created more with the aim of human interpretation than automatic processing. To capture the semantics of these tables in a coherent and structured way, it is useful to link their content to concepts in the KG. We refer to this task as *table interpretation*, mapping each row and attribute column to entities and relations respectively. These mappings can be computed by determining (1) which entities in the KG are mentioned in the table, (2) which are the types of those entities, and (3) which relations are expressed between columns (if any) [16,17,25,29,32]. After the interpretation is finished, we can use the mappings to construct facts for the KG. We call this operation *slot-filling*.

PGMs. In this paper, we employ Probabilistic Graphical Models (PGMs) to perform the interpretation. PGMs are a well-known formalism for computing joint predictions [21]. For a given set of random variables, conditional dependences between pairs of variables are expressed as edges in a graph. In these graphs, variables are connected if the value of one influences the value of another. The connection is directed if the influence is one-way, and undirected if both variables influence each other. The behaviour of the influence on every edge is expressed by a function known as the *potential function*. When performing inference in a PGM, information from the nodes is propagated through the network using the potential functions in order to determine the final distribution of the random variables.

KG Embeddings. We also make use of latent representations of the KG [20] to filter out incorrect extractions. In particular, we consider *TransE* [3], one of the most popular methods in this category. The main idea of TransE is to "embed" each entity and relation into a real-valued d-dimensional vector (where $d > 0$ is a given hyperparameter). The set of all vectors constitutes a model Θ of $|\mathcal{E}|d + |\mathcal{R}|d$ parameters which is trained so that the distance between the vectors of entities which are connected in $\mathcal{K}$ is smaller than the distance between the ones of entities which are not connected.

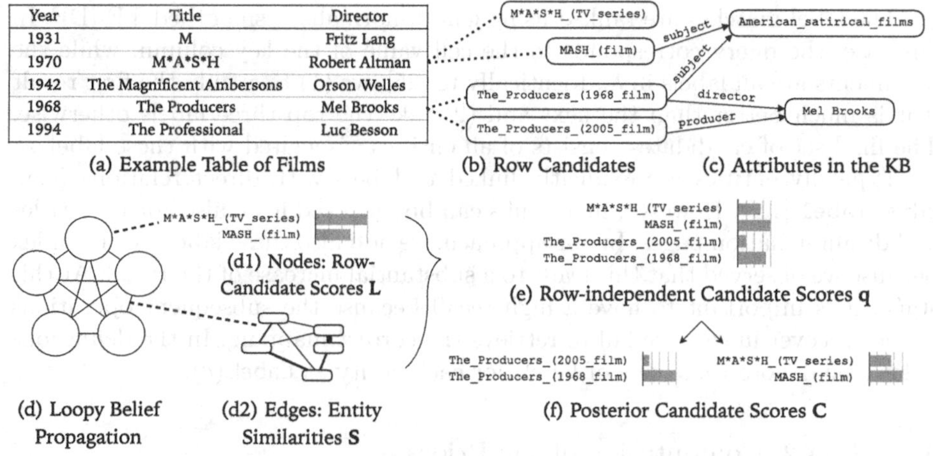

Fig. 1. Schematic representation of our method.

3 Table Interpretation

We introduce our method for performing table interpretation. Figure 1 shows the computation that takes place during the interpretation, using table (a) as a motivating example. In this case, the key-column is the second one ("title") but its content is ambiguous since the values can refer to movies, TV series, or books. For instance, the second row can refer to the TV serial `M*A*S*H` or to the movie `MASH`, as is shown in Fig. 1b. The goal of this task is to map as many rows ρ as possible to corresponding entities in $\mathcal{E}$ and each column c to one relation in $\mathcal{R}$. To this end, we perform a sequence of five operations, described below.

3.1 Step 1: Candidate Entity Selection

First, we identify the key-column (if any) using the heuristics proposed by [25], which consists of selecting the column with most unique non-numeric values breaking ties by choosing the leftmost one. This heuristics works well in practice so we apply it without modifications. Only the tables with valid key columns are considered since these are the only ones for which we can (potentially) extract factual knowledge.

For every cell in the key column, we then select a set of entity candidates. We represent this computation with the function $\mathsf{Cand}(\rho)$ which takes in input a generic row ρ and returns all entities in $\mathcal{E}$ which are potential candidates with ρ. This function is implemented by (1) indexing all the labels in $\mathcal{K}$, (2) retrieving the labels which contain the cell value of the key column, (3) returning the entities associated to the labels. Let $e \in \mathsf{Cand}(\rho)$ be a potential entity candidate for row ρ. We call the tuple (ρ, e) a *row-entity assignment.* If $\mathsf{Cand}(\rho)$ is empty, then ρ is ignored. Otherwise, the table interpretation process will determine which row-entity assignment should be selected.

The label matches are ranked using length-normalised smoothed TF-IDF. In our case, the query corresponds to the cell value of the key column, while the documents are all labels in $\mathcal{K}$. Identically to [25], we (1) take only the first result if it is much better than the next and (2) take the top three labels otherwise. The final set of candidates consists of all entities associated with these labels.

Typically entities are explicitly linked to labels with direct relations (e.g., `rdfs:label` [11]). However, more links can be retrieved if we also consider titles and disambiguation pages. In our approach, we add also these labels to the index because we observed that this leads to a substantial increase of the recall. At this stage, it is important to have a high recall because the subsequent operations cannot recover in case we fail to retrieve the correct mapping. In the definitions below, we denote these sets of labels for each entity as $\mathsf{Labels}(e)$.

3.2 Step 2: Computation of the Priors

In this step, we compute a score of the row-entity assignments by comparing all cell values in the row with all the labels of entities that are connected to the candidate entities. To this end, we first define attribute links, and related labels of an entity e as

$$\mathsf{Links}(e) = \{\langle r, v\rangle \mid \langle e, r, v\rangle \in \mathcal{F}\} \tag{1}$$

$$\mathsf{LinkLabels}(e, r) = \{l \mid \langle r, v\rangle \in \mathsf{Links}(e), l \in \mathsf{Labels}(v)\} \tag{2}$$

Intuitively, $\mathsf{Links}(e)$ contains all links of e while $\mathsf{LinkLabels}(e, r)$ represents the labels at the other end of the r-links from e. Then, we introduce the function

$$\mathsf{Match}(c, \rho, e, r) = \max_{s \in \mathsf{Cell}(c,\rho)} \max_{l \in \mathsf{LinkLabels}(e,r)} \mathsf{TokenJaccard}(s, l) \tag{3}$$

to compute the highest attainable string similarity between the cell at column c and row ρ and the values of the r-links from e. Here, $\mathsf{Cell}(i, j)$ returns the content of the cell at row i and column j in a table with n rows and m columns, while $\mathsf{TokenJaccard}$ is the Jaccard index $J(A, B) = \frac{|A \cap B|}{|A \cup B|}$ of the tokens in each string. For instance, in the table in Fig. 1 each cell is matched to each attribute of the corresponding row-entity candidates, e.g., Match(3, 4, `The_Producers_(1968_film)`, `director`) is the score that quantifies to what extent the content of the cell at coordinates (3, 4) matches the string "Mel Brooks", which is the label of the director of the film. Note that we treat the content of every cell as a string. There are some approaches that use type-specific cell and column matching methods [16,22,25,32], but a combination of our method with these techniques should be seen as future work.

We can now compute likelihood scores for mapping cells to relations (Eq. 4), and for mapping columns to relations (Eq. 5) to aggregate and normalise these scores on the row and column levels respectively:

$$\mathsf{CellScore}(c, \rho, r) = \frac{1}{|\mathsf{Cand}(\rho)|} \sum_{e \in \mathsf{Cand}(\rho)} \mathsf{Match}(c, \rho, e, r) \tag{4}$$

$$\mathsf{ColScore}(c, r) = \frac{\sum_{i=0}^{n} \mathsf{CellScore}(c, \rho_i, r)}{\sum_{i=0}^{n} \sum_{r' \in \mathcal{R}} \mathsf{CellScore}(c, \rho_i, r')} \tag{5}$$

For instance, in Fig. 1a, $\mathsf{CellScore}(4, 3, \texttt{director})$ returns the likelihood that the cell (4, 3) matches the relation `director`, while $\mathsf{ColScore}(3, \texttt{director})$ returns the aggregated scores for column 3 considering all rows in the table.

Since $\mathsf{ColScore}(c, r)$ is the likelihood score that column c maps to relation r, we can use this value to construct the prior distribution of all assignments to c. Furthermore, we can use these scores to refine the likelihood of the possible row-entity matchings. We compute such likelihood as

$$\mathsf{RowScore}(\rho, e) = \frac{1}{m} \sum_{i=0}^{m} \max_{r \in \mathcal{R}} \mathsf{ColScore}(c_i, r) \times \mathsf{Match}(c_i, \rho, e, r) \tag{6}$$

In essence, Eq. 6 computes the likelihood of an entity-row matching as the average best product that each cell matches to a certain attribute (r, e) ($\mathsf{Match}(\cdot)$) with the general likelihood that the column matches to r ($\mathsf{ColScore}(\cdot)$). We use the values of RowScore to build a prior distribution for all entity-row matches.

3.3 Step 3: Entity Similarity Scores

Both prior distributions computed with Eqs. 4 and 5 rely on the Jaccard Index. Thus, they are distributions which are ultimately built on the string similarities between the strings in the cells and the entities' labels. We use these scores to compute similarity scores between pairs of candidate entities across the rows. In the next step, we will use these similarities to compute better entity-row likelihood scores than the ones of Eq. 6.

First, we weigh all links $\langle r, v \rangle$ depending on their popularities across the entities in the table and the corresponding prior of the assignments that use them. To this end, we define the function LinkTotal as

$$\mathsf{LinkTotal}(r, v) = \sum_{i=0}^{n} \max_{e \in \mathsf{Cand}(\rho_i)} \mathsf{RowScore}(\rho_i, e)[\langle r, v \rangle \in \mathsf{Links}(e)] \tag{7}$$

where $[x]$ returns 1 if x is true or 0 otherwise. Note that since RowScore returns a value between 0 and 1, $\mathsf{LinkTotal}(\cdot)$ returns n in the best case.

Then, we represent the coverage and saliency of $\langle r, v \rangle$ by normalising the value $\mathsf{LinkTotal}(r, v)$ with respect to the table and the KG:

$$\mathsf{Cover}(r, v) = \frac{\mathsf{LinkTotal}(r, v)}{\sum_{i=1}^{n} [\langle r, v \rangle \in \cup_{e \in \mathsf{Cand}(\rho_i)} \mathsf{Links}(e)]} \tag{8}$$

$$\mathsf{Salience}(r, v) = \frac{\mathsf{LinkTotal}(r, v)}{|\{e \in \mathcal{E} \mid \langle r, v \rangle \in \mathsf{Links}(e)\}|} \tag{9}$$

Intuitively, $\mathsf{Cover}(\cdot)$ computes the popularity of $\langle r, v\rangle$ among the rows of the table, while $\mathsf{Salience}(\cdot)$ considers all entities in $\mathcal{K}$. We combine them as

$$\mathsf{LinkScore}(r, v) = \mathsf{Cover}(r, v) \times \mathsf{Salience}(r, v) \tag{10}$$

so that we can rank the attributes depending both on their coverage within the table and popularity in the KG. This combination allows us to give low ranks to attributes, like $\langle$`isA,Resource`$\rangle$, which should not be considered despite their high coverage since they are not informative. In contrast, it can boost up the score of attributes with a medium coverage in case they have a high saliency.

Finally, we use the scores from Eq. 10 to compute a similarity score between pairs of entities. We compute the similarity between entities e_1 and e_2 as

$$\mathsf{EntitySimilarity}(e_1, e_2) = \sum_{\langle r,v\rangle \in \mathsf{Links}(e_1) \cap \mathsf{Links}(e_2)} \mathsf{LinkScore}(r, v) \tag{11}$$

3.4 Step 4: Disambiguation

Now, we compute which are the row-entity assignments which maximise the coherence in the table, i.e., maximise the similarity between the entities. These assignments are determined using Loopy Belief Propagation (LBP) [21].

We model each row-entity prediction as a categorical random variable, for which the label score $\mathsf{RowScore}(\rho, e)$ is the prior distribution (Fig. 1d1). For convenience, we can view these scores as a sparse matrix $\boldsymbol{L}$ of size $n \times |\mathcal{E}|$. The variables are connected to each other with the edge potentials being defined by entity-entity similarities $\mathsf{EntitySimilarity}(e_1, e_2)$ (Fig. 1d2; equivalently represented by a matrix $\boldsymbol{S}$), which forms a complete graph. Since this graph has loops it is not possible to perform exact inference. Therefore we approximate it by executing LBP. Additionally, all our edge potentials are identical. This causes all nodes to receive identical information from each other. Instead of having separate messages for each node, we thus have a single vector-valued message that provides the belief updates for our nodes:

$$q_e = \prod_{\rho=0}^{n} \sum_{e' \in \mathsf{Cand}(\rho)} L_{\rho,e'} \times S_{e,e'} = \prod_{\rho=0}^{n} (\boldsymbol{LS})_{\rho,e} \tag{12}$$

$$C_{\rho,e} = L_{\rho,e} \times q_e \tag{13}$$

where q_e indicates how similar entity e is to all weighted candidates of all rows, and $C_{\rho,e}$ is the coherence score of entity e for row ρ (Figs. 1e and f respectively). Because the main operation consists of a single matrix multiplication, computation is fast and can be parallelized by standard matrix processing libraries.

LBP can be run for multiple iterations (in our case, replacing $L_{\rho,e'}$ by $C_{\rho,e'}$), but is not guaranteed to converge [21]. In fact, we observed that sometimes an excessive number of iterations led to suboptimal assignments. This occurred when the entity similarity scores (Eq. 11) were not accurate due to missing attributes in the KG and ended up "overriding" the more accurate priors that were computed considering only label similarities (Eq. 6) when they are combined in the following step. From our experimental analysis, we observed that in the overwhelming majority of the cases a single iteration of LBP was enough to converge. Therefore, we apply Eq. 13 only once without further iterations.

As we can see from Eq. 13, the selection of the entity for row ρ relies on two components, $\boldsymbol{L}$ and $\boldsymbol{q}$: The first takes into account to what extent the entity label matches the label of candidate entities and to what extent the labels of the attributes matches with the remaining cell values. The second considers the coherence, i.e., the mappings that maximise the similarity between the entities.

Finally, we disambiguate rows by choosing the highest-rated candidate $\hat{e}_\rho = \text{argmax}_e\ C_{\rho,e}$. Then, we re-calculate $\mathsf{ColScore}(c,r)$ with the updated set of candidates containing only the predicted entity $\mathsf{Cand}(\rho) = \{\hat{e}_\rho\}$ and disambiguate columns by choosing the highest scoring relation $\hat{r}_c = \text{argmax}_r\ \mathsf{ColScore}(c,r)$. After this last step is computed, our procedure has selected one entity per row and one relation per attribute column. In the next section, we discuss how we can extract triples from the table.

4 Slot-Filling

After the table is interpreted, we can extract partial triples of the form $\langle s, r, ?\rangle$ where s are the entities mapped to rows and r are the relations associated to columns. If the cell contains numbers or other datatypes (e.g., dates) that we can add the cell value to the KG as-is, but this is inappropriate if the content of the cell refers to an entity. In this case, we need to map the content of the cell to an entity in the KG.

The disambiguation of the content of a cell could be done by querying our label index precisely the same way as done in Sect. 3.1. However, this extraction is suboptimal since now we have available some context, i.e., $\langle s, r, ?\rangle$ that we can leverage to refine our search space. To this end, we can exploit techniques for predicting the likelihood of triples given the KG's structure, namely KG embeddings provided by the TransE algorithm [3]. Given in input e_i, i.e., the entity associated to row i and r_j, i.e., the relation associated to column j, our goal is to extract a fact of the form $\langle e_i, r_j, x\rangle$ where entity x is unknown. We proceed as follows:

1. We query the label index with the content of $\mathsf{Cell}(i,j)$ as done for the computation of $Cand(\cdot)$ in Sect. 3.1. This computation returns a list of entity candidates $\langle e_1, \ldots, e_n\rangle$ ranked based on label string similarities.
2. For each candidate $e_k \in \langle e_1, \ldots, e_n\rangle$, we compute $\mathsf{Rank}(k) = d(\boldsymbol{e_i} + \boldsymbol{r_j}, \boldsymbol{e_k})$ where d is the distance measure used to compute the TransE embeddings (we use the L_1 norm), and $\boldsymbol{e_i}, \boldsymbol{r_j}, \boldsymbol{e_k}$ are the TransE vectors of e_k, r_j, e_i respectively.
3. We return $\langle e_i, r_j, e_k\rangle$ where e_k is the entity with the lowest $\mathsf{Rank}(k)$, i.e, has the closest distance hence it is the triple with the highest likelihood score.

5 Evaluation

We implemented our method into a system called TAKCO (TAble-driven KG COmpleter). The code is available online[1].

Baselines. Since our goal is to extract novel facts from tables, we considered existing systems that perform slot-filling as baselines. In particular, we considered the systems T2K MATCH [25] and TABLEMINER+ [32] because of their state-of-the-art results. There are other systems that implement only parts of the pipeline, for instance entity disambiguation (see Sect. 6 for an overview). An important system in this category is TabEL [2], which exploits co-occurrences of anchor links to entity candidates on Wikipedia pages for predicting a coherent set of entities. Although such system can potentially return better performance on entity disambiguation, we did not include it in our analysis due its reliance on additional inputs. A comparison between the performance of our method for the subtask of entity disambiguation, and more specialized frameworks like TabEL should be seen as future work.

The system T2K MATCH implements a series of matching steps that match table rows to entities, using similarities between entity property values and the table columns. The TABLEMINER+ system consists of two phases that are alternated until a certain confidence level has been reached. Note that these approaches primarily focus on table interpretation. In contrast, we provide an end-to-end system which considers also the operation of slot-filling.

The first system is designed to work with a specific subselection of DBpedia [1] while the second system was originally built to use the Freebase API. We have performed some slight modifications to their source code so that we could perform a fair comparison. For T2K MATCH, we modified the system to be able to use an augmented set of candidates so that in some experiments we could measure precisely the performance of table interpretation. For TABLEMINER+, we modified the system so that we could use different KGs without API access.

Knowledge Graphs. Our method can work with any arbitrary KG. We consider DBpedia (so that we could compare against T2K MATCH) which is a popular KGs created from Wikipedia and other sources. We use two versions of DBpedia: The first is the triple-based version of the tabular subset used by T2K MATCH. This is a subset of DBpedia from 2014 and we consider it so that we can perform an exact comparison. It contains 3.4M entities and 28M facts. Additionally, we also use the latest version of the full KG (version 2016-10). The full DBpedia contains 15M entities (including entities without labels and redirected entities) and 110M facts. Finally, we compare our performance using Wikidata ("truthy" RDF export, acquired on Oct 2018), which has 106M entities and 1B facts. For evaluation, we map the gold standard to Wikidata using `owl:sameAs` links from DBpedia.

Testsets. To the best of our knowledge, there are two openly available datasets of tables that have been annotated for the purpose of table interpretation. The

[1] https://github.com/karmaresearch/takco.

first one is the *T2D* dataset [25], which contains a subset of the WDC Web Tables Corpus – a set of tables extracted from the CommonCrawl web scrape[2]. We use the latest available version of this dataset (v2, released 2017/02). In our experiments, we disregarded tables without any annotation. The resulting dataset contains 238 entity tables with 659 column annotations and 26106 row-entity annotations. Throughout, we refer to this dataset as *T2D-v2*.

The second dataset is *Webaroo*, proposed by [16]. Tables in this dataset were annotated with entities and relations in YAGO. While these tables are a less varied sample of the ones in the T2D, they allow us to study the behaviour of the systems on a dataset with different annotations. This dataset contains 429 entity tables with 389 and 4447 column and row-entity annotations respectively. In order to test the performance of T2K MATCH with this dataset, we "ported" the YAGO annotations to DBpedia using the Wikipedia links they refer to. Finally, we tested the scalability of our system by running it on a large set of Wikipedia tables [2]. Instructions to obtain these datasets are available in the code repository of our system.

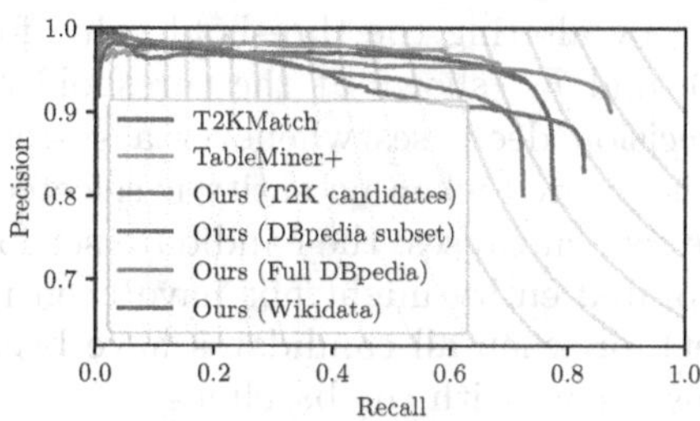

(a) Performance tradeoff, T2D-v2

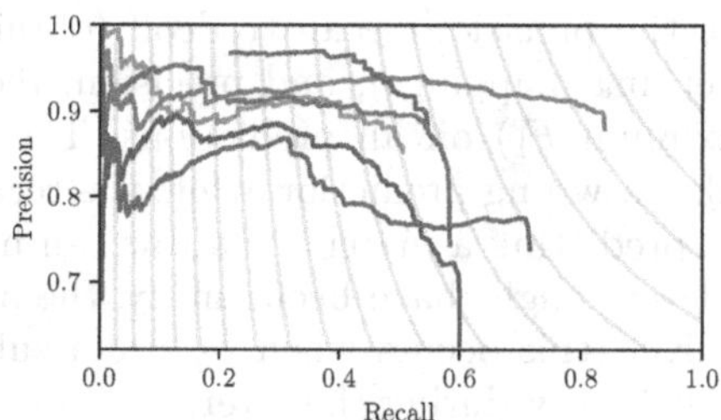

(b) Performance tradeoff, Webaroo

System	Pr.	Re.	F_1
T2KMatch	.94	.73	.82
TableMiner+	**.96**	.68	.80
Ours (T2K candidates)	.88	.72	.79
Ours (DBpedia subset)	.90	.76	.83
Ours (Full DBpedia)	.92	**.86**	**.89**
Ours (Wikidata)	.87	.82	.84

(c) Row-entity evaluation, T2D-v2

System	Pr.	Re.	F_1
T2KMatch	.88	.55	.67
TableMiner+	.85	.51	.63
Ours (T2K candidates)	.74	.58	.65
Ours (DBpedia subset)	.72	.59	.65
Ours (Full DBpedia)	**.88**	**.84**	**.86**
Ours (Wikidata)	.77	.71	.74

(d) Row-entity evaluation, Webaroo

Fig. 2. Row-entity evaluation scores and precision-recall tradeoff for the T2D-v2 and Webaroo datasets (the isolines of constant F_1 score are shown in grey). Precision, recall, and F_1 are calculated at the threshold of maximum F_1.

[2] http://webdatacommons.org/webtables/.

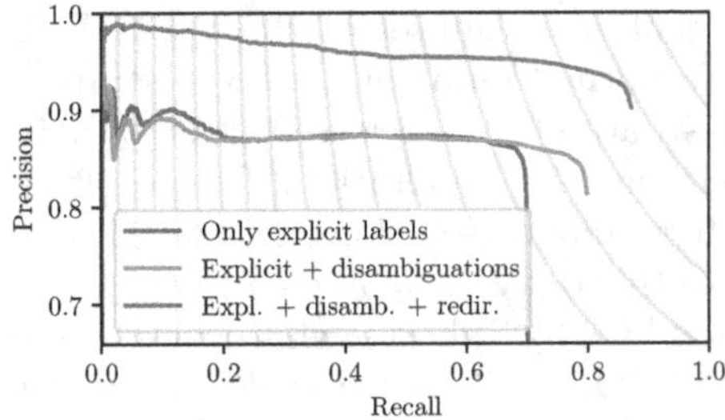

System	Pr.	Re.	F_1
Only explicit labels	.85	.69	.76
Explicit + disambiguations	.84	.79	.81
Expl. + disamb. + redir.	**.92**	**.86**	**.89**

Fig. 3. Row-entity evaluation scores and precision-recall tradeoff of our approach given different label sources, on T2D-v2.

5.1 Table Interpretation

We evaluate the performance of determining the correct row-entity assignments, which are the key output for table interpretation. Figure 2b, d and a, c report a comparison of the performance of our method against the baselines. We measure the precision/recall tradeoff (obtained by altering the threshold value for accepting mappings), and precision, recall, and F_1 (shown at the threshold of maximum F_1) on all predictions. The precision decreases whenever a system makes a wrong prediction while the recall is affected when no entity is selected. Not predicting a match for a row can have several causes: the candidate set for that row might have been empty, the annotated entity might not have been in the KG (this occurs when we use a subset), or when all candidates have been pruned away during the interpretation (this occurs with the baselines).

In these experiments, we configured our system with three different settings: First, we use the same KG and the candidates (i.e., the output of $\mathsf{Cand}(\cdot)$) used by the other two systems. We refer to this setting as "T2K candidates". Then, we use the KG subset used by T2K Match in our own label index and disambiguation ("DBpedia subset"). Finally, we use our own candidate set generation and full KG ("Full DBpedia"). By evaluating the performance of our method with these settings, we can compare the performance of our approach given the limitations of the inputs that the other systems face.

From the results reported in the figures, we can make a few considerations. First, our method returns a comparable recall but an inferior precision than the baselines if we use the set of candidates from T2K Match, but is able to match its performance in terms of F_1 when using the same KG. However, the baselines are limited with respect to KGs. In fact, T2K Match requires that DBpedia is translated into a tabular format while our method does not have this restriction. If our method is configured to use the full DBpedia KG, then it returns the highest recall with only a small loss in terms of precision. This translates in a significantly higher F_1 score than the best of the baselines. These are positive results since a high recall is important for extracting novel facts.

While the precision of our system is low in the limited-input setting, many of the errors that it makes are due to problems with the candidate set and the

KG. Therefore, we evaluated a scenario (not shown in the figures of this paper) in which we artificially expanded the candidate set to always include the gold standard. This means we are artificially making use of a "perfect" candidate index. Even with this addition, T2K MATCH is unable to use these candidates for prediction and returns the same results. In contrast, manually adding them to our system leads to both a notably higher recall and precision.

This indicates that our method is sensitive to the candidate generation, i.e., to the very first selection of candidates using the index label. To evaluate how our system behaves with richer label indices, we evaluated our method on T2D-v2 with three different label indices. The first index only uses the explicit labels of the entities. The second one includes also the labels that we obtain from redirect pages in Wikipedia. The third one adds also the labels we obtain from the disambiguation pages. The results of this experiment are reported in Fig. 3. As we can see from these results, including more labels per entity significantly improves both the precision and recall of our system.

System	Redundant			Novel		
	Pr.	Re.	F_1	Pr.	Re.	F_1
T2KMatch	.84	.82	.83	**.76**	.66	.71
TableMiner+	**.86**	.73	.79	.73	.56	.63
Ours (T2K candidates)	.81	.84	.83	.61	.71	.66
Ours (DBpedia subset)	.83	.90	.86	.59	.76	.66
Ours (Full DBpedia)	.83	**.96**	**.89**	.70	**.83**	**.76**

(a) The scores for extracting novel and redundant triples from T2D-v2, measured at the acceptance threshold of maximum F_1.

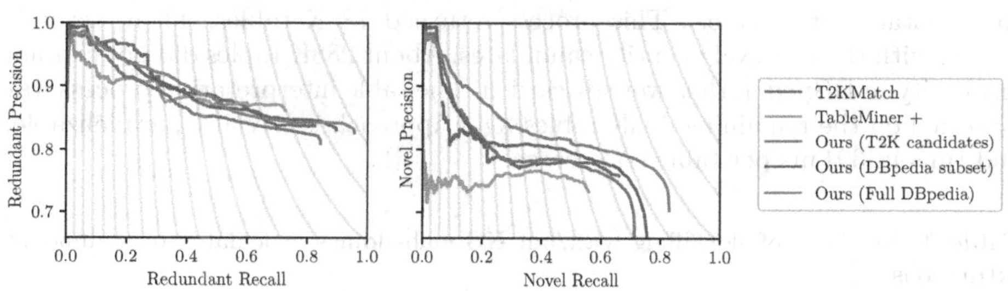

(b) The precision-recall tradeoff curve on T2D-v2.

Fig. 4. The novel and redundant precision-recall tradeoff for the T2D-v2 dataset (in gray, the isolines of constant F_1 score). Unlike the experiments in the previous figures, here the bias towards extracting known (redundant) facts is made explicit and we focus on finding novel KG facts in web tables.

5.2 Measuring Redundancy

Current systems (e.g., [25,32]) were evaluated against a set of manual annotations, and scored on the individual subtasks of table interpretation. Such evaluation did not consider the novelty of facts that the system has extracted. In other words, no difference was made between predictions of already known facts or new knowledge, but this difference is important in our context. In order to fill this gap, we need to distinguish between these cases when measuring performance.

Given in input a KG $\mathcal{K} = (\mathcal{E}, \mathcal{R}, \mathcal{F})$, an extraction technique like ours is expected to yield a new set of predicted facts $\mathcal{F}_P$ over $\mathcal{E}$ and $\mathcal{R}$ from an input source like web tables. If we have gold standard table annotations, we can generate another set of facts $\mathcal{F}_G$ and use them for evaluating how many facts in $\mathcal{F}_P$ are correct. Note that both $\mathcal{F}_P$ and $\mathcal{F}_G$ might contain facts that are either in $\mathcal{F}$ or not. So far, current techniques have been evaluated w.r.t. the set of true positives $\mathcal{F}_G \cap \mathcal{F}_P$ (correctly extracted facts) and false negatives as $\mathcal{F}_G \setminus \mathcal{F}_P$ (valid facts that were missed). These measures do not take the redundancy of the extracted facts into account, while the redundant information exceeds the novel information for benchmark datasets [14].

In Fig. 4, we show the evaluation of the correctness of *novel* and *redundant* facts separately. Crucially, our system significantly outperforms the baselines with respect to the recall of novel facts, which is paramount to KG completion. In the tradeoff curve for novel triples (Fig. 4b), we also outperform the state-of-the-art regarding precision for most threshold values.

5.3 Slot-Filling

To test the scalability of our system, we have run it on all 1.6M tables in the Wikitable dataset. The first step concerns detecting entity tables with key columns that contain entity labels. This process returned 786K tables. Then, we proceeded with the retrieval of entity candidates. About 288K tables did not contain any entity in DBpedia, thus were discarded. The table interpretation process was launched on the remaining 498K tables. Our approach is trivially parallelizable, and runs in 391 ms per table on average.

Table 1. Precision of slot-filling with/out KG embeddings, calculated on redundant extractions.

Ranking	Dataset	Prec@1	Prec@3
Only Label Index (TF-IDF score)	Wikitable	0.37	0.42
	T2D-v2	0.24	0.31
Labels + Embeddings (TransE)	Wikitable	**0.61**	**0.72**
	T2D-v2	**0.62**	**0.74**

From these tables, we extracted 2.818.205 unique facts for 1.880.808 unique slots of the form $\langle s, r, ? \rangle$. Of those slots, 823.806 already contain at least one entity o in the KG. However, we do not know whether our extractions are redundant, or t represents a new extraction that should be added to the existing ones in the KG. To determine the novelty, we queried the label index for every extracted fact and discovered that in 307.729 cases the labels were matching. We can assume these extracted facts to be redundant. From these numbers, we conclude that our extraction process has produced about 1.6M extractions for which we have no evidence of redundancy and thus can be considered as novel. A manual analysis over a sample confirmed this conclusion.

Finally, we evaluated the effectiveness of our procedure for re-ranking the extractions using the KG embeddings on the Wikitable and T2D-v2 datasets. To this end, we compare the naïve index-based ranking obtained by simply picking the top result returned from the label index against our strategy or re-ranking considering the distance of the corresponding embeddings (Sect. 4). We chose to measure the precision for the first or top-3 ranked candidates since this is a standard metric used to evaluate the performance of link prediction [20].

Since we need to know the correct entity, we restricted this analysis to the redundant extractions (i.e., the ones already in the KG) and disregarded the novel ones. Table 1 reports the results both when we consider only the best result and the top three. We see that our embedding-based ranking outperforms the index-based ranking in both cases, and predicts the correct entity at the top of the ranking in 61% of the time, compared to 37% for the Wikitable dataset. Moreover, the relatively low results obtained with the index-based ranking strategy indicate that labels are in general not reliable for disambiguating attributes.

6 Related Work

The first system for interpreting web tables was introduced by Limaye et al. [16]. The system uses a probabilistic graphical model that makes supervised predictions based on a large number of features. Subsequent work approached the problem with a task-specific knowledge graph [29,30] and sped up predictions by limiting the feature set [17] or using distributed processing [10]. Others used an entity label prior from hyperlinks on the web [2], and interpreted tables in limited domains [23].

A separate family of table interpretation systems limit themselves to attribute matching. The simplest approaches perform string similarities between the column headers and relation names or cell values and entity labels [8]. When no overlap between the table and KG can be assumed at all, the work at [22] uses supervised models based on features of the column header and cell values. Some approaches focus on matching tables to relation from Open Information Extraction [29,30] or exploit occurrences of cell value pairs in a corpus of text [5,27], and others perform supervised learning [9,22]. While several approaches have been proposed that are limited to entity linking [2,7], the focus of our work is to optimize table interpretation for novel fact extraction.

The systems evaluated in this paper are designed for open-domain table interpretation. In closed-domain settings, assumptions can reduce the redundancy of extractions. For example, the work of [23] models the incompleteness in the domain subset of the KG by estimating class probabilities based on relations between entities, which the limited domain makes tractable. The systems of [30] and [29] use a probabilistic KG created from a web corpus for supporting table search. This type of KG offers many strategies for improving the recall of new knowledge because it allows for an explicit model of low-confidence facts.

Several models use large web text corpora in addition to the information from the KG. The work by Bhagavatula et al. [2] uses the anchor text of hyperlinks on the web to create a prior for instance matching that takes the popularity of entities into account. Additionally, it exploits co-occurrences of anchor links to entity candidates on Wikipedia pages for predicting a coherent set of entities. The work of [27] creates a set of syntactic patterns from the ClueWeb09 text corpus featuring entities from relations in the KG. Given query pairs of entities from tables, the syntactic patterns from text featuring the query pair are matched to the patterns in the set. A probabilistic model then allows for the prediction of relations from the KG. A similar approach is taken by [5], who use a language model instead of extracted syntactic patterns. This approach queries a search engine with the entity pair, and classify the text that occurs between the entity mentions. A separate direction is the matching of numeric columns, either with metrics for numeric distribution similarity [19] or sophisticated ontologies of quantities and statistical models [12].

The survey at [13] discusses approaches and challenges to the slot filling task in the context of textual information extraction. Most systems use distant supervision for textual pattern learning, and some employ cross-slot reasoning to ensure the coherence of multiple extracted values. Recently, work on Universal Schemas by Riedel et al. [24] has allowed the joint factorisation of textual extractions and KB relations and this boosts slot-filling precision.

In the field of data fusion, systems explicitly aim for high recall and use a post-processing filter to improve precision. In [18], the extracted facts are filtered using machine learning models, and in [6] they are filtered using a sophisticated statistical model of the KG. In [26], the system of [25] is used to interpret a large collection of web tables, after which the extracted facts are filtered using several strategies. However, only 2.85% of web tables can be matched, which is attributed to a topical mismatch between the tables and the KG.

7 Conclusion

We investigate the problem of extending KGs using the data found in Web tables. Existing approaches have focused on overall precision and recall of facts extracted from web tables, but it is important for the purpose of KG completion that the extraction process returns as many (correct) *novel* facts as possible.

We developed and evaluated a new table interpretation method to counter this problem. Our method uses a flexible similarity criterion for the disambiguation of entity-row matches, and employs a PGM to compute new likelihood scores depending on how the various candidates are similar to each other to maximise the coherence of assignments. Because it combines the syntactic match between the tables and the KG with the coherence of the entity predictions, it can confidently predict more candidates for which the attributes in the table are not yet in the KG. Consequently, it extracts more novel facts for KG completion. For the task of slot-filling, we introduced a novel approach for attribute disambiguation based on KG embeddings, which outperforms a naive label-based approach.

We compared our method to two state-of-the art systems, and performed an extensive comparative evaluation on multiple knowledge bases. Our evaluation shows that our system achieves a higher recall during the interpretation process, which is necessary to extract novel information. Furthermore, it is able to extract more (correct) facts that are not yet in the KG.

Interesting directions for future work include the development of extensions for tables where the entity is identified by multiple columns or where rows do not necessarily describe entities. In particular, the heuristics for determining the key column of the table (and whether such a column is present) would need to be replaced by a model that reliably detects the type of table. Moreover, the inclusion of external sources can be useful to extract more novel information from the table. Finally, despite the remarkable work by different research teams to produce good benchmark datasets, there is still the need for larger and more diverse benchmarks to further challenge the state-of-the-art.

References

1. Auer, S., Bizer, C., Kobilarov, G., Lehmann, J., Cyganiak, R., Ives, Z.: DBpedia: a nucleus for a web of open data. In: Aberer, K., et al. (eds.) ASWC/ISWC -2007. LNCS, vol. 4825, pp. 722–735. Springer, Heidelberg (2007). https://doi.org/10.1007/978-3-540-76298-0_52
2. Bhagavatula, C.S., Noraset, T., Downey, D.: TabEL: entity linking in web tables. In: Arenas, M., et al. (eds.) ISWC 2015. LNCS, vol. 9366, pp. 425–441. Springer, Cham (2015). https://doi.org/10.1007/978-3-319-25007-6_25
3. Bordes, A., Usunier, N., Garcia-Duran, A., Weston, J., Yakhnenko, O.: Translating embeddings for modeling multi-relational data. In: Proceedings of NIPS, pp. 2787–2795 (2013)
4. Cafarella, M., et al.: Ten years of webtables. Proc. VLDB **11**(12), 2140–2149 (2018)
5. Cannaviccio, M., Barbosa, D., Merialdo, P.: Towards annotating relational data on the web with language models. In: Proceedings of WWW, pp. 1307–1316 (2018)
6. Dong, X.L., et al.: Knowledge vault: a web-scale approach to probabilistic knowledge fusion. In: Proceedings of KDD, pp. 601–610 (2014)
7. Efthymiou, V., Hassanzadeh, O., Rodriguez-Muro, M., Christophides, V.: Matching web tables with knowledge base entities: from entity lookups to entity embeddings. In: d'Amato, C., et al. (eds.) ISWC 2017. LNCS, vol. 10587, pp. 260–277. Springer, Cham (2017). https://doi.org/10.1007/978-3-319-68288-4_16
8. Efthymiou, V., Hassanzadeh, O., Sadoghi, M., Rodriguez-Muro, M.: Annotating web tables through ontology matching. In: Proceedings of OM at ISWC, pp. 229–230 (2016)

9. Ermilov, I., Ngomo, A.-C.N.: TAIPAN: automatic property mapping for tabular data. In: Blomqvist, E., Ciancarini, P., Poggi, F., Vitali, F. (eds.) EKAW 2016. LNCS (LNAI), vol. 10024, pp. 163–179. Springer, Cham (2016). https://doi.org/10.1007/978-3-319-49004-5_11
10. Hassanzadeh, O., Ward, M.J., Rodriguez-Muro, M., Srinivas, K.: Understanding a large corpus of web tables through matching with knowledge bases: an empirical study. In: Proceedings of OM at ISWC, pp. 25–34 (2015)
11. Hayes, P.: RDF Semantics. W3C Recommendation (2004). http://www.w3.org/TR/rdf-mt/
12. Ibrahim, Y., Riedewald, M., Weikum, G.: Making sense of entities and quantities in web tables. In: Proceedings of CIKM, pp. 1703–1712 (2016)
13. Ji, H., Grishman, R.: Knowledge base population: successful approaches and challenges. In: Proceedings of the 49th Annual Meeting of the Association for Computational Linguistics: Human Language Technologies, vol. 1, pp. 1148–1158. Association for Computational Linguistics (2011)
14. Kruit, B., Boncz, P., Urbani, J.: Extracting new knowledge from web tables: novelty or confidence? In: Proceedings of KBCOM (2018)
15. Kruit, B., Boncz, P., Urbani, J.: Extracting novel facts from tables for knowledge graph completion (extended version). arXiv e-prints arXiv:1907.00083 (2019)
16. Limaye, G., Sarawagi, S., Chakrabarti, S.: Annotating and searching web tables using entities, types and relationships. PVLDB **3**(1–2), 1338–1347 (2010)
17. Mulwad, V., Finin, T., Joshi, A.: Semantic message passing for generating linked data from tables. In: Alani, H., et al. (eds.) ISWC 2013. LNCS, vol. 8218, pp. 363–378. Springer, Heidelberg (2013). https://doi.org/10.1007/978-3-642-41335-3_23
18. Muñoz, E., Hogan, A., Mileo, A.: Using linked data to mine RDF from Wikipedia's tables. In: Proceedings of WSDM, pp. 533–542 (2014)
19. Neumaier, S., Umbrich, J., Parreira, J.X., Polleres, A.: Multi-level semantic labelling of numerical values. In: Groth, P., et al. (eds.) ISWC 2016. LNCS, vol. 9981, pp. 428–445. Springer, Cham (2016). https://doi.org/10.1007/978-3-319-46523-4_26
20. Nickel, M., Murphy, K., Tresp, V., Gabrilovich, E.: A review of relational machine learning for knowledge graphs. Proc. IEEE **104**(1), 11–33 (2016)
21. Pearl, J.: Probabilistic Reasoning in Intelligent Systems - Networks of Plausible Inference. Morgan Kaufmann Publishers Inc., Burlington (1989)
22. Pham, M., Alse, S., Knoblock, C.A., Szekely, P.: Semantic labeling: a domain-independent approach. In: Groth, P., et al. (eds.) ISWC 2016. LNCS, vol. 9981, pp. 446–462. Springer, Cham (2016). https://doi.org/10.1007/978-3-319-46523-4_27
23. Ran, C., Shen, W., Wang, J., Zhu, X.: Domain-specific knowledge base enrichment using Wikipedia tables. In: Proceedings of ICDM, pp. 349–358 (2015)
24. Riedel, S., Yao, L., McCallum, A., Marlin, B.M.: Relation extraction with matrix factorization and universal schemas. In: Proceedings of HLT-NAACL (2013)
25. Ritze, D., Lehmberg, O., Bizer, C.: Matching HTML tables to DBpedia. In: Proceedings of WIMS, p. 10 (2015)
26. Ritze, D., Lehmberg, O., Oulabi, Y., Bizer, C.: Profiling the potential of web tables for augmenting cross-domain knowledge bases. In: Proceedings of WWW, pp. 251–261 (2016)
27. Sekhavat, Y.A., Paolo, F.D., Barbosa, D., Merialdo, P.: Knowledge base augmentation using tabular data. In: Proceedings of LDOW at WWW (2014)
28. Sun, H., Ma, H., He, X., Yih, W.T., Su, Y., Yan, X.: Table cell search for question answering. In: Proceedings of WWW, pp. 771–782 (2016)

29. Venetis, P., et al.: Recovering semantics of tables on the web. PVLDB **4**, 528–538 (2011)
30. Wang, J., Wang, H., Wang, Z., Zhu, K.Q.: Understanding tables on the web. In: Atzeni, P., Cheung, D., Ram, S. (eds.) ER 2012. LNCS, vol. 7532, pp. 141–155. Springer, Heidelberg (2012). https://doi.org/10.1007/978-3-642-34002-4_11
31. Yakout, M., Ganjam, K., Chakrabarti, K., Chaudhuri, S.: InfoGather: entity augmentation and attribute discovery by holistic matching with web tables. In: Proceedings of SIGMOD, pp. 97–108 (2012)
32. Zhang, Z.: Effective and efficient semantic table interpretation using TableMiner+. Semant. Web **8**(6), 921–957 (2017)

Difficulty-Controllable Multi-hop Question Generation from Knowledge Graphs

Vishwajeet Kumar[1,3,4], Yuncheng Hua[2,4], Ganesh Ramakrishnan[3], Guilin Qi[2,6,7], Lianli Gao[5], and Yuan-Fang Li[4(✉)]

[1] IITB-Monash Research Academy, Mumbai, India
[2] School of Computer Science and Engineering, Southeast University, Nanjing, China
[3] IIT Bombay, Mumbai, India
[4] Monash University, Melbourne, Australia
yuanfang.li@monash.edu
[5] The University of Electronic Science and Technology of China, Chengdu, China
[6] Key Laboratory of Computer Network and Information Integration (Southeast University) Ministry of Education, Nanjing, China
[7] Key Laboratory of Rich-media Knowledge Organization and Service of Digital Publishing Content, SAPPRFT, Beijing, China

Abstract. Knowledge graphs have become ubiquitous data sources and their utility has been amplified by the research on ability to answer carefully crafted questions over knowledge graphs. We investigate the problem of question generation (QG) over knowledge graphs wherein, the level of difficulty of the question can be controlled. We present an end-to-end neural network-based method for automatic generation of complex multi-hop questions over knowledge graphs. Taking a subgraph and an answer as input, our transformer-based model generates a natural language question. Our model incorporates difficulty estimation based on named entity popularity, and makes use of this estimation to generate difficulty-controllable questions. We evaluate our model on two recent multi-hop QA datasets. Our evaluation shows that our model is able to generate high-quality, fluent and relevant questions. We have released our curated QG dataset and code at https://github.com/liyuanfang/mhqg.

Keywords: Question generation · Knowledge graph · Natural language processing · Transformer · Neural network

1 Introduction

Knowledge graphs (KG) have quickly become an indispensable information source for both research and practice in recent years. A great amount of effort has been invested into curating large KGs such as Freebase [3], DBPedia [2] and Wikidata [11]. Question answering (QA) [8,19], the task of answering natural-language questions over a KG, has attracted substantial research interest as it is

C. Ghidini et al. (Eds.): ISWC 2019, LNCS 11778, pp. 382–398, 2019.
https://doi.org/10.1007/978-3-030-30793-6_22

an accessible, natural way of retrieving information from KGs without the need for learning complex structural query languages such as SPARQL.

State-of-the-art KG QA models are typically based on neural networks and as a result, they are data-driven and need large amounts of training data, containing a set of triples in the form of a graph, a question and the corresponding answer. To cater to the need of training and evaluating KG QA models, a number of datasets have been created and curated over the years. These datasets include those that contain simple, single-hop information [1,4,24] as well as those that contain more complex information. These complex datasets either comprise multi-hop instances [30,34,35] or instances that are answerable only through discrete reasoning [23].

However, further improvements in KG QA have been hindered by the limited availability of data. The abundance of large-scale "simple", single-triple data does not necessarily help advance state-of-the-art. This is because, questions on such data are *easy* to answer, once correct entities and predicates are identified. In contrast, complex questions whose answering entails inference across multiple triples are naturally more difficult to answer and are therefore more valuable resources for improving KG QA models. However, complex questions are also more difficult to create, and most existing complex question datasets are created either manually or in a semi-automated manner.

Question generation (QG) over knowledge graphs poses a number of challenges. To illustrate the challenges, in Example 1 we present two subgraphs (both in visual and textual form) and the corresponding reference questions and answers from the ComplexWebQuestions [28] and the PathQuestion [35] datasets. The first example is from PathQuestion, which has the entities and predicates separated by a special token `#`, the end of the subgraph denoted by the token `<end>`, followed by the answer entity. It contains three entities connected by two predicates. The second example is from ComplexWebQuestions, which has the triples separated by the special token `<t>`. The example is a three-hop subgraph. Different from the previous example, this subgraph is not a sequence of triples but rather star-shaped, and has multiple answers.

Example 1. Two examples, each consisting of a subgraph, a question about it, together with the answer.

G:	henry_i_duke_of_guise#parents#anna_deste#spouse# jacques_de_savoie_2nd_duc_de_nemours#<end># jacques_de_savoie_2nd_duc_de_nemours
Q:	what is the name of the spouse of henry_i_duke_of_guise 's mom?
A:	jacques_de_savoie_2nd_duc_de_nemours

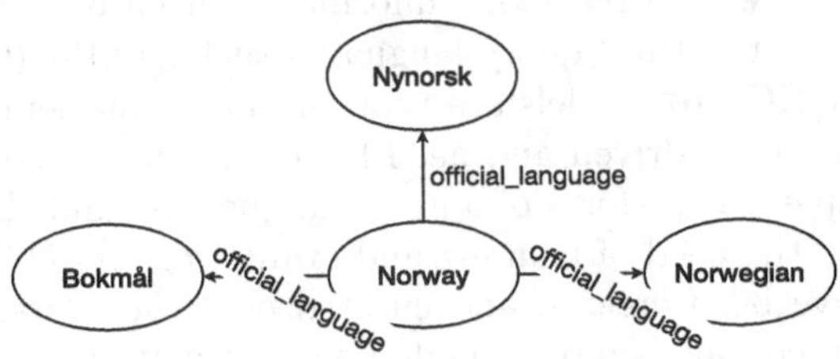

G: `Norway official_language Bokmål <t>`
`Norway official_language Norwegian <t>`
`Norway official_language Nynorsk`

Q: `what languages are spoken in norway?`
A: `Bokmål, Norwegian, Nynorsk`

We address the following challenges for QG over KGs. Firstly, the input is a graph, and not necessarily a sequence of tokens. The second graph in Example 1 contains one entity with three outgoing predicates connecting to three other entities, and is obviously not structured as a sequence. Conventional text generation methods are however based on sequence-to-sequence models such as recurrent neural networks (RNN), that assume the input to be a sequence. Such a mismatch may negatively affect the quality of QG. In the same vein, for complex, multi-hop questions, a model would need to look at different parts of the graph repeatedly to generate a syntactically fluent question. Again, this is difficult for RNN-based techniques that operate sequentially. Last but not least, it is desirable to be able to generate questions of varying difficulty levels.

In this paper, we address the important problem of automatic generation of *complex, multi-hop* questions over KGs. We propose an end-to-end, self-attentive QG method based on the Transformer [31] architecture. Our approach does not assume sequential representation of an input graph, and is naturally able to attend to different parts of a graph in an efficient manner. Moreover, we model and estimate the difficulty level of a given subgraph-question pair so that we can generate questions of varying difficulty levels.

To the best of our knowledge, this is the first work on automatic generation of complex, multi-hop questions from KGs. Our main contributions are fourfold.

1. We propose a novel model for generating complex, difficulty-controllable questions from subgraphs of multiple triples.
2. Our Transformer-based model naturally treats a subgraph (a set of triples) as a graph and avoids arbitrary *linearisation* into a sequence of triples.
3. Our evaluation over a state-of-the-art natural-language generation model on two multi-hop QA datasets shows our technique is able to generate questions of much higher quality.
4. Models, dataset and code is available[1] to facilitate reproduction and further research on KG QA research.

[1] https://github.com/liyuanfang/mhqg.

2 Related Work

In this section we briefly discuss prior work from the areas of question answering and question generation that are most related to our work.

2.1 Question Answering over Knowledge Graphs

Question Answering over Linked Data (QALD) [19] has been under intense investigation in recent years. A wide array of methods and techniques have been developed. Bordes *et al.* [4] employed Memory Networks [33] to answer simple, one-hop questions, and created the SimpleQuestions dataset that contains 100k one-hop questions. Semantic parsing has also been investigated as an effective method for answering both simple [1] and complex [34] questions. Talmor and Berant proposed [28] to decompose a complex question into simpler ones as a way of answering it. Unlike in semantic parsing where the knowledge graph is used for QA, Talmor and Berant propose to answer simple questions by performing a Web search. The final answer is computed from the sequence of answers. The results are evaluated on their own ComplexWebQuestions dataset that includes SPARQL queries, answers and text snippets as evidence. As a byproduct of these methods, the datasets WebQuestions [1] and WebQuestionsSP [34] were created. An Interpretable Reasoning Network (IRN) was proposed by Zhou, Huang and Zhu [35] to answer multi-hop (path or conjunctive) questions. Two datasets, PathQuestion and WorldCup2014, of up to three hops were created for evaluating IRN.

A different type of complex questions answering task that involve discrete reasoning has recently been proposed in CSQA [23]. Unlike multi-hop questions, questions in CSQA requires a variety of different reasoning tasks, such as logical, quantitative, qualitative, and comparative reasoning.

Interested readers are referred to a recent survey [8] for further details.

2.2 Question Generation

Question generation (QG) has recently attracted significant interests in the natural language processing (NLP) and computer vision (CV) community. Given an input (e.g. a passage of text in NLP or an image in CV), optionally also an answer, the task of QG is to generate a natural-language question that is answerable from the input. Neural network-based methods [9,12,17,18,26] are the state-of-the-art in QG. These end-to-end models do not require the manual creation of templates or rules, and are able to generate high-quality, fluent questions.

For any data-driven tasks such as question answering, the availability of large, varied and challenging datasets is crucial to their continued improvements. In fact, the recent development and interests in QALD is in part driven by the creation and release of the public datasets discussed in the previous subsection. Significant manual work has been invested in the creation (e.g. by Amazon Mechanical Turk workers) and curation (e.g. by the researchers) of these datasets.

Despite the continued efforts, constrained by available resources, these datasets are limited in their size and variability.

As a response to this issue, the (semi-)automatic generation of questions over KG has recently been investigated. Seyler et al. [25] proposed a semi-automatic method of generating multi-hop quiz questions from KG. With an entity e as the starting point, the KG is queried to find all triples with the entity as either the subject or the object, using SPARQL with patterns $\langle e\ ?p\ ?o\rangle$ and $\langle ?s\ ?p\ o\rangle$. The SPARQL queries are then verbalised from a given pattern to generate quiz questions. The notion of difficulty, which is measured from entity popularity, triple pattern selectivity and coherence, is incorporated in this work.

Inspired by QALD [19], Large-Scale Complex Question Answering Dataset (LC-QuAD) [30], a QA dataset of 5,000 multi-hop questions, was recently released. Similar to the previous work, LC-QuAD's generation is semi-automatic. The starting point is a manually curated list of DBPedia entities and predicates, a list of SPARQL templates, as well as a list of natural-language question templates, one for each SPARQL template. Given a seed entity and predicates, a two-hop subgraphs are extracted from DBPedia. The subgraphs and templates are merged to create valid SPARQL queries, and in turn natural-language questions. These questions are eventually corrected and reviewed by human users.

Different from the above works, our method is end-to-end and fully automated without the need of manually created templates or patterns. Our method only requires a subgraph (similar to a text passage and an image in other settings) and optionally an answer, from which a natural-language question is generated.

The 30M Factoid Question Answer Corpus [24] is possibly the earliest work using neural networks to generate questions over KG, and the largest dataset of single-hop questions. With SimpleQuestions [4] as the training set, they employ a standard encoder-decoder architecture to embed facts (triples), from which questions are generated. Reddy et al. [22] also uses a standard sequence-to-sequence model to generate single-hop questions from a set of keywords, extracted from a KG using rules. Elsahar et al. recently proposed a method [10] of generating single-hop questions from KG. Their method supports the generation involving unseen predicates and types, which is achieved by incorporating side information, in this case textual context from Wikipedia articles. Employing the encoder-decoder architecture with GRUs (gated recurrent units), the decoder module makes use of triple attention and textural attention to generate the next, possibly unseen token.

Our method differs from the above in a number of important ways. (1) Our model generates complex multi-hop questions, whilst all of the above neural network-based methods generate single-hop questions. (2) Our end-to-end model estimates and controls difficulty levels of generated questions. (3) We employ the Transformer [31] as our base model. The Transformer architecture allows us to naturally treat a graph as a graph, instead of a sequence of triples. Moreover, compared to variants of recurrent neural networks (e.g. LSTM [15] and GRU [6]), training on the Transformer is more efficient.

More broadly speaking, question generation from KG is a special case of text generation from KG, which has also been investigated recently [20,29,32]. These techniques encode a set of triples using either customised LSTM or GCN (graph convolutional network), and are typically evaluated on the WebNLG dataset [13]. A main difference is that these work do not take into account the answer or the difficulty level, which are important in the task of QG. Moreover, compared to RNN-based methods, our technique is more effective and efficient in handling larger contexts and is able to attend to multiple places in the context.

3 Our Approach

We model the problem of question generation over knowledge graphs as a sequence-to-sequence (Seq2Seq) learning problem. We assume a background knowledge graph $\mathcal{G}$, comprising a set of triples (facts). Given a subgraph $G = \{f_1, \ldots, f_n\} \subseteq \mathcal{G}$ of n facts, a set of entities E_A that appears in some triple(s) in G that represents the *answer*, our model will generate a natural-language question $Q = (w_1, \ldots, w_m)$, i.e. a sequence of m words, such that

$$Q^* = \arg\max_{Q} P(Q \mid G, E_A; \Theta) \quad (1)$$

$$= \arg\max_{w_1,\ldots,w_m} \prod_{i=1}^{m} P(w_i \mid w_1, \ldots, w_{i-1}, G, E_A; \Theta) \quad (2)$$

where Θ denotes model parameters.

The high-level architecture of our model can be seen in Fig. 1. It uses the Transformer as the base architecture. The encoder (Sect. 3.1) consists of a stack of Transformers, taking as input the subgraph, the answer entities and estimated difficulty level of the subgraph. Difficulty modelling and estimation is described in detail in Sect. 3.2. The decoder (Sect. 3.3) is another stack of Transformers and decodes a multi-hop question given the encoder output, conditioned on the user-specified difficulty setting.

3.1 Knowledge Graph Encoding

For a subgraph G, the encoder takes its embedding as input, which in turn is constructed from the embeddings of the triples in G. Let d_e denote the dimension of entity/relation embeddings and d_g denote the dimension of triple embeddings. At initialisation, the embedding of a triple is the concatenation of the embeddings of the subject, the predicate and the object of the triple, with the rest of the values randomly initialised to match triple embedding dimension d_g. Each answer entity in E_A is additionally embedded into a d_e-dimensional vector, learned from whether it is an answer entity through an MLP (multi-layer perceptron). Element-wise addition is then performed on the answer embedding and the original entity embedding to obtain the final embedding for each answer entity.

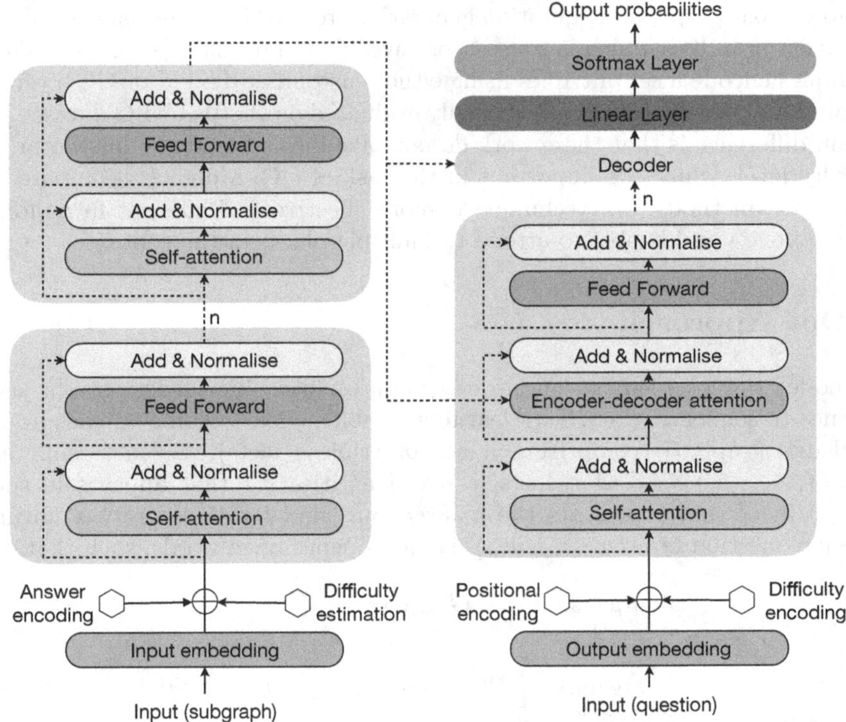

Fig. 1. The high-level architecture of our multi-hop question generation framework. The encoder stack of Transformers is on the left and the decoder stack is on the right.

Therefore, for graph G containing n triples, it is represented as a matrix $\boldsymbol{G} \in \mathbb{R}^{n \times d_g}$. Taking $\boldsymbol{G}$ as input, the Transformer encoder maps it to a sequence of continuous representations $\boldsymbol{Z} = (z_1, \cdots, z_n) \in \mathbb{R}^{n \times d_v}$.

Let $\boldsymbol{Q}, \boldsymbol{K} \in \mathbb{R}^{n \times d_k}, \boldsymbol{V} \in \mathbb{R}^{n \times d_v}$ denote the *query*, the *key* and the *value* matrices of the encoder Transformer. Given input $\boldsymbol{G}$, we use the query matrix $\boldsymbol{V}$ to soft select the relevant triples with the scaled dot-product attention:

$$\text{Att}(\boldsymbol{Q}, \boldsymbol{K}, \boldsymbol{V}) = \text{softmax}(\frac{\boldsymbol{Q}\boldsymbol{K}^T}{\sqrt{d_k}})\boldsymbol{V} \tag{3}$$

where $\boldsymbol{K}^T$ is $\boldsymbol{K}$'s transpose, $\boldsymbol{Q} = \boldsymbol{G}\boldsymbol{W}^Q, \boldsymbol{K} = \boldsymbol{G}\boldsymbol{W}^K, \boldsymbol{V} = \boldsymbol{G}\boldsymbol{W}^V$, and $\boldsymbol{W}^Q, \boldsymbol{W}^K \in \mathbb{R}^{d_g \times d_k}, \boldsymbol{W}^V \in \mathbb{R}^{d_g \times d_v}$ are trainable model parameters.

To be able to attend to information from different triples in different representation subspaces, we use the multi-head attention with k heads and aggregate them as follows:

$$\text{MultiAtt}(\boldsymbol{Q}, \boldsymbol{G}) = \text{concat}(\boldsymbol{a}_1, \ldots, \boldsymbol{a}_k)\boldsymbol{W}^O \tag{4}$$

where $\boldsymbol{W}^O \in \mathbb{R}^{kd_v \times d_g}$, and $\boldsymbol{a}_i = \text{Att}(\boldsymbol{Q}\boldsymbol{W}_i^Q, \boldsymbol{G}\boldsymbol{W}_i^K, \boldsymbol{G}\boldsymbol{W}_i^V), i \in [1, k]$ as defined in Formula 3.

Aggregated multi-head attention output is passed to a feed-forward neural net (FFNN) in each of the encoder stack of Transformers, where the output $\boldsymbol{x}$ goes through two linear transformations:

$$\text{FFNN}(\boldsymbol{x}) = \max(0, \boldsymbol{x}\boldsymbol{W}_1 + \boldsymbol{b}_1)\boldsymbol{W}_2 + \boldsymbol{b}_2 \tag{5}$$

In all the encoder layers other than 1st layer we directly feed output of the previous encoder layer as input. The output of the top of the encoder is finally transformed into two attention matrices, the keys $\boldsymbol{K}_{encdec}$ and the values $\boldsymbol{V}_{encdec}$.

The original Transformer is designed for handling sequences, and for that purpose it provides *positional encoding* to encode the position of each input token. As a subgraph does not necessarily form a sequence of triples (cf the second graph in Example 1), we do not use positional encoding in our encoder.

The subgraph embedding is augmented with the answering (entity) encoding as well as a difficulty estimation, which is described in the next subsection.

3.2 Difficulty Level Modelling and Estimation

Given a subgraph, it is desirable to generate questions of different difficulty levels in different situations. As there is no ground truth for question difficulty level, we estimate the difficulty using characteristics of the question and the subgraph, namely (1) the *confidence* of entity linking in the question, and (2) the *selectivity* of the surface forms of entities in the subgraph.

Confidence. We employ NER (named entity recognition) systems to perform entity recognition and linking. Intuitively, high confidence of an NER system about an entity-mention linking may be due to the low ambiguity of the mention and the high differentiability of the context, both of which would make the subgraph easy to understand and the generated question easy to answer. For example, given the mention "`Cold War`", if the NER system returns a higher confidence score for the entity freebase:m.034y4w than freebase:m.011l309l, a question that contains the former would be more likely to be correct, hence easier to answer.

Selectivity. On the other hand, the less selective a mention is (e.g. "`John Smith`" vs "`Elon Musk`"), the more confusing it would be for the question containing that mention. We query Wikipedia with the each mention, and use the number of returned hits as an estimation of its *selectivity*, where he higher the number of hits, the lower the selectivity, thus the more difficult the question.

Given a training instance (G, q) of a subgraph G and a question q, we denote the confidence of $Con(q)$, by averaging over all identified mentions in q and min-max normalisation over the training corpus. We denote the selectivity of the subgraph $Sel(G)$, by averaging over all entities in G and min-max normalisation. We estimate the difficulty level of a given subgraph and a question, $Dif(G, q)$, as follows:

$$\text{Dif}(G, q) = \frac{1 + Sel(G)}{1 + Con(q)} \tag{6}$$

The difficulty estimation Dif(G, q) is then normalised into the closed interval $[0, 1]$, and finally converted into a binary vector $\boldsymbol{x} \in \{0, 1\}^2$ by thresholding, where $(0, 1)$ and $(1, 0)$ represent easy and difficult respectively. We randomly observe values of around 200 instances of *easy* difficulty level and we choose the maximum of those values as threshold. We note that we use a one-hot vector to represent difficulty levels so that it is easy to generalise it to multiple difficulty levels (e.g. easy, medium, hard).

3.3 Complex Question Decoder

Our decoder is a stack of Transformer decoders, conditioned on the difficulty level of the question to be generated. Similar to the encoder, the decoder also has multiple scaled dot-product attention layers along with feed forward neural network layers. Besides the self-attention, the decoder uses the final (top in Fig. 1) encoder Transformer's output attention matrices ($\boldsymbol{K}_{encdec}$ and $\boldsymbol{V}_{encdec}$) in its encoder-decoder attention layer, which helps decoder in attending to (focusing on) important triples in the input subgraph.

The encoder-decoder attention layer works very similarly to the multi-head self attention layer described in Sect. 3.1 above. The main difference is that the encoder-decoder attention layer computes the query matrix ($\boldsymbol{Q}$) using the layer below it in the decoder and takes the key ($\boldsymbol{K}$) and values ($\boldsymbol{V}$) matrices from encoder output.

The output vector from the decoder stack is fed to a fully connected neural network (linear layer) which projects it to logits vector. Finally the softmax layer converts this logits vectors into a probability distribution over vocabulary, from which the question is decoded.

We encode difficulty into the decoder using a multi-layer perceptron *DE* consisting of an input linear layer followed by a rectified linear unit (ReLU) layer and an output linear layer. The input to DE is a length-two vector $\boldsymbol{x}$ representing a given difficulty level, as described in the previous subsection.

$$\mathrm{DE}(\boldsymbol{x}) = Linear(ReLU(\boldsymbol{W}\boldsymbol{x} + \boldsymbol{b})) \tag{7}$$

where $\boldsymbol{x}$ the difficulty level and $\boldsymbol{W} \in \mathbb{R}^{d_g \times 2}$ and $\boldsymbol{b} \in \mathbb{R}^{d_g}$ are trainable model parameters. We sum DE$(\boldsymbol{x})$ with decoder input to condition decoder to generate question of encoded difficulty.

At the decoder side, the order of question words is important. Therefore, we inject/add sequence order information to the decoder input. To represent order of the sequence we use fixed *positional encoding* with sine and cosine functions of different frequencies:

$$\mathrm{PE}_{(pos,2i)} = \sin\left(pos/10000^{2i/d_g}\right) \tag{8}$$

$$\mathrm{PE}_{(pos,2i+1)} = \cos\left(pos/10000^{2i/d_g}\right) \tag{9}$$

where *pos* is the position and i is the index of dimension.

Label Smoothing. Label smoothing [27] has shown great impact especially in Transformers with multi-head attention. Adding label smoothing reduces expected calibration error. Motivated by previous work [7], we use label smoothing for regularisation with an uncertainty of 0.1. Our label smoothing technique is based on the Kullback-Leibler divergence loss. Instead of using the vanilla one-hot question word distribution, we build a distribution that has confidence of the correct word and distributes the rest of the smoothing mass throughout the output vocabulary.

4 Evaluation

Dataset and Preprocessing. We collected data from three recent multi-hop question answering datasets: WebQuestionsSP [34], ComplexWebQuestions [28], and PathQuestion [35][2], all of which are based on Freebase.

Each instance in WebQuestionsSP and ComplexWebQuestions contains a natural-language question, a corresponding SPARQ query and the answer entity and some other auxiliary information. For each instance, we convert its SPARQL query to return a subgraph instead of the answer entity, by changing it from a `SELECT` query to a `CONSTRUCT` query. An example `CONSTRUCT` query and its returned graph from the WebQuestionsSP dataset is shown in Example 2 below. We combine these two datasets and refer to them as WQ hereinafter.

Example 2. An example `CONSTRUCT` query and the corresponding returned graph.

```
PREFIX ns: <http://rdf.freebase.com/ns/>
CONSTRUCT WHERE { FILTER (?x != ns:m.02189)
FILTER (!isLiteral(?x) OR lang(?x) = '' OR langMatches(lang(?x), 'en'))
ns:m.02189 ns:organization.organization.founders ?x .
?x ns:medicine.notable_person_with_medical_condition.condition ns:m.0g02vk .
}
```

The subgraph returned after executing the above query is given below. Note the Freebase prefix is omitted for brevity reasons.

```
m.02189 organization.organization.founders m.04xzm .
m.04xzm medicine.notable_person_with_medical_condition.condition m.0g02vk .
```

PathQuestion (referred to as PQ hereinafter) is similar to WQ. However, PQ only contains *verbalised* entities and predicates but not their Freebase IDs. As a result, we process this dataset differently.

Conceptually, each of WQ and PQ is a set of tuples $\{(Q_t, G, E_A)\}$, where Q_t is a natural-language question, G is the subgraph from which the question is derived, and E_A is the set of answer entities to question Q_t. Brief statistics of the two datasets can be found in Table 1.

[2] Retrieved from https://www.microsoft.com/en-us/download/details.aspx?id=52763, https://www.tau-nlp.org/compwebq, and https://github.com/zmtkeke/IRN/tree/master/PathQuestion respectively.

For each dataset (WQ and PQ), we split it into 80%, 10% 10% for training, validation and testing.

Table 1. Brief statistics of the collected datasets.

Dataset	# entities	# predicates	# hops	# instances
WQ [28,34]	25,703	672	2 to 100	22,989
PQ [35]	7,250	378	2, 3	9,731
Total	32,953	1,050	–	32,720

Implementation Details. We have implemented our multi-hop question generation model, denoted MHQG[3], in the PyTorch framework. For the state-of-the-art question generation model Learning to Ask (L2A) [9] used for comparison, we used its publicly available code.

We set triple embedding dimension for the Transformers to 512, i.e. $d_g = 512$. The triple embeddings are fine-tuned during training. We use 8 parallel attention heads with d_k and d_v set to 64. The dimension of encoder and decoder's fully connected feed forward neural nets is set to 2048. We set the number of layers of Transformers to six ($n = 6$ in Fig. 1) for both the encoder and the decoder.

For the WQ dasatet, we obtain the pre-trained 50-dimensional TransE [5] embeddings for Freebase from OpenKE [14]. The embedding of a triple is the 150-dimensional concatenated embeddings of its components (subject, predicate and object). For initialisation, we extend the 150-dimensional embedding vectors to 512-dimensional with random values for the remaining 362 dimensions.

As PQ only contains lexicalised entities and predicates but not their IDs, we resort to using the pre-trained 300-dimensional GloVe [21] word embeddings for this dataset. For each entity/predicate, its embedding is the average of the embeddings of its words. We extend the embedding vectors to 512-dimensional with random values for the remaining 212 dimensions. As in WQ, the triple embeddings are fine-tuned during training.

For example, for the following (2-triple) subgraph in PQ `claudius#parents#nero_claudius_drusus#nationality#roman_empire`, the embedding of the entity `roman_empire` is the average of the GloVe embeddings of words `roman` and `empire`. We mask entities in questions to a generic entity form such as "ENT1" to handle unseen entities, thus resolving the out of vocabulary issue. Entity masking also helps model learn better generalisations for similar training instances.

We use TAGME[4] for entity recognition and entity linking, and obtain the TAGME *confidence* score in difficulty estimation (Sect. 3.2).

[3] Available at https://github.com/liyuanfang/mhqg.
[4] https://tagme.d4science.org/tagme/.

We used the Adam optimiser [16] with $\beta_2 = 0.998$, initialised with learning rate 2 to optimise model parameters. The learning rate increases linearly for the first 800 training steps (warmup steps) and decreases thereafter proportionally to the inverse square root of the step number. For regularisation we apply dropout to the output of each layer with the dropout probability set to 0.1. We use beam search in the decoder with beam size of 10 for decoding question words. These parameters are empirically chosen using grid search.

All our models are trained on a single P100 GPU. We train for 15 epochs, and select the model with the minimum perplexity on the validation set to generate question on the test set for evaluation.

4.1 Results and Discussion

To the best of our knowledge, this work is the first to address multi-hop question generation from KG. Therefore, there is no other model that we can compare with directly. Existing text generation models such as GTR-LSTM [29] and GCN [20] are trained on a different KG (DBPedia instead of Freebase). Comparing them requires significant additional data preprocessing work, including entity linking, triple embedding, etc., as well as mandatory additional data (e.g. entity types) that are not available to us. As a result, we leave comparing with them to future work.

Instead, we use a state-of-the-art natural language QG model, Learning to Ask [9] (referred to as L2A hereinafter), as a baseline model for comparison. L2A is a recent LSTM-based Seq2Seq model that takes a sentence as input and generates a question. We train L2A using the linearised subgraph with 300-dimensional embeddings, which are fine-tuned during training. We use a 2 layer Bi-LSTM encoder and decoder with hidden unit size set to 600. The other hyper-parameters are set exactly the same as described in L2A [9]

We perform two experiments to evaluate the effectiveness of our proposed model: automatic evaluation using widely-used metrics including BLEU, GLEU and METEOR and human evaluation. We compare two variants of our model against L2A: with (MHQG+AE) or without (MHQG) answer encoding. The automatic evaluation is performed on the full test sets, whereas a subset of 50 randomly selected questions, 25 from each of WQ and PQ, are used in human evaluation.

The results of automatic evaluation are shown in Table 2. As can be seen, on both datasets, both our models outperform L2A substantially across all three evaluation metrics. On both datasets, our models outperform L2A on BLEU for 5.56 and 8.99 absolute points, representing a 93% and 53% respectively. On the PQ dataset, the differences in ROUGE-L and METEOR are more substantial than on the WQ dataset. Moreover, MHQG+AE, the model with answer encoding, also consistently exhibits better performance than without it.

Table 2. Results of automatic evaluation. Best results for each metric is **bolded**.

Model	WQ			PQ		
	BLEU	ROUGE-L	METEOR	BLEU	ROUGE-L	METEOR
L2A	6.01	26.95	25.24	17.00	50.38	19.72
MHQG	11.49	34.61	27.65	24.98	58.08	31.32
MHQG+AE	**11.57**	**35.53**	**29.69**	**25.99**	**58.94**	**33.16**

Table 3. Results of human evaluation, showing percentages of questions with correct syntax, semantics and difficulty level for the two datasets and each model. The numbers in parentheses are the percentage of agreement between participants. Best results for each metric is **bolded**.

Model	WQ			PQ		
	Syntax	Semantics	Difficulty	Syntax	Semantics	Difficulty
L2A	78 (97)	80 (95)	48 (59)	67 (65)	65 (73)	58 (50)
MHQG	79 (75)	83 (81)	**60** (49)	64 (75)	70 (69)	**68** (44)
MHQG+AE	**98** (73)	**97** (76)	56 (53)	**78** (70)	**74** (62)	**68** (49)

In human evaluation, four participants were asked to judge the correctness of syntax, semantics and difficulty level of the questions generated by L2A and our models. The results are averaged across the four participants and are summarised in Table 3. For all evaluation criteria, both of our models outperform L2A. Notably, on WQ, our model MHQG+AE achieves 98% and 97% of syntactic and semantic correctness respectively. Overall MHQG+AE achieves best result, except the slightly lower percentage of correct difficulty level for WQ. This is consistent with the results in automatic evaluation in Table 2, where MHQG+AE also shows best performance.

Below in Example 3 we show two questions, one easy, and one hard, generated by our model MHQG+AE on a same graph. Fro brevity reasons only the localname of the freebase predicates are shown. As can be seen, the difference in hardness is obvious, showing the effectiveness of our model in controlling question difficulty.

Example 3. An example graph with two questions of different difficulty levels generated by our model MHQG+AE.

Graph:	m.0gtqy5p location m.0r0m6 <t> m.0gtqxxq location m.0fpzwf <t> m.01vrncs places_lived m.03pnpl8 <t> m.01vrncs film.film_subject.films m.0djlxb <t> m.03pnpl8 location m.0h1k6 <t> m.0gtqxxk location m.02_286 <t> m.01vrncs places_lived m.0gtqy5p <t> m.01vrncs places_lived m.0gtqxxk <t> m.0gtqy5h location m.0wjjx<t> m.01vrncs places_lived m.0gtqxxq <t> m.01vrncs places_lived m.0gtqy5h <t>
Easy:	where did bob dylan live?
Hard:	where did the subject of the film "I'm Not There" live?

Example 4 below shows two complex, 7-hop and 4-hop, subgraphs from WQ and the questions generated on them, by L2A and our two models. As can be seen, our models generate questions of much higher quality than L2A.

Example 4. Two subgraphs and questions generated by different models.

Graph:	m.0jjl89y office_position_or_title m.0j6tpbb <t> m.0hqg6pb office_position_or_title m.0j6tpbb <t> m.03gj2 official_language m.02ztjwg <t> m.03gj2 governing_officials m.0hqg6m3 <t> m.03gj2 governing_officials m.0jjl89y <t> m.03gj2 governing_officials m.0hqg6pb <t> m.0hqg6m3 office_position_or_title m.0j6tpbb <t>
L2A:	what language is spoken in the governmental jurisdiction?
MHQG:	what is the spoken language in the country with governmental position prime minister of hungary?
MHQG+AE:	what language is spoken in the governmental jurisdiction where prime minister of hungary holds office?

Graph:	m.0d04z6 currency_used m.049p2z <t> m.0d04z6 national_anthem m.048z_y1 <t> m.0d04z6 currency_used m.049p6c <t> m.048z_y1 anthem m.011g5j <t>
L2A:	the country that contains uses what type of currency?
MHQG:	what is the currency used in the country with la bayamesa as its national anthem?
MHQG+AE:	what currency is used in the country with national anthem la bayamesa?

5 Conclusion

In this paper we present a novel technique for the automatic generation of complex, multi-hop questions from knowledge graphs. Our technique takes a subgraph as input, encodes the answer, estimates the difficulty level, and generates a natural-language question from the subgraph. We employ a Transformer-based encoder-decoder model that is conditioned on the difficulty level. Experiments were performed on three recent multi-hop question-answering datasets to assess the quality of generated questions, by both widely-used evaluation metrics and human judgements. Compared to a state-of-the-art text question generation technique, our method generates questions that are more fluent and relevant with tunable difficulty levels.

Our technique allows the generation of complex questions over a large knowledge without any manual intervention. This ability can facilitate the continued improvements of knowledge graph question answering methods by providing substantial amount of new training data with minimal cost.

We have planned a number of further research directions. Firstly, we will investigate a more refined estimation of difficulty levels, taking into account more comprehensive information such as predicates and the graph itself, but not only entities. Secondly, taking into account additional information sources such as background ontologies as entity and predicate definitions is also worth investigating.

References

1. Berant, J., Chou, A., Frostig, R., Liang, P.: Semantic parsing on freebase from question-answer pairs. In: Proceedings of the 2013 Conference on Empirical Methods in Natural Language Processing, pp. 1533–1544. Association for Computational Linguistics (2013)
2. Bizer, C., et al.: DBpedia-a crystallization point for the web of data. Web Semant.: Sci. Serv. Agents World Wide Web **7**(3), 154–165 (2009)
3. Bollacker, K., Evans, C., Paritosh, P., Sturge, T., Taylor, J.: Freebase: a collaboratively created graph database for structuring human knowledge. In: Proceedings of the 2008 ACM SIGMOD International Conference on Management of Data, pp. 1247–1250. ACM (2008)
4. Bordes, A., Usunier, N., Chopra, S., Weston, J.: Large-scale simple question answering with memory networks. arXiv preprint arXiv:1506.02075 (2015)
5. Bordes, A., Usunier, N., Garcia-Duran, A., Weston, J., Yakhnenko, O.: Translating embeddings for modeling multi-relational data. In: Advances in Neural Information Processing Systems, pp. 2787–2795 (2013)
6. Cho, K., et al.: Learning phrase representations using RNN encoder-decoder for statistical machine translation. In: Proceedings of the 2014 Conference on Empirical Methods in Natural Language Processing (EMNLP), pp. 1724–1734. Association for Computational Linguistics, Doha, Qatar, October 2014
7. Chorowski, J., Jaitly, N.: Towards better decoding and language model integration in sequence to sequence models. In: Proceedings of the Interspeech 2017, pp. 523–527 (2017)
8. Diefenbach, D., Lopez, V., Singh, K., Maret, P.: Core techniques of question answering systems over knowledge bases: a survey. Knowl. Inf. Syst. **55**(3), 529–569 (2018)
9. Du, X., Shao, J., Cardie, C.: Learning to ask: neural question generation for reading comprehension. In: ACL, vol. 1, pp. 1342–1352 (2017)
10. Elsahar, H., Gravier, C., Laforest, F.: Zero-shot question generation from knowledge graphs for unseen predicates and entity types. In: Proceedings of the 2018 Conference of the North American Chapter of the Association for Computational Linguistics: Human Language Technologies, (Long Papers), vol. 1, pp. 218–228. Association for Computational Linguistics, New Orleans, Louisiana, June 2018

11. Erxleben, F., Günther, M., Krötzsch, M., Mendez, J., Vrandečić, D.: Introducing wikidata to the linked data web. In: Mika, P., et al. (eds.) ISWC 2014. LNCS, vol. 8796, pp. 50–65. Springer, Cham (2014). https://doi.org/10.1007/978-3-319-11964-9_4
12. Fan, Z., Wei, Z., Li, P., Lan, Y., Huang, X.: A question type driven framework to diversify visual question generation. In: IJCAI, pp. 4048–4054 (2018)
13. Gardent, C., Shimorina, A., Narayan, S., Perez-Beltrachini, L.: Creating training corpora for NLG micro-planners. In: Proceedings of the 55th Annual Meeting of the Association for Computational Linguistics, (vol. 1: Long Papers), pp. 179–188. Association for Computational Linguistics, Vancouver, Canada, July 2017
14. Han, X., et al.: OpenKE: an open toolkit for knowledge embedding. In: Proceedings of the 2018 Conference on Empirical Methods in Natural Language Processing: System Demonstrations, pp. 139–144. Association for Computational Linguistics, Brussels, Belgium, November 2018
15. Hochreiter, S., Schmidhuber, J.: Long short-term memory. Neural Comput. **9**(8), 1735–1780 (1997)
16. Kingma, D.P., Ba, J.: Adam: a method for stochastic optimization. arXiv preprint arXiv:1412.6980 (2014)
17. Kumar, V.,Boorla, K., Meena, Y., Ramakrishnan, G., Li, Y.-F.: Automating reading comprehension by generating question and answer pairs. In: Phung, D., Tseng, V.S., Webb, G.I., Ho, B., Ganji, M., Rashidi, L. (eds.) PAKDD 2018. LNCS, vol. 10939, pp. 335–348. Springer, Cham (2018). https://doi.org/10.1007/978-3-319-93040-4_27
18. Li, Y., et al.: Visual question generation as dual task of visual question answering. In: Proceedings of the IEEE Conference on Computer Vision and Pattern Recognition, pp. 6116–6124 (2018)
19. Lopez, V., Unger, C., Cimiano, P., Motta, E.: Evaluating question answering over linked data. Web Semant. Sci. Serv. Agents World Wide Web **21**, 3–13 (2013)
20. Marcheggiani, D., Perez-Beltrachini, L.: Deep graph convolutional encoders for structured data to text generation. In: Proceedings of the 11th International Conference on Natural Language Generation, pp. 1–9. Association for Computational Linguistics, Tilburg University, The Netherlands, November 2018
21. Pennington, J., Socher, R., Manning, C.: GloVe: global vectors for word representation. In: Proceedings of the 2014 Conference on Empirical Methods in Natural Language Processing (EMNLP), pp. 1532–1543. Association for Computational Linguistics, Doha, Qatar, October 2014
22. Reddy, S., Raghu, D., Khapra, M.M., Joshi, S.: Generating natural language question-answer pairs from a knowledge graph using a RNN based question generation model. In: Proceedings of the 15th Conference of the European Chapter of the Association for Computational Linguistics, vol. 1, Long Papers, pp. 376–385. Association for Computational Linguistics (2017)
23. Saha, A., Pahuja, V., Khapra, M.M., Sankaranarayanan, K., Chandar, S.: Complex sequential question answering: towards learning to converse over linked question answer pairs with a knowledge graph. In: Thirty-Second AAAI Conference on Artificial Intelligence (2018)
24. Serban, I.V., et al.: Generating factoid questions with recurrent neural networks: the 30M factoid question-answer corpus. arXiv preprint arXiv:1603.06807 (2016)
25. Seyler, D., Yahya, M., Berberich, K.: Generating quiz questions from knowledge graphs. In: Proceedings of the 24th International Conference on World Wide Web, WWW 2015 Companion, pp. 113–114. ACM, New York, NY, USA (2015)

26. Song, L., Wang, Z., Hamza, W., Zhang, Y., Gildea, D.: Leveraging context information for natural question generation. In: NAACL (Short Papers), vol. 2, 569–574 (2018)
27. Szegedy, C., Vanhoucke, V., Ioffe, S., Shlens, J., Wojna, Z.: Rethinking the inception architecture for computer vision. In: Proceedings of the IEEE Conference on Computer Vision and Pattern Recognition, pp. 2818–2826 (2016)
28. Talmor, A., Berant, J.: The web as a knowledge-base for answering complex questions. In: Proceedings of the 2018 Conference of the North American Chapter of the Association for Computational Linguistics: Human Language Technologies, Vol. 1 (Long Papers), pp. 641–651. Association for Computational Linguistics (2018)
29. Trisedya, B.D., Qi, J., Zhang, R., Wang, W.: GTR-LSTM: a triple encoder for sentence generation from RDF data. In: Proceedings of the 56th Annual Meeting of the Association for Computational Linguistics, (vol. 1: Long Papers), pp. 1627–1637. Association for Computational Linguistics, Melbourne, Australia, July 2018
30. Trivedi, P., Maheshwari, G., Dubey, M., Lehmann, J.: LC-QuAD: a corpus for complex question answering over knowledge graphs. In: d'Amato, C., et al. (eds.) ISWC 2017. LNCS, vol. 10588, pp. 210–218. Springer, Cham (2017). https://doi.org/10.1007/978-3-319-68204-4_22
31. Vaswani, A., et al.: Attention is all you need. In: Advances in Neural Information Processing Systems (NIPS), pp. 5998–6008 (2017)
32. Vougiouklis, P., et al.: Neural Wikipedian: generating textual summaries from knowledge base triples. J. Web Semant. **52–53**, 1–15 (2018)
33. Weston, J., Chopra, S., Bordes, A.: Memory networks. In: Bengio, Y., LeCun, Y. (eds.) Conference Track Proceedings on 3rd International Conference on Learning Representations, ICLR 2015, San Diego, CA, USA, 7–9 May 2015 (2015)
34. Yih, W., Richardson, M., Meek, C., Chang, M.W., Suh, J.: The value of semantic parse labeling for knowledge base question answering. In: Proceedings of the 54th Annual Meeting of the Association for Computational Linguistics, (vol. 2: Short Papers), pp. 201–206. Association for Computational Linguistics (2016)
35. Zhou, M., Huang, M., Zhu, X.: An interpretable reasoning network for multi-relation question answering. In: Proceedings of the 27th International Conference on Computational Linguistics, pp. 2010–2022. Association for Computational Linguistics (2018)

Type Checking Program Code Using SHACL

Martin Leinberger[1(✉)], Philipp Seifer[2], Claudia Schon[1], Ralf Lämmel[2], and Steffen Staab[1,3]

[1] Institute for Web Science and Technologies, University of Koblenz-Landau, Koblenz, Germany
mleinberger@uni-koblenz.de

[2] The Software Languages Team, University of Koblenz-Landau, Mainz, Germany

[3] Web and Internet Science Research Group, University of Southampton, Southampton, England

Abstract. It is a strength of graph-based data formats, like RDF, that they are very flexible with representing data. To avoid run-time errors, program code that processes highly-flexible data representations exhibits the difficulty that it must always include the most general case, in which attributes might be set-valued or possibly not available. The Shapes Constraint Language (SHACL) has been devised to enforce constraints on otherwise random data structures. We present our approach, Type checking using SHACL (TyCuS), for type checking code that queries RDF data graphs validated by a SHACL shape graph. To this end, we derive SHACL shapes from queries and integrate data shapes and query shapes as types into a λ-calculus. We provide the formal underpinnings and a proof of type safety for TyCuS. A programmer can use our method in order to process RDF data with simplified, type checked code that will not encounter run-time errors (with usual exceptions as type checking cannot prevent accessing empty lists).

Keywords: SHACL · Programming with RDF · Type checking

1 Introduction

Graph-based data formats, such as RDF, have become increasingly popular, because they allow for much more flexibility for describing data items than rigidly-structured relational databases. Even when an ontology defines classes and properties, because of its open-world assumption, it is always possible to leave away required information or to add new classes and properties on the fly. Such flexibility incurs cost. Programmers cannot rely on structural restrictions of data relationships. For instance, the following T-Box axiom states that every `Student` has at least one `studiesAt` relation:

$$\texttt{Student} \sqsubseteq \geq 1\ \texttt{studiesAt}.\top \tag{1}$$

C. Ghidini et al. (Eds.): ISWC 2019, LNCS 11778, pp. 399–417, 2019.
https://doi.org/10.1007/978-3-030-30793-6_23

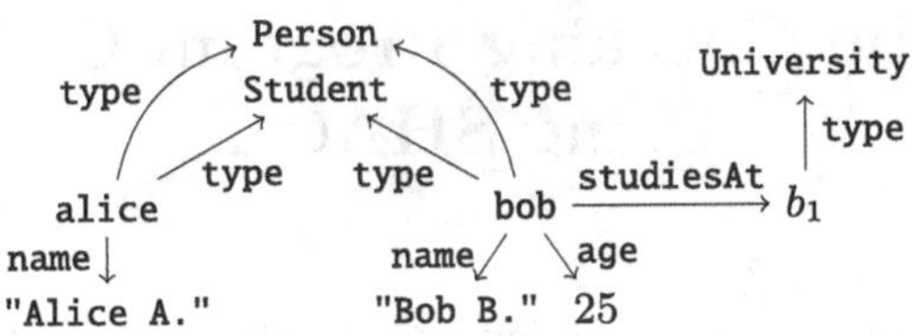

Fig. 1. Sample RDF data graph G_1.

Consider an RDF data graph such as shown in Fig. 1. The two nodes `alice` and `bob` are both instances of `Student` and `Person`. For `alice`, only the name is known. For `bob`, name, age and that he studies at b_1, which is an instance of `University`. Such a graph is a valid A-Box for the T-Box stated above. However, for a program containing a variable x representing an instance of `Student`, there is no guarantee that the place of study is explicitly mentioned in the data and can be displayed. Depending on whether x contains `alice` or `bob`, the following program may succeed or encounter a run-time error:

```
print(x.studiesAt)
```

The Shapes Constraint Language (SHACL) is a recent W3C recommendation [13] set out to allow for formulating integrity constraints. By now, a proposal for its formal semantics has been formulated by the research community [7] and SHACL shape graphs can be used to validate given data graphs. [13] itself states that:

> SHACL shape graphs [...] may be used for a variety of purposes besides validation, including user interface building, code generation and data integration.

However, it does not state *how* SHACL shape graphs might be used for these purposes. We consider the problem of writing code against an—possibly evolving—RDF data graph that is and remains conformant to a SHACL shape graph. We assume that the RDF database handles the rejection of transactions that invalidate conformance between SHACL shape graph and data graph. Then, the programming language should be able to type check programs that were written referring to a defined SHACL shape graph. Type checking should reject programs that could cause run-time errors, e.g., because they try to access an RDF property that is not guaranteed to exist without safety precautions. They should also simplify programs for which queries are guaranteed to return single values rather than lists, and they should accept programs that do not get stuck when querying conformant data graphs (with usual exceptions).

To exemplify this, consider three SHACL shapes `StudentShape`, `PersonShape` and `UniversityShape` (see Fig. 2). `StudentShape` validates all instances of `Student`, enforcing that there is at least one `studiesAt` relation, that all `studiesAt` relations point to a node conforming to the `UniversityShape` and that all instances of `Student` are also instances of `Person`. `PersonShape`

```
ex:StudentShape a sh:NodeShape;
  sh:targetClass ex:Student;
  sh:property [
    sh:path ex:studiesAt;
    sh:minCount 1;
    sh:node ex:UniversityShape ];
  sh:class ex:Person.

ex:PersonShape a sh:NodeShape;
    sh:targetClass ex:Person;
    sh:property [
      sh:path ex:name;
      sh:minCount 1;
      sh:maxCount 1 ].
ex:UniversityShape a
    sh:NodeShape;
  sh:property [
    sh:path [
      sh:inversePath;
      ex:studiesAt ];
    sh:minCount 1;
    sh:node
        ex:StudentShape ].
```

Fig. 2. SHACL constraints for RDF data graph G_1.

Listing 1. Program that may produce a run-time error.

```
map (fun x -> x.?X.age) (query {
    SELECT ?X WHERE { ?X rdf:type ex:Student.} })
```

validates all instances of `Person` and enforces the presence of exactly one `name` relation. `UniversityShape` enforces at least one incoming `studiesAt` relation and that all incoming `studiesAt` relations are from nodes conforming to the `StudentShape`. In order for G_1 to be valid with respect to the SHACL constraints above, either the statement that `alice` is an `Student` must be removed or a place of study for `alice` added. With these changes, the program above cannot fail anymore. A different program (see Listing 1) may query for all instances of `Student`. The program may then try to access the `age` relation of each query result. However, since it is possible to construct an RDF graph that is validated by the shapes above, but lacks an `age` relation on some instances of `Student`, the program is unsafe and may crash with a run-time error. Contrary to that, a similar program that accesses the `name` relation instead is guaranteed to never cause run-time errors.

Contributions. We propose a type checking procedure based on SHACL shapes being used as types. We assume that a program queries an—possibly evolving—RDF data graph that is validated by a SHACL shape graph. Our contributions are then as follow:

1. We define how SHACL shapes can be inferred from queries. As queries are the main interaction between programs and RDF data graphs, inferring types from data access is a major step in deciding which operations are safe.
2. We then use a tiny core calculus that captures essential mechanisms to define a type system. Due to its simplicity, we use a simply typed λ-calculus whose basic model of computation is extended with queries. We define how SHACL

shapes are used to verify the program through a type system and show that the resulting language is type-safe. That is, a program that passed type checking successfully does not yield run-time errors (with the usual exception of e.g., accessing the head of an empty list).

Organization. The paper first recalls basic syntax and semantics for SPARQL and SHACL in Sect. 2. Then, the paper describes how we infer SHACL shapes from queries in Sects. 3 and 4 before defining syntax and evaluation rules of the λ-calculus in Sect. 5. Then, the type system including subtyping is defined in Sect. 6 before showing its soundness in Sect. 7. Finally, we discuss related work in Sect. 8 and conclude in Sect. 9.

2 Preliminaries

2.1 SPARQL

RDF graphs are queried via the SPARQL standard [20]. We focus on a core fragment of SPARQL that features conjunctive queries (CQ) and simple path (P) expressions. We abbreviate this fragment by PCQ. That is, our queries are conjunctions of property path expressions that use variables only in place of graph nodes, not in place of path expressions[1] [3]. This is also a very widely used subset of SPARQL queries [18].

$q ::=$	$(\overline{x}) \leftarrow body$	*(query)*
$body ::=$		*(query body)*
	$body \wedge body$	(conjunction)
	$\mid pattern$	(pattern)
$pattern ::=$		*(pattern)*
	$x\ r\ v$	(subject var pattern)
	$\mid v\ r\ x$	(object var pattern)
	$\mid x\ r\ x$	(subject object var pattern)
$r ::=$	$i \mid r^{-} \mid r/r \mid r^{+}$	*(path expresssions)*

Fig. 3. Syntax of PCQs.

Syntax. We denote the set of graph nodes of an RDF graph G by N_G with $v \in N_G$ denoting a graph node. Furthermore, we assume the existence of a set of variables N_V with x representing members of this set. The metavariable r denotes a SPARQL property path expression. A property path expression

[1] As we use plain RDF, we do not differentiate between distinguished and existential variables.

allows for defining paths of arbitrary length through an RDF graph. In our case, a property path is either a simple iri (i), the inverse of a path (r^-) or a path that connects subject to object via one or more occurrences of r (r^+). Lastly, we allow for path sequences (r_1/r_2). A PCQ $q = (\overline{x}) \leftarrow body$ consists of a head ($\overline{x}$) and a *body*. We use $\overline{x}$ to denote a sequence of variables $x_1, \ldots, x_n$. In a head of a PCQ ($\overline{x}$), the sequence $\overline{x}$ represents the answer variables of the query which are a subset of all variables occurring in the body of q. We use $vars(q)$ to refer to the set of all variables occurring in q. Figure 3 summarizes the syntax.

Semantics. For query evaluation, we follow standard semantics. Evaluation of a query over a graph G is denoted by $[\![\cdot]\!]_G$ and yields a set of mappings μ, mapping variables of the query onto graph nodes. The full evaluation rules can be found in the extended technical report of the paper[2].

2.2 Shapes Constraint Language (SHACL)

The Shapes Constraint Language (SHACL) is a W3C standard for validating RDF graphs. In the following, we rely on the definitions presented by [7]. SHACL groups constraints in so-called *shapes.* A shape is referred to by a name, it has a set of constraints and defines its *target nodes.* Target nodes are those nodes of the graph that are expected to fulfill the constraints of the shape. As exemplified by `StudentShape` and `UniversityShape` (see Fig. 2), constraints may reference other shapes.

Constraint Syntax. We start by defining constraints. We follow [7], who use a logical abstraction of the concrete SHACL language. Fragments of first order logic are used to simulate node shapes whereas so called property shapes are completely abstracted away. Constraints that are used in shapes are defined by the following grammar:

$$\phi ::= \top \mid s \mid v \mid \phi_1 \wedge \phi_2 \mid \neg\phi \mid \geq_n r.\phi \tag{2}$$

where s is a shape name (indicating a reference to another shape), v is a constant (or rather a graph node), r is a property path and $n \in \mathbb{N}^+$. Additional syntactic constructs may be derived from this basic grammar, including $\leq_n r.\phi$ for $\neg(\geq_{n+1} r.\phi)$, $=_n r.\phi$ for $(\leq_n r.\phi) \wedge (\geq_n r.\phi)$ and $\phi_1 \vee \phi_2$ for $\neg(\neg\phi_1 \wedge \neg\phi_2)$. We sometimes use ϕ_s to denote the constraint belonging to a specific shape s. To improve readability, we sometimes add parenthesis to constraints although they are not explicitly mentioned in the grammar.

Constraint Evaluation. Evaluation of constraints is rather straightforward with the exception of reference cycles. Evaluation is therefore grounded using assignments σ which map graph nodes to shape names [7]. We rely on total assignments instead of partial assignments for simplicity.

---

[2] Available at https://arxiv.org/abs/1907.00855.

Definition 1 (Total Assignment). *Let G be an RDF data graph with its set of nodes N_G and let N_S a set of shape names. Then σ is a total function $\sigma : N_G \rightarrow 2^{N_S}$ mapping graph nodes v to subsets of N_S. If $s \in \sigma(v)$, then v is assigned to the shape s.*

Evaluation of a constraint ϕ for a node v of a graph G using an assignment σ is denoted $[\![\phi]\!]^{v,G,\sigma}$ and yields either true or false. The extended version contains the complete definition.

Shapes and Validation. A shape is modelled as a triple (s, ϕ, q) consisting of a shape name s, a constraint ϕ and a query for target nodes q which is either an empty set or a monadic query that has exactly one answer variable to describe all intended *target nodes.* Target nodes denote those nodes which are expected to fulfill the constraint associated with the shape. In a slight abuse of notation, we write $v \in [\![q]\!]_G$ to indicate that a node v is a target node for s in the graph G. If S is a set of shapes, we assume that for each $(s, \phi, q) \in S$, if shape name s' appears in ϕ, then there also exists a $(s', \phi', q') \in S$. To illustrate this, consider our running example again (see Fig. 2)[3]. The set S_1 containing all three shapes looks as follows:

$$\begin{aligned} S_1 = \{&(s_{Student}, \geq_1 \texttt{studiesAt}.\top \wedge \leq_0 \texttt{studiesAt}.\neg s_{University} \wedge \geq_1 \texttt{type.Person}, \\ &\quad (x_1) \leftarrow x_1 \texttt{ type Student}), \\ &(s_{Person}, =_1 \texttt{name}.\top, (x_1) \leftarrow x_1 \texttt{ type Person}), \\ &(s_{University}, \geq_1 \texttt{studiesAt}^-.\top \wedge \leq_0 \texttt{studiesAt}^-.s_{Student}, \emptyset)\} \end{aligned}$$

Intuitively, only certain assignments are of interest. Such an assignment is called a *faithful assignment.*

Definition 2 (Faithful assignment). *An assignment σ for a graph G and a set of shapes S is faithful, iff for each $(s, \phi, q) \in S$ and for each graph node $v \in N_G$, it holds that:*

- *if $v \in [\![q]\!]_G$, then $s \in \sigma(v)$.*
- *if $s \in \sigma(v)$, iff $[\![\phi]\!]^{v,G,\sigma} = true$.*

Validating an RDF graph means finding a faithful assignment. The graph is said to *conform* to the set of shapes.

Definition 3 (Conformance). *A graph G conforms to a set of shapes S iff there is a faithful assignment σ for G and S. We write $\sigma^{G,S}$ to denote that σ is a faithful assignment for G and S.*

[3] We simplified target queries in the example—in reality, the target queries should query for Student or any of its subclasses. We simplified this as we do not use any RDFS subclass relations in our examples.

Validating an RDF graph means finding a faithful assignment. In case of graph G_1 (see Fig. 1) and the set of shapes S_1, it is impossible to validate the graph. `alice` would need to be assigned to $s_{Student}$, but has no `studiesAt` relation. However, if the statement (`alice`, `type`, `Student`) is removed, then the graph is valid since a faithful assignment may assign s_{Person} to `alice` and `bob`, $s_{Student}$ solely to `bob` and $s_{University}$ to b_1.

3 Shape Inference for Queries

In this section, we describe how to infer shapes from PCQs for all variables in a given query. Given a query q with $x \in vars(q)$, let s^q_x be the globally unique shape name for variable x in query q. Then we assign the shape (s^q_x, ϕ, q_x). We discard sub- or superscripts if they are evident in context.

Our typing relation ":" for a PCQ q constructs a set of shapes S_q in the following manner: For every subject var pattern $x\ r\ v$ in the body of q (object var pattern $v\ r\ x$ respectively), we assign the constraint $\geq_1 r.v$ ($\geq_1 r^-.v$). As target nodes, we use the original query but projected on the particular variable. In case of variables on both subject and object ($x_1\ r\ x_2$), we infer two shapes $s^q_{x_1}$ and $s^q_{x_2}$. We use shape references to express the dependencies and infer the constraints $\geq_1 r.s^q_{x_2}$ and $\geq_1 r^-.s^q_{x_1}$. In case of a conjunction ($body_1 \wedge body_2$), we infer the sets of constraints for each query body individually and then combine the results using the operator $\boxtimes$. The relation $\boxtimes$ takes two sets of shapes S_{q_1} and S_{q_2} combines them into a unique set performing a full outer join on the shape names:

$$
\begin{aligned}
S_{q_1} \boxtimes S_{q_2} = \{&(s^q_{x_i}, \phi_i \wedge \phi_j, (x_i) \leftarrow body_i \wedge body_j) | (s^q_{x_i}, \phi_i, (x_i) \leftarrow body_i) \in S_{q_1} \\
&\wedge (s^q_{x_i}, \phi_j, (x_i) \leftarrow body_j) \in S_{q_2}\} \cup \\
&\{(s^q_{x_i}, \phi_i, q_i) | (s^q_{x_i}, \phi_i, q_i) \in S_{q_1} \wedge \neg\exists (s^q_{x_i}, \phi_j, q_j) \in S_{q_2}\} \cup \\
&\{(s^q_{x_j}, \phi_j, q_j) | \neg\exists (s^q_{x_j}, \phi_i, q_i) \in S_{q_1} \wedge (s^q_{x_j}, \phi_j, q_j) \in S_{q_2}\}
\end{aligned}
$$

Figure 4 contains the complete set of rules for inferring sets of shapes from PCQs.

As an example, consider the query $q = (x_1, x_2) \leftarrow x_1$ `type Student` $\wedge\ x_1$ `studiesAt` x_2 as used before. Then shape inference on the body assigns the following set of shapes:

$$
\begin{aligned}
&(1)\ x_1\ \texttt{type Student} \wedge x_1\ \texttt{studiesAt}\ x_2 : (2) \boxtimes (3) \\
&\quad = \{(s^q_{x_1}, \geq_1 \texttt{type.Student} \wedge \texttt{studiesAt}.s^q_{x_2}, (x_1) \leftarrow x_1\ \texttt{type Student} \wedge x_1\ \texttt{studiesAt}\ x_2), \\
&\qquad (s^q_{x_2}, \geq_1 \texttt{studiesAt}^-.s^q_{x_1}, (x_2) \leftarrow x_1\ \texttt{type Student} \wedge x_1\ \texttt{studiesAt}\ x_2)\} \\
&(2)\ x_1\ \texttt{type Student} : \{(s^q_{x_1}, \geq_1 \texttt{type.Student}, (x_1) \leftarrow x_1\ \texttt{type Student})\} \\
&(3)\ x_1\ \texttt{studiesAt}\ x_2 : \{(s^q_{x_1}, \geq_1 \texttt{studiesAt}.s^q_{x_2}, (x_1) \leftarrow x_1\ \texttt{studiesAt}\ x_2), \\
&\qquad (s^q_{x_2}, \geq_1 \texttt{studiesAt}^-.s^q_{x_1}, (x_2) \leftarrow x_1\ \texttt{studiesAt}\ x_2)\}
\end{aligned}
$$

$$x\ r\ v : \{(s^q_x, \geq_1 r.v, (x) \leftarrow x\ r\ v)\}\ \textbf{(R-SUB-VAR)}$$

$$v\ r\ x : \{(s^q_x, \geq_1 r^-.v, (x) \leftarrow v\ r\ x)\}\ \textbf{(R-OBJ-VAR)}$$

$$x_1\ r\ x_2 : \{(s^q_{x_1}, \geq_1 r.s^q_{x_2}, (x_1) \leftarrow x_1\ r\ x_2), (s^q_{x_2}, \geq_1 r^-.s^q_{x_1}, (x_2) \leftarrow x_1\ r\ x_2)\}\ \textbf{(R-VARS)}$$

$$\frac{body_1 : S_{q1} \qquad body_2 : S_{q2}}{body_1 \wedge body_2 : S_{q_1} \boxtimes S_{q_2}}\ \textbf{(R-CONJ)} \qquad \frac{body : S_q}{(\overline{x}) \leftarrow body : S_q}\ \textbf{(R-PROJ)}$$

Fig. 4. Inference rules for inferring a set of shapes from the body of query q.

4 Soundness of Shape Inference for Queries

Shape inference for queries is sound if the shape constraints inferred for each variable evaluate to true for all possible mappings of the variable.

Definition 4 (Soundness of shape inference). *Given an RDF graph G, a PCQ q with its variables $x_i \in vars(q)$ and the set of inferred shapes $S_q = \{(s^q_{x_i}, \phi_{x_i}, q_{s_{x_i}})^{x_i \in vars(q)}\}$, a shape constraint is sound if there exists a faithful assignment σ^{G,S_q} such that*

$$\forall x_i \in vars(q) : \forall \mu \in [\![q]\!]_G : [\![\phi_{x_i}]\!]^{\mu(x_i),G,\sigma^{G,S_q}} = true$$

We show that the faithful assignment σ^{G,S_q} can be constructed by assigning all shape names solely based on target nodes.

Theorem 1. *For any graph G, a PCQ q and the set of shapes S_q inferred from q, assignment σ^{G,S_q} is constructed such that for each shape $(s, \phi_s, q_s) \in S_q$ and for each graph node $v \in N_G$:*

1. *If $v \in [\![q_s]\!]_G$, then $s \in \sigma^{G,S_q}(v)$,*
2. *If $v \notin [\![q_s]\!]_G$, $s \notin \sigma^{G,S_q}(v)$.*

Such an assignment σ^{G,S_q} is faithful.

Proof (Sketch). Intuitively, a node v is part of the query result due to the presence of some relations for the node. The assigned constraints require the presence of the exact same relations to evaluate to true. A induction over the query evaluation rules can therefore show that (1) all nodes that are in the query result fulfill the constraint whereas (2) a node not being in the query result would also violate the constraint. ∎

The faithful assignment σ^{G,S_q} constructed in the manner as explained above is unique. This is expected as shape inference does not use negation.

Proposition 1. *The assignment σ^{G,S_q} constructed as described above is unique.*

Proof. Assume that a different faithful assignment σ'^{G,S_q} exists. There must be at least one node v for which $\sigma^{G,S_q}(v) \neq \sigma'^{G,S_q}(v)$.

1. It is impossible that there is an s such that $s \in \sigma^{G,S_q}(v)$ and $s \notin \sigma'^{G,S_q}(v)$. σ assigns shapes based on target nodes, v must be a target node for s and σ' is not faithful.
2. It cannot be that $s \notin \sigma^{G,S_q}(v)$ and $s \in \sigma'^{G,S_q}(v)$. v must fulfill the constraint ϕ_s of shape s, otherwise σ' would not be faithful. If that is the case, then σ is not faithful. This contradicts Theorem 1. ■

Given a faithful assignment $\sigma^{G,S}$ for a set of shapes S and assignment σ^{G,S_q} for an inferred set of shapes, the two assignments can be combined by simply taking the union $\sigma^{G,S}(v) \cup \sigma^{G,S_q}(v)$ for each graph node $v \in N_G$. While not true for two arbitrary assignments, it is true in this case because shape names of S and S_q are disjoint.

5 Core Language

Syntax. Our core language (Fig. 5) is a simply typed call-by-value λ-calculus. A program is a pair consisting of shapes written for the program S and a term. Terms (t) include[4] function application and if-then-else expressions. Constructs for lists are included in the language: **cons**, **nil**, **null**, **head** and **tail**. Specific to our language is a querying construct for querying an RDF graph with PCQs. To avoid confusion between PCQ query variables and program variables, we refer to the variables of a query always with the symbol l as they are treated as labels in the program. We assume labels to be either simple user-defined labels as commonly used in records, query variables or property paths. Labels are used for projection. In case of a projection for a record, the value associated with label is selected. When evaluating queries, evaluation rules turn query results into lists of records whereas answer variables are used as record labels. Lastly, in case of a projection for a graph node, the label is interpreted as a property path and the graph is traversed accordingly. Even though not explicitly mentioned in the syntax, we sometimes add parenthesis to terms for clarification. Values (*val*) include graph nodes, record values, nil and cons to represent lists, λ-abstractions and the two boolean values true and false. λ-abstractions indicate the type of their variable explicitly.

Types (T) include shape names (s) as well as type constructors for function ($T \to T$), list (T list) and record types ($\{l_i : T_i^{i \in 1...n}\}$). We assume primitive data types such as integers and strings, but omit routine details. To illustrate them, we include booleans in our syntax. As common in simply typed λ-calculi, we also require a context Γ for storing type bindings for λ-abstractions.

[4] Since they show no interesting effects, let statements and a fixpoint operator allowing for recursion, e.g., as necessary to define a `map` function are omitted. They are contained in the extended version.

$P ::=$		*(program)*	$val ::=$		*(values)*
	S, t	(program shapes and term)		v	(graph node)
				$\mid \{l_i = val_i^{i \in 1 \ldots n}\}$	(record)
$t ::=$		*(term)*		$\mid$ **nil**$[T]$	(empty list)
	$t\ t$	(application)		$\mid$ **cons** $val\ val$	(list constructor)
	$\mid$ **if** t **then** t **else** t	(if-then-else)		$\mid \lambda(x : T).t$	(abstraction)
	$\mid$ **cons** $t\ t$	(list constructor)		$\mid$ true	(true)
	$\mid$ **null** t	(test for empty list)		$\mid$ false	(false)
	$\mid$ **head** t	(head of list)			
	$\mid$ **tail** t	(tail of list)	$T ::=$		*(types)*
	$\mid$ **query** q	(query)		s	(shape name)
	$\mid t.l$	(projection)		$\mid T \rightarrow T$	(function type)
	$\mid \{l_i = t_i^{i \in 1 \ldots n}\}$	(record)		$\mid T$ list	(list type)
	$\mid x$	(variable)		$\mid \{l_i : T_i^{i \in 1 \ldots n}\}$	(record type)
	$\mid val$	(value)		$\mid$ bool	(boolean)
			$\Gamma ::=$		*(context)*
				$\emptyset$	(empty context)
				$\mid \Gamma, x : T$	(type binding)

Fig. 5. Abstract syntax of λ_{SHACL}.

As an example, remember the program in Listing 1 which queried for all instances of `Student`. Assuming that `map` is defined using basic recursion, the program can be expressed as

$$\mathbf{map}\ (\lambda(y : \{x : s_{Student}\}).y.x.\texttt{age})\ (\mathbf{query}\ (x_1) \leftarrow x\ \texttt{type Student})$$

In this program, the function (λ-abstraction) has one variable y whose type is a record. The record consists of a single label x, representing the answer variable of the query. The type of x is the shape $s_{Student}$. The term $y.x$ in the body of the function constitutes an access to the record label. Accessing the `age` in the next step constitutes a projection that traverses the graph. Type-checking rightfully rejects this program as nodes conforming to $s_{Student}$ may not have a `age` relation.

Semantics. The operational semantics is defined using a reduction relation, which extends the standard ones. As types do not influence run-time behavior, shapes do not occur in the evaluation rules. However, we define the reduction rules with respect to an RDF graph G. Reduction of lists, records and other routine terms bear no significant differences from reduction rules as, e.g., defined in [19] (c.f. Fig. 6, reduction rules for lists are only contained in the technical report). Reduction rules for queries and node projections are summarized by rules E-QUERY and E-PROJNODE in Fig. 6. A term representing a query can be directly evaluated to a list of records. Query evaluation $[\![q]\!]_G$ returns a list of mappings. As in other approaches (e.g., [2]), each query result becomes a record

$$(G \Rrightarrow S_P, t) \rightarrow (G \Rrightarrow t) \text{ (E-PROGRAM)} \qquad \frac{G \Rrightarrow t_1 \rightarrow t_1'}{G \Rrightarrow t_1 t_2 \rightarrow G \Rrightarrow t_1' t_2} \text{ (E-APP1)}$$

$$\frac{G \Rrightarrow t_2 \rightarrow t_2'}{G \Rrightarrow val_1 t_2 \rightarrow G \Rrightarrow val_1 t_2'} \text{ (E-APP2)} \qquad \frac{G \Rrightarrow t_1 \rightarrow G \Rrightarrow t_1'}{G \Rrightarrow t_1.l \rightarrow G \Rrightarrow t_1'.l} \text{ (E-PROJ)}$$

$$G \Rrightarrow (\lambda x : T.t_1) val_2 \rightarrow G \Rrightarrow [x \mapsto val_2] t_1 \text{ (E-APPABS)}$$

$$G \Rrightarrow \textbf{if true then } t_2 \textbf{ else } t_3 \rightarrow G \Rrightarrow t_2 \text{ (E-IF-TRUE)}$$

$$G \Rrightarrow \textbf{if false then } t_2 \textbf{ else } t_3 \rightarrow G \Rrightarrow t_3 \text{ (E-IF-FALSE)}$$

$$\frac{G \Rrightarrow t_1 \rightarrow t_1'}{G \Rrightarrow \textbf{if } t_1 \textbf{ then } t_2 \textbf{ else } t_3 \rightarrow G \Rrightarrow \textbf{if } t_1' \textbf{ then } t_2 \textbf{ else } t_3} \text{ (E-IF)}$$

$$\frac{G \Rrightarrow t_j \rightarrow t_j'}{\begin{array}{c} G \Rrightarrow \{l_i = val_i^{i \in 1 \ldots, j-1}, l_j = t_j, l_k = t_k^{k \in j+1 \ldots n}\} \rightarrow \\ G \Rrightarrow \{l_i = val_i^{i \in 1 \ldots, j-1}, l_j = t_j', l_k = t_k^{k \in j+1 \ldots n}\} \end{array}} \text{ (E-RCD)}$$

$$G \Rrightarrow \{l_i = val_i^{i \in 1 \ldots n}\}.l_j \rightarrow G \Rrightarrow val_j \text{ (E-PROJRCD)}$$

$$\frac{q = (l_1, \ldots, l_n) \leftarrow body \qquad [\![q]\!]_G = \{\mu_1, \ldots, \mu_m\}}{\begin{array}{c} (G \Rrightarrow \textbf{query } q) \rightarrow G \Rrightarrow \textbf{cons } \{l_i = \mu_1(l_i)^{i \in 1, \ldots, n}\}, \ldots, \\ \textbf{cons } \{l_i = \mu_m(l_i)^{i \in 1, \ldots, n}\}, \textbf{nil} \end{array}} \text{ (E-QUERY)}$$

$$\frac{[\![(x) \leftarrow l(v, x)]\!]_G = \{\mu_1, \ldots, \mu_n\}}{G \Rrightarrow v.l \rightarrow G \Rrightarrow \textbf{cons } \mu_1(x) \ldots \textbf{cons } \mu_n(x) \textbf{ nil}} \text{ (E-PROJNODE)}$$

Fig. 6. Reduction rules of λ_{SHACL}.

of the list. For each record, labels are created for each variable whereas the value of the record is the value provided by the mapping. A projection on a given graph node is evaluated as a query by turning the property path expression l into a query pattern. However, instead of a record a plain list of graph nodes is returned.

Any term t which cannot be reduced any further (i.e. no rule applies to the term anymore) is said to be in *normal form*. When evaluation is successful, then the term has been reduced to a value *val*. Any term that is in normal form but not a value is said to be stuck. As usual [19], we use "stuckness" as a simple notion of a run-time error.

6 Type System

The most distinguishing feature of the type system is the addition of shape names as types in the language. As each shape name requires a proper definition, our typing relation ":" is defined with respect to a set of shapes. Likewise, a typing context Γ is required to store type bindings for λ-abstractions. Since certain constructs such as queries create new shapes during the type checking process, the typing relation does not only assign a type to a term but also a set of newly created shapes which in turn may contain definitions of shape names that are being used as types.

For the typing rules, we require the definition function *lub* that computes the least upper bound of two types. The exact definition can be found in the technical report. Intuitively, in case of two shapes s_1 and s_2, we rely on disjunction $s_1 \vee s_2$ as a least upper bound.

Typing Rules. The typing rules for constructs unrelated to querying are mainly the standard ones as common in simply typed λ-calculi, except all rules are defined with respect to a set of shapes and return a set of newly created shapes (see Fig. 7). Basic rules, such as for boolean values (rules T-TRUE and T-FALSE) simply return empty sets of shapes as they do not create new shapes. Several rules take possible extensions of the set of shapes into account. E.g., rule T-PROGRAM takes the set of shapes as defined by the program S_P and the pre-defined set of shapes S and uses the union of both to analyze the term t.

New shapes are mainly created when either the least upper bound judgement is used or one of the two query expressions (either **query** or projections) are used (see rules T-QUERY and T-NPROJ in Fig. 7). In case of a **query** statement (rule T-QUERY), the shape inference rules as described in Sect. 3 are being used to construct the set S_q which is being returned as newly created shapes. The actual type of a query then comprises a list of records. Each record contains one label per answer variable whereas the type of each label is the respective shape name for the query variable. Likewise, projections on graph nodes (T-NODEPROJ) create a new shape name s' using a function *genName* based on the old shape name s with the appropriate constraint $\geq_1 l^-.s$. The newly created definition is returned as a set with the actual type of the expression being s list.

Subtyping. Subtyping rules are summarized in Fig. 8. We rely on a standard subtyping relation. A term t of type T_1 is also of type T_2, if $T_1 <: T_2$ is true (T-SUB). Any type is always a subtype of itself (S-RELF). If T_1 is a subtype of T_2 and T_2 is a subtype of T_3, then T_1 is also a subtype of T_3 (S-TRANS). Subtyping for lists and functions is reduced to subtyping checks for their associated types. A list T_1 list is a subtype of T_2 list if T_1 is a subtype of T_2 (S-LIST). Function types are in a subtyping relation (S-FUNC) if their domains are in a flipped subtyping relationship ("contra-variance") and their co-domains are in a subtyping relationship ("co-variance"). Record type is a subtype of another

$$\frac{S \cup S_P, \Gamma \vdash t_1 : T_1, S_1}{S, \Gamma \vdash S_P, t_1 : T_1, S_1} \text{ (T-PROGRAM)}$$

$$\frac{S, \Gamma \vdash t_1 : T_{11} \rightarrow T_{12}, S_1 \qquad S, \Gamma \vdash t_2 : T_{11}, S_2}{S, \Gamma \vdash t_1 t_2 : T_{12}, S_1 \cup S_2} \text{ (T-APP)}$$

$$\frac{\begin{array}{c} S, \Gamma \vdash t_1 : \text{bool}, S_1 \\ S, \Gamma \vdash t_2 : T_2, S_2 \qquad S, \Gamma \vdash t_3 : T_3, S_3 \qquad \mathit{lub}(T_2, T_3, S \cup S_2 \cup S_3) = T_{\mathit{lub}}, S_{\mathit{lub}} \end{array}}{S, \Gamma \vdash \textbf{if } t_1 \textbf{ then } t_2 \textbf{ else } t_3 : T_{\mathit{lub}}, S_1 \cup S_2 \cup S_3 \cup S_{\mathit{lub}}} \text{ (T-IF)}$$

$$S, \Gamma \vdash \textbf{nil}[T] : T \text{ list}, \emptyset \text{ (T-NIL)} \qquad \frac{S, \Gamma \vdash t_1 : T \text{ list}, S_1}{S, \Gamma \vdash \textbf{tail } t_1 : T \text{ list}, S_1} \text{ (T-TAIL)}$$

$$\frac{S, \Gamma \vdash t_1 : T_1, S_1 \qquad S, \Gamma \vdash t_2 : T_1 \text{ list}, S_2}{S, \Gamma \vdash \textbf{cons } t_1 \; t_2 : T_1 \text{ list}, S_1 \cup S_2} \text{ (T-CONS)}$$

$$\frac{S, (\Gamma, x : T_1) \vdash t : T_2, S_2}{S, \Gamma \vdash \lambda(x : T_1).t : T_1 \rightarrow T_2, S_2} \text{ (T-ABS)} \qquad \frac{x : T \in \Gamma}{S, \Gamma \vdash x : T, \emptyset} \text{ (T-VAR)}$$

$$S, \Gamma \vdash \text{true} : \text{bool}, \emptyset \text{ (T-TRUE)} \qquad S, \Gamma \vdash \text{false} : \text{bool}, \emptyset \text{ (T-FALSE)}$$

$$\frac{S, \Gamma \vdash t_1 : T_1 \text{ list}, S_1}{S, \Gamma \vdash \textbf{null } t_1 : \text{bool}, S_1} \text{ (T-NULL)} \qquad \frac{S, \Gamma \vdash t_1 : T_1 \text{ list}, S_1}{S, \Gamma \vdash \textbf{head } t_1 : \text{T}, S_1} \text{ (T-HEAD)}$$

$$\frac{\text{for each } i \qquad S, \Gamma \vdash t_i : T_i, S_i}{S, \Gamma \vdash \{l_i = t_i^{1 \in 1 \ldots n}\} : \{l_i : T_i^{i \in 1 \ldots n}\}, \bigcup_{i=1}^{n} S_i} \text{ (T-RCD)}$$

$$\frac{S, \Gamma \vdash t_1 : \{l_i : T_i^{i \in 1, \ldots, n}\}, S_1}{S, \Gamma \vdash t_1.l_i : T_i, S_1} \text{ (T-RCDPROJ)}$$

$$\frac{\begin{array}{c} q = (l_1, \ldots, l_n) \leftarrow \mathit{body} \\ \mathit{vars}(q) = \{l_1, \ldots, l_n, \ldots l_m\} \qquad q : S_q = \{(s^q_{l_i}, \phi^q_{l_i}, q^q_{s_{l_i}})^{i \in 1 \ldots m}\} \end{array}}{S, \Gamma \vdash \textbf{query } q : \{(l_i : s^q_{l_i})^{i \in 1 \ldots n}\} \text{ list}, S_q} \text{ (T-QUERY)}$$

$$\frac{S, \Gamma \vdash t_1 : s, S_1 \qquad \mathit{genName}(s) = s' \qquad S \cup \{s', \geq_1 l^-.s, \emptyset\} \vdash s <: s'}{S, \Gamma \vdash t_1.l : s' \text{ list}, S_1 \cup \{s', \geq_1 l^-.s, \emptyset\}} \text{ (T-NPROJ)}$$

Fig. 7. Typing rules for λ_{SHACL}.

record if (1) it has the the same plus more fields (S-RCDWIDTH), (2) it is a permutation of the supertype (S-RCDPERM) and (3) if the types of the fields are in a subtype relation (S-RCDDEPTH).

Subtyping relations between two shapes s_1 and s_2 are defined via faithful assignments. An assignment $\sigma : N_G \rightarrow 2^{N_S}$ is a function that assigns shape names to graph nodes. We require the opposite direction—a function σ_{inv} assigning nodes to shapes.

Definition 5 (Inverse assignments). *Let G be an RDF data graph, S a set of shapes and $\sigma^{G,S}$ a faithful assignment for G and S. Then $\sigma_{inv}^{G,S}$ is a total function $\sigma_{inv}^{G,S} : N_S \rightarrow 2^{N_G}$ mapping shape names to subsets of N_G such that for all graph nodes $v \in N_G$ and all shape names $s \in N_S$: $s \in \sigma^{G,S}(v)$ iff $v \in \sigma_{inv}^{G,S}(s)$*

For a given set of shapes S, two shapes s_1 and s_2 are in a subtyping relation if, for all possible RDF graphs $G \in \mathcal{G}$ and all faithful assignments $\Sigma^{G,S}$ for S and G, it holds that $\sigma_{G,S}^{inv}(s_1) \subseteq \sigma_{G,S}^{inv}(s_2)$ (S-SHAPE). That is, the sets of nodes conforming to the two shapes are in a subset relation for all possible RDF graphs conform to the set of shapes.

$$\frac{S,\Gamma \vdash t_1 : T_1, S_1 \qquad S \vdash T_1 <: T_2}{S,\Gamma \vdash t_1 : T_2, S_1} \text{ (T-SUB)} \qquad S \vdash T <: T \text{ (S-REFL)}$$

$$\frac{S \vdash T_1 <: T_2 \qquad S \vdash T_2 <: T_3}{S \vdash T_1 <: T_3} \text{ (S-TRANS)}$$

$$\frac{S \vdash T_{21} <: T_{11} \qquad S \vdash T_{12} <: T_{22}}{S \vdash T_{11} \rightarrow T_{12} <: T_{21} \rightarrow T_{22}} \text{ (S-FUNC)} \qquad \frac{S \vdash T_1 <: T_2}{S \vdash T_1 \text{ list} <: T_2 \text{ list}} \text{ (S-LIST)}$$

$$S \vdash \{l_i : T_i^{i \in 1 \ldots n+k}\} <: \{l_i : T_i^{i \in 1 \ldots n}\} \text{ (S-RCDWIDTH)}$$

$$\frac{\{k_j : T_j^{j \in 1 \ldots n}\} \text{ is a permutation of } \{l_i : T_i^{i \in 1 \ldots n}\}}{S \vdash \{k_j : T_j^{j \in 1 \ldots n}\} <: \{l_i : T_i^{i \in 1 \ldots n}\}} \text{ (S-RCDPERM)}$$

$$\frac{\text{for each } i \qquad T_i <: T_i'}{S \vdash \{l_i : T_i^{i \in 1 \ldots n}\} <: \{l_i : {T'}_i^{i \in 1 \ldots n}\}} \text{ (S-RCDDEPTH)}$$

$$\frac{\forall G \in \mathcal{G} : \forall \sigma_{G,S}^{inv} \in \Sigma_{G,S}^{inv} : \sigma_{G,S}^{inv}(s_1) \subseteq \sigma_{G,S}^{inv}(s_2)}{S \vdash s_1 <: s_2} \text{ (S-SHAPE)}$$

Fig. 8. Subtyping rules.

Algorithmic Subtyping. Algorithmic solutions to standard subtyping rules such used in Fig. 8 are, e.g., described by [19]. In the case of subtyping for shapes, algorithmic approaches similar to subsumption checking in description logics [1] can be employed. That is, s_1 must be a subtype of s_2 if it can be shown that

$$\cdots \quad \frac{S, \Gamma \vdash t_1 : t_1', T_1 \text{ list}, S_1}{S, \Gamma \vdash \textbf{head}\ t_1 : \textbf{head}\ t_1', T_1, S_1} \text{(T-HEAD)}$$

$$\frac{\begin{array}{c} S, \Gamma \vdash t_1 : t_1', s, S_1 \\ S \cup S' \cup \{s_{tmp}, =_1 l.\top, \emptyset\} \vdash s <: s_{tmp} \qquad genName(s) = s' \end{array}}{S, \Gamma \vdash t_1.l : \textbf{head}\ t_1'.l, s', S_1 \cup \{s', \geq_1 l^-.s, \emptyset\}} \text{(T-NPROJ-1)}$$

$$\frac{\begin{array}{c} S, \Gamma \vdash t_1 : t_1', s, S_1 \qquad S \cup S' \cup \{s_{tmp}, =_1 l.\top, \emptyset\} \not\vdash s <: s_{tmp} \\ S \cup S' \cup \{s_{tmp}, \geq_1 l.\top, \emptyset\} \vdash s <: s_{tmp} \qquad genName(s) = s' \end{array}}{S, \Gamma \vdash t_1.l : t_1'.l, s' \text{ list}, \{s', \geq_1 l^-.s, \emptyset\}} \text{(T-NPROJ-2)}$$

Fig. 9. Type system with type elaboration (excerpt).

no graph exists that contains a node v for which $s_1 \in \sigma^{G,S}(v)$ but $s_2 \notin \sigma^{G,S}(v)$. As of now, we compare constraint sets which is sound but incomplete. We don't know whether a complete algorithm exists, although we plan to investigate a transformation into a description logic based reasoning problem.

Type Elaboration. Types do not play any role during the evaluation of terms. They are only used during the type checking process. This is by design, as run-time type checks incur overhead and should be avoided, in particular if the type check is computationally expensive. However, the evaluation relation only evaluates terms of the form $v.l$ (node projections) into lists of graph nodes (c.f. rule E-PROJNODE of Fig. 6 and T-NPROJ of Fig. 7), even though a shape may hint that there is only one successor (e.g., `studiesAt` of shape $s_{Student}$). As the evaluation rules have no information about types, the type system must annotate or transform terms such that they can be treated differently during run-time. This process is called *type elaboration* [19]. The typing relation ":" then takes a set of shapes S and a typing context Γ and returns a term t, a type T and a set of newly introduced shapes S'. This is exemplified by the rules in Fig. 9. Most rules simply return the term without modifications (e.g., rule T-HEAD). However, in case of node projections where it can be shown that there is only a single successor, a **head** is automatically added to the term (rule T-NPROJ-1). Otherwise, the term is not modified (rule T-NPROJ-2).

7 Type Soundness

A term t is said to be well-typed if the type system assigns a type. We show the soundness of the λ_{SHACL} type system by proving that a well-typed term does not get stuck during evaluation. As with other languages, there are exceptions to this rule, e.g., down-casting in object-oriented languages, c.f. [10]. For λ_{SHACL}, this exception concerns lists. We show that if a program is well-typed, then the only way it can get stuck is by reaching a point where it tries to compute **head**

nil or **tail nil**. Furthermore, terms must be closed, meaning that all program variables are bound by function abstractions [19]. We proceed in two steps, by showing that a well-typed term is either a value or it can take a step (progress) and by showing that if that term takes a step, the result is also well-typed (preservation).

Lemma 1 (Canonical Forms Lemma). *Let val be a well-typed value. Then the following observations can be made:*

1. *If val is a value of type s, then val is of the form v.*
2. *If val is value of type $T_1 \to T_2$, then val is of the form $\lambda(x : T_1).t_2$.*
3. *If val is a value of type T list, then val is either of the form* **cons** *val... or* ***nil***.
4. *If val is a value of type $\{l_i : T_i^{i\in 1...n}\}$, then val is of the form $\{l_i = val_i^{i\in 1...n}\}$.*
5. *If val is a value of type bool, then val is either of the form true or false.*

Given Lemma 1, we can show that a well-typed term is either a value or it can take a step.

Theorem 2 (Progress). *Let t be a closed, well-typed term. If t is not a value, then there exists a term t' such that $t \to t'$. If $S, \Gamma \vdash t : T, S'$, then t is either a value, a term containing the forms* **head nil** *or* **tail nil***, or there is some t' with $t \to t'$.*

Proof (Sketch). The theorem can be shown by induction on the derivation of $S, \Gamma \vdash t : T, S$. Queries ($t =$ **query** q) are straightforward as no sub-term exists. For node projections ($t_1.l$ with the type of t_1 being a shape name), Lemma 1 tells us that it must ultimately reduce to a graph node. In that case rule E-PROJNODE applies. The full proof can be found in the tech report. ∎

Given that a well-typed term can take a step, we now need to show that taking a step according to the evaluation rules preserves the type.

Theorem 3 (Preservation). *Let t be a term and T a type. If $S, \Gamma \vdash t : T, S'$ and $t \to t'$, then $S, \Gamma \vdash t' : T, S'$.*

Proof (Sketch). As with progress, the proof is an induction over the typing relation $S, \Gamma \vdash t : T, S'$. For each term, possible ways of reducing it are distinguished and it is shown that in each case the type does not change. For queries, this is immediate. In case of node projections, t_1 either took a step, in which case the typing rule applies again, or it is a graph node v with type s. Each v' which is reached via the node projection conforms to the newly created shape s' with its constraint $\geq_1 l^-.s$. Therefore, the type is also preserved. ∎

As a direct consequence of Theorems 2 and 3, a well-typed, closed term does not get stuck during evaluation.

8 Related Work

The presented approach is generally related to the validation of RDF as well as the integration of RDF into programming languages. RDF validation has seen an increase in interest. Among them are inference-based approaches such as [16,23], in which OWL expressions are used as integrity constraints by relying on a closed-world assumption. The fact that constraints are OWL expressions puts these approaches closer to [15] than the approach described here. A validation approach that is relatively similar to SHACL is ShEx [4]. ShEx also uses shapes to group constraints, but removes property path expressions and features well-defined recursion. We chose SHACL over ShEx due to SHACL being a W3C recommendation. Due to the similarity between SHACL and ShEx, the integration process for the latter is very similar. In fact, the definition for recursion used in ShEx even simplifies some aspects as there is no need for the notion of faithful assignments.

In terms of integration of RDF into programming languages, we consider different approaches. Generic representations, e.g., the OWL API [9] or Jena [5], use types on a meta-level (e.g., *Statement*) that do not allow a static type-checker to verify a program. This leaves correctness entirely on the hands of the programmer. Mapping approaches use schematic information of the data model to create types in the target language. Type checking can offer some degree of verification. An early example of this is OWL2Java [12], a more recent one is LITEQ [14]. However, mapping approaches based on ontologies come with their own limitations. OWL relies on a open-world assumption, in which missing information is treated as incomplete data rather than constraint violations. As shown in the introduction, structural information does therefore not necessarily imply the presence of data relationships. This is problematic for type-checkers as they rely on a closed world. The most powerful approaches create new languages or extend existing ones to accomodate the specific requirements of the data model. Examples include rule-based programming [11] as well as a transformation and validation language [21]. However, both are untyped. Typed approaches to linked data is provided by [6,8]. Zhi# [17], an extension of the C# language provides an integration for OWL ontologies, albeit it only considers explicitly given statements. Contrary to that, [15,22] provides an integration of OWL ontologies also considering implicit statements. However, as shown in the introduction, programmers cannot rely on structural restrictions given by OWL ontologies whereas SHACL enforces its structural restriction with a closed-world assumption.

9 Summary and Future Work

In this paper, we have presented an approach for type checking programs using SHACL. We have shown that by using SHACL shapes as types, type safety can be achieved. This helps in writing less error-prone programs, in particular when facing evolving RDF graphs. The work can be extended in several directions.

First, an implementation of the presented approach is highly desirable. Comparably to [22], we plan on implementing the approach in Scala using compiler plugins that add new compilation phases. Shape names constitute a new form of types. As shape names are known before compilation, they can be syntactically integrated using automatically generated type aliases to a base type. This allows for type checking shape types in a separate compilation phase that runs after the standard Scala type inference and type checker phases. As there is little interaction between normal Scala types and shape types, issues only arise when code converts e.g., literals into standard Scala types. However, this can be solved through minor code transformations before the type checking phase. Lastly, transformations based on type elaboration can also run as a separate phase. As shape types do not influence run-time behavior, compilation produces standard JVM byte code. However, one noteworthy limitation of using type aliases to represent shape names is that method overloading based on shape names is not possible. Resolving this issue requires better integration techniques which remain as future work.

Second, finding sound and complete methods for deciding shape subsumption is an interesting problem that requires future research. This is an important step as it defines practical boundaries in terms of the parts of SHACL that can be used for type checking. Lastly, the supported subset of SPARQL queries is relatively small and should be extended by missing features such as union of queries or filter expressions. This raises questions about the parts of SPARQL that can be described with SHACL shapes.

References

1. Baader, F., et al. (eds.): The Description Logic Handbook: Theory, Implementation, and Applications. Cambridge University Press, Cambridge (2003)
2. Bierman, G., Meijer, E., Schulte, W.: The essence of data access in Cω. In: Black, A.P. (ed.) ECOOP 2005. LNCS, vol. 3586, pp. 287–311. Springer, Heidelberg (2005). https://doi.org/10.1007/11531142_13
3. Bischof, S., Krötzsch, M., Polleres, A., Rudolph, S.: Schema-agnostic query rewriting in SPARQL 1.1. In: Mika, P., et al. (eds.) ISWC 2014. LNCS, vol. 8796, pp. 584–600. Springer, Cham (2014). https://doi.org/10.1007/978-3-319-11964-9_37
4. Boneva, I., Labra Gayo, J.E., Prud'hommeaux, E.G.: Semantics and validation of shapes schemas for RDF. In: d'Amato, C., et al. (eds.) ISWC 2017. LNCS, vol. 10587, pp. 104–120. Springer, Cham (2017). https://doi.org/10.1007/978-3-319-68288-4_7
5. Carroll, J.J., et al.: Jena: implementing the semantic web recommendations. In: Proceedings WWW 2004, pp. 74–83. ACM (2004)
6. Ciobanu, G., et al.: Minimal type inference for linked data consumers. J. Log. Algebr. Meth. Program. **84**(4), 485–504 (2015)
7. Corman, J., Reutter, J.L., Savković, O.: Semantics and validation of recursive SHACL. In: Vrandečić, D., et al. (eds.) ISWC 2018. LNCS, vol. 11136, pp. 318–336. Springer, Cham (2018). https://doi.org/10.1007/978-3-030-00671-6_19
8. Horne, R., et al.: A verified algebra for read-write linked data. Sci. Comput. Program. **89, Part A**, 2–22 (2014)

9. Horridge, M., et al.: The OWL API: a Java API for OWL ontologies. Semant. Web **2**(1), 11–21 (2011)
10. Igarashi, A., et al.: Featherweight Java: a minimal core calculus for Java and GJ. ACM Trans. Program. Lang. Syst. **23**(3), 396–450 (2001)
11. Käfer, T., et al.: Rule-based programming of user agents for linked data. In: Proceedings Linked Data on the Web. CEUR Workshop Proceedings, CEUR-WS.org (2018)
12. Kalyanpur, A., et al.: Automatic mapping of OWL ontologies into Java. In: Proceedings Software Engineering & Knowledge Engineering (SEKE) 2004, pp. 98–103 (2004)
13. Knublauch, H., et al.: Shapes constraint language (SHACL). W3C Recommendation (2017). https://www.w3.org/TR/shacl/
14. Leinberger, M., Scheglmann, S., Lämmel, R., Staab, S., Thimm, M., Viegas, E.: Semantic web application development with LITEQ. In: Mika, P., et al. (eds.) ISWC 2014. LNCS, vol. 8797, pp. 212–227. Springer, Cham (2014). https://doi.org/10.1007/978-3-319-11915-1_14
15. Leinberger, M., Lämmel, R., Staab, S.: The essence of functional programming on semantic data. In: Yang, H. (ed.) ESOP 2017. LNCS, vol. 10201, pp. 750–776. Springer, Heidelberg (2017). https://doi.org/10.1007/978-3-662-54434-1_28
16. Motik, B., et al.: Adding integrity constraints to OWL. In: Proceedings OWLED 2007. CEUR Workshop Proceedings, vol. 258. CEUR-WS.org (2007)
17. Paar, A., Vrandečić, D.: Zhi# – OWL aware compilation. In: Antoniou, G., et al. (eds.) ESWC 2011. LNCS, vol. 6644, pp. 315–329. Springer, Heidelberg (2011). https://doi.org/10.1007/978-3-642-21064-8_22
18. Picalausa, F., Luo, Y., Fletcher, G.H.L., Hidders, J., Vansummeren, S.: A structural approach to indexing triples. In: Simperl, E., Cimiano, P., Polleres, A., Corcho, O., Presutti, V. (eds.) ESWC 2012. LNCS, vol. 7295, pp. 406–421. Springer, Heidelberg (2012). https://doi.org/10.1007/978-3-642-30284-8_34
19. Pierce, B.C.: Types and Programming Languages. The MIT Press, Cambridge (2002)
20. Prud'hommeaux, E., et al.: SPARQL query language for RDF. W3C Rec. November 2013. https://www.w3.org/TR/rdf-sparql-query/
21. Prud'hommeaux, E., et al.: Shape expressions: an RDF validation and transformation language. In: Proceedings SEMANTICS 2014, pp. 32–40. ACM (2014)
22. Seifer, P., et al.: Semantic query integration with reason. Program. J. **3**(3), 13 (2019)
23. Tao, J., et al.: Integrity constraints in OWL. In: Proceedings of the AAAI 2010. AAAI Press (2010)

Decentralized Reasoning on a Network of Aligned Ontologies with Link Keys

Jérémy Lhez[1], Chan Le Duc[1], Thinh Dong[2], and Myriam Lamolle[1(✉)]

[1] LIASD, Université Paris 8 - IUT de Montreuil, Montreuil, France
{lhez,leduc,lamolle}@iut.univ-paris8.fr
[2] University of Danang, Da Nang, Vietnam
dnnthinh@kontum.udn.vn

Abstract. Link keys are recently introduced to formalize data interlinking between data sources. They are considered as a new kind of correspondences included in ontology alignments. We propose a procedure for reasoning in a decentralized manner on a network of ontologies with alignments containing link keys. In this paper, the ontologies involved in such a network are expressed in the logic $\mathcal{ALC}$ while the alignments can contain concept, individual and link key correspondences equipped with a loose semantics. The decentralized aspect of our procedure is based on a process of knowledge propagation through the network via correspondences. This process allows to reduce polynomially global reasoning to local reasoning.

1 Introduction

Reasoning on a network of aligned ontologies has been investigated in different contexts where the semantics given to correspondences differs from one to another. To be able to develop a procedure for reasoning on a network of aligned ontologies, it is needed to equip the correspondences of the alignment with a semantics compatible with those defined in the ontologies. A simple approach to this issue consists in considering the correspondences as logical axioms expressed in the ontology language and merging all involved ontologies and the alignments into a unique ontology. In this case, the reasoning problem on such a network of aligned ontologies can be expressed as the following usual entailment:

$$\bigcup_{1 \le i \le n} O_i \cup \bigcup_{1 \le i < j \le n} A_{ij} \models \alpha \tag{1}$$

where O_i is an $\mathcal{ALC}$ ontology, A_{ij} is an alignment between O_i and O_j, and α[1] is a link key or a concept assertion/axiom.

This approach is characterized by the following two main aspects: (i) the correspondences of the alignments are semantically handled as ontology assertion/axioms, and (ii) reasoning is performed on the unique ontology in a centralized manner, *i.e.* all reasoning tasks are carried out on a single location with

[1] Consistency of the network can be reduced to the entailment (1) with $\alpha = \bot(x)$.

C. Ghidini et al. (Eds.): ISWC 2019, LNCS 11778, pp. 418–434, 2019.
https://doi.org/10.1007/978-3-030-30793-6_24

a reasoner. Such an approach is quite unexploitable in the context of the Web where numerous ontologies and alignments are located in different sites. There have been researches [1–6], which aimed to distribute reasoning over several locations. However, these approaches usually lead to an exponential blow-up of message passing between local reasoners associated with different locations [5,10]. The main reason for this exponential blow-up is due to the strong semantics of the correspondences involved in the alignments.

In this paper, we introduce a new semantics of correspondences which are weaker than the usual one and propose a procedure for reasoning on a network of aligned ontologies in a decentralized manner—that means—reasoning can be independently performed on different sites following a process of knowledge propagation through the network of the ontologies via the alignments with link keys. Usefulness of link keys in Semantic Web applications and the problem of reasoning with them in the centralized context have been investigated by Atencia and Gmati [7,8].

To illustrate our settings, we consider the following example in which knowledge is modelled in description logics. This formalism is used to encode the semantics of web languages such as OWL2.

Example 1. Consider two ontologies, denoted O_1 and O_2, where O_1 describes a terminology used by conference organizers, and O_2 stores information about researchers and conferences they have attended. In O_1, there are classes Participant, Presenter, DemoPaperPresenter; and a property present. In O_2, we can find classes Researcher, PhDStudent, Developer; and a property registerTo (*i.e.* someone registers to present a paper).

An alignment A_{12} tells us that DemoPaperPresenter is simultaneously aligned with Researcher and Developer.

$$\mathsf{DemoPaperPresenter} \rightarrow \mathsf{Researcher} \tag{2}$$

$$\mathsf{DemoPaperPresenter} \rightarrow \mathsf{Developer} \tag{3}$$

In addition, A_{12} contains a link key which says that if a participant presents in the conference the same paper as that to which a researcher registers the conference then the participant and the researcher would be the same person.

$$\{\langle \mathit{present}, \mathit{registerTo}\rangle\} \ \mathit{linkkey} \ \langle \mathit{Participant}, \mathit{Researcher}\rangle \tag{4}$$

If we now add to O_1 and O_2 the following axioms/assertion

$$O_1 : \mathsf{DemoPaperPresenter(Anna)} \tag{5}$$

$$O_1 : \mathsf{DemoPaperPresenter} \sqsubseteq \mathsf{Participant} \tag{6}$$

$$O_2 : \mathsf{PhDStudent} \sqsubseteq \mathsf{Researcher} \tag{7}$$

$$O_2 : \mathsf{Researcher} \sqsubseteq \neg\mathsf{Developer} \tag{8}$$

then a reasoner can find the entailment:

$$\begin{aligned} &O_1 \cup O_2 \cup A_{12} \models \\ &\{\langle \mathsf{present}, \mathsf{registerTo}\rangle\} \text{ linkkey } \langle \mathsf{DemoPaperPresenter}, \mathsf{PhDStudent}\rangle \end{aligned} \tag{9}$$

This entailment holds because of the axioms (6), (7) and the link key (4). If we now interpret the correspondences (2) and (3) as subsumption in the standard semantics then the network $O_1 \cup O_2 \cup A_{12}$ is inconsistent because of the assertion/axiom (5) and (8). However, if we interpret these correspondences as a means for propagating concept unsatisfiability, *i.e.* unsatisfiability of the "subsumer" implies unsatisfiability of the "subsumee", then the network is consistent. In the following sections, we show that the weakened semantics corresponding to the latter interpretation of concept correspondences leads to a substantial change of the computational complexity of algorithms for reasoning.

In addition, the weakened semantics would not be really interesting for the correspondences (2) and (3). However, it would be more relevant for correspondences between ontologies of different nature. Given two ontologies about `equipment` and `staff` and a correspondence Computer $\rightarrow$ Developer between them. With this correspondence, the weakened semantics tells us that if there is no developer then there is no computer. The standard semantics is irrelevant in this case. □

Based on the weakened semantics of alignments, we introduce in this paper the notion of consistency for a network of ontologies with alignments containing link keys (or an *ontology network* for short). Then, we propose an algorithm for checking consistency of an ontology network by reducing this task to checking consistency of each ontology which is polynomially extended. This consists in (i) propagating individual equalities of the form $a \approx b$ through all ontologies of the network via individual correspondences of the same form $a \approx b$, (ii) applying link keys in the alignments, which may lead to add new individual correspondences, (iii) propagating concept unsatisfiabilities through all ontologies of the network via concept correspondences of the form $C \rightarrow D$. We show that the complexity of the process of knowledge propagation is polynomial in the size of the network. In addition, we also prove that consistency of the ontologies and alignments extended by this process of knowledge propagation is equivalent to consistency of the network.

The remainder of the paper is organised as follows. Section 2 positions our work with respect to works on distributed reasoning in description logics. Section 3 describes the logic $\mathcal{ALC}$ with individuals, alignments, a new semantics of alignments and inference services. Section 4 provides the algorithms for propagating individual equalities, applying link keys and propagating concept satisfiabilities. We also prove that reasoning on the ontology network is reducible to reasoning on each ontology extended by the algorithms, and this reduction is polynomial in the size of the ontology network. Section 5 presents examples of the use of the algorithms. Section 6 describes the architecture of Draon in which the algorithms are implemented in a decentralized manner. We also report some experimental results. Section 7 concludes the paper and presents future work.

2 Related Work

In the literature, there have been several reasoning approaches which either (i) merge all ontologies and alignments into a unique ontology and perform reasoning over that unique ontology, or (ii) use a distributed semantics such as DDL (Distributed Description Logics) [1], E-connection [2], IDDL (Integrated Distributed Description Logics) [4], Package-based Description Logics [3] and design a distributed algorithm for reasoning. The second option consists in defining new formalisms which allow reasoning with multiple domains in a distributed way. The new semantics of these formalisms reconcile conflicts between ontologies, but they do not adequately formalize the quite common case of ontologies related with ontology alignments produced by third party ontology matchers. Indeed, these formalisms assert cross-ontology correspondences (bridge rules, links or imports) from one ontology's point of view, while often, such correspondences are expressed from a point of view that encompasses both aligned ontologies. Another issue of these non-standard semantics is that reasoners such as Drago [9], Pellet [10], an early version of Draon [11] using the distributed algorithms resulting from the corresponding semantics require an exponential number of message exchanges over network. This exponential blow-up results from exchanging model portions (the so-called distributed tableau) between modules of the reasoner located on different sites.

Recenty, Atencia and Gmati [7,8] have proposed a tableau algorithm for reasoning in the centralized context on an $\mathcal{ALC}$ ontology with link keys. They have showed that adding link keys to $\mathcal{ALC}$ does not augment the complexity of the tableau algorithm.

3 Preliminaries

The syntax and semantics of the logic $\mathcal{ALC}$ are defined below.

Definition 1 (Syntax of $\mathcal{ALC}$). *Let* $\mathbf{C}$, $\mathbf{R}$ *and* $\mathbf{I}$ *be non-empty sets of* concept names, role names *and* individuals, *respectively. The set of* $\mathcal{ALC}$-concepts *(or simply concepts) is the smallest set such that*

- *every concept name in* $\mathbf{C}$, $\top$ *and* $\bot$ *are concepts, and*
- *if* C, D *are concepts and* R *is a role name in* $\mathbf{R}$ *then* $C \sqcap D$, $C \sqcup D$, $\neg C$, $\forall R.C$ *and* $\exists R.C$ *are concepts.*

A general concept inclusion *(GCI) is an expression of the form* $C \sqsubseteq D$ *where* C, D *are concepts. A* terminology *or* TBox *is a finite set of GCIs.*

An ABox assertion *is an expression of the form* $C(a)$, $R(a, b)$, $a \approx b$ *or* $a \not\approx b$ *where* C *is a concept,* R *is a role name in* $\mathbf{R}$ *and* a, b *are individuals in* $\mathbf{I}$. *An* ABox *is a finite set of ABox assertions. A pair* $O = (\mathcal{A}, \mathcal{T})$, *where* $\mathcal{T}$ *is a TBox and* $\mathcal{A}$ *is an ABox, is called an* $\mathcal{ALC}$ ontology. *We use* $\mathsf{Voc}_I(O)$, $\mathsf{Voc}_C(O)$ *and* $\mathsf{Voc}_R(O)$ *to denote the sets of individuals, concept names and role names occurring in* O.

Definition 2 (Semantics of $\mathcal{ALC}$). *An* interpretation $\mathcal{I} = (\Delta^\mathcal{I}, \cdot^\mathcal{I})$ *is composed of a non-empty set* $\Delta^\mathcal{I}$*, called the* domain *of* $\mathcal{I}$*, and a* valuation $\cdot^\mathcal{I}$ *which maps every concept name to a subset of* $\Delta^\mathcal{I}$*, every role name to a subset of* $\Delta^\mathcal{I} \times \Delta^\mathcal{I}$ *and each individual to an element of* $\Delta^\mathcal{I}$*. The valuation is extended to constructed concepts such that, for all concepts* C, D *and role name* R*, the following is satisfied:*

$$\top^\mathcal{I} = \Delta^\mathcal{I}, \bot^\mathcal{I} = \emptyset$$
$$(C \sqcap D)^\mathcal{I} = C^\mathcal{I} \cap D^\mathcal{I}, (C \sqcup D)^\mathcal{I} = C^\mathcal{I} \cup D^\mathcal{I}$$
$$(\neg C)^\mathcal{I} = \Delta^\mathcal{I} \setminus C^\mathcal{I}$$
$$(\forall R.C)^\mathcal{I} = \{x \in \Delta^\mathcal{I} \mid \forall y.\langle x, y\rangle \in R^\mathcal{I} \Rightarrow y \in C^\mathcal{I}\}$$
$$(\exists R.C)^\mathcal{I} = \{x \in \Delta^\mathcal{I} \mid \exists y.\langle x, y\rangle \in R^\mathcal{I} \wedge y \in C^\mathcal{I}\}$$

An interpretation $\mathcal{I}$ satisfies *a* GCI $C \sqsubseteq D$*, denoted by* $\mathcal{I} \models C \sqsubseteq D$*, if* $C^\mathcal{I} \subseteq D^\mathcal{I}$*.* $\mathcal{I}$ *is a* model *of a* TBox $\mathcal{T}$ *if* $\mathcal{I}$ *satisfies every GCI in* $\mathcal{T}$*.*

An interpretation $\mathcal{I}$ *satisfies the ABox assertions*

$$C(a) \textit{ if } a^\mathcal{I} \in C^\mathcal{I}$$
$$R(a, b) \textit{ if } \langle a^\mathcal{I}, b^\mathcal{I}\rangle \in R^\mathcal{I}$$
$$a \approx b \textit{ if } a^\mathcal{I} = b^\mathcal{I}$$
$$a \not\approx b \textit{ if } a^\mathcal{I} \neq b^\mathcal{I}$$

Given an ABox assertion α*,* $\mathcal{I} \models \alpha$ *denotes that* $\mathcal{I}$ *satisfies* α*.* $\mathcal{I}$ *is a model of an ABox* $\mathcal{A}$ *if it satisfies every ABox assertion in* $\mathcal{A}$*.*

An interpretation $\mathcal{I}$ *is a model of an* $\mathcal{ALC}$ *ontology* $O = (\mathcal{A}, \mathcal{T})$ *if* $\mathcal{I}$ *is a model of* $\mathcal{T}$ *and* $\mathcal{A}$*. An ontology* O *is* consistent *if there exists a model of* O*. An ontology* O entails *a GCI, an ABox assertion, written* $O \models \alpha$*, if every model of* O *satisfies* α*.*

We need notations and definitions that will be used in the paper. We use $|S|$ to denote the cardinality of a set S. Given an $\mathcal{ALC}$ ontology $\mathcal{O} = \langle \mathcal{A}, \mathcal{T}\rangle$, we denote by $\mathsf{sub}(\mathcal{O}) = \mathsf{sub}(\mathcal{A}, \mathcal{T})$ the set of all sub-concepts occurring in $\mathcal{A}, \mathcal{T}$. The size of an ontology $\mathcal{O}$ is denoted by $|\mathcal{O}| = |\mathcal{A}| + |\mathcal{T}|$ where $|\mathcal{A}|$ is the size of all assertions, $|\mathcal{T}|$ the size of all GCIs. It holds that $|\mathsf{sub}(\mathcal{O})|$ is polynomially bounded by $|\mathcal{O}|$ since if a concept is represented as a string then a sub-concept is a substring.

To be able to define a network of aligned ontologies, we need alignments which represent semantic links between ontology entities such as individuals, concepts or roles.

Definition 3 (network of aligned ontologies). *An* $\mathcal{ALC}$ *network of aligned ontologies is a tuple* $\langle \{O_i\}_{i=1}^n, \{A_{ij}\}_{i,j=1,i\neq j}^n\rangle$ *where* O_i *is an* $\mathcal{ALC}$ *ontology with* $1 \leq i \leq n$*, and* A_{ij} *with* $1 \leq i < j \leq n$ *is an alignment containing correspondences of the following forms:*

- $C \rightarrow D$ *or* $C \leftarrow D$ *where* $C \in \mathsf{sub}(O_i)$ *and* $D \in \mathsf{sub}(O_j)$*. Such a correspondence is called concept correspondence.*

- *$a \approx b$ ($a \not\approx b$) where $a \in \mathsf{Voc}_I(O_i)$ and $b \in \mathsf{Voc}_I(O_j)$. Such a correspondence is called individual correspondence.*
- *a link key $\{\langle P_k, Q_k\rangle\}_{k=1}^n \mathsf{linkkey}\langle C, D\rangle$ where $P_k \in \mathsf{Voc}_R(O_i)$, $Q_k \in \mathsf{Voc}_R(O_j)$ for $1 \le k \le n$ and $C \in \mathsf{sub}(O_i)$ and $D \in \mathsf{sub}(O_j)$. Such a correspondence is called link key correspondence.*

Note that when we write $C \to D \in A_{ij}$ this means $C \in \mathsf{Voc}_C(O_i)$ and $D \in \mathsf{Voc}_C(O_j)$. Analogously, $C \leftarrow D \in A_{ij}$ implies $C \in \mathsf{Voc}_C(O_i)$ and $D \in \mathsf{Voc}_C(O_j)$. Semantically, $C \to D$ is different from $C \leftarrow D$. The following definition formalizes the semantics of correspondences in an alignment so that it is compatible with that of ontologies. We retain the standard semantics for individual and link key correspondences while the semantics of concept correspondences is weakened.

Definition 4 (semantics of alignments). *An $\mathcal{ALC}$ network of aligned ontologies is a tuple $\langle\{O_i\}_{i=1}^n, \{A_{ij}\}_{i,j=1,i\neq j}^n\rangle$ where O_i is an $\mathcal{ALC}$ ontologies with $1 \le i \le n$, and A_{ij} is an alignment with $1 \le i < j \le n$. Let $\mathcal{I}$ and $\mathcal{J}$ be models of O_i and O_j respectively.*

- *If $C \to D$ is in A_{ij} then $D^{\mathcal{J}} = \emptyset$ implies $C^{\mathcal{I}} = \emptyset$.*
- *If $a \approx b$ is in A_{ij} then $a^{\mathcal{I}} = a^{\mathcal{J}}$.*
- *If $a \not\approx b$ is in A_{ij} then $a^{\mathcal{I}} \neq a^{\mathcal{J}}$.*
- *If $\{\langle P_k, Q_k\rangle\}_{k=1}^n \mathsf{linkkey}\langle C, D\rangle$ is in A_{ij} then $(a_k^i)^{\mathcal{I}} = (a_k^j)^{\mathcal{J}}$, $\langle a^{\mathcal{I}}, (a_k^i)^{\mathcal{I}}\rangle \in P_k^{\mathcal{I}}$, $\langle b^{\mathcal{J}}, (a_k^j)^{\mathcal{J}}\rangle \in Q_k^{\mathcal{J}}$ for all $1 \le k \le n$, $a^{\mathcal{I}} \in C^{\mathcal{I}}$, $b^{\mathcal{J}} \in D^{\mathcal{J}}$ imply $a^{\mathcal{I}} = b^{\mathcal{J}}$.*

The notion of consistency for a network of aligned ontologies can be naturally introduced thanks to the semantics of ontologies and alignments involved in the network.

Definition 5 (network consistency). *Let $\langle\{O_i\}_{i=1}^n, \{A_{ij}\}_{i,j=1,i\neq j}^n\rangle$ be a network of aligned ontologies in $\mathcal{ALC}$. The network is consistent if there is a model $\mathcal{I} = \{\mathcal{I}_i\}_{i=1}^n$ where $\mathcal{I}_i = \langle\Delta^{\mathcal{I}_i}, \cdot^{\mathcal{I}_i}\rangle$ is a model of O_i for all $1 \le i \le n$ such that*

1. *For each correspondence $a \approx b$ in A_{ij} with $1 \le i < j \le n$, $a^{\mathcal{I}_i} = b^{\mathcal{I}_j}$. For each correspondence $a \not\approx b$ in A_{ij} with $1 \le i < j \le n$, $a^{\mathcal{I}_i} \neq b^{\mathcal{I}_j}$.*
2. *For each correspondence $C \to D$ in A_{ij} with $1 \le i < j \le n$, if $D^{\mathcal{I}_j} = \emptyset$ then $C^{\mathcal{I}_i} = \emptyset$.*
3. *For each correspondence $\{\langle P_k, Q_k\rangle\}_{k=1}^n \mathsf{linkkey}\langle C, D\rangle$ in A_{ij} with $1 \le i < j \le n$, if $(a_k^i)^{\mathcal{I}_i} = (a_k^j)^{\mathcal{I}_j}$, $\langle a^{\mathcal{I}_i}, (a_k^i)^{\mathcal{I}_i}\rangle \in P_k^{\mathcal{I}_i}$, $\langle b^{\mathcal{I}_j}, (a_k^j)^{\mathcal{I}_j}\rangle \in Q_k^{\mathcal{I}_j}$ for all $1 \le k \le n$, $a^{\mathcal{I}_i} \in C^{\mathcal{I}_i}$, $b^{\mathcal{I}_j} \in D^{\mathcal{I}_j}$ then $a^{\mathcal{I}_i} = b^{\mathcal{I}_j}$.*

A network $N = \langle\{O_i\}_{i=1}^n, \{A_{ij}\}_{i,j=1,i\neq j}^n\rangle$ entails *a link key α, written $N \models \alpha$, if every model of N satisfies α. In particular, an alignment A_{ij} is called clash-free if $\{a \approx b, a \not\approx b\} \not\subseteq A_{ij}$.*

We finish this section by proving the following lemma which allows to reduce link key entailment to consistency of the network of aligned ontologies.

Lemma 1 (Reduction of link key entailment to consistency). *Let $\langle\{O_1, O_2\}, A_{12}\rangle$ be a network of aligned ontologies in $\mathcal{ALC}$. It holds that*

$$\langle\{O_1, O_2\}, A_{12}\rangle \models (\{\langle P_i, Q_i\rangle\}_{i=1}^{m} \textsf{linkkey}\ \langle C, D\rangle) \text{ iff } \langle\{O_1', O_2'\}, A_{12}'\rangle \text{ is inconsistent}$$

with $O_1' = O_1 \cup \{C(x)\} \cup \{P_i(x, z_i)\}_{i=1}^{n}$, $O_2' = O_2 \cup \{D(y)\} \cup \{Q_i(y, z_i')\}_{i=1}^{n}$, $A_{12}' = A_{12} \cup \{z_i \approx z_i'\}_{i=1}^{n} \cup \{x \not\approx y\}$, $x, z_1, \cdots, z_n$ *are new individuals in* O_1 *and* $y, z_1', \cdots, z_n'$ *are new individuals in* O_2.

Proof. Let $\lambda = \{\langle P_i, Q_i\rangle\}_{i=1}^{n}$ $\textsf{linkkey}$ $\langle C, D\rangle$. Assume that $\langle\{O_1, O_2\}, A_{12}\rangle \models \lambda$. We show that $\langle\{O_1', O_2'\}, A_{12}'\rangle$ is inconsistent. By contradiction, assume that $\langle\{O_1', O_2'\}, A_{12}'\rangle$ has a model $\mathcal{I} = \langle\mathcal{I}_1, \mathcal{I}_2\rangle$, *i.e.* O_1' and O_2' have models $\mathcal{I}_1$ and $\mathcal{I}_2$ satisfying Definition 5. This implies that $\mathcal{I}_1$ and $\mathcal{I}_2$ are models of O_1 and O_2. Hence, $x^{\mathcal{I}_1} \in C^{\mathcal{I}_1}$, $y^{\mathcal{I}_2} \in D^{\mathcal{I}_2}$, $\langle x^{\mathcal{I}_1}, z_i^{\mathcal{I}_1}\rangle \in P_i^{\mathcal{I}_1}$, $\langle y^{\mathcal{I}_2}, {z'}_i^{\mathcal{I}_2}\rangle \in Q_i^{\mathcal{I}_2}$,

Algorithm 1. Propagating individual equalities

function PROPAGATEEQUAL(O_i, O_j, A_{ij})
  while A_{ij} or O_i or O_j is unstationary **do**
    if O_i or O_j is inconsistent or A_{ij} is not clash-free **then**
      return false
    end if
    for $a_i^1 \approx a_j^1 \in A_{ij}$, $a_i^2 \approx a_j^2 \in A_{ij}$ **do**
      for $O_k \models a_k^m \approx a_k^h$, $k \in \{i, j\}$, $m, h \in \{1, 2\}$, $m \neq h$ **do**
        $A_{ij} \leftarrow A_{ij} \cup \{a_i^h \approx a_j^m, a_i^m \approx a_j^h\}$
        $O_k \leftarrow O_k \cup \{a_k^1 \approx a_k^2\}$
      end for
    end for
    for each $\{\langle P_k, Q_k\rangle\}_{k=1}^{n}\textsf{linkkey}\langle C, D\rangle \in A_{ij}$ **do**
      for $a_k^i \approx a_k^j \in A_{ij}$, $a \in \textsf{Voc}_I(O_i)$, $b \in \textsf{Voc}_I(O_j)$, $P_k(a', {a'}_k^i) \in O_i$,
       $Q_k(b', {a'}_k^j) \in O_j$, $O_i \models a \approx a'$, $O_i \models a_k^i \approx {a'}_k^i$, $O_j \models b \approx b'$
       $O_j \models a_k^j \approx {a'}_k^j$ for all $1 \leq k \leq n$ **do**
        if $O_i \cap \{C(a), \neg C(a)\} = \emptyset$ **then**
          $O_i \leftarrow O_i \cup \{(C \sqcup \neg C)(a)\}$
        end if
        if $O_j \cap \{D(b), \neg D(b)\} = \emptyset$ **then**
          $O_j \leftarrow O_j \cup \{(D \sqcup \neg D)(b)\}$
        end if
      end for
      for $a_k^i \approx a_k^j \in A_{ij}$, $O_i \models C(a)$, $O_j \models D(b)$, $P_k(a', {a'}_k^i) \in O_i$,
       $Q_k(b', {a'}_k^j) \in O_j$, $O_i \models a \approx a'$, $O_i \models a_k^i \approx {a'}_k^i$, $O_j \models b \approx b'$
       $O_j \models a_k^j \approx {a'}_k^j$ for all $1 \leq k \leq n$ **do**
        $A_{ij} \leftarrow A_{ij} \cup \{a \approx b\}$
      end for
    end for
  end while
  return true
end function

Algorithm 2. Propagating concept unsatisfiability

function PROPAGATEUNSAT(O_i, O_j, A_{ij})
  while A_{ij} or O_i or O_j is unstationary **do**
    if O_i or O_j is inconsistent or A_{ij} is not clash-free **then**
      return false
    end if
    for each $D \rightarrow C \in A_{ij}$ **do**
      if $O_j \models C \sqsubseteq \bot$ **then**
        $O_i \leftarrow O_i \cup \{D \sqsubseteq \bot\}$
      end if
    end for
    for each $D \leftarrow C \in A_{ij}$ **do**
      if $O_i \models D \sqsubseteq \bot$ **then**
        $O_j \leftarrow O_j \cup \{C \sqsubseteq \bot\}$
      end if
    end for
    for $C_i^1 \rightarrow C_j^1 \in A_{ij}, C_i^2 \leftarrow C_j^2 \in A_{ij}$ **do**
      for $O_j \models C_j^1 \sqsubseteq C_j^2$ **do**
        $A_{ij} \leftarrow A_{ij} \cup \{C_i^1 \rightarrow C_j^2, C_i^2 \leftarrow C_j^1\}$
      end for
    end for
    for $C_i^1 \leftarrow C_j^1 \in A_{ij}, C_i^2 \rightarrow C_j^2 \in A_{ij}$ **do**
      for $O_i \models C_i^1 \sqsubseteq C_i^2$ **do**
        $A_{ij} \leftarrow A_{ij} \cup \{C_i^1 \rightarrow C_j^2, C_i^2 \leftarrow C_j^1\}$
      end for
    end for
  end while
  return true
end function

$z_i^{\mathcal{I}_1} = z_i'^{\mathcal{I}_2}$ and $x^{\mathcal{I}_1} \neq y^{\mathcal{I}_2}$. This implies that $\mathcal{I} \not\models \lambda$. Thus, we have a model $\mathcal{I}$ of $\langle\{O_1', O_2'\}, A_{12}'\rangle$ such that $\mathcal{I} \not\models \lambda$. Therefore, $\langle\{O_1, O_2\}, A_{12}\rangle \not\models \lambda$, which contradicts the assumption.

Assume now that $\langle\{O_1, O_2\}, A_{12}\rangle \not\models \lambda$. Let us show that $\langle\{O_1', O_2'\}, A_{12}'\rangle$ is consistent. Since $\langle\{O_1', O_2'\}, A_{12}'\rangle \not\models \lambda$, then there exists an interpretation $\mathcal{I} = \langle\mathcal{I}_1, \mathcal{I}_2\rangle$ such that $\mathcal{I} \models \langle\{O_1', O_2'\}, A_{12}'\rangle$ and $\mathcal{I} \not\models \lambda$.

Since $\mathcal{I} \not\models \lambda$, by the semantics of link keys, there exist $\delta, \delta_1, \ldots, \delta_n \in \Delta_1^{\mathcal{I}_1}$ and $\delta', \delta_1', \ldots, \delta_n' \in \Delta_2^{\mathcal{I}_2}$ such that $\delta \in C^{\mathcal{I}_1}$, $\delta' \in D^{\mathcal{I}_2}$, $(\delta, \delta_1) \in P_1^{\mathcal{I}_1}, (\delta', \delta_1') \in Q_1^{\mathcal{I}_2}, \ldots, (\delta, \delta_n) \in P_n^{\mathcal{I}_1}, (\delta', \delta_n) \in Q_n^{\mathcal{I}_2}$, $\delta_1 = \delta_1', \ldots, \delta_n = \delta_n'$ and $\delta \neq \delta'$. Let us extend $\mathcal{I}$ by defining $x^{\mathcal{I}_1} = \delta$, $y^{\mathcal{I}_2} = \delta'$, $z_1^{\mathcal{I}_1} = \delta_1, \ldots, z_n^{\mathcal{I}_1} = \delta_n$, $z_1'^{\mathcal{I}_2} = \delta_1', \ldots, z_n'^{\mathcal{I}_2} = \delta_n'$. Then, $\mathcal{I}$ is a model of $\langle\{O_1', O_2'\}, A_{12}'\rangle$. Therefore, $\langle\{O_1', O_2'\}, A_{12}'\rangle$ is consistent. □

This lemma can be extended to a general network of aligned ontologies containing more than two ontologies.

4 An Algorithm for a Network of Aligned Ontologies

The algorithm for deciding consistency of a network of aligned ontologies deals with pair by pair of ontologies in the network. For each pair of ontologies and an alignment between them, the algorithm repeats the following three tasks: propagating individual equalities from one ontology to the other via individual correspondences; applying link key correspondences which may lead to adding new individual correspondences; and propagating concept unsatisfiabilities from one ontology to the other via concept correspondences. The execution of a task may trigger the execution of another task. The execution of these tasks may lead to a change of ontologies and alignments in the network. The algorithm terminates on the pair of ontologies when the ontologies and the alignment reach stationarity. The first and second tasks are described in Algorithm 1 while the third one is outlined in Algorithm 2.

The following lemma establishes that the propagation performed by Algorithms 1 and 2 and consistency of the pair of the extended ontologies suffice to decide consistency of the network composed of the initial ontologies and the alignment.

Lemma 2 (reduction for a pair). *Let O_1, O_2 be two consistent ontologies and A_{12} be an alignment. We use $\widehat{O_1}$, $\widehat{O_2}$ and $\widehat{A_{12}}$ to denote the resulting ontologies and alignment obtained by calling* $\mathsf{propagatePair}(O_1, O_2, A_{12})$. *It holds that $\widehat{O_1}, \widehat{O_2}$ are consistent and $\widehat{A_{12}}$ is clash-free iff the network $\langle\{O_1, O_2\}, \{A_{12}\}\rangle$ is consistent.*

Before providing a complete proof of the lemma, we summarize the main arguments. The soundness of the if-direction of Lemma 2 is straightforward since Algorithms 1 and 2 add only logical consequences of the network to the ontologies and alignments. The soundness of the only-if-direction of the lemma is based on the following elements: (i) consistency of the extended ontologies and clash-freeness of the extended alignments imply consistency of the initial ontologies and clash-freeness of the initial alignments; (ii) Algorithms 1 and 2 make explicit all individual equalities, and thus eventual clashes of the kind $a \approx b, a \not\approx b$ must be discovered. This ensures that two models of the extended ontologies satisfy individual correspondences; (iii) Algorithms 1 and 2 apply link keys until they are not applicable over the initial individuals in the ontologies. Since models of an $\mathcal{ALC}$ ontology are tree-shaped and $\mathcal{ALC}$ does not allow for inverse roles, satisfaction of the link keys over the initial individuals is sufficient; and (iv) Algorithms 1 and 2 propagate concept unsatisfiabilities. If the "subsumer" of a concept correspondence is satisfiable then a model of the ontology can be extended such that the interpretation of the subsumer in this model is not empty. This implies that the concept correspondence is satisfied.

Proof. "If-direction". Assume that the network $\langle\{O_1, O_2\}, \{A_{12}\}\rangle$ is consistent. By definition, O_i has a model $\mathcal{I}_i$ with $1 \leq i \leq 2$ such that they satisfy all correspondences $\alpha \in A_{12}$. We show that $\mathcal{I}_1$ is a model of $\widehat{O_1}$. For this, we have to prove that:

- $a_0^{\mathcal{I}_1} = a_n^{\mathcal{I}_1}$ if $a_0 \approx a_n$ is added to O_1 by Line 9 in Algorithm 1. We have $a_0 \approx a_n$ is added to O_1 if Algorithm 1 discovers a sequence of equalities $a_0 \approx a_1, \cdots, a_{n-1} \approx a_n$ such that $a_i \approx a_{i+1} \in \widehat{O_1} \cup \widehat{O_2} \cup \widehat{A_{12}}$ for $0 \leq i \leq n-1$. This sequence of equalities implies $a_0^{\mathcal{I}_1} = a_n^{\mathcal{I}_1}$. Note that if there is some $a \approx b \in A_{ij}$ then $\Delta^{\mathcal{I}_1} \cap \Delta^{\mathcal{I}_2} \neq \emptyset$ according to Definition 4. By using the same argument, we can show $a_0^{\mathcal{I}_2} = a_n^{\mathcal{I}_2}$ if $a_0 \approx a_n$ is added to O_2 by Line 9 in Algorithm 1.
- $C_0^{\mathcal{I}_1} = \emptyset$ if $C_0 \sqsubseteq \bot$ is added to O_1 by Line 8 in Algorithm 2. We have $C_0 \sqsubseteq \bot$ is added to O_1 if Algorithm 1 discovers a sequence $C_0 \Rightarrow C_1, \cdots, C_{n-1} \Rightarrow C_n$ such that $\widehat{O_1} \models C_i \Rightarrow C_{i+1}$ or $\widehat{O_2} \models C_i \Rightarrow C_{i+1}$ or $C_i \Rightarrow C_{i+1} \in \widehat{A_{12}}$ for $0 \leq i \leq n-1$, and $\widehat{O_i} \models C_n^{\mathcal{I}_i} \sqsubseteq \bot$ $(i \in \{1, 2\})$ where "$\Rightarrow$" represents "$\longrightarrow$" or "$\sqsubseteq$" and $C \leftarrow D = D \Rightarrow C$, $C \sqsupseteq D = D \Rightarrow C$. This implies $C_i^{\mathcal{I}_i} = \emptyset$ for $1 \leq i \leq n$. By using the same argument, we can show $C_0^{\mathcal{I}_2} = \emptyset$ if $C_0 \sqsubseteq \bot$ is added to O_2 by Line 13 in Algorithm 2.
- The concepts $(C \sqcup {\sim}C)(a)$ and $(D \sqcup {\sim}D)(b)$ added by Lines 17 and 20 in Algorithm 2 do not change consistency since they are tautologies.

"Only-If-direction". Since $\widehat{O_i}$ is consistent, according to [12], $\widehat{O_i}$ has a tree-shaped model $\mathcal{I}_i$ where each interpretation domain Δ_i of $\mathcal{I}_i$ is composed of a set of initial individuals I^i_{old} and a set of new individuals I^i_{new} for $1 \leq i \leq 2$. Since $O_i \subseteq \widehat{O_i}$, $\mathcal{I}_i$ is a model of O_i with $1 \leq i \leq 2$. We will extend $\mathcal{I}_1$ and $\mathcal{I}_2$ so that they satisfy the correspondences in A_{12}.

- If $a \approx b \in \widehat{A_{12}}$ then $a^{\mathcal{I}} = a^{\mathcal{J}}$ for all models $\mathcal{I}$ and $\mathcal{J}$ of O_1 and O_2 respectively due to Definition 4. We define $a^{\mathcal{I}_1} = a^{\mathcal{I}_2}$. Thus, $a^{\mathcal{I}_1} = a^{\mathcal{I}_2}$ for each $a \approx b \in A_{12}$ since $A_{12} \subseteq \widehat{A_{12}}$. By construction, $\mathcal{I}_1$ and $\mathcal{I}_2$ satisfy all of the individual correspondences in A_{12} according to Definition 4.
- If $a \not\approx b \in \widehat{A_{12}}$ then $a \approx b \notin \widehat{A_{12}}$ since $\widehat{A_{12}}$ is clash-free.
- Let $C_h \rightarrow D_h \in A_{12}$. If $\widehat{O_2} \models D_h \sqsubseteq \bot$ then $C_h \sqsubseteq \bot$ is added to $\widehat{O_1}$ by Algorithm 2. Hence, $D_h^{\mathcal{I}_2} = \emptyset$ implies $C_h^{\mathcal{I}_1} = \emptyset$. Note that if $\widehat{O_2} \models D_h \sqsubseteq \bot$ then $\widehat{O_2'} \models D_h \sqsubseteq \bot$ for all $\widehat{O_2} \subseteq \widehat{O_2'}$.

  Assume that $\widehat{O_2} \not\models D_h \sqsubseteq \bot$. Thus, $\widehat{O_2} \cup \{D_h(x_h)\}$ is consistent where x_h is a new individual. According to [12], $\widehat{O_2} \cup \{D_h(x_h)\}$ has a tree-shaped model $\mathcal{I}_2'$ of $\widehat{O_2} \cup \{D_h(x_h)\}$. We show that if $\widehat{O_2} \cup \{D_1(x_1)\}$ and $\widehat{O_2} \cup \{D_2(x_2)\}$ are consistent with new individual x_1, x_2 then $\widehat{O_2} \cup \{D_1(x_1), D_2(x_2)\}$ is consistent. Indeed, running the standard tableau algorithm in [12] on $\widehat{O_2} \cup \{D_1(x_1)\}$ can build a set $\mathbf{T}$ of completion trees rooted at the initial individuals in $\widehat{O_2}$ and a completion tree T_{x_1} rooted at x_1. Analogously, if the standard tableau algorithm runs on $\widehat{O_2} \cup \{D_2(x_2)\}$, it can build a set $\mathbf{T}$' of completion trees rooted at the initial individuals in $\widehat{O_2}$ and a completion tree T_{x_2} rooted at x_2. All trees are clash-free and complete. Hence, $\mathbf{T} \cup \{T_{x_1}, T_{x_2}\}$ can represent a model of $\widehat{O_2} \cup \{D_1(x_1), D_2(x_2)\}$.

  Therefore, we can run the standard tableau algorithm in [12] on $\widehat{O_2} \cup \{D_i(x_i)\}_{i=1}^m$ to obtain a tree-shaped model $\mathcal{J}_2$ of $\widehat{O_2} \cup \{D_i(x_i)\}_{i=1}^m$ where

x_h is a new individual and $\widehat{O_2} \not\models D_h \sqsubseteq \bot$ for $1 \leq h \leq m$.

By using the same argument, we can obtain a tree-shaped model $\mathcal{J}_1$ of $\widehat{O_1} \cup \{D'_1(x'_1), \cdots, D'_{m'}(x'_{m'})\}$. By construction, $\mathcal{J}_1$ and $\mathcal{J}_2$ satisfy all of the concept correspondences in A_{12} according to Definition 4. In addition, they remain to satisfy all of the individual correspondences in A_{12}. For the sake of the simplicity, we rename $\mathcal{J}_1$ and $\mathcal{J}_2$ to $\mathcal{I}_1$ and $\mathcal{I}_2$.

- Assume that $\{\langle P_k, Q_k\rangle\}_{k=1}^{n}\mathsf{linkkey}\langle C, D\rangle$ is a link key in A_{12} and $(a_k^1)^{\mathcal{I}_1} = (a_k^2)^{\mathcal{I}_2}$, $\langle a^{\mathcal{I}_1}, (a_k^1)^{\mathcal{I}_1}\rangle \in P_k^{\mathcal{I}_1}$, $\langle b^{\mathcal{I}_2}, (a_k^2)^{\mathcal{I}_2}\rangle \in Q_k^{\mathcal{I}_2}$ for all $1 \leq k \leq n$, $a^{\mathcal{I}_1} \in C^{\mathcal{I}_1}$, $b^{\mathcal{I}_2} \in D^{\mathcal{I}_2}$.
  1. If $(a_k^1)^{\mathcal{I}_1} = (a_k^2)^{\mathcal{I}_2}$ then there is a sequence $a_0 \approx a_1, \cdots, a_{m-1} \approx a_m$ (discovered by Algorithm 1) such that $a_i \approx a_{i+1} \in \widehat{O_1} \cup \widehat{O_2} \cup \widehat{A_{12}}$ for $0 \leq i \leq m-1$ with $a_k^1 = a_0, a_k^2 = a_m$. This implies that $a_k^1 \approx a_k^2 \in \widehat{A_{12}}$ for $1 \leq k \leq n$.
  2. Since $\mathcal{I}_1$ and $\mathcal{I}_2$ are tree-shaped whose roots are the old individuals, the condition of the link key holds only if all individuals a_k^1, a_k^2 for $1 \leq k \leq n$, and a, b are contained $I_{old}^1 \cup I_{old}^2$. Hence, $\langle a^{\mathcal{I}_1}, (a_k^1)^{\mathcal{I}_1}\rangle \in P_k^{\mathcal{I}_1}$ iff $P_k(a', a'^1_k) \in O_i$ with $O_i \models a \approx a'$, $O_i \models a_k^1 \approx a'^1_k$ for $1 \leq k \leq n$ where a, a' and a_k^1, a'^1_k are old individuals. Analogously, $\langle b^{\mathcal{I}_2}, (a_k^2)^{\mathcal{I}_2}\rangle \in Q_k^{\mathcal{I}_2}$ iff $Q_k(b', a'^2_k) \in O_j$ with $O_j \models b \approx b'$, $O_j \models a_k^2 \approx a'^2_k$ for $1 \leq k \leq n$ where b, b' and a_k^2, a'^2_k are old individuals.
  3. Since $a^{\mathcal{I}_1} \in C^{\mathcal{I}_1}$ and $(C \sqcup \neg C)(a) \in O_1$ (Line 17, Algorithm 1), we have $\widehat{O_1} \models C(a)$. Analogously, from $b^{\mathcal{I}_2} \in D^{\mathcal{I}_2}$ and $(D \sqcup \neg D)(b) \in O_2$ (Line 20, Algorithm 1), we obtain $\widehat{O_2} \models D(b)$.

  Therefore, the 3 items above trigger Line 26 in Algorithm 1 which adds to $\widehat{A_{12}}$ the assertion $a \approx b$. Thus, we obtain $a^{\mathcal{I}_1} \approx b^{\mathcal{I}_2}$.

Algorithm 3. Complete propagation over the whole network

```
function PROPAGATEOVERNETWORK(⟨{O_i}_{i=1}^n, {A_ij}_{i,j=1,i≠j}^n⟩)
    while O_i, O_j, A_ij are unstationary for all 1 ≤ i < j ≤ n do
        for 1 ≤ i < j ≤ n do
            while O_i, O_j, A_ij are unstationary do
                if propagateEqual(O_i, O_j, A_ij) returns false then
                    return false
                end if
                if propagateUnsat(O_i, O_j, A_ij) returns false then
                    return false
                end if
            end while
        end for
    end while
    return true
end function
```

We have proven that $\mathcal{I}_1$ and $\mathcal{I}_2$ are models of O_1 and O_2 which satisfy all of the correspondences in A_{12}. □

We can observe that Algorithms 1 and 2 can be implemented in a decentralized manner since each call for checking ontology entailment or consistency can be sent to a local reasoner associated with the ontology located on a different site.

To check consistency of a network of aligned ontologies, it is needed to run Algorithms 1 and 2 on each pair of ontologies with the alignment between them until all ontologies and alignments are stationary. Note that saturating a pair of ontologies with the alignment can make a saturated pair of ontologies unsaturated. This is due to the fact that an ontology can be shared by several pairs of ontologies.

The following theorem is a consequence of Lemma 2.

Theorem 1 (reduction for network). *Let $\langle\{O_i\}_{i=1}^n, \{A_{ij}\}_{i,j=1,i\neq j}^n\rangle$ be a network of aligned ontologies. We use $\widehat{O_i}$ and $\widehat{A_{ij}}$ to denote the resulting ontologies and alignments obtained by calling* propagateOverNetwork($\langle\{O_i\}_{i=1}^n$, $\{A_{ij}\}_{i,j=1,i\neq j}^n\rangle$). *It holds that $\widehat{O_i}$ is consistent for all $1 \leq i \leq n$ and $\widehat{A_{ij}}$ is clash-free for all $1 \leq i < j \leq n$ iff the network $\langle\{O_i\}_{i=1}^n, \{A_{ij}\}_{i,j=1,i\neq j}^n\rangle$ is consistent.*

We now investigate the complexity of the algorithms. Under the hypothesis in which a call to reasoners associated with ontologies is considered as an oracle, *i.e.* an elementary operation, our algorithms are tractable.

Theorem 2. *Let $\langle\{O_i\}_{i=1}^n, \{A_{ij}\}_{i,j=1,i\neq j}^n\rangle$ be a network of aligned ontologies. The algorithm* propagateOverNetwork($\langle\{O_i\}_{i=1}^n, \{A_{ij}\}_{i,j=1,i\neq j}^n\rangle$) *runs in polynomial time in the size of the network if each check of entailment or consistency occurring in the algorithms is considered as an oracle.*

Proof. The complexity of the algorithm propagateOverNetwork depends on the complexity of propagateEqual, propagateUnsat. When running these algorithms, each ontology is monotonically extended. It is straightforward to obtain that the number of axioms of the form $C \sqsubseteq \bot$ added to ontologies O_i and O_j is bounded by a polynomial function in the size of initial alignments since C must occur in initial correspondences. Analogously, the number of individuals correspondences $a \approx b$ added to alignments A_{ij} is bounded by a polynomial function in the size of initial alignments since a, b must occur in initial correspondences. This implies that the number of iterations of the *while* loops in Algorithms 1, 2 and 3 is bounded by a polynomial function in the size of initial alignments.

In addition, the number of iterations of the *for* loops in Algorithms 1, 2 and 3 is bounded by a polynomial function in the size of initial alignments, the size of ontologies and the number of ontologies and alignments included in the network. This observation completes the proof. □

5 Examples

This section provides some examples for showing the difference of the standard semantics from the new one in terms of reasoning and how to use the algorithms presented in Sect. 4.

Example 2. The ontologies and alignment in Example 1 can be rewritten as follows :

$$O_1 = \{DP \sqsubseteq P, DP(a)\}, O_2 = \{PS \sqsubseteq R, R \sqsubseteq \neg D\},$$
$$A_{12} = \{DP \rightarrow R, DP \rightarrow D, \langle pr, re\rangle \mathsf{linkkey}\langle P, R\rangle\}$$

If the correspondences are considered as standard subsumptions then the ontology $O_1 \cup O_2 \cup A_{12}$ is inconsistent. Indeed, assume that there is a model $\mathcal{I} = \langle \Delta^{\mathcal{I}}, \cdot^{\mathcal{I}}\rangle$ of the ontology. This implies that $a^{\mathcal{I}} \in DP^{\mathcal{I}}$, $DP^{\mathcal{I}} \subseteq R^{\mathcal{I}}$ and $DP^{\mathcal{I}} \subseteq D^{\mathcal{I}}$. Thus, $a^{\mathcal{I}} \in R^{\mathcal{I}} \cap D^{\mathcal{I}}$. However, we have $R^{\mathcal{I}} \subseteq \Delta^{\mathcal{I}} \setminus D^{\mathcal{I}}$, which is a contradiction.

If we now interpret the correspondences under the semantics given in Definition 4 then there is no propagation needed according to Algorithms 1 and 2. It is obvious that O_1 and O_2 are consistent, and the network $\langle\{O_1, O_2\}, A_{12}\rangle$ is consistent under the semantics given in Definition 4.

Example 3. In this example, we reduce the two correspondences in Example 2 to one as follows.

$$O_1 = \{DP \sqsubseteq P, DP(a)\}, O_2 = \{PS \sqsubseteq R, R \sqsubseteq \neg D\},$$
$$A_{12} = \{DP \rightarrow R \sqcap D, \langle pr, re\rangle \mathsf{linkkey}\langle P, R\rangle\}$$

We now interpret the correspondence under the semantics given in Definition 4. Since $O_2 \models R \sqcap D \sqsubseteq \bot$, Algorithm 2 propagates unsatisfiability of $R \sqcap D$ to O_1 via the correspondence $DP \rightarrow R \sqcap D$. Hence, it adds $DP \sqsubseteq \bot$ to O_1. This leads to inconsistency of $\widehat{O_1}$. Therefore, the network $\langle\{O_1, O_2\}, A_{12}\rangle$ is not consistent.

Example 4. The ontologies and alignment in Example 1 can be rewritten as follows :

$$O_1 = \{DP \sqsubseteq P, DP(a)\}, O_2 = \{PS \sqsubseteq R, R \sqsubseteq \neg D\},$$
$$A_{12} = \{DP \rightarrow R, DP \rightarrow D, \langle pr, re\rangle \mathsf{linkkey}\langle P, R\rangle\}$$

We consider whether $\langle\{O_1, O_2\}, A_{12}\rangle \models \lambda$ where $\lambda = \langle pr, re\rangle \mathsf{linkkey}\langle P, R\rangle$. Due to Lemma 1, we extend O_1, O_2 and A_{12} by adding to O_1 assertions $DP(x), pr(x, x_1)$, to O_2 assertions $PS(y), re(y, y_1)$, and to A_{12} assertions $x_1 \approx y_1, x \not\approx y$. Let $\widehat{O_1}, \widehat{O_2}$ and $\widehat{A_{12}}$ be the extended ontologies and alignment.

If there are models $\mathcal{I}_1$ and $\mathcal{I}_2$ of $\widehat{O_1}, \widehat{O_2}$ then, we have $x \in DP^{\mathcal{I}_1}$ and $y \in PS^{\mathcal{I}_2}$, and $DP^{\mathcal{I}_1} \subseteq P^{\mathcal{I}_1}$ and $PS^{\mathcal{I}_2} \subseteq R^{\mathcal{I}_2}$.

Thus, the link key $\langle pr, re\rangle \mathit{linkkey}\langle P, R\rangle$ is applicable, and Algorithm 1 adds $x \approx y$ to $\widehat{A_{12}}$. This leads to a clash in $\widehat{A_{12}}$ and thus the network $\langle\{\widehat{O_1}, \widehat{O_2}\}, \widehat{A_{12}}\rangle$ is not consistent. Therefore, $\langle\{O_1, O_2\}, A_{12}\rangle \models \lambda$ holds.

6 Implementation and Experimental Results

An implementation of the proposed algorithms has been integrated within a reasoner written in Java, called Draon [11], which already allowed to reason in a decentralized manner on a network of aligned ontologies under the IDDL semantics [5]. Algorithms 1, 2 and 3 can be naturally implemented such that reasoning tasks on ontologies can be independently performed by different reasoners located on different sites.

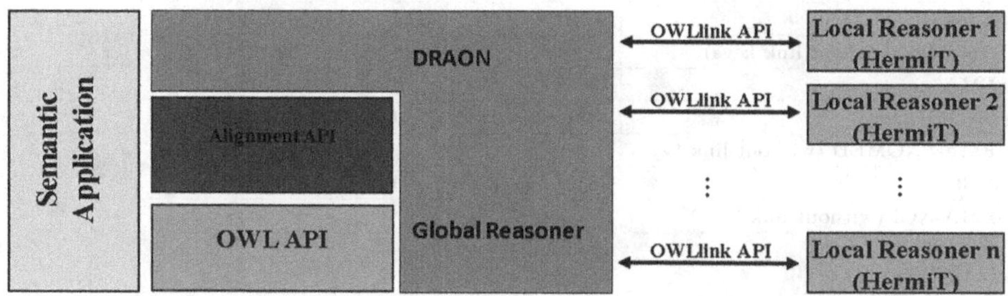

Fig. 1. Architecture of Draon

The architecture of Draon is despicted in Fig. 1. A global reasoner implements Algorithm 3. This global reasoner loads alignments and executes Algorithm 3. It propagates assertion/axioms to local reasoners located on different sites. Then it asks local reasoners to check entailment and consistency of the ontology associated with each local reasoner. The global reasoner and each local reasoner use HermiT [13] as OWL reasoner. The communication between the global reasoner and all local reasoners is based on OWLLink [14]. When connecting to a local reasoner, the global reasoner creates a Java thread which deals with the communication between them. Data shared by the threads are synchronized and protected by using semaphores. Note that we can replace HermiT with any OWL reasoner since OWLLink supports a generic OWL reasoner.

Table 1 provides information on the ontologies and alignments used for the experiments. These datasets are taken from OAEI2012[2] and OAEI2018[3] Campaigns. We have chosen small ontologies and alignments such as `iasted.owl`, `sigkdd.owl`, `iasted-sigkdd.rdf` to test our algorithm on alignments with link keys since they are well understood and manually checkable. This allows us to create manually relevant link keys (to our best knowledge, there is no system which can generate link keys expressed in the alignment syntax). In addition, we have selected large ontologies and alignment such as SNOMED, FMA, FMA-SNOMED in order that the difference between the reasoning complexities of the two semantics IDDL (implemented in Draon) and APPROX (the new semantics introduced in the paper) is more noticeable.

[2] cs.ox.ac.uk/isg/projects/SEALS/oaei/2012/.
[3] oaei.ontologymatching.org/2018/conference.

Table 1. Ontologies and alignments without link keys and their characteristics

	Concepts	Roles	Individuals	Axioms/Correspondences
Iasted	141	38	6	551
Sigkdd	50	18	5	210
iast-sigkdd (without link keys)				15
Conference	60	46	2	414
Ekaw	74	33	4	351
conference-ekaw (without link keys)				27
Cmt	30	49	3	327
Edas	104	30	117	1025
cmt-edas (without link keys)				14
FMA	10157	0	0	47467
SNOMED	13412	18	0	47104
FMA-SNOMED (without link keys)				9139
NCI	25591	87	0	135556
FMA-NCI (without link keys)				3038

We use two remote DELL servers with Intel 3.4 GHz Processor 8 cores and 32 Gb RAM on which two HermiT-based local reasoners are running. The global reasoner is also launched on a third computer with the same configuration.

We run Draon to check consistency of several networks of ontologies each of which is composed of ontologies and alignment described in Table 1. The results are put in Table 2 which shows execution times of Draon under the two different semantics IDDL and APPROX. The difference of the performances in time results from the fact that reasoning under IDDL may require in the worst case an exponential number of message exchanges between the global reasoner and the local reasoners while reasoning under APPROX needs at most a polynomial number of message exchanges.

Table 3 provides first experimental results when running Draon to check consistency of networks containing small ontologies and alignment with link keys. The alignments in this table are obtained by adding to the corresponding alignments in Table 2 some link keys manually created.

Table 2. Execution time for checking consistency of ontology networks according to different semantics

Ontology 1	Ontology 2	Alignment	IDDL	APPROX
Iasted	Sigkdd	iasted-sigkdd (without link keys)	3.5 s	9 ms
Conference	Ekaw	conference-ekaw (without link keys)	7.5 s	11 ms
Cmt	Edas	cmt-edas (without link keys)	7.5 s	16 ms
FMA	SNOMED	FMA-SNOMED (without link keys)	>15 min	81 s
FMA	NCI	FMA-NCI (without link keys)	>15 min	10 s

Table 3. Execution time (in milliseconds) for checking consistency of ontology networks with link keys

Ontology 1	Ontology 2	Alignment	Consistency in APPROX
Iasted	Sigkdd	iast-sigkdd (with link keys)	9 ms
Conference	Ekaw	conference-ekaw (with link keys)	11 ms
Cmt	Edas	cmt-edas (with link keys)	17 ms

7 Conclusion and Future Work

We have presented a new semantics of alignments which is weaker than the standard semantics. This weakened semantics of alignments allows us to express correspondences between ontologies of different nature on the one hand and to propose an efficient algorithm for reasoning on a network of ontologies with alignments containing link keys on the other hand. This new kind of correspondences is useful for establishing data links between heterogeneous datasets. The complexity of the proposed algorithm is polynomial in the size of the network if each call for checking ontology entailment or consistency is considered as an oracle. We have integrated an implementation of our algorithm within a distributed reasoner, called Draon, and reported some experimental results.

Our algorithm can be extended to deal with ontologies expressed in a more expressive Description Logic than $\mathcal{ALC}$ in condition that the new logic does not allow for inverse roles. This restriction on expressiveness prevents the current algorithm from merging individuals which are initially not in the ontology. Another extension of the current work aims to add role correspondences to alignments. This may require the algorithm to support ontologies allowing for hierarchy of roles and the negation of roles. We plan to carry out experiments of Draon on ontologies and alignments located on a large number of nodes equipped with a local reasoner. New evaluations of Draon on alignments with a large number of link keys are also expected.

Acknowledgements. This work has been partially supported by the ANR project Elker (ANR-17-CE23-0007-01).

References

1. Borgida, A., Serafini, L.: Distributed description logics: assimilating information from peer sources. J. Data Semant. (1), 153–184 (2003)
2. Grau, B.C., Parsia, B., Sirin, E.: Combining OWL ontologies using $\mathcal{E}$-connections. J. Web Semant. **4**(1), 40–59 (2006)
3. Bao, J., Caragea, D., Honavar, V.G.: A distributed tableau algorithm for package-based description logics. In: Proceedings of the ECAI Workshop on on Context Representation and Reasoning (2006)

4. Zimmermann, A., Euzenat, J.: Three semantics for distributed systems and their relations with alignment composition. In: Cruz, I., et al. (eds.) ISWC 2006. LNCS, vol. 4273, pp. 16–29. Springer, Heidelberg (2006). https://doi.org/10.1007/11926078_2
5. Zimmermann, A., Le Duc, C.: Reasoning with a network of aligned ontologies. In: Calvanese, D., Lausen, G. (eds.) RR 2008. LNCS, vol. 5341, pp. 43–57. Springer, Heidelberg (2008). https://doi.org/10.1007/978-3-540-88737-9_5
6. Adjiman, P., Chatalic, P., Goasdoué, F., Rousset, M., Simon, L.: Distributed reasoning in a peer-to-peer setting: application to the semantic web. J. Artif. Intell. Res. **25**, 269–314 (2006)
7. Atencia, M., David, J., Euzenat, J.: Data interlinking through robust linkkey extraction. In: Schaub, T., Friedrich, G., O'Sullivan, B., (eds.) Proceedings 21st European Conference on Artificial Intelligence (ECAI), Praha (CZ), Amsterdam (NL), pp. 15–20. IOS Press (2014)
8. Gmati, M., Atencia, M., Euzenat, J.: Tableau extensions for reasoning with link keys. In: Proceedings of the 11th International Workshop on Ontology Matching, Kobe, Japan, pp. 37–48 (2016)
9. Sirin, E., Parsia, B., Grau, B.C., Kalyanpur, A., Katz, Y.: Pellet: a pratical OWL-DL reasoner. J. Web Semant. **5**(2), 51–53 (2007)
10. Serafini, L., Tamilin, A.: DRAGO: distributed reasoning architecture for the semantic web. In: Gómez-Pérez, A., Euzenat, J. (eds.) ESWC 2005. LNCS, vol. 3532, pp. 361–376. Springer, Heidelberg (2005). https://doi.org/10.1007/11431053_25
11. Le Duc, C., Lamolle, M., Zimmermann, A., Curé, O.: DRAOn: a distributed reasoner for aligned ontologies. In: Informal Proceedings of the 2nd International Workshop on OWL Reasoner Evaluation (ORE-2013), Ulm, Germany, 22 July 2013, pp. 81–86 (2013)
12. Horrocks, I., Sattler, U., Tobies, S.: Reasoning with individuals for the description logic $\mathcal{SHIQ}$. In: McAllester, D. (ed.) CADE 2000. LNCS, vol. 1831, pp. 482–496. Springer, Heidelberg (2000). https://doi.org/10.1007/10721959_39
13. Shearer, R., Motik, B., Horrocks, I.: HermiT: a highly-efficient OWL reasoner. In: Ruttenberg, A., Sattler, U., Dolbear, C., (eds.) Proceedings of the 5th International Workshop on OWL: Experiences and Directions (OWLED 2008 EU), Karlsruhe, Germany, 26–27 October 2008
14. Liebig, T., Luther, M., Noppens, O., Wessel, M.: Owllink. Semant. Web **2**(1), 23–32 (2011)

Ontology Completion Using Graph Convolutional Networks

Na Li[1(✉)], Zied Bouraoui[2(✉)], and Steven Schockaert[3(✉)]

[1] State Key Laboratory for Novel Software Technology, Nanjing University, Nanjing, China
dg1733007@smail.nju.edu.cn

[2] CRIL - CNRS & University of Artois, Lens, France
zied.bouraoui@cril.fr

[3] Cardiff University, Cardiff, UK
SchockaertS1@Cardiff.ac.uk

Abstract. Many methods have been proposed to automatically extend knowledge bases, but the vast majority of these methods focus on finding plausible missing facts, and knowledge graph triples in particular. In this paper, we instead focus on automatically extending ontologies that are encoded as a set of existential rules. In particular, our aim is to find rules that are plausible, but which cannot be deduced from the given ontology. To this end, we propose a graph-based representation of rule bases. Nodes of the considered graphs correspond to predicates, and they are annotated with vectors encoding our prior knowledge about the meaning of these predicates. The vectors may be obtained from external resources such as word embeddings or they could be estimated from the rule base itself. Edges connect predicates that co-occur in the same rule and their annotations reflect the types of rules in which the predicates co-occur. We then use a neural network model based on Graph Convolutional Networks (GCNs) to refine the initial vector representation of the predicates, to obtain a representation which is predictive of which rules are plausible. We present experimental results that demonstrate the strong performance of this method.

Keywords: Knowledge base completion · Rule induction · Graph Convolutional Networks · Commonsense reasoning

1 Introduction

Many approaches have been proposed in recent years for the problem of finding plausible missing facts in knowledge graphs, typically by learning vector space representations of the entities and relations that are predictive of plausible triples [7,26,32,42,47]. Beyond knowledge graphs, however, ontologies also play an important role on the Web [18]. For the ease of presentation, in this paper we will consider ontologies which are encoded as sets of existential rules [4], although our model would be straightforward to adapt to other formalisms

C. Ghidini et al. (Eds.): ISWC 2019, LNCS 11778, pp. 435–452, 2019.
https://doi.org/10.1007/978-3-030-30793-6_25

such as description logics [2]. Similar to knowledge graphs, existing ontologies are often incomplete, hence there is a need for methods that can automatically predict plausible missing rules for a given ontology. For some ontologies, where we have a large database of facts (often called an ABox), plausible rules can be learned similarly to how rules are learned in inductive logic programming and statistical relational learning [10,30,39,43]. However, for many commonly used ontologies, such a database of facts is not available. In this paper, we therefore address the challenge of predicting plausible missing rules based only on the rules that are in a given ontology (along with word embeddings in some variants of our proposed model).

This problem has thus far hardly received any attention, with the exception of [9]. The main underlying idea behind the approach from [9], which we will build on in this paper, is that ontologies often contain large sets of rules which only differ in one predicate. As a simple example, consider the following rules

$$\mathit{Beer}(x) \rightarrow R(x)$$
$$\mathit{Gin}(x) \rightarrow R(x)$$

Without knowing what the predicate R represents, we can infer that the following rule is also valid:

$$\mathit{Wine}(x) \rightarrow R(x)$$

This is intuitively because almost all natural properties which beer and gin have in common are also satisfied by wine. To formalize this intuition, [9] considered the notion of rule templates.

A rule template ρ is a second-order predicate, which corresponds to a rule in which one predicate occurrence has been replaced by a placeholder. For example, in the above example, we can consider a template ρ such that $\rho(P)$ holds if the rule $P(x) \rightarrow R(x)$ is valid, meaning that we would expect this rule to be entailed by the ontology if the ontology were complete. Given such a template ρ, we can consider the set of all instances $P_1, ..., P_n$ such that the corresponding rules $\rho(P_1), ..., \rho(P_n)$ are entailed by the given ontology. The main strategy for finding plausible rules proposed in [9] then essentially consists in finding predicates P which are similar to $P_1, ..., P_n$. More precisely, the predicates are represented as vectors and it is assumed that each template ρ can be modelled as a Gaussian distribution over the considered vector space, i.e. the probability that $\rho(P)$ is a valid rule is considered to be proportional to $\mathcal{G}_\rho(\mathbf{p})$, with $\mathbf{p}$ the vector representation of P and $\mathcal{G}_\rho$ the Gaussian distribution modelling ρ. In addition to the templates described above, which are called *unary templates*, [9] also considered *binary templates*, which correspond to rules in which two predicate occurrences have been replaced by a placeholder. While unary templates enable a strategy known as interpolation, using binary templates leads to a form of analogical reasoning, both of which are well-established commonsense reasoning principles.

A critical aspect of this strategy for ontology completion is how the vector representation of the predicates is obtained. The approach from [9] relies on the combination of two types of vectors: (i) the word vector of the predicate name, obtained from a standard pre-trained word embedding [28]; (ii) a vector representation which is learned from the ontology itself, using a variant of the AnalogySpace method [40]. However, there are important limitations with this strategy. For instance, it is not clear why the predicates that satisfy a given template should follow a Gaussian distribution in the considered vector space. Moreover, the way in which the predicate representations are constructed does not maximally take advantage of the available information. In particular, the approach based on the AnalogySpace method only relies on the known instances of the unary templates, i.e. binary templates are completely ignored for constructing the vector representations of the predicates. This is clearly sub-optimal, as knowing that $\rho(P, R)$ is a valid rule, for a given binary template ρ, intuitively tells us something about the semantic relationship between the predicates P and R, which should in turn allow us to improve our representation of P and R.

In this paper, we introduce a new method for predicting plausible rules which addresses both concerns. Our model is based on Graph Convolutional Networks (GCNs), a popular neural network architecture for graph-structured data [12,22,37]. We start from a graph-based representation of the rule base, in which the nodes correspond to predicates. Each node is annotated with a vector representation of the corresponding predicate. In this paper, we will use the vector representations from [9] for this purpose. Crucially, however, rather than using these vectors directly for making predictions as in [9], in our case they are merely used for initializing the GCN. Edges are annotated with the binary templates that are satisfied by the corresponding pair of predicates. We then propose a GCN model, which iteratively refines the vector encoding of the nodes, taking advantage of the edge annotations based on the binary templates. The resulting node vectors are then used to predict which predicates satisfy the different unary templates and which pairs of predicates satisfy the different binary templates, and thus to predict which rules are plausible. Note in particular, that our aim is to *learn* a vector representation of the predicates which is predictive of plausible rules, rather than relying on assumptions about a given vector representation. Our experimental results confirm that this approach is able to substantially outperform the method from [9].

2 Related Work

Within the area of knowledge base completion, we can broadly distinguish between two classes of methods: methods focused on finding plausible facts and methods focused on finding plausible rules.

Predicting Facts. In the last few years, there has been a large amount of work on finding missing triples in knowledge graphs. A popular strategy for this task is to rely on knowledge graph embedding, which aims to identify plausible triples by representing entities as vectors in a low-dimensional vector space and learning a parametrized scoring function for each relation. For instance, in the influential TransE model, relations are modelled as translations between the embeddings of entities [7], that is, $\mathbf{e}_h + \mathbf{e}_r \approx \mathbf{e}_t$, if $(h,\ r,\ t)$ holds. Some other well-known approaches make use of bilinear scoring functions. For example, in [47] the authors propose to learn entity embeddings such that $\mathbf{e}_h^{\mathrm{T}}\mathbf{R}_r\mathbf{e}_t$ is higher for correct triples (h, r, t) than for incorrect triples. Here $\mathbf{e}_h$ and $\mathbf{e}_t$ are the embeddings of the entities h and t, and $\mathbf{R}_r$ is a diagonal matrix representing the relation r. The ComplEx model [42] is an extension of [47] in the complex space. A different strategy consists in learning latent soft clusters of predicates to predict missing facts in relational data, for example by using Markov logic network [23] or by applying neural network models [35,39]. Several rule-based approaches have also been proposed, where observed regularities in the given knowledge graph are summarized as a weighted set of rules, which is then used to derive plausible missing facts. For instance, a soft inference procedure was proposed in [25] to infer different relations by tuning the weights associated with random walks that follow different paths through the graph. [15] proposed a novel method with iterative guidance from soft rules with various confidence levels extracted automatically from the knowledge graph. The aforementioned strategies all rely on exploiting statistical regularities in the given knowledge graph. There are also several ways in which external knowledge can be used to predict missing facts. One possibility is to rely on information extraction from text corpora [1,24]. In this setting, one can distinguish between methods based on a generic question answering system [44] and methods which use the given knowledge bases as a distant supervision signal [29,33]. Apart from directly relying on text corpora, some approaches have instead relied on pre-trained entity embeddings, which can be learned from open-domain resources such as Wikipedia, WikiData or BabelNet [11,19]. For instance [8] focused on finding missing instances of concepts in the context of ontologies, by modelling these concepts as Gaussians in a given vector space. This problem of ABox induction was also considered in [6], which instead relied on kernels for structured data to capture similarities between entities. A similar problem was also considered in [31], which relied on features that were directly derived from Wikipedia. Finally, various approaches have also been proposed to combine the two main aforementioned strategies, for example by incorporating textual descriptions of entities when learning knowledge graph embeddings [20,45,46,48], or by incorporating relation extraction methods [34,41].

Predicting Rules. The problem of learning rules, in the context of ontologies, has been approached from two different angles. First, we can identify methods that induce rules based on the given (relational) facts, e.g. based on ideas from the field of Statistical Relational Learning. For example, [10] proposed a system inspired by inductive logic programming, while [43] introduced statistical schema induction to mine association rule from RDF data and then generate ontologies. More recently, [39] used so-called Lifted Relational Neural Networks to learn rules in an implicit way. In [30], meta-rules were found automatically by meta-interpretive learning. Some other methods, e.g. [3], used Formal Concept

Analysis. What all these approaches have in common is that a sufficiently large database is required to be able to learn rules from a given ontology, which is however, not the case for the majority of available ontologies on the Web. The second class of methods is concerned with predicting rules directly from the ontology itself, which did not receive much attention yet. From a purely theoretical side, this problem has been studied in a propositional setting in [38], where methods based on interpolation and extrapolation of rules were proposed. However, the implementation of these methods requires some background knowledge (e.g. a betweenness relation is required to apply interpolation), which is not often available. In [5], a method that implements a kind of similarity based reasoning using Markov logic has been proposed in order to find plausible rules. The idea of similarity based reasoning has been also pursued in logic programming to extend the unification mechanism [27,36]. As already mentioned in Sect. 1, [9] recently proposed a method that relies on the notion of rule templates and the estimation of Gaussian distributions over predicate embeddings to make predictions.

Graph Convolutional Networks. In this paper, we use a variant of Graph Convolutional Networks (GCNs) to learn a vector representation of the predicates that occur in our rule base which is suitable for predicting plausible rules. GCNs are a generalization of Convolutional Neural Networks (CNNs). Whereas the latter require data with a regular structure, such as images or sequences, GCNs allow for irregular graph-structured data. GCNs can learn to extract features from the given node representations, and compose these features to construct highly expressive node vectors. These node vectors can then be used in a wide variety of graph-related tasks, such as graph classification [12] and graph generation [14]. Recently, researchers have applied GCNs to find missing facts in knowledge bases [16,37]. For example, [16] use GCNs for the standard triple classification and out-of-knowledge-base entity problems. Schlichtkrull et al. [37] model multi-relational data using GCNs for entity classification and link prediction. However, to our knowledge, this paper is to first to use GCNs for rule base completion.

3 A GCN Model for Rule Induction

Let $\mathcal{R}$ be a rule base, i.e. a set of rules. Our aim is to find additional rules that intuitively appear to be plausible, even if they cannot be deduced from $\mathcal{R}$. Throughout our description, we will assume that $\mathcal{R}$ contains existential rules [4], i.e. rules of the following form:

$$r_1(\mathbf{x_1}) \wedge ... \wedge r_n(\mathbf{x_n}) \rightarrow \exists \mathbf{y} \,.\, s_1(\mathbf{z_1}) \wedge ... \wedge s_m(\mathbf{z_m}) \qquad (1)$$

where $\mathbf{x_1}, ..., \mathbf{x_n}, \mathbf{y}, \mathbf{z_1}, ..., \mathbf{z_m}$ are tuples of variables. We consider existential rules because they are an expressive and well-studied framework for representing ontologies. However, because our method treats these rules as purely syntactic objects, it is in fact not tied to any particular logical framework or semantics. We could readily apply the same method to description logics, for instance.

3.1 Graph Representation of the Rule Base

Before we introduce our proposed method in Sect. 3.2, we now first describe how the rule base $\mathcal{R}$ can be encoded as a graph.

Rule Templates. As mentioned in Sect. 1, our graph encoding of the rule base will rely on the notion of rule templates from [9]. Rule templates are second-order predicates, which correspond to a rule in which one (for unary templates) or two (for binary templates) occurrences of a predicate have been replaced by a placeholder. For a unary template ρ and a predicate P, we write $\rho(P)$ to denote the rule that is obtained by instantiating the placeholder with P, and similar for binary templates. We say that P satisfies ρ if $\rho(P)$ is a valid rule in the considered domain. If $\mathcal{R}$ were complete, then P would satisfy ρ iff $\mathcal{R}$ entails $\rho(P)$. In general, however, the rule base $\mathcal{R}$ is incomplete, which means that it only partially specifies which predicates satisfy the template ρ. In particular, suppose that $P_1, ..., P_n$ are all the predicates for which $\rho(P_i)$ can be deduced from the given rule base $\mathcal{R}$. Then $P_1, ..., P_n$ are the only predicates which are known to satisfy the template ρ. The problem we consider below is to identify additional predicates P which are likely to satisfy ρ, or equivalently, identify rules of the form $\rho(P)$ which are valid in the considered domain but missing from the given rule base. However, rather than considering this problem for a single template, we consider all the possible templates that occur in $\mathcal{R}$.

Let θ be an existential rule of the form (1). Then θ is associated with the following unary templates:

$$\rho_1(\star) = \star(\mathbf{x_1}) \wedge ... \wedge r_n(\mathbf{x_n}) \rightarrow \exists \mathbf{y}.s_1(\mathbf{z_1}) \wedge ... \wedge s_m(\mathbf{z_m})$$

$$...$$

$$\rho_{n+m}(\star) = r_1(\mathbf{x_1}) \wedge ... \wedge r_n(\mathbf{x_n}) \rightarrow \exists \mathbf{y}.s_1(\mathbf{z_1}) \wedge ... \wedge \star(\mathbf{z_m})$$

as well as the following binary templates:

$$\rho_{1,2}(\star, \bullet) = \star(\mathbf{x_1}) \wedge \bullet(\mathbf{x_2}) \wedge ... \wedge r_n(\mathbf{x_n}) \rightarrow \exists \mathbf{y}.s_1(\mathbf{z_1}) \wedge ... \wedge s_m(\mathbf{z_m})$$

$$...$$

$$\rho_{1,n+m}(\star, \bullet) = \star(\mathbf{x_1}) \wedge r_2(\mathbf{x_2}) \wedge ... \wedge r_n(\mathbf{x_n}) \rightarrow \exists \mathbf{y}.s_1(\mathbf{z_1}) \wedge ... \wedge \bullet(\mathbf{z_m})$$

$$...$$

$$\rho_{n+m-1,n+m}(\star, \bullet) = r_1(\mathbf{x_1}) \wedge ... \wedge r_n(\mathbf{x_n}) \rightarrow \exists \mathbf{y}.s_1(\mathbf{z_1}) \wedge ... \wedge \star(\mathbf{z_{m-1}}) \wedge \bullet(\mathbf{z_m})$$

In addition to these templates, we also consider typed templates. In particular, assume that the predicates are organized in a taxonomy and let ρ be a rule template that was obtained by replacing the predicate P in the rule θ by a placeholder. Let Q be a parent of P in the taxonomy (i.e. we have that $\mathcal{R}$ contains the rule $P(x) \rightarrow Q(x)$). Then the corresponding typed version of ρ, denoted by ρ^Q, is satisfied by those predicates P' that satisfy ρ and that also have Q as a direct parent.

We denote respectively by $\mathcal{L}_1(\theta)$ and $\mathcal{L}_2(\theta)$ the set of all unary and binary templates that can be obtained from the rule θ (including both typed and untyped templates). We also let $\mathcal{L}_1(\mathcal{R}) = \bigcup_{\theta \in \mathcal{R}} \mathcal{L}_1(\theta)$ and $\mathcal{L}_2(\mathcal{R}) = \bigcup_{\theta \in \mathcal{R}} \mathcal{L}_2(\theta)$ be respectively the set of all unary and binary templates that can be obtained from the set of rules $\mathcal{R}$.

Graph Representation. We encode the rule base $\mathcal{R}$ as a graph $\mathcal{G}_{\mathcal{R}} = (\mathcal{P}_{\mathcal{R}}, \mathcal{E})$ where $\mathcal{P}_{\mathcal{R}}$ is a set of all predicates that occur in $\mathcal{R}$ and $\mathcal{E}$ contains all pairs of predicates (P, Q) that co-occur in at least one rule in $\mathcal{R}$. To capture the knowledge encoded in the rule base (as well as potentially some external knowledge), we use two labelling functions. The node labelling function η maps each predicate P from $\mathcal{P}_{\mathcal{R}}$ onto a real valued vector $\eta(P) \in \mathbb{R}^d$. This vector can be viewed as the input encoding of the predicate P and can be defined in different ways (see below). The edge labelling function ξ maps each pair of predicates (P, Q) from $\mathcal{E}$ onto a binary vector $\xi(P, Q) \in \{0, 1\}^m$, where $m = |\mathcal{L}_2(\mathcal{R})|$. In particular, let $\rho_1, ..., \rho_m$ be an enumeration of all binary templates from $\mathcal{L}_2(\mathcal{R})$. The ith coordinate of the vector $\xi(P, Q)$ is 1 iff the rule $\rho_i(P, Q)$ occurs in $\mathcal{R}$.

Node Vectors. To construct the input encoding $\eta(P)$ of predicate P, we will either use a vector $\eta_w(P)$ derived from the name of predicate P using a standard pre-trained word embedding, or a vector $\eta_t(P)$ that encodes which of the unary templates from $\mathcal{L}_1(\mathcal{R})$ are satisfied by P. Specifically, to obtain the vector $\eta_w(P)$, we first tokenize the predicate name using a small set of simple heuristics, based on standard ontology naming conventions[1]. For example, the predicate name *RedWine* gives the following list of words: (*red*, *wine*). Let $(w_1, ..., w_n)$ be the list of words thus obtained, then the vector representation $\eta_w(P)$ of P is simply obtained by averaging the vector representations of these words. Namely, $\eta_w(P) = \frac{1}{n}(\mathbf{w_1} + ... + \mathbf{w_n})$, where $\mathbf{w_i}$ denotes for the vector representation of word w_i in the word embedding. Even though this averaging strategy may seem naive, it is known to be surprisingly effective for capturing the meaning of phrases and sentences [17].

The vector $\eta_t(P)$, encoding knowledge about P derived from the unary templates, is constructed as follows. First, we consider a binary vector $\eta_t^B(P) \in \{0, 1\}^k$ with $k = |\mathcal{L}_1(\mathcal{R})|$, whose i^{th} coordinate is 1 iff the ith unary template, in some arbitrary but fixed enumeration of the unary templates, is satisfied by P. In other words, η_t^B is thus the counterpart of ξ for unary templates. We then define $\eta_t(P) \in \mathbb{R}^l$ as the a low-dimensional approximation of η_t^B, obtained using singular value decomposition (SVD) as in [9]. In particular, let X be a matrix with one row for each predicate, where the row corresponding to P is given by the vector $\eta_t^B(P_i)$. Let $X = U \Sigma V^T$ be the singular value decomposition of X. Then $\eta_t(P)$ is given by the first l columns of the row corresponding to P in the matrix $U\Sigma$. This use of the singular value decomposition is a well-known technique to compress the information encoded in the vectors $\eta_t^B(P)$ into a lower-dimensional representation. Note that the vectors $\eta_t(P)$ and $\eta_t(Q)$ will be similar if the sets of unary templates satisfied by P and Q are similar.

[1] http://wiki.opensemanticframework.org/index.php/Ontology_Best_Practices.

3.2 GCN Model

Background. Graph Convolutional Networks (GCNs) produce node-level embeddings of graphs, by iteratively exchanging the current vector representations of the nodes along the edges of the graph. GCNs are thus essentially message-passing models. Let us write $\mathbf{h}_i^{(0)}$ for the initial vector representation of node n_i. A GCN iteratively refines this representation based on the following propagation rule [13]:

$$\mathbf{h}_i^{(l+1)} = \sigma\left(\sum_{j \in \mathcal{N}_i} f\left(\mathbf{h}_i^{(l)}, \mathbf{h}_j^{(l)}\right)\right) \tag{2}$$

where $\mathcal{N}_i$ is the neighborhood of n_i, i.e. the set of nodes that are incident with n_i. Furthermore, $f(\cdot,\cdot)$ is a transformation function, which is used to combine the current representation of n_i with the current representation of a given neighbor n_j. Both linear and non-linear transformations can be used for this purpose, but we will restrict ourselves to linear transformations in this paper. These transformed representations are intuitively viewed as messages which are sent from the neighbors of n_i. These messages are then aggregated (using a summation) after which a non-linear activation function σ is used. We will use the ReLU function for this purpose, defined by $\sigma(x) = \max(0, x)$.

Model Description. The standard formulation in (2) does not take into account edge labels, which play an important role in our setting as they encode the nature of the relationship between the (predicates corresponding to the) two nodes. Let us write $\mathcal{N}_P^{\rho_i}$ for the set of all nodes Q that are connected with P in our graph for which (P, Q) is an instance of the binary template ρ_i, i.e. $(P, Q) \in \mathcal{E}_{\mathcal{R}}$ and the ith component of $\xi(P, Q)$ is 1.

We specifically consider the following variant:

$$\mathbf{h}_P^{(l+1)} = \sigma\left(\mathbf{W}_0^{(l)}\mathbf{h}_P^{(l)} + \sum_{\rho \in \mathcal{L}_2(\mathcal{R})} \sum_{Q \in \mathcal{N}_P^{\rho}} \frac{1}{|\mathcal{N}_P^{\rho}|}\mathbf{W}_\rho^{(l)}\mathbf{h}_Q^{(l)}\right) \tag{3}$$

where we write $\mathbf{h}_P^{(l)}$ for the embeddings of the (node corresponding to) predicate P. In the input layer, $\mathbf{h}_P^{(0)}$ is the vector representation of the node P given by the label $\eta(P)$. The matrix $\mathbf{W}_\rho^{(l)}$ encodes a template-specific linear transformation, which together with the node transformation $\mathbf{W}_0^{(l)}$ defines the l-th layer of our model.

We now describe how the GCN model can be used to predict plausible instances of the considered unary and binary templates. Note that each such a prediction corresponds to the prediction of a plausible rule, as mentioned in Sect. 3.1.

Unary Template Prediction. We treat the problem of predicting plausible instances of unary templates as a multi-label node classification problem. To this end, we add an output layer to the GCN which has one neuron for each unary template and each predicate, i.e. for each predicate-template combination we make a prediction about whether the template applies to that predicate. We use a sigmoid activation function for this output layer and we use the cross-entropy loss function to train the model:

$$J = -\sum_{\rho \in \mathcal{L}_1(\mathcal{R})} \sum_{Q \in \mathcal{P}_{\mathcal{R}}} y_Q^\rho \log(p_Q^\rho) + (1 - y_Q^\rho) \log(1 - p_Q^\rho)$$

where $p_Q^\rho \in [0, 1]$ is the model's prediction that predicate Q satisfies template ρ and $y_Q^\rho \in \{0, 1\}$ is the corresponding ground truth, i.e. $y_Q^\rho = 1$ iff $\rho(Q)$ can be entailed from $\mathcal{R}$. Note that when training this model, we thus implicitly assume that the rule base $\mathcal{R}$ is complete. However, the capacity of the GCN model is not sufficient to perfectly satisfy this training objective, which means that it will make some mistakes and predict some rules which are, in fact, not entailed by $\mathcal{R}$. These "mistakes" then correspond to the rules which we view to be plausible. Indeed, the reason why the GCN model predicts such a rule $\rho(P)$ is it is not able to separate P from the predicates that are known to satisfy ρ, which suggests that P is semantically similar to such predicates, and thus that $\rho(P)$ should be considered as plausible.

For the ease of presentation, in the formulation of the loss function above, we assumed that all templates are untyped. For typed templates, rather than considering all predicates $Q \in \mathcal{P}_{\mathcal{R}}$, we only consider those of the correct type. Furthermore, in the experiments, we add the following regularization term to the loss function, which we empirically found to be helpful:

$$J_{reg} = \sum_{\rho \in \mathcal{L}_2(\mathcal{R})} \sum_{(Q,S) \in \mathcal{N}_P^\rho} \|\mathbf{h}_Q - \mathbf{h}_S\|_2^2$$

where we write $\mathbf{h}_P$ for the embedding of predicate P in the final layer. Note that this regularization is thus only applied to the final embeddings, i.e. the layer before the classification layer, instead of all layers.

The intuitive justification is that predicates which often co-occur in the same rule are likely to be semantically related. This is particularly useful because the majority of the rules in a typical ontology are basic subsumption rules of the form $P(x) \rightarrow Q(x)$. In some cases, we do not have much information about the parent concept Q (e.g. because Q is an abstract concept), in which case the regularization term will encourage its representation to be close to the average of the representations of its children. Conversely, it may also be the case that we instead do not have much information about P (e.g. because it is too specialized), in which case the regularization term would encourage the representation of P to stay close to the representation of its parent.

Binary Template Prediction. We view the problem of predicting binary template instances as a link prediction problem. For each pair of predicates (P, Q) from

$\mathcal{P}_\mathcal{R}$ and each binary template $\rho \in \mathcal{L}_2(\mathcal{R})$, the task is to predict whether (P, Q) satisfies ρ. To this end, we need a scoring function for each template ρ such that $s_\rho(P, Q)$ is high for valid pairs (P, Q) and low for other pairs. In principle, any of the scoring functions that have been proposed for knowledge graph embedding could be used for this purpose. In our experiments, we will use the following bilinear scoring function [47]:

$$s(P, \rho, Q) = \mathbf{h}_P^T \mathbf{R}_\rho \mathbf{h}_Q,$$

where $\mathbf{h}_P$ and $\mathbf{h}_Q$ are the final-layer vector representations of the predicates, as before. Furthermore, $\mathbf{R}_\rho$ is a diagonal matrix which corresponds to the representation that is learned for the binary template ρ. Note that while this scoring function is symmetric, this symmetry is broken in practice when using typed binary templates. This is because the only situation in which both the rules $\rho(P, Q)$ and $\rho(Q, P)$ would be considered is when they are of the same type (i.e. they have the same parent), which is almost never the case. In order to train the model, we sample negative examples by randomly corrupting one of the predicates in positive examples. We apply a sigmoid function to the scoring function and then again train the model using a cross-entropy loss.

4 Model Evaluation

In this section, we experimentally evaluate our method[2], comparing it against the method from [9] as our baseline.

Methodology. The datasets we consider are constructed from the OWL version of the following ontologies: SUMO[3], which is a large open domain ontology, as well as Wine[4], Economy[5], Transport[6] and Olympics[7], which are smaller domain-specific ontologies. These OWL ontologies were then converted into existential rules (where we simply omitted those OWL axioms that cannot be expressed in this way). In the experiments, we use a standard pre-trained 300-dimensional word embedding learned using Skip-gram on the 100B words Google News corpus[8].

To evaluate the performance of our model, we split the considered rule bases into training and test sets. We use 10-fold cross validation for the small ontologies, while for the larger SUMO ontology, we use a fixed 2/3 split for training and 1/3 for testing. After splitting each rule base, we applied Pellet Reasoner[9]

[2] Implementation and data are available at https://github.com/bzdt/GCN-based-Ontology-Completion.git.
[3] http://www.adampease.org/OP/.
[4] https://www.w3.org/TR/2003/PR-owl-guide-20031215/wine.
[5] http://reliant.teknowledge.com/DAML/Economy.owl.
[6] http://reliant.teknowledge.com/DAML/Transportation.owl.
[7] http://swat.cse.lehigh.edu/resources/onto/olympics.owl.
[8] https://code.google.com/archive/p/word2vec/.
[9] https://github.com/stardog-union/pellet.

Table 1. Parameter settings for *GCN* models.

		Wine		Economy		Olympics		Transport		SUMO	
		UT	BT	UT	BT	UT	BT	UT	BT	UT	BT
GCN_{mf}	lr	0.01	0.001	0.01	0.001	0.01	0.001	0.01	0.001	0.01	0.001
GCN_{mf}	hid	32	32	64	32	32	32	64	32	32	32
GCN_{mf}	ly	3	4	3	4	3	4	3	4	5	5
GCN_{mf}	l2	0	0.1	0	0.1	0	0.1	0	0.1	0	0.1
GCN_{we}	lr	0.01	0.001	0.01	0.001	0.01	0.001	0.01	0.001	0.01	0.001
GCN_{we}	hid	32	32	64	32	32	32	64	32	32	32
GCN_{we}	ly	3	4	3	4	3	4	3	4	5	5
GCN_{we}	l2	0	0.1	0	0.1	0	0.1	0	0.1	0	0.1
GCN_{cm}	lr	0.01	0.001	0.01	0.001	0.01	0.001	0.01	0.001	0.01	0.001
GCN_{cm}	hid	32	32	64	32	32	32	64	32	32	32
GCN_{cm}	ly	3	4	3	4	3	4	3	4	5	6
GCN_{cm}	l2	0.1	0.1	0	0.1	0	0.1	0	0.1	0	0.1
GCN_{con}	lr	0.01	0.001	0.01	0.001	0.01	0.001	0.01	0.001	0.01	0.001
GCN_{con}	hid	32	128	64	32	64	64	32	64	32	32
GCN_{con}	ly	3	4	3	4	4	4	3	4	5	6
GCN_{con}	l2	0	0.1	0	0.1	0	0.1	0	0.1	0	0.1

to determine all rules that can be derived from each training split. Subsequently, we removed from the corresponding test split all rules that could be derived from the training split. The derived rules are kept in the training split, i.e. we apply our model to the deductive closure of the rules in the training data.

Clearly, because it is based on rule templates, our GCN model can only predict rules that correspond to instances of rule templates which occur in the training data. Our evaluation therefore focuses on predicting, for all of the unary (resp. binary) templates found in the training data, which predicates (resp. pairs of predicates) are likely to satisfy them, beyond those instances that are already found in the training data. Furthermore, we can only make predictions about predicates that occur in the training data, so any predicates that only appear in the test split are also ignored.

For evaluation purposes, we assume that a prediction is correct iff the corresponding rule can be derived from the given ontology (i.e. training and test split). This is clearly a simplifying assumption, given that our starting point is that some valid rules are actually missing. As a result, the reported evaluation scores should be viewed as a lower approximation of the performance of the methods (given that some predictions which are assessed to be false may actually be correct rules that were missing in the original ontology). Importantly, however, this still allows us to compare the relative performance of different methods. This evaluation strategy follows common practice in the context of knowledge base completion (e.g. the standard benchmarks for knowledge graph completion also rely on this simplifying assumption).

We choose the number of layers according to the size of the ontology. For small ontologies (e.g. Wine), a limited number of layers is preferable to avoid overfitting, while for larger ontologies (e.g. SUMO), it makes sense to use more layers as more training data is available for these cases. Specifically, for unary template prediction, we use a model consisting of 3 GCN layers for the small datasets (which includes the output layer), and 5 GCN layers for SUMO. For the first two layers we use a ReLU activation function, while sigmoid is used for the output layer. Regardless of the number of GCN layers, sigmoid is always used for the last layer and ReLU for the other layers. For the binary template prediction, we use 2 GCN layers with ReLU activation for the small datasets, and 3 GCN layers for SUMO. This is followed by a scoring layer and a fully connected layer using sigmoid. Crucially, to avoid overfitting and encourage the model to generalize beyond the given instances of the templates, we apply dropout (dropout rate = 0.5) to the hidden layers. We also use L2-norm regularization, which encourages the model to focus on the most informative binary templates only when aggregating the messages (noting that the model would converge to $\mathbf{W}_{\rho}^{(l)} = 0$ if template ρ were not informative). We have implemented the model in the Deep Graph Library (DGL)[10], using the Adam optimizer [21] for training. We considered four variants of the GCN model:

- GCN_{mf} uses the $\eta_t(P)$ vector based on SVD decomposition as initial representation of P.
- GCN_{we} uses the predicate representations $\eta_w(P)$ obtained from the word embedding as input vectors.
- GCN_{cm} combines the two independent models, i.e. it trains models for both $\eta_t(P)$ and $\eta_w(P)$ independently, and combines their predictions. We calculate the performance measures of the union set of the rules predicted using both models. For a given rule, as long as one of the two models predicts it correctly, it is considered a correct prediction.
- GCN_{con} combines the two representations, i.e. it uses the concatenation of $\eta_t(P)$ and $\eta_w(P)$ as the input encoding of P.

As our baseline, we consider the model from [9], which we will refer to as BRI. We consider four variants of this model, being direct counterparts to the four variants of our model:

- BRI_{mf} uses the $\eta_t(P)$ vector to represent predicates.
- BRI_{we} uses the representation $\eta_w(P)$ based on word vectors.
- BRI_{cm} combines the predictions of the BRI_{mf} and BRI_{we} models.
- BRI_{con} uses the concatenation of $\eta_t(P)$ and $\eta_w(P)$.

To tune the parameters of the models, we randomly select 10% of the training data as a validation set. The parameters to be tuned include the learning rate

[10] https://docs.dgl.ai.

Table 2. Results of the rule induction experiments.

		Wine		Economy		Olympics		Transport		SUMO	
		UT	BT	UT	BT	UT	BT	UT	BT	UT	BT
BRI_{mf}	Pr	0.030	0.583	0.091	0.992	0.150	0.286	0.000	0.600	0.534	1.000
BRI_{mf}	Rec	0.045	0.180	0.070	0.309	0.108	0.191	0.000	0.173	0.201	0.072
BRI_{mf}	F1	0.032	0.259	0.075	0.445	0.114	0.214	0.000	0.251	0.292	0.134
BRI_{we}	Pr	0.118	0.400	0.093	0.993	0.307	0.286	0.000	1.000	0.791	0.969
BRI_{we}	Rec	0.311	0.073	0.294	0.599	0.225	0.238	0.000	0.464	0.287	0.328
BRI_{we}	F1	0.159	0.124	0.138	0.742	0.234	0.257	0.000	0.609	0.421	0.490
BRI_{cm}	Pr	0.118	0.700	0.089	**0.992**	0.407	0.250	0.000	**1.000**	0.802	0.971
BRI_{cm}	Rec	0.331	0.234	0.297	**0.627**	0.325	0.250	0.000	**0.538**	0.316	0.348
BRI_{cm}	F1	0.162	0.330	0.135	**0.765**	0.334	0.250	0.000	**0.667**	0.453	0.513
BRI_{con}	Pr	0.094	0.600	0.072	0.855	0.200	0.286	0.000	0.367	0.250	0.750
BRI_{con}	Rec	0.102	0.288	0.101	0.267	0.050	0.191	0.000	0.132	0.002	0.015
BRI_{con}	F1	0.085	0.364	0.083	0.387	0.079	0.214	0.000	0.187	0.005	0.030
GCN_{mf}	Pr	0.489	0.475	**0.750**	0.733	0.278	0.286	0.010	0.400	0.543	0.732
GCN_{mf}	Rec	0.349	0.244	**0.153**	0.180	0.292	0.286	0.018	0.077	0.421	0.409
GCN_{mf}	F1	0.334	0.313	**0.243**	0.269	0.273	0.286	0.013	0.125	0.474	0.524
GCN_{we}	Pr	0.645	0.900	0.172	0.911	0.350	0.429	0.020	0.850	0.719	0.836
GCN_{we}	Rec	0.259	0.356	0.218	0.526	0.392	0.429	0.033	0.267	0.396	0.493
GCN_{we}	F1	0.355	0.488	0.183	0.651	0.328	0.429	0.021	0.387	0.510	0.620
GCN_{cm}	Pr	0.465	0.875	0.175	0.891	**0.465**	0.429	0.118	0.850	**0.778**	**0.884**
GCN_{cm}	Rec	0.382	0.444	0.232	0.591	**0.533**	0.429	0.033	0.313	**0.437**	**0.516**
GCN_{cm}	F1	0.353	0.563	0.189	0.688	**0.463**	0.429	0.036	0.434	**0.559**	**0.651**
GCN_{con}	Pr	**0.416**	**0.900**	0.163	0.912	0.233	**0.857**	**0.371**	0.454	0.692	0.812
GCN_{con}	Rec	**0.356**	**0.476**	0.245	0.585	0.267	**0.762**	**0.044**	0.139	0.374	0.485
GCN_{con}	F1	**0.356**	**0.607**	0.191	0.698	0.242	**0.786**	**0.077**	0.201	0.485	0.607

(chosen from {0.1, 0.01, 0.001}) for Adam optimization, the number of units in the hidden layers (chosen from {16, 32, 64, 128, 256}), the dimensionality of the input encodings of the predicates in cases where we use the SVD based method (chosen from {20, 30, 40, 50, 100}) and the threshold for classification and the hyperparameter for L2 regularization. Table 1 reports the different settings that were selected. The trade-off hyperparameters of the regularizer J_{reg} for unary template prediction are 0.01 for the Economy and Transport ontologies and 0.1 for Wine and Olympics ontologies. We use the same parameters for each fold. For instance, for the Wine ontology, the number of units is 32 and we use a 40-dimensional input encoding of the predicates. The hyperparameter for L2 is set to 0 for the unary template prediction and to 0.1 for binary template prediction respectively.

Quantitative Evaluation. Table 2 reports the performance of the different models in terms of precision (Pr), recall (Rec) and F1 score. Note that both unary template predictions and binary template predictions are the multi-label classification tasks. However, what matters in the prediction is not how many nodes or links are classified correctly, but how successful the models are at predicting missing rules. Therefore, the precision, recall and F1 scores are computed w.r.t. the number of correctly predicted rules instead. In all cases, we use micro-averaging to calculate the overall precision, recall and F1 scores.

The results in Table 2 show that the GCN model is indeed able to outperform the BRI model from [9]. The table separately shows the performance of models which only rely on unary templates (UT) for predicting plausible rules and models which only rely on binary templates (BT). As can be seen, for UT, the GCN models consistently, and often substantially, outperform the BRI counterparts, which demonstrates that the GCN models are able to improve the representation of the predicates by propagating and incorporating the information received from related predicates. In the case of the BT results, the GCN models perform best on the Wine, Olympics and SUMO ontologies, but they perform less well on the Economy and Transport ontologies. This can be explained by the fact that the number of examples we have for each binary template in these cases is much lower, which can result in overfitting on the training data. In contrast, for SUMO, which is by far the largest ontology, the outperformance of our model is consistent and very substantial. Finally, when comparing the GCN_{mf} and GCN_{we} variants, we clearly see that using word embeddings to initialize the node vectors leads to the best results, although both models are outperformed by the concatenation based model GCN_{con} or the combined model GCN_{cm}. Comparing the performance of GCN_{cm} and GCN_{con}, we can see that the concatenation model GCN_{con} generally performs better. Interestingly, the difference in performance between GCN_{cm} and GCN_{con} is more mixed.

Qualitative Analysis. We illustrate the performance of the GCN model by discussing some examples of predicted rules. As an example from the UT setting, our model was able to correctly predict the following rule from the Wine ontology:

$$DryRedWine(x) \rightarrow TableWine(x)$$

by using the template $\rho(\star) = \star(x) \rightarrow TableWine(x)$. The instances of this template that were given in the training data are *RedTableWine*, *DryWhiteWine* and *Burgundy*. Based on these instances, the BRI model was not able to predict that *DryRedWine* is also a plausible instance. The GCN models, however, were able to exploit edges (i.e. binary templates) corresponding to the following rules:

$$\begin{aligned} Merlot(x) &\rightarrow DryRedWine(x) \\ Merlot(x) &\rightarrow RedTableWine(x) \\ DryRedWine(x) &\rightarrow DryWine(x) \\ DryWhiteWine(x) &\rightarrow DryWine(x) \\ Burgundy(x) &\rightarrow DryWine(x) \end{aligned}$$

As an example from the BT setting, the GCN model was able to correctly predict the following rule from the Olympics ontology:

$$WomansTeam(x) \rightarrow \exists y \,.\, hasMember(x, y) \wedge Woman(y)$$

based on the following rules from the training data:

$$MensTeam(x) \rightarrow \exists y\,.\,hasMember(x,y) \wedge Man(y)$$
$$MixedTeam(x) \rightarrow \exists y\,.\,hasMember(x,y) \wedge Woman(y)$$

This illustrates the ability of models based on binary templates to perform analogical reasoning. Note that this rule cannot be predicted in the setting where only unary templates are used.

From a practical perspective, an important question is whether our model is able to find rules which are missing from the existing ontologies, rather than merely identifying held-out rules (as we did in the experiments above). Here we present some examples of rules that were predicted by our model, but which cannot be deduced from the full ontologies. These predictions are based on a GCN model that was trained on the full ontologies. Some of the rules we obtained are as follows:

$$Cycle(x) \rightarrow LandVehicle(x)$$
$$AgriculturalProduct(x) \rightarrow Product(x) \wedge Exporting(x)$$
$$CargoShip(x) \rightarrow Ship(x) \wedge DryBulkCargo(x)$$

As can be seen, these rules intuitively make sense, which suggests that our approach could indeed be useful to suggest missing rules in a given ontology. Since there exists rule $Bicycle(x) \rightarrow Cycle(x)$ in the Transport ontology, which makes $Cycle(x) \rightarrow LandVehicle(x)$ plausible. $AgriculturalProduct(x) \rightarrow Product(x) \wedge Exporting(x)$ is plausible, here "Exporting", according to the Economy ontology, is employed in international trade, because of the rules $Exporting(x) \rightarrow ChangeOfPossession(x)$ and $Exporting(x) \rightarrow FinancialTransaction(x)$.

5 Conclusion

In this paper, we proposed a method for predicting plausible missing rules from a given ontology (or rule base) based on Graph Convolutional Networks (GCNs). To this end, we introduced an encoding of the ontology as a graph. We then introduced a GCN model that can take advantage of this graph encoding to predict rules in a more faithful way than existing methods. This is essentially due to the fact that the GCN model is able to derive structural features from the rule base, to learn much richer representations of predicates than those that are used in existing approaches.

The problem considered in this paper is not yet as mature as related topics such as knowledge graph completion, and accordingly there are still several important and interesting avenues for future work. One natural extension of our current approach would be to use a joint prediction framework, which would ensure that the collection of rules predicted by the model is consistent with the given rule base. Essentially, such an approach would be able to use the requirement that the set of rules needs to be logically consistent as a kind of additional supervision signal. More generally, there is a clear benefit in developing methods that can integrate induction (in the sense of predicting plausible rules) and deduction in a tighter way. In terms of the technical details of our GCN model, one area that could be improved is that the parameters which are learned for each of the binary templates are currently independent from each other, which can lead to overfitting, given the small number of instances of many templates. As a possible alternative, the edge labels could be replaced by a low rank approximation of the current binary vectors.

Acknowledgements. Steven Schockaert was supported by ERC Starting Grant 637277. Zied Bouraoui was supported by CNRS PEPS INS2I MODERN.

References

1. Alfarone, D., Davis, J.: Unsupervised learning of an IS-A taxonomy from a limited domain-specific corpus. In: Proceedings IJCAI, pp. 1434–1441 (2015)
2. Baader, F., Calvanese, D., McGuinness, D.L., Nardi, D., Patel-Schneider, P.F. (eds.): The Description Logic Handbook: Theory, Implementation, and Applications. Cambridge University Press, New York (2003)
3. Baader, F., Ganter, B., Sertkaya, B., Sattler, U.: Completing description logic knowledge bases using formal concept analysis. In: Proceedings IJCAI, vol. 7, pp. 230–235 (2007)
4. Baget, J., Leclère, M., Mugnier, M., Salvat, E.: On rules with existential variables: walking the decidability line. Artif. Intell. **175**(9–10), 1620–1654 (2011). https://doi.org/10.1016/j.artint.2011.03.002
5. Beltagy, I., Chau, C., Boleda, G., Garrette, D., Erk, K., Mooney, R.: Montague meets Markov: deep semantics with probabilistic logical form. In: Proceedings of *SEM13, pp. 11–21 (2013)
6. Bloehdorn, S., Sure, Y.: Kernel methods for mining instance data in ontologies. In: Aberer, K., et al. (eds.) ASWC/ISWC -2007. LNCS, vol. 4825, pp. 58–71. Springer, Heidelberg (2007). https://doi.org/10.1007/978-3-540-76298-0_5
7. Bordes, A., Usunier, N., Garcia-Duran, A., Weston, J., Yakhnenko, O.: Translating embeddings for modeling multi-relational data. In: Proceedings NIPS, pp. 2787–2795 (2013)
8. Bouraoui, Z., Jameel, S., Schockaert, S.: Inductive reasoning about ontologies using conceptual spaces. In: Proceedings AAAI, pp. 4364–4370 (2017)
9. Bouraoui, Z., Schockaert, S.: Automated rule base completion as Bayesian concept induction. In: Proceedings of the Thirty-Third AAAI Conference on Artificial Intelligence, Honolulu, Hawaii, USA, 27 January–1 February (2019)
10. Bühmann, L., Lehmann, J., Westphal, P.: Dl-learner–a framework for inductive learning on the semantic web. J. Web Semant. **39**, 15–24 (2016)
11. Camacho-Collados, J., Pilehvar, M.T., Navigli, R.: Nasari: integrating explicit knowledge and corpus statistics for a multilingual representation of concepts and entities. Artif. Intell. **240**, 36–64 (2016)
12. Duvenaud, D.K., et al.: Convolutional networks on graphs for learning molecular fingerprints. In: Advances in Neural Information Processing Systems, pp. 2224–2232 (2015)

13. Gilmer, J., Schoenholz, S.S., Riley, P.F., Vinyals, O., Dahl, G.E.: Neural message passing for quantum chemistry. In: Proceedings of the 34th International Conference on Machine Learning, vol. 70, pp. 1263–1272. JMLR. org (2017)
14. Grover, A., Zweig, A., Ermon, S.: Graphite: iterative generative modeling of graphs. arXiv preprint arXiv:1803.10459 (2018)
15. Guo, S., Wang, Q., Wang, L., Wang, B., Guo, L.: Knowledge graph embedding with iterative guidance from soft rules. In: Thirty-Second AAAI Conference on Artificial Intelligence (2018)
16. Hamaguchi, T., Oiwa, H., Shimbo, M., Matsumoto, Y.: Knowledge transfer for out-of-knowledge-base entities: a graph neural network approach. arXiv preprint arXiv:1706.05674 (2017)
17. Hill, F., Cho, K., Korhonen, A.: Learning distributed representations of sentences from unlabelled data. In: Proceedings NAACL-HLT, pp. 1367–1377 (2016)
18. Horrocks, I.: Ontologies and the semantic web. Commun. ACM **51**(12), 58–67 (2008). https://doi.org/10.1145/1409360.1409377
19. Jameel, S., Bouraoui, Z., Schockaert, S.: MEmbER: max-margin based embeddings for entity retrieval. In: Proceedings SIGIR, pp. 783–792 (2017)
20. Jameel, S., Schockaert, S.: Entity embeddings with conceptual subspaces as a basis for plausible reasoning. In: ECAI, pp. 1353–1361 (2016)
21. Kingma, D.P., Ba, J.: Adam: a method for stochastic optimization. arXiv preprint arXiv:1412.6980 (2014)
22. Kipf, T.N., Welling, M.: Semi-supervised classification with graph convolutional networks. arXiv preprint arXiv:1609.02907 (2016)
23. Kok, S., Domingos, P.: Statistical predicate invention. In: Proceedings ICML, pp. 433–440 (2007)
24. Kozareva, Z., Hovy, E.: A semi-supervised method to learn and construct taxonomies using the web. In: Proceedings EMNLP, pp. 1110–1118 (2010)
25. Lao, N., Mitchell, T., Cohen, W.W.: Random walk inference and learning in a large scale knowledge base. In: Proceedings EMNLP, pp. 529–539 (2011)
26. Lin, Y., Liu, Z., Luan, H., Sun, M., Rao, S., Liu, S.: Modeling relation paths for representation learning of knowledge bases. In: Proceedings of the 2015 Conference on Empirical Methods in Natural Language Processing, pp. 705–714 (2015)
27. Medina, J., Ojeda-Aciego, M., Vojtáš, P.: Similarity-based unification: a multi-adjoint approach. Fuzzy Sets Syst. **146**, 43–62 (2004)
28. Mikolov, T., Sutskever, I., Chen, K., Corrado, G.S., Dean, J.: Distributed representations of words and phrases and their compositionality. In: Proceedings of the 27th Annual Conference on Neural Information Processing Systems, pp. 3111–3119 (2013)
29. Mintz, M., Bills, S., Snow, R., Jurafsky, D.: Distant supervision for relation extraction without labeled data. In: Proceedings ACL, pp. 1003–1011 (2009)
30. Muggleton, S.H., Lin, D., Tamaddoni-Nezhad, A.: Meta-interpretive learning of higher-order dyadic datalog: predicate invention revisited. Mach. Learn. **100**(1), 49–73 (2015)
31. Neelakantan, A., Chang, M.: Inferring missing entity type instances for knowledge base completion: new dataset and methods. In: Proceedings NAACL, pp. 515–525 (2015)
32. Qian, W., Fu, C., Zhu, Y., Cai, D., He, X.: Translating embeddings for knowledge graph completion with relation attention mechanism. In: IJCAI, pp. 4286–4292 (2018)

33. Riedel, S., Yao, L., McCallum, A.: Modeling relations and their mentions without labeled text. In: Balcázar, J.L., Bonchi, F., Gionis, A., Sebag, M. (eds.) ECML PKDD 2010. LNCS, vol. 6323, pp. 148–163. Springer, Heidelberg (2010). https://doi.org/10.1007/978-3-642-15939-8_10
34. Riedel, S., Yao, L., McCallum, A., Marlin, B.M.: Relation extraction with matrix factorization and universal schemas. In: Proceedings HLT-NAACL, pp. 74–84 (2013)
35. Rocktäschel, T., Riedel, S.: Learning knowledge base inference with neural theorem provers. In: Proceedings of the 5th Workshop on Automated Knowledge Base Construction, pp. 45–50 (2016)
36. Rocktäschel, T., Riedel, S.: End-to-end differentiable proving. In: Proceedings NIPS, pp. 3791–3803 (2017)
37. Schlichtkrull, M., Kipf, T.N., Bloem, P., van den Berg, R., Titov, I., Welling, M.: Modeling relational data with graph convolutional networks. In: Gangemi, A., et al. (eds.) ESWC 2018. LNCS, vol. 10843, pp. 593–607. Springer, Cham (2018). https://doi.org/10.1007/978-3-319-93417-4_38
38. Schockaert, S., Prade, H.: Interpolative and extrapolative reasoning in propositional theories using qualitative knowledge about conceptual spaces. Artif. Intell. **202**, 86–131 (2013)
39. Šourek, G., Manandhar, S., Železný, F., Schockaert, S., Kuželka, O.: Learning predictive categories using lifted relational neural networks. In: Cussens, J., Russo, A. (eds.) ILP 2016. LNCS, vol. 10326, pp. 108–119. Springer, Cham (2017). https://doi.org/10.1007/978-3-319-63342-8_9
40. Speer, R., Havasi, C., Lieberman, H.: AnalogySpace: reducing the dimensionality of common sense knowledge. In: Proceedings AAAI, pp. 548–553 (2008)
41. Toutanova, K., Chen, D., Pantel, P., Poon, H., Choudhury, P., Gamon, M.: Representing text for joint embedding of text and knowledge bases. In: Proceedings of EMNLP-15, pp. 1499–1509 (2015)
42. Trouillon, T., Welbl, J., Riedel, S., Gaussier, É., Bouchard, G.: Complex embeddings for simple link prediction. In: Proceedings ICML, pp. 2071–2080 (2016)
43. Völker, J., Niepert, M.: Statistical schema induction. In: Antoniou, G., et al. (eds.) ESWC 2011. LNCS, vol. 6643, pp. 124–138. Springer, Heidelberg (2011). https://doi.org/10.1007/978-3-642-21034-1_9
44. West, R., Gabrilovich, E., Murphy, K., Sun, S., Gupta, R., Lin, D.: Knowledge base completion via search-based question answering. In: Proceedings WWW, pp. 515–526 (2014)
45. Xiao, H., Huang, M., Meng, L., Zhu, X.: SSP: semantic space projection for knowledge graph embedding with text descriptions. In: Proceedings AAAI, vol. 17, pp. 3104–3110 (2017)
46. Xie, R., Liu, Z., Jia, J., Luan, H., Sun, M.: Representation learning of knowledge graphs with entity descriptions. In: Proceedings of AAAI, pp. 2659–2665 (2016)
47. Yang, B., Yih, W., He, X., Gao, J., Deng, L.: Embedding entities and relations for learning and inference in knowledge bases. In: Proceedings of ICLR-15 (2015)
48. Zhong, H., Zhang, J., Wang, Z., Wan, H., Chen, Z.: Aligning knowledge and text embeddings by entity descriptions. In: EMNLP, pp. 267–272 (2015)

Non-parametric Class Completeness Estimators for Collaborative Knowledge Graphs—The Case of Wikidata

Michael Luggen[1(✉)], Djellel Difallah[2], Cristina Sarasua[3], Gianluca Demartini[4], and Philippe Cudré-Mauroux[1]

[1] University of Fribourg, Fribourg, Switzerland
{michael.luggen,philippe.cudre-mauroux}@unifr.ch
[2] New York University, New York, USA
djellel@nyu.edu
[3] University of Zurich, Zurich, Switzerland
sarasua@ifi.uzh.ch
[4] University of Queensland, Brisbane, Australia
demartini@acm.org

Abstract. Collaborative Knowledge Graph platforms allow humans and automated scripts to collaborate in creating, updating and interlinking entities and facts. To ensure both the completeness of the data as well as a uniform coverage of the different topics, it is crucial to identify underrepresented classes in the Knowledge Graph. In this paper, we tackle this problem by developing statistical techniques for class cardinality estimation in collaborative Knowledge Graph platforms. Our method is able to estimate the completeness of a class—as defined by a schema or ontology—hence can be used to answer questions such as "Does the knowledge base have a complete list of all {Beer Brands—Volcanos—Video Game Consoles}?" As a use-case, we focus on Wikidata, which poses unique challenges in terms of the size of its ontology, the number of users actively populating its graph, and its extremely dynamic nature. Our techniques are derived from species estimation and data-management methodologies, and are applied to the case of graphs and collaborative editing. In our empirical evaluation, we observe that (i) the number and frequency of unique class instances drastically influence the performance of an estimator, (ii) bursts of inserts cause some estimators to overestimate the true size of the class if they are not properly handled, and (iii) one can effectively measure the convergence of a class towards its true size by considering the stability of an estimator against the number of available instances.

Keywords: Knowledge Graph · Class completeness · Class cardinality · Estimators · Edit history

C. Ghidini et al. (Eds.): ISWC 2019, LNCS 11778, pp. 453–469, 2019.
https://doi.org/10.1007/978-3-030-30793-6_26

1 Introduction

Knowledge Graphs (KGs) play a critical role in several tasks including speech recognition, entity linking, relation extraction, semantic search, or fact-checking. Wikidata [20] is a free KG that is collaboratively curated and maintained by a large community of thousands of volunteers. With currently more than 55M data items and over 5.4K distinct properties that help describe these data items, Wikidata is the bridge between many Wikimedia projects (e.g., Wikipedia, Wikimedia Commons, and Wiktionary), as well as the interlinking hub of many other Linked Data sources. Its data is consumed by end-user applications such as Google Search, Siri, and applications to browse scholarly information[1].

Being a collaborative, crowdsourced effort, Wikidata's data is highly dynamic. Editors can create items individually (e. g. a new instance representing a natural disaster that just happened), or in bulk (e. g. importing data about all the pieces of art in a city) about any topic that satisfies the notability criteria defined by the community[2]. The open curation process leads to a KG evolving dynamically and at various speeds. While such a process is beneficial for data diversity and freshness, it does not guarantee the total (or even partial) *completeness* of the data. Given that previous research has shown that data consumers identify completeness as one of the key data quality dimensions [22], together with accuracy and freshness, it is of utmost importance to provide mechanisms to measure and foster data completeness in collaborative KGs.

In that context, the Wikidata community has already endorsed a series of initiatives and tools that encourage efforts towards population completeness [24]. For instance, there are WikiProjects[3] that aim at populating Wikidata with bibliographic references, genes, or notable women.

With such a decentralized approach of independently-run data entry and import efforts, it has become very difficult to understand and measure what is still missing in Wikidata. While there is related work that measures the completeness of item descriptions in Wikidata (see Sect. 2), there is (to the best of our knowledge) no systematic approach to measure *class completeness* other than by manually checking for candidate entities and facts to be inserted in the KG.

In this paper, we focus on the specific problem of *estimating class completeness* in a collaborative KG and experimentally evaluate our methods over Wikidata. We limit our work to the family of finite classes, where the number of instances in such classes is fixed. We take a data-driven approach to that problem by leveraging models from statistics and ecology used to estimate the size of species [4]. We propose methods to calculate the cardinality of classes and build estimates for the class convergence to the true value. We note that while we focus our empirical study on Wikidata, our proposed methodology is applicable to any other collaborative graph dataset with analogous characteristics, where the action log describing its evolution is available. By calculating the expected

[1] Scholia https://tools.wmflabs.org/scholia/.
[2] Wikidata's Notability https://www.wikidata.org/wiki/Wikidata:Notability.
[3] Wikidata WikiProjects https://www.wikidata.org/wiki/Wikidata:WikiProjects.

class cardinality, we are able to measure class completeness given the number of instances currently present in the KG for that class. We evaluate different class size estimation methods against classes whose sizes are known through trustworthy third-party sources (e.g., the number of municipalities in the Czech Republic) and for which a complete ground truth exists. We then apply these methods to other classes in order to generate completeness estimates for other parts of the KG.

The main contributions of this paper are as follows:

- We show how the edit history of a KG can be used to inform statistical methods adapted from species estimators (Sect. 3);
- We evaluate the effectiveness of statistical methods to estimate the class size and KG completeness based on repeated sampling (Sect. 4);
- We provide tools to make Wikidata end-users (both human and applications) aware of the incompleteness of many subparts in Wikidata (Sect. 4.4).

2 Related Work

Data Completeness in Knowledge Graphs is one of the most important data quality dimensions for Linked Data [24]; it has also been acknowledged as a key data quality indicator by the Wikidata community[4]. Different data cleaning methods proposed by the research community have focused on different types of completeness. For example, ReCoin [1] measures the relative completeness that item descriptions have, compared to other items of the same type. It keeps track of used properties and encourages editors to add new statements and foster more homogeneous item descriptions. Galárraga et al. [9] investigate different signals to predict the completeness of *relations* in KGs. The work of Soulet et al. [17] introduces a method to estimate the lower bound of completeness in a KG. The completeness is estimated through the missing facts to reach a distribution according to Benfords Law. Kaffee et al. [12] study label completeness across languages. The work by Wulczyn et al. [23] encourages Wikipedia editors to write different language versions of existing articles. Tanon et al. [18] uses association rules to identify missing statements, while Darari et al. [6] provide means to describe and reason over RDF statement completeness. To complement these methods, in this paper we consider the problem of class completeness in the KG.

Cardinality Estimation in Databases. Estimating the cardinality of a table in relational databases is key to query performance optimization. This requires a combination of database technology and statistical methods and allows to compute the cost of database operations that are then used for optimization strategies (e.g., storage allocation and data distribution) [13]. Similarly, cardinality estimation is key to optimize query execution in RDF triplestores. The key difference with relational databases is the presence of many self-joins in queries over

[4] Wikidata Quality RFC https://www.wikidata.org/wiki/Wikidata:Requests_for_comment/Data_quality_framework_for_Wikidata.

RDF data. This requires custom cardinality estimation techniques for SPARQL queries over RDF data [14]. In distributed databases, cardinality estimation is also a necessary step to optimize query execution. The key aspect is estimating the size of non-materialized views in a way that is accurate and provides statistical bounds [15]. Our work addresses the different problem of determining the cardinality of a class in a KG leveraging its edit history.

Data Completeness in Crowdsourcing. The problem of counting items and individuals also arises in a crowdsourcing setting. Previous work [7] developed models to estimate the size of the crowd in Amazon MTurk by taking into account the propensity of a worker to participate in an online survey or micro-tasks, respectively. That work used *capture-recapture*, a technique based on repeated observations of the same worker participating in tasks. In our class size estimation method, we estimate the size of data (not crowds) based on observations made through another form of crowdsourcing, i.e., volunteering.

In a similar setting, Trushkowsky et al. [19] tackled the problem of enumerating the list of all instances in a specific class through paid crowdsourcing. The crowd workers were explicitly asked to provide a list of distinct items, for example, "input the list of all ice cream flavors". Similar to our work, the authors used *capture-recapture* techniques but also had to deal with aspects unique to a crowdsourcing environment. For instance, they introduced a "pay-as-you-go" method to estimate the cost-benefit ratio of crowdsourcing additional tasks to complement the current list. They looked at both open-world and closed-world assumptions where the cardinality of the set is either known (e.g., "list of US states") or unknown and possibly unbounded (e.g, "ice cream flavors"). Their methods are based on techniques borrowed from ecology research to count the number of animals of a certain species, which we describe next.

Species Richness Methods. In the field of ecology and bio-statistics, several capture-recapture techniques have been proposed to estimate the number of existing species [2,21]. The idea of capture-recapture is to draw a sample at random from a population and to estimate the number of unobserved items based on the frequency of the observed items. Such approaches work well for closed populations, but different techniques are required when we allow for open populations. Open vs. closed population problems have fundamentally different questions to answer. The former focus on estimating the rates of arrival and departure, the latter is about size and propensity of capture. We restrict our work to the realm of closed classes since it was shown that if a closed population method is utilized when in fact there is a process of arrival/departure, then closed estimators tend to overestimate. For example, the open-world-safe estimator "Chao92" [4] provides more accurate estimations when more evidence is available from a class. We present our results based on this and other estimators in Sect. 4.

In our work, we look at the problem of estimating the size of a given class (e.g., Volcanos) or composite classes (e.g., Paintings drawn by Vincent van Gogh) in Wikidata. We tap into the edit patterns of Wikidata volunteers [16], and apply capture-recapture techniques to estimate the completeness of a given class.

3 Class Completeness Estimators

In this section, we introduce the family of estimators we leverage to tackle the class estimation problem in collaborative KGs. First, we introduce the problem statement and the assumptions that we make in the context of Wikidata by defining the notion of *class* in Wikidata. Next, we introduce several statistical estimators ordered by complexity and show how they build upon each other. In this paper, we refer to entities as all the instances of a particular class e.g., "Cathedrals in Mexico".

3.1 Problem Definition

Given a finite class C of instances $I_C = \{I_1, ..., I_N\}$, our goal is to estimate the number of instances of C i.e., $N = |I_C|$. We note D the current count of instances of a given class in the knowledge graph. A class is complete once D is equal to the true class size N.

The capture-recapture data collection protocol that we follow is based on n observations recorded during k successive *sample periods.* Each observation relates to a direct or indirect change made to an instance of a specific class during the sample period (i.e., one month). In practice, we extract *mentions* from the edits in the knowledge graph. An edit is a change that either adds, modifies or deletes a statement involving one or more entities. Every reference of an entity in the *subject* or *object* position of a statement defines a mention for the class that the mentioned entity belongs to. In the end, each mention is composed of an entity (also called *instance* because it belongs to a class), the class the instance belongs to, and a timestamp.

3.2 Interpreting Edit Activity Related to Classes

Given the edit history of a KG, we extract mentions as described in Listing 1.1: For every edit, we create a mention if one of the entities referenced belongs to a class. This is done on a per class basis.

Listing 1.1. Query on the Wikidata Graph illustrating the relation between edits and mentions on the example of the Single Domain class *City* (Q515). (The properties referenced with the *edit* prefix are not available in the public Wikidata endpoint.)

```
SELECT ?instance ?timestamp
WHERE { ?instance wdt:P31/wdt:P279* wd:Q515.
        { ?mention edit:subject ?instance. }
        UNION
        { ?mention edit:object  ?instance. }
        ?mention edit:timestamp ?timestamp.
}
```

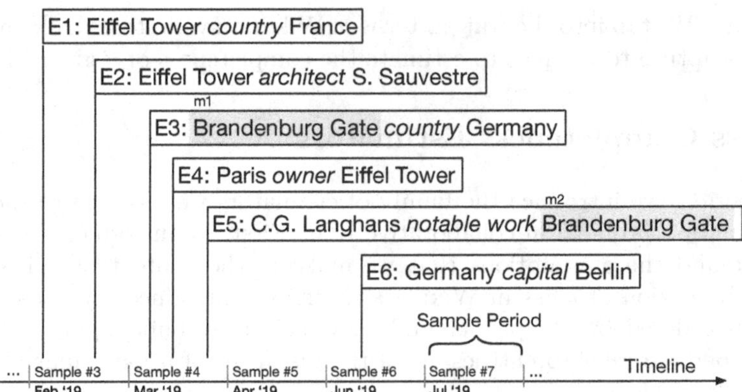

Fig. 1. The edits (E_i) of the Knowledge Graph (representing new edges) are leveraged to identify mentions. The source and target of each edge are collected to create a mention from the entity involved. Sample period #4 contains 3 *edits*, in which we identify 6 *mentions*, from which we extract 2 *observations* for class monument (despite the 3 mentions of entities of that class because m_1 and m_2 are only counted once), 1 observation for class country, 1 observation for class city and 1 observation for class person.

We show in Fig. 1 how the mentions get aggregated per sample period on the overall timeline. In a given sample period, we count one observation per instance having at least one mention. With X_i being the frequency of observations relating to instance I_i, we compute the frequency of frequencies $f_i = \sum_{j=1}^{N} \mathbb{1}[X_j = i]$, for $1 \leq i \leq k$. For example, f_1 is the number of instances observed only once (singletons), f_2 is the number of instances observed twice (doubletons) etc. With this notation, f_0 represents the number of instances that we never observed and we seek to estimate. Each instance $I_i \in I_C$ of a given class has a unique probability p_i of being mentioned, with $\sum p_i = 1$.

To be able to leverage the statistical techniques described below, the distribution of classes among the observations is supposed to follow a stationary multinomial distribution with unknown parameter $p_1, ..., p_N$. This leads to the following assumptions:

1. The classes of interest are closed and countable as of the beginning of the experiment;
2. The observations are independent events;
3. In a class, the observations are at random and "with replacement";
4. The probability of observing an instance within a class does not change over time.

First, by assuming that classes are closed, we reduce the scope of the questions we can answer. Tracking the changes (growth and shrinkage) of an open class such as "Events in Paris" or "Sitting Presidents" would require a different approach, data, and assumptions. Second, using a large number of edits made by different volunteers and scripts introduces a number of corner cases that we need to work with. It is for example possible to observe dependant actions, for example: systematically adding "Name" followed by "Date of Birth" or editors correcting each other. While our assumption is a simplifying one, we have not observed any significant correlations in the edits. This stems from the fact that the volunteers are not restricted on which edits they perform and what entities or classes they need to focus on. The third assumption comes in contrast to the work in [19] where crowd workers were asked to list items that belong to a particular class. Hence, a given crowd worker is answering from a population of possible items (i.e., sampling "without replacement"). In our case, Wikidata editors can create edits which repeatedly mention the same entity in the context of their work. Finally, the fourth assumption is based on the fact that the observations we make are created through indirect references and are not directly related to the classes themselves.

3.3 Non-parametric Estimators

The intuition behind the estimators that we consider is based on the frequency of edits involving entities of a given class. To estimate the true class size we consider non-parametric methods that primarily use the frequencies of observations among instances. Non-parametric methods do not assume any probability distribution of p_i among the instances of a given class.

Jackknife Estimators [Jack1]. Jackknife (or "leave-one-out") methods have been used to develop species richness estimators [11]. Similarly to k-fold cross validation, we use observations from $k-1$ periods by removing observations from one sample period from the data at a time and average the resulting pseudo-estimates made on each sub-fold. We write f_1^i to denote the instances observed only once in period i. We note that the number of distinct elements obtained when dropping period i becomes $D_{-i} = D - f_1^i$.

We compute a pseudo estimate for each sub-sample of observations obtained by dropping the $i-th$ period using $\hat{N}_{-i} = kD - (k-1)D_{-i}$, and averaging across k. A closed form of the first and second order Jackknife estimators is given by Eqs. (1) and (2) respectively [3]. We observe that $\hat{N}_{\text{JACK1}}$ implies that the number of unseen instances is approximately the same as the number of singletons after a large number of sampling periods.

$$\hat{N}_{\text{JACK1}} = D + \frac{k-1}{k} f_1 \tag{1}$$

$$\hat{N}_{\text{JACK2}} = D + \frac{2k-3}{k} f_1 - \frac{(k-2)^2}{k(k-1)} f_2 \tag{2}$$

Sample Coverage and the Good-Turing Estimator [N1-UNIF]. The following methods are based on the concept of *sample coverage* which is a measure of sample completeness.

$$S = \sum^{N} p_i \mathbb{1}[X_i > 0] \tag{3}$$

Since the probabilities of observing the instances as well as the population size are unknown, a popular estimate of the sample coverage is given by the Good-Turing Estimator [10] Eq. (4). Effectively, this estimator relies on the complement of the ratio of singletons among the sample data and as an indicator of true sample coverage. For example, if in past sample periods we have seen each instance only once, the probability of observing a new instance by collecting a new sample is 1. Conversely, if all the instances were seen more than once, i.e., $f_1 = 0$ the probability of seeing a new instance in a new sample is reduced to 0.

$$\hat{S} = 1 - \frac{f_1}{n} \tag{4}$$

If all instances have the same probability of being observed, the population size using the Good-Turing sample coverage is given by:

$$\hat{N}_{\text{N1-UNIF}} = \frac{D}{\hat{S}} = \frac{D}{1 - \frac{f_1}{n}} \tag{5}$$

We draw the attention of the reader to the trade-off that singletons and popular instances create. Typically, frequency counts will be heavily unbalanced and will tend to over or under-estimate the true population size.

Singleton Outliers Reduction [SOR]. To mitigate the effect of the singletons on a class, a popular approach is to threshold the number of singleton elements. Trushkowsky et al. [19] proposed to limit the number of singletons introduced by a given contributor to two standard deviations above the mean of singletons introduces by other workers. We adapt this method to our scenario by limiting the f_1 count to fall within two standard deviations above the mean. The rationale behind our choice is to strike a balance between low and high dispersion of f_1 frequencies with respect to the set F of all frequencies that we observe.

$$\hat{N}_{\text{SOR}} = \frac{D}{1 - \frac{\tilde{f}_1}{n}} \tag{6}$$

with,

$$\begin{aligned} \tilde{f}_1 &= \min\Big\{ f_1, 2\sigma + \mu \Big\} \\ \mu &= \sum_{\forall j > 1}^{F} \frac{f_j}{|F| - 1} \\ \sigma &= \sqrt{\sum_{\forall j > 1}^{F} \frac{(f_j - \mu)^2}{|F| - 2}} \end{aligned} \tag{7}$$

Abundance-Based Coverage Estimator [Chao92]. The work by Chao and Lee [4] (hereon *chao92*) uses the concept of sample coverage introduced above and assumes that the probabilities of capture can be summarized by their mean i.e., $\bar{p} = \sum p_i/N = 1/N$ and their coefficient of variation (or γ) with $\gamma^2 = [N^{-1}\sum_i(p_i - \bar{p_i})^2]/\bar{p}^2$.

However, since we do not have access to the probabilities p_i and N, the coefficient of variation is in turn estimated by using $\hat{N}_{\text{UNIF}}$ (via the Good-Turing estimator of sample coverage), and p_i's with the observed data and corresponding f_i.

$$\gamma^2 = \max\Big\{\hat{N}_{\text{UNIF}} \sum_{i=1}^{k} \frac{i(i-1)f_i}{[n(n-1)]-1}, 0\Big\} \tag{8}$$

The *chao92* estimator is given by Eq. (9). We note that if the coefficient of variation is close the zero, the estimator reduces to Eq. (5) indicating an equiprobable scenario. Conversely, as γ grows, signaling more variability in the probabilities of capture, we add a factor proportional to the number of singletons to the equiprobable estimate. We note that a high *estimated* coefficient of variation combined with a high number of singletons might result in significant overestimation.

$$\hat{N}_{\text{CHAO92}} = \frac{D}{\hat{S}} + \frac{n(1-\hat{S})}{\hat{S}}\gamma^2 = \frac{D + f_1\gamma^2}{\hat{S}} \tag{9}$$

3.4 Evaluation Metrics

We evaluate the robustness and convergence of our estimators using the following metrics.

Error Metric. To evaluate the performance of the estimators in a controlled setting, we leverage the error metric introduced in [19]. For reference, the ϕ error metric aims at capturing the bias of the estimates as the absolute distance from the ground truth, if available. The sample order weighs the bias terms, that is, more recent errors get penalized more heavily. Conducting such an evaluation requires the ground truth value of the class size N, as well as the estimates calculated on the time-ordered sample periods.

$$\phi = \frac{\sum_{i=1}^{k}\left|\hat{N}_i - N\right| i}{\sum i} = \frac{2\sum_{i=1}^{k}|\hat{N}_i - N|}{k(k+1)} \tag{10}$$

Convergence Metric. Conversely, we introduce a new metric ρ that aims at evaluating the convergence of a given estimate. This metric acts as the main measurement tool in a real scenario where we do not have access to the ground truth, e.g. when performing large-scale analyses of completeness across classes. The metric is derived from ϕ, as we look for stability and close distance between the estimate and the number D of distinct values. In contrast to the error metric, only the last w observed samples out of the full set of samples are used in the convergence metric. The closer the metric is to zero, the more confident we are that the class has converged to its complete set.

$$\rho = \frac{\sum_{i=k-w}^{k} \frac{|\hat{N}_i - D_i|}{D_i}}{w} \tag{11}$$

In the following section, we evaluate the presented estimators on a set of eight classes from Wikidata. We report our findings using the error and convergence metrics for the following estimators: Jack1 ($\hat{N}_{\text{JACK1}}$)[5], N1-UNIF ($\hat{N}_{\text{N1-UNIF}}$), SOR ($\hat{N}_{\text{SOR}}$) and Chao92 ($\hat{N}_{\text{CHAO92}}$).

4 Experimental Evaluation

We discuss the results of an extensive experimental evaluation of the estimators introduced in Sect. 3 below, starting with the description of the dataset we used. We obtain the full edit history of the Knowledge Graph and collect the observations for all the classes we found in Wikidata. We then selected a sub-sample of classes for which we have meaningful characteristics regarding the number of observations spread over time. From this set, we randomly selected classes and searched for an independent authoritative source that reports their true cardinality. We set the sample period to 30 days, which results in at least one observation per sample period on most classes we selected. We use the last four samples ($w = 4$ which equals roughly 4 Months) of our results to calculate the convergence metric. Note that if an instance was not assigned the correct class we are not able to count it and we consider it as missing. This is a desirable effect since a declarative query on Wikidata requesting the full list of a class will not return such instances either.

4.1 Data

To evaluate our class completeness estimation methods, we use two different datasets from Wikidata: First, we use the *entity graph*, provided by the Wikidata JSON dumps as of Aug 18, 2018[6]. The JSON dump contains the actual node descriptions and the edges between the nodes. Second, we use *the edit history* as of Oct 1, 2018 provided in the Wikibase XML Dump[7]. The edit history provides the list of all actions performed on the KG including the creation of new items, the update of labels and other values, as well as reverted edits[8]. For each action, the XML dump provides the item changed, the user who made the change, the timestamp, a comment describing the action, and a pointer to the state of the graph before this action.

[5] We do not report on Jack2 as it has been shown to over-estimate the population size when the sample size is large [5], which we have experienced as well.

[6] JSON Dump: https://doi.org/10.5281/zenodo.3268725.

[7] Edit History: https://dumps.wikimedia.org/wikidatawiki/latest/.

[8] List of all Wikibase actions: https://www.mediawiki.org/wiki/Wikibase/API/en.

Dataset Description: Entity Degree Distribution. To explore the characteristics of the dataset, we look at the graph as a whole (Fig. 2) and observe the constant overall growth of entities with different in and out-degrees at different points in time.

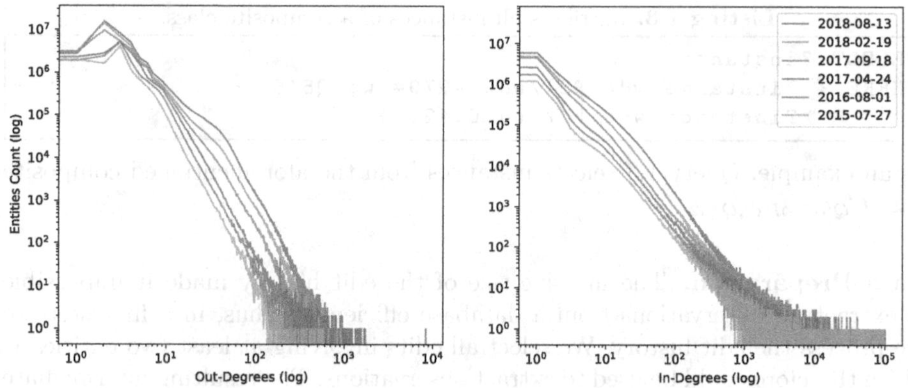

Fig. 2. The evolution of Wikidata: a temporal view on how the in- and out-degree distributions have evolved since the inception of the project.

Classes and Instances in the Case of Wikidata. Wikidata can be interpreted as an RDF graph [8], with a data model that differentiates between entities (including classes and instances) and properties. We define classes and instances in the Wikidata graph $G = (V, E)$ as follows:

Single Domain Classes. In Wikidata, edges with the explicit label E_{P31}: instanceOf and E_{P279}: subclassOf explicitly define classes.[9] The target vertex V_t which can be reached by following the edge with label E_{P31}: instanceOf from the source vertex V_s are part of the classes C. Super classes collect all instances of a class C which follow the edge E_{P279}: subclassOf once or multiple times.

Listing 1.2. Retrieves all instances of a specified single domain.

```
SELECT ?instance
WHERE { ?instance wdt:P31/wdt:P279* wd:Q515. }
```

To extract all instances of class C_{Q515} : *City* we issue Query 1.2 against the Wikidata endpoint.

[9] https://www.wikidata.org/wiki/Wikidata:WikiProject_Ontology/Classes.

Composite Classes. We create composite classes by joining a class C on one or multiple properties E and their target instances V. As an example, we can join class C_{Q515}: City with property E_{P17}: country and target V_{Q142}: France on the instances of C_{Q515}. The result is a composite class of all Cities in France $C_{Q515 \bowtie P17,Q142}$.

Listing 1.3. Retrieves all instances of a composite class.

```
SELECT ?instance
WHERE { ?instance wdt:P31/wdt:P279* wd:Q515.
        ?instance wdt:P17 wd:Q142. }
```

As an example, Query 1.3 selects instances from the aforementioned composite class $C_{Q515 \bowtie P17,Q142}$.

Data Preparation. The massive size of the edit history made it impossible to extract all observations from a database efficiently. Thus, in a first step we pre-process the edit history. We select all edits involving at least two entities V which therefore could be used to extract observations. The resulting intermediate data provides more than 161 million edits containing the source entity V_s, the property label of the connecting E, the target entity V_t, as well as the timestamp and the user. In a second step, we pre-processed the JSON Dump into an in-memory graph to get fast access to all instances V and properties E (with property labels) of the Wikidata Graph. This gives us information on which entity V belongs to which class C. Finally, to extract the observations pointing to an entity, we join the Wikidata edits with the in-memory Graph.

We filter out the observations belonging to a specific class C by joining the observations pointing to an entity which in turn point to a class. The resulting data, grouped by class, consists of 370 million distinct observations.

4.2 Results

Figure 3 shows the results of the various estimators we consider. The top part of each plot represents the results of the estimators for a specific domain, as well as the lower bound given by the absolute number of *distinct* instances observed. The x-axis represents the number of sample periods that we obtain in chronological order to perform the class size estimation. At each sample period, we run an estimator using all the data samples collected so far. The dashed line indicates the ground truth size. The bottom part of each plot shows a comparison of two indicators: *Distinct*, the distinct number of instances up to the sample period and f_1, the proportion of instances observed exactly once, both normalized to the distinct number of instances retrieved in the end. These indicators are key to our methods and serve the purpose of explaining the behavior of each estimator with respect to the properties of the samples. In the following, we discuss these results and highlight key properties of each set of observations.

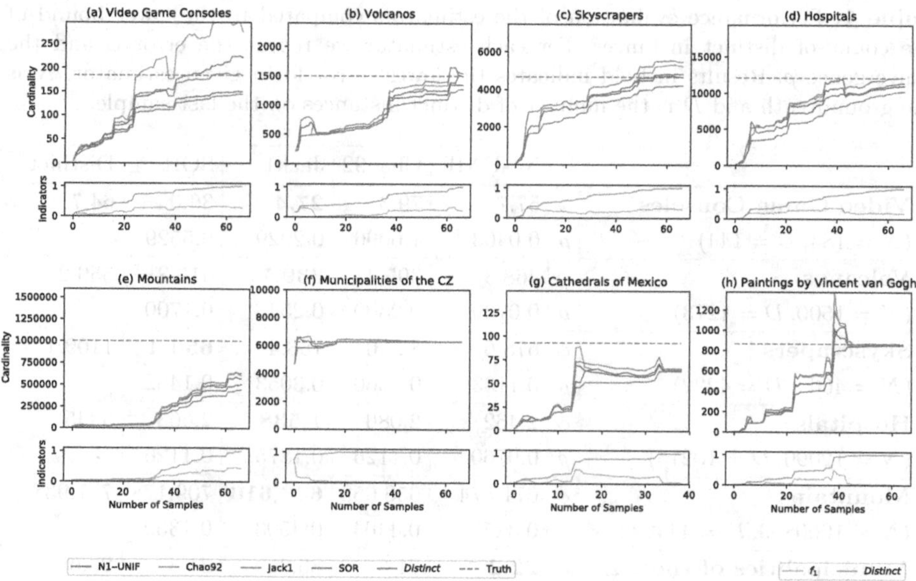

Fig. 3. Estimators used on Single Domain (a)–(f) and Composite classes (g)–(h).

Size Estimates on Single Domain Classes. First, we inspect the results of estimating the size of a class when the query involves a single class definition. The first five figures show incomplete classes. In Fig. 3(a) we show the results for the small-sized class Video Game Consoles ($N = 184$)[10]. We note how Chao92 is particularly intolerant to the small class size and overestimates. Figure 3(b) shows the estimators for the class Volcanos ($N = 1500$)[11]. Figure 3(c), for Skyscrapers ($N = 4669$)[12], shows a class that is almost complete. The estimators are overshooting, because the f_1 on the available instances is high. In Fig. 3(d) Hospitals ($N = 12090$)[13], we observe how large classes also bring larger numbers of observations. This in turn helps the estimators to get stable before completeness is reached. A massive class is represented with Fig. 3(e) Mountains ($N = 1000809$)[14]. We are aware that the ground truth, even if well researched by the source, is still rather suggestive. Nevertheless, the estimators suggest that there are missing instances. Finally, Fig. 3(f) Municipalities of the Czech Republic ($N = 6258$)[15] shows a class which was complete early (around Sample 10). All estimators slowly converge to the ground truth.

---

10 https://en.wikipedia.org/wiki/List_of_home_video_game_consoles.

11 https://www.usgs.gov/faqs/how-many-active-volcanoes-are-there-earth.

12 http://www.skyscrapercenter.com/.

13 https://gateway.euro.who.int/en/indicators/hfa_471-5011-number-of-hospitals/.

14 https://peakvisor.com/en/news/how_many_mountains_on_earth.html.

15 https://www.oecd.org/regional/regional-policy/Subnational-governments-in-OECD-Countries-Key-Data-2018.pdf.

Table 1. Performance evaluation of the estimators compared to the lower bound of the count of distinct instances. For each estimator we report the error ϕ and the convergence ρ. Results in bold indicates the lowest error for a given estimator. N is the groundtruth and D is the number of distinct instances on the last sample.

		N1-UNIF	Chao92	Jack1	SOR	Distinct
Video Game Consoles	ϕ	57.7	79.3	**27.4**	36.0	64.7
$(N = 184, D = 144)$	ρ	0.0403	1.0096	0.2929	0.5529	
Volcanos	ϕ	468.3	395.4	**339.7**	415.8	550.2
$(N = 1500, D = 1273)$	ρ	0.0739	0.2300	0.2545	0.1700	
Skyscrapers	ϕ	678.6	826.0	758.4	**650.4**	1109.1
$(N = 4669, D = 4222)$	ρ	0.1133	0.2560	0.3053	0.1482	
Hospitals	ϕ	2,462	2,080	**1,538**	2,663	3945
$(N = 12090, D = 10215)$	ρ	0.0760	0.1126	0.1875	0.1126	
Mountains	ϕ	671,874	656,653	**643,616**	709,178	751,938
$(N = 1000809, D = 444222)$	ρ	0.3255	0.4404	0.4503	0.1359	
Municipalities of the CZ	ϕ	**22.2**	31.3	86.3	31.3	26.6
$(N = 6258, D = 6256)$	ρ	0.0002	0.0008	0.0029	0.0008	
Cathedrals of Mexico	ϕ	37.2	35.0	**31.7**	36.6	43.1
$(N = 93, D = 63)$	ρ	0.0159	0.0162	0.0463	0.0162	
Paintings by V. van Gogh	ϕ	184.8	183.1	**173.0**	189.1	204.9
$(N = 864, D = 848)$	ρ	0.0027	0.0028	0.0119	0.0028	

Size Estimates on Composite Classes. As composite classes are by definition a subset of instances, compared to single domain classes, the associated observations can also drop to low numbers. Figure 3(g) shows such a case where the number of observations involving instances of a $C_{Q2977 \bowtie P17,Q96}$ Cathedrals in Mexico ($N = 93$)[16] is $n = 387$. Figure 3(h) $C_{Q3305213 \bowtie P170,Q5582}$ Paintings by Vincent van Gogh ($T = 864$)[17] is an example which displays the different phases of an estimator can encounter until class completeness. Starting by growing slowly at first with the addition of the first few elements. We observe intermittent overshooting when a large number of instances are added in a batch process. The final phase is a fast convergence towards the value of the ground truth.

Performance Evaluation. For all our experiments, we computed the error and convergence metrics introduced in Sect. 3.4 to obtain quantitative measurements on how the estimators perform and how they can be used. Table 1 summarizes the evaluation results across all classes considered in our work. We observe that Jack1 and SOR consistently achieve the lowest error rate across all classes.

---
[16] https://en.wikipedia.org/wiki/List_of_cathedrals_in_Mexico.
[17] https://de.wikipedia.org/wiki/Vincent_van_Gogh#cite_note-Thomson_84-1.

Table 2. Lists of 10 randomly picked examples. Left with a low ρ suggesting a complete class, and right a high ρ suggesting an incomplete class.

	SOR $\rho < 0.001$	Distinct		SOR $\rho > 0.1$	Distinct
municipality of Japan	0.0000	739	urban beach	0.1759	683
Philippine TV series	0.0009	822	hydroelectric power station	0.2975	2,936
Landgemeinde of Austria	0.0000	1,116	aircraft model	0.1800	3,919
district of China	0.0009	975	motorcycle manufacturer	0.1758	690
nuclear isomer	0.0002	1,322	local museum	0.1760	1,150
international border	0.0000	529	waterfall	0.1942	5,322
commune of France	0.0001	34,937	race track	0.2783	946
village of Burkina Faso	0.0005	2,723	film production company	0.2107	2,179
supernova	0.0005	5,906	red telephone box	0.3469	2,716
township of Indiana	0.0002	999	mountain range	0.2390	21,390

4.3 Discussion

Our experimental results unveiled key properties in terms of the sensitivity and conditions under which some estimators perform better than others. Generally speaking, all estimators beat the lower bound of distinct numbers in the error metric ϕ. The exception is the class (Municipalities of the CZ) which converged early on, and for which N1-UNIF still beats the error of the distinct values. However, the other estimators lose against the lower bound (distinct) in this example on the number of instances because they over estimate the class size in the early samples before the class reaches completeness. We observe that more conservative estimators N1-UNIF, Chao92 perform worse then Jack1 and SOR for incomplete classes, which is why we recommend the last two in the end for the estimation of the class size. The convergence metric can be used as an indicator to distinguish complete from incomplete classes without requiring the knowledge of the real class size. In Table 1, we see how the convergence metrics ρ are low (<0.001) for complete classes. On the other hand for incomplete classes ρ is comparatively high (>0.1). Table 2 lists ten randomly-picked classes, along with the convergence on *SOR* and the number of distinct instances, for a low and high ρ values suggesting complete and incomplete classes respectively. These lists illustrate how our convergence metric can be leveraged to identify gaps in the KG.

4.4 Additional Material and Tools

The results on all classes in Wikidata are available at http://cardinal.exascale.info. We also release our Python code implementing the data processing pipeline, all estimators and metrics as an open source package[18]. This includes tools to seek for incomplete classes based on the convergence metric. Finally, we provide the pre-processed data at every step of the processing pipeline, as well as the final results for each dataset.

[18] https://github.com/eXascaleInfolab/cardinal/.

5 Conclusions and Future Work

In this work, we introduced a methodology to estimate class sizes in a collaborative KG and evaluated it over Wikidata. We showed how collaborative editing dynamics create a trove of information that can be mined to extract information about data access, edits, data linkage, and overall graph growth. We relied on the edit history over six years of activity in Wikidata to collect capture-recapture observations related to a particular entity within the class of interest. We reviewed, applied, and evaluated a battery of non-parametric statistical techniques that leverage frequency statistics collected from the data to estimate the completeness of a given class.

Our experimental results show that many estimators yield accurate estimates when provided with enough observations that reflect the actual underlying distribution of the instances of a class. However, some estimators like Chao92 tend to be less robust to bursts of newly discovered instances. Finally, based on our results, we provided a set of practical recommendations to use convergence metric in conjunction with estimators to decide whether a particular class is complete or to perform large-scale completeness analyses. Our work has direct implications for both Wikidata editors and data consumers. We can provide convergence statistics on the estimated class completeness by domains to point to knowledge gaps. Such statistics could aid newcomers, who often feel insecure about what to edit, to decide what to contribute or what to focus on.

In future work, we plan to leverage statistics on page views showing the attention that specific groups of items receive within the KG to inform estimators. We would also like to develop parametric models that assume a particular edit probability distribution. This is especially applicable to domains with a considerable bias towards popular entities such as Humans and Musicians. Another area of potential development is the usage of completeness estimators to detect systematic errors in Wikidata: While exploring the data, we have observed many cases of misclassification, which we conjecture as being the result of the growing complexity of the Wikidata ontology that includes more than forty thousand classes at the time of writing.

Acknowledgements. This project has received funding from the European Research Council (ERC) under the European Union's Horizon 2020 research and innovation programme (grant agreement 683253/GraphInt). It is also supported by the Australian Research Council (ARC) Discovery Project (Grant No. DP190102141).

References

1. Balaraman, V., Razniewski, S., Nutt, W.: Recoin: relative completeness in Wikidata. In: Companion Proceedings of the The Web Conference, pp. 1787–1792 (2018)
2. Bunge, J., Fitzpatrick, M.: Estimating the number of species: a review. J. Am. Stat. Assoc. **88**(421), 364–373 (1993)
3. Burnham, K.P., Overton, W.S.: Robust estimation of population size when capture probabilities vary among animals. Ecology **60**(5), 927–936 (1979)

4. Chao, A., Lee, S.M.: Estimating the number of classes via sample coverage. J. Am. Stat. Assoc. **87**(417), 210–217 (1992)
5. Chiu, C.H., Wang, Y.T., Walther, B.A., Chao, A.: An improved nonparametric lower bound of species richness via a modified good-turing frequency formula. Biometrics **70**(3), 671–682 (2014)
6. Darari, F., Nutt, W., Pirrò, G., Razniewski, S.: Completeness management for RDF data sources. ACM Trans. Web **12**(3), 18:1–18:53 (2018)
7. Difallah, D., Filatova, E., Ipeirotis, P.: Demographics and dynamics of mechanical Turk workers. In: WSDM, pp. 135–143. ACM (2018)
8. Erxleben, F., Günther, M., Krötzsch, M., Mendez, J., Vrandecic, D.: Introducing Wikidata to the linked data web. In: ISWC, pp. 50–65 (2014)
9. Galárraga, L., Razniewski, S., Amarilli, A., Suchanek, F.M.: Predicting completeness in knowledge bases. In: WSDM, pp. 375–383 (2017)
10. Good, I.J.: The population frequencies of species and the estimation of population parameters. Biometrika **40**(3–4), 237–264 (1953)
11. Heltshe, J.F., Forrester, N.E.: Estimating species richness using the jackknife procedure. Biometrics **39**, 1–11 (1983)
12. Kaffee, L., Simperl, E.: The human face of the web of data: a cross-sectional study of labels. In: SEMANTICS, pp. 66–77 (2018)
13. Mannino, M.V., Chu, P., Sager, T.: Statistical profile estimation in database systems. ACM Comput. Surv. **20**(3), 191–221 (1988)
14. Neumann, T., Moerkotte, G.: Characteristic sets: accurate cardinality estimation for RDF queries with multiple joins. In: ICDE, pp. 984–994. IEEE (2011)
15. Papapetrou, O., Siberski, W., Nejdl, W.: Cardinality estimation and dynamic length adaptation for bloom filters. Distrib. Parallel Databases **28**(2–3), 119–156 (2010)
16. Sarasua, C., Checco, A., Demartini, G., Difallah, D., Feldman, M., Pintscher, L.: The evolution of power and standard Wikidata editors: comparing editing behavior over time to predict lifespan and volume of edits. Comput. Support. Coop. Work (CSCW) (2018). https://doi.org/10.1007/s10606-018-9344-y
17. Soulet, A., Giacometti, A., Markhoff, B., Suchanek, F.M.: Representativeness of knowledge bases with the generalized Benford's law. In: Vrandečić, D., et al. (eds.) ISWC 2018. LNCS, vol. 11136, pp. 374–390. Springer, Cham (2018). https://doi.org/10.1007/978-3-030-00671-6_22
18. Pellissier Tanon, T., Stepanova, D., Razniewski, S., Mirza, P., Weikum, G.: Completeness-aware rule learning from knowledge graphs. In: d'Amato, C., et al. (eds.) ISWC 2017. LNCS, vol. 10587, pp. 507–525. Springer, Cham (2017). https://doi.org/10.1007/978-3-319-68288-4_30
19. Trushkowsky, B., Kraska, T., Franklin, M.J., Sarkar, P.: Crowdsourced enumeration queries. In: ICDE, pp. 673–684. IEEE (2013)
20. Vrandečić, D., Krötzsch, M.: Wikidata: a free collaborative knowledgebase. Commun. ACM **57**(10), 78–85 (2014)
21. Walther, B., Morand, S.: Comparative performance of species richness estimation methods. Parasitology **116**(4), 395–405 (1998)
22. Wang, R.Y., Strong, D.M.: Beyond accuracy: what data quality means to data consumers. J. Manag. Inf. Syst. **12**(4), 5–33 (1996)
23. Wulczyn, E., West, R., Zia, L., Leskovec, J.: Growing Wikipedia across languages via recommendation. In: WWW, pp. 975–985 (2016)
24. Zaveri, A., Rula, A., Maurino, A., Pietrobon, R., Lehmann, J., Auer, S.: Quality assessment for linked data: a survey. Semant. Web J. **7**, 63–93 (2015)

Pretrained Transformers for Simple Question Answering over Knowledge Graphs

Denis Lukovnikov[1(✉)], Asja Fischer[2], and Jens Lehmann[1,3]

[1] University of Bonn, Bonn, Germany
{lukovnik,jens.lehmann}@cs.uni-bonn.de
[2] Ruhr University Bochum, Bochum, Germany
asja.fischer@rub.de
[3] Fraunhofer IAIS, Dresden, Germany
jens.lehmann@iais.fraunhofer.de

Abstract. Answering simple questions over knowledge graphs is a well-studied problem in question answering. Previous approaches for this task built on recurrent and convolutional neural network based architectures that use pretrained word embeddings. It was recently shown that finetuning pretrained transformer networks (e.g. BERT) can outperform previous approaches on various natural language processing tasks. In this work, we investigate how well BERT performs on SimpleQuestions and provide an evaluation of both BERT and BiLSTM-based models in limited-data scenarios.

1 Introduction

Question Answering (QA) over structured data aims to directly provide users with answers to their questions (stated in natural language), computed from data contained in the underlying database or knowledge graph (KG). To this end, a knowledge graph question answering (KGQA) system has to understand the intent of the given question, formulate a query, and retrieve the answer by querying the underlying knowledge base. The task of translating natural language (NL) inputs to their logical forms (queries) is also known as semantic parsing. In this work, we focus on answering simple questions (requiring the retrieval of only a single fact) over KGs such as Freebase [2].

The availability of large quantities of high-quality data is essential for successfully training neural networks on any task. However, in many cases, such datasets can be difficult and costly to construct. Fortunately, the lack of data can be mitigated by relying on transfer learning from other tasks with more data. In transfer learning, (neural network) models are first trained on a different but related task, with the goal of capturing relevant knowledge in the pretrained model. Then, the pretrained model is finetuned on the target task, with the goal of reusing the knowledge captured in the pretraining phase to improve performance on the target task.

C. Ghidini et al. (Eds.): ISWC 2019, LNCS 11778, pp. 470–486, 2019.
https://doi.org/10.1007/978-3-030-30793-6_27

Recently proposed transfer learning methods [5,8,10,15,17,18] show that significant improvement on downstream natural language processing (NLP) tasks can be obtained by finetuning a neural network that has been trained for language modeling (LM) over a large corpus of text data without task-specific annotations. Models leveraging these techniques have also shown faster convergence and encouraging results in a few-shot or limited-data settings [8]. Owing to their benefit, the use of this family of techniques is an emerging research topic in the NLP community [10]. However, it has received little attention in KGQA research so far.

The main focus of our work is to investigate transfer learning for question answering over knowledge graphs (KGQA) using models pretrained for language modeling. For our investigation, we choose BERT [5] as our pretrained model used for finetuning, and investigate transfer from BERT using the SimpleQuestions [3] task. BERT is a deep transformer [20] network trained on a masked language modeling (MLM) task as well as a subsequent sentence pair classification task. We use SimpleQuestions because it is a very well-studied dataset that characterizes core challenges of KGQA, and is, to the best of our knowledge, the largest gold standard dataset for KGQA. The large size of the dataset is particularly appealing for our study, because it allows us to investigate performance for a wider range of sizes of the data used for training. Promising results with BERT for KGQA have been very recently reported on other KGQA datasets [12]. However, we found a thorough investigation of the impact of data availability and an analysis of internal model behavior to be missing, which would help to better understand model behavior in applications of KGQA.

The contributions of this work are as follows:

- We demonstrate for the first time the use of a pretrained transformer network (BERT) for simple KGQA. We also propose a simple change in our models that yields a significant improvement in entity span prediction compared to previous work.
- We provide a thorough evaluation of pretrained transformers on SimpleQuestions for different amounts of data used in training and compare with a strong baseline based on bidirectional Long-Short-Term-Memory [7] (BiLSTM). To the best of our knowledge, our work is the first to provide an analysis of performance degradation with reduced training data sizes for SimpleQuestions and KGQA in general.
- We try to provide an understanding of the internal behavior of transformer-based models by analyzing the changes in internal attention behavior induced in the transformer during finetuning.

We perform our study using the general framework used in recent works [13, 16], where simple question interpretation is decomposed into (1) entity span detection, (2) relation classification, and (3) a heuristic-based post-processing step to produce final predictions. In this work, we particularly focus on the first two subtasks, providing detailed evaluation results and comparison with a baseline as well as [13].

2 Approach

We follow the general approach outlined in BuboQA [13], which decomposes simple question interpretation into two separate learning problems: (1) entity span detection and (2) relation classification. Recent works on SimpleQuestions show that this general approach, followed by a heuristic-based entity linking and evidence integration step can achieve state-of-the-art performance [13,16], compared to earlier works [4,6,11,24] that investigated more complicated models.

In summary, our approach follows the following steps at test time:

1. Entity Span Detection and Relation Prediction: The fine-tuned BERT model is used to perform sequence tagging to both (1) identify the span s of the question q that mentions the entity (see Sect. 2.2) and (2) predict the relation r used in q (see Sect. 2.3). In the example "*Where was Michael Crichton born?*", s would be the span "*Michael Crichton*". The tagger is trained using annotations automatically generated from the training data and entity labels in Freebase.
2. Entity Candidate Generation: We retrieve entities whose labels are similar to the predicted entity span s using an inverted index[1] and rank them first by string similarity (using `fuzzywuzzy`) and then by the number of outgoing relations. For our example, the resulting set of entity candidates will contain the true entity for Michael Crichton, the writer (corresponding to Freebase URI http://www.freebase.com/m/056wb). Note that the true entity does not necessarily rank highest after the retrieval phase.
3. Query Ranking: Given the relations predicted in Step 1, and the set of entities from Step 2, the entity-relation pairs are re-ranked as detailed in Sect. 2.4. After ranking entity-relation pairs, we take the top-scoring pair, from which we can trivially generate a query to retrieve the answer from the KG.

Whereas previous works experimented with recurrent and convolutional neural network (RNN resp. CNN) architectures, we investigate an approach based on transformers. Several existing works train separate models for the two learning tasks, i.e. entity span detection and relation prediction. Instead, we train a single network for both tasks simultaneously.

2.1 Background: Transformers and BERT

Transformers: Transformer [20] networks have been recently proposed for NLP tasks and are fundamentally different from the previously common RNN and CNN architectures. Compared to RNNs, which maintain a recurrent state, transformers use multi-head self-attention to introduce conditioning on other timesteps. This enables the parallel computation of all feature vectors in a transformer layer, unlike RNNs, which process the input sequence one time step at a

[1] The inverted index maps words to entities whose labels contain that word.

time. And unlike RNNs, which have to store information useful for handling long-range dependencies in its hidden state, the transformer can access any timestep directly using the self-attention mechanism.

More specifically, transformers consists of several layers of multi-head self-attention with feedforward layers and skip connections. Multi-head self-attention is an extension of the standard attention mechanism [1], with two major differences: (1) attention is applied only within the input sequence and (2) multiple attention heads enable one layer to attend to different places in the input sequence.

Let the transformer consist of L layers, each ($l \in \{1, \ldots, L\}$) producing N output vectors $\mathbf{x}_1^{l+1}, \ldots, \mathbf{x}_N^{l+1}$, which are then used as inputs in the $l+1$-th transformer layer. The inputs $\mathbf{x}_1^1, \ldots, \mathbf{x}_N^1$ to the first transformer layer are the embeddings of the input tokens $x_1, \ldots, x_T$.

The attention scores of the l-th layer are computed as follows:

$$a_{l,h,i,j} = (\mathbf{x}_i^l W_Q^{(l,h)})^\top (\mathbf{x}_j^l W_K^{(l,h)}), \tag{1}$$

$$\alpha_{l,h,i,j} = \frac{e^{a_{h,l,i,j}}}{\sum_{k=1}^{N} e^{a_{h,l,i,k}}}, \tag{2}$$

where $\alpha_{l,h,i,j}$ is the self-attention score for head $h \in \{1, \ldots, M\}$ in layer l between position i (corresponding to $\mathbf{x}_i^l$) and position j (corresponding to $\mathbf{x}_j^l$) and is implemented as a softmax of dot products between the input vectors $\mathbf{x}_i^l$ and $\mathbf{x}_j^l$, after multiplication with the so called query and key projection matrices for head h of layer l ($W_Q^{(l,h)}$ and $W_K^{(l,h)}$, respectively).

Intermediate representation vectors for each input position are computed as the concatenation of the M heads' summary vectors, each computed as a $\alpha_{l,h,i,j}$-weighted sum of input vectors $\mathbf{x}_1^l, \ldots, \mathbf{x}_N^l$, which are first projected using the matrix $W_V^{(l,h)}$:

$$\mathbf{h}_i^l = [\sum_{j=1}^{N} \alpha_{l,h,i,j} \cdot \mathbf{x}_j^l W_V^{(l,h)}]_{h=1..M} \,. \tag{3}$$

The output of the l-th transformer layer (which is also the input to the $l+1$-th layer) is then given by applying a two-layer feedforward network with a ReLU activation function on $\mathbf{h}_i^l$, that is:

$$\mathbf{x}_i^{l+1} = \max(0, \mathbf{h}_i^l W_1^{(l)} + b_1^{(l)}) W_2^{(l)} + b_2^{(l)}. \tag{4}$$

For more details, that were omitted here, we refer the reader to the work of Vaswani et al. [20] and other excellent resources, like the Illustrated Transformer[2].

[2] http://jalammar.github.io/illustrated-transformer/.

BERT: Following previous work on transfer learning form pretrained transformer-based language models [17], Devlin et al. [5] pretrain transformers on a large collection of unsupervised language data, leading to a model called BERT. However, in contrast to a classical, left-to-right language model used by OpenAI-GPT [17], BERT builds on pretraining a masked language model (MLM). The MLM pretraining is done by randomly masking words, i.e. by randomly replacing them with `[MASK]` tokens, feeding the resulting partially masked sequence into the model and training the model to predict the words that have been masked out, given the other words. This enables BERT's feature vectors to include information both from the preceding tokens as well as the following tokens, whereas the left-to-right LM pretraining of OpenAI-GPT constrained the model to look only at the past. In addition to the MLM task, BERT is also pre-trained on a sentence pair classification task. Specifically, it is trained to predict whether one sentence follows another in a text. This pre-training task is useful for downstream tasks such as entailment, which is formulated as classification of sentence pairs, but also for single sentence classification.

BERT for text works as follows. Given a sentence (e.g. "What songs have Nobuo Uematsu produced"), it is first tokenized to (sub) word level using a WordPiece [21] vocabulary (→ ["What", "songs", "have", "no", "#buo", "u", "#ema", "#tsu", "produced"]). More common words are taken as words ("What", "songs", "have"), while uncommon words are split into subword units ("nobuo" → ["no", "#buo"]). This method significantly reduces vocabulary size and the amount of rare words without dramatically increasing sequence length. The input sequence is also padded with a `[CLS]` token at the beginning and a `[SEP]` token at the end.

The WordPiece token sequence is then embedded into a sequence of vectors. Position[3] (and sequence type[4]) embedding vectors are added to the token embeddings. The resulting embedding vectors are fed through the transformer, which uses several layers of multi-head self-attention and feedfoward layers, as described above. The output vectors for each token can be used for sequence tagging tasks, while the vector associated with the `[CLS]` token at the beginning of the sequence is assumed to capture relevant information about the input sequence as a whole, since it has been pre-trained for sentence pair classification.

2.2 Entity Span Prediction

In this step, we intend to identify the span of tokens in the input question referring to the subject entity mentioned in it. Previous works treated this problem as a binary I/O sequence tagging problem, and explored the use of BiLSTM, conditional random fields (CRFs), and combined BiLSTM-CRF taggers. The sequence tagging model is trained to classify each token in the input sequence

[3] The use of self-attention requires explicit position indication since this information can not be implicitly inferred, like in RNNs.

[4] BERT uses two sequence types: first-sentence and second-sentence, where the latter is only used for sentence-pair inputs and is thus irrelevant for our task.

as belonging to the entity span (I) or not (O). Instead, we treat span prediction as a classification problem, where we predict the start and end positions of the entity span using two classifier heads. This approach assumes that only one entity is mentioned in the question and that its mention is a single contiguous span. Formally, the start-position classifier has the following form:

$$p(i = \texttt{START}|x_1, \ldots, x_N) = \frac{e^{\mathbf{x}_i^{L+1\top} \mathbf{w}_{\texttt{START}}}}{\sum_{j=1}^{N} e^{\mathbf{x}_j^{L+1\top} \mathbf{w}_{\texttt{START}}}}, \tag{5}$$

where $\mathbf{x}_i^{L+1}$ is the feature vector produced by BERT's topmost (L-th) layer for the i-th token of the sequence and $\mathbf{w}_{\texttt{START}}$ is the parameter vector of the start position classifier. End position prediction works analogously, applying a different parameter vector, $\mathbf{w}_{\texttt{END}}$.

2.3 Relation Prediction

Relation prediction can be considered a sequence classification task since the SimpleQuestions task assumes there is only a single relation mentioned in the question. Thus, for relation prediction, we use BERT in the sequence classification setting where we take the feature vector $\mathbf{x}_{\texttt{CLS}}^{L+1} = \mathbf{x}_1^{L+1}$ produced for the [CLS][5] token at the beginning of the input sequence and feed it through a softmax output layer to get a distribution over possible relations:

$$p(r = R_i|x_1, \ldots, x_N) = \frac{e^{\mathbf{x}_{\texttt{CLS}}^{L+1\top} \mathbf{w}_{R_i}}}{\sum_{k=1}^{N_R} e^{\mathbf{x}_{\texttt{CLS}}^{L+1\top} \mathbf{w}_{R_k}}}, \tag{6}$$

where $\mathbf{w}_{R_i}$ is the vector representation of relation R_i[6].

Previous works [16,23,24] propose using the question *pattern* instead of the full original question in order to reduce noise and overfitting. They do this by replacing the predicted entity span with a placeholder token. Doing this would require training a separate model for relation prediction and introduce dependency on entity span prediction. In our BERT-based approach, we chose to train a single model to perform both entity span prediction and relation prediction in a single pass. Thus, we do *not* replace the entity span for relation prediction. We also experimented with training a separate transformer with (1) setting the attention mask for all self-attention heads such that the entity tokens are ignored and (2) replacing the entity mention with a [MASK] token. However, both methods failed to improve relation classification accuracy in our experiments.

Training a separate relation classifier network without entity masking yields results equivalent to simply training a single network for both entity span prediction and relation prediction.

---

[5] Before using BERT, the input sequence is first tokenized into WordPieces, a [CLS] token at the beginning and a [SEP] token is added at the end.

[6] The vector $\mathbf{w}_{R_i}$ is a trainable parameter vector, unique for relation R_i (and is thus not presented by subsymbolic encodings as it is for example the case in [11,24]).

2.4 Logical Form Selection

To get the final logical forms, we take the top K (where K = 50 in our experiments) entity candidates during entity retrieval and for each, we take the highest-scored relation that is connected to the entity in the knowledge graph. We rank the entity-predicate candidate pairs first based on the string similarity of any of their entity labels/aliases with the identified span, breaking ties by favouring entity-predicate pairs with predicates with higher prediction probability under the BERT model, and the remaining ties are broken by entity in-degree (the number of triples the entity participates in as an object).

3 Experimental Setup

We use the small uncased pretrained BERT model from a PyTorch implementation of BERT[7]. The whole transformer network and original embeddings were finetuned during training. For training, the Adam optimizer [9] was employed and we experimented with different learning rate schedules. Most of the final results reported use a cosine annealing learning rate schedule with a short warmup phase of approximately 5% of total training updates. We indicate if reported results rely on a different schedule.

We used PyTorch 1.0.1 and trained on single Titan X GPU's. The source code is provided at https://github.com/SmartDataAnalytics/semparse-sq.

3.1 Metrics

To evaluate the entity span prediction model, we compute the average[8] F1 and span accuracy[9] on word level. Since BERT operates on subword-level (WordPiece), we first need to obtain word-level metrics. To do this, we first transform the predictive distributions over subword units to distributions over words by summing the probabilities assigned to subword units of a word. Then, we take the argmax over the resulting distribution over words.

We also compute F1 on word level over the entire dev/test datasets to compare our numbers to BuboQA [13]. Even though the difference between the dataset-wide F1 and the averaged F1 is small, we believe the latter is more informative, since the contribution of every example is equal and independent of the span lengths.[10] (lower entropy of the predictive categorical distribution).

For relation classification, we report classification accuracy.

[7] https://github.com/huggingface/pytorch-pretrained-BERT.

[8] F1, precision and recall are computed separately for each example based on span overlaps and then averaged across all examples in the dev/test set.

[9] Span accuracy is one only for examples where all token memberships are predicted correctly.

[10] The implementation of F1 in BuboQA's evaluation code seems to be computing F1 based on precision and recall computed over the dataset as a whole, thus letting examples with longer spans contribute more towards the final score.

3.2 Baseline

As a baseline, we use a BiLSTM start/end classifier for entity span prediction and a BiLSTM sequence classifier for relation prediction. The BiLSTM start/end classifier works on word level and uses the same Glove [14] embeddings as BuboQA [13]. We use the same output layer form as our BERT-based model, where instead of performing a binary I/O tagging of the input sequence, we simply predict the beginning and end positions of the span using a softmax over sequence length (see also Eq. 5). Using this small change significantly improves the performance of our baseline for entity span prediction, as shown in Sect. 4.

For relation classification, we use a different BiLSTM, taking the final state as the question representation vector and using it in a classifier output as in BuboQA [13] – comprising of an additional forward layer, a ReLU, a batch normalization layer and a softmax output layer. We did not replace the entity mentions with an entity placeholder (like [16]), and instead fed the original sequences into the relation classification encoder.

Even though these BiLSTM baselines are quite basic, previous work has shown they can be trained to obtain state-of-the-art results [13,16].

Both BiLSTMs were trained using a cosine annealing learning rate schedule as the one used to train our BERT-based model.

As shown in Sect. 4, our baselines perform better than or on par with equivalent networks used in BuboQA [13].

3.3 Effect of Limited Training Data

In order to further illustrate the usefulness of fully pretrained models for SimpleQuestions and KGQA, we perform a series of experiments to measure how performance degrades when fewer examples are available for training. SimpleQuestions is a fairly large dataset containing 75k+ training examples. With abundant training data available, a randomly initialized model is likely to learn to generalize well, which might make the advantage of starting from a fully pretrained model less pronounced. The large size of SimpleQuestions makes it possible to study a wider range of limited-data cases than other, smaller datasets.

We run experiments for both BERT and our baseline BiLSTM with different fractions of the original 75k+ training examples retained for training. Examples are retained such that the number of relations not observed during training is minimized, favouring the removal of examples with most frequently occurring relations. We assume that this strategy, compared to random example selection, should not have a big effect on entity span prediction accuracy but should minimize errors in relation prediction due to unseen relation labels, and create more balanced datasets for more informative performance assessment. We report span accuracy and relation accuracy on the validation set of SimpleQuestions as a function of the fraction of data retained in Table 3. For relation prediction, we only report experiments where the retained examples cover all relations observed in the full training dataset at least once.

4 Results and Analysis

For the two learning tasks, we observe significant improvements from using BERT, as shown in Table 1a for entity span prediction and Table 1b for relation prediction (see Sect. 4.1). Section 4.2 talks about experiments with fewer training data, Sect. 4.3 shows component performance on the test set. Final results for the whole simple QA task are discussed in Sect. 4.4. Finally, we conclude with an analysis of the attentions in the transformer in Sect. 4.5.

4.1 Full Data Results

From Table 1a, we can see that BERT outperforms our BiLSTM baseline by almost 2% accuracy (evaluated on validation set), although the difference in F1 is smaller. Compared to BuboQA [13], we obtain much higher dataset-wide F1 scores, which we attribute to our start/end prediction rather than I/O tagging used by previous works, including BuboQA.

The improvement is less pronounced in relation classification accuracies (see Table 1b), where our baseline BiLSTM achieves the same results as those reported by BuboQA [13] for a CNN. Our BERT-based classifier beats our BiLSTM by almost 1% accuracy.

Table 1. Component performance evaluation results, trained on all available training data, measured on validation set. (a) Entity span prediction performance, measured by span accuracy, average span F1 and dataset-wide F1 (F1*), all on word level. (b) Relation prediction performance, measured by accuracy (R@1).

	Accuracy	Avg. F1	F1*
BiLSTM [13]	–	–	93.1
CRF [13]	–	–	90.2
BiLSTM (ours)	93.8	97.0	97.1
BERT (ours)	95.6	97.8	97.9

(a) Entity span prediction.

	Accuracy
BiGRU [13]	82.3
CNN [13]	82.8
BiLSTM (ours)	82.8
BERT (ours)	83.6

(b) Relation prediction.

Table 2 shows entity retrieval performance for different numbers of candidates, compared against the numbers reported in [13]. The recall at 50 is 2.71% higher. Please note that we also use entity popularity during retrieval to break ties that occur when multiple retrieved entities have the same name (and thus the same string similarity—the main sorting criterion).

4.2 Effect of Limited Training Data

From the limited-data experiments for entity span prediction shown in Table 3 (top part), we can conclude that a pretrained transformer is able to generalize

Table 2. Entity recall on validation set.

R@N	BiLSTM [13]	BiLSTM (ours)	BERT (ours)
1	67.8	76.45	77.17
5	82.6	87.46	88.18
20	88.7	91.47	92.13
50	91.0	93.07	93.71
150	–	94.88	95.40

much better with fewer examples. In fact, with only 1% of the original training data used (757 examples), BERT reaches a best span prediction accuracy of 85.4% on the validation set, corresponding to an average F1 of 93.2. In contrast, our BiLSTM baseline achieves only 74.0% span prediction accuracy on the validation set, corresponding to 88.6 F1. In an extremely data-starved scenario, with only 0.03% of the original dataset—corresponding to just 22 training examples—the best validation accuracy we observed for BERT was 62.5%, corresponding to 80.9 F1. In the same setting, we were not able to obtain more than 33.1% accuracy with our BiLSTM baseline. Overall, we can clearly see that the degradation in performance with less data is much stronger for our Glove-based BiLSTM baseline.

Limited-data experiments for relation prediction (shown in Table 3) (bottom part) reveals that relation classification is more challenging for both our BiLSTM and BERT-based models. However here too, BERT seems to degrade more gracefully than our Glove+BiLSTM baseline.

Table 3. Entity span detection accuracies (top half) and relation prediction accuracies (bottom half) as a function of fraction of training data retained. Evaluated on the entire validation set. (*) indicates a cosine learning rate schedule with restarts—in extremely low data scenarios for relation classification, this seems to yield better results than the cosine learning rate schedule without restarts that is used everywhere else.

		0.03% (22)	0.2% (151)	1% (757)	2.5% (1k9)	5% (3k8)	10% (7k6)	25% (18k9)	50% (37k9)	75% (56k8)	100% (75k7)
Entity span	BiLSTM	33.1	64.5	74.0	78.1	82.5	85.5	90.1	92.0	93.4	93.8
	BERT	62.5	79.1	85.4	88.9	90.8	92.4	94.2	94.9	95.5	95.6
Relation	BiLSTM	–	–	–	26.5	41.0	56.3	72.4	79.0	81.3	82.8
	BERT	–	–	–	29.6*	48.6	67.5	76.5	80.1	82.6	83.6

4.3 Performance on Test Set

After identifying good hyperparameters for both our BiLSTM baseline and our BERT-based model using the validation set, we evaluated our models using the same evaluation metrics on the test set. Results for both entity span prediction and relation prediction on the test set are reported in Table 4.[11] As shown in Table 4, the test set results are close to the validation set results for both models.

Table 4. Component results on test set.

	Entity span		Relation
	Accuracy	Avg. F1	Accuracy
BiLSTM	93.2	96.7	82.4
BERT	95.2	97.5	83.5

4.4 Final Results

In Table 5, we compare our final predictions against previous works on SimpleQuestions. With our simple entity linking and logical form selection procedure (see Sect. 2.4), we achieve 77.3% accuracy on the test set of SimpleQuestions, beating all but one of the existing approaches. We suspect that the final score can be further improved by finding better rules for logical form selection, however that is not the goal of this study.

Investigating the entity and relation prediction accuracies separately, we find accuracies of 82.7% for entities and 86.6% for relations. Comparing the 86.6% for relation accuracy after re-ranking (Sect. 2.4) to the 83.5% (Table 4) relation accuracy before the re-ranking confirms that re-ranking has helped to reduce

Table 5. Final accuracy for the full prediction task on the test set of SimpleQuestions. ([19] is not included in the comparison because neither [13] or [16] could reproduce the reported results (86.8%)).

Approach	Accuracy
MemNN [3]	61.6
Attn. LSTM [6]	70.9
GRU [11]	71.2
BuboQA [13]	74.9
BiGRU [4]	75.7
Attn. CNN [23]	76.4
HR-BiLSTM [24]	77.0
BiLSTM-CRF [16]	78.1
BERT (ours)	77.3

[11] Note that the test set contains "unsolvable" entries, where the correct entity span has not been identified in pre-processing. For these examples, we set the accuracy and F1 to zero.

errors. By analyzing the 22.7% of test examples that were predicted incorrectly, it turned out that in 35% of those cases both a wrong relation and a wrong entity had been predicted, in 41% only the entity was wrong and 24% had only a wrong relation. Of all the cases where the entity was predicted wrong, in 28.6% cases this resulted from the correct entity missing in the candidate set. Entity retrieval errors are also correlated with relation errors: of the cases where the correct entity was not among the retrieved candidates, 71.2% had a wrongly predicted relation, against 55.7% for cases where the correct entity was among the candidates.

4.5 Attention Analysis

One of the advantages of using transformers is the ability to inspect the self-attention weights that the model uses to build its representations. Even though this does not completely explain the rules the model learned, it is a step towards explainable decision making in deep learning, and a qualitative improvement upon RNNs. In an attempt to understand how the model works, before and after fine-tuning, we manually inspected the attention distributions used by the transformer network internally during the encoding process.

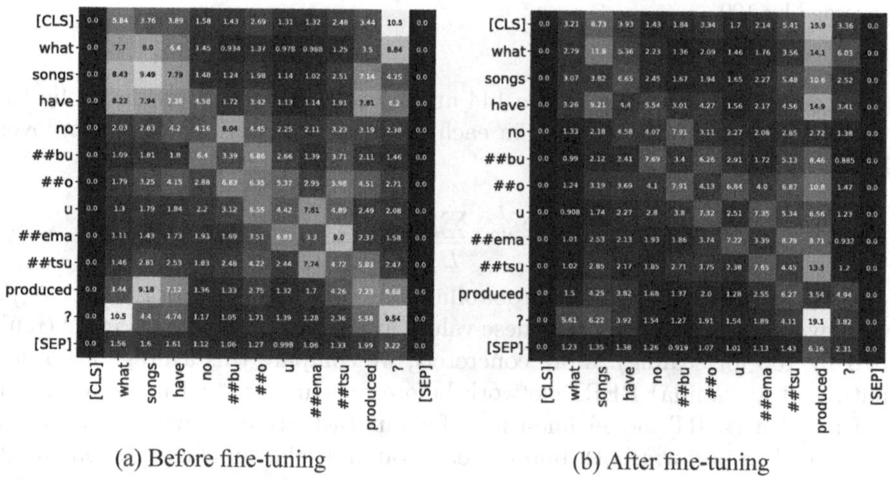

(a) Before fine-tuning (b) After fine-tuning

Fig. 1. Average attention distribution for the example "*What songs have Nobuo Uematsu produced?*", (a) before training on our tasks (vanilla pretrained BERT) , and (b) after training on our tasks (finetuned BERT). The numbers are scaled to values between 0 and 100, and are computed by averaging of the attention distributions over all heads in all layers, and multiplying the average by 100. We set the scores for [CLS] and [SEP] tokens to zero in the plots since they always receive a much higher average attention weight than the actual words from the sentence and thus would dominate the plot.

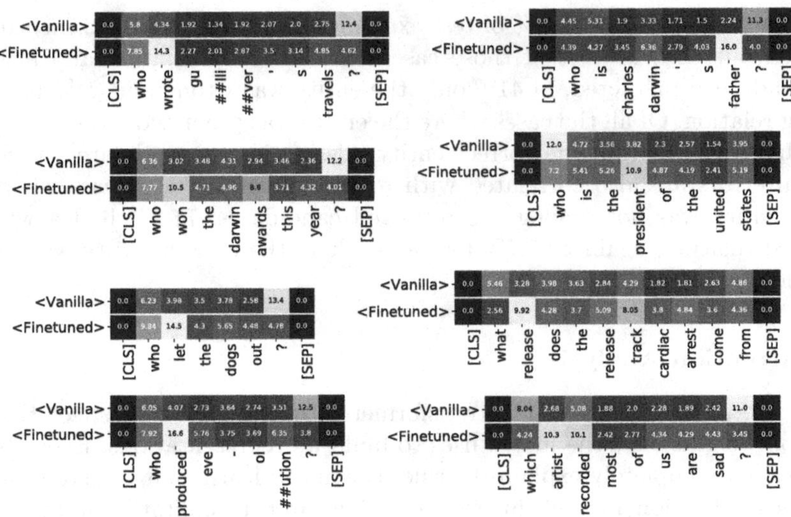

Fig. 2. Average attention distributions for the [CLS] token for several examples. <**Vanilla**> is pretrained BERT before finetuning. <**Finetuned**> is BERT finetuned on our tasks. The numbers are scaled to values between 0 and 100, and are computed by averaging of the attention distributions over all heads in all layers, and multiplying the average by 100.

We compute the average of the 144 attention distributions produced by the $M = 12$ different attention heads in each of the $L = 12$ layers of the employed BERT network:

$$\beta_{i,j} = \frac{\sum_{l=1}^{L} \sum_{h=1}^{M} \alpha_{l,h,i,j}}{L \cdot M}, \tag{7}$$

where $\alpha_{l,h,i,j}$ are the attention probabilities as computed in Eq. 2, Here, $\beta_{i,j}$'s are the average attention scores; these values are displayed in Figs. 1 and 2 (multiplied by 100 for scaling). More concretely, we compare this average attention signature of a (vanilla) BERT network before fine-tuning it with the attention signature of a BERT model fine-tuned for our tasks (recall that we trained a single model to perform both border detection and relation classification simultaneously). By comparing the attentions before and after training on our tasks, we can identify differences in internal behavior of the model that arose during training.

In Fig. 1, the average of all attention distributions is shown for an example question for two versions of the transformer model: pre-trained (vanilla) BERT and BERT fine-tuned for our tasks. While in general, the average attention distribution roughly follows the same patterns after fine-tuning, we can see that the behavior of the attention mechanism responsible for building the representation of the [CLS] token is significantly different. We found that, before fine-tuning, the representation building of the [CLS] token generally focuses on punctuation and less strongly, on other words. After finetuning, [CLS]'s representation is strongly focused on words that characterise the relation conveyed by the sentence. For example, for the question "*Who wrote Gulliver's travels?*" (see Fig. 2, first example), the attention is shifted towards the word "*wrote*", which specifies the authorship relationship of the intended answer with the subject entity (*Gulliver's Travels*) mentioned in the question. We provide several other examples of this kind of attention change in Fig. 2.

This change in internal attention behavior can be explained by the fact that sequence classification for relation prediction is done based on the representation built for the [CLS] token and attending to relation-specifying words more would produce more useful features for the classifier.

5 Related Work

Bordes et al. [3] propose a memory network (MemNN)-based solution to SimpleQuestions. They use bag-of-words representations for triples and question and train a model that predicts the right triple by minimizing a margin-based ranking loss as defined in the section above. They compute scores between questions and whole triples, including the triple objects. However, triple objects are answers and thus might not be present in the question, which may affect the performance adversely. The same work introduces the SimpleQuestions dataset, consisting of approximately 100,000 question-answer pairs.

Follow-up works on SimpleQuestions typically predict the subject entity and predicate separately, (unlike [3], which ranks whole triples). [6] explore fully character-level encoding of questions, entities and predicates, and use an attention-based decoder [1]. [11] explore building question representations on both word- and character-level. [24] explore relation detection in-depth and propose a hierarchical word-level and symbol-level residual representation. Both [4] and [11] improve upon them by incorporating structural information such as entity type for entity linking. [4] and [23] propose an auxiliary BiRNN+CRF sequence labeling model to determine the span of the entity. The detected entity span is then used for filtering entity candidates. Further, [13] investigates different RNN and CNN-based relation detectors and a BiLSTM and CRF-based entity mention detectors. [16] estimates the upper-bound on accuracy for SimpleQuestions, which is less than 83.4% due to unresolvable ambiguities (which is caused by the question lacking information to correctly disambiguate entities). Both [16] and [13] first identify the entity span, similarly to previous works, but disambiguate the entity without using neural networks. With extensive hyperparameter tuning, relatively basic models and simple heuristics, [16] outperformed previous approaches.

[22] proposes a semi-supervised method for semantic parsing based on a structured variational autoencoder that treats logical forms as tree-structured latent variables, and also performs experiments in limited data settings (on ATIS and DJANGO).

6 Conclusion

As demonstrated by our experiments, BERT significantly outperforms a strong BiLSTM baseline on the learning problems of relation classification and entity span prediction for simple questions. Moreover, the pre-trained transformer shows less performance decrease when confronted with fewer training data, as can be seen in our limited-data study, which to the best of our knowledge is the first ever conducted for the SimpleQuestions data set. The final results on the whole SimpleQuestions task are competitive with the current state-of-the-art.

Our comparison of a fully pre-trained transformer to a BiLSTM-based model where only the word embeddings have been pretrained (Glove) might not yield a fair comparison between the two architectures (transformer vs BiLSTM). Further insights could be gained by analyzing the performance of a BiLSTM, which has also been pretrained as a language model (maybe combined with other tasks) in future. Here instead, our aim was to provide evidence that the use of neural networks pre-trained as language model is beneficial for knowledge graph-based question answering like answering SimpleQuestions, a usecase not included in the original BERT evaluation and, to the best of our knowledge, not yet explored in the literature.

Even though BERT improves upon our BiLSTM baseline on SimpleQuestions, the improvements in the full data scenario might not justify the significantly longer training and inference times and memory requirements. These practical concerns, however, could be mitigated by practical tweaks and future research. Furthermore, with fewer data the performance increases w.r.t. the baseline become more spectacular, indicating that using pre-trained networks like BERT might be essential for achieving reasonable performance in limited data scenarios. Such scenarios are common for datasets with more complex questions. Therefore, we believe pretrained networks like BERT can have a bigger impact for complex KGQA (even when training with all data available).

Acknowledgement. We acknowledge support by the European Union H2020 Framework Project Cleopatra (GA no. 812997). Furthermore, this work has been supported by the Fraunhofer Cluster of Excellence "Cognitive Internet Technologies" (CCIT).

References

1. Bahdanau, D., Cho, K., Bengio, Y.: Neural machine translation by jointly learning to align and translate. arXiv preprint arXiv:1409.0473 (2014)
2. Bollacker, K., Evans, C., Paritosh, P., Sturge, T., Taylor, J.: Freebase: a collaboratively created graph database for structuring human knowledge. In: Proceedings of the 2008 ACM SIGMOD International Conference on Management of Data, pp. 1247–1250. ACM (2008)
3. Bordes, A., Usunier, N., Chopra, S., Weston, J.: Large-scale simple question answering with memory networks. arXiv preprint arXiv:1506.02075 (2015)
4. Dai, Z., Li, L., Xu, W.: CFO: conditional focused neural question answering with large-scale knowledge bases. In: Proceedings of the 54th Annual Meeting of the

Association for Computational Linguistics (Volume 1: Long Papers), vol. 1, pp. 800–810 (2016)
5. Devlin, J., Chang, M.W., Lee, K., Toutanova, K.: Bert: pre-training of deep bidirectional transformers for language understanding. arXiv preprint arXiv:1810.04805 (2018)
6. He, X., Golub, D.: Character-level question answering with attention. In: Proceedings of the 2016 Conference on Empirical Methods in Natural Language Processing, pp. 1598–1607 (2016)
7. Hochreiter, S., Schmidhuber, J.: Long short-term memory. Neural Comput. **9**(8), 1735–1780 (1997)
8. Howard, J., Ruder, S.: Universal language model fine-tuning for text classification. In: Proceedings of the 56th Annual Meeting of the Association for Computational Linguistics (Volume 1: Long Papers), pp. 328–339 (2018)
9. Kingma, D.P., Ba, J.: Adam: a method for stochastic optimization. arXiv preprint arXiv:1412.6980 (2014)
10. Liu, X., He, P., Chen, W., Gao, J.: Multi-task deep neural networks for natural language understanding. arXiv preprint arXiv:1901.11504 (2019)
11. Lukovnikov, D., Fischer, A., Lehmann, J., Auer, S.: Neural network-based question answering over knowledge graphs on word and character level. In: Proceedings of the 26th International Conference on World Wide Web, pp. 1211–1220. International World Wide Web Conferences Steering Committee (2017)
12. Maheshwari, G., Trivedi, P., Lukovnikov, D., Chakraborty, N., Fischer, A., Lehmann, J.: Learning to rank query graphs for complex question answering over knowledge graphs. In: International Semantic Web Conference. Springer, Heidelberg (2019)
13. Mohammed, S., Shi, P., Lin, J.: Strong baselines for simple question answering over knowledge graphs with and without neural networks. In: Proceedings of the 2018 Conference of the North American Chapter of the Association for Computational Linguistics: Human Language Technologies, Volume 2 (Short Papers), vol. 2, pp. 291–296 (2018)
14. Pennington, J., Socher, R., Manning, C.: Glove: global vectors for word representation. In: Proceedings of the 2014 Conference on Empirical Methods In Natural Language Processing (EMNLP), pp. 1532–1543 (2014)
15. Peters, M.E., et al.: Deep contextualized word representations. In: Proceedings of NAACL (2018)
16. Petrochuk, M., Zettlemoyer, L.: Simplequestions nearly solved: a new upperbound and baseline approach. In: Proceedings of the 2018 Conference on Empirical Methods in Natural Language Processing (2018)
17. Radford, A., Narasimhan, K., Salimans, T., Sutskever, I.: Improving language understanding by generative pre-training (2018)
18. Radford, A., Wu, J., Child, R., Luan, D., Amodei, D., Sutskever, I.: Language models are unsupervised multitask learners. Technical report (2019)
19. Ture, F., Jojic, O.: No need to pay attention: simple recurrent neural networks work! In: Proceedings of the 2017 Conference on Empirical Methods in Natural Language Processing, pp. 2866–2872 (2017)
20. Vaswani, A., et al.: Attention is all you need. In: Advances in Neural Information Processing Systems, pp. 5998–6008 (2017)
21. Wu, Y., et al.: Google's neural machine translation system: bridging the gap between human and machine translation. arXiv preprint arXiv:1609.08144 (2016)

22. Yin, P., Zhou, C., He, J., Neubig, G.: StructVAE: tree-structured latent variable models for semi-supervised semantic parsing. In: Gurevych, I., Miyao, Y. (eds.) Proceedings of the 56th Annual Meeting of the Association for Computational Linguistics, ACL 2018, Melbourne, Australia, 15–20 July 2018, Volume 1: Long Papers, pp. 754–765. Association for Computational Linguistics (2018). https://aclanthology.info/papers/P18-1070/p18-1070
23. Yin, W., Yu, M., Xiang, B., Zhou, B., Schütze, H.: Simple question answering by attentive convolutional neural network. In: Proceedings of COLING 2016, the 26th International Conference on Computational Linguistics: Technical Papers, pp. 1746–1756 (2016)
24. Yu, M., Yin, W., Hasan, K.S., dos Santos, C., Xiang, B., Zhou, B.: Improved neural relation detection for knowledge base question answering. In: Proceedings of the 55th Annual Meeting of the Association for Computational Linguistics (Volume 1: Long Papers), vol. 1, pp. 571–581 (2017)

Learning to Rank Query Graphs for Complex Question Answering over Knowledge Graphs

Gaurav Maheshwari[1,3(✉)], Priyansh Trivedi[1,3], Denis Lukovnikov[1], Nilesh Chakraborty[1], Asja Fischer[2], and Jens Lehmann[1,3]

[1] Smart Data Analytics (SDA) Group, Bonn, Germany
[2] Ruhr-University, Bochum, Germany
[3] Fraunhofer IAIS, Dresden, Germany
Gaurav.Maheshwari@iais.fraunhofer.de

Abstract. In this paper, we conduct an empirical investigation of neural query graph ranking approaches for the task of complex question answering over knowledge graphs. We propose a novel self-attention based *slot matching* model which exploits the inherent structure of query graphs, our logical form of choice. Our proposed model generally outperforms other ranking models on two QA datasets over the DBpedia knowledge graph, evaluated in different settings. We also show that domain adaption and pre-trained language model based transfer learning yield improvements, effectively offsetting the general lack of training data.

1 Introduction

Knowledge graph question answering (KGQA), where natural language questions like "What is the population of the capital of Germany?" can be answered by lookup and composition of one or many facts from a knowledge graph (KG), has garnered significant interest in the Natural Language Processing (NLP) and Semantic Web community.

Numerous approaches [2,7,22] use semantic parsing to create an *ungrounded* expression of a given natural language question (NLQ), and then ground it w.r.t. a target KG. Here, *grounding* refers to linking elements in the expression with elements (i.e. entities and predicates) in the KG. While this approach suits the non-trivial task of handling wide syntactic and semantic variations of a question during parsing, it needs to handle lexical as well as structural mismatch between the generated expression and the target KG during grounding. For instance, the predicate $mother(x_a, x_b)$, parsed from a question, might be represented as $parent(x_a, x_b) \wedge gender(x_a, female)$ in a KG. Failing to anticipate and tackle these issues can lead to undesirable situations where the system generates expressions which are illegal w.r.t. the given KG.

G. Maheshwari, P. Trivedi, D. Lukovnikov and N. Chakraborty—These four authors contributed equally.

C. Ghidini et al. (Eds.): ISWC 2019, LNCS 11778, pp. 487–504, 2019.
https://doi.org/10.1007/978-3-030-30793-6_28

We focus on an alternate family of approaches [23,24] which, given an NLQ, first generate a list of formal expressions describing possible candidate queries which are in accordance with the KG structure, and then rank them w.r.t. the NLQ. We use a custom grammar called *query graph* to represent these candidate expressions, comprised of paths in the KG along with some auxiliary constraints. In this work, we propose a novel *slot matching* model for ranking query graphs. The proposed model exploits the structure of query graphs by using attention to compute different representations of the question for each predicate in the query graph. We compare our models against several baseline models by evaluating them over two DBpedia [12] based KGQA datasets namely, LC-QuAD [20] and QALD-7 [21].

Furthermore, we appropriate bidirectional transformers (BERT) [6] to be used in the slot matching configuration, thereby enabling the use of large-scale pre-trained language models for the task. To the best of our knowledge, this is the first work that explores their use for KGQA.

Finally, we also investigate the potential of transfer learning in KGQA by fine-tuning models trained on LC-QuAD on the much smaller QALD-7 dataset, resulting in a significant improvement in performance on the latter. We thereby demonstrate the efficacy of simple transfer learning techniques for improving performance of KGQA on target domains that lack training data.

The major contributions of this work are summarized as follows:

- A novel ranking model which exploits the structure of query graphs, and uses multiple attention scores to explicitly compare each predicate in a query graph with the natural language question.
- An investigation of fine-tuning based transfer learning across datasets and the use of pre-trained language models (BERT [6]) for the KGQA task.

Our experiments show that the proposed slot-matching model outperforms the baseline models, and that it can be combined with transfer learning techniques to offset the lack of training data in target domain. We have made the source code of our system, and the experiments publicly available at https://github.com/AskNowQA/KrantikariQA.

2 Related Work

In this section we briefly summarize existing approaches for KGQA and transfer learning techniques relevant to the use of pretrained language models for downstream tasks.

2.1 KG Question Answering

Traditional semantic parsing based KGQA approaches [2,5,7,8,19,22] aim to learn semantic parsers that generate *ungrounded* logical form expressions from NLQs, and subsequently ground the expressions semantically by querying the KG.

In recent years, several papers have taken an alternate approach to semantic parsing by treating KGQA as a problem of semantic graph generation and ranking of different candidate graphs. [1] compare a set of manually defined query templates against the NLQ and generate a set of grounded query graph candidates by enriching the templates with potential predicates. Notably, [23] create grounded *query graph* candidates using a staged heuristic search algorithm, and employ a neural ranking model for scoring and finding the optimal semantic graph. The approach we propose in this work is closely related to this. [24] use a hierarchical representation of KG predicates in their neural query graph ranking model. They compare their results against a local sub-sequence alignment model with cross-attention [16] (originally proposed for the natural language inferencing task [3]). We adapt the models proposed by both [16] and [24] to our task, and compare them against the ranking model we propose (See Sect. 4.2).

2.2 Transfer Learning from Pre-trained Language Models

Recently, multiple approaches have been proposed exploiting transfer learning from pre-trained language models for downstream NLP tasks. They typically use a (downstream) task-agnostic architecture that undergoes time-consuming pre-training over large-scale general-domain corpus, and then is fine-tuned for different target tasks separately. [10] propose an innovative mechanism of fine-tuning long-short-term-memory (LSTMs) [9] and a wide repertoire of regularization techniques which prevent overfitting and catastrophic forgetting. The use of transformers in a similar transfer learning setting was proposed by [18]. The architecture was augmented by [6] enabling bidirectional training of transformers by masking random tokens in the input sequence, and training the model to predict those missing words. Generally, these approaches have achieved state-of-the-art results over multiple NLP tasks, including text classification, reading comprehension, named entity recognition. Motivated by their success, we investigate the effect of leveraging these transfer learning approaches for KGQA (as described in Sect. 5.3). Parallel to our work, [14] also explored the use of pre-trained transformer for the task of simple question answering over KG. They showed that with a fraction of training data, using pre-trained language models can achieve almost similar performance to those trained from scratch.

3 Background

In this section we will give a formal definition of the task of KGQA and a description of the employed query graph language.

3.1 Problem Formulation

Let $K \subseteq (\mathcal{E} \times \mathcal{P} \times (\mathcal{E} \cup \mathcal{L}))$ be a KG where $\mathcal{E} = \{e_1 \ldots e_{n_e}\}$ is the set of entities, $\mathcal{L}$ is the set of all literal values, and $\mathcal{P} = \{p_1 \ldots p_{n_p}\}$ is the set of predicates connecting two entities, or an entity with a literal.

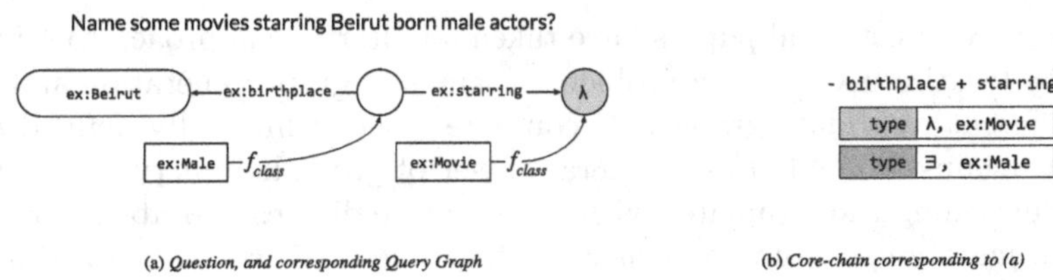

Fig. 1. A question and its corresponding query graph (a), and core chain (b).

Given K, and a natural language question Q, the KGQA task can be defined as generating an expression in a formal query language, which returns the intended answer $a \in A$ when executed over K. Here, A is the set of all answers a KGQA system can be expected to retrieve, consisting of (i) a subset of entities (e_i) or literals (l_i) from K, (ii) the result of an arbitrary aggregation function ($f : \{e_i\} \cup \{l_i\} \mapsto \mathbb{N}$), or (iii) a boolean ($T/F$) variable depending on whether the subgraph implied by Q is a subset of K.

In contrast, answering *simple questions* is a subset of the above KGQA task where (i) the answer set can only contain A, a subset of entities (e_i) or literals (l_i), and (ii) members of the answer set must be directly connected to the topic entity with a predicate $p_i \in \mathcal{P}$. This work aims to solve the aforementioned KGQA task, which implicitly includes answering simple questions as well.

3.2 Query Graphs

We use query graphs as the intermediary query language to express candidates of formal KG queries given an NLQ. They represent a path in K as a directed acyclic labeled graph. We borrow the augmentations made to the query graph grammar in [23], which makes the conversion from query graph expressions to executable queries trivial, and slightly modify it to suit our use case. In the subsequent paragraphs we detail the modified query graph grammar we employ.

Elements of a Query Graph: A query graph consists of a combination of nodes $n \in \{$*grounded entity, existential variable, lambda variable, auxiliary function*$\}$, connected with labeled, directed edges representing predicates from the set of predicates $\mathcal{P}$ of K. We define each of the aforementioned elements in detail below by the help of a running example, answering the question "*Name some movies starring Beirut born male actors?*":

- **Grounded Entities:** Grounded entities correspond to entities of K mentioned in the NLQ. Each query graph has at least one grounded entity. In the case of our example, ex:Beirut is the grounded entity represented by the rounded rectangle in Fig. 1a.
- **Existential Variables:** Existential variables are ungrounded nodes, i.e. they do not correspond to an explicit entity mentioned in the NLQ but are instead placeholders for intermediate entities in the KG path. They help disambiguate

the structure of query graphs by the means of auxiliary functions (described below). In our example, we have one existential variable which is represented by a circle and stands for entities like ex:Keanu_Reeves and ex:Nadine_Labaki.
- **Lambda Variables:** Similar to *existential variables*, they are ungrounded nodes acting as a placeholder for a set of entities which are the potential answer to the query. The are represented by shaded circles in our example, and can have entities like ex:John_Wick (a movie) and ex:Rain (a TV series) mapped to it.
- **Auxiliary Functions:** Auxiliary functions are applied over the set of entities mapped to any ungrounded node (i.e. *grounded* and *existential variables*) in the query graph. In our grammar, they can be of two types, namely, the cardinality function or a class constraint $f_{class} : \{e \in E | (e, \text{rdf:type}, class) \in K\}$ where $(class, \text{rdf:type}, \text{owl:Class}) \in K$. In our example, we can apply the class constraint function over the entities mapped to the existential variable to only include male actors, and to the entities mapped to the lambda variable, represented by rectangle, to only include movies. The cardinality constraint can be used for NLQs like "*How many movies have casted Beirut born male actors?*" by imposing a count constraint over the lambda variable.

Finally, a new flag is defined which determines whether the query graph is used to fetch the value of the lambda variable, or to verify whether the graph is a valid subset of the target KG. The latter is used in the case of Boolean queries like "*Did Keanu Reeves act in John Wick?*" We represent this decision with a flag instead of another node or constraint in the graph as it doesn't affect the execution of the query graph, but in the case of a Boolean query only inquires, post execution, whether the query had a valid solution.

Query Graph Representation: We represent the query graphs in a linear form so as to easily encode them in our ranking models. We linearize the directed graph by starting from one of the grounded entities and using +, − signs to denote the outgoing and incoming edges, respectively. We represent auxiliary functions with another flag along with the linearized chain. Externalizing the auxiliary functions enables us to remove the ungrounded nodes from the core chain, which is now composed of the grounded entity and relations prefixed by +, − signs. Finally, we replace the URIs of the grounded entities and predicates with their corresponding surface forms. Hereafter, we refer to this linearized representation as the *core chain* of a query graph. This representation also ensures that the query graph maintains textual similarity to the source NLQ, enabling us to use a wide variety of text similarity based approaches for ranking them. Figure 1b illustrates the core chain corresponding to the query graph in our running example. In our preliminary analysis we found that removing mentions of grounded entities in the core chain increased the performance of our approach. We thus exclude the grounded entities from the final core chain representation. Since the grounded entities are the same for a given NLQ, no information is lost from the core chain candidate set upon doing this.

4 Approach Overview

We treat KGQA as the task of generating and ranking query graph candidates w.r.t. a given NLQ. For instance, given the question "What is the population of the capital of Germany?", we would like a ranking model to assign a higher score to "`+ capital + population`" than "`+ capital + mayor`", where "+" indicates that the relation must be followed in the forward direction. More formally, given a question Q and a set of candidate core chains $C^1 \dots C^N$, we select the most plausible core chain as follows:

$$C^* = \underset{C^i}{\operatorname{argmax}} \; \mathsf{sim}(Q, C^i) \; , \tag{1}$$

where $\mathsf{sim}(\cdot,\cdot)$ is a function assigning a score to a pair of a NLQ and a core chain. We implement $\mathsf{sim}(\cdot,\cdot)$ as the dot product of two vectors produced by the encoder $\mathsf{enc}^{\mathsf{q}}(Q)$ and the core chain encoder $\mathsf{enc}^{\mathsf{c}}(C^n)$ respectively, i.e.,

$$\mathsf{sim}(Q, C^n) = \mathsf{enc}^{\mathsf{q}}(Q) \cdot \mathsf{enc}^{\mathsf{c}}(C^n) \; . \tag{2}$$

We train our ranking model with a pairwise loss function that maximizes the difference between the score of correct (positive) and incorrect (negative) pairs of NLQs and core chains, that is

$$L = \max(0, \gamma - \mathsf{sim}(Q, C^+) + \mathsf{sim}(Q, C^-)) \; , \tag{3}$$

where $\mathsf{sim}(Q, C^+)$ and $\mathsf{sim}(Q, C^-)$ are the scores for the correct and incorrect question-core chain pair, respectively.

We assume the entities mentioned in the NLQ to be given (but do not require exact entity spans i.e which tokens in the question correspond to which entity). In the next section (Sect. 4.1), we outline a mechanism for generating core chain candidates. Following that, we describe a novel core chain ranking model in Sect. 4.2. Furthermore, for a fully functioning QA system, additional auxiliary functions needs to be predicted. We define them, and outline our method of predicting them in Sect. 4.3.

4.1 Core Chain Candidate Generation

Core chains, as described in the previous section, are linearized subsets of query graphs which represent a path consisting of entities and predicates without the additional constraints. Working under the assumption that the information required to answer the question is present in the target KG, and that we know the entities mentioned in the question, we collect all the plausible paths of up to two hops from an arbitrary grounded entity node[1] to generate the core chain candidate set. Here, we use the term *hop* to collectively refer to a KG relation along with the corresponding +/− sign indicating whether the relation is incoming or outgoing w.r.t. the entity.

[1] Entity that has been linked in the question.

We retrieve candidate core chains by collecting all predicates (one-hop chains) and paths of two predicates (two-hop chains) that can be followed from an arbitrary grounded node. In this process, predicates are followed in both outgoing and incoming direction (and marked with a + and − in the chain, respectively). We further restrict our candidate set of core chains as follows: if two entities have been identified in the question, we discard the core chains which do not contain both the entities as grounded nodes. When applied, this step substantially decreases the candidate set while retaining all the relevant candidates. Finally, we drop the mention of entities from the core chain since every core chain thus generated will contain the same entities in the same position, and doing so leads to no information loss. Doing so enables our ranking models to retain the focus on comparing the predicates of the core chain to the question.

Although we limit the core chains to a length of two hops for the purposes of this study, this approach can easily be generalized to longer core chains. However, it may result in an additional challenge of handling a larger number of candidate core chains.

4.2 Slot Matching Model

To exploit the specific structure of the task, we propose an encoding scheme which partitions core chains into the aforementioned *hops*, and creates multiple, hop-specific representations of the NLQ, which we call *slots*. We then compare the hop (segments of a core-chain) representations with their corresponding slot (an encoded representation of the NLQ) to get the final score.

First, the question $Q = \{q_1 \dots q_T\}$ is encoded using a bidirectional LSTM (LSTM^q) resulting in the question encoding

$$[\hat{\mathbf{q}}_1 \dots \hat{\mathbf{q}}_T] = \mathsf{LSTM}^q(Q) \ . \tag{4}$$

Now, consider a core chain consisting of M hops. For each hop $j = 1, \dots, M$, we define a trainable slot attention vector $\mathbf{k_j}$ which is used to compute attention weights $\alpha_{t,j}$, individually for every hop j, over all the words $q_t, t = 1, \dots, T$ of Q. Then, a set of fixed-length question representations $\mathbf{q}_j$ are computed using the corresponding attention weights $\alpha_{t,j}$, that is

$$\alpha_{t,j} = softmax(\{< \hat{\mathbf{q}}_l, \mathbf{k}_j >\}_{l=1 \dots T})_t \ , \tag{5}$$

$$\mathbf{q}_j = \sum_{t=1}^{T} \alpha_{t,j} \cdot \hat{\mathbf{q}}_t \ . \tag{6}$$

We represent the core chains by separately encoding each hop by another LSTM (LSTM^c)

$$\mathbf{c}_j = \mathsf{LSTM}^c(C_j) \ , \tag{7}$$

where $C_j = [c_{j,1} \dots c_{j,T'_j}]$ is the sequence of words in the surface from of the predicate along with the +/− signs, corresponding to the jth hop of the core

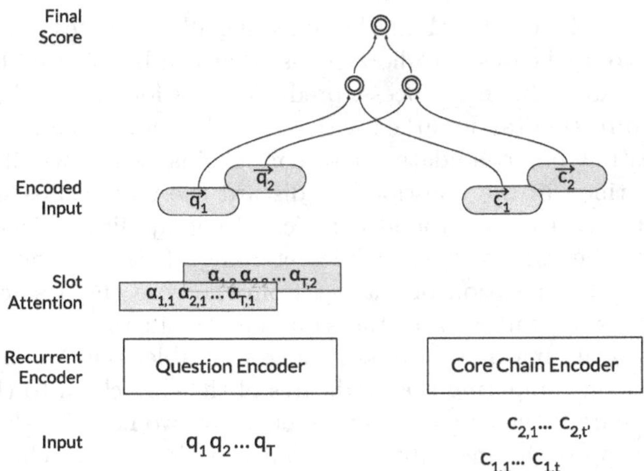

Fig. 2. The slot matching model uses parameterized attention vectors to create j representations of the question, and compares each of them correspondingly with the j hops in a core chain. Here t and t' represent the number of words in each hop of the core chain, and $c_{t,1}$ is the tth word in the first hop.

chain. Finally, $\mathbf{q}_1, \ldots, \mathbf{q}_M$ and $\mathbf{c}_1, \ldots, \mathbf{c}_M$ are concatenated to yield our final representation of the NLQ and the query graph ($\mathsf{enc}^\mathsf{q}(Q)$ and $\mathsf{enc}^\mathsf{c}(C)$), respectively, which is used in score function given in Eq. 2, i.e.

$$[\mathbf{q}_1, \ldots \mathbf{q}_M] = \mathsf{enc}^\mathsf{q}(Q) \tag{8}$$
$$[\mathbf{c}_1, \ldots \mathbf{c}_M] = \mathsf{enc}^\mathsf{c}(C)\ . \tag{9}$$

Figure 2 summarizes the proposed approach.

Note that the model proposed here is not the same as *cross attention* between the input sequences (as described by [16] which we also experiment with) as, in our case the attention weights aren't affected by the predicates in the core chain, as the encoder attempts to focus on *where* a predicate is mentioned in Q, and not *which* predicate is mentioned. In Sect. 5.1, we discuss advantages of *slot based attention* over *cross attention* in further detail.

Using Transformers in the Slot Matching Configuration: [6] demonstrate that the use of pre-trained bidirectional transformers (BERT) can provide improvements for numerous downstream NLP tasks. Motivated by their findings, we investigate whether they can positively impact the performance on our KGQA task as well.

In this subsection, we describe how we use BERT to encode the NLQ and the core chains in the slot matching model. In the simplest approach, we would simply replace the LSTM in Eqs. (4) and (7) with pre-trained transformers and keep the rest of the model unchanged.

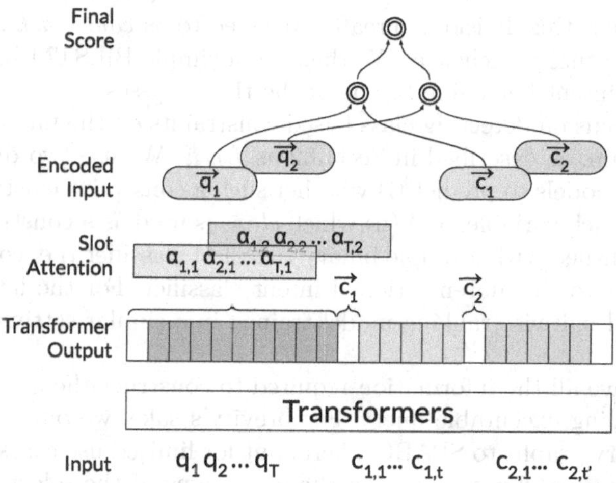

Fig. 3. Illustration of the transformer model in the slot matching configuration.

However, [6,18] prescribe converting structured inputs into an single ordered sequence. We thus concatenate our inputs: (i) a question $Q = [q_1 \dots q_T]$ of length T, and (ii) the M hops of a core chain $C = \big[\, [\, c_{1,1} \dots c_{1,T_1'} \,] \cdots [\, c_{M,1} \dots c_{M,T_M'} \,] \,\big]$ into a sequence of length $l = T + \sum_{j=1}^{M} T_j'$ (excluding sequence delimiters), and pass it through the transformer. Concretely, we use [6]'s input encoding scheme: we (1) prepend the sequence with a `[CLS]` token, (2) append the `[SEP]` separator token at the end of the question and (3) separate the different predicate surface forms in the appended candidate core chain with the same `[SEP]` token. The input to the transformer corresponding to our previous example then looks like this: "`[CLS]` *Name some movies starring Beirut born male actors* `[SEP]` + *capital* `[SEP]` + *population* `[SEP]`". [6] use the output of the transformer at first position (corresponding to the `[CLS]` token) for classification. Instead, for our slot matching transformer, we replace $[\hat{\mathbf{q}}_1 \dots \hat{\mathbf{q}}_T]$ in Eq. (4) with the question portion of the transformer's outputs. Applying Eqs. (5) and (6) as before yields a set of slot-specific question encodings $\mathbf{q}_1, \dots, \mathbf{q}_M$. Slot-specific hop encodings $\mathbf{c}_1, \dots, \mathbf{c}_M$ are obtained from the same sequence of output vectors of the transformer by taking the representation at the `[SEP]` delimiter preceding the jth hop. Given these encodings, the score for a question-chain pair is computed as before. The model is depicted in Fig. 3.

4.3 Predicting Auxiliary Functions

In this section, we describe our approach towards learning to predict the auxiliary functions used for constructing a complete query graph. We begin by predicting the intent of the question. In both the datasets considered in our experiments, a question can ask for the cardinality of the lambda variable, ask whether a certain fact exists in the KG, or simply ask for the set of values in the lambda variable. Further, this division, hereafter referred to as *count*, *ask* and *set* based questions, is mutually exclusive. We thus use a simple BiLSTM based classifier to predict the intent belonging to one of the three classes.

Next, we focus on detecting class based constraints on the ungrounded nodes of the core chain, as described in Sect. 3.2 as f_{class}. We use two different, separately trained models to predict (i) whether such a constraint exists in the NLQ, and if so, on which variable, and (ii) which *class* is used as a constraint. The former is accomplished with a simple binary BiLSTM classifier (i.e. constraint exist or not), similar to the aforementioned intent classifier. For the latter, we use a BiLSTM based pairwise ranking model trained in a similar setting as described in Eq. 3.

We now have all the information required to construct the query graph, and the corresponding executable query. For brevity's sake, we omit the algorithm to convert query graphs to SPARQL here, but for limited use cases such as ours, simple template matching (based on the +/− signs of the selected core chain, the class constraint, and the result of the intent classifier) shall suffice.

5 Experiments

In a first set of experiments we compare the KGQA performance of the proposed slot matching model with some baseline models as described in the following section. After that, we describe experiments investigating transfer learning across KGQA datasets and from pre-trained transformers.

5.1 Approach Evaluation

Our first experiment focuses on investigating the performance of the **Slot Matching (LSTM)** model. As a baseline we use a simple neural ranking model where we replace $\mathsf{enc}^{\mathsf{q}}$ and $\mathsf{enc}^{\mathsf{c}}$ with a single layered bidirectional LSTM (**BiLSTM**). We also compare our model to those proposed by [16] (decomposable attention model, or **DAM**), [24] (hierarchical residual model, or **HRM**), and [11] which uses a multi-channel convolutional neural network (**CNN**).

Datasets. Our models are trained and evaluated over the following two KGQA datasets:

LC-QuAD [20] is a gold standard question answering dataset over the DBpedia 04-2016 release, having 5000 NLQ and SPARQL pairs. The coverage of our grammar covers all kinds of questions in this dataset.

QALD-7 [21] is a long running challenge for KGQA over DBpedia. While currently its 9th version is available, we use QALD-7 (Multilingual) for our purposes, as it is based on the same DBpedia release as that of LC-QuAD. QALD-7 is a gold-standard dataset having 220 and 43 training and test questions respectively along with their corresponding SPARQL queries. Some of the questions in the dataset are outside the scope of our system. We nonetheless consider all the questions in our evaluation.

Table 1. Performance on LC-Quad and QALD-7. The reported metrics are core chain accuracy (CCA), mean reciprocal rank (MRR) of the core chain rankings, as well as precision (P), recall (R), and the F1 of the execution results of the whole system.

	LC-QuAD					QALD-7				
	CCA	MRR	P	R	F1	CCA	MRR	P	R	F1
BiLSTM [9]	0.61	0.70	0.63	0.75	0.68	0.28	0.41	0.20	0.36	0.26
CNN [11]	0.44	0.55	0.49	0.61	0.54	0.31	**0.45**	0.20	0.33	0.25
DAM [16]	0.57	0.66	0.59	0.72	0.65	0.28	0.40	0.20	0.36	0.26
HRM [24]	0.62	0.71	0.64	0.77	0.70	0.28	0.40	0.15	0.31	0.20
Slot-Matching (LSTM)	**0.63**	**0.72**	**0.65**	**0.78**	**0.71**	**0.31**	0.44	**0.28**	**0.44**	**0.34**

Evaluation Metrics. We measure the performance of the proposed methods in terms of their ability to find the correct core chain, as well as the execution results of the whole system. For core chain ranking, we report Core Chain Accuracy (CCA) and Mean Reciprocal Rank (MRR). Based on the execution results of the whole system (including auxiliary functions), we also report Precision (P), Recall (R), and F1.

Training. Our models are trained with negative sampling, where we sample 1000 negative core chains per question, along with the correct one, for every iteration. We train our models for a maximum of 300 epochs, using a 70-10-20 split as train, validation and test data over LC-QuAD [2] QALD-7 has a predefined train-test split, and we use one eighth of the train data for validation. We embed the tokens using Glove embeddings [17], and keep the relevant subset of the embeddings trainable in the model. We use Adam optimizer with an initial learning rate of 0.001 and set the margin (γ) in the pairwise loss function as 1.

We share parameters between $\mathsf{enc}^{\mathsf{q}}$ and $\mathsf{enc}^{\mathsf{c}}$ in the BiLSTM, CNN and DAM models, since in these models, input sequences are processed in the same manner, while the same does not hold for the slot matching, or HRM. We illustrate the impact of this choice on model performance towards the end of this section (Table 1).

Results. In our experiments, the slot matching model performs the best among the ones compared, suggesting that different attention scores successfully create suitably weighted representations of the question, corresponding to each hop. This is further reinforced upon visualizing attention scores, as presented in Fig. 4, where we notice that the different attention *slots* focus on different predicate spans in the question. While the decomposable attention model (DAM) proposed by [16] also uses attention, its performance generally lags behind the

[2] That is, we use the first 70% of dataset, as made available on https://figshare.com/projects/LC-QuAD/21812 by [20], to train our models. Next 10% is used to decide the best hyperparamters. The metrics we report in the rest of this section are based on the model's performance on the last 20% of it.

slot matching model. DAM's cross-attention between question and core chain leads to a summarized question representation that is dependent on the candidate core chain and vice versa. On the other hand, the slot matching approach merely attempts to learn to extract important, relation-specific parts of the NLQ, prior to seeing a specific core chain, which judging by our experiments seems to be a better model bias and might help generalizing. The hierarchical residual model (HRM) [24] is second best in our comparison, suggesting that pooling relation and word level encodings is a promising strategy to form core chain representations. The competitive performance of the BiLSTM model is in coherence with recent findings by [15], that a simple recurrent model can perform almost as well as the best performing alternative.

All models generally exhibit poor performance over QALD-7, which is understandable given the fact that QALD-7 has only 220 examples in the training set, which is 20 times smaller than LC-QuAD. We will show in the next section that transfer learning across datasets is a viable strategy in this case to improve model performance.

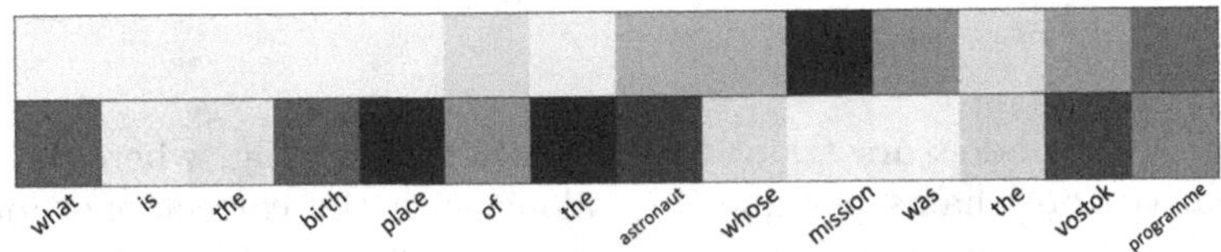

Fig. 4. Visualized attention weights (darker color corresponds to larger attention weights) of the slot matching question encoder for the question "*What is the birth place of the astronaut whose mission was the vostok programme?*" The two rows represent different slot attention scores. One can see that first puts a higher weight on *mission* while the second (beside others) on *birth place.* (Color figure online)

Error Analysis: We now illustrate the effect of different characteristics of the test data on the model performance.

Effect of Number of Core Chain Candidates: In our ranking based approach, the difficulty of selecting the correct core chain depends on the number of core chain candidates, which can be disproportionately large for questions about well-connected entities in DBpedia (e.g. `dbr:United_States`). In order to investigate its effect, we plot the core chain accuracy (CCA) vs. the number of core chain candidates, for all the models we experiment with, in Fig. 5a. Upon inspection, we find the core chain accuracy to be inversely correlated to the number of core chain candidates. Specifically, we find that the performance of the BiLSTM, HRM and the slot pointer model (the three best performing ones in Exp. 5.1) remain almost the same for as many as 2000 core chain candidates per question. Thereafter, the BiLSTM and HRM models' accuracy declines faster than that of the proposed slot matching model, giving a competitive edge to the latter.

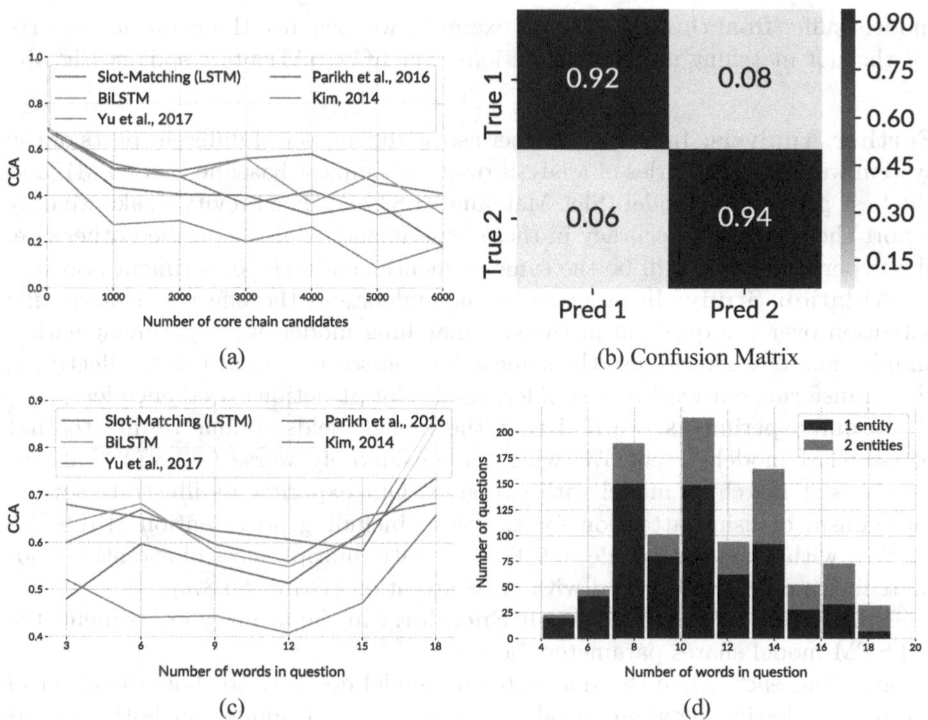

Fig. 5. Here, (a) shows the decrease in accuracy with increasing number of candidates for all the rankings models in Sect. 5.1; (b) is a confusion matrix representing the number of hops in true and predicted core chains for the test data of LC-QuAD for the slot matching model. (c) The relation of model accuracy w.r.t. question length. And (d) a histogram depicting the distribution of questions in LC-QuAD's test split w.r.t. their question lengths. Here, the proportion of questions with two entity mentions are depicted with red color. (Color figure online)

Effect of Length of Questions: We noticed that it is relatively easier for the models to answer longer questions. To better understand this phenomenon, we plot the core chain accuracy w.r.t. the length of questions for all the models in Fig. 5c, and the frequency of questions w.r.t. their lengths in Fig. 5d.

We find that longer questions are more likely to contain two entity mentions than just one. This hints to the fact that the number of candidate core chains reduces accordingly, as every valid core chain candidate must include all entity mentions of the question, which simplifies the ranking process as detailed in Sect. 4.1.

Effect of Length of Core Chains: Inherent biases in the data might make our models more inclined to assign higher ranks to paths of a certain length, at the expense of selecting the correct path. We thus compose a confusion matrix representing the number of hops in the ground-truth and predicted core chains, which we hypothesize can help detect these biases. We find that none of our models suffer from this issue. As an example, we visualize the confusion matrix for the slot matching model's predictions over LC-QuAD's test split in Fig. 5b.

Further Analysis: In order to better assess the impact of different parts of the system we perform a series of analysis over the simplest baseline (BiLSTM), and the best performing model (Slot Matching (LSTM)). For brevity's sake we only report the core chain accuracy in these experiments. Unless specified otherwise, the hyperparameters will be the same as mentioned in the experiment above.

Ablation Study: In order to better understand the effect of slot-specific attention over the question in the slot matching model, we experiment with a simpler model where we use the same attention scores for each slot. Effectively, this transforms our enc^q to a simpler, single-slot attention based encoder.

In our experiments, we find that the model yields similar results to that of BiLSTM model, i.e. 60.3%, which is considerably worse (−2.8%) than the regular slot matching model with two slots. Our experiments illustrate several mechanism of using attention for the task, including no attention (BiLSTM, 61.4%), with attention (single slot, 60.3%), with multiple slots of attention (slot matching model, 63.1%), and with cross attention (DAM, 56.8%).

Parameter Sharing between Encoders: In the primary experiment, the BiLSTM model shares parameters between enc^q and enc^c, while the slot matching model doesn't. To show the effect of parameter sharing between encoders, we retrain both models in both settings (with and without parameter sharing).

Sharing encoders leads to a *decrease* of 2.9% (60.4% from 63.1%) in CCA of the slot matching model. Conversely, sharing encoders *increases* the performance of the BiLSTM model by 3.1% (61.4% from 58.3%). In the BiLSTM's case, learning a mapping that captures the equivalence of questions and core chains is not hindered by sharing parameters because the model structure is the same on both sides (simple encoders). Sharing parameters in this case could help because of the decrease in the total number of parameters. In the case of the slot matching model, however, sharing the parameters of the encoders would require the encoder to be usable for both the attention-based summary of the question encoder as well as the simple encoder for each hop (where the latter processes much shorter sequences) which leads to a performance bottle neck.

5.2 Transfer Learning Across KGQA Datasets

As mentioned above, all models generally show poor performance when trained solely on QALD-7 due to a more varied and significantly smaller dataset. Therefore, we hypothesize that pre-training the models on the much larger LC-QuAD dataset might lead to a significant increase in performance. To that end, we perform the following fine-tuning experiment: we pre-train our ranking models over LC-QuAD, and then fine-tune and evaluate them over QALD-7. We set the initial learning rate to 0.0001 (which is an order of magnitude less than in the experiments in Sect. 5.1), and experiment with custom learning rate schedules, namely *slanted triangular learning rate* (sltr) proposed in [10], and *cosine annealing* (cos) proposed in [13]. We keep the hyperparameters of *sltr* unchanged, and set the number of cycles for *cos* to 3 based on the performance on the validation set.

Table 2. CCA for the fine-tuning experiment where we pre-train on LC-QuAD and fine-tune over QALD-7. The initial learning rate is 10^{-3} for all configurations.

Learning rate	BiLSTM	Slot matching (LSTM)
constant	0.37	0.37
sltr	**0.39**	**0.42**
cos	0.25	0.28

We conduct the experiment on the BiLSTM and the Slot Matching (LSTM) ranking model, and only report the *core chain accuracies* (CCA) as the rest of the system remains unchanged for the purposes of this experiment.

We find that *fine-tuning* a ranking model trained over LC-QuAD leads to a substantial (~11%) increase in performance on QALD-7 compared to non-pre-trained models. Interestingly, we find that the results of the fine-tuning experiment are sensitive to the learning rate schedule used. While constant learning rate provides a relatively comparable performance w.r.t. *sltr*, using the cosine annealing schedule adversely affects model performance.

We report the results of this experiment in Table 2. In summary we conclude that transferring models across KGQA datasets via simple fine-tuning is a viable strategy to compensate for the lack of training samples in the target dataset.

5.3 Transfer Learning with Pre-trained Transformers

For our transformer based slot matching model, we use a transformer, initialized with the weights of BERT-Small[3], instead of an LSTM, as discussed in Sect. 4.2. The transformer has 12 layers of hidden size 768 and 12 attention heads per layer. Following [6], we set dropout to 0.1. We train using Adam with initial learning rate 0.00001. Table 3 shows the performance of the pre-trained transformer (**BERT**), used as in [6] as well as the pre-trained transformer in the slot matching configuration (**Slot Matching (BERT)**). For BERT, we follow the sequence pair classification approach described by [6].

Table 3. CCA for slot matching model, as proposed in Sect. 4.2 initialized with the weights of BERT-Small, compared with regular transformers initialized with the same weights.

	QALD-7	LC-QuAD
BERT	**0.23**	0.67
Slot matching (BERT)	0.18	**0.68**

[3] as provided by the authors at https://github.com/google-research/bert.

Through this experiment we find that using pre-trained weights immensely improves model performance, as both transformer based models outperform the ones in Sect. 5.1. Additionally, we find that the augmentations we propose in Sect. 4.2 are beneficial for the task, improving CCA on LC-QuAD by 1.4% relative to regular pre-trained transformers. However, both models exhibit poor performance over QALD-7, suggesting that these models need substantial amounts of data to be properly fine-tuned for the task. We thus conclude that using pre-trained transformers in the slot matching setting is advantageous for the task, if ample training data is available at hand.

6 Conclusion and Future Work

In this work, we studied the performance of various neural ranking models on the KGQA task. First, we propose a novel task-specific ranking model which outperforms several existing baselines in our experiments over two datasets. An error analysis shows that the model performs especially well on smaller candidate sets and for longer questions which highlights its high potential for answering complicated questions. Second, we present an extensive study of the use of transfer learning for KGQA. We show that pre-training models over a larger task-specific dataset and fine-tuning them on a smaller target set leads to an increase in model performance. We thereby demonstrate the high potential of these techniques for offsetting the lack of training data in the domain. Finally, we propose mechanisms to effectively employ large-scale pre-trained state of the art language models (BERT [6]) for the KGQA task, leading to an impressive performance gain on the larger dataset.

We aim to extend this work by incorporating a three phased domain adaption strategy as proposed in [10] for the KGQA task. We will study the effect of pretraining our ranking models with synthetically generated datasets, aiming for consistent coverage of relations involved in the ranking process. Further, we intend to explore differentiable formal query execution mechanisms [4] enabling answer supervision based training of our model.

Acknowledgements. This work has been supported by the Fraunhofer-Cluster of Excellence "Cognitive Internet Technologies" (CCIT).

References

1. Bast, H., Haussmann, E.: More accurate question answering on freebase. In: Proceedings of the 24th ACM International on Conference on Information and Knowledge Management, pp. 1431–1440. ACM (2015)
2. Berant, J., Liang, P.: Semantic parsing via paraphrasing. In: Proceedings of the 52nd Annual Meeting of the Association for Computational Linguistics (Volume 1: Long Papers), pp. 1415–1425. Association for Computational Linguistics (2014). https://doi.org/10.3115/v1/P14-1133

3. Bowman, S.R., Angeli, G., Potts, C., Manning, C.D.: A large annotated corpus for learning natural language inference. In: Proceedings of the 2015 Conference on Empirical Methods in Natural Language Processing (EMNLP). Association for Computational Linguistics (2015)
4. Cohen, W.W.: TensorLog: a differentiable deductive database. arXiv preprint arXiv:1605.06523 (2016)
5. Cui, W., Xiao, Y., Wang, H., Song, Y., Hwang, S.w., Wang, W.: KBQA: learning question answering over QA corpora and knowledge bases. Proc. VLDB Endow. **10**(5), 565–576 (2017). https://doi.org/10.14778/3055540.3055549
6. Devlin, J., Chang, M.W., Lee, K., Toutanova, K.: Bert: pre-training of deep bidirectional transformers for language understanding. arXiv preprint arXiv:1810.04805 (2018)
7. Dubey, M., Dasgupta, S., Sharma, A., Höffner, K., Lehmann, J.: AskNow: a framework for natural language query formalization in SPARQL. In: Sack, H., Blomqvist, E., d'Aquin, M., Ghidini, C., Ponzetto, S.P., Lange, C. (eds.) ESWC 2016. LNCS, vol. 9678, pp. 300–316. Springer, Cham (2016). https://doi.org/10.1007/978-3-319-34129-3_19
8. Fader, A., Zettlemoyer, L., Etzioni, O.: Open question answering over curated and extracted knowledge bases. In: Proceedings of the 20th ACM SIGKDD International Conference on Knowledge Discovery and Data Mining, pp. 1156–1165. ACM (2014)
9. Hochreiter, S., Schmidhuber, J.: Long short-term memory. Neural Comput. **9**(8), 1735–1780 (1997)
10. Howard, J., Ruder, S.: Universal language model fine-tuning for text classification. In: Proceedings of the 56th Annual Meeting of the Association for Computational Linguistics (Volume 1: Long Papers), vol. 1, pp. 328–339 (2018)
11. Kim, Y.: Convolutional neural networks for sentence classification. arXiv preprint arXiv:1408.5882 (2014)
12. Lehmann, J., et al.: Dbpedia-a large-scale, multilingual knowledge base extracted from Wikipedia. Seman. Web **6**(2), 167–195 (2015)
13. Loshchilov, I., Hutter, F.: SGDR: stochastic gradient descent with warm restarts. arXiv preprint arXiv:1608.03983 (2016)
14. Lukovnikov, D., Fischer, A., Lehmann, J.: Pretrained transformers for simple question answering over knowledge graphs. In: International Semantic Web Conference. Springer, Heidelberg (2019)
15. Mohammed, S., Shi, P., Lin, J.: Strong baselines for simple question answering over knowledge graphs with and without neural networks. arXiv preprint arXiv:1712.01969 (2017)
16. Parikh, A., Täckström, O., Das, D., Uszkoreit, J.: A decomposable attention model for natural language inference. In: Proceedings of the 2016 Conference on Empirical Methods in Natural Language Processing, pp. 2249–2255. Association for Computational Linguistics (2016). https://doi.org/10.18653/v1/D16-1244, http://www.aclweb.org/anthology/D16-1244
17. Pennington, J., Socher, R., Manning, C.D.: GloVe: global vectors for word representation. In: Empirical Methods in Natural Language Processing (EMNLP), pp. 1532–1543 (2014). http://www.aclweb.org/anthology/D14-1162
18. Radford, A., Narasimhan, K., Salimans, T., Sutskever, I.: Improving language understanding by generative pre-training (2018). https://s3-us-west-2.amazonaws.com/openai-assets/research-covers/language-unsupervised/language_understanding_paper.pdf

19. Reddy, S., Täckström, O., Petrov, S., Steedman, M., Lapata, M.: Universal semantic parsing. In: Proceedings of the 2017 Conference on Empirical Methods in Natural Language Processing, pp. 89–101. Association for Computational Linguistics (2017). http://aclweb.org/anthology/D17-1009
20. Trivedi, P., Maheshwari, G., Dubey, M., Lehmann, J.: LC-QuAD: a corpus for complex question answering over knowledge graphs. In: d'Amato, C., et al. (eds.) ISWC 2017. LNCS, vol. 10588, pp. 210–218. Springer, Cham (2017). https://doi.org/10.1007/978-3-319-68204-4_22
21. Usbeck, R., Ngomo, A.-C.N., Haarmann, B., Krithara, A., Röder, M., Napolitano, G.: 7th open challenge on question answering over linked data (QALD-7). In: Dragoni, M., Solanki, M., Blomqvist, E. (eds.) SemWebEval 2017. CCIS, vol. 769, pp. 59–69. Springer, Cham (2017). https://doi.org/10.1007/978-3-319-69146-6_6
22. Xu, K., Zhang, S., Feng, Y., Zhao, D.: Answering natural language questions via phrasal semantic parsing. In: Zong, C., Nie, J.Y., Zhao, D., Feng, Y. (eds.) Natural Language Processing and Chinese Computing. Communications in Computer and Information Science, vol. 496, pp. 333–344. Springer, Berlin (2014). https://doi.org/10.1007/978-3-662-45924-9_30
23. Yih, W.T., Chang, M.W., He, X., Gao, J.: Semantic parsing via staged query graph generation: question answering with knowledge base. In: Proceedings of the 53rd Annual Meeting of the Association for Computational Linguistics and the 7th International Joint Conference on Natural Language Processing (Volume 1: Long Papers), vol. 1, pp. 1321–1331 (2015)
24. Yu, M., Yin, W., Hasan, K.S., dos Santos, C., Xiang, B., Zhou, B.: Improved neural relation detection for knowledge base question answering. In: Proceedings of the 55th Annual Meeting of the Association for Computational Linguistics (Volume 1: Long Papers), pp. 571–581. Association for Computational Linguistics (2017). https://doi.org/10.18653/v1/P17-1053, http://www.aclweb.org/anthology/P17-1053

THOTH: Neural Translation and Enrichment of Knowledge Graphs

Diego Moussallem[1(✉)], Tommaso Soru[2], and Axel-Cyrille Ngonga Ngomo[1]

[1] Data Science Group, University of Paderborn, Paderborn, Germany
{diego.moussallem,axel.ngonga}@upb.de
[2] AKSW Research Group, University of Leipzig, Leipzig, Germany
tsoru@informatik.uni-leipzig.de

Abstract. Knowledge Graphs are used in an increasing number of applications. Although considerable human effort has been invested into making knowledge graphs available in multiple languages, most knowledge graphs are in English. Additionally, regional facts are often only available in the language of the corresponding region. This lack of multilingual knowledge availability clearly limits the porting of machine learning models to different languages. In this paper, we aim to alleviate this drawback by proposing THOTH, an approach for translating and enriching knowledge graphs. THOTH extracts bilingual alignments between a source and target knowledge graph and learns how to translate from one to the other by relying on two different recurrent neural network models along with knowledge graph embeddings. We evaluated THOTH extrinsically by comparing the German DBpedia with the German translation of the English DBpedia on two tasks: fact checking and entity linking. In addition, we ran a manual intrinsic evaluation of the translation. Our results show that THOTH is a promising approach which achieves a translation accuracy of 88.56%. Moreover, its enrichment improves the quality of the German DBpedia significantly, as we report +18.4% accuracy for fact validation and +19% F_1 for entity linking.

1 Introduction

A recent survey estimates that more than 3.7 billion humans use the internet every day and produce nearly 2.5 quintillion bytes of data on the Web each day.[1] The availability of such large amounts of data is commonly regarded as one of the motors for the current lapses in the development of Artificial Intelligence (AI)-powered solutions. In this paper, we focus on the portion of data made available in the form of Knowledge Graph (KG). Recent works have shown the benefits of exploiting KGs to improve Natural Language Processing (NLP) tasks such as Natural Language Inference (NLI) [20] and Question Answering (QA) [35]. A given KG (especially Resource Description Framework (RDF) KG) commonly stores knowledge in triples. Each triple consists of (i) a subject—often an entity,

[1] https://tinyurl.com/statswebdata.

C. Ghidini et al. (Eds.): ISWC 2019, LNCS 11778, pp. 505–522, 2019.
https://doi.org/10.1007/978-3-030-30793-6_29

(ii) a relation—often called property—and (iii) an object—an entity or a literal.[2] For example, `<Edmund_Hillary, birthPlace, Auckland>`,[3] represents the information that "Edmund Hillary was born in Auckland".

Considerable amounts of partly human effort has been invested in making KGs available across languages. However, even popular KGs like DBpedia and Wikidata are largest in their English version [25]. Additionally, region-specific facts are often limited to the KG specific to the region from which they emanate or to the KG in the language spoken in said region [1]. This lack of multilingual knowledge availability limits the porting of Machine Learning (ML) models to different languages. The Semantic Web (SW) community has been trying to alleviate this bottleneck by creating different approaches for enriching the Linked Open Data (LOD) cloud with multilingual content. However, it is a difficult endeavor as the majority of ML algorithms for extracting knowledge from raw data only support English.

Previous works have tried to address this problem by using Machine Translation (MT) systems [2,27]. However, these works focused only on translating the labels of domain-specific KGs from English into a target language. This kind of approach ignores an essential part of a KG, namely its graph structure. For example, while translating a highly ambiguous label such as *Kiwi*, an MT system has to predict in which domain this word has to be translated in the target language. Otherwise, the translation of *Kiwi* can be the common term for inhabitants of New Zealand,[4] a fruit,[5] a bird,[6] or a computer program.[7] These domains can be derived in KGs through predicates such as type predicates (i.e., `rdf:type` in RDF). Clearly, taking the graph structure of KG into account can support an MT system when spotting the correct translation for ambiguous labels.

RDF KGs rely on Uniform Resource Identifier (URI)s for the unique identification of relations (predicates) and resources (entities).[8] While some KGs use encoded URIs with numeric IDs (e.g., Wikidata), most KGs use language-based URIs, which allows humans to derive the semantics behind the URI by reading it. For example, the Multilingual KG DBpedia is composed of independent KGs in different languages interlinked by `owl:sameAs` relations. We argue that if a KG uses human-legible URI, then an enrichment approach for language-based KGs should not simply translate only the labels of its resources and maintain or change its URI prefixes by adding a language code. It should also be able to generate correct URIs during the translation process. For instance, changing an English DBpedia resource `<http://dbpedia.org/resource/United_Kingdom>` to a German DBpedia resource `<http://`**`de`**`.dbpedia.org-`

[2] a string or a value with a unit.

[3] http://dbpedia.org/page/Edmund_Hillary.

[4] http://dbpedia.org/resource/Kiwi_(people).

[5] http://dbpedia.org/resource/Kiwifruit.

[6] http://dbpedia.org/resource/Kiwi.

[7] http://dbpedia.org/resource/KiwiIRC.

[8] https://www.w3.org/TR/cooluris.

/resource/**United_Kingdom**> is inherently incorrect since this entity already exists with another URI in the German DBpedia (i.e., <http://de.dbpedia.org/resource/Vereinigtes_Königreich>.). Consequently, a simple translation of labels without a translation of URIs would assign a supplementary URI to an existing resource, hence breaking the uniqueness of URIs within single KGs. Thus, an approach for translating KGs must be capable of translating labels and URIs. In this work, we focus on translating and enriching KGs with language-based URIs to provide KGs in different languages. To this end, we present THOTH, an approach which considers the graph structure of the KG while translating its URIs along with their labels. First, THOTH extracts bilingual alignments between a source and target KG using SPARQL queries. Afterwards, THOTH uses the acquired bilingual knowledge to train two different Neural Machine Translation (NMT) models based on an Recurrent Neural Network (RNN), (1) triple- and (2) text-based. The triple-based RNN model is trained only on triples represented by <resource,predicate,resource> while the text-based RNN model, is trained on generic bilingual parallel corpora and is able to translate triples which contain literals (texts), i.e., <resource,predicate,literal>. Both models are enriched with Knowledge Graph Embeddings (KGE) created from the source and target KGs. We envision that THOTH can benefit and support the multilinguality in the LOD cloud and the SW.

With this aim, we apply THOTH on the English and German DBpedia [4]. We hence evaluate the enriched German DBpedia both extrinsically and intrinsically. The extrinsic evaluation is carried out on the tasks of fact checking and Entity Linking (EL). The intrinsic evaluation is carried out by means of a manual error analysis of a sample of the data. The main contributions of this paper can be summarized as follows:

- We present a novel approach based on Neural Network (NN)s along with KGEs for translating and enriching KGs across languages.
- THOTH is a promising approach which achieves a translation accuracy of 88.56% across all elements of a triple. Also, its enrichment improves the quality of the original German DBpedia significantly in both the fact checking and the EL tasks: We achieve improvements of 18.4% for fact validation and 19% for EL.

The version of THOTH used in this paper and also all experimental data are publicly available.[9]

2 Related Work

A wide range of works have investigated the enrichment of KGs through different techniques, for example, MT [16], cross-lingual knowledge interlinking and alignment [11], natural language generation [21] and KGE [12]. In this section,

[9] https://github.com/dice-group/THOTH.

we briefly describe recent approaches which exploited the enrichment of KGs from the MT aspect and also worked on the development of KGE which is an important part of our approach.

KG Translation. According to a recent survey [30], the translation of KGs has been carried out through a localization task which relies on Statistical Machine Translation (SMT) systems for translating the labels of KGs and domain-specific ontologies into target languages. Recently, Arčan and Buitelaar [3] performed the translation of domain-specific expressions from medical and financial domains represented by English KGs into other languages by relying on an NMT architecture. They showed that the results of NMT surpassed the SMT. As a way of overcoming the weakness of previous works, Feng et al. [16] presented an NN approach, which learns continuous triple representation with a gated NN for translating an English KG into Chinese. The authors built their approach upon a subset of Freebase [7] and mapped the source and target triples in the same semantic vector space. Consequently, their technique was capable of learning the KG structure for translating the terms. Their adapted NN approach improved the translation accuracy over a strong NMT baseline and showed that considering a KG structure is essential for performing a KG translation and leads to a better disambiguation quality for ambiguous terms.

Knowledge Graph Embeddings. Manifold approaches interpret relationships as displacements operating on low-dimensional embeddings of entities, e.g. TransE [8]. More recently, Nickel et al. [31] proposed HolE, which relies on holographic models of associative memory by employing a circular correlation to create compositional representations. Ristoski and Paulheim [33] presented RDF2Vec, which uses language modeling approaches for unsupervised feature extraction from sequences of words and adapts them to RDF graphs. RDF2Vec has been extended to reduce the computational time and bias of random walking [13]. In its subsequent extension, Cochez et al. [14] exploited the Global Vectors algorithm in RDF2Vec for computing embeddings from the co-occurrence matrix of entities and relations without generating the random walks. However, Joulin et al. [19] showed recently that a simple Bag-of-Words (BoW) based approach with the *fastText* algorithm [18] generates surprisingly good KGE while achieving state-of-the-art results.

3 Preliminaries

In the following, we present preliminary concepts of NMT and KGE for a better understanding of THOTH approach.

Neural Machine Translation. In this work, we use the RNN architecture. It consists of an encoder and a decoder, i.e., a two-tier architecture where the encoder reads an input sequence $x = (x_1, ..., x_n)$ and the decoder predicts a target sequence $y = (y_1, ..., y_n)$. Encoder and decoder interact via a soft-attention mechanism [5,26], which comprises one or multiple attention layers. We follow the notations from Tang et al. [36] in the subsequent sections: h_i^l corresponds to the hidden state at step i of layer l. h_{i-1}^l represents the hidden state at the previous step of layer l while h_i^{l-1} means the hidden state at i of $l-1$ layer. $E \in \mathbb{R}^{m \times K_x}$ is a word embedding matrix, $W \in \mathbb{R}^{n \times m}$, $U \in \mathbb{R}^{n \times n}$ are weight matrices, with m being the word embedding size and n the number of hidden units. K_x is the vocabulary size of the source language. Thus, E_{x_i} refers to the embedding of x_i, and $e_{pos,i}$ indicates the positional embedding at position i. In RNN models, networks change as new inputs (previous hidden state and the token in the line) come in, and each state is directly connected to the previous state only. Therefore, the path length of any two tokens with a distance of n in RNNs is exactly n. Its architecture enables adding more layers, whereby two adjoining layers are usually connected with residual connections in deeper configurations. Equation 1 displays h_i^l, where f_{rnn} is usually a function based on Gated recurrent unit (GRU) or Long Short-Term Memories (LSTM). The first layer is then represented as $h_i^0 = f_{rnn}(WE_{x_i}, Uh_{i-1}^0)$. Additionally, the initial state of the decoder is commonly initialized with the average of the hidden states or the last hidden state of the encoder.

$$h_i^l = h_i^{l-1} + f_{rnn}(h_i^{l-1}, h_{i-1}^l) \tag{1}$$

Knowledge Graph Embeddings. The underlying concept of KGE is that, in a given KG, each subject entity h or object entity t can be associated with a vector in a continuous vector space whereby its relation r can be modelled as displacement vectors $(h + r = t)$ while preserving the inherent structure of the KG. In fastText [19], the model is based on BoW representation which considers the subject entities h and object entities t along with their relation r as a unique discrete token. Thus, fastText models the co-occurrences of entities and its relations with a linear classifier and standard cost functions. Hence, it allows theoretically creating either a structure-based or semantically-enriched KGE. Therefore, we use fastText models in our experiments.[10] The aim of the algorithm is represented by the following equation:

$$-\frac{1}{N}\sum_{n=1}^{N} y_n \log(f(WVz_n)), \tag{2}$$

The normalized BoW of the x_n input set is represented as z_n, y_n as the label. V is a matrix, which is used as a look-up table over the discrete tokens and a matrix W is used for the classifier. The representations of the discrete tokens are averaged into BoW representation, which is in turn fed to a linear classifier. f is used to compute the probability distribution over the classes, and N input sets for discrete tokens.

[10] We could not use RDF2Vec in our work as its code was incomplete.

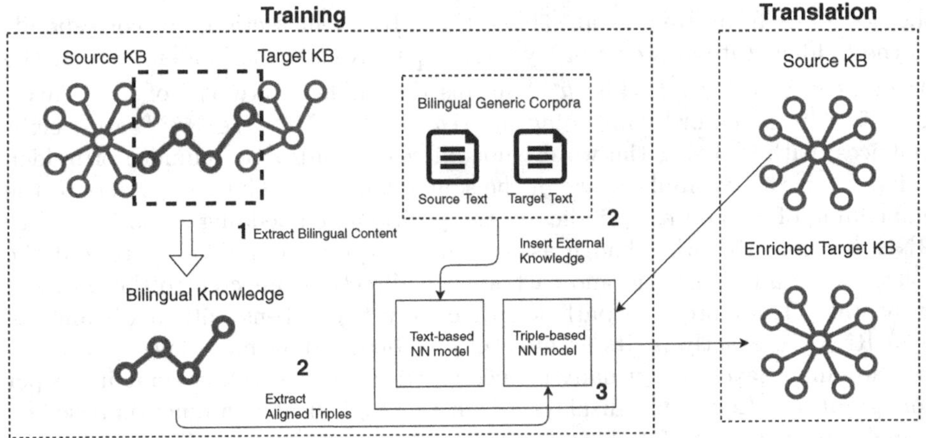

Fig. 1. Overview of THOTH.

4 The THOTH Approach

NNs have shown an impressive capability of parsing and translating natural language sentences. For example, the application of NN within MT systems led to a remarkable performance over well-established Phrase-based SMT approaches [22]. Consequently, the interest in NMT for devising new solutions to translation problems increased. The underlying idea behind our approach, THOTH, is based on the formal description of a translation problem as follows: *Given that KGs are composed of facts extracted from text, we can consider the facts (i.e., triples) as sentences where URIs are tokens and train a NMT model to translate the facts from one language into another.* The enrichment process implemented by THOTH consists of two phases. The data gathering and preprocessing steps occur in the training phase, while the enrichment per se is carried out during the translation phase and consists of two steps: (1) translation and (2) enrichment. All steps carried out in THOTH are language-agnostic, which allow the use of other language-based KGs. An overview can be found in Fig. 1.

4.1 Training Phase

While devising our approach, we perceived that one crucial requirement is that all resources and predicates in the source and target KGs must have at least one label via a common predicate such as `rdfs:label`.[11] This avoids the generation of inadequate resources. After establishing this, we divide THOTH into two models in order to take into account the challenge of translating datatype property values (i.e., texts) and object property values (i.e., entities). Trying to tackle both kinds of statements with a single model is likely to fail as labels can easily reach a length of 50 characters. Therefore, we divide the data gathering process into two blocks in order to be able to train 2 models.

[11] https://www.w3.org/TR/webont-req/#section-requirements.

```
1 SELECT *
2    WHERE {
3        ?s1 ?p1 ?o1 .
4        ?s2 ?p2 ?o2 .
5        ?s1 owl:sameAs ?s2 .
6        ?o1 owl:sameAs ?o2 .
7 FILTER(?p1 != owl:sameAs && ?p2 != owl:sameAs)
8 } ORDER BY ?s1 ?o1 LIMIT 1000000
```

Listing 1.1. A SPARQL query for retrieving aligned bilingual triples

```
EN: dbr:crocodile_dundee_ii dbo:country dbr:united_states
DE: dbr_de:crocodile_dundee_ii dbo:country dbr_de:vereinigte_staaten
EN: dbr:til_there_was_you dbo:writer dbr:winnie_holzman
DE: dbr_de:zwei_singles_in_l.a. dbo:writer dbr_de:winnie_holzman
```

Listing 1.2. Sample of the triple-based training data

Data Gathering Process. First, we upload the source and target KG into a SPARQL endpoint and query both graphs by looking for resources which have the same "identity". Identical resources are usually connected via `owl:sameAs` links. However, aligned triples must not contain `owl:sameAs` as predicates in themselves (see line 7 in Listing 1.1). Second, we perform another SPARQL query for gathering only the labels of the aligned resources. Thus, we generate two bilingual training files, one with triples and another with labels (see Listing 1.2 for an example). Once both training files are created, we split them into training, development, and test sets.

Preprocessing. Before we start training the triple- and text-based models, we tokenize both training data files. Subsequently, we apply Byte Pair Encoding (BPE) models on them for dealing with out-of-vocabulary (OOV) words [34]. BPE is a form of data compression that iteratively replaces the most frequent pair of bytes in a sequence with a single, unused byte. The symbol vocabulary is initialized with the character vocabulary, and each word is represented as a sequence of characters-plus a special end-of-word symbol, which allows restoring the original tokenization after the translation step. For example, suppose we have the entity or label "Auckland", after the BPE, i.e., the sub- word information, it becomes Au■ ck■ la■ nd.[12] Applying BPE on the training data allows the translation models to translate words and sub-words and consequently improve their translation performance. It is a well-known technique from the MT community for handling the open vocabulary problem.

Knowledge Graph Embeddings. Based on recent findings [28], we generate KGEs from the aligned triples along with their labels by using *fastText*. We rely on multinomial logistic regression [6] as a classifier in a supervised training imple-

[12] The black squares represents how the model splits the frequent tokens in a sequence for a better translation process.

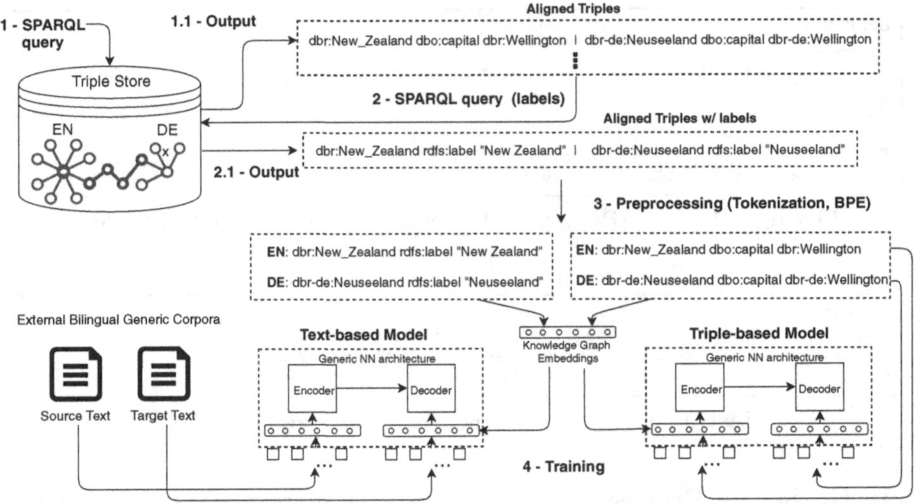

Fig. 2. Training phase overview

mented in *fastText*. It assigns the entity's URI to its surface forms. For example, the triple with literal, `<dbr:ISWC, rdfs:label, International Semantic Web Conference>` becomes `<__label__dbr:ISWC International Semantic Web Conference>` for training the KGE[13]. This technique enables the NN to retrieve from KGE the surface form of the entities through their URIs.

Training. Both triple- and text-based models rely on a standard RNN model described in Sect. 3. The difference between both models is the training data format. The Triple-based model is trained only with the aligned triples, while the text-based was trained with an external generic bilingual corpora. Additionally, both models are augmented with a KGE model. The idea of using KGE is to maximize the vector values of the triple-based and text-based NMT embeddings layers while training their models. An overview of the training phase can be found in Fig. 2 for a better understanding.

4.2 Translation Phase

Here, THOTH expects the entire source KG as an input to be translated and enriched into the target language as an output. To this end, THOTH first relies on a script which is responsible for splitting the KG triples which comprises only the resources in one file and the triples which contain literals as objects in a different file. Once the division is done, and two set files are generated, THOTH starts translating the triples only with resources. After that, THOTH has to deal with the triples which have labels, and they are handled

[13] More than one surface forms can be assigned to the entities.

differently. The subject and predicate of the triples are sent to the Triple-based model along with a special character in the place of its object. For example, suppose THOTH is parsing the following triple, <dbr:ISWC, rdfs:label, International Semantic Web Conference>, it is sent to the Triple-based model as <dbr:ISWC, rdfs:label, ▲. This special character simply tells the model to ignore the value and copy it to the target. In turn, the Text-based NMT model translates only the object; in this case, the label *International Semantic Web Conference*. We argue that the Text-based model can translate the labels correctly since its model was augmented with a KGE model representing the URIs of both KGs, source and target. We hence hypothesize that since neural models learn translations in a continuous vector space, they can assimilate and link the labels with the entities and correctly translate the labels. Afterwards, subject and predicate are attached with their object literal in a triple again. Finally, the two different files are combined into one again resulting in a translated KG. Once the translation step is complete, THOTH gets the translated KG, and the original target (German) KG used in the training part and combines both into a single KG. The idea here is to enrich the original KG with translated triples. When conflicts of values, for example, the triples match partially, and duplicated triples appear between the original KG and the translated KG, we opt to maintain the triples from the original KG as THOTH's aim is not to produce a newly translated KG but enrich the original one.

5 Evaluation

5.1 Goals

In our evaluation, we plan to address the following research questions:

Q1: Can NNs along with KGE support a full (triples and labels) translation of KGs?
Q2: How accurate are the triples generated by THOTH?
Q3: Can an artificially enriched KG improve the performance of a system on NLP tasks?

To this end, we designed our evaluation in three-fold set. First, we measure the performance of THOTH using an automatic MT evaluation metric, BLEU, along with its translation accuracy. Second, we evaluated THOTH extrinsically by comparing the German DBpedia with the German translation of the English DBpedia on two tasks: Fact Validation and Entity Linking. Third, we ran a manual intrinsic evaluation of the translation. We choose German as a target language because of the abundance of benchmarking systems and datasets for this pair.

5.2 Experimental Setup

In our experiments, we based the parameters on previous literature [24]. Both the triple-based and the text-based NMT models are built upon an RNN architecture using a bi-directional 2-layer LSTM encoder-decoder model with attention mechanism [5]. The training uses a batch size of 32 and the stochastic gradient descent with an initial learning rate of 0.0002. We set the dimension of the word embeddings to 500 and the internal embeddings of hidden layers to size 500. The dropout is set to 0.3 (naive). We use a maximum sentence length of 50, a vocabulary of 50,000 words and a beam size of 5. All experiments are performed with the OpenNMT framework [23]. In addition, we encode the triples and words using BPE [34] with 32,000 merge operations.

For training the text-based model, our training set consists of a merge of all parallel training data provided by the Workshop on Machine Translation (WMT) tasks[14], obtaining after preprocessing a corpus of five million sentences with 79M running words. In the triple-based model, we use the bilingual alignments from the English, and German versions of DBpedia[15] for training. This alignment contains 346,373 subjects, 292 relations and 208,079 objects in 1,012,681 triples. We divide this data into 80% training, 10% development and 10% test. Overall, the English KG contains 4.2 million entities, 661 relations, and 2.1 million surface forms, while the German version has 1 million entities, 249 relations, and 0.5 million surface forms. Additionally, we train the KGE on both DBpedia versions using the *fastText* algorithm (Eq. 2) with a vector dimension size of 500 and a window size of 50 by using 12 threads with hierarchical softmax.

The overall enrichment quality of THOTH is measured by working through different steps. Firstly, we evaluate the translations automatically by computing a translation accuracy with BLEU [32] score which is a cost-effective and standard MT evaluation metric. BLEU uses a modified precision metric to compare the MT output with the reference (i.e., human) translation. This automatic evaluation is done with a bilingual aligned triples test set. In the subsequent evaluation steps, we investigate THOTH's performance on a full KG translation setting. In this case, we use THOTH models for translating and enriching all Concise Bounded Description (CBD) resources of English DBpedia to an enriched-German DBpedia version. The further extrinsic evaluation steps are described below.

Fact Validation Task. In line with the data quality metrics proposed in Zaveri et al. [39], our KG translation approach can address the dimension of the completeness of KGs. An area in which completeness has a significant impact is fact validation. Hence, fact validation benchmarks can be used as a proxy for measuring our translation quality as they provide both true and false facts. We selected FactBench—a multilingual benchmark dataset for the evaluation of fact validation algorithms [17]—for our experiments. FactBench contains positive and negative facts. We only use the 750 positive facts distributed over 10 relations as reference data in our experiment. Our aim is to check the number of true facts which existed in the original KG (i.e., in the German version of DBpedia)

[14] http://www.statmt.org/wmt18/translation-task.html.

[15] We selected the subsets of mapping-based objects and labels to evaluate the quality of our approach since they are the most used ones for training Linked-Data NLP approaches.

and how many true triples THOTH was able to add to the KG through enrichment. We used 5 of the 10 predicates in our evaluation data set, i.e., `award`, `birthplace`, `deathplace`, `leader`, `starring` because the other predicates do not lead to sufficient training data. Overall, our evaluation dataset consists of a total count of 375 facts.

NLP Task. One of the most important NLP techniques for extracting knowledge automatically from unstructured data is Entity Linking, also known as Named Entity Disambiguation (NED). The goal of an EL approach is as follows: Given a piece of text, a reference knowledge graph K and a set of entity mentions in that text, map each entity mention to the corresponding resource in K. Our idea here is to exploit the graphs connections from the enriched-German DBpedia (THOTH) KG to improve a given EL system on a disambiguation task. We chose MAG, a multilingual EL system introduced by [29], which is language- and KG-agnostic. MAG does not require any training while showing competitive results. Also, we selected GERBIL [37] as a benchmarking platform because it has been widely used for evaluating different NLP tasks. In this task, we had to make the URIs of the gold standard datasets lowercase before performing our experiment since the THOTH translation models produces lower-cased URIs. The URI case sensitivity is dependent on the implementation of the web server[16]. Thus, converting all URIs to lowercase is valid and does not produce false results. As the evaluation is on the German language, we uploaded four German datasets to GERBIL (see Table 1). The **VoxEL** dataset is a manually annotated gold standard. This dataset has two versions: (i) a strict version *VoxEL-strict* where entities correspond to a restricted definition of entity, as a mention of a person, place or organization, and (ii) a relaxed version *VoxEL-relaxed*, where a broader selection of mentions referring to entities described by Wikipedia is maintained. The **N³ news.de** dataset is a real-world dataset collected from 2009 to 2011, which contains documents from the German news portal `news.de`. Finally, **DBpedia Abstracts** is a large, multilingual corpus generated from enriched Wikipedia data of annotated Wikipedia abstracts [9]. This corpus stems from Wikipedia annotations which were created manually.[17]

Table 1. Dataset statistics.

Corpus	Language	Topic	Documents	Entities
VoxEL-strict	German	News	15	204
VoxEL-relaxed	German	News	15	674
N^3 news.de	German	News	53	627
German Abstract	German	Mixed	38,197	346,448

[16] https://tools.ietf.org/html/rfc3986#section-3.1.

[17] We reduced our testset to the first subset of provided abstracts due to evaluation platform limits.

5.3 Results

In this section, we report the results of THOTH's enrichment in the German DBpedia on the settings mentioned above. Also, we aim to answer the three research questions defined in Sect. 5.1 and carried out a thorough manual analysis of our results.

Translation Results. We evaluated our translation on the test set of the bilingual data we extracted via SPARQL queries (see Sect. 5.2). To this end, we used the THOTH models for translating source English triples to German triples. First, we computed the BLEU score by comparing THOTH's output with the corresponding target (German) side of the bilingual test set. THOTH achieved a BLEU score of 65.47, which is superior to the state-of-the-art translation scores achieved on natural language [15].

Given that it is not possible to infer the quality of a given translation only relying on one automatic evaluation metric, we created an additional evaluation script which computes the exact string match of subjects, predicates, and objects between an output and a reference translation triple. Additionally, we also computed the overall triple accuracy. For example, given the following triple from THOTH's output, `<dbr_de:iago_falque dbo:club dbr_de:fc_turin>`, we measure if its subject, predicate and object are equal to the ones of the reference translation; in this case, we found it to be the same. However, in the case where some of them are different, the accuracy of the triple is 0 because the meaning of the triple is wrong in comparison to its reference. Figure 3 depicts the accuracy results of THOTH's output in comparison to the German test set. THOTH achieved up to 80% accuracy for subjects, predicates, and objects. As expected, THOTH's accuracy decreased to 68.83% while measuring entire triples. We analyzed the results manually to understand this drop in the performance. Our manual analysis suggests that the poorer performance w.r.t. triples is linked to the partially weak disambiguation power of the underlying KGE

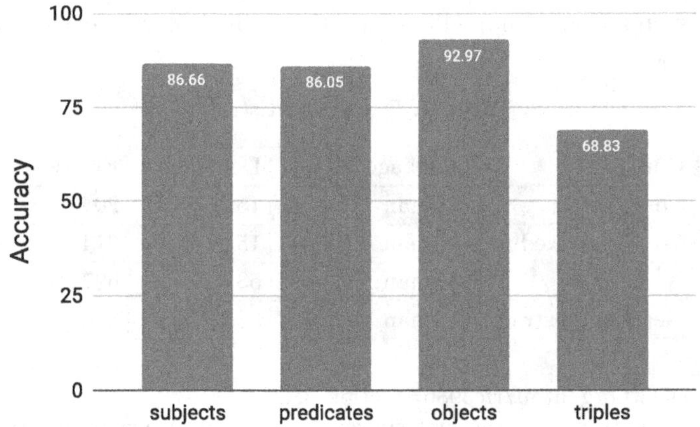

Fig. 3. Overall translation accuracy

model, which assigned the same vector value for similar predicates. We discuss this particular challenge along with other findings in Sect. 5.4. Regarding **Q1**, our results confirm that NNs along KGE can support a full KG translation by considering the consistent quality of THOTH translations.

Fact Validation Results. Here, we used THOTH to translate the entire English DBpedia to German. In this case, we do not have a gold standard translation to compare automatically. Therefore, we evaluated the THOTH's enrichment capability in the perspective of a fact-validation task. The main goal here was to check if THOTH could enrich the original German KG with new correct facts which were not present in its original version. Figure 4 reports an improvement of 18.4% across all predicates. Interestingly, the original German DBpedia KG did not contain any fact with the predicate `award` from the FactBench dataset. However, after THOTH's enrichment, its coverage of FactBench increased to 28%. We also noticed an improvement of 48% w.r.t. the `leader` predicate. Further (even if smaller) increases can be seen in the `birthPlace`, `deathPlace`, and `starring` predicates, where we achieve an average enhancement of 4%. Delving into the data shows that the predicates which got modest improvements are the most mapped by the German DBpedia from Wikipedia[18]. Consequently, these predicates are present in abundance in the original German KG. Overall, it becomes clear that THOTH achieves the task of improving the quality of KGs w.r.t. their completeness. Additionally, we can answer **Q2** with the results of THOTH on the fact-validation task, where it achieved an increase of +18.4% accuracy. THOTH obviously led to a significant increase in the number of correct facts in the original KG.

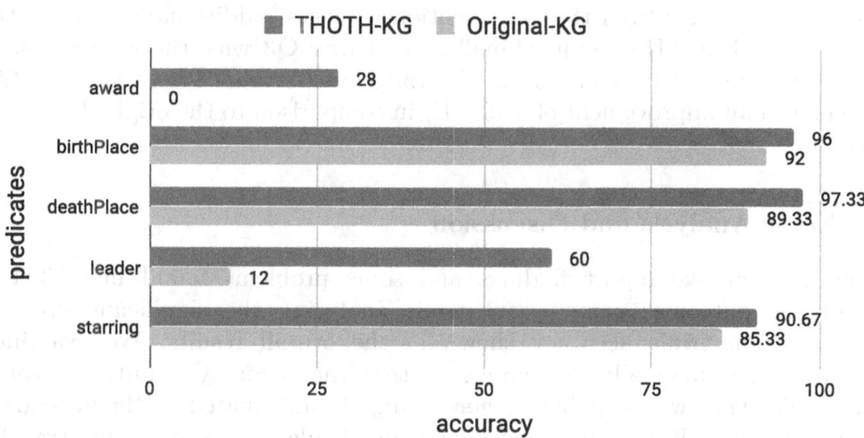

Fig. 4. A comparison between the enriched-German DBpedia (THOTH) KG with the original German DBpedia on the validation of facts.

[18] http://mappings.dbpedia.org/server/statistics/de/.

Table 2. Micro results in a comparison between German DBpedia KG with Enriched-German DBpedia (THOTH) KG in MAG.

Datasets	MAG-DBpedia-KG			MAG-THOTH-KG		
	F-measure	Precision	Recall	F-measure	Precision	Recall
German abstracts	0.78	0.79	0.76	**0.97**	**0.99**	**0.96**
N^3 news.de	0.77	0.78	0.76	**0.98**	**0.99**	**0.97**
VoxEL-strict	0.40	0.46	0.35	**0.70**	**0.81**	**0.61**
VoxEL-relaxed	0.57	0.57	0.57	**0.64**	**0.64**	**0.64**

Entity Linking Results. For this evaluation, we used the optimal parameter configuration for MAG described by Moussallem et al. [29]. Table 2 reports the results of MAG in two configuration sets, one with original German DBpedia and another with the *Enriched-German DBpedia (THOTH)* as reference KGs. The version of MAG running on the translated KG achieves significantly better results than that running on the original KG. The average improvement across all datasets is around 19% in F-measure. The results of the *German abstracts* data set and N^3 *news.de* are surprisingly high. We sampled the results manually, and we could establish that the results were correct. We also investigated the creation of both benchmarking datasets, and we concluded that at the time of their creation, the links used in both were based on the English DBpedia as an auxiliary KG. Therefore, when THOTH translated the English KG to German and enriched the original German DBpedia with English knowledge, MAG was able to get very high HITS scores for many resources. For example, the HITS score of dbr_de:Frankreich (dbr:France) increased around 50% from 0.08 to 0.12. The superior results of MAG using the enriched knowledge on the VoXEL datasets (which do not suffer from the aforementioned biases) additionally confirm the pertinence of THOTH's results. Finally, we answer **Q3** with the EL results, as they proved that MAG while using the *Enriched-German DBpedia (THOTH)* KG achieved an improvement of +19% F_1 in comparison to the original German DBpedia.

5.4 Error Analysis and Discussion

In this section, we report findings and some problems found in THOTH. One of the outcomes came about while analyzing the significant drop in the translation triple accuracy shown in the overall results. We examined the translations manually and perceived that the accuracy mainly decreased because THOTH was capable of generating disambiguated URIs instead of the correct ones. For example, the following triple in the reference translation `<dbr_de:don_getty dbo:birthplace dbr_de:westmount>` did not match with the following output, `<dbr_de:don_getty dbo:birthplace dbr_de:westmount_(québec)>`, simply because THOTH generated a different object URI. Although the output object has a different URI, it is correct because the birthplace of Don Getty was Westmount in Québec. However, this more explicit URI led to an error and consequently decreased the translation accuracy. It is a fascinating example because we could see that the NN models along with the KGE were able to understand the KGs graph structure and predict a disambiguated URI based on the knowledge from the English DBpedia. Additionally, no similar example was present in the training set, indicating that the BPE model learned correctly to translate the URIs.

Besides the aforementioned results, we noticed some mistranslations of similar predicates which were responsible for decreasing the accuracy of triple translation. For example, the following English source triple `dbr:zenyattà_mondatta dbo:artist dbr:the_police` was translated into `dbr_de:zenyattà_mondatta dbo:producer dbr_de:the_police`. This example shows that THOTH translated the subject and object correctly. However, the predicate was incorrect and was mistranslated from dbo:artist to dbo:producer. A similar problem occurred while translating the triple, `dbr:albert_einstein dbo:citizenship dbr:Switzerland` to `dbr:albert_einstein dbo:birthplace dbr:der_Schweiz`. After a manual analysis, we identified that both cases happened because THOTH could not distinguish the predicates which share the same domain and range. In a more in-depth analysis, we perceived that the predicates mentioned above are very close to each other in the vector space thus complicating the disambiguation process of NN models. The performance of THOTH was not affected by these false triples since they were automatically removed from the *Enriched-German DBpedia (THOTH)* dataset in the enrichment step. After this manual analysis of the results, we believe that addressing the problem of similar predicates (e.g., through novel embedding techniques) can enhance the translation quality of THOTH.

6 Conclusion

In this paper, we introduced a neural approach named THOTH for translating and enriching KGs from different languages. THOTH relies on two different RNN-based NMT models along with KGEs for translating triples and texts jointly. We carried out an extensive evaluation set for certifying the quality of our approach. Our results show that THOTH is a promising approach which achieves a translation accuracy of 88.56%. Moreover, its enrichment improves the quality of the German DBpedia significantly, as we report +18.4% accuracy for fact validation and +19% F_1 for entity linking. As future work, we plan to investigate the application of sub-graphs [10] for improving the disambiguation of similar predicates. Additionally, we aim to exploit other NN architectures, such as Transformer [38], for improving THOTH's performance. Moreover, we plan to apply THOTH in the context of low-resource KG scenarios with Asian and African languages as well as apply THOTH on the Wikidata KG.

Acknowledgments. This work has been supported by the German Federal Ministry of Transport and Digital Infrastructure (BMVI) in the projects LIMBO (no. 19F2029I) and OPAL (no. 19F2028A) as well as by the Brazilian National Council for Scientific and Technological Development (CNPq) (no. 206971/2014-1).

References

1. Palmero Aprosio, A., Giuliano, C., Lavelli, A.: Towards an automatic creation of localized versions of DBpedia. In: Alani, H., et al. (eds.) ISWC 2013. LNCS, vol. 8218, pp. 494–509. Springer, Heidelberg (2013). https://doi.org/10.1007/978-3-642-41335-3_31
2. Arcan, M., Buitelaar, P.: Ontology label translation. In: HLT-NAACL, pp. 40–46 (2013)
3. Arcan, M., Buitelaar, P.: Translating domain-specific expressions in knowledge bases with neural machine translation. arXiv preprint arXiv:1709.02184 (2017)
4. Auer, S., Bizer, C., Kobilarov, G., Lehmann, J., Cyganiak, R., Ives, Z.: DBpedia: a nucleus for a web of open data. In: Aberer, K., et al. (eds.) ASWC/ISWC -2007. LNCS, vol. 4825, pp. 722–735. Springer, Heidelberg (2007). https://doi.org/10.1007/978-3-540-76298-0_52
5. Bahdanau, D., Cho, K., Bengio, Y.: Neural machine translation by jointly learning to align and translate. arXiv preprint arXiv:1409.0473 (2014)
6. Böhning, D.: Multinomial logistic regression algorithm. Ann. Inst. Stat. Math. **1**, 197–200 (1992)
7. Bollacker, K., Evans, C., Paritosh, P., Sturge, T., Taylor, J.: Freebase: a collaboratively created graph database for structuring human knowledge. In: Proceedings of the 2008 ACM SIGMOD International Conference on Management of Data, pp. 1247–1250. ACM (2008)
8. Bordes, A., Usunier, N., Garcia-Duran, A., Weston, J., Yakhnenko, O.: Translating embeddings for modeling multi-relational data. In: Advances in Neural Information Processing Systems, pp. 2787–2795 (2013)
9. Brümmer, M., Dojchinovski, M., Hellmann, S.: DBpedia abstracts: a large-scale, open, multilingual NLP training corpus. In: Proceedings of the Tenth International Conference on Language Resources and Evaluation (LREC 2016). European Language Resources Association (ELRA), Paris, May 2016
10. Cao, Z., Wang, L., de Melo, G.: Link prediction via subgraph embedding-based convex matrix completion. In: Proceedings of the 32nd AAAI Conference on Artificial Intelligence (AAAI 2018). AAAI Press (2018)
11. Chen, M., Tian, Y., Yang, M., Zaniolo, C.: Multilingual knowledge graph embeddings for cross-lingual knowledge alignment. In: Proceedings of the 26th International Joint Conference on Artificial Intelligence, pp. 1511–1517. AAAI Press (2017)
12. Chen, M., Tian, Y., Yang, M., Zaniolo, C.: Multilingual Knowledge Graph Embeddings for Cross-lingual Knowledge Alignment. In: Proceedings of the 26th International Joint Conference on Artificial Intelligence (IJCAI), pp. 1–10. AAAI Press (2017)
13. Cochez, M., Ristoski, P., Ponzetto, S.P., Paulheim, H.: Biased graph walks for RDF graph embeddings. In: Proceedings of the 7th International Conference on Web Intelligence, Mining and Semantics, p. 21. ACM (2017)
14. Cochez, M., Ristoski, P., Ponzetto, S.P., Paulheim, H.: Global RDF vector space embeddings. In: d'Amato, C., et al. (eds.) ISWC 2017. LNCS, vol. 10587, pp. 190–207. Springer, Cham (2017). https://doi.org/10.1007/978-3-319-68288-4_12
15. Edunov, S., Ott, M., Auli, M., Grangier, D.: Understanding back-translation at scale. arXiv preprint arXiv:1808.09381 (2018)
16. Feng, X., Tang, D., Qin, B., Liu, T.: English-Chinese knowledge base translation with neural network. In: Proceedings of COLING 2016, the 26th International Conference on Computational Linguistics: Technical Papers, pp. 2935–2944 (2016)

17. Gerber, D., et al.: Defacto—temporal and multilingual deep fact validation. Web Semant. Sci. Serv. Agents World Wide Web **35**, 85–101 (2015)
18. Joulin, A., Grave, E., Bojanowski, P., Mikolov, T.: Bag of tricks for efficient text classification. In: Proceedings of the 15th Conference of the European Chapter of the Association for Computational Linguistics: Volume 2, Short Papers, vol. 2, pp. 427–431 (2017)
19. Joulin, A., Grave, E., Bojanowski, P., Nickel, M., Mikolov, T.: Fast linear model for knowledge graph embeddings. arXiv preprint arXiv:1710.10881 (2017)
20. K M, A., Basu Roy Chowdhury, S., Dukkipati, A.: Learning beyond datasets: knowledge graph augmented neural networks for natural language processing. In: Proceedings of the 2018 Conference of the North American Chapter of the Association for Computational Linguistics: Human Language Technologies, Volume 1 (Long Papers), pp. 313–322. Association for Computational Linguistics (2018). http://aclweb.org/anthology/N18-1029
21. Kaffee, L.-A., et al.: Mind the (language) gap: generation of multilingual Wikipedia summaries from Wikidata for ArticlePlaceholders. In: Gangemi, A., et al. (eds.) ESWC 2018. LNCS, vol. 10843, pp. 319–334. Springer, Cham (2018). https://doi.org/10.1007/978-3-319-93417-4_21
22. Kalchbrenner, N., Blunsom, P.: Recurrent continuous translation models. In: EMNLP, vol. 3, p. 413 (2013)
23. Klein, G., Kim, Y., Deng, Y., Senellart, J., Rush, A.M.: OpenNMT: Open-Source Toolkit for Neural Machine Translation. ArXiv e-prints (2017)
24. Klein, G., Kim, Y., Deng, Y., Senellart, J., Rush, A.: OpenNMT: open-source toolkit for neural machine translation. In: Proceedings of ACL 2017, System Demonstrations, pp. 67–72 (2017)
25. Lakshen, G.A., Janev, V., Vraneš, S.: Challenges in quality assessment of Arabic DBpedia. In: Proceedings of the 8th International Conference on Web Intelligence, Mining and Semantics, p. 15. ACM (2018)
26. Luong, T., Pham, H., Manning, C.D.: Effective approaches to attention-based neural machine translation. In: Proceedings of the 2015 Conference on Empirical Methods in Natural Language Processing, pp. 1412–1421. Association for Computational Linguistics (2015). https://doi.org/10.18653/v1/D15-1166. http://aclweb.org/anthology/D15-1166
27. McCrae, J.P., Arcan, M., Asooja, K., Gracia, J., Buitelaar, P., Cimiano, P.: Domain adaptation for ontology localization. Web Semant. Sci. Serv. Agents World Wide Web **36**, 23–31 (2016)
28. Moussallem, D., Arčan, M., Ngomo, A.C.N., Buitelaar, P.: Augmenting neural machine translation with knowledge graphs. arXiv preprint arXiv:1902.08816 (2019)
29. Moussallem, D., Usbeck, R., Röeder, M., Ngomo, A.C.N.: MAG: a multilingual, knowledge-base agnostic and deterministic entity linking approach. In: Proceedings of the Knowledge Capture Conference, p. 9. ACM (2017)
30. Moussallem, D., Wauer, M., Ngomo, A.C.N.: Machine translation using semantic web technologies: a survey. J. Web Semant. **51**, 1–19 (2018)
31. Nickel, M., Rosasco, L., Poggio, T.A., et al.: Holographic embeddings of knowledge graphs. In: AAAI, pp. 1955–1961 (2016)
32. Papineni, K., Roukos, S., Ward, T., Zhu, W.J.: BLEU: a method for automatic evaluation of machine translation. In: Proceedings of the 40th Annual Meeting on Association for Computational Linguistics, pp. 311–318. Association for Computational Linguistics (2002)

33. Ristoski, P., Paulheim, H.: RDF2Vec: RDF graph embeddings for data mining. In: Groth, P., et al. (eds.) ISWC 2016. LNCS, vol. 9981, pp. 498–514. Springer, Cham (2016). https://doi.org/10.1007/978-3-319-46523-4_30
34. Sennrich, R., Haddow, B., Birch, A.: Neural machine translation of rare words with subword units. In: Proceedings of the 54th Annual Meeting of the Association for Computational Linguistics (Volume 1: Long Papers), pp. 1715–1725. Association for Computational Linguistics (2016)
35. Sorokin, D., Gurevych, I.: Modeling semantics with gated graph neural networks for knowledge base question answering. In: Proceedings of the 27th International Conference on Computational Linguistics, pp. 3306–3317. Association for Computational Linguistics (2018). http://aclweb.org/anthology/C18-1280
36. Tang, G., Müller, M., Rios, A., Sennrich, R.: Why self-attention? A targeted evaluation of neural machine translation architectures. In: Proceedings of the 2018 Conference on Empirical Methods in Natural Language Processing, pp. 4263–4272 (2018)
37. Usbeck, R., et al.: GERBIL: general entity annotator benchmarking framework. In: Proceedings of the 24th International Conference on World Wide Web, WWW 2015, Florence, Italy, 18–22 May 2015, pp. 1133–1143 (2015)
38. Vaswani, A., et al.: Attention is all you need. In: Advances in Neural Information Processing Systems, pp. 5998–6008 (2017)
39. Zaveri, A., Rula, A., Maurino, A., Pietrobon, R., Lehmann, J., Auer, S.: Quality assessment for linked data: a survey. Semant. Web **7**(1), 63–93 (2016)

Entity Enabled Relation Linking

Jeff Z. Pan[1,2,3](✉), Mei Zhang[1], Kuldeep Singh[4], Frank van Harmelen[5], Jinguang Gu[1], and Zhi Zhang[1]

[1] College of Computer Science and Technology, Wuhan University of Science and Technology, Wuhan 430065, China
zhangmeiontoweb@gmail.com, simon@wust.edu.cn, wustzz@sina.com

[2] Department of Computer Science, The University of Aberdeen, Aberdeen, UK
jeff.z.pan@abdn.ac.uk

[3] Edinburgh Research Centre, Huawei, Edinburgh, UK

[4] Nuance Communications Deutschland GmbH, Munich, Germany
kuldeep.singh1@nuance.com

[5] Vrije Universiteit Amsterdam, Amsterdam, The Netherlands
frank.van.harmelen@vu.nl

Abstract. Relation linking is an important problem for knowledge graph-based Question Answering. Given a natural language question and a knowledge graph, the task is to identify relevant relations from the given knowledge graph. Since existing techniques for entity extraction and linking are more stable compared to relation linking, our idea is to exploit entities extracted from the question to support relation linking. In this paper, we propose a novel approach, based on DBpedia entities, for computing relation candidates. We have empirically evaluated our approach on different standard benchmarks. Our evaluation shows that our approach significantly outperforms existing baseline systems in both recall, precision and runtime.

Keywords: Question answering · Semantic Web · Semantic search · Predicate linking · Knowledge Graph

1 Introduction

Over the past years, the number and size of Knowledge Graphs (KG) [24] in the Semantic Web has increased significantly. Among them, well known ones include DBpedia [1], Yago [32], Freebase [5] and Wikidata [37]. To make such information easily available, many question answering (QA) systems over KGs have been created in the last years [4,12,16]. The research community has addressed the problem of question answering over KGs via two different approaches. Firstly, researchers have developed end-to-end QA systems such as [8,16] that use deep learning and machine learning models to directly predict mapping/linking of entities and relations in the input question to their KG occurrences to extract correct answers. These end to end QA systems are frequently developed for question answering over Freebase due to the availability of large training data

C. Ghidini et al. (Eds.): ISWC 2019, LNCS 11778, pp. 523–538, 2019.
https://doi.org/10.1007/978-3-030-30793-6_30

in benchmarks (e.g. the SimpleQuestion benchmark [6] for Freebase, containing 100.000 questions). However, for DBpedia the availability of training data is limited to at most 5000 questions [34]). Therefore, researchers have focused on QA systems based on semantic parsing that heavily rely on semantics associated with natural language understanding of the input question. Semantic parsing based QA (SQA) systems implement a sequence of tasks (often referred to the QA pipeline [26]) to translate natural language questions to their corresponding SPARQL query. These systems over DBpedia implement independent component(s) in the architecture for entity and relation linking [26,29], that is, to link the extracted entities and relations from the input question to their knowledge graph occurrences. While doing so, most QA systems face the following challenges: (i) how to deal with the extraction of entity and relation candidates in the question, and (ii) how to link the relation and entity candidates to the knowledge graph. The third approach is the collaborative QA systems which promotes reusability of QA components.

In this paper, we address the challenge of relation linking. Recently, to build SQA systems in a collaborative effort, many frameworks such as Qanary [7], OKBQA[1] [14] and Frankenstein [31] are developed that use modular approaches for building QA systems by reusing existing independently released tools. Several independent entity and relation linking tools such as DBpedia Spotlight [17], AGDISTIS [36], SIBKB [30], ReMatch [18] and Tag Me [10] are reused in these frameworks. Following this approach, in this paper, we will develop a new relation linking component, embed it in an existing framework (in our case Frankenstein) and compare its performance against the state of the art. We focus on *relation* linking because independent *entity* linking tools already perform well when they are applied to QA frameworks like Frankenstein, while on the other hand all the existing independent relation linking tools fail miserably both in terms of precision and runtime [31]. This failure of relation linking tools impact the overall performance of the QA frameworks. Recently released studies by Singh et. al. [28,31][2] have concluded that one of the main reasons behind relational linking tool having limited performance is that the existing relation linking tools focus more on identifying relations in the original question, while completely ignoring the context of the entities that co-occur with these relations.

Therefore, in this paper, we propose to make use of entities appearing in questions to support the task of relation linking over the DBpedia knowledge graph. More precisely, properties that are logically connected to the target entities (as domains or ranges) are called the *candidate property list* (or simply *property list*). This property list can then be used to expand the set of relation candidates which can be used for the construction of SPARQL queries in the QA pipeline. Our evaluations later in this paper will show that the use of logically connected property candidates leads to substantial gains in not only recall, precision but also runtime.

---

[1] http://www.okbqa.org/.

[2] Authors evaluated five independent relation linking tools for DBpedia and other 18 entity linking tools.

For example, given an input question "Which comic characters are painted by Bill Finger?", we can extract the relation phrase `are painted by` and the entity phrase `Bill Finger`. Typically, existing relation linking approaches [18,30] would directly extract the relation phrase in the question, while ignoring the entities (Bill Finger in this case) and expand the relation candidate using a synonym list, such as "painter". These tools then attempt to map the relation candidate to DBpedia relations. However, this mapping leads them to provide `dbo:painter`[3], leading to an empty answer to the resulting SPARQL query. The SPARQL query returns null because `dbo:painter` is not the correct property of the entity `Bill Finger`. Instead, we assume that the entity `Bill Finger` is already linked to its DBpedia mention and acts as one of the inputs besides the natural language question. We construct a property list (see more details in the next sections) by collecting all properties of the DBpedia entity `dbr:Bill_Finger`[4], including properties that have some types of `dbr:Bill_Finger` as domains or ranges. We then further make use of the property list, including ranking of the list and making sure that the range of the chosen property is compatible with `comic characters`. At the end, we get `dbo:creator` as a candidate relation. When we apply this result to the SPARQL query corresponding to the question, we can conclude that `dbo:creator` is the best choice. In this way, we eliminate the requirement for large training data by focusing on the structure of the DBpedia knowledge graph (in terms of entities and their associated properties), and by considering the context of the relation consisting of the entities in the question.

Based on the above idea, we propose and implement a new relation linking framework (Entity Enabled Relation Linking, EERL) for factoid questions using DBpedia. The contributions of this paper can be summarised as follows: Firstly, a novel approach for generating and ranking candidate relations to be used in QA systems. Secondly, an efficient implementation of this approach in the EERL framework, that can be deployed as part of a larger QA pipeline; and thirdly, an in-depth evaluation of our approach using a set of questions from two benchmarking datasets having more than 5000 diverse questions. Our evaluation shows a large improvement over the state of the art in both precision, recall and the runtime.

As most existing works in the literature, we test our approach on DBpedia. However, there is no specific assumption in our work on the structure or schema of the underlying knowledge graph, and our method should be equally applicable and can be extended to any other knowledge graph.

The rest of the paper is organised into the following sections: Section 2 presents our problem statement, Sect. 3 describes some of the major contributions in relation linking used in question answering, Sect. 4 presents our approach for the identified problem. Section 5 describes our experimental setting and our evaluation results. Finally Section 6 presents some of the key discussion points considering our approach, and we conclude the paper in Sect. 7.

[3] dbo is bound to http://dbpedia.org/ontology/.
[4] dbr is bound to http://dbpedia.org/resource/.

2 Background

2.1 Knowledge Graph

More formally, we define a knowledge graph [23,24] $\mathcal{G} = \mathcal{T} \cup \mathcal{A}$ consisting of a data sub-graph $\mathcal{A}$ (or ABox) and a schema sub-graph $\mathcal{T}$ (or TBox). Facts in the ABox are represented as triples of the following two forms:

- *Relation assertion* (h,r,t), where h (t) is the head (tail) entity, and r the relation; e.g., (`dbr:Barack_Obama`, `dbp:birthPlace`, `dbr:Hawaii`) is a relation assertion.
- *Type assertion* (e, rdf:type, C), where e is an entity, rdf:type is the instance-of relation from the standard W3C RDF specification and C is a type; e.g., (`dbr:Bill_Finger`, rdf:type, `dbo:Person`) is a type assertion.

A TBox includes type inclusion axioms, such as (`dbo:Person rdfs:subClassOf dbo:Agent`), and relation axioms, such as ((`dbp:birthPlace rdfs:domain dbo:` Person)) and (`dbp:birthPlace rdfs: range dbo:Place`). There can be other kinds of type and relation axioms defined in the W3C standard knowledge graph schema language OWL, which is based on Description Logics. We refer the readers to [2] for more details on Description Logic. In the rest of the paper, we use E($\mathcal{A}$) (resp. R($\mathcal{T}$)) to refer to the set of entities (resp. relations) in $\mathcal{A}$ (resp. $\mathcal{T}$). Note that the set of relations in $\mathcal{A}$ is a subset of the set of relations in $\mathcal{T}$, some of which might not have instances in $\mathcal{A}$.

2.2 Problem Statement

Firstly, let us formalise the problem of relation linking for factoid questions, before proposing our new research problem. Given the schema $\mathcal{T}$ of a knowledge graph $\mathcal{G} = \mathcal{T} \cup \mathcal{A}$ and an input natural language question q, the task of entity linking is to identify a set of relations $R_q \subseteq$ R($\mathcal{T}$) for the set of relation phrases in q.

In this paper, we propose a variant of the problem of relation linking for factoid questions, based on entities identified within these questions. Formally, given a knowledge graph $\mathcal{G} = \mathcal{T} \cup \mathcal{A}$, an input natural question q and a set of entities $E_q \subseteq$ E($\mathcal{A}$) identified in q, the task of *entity enabled relation linking* is to identify a set of relations $R_q \subseteq$ R($\mathcal{T}$) for the set of relation phrases in q based on the entities E_q.

Note that entities in the ABox $\mathcal{A}$ of $\mathcal{G}$ as well as their interconnections are not taken into account in the task of (pure) relation linking, but in entity enabled relation linking, which, in fact, also takes into account the implicit connections between the entities in $\mathcal{A}$. This makes entity enabled relation linking a (much) harder problem than (pure) relation linking.

3 Related Work

Given a natural language question and a knowledge graph, the task of relation linking is to identify relevant relations from the given knowledge graph for the relation phrases from the question. There are a variety of resources and systems for relation linking over DBpedia.

PATTY [20]**:** PATTY is a large resource for textual patterns that denote binary relations between entities. Its a two column large knowledge source, where one column represents natural language relational patterns, and the another column contains associated DBpedia predicates. However, PATTY cannot be used directly as a component for relation linking in a QA system and needs to be modified based on individual developers' requirements.

BOA [11]**:** BOA can be used to extract natural language representations of predicates independent of the language, if provided with a Named Entity Recognition service. Like PATTY, BOA also needs to be modified before using directly in a QA system.

SIBKB [30]**:** SIBKB provides searching mechanisms for linking natural language relations to knowledge graphs. The tool uses PATTY as the underlying knowledge source and proposes a novel approach based on semantic similarities of the words with DBpedia predicates for an independent relation linking tool that accepts question as input and provides DBpedia properties as output.

Rematch [18]**:** The ReMatch system is an independently reusable tool, for matching natural language relations to KB properties. This tool employs dependency parse characteristics with adjustment rules and then carries out a match against KG properties enhanced with the lexicon Wordnet. However, the run time is relatively slow for each question.

EARL [3]**:** EARL is the most recent approach for the joint entity and relation linking. This tool treats entity and relations linking as a single step. At first, it aims to identify entities in the question and, following a graph traversal approach, identifies the relation associated with the entities. EARL determines the best semantic connection between all keywords of the question by exploiting the connection density between entity and relation candidates.

The work by Usbeck et al. [36] proposes an entity linking tool AGDISTIS that is most closely related to our approach. AGDISTIS combines the HITS algorithm with label expansion strategies and string similarity measures. Similar to our approach where we rely on linked URIs of entities in a question besides the question as input, AGDISTIS accepts a natural language question (or sentence) and recognised entities as inputs to provide disambiguated entity URIs. However, unlike our approach, it is restricted to entity linking and does not perform relation linking. Furthermore, TBSL QA system [35] uses entities in the query Q to generate templates that are later filled with properties from the graph which is quite similar to our idea of the use of entities in finding correct predicate. TBSL uses external resource BOA to find the correct matching besides string matching to get the correct relations. Our approach goes a step ahead and heavily relies on ontology reasoning to find the correct predicate(s) for the given entity without using any external knowledge resource. This demonstrates the power of exploiting knowledge encoded in the knowledge graph itself. Furthermore, using entities to map the relations in a question is new in QA relation linking but this has been well studied in ontology mapping (alignment). For example, in mapping tables to ontologies, some approaches such as [19] create a candidate list of the properties and rank them after linking the entities in the table cells. Furthermore, there are also efforts developing rich schema for question answering in e.g., legal domain [9].

4 Approach

In this section, we describe our approach to use entities in E_q for relation linking.

4.1 Preliminaries and Proposed Hypothesis

To evaluate our novel approach for addressing relation linking problem, we have analysed 100 randomly chosen question answering pairs from the benchmarking datasets of Sect. 5. While analysing the SPARQL query associated with the input questions, We observe that most of predicates of these queries (i.e. the KG relations for the natural language relations occurring in the input question) are the properties of the entities in the questions. For example, given a question "**Which comic characters are painted by Bill Finger ?**" (a question from the LC-QuAD dataset [34]), the SPARQL query of this question is:

```
"SELECT␣DISTINCT␣?uri␣WHERE{
?uri␣␣http://dbpedia.org/ontology/creator
http://dbpedia.org/resource/Bill_Finger.
?uri␣https://www.w3.org/1999/02/22-rdf-syntaxns#type
http://dbpedia.org/ontology/ComicsCharacter.}␣"
```

In this query, the predicate `dbo:creator` of the associated entity `dbr:Bill_Finger` is one of the property of `dbr:Bill_Finger` in DBpedia. Furthermore, it is often a case that there is no natural language label of a relation in the question. For example, the question "**How many shows does HBO have ?**" (a question from LC-QuAD dataset [34]) contains no natural language relation label. Such questions are called questions with hidden relations [28]. The SPARQL Query of this question is:

```
"SELECT␣DISTINCT␣COUNT(?uri)␣WHERE{
?uri␣http://dbpedia.org/ontology/channel
http://dbpedia.org/resource/HBO␣.
?uri␣https://www.w3.org/1999/02/22-rdf-syntaxns#type
http://dbpedia.org/ontology/TelevisionShow␣.}"
```

Here, the predicate `dbo:channel` is not the property of `dbr:HBO` explicitly, but rather a property from the type `dbo:Broadcaster` of `dbr:HBO`, where `dbo:Broad caster` is a range of `dbo:channel`.

Hypothesis: Based on this analysis, we propose the following hypothesis: *"The relations in questions are properties of the entities occurring in the question or properties of the types of these entities."* This hypothesis is surprisingly simple, but to the best of our knowledge this simple hypothesis has not yet been exploited in any of the current state of the art approaches for QA relation linking.

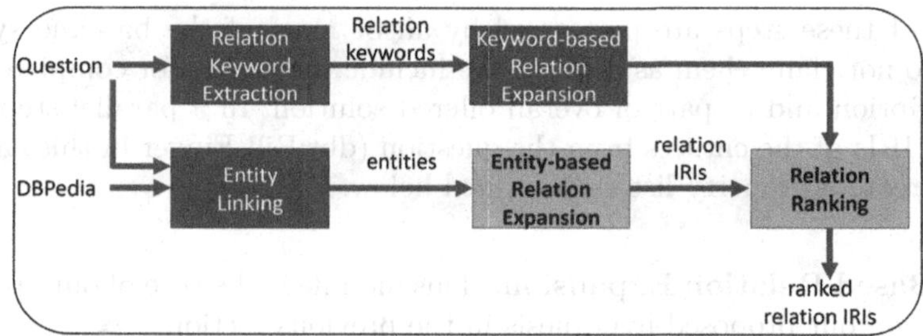

Fig. 1. Conceptual Architecture of our EERL Framework. All of the baseline relation linking frameworks found in the literature share the top part of the pipeline. Our contribution in the EERL framework is the additional entity-based part of the pipeline in the bottom half of the image.

Based on this hypothesis, we developed an approach that follows five main steps (see Fig. 1): (1) RELATION KEYWORD EXTRACTION: to extract natural language relation keywords from the question, (2) KEYWORD-BASED RELATION EXPANSION: to expand extracted relation keywords using background knowledge, (3)ENTITY LINKING: link the entities in natural language questions to DBpedia IRIs, (4) ENTITY-BASED RELATION EXPANSION: to use entities in E_q to form candidate property list, and then (5) RELATION RANKING: to rank the candidates in property list to get the best relations R_q. We implemented our approach in proposed EERL framework which is described in next section.

4.2 EERL Framework

Our EERL framework consists of five different modules as illustrated in the Fig. 1. The framework has two inputs: a natural language question q and the DBpedia knowledge graph.

Relation Keyword Extractor. The first module is the Relation Keyword Extractor that extracts relation phrases from the input question.

Example: In the question "Which comic characters are painted by Bill Finger?", we extract the "painted by" phrase. We utilize TexRazor API[5] which provides us with relation phrasess and reused the implementation of this module from the work of [30].

Keyword-Based Relation Expansion. In the second module "Keyword-based Relation Expansion", we expand the relation phrase "painted by" using background knowledge from PATTY [20] to get a list of associated relation phrases. We first convert "painted by" in a vector using Glove [25] and then used the vector representation of PATTY created by [30] to get the most suitable relation phrase. For the given example, this step provides us with "painter".

[5] https://www.textrazor.com/docs/rest.

Both of these steps are performed by all or most of the baseline systems, and we do not claim them as novelty. We include them only for completeness of our description and as part of overall offered solution. In a parallel step, input DBpedia IRIs of the entities from the question (dbr:Bill_Finger in this case) are used to create a property list as described below.

Entity-Based Relation Expansion. This module is the core of our approach, and relies on our proposed hypothesis in the previous section.

Given a KG $\mathcal{G} = \mathcal{T} \cup \mathcal{A}$, the entities in a knowledge graph are the nodes of the $\mathcal{G}$. These nodes are connected to other nodes (i.e. other entities) via directed labeled edges. We divide these edges into two categories: explicit and implicit relations.

Explicit Relations. Explicit relations are the properties of entities which can be fetched from $\mathcal{A}$. For example, in the sentence: **The spouse of Barack Obama is Michelle Obama**, represented in RDF as the triple (`dbr:Barack_Obama`, `dbo:spouse`,`dbr:Michelle_Obama`), `dbo:spouse` is the property of `dbr:Barack_Obama`.

Implicit Relations. Implicit relations are the relations between entities that can be derived from $\mathcal{T}$. For instance, from the sentence "Barack Obama is born in Honolulu", the explicit relation is `dbo:birthPlace`. There is also an implicit relation `dbo:HomeTown`, which is introduced by the type `dbo:Agent` of the entity `dbr:Barack`: `(dbr:Barack_Obama,rdfs:type,dbo:Agent)` and `(dbo:HomeTown, rdfs:domain, dbo:Agent)`.

We utilise both explicit and implicit relations to extract right set of relations. We first expand the potential relation candidates using explicit relations, and then further expand it with implicit relations.

Expansion 1: In this step, we fetch the property set from the instance triples in $\mathcal{A}$. To avoid large scale retrieval, we just retrieve the ontologies associated with the entity of the question rather retrieving all the ontologies of DBpedia. For each entity e in the input question, we retrieve all explicit properties from the associated ontology of this entity. We add these explicit properties to the list P1, and we call this list the *explicit property list* (EPL).

Example: Given the question "Which comic characters are painted by Bill Finger?" (a question from LC-QuAD dataset). If we do not use expansion 1, we would just get `dbo:painter` as the relation. When we apply expansion 1 to it, we also get the relation result `dbo:creator` which is derived from the explicit property list of `dbr:Bill_Finger`. As we illustrated above, `dbo:creator` is indeed the right answer.

Expansion 2: Based on Expansion 1, we add another iteration which is based on reasoning to gather the implicit property list from $\mathcal{T}$. To get the implicit property list, we first get domains and ranges from the schema $\mathcal{T}$. There are two kinds of domains and ranges. The first is global domains and ranges, and the second is the local domains and ranges. Global domains and ranges are usual RDFS domains and ranges. In description logic form, they can be represented as

$\top \sqsubseteq \forall r^{-}.GD$ (GD is a global domain of the property r), $\top \sqsubseteq \forall r.GR$ (GR is a global range of the property r), Local domains and ranges is similar but the left hand side $\top$ can be replaced by a type (such as C): $C \sqsubseteq \forall r^{-}.GD$ (GD is a local domain of the property r w.r.t. C entities), $C \sqsubseteq \forall r.GR$ (GR is a local range of the property r w.r.t. C entities). Both global and local domains and ranges can be inferred from $\mathcal{T}$. Given $\mathcal{T}$ is often fixed, so all the global and local domains and ranges can be computed offline. Given an entity e from an input question q, we add all the properties related (through global/local domains or range) to some types of e to the list P2, called the *implicit property list* (IPL).

To consider all the possibilities of relation expansion, we combine expansions of type 1 and type 2 above.

Example: Consider the question "How many shows does HBO have?". If we just use expansion 1, we will obtain the explicit property list of `dbr:HBO`. In this list, the `dbo:producer` ranks the highest. However, if we apply expansion 2 to this question, we do not only get the explicit property list of dbr:HBO, but also get the implicit property list of `dbr:HBO`. Because the `rdf:type` of `dbr:HBO` includes `dbo:Broadcaster`, and `dbo:Broadcaster` is a global range of `dbo:channel`.

It turns out that `dbo:channel` is the desired answer (and not `dbo:producer`) (Fig. 2).

Relation Candidate Ranking: Once we expand the explicit and implicit relations, we get all the possible relation candidates in the property list P. The next step for our framework is to select the best relations from these candidates which constitutes the final module of the EERL framework. In the EERL system, we reuse the approach of SIBKB to ranking candidates.

In the following, we will focus on strategies for re-ranking the candidates from the explicit property list EPL and the implicit property list IPL.

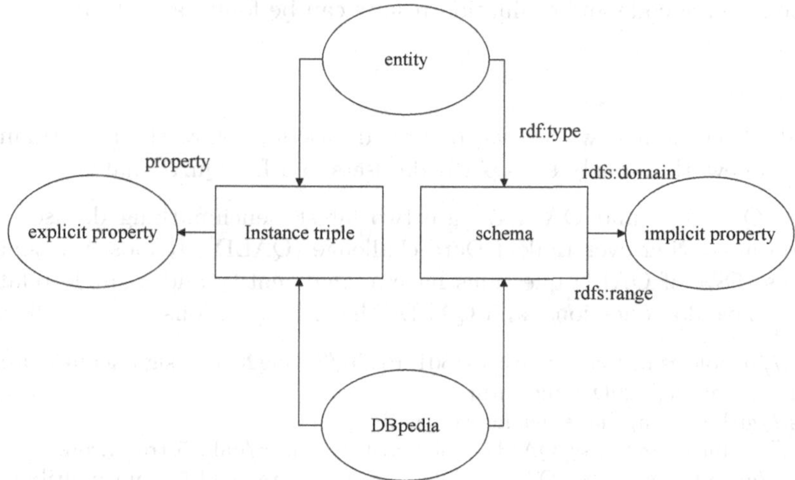

Fig. 2. The process of getting explicit property list and implicit property list

Existence Re-ranking and Extending: We perform re-ranking by extending the candidate list according to the existence of relations in the explicit property list EPL or the implicit property list IPL. From the candidate ranking step of SIBKB, we can get a K-V list. This list is ranked by the sum of similarity sum(Va). We use the principle that if relations k in relation list K matches property p in EPL or in IPL, then we will add a high weight value w1 into K-V list, which can be formalised as $R[k] = Va + w1$. If not, we will extend the K-V list by adding the property p to it with w1, which is $R[p] = w$.

LD Re-ranking: We leverage the levenshtein distance LD[6] for re-ranking and extending the candidate list. We calculate LD between extracted words from the lists EW and the words from the property candidate list PCL (both explicit property list EPL and implicit property list IPL). We restrict LD to a range (0, 1). Then we identify the p in EPL and IPL with the shortest levenshtein distance to the extracted relation word EW, and give a weight value w2 to p, which is $R(p) = Va + w2$. For the weight value w2, the higher the weight value w2 the smaller the Levenshtein distance LD. Please note, for w1, w2 and w3, we define it empirically, and then through the results of the evaluation to adjust them.

Synonym Re-ranking and Extending: If the length of the extracted words string len(ew) is 1, we'll get Synonyms set S(ew) of ew first, then calculate the distance between the property candidate list PCL and s(ew) in S(ew). Similar to LD re-ranking, we restrict the distance LD in a range (0,1), identity the property p with levenshtein distance, then add a weight value w3, for the whole process $w3 = K/ld$ which can be formalised as $ld = l - distance(s(ew), p)$. $R[p] = Va + w3$.

5 Experiments

In this section, we present the experimental results to validate our approach. The open source code and evaluation results can be found at Github.[7]

5.1 Datasets

For evaluation studies, we leveraged three datasets to show the performance of EERL framework, namely the QALD datasets and LC-QuAD dataset.

QALD: QALD-5[8] and QALD-7[9] are two latest benchmarking datasets from Question answering over Linked Data challenge (QALD). It mostly has simple questions (58% of QALD questions have a single entity and a single relation). QALD-5 have 350 questions, and QALD-7 has 215 questions.

[6] https://people.cs.pitt.edu/~kirk/cs1501/Pruhs/Spring2006/assignments/editdistance/Levenshtein\%20Distance.htm.

[7] https://github.com/zhangmeiontoweb/EERL.

[8] https://github.com/ag-sc/QALD/blob/master/5/data/qald-5_train.json.

[9] https://github.com/ag-sc/QALD/blob/master/7/data/qald-7-train-multilingual.json.

LC-QuAD: LC-QuAD[10] has 5000 questions for QA over DBpedia and 80 percent of its questions are complex i.e. questions with more than one entity and one relation. It is a manually fully-annotated, with all keywords classified as entity or predicate, and mapped to the URIs of DBpedia. Please note, there are three kinds of questions which are not considered for evaluation: (1) the questions that are not fit for our hypothesis, i.e. questions for which relations are not the property of given entities (2) for QALD dataset, we exclude questions that don't give the SPARQL (3) in LC-QuAD dataset, the given relations for the questions which are not correct for the current DBpedia version. As we use the latest DBpedia version to retrieve the relation candidates, such questions from LC-QuAD has been ignored.

Baseline Relation Linking Tools. Various relation linking approaches have been evaluated on these datasets. SIBKB [30], ReMatch [18], and EARL [3] have been evaluated over QALD-7 and QALD-5. We therefore compare our results for the same experiment settings. We then report our results for complete LC-QuAD dataset comparing it to the baselines.

Table 1. Performance of EERL framework compared to various relation linking tools

QA Component	Dataset	Precision	Recall	F-score
SIBKB	QALD-5	0.27	0.34	0.29
ReMatch	QALD-5	0.36	0.39	0.37
EARL	QALD-5	0.17	0.21	0.19
EERL	QALD-5	**0.43**	**0.49**	**0.45**
SIBKB	QALD-7	0.33	0.35	0.34
ReMatch	QALD-7	0.35	0.38	0.37
EARL	QALD-7	0.30	0.31	0.30
EERL	QALD-7	**0.42**	**0.46**	**0.43**
SIBKB	LC-QuAD	0.15	0.18	0.16
ReMatch	LC-QuAD	0.18	0.20	0.19
EARL	LC-QuAD	0.20	0.25	0.21
EERL	LC-QuAD	**0.53**	**0.58**	**0.55**

5.2 Experimental Settings

We executed our experiments on one virtual server, with eight cores and 32 GB RAM running on the Ubuntu 16.04.3 operating system. We have reused the open source implementation of the Frankenstein Resource Platform[11] [27] and integrated our EERL framework in it for executing the different experiments. As DBpedia IRIs of the entities are also our inputs besides the natural language question, we use gold annotated linked named entities as input.

[10] https://figshare.com/articles/Full_Annotated_LC_QuAD_dataset/5-782197.
[11] https://github.com/WDAqua/Frankenstein.

5.3 Result and Analysis

Metrics: The following evaluation metrics per relation linking approach have been used: *(i)* `Micro Precision (MP)`: For a given tool, the ratio of correct answers vs. total number of answers retrieved for a particular question. *(ii)* `Precision`: The average of the Micro Precision over all questions by a relation linking tool. *(iii)* `Micro Recall (MR)`: The number of correct answers retrieved by a component vs. gold standard answers for given question. *(iv)* `Recall (R)`: The average of Micro Recall over all questions for a given relation linking tool. *(v)* `Micro F-score (MF)`: Harmonic mean of MP and MR for each question. *(vi)* `F-score`: Harmonic mean of P and R for each component.

Evaluation: We evaluate our system with three metrics, they are Precision, Recall, F-score. Table 1 summarises the results of our framework compared to the baseline for the different datasets. Our framework significantly outperforms the baselines for relation linking for QALD-5 340 questions. We then extended our evaluation to QALD-7, where our framework EERL also achieves the highest performance in terms of Precision, Recall and F-score.

We then extended our performance evaluation to complex questions, and utilised the LC-QuAD dataset in two settings. In the first setting, we evaluated our performance for all the 5000 questions. We achieved significantly high Precision, Recall and F-score values for complex questions, as illustrated in Table 1. Singh et al. [31] have evaluated five relation linking approaches for 3253 questions of LC-QuAD including SIBKB, Rematch and other three tools which Frankenstein offers in its architecture. Table 1 also summarises our results compared to the best performing tool from [31], where we achieve a significant increase in performance with our EERL framework. Besides, Table 1 shows that the EERL system enhanced largely with our approach compare to all baselines across datasets.

Execution Time: Execution time is also an important KPI to evaluate our approach. Table 2 shows the execution time that each system uses for the QALD-7 and LC-QuAD datasets. The results show that our approach also significantly improves the run time. Please note, for runtime calculation, time needed for entity recognition has been cut and only the time taken by each tool to link the relation is reported in the Table 2.

Error Analysis: Even though we achieve a relative higher performance compared with state-of-the-art, we find room for improvement in our EERL framework. From the experimental results, we deduce that the errors are caused by two factors. The first factor is the effectiveness of our hypothesis. We assume that a relation in the query is the property of the entity while some of the questions' relations don't appear in the property list. And this is the main reason why our system doesn't perform better on the QALD-5 and QALD-7 datasets compared to its performance on LC-QuAD. The second reason for failure is the ranking method. We observe from the results that for many questions containing two relations, the performance of our ranking methods is limited.

Table 2. Run time (avgerage seconds/question)

System	QALD-7	LC-QuAD
SIBKB	1.1	2.2
ReMatch	110	130
EERL	**1.3**	**1.8**

6 Discussion

From Table 1, we can infer that the SIBKB, ReMatch, and EARL systems have very limited performance. Our EERL system not only outperforms these systems, it also does not show a sharp decline in performance on complex questions. In fact, for complex questions our approach performs better than on the simple questions of the QALD dataset. One primary reason for this behaviour is the presence of more context about the entities in the complex questions, because complex questions usually contain two entities. Our approach utilizes this context to correctly predict the DBpedia relation.

Furthermore our proposed EERL framework also can give its result within a reasonable time. Our results show that, by using the property candidate list as the relation candidates, (i) we can narrow the relation range and this will speed up the process of retrieving relation candidates; and (ii) this approach can be used as a ranking method to rank the relation candidates to prevent filtering the correct candidates. We believe that our approach can be reused in other relation linking systems, and it could easily be extended to other knowledge graphs. This is due to the fact that other knowledge graphs have similar structure as DBpedia and they use common knowledge source (i.e. Wikipedia). Hence, our approach should work equally well for the KGs having clear separation of A box and T-Box concepts. We agree, few knowledge graphs (such as Wikidata) do not have clear and correct definition of domain and ranges, neither a well defined Ontology. Our approach will find limitation in such scenario. For knowledge graphs with no 'TBoxes or very incomplete TBoxes, ontology learning of domains and ranges might help, but it has been out of scope for this paper.

However, to further improve the EERL framework, we plan to optimise our approach in three possible ways. Firstly, we analysed our results, and found that over half of the wrong results were due to the wrong extracted relation words. Relation extraction from free text has been a long standing field of natural language processing research. We plan to utilise some of its techniques to extract the correct natural language label for the relation. Secondly, the similarity algorithm is a method for calculating the similarity between possible candidates and the recognised relation words. We plan to utilise external knowledge sources such as Wordnet[12] to provide a list of synonyms for relation labels. Finally, existing datasets for question answering over DBpedia do not contain large number of questions. With the availability of larger datasets, we plan to employ machine learning techniques for proposing a ranking model for the candidate relations.

[12] https://wordnet.princeton.edu/.

7 Conclusions

In this paper, we have proposed a novel approach which can directly link the natural language relation of the question to its mention in the DBpedia. Unlike previous work in this domain, we utilize the contextual information provided by the entities in the question to find the relation in the knowledge graph. Our approach can choose the best property to match the entities by ranking the similarity between the entities' property list and extracted relation words from question. In our approach we jointly utilize the relation and property list to ensure the integrity of the question information. This has also impacted the performance, and we outperform the existing baseline approaches for relation linking. We hope, our work sets a foundation for the research community to exploit (approximate) ontology reasoning [13,15,21–23,33] in finding correct predicates for the questions and then applying machine learning approaches on top of it for better results. Our framework is reusable, and we have integrated it to Frankenstein framework for its reusability in creating collaborative question answering systems.

Acknowledgements. This work has been supported by the National Natural Science Foundation of China (61673304) and the Key Projects of National Social Science Foundation of China (11&ZD189).

References

1. Auer, S., Bizer, C., Kobilarov, G., Lehmann, J., Cyganiak, R., Ives, Z.: DBpedia: a nucleus for a web of open data. In: Aberer, K., et al. (eds.) ASWC/ISWC -2007. LNCS, vol. 4825, pp. 722–735. Springer, Heidelberg (2007). https://doi.org/10.1007/978-3-540-76298-0_52
2. Baader, F., Calvanese, D., McGuinness, D.L., Nardi, D., Patel-Schneider, P.F. (eds.): The Description Logic Handbook: Theory, Implementation, and Applications. Cambridge University Press, Cambridge (2003)
3. Banerjee, D., Dubey, M., Chaudhuri, D., Lehmann, J.: Joint entity and relation linking using EARL. In: ISWC (2018)
4. Bast, H., Haussmann, E.: More accurate question answering on freebase. In: Proceedings of the 24th ACM International on Conference on Information and Knowledge Management, CIKM 2015, pp. 1431–1440. ACM, New York (2015)
5. Bollacker, K.D., Cook, R.P., Tufts, P.: Freebase: a shared database of structured general human knowledge. In: AAAI (2007)
6. Bordes, A., Usunier, N., Chopra, S., Weston, J.: Large-Scale Simple Question Answering with Memory Networks. CoRR, abs/1506.02075 (2015)
7. Both, A., Diefenbach, D., Singh, K., Shekarpour, S., Cherix, D., Lange, C.: Qanary – a methodology for vocabulary-driven open question answering systems. In: Sack, H., Blomqvist, E., d'Aquin, M., Ghidini, C., Ponzetto, S.P., Lange, C. (eds.) ESWC 2016. LNCS, vol. 9678, pp. 625–641. Springer, Cham (2016). https://doi.org/10.1007/978-3-319-34129-3_38
8. Dai, Z., Li, L., Xu, W.: CFO: conditional focused neural question answering with large-scale knowledge bases. In: ACL (2016)

9. Fawei, B.J., Pan, J.Z., Kollingbaum, M.J., Wyner, A.Z.: A criminal law and procedure ontology for legal question answering. In: JIST (2018)
10. Ferragina, P., Scaiella, U.: TAGME: on-the-fly annotation of short text fragments (by Wikipedia entities). In: CIKM, pp. 1625–1628 (2010)
11. Gerber, D., Ngomo, A.-C.N.: Bootstrapping the linked data web. In: 1st Workshop on Web Scale Knowledge Extraction@ ISWC (2011)
12. Höffner, K., Walter, S., Marx, E., Usbeck, R., Lehmann, J., Ngomo, A.-C.N.: Survey on challenges of question answering in the semantic web. In: Semantic Web (2017)
13. Hogan, A., Pan, J.Z., Polleres, A., Decker, S.: SAOR: template rule optimisations for distributed reasoning over 1 billion linked data triples. In: Patel-Schneider, P.F., et al. (eds.) ISWC 2010. LNCS, vol. 6496, pp. 337–353. Springer, Heidelberg (2010). https://doi.org/10.1007/978-3-642-17746-0_22
14. Kim, J., Choi, G., Kim, J.-U., Kim, E.-K., Choi, K.-S.: The open framework for developing knowledge base and question answering system. In: COLING, pp. 161–165 (2016)
15. Lecue, F., Pan, J.Z.: Consistent knowledge discovery from evolving ontologies. In: Proceedings of 29th AAAI Conference on Artificial Intelligence (AAAI-2015) (2015)
16. Lukovnikov, D., Fischer, A., Lehmann, J., Auer, S.: Neural network-based question answering over knowledge graphs on word and character level. In: WebConf, pp. 1211–1220 (2017)
17. Mendes, P.N., Jakob, M., García-Silva, A., Bizer, C.: DBpedia spotlight: shedding light on the web of documents. In: I-SEMANTICS, pp. 1–8 (2011)
18. Mulang, I.O., Singh, K., Orlandi, F.: Matching natural language relations to knowledge graph properties for question answering. In: Semantics (2017)
19. Mulwad, V., Finin, T., Joshi, A.: Semantic message passing for generating linked data from tables. In: Alani, H., et al. (eds.) ISWC 2013. LNCS, vol. 8218, pp. 363–378. Springer, Heidelberg (2013). https://doi.org/10.1007/978-3-642-41335-3_23
20. Nakashole, N., Weikum, G., Suchanek, F.M.: PATTY: a taxonomy of relational patterns with semantic types. In: EMNLP-CoNLL (2012)
21. Pan, J.Z., Ren, Y., Zhao, Y.: Tractable approximate deduction for OWL. Artif. Intell. 95–155
22. Pan, J.Z., Thomas, E.: Approximating OWL-DL ontologies. In: The Proceedings of the 22nd National Conference on Artificial Intelligence (AAAI-2007), pp. 1434–1439 (2007)
23. Pan, J.Z., et al. (eds.): Reasoning Web: Logical Foundation of Knowledge Graph Construction and Querying Answering. Springer, Heidelberg (2017). https://doi.org/10.1007/978-3-319-49493-7
24. Pan, J.Z., Vetere, G., Gomez-Perez, J.M., Wu, H. (eds.): Exploiting Linked Data and Knowledge Graphs for Large Organisations. Springer, Heidelberg (2016). https://doi.org/10.1007/978-3-319-45654-6
25. Pennington, J., Socher, R., Manning, C.: Glove: global vectors for word representation. In: Proceedings of the 2014 Conference on Empirical Methods in Natural Language Processing (EMNLP), pp. 1532–1543 (2014)
26. Singh, K.: Towards dynamic composition of question answering pipelines. Ph.D. thesis, University of Bonn, Germany (2019)

27. Singh, K., Both, A., Sethupat, A., Shekarpour, S.: Frankenstein: a platform enabling reuse of question answering components. In: Gangemi, A., et al. (eds.) ESWC 2018. LNCS, vol. 10843, pp. 624–638. Springer, Cham (2018). https://doi.org/10.1007/978-3-319-93417-4_40
28. Singh, K., Lytra, I., Radhakrishna, A.S., Shekarpour, S., Vidal, M.-E., Lehmann, J.: No one is perfect: analysing the performance of question answering components over the DBpedia knowledge graph. CoRR, abs/1809.10044 (2018)
29. Singh, K., et al.: QAESTRO – semantic-based composition of question answering pipelines. In: Benslimane, D., Damiani, E., Grosky, W.I., Hameurlain, A., Sheth, A., Wagner, R.R. (eds.) DEXA 2017. LNCS, vol. 10438, pp. 19–34. Springer, Cham (2017). https://doi.org/10.1007/978-3-319-64468-4_2
30. Singh, K., et al.: Capturing knowledge in semantically-typed relational patterns to enhance relation linking. In: K-CAP, pp. 31:1–31:8 (2017)
31. Singh, K., et al.: Why reinvent the wheel: let's build question answering systems together. In: WebConf, pp. 1247–1256 (2018)
32. Suchanek, F.M., Kasneci, G., Weikum, G.: Yago: a core of semantic knowledge. In: WWW, pp. 697–706 (2007)
33. Thomas, E., Pan, J.Z., Ren, Y.: TrOWL: tractable OWL 2 reasoning infrastructure. In: Aroyo, L., et al. (eds.) The Semantic Web: Research and Applications, ESWC 2010. Lecture Notes in Computer Science, vol. 6089, pp. 431–435. Springer, Berlin (2010). https://doi.org/10.1007/978-3-642-13489-0_38
34. Trivedi, P., Maheshwari, G., Dubey, M., Lehmann, J.: LC-QuAD: a corpus for complex question answering over knowledge graphs. In: d'Amato, C., et al. (eds.) ISWC 2017. LNCS, vol. 10588, pp. 210–218. Springer, Cham (2017). https://doi.org/10.1007/978-3-319-68204-4_22
35. Unger, C., Bühmann, L., Lehmann, J., Ngomo, A.-C.N., Gerber, D., Cimiano, P.: Template-based question answering over RDF data. In: WebConf, pp. 639–648. ACM (2012)
36. Usbeck, R., et al.: AGDISTIS - graph-based disambiguation of named entities using linked data. In: Mika, P., et al. (eds.) ISWC 2014. LNCS, vol. 8796, pp. 457–471. Springer, Cham (2014). https://doi.org/10.1007/978-3-319-11964-9_29
37. Vrandecic, D., Krötzsch, M.: Wikidata: a free collaborative knowledge base. Commun. ACM **57**(10), 78–85 (2014)

SHACL Constraints with Inference Rules

Paolo Pareti[1(✉)], George Konstantinidis[1], Timothy J. Norman[1], and Murat Şensoy[2]

[1] University of Southampton, Southampton, UK
pp1v17@soton.ac.uk
[2] Özyeğin University, Istanbul, Turkey

Abstract. The Shapes Constraint Language (SHACL) has been recently introduced as a W3C recommendation to define constraints that can be validated against RDF graphs. Interactions of SHACL with other Semantic Web technologies, such as ontologies or reasoners, is a matter of ongoing research. In this paper we study the interaction of a subset of SHACL with inference rules expressed in datalog. On the one hand, SHACL constraints can be used to define a "schema" for graph datasets. On the other hand, inference rules can lead to the discovery of new facts that do not match the original schema. Given a set of SHACL constraints and a set of datalog rules, we present a method to detect which constraints could be violated by the application of the inference rules on some graph instance of the schema, and update the original schema, i.e, the set of SHACL constraints, in order to capture the new facts that can be inferred. We provide theoretical and experimental results of the various components of our approach.

1 Introduction

Information about the type of data contained in a dataset is a critical piece of information both to understand data, and to interface with databases. While the relational model explicitly defines a schema, graph data representations are inherently schemaless, in the sense that any RDF triple could, in principle, be stored in any RDF triplestore. The Shapes Constraint Language (SHACL) [10], is a W3C recommendation recently introduced to define properties of RDF datasets. SHACL allows the definition of constraints that can be validated against RDF graphs. Such constraints can be seen as the schema of the graphs that do not violate them. Schemas are not static objects, and they can evolve over time to reflect changes in the datasets they model. One important source of change in graph datasets comes from the application of inference rules. Inference rules can be used to reason about ontological properties, such as class membership. They can also be used for non-ontological types of inference, such as aggregating sensor data to detect important facts such as the presence of a fire, or the temperature of a room. This paper focuses on datalog rules [6] without negation (the exact subset of datalog that we consider is defined in Sect. 2).

The application of inference rules might generate new facts, not captured by the original schema definition. Given a set of SHACL constraints and a set of

C. Ghidini et al. (Eds.): ISWC 2019, LNCS 11778, pp. 539–557, 2019.
https://doi.org/10.1007/978-3-030-30793-6_31

inference rules, we would like to determine whether a graph, initially valid with respect to the SHACL constraints, remains valid after computing its closure with the inference rules. If constraint violations can occur, a domain expert could decide whether to remove the inference rules that cause these violations, or to update the violated SHACL constraints. Updating the violated constraints to account for the new facts that can be produced via inference effectively creates a new schema.

This research is motivated by use cases in the area of Occupational Health and Safety (OHS), and in particular in the mining sector. In these areas, schemas are used to model and understand the underlying data sources, and to ensure interoperability between different applications. Inference rules, usually developed separately, are used to aggregate raw sensor data into more useful abstractions and encode OHS policies (e.g. to detect unsafe working environments). At the moment, domain experts are needed to define such rules. However this process is slow, expensive and error prone. Our research aims to better inform experts about the effects of applying certain rules (which could affect the schema, and thus interoperability) and automatically detect conflicts between rules and schemas. For example, as schemas frequently change (e.g. sensors malfunction, or new ones are deployed), it is essential to automatically detect schema changes that render important rules (and policies) no longer applicable, on unforeseen datasets.

In this paper we present an approach that models *triplestore schemas* as triplets of sets: a set of triple patterns that can be appropriately instantiated by RDF triples, a set of positions in those triples that cannot be instantiated by literal values (e.g. object positions in triples), and a set of existential validity rules (such as tuple-generating dependencies [8]) which must hold on the instatiated triples in order for our graph to be valid. Our triplestore schema captures a fragment of SHACL, but abstracts away from its particular syntax and can be used as a logical tool to model properties of RDF graphs in general. However, it is not meant to provide a complete formal semantic representation of the core SHACL components, such as the one presented in [7].

Furthermore, we investigate how our triplestore schemas interact with inference rules and evolve into new schemas, that we call *schema consequences*; these are schemas that model all possible RDF graphs extended with the inferred facts. Given an input schema S, we want to reason about the applicability of inference rules on all potential instances of S, and compute the schema consequence. This problem proves challenging even without taking existential validity rules into account in our schemas; i.e., for what we call our *simple* schema consequence. To reason with inference rules in this version of the problem we have to make use of the notion of a "canonical" instance of S, representative of all other instances. For this, we first explore such an instance known as the *critical instance* and investigated in relational databases [13]; running the inference rules on this graph enables us to produce our schema consequence. However, the critical instance is inefficient, as it has a very large size, and so we turn our attention to finding a much smaller representative instance, that we call the *sandbox* graph. We then present a novel query rewriting algorithm that can compute the simple schema consequence on the sandbox graph, much more efficiently than in the critical instance case.

Building on top of our simple schema consequence we use a novel combination of techniques, variations of datalog rewriting [1] and the Chase algorithm [4], to produce our *existential-preserving* schema consequence, a triplestore schema the identifies and removes from its description the existential validity rules that could potentially be violated on some instance produced by the inference rules. We provide both theoretical and experimental evaluations of our approach.

2 Background

We consider triplestores containing a single RDF *graph.* Such a graph is a set of *triples* $\mathbb{U} \times \mathbb{U} \times (\mathbb{U} \cup \mathbb{L})$ where $\mathbb{U}$ is the set of all IRIs and $\mathbb{L}$ the set of all literals. Although we do not explicitly discuss blank nodes, it should be noted that, for the purpose of this paper, when they occur in a graph they can be treated exactly as IRIs. We use the term *constants* to refer to both literals and IRIs. A *graph pattern* is a set of *triple patterns* defined in: $(\mathbb{U} \cup \mathbb{V}) \times (\mathbb{U} \cup \mathbb{V}) \times (\mathbb{U} \cup \mathbb{L} \cup \mathbb{V})$, where $\mathbb{V}$ the set of all variables. Given a pattern P, $vars(P)$ and $const(P)$ are the sets of variables and constants in the elements of P, respectively. We represent IRIs as namespace-prefixed strings of characters, where a namespace prefix is a sequence of zero or more characters followed by a colon e.g. `:a`; literals as strings of characters enclosed in double-quotes, e.g. `"1"`; and variables as strings of characters prefixed by a question-mark, e.g. `?v`. The first, second and third elements of a triple t are called, respectively, *subject*, *predicate* and *object*, and are denoted by $t[x]$, $x \in \tau$ with $\tau = \{1, 2, 3\}$ throughout the paper.

A *variable substitution* is a partial function $\mathbb{V} \nrightarrow \mathbb{V} \cup \mathbb{U} \cup \mathbb{L}$. A *mapping* is a variable substitution defined as $\mathbb{V} \nrightarrow \mathbb{U} \cup \mathbb{L}$. Given a mapping m, if $m(?v) = n$, then we say m contains *binding* $?v \rightarrow n$. The domain of a mapping m is the set of variables $dom(m)$. Given a triple or a graph pattern p and a variable substitution m we abuse notation and denote by $m(p)$ the pattern generated by substituting every occurrence of a variable $?v$ in p with $m(?v)$ if $?v \in dom(m)$ (otherwise $?v$ remains unchanged in $m(p)$). A *grounding* is a mapping that transforms a graph pattern into a graph.

Given a graph pattern P and a graph I, we denote the SPARQL evaluation of P over I as the set of mappings $[\![P]\!]_I$, as defined in [14]. A graph pattern *matches* a graph if its evaluation on the graph returns a non-empty set of mappings. We consider inference rules $A \rightarrow C$, where A and C are graph patterns, and can be expressed as SPARQL `construct` queries. Note that essentially both A and C in an inference rule are conjunctive queries [1]. The *consequent* C of the rule is represented in the `construct` clause of the query, which is instantiated using the bindings obtained by evaluating the *antecedent* A, expressed in the `where` clause. For technical reasons, we restrict the subset of datalog that we consider with the requirement that each triple pattern in the consequent C of a rule: (1) has a constant in the predicate position; and (2) does not have the same variable in the subject and object position. A single application of an inference rule $r : A \rightarrow C$ to a dataset I, denoted by $r(I)$, is $I \cup \bigcup_{m \in [\![A]\!]_I} \{m(C), \text{ if } m(C) \text{ is a valid RDF a graph}\}$. These rules capture datalog [1] and subsets of rule notations such as SPIN and SWRL can be represented in this format [3]. The closure of a dataset I under a set of inference rules R, denoted by $clos(I, R)$, is the unique dataset obtained by repeatedly applying all the rules in R until no new statement is inferred, that is, $clos(I, R) = \bigcup_{i=0}^{i=\infty} I_i$, with $I_0 = I$, and $I_{i+1} = \bigcup_{r \in R}\{r(I_i)\}$.

The Shapes Constraint Language (SHACL) defines constraints that can be validated against RDF graphs. An example of a constraint is the requirement for an RDF term to be an IRI. The nodes of an RDF graph against which such constraints are validated are called *focus nodes*. At the core of the SHACL language is the concept of *shapes*. A shape groups together a set of constraints, and defines which focus nodes it should apply to. A shape could either directly target specific nodes, such as all the elements of a class, or it could be referenced by other shapes. For example, it is possible to define the shape of a "well-formed email address", and then specify that every entity of type "person" must have at least one email address that satisfies this shape. In this paper we prefix SHACL terms with the namespace sh:.

Given a schema S, we denote with $\mathbb{I}(S)$ the set of instances of S, which are the graphs that S models. We say that two schemas S and S' are semantically equivalent if they model the same set of instances; i.e. if $\mathbb{I}(S) = \mathbb{I}(S')$. Naturally, the interpretation of SHACL constraints as a schema is based on SHACL validation. We say that a graph is an instance of a SHACL schema, defined by its set of constraints, if the graph does not violate the SHACL constraints.

3 Problem Definition

In this section we are going to present our definition of a *triplestore schema*, a simple representation that captures a powerful fragment of SHACL. A set of SHACL shapes S belongs to this fragment if and only if there exists a triplestore schema S' such that $\mathbb{I}(S) = \mathbb{I}(S')$ (the set of instances of a triplestore schema will be defined later in this section). An important characteristic of this fragment (discussed later) is that its existential validity rules must have atomic antecedents and consequents. This is sufficient to model common constraints for RDF validation, such as the Data Quality Test Patterns TYPEDEP, TYPRODEP, PVT, RDFS-DOMAIN and RDFS-RANGE in the categorisation by Kontokostas et al. [11].

The two main components of triplestore schemas are: (1) a set of abstract triple patterns, that intend to model all different triples/instantiations of those patterns; and (2) a set of existential validity constraints that represent "if-then" statements of SHACL shapes. Abstracting away from the particulars of the SHACL syntax, on one hand, simplifies our approach and, on the other hand, makes it applicable to the fragments of other languages (e.g. ShEx [15]) which can be converted into our triplestore schema. Once we have a triplestore schema in place, we define our problem of how do instances of such a schema interact with a set of datalog inference rules. In particular, we would like to reason at the schema level and decide if there is a potential instance graph of our schema on which our datalog rules would infer facts that violate the validity constraints.

3.1 From SHACL to Triplestore Schemas

Our work is inspired by Internet of Things (IoT) settings and as our running example we consider a dataset of a mining company. The SHACL schema, S_1, for this mine dataset is presented in Fig. 1. This repository collects data from sensors carried by workers and deployed in the mine. Data is modelled according to the Semantic Sensor Network Ontology (SSN) [12], with namespace prefix s:. In SSN, sensor measurements are called *observations*. The *result* of an observation (e.g. "20") relates to a particular *observed property* (e.g. temperature) of a particular *feature of interest* (e.g. a room). In our example the mine contains two types of sensors. The first is a carbon monoxide (CO) detector, which records value "0" if the CO concentration is within the allowed limits, and "1" otherwise. The second is an RFID reader used to locate personnel in the mine by sensing the nearby RFID tags carried by the mine workers. SHACL shape :s0 specifies that the collected sensor data will only refer to those two sensor types. The dataset of the mine is expected to contain a list of known personnel RFID tags, and information on who is currently carrying them. Shape :s1 specifies that for every personnel tag, we know who it is carried by. Shapes :s2 and :s3 restrict features of interest to being IRIs and measurement results to be IRIs or literals. Shape :s4 declares that the sensor data contains instances of only two classes, namely sensor observations, and personnel tags.

```
:s0   a                      sh:NodeShape ;
      sh:targetObjectsOf     sn:observedProperty ;
      sh:in                  ( :COLevel :TagID ) .
:s1   a                      sh:NodeShape ;
      sh:targetClass         :PersonnelTag ;
      sh:property            [ sh:minCount  1 ;
                               sh:path       :carriedBy ] .
:s2   a                      sh:NodeShape ;
      sh:targetObjectsOf     sn:hasFeatureOfInterest ;
      sh:nodeKind            sh:IRI .
:s3   a                      sh:NodeShape ;
      sh:targetObjectsOf     sn:hasResult ;
      sh:nodeKind            sh:IRIOrLiteral .
:s4   a                      sh:NodeShape ;
      sh:targetObjectsOf     rdf:type ;
      sh:in                  ( sn:Observation :PersonnelTag ) .
```

Fig. 1. Schema S_1.

```
?v1 sn:observedProperty :COLevel .   ?v5 :carriedBy ?v6 .
?v2 sn:observedProperty :TagID .     ?v7 sn:hasFeatureOfInterest ?v8 .
?v3 rdf:type sn:Observation .        ?v9 sn:hasResult ?v10 .
?v4 rdf:type :PersonnelTag .
```

Fig. 2. Graph pattern S_1^G.

When using SHACL as a schema language, we would like the constraints to describe the type of data contained in a dataset as accurately as possible. SHACL constraints usually target only a limited number of predicates in an RDF graph, and triples with predicates other than the targeted ones could be present in the graph without causing violations. However, for our purposes we adopt a closed-world view of the available vocabulary of predicates, and we would like to restrict valid graphs to only contain a fixed set of predicates. This vocabulary restriction can be specified by an appropriate SHACL constraint that uses the `sh:closed` component. We assume, therefore, that all SHACL schemas that we work with contain a component that specifies that valid instances of this schema do not contain predicates other than the ones that appear in the SHACL shapes. This is inline with relational databases where the discovery of completely new types of facts (i.e. triples with unforseen predicates) would be reflected by a corresponding change in the original schema.

In our running example, instances of schema S_1 would contain triples matching the triples patterns of graph pattern S_1^G displayed in Fig. 2, where each variable can be appropriately instantiated by an IRI or a literal. In fact, exactly such a set of triple patterns will be the first element of our representation of triple-store schemas, called a *schema graph*, defined below. Note that valid instances of our schema might contain multiple instantiations of some, but not necessarily all of the predicates defined in the schema graph, and they cannot contain other kinds of triples (e.g. undefined predicates). We use different variables in S_1^G to denote the fact that variables in a schema graph act as wildcards, and are not meant to join triple patterns together.

In addition to the schema graph, a second part of our schema representation will be the subset of variables from the schema graph, called the *no-literal set*, where literals can not occur in valid instances. For example, we cannot instantiate variables `?v7` and `?v8` of triple pattern [`?v7`, `sn:hasFeatureOfInterest`, `?v8`] from Fig. 2 with a literal; in the case of `?v7`, because we would not generate a valid `RDF` triple, and in the case of `?v8`, because it would violate shape `:s2`.

The last part of our schema representation will translate SHACL constraints to "if-then" statements like the following, which corresponds to shape `:s1` of schema S_1:

e_1 = [`?v1`, `rdf:type`, `:PersonnelTag`] $\rightarrow^{\exists}$ [`?v1`, `:carriedBy`, `?v2`]

These constraints are essentially *existential rules* [2], also expressible as tuple-generating dependencies (TGDs) [8]. For all practical purposes, the part of SHACL that we consider, when translatable to existential rules, falls into a language known as linear weakly-acyclic TGDs [8] with a single atom in the consequent. Linear means that these rules have only one atom (one triple pattern) in the antecedent, and *weakly-acyclic* is a property that guarantees that forward-chaining algorithms, such as the Chase [4], terminate. Formally, we define an existential rule as a formula of the form: $a \rightarrow^{\exists} c$, where a and c, respectively the antecedent and the consequent of the rule, are triple patterns. The consequent specifies which triples must exist in a graph whenever the antecedent holds in that graph. We say that an existential rule $a \rightarrow^{\exists} c$ is *violated* on a graph I if there exists a mapping $m \in [\![\{a\}]\!]_I$ such that $[\![m(c)]\!]_I = \varnothing$ (i.e. $m(c)$ is not in I), and *satisfied* otherwise. Note that if $m(c)$ is a ground triple, and $m(c) \in I$, then $[\![m(c)]\!]_I$ is not empty, as it contains the empty mapping [14]. Given a set of existential rules E, we use $violations(E, I)$ to refer to the set of pairs $\langle m, e\rangle$, where $e \in E$ and mapping m causes e to be violated on instance I.

We are now ready to define our triplestore schemas. A triplestore schema (or from now on, just *schema*) S, is a tuple $\langle S^G, S^{\Delta}, S^{\exists}\rangle$, where S^G, called a *schema graph*, is a set of triple patterns where every variable occurs at most once, S^{Δ} is a subset of the variables in S^G which we call the *no-literal* set, and $S^{\exists}$ is a set of existential rules. Intuitively, S^G defines the type of triples that can appear in a graph, where variables act as wildcards, which can be instantiated with any constant element. To account for the restrictions imposed by the RDF data model, the no-literal set S^{Δ} defines which variables cannot be instantiated with literals, thus S^{Δ} must at least include all variables that occur in the subject or predicate position in S^G. For example, if $\langle$`?v1`, `sn:hasResult`, `?v2`$\rangle \in S'^G$ and `?v2` $\notin S'^{\Delta}$, then the instances of schema S' can contain any triple that has `sn:hasResult` as a predicate. If $\langle$`?v3`, `rdf:type`, `:Observation`$\rangle \in S'^G$ and `?v3` $\in S'^{\Delta}$, the instances of S' can contain any entity of type `:Observation`. While S^G and S^{Δ} together define the set of all the possible triples that can be found in a graph, not all combinations of such triples are valid instances of the schema. The set of existential rules $S^{\exists}$ defines further requirements that instances of the schema must satisfy. Formally, a graph I is an *instance* of a triplestore schema $\langle S^G, S^{\Delta}, S^{\exists}\rangle$ if and only if $violations(S^{\exists}, I) = \varnothing$ and for every triple t^I in I there exists a triple pattern t^S in S^G, such that t^I is an *instantiation* of t^S w.r.t S^{Δ}; that is, there exists a mapping m such that (1) $m(t^S) = t^I$ and (2) m does not bind any variable in S^{Δ} to a literal.

For our SHACL to triplestore schema translation we direct the reader to our external appendix[1] and our implementation in our code repository.[2]

3.2 Inference Rules and Schema Consequences

We are interested in the effect that inference rules (not to be confused with existential rules) have on RDF graphs, and their interaction with existential rules. Inference rules are used to compute the *closure* of instances of our original schema as defined in Sect. 2. As an example consider the of inference rules

[1] https://github.com/paolo7/ISWC2019-appendix/raw/master/Appendix.pdf.
[2] https://github.com/paolo7/ISWC2019-code.

```
:o1 sn:observedProperty :TagID ;
  sn:hasFeatureOfInterest :room1 ;
  sn:hasResult :WID1 .
:o2 sn:observedProperty:TagID ;
  sn:hasFeatureOfInterest:room2 ;
  sn:hasResult :WID2 .
:o3 sn:observedProperty :COLevel ;
  sn:hasFeatureOfInterest :room2 ;
  sn:hasResult "1" .
:WID1 a :PersonnelTag ;
  :carriedBy :Alex .
```

Fig. 3. Instance I_1.

$R_1 = \{r_1, r_2, r_3\}$ below. Rule r_1 states that the RFIDs recorded by the sensors should be interpreted as personnel tags, and it records the location of where they are detected. Rule r_2 states that locations with a high carbon monoxide (CO) concentration should be off-limits. Rule r_3 states that if someone is located in an off-limits area, then they are trespassing in that area.

r_1 = { [?v1, sn:observedProperty, :TagID],
[?v1, sn:hasResult, ?v2],
[?v1, sn:hasFeatureOfInterest, ?v3] }
→ { [?v2, rdf:type, :PersonnelTag], [?v2, :isLocatedIn, ?v3] }
r_2 = { [?v1, sn:observedProperty, :COLevel],
[?v1, sn:hasResult, "1"],
[?v1, sn:hasFeatureOfInterest, ?v2] }
→ { [?v2, rdf:type, :OffLimitArea] }
r_3 = { [?v1, :isLocatedIn, ?v2],
[?v2, rdf:type, :OffLimitArea] }
→ { [?v1, :isTrespassingIn, ?v2] }

In our example, an emergency response application might need to know who is carrying each personnel RFID tag, in order to compute an emergency response plan. In this case, it is important to know which existential rules the application of a set of inference rules can violate. Once potential violations are detected, a domain expert could, for example, decide whether to relax (i.e. remove) the violated existential rules, or to remove the inference rules that cause the violations.

Thus, an example of the central question we address in this paper is: is e_1 guaranteed to remain valid in instances of schema S_1 under closure with inference rules R_1? The answer to this question is *no*, as demonstrated by graph I_1, which is a valid instance of S_1. This instance contains two records of miner tags being detected, namely :WID1 and :WID2. While we know that :WID1 is being carried by worker :Alex, we do not have any such information about tag :WID2.

Rule r_1 will deduce that :WID2 is a personnel tag, by inferring triples [:WID2, rdf:type, :PersonnelTag] and [:WID2, :isLocatedIn, :room2] from instance I_1. However, since there is no information on who is carrying tag :WID2, existential rule e_1 is violated. A domain expert analysing this conflict can then decide to either relax e_1, to state that there is not always information on who is carrying a personnel tag, or to remove rule r_1, to state that not all RFIDs recorded by the sensors are personnel tags. Rule r_2 is triggered by observation :o3, inferring triple [:room2, rdf:type, :OffLimitArea]. The IRI :OffLimitArea is not one of the types allowed in the original schema. Therefore, we might want to either revise rule r_2, or extend schema S_1 to allow for instances of this type. Facts inferred by rules r_1 and r_2 together trigger rule r_3, which will infer [`:WID2`, `:isTrespassingIn`, `:room2`]; i.e., that the person carrying the RFID tag `:WID2` is trespassing in dangerous area `:room2`. These new facts contain the new predicate `:isTrespassingIn`, and thus violate our closed-world interpretation of schema S_1 (as captured by our schema graph patterns). Hence, if one wants to retain all inference rules R_1 in our mine repository, an alteration of the original schema (and its schema graph) is required.

In this paper we deal with predicting these kinds of constraint violation, and computing an updated schema that accounts for them, without looking at specific instances such as I_1. Given a schema $S : <S^G, S^{\Delta}, S^{\exists}>$ and a set of inference rules R, we want to compute a new schema, called *schema consequence*, which captures all the inferences of the set of rules R on any potential instance of S. By computing an updated triplestore schema, once a violation is detected, our approach gives preference to maintaining inference rules over maintaining the original schema, essentially choosing to alter the schema graph and/or the existential rules. This is not an inherent limitation of our approach, which could be easily transformed to a method that maintains the original schema and chooses to reject conflicting inference rules.

To present our problem incrementally, we first compute a *simple* schema consequence which does not take existential rules into account (i.e. it only deals with S^G and S^{Δ} of our triplestore schema) and then we extend our solution to take $S^{\exists}$ into account in our *existentially-preserving* schema consequence.

The simple interpretation of a schema consequence captures the type of triples that the closure of an instance of the schema could potentially contain. Given a schema S and a set of inference rules R, a schema S' is a *simple schema consequence* of S with respect to R, denoted $con(S, R)$, if $\mathbb{I}(S') = \bigcup_{I \in \mathbb{I}(S)} \{I' | I' \subseteq clos(I, R)\}$. It is important to note that every subset of an instance's closure is still an instance of the simple schema consequence. Thus a simple schema consequence can contain the consequence of an inference rule application without containing a set of triples matching the antecedent, or vice versa. This situation is commonly encountered when some triples are deleted after an inference is made. Effectively, this definition does not assume that all the triples in an instance's closure are retained. One use of this schema consequence is to discover whether certain important facts (e.g. personnel trespassing in a dangerous area) can be inferred from the given schema (e.g. available sensor data streams) and set of inference rules (e.g. sensor data aggregation rules). Another use is to compute which inference rules are *applicable* on a schema, which means that they will be triggered on at least one instance of that schema.

Given a schema S and a set of inference rules R, a schema S' is an existential-preserving schema consequence of S with respect to R, denoted $con^{ex}(S, R)$, if and only if $\mathbb{I}(S') = \bigcup_{I \in \mathbb{I}(S)} \{I' | I' \subseteq clos(I, R) \wedge violations(S^{\exists}, I') = violations(S^{\exists}, clos(I, R))\}$. In other words, instances of an existential-preserving schema consequence are generated by computing the closure of an instance of the original schema under the inference rules, and then discarding a set of triples as long as doing so does not generate new violations of existential rules $S^{\exists}$. This allows us to detect which existential rules can be violated by the application of inference rules (and not just by arbitrary triple deletions). Our approaches to compute simple and existential-preserving schema consequences are presented, respectively, in Sects. 4 and 5.

4 Computing the Simple Schema Consequence

We compute $con(S, R)$ iteratively, on a rule-by-rule basis. In correspondence to a single application $r(I)$, of an inference rule r on an instance I, we define a *basic consequence* of a schema S by an inference rule r, denoted by $r(S)$, as a finite schema S' for which $\mathbb{I}(S') = \bigcup_{I \in \mathbb{I}(S)} \{I' | I' \subseteq r(I)\}$. It is now easy to see that the consequence schema for a set of inference rules $con(S, R)$ is obtained by repeatedly executing $r(S)$ for all $r \in R$ until no new pattern is inferred. Formally, $con(S, R) = \bigcup_{i=0}^{i=n} S_i$, with $S_0 = S$, and $S_{i+1} = \bigcup_{r \in R} \{r(S_i)\}$, and $S_n = S_{n-1}$ (modulo variable names). In this section we focus on computing a single basic schema consequence $r(S)$, and describe two approaches for this, namely Schema Consequence by Critical Instance (`critical`(S, r)), and Schema Consequence by Query Rewriting (`score`(S, r)).

Given a schema S and an inference rule $r : A \rightarrow C$, our approach to compute the basic schema consequence for r on S is based on evaluating A, or an appropriate rewriting thereof, on a "canonical" instance of S, representative of all instances modelled by the schema. The mappings generated by this evaluation are then (1) filtered (in order to respect certain literal restrictions in RDF) and (2) applied appropriately to the consequent C to compute the basic schema consequence.

We present two approaches, that use two different canonical instances. The first instance is based on the concept of a *critical instance*, which has been investigated in the area of relational databases before [13] (and similar notions in the area of Description Logics [9]). Adapted to our RDF setting, the critical instance would be created by substituting the variables in our schema, in all possible ways, with constants chosen from the constants in S^G and A as well as a new constant not in S^G or A. In [13] this instance is used in order to decide Chase termination; Chase is referred to rule inference with *existential* variables, more expressive than the ones considered here and for which the inference might be infinite (see [4] for an overview of the Chase algorithm). Although deciding termination of rule inference is slightly different to computing the schema consequence, we show how we can take advantage of the critical instance in order to solve our problem. Nevertheless, this approach, that we call `critical`, creates prohibitively large instances when compared to the input schema. Thus, later on in this section we present a rewriting-based approach, called `score`, that runs a rewriting of the inference rule on a much smaller canonical instance of the same size as S^G.

The Critical Approach. For both versions of our algorithms we will use a new IRI $:\lambda$ such that $:\lambda \notin const(S^G) \cup const(A)$. Formally, the critical instance $\mathbb{C}(S, A \rightarrow C)$ is the set of triples:

$$\{t|\text{ triple } t \text{ with } t[i] = \left\{ \begin{array}{ll} c & \text{if } t^S[i] \text{ is a variable and:} \\ & \text{(1) } c \text{ is a IRI or} \\ & \text{(2) } i = 3 \text{ and } t^S[i] \notin S^{\Delta} \\ t^S[i] & \text{if } t^S[i] \text{ is not a variable} \end{array} \right\},$$
$$t^S \in S^G, i \in \tau, c \in const(S^G) \cup const(A) \cup \{:\lambda\}\}$$

The critical instance replaces variables with IRIs and literals from the set $const(S^G) \cup const(A) \cup \{:\lambda\}$, while making sure that the result is a valid RDF graph (i.e. literals appear only in the object position) and that it is an instance of the original schema (i.e. not substituting a variable in S^{Δ} with a literal). In order to compute the triples of our basic schema consequence for inference rule r we evaluate A on the critical instance, and post-process the mappings $[\![A]\!]_{\mathbb{C}(S,r)}$ as we will explain later. Before presenting this post-processing of the mappings we stress the fact that this approach is inefficient and as our experiments show, non scalable. For each triple t in the input schema S, up to $|const(S^G) \cup const(A) \cup \{:\lambda\}|^{vars(t)}$ new triples might be added to the critical instance.

The Score Approach. To tackle the problem of efficiency we present an alternative solution based on query rewriting, called `score`. This solution uses a small instance called the *sandbox* instance which is obtained by taking all triple patterns of our schema graph S^G and substituting all variables with the same new IRI $:\lambda$. This results in an instance with the same number of triples as S^G. The main property that allows us to perform this simplification is the fact that variables in S^G are effectively independent from each other. Formally, a sandbox graph $\mathbb{S}(S)$ is the set of triples:

$$\{t|\text{ triple } t \text{ with } t[i] = \left\{ \begin{array}{ll} :\lambda & \text{if } t^S[i] \text{ is a variable,} \\ t^S[i] & \text{else} \end{array} \right\}, t^S \in S^G, i \in \tau\}$$

Contrary to the construction of the critical instance, in our sandbox graph, variables are never substituted with literals (we will deal with RDF literal peculiarities in a post-processing step). Also notice that $\mathbb{S}(S) \in \mathbb{I}(S)$ and $\mathbb{S}(S) \subseteq \mathbb{C}(S, r)$. As an example, consider the sandbox graph $\mathbb{S}(S_1)$ of schema S_1 from Sect. 3.1:

```
:λ sn:observedProperty :COLevel .  :λ :carriedBy :λ .
:λ sn:observedProperty :TagID .    :λ sn:hasFeatureOfInterest :λ .
:λ rdf:type sn:Observation .       :λ sn:hasResult :λ .
:λ rdf:type :PersonnelTag .
```

The critical instances $\mathbb{C}(S_1, r_1)$, $\mathbb{C}(S_1, r_2)$ and $\mathbb{C}(S_1, r_3)$ from our example would contain all the triples in $\mathbb{S}(S_1)$, plus any other triple obtained by substituting some variables with constants other than $:\lambda$. For example, $\mathbb{C}(S_1, r_2)$ would contain the triple [$:\lambda$, `sn:hasResult`, `:OffLimitArea`]}.

In order to account for all mappings produced when evaluating A on $\mathbb{C}(S, r)$ we will need to evaluate a different query on our sandbox instance, essentially by appropriately rewriting A into a new query. To compute mappings, we consider a rewriting $\mathbb{Q}(A)$ of A, which expands each triple pattern t_A in A into the union of the 8 triple patterns that can be generated by substituting any number of elements in t_A with $:\lambda$. Formally, $\mathbb{Q}(A)$ is the following conjunction of disjunctions of triple patterns, where $\bigwedge$ and $\bigvee$ denote a sequence of conjunctions and disjunctions, respectively:

$$\mathbb{Q}(A) = \bigwedge_{t \in A} \left(\bigvee_{\substack{x_1 \in \{:\lambda, t[1]\} \\ x_2 \in \{:\lambda, t[2]\} \\ x_3 \in \{:\lambda, t[3]\}}} \langle x_1, x_2, x_3 \rangle \right)$$

When translating this formula to SPARQL we want to select mappings that contain a binding for all the variables in the query, so we explicitly request all of them in the select clause. For example, consider graph pattern $A_1 = \{\langle$?v3, :a, ?v4$\rangle, \langle$?v3, :b, :c$\rangle\}$, which is interpreted as query:

```
SELECT ?v3 ?v4 WHERE { ?v3 :a ?v4 . ?v3 :b :c }
```

Query rewriting $\mathbb{Q}(A_1)$ then corresponds to:

```
SELECT ?v3 ?v4 WHERE {
  { {?v3 :a ?v4} UNION {:λ :a ?v4} UNION {?v3 :λ ?v4}
    UNION {?v3 :a :λ} UNION {:λ :λ ?v4} UNION {:λ :a :λ}
    UNION {?v3 :λ :λ} UNION {:λ :λ :λ} }
  { {?v3 :b :c} UNION {:λ :b :c} UNION {?v3 :λ :c}
    UNION {?v3 :b :λ} UNION {:λ :λ :c} UNION {:λ :b :λ}
    UNION {?v3 :λ :λ} UNION {:λ :λ :λ} } }
```

Below we treat $\mathbb{Q}(A)$ as a union of conjunctive queries, or UCQ [1], and denote $q \in \mathbb{Q}(A)$ to be a conjunctive query within it.

We should point out that in this section we present a generic formulation of both approaches that is applicable to schema graphs having variables in the predicate position. If variables cannot occur in this position, such as in the triplestore schemas representation of SHACL constraints, these approaches could be optimised; for example by removing from $\mathbb{Q}(A)$ all the triples patterns that have $:\lambda$ in the predicate position.

Having defined how the `critical` and `score` approaches compute a set of mappings, we now describe the details of the last two phases required to compute a basic schema consequence.

Filtering the Mappings. This phase deals with processing the mappings computed by either `critical` or `score`, namely $[\![A]\!]_{\mathbb{C}(S,r)}$ or $[\![\mathbb{Q}(A)]\!]_{\mathbb{S}(S)}$. It should be noted that it is not possible to simply apply the resulting mappings on the consequent of the inference rule, as such mappings might map a variable in the subject or predicate position to a literal, thus generating an invalid triple pattern. Moreover, it is necessary to determine which variables should be included in the no-literal set of the basic schema consequence. The schema S' (output of our approaches) is initialised with the same graph and no-literal set as S, and with an empty set of existential rules. Formally S' is initialised to $\langle S^G, S^\Delta, \varnothing\rangle$. We then incrementally extend S' on a mapping-by-mapping basis until all the mappings have been considered, at which point, S' is the final output of our basic schema expansion.

For each mapping m in $[\![A]\!]_{\mathbb{C}(S,r)}$ or $[\![\mathbb{Q}(A)]\!]_{\mathbb{S}(S)}$, we do the following. We create a temporary no-literal set Δ^m. This set will be used to keep track of which variables could not be bound to any literals if we evaluated our rule antecedent A on the instances of S, or when instantiating the consequence of the rule. We initialise Δ^m with the variables of our inference rule $A \rightarrow C$ that occur in the subject or predicate position in some triple of A or C, as we know that they cannot be matched to, or instantiated with literals.

We then consider the elements that occur in the object position in the triples t_A of A. We take all the rewritings t_q of t_A in $\mathbb{Q}(A)$ (if using `critical`, it would be enough to consider a single rewriting t_q with $t_q = t_A$). Since the mapping m has been computed over the canonical instance ($\mathbb{S}(S)$ or $\mathbb{C}(S,r)$ depending on the approach), we know that there exists at least one t_q such that $m(t_q)$ belongs to the canonical instance. We identify the set of schema triples $t^S \in S$ that model $m(t_q)$, for any of the above t_q. Intuitively, these are the schema triples that enable t_A, or one of its rewritings, to match the canonical instance with mapping m. If $t_A[3]$ is a literal l, or a variable mapped to a literal l by m, we check if there exists any t^S from the above such that $t^S[3] = l$ or $t^S[3]$ is a variable that allows literals (not in S^Δ). If such a triple pattern does not exist, then $m(A)$ cannot be an instance of S since it has a literal in a non-allowed position, and therefore we filter out m. If $t_A[3]$ is a variable mapped to $:\lambda$ in m, we check whether in any of the above t^S, $t^S[3]$ is a variable that allows literals (not in S^Δ). If such t^S cannot be found, we add variable $t_A[3]$ to Δ^m. Intuitively, this models the fact that $t_A[3]$ could not have been bound to literal elements under this mapping. Having considered all the triples $t_A \in A$ we filter out mapping m if it binds any variable in Δ^m to a literal. If m is not filtered out, we say that inference rule r is applicable, and we use m to expand S'.

Schema Expansion. For each mapping m that is not filtered out, we compute the substitution s^m, which contains all the bindings in m that map a variable to a value other than $:\lambda$, and for every binding $?v \rightarrow :\lambda$ in m, a variable substitution $?v \rightarrow ?v^*$ where $?v^*$ is a new variable. We then add triple patterns $s^m(m(C))$ to S'^G and then add the variables $s^m(\Delta^m) \cap vars(S'^G)$ to S'^Δ. Although the schema consequences produced by `score`(S,r) and `critical`(S,r) might not be identical, they are semantically equivalent (i.e. they model the same set of instances). This notion of equivalence is captured by Theorem 1.

Theorem 1. *For all rules* $r : A \rightarrow C$ *and triplestore schemas* S, $\mathbb{I}(score(S,r)) = \mathbb{I}(critical(S,r))$.

The `score` approach (and by extension `critical`, via Theorem 1) is sound and complete. The following theorem captures the this notion by stating the semantic equivalence of `score`(S,r) and $r(S)$. For our proofs, we refer the reader to our Appendix (see footnote 1).

Theorem 2. *For all rules* $r : A \rightarrow C$ *and triplestore schemas* S, $\mathbb{I}(\mathit{score}(S, r)) = \mathbb{I}(r(S))$.

Termination. It is easy to see that our approaches terminate since our datalog rules do not contain existential variables, and do not generate new IRIs or literals (but just new variable names). After a finite number of iterations, either approach will only generate isomorphic (and thus equivalent) triple patterns.

5 Computing the Existential-Preserving Schema Consequence

In order to compute the existential-preserving schema consequence we are going to build on the result of our simple schema consequence. Recall the definition of schema consequences from Sect. 3.2 and note that given a schema $S = \langle S^G, S^\Delta, S^\exists \rangle$ and a set of inference rules R such that $con(S, R) = \langle S'^G, S'^\Delta, \varnothing \rangle$ then $con^{ex}(S, R) = \langle S'^G, S'^\Delta, S'^\exists \rangle$ for some $S'^\exists \subseteq S^\exists$; that is, the output schema graph and no-literal set of the existential-preserving schema consequence are the same as those of the simple one.

Our first step is to compute the schema graph and no-literal set of the existential preserving schema consequence, as in Sect. 4. Next, and in the rest of this section, we want to compute the set of existential rules $S'^\exists$ that are still valid on all possible "closure" instances (instances of the original schema closed under R), or complementary, those existential rules that are violated on some "closure" instance.

Starting from an instance I of S, which by definition satisfies $S^\exists$, an existential rule might become violated by the inference rules due to new facts added by the closure. Thus, the aim of the algorithm is to find an instance I of S, that can "trigger" an existential rule $a \rightarrow^\exists c$ by mapping its antecedent a on $clos(I, R)$. For every existential rule, we want to construct I in a "minimal" way, so that if $clos(I, R)$ satisfies the rule e then there is no proper subset I' of I which is still an instance of S and does not satisfy the rule. By considering all such minimal instances I for every existential rule, we can determine if the rule is violated or not on any potential closure of an instance.

We can achieve finding these violating instances if they exist, intituitively, by starting from triples that are: (1) groundings of the inference rules' antecedents; (2) instances of the original schema S; and (3) which produce, via the closure, a fact on which we can map a. To find the minimal number of inference rules' antecedents that we have to ground, we can reason "backwards" starting from an inference rule antecedent A whose consequent can trigger e, and compute inference rules' antecedents that can compute A. We have implemented this backward-chaining reasoning in a way similar to query rewriting in OBDA [5], and the Query-Sub-Query algorithm in datalog [1]. We don't provide the specifics of the algorithm but emphasize that it terminates by relying on a notion of minimality of the rewritings produced. A rewriting produced by our algorithm is essentially a "transitive" antecedent via our inference rules, which can produce A.

Algorithm 1. Computation of the existential rules in $con^{ex}(S, R)$

1: **procedure** RETAINEDEXISTENTIALS($S : \langle S^G, S^\Delta, S^\exists \rangle, R$)
2: $V \leftarrow \varnothing$
3: **for each** $e : a \rightarrow^\exists c \in S^\exists$ **do**
4: **for each** $r : A \rightarrow C \in R$ **do**
5: **if** $[\![\mathbb{Q}(a)]\!]_{\mathbb{S}(C)} \neq \varnothing$ **then**
6: $W \leftarrow$ all rewritings of the antecedent of $r : A \rightarrow C$ with rules R
7: **for each** $w : A^w \rightarrow C \in W$ **do**
8: $M^w \leftarrow [\![\mathbb{Q}(A^w)]\!]_{\mathbb{S}(S)}$
9: **for each** $m^w \in M^w$ **do**
10: $\tilde{m}^w \leftarrow$ all mappings in m^w that do not map a variable to $:\lambda$
11: $g \leftarrow$ mapping from the $vars(\tilde{m}(A^w))$ to new `IRIs`
12: $I^g \leftarrow g(\tilde{m}(A^w))$
13: $I^{g'} \leftarrow \varnothing$
14: **while** $I^g \neq I^{g'}$ **do**
15: $I^{g'} \leftarrow I^g$
16: **for each** $e' : a' \rightarrow^\exists c' \in S^\exists$ **do**
17: $M^{e'} \leftarrow [\![\mathbb{Q}(a')]\!]_{\mathbb{S}(I^g)}$
18: **for each** $m' \in M^{e'}$ **do**
19: **if** $[\![\mathbb{Q}(m'(c'))]\!]_{\mathbb{S}(I^g)} \neq \varnothing$ **then**
20: $g^e \leftarrow$ mapping from $vars(m'(c))$ to new `IRIs`
21: $I^g \leftarrow I^g \cup g^e(m'(c))$
22: $I^g \leftarrow clos(I^g, R)$
23: $M^I \leftarrow [\![\mathbb{Q}(a)]\!]_{\mathbb{S}(I^g)}$
24: **for each** $m^I \in M^I$ **do**
25: **if** $[\![\mathbb{Q}(m^I(c))]\!]_{\mathbb{S}(I^g)} \neq \varnothing$ **then**
26: $V \leftarrow V \cup \{e\}$
return $S^\exists \setminus V$

By instantiating these rule antecedents in one rewriting, that is also an instance of $\langle S^G, S^\Delta, \varnothing \rangle$, and "closing" it existentially[3] with $S^\exists$ we produce a "minimal" instance of the original schema on the closure of which we know we can find A. This A is the antecedent of an inference rule that can infer facts matching the antecedent of e, and thus, after applying this rule, we can check the satisfaction or violation of e. Our rewritings' groundings are representative of all possible instances whose closure can lead to a fact that the antecedent of e maps to. If e is valid in all these instances then e can not be violated in any closure of an instance of S, and thus we retain it from $S^\exists$.

The pseudocode for our algorithm can be seen in Algorithm 1. For each existential rule e we consider each inference rule $r : A \rightarrow C$ such that inferring C could trigger e (lines 3–5). We then compute all the rewritings W of A by means of backward-chaining the rules in R. For each such rewriting A^w, we want to see if we can match it on the instances of S. We do so by reusing the `score` approach, computing the set of mappings $M^w = [\![\mathbb{Q}(A^w)]\!]_{\mathbb{S}(S)}$. If M^w is empty,

[3] For this step we implement a version of the Chase algorithm [4].

then there is no instance of S on which A^w would match. Otherwise, we consider whether this potential match could violate the existential rule e (lines 10–26). For each mapping $m^w \in M^w$ we compute the instance I^g, grounding of A^w, by first applying to A^w all mappings in m^w that do not map a variable to :λ, and then mapping any remaining variable to new IRIs (lines 10–12). To make sure that I^g is an instance of S we perform the Chase on I^g using the existential rules. Lines 13 to 21 exactly implement the well-known Chase algorithm [4] to compute existential closure using our own `score` approach. Finally, we compute the closure on I^g with the inference rules R and, if it violates e, we add e to the set V of the existential rules that can be violated (lines 22–26). The output of our algorithm ($S'^{\exists}$) is $S^{\exists} \backslash V$.

6 Experimental Evaluation

We developed a Java implementation of our algorithms. This allowed us to test their correctness with a number of test cases, and to assess their scalability using synthetic schemas of different sizes. We present here two experiments. In the first, we compare the time to compute the simple schema consequence, on different sized schemas, using the `score` and `critical` approaches. In the second, we show the overhead in computational time to compute the existential-preserving schema consequence. Since this overhead is the same, regardless of which approach we use to compute the simple schema consequence, we only consider `score` in this experiment.

We developed a synthetic schema and an inference rule generator that is configurable with 8 parameters: $\pi_C, |P|, |U|, |L|, |S^G|, |R|, |S^{\exists}|, n_A$, which we now describe. To reflect the fact that triple predicates are typically defined in vocabularies, our generator does not consider variables in the predicate position. Random triple patterns are created as follows. Predicate IRIs are randomly selected from a set of IRIs P. Elements in the subject and object position are instantiated as constants with probability π_C, or else as new variables. Constants in the subject positions are instantiated with a random IRI, and constants in the object position with a random IRI with 50% probability, or otherwise with a random literal. Random IRIs and literals are selected, respectively, from sets U and L ($U \cap P = \varnothing$). We consider chain rules where the triples in the antecedent join each other to form a list where the object of a triple is the same as the subject of the next. The consequent of each rule is a triple having the subject of the first triple in the antecedent as a subject, and the object of the last triple as object. An example of such inference rule generated by our experiment is: $\{\langle$?v0, :m1, ?v1$\rangle, \langle$?v1, :m3, ?v2$\rangle\} \rightarrow \{\langle$?v0, :m2, ?v2$\rangle\}$ In each run of the experiment we populate a schema $S = \langle S^G, S^{\Delta}, S^{\exists} \rangle$ and a set of inference rules R having n_A triples in the antecedent. To ensure that some inference rules in each set are applicable, half of the schema is initialized with the antecedents triples of randomly selected inference rules. The other half is populated with random triple patterns. Each existential rule of schema S is created as follows. Its antecedent is selected randomly from all the consequents of the inference rules, while its

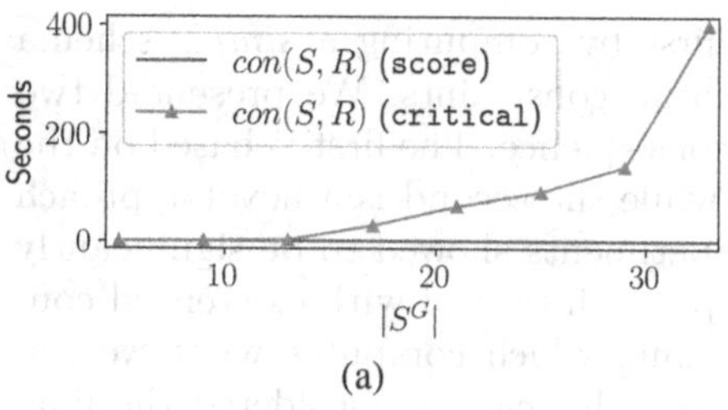

(a)

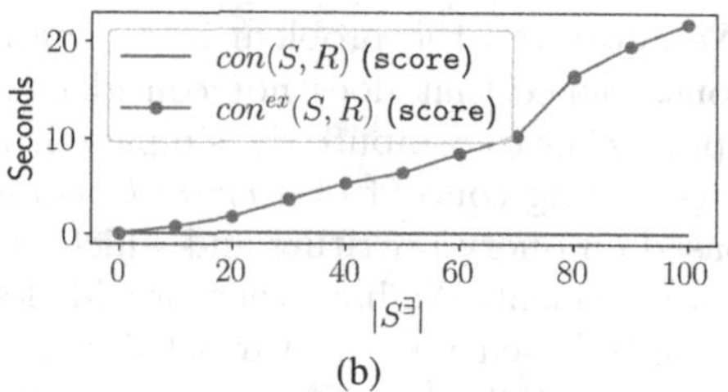

(b)

Fig. 4. (a) Average time to compute $con(S, R)$ using `score` and `critical` as the schema size $|S^G|$ grows. The other parameters are: $|P| = 1.5|S^G|$, $\pi_C = 0.1$, $|U| = |L| = |S^G|$, $|R| = 4$, $n_A = 2$, $|S^\exists| = 0$. (b) Average time to compute $con(S, R)$ and $con^{ex}(S, R)$ using the `score` approach as the number of existential rules $|S^\exists|$ increases. The other parameters are $|S| = 100$, $|P| = 110$, $\pi_C = 0.1$, $|U| = |L| = |S^G|$, $|R| = 20$, $n_A = 2$.

consequence is selected randomly from all the antecedents of all the inference rules. This is done to ensure the relevance of the existential rules, and increase the likelihood of interactions with the inference rules. We initialize S^Δ with all the variables in the subject and predicate position in the triples of S. The code for these experiments is available on GitHub (see footnote 2). We run the experiments on a standard Java virtual machine running on Ubuntu 16.04 with 15.5 GB RAM, an Intel Core i7-6700 Processor. Average completion times of over 10 min have not been recorded.

The results of the first experiment are displayed in Fig. 4(a). This figure shows the time to compute the schema consequence for different schema sizes $|S|$ using `score` and `critical`. The parameters have been chosen to be small enough to accommodate for the high computational complexity of the `critical` approach. This figure shows that `score` is orders of magnitude faster, especially on large schema sizes. The `critical` approach, instead, does not scale (times out) beyond schemas with over 33 triples. Figure 4(b) shows the increase of computation time as schemas with more existential rules are considered. The results of the second experiment show how our approach to compute the existential-preserving schema consequence can scale to a large number of existential rules on a large input schema in a matter of seconds.

7 Conclusion

SHACL constraints can can be used to define the schema of graph datasets. However, the application of inference rules could cause the violation of such constraints, and thus require a change in the schema. In this paper we address the problem of computing the *schema consequence* of a schema S and a set of rules R; that is, the evolved schema of the graphs, instances of S, closed under inference rules R. To address this problem we introduced our notion of a *triplestore schema*, which captures a fragment of SHACL, and can also be used as a standalone logical tool to model properties of RDF graphs in general.

We addressed the problem incrementally, first by computing a *simple* schema consequence that does not consider existential constraints. We presented two approaches to compute the simple schema consequence. The first is based on the pre-existing concept of a *critical instance*, while the second is a novel approach based on query rewriting and which our experiments showed to be significantly more efficient. We have then provided an approach to deal with existential constraints based on backward-chaining reasoning, which computes what we call an *existential-preserving* schema consequence. This can be considered the final output of our approach, which a domain expert can use to update the schema of an RDF dataset, if they choose to retain all the inference rules considered. The machinery we developed in the form of the simple schema consequence, can also have other applications, such as determining which rules are applicable on a dataset and, if they are, what kind of triples they can infer.

Acknowledgments. This work was supported by an Institutional Links grant, ID 333778, under the Newton-Katip Çelebi Fund. The grant is funded by the UK Department for Business, Energy and Industrial Strategy and the Scientific and Technological Research Council of Turkey (TUBITAK) under grant 116E918, and delivered by the British Council.

References

1. Abiteboul, S., Hull, R., Vianu, V.: Foundations of Databases: The Logical Level. Addison-Wesley Longman Publishing Co., Inc. (1995)
2. Baget, J.F., Leclère, M., Mugnier, M.L., Salvat, E.: On rules with existential variables: walking the decidability line. Artif. Intell. **175**(9–10), 1620–1654 (2011)
3. Bassiliades, N.: SWRL2SPIN: a tool for transforming SWRL rule bases in OWL ontologies to object-oriented SPIN rules. CoRR (2018). http://arxiv.org/abs/1801.09061
4. Benedikt, M., et al.: Benchmarking the chase. In: Proceedings of the 36th ACM SIGMOD-SIGACT-SIGAI Symposium on Principles of Database Systems, pp. 37–52. ACM (2017)
5. Calvanese, D., et al.: Ontologies and databases: the *DL-Lite* approach. In: Tessaris, S., et al. (eds.) Reasoning Web 2009. LNCS, vol. 5689, pp. 255–356. Springer, Heidelberg (2009). https://doi.org/10.1007/978-3-642-03754-2_7
6. Ceri, S., Gottlob, G., Tanca, L.: What you always wanted to know about datalog (and never dared to ask). IEEE Trans. Knowl. Data Eng. **1**(1), 146–166 (1989)
7. Corman, J., Reutter, J.L., Savković, O.: Semantics and validation of recursive SHACL. In: Vrandečić, D., et al. (eds.) ISWC 2018. LNCS, vol. 11136, pp. 318–336. Springer, Cham (2018). https://doi.org/10.1007/978-3-030-00671-6_19
8. Fagin, R., Kolaitis, P.G., Miller, R.J., Popa, L.: Data exchange: semantics and query answering. Theor. Comput. Sci. **336**(1), 89–124 (2005)
9. Glimm, B., Kazakov, Y., Liebig, T., Tran, T.K., Vialard, V.: Abstraction refinement for ontology materialization. In: International Semantic Web Conference, pp. 180–195 (2014)
10. Knublauch, H., Kontokostas, D.: Shapes constraint language (SHACL). In: W3C Recommendation, W3C (2017). https://www.w3.org/TR/shacl/

11. Kontokostas, D., et al.: Test-driven evaluation of linked data quality. In: Proceedings of the 23rd International Conference on World Wide Web, WWW 2014, pp. 747–758. ACM (2014)
12. Lefrançois, M., Cox, S., Taylor, K., Haller, A., Janowicz, K., Phuoc, D.L.: Semantic sensor network ontology. In: W3C Recommendation, W3C (2017). https://www.w3.org/TR/2017/REC-vocab-ssn-20171019/
13. Marnette, B.: Generalized schema-mappings: from termination to tractability. In: Proceedings of the Twenty-Tighth ACM SIGMOD-SIGACT-SIGART Symposium on Principles of Database Systems, pp. 13–22. ACM (2009)
14. Pérez, J., Arenas, M., Gutierrez, C.: Semantics and complexity of SPARQL. ACM Trans. Database Syst. **34**(3), 16:1–16:45 (2009)
15. Prud'hommeaux, E., Labra Gayo, J.E., Solbrig, H.: Shape expressions: an RDF validation and transformation language. In: Proceedings of the 10th International Conference on Semantic Systems, SEM 2014, pp. 32–40. ACM (2014)

Query-Based Entity Comparison in Knowledge Graphs Revisited

Alina Petrova(✉), Egor V. Kostylev, Bernardo Cuenca Grau, and Ian Horrocks

Department of Computer Science, University of Oxford, Oxford, UK
{alina.petrova,egor.kostylev,bernardo.cuenca.grau, ian.horrocks}@cs.ox.ac.uk

Abstract. Large-scale knowledge graphs are increasingly being used in applications, and there is a growing need for tools that can effectively support users in analysis and exploration tasks. One such important task is entity comparison—to describe in an informative way the similarities between two given entities as described in a knowledge graph. In our previous work the result of entity comparison is modelled as a similarity query—that is, a SPARQL query having the input entities as part of the answer over the input graph; for instance, one can describe the similarity between two companies such as Telenor and Vodafone in the YAGO graph as a query asking for all telecom companies based in Europe. In this paper, we extend the results of our prior work in different ways. First, we expand the language of similarity queries to consider a richer fragment of SPARQL allowing for numeric filter expressions; this enables us to express that Telenor and Vodafone are also similar in that they both have at least 30,000 employees. We then propose algorithms for computing similarity queries satisfying certain additional desirable properties, such as being as specific as possible. Such algorithms are, however, impractical; hence, we also propose and implement a scalable algorithm that is guaranteed to compute a similarity query, but not necessarily a most specific one.

1 Introduction

Large-scale knowledge graphs are increasingly being used in applications, and there is a growing need for tools that can effectively support users in analysis and exploration tasks. One such important task is *entity comparison*—to describe in an informative way the similarities and differences between two given entities as outlined in a knowledge graph. This is in stark contrast to the computation of a similarity measure, where the output is a number indicating how similar the given entities are likely to be rather than a human-readable explanation.

To make our discussion concrete, consider a small excerpt from the YAGO knowledge graph [19] (in RDF format) about European companies that is depicted in Fig. 1. We would like a tool to assist us in comparing Telenor with

C. Ghidini et al. (Eds.): ISWC 2019, LNCS 11778, pp. 558–575, 2019.
https://doi.org/10.1007/978-3-030-30793-6_32

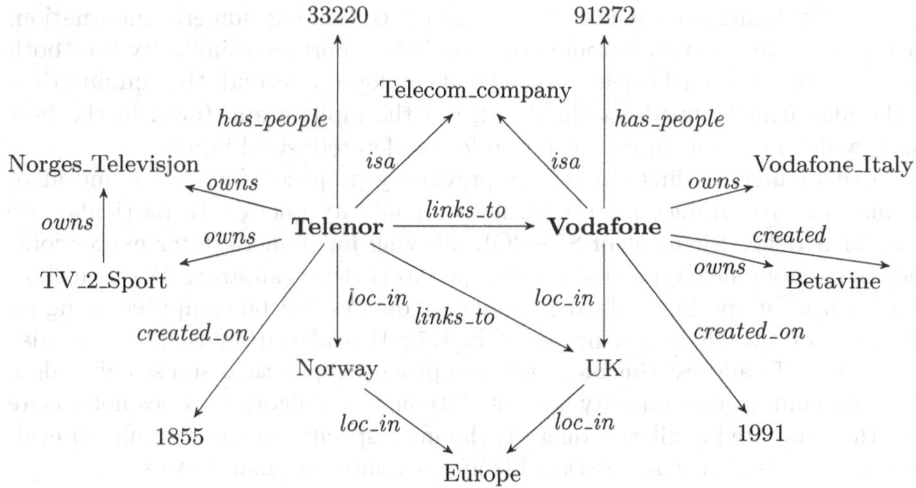

Fig. 1. An excerpt of the YAGO knowledge graph

Vodafone. In particular, the tool should be able to automatically report that Telenor and Vodafone are similar in that they are both telecom companies located in Europe which own other companies, have at least 25 years of operating experience and more than 30,000 employees on payroll; however, they are different in that Telenor is located in Norway whereas Vodafone is based in the UK.

Entity comparison is used routinely across multiple domains and applications, from online shopping to food and nutrition comparison widgets, to Facebook's 'see what you have in common' pages. Existing tools typically focus on a constrained application domain (e.g., used cars) and provide a side-by-side comparison of the given entities based on a fixed set of relevant attributes (e.g., price, engine size, or colour). We are, however, interested in the generic entity comparison support in knowledge graphs, in which case it is no longer possible to fix a relevant set of attributes or relationships upfront.

In our previous work, we proposed a logical framework for entity comparison in knowledge graphs represented in RDF format [17]. The description of similarities and differences is given in terms of SPARQL queries in the conjunctive fragment. In particular, a *similarity query* is a query containing the two given entities to compare as answers. A more specific such query is seen as more informative: for example, knowing that both Vodafone and Telenor are telecom companies is more informative than just knowing that they are both companies.

We previously showed that, for any given RDF graph and pair of entities to compare, there exists a unique most specific similarity query (MSSQ), which can be computed in polynomial time in the size of the input graph [17]. The algorithm in that work, however, has two important practical limitations. First, it was designed for a fragment of SPARQL without numeric filter expressions, which significantly limits its applicability to graphs containing numeric information; for instance, the algorithm would not be able to report as a similarity that both Vodafone and Telenor have at least 30,000 employees. Second, the running time of the algorithm is quadratic in the size of the input graph (even in the best case), which makes it impractical even for moderately-sized inputs.

In this paper, we first extend the previously proposed framework and algorithms so as to produce more informative similarity queries. In particular, we consider a richer fragment of SPARQL allowing for numeric filter expressions, and also study a new type of similarity queries that we call *exact*. We then show that both most-specific and exact similarity queries can be computed using an extension of the algorithm proposed in [17]; this algorithm is, however, also impractical. To address this issue, we then propose a practical and scalable algorithm for computing similarity queries. Although our algorithm does not ensure that the computed similarity query is the most specific one, our empirical evaluation suggests that it is a reasonable approximation in many cases.

2 Preliminaries

Let $\mathbf{U}$, $\mathbf{L}$, and $\mathbf{B}$ be pairwise disjoint, countably infinite sets of *IRIs*, *literals*, and *blank nodes*, respectively. We assume that $\mathbf{L}$ includes all integers $\mathbb{Z}$. We will refer to IRIs and literals collectively as *entities*. An *RDF triple* (or simply a *triple*) is a tuple (s, p, o) from $(\mathbf{U} \cup \mathbf{B}) \times \mathbf{U} \times (\mathbf{U} \cup \mathbf{L} \cup \mathbf{B})$, where s is called the *subject*, p the *predicate*, and o the *object*. An (*RDF*) *graph* is a finite set of triples.

Let $\mathbf{X}$ be a countable infinite set of variables disjoint from $\mathbf{U}$, $\mathbf{B}$, and $\mathbf{L}$. A *term* is an element from $\mathbf{U} \cup \mathbf{L} \cup \mathbf{X}$. A *triple pattern* is a triple of terms from the set $(\mathbf{U} \cup \mathbf{X}) \times (\mathbf{U} \cup \mathbf{X}) \times (\mathbf{U} \cup \mathbf{L} \cup \mathbf{X})$. A *basic graph pattern* is a non-empty finite set of triple patterns. An *arithmetic comparison* is an expression of the form $(?Y \lhd n)$, where $?Y$ is a variable in $\mathbf{X}$, n is an integer (i.e., a literal), and $\lhd$ is a comparison symbol in $\{<, \leq, >, \geq\}$. A (*arithmetic*) *filter condition* is a finite (possibly empty) set of arithmetic comparisons. For E an expression such as a pattern or a filter condition we denote with $\mathsf{var}(E)$ and $\mathsf{term}(E)$ the sets of variables and terms, respectively, occurring in E. A basic graph pattern P is *connected* if for every pair $t, t' \in \mathsf{term}(P)$ there is a sequence of triple patterns $T_1, \ldots, T_m$ in P such that $t \in \mathsf{term}(T_1)$, $t' \in \mathsf{term}(T_m)$ and $\mathsf{term}(T_i) \cap \mathsf{term}(T_{i+1}) \neq \emptyset$ for all $i = 1, \ldots, m-1$.

In this paper, we concentrate on (SPARQL) queries of a very specific form. In particular, in the context of this paper, a *query* is an expression of the form

$$\text{SELECT } ?X \text{ WHERE } P \text{ FILTER } C, \tag{1}$$

where P is a connected basic graph pattern, $?X \in \mathsf{var}(P)$ is the *answer variable* of the query and C is a filter condition satisfying $\mathsf{var}(C) \subseteq \mathsf{var}(P)$. Such queries essentially correspond to connected monadic conjunctive queries with arithmetic comparisons (CQACs) [15] restricted to signatures over a single ternary relation and using no comparisons between variables.

A *valuation* of a finite set of variables $?\bar{X}$ from $\mathbf{X}$ is a mapping from $?\bar{X}$ to $\mathbf{U} \cup \mathbf{L} \cup \mathbf{B}$. An element from $\mathbf{U} \cup \mathbf{L} \cup \mathbf{B}$ is an *answer* to a query Q of the form (1) over a graph G if there exists a valuation ν of $\mathsf{var}(P)$ so that $\nu(P) \subseteq G$ and $\nu(?Y) \lhd n$ holds for each comparison $(?Y \lhd n)$ in C. We denote by $[Q]_G$ the set of all answers to Q over G. A query Q_1 is *subsumed* by a query Q_2, written $Q_1 \subseteq Q_2$, if $[Q_1]_G \subseteq [Q_2]_G$ for every graph G. Query Q_1 is *strictly subsumed* by query Q_2, denoted by $Q_1 \subset Q_2$, if $Q_1 \subseteq Q_2$ and $Q_2 \not\subseteq Q_1$. Finally, Q_1 and Q_2 are *equivalent*, denoted by $Q_1 \equiv Q_2$, if $Q_1 \subseteq Q_2$ and $Q_2 \subseteq Q_1$. Subsumption and equivalence allow us to compare queries relative to their specificity, so we sometimes say that Q_1 is *(strictly) more specific* than Q_2 if Q_1 is (strictly) subsumed by Q_2.

We conclude this section with an observation that we restrict the filter conditions to only arithmetic comparisons between variables and constants. This is justified by the fact that all other comparisons, such as general inequalities between variables and IRIs, have very little meaning in the context of entity comparisons, and moreover may flood similarity queries hiding the essential parts.

3 Entity Comparison Using Similarity Queries

There are two main proposals for capturing similarities between entities in the literature: either by queries [17] that have given entities as answers or by explicit paths in the graph originating in given entities and converging into the same node [6,11,14]. As discussed in our previous work [17], queries contain variables, which allows us to represent similarities at a higher level of abstraction, so we adopt the first approach. We start by extending the notions of similarity and most specific similarity queries of [17] to also consider filter conditions.

Definition 1. *A query Q is a* similarity query *for entities a and b in a graph G if $\{a, b\} \subseteq [Q]_G$. A similarity query Q for a and b in G is* most specific *(*MSSQ*) for a and b if there is no similarity query Q' for a and b in G such that $Q' \subset Q$.*

For example, the following query Q_{ex} asking for all telecom companies located in Europe is a similarity query for Vodafone and Telenor in the graph in Fig. 1:

$$\textsc{Select}\ ?X\ \ \textsc{Where}\ \{(?X, \mathit{isa}, \mathit{Telecom\_company}),\\ (?X, \mathit{loc\_in}, ?Y),\ (?Y, \mathit{loc\_in}, \mathit{Europe}))\}.$$

Query Q_{ex} is, however, not an MSSQ since the following query Q'_{ex} is also a similarity query, and it is strictly more specific as it adds the information that both companies were created between 1855 and 1991:

$$\textsc{Select}\ ?X\ \ \textsc{Where}\ \{(?X, \mathit{isa}, \mathit{Telecom\_company}),\\ (?X, \mathit{loc\_in}, ?Y),\ (?Y, \mathit{loc\_in}, \mathit{Europe}), (?X, \mathit{created\_on}, ?Z)\}\\ \textsc{Filter}\ \{(?Z \leq 1991),\ (?Z \geq 1855)\}.$$

It is not difficult to see that a similarity query exists, provided the input entities appear at the same position (i.e., subject, predicate, or object) in the input graph. Moreover, as the above example suggests, there may be multiple (even infinitely many) similarity queries for a pair of entities in a graph. We next show, however, that MSSQs are unique modulo equivalence. Intuitively, this is the case because the conjunction of similarity queries is also a similarity query.

Proposition 1. *MSSQs are unique up to equivalence.*

Proof. Let a and b be entities in a graph G. Consider two arbitrary MSSQs $Q_i = \text{SELECT } ?X \text{ WHERE } P_i \text{ FILTER } C_i$, $i \in \{1, 2\}$, for a and b in G. Then query

$$Q = \text{SELECT } ?X \text{ WHERE } P_1 \cup P_2 \text{ FILTER } C_1 \cup C_2$$

is a similarity query, which is also more specific than both Q_1 and Q_2. Note that $P_1 \cup P_2$ is connected because P_1 and P_2 are both connected and both mention $?X$. Therefore, Q_1, Q_2, and Q are all equivalent MSSQs. □

The notion of MSSQ relies on query subsumption, which is a data-independent relationship between queries. It would clearly also make sense to look for similarity queries that are as discriminating for input entities a and b as possible over the specific input graph G at hand—that is, those similarity queries that return only a and b as answers when evaluated over G.

Definition 2. *A query Q is an* exact similarity query (ESQ) *for entities a and b in a graph G if $\{a, b\} = [Q]_G$.*

For instance, our example query Q_{ex} is an ESQ for the example graph from Fig. 1 because Vodafone and Telenor are the only telecom companies in Europe represented in the graph. However, as already discussed, Q_{ex} is not an MSSQ because it is not minimal with respect to subsumption. Furthermore, if we were to consider the whole of YAGO instead of our example excerpt, Q_{ex} would certainly no longer be an ESQ since YAGO contains many other European telecom companies. So, MSSQs and ESQs are incomparable in general. The following proposition, however, establishes a useful link between ESQs and MSSQs, which we exploit in the algorithms proposed in following sections.

Proposition 2. *If Q is an MSSQ for entities a and b in a graph G such that $[Q]_G \neq \{a, b\}$, then no ESQ for a and b in G exists.*

Proof. Let Q' be an ESQ for a and b in G—that is, Q' is a similarity query with $[Q']_G = \{a, b\}$. So, Q' is a similarity query that is not subsumed by the MSSQ Q, which contradicts Proposition 1. □

4 Computing Most Specific and Exact Similarity Queries

In this section, we present an algorithm that computes an MSSQ, if one exists, and reports failure otherwise. We also show how a simple modification of this algorithm can be used for computing an ESQ. Our algorithm for MSSQ extends the one in [17], where changes are needed to deal with filter conditions.

Our algorithm relies on the following notion of the (tensor) product graph.

Algorithm 1. COMPUTE_MSSQ

Input: graph G, entities a and b in G
Output: MSSQ for a and b in G, or *fail*

1 compute $G \times G$;
2 **if** $\langle a, b\rangle$ does not occur in a triple in $G \times G$ **then return** *fail*;
3 compute the connected component $G_\times$ of $\langle a, b\rangle$ in $G \times G$;
4 **let** P be the pattern obtained from $G_\times$ by replacing each pair $\langle c_1, c_2\rangle$ with either variable $?X_{c_1,c_2}$, if $c_1 \neq c_2$ or $c_1 \in \mathbf{B}$, or with c_1 otherwise;
5 **if** $a = b$ **then**
6 add to P all triple patterns obtained from triple patterns already in P by replacing at least one occurrence of a with $?X_{a,a}$;
7 **let** C be $\{(?X_{n_1,n_2} \leq \max(n_1, n_2)), (?X_{n_1,n_2} \geq \min(n_1, n_2)) \mid ?X_{n_1,n_2} \in \mathsf{var}(P); n_1, n_2 \in \mathbb{Z}\}$;
8 **return** SELECT $?X_{a,b}$ WHERE P FILTER C.

Definition 3. *Given triples* $\tau_1 = (s_1, p_1, o_1)$ *and* $\tau_2 = (s_2, p_2, o_2)$*, let*

$$\tau_1 \times \tau_2 = (\langle s_1, s_2\rangle, \langle p_1, p_2\rangle, \langle o_1, o_2\rangle).$$

The product $G_1 \times G_2$ *of graphs* G_1 *and* G_2 *is the set* $\{\tau_1 \times \tau_2 \mid \tau_1 \in G_1, \tau_2 \in G_2\}$.

Algorithm COMPUTE_MSSQ (given in Algorithm 1) accepts as input a graph G, and entities a and b in G. In the first step, it computes the product graph $G \times G$ and checks whether the node $\langle a, b\rangle$ occurs in $G \times G$; if it does not, then the algorithm determines that a similarity query (and hence an MSSQ) for a and b in G does not exist, and reports failure. In contrast, if $\langle a, b\rangle$ occurs in the product graph $G \times G$, then the algorithm computes the connected component of $\langle a, b\rangle$ in the product graph and constructs the output query based on it. Specifically, the algorithm computes the pattern P in the query by replacing each element of a product triple in $G \times G$ with either a constant or a variable (uniquely associated with the element), and the filter condition C by adding suitable inequalities for those variables representing pairs of numeric literals in the product graph.

Since the size of $G \times G$ is quadratic in the size of G, the algorithm works in polynomial time. Correctness is established by the following theorem.

Theorem 1. COMPUTE_MSSQ *is a polynomial time procedure that returns an MSSQ for its input entities and graph, if it exists, or fail otherwise.*

Proof. First, recall that a similarity query of entities a and b in a graph G exists if and only if both a and b appear in the same position in triples in G, which happens precisely when $\langle a, b\rangle$ appears in a triple in $G \times G$ by construction. So, if COMPUTE_MSSQ returns *fail* in line 2 then there is no MSSQ for a and b.

Next, algorithm COMPUTE_MSSQ extends our previously proposed algorithm from [17] that computes a most specific similarity query without filter conditions for two entities in an RDF graph. So, if the MSSQ (in the extended language) does not contain integers, then COMPUTE_MSSQ returns this MSSQ, with the filter condition C being empty. If the MSSQ contains integers, then the algorithm first generates the most specific basic graph pattern P in lines 1–6 as before and then computes the filter condition C in line 7; moreover, C contains the arithmetic comparisons for all possible numeric variables in P, and these comparisons are constrained in the tightest way possible by the integer values.

Finally, as already mentioned, all steps can be done in polynomial time. □

The correctness of the algorithm implies that an MSSQ is always guaranteed to exist whenever a similarity query exists for the given input. Furthermore, checking whether a similarity query exists can be done efficiently.

Despite running in polynomial time, Algorithm 1 is impractical. Indeed, real-life graphs G of interest tend to contain millions of triples, and the algorithm explicitly constructs the product graph $G \times G$, which is of quadratic size in the size of G. Moreover, large MSSQs are often incomprehensible and practically useless for entity comparison. Hence, it makes sense to design *approximation algorithms*, which, on the one hand, construct reasonably specific similarity queries and, on the other hand, can scale to large input graphs. In Sect. 5 we devise one such algorithm. We next show, however, that checking whether a query (e.g., a query output by an approximation algorithm) is an MSSQ is computationally hard.

Theorem 2. *The problem of checking whether a query is an MSSQ for two entities in a graph is* Π_2^P*-complete.*

Proof (Sketch). To check whether a query Q is an MSSQ for entities a and b in a graph G, we proceed as follows. First, we apply Algorithm 1 to obtain (in polynomial time) an MSSQ Q' for a and b in G. By Proposition 1, Q is an MSSQ if and only if it is equivalent to Q'. So, second, we check equivalence of Q and Q'; since all MSSQs are essentially CQACs, the check is feasible in Π_2^P [15].

In turn, the lower bound is obtained by reduction of the equivalence problem for connected CQACs with a restricted form of comparisons, which can be shown to be Π_2^P-complete by a similar technique as in [15]. The idea of the reduction is to first construct a graph G with entities a and b using the first CQAC q_1 such that q_1 corresponds to an MSSQ for a and b in G; then, to rewrite the second CQAC q_2 into a query Q syntactically compatible with G; and finally to show that Q is the MSSQ for a and b in G if and only if q_1 and q_2 are equivalent. □

We next observe that Algorithm 1 can be easily modified to compute an ESQ, if one exists. Indeed, let algorithm COMPUTE_ESQ be the same as COMPUTE_MSSQ except that it additionally evaluates the constructed query at the end, and returns the query only if the result is precisely a, b, and *fail* otherwise.

Theorem 3. COMPUTE_ESQ *is a procedure that returns an ESQ for its input entities and graph if it exists, or fail otherwise.*

Proof. If the algorithm returns a query Q, then Q is an ESQ for the input entities a and b in the input graph G since this is explicitly checked in the last step. Assume now that the algorithm returns *fail*; we argue that no ESQ exists.

If it returns *fail* in line 2, then by the correctness of Algorithm 1 we can conclude that no similarity query (and hence no ESQ) exists for a and b in G. In turn, if the algorithm returns *fail* in the last step, we know that the constructed query Q is not an ESQ. Furthermore, by the correctness of Algorithm 1, we know that Q is an MSSQ for a and b in G, so, by Proposition 2, no ESQ exists. □

Note that the evaluation step in COMPUTE_ESQ does not work in (deterministic) polynomial time. As the following proposition says, no ESQ can be computed in polynomial time (assuming P $\neq$ NP).

Theorem 4. *The problem of checking whether an ESQ for two entities in a graph exists is* CONP*-complete.*

Proof (Sketch). The upper bound follows from the algorithm: first it computes, in polynomial time, a candidate query Q and then universally guesses an entity different from a and b verifying that it is not an answer to Q. The last can be done in CONP by usual query evaluation algorithms.

The lower bound is obtained by reduction of the CONP-complete problem of checking whether there exists a *difference* comparison-free query Q for an entity a relative to an entity b in an RDF graph G—that is, such that Q has the empty filter condition and has a as an answer over G but not b [17]. In particular, given G, a, and b as instance to the difference existence problem, consider the graph $G' = G \cup \{(a, d, c), (b, d, c)\}$ for fresh entities d and c not occurring in G. Then it is not difficult to check that there exists a difference query for a relative to b in G if and only if there exists an ESQ for a and a in G'. □

We conclude the section with the complexity of checking if a query is an ESQ.

Theorem 5. *The problem of checking whether a query is an ESQ for two entities in a graph is* DP*-complete.*

Proof (Sketch). To establish the upper bound, consider the algorithm that checks in NP that both input entities are answers to the query on the input graph and checks in CONP that there are no other answers. For the lower bound, we first show that the verification problem for comparison-free difference queries is DP-hard, and then reduce this problem to ESQ verification in a way very similar to the one presented in the proof of Theorem 4. □

5 Computing Approximated MSSQs

As discussed in Sect. 4, algorithm COMPUTE_MSSQ is impractical even for moderately-sized input graphs G since the algorithm computes upfront the product graph $G \times G$ of the input graph G with itself, which is of quadratic size. In this section, we propose a practical algorithm that computes a similarity query for two entities in a graph (if one exists). Although the query computed by the algorithm is not guaranteed to be an MSSQ, we will verify empirically in Sect. 6 that it is a reasonable approximation in practice. Before going to the details, we make two important observations. First, in the rest of the paper we concentrate on MSSQs leaving similar treatment of ESQs for future work. Second, the theoretical framework and the exact algorithm COMPUTE_MSSQ treat subjects, predicates, and objects in the same way; however, in practice we would like to compare subject and object entities, considering predicates as relations, and hence our approximation algorithm assumes that the compared entities appear in the graph either both as subjects or both as objects at least once (and hence an MSSQ exists).

Our algorithm relies on the notion of a *similarity tree* for entities a and b in a graph G, which we define next. Roughly speaking, a similarity tree is a labelled directed tree, where each node is labelled with a pair of sets of entities (appearing in subject and object positions in G), with the first set in a pair corresponding to a and the second to b; the root node is labelled with the pair $(\{a\}, \{b\})$. Each edge in the tree is labelled with two sets of entities (appearing in the predicate position in triples from G) and a direction of triples. Furthermore, we require that the tree is consistent with the structure of G in that each edge in the tree is justified by corresponding triples in G.

Definition 4. *A* pair tree *is a rooted labelled directed tree such that*

- *each node v is labelled with a pair (V_1, V_2), where each V_i is a non-empty set of entities satisfying either $V_1 \cap V_2 = \emptyset$ or $V_1 = V_2 = \{c\}$ for an entity c;*
- *each edge e is labelled with a tuple (E_1, E_2, dir), where each E_i is a set of entities satisfying either $E_1 \cap E_2 = \emptyset$ or $E_1 = E_2 = \{c\}$ for an entity c, and where $\mathsf{dir} \in \{\rightarrow, \leftarrow\}$.*

An edge $e = (v, v')$ in a pair tree $\mathcal{T}$ is justified *in a graph G if the following properties hold for both $i = 1, 2$, where (V_1, V_2), (E_1, E_2, dir), and (V_1', V_2') are labels of v, e, and v', respectively:*

- *for each entity $c \in V_i$ there is a triple* justifying *e in G for c—that is, a triple (s, p, o) such that $p \in E_i$ and either $s = c$ and $o \in V_i'$ when dir is $\rightarrow$, or $s \in V_i'$ and $o = c$ otherwise.*

Pair tree $\mathcal{T}$ is a similarity tree *for entities a and b in graph G if the root is labelled with $(\{a\}, \{b\})$ and all edges in $\mathcal{T}$ are justified in G.*

Consider Fig. 2, where a graph G_{ex} and two pair trees $\mathcal{T}_1$ and $\mathcal{T}_2$ are depicted (for brevity, g, f, and r in the trees abbreviate $(\{g\}, \{g\})$, $\{f\}, \{f\}$, and $\{r\}, \{r\}$, respectively). Note that the roots in both trees are labelled by $(\{a\}, \{b\})$. In $\mathcal{T}_1$ the edge between the root and the node labelled $(\{c\}, \{d, d'\})$ is justified: for both a and b there exists a triple in G that has this entity as the subject, f as the predicate, and c and d (or d'), respectively, as the object. However, neither of the other two edges in $\mathcal{T}_1$ is justified, because of the $\{d, d'\}$ component in the parent node label: there are no triples (g, r, d') and (d, f, d) in G. In contrast, every edge in $\mathcal{T}_2$ is justified, and hence $\mathcal{T}_2$ is a similarity tree.

Similarity trees are relevant since they have corresponding similarity queries.

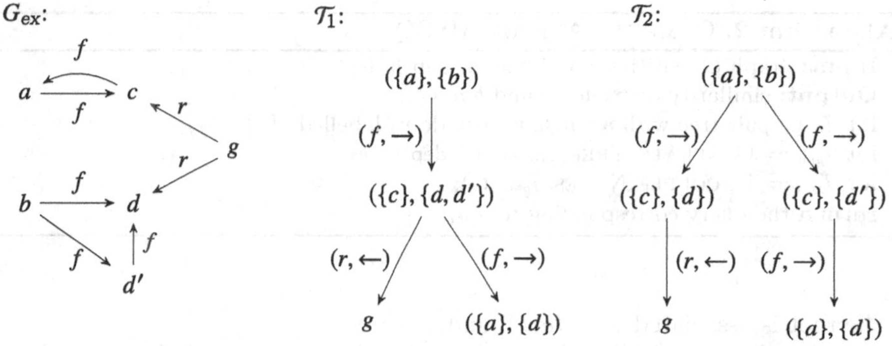

Fig. 2. An example graph G_{ex} and two pair trees $\mathcal{T}_1$ and $\mathcal{T}_2$

Definition 5. *Let $\mathcal{T}$ be a similarity tree for entities a, b in a graph G. For each node or edge u in $\mathcal{T}$ labelled with (L_1, L_2) or (L_1, L_2, dir), respectively, let t_u be*

- *a variable $?X$ if u is the root of the tree;*
- *the entity c if $L_1 \cap L_2 = \{c\}$; and*
- *a fresh variable otherwise.*

The query corresponding *to $\mathcal{T}$ is* SELECT $?X$ WHERE P FILTER C *with*

- *P containing, for each edge $e = (v, v')$ in $\mathcal{T}$, the triple pattern $(t_v, t_e, t_{v'})$ or $(t_{v'}, t_e, t_v)$ if e is labelled with $\rightarrow$ or $\leftarrow$, respectively; and*
- *C containing, for each node v in $\mathcal{T}$ labelled (V_1, V_2) with each V_i consisting of only integers, the arithmetic comparisons $(t_v \geq min)$ and $(t_v \leq max)$, where min and max are the minimal and the maximal, respectively, values in $V_1 \cup V_2$.*

The query corresponding to the similarity tree $\mathcal{T}_2$ from Fig. 2 is

$$Q_{sim} = \text{SELECT } ?X \text{ WHERE } \{(?X, f, ?Y_1), (g, r, ?Y_1), (?X, f, ?Y_2), (?Y_2, f, ?Y_3)\}.$$

The following proposition establishes that the query corresponding to a similarity tree is indeed a similarity query.

Proposition 3. *The query corresponding to a similarity tree for entities a and b in a graph G is a similarity query for a and b in G.*

Proof (Sketch). Given a similarity tree $\mathcal{T}$ for a and b in G, let us first traverse $\mathcal{T}$ from the root to the leaves and recursively associate each node and edge in $\mathcal{T}$ with a pair of entities such that the first is from the first component of the label of the node or edge and the second is from the second component, as well as the following holds:

Algorithm 2. COMPUTE_APPROX_MSSQ

```
Input: graph G, entities a and b in G, depth dep
Output: similarity query for a and b in G
1 let T_0 be pair tree with a single root node v_0 labelled ({a}, {b});
2 let T_gen := GENERATE_TREE(T_0, v_0, G, dep);
3 let T_sim := UNCOUPLE_NODES(T_gen, G);
4 return the query corresponding to T_sim.
```

- the root is associated with (a, b), and,
- for each edge $e = (v, v')$ with v associated with (c_a, c_b), e and v' are associated with pairs of entities (d_a, d_b) and (c'_a, c'_b), respectively, from the labels of e and v' such that the triples (c_a, d_a, c'_a) and (c_b, d_b, c'_b), if e is labelled by $\rightarrow$, or the triples (c'_a, d_a, c_a) and (c'_b, d_b, c_b) otherwise, justify e in G for c_a and c_b, respectively (such justifying triples exist by Definition 4).

Let Q be the query corresponding to similarity tree $\mathcal{T}$. Consider the valuations ν_a and ν_b that send $?X$ to a and b, respectively, and every other variable $?Y$ of Q to the entities c_a and c_b, respectively, in the pair (c_a, c_b) associated to the node or edge u such that t_u is $?Y$ according to Definition 5. It is immediate to check that valuations ν_a and ν_b justify a and b as answers to Q, as required. □

We are ready to present algorithm COMPUTE_APPROX_MSSQ (given in Algorithm 2), which computes a similarity query of a given depth dep (i.e., a natural number) for given entities a and b in a given graph G according to the three steps described next. In the first step (line 2), we create a preliminary pair tree $\mathcal{T}_{gen}$. For example, for the input graph G_{ex} from Fig. 2, for the entities a and b in that graph and for depth 2 the pair tree $\mathcal{T}_{gen}$ is $\mathcal{T}_1$. As in this example, $\mathcal{T}_{gen}$ may not yet be a similarity tree. Hence, in the second step (line 3), we uncouple some of the nodes in $\mathcal{T}_{gen}$, making all edges in the tree justified, and thus creating a similarity tree $\mathcal{T}_{sim}$. For example, we uncouple the node from $\mathcal{T}_1$ labelled $(\{c\}, \{d, d'\})$ into two new nodes, labelled $(\{c\}, \{d\})$ and $(\{c\}, \{d'\})$, respectively. The former becomes the parent node for the node labelled g, while the latter becomes the parent node for the node labelled $(\{a\}, \{d\})$. As the result, in this example $\mathcal{T}_{sim}$ is $\mathcal{T}_2$. Finally (in step 4), we turn $\mathcal{T}_{sim}$ into a similarity query corresponding to this tree; for example we turn $\mathcal{T}_2$ into Q_{sim}.

Let us look at each of the steps in more detail. In the first step (line 2), the algorithm constructs, by means of the recursive subroutine GENERATE_TREE, a pair tree $\mathcal{T}_{gen}$ of depth at most dep. In particular, in lines 1–2 of COMPUTE_APPROX_MSSQ a root labelled $(\{a\}, \{b\})$ is created and passed to the recursion. When a node v in $\mathcal{T}$ labelled (V_1, V_2) is received in a recursive call of GENERATE_TREE, the following extensions are performed, where $(s, p, o)^{\rightarrow}$ and $(s, p, o)^{\leftarrow}$ denote (s, p, o) and (o, p, s), respectively:

- first, for each direction $\mathsf{dir} \in \{\rightarrow, \leftarrow\}$ and each pair of entities c, d such that, for both $i = 1, 2$, there are triples $(c_i, d, c)^{\mathsf{dir}} \in G$ with $c_i \in V_i$, a new edge labelled $(\{d\}, \{d\}, \mathsf{dir})$ from v to a new node labelled $(\{c\}, \{c\})$ is added to $\mathcal{T}$;
- second, for each $\mathsf{dir} \in \{\rightarrow, \leftarrow\}$ and each entity c such that, for both $i = 1, 2$, there exists $(c_i, d_i, c)^{\mathsf{dir}} \in G$ with $c_i \in V_i$ the sets

$$E_i = \{d_i \mid (c_i, d_i, c)^{\mathsf{dir}} \in G \text{ for } c_i \in V_i\}$$

  are considered; if the sets $E_1 \setminus E_2$ and $E_2 \setminus E_1$ (i.e., the sets of edge entities not covered in the previous case) are both non-empty, then an edge labelled $(E_1 \setminus E_2,\ E_2 \setminus E_1,\ \mathsf{dir})$ from v to a new node labelled $(\{c\}, \{c\})$ is added;
- third, for each $\mathsf{dir} \in \{\rightarrow, \leftarrow\}$ and each d such that, for both $i = 1, 2$, there are triples $(c_i, d, c_i')^{\mathsf{dir}} \in G$ with $c_i \in V_i$ the sets

$$V_i' = \{c_i' \mid (c_i, d, c_i')^{\mathsf{dir}} \in G \text{ for } c_i \in V_i\}$$

  are considered; if $V_1' \setminus V_2'$ and $V_2' \setminus V_1'$ (i.e., the sets of not covered node entities) are non-empty, then an edge labelled $(\{d\}, \{d\}, \mathsf{dir})$ from v to a new node v' labelled $(V_1' \setminus V_2',\ V_2' \setminus V_1')$ is added; moreover, if the depth of v is non-zero, then GENERATE_TREE is recursively called for v';
- finally, for both $\mathsf{dir} \in \{\rightarrow, \leftarrow\}$ the sets

$$E_i = \{d_i \mid (c_i, d_i, c_i')^{\mathsf{dir}} \in G \text{ for } c_i \in V_i\} \text{ and}$$
$$V_i' = \{c_i' \mid (c_i, d_i, c_i')^{\mathsf{dir}} \in G \text{ for } c_i \in V_i \text{ and } d_i \in E_i \setminus E_{3-i}\}$$

  are considered for both $i = 1, 2$; if the sets $E_1 \setminus E_2$, $E_2 \setminus E_1$, $V_1' \setminus V_2'$, and $V_2' \setminus V_1'$ are all non-empty, then an edge labelled $(E_1 \setminus E_2,\ E_2 \setminus E_1,\ \mathsf{dir})$ from v to a new node v' labelled $(V_1' \setminus V_2',\ V_2' \setminus V_1')$ is added; moreover, if the depth of v is non-zero, then GENERATE_TREE is called for v'.

After all these extensions, $\mathcal{T}$ is returned to the previous level of recursion.

As mentioned above, the resulting $\mathcal{T}_{gen}$ is a pair tree; however, it may not be a similarity tree for a and b, since some edges may not be justified in G. So, in the second step (line 3) of COMPUTE_APPROX_MSSQ, pair tree $\mathcal{T}_{gen}$ is refined from the leaves upwards using subroutine UNCOUPLE_NODES, which ensures that each edge in the tree is suitably justified, and hence yields a similarity tree $\mathcal{T}_{sim}$ for a and b in G. In particular, this subroutine considers nodes of its input pair tree $\mathcal{T}$ from leaves to the root, and for each node v under consideration and each child v' of v—that is, a node with an edge $e = (v, v')$—the following is performed, where (V_1, V_2), (E_1, E_2, dir), and (V_1', V_2') are labels of v, e, and v', respectively:

- a node v^* and an edge (v^*, v') labelled (V_1^*, V_2^*) and $(E_1^*, E_2^*, \mathsf{dir})$, respectively, are added to $\mathcal{T}$, for maximal sets $V_i^* \subseteq V_i$ and $E_i^* \subseteq E_i$, $i = 1, 2$, with (v^*, v') justified by G;
- if v is not the root then an edge (v_p, v^*) labelled as the incoming edge (v_p, v) to v is added to $\mathcal{T}$;

– when all children of v are processed, each group of children with the same label are merged to one, and v is removed.

Note that, by construction, the resulting $\mathcal{T}_{sim}$ is a pair tree as well; moreover, we will see that, contrary to $\mathcal{T}_{gen}$, it is a similarity tree.

Finally, in the last step (line 4), algorithm COMPUTE_APPROX_MSSQ constructs the query corresponding to the similarity tree according to Definition 5, which is guaranteed to be a similarity query by Proposition 3.

Overall, we arrive to the following correctness theorem.

Theorem 6. *For each positive integer* dep, COMPUTE_APPROX_MSSQ *computes a similarity query for entities a and b in a graph G.*

Proof (Sketch). The claim follows from the construction and Proposition 3. Indeed, the pair tree $\mathcal{T}_{sim}$ is a similarity tree for input G, a, and b because the root is labelled with $(\{a\}, \{b\})$, while all the edges are processed in UNCOUPLE_NODES in the bottom-up manner and explicitly verified to be justified by G. □

We next briefly discuss the running time of the algorithm. One execution of the GENERATE_TREE subroutine runs in $\mathcal{O}(\rho \cdot |G|)$, where ρ is the number of different entities appearing in the predicate position in triples from G. GENERATE_TREE is recursively called at most $(2\rho)^{\mathsf{dep}-1}$ times, hence the full runtime of these calls is $\mathcal{O}(\rho^{\mathsf{dep}} \cdot |G|)$. Then the subroutine UNCOUPLE_NODES performs a check on $\mathcal{O}(\rho^{\mathsf{dep}} \cdot |G|)$ pair tree nodes, each check being in $\mathcal{O}(|G|)$. Hence, COMPUTE_APPROX_MSSQ runs in $\mathcal{O}(\rho^{\mathsf{dep}} \cdot |G|^2)$ in the worst case. Note that ρ for a graph G is typically much smaller in practice than the number of triples in G (e.g., $\rho = 128$ for full YAGO), and the checks in UNCOUPLE_NODES are made for all triples in G containing the current entity, which usually constitute only a small fraction of G. This makes the algorithm suitable for real-case scenarios, which we will demonstrate in the next section.

Finally, we observe that it is possible to find an example where the approximating SQ has arbitrary many answers while the MSSQ has just two (i.e., the input entities). So, there is no constant approximation ratio for our algorithm. However, the same can be said about any approximation algorithm that outputs a SQ that is not an MSSQ, so we cannot hope for such theoretical guarantees. Instead, we evaluate the quality of our approximation empirically in Sect. 6.

6 Evaluation

We implemented our two similarity algorithms COMPUTE_MSSQ and COMPUTE_APPROX_MSSQ in Python. We then evaluated the performance of our implementations and estimated to what extent the similarity queries computed by algorithm COMPUTE_APPROX_MSSQ approximate MSSQs computed by algorithm COMPUTE_MSSQ in practical cases. We used the following three RDF graphs (datasets) in our experiments:

Table 1. Runtime (in seconds) and output query size (in number of triples) of COMPUTE_APPROX_MSSQ on the LUBM1, TFG, and YAGO graphs

		Runtime				Size
RDF graph	Depth	Avg	Median	Max	Timeouts	Avg
LUBM1	1	0.000851	0.000346	0.006910	–	1.88
	2	0.002690	0.000971	0.036051	–	11.25
	3	0.072132	0.001389	2.101702	–	463.00
	4	0.348439	0.002058	8.558924	–	3235.02
TFG	1	0.000811	0.000356	0.045334	–	0.75
	2	0.001115	0.000373	0.045334	–	3.54
	3	0.058080	0.000415	3.540030	–	592.86
	4	67.203592	11.308518	352.100547	–	35904.21
YAGO	1	0.000918	0.000327	0.056005	–	0.73
	2	0.006476	0.000338	0.175918	–	7.81
	3	8.318439	0.000347	461.952534	–	149.63
	4	84.950921	0.640530	488.342738	3	1287.67

– the synthetic graph LUBM1 [12] consisting of 100,543 triples over 26,437 entities, out of which 17 appear in the predicate positions;
– a subset of the anonymised Twitter follower graph (TFG) [18] consisting of 713,319 triples over 404,719 entities, only one of which (i.e., entity *follows*) appears in the predicate positions; and
– a subset of YAGO graph [19] consisting of 1,069,072 triples over 604,905 entities, out of which 42 appear in the predicate positions.

The graphs are different in size and nature: YAGO has a rich set of property entities, while TFG uses only one; LUBM1 has a regular structure and resembles data typically encountered in databases, whereas YAGO is more heterogeneous.

All experiments were performed on a MacBook Air laptop with macOS 10.14, 1.6 GHz Intel Core i5 processor, and 16 GB 2133 MHz LPDDR3 memory.

6.1 Performance Analysis

We evaluated the runtime of our implementation of COMPUTE_APPROX_MSSQ for increasing values of the depth parameter. For this, we randomly selected 100 pairs of entities in each graph and, for each such pair, we ran the implemented algorithm for values of the depth parameter ranging from 1 to 4. For each graph and each depth value, we recorded the average, median and maximum runtime as well as the average number of triple patterns in a query amongst all the selected pairs of entities. We limited the maximum depth to 4, since queries beyond that depth are very difficult to comprehend due to their size and structure; indeed, psychologists established precise limitations in the human capacity to store and process information, where experiments show that most people would have trouble keeping in memory chains of related pieces of information longer than 4 [8].

Our results for LUBM1, TFG, and YAGO are summarised in Table 1. We can observe that our similarity queries can be computed efficiently with sub-second average running times in most cases; in contrast our implementation of exact COMPUTE_MSSQ timed out in all cases. The average runtime becomes larger for depth 4 for larger datasets, such as TFG and YAGO; in case of YAGO the algorithm reached 3 timeouts for 500 s threshold. However, we can also observe that output queries tend to become very large (and hence difficult to interpret, verbalise, and comprehend) for depths greater than 3. Therefore, it is only practical to consider approximated MSSQs of depth up to 3, for which our algorithm can always compute a similarity query.

6.2 Query Specificity Analysis

In this section we report the results of an experiment that aims to estimate how different the similarity queries computed using COMPUTE_APPROX_MSSQ are from the actual MSSQs computed by the exact algorithm COMPUTE_MSSQ. Unfortunately, our implementation of COMPUTE_MSSQ timed out and hence failed to produce a query for all inputs in our datasets; thus, a direct comparison of the answers to the similarity queries produced by the algorithms is not feasible. To circumvent this limitation, we have designed an experiment consisting of the following steps for each of the LUBM1, TFG, and YAGO graphs:

1. we first created 40 random connected graphs, called *pattern graphs*, such that each of them consists of 4 triples, and exactly 20 are acyclic;
2. for each pattern graph G, we created its copy G' with all entities renamed to fresh entities;
3. we then picked an entity a from each such G at random and the corresponding a' in the copy G' and ran both algorithms on $G \cup G'$ as a graph and a, a' as input entities; the approximation algorithm was run for depths 1 to 3;
4. finally, we evaluated the resulting queries on the considered graph (LUBM1, TFG, or YAGO) and compared the answers.

Intuitively, each pattern graph G represents a 'pattern' that may occur in the real data (and hence a pattern that will be reflected in the MSSQ). The approximation algorithm COMPUTE_APPROX_MSSQ constructs a tree-like query where variables in the predicate positions of triple patterns occur at most once, and hence the query returned by COMPUTE_APPROX_MSSQ on a graph $G \cup G'$ may not faithfully reflect the data pattern encoded by G. By evaluating the resulting queries in step 4 we are also assessing how common each pattern is in the graph (based on the number of answers to the MSSQ) as well as how faithfully the approximated query reflects the pattern.

Our results are summarised in Table 2. As can be seen from the average percentage of entities contained in query answer sets, similarity queries computed by COMPUTE_APPROX_MSSQ become more specific and closer to MSSQs as

Table 2. Average number of answers (avg) and average percentage of all entities in answers (%) to MSSQs and the approximating queries, computed over acyclic (A) and cyclic (C) pattern graphs and evaluated on the LUBM1, TFG, and YAGO graphs

RDF graph		MSSQs		Approximations					
		Avg	%	dep = 1		dep = 2		dep = 3	
				Avg	%	Avg	%	Avg	%
LUBM1	A	7983.15	30.20	12157.45	45.97	10360.35	39.19	10332.05	39.08
	C	33.65	0.13	6697.00	25.33	2960.45	11.20	2522.35	9.54
TFG	A	156566.47	38.69	161958.50	40.02	161345.60	39.87	156566.47	38.69
	C	42838.20	10.58	83284.95	20.59	82541.10	20.39	78122.65	19.30
YAGO	A	147284.37	24.51	207236.80	34.26	175541.00	29.02	169331.26	27.99
	C	7175.25	1.19	83641.85	13.83	44372.90	7.34	41518.15	6.86

the depth grows. Unsurprisingly, the approximating queries evaluated on the TFG graph are almost identical to MSSQs, since the graph contains a single relation. The approximation error consistently goes below 10% for both cyclic and acyclic pattern graphs for depth 3 on all datasets, as can be seen from the percentage for MSSQs and approximated queries of dep = 3. This makes COMPUTE_APPROX_MSSQ suitable for real-world applications of entity comparison.

7 Related Work

Exploring relationships between entities in RDF graphs is a recent and growing research topic. Some approaches focus on general relatedness and connectedness of entities. They explore paths connecting given entities together and analyse patterns in these paths [1,6,11,14,16]. More generic approaches look at patterns that are common for several entities in a graph. An approach by El Hassad et al. [9,10] attempts to find commonalities between Web resources by computing the least general generalisation (lgg) of the RDF data containing these resources. The computation is based on the RDFS entailment rules, and an lgg is itself an RDF graph that entails subgraphs of the input RDF dataset that contain the target Web resources. To the best of our knowledge, our recent work [17] is the only one focussing not only on patterns common for input entities (see Sect. 3), but also on patterns that differentiate input entities from each other.

The problem of computing similarity and difference queries can be viewed as an instance of the query reverse engineering (QRE) problem; in case of exact similarities, the problem becomes an instance of the definability problem, a more restricted version of QRE. In particular, the QRE problem for a query language takes as input a dataset and two disjoint sets of positive and negative example tuples of constants, and decides whether there exists a query in the language whose answers over the dataset contain all the positive examples but none of the negative examples. The definability problem is the same except there are no negative examples, but the answers to the query should be exactly the positive examples. Both problems have been studied for various query languages [5,13, 20,22,23], including SPARQL [2] and CQs [4,21]. Hence, our work contributes to the field by setting complexity bounds for monadic unary CQACs.

Finally, computing MSSQs is related to the problem of finding the least common subsumer for description logic (DL) concepts [3,7], which, for two individuals and a set of concept and role names, requires to compute a DL concept that contains both individuals and is most specific modulo concept subsumption.

8 Conclusion and Future Work

We investigated the problem of entity comparison in knoweldge graphs, taking as the basis our recently proposed framework [17], in which entity comparison is modelled via similarity queries. In particular, we extended the language of similarity queries to consider a richer fragment of SPARQL allowing for numeric filter expressions, and studied the complexity of computing various similarity queries in this fragment. We also proposed and implemented a scalable algorithm that is guaranteed to compute a similarity query and can be used on large knowledge graphs. An immediate step of future research is to study difference queries in the extended query language, and to create scalable algorithms for computing difference queries that are as generic as possible for the given entities in a graph. Another important problem is to present similarity and difference queries to the user in a comprehensible way, which is not trivial given their size and complicated structure. Possible solutions include splitting the queries into subqueries and ranking, visualising or verbalising them, and allowing the users to iteratively expand only the parts of queries they are interested in. Once these problems are solved, a comprehensive entity comparison tool would be possible.

Acknowledgements. This research was supported by the SIRIUS Centre for Scalable Data Access and the EPSRC projects DBOnto, MaSI^3, and ED^3.

References

1. Aebeloe, C., Montoya, G., Setty, V., Hose, K.: Discovering diversified paths in knowledge bases. Proc. VLDB Endow. **11**(12), 2002–2005 (2018)
2. Arenas, M., Diaz, G.I., Kostylev, E.V.: Reverse engineering SPARQL queries. In: Proceedings of WWW, pp. 239–249 (2016)
3. Baader, F., Turhan, A.-Y.: On the problem of computing small representations of least common subsumers. In: Jarke, M., Lakemeyer, G., Koehler, J. (eds.) KI 2002. LNCS (LNAI), vol. 2479, pp. 99–113. Springer, Heidelberg (2002). https://doi.org/10.1007/3-540-45751-8_7
4. Barceló, P., Romero, M.: The complexity of reverse engineering problems for conjunctive queries. In: Proceedings of ICDT, pp. 7:1–7:17 (2017)
5. Bonifati, A., Ciucanu, R., Lemay, A.: Learning path queries on graph databases. In: Proceedings of EDBT, pp. 109–120 (2015)

6. Cheng, G., Zhang, Y., Qu, Y.: Explass: exploring associations between entities via top-K ontological patterns and facets. In: Mika, P., et al. (eds.) ISWC 2014. LNCS, vol. 8797, pp. 422–437. Springer, Cham (2014). https://doi.org/10.1007/978-3-319-11915-1_27
7. Colucci, S., Donini, F.M., Giannini, S., Di Sciascio, E.: Defining and computing least common subsumers in RDF. Web Semant. **39**, 62–80 (2016)
8. Cowan, N.: The magical number 4 in short-term memory: A reconsideration of mental storage capacity. Behav. Brain Sci. **24**(1), 87–114 (2001)
9. El Hassad, S., Goasdoué, F., Jaudoin, H.: Learning commonalities in RDF. In: Blomqvist, E., Maynard, D., Gangemi, A., Hoekstra, R., Hitzler, P., Hartig, O. (eds.) ESWC 2017. LNCS, vol. 10249, pp. 502–517. Springer, Cham (2017). https://doi.org/10.1007/978-3-319-58068-5_31
10. El Hassad, S., Goasdoué, F., Jaudoin, H.: Learning commonalities in SPARQL. In: d'Amato, C., et al. (eds.) ISWC 2017. LNCS, vol. 10587, pp. 278–295. Springer, Cham (2017). https://doi.org/10.1007/978-3-319-68288-4_17
11. Fionda, V., Pirrò, G.: Explaining and querying knowledge graphs by relatedness. Proc. VLDB Endow. **10**(12), 1913–1916 (2017)
12. Guo, Y., Pan, Z., Heflin, J.: LUBM: a benchmark for OWL knowledge base systems. Web Semant. **3**(2–3), 158–182 (2005)
13. Gutiérrez-Basulto, V., Jung, J.C., Sabellek, L.: Reverse engineering queries in ontology-enriched systems: The case of expressive horn description logic ontologies. In: Proceedings of IJCAI, pp. 1847–1853 (2018)
14. Heim, P., Hellmann, S., Lehmann, J., Lohmann, S., Stegemann, T.: RelFinder: Revealing relationships in RDF knowledge bases. In: Chua, T.-S., Kompatsiaris, Y., Mérialdo, B., Haas, W., Thallinger, G., Bailer, W. (eds.) SAMT 2009. LNCS, vol. 5887, pp. 182–187. Springer, Heidelberg (2009). https://doi.org/10.1007/978-3-642-10543-2_21
15. Klug, A.: On conjunctive queries containing inequalities. J. ACM **35**(1), 146–160 (1988)
16. Lehmann, J., Schüppel, J., Auer, S.: Discovering unknown connections - the DBpedia relationship finder. Proc. CSSW **113**, 99–110 (2007)
17. Petrova, A., Sherkhonov, E., Cuenca Grau, B., Horrocks, I.: Entity comparison in RDF graphs. In: d'Amato, C., et al. (eds.) ISWC 2017. LNCS, vol. 10587, pp. 526–541. Springer, Cham (2017). https://doi.org/10.1007/978-3-319-68288-4_31
18. Rossi, R.A., Gleich, D.F.: A dynamical system for PageRank with time-dependent teleportation. Internet Math. **10**(1), 188–217 (2014)
19. Suchanek, F.M., Kasneci, G., Weikum, G.: YAGO: A large ontology from Wikipedia and Wordnet. Web Semant. **6**(3), 203–217 (2008)
20. Tan, W.C., Zhang, M., Elmeleegy, H., Srivastava, D.: Reverse engineering aggregation queries. PVLDB **10**(11), 1394–1405 (2017)
21. ten Cate, B., Dalmau, V.: The product homomorphism problem and applications. In: Proceedings of ICDT, pp. 161–176 (2015)
22. Weiss, Y.Y., Cohen, S.: Reverse engineering SPJ-queries from examples. In: Proceedings of PODS, pp. 151–166 (2017)
23. Zhang, M., Elmeleegy, H., Procopiuc, C.M., Srivastava, D.: Reverse engineering complex join queries. In: Proceedings of SIGMOD, pp. 809–820 (2013)

Anytime Large-Scale Analytics of Linked Open Data

Arnaud Soulet[1,2(✉)] and Fabian M. Suchanek[2]

[1] Université de Tours, LIFAT, Blois, France
arnaud.soulet@univ-tours.fr
[2] Telecom Paris, Institut Polytechnique de Paris, Paris, France
{soulet,suchanek}@telecom-paris.fr

Abstract. Analytical queries are queries with numerical aggregators: computing the average number of objects per property, identifying the most frequent subjects, etc. Such queries are essential to monitor the quality and the content of the Linked Open Data (LOD) cloud. Many analytical queries cannot be executed directly on the SPARQL endpoints, because the fair use policy cuts off expensive queries. In this paper, we show how to rewrite such queries into a set of queries that each satisfy the fair use policy. We then show how to execute these queries in such a way that the result provably converges to the exact query answer. Our algorithm is an anytime algorithm, meaning that it can give intermediate approximate results at any time point. Our experiments show that the approach converges rapidly towards the exact solution, and that it can compute even complex indicators at the scale of the LOD cloud.

1 Introduction

The Linked Open Data (LOD) cloud accumulates more and more triplestores, which are themselves more and more voluminous. Several statistical indicators have been proposed to monitor the content and the quality of the data: Mapping methods [3,11,29] provide statistical indicators to summarize the property and class usage and the links between them. Other indicators evaluate the completeness of the data [16,24] or the representativeness of the properties [34]. However, the increase in volume that makes these indicators more necessary also makes them harder to compute. The most recent methods adopt distributed architectures [14,33] that centralize the data, and then execute the indicator queries on that centralized data repository. To compute the exact query result, these approaches thus require the materialization of the entire LOD cloud. This is expensive in both storage space and processing time.

It would thus be interesting to calculate these indicators not on a centralized data repository, but directly from the SPARQL endpoints. Unfortunately, computing large-scale analytical indicators with SPARQL queries is very challenging. First, these queries concern hundreds of triplestores – while federated query processing [30] already has difficulties coping with a dozen of them. Second, existing engines assume that the SPARQL endpoints have no usage limits.

C. Ghidini et al. (Eds.): ISWC 2019, LNCS 11778, pp. 576–592, 2019.
https://doi.org/10.1007/978-3-030-30793-6_33

However, public SPARQL endpoints have relatively strict fair use policies, which cut off queries that are too expensive. As it turns out, statistical indicators are usually exactly among the most expensive queries. For instance, computing the proportion of each property of the LOD cloud involves every single triple of every single triplestore – an impossibility to compute under current fair use policies.

This paper proposes to relax the notion of exact query answers, and to compute *approximate query answers* instead. Given an analytical query and a set of triplestores, we propose to split the query into a series of smaller queries that each respect the fair use policies. We have developed an algorithm that aggregates these query answers into an approximate answer. Our algorithm is an anytime algorithm, meaning that the approximate answer can be read off at any time, and provably converges to the exact answer over time. In this way, our approach does not only avoid the large storage requirements of centralized solutions, but it also delivers a first answer very quickly, while at the same time respecting the fair use policies. More specifically, our contributions are as follows:

- We provide an algebraic formalization of analytical queries in the context of fair use policies.
- We propose a parallelizable anytime algorithm whose results are proportional to the exact query answer and provably converge to it.
- We show the efficiency of our approach by computing complex indicators on a large part of the LOD cloud.

This paper is organized as follows. Section 2 reviews related work. Section 3 introduces the notions of analytical queries and fair use policies. Section 4 presents our algorithm. Section 5 provides experimental results, before Sect. 6 concludes.

2 Related Work

Centralized Query Answering. Several architectures have been proposed to handle SPARQL queries on large volumes of data. Some approaches use the Pig Latin language [22,23], others use Spark [32], and again others HBase [15]. For analytical queries, groupings and aggregates are the most important aspects. Several architectures have been specifically designed for this use case:

LODStats [3] is inspired by approaches for querying RDF streams [5,8]. It parallelizes streaming and sorting techniques to efficiently process RDF data. More recent methods either use HDFS (LODOP [14]) or store the data in memory (DistLODStats [33] via Spark). Exact rewriting rules have also been proposed to optimize the execution of such queries with groupings and aggregates in RDF data [11]. All of these approaches centralize the data. This does not just come with high download cost and high disk storage requirements, but also long execution times. Our method, in contrast, does not centralize the data and computes a continuous approximation of the query answer.

Federated Query Answering. Federated query systems avoid the centralization of the data by executing SPARQL queries directly over several endpoints [30]. Some of these approaches are dedicated in particular to aggregate queries [20]. These systems decompose a query into a set of queries that are executed on each triplestore. Then the results are recombined to yield the final query answer. A recent study analyzes the large-scale performance of these approaches [31]. Some systems are specifically dedicated to privacy [21] or authorization constraints [12]. However, none of these systems is able to respect the fair use policies of SPARQL endpoints. Much like on the Deep Web [7], queries that do not respect this policy will simply fail. This issue is even more important in the case of analytical queries, which concern many public endpoints, and potentially all entities in each of them. Our approach, in contrast, makes sure that the federated queries satisfy the fair use policy, while at the same time guaranteeing that the recombined result tends towards the exact answer.

Query Answering by Samples. Several works aim at computing aggregates by sampling the data directly. With regard to RDF graphs, only [17,25] samples the data to study its statistics. This approach requires a partial centralization of the data and offers no theoretical guarantee on the exactness of the result. Our approach, in contrast, provably converges to a result proportional to the exact answer. Finally, there are several proposals about sampling operators in the database field [27,28]. Unfortunately, these operators cannot be used in our scenario, because they are not implemented by SPARQL endpoints. Similarly, there are anytime approaches [19] to compute aggregates in databases, but these work designed for centralized data directly modify the query execution plan and the read-access to the data.

3 Preliminaries

3.1 Basic Definitions

This work relies on the SPARQL algebra framework [13], whose notations are mainly inspired from traditional relational algebra [1]. In all of the following our sets are multi-sets, i.e., they can contain the same element several times. In the algebraic framework, a relation $T[A_1, .., A_n]$ consists of a name T, attribute names $A_1, ..., A_n$ (the *schema*) and a set of n-tuples. For ease of notation, we will often identify a relation with its set of tuples. A triplestore is a relation with the 3 attributes subject, property, and object (which we omit because they are always the same). The Linked Open Data (LOD) cloud is a set of triplestores $\{T_1, \dots, T_N\}$. For instance, Table 1 shows two small triplestores T_{Caesar} and T_{daVinci}, which contain 16 triples with 2 properties.

The following operators are defined on relations: The *Cartesian product* of two relations R and S is defined as $R \times S = \{(t, u) | t \in R \wedge u \in S\}$. The *union*, the *intersection* and the *difference* of two relations R and S with the same schema are defined as $R \cup S$, $R \cap S$ and $R - S$, respectively. Given a relation R and a boolean formula f, the *selection* $\sigma_f(I) = \{t | t \in I \wedge f(t)\}$ selects the tuples of R that satisfy the logical formula f. Given a relation R with at least the attributes $A_1, ...A_n$, the *extended projection* $\pi_{A_1,...,A_n}(R) =$

Table 1. A toy example with 2 triplestores with FOAF properties

T_{Caesar}

subj	prop	obj
Gaius	**parentOf**	Julius
Gaius	**parentOf**	JuliaTheE.
Gaius	**parentOf**	JuliaTheY.
Marcus	**parentOf**	Atia
JuliaTheY.	**parentOf**	Atia
Gaius	**gender**	male
Julius	**gender**	male
JuliaTheE.	**gender**	female
JuliaTheY.	**gender**	female
Marcus	**gender**	male
Atia	**gender**	female

T_{daVinci}

subj	prop	obj
Piero	**parentOf**	Leonardo
Caterina	**parentOf**	Leonardo
Piero	**gender**	male
Caterina	**gender**	female
Leonardo	**gender**	male

$\{t[A_1, \ldots, A_n] | t \in R\}$ preserves only the attributes $A_1, \ldots, A_n$ of R. Besides, the projection also allows extending the relation by arithmetic expressions and the (re)naming of expressions. For instance, $\pi_{A+B \rightarrow B', C \rightarrow C'}(R)$ creates a new relation where the first attribute called B' results from the arithmetic expression $A + B$ and the second attribute corresponds to C, but was renamed to C'. Given a relation R with at least the attributes $A_1, \ldots, A_n, B$, and given an aggregation function `AGG` (which can be `COUNT`, `SUM`, `MAX`, `MIN`), a *grouping* $\gamma_{A_1,\ldots,A_n,\texttt{AGG}(B)}(R) = \{(a_1, \ldots, a_n, \texttt{AGG}(\pi_B(\sigma_{A_1=a_1 \wedge \cdots \wedge A_n=a_n}(R)))$ $|(a_1, \ldots, a_n) \in \pi_{A_1,\ldots,A_n}(R)\}$ groups tuples of I by $A_1, \ldots A_n$ and computes `AGG` on the attribute B. Our approach currently does not support an aggregation operator to compute the median. However, our approach will work for the average, which can be decomposed into `SUM` and `COUNT` aggregates. The expression $\gamma_{A_1,\ldots,A_n}(R)$ has the same effect as a projection on $A_1, \ldots, A_n$, but it does not retain duplicates. Finally, a *query* q is a function from one relation to another one. The set of attributes of the result of q is denoted by $\mathbf{sch}(q)$.

3.2 Analytical Queries

Our definition of analytical queries is inspired by multi-dimensional queries in online analytical processing (OLAP) [9,10]:

Definition 1 (Analytical query). *An analytical query is a query of the form* $\gamma_{A_1,\ldots,A_n,\texttt{AGG}(B)}(q(T))$, *where* q *is a query such that* $\{A_1, \ldots, A_n, B\} \subseteq \mathbf{sch}(q)$.

For example, the following analytical query counts, for each property p and each integer i how many subjects have exactly i objects for property p:

$$\alpha_{card} \equiv \gamma_{prop,card,\texttt{COUNT}(subj)\rightarrow count}(\gamma_{subj,prop,\texttt{COUNT}(obj)\rightarrow card}(T))$$

In this query, $A_1 = prop$ and $A_2 = card$ are two aggregate attributes; *subj* is the measure attribute B; `COUNT` is the aggregate function, and

$\gamma_{subj,prop,\texttt{COUNT}(obj)\rightarrow card}(T)$ is the query q. In this case, the aggregation is computed on the view $\gamma_{subj,prop,\texttt{COUNT}(obj)\rightarrow card}(T)$, which contains the number of objects for each pair of a subject and a property. Table 2 shows how this query is executed on $T_{\text{Caesar}} \cup T_{\text{daVinci}}$ from Table 1: The result tells us that there are 4 subjects with 1 child, 1 subject with 3 children, and 9 subjects with 1 gender. This information is particularly useful for discovering maximum cardinality constraints [26] (e.g., that there is at most one **gender** for a subject).

Table 2. Execution of the analytical query α_{card} on $T_{\text{Caesar}} \cup T_{\text{daVinci}}$

$\alpha_{card}(T_{\text{Caesar}})$

prop	card	count
gender	1	6
parentOf	1	2
parentOf	3	1

$+$

$\alpha_{card}(T_{\text{daVinci}})$

prop	card	count
gender	1	3
parentOf	1	2

$\rightarrow$

$\alpha_{card}(T_{\text{Caesar}} \cup T_{\text{daVinci}})$

prop	card	count
gender	1	9
parentOf	1	4
parentOf	3	1

Table 3. Examples of analytical queries

Cardinality distribution per property and subject:

$$\alpha_{card} \equiv \gamma_{prop,card,\texttt{COUNT}(subj)\rightarrow count}(\gamma_{subj,prop,\texttt{COUNT}(obj)\rightarrow card}(T))$$

First significant digit distribution per property:

$$\alpha_{FSD} \equiv \gamma_{prop,fsd,\texttt{COUNT}(obj)\rightarrow count}(\gamma_{obj,prop,\texttt{FSD}(\texttt{COUNT}(subj))\rightarrow fsd}(T))$$

Co-class usage per property:

$$\alpha_{att} \equiv \gamma_{p,o',o'',\texttt{COUNT}(*)\rightarrow count}(\sigma_{s=s'=s''\wedge p'=p''=\texttt{rdf:type}}(T \times T' \times T''))$$

Maximum value for each numerical property:

$$\alpha_{max} \equiv \gamma_{prop,\texttt{MAX}(obj)\rightarrow max}(\sigma_{\texttt{datatype}(prop)\in\{int,float\}}(T))$$

Property usage: $\alpha_{prop} \equiv \gamma_{prop,\texttt{COUNT}(*)\rightarrow count}(T)$

Class usage: $\alpha_{class} \equiv \gamma_{obj,\texttt{COUNT}(*)\rightarrow count}(\sigma_{prop=\texttt{rdf:type}}(T))$

Our definition of analytical queries is very general: It allows the computation of arbitrary aggregations on arbitrary views on the data. With this, our definition is more expressive than most of the proposals in the literature, which have often focused on statistics that concern individual triples [3,11]. Table 3 shows more examples of analytical queries. The second query α_{FSD} uses the function FSD, which, given a number (e.g., 42) returns the first significant digit of that number (here: 4). The query α_{FSD} then calculates for each property the distribution of the first significant digits of the fact number per object. This query is particularly useful for estimating the representativeness of a knowledge base by exploiting Benford's law [34]. We will use this query in Sect. 5 to evaluate the representativeness of the LOD cloud. The query α_{att} counts the number of subjects at the intersection of two classes (here, obj' and obj'') for each property. Such statistics are useful for identifying the obligatory attributes for a given class [24]. Finally, the last three queries come from [3]. They return the usage of properties and classes as well as the maximum value for numerical properties.

As said above, these last three queries are less sophisticated because their inner query q is a simple filter.

In the following, we will often have to combine the results of analytical queries from several relations:

Definition 2 (Aggregator). *The aggregator version of an analytical query* $\alpha(T) \equiv \gamma_{A_1,\ldots,A_n,\mathtt{AGG}(B)}(q(T))$*, denoted* $\widetilde{\alpha}(T)$*, is* $\gamma_{A_1,\ldots,A_n,\widetilde{\mathtt{AGG}}(B)}(T)$*, where* $\widetilde{\mathtt{COUNT}} = \mathtt{SUM}$ *and* $\widetilde{\mathtt{AGG}} = \mathtt{AGG}$ *otherwise.*

For example, with MAX as aggregate function, we have $\widetilde{\alpha}_{max} \equiv \gamma_{prop,\mathtt{MAX}(obj)\rightarrow max}(T)$ (because $\widetilde{\mathtt{MAX}} = \mathtt{MAX}$). The aggregator version of a query serves to combine the results of an analytical query on two triplestores. For example, we can compute $\widetilde{\alpha}_{card}(\alpha_{card}(T_{\mathrm{Caesar}}) \cup \alpha_{card}(T_{\mathrm{daVinci}}))$. In this expression, $\widetilde{\alpha}_{card}$ will just copy all rows of its argument, and merge any two rows that concern the same property and the same cardinality by summing up the two count values. Since T_{Caesar} and T_{daVinci} have no subject in common, the result is equivalent to $\alpha_{card}(T_{\mathrm{Caesar}} \cup T_{\mathrm{daVinci}})$ (see again Table 2). Thus, instead of computing α_{card} on the union of T_{Caesar} and T_{daVinci}, we can compute α_{card} on each of the triplestores and aggregate the results by $\widetilde{\alpha}_{card}$.

3.3 Fair Use Policy

The fair use policy of a triplestore T, denoted by $\mathcal{P}_T$, is the set of limits imposed by the data provider. Formally, $Q \models \mathcal{P}_T$ means that the set of queries Q satisfies the fair use policy of T. The execution time between two queries is often an important criterion for such policies. Let Q be a set of queries. Given two queries $q_1 \in Q$ and $q_2 \in Q$, $\mathtt{t}(q_1, q_2)$ denotes the delay between the execution of two queries. For instance, for DBpedia[1], there is a limit on the number of connections per second you can make, as well as restrictions on result set sizes and query time. The restriction on the result set size is usually not a problem: We can simply execute the same query several times, and use the OFFSET clause to retrieve different parts of the result. It is the restriction on the query execution time that usually spoils the query, because the query will use up the time budget and then abort without a result.

To deal with this difficulty, our approach requires the policies to have two properties. First, a policy $\mathcal{P}$ is *monotone* iff for all $Q_1 \models \mathcal{P}$ and $Q_2 \models \mathcal{P}$, there exists a delay d such that $Q_1 \cup Q_2 \models \mathcal{P}$ if $min_{q_1 \in Q_1, q_2 \in Q_2} \mathtt{t}(q_1, q_2) \geq d$. A monotone behavior for a policy means that if some queries have been successfully executed, it will be possible to execute them again (observing a delay d). Consequently, if a query is rejected because the query number per time limit is reached, the monotone property guarantees that we can successfully fire a new query after a short waiting time. Second, a policy $\mathcal{P}$ is *consistent* iff any query q that satisfies the policy of a triplestore T also satisfies the policy on a smaller portion: $\forall T' \subseteq T : (q(T) \models \mathcal{P}) \Rightarrow (q(T') \models \mathcal{P})$. A consistent behavior for a policy means that if a query has been successfully executed on a set of triples,

[1] https://wiki.dbpedia.org/public-sparql-endpoint.

Table 4. $\alpha_{card}(T_{\text{Caesar}} \cup T_{\text{daVinci}})$ and its approximation

α_{card}

prop	card	count
gender	1	9
parentOf	1	4
parentOf	3	1

→ $\overline{\alpha_{card}}$

...	count
...	$9/14 = 0.64$
...	$4/14 = 0.29$
...	$1/14 = 0.07$

(a) α_{card}

$A_{\alpha_{card}}$

prop	card	count
gender	1	4
parentOf	1	2

→ $\overline{A_{\alpha_{card}}}$

...	count
...	$4/6 = 0.66$
...	$2/6 = 0.33$

(b) Approximation of α_{card}

the same query can be executed on a subset of these triples. In the following, we assume that all policies are both monotone and consistent. In practice, we found that these two assumptions are satisfied by most triplestores, including DBpedia. The following sections will show how to use these properties in order to overcome the restriction on query time.

3.4 Problem Statement

In most cases, it is not possible to execute an analytical query directly on the SPARQL endpoint of a large triplestore due to the fair use policy. For instance, α_{card} executed on DBpedia with the public SPARQL endpoint leads to a timeout error. Therefore, our goal is to split an analytical query into a set of queries that each respect the policy. Then, we will combine the different answers in order to approximate the original query answer. We formalize the notion of approximation by introducing a distance between two analytical queries:

Definition 3 (Distance). *Given two relations $R_1[A_1, \ldots, A_n, B]$ and $R_2[A_1, \ldots, A_n, B]$ where B is a numerical attribute, the distance between R_1 and R_2, denoted by $||R_1 - R_2||_2$, is the Euclidean distance between the normalized vectors of values stemming from each group $\langle a_1, \ldots, a_n, v\rangle$:*

$$||R_1 - R_2||_2 = \sqrt{\sum_{\langle a_1,\ldots,a_n\rangle \in \gamma_{A_1,\ldots,A_n}(R_1 \cup R_2)} (v_{R_1} - v_{R_2})^2}$$

where the value v_R is computed as $\pi_B(\sigma_{A_1=a_1 \wedge \cdots \wedge A_n=a_n}(R))$ divided by $\gamma_{\text{SUM}(B)}(R)$. If R does not contain a tuple $\langle a_1, \ldots, a_n, \cdot\rangle$, v_R is zero.

This distance computes the Euclidean distance between the normalized relations $\overline{R_1}$ and $\overline{R_2}$ where $\overline{R} = \gamma_{A_1,\ldots,A_n,B\times s^{-1}}(R)$, with $s = \gamma_{\text{SUM}(B)}(R)$. The rest of this work could be naturally extended to any distance between $\overline{R_1}$ and $\overline{R_2}$. In the sequel, we will compute the distance between the exact result of an analytical query and an approximate answer. Then the normalization will make sure that two proportional analytical queries will be judged equivalent. For instance, in Table 4, $A_{\alpha_{card}}$ (which contains only 4 subjects with 1 gender, and 2 subjects with 1 child) is an approximation of the analytical query α_{card} executed on $T_{\text{Caesar}} \cup T_{\text{daVinci}}$ with $||A_{\alpha_{card}} - \alpha_{card}||_2 = \sqrt{0.02^2 + 0.04^2 + -0.07^2} = 0.083$. In practice, the proportionality of results is often as important as absolute values

– e.g., for ranking groups $\langle a_1, \ldots, a_n \rangle$. Besides, it is possible to reconstruct the absolute values, if necessary, by querying the triplestore to obtain the absolute value for one group $\langle a_1, \ldots, a_n \rangle$. For instance, the approximation $A_{\alpha_{card}}$ ranks $\langle$`gender`$, 1\rangle$ and $\langle$`parentOf`$, 1\rangle$ in the same order as α_{card}. By computing the absolute value of *count* for $\langle$`gender`$, 1\rangle$ (here: 9), it is possible to also estimate the count value for $\langle$`parentOf`$, 1\rangle$: $9 \times 0.33/0.66 = 4.5$, which slightly overestimates the correct value of 4.

With this, we can now state our goal: Given a set of triplestores $LOD = \{T_1, \ldots, T_N\}$ with monotone and consistent policies and an analytical query α, find a set of queries $Q = \{q_1, \ldots, q_k\}$ such that $Q \models \mathcal{P}_{LOD}$ and $\lim_{k \to +\infty} ||F(q_1(T), \ldots, q_k(T)) - \alpha(T)||_2 = 0$, where F is a query aggregator and $T = T_1 \cup \cdots \cup T_N$.

4 Our Approach

In Sect. 4.1, we show how to rewrite an analytical query to satisfy a fair use policy. In Sect. 4.2, we will use this rewriting strategy to develop an algorithm that scales to the LOD cloud.

4.1 Analytical Query Rewriting

Partitioning. In the following, we will first treat analytical queries on a single triplestore. The key idea of our approach is to partition the input triplestore so that the analytical query can be executed on each part. Of course, the size of each part of the partition has to be small enough for the query to satisfy the fair use policy of the triplestore (*policy constraint*). At the same time, the partitioning must not corrupt the reconstruction of the correct result of the query on the entire triplestore (*validity constraint*). In our running example, it is possible to partition the triplestore according to the subject (shown on the left-hand side of Table 5) to calculate the number of subjects per cardinality and property with α_{card}. On the other hand, it is not possible to partition it according to the objects (shown on the right-hand side of Table 5), because it would not be feasible to reconstruct the number of objects associated with each subject: The three children of Gaius would be in separate groups, and we would wrongly count 3 times that Gaius had only one child.
The notion of α-partition attributes formalizes this compromise on the partition:

Definition 4 (α-partition). *Given an analytical query of the form* $\alpha(T) \equiv \gamma_{A_1,\ldots,A_n,\texttt{AGG}(B)}(q(T))$*, a set of attributes* $\{P_1, \ldots, P_m\} \subseteq \mathbf{sch}(T)$ *is an* α*-partition if it satisfies the following two constraints:*

1. ***Validity constraint:***
   $\alpha(T) = \gamma_{A_1,\ldots,A_n,\texttt{AGG}(B)}(\bigcup_{\langle p_1,\ldots,p_m\rangle \in \gamma_{P_1,\ldots,P_m}(T)} q(\sigma_{P_1=p_1 \wedge \cdots \wedge P_m=p_m}(T)))$
2. ***Policy constraint:***
   $q(\sigma_{P_1=p_1 \wedge \cdots \wedge P_m=p_m}(T)) \models \mathcal{P}$ *for all* $\langle p_1, \ldots, p_m\rangle \in \gamma_{P_1,\ldots,P_m}(T)$.

Table 5. Examples of partitions on T_{Caesar}

Partition on *subj*

subj	prop	obj
Gaius	`parentOf`	Julius
Gaius	`parentOf`	JuliaTheE.
Gaius	`parentOf`	JuliaTheY.
Gaius	`gender`	male
Marcus	`parentOf`	Atia
Marcus	`gender`	male
JuliaTheY.	`parentOf`	Atia
JuliaTheY.	`gender`	female
Julius	`gender`	male
JuliaTheE.	`gender`	female
Atia	`gender`	female

Partition on *obj*

subj	prop	obj
Gaius	`parentOf`	Julius
Gaius	`parentOf`	JuliaTheE.
Gaius	`parentOf`	JuliaTheY.
Marcus	`parentOf`	Atia
JuliaTheY.	`parentOf`	Atia
Marcus	`gender`	male
Julius	`gender`	male
Gaius	`gender`	male
JuliaTheY.	`gender`	female
JuliaTheE.	`gender`	female
Atia	`gender`	female

In our running example, the partitioning by subjects $\gamma_{subj}(T_{\text{Caesar}}) = \{Gaius, Marcus, JuliaTheY., \dots\}$ or by properties $\gamma_{prop}(T_{\text{Caesar}}) = \{\texttt{parentOf}, \texttt{gender}\}$ are two valid partitions. We can also combine several α-partitions:

Property 1. *Given an analytical query of the form $\alpha(T) \equiv \gamma_{A_1,\dots,A_n,\texttt{AGG}(B)}(q(T))$, and two α-partitions $P \subseteq \mathbf{sch}(T)$ and $Q \subseteq \mathbf{sch}(T)$, $P \cup Q$ is also an α-partition.*

This property follows from the fact that we consider only consistent fair use policies. The partition $P \cup Q$ leads to a smaller set of triples in each group than groups resulting from P or Q. In our running example, as $\{subj\}$ and $\{prop\}$ are two α_{card}-partitions, $\{subj, prop\}$ is also an α_{card}-partition. It leads to the groups $\gamma_{subj,prop}(T_{\text{Caesar}}) = \{\langle Gaius, \texttt{parentOf}\rangle, \langle Gaius, \texttt{gender}\rangle, \langle Marcus, \texttt{parentOf}\rangle, \dots\}$.

Rewriting. At this point, we could consider running the inner query q on each part of an α-partition, and then aggregate the results. However, this would require a large storage capacity. In our running example, let us consider the α-partition *prop*: $\gamma_{prop}(T_{\text{Caesar}}) = \{\texttt{gender}, \texttt{parentOf}\}$. We would have to store 9 (= 6 + 3) rows materializing the result from the query $q = \gamma_{subj,prop,\texttt{COUNT}(obj)\rightarrow card}(R)$ applied on each part $\sigma_{prop=gender}(T_{\text{Caesar}})$ and $\sigma_{prop=parentOf}(T_{\text{Caesar}})$. The following property shows that it is possible to apply the analytical query directly on each part instead:

Property 2 (Partition rewriting). *An analytical query of the form $\alpha(T) \equiv \gamma_{A_1,\dots,A_n,\texttt{AGG}(B)}(q(T))$ with an α-partition $\{P_1, \dots, P_m\} \subseteq \mathbf{sch}(T)$ can be computed as follows:*

$$\alpha(T) \equiv \widetilde{\alpha}\left(\bigcup_{\langle p_1,\dots,p_m\rangle \in \gamma_{P_1,\dots,P_m}(T)} \alpha(\sigma_{P_1=p_1 \wedge \dots \wedge P_m=p_m}(T)) \right)$$

This property follows from Definition 1 with the following rewriting rule (for an α-partition): $\alpha(T \cup T') = \widetilde{\alpha}(\alpha(T) \cup \alpha(T'))$. With the above example, we obtained three rows (instead of 9), split into 2 parts: $\alpha_{card}(\sigma_{prop=gender}(T_{\text{Caesar}})) = \{\langle gender, 1, 6\rangle\}$ and $\alpha_{card}(\sigma_{prop=parentOf}(T_{\text{Caesar}})) = \{\langle parentOf, 1, 2\rangle, \langle parentOf, 3, 1\rangle\}$. The query $\widetilde{\alpha}_{card}$ merges them into one result.

Approximating. Property 2 gives us an exact method for answering an analytical query. This method can be parallelized by running the queries corresponding to different parts in parallel. However, the computation risks being slow if the number of parts is high. If one interrupts the query execution, the intermediate result will be biased by the order in which the parts of T were queried. We propose to remedy both problems by drawing the parts randomly. For this purpose, we rely on the sampling operator $\psi_k(R)$ [28], which randomly draws k tuples from R (with replacement). We can then reformulate Property 2 as follows:

Property 3 (Sampling approximation). *An analytical query of the form* $\alpha(T) \equiv \gamma_{A_1,\ldots,A_n,\texttt{AGG}(B)}(q(T))$ *can be approximated by sampling k groups resulting from an* α*-partition* $\{P_1, \ldots, P_m\} \subseteq \mathbf{sch}(T)$*:*

$$\lim_{k \to +\infty} \left\| \widetilde{\alpha} \left(\bigcup_{\langle p_1,\ldots,p_m\rangle \in \psi_k(\gamma_{P_1,\ldots,P_m}(T))} \alpha(\sigma_{P_1=p_1 \wedge \cdots \wedge P_m=p_m}(T)) \right) - \alpha(T) \right\|_2 = 0$$

This follows from the fact that a uniform random sampling tends to the original distribution when its size increases. This result is very important because it provides an efficient method for approximating an analytical query. First, the sampling operator avoids materializing the partition, which would incur a cost of computation that might not satisfy the fair use policy. Second, because of the replacement, the same part may be drawn several times. Interestingly, this does not prevent a correct approximation of the result. On the contrary, this replacement is interesting because it avoids the necessity to remember which parts have already been drawn – thus leading to lower space complexity. In our running example, consider the α_{card}-partition $\{subj\}$, which leads to $\gamma_{subj}(T_{\text{Caesar}} \cup T_{\text{daVinci}}) = \{$*Gaius, Marcus, JuliaTheY., Julius, JuliaTheE., Atia, Piero, Caterina, Leonardo*$\}$. We can randomly draw 4 groups: Marcus, JuliaTheE., JuliaTheY. and Leonardo. We obtain $\alpha_{card}(\sigma_{subj=Marcus}(T_{\text{Caesar}})) = \{\langle gender, 1, 1\rangle, \langle parentOf, 1, 1\rangle\}$ (idem for JuliaTheY.) and $\alpha_{card}(\sigma_{subj=JuliaTheE.}(T_{\text{Caesar}})) = \{\langle gender, 1, 1\rangle\}$ (idem for Leonardo). We can then construct the approximation $A_{\alpha_{card}}$ (see Table 4) by aggregating these four results with $\widetilde{\alpha}_{card}$. Even if Property 3 provides no guarantee on the convergence speed, we will see in the experimental section that in practice this convergence is fast.

4.2 Anytime Algorithm

In this section, we show how to algorithmically implement Property 3 efficiently at LOD scale. For this, we have two main challenges to overcome. First, each

Algorithm 1. SAMPLE-AND-AGGREGATE

Input: A set of triplestores $LOD = \{T_1, \ldots, T_N\}$, an analytical query α and a compatible α-partition$\{P_1, \ldots, P_m\}$
Output: An approximate answer of $\alpha(T_1 \cup \cdots \cup T_N)$

1: $Ans_0 := \emptyset$
2: $k := 0$
3: Define weights $\omega(T) = |\gamma_{P_1,..,P_n}(T)|$ for all $T \in LOD$
4: **repeat**
5: Draw a triplestore $T \sim \omega(LOD)$
6: Draw a tuple $\langle p_1, \ldots, p_m \rangle \sim u(\gamma_{P_1,..,P_n}(T))$
7: $Ans_{k+1} := \widetilde{\alpha}(Ans_k \cup \alpha(\sigma_{P_1=p_1 \wedge \cdots \wedge P_m=p_m}(T)))$
8: $k := k + 1$
9: **until** The user stops the process
10: **return** Ans_k

query q has to be executed on a set of triplestores and not on a single triplestore. Second, the sampling operator is not natively implemented in SPARQL.

Let us consider the first problem: If we have the set of triplestores $LOD = \{T_1, \ldots, T_N\}$, we have to create $T = \bigcup_{i \in [1..N]} T_i$ (e.g., $T_{\text{Caesar}} \cup T_{\text{daVinci}}$ in our example of Table 1). Thus, a single query has to be run on N triplestores, which is very expensive. In practice, however, a part usually resides in a single triplestore. We formalize this notion as follows:

Definition 5 (Compatible α-partition). *Given a set of triplestores $LOD = \{T_1, \ldots, T_N\}$, an α-partition $\{P_1, \ldots, P_m\}$ is compatible with LOD if for all $\langle p_1, \ldots, p_m \rangle \in \gamma_{P_1,\ldots,P_n}(T)$, there exists $T \in LOD$ such that $\sigma_{P_1=p_1 \wedge \cdots \wedge P_m=p_m}$ $(T_1 \cup \cdots \cup T_N) \subseteq T$.*

Let us consider again our running example $T = T_{\text{Caesar}} \cup T_{\text{daVinci}}$. It is clear that the partition $\gamma_{subj}(T) = \{Gaius, Marcus, \ldots\}$ is compatible with $\{T_{\text{Caesar}}, T_{\text{daVinci}}\}$ because each part $\sigma_{subj=x}(T)$ is entirely contained in the tuples of one triplestore. In the following, we make the assumption that all α-partitions are compatible with the LOD cloud. In some cases, α-partitions are provably compatible with the LOD cloud (see Sects. 5.1 and 5.2), unless two triplestores contain the same triple. But even if our assumption does not hold for a small proportion of parts, this does not significantly degrade the overall quality of the approximation.

We use the idea of compatible partitions in Algorithm 1. It takes as input a set of triplestores $LOD = \{T_1, \ldots, T_N\}$, an analytical query α and a compatible α-partition $\{P_1, ..., P_n\}$. It returns an approximation of this analytical query that can be requested at any time. The main loop (Lines 4–9) is repeated until the user stops the process in order to obtain the last answer Ans_k (Line 10). Each iteration refines the previous answer using a sampling phase and an aggregation phase. The sampling phase is implemented as follows: We first compute a weight for each triplestore corresponding to the partition size (Line 3). If the size of a partition is not computable, we can use the size of the triplestore as a pessimistic estimate. The sampling draws a fragment at random[2] by first choosing a triplestore T in proportion to its number of fragments $\omega(T)$ (Line 5) and then uniformly drawing a fragment from this triplestore (Line 6). This uniform drawing is implemented by using the query $\gamma_{P_1,\ldots,P_n}(T)$ with `LIMIT 1 OFFSET` r, where r is a random number uniformly drawn from $[0..\omega(T)]$. The draw is rejected if the answer is empty (i.e., $r > |\gamma_{P_1,\ldots,P_n}(T)|$) due to a pessimistic estimate in Line 3. Finally, the aggregation phase (Line 7) merges the previous answer Ans_k with the query on the fragment that has just been selected $\alpha(\sigma_{P_1=p_1\wedge\cdots\wedge P_m=p_m}(T))$. With Property 3, it is easy to show that our algorithm is correct:

Theorem 1 (Correctness). *Given a set of triplestores* $LOD = \{T_1,\ldots,T_N\}$ *with monotone policies, an analytical query* α *and a compatible* α*-partition* $\{P_1,\ldots,P_m\}$*, Algorithm 1 returns an approximate answer* Ans_k *of* $\alpha(T_1 \cup \cdots \cup T_N)$ *that aggregates* k *queries* $q(\sigma_{P_1=p_1\wedge\cdots\wedge P_m=p_m}(T_i)) \models \mathcal{P}$ *such that* $\lim_{k\to+\infty} ||Ans_k - \alpha(T_1 \cup \cdots \cup T_N)||_2 = 0$.

This theorem means that the user can obtain an approximation with any desired precision by granting a sufficient time budget. Our method is therefore an anytime algorithm [35]. Another advantage of this algorithm is that it is easily parallelizable. It is possible to execute M sampling phases in parallel (to reduce the time complexity linearly). In this case, the aggregation phase must either group together the results in a unique answer Ans_k, or maintain M answers $Ans_k^{(i)}$ in parallel, which will then be merged in the end (i.e., $Ans_k = \widetilde{\alpha}\left(\bigcup_{i\in[1..M]} Ans_k^{(i)}\right)$). The first solution saves storage space, but the second solution also has a reasonable space complexity. This is because there is no intermediate result to store:

Property 4 (Space complexity). *Given a set of triplestores* $LOD = \{T_1,\ldots,T_N\}$*, an analytical query* α*, and a compatible* α*-partition, Algorithm 1 requires* $O(|\alpha(T_1 \cup \cdots \cup T_N)|)$ *space.*

This property is crucial, because it means that the number of iterations (and thus the achieved precision) does not influence the required storage space.

5 Experiments

The goal of this experimental section is to answer the following questions: (i) How fast does our algorithm converge to the exact result? and (ii) How does the method perform on the LOD to approximate simple and complex analytical queries? We have implemented our algorithm in Java in a multi-threaded version to perform multiple parallel samplings. The result of each thread is aggregated with a relational database. For the time measurements, we did not count the preprocessing step executed once for all threads (Line 3 of Algorithm 1) because

[2] Given a set Ω with a probability distribution P, $x \sim P(\Omega)$ denotes that the element $x \in \Omega$ is drawn at random with a probability $P(x)$.

it does not take longer than a few minutes. All experimental data (the list of endpoints and the experimental results), as well as the source code, are available at https://github.com/asoulet/iswc19analytics.

5.1 Efficiency of the Approach

This section evaluates the convergence speed of our algorithm with the query α_{prop} (Table 3). We ran the experiment on DBpedia, because its triplestore is small enough (58,333 properties for 438,336,518 triples) to compute the exact answer to the query. We evaluate our algorithm with the partition $\{subj, prop, obj\}$. We use only 8 threads to avoid overwhelming DBpedia with too many queries and violating its fair use policy. To estimate the difference between our approximation and the exact query, we use 3 evaluation measures: the L1-norm, the L2-norm and the Kullback–Leibler divergence. We compute the proportion of top-k properties that are truly in the most $k \in \{50, 100\}$ used properties in the ground truth. We also count the number of sampled queries and the size of the approximate answer (number of approximated properties). We repeated the experiments 5 times, and report the arithmetic mean of the different measurements every minute. We cut off the computation after 100 min.

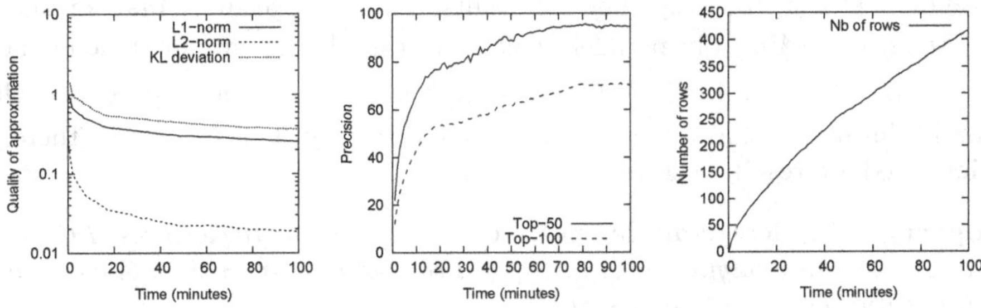

Fig. 1. Performance of our algorithm for the query α_{prop} on DBpedia

Figure 1 (left) plots the approximation quality over time (lower is better). As expected, we observe that the approximation converges to the exact query. Interestingly, this convergence is very fast (note that y-axis is a logscale). From the first minutes on, the frequency estimation of the properties is sufficiently close to the final result to predict the order of the most frequent properties (see Fig. 1, middle). Figure 1 (right) shows the size of the approximate answer (i.e., the number of tuples). Of course, the size increases to tend to the size of the result of the exact query (which is 58,333). However, during the first 100 min, the number of rows remains very small (just 415). Indeed, the final approximation has been calculated with a very low communication cost of only 3,485 triples (0.0008% of DBpedia).

5.2 Use Case 1: Property and Class Usage on the LOD Cloud

In the following, we tested our algorithm on the scale of the LOD cloud. We used https://lod-cloud.net/ to retrieve all SPARQL endpoints of the LOD cloud that contain the property `rdf:type` (which is required for our queries, see Table 3). This yielded 114 triplestores that were functional, including LinkedGeoData [4], DBpedia [2], EMBL-EBI [18] and Bio2RDF [6]. Together, these triplestores contain more than 51.2 billion triples.

Our first experiment evaluates our algorithm on the queries α_{prop} and α_{class}, which measure property usage and class usage, respectively (see Table 3 again). We used again $\gamma_{subj,prop,obj}(T)$ as partition, and the algorithm ran with 32 parallel sampling threads. To obtain an estimation of the ground truth, we ran the algorithm for 250 h. After this time, the result does not change much any more, and we thus believe that we are not too far off the real ground truth. We then measured the precision of the result after every minute of execution with respect to our assumed ground truth.

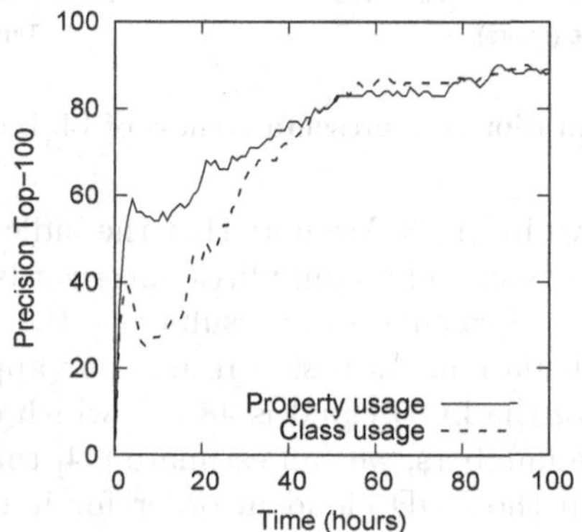

Fig. 2. Property and class usage (queries α_{prop} and α_{class}) on the LOD cloud

Figure 2 shows the top-100 precision for both queries. We observe that both queries have the same behavior: After 25 h, 50% of the 100 most used properties and classes are found by our algorithm. After 100 h, 90 properties (or classes) are accurately found with a sample of only 179k triples. These approximations require less than 3k rows as storage cost and 179k queries as communication cost – i.e., 0.00035% of the cost of a traditional data centralization approach.

5.3 Use Case 2: Representativeness of the LOD

Our next experiment evaluates our algorithm on a very complex query, α_{FSD}. This query yields, for each property, a distribution over the frequency of the first significant digit of the number of objects per subject. We used the method proposed in [34] to convert this distribution into a score between 0 and 1 that measures the "representativeness" of the triplestores. A score of 1 means that the data is representative of the distribution in the real world (see [34] for details). We also computed the proportion of the LOD cloud that conforms to Benford's law, and the number of distinct properties that are stored, and that are involved in the calculation of the representativeness. We partitioned by subject, $\gamma_{subj}(T)$, and used again 32 parallel sampling threads during 100 h.

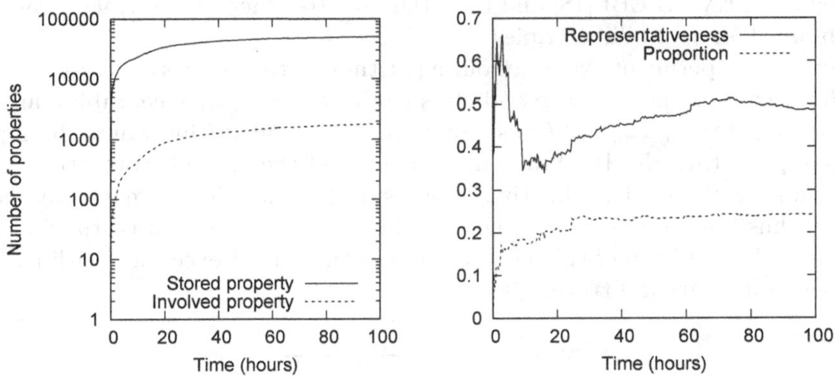

Fig. 3. Computation of representativeness of Linked Open Data

The results are shown in Fig. 3. We note that the indicators converge rapidly to a first approximation that evolves only little afterwards. In particular, 60.7% of the properties needed to calculate the results (see the solid line) are already known after 20 h of calculation. As a side result, our approach estimates that the representativeness of the LOD cloud is 48.7%, which concerns 24.2% of the LOD cloud. From these numbers, we can estimate [34] that at least 13.1 billion triples are missing from the LOD cloud in order for it to be a representative sample of reality.

6 Conclusion

In this paper, we have presented a new paradigm for computing analytical queries on Linked Open Data: Instead of centralizing the data, we aggregate the results of queries that are fired directly on the SPARQL endpoints. These queries compute only small samples, so that they have short execution times, and thus respect the fair use policies of the endpoints. Our algorithm is an anytime algorithm, which can deliver approximate results already after a very short execution time, and which provably converges to the exact result over time. The algorithm is easily parallelizable, and requires only linear space (in the size of the query answer). In our experiments, we have shown that our approach scales to the size of the LOD cloud. We have also seen that it rapidly delivers a good approximation of the exact query answer. For future work, we aim to investigate how our approach could be endowed with OWL reasoning capabilities, to respect equivalences between resources.

Acknowledgements. This work was partially supported by the grant ANR-16-CE23-0007-01 ("DICOS").

References

1. Abiteboul, S., Hull, R., Vianu, V.: Foundations of Databases: the Logical Level. Addison-Wesley Longman Publishing Co., Inc, Boston (1995)
2. Auer, S., Bizer, C., Kobilarov, G., Lehmann, J., Cyganiak, R., Ives, Z.: DBpedia: a nucleus for a web of open data. In: Aberer, K., et al. (eds.) ASWC/ISWC -2007. LNCS, vol. 4825, pp. 722–735. Springer, Heidelberg (2007). https://doi.org/10.1007/978-3-540-76298-0_52
3. Auer, S., Demter, J., Martin, M., Lehmann, J.: LODStats – an extensible framework for high-performance dataset analytics. In: ten Teije, A., et al. (eds.) EKAW 2012. LNCS, vol. 7603, pp. 353–362. Springer, Heidelberg (2012). https://doi.org/10.1007/978-3-642-33876-2_31
4. Auer, S., Lehmann, J., Hellmann, S.: LinkedGeoData: adding a spatial dimension to the web of data. In: Bernstein, A., et al. (eds.) ISWC 2009. LNCS, vol. 5823, pp. 731–746. Springer, Heidelberg (2009). https://doi.org/10.1007/978-3-642-04930-9_46
5. Barbieri, D.F., Braga, D., Ceri, S., Valle, E.D., Grossniklaus, M.: Querying RDF streams with c-SPARQL. ACM SIGMOD Rec. **39**(1), 20–26 (2010)
6. Belleau, F., Nolin, M.A., Tourigny, N., Rigault, P., Morissette, J.: Bio2RDF: towards a mashup to build bioinformatics knowledge systems. J. Biomed. Inf. **41**(5), 706–7016 (2008)
7. Bienvenu, M., Deutch, D., Martinenghi, D., Senellart, P., Suchanek, F.M.: Dealing with the deep web and all its quirks. In: VLDS (2012)
8. Bolles, A., Grawunder, M., Jacobi, J.: Streaming SPARQL - extending SPARQL to process data streams. In: Bechhofer, S., Hauswirth, M., Hoffmann, J., Koubarakis, M. (eds.) ESWC 2008. LNCS, vol. 5021, pp. 448–462. Springer, Heidelberg (2008). https://doi.org/10.1007/978-3-540-68234-9_34
9. Chaudhuri, S., Dayal, U.: An overview of data warehousing and OLAP technology. ACM Sigmod Rec. **26**(1), 65–74 (1997)
10. Codd, E.F., Codd, S.B., Salley, C.T.: Providing OLAP (on-line analytical processing) to user-analysts: an IT mandate. Codd Date **32** (1993)
11. Colazzo, D., Goasdoué, F., Manolescu, I., Roatiş, A.: RDF analytics: lenses over semantic graphs. In: WWW (2014)
12. Costabello, L., Villata, S., Vagliano, I., Gandon, F.: Assisted policy management for SPARQL endpoints access control. In: ISWC Demo (2013)
13. Cyganiak, R.: A relational algebra for SPARQL. Digital Media Systems Laboratory HP Laboratories Bristol. HPL-2005-170 **35** (2005)
14. Forchhammer, B., Jentzsch, A., Naumann, F.: LODOP - multi-query optimization for linked data profiling queries. In: PROFILES@ESWC (2014)
15. Franke, C., Morin, S., Chebotko, A., Abraham, J., Brazier, P.: Distributed semantic web data management in HBase and MySQL cluster. In: CLOUD (2011)
16. Galárraga, L., Razniewski, S., Amarilli, A., Suchanek, F.M.: Predicting completeness in knowledge bases. In: WSDM (2017)
17. Gottron, T.: Of sampling and smoothing: approximating distributions over linked open data. In: PROFILES@ ESWC (2014)
18. Goujon, M., et al.: A new bioinformatics analysis tools framework at EMBL-EBI. Nucleic Acids Res. **38**(Suppl_2), W695–W699 (2010)

19. Hellerstein, J.M., Haas, P.J., Wang, H.J.: Online aggregation. ACM Sigmod Rec. **26**, 171–182 (1997)
20. Ibragimov, D., Hose, K., Pedersen, T.B., Zimányi, E.: Processing aggregate queries in a federation of SPARQL endpoints. In: Gandon, F., Sabou, M., Sack, H., d'Amato, C., Cudré-Mauroux, P., Zimmermann, A. (eds.) ESWC 2015. LNCS, vol. 9088, pp. 269–285. Springer, Cham (2015). https://doi.org/10.1007/978-3-319-18818-8_17
21. Khan, Y., et al.: SAFE: policy aware SPARQL query federation over RDF data cubes. In: Workshop on Semantic Web Applications for Life Sciences (2014)
22. Kim, H., Ravindra, P., Anyanwu, K.: From SPARQL to MapReduce: the journey using a nested triplegroup algebra. VLDB J. **4**(12), 1426–1429 (2011)
23. Kotoulas, S., Urbani, J., Boncz, P., Mika, P.: Robust runtime optimization and skew-resistant execution of analytical SPARQL queries on pig. ISWC 2012. LNCS, vol. 7649, pp. 247–262. Springer, Heidelberg (2012). https://doi.org/10.1007/978-3-642-35176-1_16
24. Lajus, J., Suchanek, F.M.: Are all people married? Determining obligatory attributes in knowledge bases. In: WWW (2018)
25. Manolescu, I., Mazuran, M.: Speeding up RDF aggregate discovery through sampling. In: Workshop on Big Data Visual Exploration (2019)
26. Muñoz, E., Nickles, M.: Statistical relation cardinality bounds in knowledge bases. In: Hameurlain, A., Wagner, R., Benslimane, D., Damiani, E., Grosky, W.I. (eds.) Transactions on Large-Scale Data- and Knowledge-Centered Systems XXXIX. LNCS, vol. 11310, pp. 67–97. Springer, Heidelberg (2018). https://doi.org/10.1007/978-3-662-58415-6_3
27. Nirkhiwale, S., Dobra, A., Jermaine, C.: A sampling algebra for aggregate estimation. VLDB J. **6**(14), 1798–1809 (2013)
28. Olken, F.: Random sampling from databases. Ph.D. thesis, University of California, Berkeley (1993)
29. Pietriga, E., et al.: Browsing linked data catalogs with LODAtlas. In: Vrandečić, D., et al. (eds.) ISWC 2018. LNCS, vol. 11137, pp. 137–153. Springer, Cham (2018). https://doi.org/10.1007/978-3-030-00668-6_9
30. Quilitz, B., Leser, U.: Querying distributed RDF data sources with SPARQL. In: Bechhofer, S., Hauswirth, M., Hoffmann, J., Koubarakis, M. (eds.) ESWC 2008. LNCS, vol. 5021, pp. 524–538. Springer, Heidelberg (2008). https://doi.org/10.1007/978-3-540-68234-9_39
31. Saleem, M., Hasnain, A., Ngomo, A.C.N.: LargeRDFBench: a billion triples benchmark for SPARQL endpoint federation. J. Web Semant. **48**, 85–125 (2018)
32. Schätzle, A., Przyjaciel-Zablocki, M., Skilevic, S., Lausen, G.: S2RDF: RDF querying with SPARQL on spark. VLDB J. **9**(10), 804–815 (2016)
33. Sejdiu, G., Ermilov, I., Lehmann, J., Mami, M.N.: DistLODStats: distributed computation of RDF dataset statistics. In: Vrandečić, D., et al. (eds.) ISWC 2018. LNCS, vol. 11137, pp. 206–222. Springer, Cham (2018). https://doi.org/10.1007/978-3-030-00668-6_13
34. Soulet, A., Giacometti, A., Markhoff, B., Suchanek, F.M.: Representativeness of knowledge bases with the generalized Benford's Law. In: Vrandečić, D., et al. (eds.) ISWC 2018. LNCS, vol. 11136, pp. 374–390. Springer, Cham (2018). https://doi.org/10.1007/978-3-030-00671-6_22
35. Zilberstein, S.: Using anytime algorithms in intelligent systems. AI Mag. **17**(3), 73 (1996)

Absorption-Based Query Answering for Expressive Description Logics

Andreas Steigmiller(✉) and Birte Glimm

Ulm University, Ulm, Germany
{andreas.steigmiller,birte.glimm}@uni-ulm.de

Abstract. Conjunctive query answering is an important reasoning task for logic-based knowledge representation formalisms, such as Description Logics, to query for instance data that is related in certain ways. Although many knowledge bases use language features of more expressive Description Logics, there are hardly any systems that support full conjunctive query answering for these logics. In fact, existing systems usually impose restrictions on the queries or only compute incomplete results.

In this paper, we present a new approach for answering conjunctive queries that can directly be integrated into existing reasoning systems for expressive Description Logics. The approach reminds of *absorption*, a well-known preprocessing step that rewrites axioms such that they can be handled more efficiently. In this sense, we rewrite the query such that entailment can dynamically be checked in the dominantly used tableau calculi with minor extensions. Our implementation in the reasoning system Konclude outperforms existing systems even for queries that are restricted to the capabilities of these other systems.

1 Introduction

A distinguished feature of logic-based knowledge representation formalisms, such as Description Logics (DLs), is the ability to use automated reasoning techniques to access implicit knowledge of explicitly stated information. In particular, a DL knowledge base can be seen as a collection of explicitly stated information that describes a domain of interest, i.e., individuals/entities and their features. Roles are used to state the relationship between individuals, concepts represent sets of individuals with common characteristics, and axioms relate concepts or roles to each other, e.g., by specifying sub-concept relationships, or state facts about an individual/a pair of individuals. Since the DL $\mathcal{SROIQ}$ [10] is the logical underpinning of the second and current iteration of the well-known Web Ontology Language (OWL), its language features are often used in practice for modelling ontologies. Consequently, reasoning systems that support $\mathcal{SROIQ}$ are required to work with these ontologies. So far, most reasoners for expressive DLs, such as

A. Steigmiller—Funded by the German Research Foundation (Deutsche Forschungsgemeinschaft, DFG) in project number 330492673.

C. Ghidini et al. (Eds.): ISWC 2019, LNCS 11778, pp. 593–611, 2019.
https://doi.org/10.1007/978-3-030-30793-6_34

$\mathcal{SROIQ}$, are based on variants of tableau algorithms since they are easily extensible and adaptable to the expressive language features. Moreover, many developed optimisation techniques allow these systems to efficiently handle standard reasoning tasks (e.g., consistency checking, classification, instance retrieval, etc.) for many real-world ontologies. To satisfy all user demands, more sophisticated reasoning tasks such as conjunctive query answering are also often required. Such queries consist of a conjunction of concept and role facts, where variables may be used in place of individuals. Such variables may be existentially quantified (aka non-distinguished variables) or answer variables (aka distinguished variables). For the answer variables, the reasoner has to deliver bindings to named individuals of the knowledge base such that the query, instantiated with the bindings, is entailed by the knowledge base. For existential variables, it is only required that there exists a binding to any, possibly anonymous individual in each model.

To the best of our knowledge, current reasoning systems support conjunctive queries for expressive DLs only with limitations. This is due to several reasons. First, decidability of conjunctive query entailment, to which query answering is typically reduced, is still open in $\mathcal{SROIQ}$. Second, while the decidability and the worst-case complexity has been shown for many sub-languages (e.g., [3,15,18]), the used techniques are often not directly suitable for practical implementations. For the DLs $\mathcal{SHIQ}$ and $\mathcal{SHOQ}$, approaches have been developed that reduce conjunctive query answering to instance checking (e.g, [5,7,11]), which is not goal-directed and often requires many unnecessary entailment checks. Moreover, some of these reduction techniques require language features (e.g., role conjunctions) which are not available in OWL 2 and, hence, usually not supported by reasoning systems.

Even for queries with only answer variables (conjunctive instance queries), existing approaches (e.g., [9,13,19]) are often impractical since they are based on the above described reduction to instance checking. Moreover, by only using existing reasoning systems as black-boxes, the possibility to optimise conjunctive query answering is limited. Recently, query answering has been improved by lower and upper bound optimisations that utilise model abstractions built by a reasoner [6] or delegate work to specialised procedures [16,25]. Furthermore, it is possible to determine for which queries the answers from specialised systems can be complete although not all used language features are completely handled [23]. However, the specialised procedures are still used as a black-box and delegating all work to them is not possible in general. Hence, practical conjunctive query answering techniques for expressive DLs are still needed.

In this paper, we present an approach that encodes the query such that entailment can efficiently be detected in the model construction process with minor extensions to the tableau calculus. The encoding serves to identify individuals involved in satisfying the query and guides the search for a model where the query is not entailed. We refer to this technique as *absorption-based query answering* since it reminds of the absorption technique for nominal schemas [21]. The approach is correct and terminates for DLs for which decidability of conjunctive query answering is known (e.g., $\mathcal{SHIQ}$, $\mathcal{SHOQ}$). For the challenging combination of nominals,

Table 1. Core features of $\mathcal{SROIQ}$ ($\#M$ denotes the cardinality of the set M)

		Syntax	Semantics
Individuals:	Individual	a	$a^{\mathcal{I}} \in \Delta^{\mathcal{I}}$
Roles:	Atomic role	r	$r^{\mathcal{I}} \subseteq \Delta^{\mathcal{I}} \times \Delta^{\mathcal{I}}$
	inverse role	r^-	$\{\langle\gamma, \delta\rangle \mid \langle\delta, \gamma\rangle \in r^{\mathcal{I}}\}$
Concepts:	Atomic concept	A	$A^{\mathcal{I}} \subseteq \Delta^{\mathcal{I}}$
	Nominal	$\{a\}$	$\{a^{\mathcal{I}}\}$
	Top	$\top$	$\Delta^{\mathcal{I}}$
	Bottom	$\bot$	$\emptyset$
	Negation	$\neg C$	$\Delta^{\mathcal{I}} \setminus C^{\mathcal{I}}$
	Conjunction	$C \sqcap D$	$C^{\mathcal{I}} \cap D^{\mathcal{I}}$
	Disjunction	$C \sqcup D$	$C^{\mathcal{I}} \cup D^{\mathcal{I}}$
	Existential restriction	$\exists R.C$	$\{\delta \mid \exists\gamma \in C^{\mathcal{I}} : \langle\delta, \gamma\rangle \in R^{\mathcal{I}}\}$
	Universal restriction	$\forall R.C$	$\{\delta \mid \langle\delta, \gamma\rangle \in R^{\mathcal{I}} \rightarrow \gamma \in C^{\mathcal{I}}\}$
	Number restriction, $\bowtie \in \{\leqslant, \geqslant\}$	$\bowtie n\, R.C$	$\{\delta \mid \#\{\langle\delta, \gamma\rangle \in R^{\mathcal{I}} \text{ and } \gamma \in C^{\mathcal{I}}\} \bowtie n\}$
Axioms:	General concept inclusion	$C \sqsubseteq D$	$C^{\mathcal{I}} \subseteq D^{\mathcal{I}}$
	Role inclusion	$R \sqsubseteq S$	$R^{\mathcal{I}} \subseteq S^{\mathcal{I}}$
	Role chains	$R_1 \circ \ldots \circ R_n \sqsubseteq S$	$R_1^{\mathcal{I}} \circ \ldots \circ R_n^{\mathcal{I}} \subseteq S^{\mathcal{I}}$
	Concept assertion	$C(a)$	$a^{\mathcal{I}} \in C^{\mathcal{I}}$
	Role assertion	$R(a, b)$	$\langle a^{\mathcal{I}}, b^{\mathcal{I}}\rangle \in R^{\mathcal{I}}$
	Equality assertion	$a \approx b$	$a^{\mathcal{I}} = b^{\mathcal{I}}$

inverse roles, and number restrictions, termination is only guaranteed if a limited number of new nominals is generated. The technique seems well-suited for practical implementations since (i) it only requires minor extensions to tableau algorithms, (ii) can easily be combined with other well-known (query answering) optimisation techniques, and (iii) real-world ontologies hardly require the generation of (many) new nominals. In fact, we implemented the proposed technique in the reasoning system Konclude [22] with encouraging results.

The paper is organised as follows: Sect. 2 gives a brief introduction into DLs and reasoning. Section 3 describes the absorption-based query entailment checking technique, for which reductions from query answering are sketched in Sect. 4. Section 5 discusses the implementation and evaluation results. Additional explanations, examples, and evaluation results can be found in an accompanying technical report [20].

2 Preliminaries

Due to space restrictions, we only give a brief introduction into DLs and reasoning techniques (see, e.g., [1], for more details).

2.1 Description Logics and Conjunctive Queries

The syntax of DLs is defined using a vocabulary consisting of countably infinite pairwise disjointed sets N_C of *atomic concepts*, N_R of *atomic roles*, and N_I of *individuals*. A role is either atomic or an *inverse role* r^-, $r \in N_R$. The syntax and semantics of complex *concepts* and *axioms* are defined in Table 1. Note that we omit the presentation of some features (e.g., datatypes) and restrictions (e.g., number restrictions may not use "complex roles", i.e., roles that occur on the right-hand side of role chains) for brevity. A knowledge base/ontology $\mathcal{K}$ is a finite set of axioms. An *interpretation* $\mathcal{I} = (\Delta^{\mathcal{I}}, \cdot^{\mathcal{I}})$ consists of a non-empty *domain* $\Delta^{\mathcal{I}}$ and an *interpretation function* $\cdot^{\mathcal{I}}$. We say that $\mathcal{I}$ *satisfies* a general concept inclusion (GCI) $C \sqsubseteq D$, written $\mathcal{I} \models C \sqsubseteq D$, if $C^{\mathcal{I}} \subseteq D^{\mathcal{I}}$ (analogously for other axioms as shown in Table 1). If $\mathcal{I}$ satisfies all axioms of a knowledge base $\mathcal{K}$, $\mathcal{I}$ is a *model* of $\mathcal{K}$ and $\mathcal{K}$ is *consistent/satisfiable* if it has a model.

A *conjunctive query* $Q(X, Y)$ consists of a set of *query terms* $q_1, \ldots, q_k$, where X denotes the tuple of answer variables, Y the tuple of existential variables (disjoint to X), and each q_i is either a concept term $C(z)$ or a role term $r(z_1, z_2)$ with $z, z_1, z_2 \in \mathsf{vars}(Q)$, where $\mathsf{vars}(Q)$ is the set of variable names occurring in $Q(X, Y)$. A *Boolean query* $Q(\langle\rangle, Y)$, short Q, is a query without answer variables. To simplify the handling of inverse roles, we consider $r(x, y)$ as equivalent to $r^-(y, x)$. For an interpretation $\mathcal{I} = (\Delta^{\mathcal{I}}, \cdot^{\mathcal{I}})$ and a total function $\pi : \mathsf{vars}(Q) \mapsto \Delta^{\mathcal{I}}$, we say that π is a *match* for $\mathcal{I}$ and Q if, for every $C(z) \in Q$, $\pi(z) \in C^{\mathcal{I}}$ and, for every $r(z_1, z_2) \in Q$, $\langle \pi(z_1), \pi(z_2) \rangle \in r^{\mathcal{I}}$. We say that an n-ary tuple of the form $\langle a_1, \ldots, a_n \rangle$ with $a_1, \ldots, a_n$ individuals of $\mathcal{K}$ is an *answer* for $Q(\langle x_1, \ldots, x_n \rangle, Y)$ w.r.t. $\mathcal{K}$ if, for every model $\mathcal{I} = (\Delta^{\mathcal{I}}, \cdot^{\mathcal{I}})$ of $\mathcal{K}$, there exists a match π for $\mathcal{I}$ and Q with $\pi(x_i) = a_i^{\mathcal{I}}$ for $1 \leq i \leq n$. If a query $Q(X, Y)$ ($Q(\langle\rangle, Y)$) has an answer (the empty answer $\langle\rangle$) w.r.t. $\mathcal{K}$, then we say that $\mathcal{K}$ *entails* Q and with *query answering* (*query entailment checking*) we refer to the reasoning task that computes all answers (the entailment of the empty answer). W.l.o.g. we use individual names only in nominal concepts and we assume that all variables are connected via role terms.

2.2 Tableau Algorithm

A tableau algorithm decides the consistency of a knowledge base $\mathcal{K}$ by trying to construct an abstraction of a model for $\mathcal{K}$, a so-called *completion graph.* A completion graph G is a tuple $(V, E, \mathcal{L}, \dot{\neq})$, where each node $v \in V$ (edge $\langle v, w \rangle \in E$) represents one or more (pairs of) individuals. Each node v (edge $\langle v, w \rangle$) is labelled with a set of concepts (roles), $\mathcal{L}(v)$ ($\mathcal{L}(\langle v, w \rangle)$), which the individuals represented by v ($\langle v, w \rangle$) are instances of. The relation $\dot{\neq}$ records inequalities between nodes. We call $C \in \mathcal{L}(v)$ ($r \in \mathcal{L}(\langle v, w \rangle)$) a *concept (role) fact*, which we write as $C(v)$ ($r(v, w)$). A node v is a *nominal node* if $\{a\} \in \mathcal{L}(v)$ for some individual a and a *blockable node* otherwise.

A completion graph is initialised with one node for each individual in the input knowledge base. Concepts and roles are added to the node and edge labels as specified by concept and role assertions. Complex concepts are then decomposed using expansion rules, where each rule application can add new concepts to node labels and/or new nodes and edges, thereby explicating the structure of a model. The rules are applied until either the graph is *fully expanded* (no more rules are applicable), in which case the graph can be used to construct a model that is a *witness* to the consistency of $\mathcal{K}$, or an obvious contradiction (called a *clash*) is discovered (e.g., a node v with $C, \neg C \in \mathcal{L}(v)$), proving that the completion graph does not correspond to a model. $\mathcal{K}$ is *consistent* if the

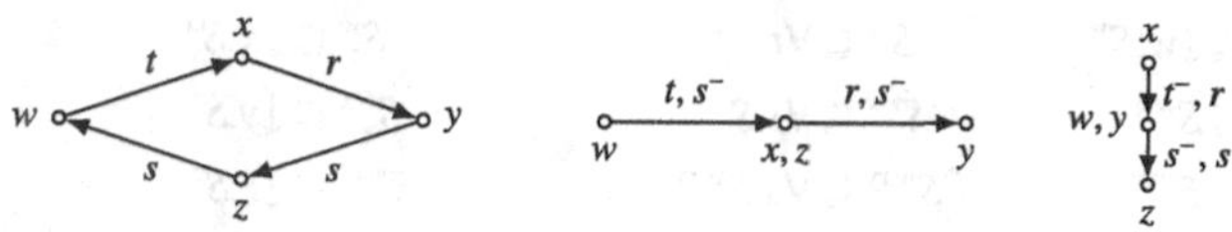

Fig. 1. Visualisation of the query of Example 1 and two possible foldings

rules (some of which are non-deterministic) can be applied such that they build a fully expanded, clash-free completion graph. Cycle detection techniques such as *pairwise blocking* [10] prevent the infinite generation of new nodes.

For handling axioms of the form $A \sqsubseteq C$, where A is atomic, one typically uses special *lazy unfolding* rules in the tableau algorithm, which add C to a node label if it contains the concept A. Axioms of the form $C \sqsubseteq D$, where C is not atomic, cannot directly be handled with lazy unfolding rules. Instead, they are internalised to $\top \sqsubseteq \neg C \sqcup D$. Given that $\top$ is satisfied at each node, the disjunction is then present in all node labels. To avoid the non-determinism introduced by internalisation, one typically uses a preprocessing step called *absorption* to rewrite axioms into (possibly several) simpler concept inclusion axioms that can be handled by lazy unfolding. Binary absorption [12] utilises axioms of the form $A_1 \sqcap A_2 \sqsubseteq C$ for absorbing more complex axioms. This requires a binary unfolding rule that adds C to node labels if A_1 and A_2 are present.

3 Absorption-Based Query Entailment Checking

Since query answering is typically reduced to query entailment checking, we first focus on a decision procedure for the latter. With the exception of role relationships between nominals/individuals, DLs allow only for expressing tree-shaped structures [8,24]. Even with nominals/individuals, forest-shaped models exists [18]. Hence, we can check query entailment by "folding" the relational structure of (parts of) the query into a tree-shaped form by identifying variables. The resulting queries (query parts), called foldings, can then be expressed as DL concepts (possibly using role conjunctions). Such query concepts can be used to check query entailment: we have that a query (part) is not entailed if a completion graph exists that satisfies none of its foldings.

Example 1. Consider the cyclic Boolean query $Q_1 = \{t(w,x), r(x,y), s(y,z), s(z,w)\}$ (cf. Fig. 1, left-hand side). There are different (tree-shaped) foldings of the query, e.g., by identifying x and z or w and y (cf. Fig. 1, middle and right-hand side). The foldings can be expressed as $\exists(t \sqcap s^-).\exists(r \sqcap s^-).\top$ and $\exists(t^- \sqcap r).\exists(s^- \sqcap s).\top$, respectively.

If we add, for each concept C that represents a folding of the query, the axiom $C \sqsubseteq \bot$ to the knowledge base, then consistency checking reveals query entailment. Note that the tableau algorithm decides for each node whether (sub-)concepts of the foldings are satisfied (due to the internalisation to $\top \sqsubseteq \neg C \sqcup \bot$) and adds corresponding (sub-)concepts or their negations to the node labels and, hence,

$\top \sqsubseteq \downarrow w.S^w$	$S^w \sqsubseteq \forall t.S^w_t$	$S^w_t \sqsubseteq \downarrow x.S^x$	
$S^w_t \sqcap S^x \sqsubseteq S^{wx}$	$S^{wx} \sqsubseteq \forall r.S^{wx}_r$	$S^{wx}_r \sqsubseteq \downarrow y.S^y$	
$S^{wx}_r \sqcap S^y \sqsubseteq S^{wxy}$	$S^{wxy} \sqsubseteq \forall s.S^{wxy}_s$	$S^{wxy}_s \sqsubseteq \downarrow z.S^z$	
$S^{wxy}_s \sqcap S^z \sqsubseteq S^{wxyz}$	$S^{wxyz} \sqsubseteq \forall s.S^{wxyz}_s$	$S^{wxyz}_s \sqcap S^w \sqsubseteq S^{wxyzw}$	$S^{wxyzw} \sqsubseteq \bot$

Fig. 2. The axioms for absorbing the query Q_1 of Example 2

the expansion of nodes is not blocked too early w.r.t. deciding query entailment. Unfortunately, state-of-the-art reasoners do not support role conjunctions and there can be many foldings of a query (especially if the query has several nested cycles or uses role terms with complex roles).

Here we propose to dynamically match and fold the query onto the completion graph. This is achieved by 'absorbing' a query into several simple axioms that can efficiently be processed, where intermediate states encode the parts of the query that are already satisfied. The intermediate states are tracked in the form of so-called *query state concepts* (written S, possibly with sub-/superscripts), which can be seen as fresh atomic concepts with a set of associated bindings of query variables to nodes in the completion graph. To realise this, we extend the tableau algorithm to *create variable bindings* (to match a variable to a node in the completion graph), to *propagate variable bindings* in the process of folding the query onto the completion graph, and to *join variable bindings*. Creating and propagating variable bindings according to the role terms of a query ultimately allows us to detect when cycles are closed.

For the creation of variable bindings, we borrow the $\downarrow$ binders from Hybrid Logics [2]. Informally, a concept of the form $\downarrow x.C$ in the label of a node v instructs the tableau algorithm to create a binding $\{x \mapsto v\}$, which binds x to the node v, and to store the binding for the sub-concept C. For the propagation of bindings, we extend the $\forall$-rule of the tableau algorithm. For example, if $\forall r.C$ is in the label of a node v and the variable binding $\{x \mapsto v\}$ is associated with it, then the tableau algorithm associates $\{x \mapsto v\}$ with C for all r-successors of v. Additionally, propagation can happen within node labels, e.g., if $S \in \mathcal{L}(v)$ with the associated binding $\{x \mapsto v\}$ and the knowledge base contains $S \sqsubseteq C$, we add C to $\mathcal{L}(v)$ and associate it with $\{x \mapsto v\}$. Finally, for joining bindings, we extend the binary unfolding rule. For example, for an axiom $S_1 \sqcap S_2 \sqsubseteq C$ and $S_1, S_2 \in \mathcal{L}(v)$ associated with $\{x \mapsto v, y \mapsto w\}$ and $\{x \mapsto v, z \mapsto w\}$, respectively, we add C associated with the joined bindings $\{x \mapsto v, y \mapsto w, z \mapsto w\}$ to $\mathcal{L}(v)$. With these basic adaptations, we can capture the query in several simple types of axioms: $S_1 \sqsubseteq \downarrow x.S_2$ for creating bindings, $S_1 \sqsubseteq S_2$ and $S_1 \sqsubseteq \forall r.S_2$ for propagating bindings, and $S_1 \sqcap S_2 \sqsubseteq S_3$ for joining bindings, where $S_{(i)}$ are query state concepts and r is a role. The resulting axioms can usually be processed quite efficiently.

3.1 Query Absorption

Before presenting a formal algorithm, we demonstrate how the concepts and axioms for a query are obtained by means of an example. We call this process *absorbing a query*.

Algorithm 1. absorbQ($Q, \mathcal{K}$)

Input: A query Q and a knowledge base $\mathcal{K}$ that is extended via side effects

$z \leftarrow$ choose one variable from vars(Q)
$S^z \leftarrow$ fresh query state concept
$\mathcal{K} \leftarrow \mathcal{K} \cup \{\top \sqsubseteq {\downarrow}z.S^z\}$
$V_{LS}(z) \leftarrow S^z$
for each $q \in Q$ **do**
  if $q = C(x)$ or $q = r(x, y)$, $z \neq x$ **then**
    choose $q_1, q_2, \ldots, q_n \in Q$ with $q_1 = r_1(z, y_1), q_2 = r_2(y_1, y_2), \ldots, q_n = r_n(y_{n-1}, x)$
    for $1 \leq i \leq n$ **do**
      absorbRT($q_i, V_{LS}, \mathcal{K}$)
    end for
  end if
  if $q = C(x)$ **then**
    absorbCT($C(x), V_{LS}, \mathcal{K}$)
    $z \leftarrow x$
  end if
  if $q = r(x, y)$ **then**
    absorbRT($r(x, y), V_{LS}, \mathcal{K}$)
    $z \leftarrow y$
  end if
end for
$S^{z_1 \ldots z_m z} \leftarrow V_{LS}(z)$
$\mathcal{K} \leftarrow \mathcal{K} \cup \{S^{z_1 \ldots z_m z} \sqsubseteq \bot\}$

Algorithm 2. absorbCT($C(x), V_{LS}, \mathcal{K}$)

$S^{x_1 \ldots x_n x} \leftarrow V_{LS}(x)$
$F_C^x \leftarrow$ fresh atomic concept
$S_C^{x_1 \ldots x_n x} \leftarrow$ fresh query state concept
$\mathcal{K} \leftarrow \mathcal{K} \cup \{S^{x_1 \ldots x_n x} \sqsubseteq \neg C \sqcup F_C^x\}$
$\mathcal{K} \leftarrow \mathcal{K} \cup \{S^{x_1 \ldots x_n x} \sqcap F_C^x \sqsubseteq S_C^{x_1 \ldots x_n x}\}$
$V_{LS}(x) \leftarrow S_C^{x_1 \ldots x_n x}$

Algorithm 3. absorbRT($r(x, y), V_{LS}, \mathcal{K}$)

$S^{x_1 \ldots x_n x} \leftarrow V_{LS}(x)$
$S_r^{x_1 \ldots x_n x} \leftarrow$ fresh query state concept
$\mathcal{K} \leftarrow \mathcal{K} \cup \{S^{x_1 \ldots x_n x} \sqsubseteq \forall r.S_r^{x_1 \ldots x_n x}\}$
if $V_{LS}(y)$ is undefined **then**
  $S^y \leftarrow$ fresh query state concept
  $\mathcal{K} \leftarrow \mathcal{K} \cup \{S_r^{x_1 \ldots x_n x} \sqsubseteq {\downarrow}y.S^y\}$
  $V_{LS}(y) \leftarrow S^y$
end if
$S^{y_1 \ldots y_m y} \leftarrow V_{LS}(y)$
$S^{z_1 \ldots z_k} \leftarrow$ fresh query state concept with $z_1 \ldots z_k = x_1 \ldots x_n x\, y_1 \ldots y_m y$
$\mathcal{K} \leftarrow \mathcal{K} \cup \{S_r^{x_1 \ldots x_n x} \sqcap S^{y_1 \ldots y_m y} \sqsubseteq S^{z_1 \ldots z_k}\}$
$V_{LS}(y) \leftarrow S^{z_1 \ldots z_k}$

Example 2 (Example 1 cont.). Consider again $Q_1 = \{t(w, x), r(x, y), s(y, z), s(z, w)\}$. We first pick a starting variable, say w, and introduce the axiom $\top \sqsubseteq {\downarrow}w.S^w$, which triggers, for all nodes, that a binding for w is created. We use the (fresh) query state concept S^w to indicate that w is bound. Since it is convenient to continue with a role term containing w, we choose $t(w, x)$ and propagate the bindings for w to t-successors using the axiom $S^w \sqsubseteq \forall t.S_t^w$ (again S_t^w is fresh and indicates the state that bindings for w have been propagated via t). Nodes to which S_t^w (with the bindings for w) is propagated are suitable bindings for x. This is captured by the axiom $S_t^w \sqsubseteq {\downarrow}x.S^x$. Since S_t^w may be propagated from different nodes, we join the propagated bindings for w and the newly created bindings for x using the axiom $S_t^w \sqcap S^x \sqsubseteq S^{wx}$, for which the extended tableau algorithm attaches the joined bindings to the fresh concept S^{wx}. We proceed analogously for $r(x, y), s(y, z)$, and $s(z, w)$ (see Fig. 2 for all created axioms). Nodes to which the concept S_s^{wxyz} is propagated, potentially close the cycle in the query. The axiom $S_s^{wxyz} \sqcap S^w \sqsubseteq S^{wxyzw}$ checks whether a join is possible. In case it is, the query is satisfied and a clash is triggered by the axiom $S^{wxyzw} \sqsubseteq \bot$. In this case, backtracking is potentially triggered to try other non-deterministic choices which might yield a complete and clash-free completion graph that is a counter example for the query entailment.

The next example demonstrates how concept terms in the query are handled.

Table 2. Tableau rule extensions for creating and propagating variable mappings

$\downarrow$-rule:	if	$\downarrow x.C \in \mathcal{L}(v)$, v not indirectly blocked, and $C \notin \mathcal{L}(v)$ or $\{x \mapsto v\} \notin \mathcal{M}(C, v)$
	then	$\mathcal{L}(v) = \mathcal{L}(v) \cup \{C\}$ and $\mathcal{M}(C, v) = \mathcal{M}(C, v) \cup \{\{x \mapsto v\}\}$
$\forall$-rule:	if	$\forall r.C \in \mathcal{L}(v)$, v not indirectly blocked, there is an r-neighbour w of v with $C \notin \mathcal{L}(w)$ or $\mathcal{M}(\forall r.C, v) \not\subseteq \mathcal{M}(C, w)$
	then	$\mathcal{L}(w) = \mathcal{L}(w) \cup \{C\}$ and $\mathcal{M}(C, w) = \mathcal{M}(C, w) \cup \mathcal{M}(\forall r.C, v)$
$\sqsubseteq_1$-rule:	if	$S^{x_1 \ldots x_n} \sqsubseteq C \in \mathcal{K}$, $S^{x_1 \ldots x_n} \in \mathcal{L}(v)$, v not indirectly blocked, and $C \notin \mathcal{L}(v)$ or $\mathcal{M}(S^{x_1 \ldots x_n}, v) \not\subseteq \mathcal{M}(C, v)$
	then	$\mathcal{L}(v) = \mathcal{L}(v) \cup \{C\}$ and $\mathcal{M}(C, v) = \mathcal{M}(C, v) \cup \mathcal{M}(S^{x_1 \ldots x_n}, v)$
$\sqsubseteq_2$-rule:	if	$S^{x_1 \ldots x_n} \sqcap A \sqsubseteq C \in \mathcal{K}$, $\{S^{x_1 \ldots x_n}, A\} \subseteq \mathcal{L}(v)$, v not indirectly blocked, and $\mathcal{M}(S^{x_1 \ldots x_n}, v) \not\subseteq \mathcal{M}(C, v)$
	then	$\mathcal{L}(v) = \mathcal{L}(v) \cup \{C\}$ and $\mathcal{M}(C, v) = \mathcal{M}(C, v) \cup \mathcal{M}(S^{x_1 \ldots x_n}, v)$
$\sqsubseteq_3$-rule:	if	$S_1^{x_1 \ldots x_n} \sqcap S_2^{y_1 \ldots y_m} \sqsubseteq C \in \mathcal{K}$, $\{S_1^{x_1 \ldots x_n}, S_2^{y_1 \ldots y_m}\} \subseteq \mathcal{L}(v)$, v not indirectly blocked, and $(\mathcal{M}(S_1^{x_1 \ldots x_n}, v) \bowtie \mathcal{M}(S_2^{y_1 \ldots y_m}, v)) \not\subseteq \mathcal{M}(C, v)$
	then	$\mathcal{L}(v) = \mathcal{L}(v) \cup \{C\}$ and $\mathcal{M}(C, v) = \mathcal{M}(C, v) \cup (\mathcal{M}(S_1^{x_1 \ldots x_n}, v) \bowtie \mathcal{M}(S_2^{y_1 \ldots y_m}, v))$

Example 3 (Example 2 cont.). Let $Q_2 = Q_1 \cup \{C(x)\}$. We again pick w as starting node and then process $t(w, x)$, which (again) yields the first four axioms in Fig. 2. Assume we next process $C(x)$. At the state S^{wx}, the tableau algorithm can either satisfy $\neg C$ (which indicates that the query is not satisfied with the bindings for w and x) or we have to assume a query state where also $C(x)$ is satisfied. This is achieved by adding the axiom $S^{wx} \sqsubseteq \neg C \sqcup F_C^x$, where F_C^x is a fresh concept. Note that we want to keep the number of modified tableau rules minimal. Hence, when applied to $\neg C \sqcup F_C^x$, the $\sqcup$-rule does not propagate bindings. In case, the disjunct F_C^x is chosen, we join its empty set of variable bindings with those for S^{wx} using the axiom $S^{wx} \sqcap F_C^x \sqsubseteq S_C^{wx}$, which is handled by the extended binary unfolding rule. For the next role term $r(x, y)$, we then add $S_C^{wx} \sqsubseteq \forall r.S_r^{wx}$ and continue as in Example 2.

Algorithm 1 formalizes the query absorption process and extends the given knowledge base $\mathcal{K}$ via side effects. The functions absorbCT (Algorithm 2) and absorbRT (Algorithm 3) handle concept and role terms, respectively. The functions use a mapping V_{LS} from variables to the last query state concepts, i.e., each variable in the query is mapped to the last introduced query state concept for that variable such that we can later continue or incorporate the propagation for that variable. In the examples, we always chose an adjacent next query term that contained the current variable z. In case a non-adjacent term is chosen, Lines 6–11 ensure the connection to the current variable (which exists as we consider connected queries, see Sect. 2). In our example, if we were to choose $s(y, z)$ as first term in Line 5 (with w as starting variable), Lines 6–11 ensure

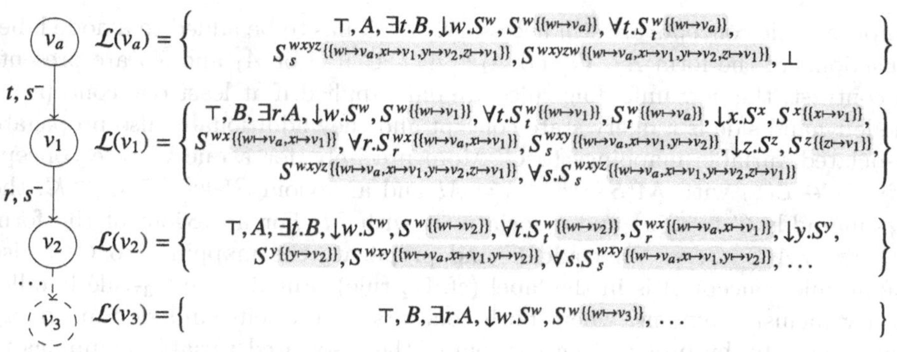

v_a —(t, s^-)→ v_1 —(r, s^-)→ v_2 ··· → v_3

$$\mathcal{L}(v_a) = \left\{ \begin{array}{c} \top, A, \exists t.B, \downarrow w.S^w, S^{w\{\{w \mapsto v_a\}\}}, \forall t.S_t^{w\{\{w \mapsto v_a\}\}}, \\ S_s^{wxyz\{\{w \mapsto v_a, x \mapsto v_1, y \mapsto v_2, z \mapsto v_1\}\}}, S^{wxyzw\{\{w \mapsto v_a, x \mapsto v_1, y \mapsto v_2, z \mapsto v_1\}\}}, \bot \end{array} \right\}$$

$$\mathcal{L}(v_1) = \left\{ \begin{array}{c} \top, B, \exists r.A, \downarrow w.S^w, S^{w\{\{w \mapsto v_1\}\}}, \forall t.S_t^{w\{\{w \mapsto v_1\}\}}, S_t^{w\{\{w \mapsto v_a\}\}}, \downarrow x.S^x, S^{x\{\{x \mapsto v_1\}\}}, \\ S^{wx\{\{w \mapsto v_a, x \mapsto v_1\}\}}, \forall r.S_r^{wx\{\{w \mapsto v_a, x \mapsto v_1\}\}}, S_s^{wxy\{\{w \mapsto v_a, x \mapsto v_1, y \mapsto v_2\}\}}, \downarrow z.S^z, S^{z\{\{z \mapsto v_1\}\}}, \\ S^{wxyz\{\{w \mapsto v_a, x \mapsto v_1, y \mapsto v_2, z \mapsto v_1\}\}}, \forall s.S_s^{wxyz\{\{w \mapsto v_a, x \mapsto v_1, y \mapsto v_2, z \mapsto v_1\}\}} \end{array} \right\}$$

$$\mathcal{L}(v_2) = \left\{ \begin{array}{c} \top, A, \exists t.B, \downarrow w.S^w, S^{w\{\{w \mapsto v_2\}\}}, \forall t.S_t^{w\{\{w \mapsto v_2\}\}}, S_r^{wx\{\{w \mapsto v_a, x \mapsto v_1\}\}}, \downarrow y.S^y, \\ S^{y\{\{y \mapsto v_2\}\}}, S^{wxy\{\{w \mapsto v_a, x \mapsto v_1, y \mapsto v_2\}\}}, \forall s.S_s^{wxy\{\{w \mapsto v_a, x \mapsto v_1, y \mapsto v_2\}\}}, \ldots \end{array} \right\}$$

$$\mathcal{L}(v_3) = \left\{ \top, B, \exists r.A, \downarrow w.S^w, S^{w\{\{w \mapsto v_3\}\}}, \ldots \right\}$$

Fig. 3. Clashed completion graph for Example 4 with propagated variable mappings

that we process, for example, $t(w, x)$ and $r(x, y)$ before we process $s(y, z)$ in Line 17. Clearly, the presented algorithm can further be optimised, e.g., by not creating binder concepts for variables that are not required in joins, but it is already quite convenient to show the principle of the approach.

3.2 Tableau Rules and Blocking Extensions

As outlined in the previous sections, minor extensions and adaptations of the tableau algorithm are required for creating, propagating, and joining bindings as well as for ensuring a correct blocking. First, we discuss the required rule extensions and define the notion of variable mappings:

Definition 1 (Variable Mapping). *A* variable mapping *μ is a (partial) function from variable names to nodes and we refer to the set of elements on which μ is defined as the* domain, *written* $\mathsf{dom}(\mu)$, *of μ. We say that two variable mappings μ_1 and μ_2 are* compatible *if $\mu_1(x) = \mu_2(x)$ for all $x \in \mathsf{dom}(\mu_1) \cap \mathsf{dom}(\mu_2)$.*

For an extended completion graph $G = (V, E, \mathcal{L}, \dot{\neq}, \mathcal{M})$ and $v \in V$, we denote with $\mathcal{M}(C, v)$ the sets of variable mappings that are associated with a concept C in $\mathcal{L}(v)$.

The $\downarrow$-rule creates and associates variable mappings with concept facts in the completion graph, which we then propagate to other concept facts w.r.t. the axioms from the query absorption by using the extensions of expansion rules depicted in Table 2. In particular, the application of the $\forall$-rule to a concept fact $\forall r.C(v)$ now also propagates mappings that are associated with $\forall r.C(v)$ to the concept C in the labels of the r-neighbours. If complex roles have to be handled, one can, for example, use an unfolding of the universal restriction according to the automata for role inclusion axioms [10].

The remaining rules of Table 2 handle the (lazy) unfolding of the new query state concepts in node labels. Please note that the standard unfolding rules for simple atomic concepts are still necessary, i.e., C has to be added to a node label for axioms of the form $A \sqsubseteq C$ and $A_1 \sqcap A_2 \sqsubseteq C$ if A or A_1 and A_2 are present. In contrast, the new unfolding rules are only applied if at least one concept on the left-hand side is a query state concept and they additionally also propagate associated variable mappings to C. More precisely, for a query state concept $S^{x_1 \ldots x_n} \in \mathcal{L}(v)$ with $\mathcal{M}(S^{x_1 \ldots x_n}, v) = M$ and an axiom $S^{x_1 \ldots x_n} \sqsubseteq C \in \mathcal{K}$, the $\sqsubseteq_1$-rule adds C to $\mathcal{L}(v)$ and associates it with M. For an axiom of the form $S^{x_1 \ldots x_n} \sqcap A \sqsubseteq C$, we only add C and propagate the mappings to C if also the atomic concept A is in the label (cf. $\sqsubseteq_2$-rule). Finally, the $\sqsubseteq_3$-rule handles binary inclusion axioms, where both concepts on the left-hand side are query state concepts, by propagating the join of the associated variable mappings to the implied concept.

Definition 2 (Variable Mapping Join). *A variable mapping $\mu_1 \cup \mu_2$ is defined by setting $(\mu_1 \cup \mu_2)(x) = \mu_1(x)$ if $x \in \mathsf{dom}(\mu_1)$, and $(\mu_1 \cup \mu_2)(x) = \mu_2(x)$ otherwise. The* join *$\mathcal{M}_1 \bowtie \mathcal{M}_2$ between the sets of variable mappings $\mathcal{M}_1$ and $\mathcal{M}_2$ is defined as follows:*

$$\mathcal{M}_1 \bowtie \mathcal{M}_2 = \{\mu_1 \cup \mu_2 \mid \mu_1 \in \mathcal{M}_1, \mu_2 \in \mathcal{M}_2 \text{ and } \mu_1 \text{ is compatible with } \mu_2\}.$$

By applying the rules of Table 2 (in addition to the standard tableau rules) for a knowledge base that is extended by the axioms from the query absorption, we get associations of variable mappings with query state concepts such that they indicate which parts of a query (and how these parts) are satisfied in the completion graph.

Example 4 (Example 2 cont.). Assume we extend $\mathcal{K}_1 = \{A(a), A \sqsubseteq \exists t.B, B \sqsubseteq \exists r.A, t \sqsubseteq s^-, r \sqsubseteq s^-\}$ with the axioms from absorbing Q_1 in Fig. 2 and test the consistency with a tableau algorithm extended by the rules of Table 2. We observe that the constructed completion graph contains a clash and, consequently, Q_1 is entailed (cf. Fig. 3). More precisely, we create a node for the individual a and add A to its node label (due to $A(a)$). Now, we alternately create t- and r-successors (due to $A \sqsubseteq \exists t.B$ and $B \sqsubseteq \exists r.A$), where the t-successors are labelled with B and the r-successors with A. Due to $t \sqsubseteq s^-$ and $r \sqsubseteq s^-$, we add s^- to each edge label. It is obvious to see that the folding $\exists(t \sqcap s^-).\exists(r \sqcap s^-).\top$ of Q_1 (cf. Example 1 and Fig. 1) is satisfied for each node that instantiates A.

Due to $\top \sqsubseteq {\downarrow}w.S^w$ from the absorption, we add S^w to each node label and associate S^w with a mapping from w to the node. In particular, for v_a representing the individual a, we associate $\{w \mapsto v_a\}$ with S^w. Note that $\{w \mapsto v_a\} \in \mathcal{M}(S^w, v_a)$ is shown as $S^{w\{\{w \mapsto v_a\}\}}$ in Fig. 3, i.e., we list the set of associated mappings as a second super-script highlighted in grey. To satisfy the axiom $S^w \sqsubseteq \forall t.S^w_t$, we unfold S^w to $\forall t.S^w_t$ and we also keep the variable mappings, i.e., we have $\{w \mapsto v_a\} \in \mathcal{M}(\forall t.S^w_t, v_a)$. Now, the application of the $\forall$-rule propagates $\{w \mapsto v_a\}$ to $S^w_t \in \mathcal{L}(v_1)$. There, we unfold S^w_t to the binder concept for x, i.e., ${\downarrow}x.S^x$. Note that the unfolding would propagate the

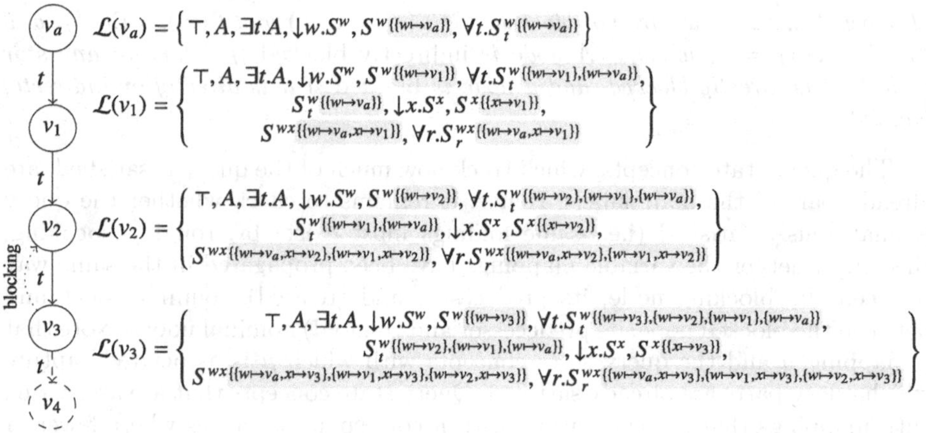

$$\mathcal{L}(v_a) = \left\{ \top, A, \exists t.A, \downarrow w.S^w, S^{w\{\{w \mapsto v_a\}\}}, \forall t.S_t^{w\{\{w \mapsto v_a\}\}} \right\}$$

$$\mathcal{L}(v_1) = \left\{ \begin{array}{c} \top, A, \exists t.A, \downarrow w.S^w, S^{w\{\{w \mapsto v_1\}\}}, \forall t.S_t^{w\{\{w \mapsto v_1\},\{w \mapsto v_a\}\}}, \\ S_t^{w\{\{w \mapsto v_a\}\}}, \downarrow x.S^x, S^{x\{\{x \mapsto v_1\}\}}, \\ S^{wx\{\{w \mapsto v_a, x \mapsto v_1\}\}}, \forall r.S_r^{wx\{\{w \mapsto v_a, x \mapsto v_1\}\}} \end{array} \right\}$$

$$\mathcal{L}(v_2) = \left\{ \begin{array}{c} \top, A, \exists t.A, \downarrow w.S^w, S^{w\{\{w \mapsto v_2\}\}}, \forall t.S_t^{w\{\{w \mapsto v_2\},\{w \mapsto v_1\},\{w \mapsto v_a\}\}}, \\ S_t^{w\{\{w \mapsto v_1\},\{w \mapsto v_a\}\}}, \downarrow x.S^x, S^{x\{\{x \mapsto v_2\}\}}, \\ S^{wx\{\{w \mapsto v_a, x \mapsto v_2\},\{w \mapsto v_1, x \mapsto v_2\}\}}, \forall r.S_r^{wx\{\{w \mapsto v_a, x \mapsto v_2\},\{w \mapsto v_1, x \mapsto v_2\}\}} \end{array} \right\}$$

$$\mathcal{L}(v_3) = \left\{ \begin{array}{c} \top, A, \exists t.A, \downarrow w.S^w, S^{w\{\{w \mapsto v_3\}\}}, \forall t.S_t^{w\{\{w \mapsto v_3\},\{w \mapsto v_2\},\{w \mapsto v_1\},\{w \mapsto v_a\}\}}, \\ S_t^{w\{\{w \mapsto v_2\},\{w \mapsto v_1\},\{w \mapsto v_a\}\}}, \downarrow x.S^x, S^{x\{\{x \mapsto v_3\}\}}, \\ S^{wx\{\{w \mapsto v_a, x \mapsto v_3\},\{w \mapsto v_1, x \mapsto v_3\},\{w \mapsto v_2, x \mapsto v_3\}\}}, \forall r.S_r^{wx\{\{w \mapsto v_a, x \mapsto v_3\},\{w \mapsto v_1, x \mapsto v_3\},\{w \mapsto v_2, x \mapsto v_3\}\}} \end{array} \right\}$$

Fig. 4. Expansion blocked completion graph for Example 5 with variable mappings

associated variable mapping(s) to the binder concept, but they are not depicted in the figures since they are not further used by the $\downarrow$-rule. In fact, the $\downarrow$-rule just creates a new variable mapping $\{x \mapsto v_1\}$ that is then joined by the $\sqsubseteq_3$-rule with $\{w \mapsto v_a\}$ such that we have $\{w \mapsto v_a, x \mapsto v_1\} \in \mathcal{M}(S^{wx}, v_1)$. These steps are repeated until we have $\{w \mapsto v_a, x \mapsto v_1, y \mapsto v_2, z \mapsto v_1\} \in \mathcal{M}(S_s^{wxyz}, v_a)$. Since $\{w \mapsto v_a\}$ is compatible with $\{w \mapsto v_a, x \mapsto v_1, y \mapsto v_2, z \mapsto v_1\}$, the $\sqsubseteq_3$-rule adds the latter variable mapping to $\mathcal{M}(S^{wxyzw}, v_a)$. Finally, the $\sqsubseteq_1$-rule adds $\bot$ to $\mathcal{L}(v_a)$. (In the figures, we again omit the variable mappings that would be associated with $\bot$ due to the unfolding since they are not relevant.) Since all facts and variable mappings are derived deterministically, no non-deterministic alternatives have to be evaluated and entailment of Q_1 is correctly determined.

As one can see from the example, the variable mappings associated with query state concepts directly correspond to foldings of the query. In particular, variables that are mapped to the same node correspond to the folding where the corresponding variables are identified. In addition, if a variable is mapped to a nominal node, then the mapping basically represents the "folding" that is obtained by replacing the variable with the associated nominal/individual (and folding up the remaining terms).

Without further optimisations, we create new bindings for every node and, due to complex roles and/or nominals, variable mappings might be propagated arbitrarily far through a completion graph. At first sight, this seems problematic for blocking. The correspondence with foldings, however, helps us to find a suitable extension of the typically used pairwise blocking technique [10] defined as follows:

Definition 3 (Pairwise Blocking). *Let* $G = (V, E, \mathcal{L}, \dot{\neq}, \mathcal{M})$ *be a completion graph. We say that a node* v *with predecessor* v' *is* directly blocked *if there exists an ancestor node* w *of* v *with predecessor* w' *such that (1)* v, v', w, w' *are* *all blockable, (2) w, w' are not blocked, (3) $\mathcal{L}(v) = \mathcal{L}(w)$ and $\mathcal{L}(v') = \mathcal{L}(w')$, and (4) $\mathcal{L}(\langle v', v\rangle) = \mathcal{L}(\langle w', w\rangle)$. A node is* indirectly blocked *if it has an ancestor node that is directly blocked, and a node is* blocked *if it is directly or indirectly blocked.*

The query state concepts, which track how much of the query is satisfied, are already part of the node labels. Hence, it remains to check whether the query is analogously satisfied (i.e., same foldings must exist) by, roughly speaking, checking whether the variable mappings have been propagated in the same way between the blocking node, its predecessor and (related) nominal nodes and between the blocked node, its predecessor and (related) nominal nodes. Note that a mapping μ and the query state concepts with which μ is associated capture which query parts are already satisfied. Query state concepts that are associated with mappings that are compatible with μ correspond to states where fewer or additional query parts are satisfied. The following notion captures such related query state concepts for a mapping μ and a node v of a completion graph:

Definition 4. *Let $G = (V, E, \mathcal{L}, \dot{\neq}, \mathcal{M})$ be a completion graph. For $v \in V$ and a mapping μ, we set* $\mathsf{states}(v, \mu) = \{C \in \mathcal{L}(v) \mid \mu_v \in \mathcal{M}(C, v)$ *is compatible with* $\mu\}$.

Note that we do not limit states to query state concepts only to enable more absorption optimisations (see [20] for details). We formally capture (query state) concepts associated with a mapping and their relation to blocking with the notion of *analogous propagation blocking* and *witness mappings*:

Definition 5 (Analogous Propagation Blocking). *Let $G = (V, E, \mathcal{L}, \dot{\neq}, \mathcal{M})$ be a completion graph and $o_1, ..., o_n \in V$ all the nominal nodes in G. We say that a node v with predecessor v' is* directly blocked *by w with predecessor w' if v is pairwise blocked by w and, for each mapping $\mu \in \mathcal{M}(C, v) \cup \mathcal{M}(C, v') \cup \mathcal{M}(C, o_1) \cup ... \cup \mathcal{M}(C, o_n)$, $C \in \mathcal{L}(v) \cup \mathcal{L}(v') \cup \mathcal{L}(o_1) \cup ... \cup \mathcal{L}(o_n)$, there exists a* witness mapping *$\mu' \in \mathcal{M}(D, w) \cup \mathcal{M}(D, w') \cup \mathcal{M}(D, o_1) \cup ... \cup \mathcal{M}(D, o_n)$, $D \in \mathcal{L}(w) \cup \mathcal{L}(w') \cup \mathcal{L}(o_1) \cup ... \cup \mathcal{L}(o_n)$ and vice versa such that* $\mathsf{states}(v, \mu) = \mathsf{states}(w, \mu')$, $\mathsf{states}(v', \mu) = \mathsf{states}(w', \mu')$, *and* $\mathsf{states}(o_i, \mu) = \mathsf{states}(o_i, \mu')$ *for $1 \leq i \leq n$.*

Example 5. (Example 2 cont.). For testing entailment of Q_1 over $\mathcal{K}_2 = \{A(a),\ A \sqsubseteq \exists t.A,\ t \circ t \sqsubseteq t\}$, we can capture the transitivity of t by extending the axioms of Fig. 2 with $S_t^w \sqsubseteq \forall t.S_t^w$ (cf. [10]). For the resulting axioms, the tableau algorithm creates a completion graph as depicted in Fig. 4, where the query is not entailed. Due to the cyclic axiom $A \sqsubseteq \exists t.A$, the tableau algorithm successively builds t-successors until blocking is established. Note that new variable mappings are created for all nodes and all mappings are propagated to all descendants due to the transitive role t. Hence, we not only have mappings with new bindings for each new successor, but also an increasing number of mappings. Nevertheless, v_3 is already directly blocked by v_2 using analogous propagation blocking since all pairwise blocking conditions are satisfied (e.g., $\mathcal{L}(v_3) = \mathcal{L}(v_2)$, $\mathcal{L}(v_2) = \mathcal{L}(v_1)$) and we have for each variable mapping a witness

Table 3. Witness mappings for testing analogous propagation blocking for Example 5

μ	μ'	$\mathsf{states}(v_3, \mu) = \mathsf{states}(v_2, \mu')$	$\mathsf{states}(v_2, \mu) = \mathsf{states}(v_1, \mu')$
$\{w \mapsto v_3\}$	$\{w \mapsto v_2\}$	$\{S^w, \forall t.S_t^w, S^x\}$	$\{S^x\}$
$\{w \mapsto v_2\}$	$\{w \mapsto v_1\}$	$\{\forall t.S_t^w, S_t^w, S^x, S^{wx}, \forall r.S_r^{wx}\}$	$\{S^w, \forall t.S_t^w, S^x\}$
$\{w \mapsto v_1\}, \{w \mapsto v_a\}$	$\{w \mapsto v_a\}$	$\{\forall t.S_t^w, S_t^w, S^x, S^{wx}, \forall r.S_r^{wx}\}$	$\{\forall t.S_t^w, S_t^w, S^x, S^{wx}, \forall r.S_r^{wx}\}$
$\{x \mapsto v_3\}$	$\{x \mapsto v_2\}$	$\{S^w, \forall t.S_t^w, S_t^w, S^x, S^{wx}, \forall r.S_r^{wx}\}$	$\{S^w, \forall t.S_t^w, S_t^w\}$
$\{w \mapsto v_a, x \mapsto v_3\}$, $\{w \mapsto v_1, x \mapsto v_3\}$	$\{w \mapsto v_a, x \mapsto v_2\}$	$\{\forall t.S_t^w, S_t^w, S^x, S^{wx}, \forall r.S_r^{wx}\}$	$\{\forall t.S_t^w, S_t^w\}$
$\{w \mapsto v_2, x \mapsto v_3\}$	$\{w \mapsto v_1, x \mapsto v_2\}$	$\{\forall t.S_t^w, S_t^w, S^x, S^{wx}, \forall r.S_r^{wx}\}$	$\{S^w, \forall t.S_t^w\}$
$\{x \mapsto v_2\}$	$\{x \mapsto v_1\}$	$\{S^w, \forall t.S_t^w, S_t^w\}$	$\{S^w, \forall t.S_t^w, S_t^w, S^x, S^{wx}, \forall r.S_r^{wx}\}$
$\{w \mapsto v_a, x \mapsto v_2\}$, $\{w \mapsto v_1, x \mapsto v_2\}$	$\{w \mapsto v_a, x \mapsto v_1\}$	$\{\forall t.S_t^w, S_t^w\}$	$\{\forall t.S_t^w, S_t^w, S^x, S^{wx}, \forall r.S_r^{wx}\}$

mapping as shown in Table 3. For example, for the mapping $\{w \mapsto v_3\}$, we have $\mathsf{states}(v_3, \{w \mapsto v_3\}) = \{S^w, \forall t.S_t^w, S^x\}$ and $\mathsf{states}(v_2, \{w \mapsto v_3\}) = \{S^x\}$ due to the compatible mappings $\{x \mapsto v_3\}$ and $\{x \mapsto v_2\}$, respectively (cf. first row of Table 3). A witness for $\{w \mapsto v_3\}$ is $\{w \mapsto v_2\}$ since $\mathsf{states}(v_2, \{w \mapsto v_2\}) = \{S^w, \forall t.S_t^w, S^x\}$ and $\mathsf{states}(v_1, \{w \mapsto v_2\}) = \{S^x\}$.

To avoid considering all nominal nodes in blocking tests, one could obtain restricted sets of relevant nominal nodes by "remembering" nominal nodes over which variable mappings have been propagated, by tracking the usage of nominals for descendants or by indexing variable mappings propagated over nominal nodes.

3.3 Correctness and Termination Sketches

As long as no new nominals are generated, a tableau algorithm with the presented extensions terminates since the sets of (query state) concepts that are used by analogous propagation blocking are bounded by the number of concepts occurring in the knowledge base and in the query absorption. Hence, we eventually have variable mappings that are associated with the same set of concepts for the nodes relevant for determining blocking. At the same time, analogous propagation blocking delays blocking sufficiently to guarantee that the completion graph is expanded enough to show (non-)entailment of the query. In addition, we observe that the query state concepts with their associated variable mappings correspond to concepts that represent satisfied (parts of) foldings of the query. Hence, correctness of the algorithm can be shown by transforming a fully expanded and clash-free completion graph with propagated variable mappings to a fully expanded and clash-free completion graph, where instead the correspondingly satisfied (sub-)concepts of folding are in the node labels and vice versa. Further details are provided in the accompanying technical report [20].

4 Optimized Query Answering Reduction

Instead of naively grounding conjunctive queries with answer variables (e.g., by adding nominal concept terms), leading to (exponentially) many query entailment checks, we can modify the presented absorption algorithm such that it delivers (candidates for) answers. For this, we extend the knowledge base by assertions of the form $O(a)$ for each individual a, where O is a fresh atomic concept that allows for distinguishing known and anonymous individuals. We then extend the query with concept terms of the form $O(x)$ for each answer variable x and absorb the query as presented in Sect. 3, but omit the implication of $\bot$ from the last query state concept. If the tableau algorithm succeeds to construct a fully expanded and clash-free completion graph, then the variable mappings that are propagated to and associated with the last query state concept in node labels encode the answer candidates. Moreover, by analysing whether variable mappings have been propagated deterministically, i.e., mappings that do not depend on non-deterministic decisions, we can already identify which of the candidates are certain answers. For the non-deterministically derived/propagated variable mappings, we have to verify the obtained answer candidates with corresponding query entailment checks. If most consequences of the knowledge base can be derived deterministically, then we often also get the answers by only extracting them from the propagated variable mappings, i.e., the approach mimics a one-pass behaviour for "relatively simple and mostly deterministic" ontologies.

The presented query answering approach can further be extended to exploit realisation results. In fact, query terms with only answer variables (and only atomic concepts) correspond to (atomic) concept and role instance retrieval queries, which are typically answered by the realisation service. Hence, we resolve these parts of a query via realisation and interpret the answers as an upper bound for the entire query. Then, we absorb the remaining part of the query by using restricted binder concepts for answer variables such that the $\downarrow$-rule only creates a binding if the binder concept is in the label of a node that represents an individual from the determined upper bound of the corresponding variable. This reduces the propagation work in completion graphs since only the remaining query terms have to be considered and only certain bindings are created.

5 Implementation and Experiments

We implemented the presented query answering approach into the tableau-based reasoning system Konclude [22], which supports the DL $\mathcal{SROIQ}$ with nominal schemas, i.e., an extension of the nominal constructor by variables for natively representing rule-based knowledge in ontologies. Axioms with nominal schemas are also absorbed in Konclude such that variable bindings are appropriately propagated through the completion graph [21], which we reuse to some extent for the query answering extension. A major difference is, however, that bindings for variables are now also created/allowed for anonymous individuals, i.e., blockable nodes in completion graphs, which requires the more sophisticated blocking technique. In addition, specialised binder concepts are used to be able to restrict the creation of bindings to determined candidates as described in Sect. 4. Furthermore, Konclude uses variants of completion graph caching techniques such that only those parts of completion graphs have to be constructed

Table 4. Statistics for evaluated ontologies with query entailment checking (EC) times in seconds

Ontology	DL	#Axioms	#C	#P	#I	#Assertions	#Q	EC avg/max [s]
DMKB	$\mathcal{SROIQ}$	4,945	697	177	653	1,500	50	0.30 / 1.08
Family	$\mathcal{SROIQ}(\mathcal{D})$	317	61	87	405	1,523	50	180.32 / $\geq$ 300.00
Finance$_{\setminus\mathcal{D}}$	$\mathcal{ALCROIQ}$	1,391	323	247	2,466	2,809	50	0.15 / 0.33
FMA3.1$_{\setminus\mathcal{D}}$	$\mathcal{ALCOIN}$	86,898	83,284	122	232,647	501,220	50	0.10 / 0.83
GeoSkills$_{\setminus\mathcal{D}}$	$\mathcal{ALCHOIN}$	738	603	23	2,592	5,985	50	0.13 / 0.25
OBI	$\mathcal{SROIQ}(\mathcal{D})$	6,216	2,826	116	167	235	50	0.06 / 0.34
UOBM(1)	$\mathcal{SHOIN}(\mathcal{D})$	206	69	44	24,858	257,658	50	0.77 / 7.12
Wine	$\mathcal{SHOIN}(\mathcal{D})$	643	214	31	367	903	50	0.08 / 0.29

that are (potentially) relevant for satisfiability tests, which has been adapted for query answering. The cached graphs are also indexed to quickly resolve candidates for answer variables. We further collect approximative statistics of how (often) concept and role facts are derived in the consistency test (e.g., whether they are derived (non-)deterministically and/or only for nominal nodes) in order to absorb the query terms in an order that ideally leads to few and cheap propagations (e.g., by preferring propagations over role terms with few and mostly deterministically derived instances).

At the moment, Konclude may not terminate for $\mathcal{SROIQ}$ ontologies if the absorption of the query leads to propagations over new nominal nodes. However, this does not seem problematic in practice. For example, the ORE2015 dataset [17] contains 1920 ontologies (with trivial ontologies already filtered out), but only 399 use all problematic language features (36 with unqualified, 281 with qualified, and 82 with functional number restrictions). Konclude never applied the new nominal rule in the consistency checks for these 399 ontologies, but we terminated the reasoner (and, hence, the analysis of the new nominal generation) for 4 ontologies after reaching the time limit of 5 min. Even if new nominals have to be generated repeatedly by the tableau algorithm, it would further be required that the query propagates differently over new nominal and blockable nodes such that blocking cannot be established.

For evaluating (the limits of) the presented query entailment checking approach,[1] we generated and/or hand-crafted 400 cyclic and non-trivial queries for interesting ontologies, such as DMKB, FMA, OBI, UOBM [14], i.e., ontologies from well-known repositories that use many features of $\mathcal{SROIQ}$ and have at least 100 individuals. Table 4 shows some metrics for these ontologies as well as the average and maximum query entailment checking times (last column). Note that the columns #C, #P, #I, and #Q denote the number of classes, properties, individuals, and queries and that the assertions are not counted to the number of axioms. In summary (see [20] for details), the entailment for most queries (90%) can be decided in under one second by using one core of a Dell PowerEdge R420

[1] Source code, evaluation data, all results, and a Docker image (koncludeeval/abqa) for easily reproducing the evaluations are available online, e.g., at https://zenodo.org/record/3266160.

Table 5. Ontologies with evaluated query answering times in seconds

Ontology	DL	#Axioms	#Assertions	#Q	Konclude	OWL BGP	PAGOdA	Pellet
$\text{ChEMBL}_{1\%}$	$\mathcal{SRIQ}(\mathcal{D})$	3,171	2,884,896	6	0.3	1800.0	0.7	17.7
FLY	$\mathcal{SRI}$	20,715	1,606	11	4.7	3300.0	20.3	3300.0
LUBM(1)	$\mathcal{ALEHI}^{+}(\mathcal{D})$	93	100,543	35	1.2	16.8	5.4	11.2
$\text{Reactome}_{10\%}$	$\mathcal{SHIN}(\mathcal{D})$	600	1,314,640	7	0.4	2100.0	14.4	33.8
$\text{Uniprot}_{1\%}$	$\mathcal{ALCHOIQ}(\mathcal{D})$	608	1,112,441	13	0.3	3900.0	2.7	307.8
UOBM(1)	$\mathcal{SHIN}(\mathcal{D})$	246	257,658	20	6.6	6000.0	22.7	972.7
ALL				92	13.6	17116.8	66.1	4643.2

server with two Intel Xeon E5-2440 CPUs at 2.4 GHz and 144 GB RAM under a 64bit Ubuntu 16.04.5 LTS. However, Konclude reached the time limit of 5 min for several queries of the Family ontology since complex roles caused propagations to many nodes such that blocking tests became quite involved. Due to the fact that many state-of-the-art reasoners such as HermiT [4] and Pellet [19] cannot even classify the Family ontology within 5 min, it can be seen as particularly difficult. It also has to be considered that typical real-world queries are often not Boolean and it is usually possible to identify individuals that could be affected by the query (e.g., from answer variables) such that only certain parts of completion graphs have to be considered for the remaining (entailment) computations (with appropriate completion graph caching techniques). To further improve the performance, one could, however, also use a representative propagation of variable mappings [21] for entailment checks and/or index more precisely which nodes constitute blocker candidates.

To further compare our query answering approach with existing systems, we used the ontologies and (non-trivial) queries from the PAGOdA evaluation [25] (cf. Table 5). (See footnote 1). Note that we excluded trivial concept and role instance retrieval queries since they can be handled by (concept and role) realisation, for which already corresponding evaluations exist (see, e.g., [17]). Since these expressive ontologies easily become problematic for several reasoning systems, we used the smallest versions of the available datasets.

We compared the absorption-based query answering approach with OWL BGP [6], PAGOdA, and Pellet, which are systems that are based on fully-fledged $\mathcal{SROIQ}$ reasoners and, hence, principally capable of answering (restricted) conjunctive queries w.r.t. knowledge bases that are formulated with more expressive DLs. Note that OWL BGP as well as PAGOdA use a fully-fledged reasoner (usually HermiT) in form of a black-box, but try to reduce the calls to the reasoner with different (lower and upper bound) optimisations. OWL BGP can mostly be considered as an adapter that enables to answer conjunctive instance queries, whereas PAGOdA tries to delegate most of the workload to a more efficient datalog engine. We tried to separate the preprocessing (i.e., loading, consistency checking, classification, etc.) from the actual query answering time. Since we could not find a simple way to realise this for Pellet, we interpreted the fastest query answering response as preprocessing/preparation time. As far it has been configurable, we used only one core of the Dell PowerEdge R420 server for each reasoner to facilitate the comparison. Moreover, we used for each query a new instance of the reasoner with a time limit of 5 min. If a reasoner did not finish the preprocessing within the time limit, then we also interpreted the response time for the query answering task as a timeout, i.e., as 5 min.

The query answering times accumulated per ontology are depicted in Table 5. By considering the accumulated times over all ontologies (last row), one can say that Konclude outperforms the other systems for the evaluated ontologies and queries. In fact, Konclude is faster than the other systems for all ontologies. Although PAGOdA can answer all queries for all evaluated ontologies, it is clearly slower than Konclude for $\text{Reactome}_{10\%}$ and the FLY ontology. For FLY, PAGOdA had to fall back to the fully-fledged reasoner, i.e., HermiT, for one query and these calls consumed most of the time. PAGOdA and Konclude returned the same answers for all queries,[2] whereas some answers are incomplete for OWL BGP and Pellet due to their restrictions w.r.t. existential variables. Pellet and especially OWL BGP are significantly slower than Konclude and PAGOdA. On the one hand, this is due to the fact that Pellet and HermiT cannot handle these ontologies as easily as Konclude and they do not have optimisations to delegate parts of the reasoning to more specialised systems (such as PAGOdA). On the other hand, our query answering is much "deeper integrated" into the reasoning system and, hence, it can better utilise the internal data structures and can profit more from corresponding (reduction) optimisations. Also preprocessing (i.e., loading, consistency checking, etc.) is significantly faster for Konclude than for the other systems (it required at most half of their time).

6 Conclusions

We presented a new query answering approach based on the well-known absorption optimisation that works well for several more expressive Description Logics and can nicely be integrated into state-of-the-art tableau-based reasoning systems. More precisely, the approach rewrites/absorbs a conjunctive query into several simple axioms such that minor extensions of the tableau algorithm appropriately create and propagate bindings for variables through completion graphs, which then basically encode the satisfied foldings of a query. Soundness, completeness, and termination is guaranteed as long as only a limited number of new nominals has to be introduced in the reasoning process, which seems always the case in practice.

The deep integration facilitates special optimisations that closely interact with other reasoning services and utilise the internal data structures of the reasoner, which results in a good performance. In fact, we integrated the presented query answering approach into the reasoning system Konclude and evaluated it with several real-world as well as benchmark ontologies. The comparison with

[2] PAGOdA ignores the cardinality of answers by evaluating all SPARQL queries as they have the DISTINCT modifier.

state-of-the-art, but restricted query answering systems shows that our approach often achieves competitive performance or even outperforms these other systems.

References

1. Baader, F., Calvanese, D., McGuinness, D., Nardi, D., Patel-Schneider, P. (eds.): The Description Logic Handbook: Theory, Implementation, and Applications, 2nd edn. Cambridge University Press, Cambridge (2007)
2. Blackburn, P., Seligman, J.: Hybrid languages. J. Logic Lang. Inf. **4**(3), 251–272 (1995)
3. Calvanese, D., Eiter, T., Ortiz, M.: Answering regular path queries in expressive description logics: an automata-theoretic approach. In: Proceedings of National Conference on Artificial Intelligence (2007)
4. Glimm, B., Horrocks, I., Motik, B., Stoilos, G., Wang, Z.: HermiT: an OWL 2 reasoner. J. Autom. Reasoning **53**(3), 1–25 (2014)
5. Glimm, B., Horrocks, I., Sattler, U.: Unions of conjunctive queries in SHOQ. In: Proceedings of International Conference on Principles of Knowledge Representation and Reasoning (2008)
6. Glimm, B., Kazakov, Y., Kollia, I., Stamou, G.: Lower and upper bounds for SPARQL queries over OWL ontologies. In: Proceedings of National Conference on Artificial Intelligence (2015)
7. Glimm, B., Lutz, C., Horrocks, I., Sattler, U.: Conjunctive query answering for the description logic SHIQ. J. Artif. Intell. Res. **31**, 157–204 (2008)
8. Grädel, E.: Why are modal logics so robustly decidable? In: Current Trends in Theoretical Computer Science, Entering the 21th Century, vol. 2, pp. 393–408. World Scientific (2001)
9. Haarslev, V., Möller, R., Wessel, M.: Querying the semantic web with Racer+nRQL. In: Proceedings of KI-2004 International Workshop on Applications of Description Logics (2004)
10. Horrocks, I., Kutz, O., Sattler, U.: The even more irresistible SROIQ. In: Proceedings International Conference on Principles of Knowledge Representation and Reasoning. AAAI Press (2006)
11. Horrocks, I., Tessaris, S.: Querying the semantic web: a formal approach. In: Horrocks, I., Hendler, J. (eds.) ISWC 2002. LNCS, vol. 2342, pp. 177–191. Springer, Heidelberg (2002). https://doi.org/10.1007/3-540-48005-6_15
12. Hudek, A.K., Weddell, G.E.: Binary absorption in tableaux-based reasoning for description logics. In: Proceedings of International Workshop on Description Logics, vol. 189. CEUR (2006)
13. Kollia, I., Glimm, B.: Optimizing SPARQL query answering over OWL ontologies. J. Artif. Intell. Res. **48**, 253–303 (2013)
14. Ma, L., Yang, Y., Qiu, Z., Xie, G., Pan, Y., Liu, S.: Towards a complete OWL ontology benchmark. In: Sure, Y., Domingue, J. (eds.) ESWC 2006. LNCS, vol. 4011, pp. 125–139. Springer, Heidelberg (2006). https://doi.org/10.1007/11762256_12
15. Ortiz, M., Calvanese, D., Eiter, T.: Data complexity of query answering in expressive description logics via tableaux. J. Autom. Reasoning **41**(1), 61–98 (2008)
16. Pan, J.Z., Thomas, E., Zhao, Y.: Completeness guaranteed approximation for OWL-DL query answering. In: Proceedings of International Workshop on Description Logics, vol. 477. CEUR (2009)

17. Parsia, B., Matentzoglu, N., Gonçalves, R.S., Glimm, B., Steigmiller, A.: The OWL reasoner evaluation (ORE) 2015 competition report. J. Autom. Reasoning **59**(4), 455–482 (2017)
18. Rudolph, S., Glimm, B.: Nominals, inverses, counting, and conjunctive queries or: why infinity is your friend!. J. Artif. Intell. Res. **39**, 429–481 (2010)
19. Sirin, E., Parsia, B., Cuenca Grau, B., Kalyanpur, A., Katz, Y.: Pellet: a practical OWL-DL reasoner. J. Web Semant. **5**(2), 51–53 (2007)
20. Steigmiller, A., Glimm, B.: Absorption-based query answering for expressive description logics - technical report. Technical report, Ulm University, Ulm, Germany (2019). https://www.uni-ulm.de/fileadmin/website_uni_ulm/iui.inst.090/Publikationen/2019/StGl2019-ABQA-TR-ISWC.pdf
21. Steigmiller, A., Glimm, B., Liebig, T.: Reasoning with nominal schemas through absorption. J. Autom. Reason. **53**(4), 351–405 (2014)
22. Steigmiller, A., Liebig, T., Glimm, B.: Konclude: system description. J. Web Semantics **27**(1), 78–85 (2014)
23. Stoilos, G., Stamou, G.: Hybrid query answering over OWL ontologies. In: Proceedings of European Conference on Artificial Intelligence (2014)
24. Vardi, M.Y.: Why is modal logic so robustly decidable? In: Proceedings of DIMACS Workshop on Descriptive Complexity and Finite Models, vol. 31. American Mathematical Society (1997)
25. Zhou, Y., Cuenca Grau, B., Nenov, Y., Kaminski, M., Horrocks, I.: PAGOdA: pay-as-you-go ontology query answering using a datalog reasoner. J. Artif. Intell. Res. **54**, 309–367 (2015)

TransEdge: Translating Relation-Contextualized Embeddings for Knowledge Graphs

Zequn Sun[1], Jiacheng Huang[1], Wei Hu[1(✉)], Muhao Chen[2], Lingbing Guo[1], and Yuzhong Qu[1]

[1] State Key Laboratory for Novel Software Technology, Nanjing University, Nanjing, Jiangsu, China
zqsun.nju@gmail.com, jchuang.nju@gmail.com, lbguo.nju@gmail.com, {whu,yzqu}@nju.edu.cn

[2] Department of Computer Science, University of California, Los Angeles, CA, USA
muhaochen@ucla.edu

Abstract. Learning knowledge graph (KG) embeddings has received increasing attention in recent years. Most embedding models in literature interpret relations as linear or bilinear mapping functions to operate on entity embeddings. However, we find that such relation-level modeling cannot capture the diverse relational structures of KGs well. In this paper, we propose a novel edge-centric embedding model TransEdge, which contextualizes relation representations in terms of specific head-tail entity pairs. We refer to such contextualized representations of a relation as edge embeddings and interpret them as translations between entity embeddings. TransEdge achieves promising performance on different prediction tasks. Our experiments on benchmark datasets indicate that it obtains the state-of-the-art results on embedding-based entity alignment. We also show that TransEdge is complementary with conventional entity alignment methods. Moreover, it shows very competitive performance on link prediction.

Keywords: Knowledge graphs · Contextualized embeddings · Entity alignment · Link prediction

1 Introduction

A knowledge graph (KG) is a multi-relational graph, whose nodes correspond to entities and directed edges indicate the specific relations between entities. For example, Fig. 1(a) shows a snapshot of the graph-structured relational triples in DBpedia. In KGs, each labeled edge is usually represented by a relational triple in the form of (`head`, `relation`, `tail`)[1], meaning that the two entities `head` and

[1] In the following, (`head`, `relation`, `tail`) is abbreviated as (h, r, t).

C. Ghidini et al. (Eds.): ISWC 2019, LNCS 11778, pp. 612–629, 2019.
https://doi.org/10.1007/978-3-030-30793-6_35

`tail` hold a specific `relation`. So, a typical KG can be defined as a triple $\mathcal{K} = (\mathcal{E}, \mathcal{R}, \mathcal{T})$, where $\mathcal{E}$ is the set of entities (i.e., nodes), $\mathcal{R}$ is the set of relations (i.e., edge labels), and $\mathcal{T} = \mathcal{E} \times \mathcal{R} \times \mathcal{E}$ denotes the set of relational triples (i.e., labeled edges). Each entity or relation is usually denoted by a URI. For example, the URI of New Zealand in DBpedia is `dbr : New_Zealand`[2]. However, such discrete and symbolic representations of KGs fall short of supporting the efficient knowledge inference [31]. Thus, learning continuous and low-dimensional embedding representations for KGs has drawn much attention in recent years and facilitated many KG-related tasks, such as link prediction [2,8,14,17,27,29,32, 34,35], entity alignment [3,4,9,25,26,33] and entity classification tasks [5,15,22].

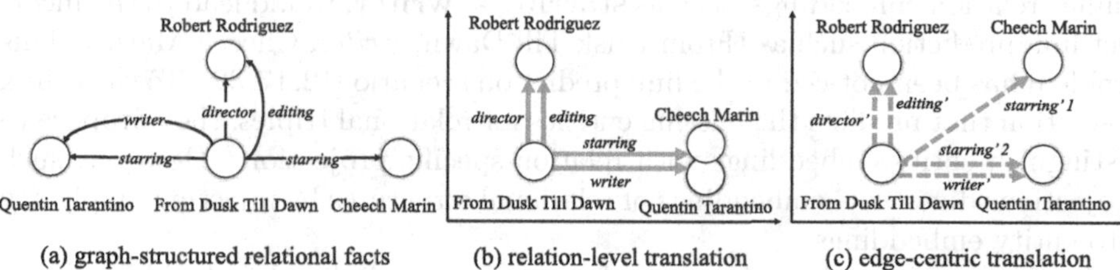

Fig. 1. (a) A snapshot of the relational facts of "From Dusk Till Dawn" in DBpedia. Circles represent entities and directed edges have labels. (b) Illustration of the relation-level translation between entity embeddings, where circles represent entity embeddings, and bold gray arrows denote the translation vectors of relations. (c) Illustration of the proposed edge-centric translation, where the dotted arrows denote the contextualized representations, i.e., edge embeddings. For example, *starring'* 1 and *starring'* 2 are two contextualized representations of the relation *starring*.

KG embedding seeks to encode the entities and relations into vector spaces, and capture semantics by the geometric properties of embeddings. To model the relational structures of KGs, most embedding models in literature interpret relations as linear or bilinear mapping functions operating on entity embeddings, such as the relation translation in TransE [2], the relation matrix factorization in DistMult [34], and the relation rotation in RotatE [27]. We refer to this kind of models as relation-level embedding. However, such relation-level models represent each relation with one embedding representation for all related head-tail entity pairs, which cannot well reflect the complex relational structures of KGs. As shown in Fig. 1(a), different entity pairs may share the same relation while one entity pair may hold different relations. The relation-level embedding cannot distinguish the different contexts of relations, which would lead to indistinguishable embeddings and incorrect relation inference.

Specifically, we take the translational KG embedding model TransE [2] as an example to explicate the aforementioned issue. TransE interprets relations as translation vectors between entity embeddings. For example, given a relational triple (h, r, t), TransE expects $\mathbf{h} + \mathbf{r} \approx \mathbf{t}$ to hold, where the boldfaced

[2] http://dbpedia.org/resource/New_Zealand.

letters denote the embeddings of entities and relations. The relation embedding **r** serves as a translation vector from **h** to **t**. However, such relation translation encounters issues when facing more complex relations. For example, considering the relational triples in Fig. 1(a): (From Dusk Till Dawn, *starring*, Quentin Tarantino) and (From Dusk Till Dawn, *starring*, Cheech Marin), translational KG embeddings would have **Quentin Tarantino** $\approx$ **Cheech Marin**, as shown in Fig. 1(b). In other words, the different entities getting involved in the same relation would be embedded very closely by the same relation translation. Such indistinguishable entity embeddings go against accurate embedding-based entity alignment. Quentin Tarantino and Cheech Marin would be mistaken for an aligned entity pair due to the high similarity of their embeddings. Besides, the similar relation embeddings, such as **starring** $\approx$ **writer**, would lead to the incorrect link prediction such as (From Dusk Till Dawn, *writer*, Cheech Marin). This problem has been noticed in the link prediction scenario [12,17,32]. Towards link prediction that predicts the missing entities for relational triples, they propose to distinguish entity embeddings with relation-specific projections. However, such projections divest KG embeddings of relational structures by injecting ambiguity into entity embeddings.

In this paper, we introduce an edge-centric translational embedding model TransEdge, which differentiates the representations of a relation between different entity-specific contexts. This idea is motivated by the graph structures of KGs. Let us see Fig. 1(a). One head-tail entity pair can hold different relations, i.e, one edge can have different labels. Also, different edges can have the same label, indicating that there are multiple head-tail entity pairs having the same relation. Thus, it is intuitive that entities should have explicit embeddings while relations should have different contextualized representations when translating between different head-tail entity pairs. Thus, we propose to contextualize relations as different edge embeddings. The context of a relation is specified by its head and tail entities. We study two different methods, i.e., context compression and context projection, for computing edge embeddings given the edge direction (head and tail entity embeddings) and edge label (relation embeddings). To capture the KG structures, we follow the idea of translational KG embeddings and build translations between entity embeddings with edge embeddings. This modeling is simple but has appropriate geometric interpretations as shown in Fig. 1(c). Our main contributions are listed as follows:

(1) We propose a novel KG embedding model TransEdge. Different from existing models that learn one simple embedding per relation, TransEdge learns KG embeddings by contextualizing relation representations in terms of the specific head-tail entity pairs. We refer to such contextualized representations of a relation as edge embeddings and build edge translations between entity embeddings to capture the relational structures of KGs. TransEdge provides a novel perspective for KG embedding (Sect. 3).
(2) We evaluate TransEdge on two tasks: entity alignment between two KGs and link prediction in a single KG. Experimental results on five datasets show that TransEdge obtains the state-of-the-art results on entity align-

ment. It also achieves very competitive performance (even the best Hits@1) on link prediction with low computational complexity. These experiments verify the good generalization of TransEdge. To the best of our knowledge, TransEdge is the first KG embedding model that achieves the best Hits@1 performance on both embedding-based entity alignment and link prediction (Sect. 4).

2 Related Work

In recent years, various KG embedding models have been proposed. The most popular task to evaluate KG embeddings is link prediction. Besides, embedding-based entity alignment also draws much attention recently. In this section, we discuss these two lines of related work.

2.1 KG Embeddings Evaluated by Link Prediction

We divide existing KG embedding models evaluated by link prediction into three categories, i.e., *translational*, *bilinear* and *neural* models. TransE [2] introduces the translational KG embeddings. It interprets relations as translation vectors operating on entity embeddings. Given a relational triple (h, r, t), TransE defines the following energy function to measure the error of relation translation: $f_{\text{TransE}}(h, r, t) = ||\mathbf{h}+\mathbf{r}-\mathbf{t}||$, where $||\cdot||$ denotes either the L_1 or L_2 vector norm. To resolve the issues of TransE on modeling complex relations, some improved translational models have been put forward, including TransH [32], TransR [17] and TransD [12]. Their key idea is to let entities have relation-specific embeddings by transformations operating on entity embeddings, such as the hyperplane projection in TransH and the space projection in TransR and TransD. We argue that such transformations introduce ambiguity to entity embeddings as they separate the original entity embedding into many dispersive relation-specific representations. For example, for each relation r, entity h would hold a representation $\mathbf{h}_r$. These dispersive representations compromise the semantic integrity in KGs as each relation is modeled separately in the relation-specific hyperplane or space. The general entity embeddings $\mathbf{h}$ and $\mathbf{t}$ are not explicitly translated by relation vectors. Although our model can also be viewed as a kind of translational KG embedding, we introduce the edge-centric model that contextualizes relations with edge embeddings.

Besides, there are some *bilinear* models that exploit similarity-based functions to compute the energy of relational triples. DistMult [34] and ComplEx [29] use the bilinear Hadamard product to compute energy. HolE [20] substitutes the Hadamard product with circular correlation. Analogy [18] imposes analogical properties on embeddings. SimplE [14] proposes an enhancement of Canonical Polyadic (CP) decomposition to compute energy. CrossE [35] exploits to simulate the crossover interactions between entities and relations. RotatE [27] defines each relation as a rotation from the head entity to the tail in the complex-valued embedding space. Recently, there are also some *neural* embedding models including ProjE [24], ConvE [8], R-GCN [23] and ConvKB [19]. These bilinear and neural models achieve superior results on link prediction at the cost of much higher model complexity. Besides, many of these embedding models also have the identified shortcomings, such as HolE and ProjE.

2.2 KG Embeddings for Entity Alignment

Recently, several embedding-based entity alignment models have been proposed. MTransE [4] captures two KG-specific vector spaces and jointly learns a transformation between them. IPTransE [36] employs PTransE [16] to embed two KGs into a unified vector space. It iteratively updates alignment information through a self-training technique. JAPE [25] incorporates attribute embeddings for entity alignment. BootEA [26] solves the entity alignment problem in a bootstrapping manner. KDCoE [3] co-trains description embeddings and structure embeddings to incorporate both the literal and structural information of KGs for entity alignment. GCN-Align [33] employs graph convolutional networks to learn KG embeddings for entity alignment. AttrE [30] regards literal values as "virtual entities" and uses TransE to embed the attribute triples for entity alignment. Note that, some of these models exploit additional resources in KGs for entity alignment, such as relation paths (IPTransE), textual descriptions (KDCoE) and literal values (AttrE). By contrast, the proposed TransEdge leverages the basic relational structures for KG embedding, without using additional resources.

3 Edge-Centric Knowledge Graph Embedding

TransEdge embeds the entities and relations of KGs in a d-dimensional vector space. Unlike the conventional relation-level models, for a relational triple, the head and tail entity embeddings in TransEdge hold an edge translation. Figure 2 illustrates the main idea. The contextualization operator ψ takes as input the combined embeddings of the head and tail entities (edge direction) as well as the relation embedding (edge label) to compute edge embeddings.

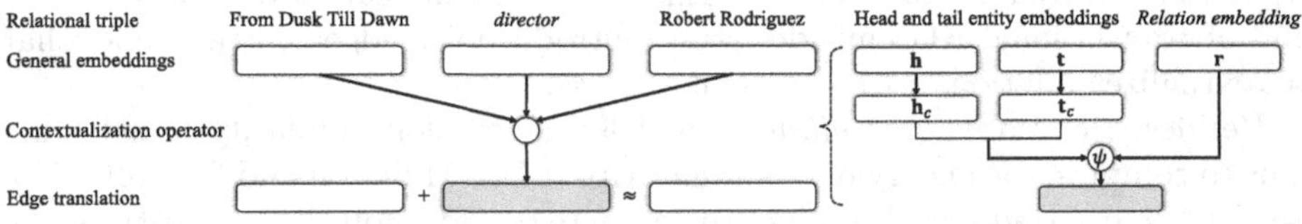

Fig. 2. Illustration of the key idea of relation-contextualized KG embeddings. The white boxes denote the general embeddings of entities and relations, and the gray boxes denote the contextualized representation for this relation, i.e., the edge embedding. $\mathbf{h}_c$ and $\mathbf{t}_c$ are the interaction embeddings for entities. ψ is a contextualization operator.

3.1 Formulation of Energy Function

Like TransE, we define an energy function to measure the error of edge translation between entity embeddings. For simplicity, the energy of a relational triple (h, r, t) in TransEdge is written as follows:

$$f(h,r,t) = ||\mathbf{h} + \psi(\mathbf{h}_c, \mathbf{t}_c, \mathbf{r}) - \mathbf{t}||. \quad (1)$$

The edge embedding $\psi(\mathbf{h}_c, \mathbf{t}_c, \mathbf{r})$ corresponds to a translation vector between the head to tail entity embeddings. In TransEdge, we learn a general embedding for each entity, such as $\mathbf{h}$ for h. General embeddings capture the geometric positions and relational semantics of entities in the vector space. We also introduce interaction embeddings for entities, such as $\mathbf{h}_c$ for h, which are used to encode their participation in the calculation of edge embeddings. Separating the interaction embeddings from general ones can avoid the interference of such two different information.

3.2 Contextualization Operation

The calculation of edge embeddings $\psi(\mathbf{h}_c, \mathbf{t}_c, \mathbf{r})$ should involve the information of both the head and tail entities (edge direction), as well as the relations (edge label). We study two different methods shown in Fig. 3, which are discussed in detail below.

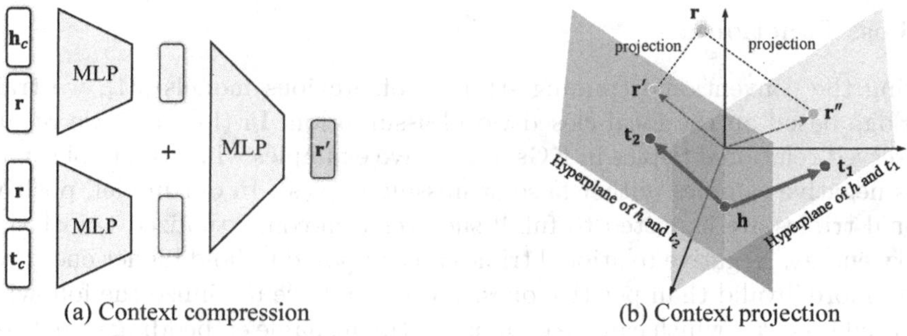

Fig. 3. Illustration of the proposed contextualization operations.

Context Compression. This method uses multilayer perceptrons (MLPs) to compress the embeddings of the edge direction and label. Specifically, given a MLP with one hidden layer (i.e., two layers in total plus the output layer) and the input vector $\mathbf{v}^{(0)}$, each layer is calculated with a set of weight matrices $\mathbf{W}$ and vectors $\mathbf{b}$:

$$\mathbf{v}^{(1)} = \sigma\big(\mathbf{W}^{(1)}\,\mathbf{v}^{(0)} + \mathbf{b}^{(1)}\big), \;\; \mathbf{v}^{(2)} = \sigma\big(\mathbf{W}^{(2)}\,\mathbf{v}^{(1)} + \mathbf{b}^{(2)}\big), \quad (2)$$

where $\sigma()$ is the activation function like tanh(). Finally, $\text{MLP}(\mathbf{v}^{(0)}) = \mathbf{v}^{(2)}$. As illustrated in Fig. 3(a), given a relational triple (h, r, t), we concatenate $\mathbf{h}_c$ and $\mathbf{r}$ as input and feed it to a MLP to get a combined representation. $\mathbf{t}_c$ and $\mathbf{r}$ are encoded in the same way. Finally, we employ another MLP to combine them. The three MLPs capture the non-linear combination of the representations of edge direction and label. Let MLP() denote a MLP. The edge embedding is calculated as follows:

$$\psi(\mathbf{h}_c, \mathbf{t}_c, \mathbf{r}) = \text{MLP}_1(\text{MLP}_2([\mathbf{h}_c; \mathbf{r}]) + \text{MLP}_3([\mathbf{r}; \mathbf{t}_c])), \tag{3}$$

where $[\mathbf{h}_c; \mathbf{r}] = \text{CONCAT}(\mathbf{h}_c, \mathbf{r}) \in \mathbb{R}^{2d}$, which concatenates the given vectors.

Context Projection. Projecting embeddings onto hyperplanes [7,32] has shown promising effects on the processing of disparate feature representations. Here, we regard the edge direction and label representations as orthogonal features and project the label representation onto the hyperplane of the edge direction representations, as illustrated in Fig. 3(b). Given two relational triples (h, r, t_1) and (h, r, t_2), $\mathbf{r}'$ and $\mathbf{r}''$ are two edge embeddings for $\mathbf{r}$ projected on hyperplanes. Let $\mathbf{w}_{(h,t)}$ be the normal vector of such hyperplane. The edge embedding for (h, r, t) is calculated by vector projection as follows:

$$\psi(\mathbf{h}_c, \mathbf{t}_c, \mathbf{r}) = \mathbf{r} - \mathbf{w}_{(h,t)}^\top \mathbf{r}\, \mathbf{w}_{(h,t)}. \tag{4}$$

We use a MLP to compute the normal vector based on the concatenated embeddings of head and tail entities. Formally, $\mathbf{w}_{(h,t)} = \text{MLP}([\mathbf{h}_c; \mathbf{t}_c])$, s.t. $||\mathbf{w}_{(h,t)}|| = 1$.

3.3 Loss Function

Following the conventional training strategy of previous models [31], we train TransEdge based on the local-closed world assumption. In this case, we regard the observed relational triples in KGs as positive examples while the unobserved ones as negative samples (either false or missing triples). In our model, positive relational triples are expected to fulfill such relation-contextualized translation with low energy. Negative relational triples are supposed to hold higher energy as they are more invalid than positive ones. To this end, we minimize the following limit-based loss [26], which can create more distinguishable embedding structures than the conventional marginal ranking loss:

$$\mathcal{L} = \sum_{(h,r,t)\in\mathcal{T}} [f(h, r, t) - \gamma_1]_+ + \sum_{(h',r',t')\in\mathcal{T}^-} \alpha\, [\gamma_2 - f(h', r', t')]_+, \tag{5}$$

where $[x]_+ = \max(0, x)$. γ_1, γ_2 are the hyper-parameters to control the energy of triples, s.t. $\gamma_1 < \gamma_2$. α is a hyper-parameter to balance the positive and negative samples. $\mathcal{T}^-$ denotes the set of negative triples, which can be generated by some heuristic strategies. Here, we choose the truncated negative sampling [26], which generates negative triples by replacing either the head or tail entities of positive relational triples with some random neighbors of these entities.

3.4 Implementation for Entity Alignment

Given a source KG $\mathcal{K}_1 = (\mathcal{E}_1, \mathcal{R}_1, \mathcal{T}_1)$ and a target KG $\mathcal{K}_2 = (\mathcal{E}_2, \mathcal{R}_2, \mathcal{T}_2)$, entity alignment seeks to find entities from different KGs that refer to the same real-world object. Embedding-based entity alignment helps overcome the semantic heterogeneity in different KGs and receives increasing attention recently.

For entity alignment, we let each entity pair in seed alignment (i.e., training data) share the same embedding (called parameter sharing), to reconcile $\mathcal{K}_1$ and $\mathcal{K}_2$. In this way, the two KGs are merged into one and we can use TransEdge to learn entity embeddings from this "combined KG". For training, semi-supervised strategies, such as self-training and co-training, have been widely used for embedding-based entity alignment [3,26,36]. This is because the size of seed alignment is usually small. For example, as investigated in [4], in Wikipedia, the inter-lingual links cover less than 15% entity alignment. To cope with this problem, we use the bootstrapping strategy [26] to iteratively select the likely-aligned entity pairs, which we denote by $\mathcal{D} = \{(e_1, e_2) \in \mathcal{E}_1 \times \mathcal{E}_2 | \cos(\mathbf{e}_1, \mathbf{e}_2) > s\}$, where s is the similarity threshold. As errors in the newly-found entity alignment are unavoidable, we do not make each newly-found entity pair share the same embedding. Instead, we minimize the following loss to let the proposed entity alignment has a small embedding distance (i.e., high similarity):

$$\mathcal{L}_{\text{semi}} = \sum_{(e_1,e_2)\in\mathcal{D}} ||\mathbf{e}_1 - \mathbf{e}_2||. \tag{6}$$

In the test phase, given an entity to be aligned in $\mathcal{K}_1$, we rank entities in $\mathcal{K}_2$ as its counterpart candidates in descending order based on the cosine similarity of entity embeddings. The right counterpart is expected to have a top rank.

The parameters of TransEdge are initialized using the Xavier initializer [10]. The embedding loss $\mathcal{L}$ on $\mathcal{T}_1 \cup \mathcal{T}_2$ and the semi-supervised training loss $\mathcal{L}_{\text{semi}}$ are jointly optimized using a stochastic gradient descent algorithm AdaGrad. We enforce the L_2 norm of KG embeddings to 1 to reduce the trivial learning by artificially increasing the embedding norms [2]. The variants of TransEdge that use context compression (CC) and context projection (CP) are denoted by TransEdge-CC and TransEdge-CP, respectively. For ablation study, we also develop the degraded variants of TransEdge without using semi-supervised training, which are marked by the suffix (w/o semi).

3.5 Implementation for Link Prediction

Link prediction is the task of inferring the missing head or tail entities when given incomplete relational triples. For example, given (__, *capitalOf*, New Zealand), the link prediction models are expected to rank the right head entity Wellington at the first place. Link prediction is a key task for KG completion and has been widely used as an evaluation task by many previous KG embedding models.

The embeddings are learned by minimizing $\mathcal{L}$. The parameters are initialized using the Xavier initializer and the loss is also optimized using AdaGrad. In the test phrase, for head prediction $(\_, r, t)$, we create a set of candidate triples by replacing $\_$ with all possible entities. The candidate triples can be ranked in ascending order according to their energy calculated using Eq. (1). The right candidate triple is expected to have a top rank. Tail prediction $(h, r, \_)$ can be done in the same way.

3.6 Complexity Analysis

In general, TransEdge learns two embeddings for each entity. We provide a complexity comparison in Table 1, where n_e and n_r denote the numbers of entities and relations, respectively, and d is the embedding dimension. As our model introduces additional parameters for embedding entities. its complexity is $O(2n_e d + n_r d)$, which is more than that of TransE. However, it is less than the complexity of TransD. Note that, the parameter complexity of TransEdge grows linearly with the number of entities and the embedding dimension.

Table 1. Complexity comparison of translational embedding models

Model	#Embeddings
TransE [2]	$O(n_e d + n_r d)$
TransH [32]	$O(n_e d + 2n_r d)$
TransR [17]	$O(n_e d + n_r d^2)$
TransD [12]	$O(2n_e d + 2n_r d)$
TransEdge (this paper)	$O(2n_e d + n_r d)$

4 Experiments

We assess TransEdge on two popular embedding-based tasks: entity alignment between two KGs and link prediction in one KG. The source code of TransEdge is available online[3].

4.1 Task 1: Embedding-Based Entity Alignment

Datasets. To evaluate TransEdge on various scenarios of entity alignment, we choose the following datasets: (1) DBP15K [25] is extracted from the multilingual DBpedia. It contains three cross-lingual entity alignment datasets: $\text{DBP}_{\text{ZH-EN}}$ (Chinese to English), $\text{DBP}_{\text{JA-EN}}$ (Japanese to English) and $\text{DBP}_{\text{FR-EN}}$ (French to English). Each dataset has 15 thousand aligned entity pairs. (2) DWY100K [26] has two large-scale monolingual datasets, DBP-WD and DBP-YG, sampled from DBpedia, Wikidata and YAGO3. Each dataset has 100 thousand aligned entity pairs. For a fair comparison, we reuse their original dataset splits in evaluation.

[3] https://github.com/nju-websoft/TransEdge.

Competitive Models. For comparison, we choose the following state-of-the-art embedding-based entity alignment models: MTransE [4], IPTransE [36], JAPE [25], BootEA [26] and its non-bootstrapping version AlignE, as well as GCN-Align [33]. We do not compare with some other models like KDCoE [3] and AttrE [30], since they require additional resources (e.g., textual descriptions and attribute values) that do not present in our problem setting as well as other competitors'. Furthermore, the character-based literal embedding used in AttrE [30] is unsuited to cross-lingual entity alignment as the characters of different languages (such as Chinese and English) can be very heterogeneous. Our goal is to exploit the basic relational structures of KGs for entity alignment.

To further understand the benefits and limitations of KG embeddings for entity alignment, we extend several representative embedding models that are used for link prediction as the competitors, including: three translational models TransH [32], TransR [17] and TransD [12]; two bilinear models HolE [20] and SimplE [14]; and two neural models ProjE [24] and ConvE [8]. Note that ComplEx [29] is very similar to HolE [27]. So, we pick HolE as the representative. We do not include Analogy [18] and ConvKB [19], because we find that these methods do not perform well on the datasets. Similar to TransEdge, we merge two KGs into one via parameter sharing and use these models to learn embeddings. We refer the open-source KG embedding framework OpenKE [11] to implement TransH, TransR, TransD and HolE, while SimplE, ProjE and ConvE are implemented based on their code.

Experimental Settings. We have tuned a series of hyper-parameters. For example, we select the learning rate among {0.001, 0.005, 0.01, 0.02} and the positive margin γ_1 among $\{0.1, 0.2, \cdots, 0.5\}$. The selected setting of hyper-parameters is reported as follows. For TransEdge-CC, $\gamma_1 = 0.3$, $\gamma_2 = 2.0$, $\alpha = 0.3$, $s = 0.75$, $d = 75$. For TransEdge-CP, $\gamma_1 = 0.2$, $\gamma_2 = 2.0$, $\alpha = 0.8$, $s = 0.7$, $d = 75$. The activation function is tanh() for MLPs. For DBP15K, we generate 20 negative samples for each relational triple and the batch size is $2,000$. For DWY100K, we generate 25 negative samples for each relational triple and the batch size is $20,000$. We adopt L_2-norm in the energy function. The learning rate is 0.01 and the training is terminated using early stop based on the Hits@1 performance to avoid overfitting. We use CSLS [6] as similarity measure. We choose three widely-used metrics: Hits@k, mean rank (MR) and mean reciprocal rank (MRR). Higher Hits@k and MRR values, and lower MR values indicate better performance. Note that, Hits@1 is equivalent to precision, and MRR is more robust than MR since MRR is more able to tolerate a few poorly-ranked correct candidates.

Entity Alignment Results. The results of entity alignment are depicted in Tables 2 and 3. We can see that TransEdge consistently achieves the best for all the metrics on the five datasets. For example, on $\text{DBP}_{\text{ZH-EN}}$, TransEdge-CP (w/o semi) achieves an improvement of 0.187 on Hits@1 against AlignE. If compared with its bootstrapping version BootEA, TransEdge-CP (w/o semi)

Table 2. Entity alignment results on DBP15K

	DBP_{ZH-EN}				DBP_{JA-EN}				DBP_{FR-EN}			
	Hits@1	Hits@10	MRR	MR	Hits@1	Hits@10	MRR	MR	Hits@1	Hits@10	MRR	MR
MTransE [4] †	0.308	0.614	0.364	154	0.279	0.575	0.349	159	0.244	0.556	0.335	139
IPTransE [36] ‡	0.406	0.735	0.516	–	0.367	0.693	0.474	–	0.333	0.685	0.451	–
JAPE [25] †	0.412	0.745	0.490	64	0.363	0.685	0.476	99	0.324	0.667	0.430	92
AlignE [26]	0.472	0.792	0.581	–	0.448	0.789	0.563	–	0.481	0.824	0.599	–
BootEA [26]	0.629	0.848	0.703	–	0.622	0.854	0.701	–	0.653	0.874	0.731	–
GCN-Align [33]	0.413	0.744	–	–	0.399	0.745	–	–	0.373	0.745	–	–
TransH [32] △	0.377	0.711	0.490	52	0.339	0.681	0.462	59	0.313	0.668	0.433	47
TransR [17] △	0.259	0.529	0.349	299	0.222	0.440	0.295	315	0.059	0.225	0.116	502
TransD [12] △	0.392	0.729	0.505	48	0.356	0.695	0.468	58	0.323	0.694	0.447	43
HolE [20] △	0.250	0.535	0.346	488	0.256	0.517	0.343	560	0.149	0.465	0.251	1133
SimplE [14] ◇	0.317	0.575	0.405	453	0.255	0.525	0.346	409	0.147	0.438	0.241	397
ProjE [24] ◇	0.290	0.527	0.374	705	0.273	0.475	0.345	919	0.283	0.527	0.368	659
ConvE [8] ◇	0.169	0.329	0.224	1123	0.192	0.343	0.246	1081	0.240	0.459	0.316	694
TransEdge-CC (w/o semi)	0.622	0.868	0.711	65	0.601	0.863	0.696	56	0.617	0.891	0.716	38
TransEdge-CP (w/o semi)	0.659	0.903	0.748	50	0.646	0.907	0.741	36	0.649	0.921	0.746	25
TransEdge-CC	0.669	0.871	0.744	66	0.645	0.859	0.722	67	0.666	0.893	0.749	40
TransEdge-CP	**0.735**	**0.919**	**0.801**	**32**	**0.719**	**0.932**	**0.795**	**25**	**0.710**	**0.941**	**0.796**	**12**

† Hits@k and MR results are taken from [25] while MRR results are taken from [26]. ‡ Results are taken from [26]. △ Results are produced by ourselves using OpenKE [11]. ◇ Results are produced by ourselves using their source code. – denotes unreported results in their papers. Unmarked results are taken from their own papers. Best results are marked in boldface, and same in the following tables.

still achieves a gain of 0.030 while the improvement of TransEdge-CP reaches 0.106. We can see that BootEA is a very competitive model due to its powerful bootstrapping strategy. However, our semi-supervised variants TransEdge-CC and TransEdge-CP significantly outperform BootEA on DBP15K. This is due to the ability of TransEdge on preserving KG structures.

On DBP15K, both TransEdge-CC and TransEdge-CP show good performance. TransEdge-CC (w/o semi) still obtains superior results than AlignE and TransEdge-CC also outperforms BootEA. Furthermore, we find that TransEdge-CP achieves better results than TransEdge-CC. We think that this is because the context projection has a good geometric interpretation, as shown in Fig. 2(b), which helps capture better and more solid relational structures of KGs for entity alignment. We can also see that the proposed semi-supervised training for entity alignment brings remarkable improvement. For example, on DBP_{ZH-EN}, it increases the Hits@1 scores of TransEdge-CP from 0.659 (w/o semi) to 0.735. These results indicate that the proposed context compression and projection can both accurately compute the edge embeddings. The proposed semi-supervised training also contributes to the performance improvement.

We notice that, on DWY100K, the improvement of TransEdge is not so large as that on DBP15K. For example, on DBP-WD, TransEdge-CP only achieves an improvement of 0.040 on Hits@1 against BootEA. We think this is because the two KGs in DBP-WD or DBP-YG have aligned relational structures and their entities are one to one aligned. But in DBP15K, there are many noisy

Table 3. Entity alignment results on DWY100K

	DBP-WD				DBP-YG			
	Hits@1	Hits@10	MRR	MR	Hits@1	Hits@10	MRR	MR
MTransE [4] ‡	0.281	0.520	0.363	–	0.252	0.493	0.334	–
IPTransE [36] ‡	0.349	0.638	0.447	–	0.297	0.558	0.386	–
JAPE [25] ‡	0.318	0.589	0.411	–	0.236	0.484	0.320	–
AlignE [26] ‡	0.566	0.827	0.655	–	0.633	0.848	0.707	–
BootEA [26] ‡	0.748	0.898	0.801	–	0.761	0.894	0.808	–
GCN-Align [33] ▽	0.479	0.760	0.578	1988	0.601	0.841	0.686	299
TransH [32] △	0.351	0.641	0.450	117	0.314	0.574	0.402	90
TransR [17] △	0.013	0.062	0.031	2773	0.010	0.052	0.026	2852
TransD [12] △	0.362	0.651	0.456	152	0.335	0.597	0.421	90
HolE [20] △	0.223	0.452	0.289	811	0.250	0.484	0.327	437
SimplE [14] ◇	0.169	0.328	0.223	3278	0.131	0.282	0.183	3282
ProjE [24] ◇	0.312	0.504	0.382	2518	0.366	0.573	0.436	1672
ConvE [8] ◇	0.403	0.628	0.483	1428	0.503	0.736	0.582	837
TransEdge-CC (w/o semi)	0.687	0.910	0.767	70	0.759	0.935	0.822	24
TransEdge-CP (w/o semi)	0.692	0.898	0.770	106	0.726	0.909	0.792	46
TransEdge-CC	0.732	0.926	0.803	**65**	0.784	**0.948**	**0.844**	**22**
TransEdge-CP	**0.788**	**0.938**	**0.824**	72	**0.792**	0.936	0.832	43

▽: Results are produced using its code. Other marks mean the same in Table 2.

entities that have no counterparts. Thus, DWY100K is relatively simple for entity alignment. On datasets with noisy entities, TransEdge gives a big advantage to others, which indicates the robustness of TransEdge.

It is interesting to see that some modified models also demonstrate competitive performance on entity alignment. ConvE even outperforms some alignment-oriented embedding models such as MTransE, IPTransE and JAPE on the DWY100K datasets, which indicates the potential of deep learning techniques. We also notice that the performance of TransR is very unstable. It achieves promising results on $\text{DBP}_{\text{ZH-EN}}$ and $\text{DBP}_{\text{JA-EN}}$ but fails on the other three datasets. We take a closer look at the five datasets and discover that $\text{DBP}_{\text{ZH-EN}}$ and $\text{DBP}_{\text{JA-EN}}$ contain some relation alignment. When TransR performs relation-specific projections on entities, the relation alignment would pass some alignment information to entities. The requirement of relation alignment limits the applicability of TransR to entity alignment. We can conclude that not all embedding models designed for link prediction are suitable for entity alignment.

4.2 Task 2: Embedding-Based Link Prediction

Datasets. We use two benchmark datasets FB15K-237 [28] and WN18RR [8] for link prediction. They are the improved versions of FB15K [2] and WN18 [2], respectively. As found in [8,28], FB15K and WN18 contain many symmetric triples that are easy to infer by learning some trivial patterns. Thus, the work in [8,28] creates FB15K-237 and WN18RR by removing inverse relations from the testing sets. So, FB15K-237 and WN18RR are more difficult, and both of them have gradually become the most popular benchmark datasets for link prediction in recent studies [8,19,27,35]. FB15K-237 contains 14,541 entities, 237 relations and 310,116 relational triples. WN18RR has 40,943 entities, 11 relations and 93,003 relational triples. For a fair comparison, we reuse the original training/validation/test splits of the two datasets in evaluation.

Competitive Models. For comparison, we choose a wide range of embedding models for link prediction as the competitors, including five translational models, seven bilinear models and five neural models, as listed in Table 4. For the sake of fairness and objectivity, we report the published results of them as many as possible. But there still exist some results unavailable in the reference papers. If some models have not been evaluated on FB15K-237 or WN18RR, we use their released code to produce the results by ourselves.

Experimental Settings. We have tuned hyper-parameter values by a careful grid search. The selected setting for hyper-parameters is as follows. For FB15K-237, $\gamma_1 = 0.4$, $\gamma_2 = 0.9$, $\alpha = 0.4$, $d = 200$. The batch size is 200 and the learning rate is 0.005. We generate 10 negative samples for each triple. For WN18RR, $\gamma_1 = 0.2$, $\gamma_2 = 2.7$, $\alpha = 0.8$, $d = 500$. The batch size is 2,000 and the learning rate is 0.01. We sample 30 negatives for each triple. The activation function is still tanh() for MLPs. We use L_2-norm in our energy function. When evaluating the ranking lists, we use the filtered setting [2], i.e., given a candidate triple list, we remove from the list all other positive triples that appear in the training/validation/test data. Then, we get a new filtered ranking list and the right triple is expected to have a high rank. By convention, we report the average results of head prediction and tail prediction. Same as embedding-based entity alignment, we use Hits@k, MR and MRR.

Link Prediction Results. Table 4 gives the link prediction results on FB15K-237 and WN18RR. We can see that TransEdge significantly outperforms the translational models TransE, TransH, TransR and PTransE. This is because the proposed edge-centric translation can distinguish the different contexts of relations, while the relation translation of the aforementioned models usually leads to indistinguishable relation embeddings when modeling complex relational structures. When compared with the bilinear and neural models, especially with the very latest model RotatE [27], TransEdge-CP still achieves the best Hits@1 scores on both datasets. The best Hits@1 performance shows that TransEdge-CP can precisely capture the relational structures of KGs for link prediction, rather than put all possible candidates with similar and ambiguous ranks. We can also see that TransEdge-CC obtains the best MR result on WN18RR. Considering that WN18RR only has 11 relations but 40,943 entities, we think this is because the MLPs can well fit such complex relational structures. Although the scores of

Table 4. Link prediction results on FB15K-237 and WN18RR

Model	Type	FB15K-237				WN18RR			
		Hits@1	Hits@10	MRR	MR	Hits@1	Hits@10	MRR	MR
TransE [2] †	Trans.	–	0.436	0.269	285	–	0.453	0.412	5429
TransH [32] †	Trans.	–	0.453	0.281	292	–	0.429	0.435	5102
TransR [17] ‡▽	Trans.	–	0.429	0.162	337	0.017	0.257	0.094	3708
TransD [12] ‡▽	Trans.	–	0.428	0.162	305	0.015	0.139	0.060	6644
PTransE [16] △	Trans.	0.210	0.501	0.314	299	0.272	0.424	0.337	5686
DistMult [34] §	Bilinear	0.155	0.419	0.241	254	0.390	0.490	0.430	5110
HolE [20] ♮▽	Bilinear	0.133	0.391	0.222	–	0.284	0.346	0.308	4874
ComplEx [29] §	Bilinear	0.158	0.428	0.247	339	0.410	0.510	0.440	5261
Analogy [18] ♯▽	Bilinear	0.131	0.405	0.219	–	0.389	0.441	0.407	3836
ProjE [24]	Neural	–	0.461	0.294	246	–	0.474	0.453	4407
ConvE [8]	Neural	0.239	0.491	0.316	246	0.390	0.480	0.460	5277
R-GCN [23]	Neural	0.153	0.414	0.248	–	–	–	–	–
ConvKB [19]	Neural	–	0.517	**0.396**	257	–	0.525	0.248	2554
CACL [21]	Neural	–	0.487	0.349	235	–	0.543	0.472	3154
SimplE [14] □	Bilinear	0.225	0.461	0.230	–	–	–	–	–
CrossE [35] ◇	Bilinear	0.211	0.474	0.299	–	0.373	0.394	0.374	6091
RotatE [27]	Bilinear	0.241	**0.533**	0.338	**177**	0.428	**0.571**	**0.476**	3340
TransEdge-CC	Trans.	0.227	0.482	0.310	305	0.411	0.516	0.439	**2452**
TransEdge-CP	Trans.	**0.243**	0.512	0.333	219	**0.433**	0.487	0.451	4866

†: Results are taken from [21]. ‡: Results of FB15K-237 are taken from [1]. ▽: Results on WN18RR are produced using OpenKE [11]. △: Results are produced using its source code. §: Results are taken from [8]. ♮: Results are taken from [23]. ♯: Results are taken from [35]. □: Results are produced using the published source code. We do not include its results of WN18RR because we find them not promising. ◇: Results of WN18RR are produced using its source code.

TransEdge by other metrics such as Hits@10 and MRR fall behind ConvKB and RotatE, the model complexity of TransEdge is lower than them. For example, the convolution operation of ConvE and ConvKB is more complicated than the matrix multiplication used in the MLPs of TransEdge. Besides, the Euclidean vector space of real numbers generated by TransEdge is simpler than the complex vector space of ComplEx and RotatE.

4.3 Analysis on Complex Relational Structures in KGs

One Entity Pair with Multiple Relations. For further comparison, we evaluate TransEdge on KGs with double relations. We create a dummy relation r' for each relation r and add a dummy triple (h, r', t) for (h, r, t). The dummy relations and triples would not change the relational structures of KGs, but they would exacerbate the effects of the cases of one entity pair with multiple relations. We compare TransEdge (w/o semi) with the relation-level translational model MTransE [4]. Due to space limitation, we report the Hits@1 results on DBP15K

Table 5. Entity alignment results on DBP15K with double relations

	$\text{DBP}_{\text{ZH-EN}}$ (double)		$\text{DBP}_{\text{JA-EN}}$ (double)		$\text{DBP}_{\text{FR-EN}}$ (double)	
	Hits@1	Hits@1↓	Hits@1	Hits@1↓	Hits@1	Hits@1↓
MTransE [4]	0.230	25.32%	0.232	16.85%	0.208	14.75%
TransEdge-CC (w/o semi)	0.601	3.38%	0.578	3.82%	0.585	5.18%
TransEdge-CP (w/o semi)	**0.652**	**1.06%**	**0.623**	**3.56%**	**0.641**	**1.23%**

and the decrease rates (marked as Hits@1↓) compared with their performance in Table 2. The results are listed in Table 5. We can see that the performance of TransEdge shows less variation than MTransE. This indicates that the complex relational structures can indeed hinder entity alignment performance while TransEdge has superior performance on modeling such structures.

Multiple Entity Pairs with One Relation. Figure 4 shows the 2D visualization for the embeddings of some entity pairs with the same relation *capital* in DBP-WD. We project these embeddings into two dimensions using PCA. We can see that the embeddings of TransEdge show flexible and robust relational structures. The translation vectors of *capital* are different in directions when involved in different contexts. For the embeddings of MTransE, the translation vectors are almost parallel. This means that, if several entities get involved in the same relational triple, they would be embedded very similarly by the same relational translation, which hinders the entity alignment performance. This experiment bears out the intuition of TransEdge illustrated by Fig. 1.

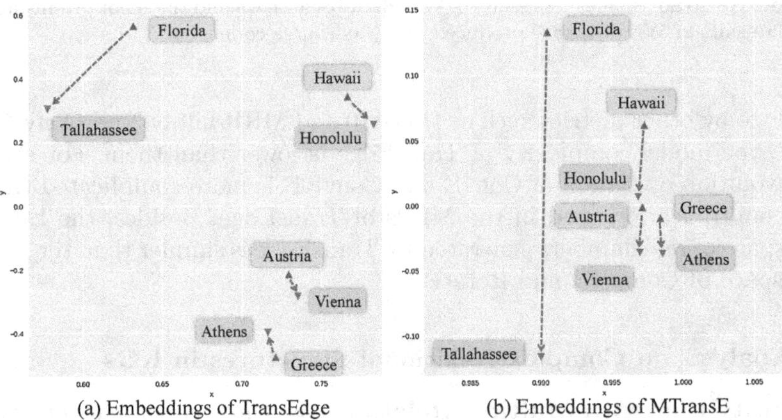

Fig. 4. 2D embedding projection of some countries (or states) and their *capital* cities. The green arrows denote the translation vectors between entities. (Color figure online)

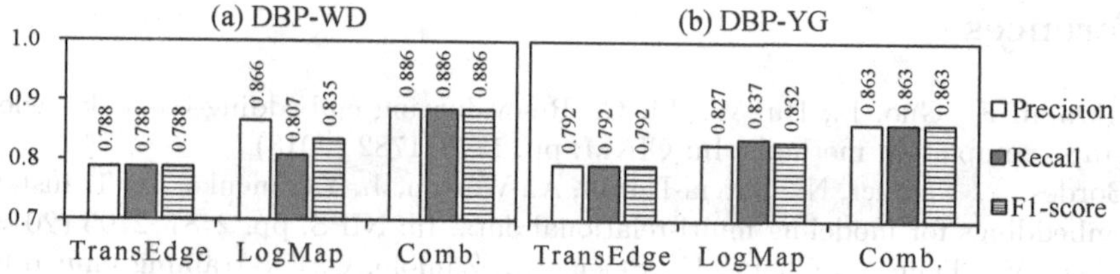

Fig. 5. Results of TransEdge, LogMap [13] and their combination on DWY100K.

4.4 Comparison with Conventional Entity Alignment Method

Conventional entity alignment methods usually exploit literal attributes like names and comments, or OWL logics, to identify similar entities, which are quite different from TransEdge. We further compare TransEdge-CP with LogMap [13], a popular and accessible conventional entity alignment method. We use its web front-end system[4] to obtain its performance on the monolingual datasets DBP-WD and DBP-YG. We also design a strategy to combine TransEdge-CP and LogMap, which combines their produced entity alignment (i.e., Hits@1 alignment for TransEdge) by voting based on the predicted similarity. We report the conventional precision, recall and F1-score results in Fig. 5. Note that, for embedding-based entity alignment, recall and F1-score are equal to precision, because we can always get a candidate list for each input entity based on their embeddings. We can see that LogMap shows very competitive performance and it outperforms TransEdge and the other embedding-based models. However, we find that the combined results achieve the best. This shows that TransEdge is complementary with conventional entity alignment methods.

5 Conclusion and Future Work

In this paper, we proposed a relation-contextualized KG embedding model. It represents relations with context-specific embeddings and builds edge translations between entities to preserve KG structures. We proposed context compression and projection to compute edge embeddings. Our experiments on standard datasets demonstrated its effectiveness on entity alignment and link prediction. For future work, we plan to study techniques like language models to represent multi-hop relation contexts. We also want to incorporate other proximity measures into the preserved KG structures, such as attribute similarity.

Acknowledgments. This work is funded by the National Natural Science Foundation of China (No. 61872172), and the Key R&D Program of Jiangsu Science and Technology Department (No. BE2018131).

---

[4] http://krrwebtools.cs.ox.ac.uk/logmap/.

References

1. Akrami, F., Guo, L., Hu, W., Li, C.: Re-evaluating embedding-based knowledge graph completion methods. In: CIKM, pp. 1779–1782 (2018)
2. Bordes, A., Usunier, N., García-Durán, A., Weston, J., Yakhnenko, O.: Translating embeddings for modeling multi-relational data. In: NIPS, pp. 2787–2795 (2013)
3. Chen, M., Tian, Y., Chang, K., Skiena, S., Zaniolo, C.: Co-training embeddings of knowledge graphs and entity descriptions for cross-lingual entity alignment. In: IJCAI, pp. 3998–4004 (2018)
4. Chen, M., Tian, Y., Yang, M., Zaniolo, C.: Multilingual knowledge graph embeddings for cross-lingual knowledge alignment. In: IJCAI, pp. 1511–1517 (2017)
5. Cochez, M., Ristoski, P., Ponzetto, S.P., Paulheim, H.: Global RDF vector space embeddings. In: d'Amato, C., et al. (eds.) ISWC 2017. LNCS, vol. 10587, pp. 190–207. Springer, Cham (2017). https://doi.org/10.1007/978-3-319-68288-4_12
6. Conneau, A., Lample, G., Ranzato, M., Denoyer, L., Jégou, H.: Word translation without parallel data. In: ICLR (2018)
7. Dasgupta, S.S., Ray, S.N., Talukdar, P.: HyTE: hyperplane-based temporally aware knowledge graph embedding. In: EMNLP, pp. 2001–2011 (2018)
8. Dettmers, T., Minervini, P., Stenetorp, P., Riedel, S.: Convolutional 2D knowledge graph embeddings. In: AAAI, pp. 1811–1818 (2018)
9. Gentile, A.L., Ristoski, P., Eckel, S., Ritze, D., Paulheim, H.: Entity matching on web tables: a table embeddings approach for blocking. In: EDBT, pp. 510–513 (2017)
10. Glorot, X., Bengio, Y.: Understanding the difficulty of training deep feedforward neural networks. AISTATS **9**, 249–256 (2010)
11. Han, X., et al.: OpenKE: an open toolkit for knowledge embedding. In: EMNLP (Demonstration), pp. 139–144 (2018)
12. Ji, G., He, S., Xu, L., Liu, K., Zhao, J.: Knowledge graph embedding via dynamic mapping matrix. In: ACL, pp. 687–696 (2015)
13. Jiménez-Ruiz, E., Grau, B.C., Zhou, Y., Horrocks, I.: Large-scale interactive ontology matching: algorithms and implementation. In: ECAI, pp. 444–449 (2012)
14. Kazemi, S.M., Poole, D.: Simple embedding for link prediction in knowledge graphs. In: NeurIPS, pp. 4289–4300 (2018)
15. Krompaß, D., Baier, S., Tresp, V.: Type-constrained representation learning in knowledge graphs. In: Arenas, M., et al. (eds.) ISWC 2015. LNCS, vol. 9366, pp. 640–655. Springer, Cham (2015). https://doi.org/10.1007/978-3-319-25007-6_37
16. Lin, Y., Liu, Z., Luan, H.B., Sun, M., Rao, S., Liu, S.: Modeling relation paths for representation learning of knowledge bases. In: ACL, pp. 705–714 (2015)
17. Lin, Y., Liu, Z., Sun, M., Liu, Y., Zhu, X.: Learning entity and relation embeddings for knowledge graph completion. In: AAAI, pp. 2181–2187 (2015)
18. Liu, H., Wu, Y., Yang, Y.: Analogical inference for multi-relational embeddings. In: ICML, pp. 2168–2178 (2017)
19. Nguyen, D.Q., Nguyen, T.D., Nguyen, D.Q., Phung, D.Q.: A novel embedding model for knowledge base completion based on convolutional neural network. In: NAACL-HLT, pp. 327–333 (2018)
20. Nickel, M., Rosasco, L., Poggio, T.A.: Holographic embeddings of knowledge graphs. In: AAAI, pp. 1955–1961 (2016)
21. Oh, B., Seo, S., Lee, K.: Knowledge graph completion by context-aware convolutional learning with multi-hop neighborhoods. In: CIKM, pp. 257–266 (2018)

22. Ristoski, P., Paulheim, H.: RDF2Vec: RDF graph embeddings for data mining. In: Groth, P., et al. (eds.) ISWC 2016. LNCS, vol. 9981, pp. 498–514. Springer, Cham (2016). https://doi.org/10.1007/978-3-319-46523-4_30
23. Schlichtkrull, M., Kipf, T.N., Bloem, P., van den Berg, R., Titov, I., Welling, M.: Modeling relational data with graph convolutional networks. In: Gangemi, A., et al. (eds.) ESWC 2018. LNCS, vol. 10843, pp. 593–607. Springer, Cham (2018). https://doi.org/10.1007/978-3-319-93417-4_38
24. Shi, B., Weninger, T.: ProjE: embedding projection for knowledge graph completion. In: AAAI, pp. 1236–1242 (2017)
25. Sun, Z., Hu, W., Li, C.: Cross-lingual entity alignment via joint attribute-preserving embedding. In: d'Amato, C., et al. (eds.) ISWC 2017. LNCS, vol. 10587, pp. 628–644. Springer, Cham (2017). https://doi.org/10.1007/978-3-319-68288-4_37
26. Sun, Z., Hu, W., Zhang, Q., Qu, Y.: Bootstrapping entity alignment with knowledge graph embedding. In: IJCAI, pp. 4396–4402 (2018)
27. Sun, Z., Deng, Z.H., Nie, J.Y., Tang, J.: RotatE: knowledge graph embedding by relational rotation in complex space. In: ICLR (2019)
28. Toutanova, K., Chen, D., Pantel, P., Poon, H., Choudhury, P., Gamon, M.: Representing text for joint embedding of text and knowledge bases. In: EMNLP, pp. 1499–1509 (2015)
29. Trouillon, T., Welbl, J., Riedel, S., Gaussier, É., Bouchard, G.: Complex embeddings for simple link prediction. In: ICML, pp. 2071–2080 (2016)
30. Trsedya, B.D., Qi, J., Zhang, R.: Entity alignment between knowledge graphs using attribute embeddings. In: AAAI (2019)
31. Wang, Q., Mao, Z., Wang, B., Guo, L.: Knowledge graph embedding: a survey of approaches and applications. IEEE Trans. Knowl. Data Eng. **29**(12), 2724–2743 (2017)
32. Wang, Z., Zhang, J., Feng, J., Chen, Z.: Knowledge graph embedding by translating on hyperplanes. In: AAAI, pp. 1112–1119 (2014)
33. Wang, Z., Lv, Q., Lan, X., Zhang, Y.: Cross-lingual knowledge graph alignment via graph convolutional networks. In: EMNLP, pp. 349–357 (2018)
34. Yang, B., Yih, W., He, X., Gao, J., Deng, L.: Embedding entities and relations for learning and inference in knowledge bases. In: ICLR (2015)
35. Zhang, W., Paudel, B., Zhang, W., Bernstein, A., Chen, H.: Interaction embeddings for prediction and explanation in knowledge graphs. In: WSDM, pp. 96–104 (2019)
36. Zhu, H., Xie, R., Liu, Z., Sun, M.: Iterative entity alignment via joint knowledge embeddings. In: IJCAI, pp. 4258–4264 (2017)

Unsupervised Discovery of Corroborative Paths for Fact Validation

Zafar Habeeb Syed[1(✉)], Michael Röder[1,2], and Axel-Cyrille Ngonga Ngomo[1,2]

[1] Data Science Group, Paderborn University, Paderborn, Germany
zsyed@mail.uni-paderborn.de, {michael.roeder,axel.ngonga}@upb.de
[2] Institute for Applied Informatics, Leipzig, Germany

Abstract. Any data publisher can make RDF knowledge graphs available for consumption on the Web. This is a direct consequence of the decentralized publishing paradigm underlying the Data Web, which has led to more than 150 billion facts on more than 3 billion things being published on the Web in more than 10,000 RDF knowledge graphs over the last decade. However, the success of this publishing paradigm also means that the validation of the facts contained in RDF knowledge graphs has become more important than ever before. Several families of fact validation algorithms have been developed over the last years to address several settings of the fact validation problems. In this paper, we consider the following fact validation setting: Given an RDF knowledge graph, compute the likelihood that a given (novel) fact is true. None of the current solutions to this problem exploits RDFS semantics—especially domain, range and class subsumption information. We address this research gap by presenting an *unsupervised approach* dubbed COPAAL, that extracts paths from knowledge graphs to corroborate (novel) input facts. Our approach relies on a mutual information measure that takes the RDFS semantics underlying the knowledge graph into consideration. In particular, we use the information shared by predicates and paths within the knowledge graph to compute the likelihood of a fact being corroborated by the knowledge graph. We evaluate our approach extensively using 17 publicly available datasets. Our results indicate that our approach outperforms the state of the art *unsupervised* approaches significantly by up to 0.15 AUC-ROC. We even outperform *supervised* approaches by up to 0.07 AUC-ROC. The source code of COPAAL is open-source and is available at https://github.com/dice-group/COPAAL.

1 Introduction

The participatory paradigm underlying the Data Web has led to more than 150 billion facts on more than 3 billion things being published on the Web in more than 10,000 RDF knowledge graphs.[1] For example, DBpedia [2], YAGO [20] and WikiData [13] contain information about millions of entities and comprise billions of facts about these entities. These facts are used in the backend of a growing number of applications including in-flight applications [13], community-support

[1] http://lodstats.aksw.org/.

C. Ghidini et al. (Eds.): ISWC 2019, LNCS 11778, pp. 630–646, 2019.
https://doi.org/10.1007/978-3-030-30793-6_36

systems [1] and even personal assistants such as Apple's Siri [13]. Ensuring the veracity of the facts contained in knowledge graphs is hence of critical importance for an increasing number of end users and applications. Manual solutions to the computation of the veracity of facts are clearly an impractical feat due to the volume and the velocity of the data of the Data Web.[2] Consequently, automated solutions to this computation, dubbed *fact validation* [11,17] (also called *fact checking* in some of the literature, e.g., [8]) have been devised over the last years.

The goal of fact validation can be summarized as follows: *Given a fact, compute the likelihood that the given fact is true.* Two main families of approaches have been devised to address this problem (see Sect. 2 for more details). The first family of approaches encompasses solutions which verbalize the input fact and use textual evidence (e.g., large corpora such as the Web or Web crawls) to find statements which support or refute the input fact [8,22,24]. We focus on the second family of approaches. These approaches use a knowledge graph $\mathcal{G}$ as background knowledge and use the facts contained therein to evaluate the likelihood that the given fact is true [5,9,18]. These approaches use sets of facts as evidence to compute the likelihood of a given fact. For example, when using DBpedia version 2016-10 as background knowledge, they might use facts such as (`Barack_Obama`, `birthPlace`, `Hawaii`) and (`Hawaii`, `country`, `United_States_of_America`) to conclude that (`Barack_Obama`, `nationality`, `United_States_of_America`) holds—a fact which is not to be found in the background knowledge base.

Our work is based on the following *observation*: While most approaches which use a knowledge graph as background knowledge have been deployed on RDF knowledge graphs, none has made use of the semantics of the accompanying schema in RDFS to the full. In particular, none of the state-of-the-art approaches makes use of the combination of domain, range and subsumption hierarchy expressed in the schema of most RDF datasets in RDFS. However, the RDFS schema contains crucial information (e.g., type information) necessary to detect facts which can be used to validate or invalidate other facts.

In this paper, we address this research gap by presenting an unsupervised fact validation approach for RDF knowledge graphs which identifies paths that support a given fact (s, p, o). This approach is based on the insight that the predicate p (e.g., `nationality`) carries mutual information with a set of other paths (e.g., paths pertaining to `birthPlace` and `country`) in the background knowledge graph $\mathcal{G}$. Hence, the presence of certain sets of paths in $\mathcal{G}$ that begin in s and end in o can be regarded as evidence which *corroborates the veracity* of (s, p, o). Our approach is the first to take the *domain* and *range* information of p, the type of s and o as well as the subsumption relations between types in the RDFS schema of $\mathcal{G}$ into consideration while identifying these paths. Our results show conclusively that using this information leads to significantly higher AUC-ROC results on 17 benchmark datasets.

Our approach has several advantages over the state of the art: (i) It uses data which can be directly queried via SPARQL from $\mathcal{G}$, i.e., there is no *need to*

[2] See https://lod-cloud.net/ for data on the growth of the Linked Open Data Cloud.

alter the representation mechanism of $\mathcal{G}$ or to use an internal representation of $\mathcal{G}$ in our implementation. Moreover, our approach can exploit the large body of work on scaling up triple stores to competitive runtimes. (ii) The proposed co-occurrence measure for the similarity calculation between predicates and paths is *not bound to path lengths and can hence be exploited to detect paths of any finite length.* (iii) Our approach is *completely unsupervised* and neither training nor labeled data is required.

The rest of the paper is organized as follows: Sect. 2 present details pertaining to related fact validation approaches. In Sect. 3, we present a brief overview of the formal notation used in this paper. We also introduce the formal specification we use throughout this work. Section 4 details the formal model underlying our approach. In particular, it gives a formal specification of corroborative paths and how they can be used to measure the likelihood of a fact being true. Section 5 provides the details of our implementation. We present our experimental setup in Sect. 6 and discuss our results in Sect. 7. Finally, we conclude in Sect. 8.

2 Related Work

Approaches to fact validation can be broadly classified into two categories: (i) approaches that use unstructured *textual* sources [8,22,24] and (ii) approaches that use *structured* information sources [3,17–19]. The latter—in particular approaches that use a given knowledge graph for fact validation—are more relevant to the work presented herein. Several approaches view a given knowledge graph as labeled graph connecting nodes (entities) and edges (relations). Given an input triple (s, p, o), the goal is then to search for paths of length up to a given threshold k and use them to validate/invalidate the given input triple. For instance, in [5,18] a knowledge graph is viewed as undirected network of paths. The task is then to find shortest paths that connect s and o and are semantically related to p. These approaches are *unsupervised* and do not require prior training data. However, these approaches do not take into consideration the *terminological information* (in particular the semantics of RDFS) of the input knowledge graph while defining semantic proximity metrics. Other approaches view KBs as graphs and search for *metapaths* to extract features [9,21,25]. These features are then used to train a classification model to label unseen facts as true or false. However, these approaches require training data in the form of labeled *metapaths* and hence required significantly more human effort that the approach presented herein. In PredPath [17], the authors propose a novel method to automatically extract metapaths—called *anchored predicate* paths—given a set of labeled examples. To achieves this goal, PredPath uses the `rdf:type` information contained in the input knowledge graph. However, the *anchored predicate paths* used for learning features are selected based on the type information of *subject* and *object* irrespective of the *predicate* connecting them. This means that they do not consider the domain, range and class subsumption provided by the RDFS schema of the given knowledge graph. Consequently, their ability to generalize over paths is limited as shown in Sect. 7 of this paper. Additionally, PredPath requires labeled training data. Hence, porting it to previously unseen predicates is significantly more demanding that porting our approach, which is fully unsupervised.

Alternative to graph models, several approaches encode the entities and relations in a KB using vector embeddings [3,12,19,23]. The fact validation problem is then formulated as calculating the similarity between the entities and predicate of a given input triple. Embedding-based methods for link prediction address a related but different problem. Given a KG $\mathcal{G}$, they compute a score function, which expresses how likely it is that any triple whose subject, predicate and object belong to the input graph $\mathcal{G}$ should belong to $\mathcal{G}$ [14]. Fact validation approaches addresses a different but related goal: Given a graph $\mathcal{G}$ and a triple t, they aim to compute the likelihood that t is true [8,18,22]. A core repercussion of these two different problem formulations are the runtimes and the applications of link prediction and fact checking. While fact validation algorithms are used in online scenarios embedding-based algorithms are often used offline. Approaches such as [6,7] mine Horn rules that can be used for knowledge base completion tasks. However, they often fail to scale to large knowledge graphs.

Our approach, is inspired by approaches that discover metapaths. We propose a novel approach for finding paths which corroborate a given triple (s, p, o). In addition, we present a novel measure to calculate association strength these paths and the input triple. In contrast to approaches based on metapaths, our approach does not need training examples and does not require any supplementary effort to deployed to previously unseen relations.

3 Preliminaries

Throughout this paper, we consider RDF knowledge graphs with RDFS semantics. We use the notation presented in Table 1.

Table 1. List of symbols

Notation	Description
$\mathcal{G}$	A knowledge graph
$\mathbb{B}, \mathbb{C}, \mathbb{E}, \mathbb{L}, \mathbb{P}$	Set of all blank nodes, RDFS classes, RDF resources, Literals and RDF predicates, respectively
$\pi^k(v_0, v_k)$	*Directed path* of length k between nodes v_0 and v_k in $\mathcal{G}$
$\mu^k(v_0, v_k)$	*Undirected path* of length k between nodes v_0 and v_k in $\mathcal{G}$
$\Pi^k(p)$	Set of *corroborative paths* for a predicate p
$\Pi^k_{(t_x, t_y)}$	Set of *typed directed paths* of length k between nodes v_0 and v_k in $\mathcal{G}$
$M^k_{(t_x, t_y)}$	Set of *typed undirected paths* of length k between nodes v_0 and v_k in $\mathcal{G}$
$\vec{q}$	Vector of k predicates in $\mathcal{G}$
$\Pi^k_{(t_x, t_y), \vec{q}}$	Set of $\vec{q}$-restricted typed *directed paths* of length k between nodes v_0 and v_k in $\mathcal{G}$
$M^k_{(t_x, t_y), \vec{q}}$	Set of $\vec{q}$-restricted typed *undirected paths* of length k between nodes v_0 and v_k in $\mathcal{G}$
$\gamma(x)$	Function mapping each element of $\mathbb{E} \cup \mathbb{P} \cup \mathbb{B} \cup \mathbb{L}$ to its type
$\lambda(t_x)$	Function mapping the type t_x to a set of resources that are instances of this type
$D(p)$	The domain of the predicate p
$R(p)$	The range of the predicate p

3.1 Knowledge Graph

Definition 1. *An RDF knowledge graph $\mathcal{G}$ is a set of RDF triples, i.e.,*

$$\mathcal{G} = \{(s, p, o) | s \in \mathbb{E} \cup \mathbb{B}, p \in \mathbb{P}, o \in \mathbb{E} \cup \mathbb{B} \cup \mathbb{L}\}, \tag{1}$$

where $\mathbb{E}$ is the set of all RDF resources, $\mathbb{B}$ is the set of all blank nodes, $\mathbb{P} \subseteq \mathbb{E}$ is the set of all RDF predicates and $\mathbb{L}$ represents the set of all literals.

Intuitively, an RDF knowledge graph can be understood as an edge-labeled directed graph in which the node s is connected to the node o via an edge with the label p iff the triple $(s, p, o) \in \mathcal{G}$. This is the approach we use to display knowledge graphs graphically (see, e.g., Fig. 1). We use the notation $s \xrightarrow{p} o$ to denote that $(s, p, o) \in \mathcal{G}$. We denote the set of all RDFS classes as $\mathbb{C}$ (with $\mathbb{C} \subseteq \mathbb{E}$). For $A \in \mathbb{C}$ and $B \in \mathbb{C}$, we write $A \sqsubseteq B$ to signify that $A^{\mathcal{I}} \subseteq B^{\mathcal{I}}$ for any interpretation $\cdot^{\mathcal{I}}$.

Example 1. An excerpt of an example RDF knowledge graph—which we will use as a running example—is displayed in Fig. 1. The example shows a subgraph extracted from DBpedia[3] consisting of nodes (resources) (e.g., `Barack Obama` and `United States`) and edges (relations) connecting these entities either directly or via intermediate nodes (e.g., `birthplace`).

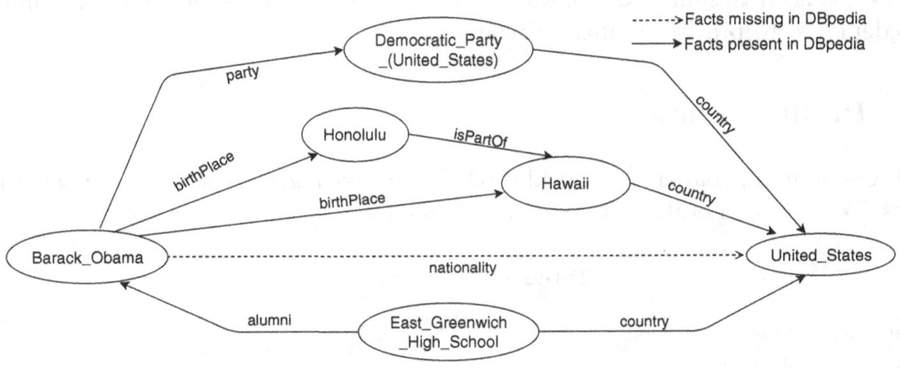

Fig. 1. A subgraph of DBpedia version 10-2016.

Definition 2. *Path: A path of length k in a knowledge graph $\mathcal{G}$ is a cycle-free sequence of triples from $\mathcal{G}$ of the form $(v_0, p_1, v_1), (v_1, p_2, v_2), ..., (v_{k-1}, p_k, v_k)$.*

This means in particular that $\forall i, j \in [0, k], i \neq j \rightarrow v_i \neq v_j$. We use $\pi^k(v_0, v_k)$ to denote paths between v_0 and v_k. For the sake of legibility, we use the notation $v_0 \xrightarrow{p_1} \dots \xrightarrow{p_{k-1}} v_k$ to denote paths. Note that several paths can exist between v_0 and v_k. For example, `BarackObama` $\xrightarrow{\texttt{birthPlace}}$ `Hawaii` $\xrightarrow{\texttt{country}}$ `USA` and `BarackObama` $\xrightarrow{\texttt{party}}$ `DemocraticParty` $\xrightarrow{\texttt{country}}$ `USA` are both paths of length 2 between the resources `BarackObama` and `USA` in our running example.

[3] http://downloads.dbpedia.org/2016-10/.

Definition 3. *Undirected path: An undirected path of length k in a graph $\mathcal{G}$ is a cycle-free sequence of triples of the form $(v_0, p_1, v1), (v_1, p_2, v_2), ..., (v_{k-1}, p_k, v_k)$ where $\forall i \in [0, k-1]$ $(v_i, p_{i+1}, v_{i+1}) \in \mathcal{G} \vee (v_{i+1}, p_{i+1}, v_i) \in \mathcal{G}$.*

Again, this means that $\forall i, j \in [0, k], i \neq j \rightarrow v_i \neq v_j$. We denote undirected paths with $\mu^k(v_0, v_k)$. For example, BarackObama $\xleftarrow{\texttt{alumni}}$ GreenwichHighSchool $\xrightarrow{\texttt{country}}$ USA is an undirected path of length 2 between BarackObama and USA in our example.

4 Corroborative Paths

4.1 Intuition

In this paper, we address the *following problem*: Given an RDF knowledge graph $\mathcal{G}$ and a triple (s, p, o), compute the likelihood that (s, p, o) is true. For example, we would have good reasons to believe that BarackObama is a citizen of the USA given that BarackObama was born in Hawaii and Hawaii is located in the USA. Clearly, we cannot formally infer that x is a national of z by virtue of the existence of $x \xrightarrow{\texttt{birthplace}} y \xrightarrow{\texttt{country}} z$. Still, this path is a strong indicator (i.e., strongly corroborates) triples of the form $x \xrightarrow{\texttt{nationality}} z$. The *basic intuition behind our work* is correspondingly that the existence of certain paths $\pi^k(s, o)$ between s and o is a strong indicator for the correctness (i.e., corroborate the existence) of (s, p, o) and can hence be used to compute its likelihood.

4.2 Formal Model

Let γ be a function which maps each element of $\mathbb{E} \cup \mathbb{P} \cup \mathbb{B} \cup \mathbb{L}$ to its type. For example, γ(BarackObama) = Person $\sqcap$ Agent $\sqcap$ Politician $\sqcap$ President and γ(UnitedStates) = Place $\sqcap$ Location $\sqcap$ Country $\sqcap$ PopulatedPlace in our running example.[4] Further, let λ be a function which maps a given type t_x to a set of resources that are instances of t_x by virtue of RDFS semantics. Extending the formal model in [17], we now define the set $\Pi^k_{(t_x,t_y)}$ of typed paths of length k between pairs of resources of type t_x and t_y in a knowledge graph $\mathcal{G}$ as follows:

$$\Pi^k_{(t_x,t_y)} = \{\pi^k(v_0, v_k) \mid \gamma(v_0) \sqsubseteq t_x \wedge \gamma(v_k) \sqsubseteq t_y\}. \quad (2)$$

For t_x = {Person} and t_y = {Place}, the path BarackObama $\xrightarrow{\texttt{birthPlace}}$ Hawaii $\xrightarrow{\texttt{country}}$ USA is an element of the set $\Pi^2_{(t_x,t_y)}$ in our running example. We define the set $M^k_{(t_x,t_y)}$ of typed undirected paths analogously.

[4] We use $\sqcap$ to denote the conjunction of classes. Note that given that President $\sqsubseteq$ Person $\sqsubseteq$ Agent, we could write the type BarackObama in an abbreviated form. Similar considerations holds for the type of UnitedStates. We chose to write the types out to remain consistent with the output of our example knowledge graph, DBpedia 2016-10.

Let $\vec{q} = q_1, \ldots, q_k$ be a vector of properties of length k. We define the set of $\vec{q}$-restricted typed paths $\Pi^k_{(t_x,t_y),\vec{q}} \subseteq \Pi^k_{(t_x,t_y)}$ as follows:

$$\begin{aligned}\Pi^k_{(t_x,t_y),\vec{q}} =& \{\pi^k(v_0, v_k) \mid \pi^k(v_0, v_k) \in \Pi^k_{(t_x,t_y)},\\ & \forall i \in [0, k-1] : (v_i, p_{i+1}, v_{i+1}) \in \pi^k(v_0, v_k) \rightarrow p_{i+1} = q_{i+1}\}.\end{aligned} \tag{3}$$

Put simply, this is the set of typed paths such that the sequence of properties in each path is exactly $\vec{q}$. For example, let t_x={`Person`}, t_y = {`Place`} and $\vec{q}$ = (`birthPlace`, `country`). Then the path `BarackObama` $\xrightarrow{\texttt{birthPlace}}$ `Hawaii` $\xrightarrow{\texttt{country}}$ `USA` is the only element of $\Pi^2_{(t_x,t_y),\vec{q}}$ in our running example. We call the elements of $\Pi^k_{(t_x,t_y),\vec{q}}$ *similar* as they share a sequence of predicates (i.e., $\vec{q}$). We define sets of $\vec{q}$-restricted undirected typed paths $M^k_{(t_x,t_y),\vec{q}}$ analogously to $\Pi^k_{(t_x,t_y),\vec{q}}$.

We can now use restricted typed paths to compute how well a predicate is corroborated in a knowledge graphs as follows: Let $D(p)$ be the domain of p and $R(p)$ be its range. Given that we assume RDF knowledge graphs, we can safely assume the existence of an RDFS class hierarchy for the said graph (defined via the `rdf:type` predicate). Consequently, we can derive the following important condition on paths $\pi^k(s, o)$ which are to corroborate the correctness of (s, p, o): *Only typed paths in* $\Pi^k_{(D(p),R(p))}$ *can corroborate facts with the predicate* p. This particular insight is one of the major differences between this and previous works (see Sect. 2), in which the consequences of RDFS semantics were not taken into consideration. In particular, while previous approaches [17] used at most $\gamma(s)$ and $\gamma(o)$ to measure the strength of the association between paths and predicates, we use $D(p)$ and $R(p)$ as well as the RDFS class hierarchy in the input knowledge graph $\mathcal{G}$ to determine the degree to which a path $\pi^k(s, o)$ corroborates a predicate p.

Given an RDF knowledge graph $\mathcal{G}$, we hence define the *corroborative paths* for a predicate p formally as follows:

$$\Pi^k(p) = \bigcup_{j=1}^{k} \Pi^j_{(D(p),R(p))}. \tag{4}$$

Simply put, *corroborative paths* in $\Pi^k(p)$ are paths of length at most k that carry similar information to p.

4.3 Association Strength

We base our computation of the strength of the association between $\Pi^j_{(t_x,t_y),\vec{q}}$ and p on their normalized pointwise mutual information [4]. To this end, we define probability $\mathcal{P}(\Pi^j_{(t_x,t_y),\vec{q}})$ of pairs of instances of t_x resp. t_y being connected via a $\vec{q}$-restricted path of length j is as follows:

$$\frac{\left|\{(a, b) : \gamma(a) \sqsubseteq t_x \wedge \gamma(b) \sqsubseteq t_y \wedge (\exists \pi^j(a, b) \in \Pi^j_{(t_x,t_y),\vec{q}})\}\right|}{|\lambda(t_x)| \cdot |\lambda(t_y)|}. \tag{5}$$

The probability $\mathcal{P}(p)$ of the predicate p linking resources of type t_x and t_y is

$$\frac{|\{(a,p,b) : \gamma(x) \sqsubseteq t_x \wedge \gamma(y) \sqsubseteq t_y \wedge (a,p,b) \in \mathcal{G}\}|}{|\lambda(t_x)| \cdot |\lambda(t_y)|} \tag{6}$$

Finally, the joint probability $\mathcal{P}(\Pi^j_{(t_x,t_y),\vec{q}}, p)$ is defined as

$$\frac{\left|\{(a,b) : \gamma(a) \sqsubseteq t_x \wedge \gamma(b) \sqsubseteq t_y \wedge (\exists \pi^j(a,b) \in \Pi^j_{(t_x,t_y),\vec{q}}) \wedge (a,p,b) \in \mathcal{G}\}\right|}{|\lambda(t_x)| \cdot |\lambda(t_y)|}. \tag{7}$$

We could now compute the NPMI of $\Pi^j_{(t_x,t_y),\vec{q}}$ and p as defined in [4]. However, a direct implementation of the original definition of the NPMI would be expensive as it would require deduplicating the sets of pairs (a,b) connected by the paths in $\Pi^j_{(t_x,t_y)}$.[5] Hence, our approach implements an approximation of the NPMI based on counting the number of paths which connect pairs (a,b) instead of the pairs themselves. We hence end up with the following approximations (note that these values are not probabilities):

$$\widehat{\mathcal{P}}(\Pi^j_{(t_x,t_y),\vec{q}}) = \frac{|\Pi^j_{(t_x,t_y),\vec{q}}|}{|\lambda(t_x)| \cdot |\lambda(t_y)|} \tag{8}$$

$$\widehat{\mathcal{P}}(\Pi^j_{(t_x,t_y),\vec{q}}, p) = \frac{|\{\pi^j(a,b) \in \Pi^j_{(t_x,t_y),\vec{q}} : (a,p,b) \in \mathcal{G}\}|}{|\lambda(t_x)| \cdot |\lambda(t_y)|}. \tag{9}$$

These approximations can be computed by using SPARQL queries without `DISTINCT` clause, which makes the computation an order of magnitude faster (see Table 7 for some of the scores returned by this function). Note that $\mathcal{P}(p)$ remains unchanged and the number of paths $a \xrightarrow{p} b$ is exactly equal to the number of pairs (a,b) connected by p. Based on these approximations we can now approximate the NPMI of $\Pi^j_{(t_x,t_y),\vec{q}}$ and p as follows:

$$\widehat{\text{NPMI}}(\Pi^j_{(t_x,t_y),\vec{q}}, p) = \frac{\log\left(\frac{\widehat{\mathcal{P}}\left(\Pi^j_{(t_x,t_y),\vec{q}}, p\right)}{\widehat{\mathcal{P}}\left(\Pi^j_{(t_x,t_y)}\right) \cdot \mathcal{P}(p)}\right)}{-\log\left(\widehat{\mathcal{P}}\left(\Pi^j_{(t_x,t_y),\vec{q}}, p\right)\right)} \tag{10}$$

5 Method and Implementation

This section presents our implementation of the formal model presented above in detail. In particular, we show how some of the core computations of our model can be implemented using SPARQL queries, ensuring practicable runtimes for our approach. As above, we explain the approach using directed paths for the sake of legibility. The approach was also implemented using undirected paths. An evaluation of the performance of the approach with directed and undirected paths is presented in Sect. 7.

[5] Preliminary experiments suggest a 20-fold increase in runtime without any significant increase in AUC-ROC.

5.1 Algorithm

Given an input triple $t = (s, p, o)$, a knowledge graph $\mathcal{G}$ and a maximum path length k, our implementation begins by identifying a set of *paths* of varying lengths connecting s and o, respectively. For each path, it calculates a score, which explicates the degree to which the path corroborate t. Finally, the scores are amalgamated to a single score τ which expresses the veracity of t. The complete algorithm is shown in Algorithm 1 and can be separated into the 4 steps (i) Initialization, (ii) Path discovery, (iii) Path scoring and (iv) Veracity calculation.

Algorithm 1. COPAAL - Corroborative Fact Validation

```
Input  : The input triple $t = (s, p, o)$, the knowledge graph $\mathcal{G}$ and
         the maximum path length $k$
Output: A veracity score $\tau$ for $t$
// Initialization
prune($G$)
$c_{D(p)} \leftarrow$ countInstances($D(p)$)
$c_{R(p)} \leftarrow$ countInstances($R(p)$)
$c_p \leftarrow$ countTriples($p$)
List $Z \leftarrow \{\}$; List $\mathcal{Q} \leftarrow \{\}$
// Path Discovery
for $j = 1$ to $k$ do
    $QT \leftarrow$ generateQueryTemplates($j$)
    for $qt \in QT$ do
        $sq \leftarrow qt(v_o = s, v_k = o)$
        $Q \leftarrow$ execute($sq$)
        prune($Q$)
        for $\vec{q} \in Q$ do
            $\mathcal{Q}$.add(($qt, \vec{q}$))
        end
    end
end
// Path scoring
for $(qt, \vec{q}) \in \mathcal{Q}$ do
    $sq \leftarrow$ generatePathCountQuery ($qt, \pi^j(s, o), D(p), R(p)$)
    $c_\Pi \leftarrow$ execute($sq$)
    $sq \leftarrow$ generateCoocCountQuery ($sq, t$)
    $c_{\Pi,p} \leftarrow$ execute($sq$)
    $Z$.add(calcNPMI($c_{\Pi,p}, c_\Pi, c_p, c_{D(p)}, c_{R(p)}$))
end
// Veracity calculation
$\tau \leftarrow 1$
for $\zeta \in Z$ do
    $\tau \leftarrow \tau \times (1 - \zeta)$
end
return $1 - \tau$
```

Initialization. Firstly, we prune $\mathcal{G}$ by removing all nodes from domain outside the union of (i) base namespace(s) of $\mathcal{G}$, (ii) the namespace for RDF, RDFS and OWL. We carry out this preprocessing because we are interested in relations (edges) that are defined by the ontology of the given $\mathcal{G}$ (line 1). Thereafter, the domain $D(p)$ and range $R(p)$ of the given triple's predicate p are determined.[6] The number of instances of these two types as well as the number of triples containing p as predicate are retrieved via SPARQL count queries (lines 2–4).

Path Discovery. In the second step, the properties of all paths $\pi^j(s, o)$ (i.e., their $\vec{q}$ restrictions) of length $j \in [1, k]$ between s and o are retrieved. To this end, we generate SPARQL[7] query templates (line 7). The query template which retrieves directed paths of length $j = 2$ between `?v0` and `?v2` from an RDF graph is:

```
SELECT ?p1 ?p2
WHERE {
    ?v0 ?p1 ?v1 .
    ?v1 ?p2 ?v2 .
}
```

Note that the query has to be modified with `UNION` to cover *undirected paths*. Still, a single query can be used to detect paths of any length. Hence, our approach generates k queries in this step.

After generating all necessary query templates up to the given length k, we replace the variables `?v0` and `?vj` with s and o respectively in the query (line 9). We prune the results of the query (line 11) by removing results containing predicates which define the terminology (e.g., class membership through `rdf:type`, class hierarchy through `rdfs:subClassOf`).[8] The remaining $\vec{q}$-restrictions are stored as pairs together with the template which was used to retrieve them in the list $\mathcal{Q}$ (line 12–14). We store the template to ensure that we can reconstruct the direction of the predicates in case undirected paths are used.

Path Scoring. Pairs in $\mathcal{Q}$ are used to define the $\vec{q}$-restricted typed path sets $\Pi^j_{(D(p),R(p)),\vec{q}}$. For each of these pairs, a score ζ is calculated based on the NPMI approximation in Eq. 10 (lines 16–23). For the sake of efficiency, we use SPARQL queries to obtain the necessary counts of typed paths which are generated based on the query template and $\vec{q}$ (line 18). However, as pointed out in [7], a direct translation of the needed counts into queries leads to time-consuming computa-

---

[6] If $D(p)$ or $R(p)$ are not available, the types of the given subject or object will be used, respectively.

[7] https://www.w3.org/TR/rdf-sparql-query/.

[8] We are aware that the terminology (especially concept similarity scores) used in G can potentially inform the fact validation process further. Studying the integration of assertional and terminological information will be the object of future work and is out of the scope of this paper.

tions[9] which require optimization. Therefore, we generate the SPARQL queries needed for our counts with a recursive structure. Listing 1.1 shows a sample query used to count the number of paths ?vo $\xrightarrow{birthPlace}$?v1 $\xrightarrow{country}$?v2 between entities with the types Person and Country, respectively.

Listing 1.1. SPARQL query to count all paths of an example $\vec{q}$

```
SELECT SUM(?b1*?b2) as ?sum WHERE {
  SELECT COUNT(?v1) as ?b2, ?b1 WHERE {
    ?v0 <http://dbpedia.org/ontology/birthPlace> ?v1 .
    ?v0 a <http://dbpedia.org/ontology/Person> .
    {
      SELECT COUNT(?v2) as ?b1, ?v1 WHERE {
        ?v1 <http://dbpedia.org/ontology/country> ?v2 .
        ?v2 a <http://dbpedia.org/ontology/Country> .
      } GROUP BY ?v1
    }
  } GROUP BY ?v0 ?b1
}
```

Veracity Calculation. We treat the association strength of each $\vec{q}$-restricted typed path as the confidence with which the path supports the existence of the input predicate p. We hence combine the ζ values by checking whether at least one path supports p. Let Z be the set of scores of all single paths, the veracity score τ can be calculated with the following equation (see lines 23–28):

$$q\tau = 1 - \prod_{\zeta \in Z} (1 - \zeta). \tag{11}$$

6 Experiments and Results

In this section, we provide details of the data and hardware we used in our experiments. We compare the results of our approach with those achieve by state-of-the-art approaches in the subsequent section.

6.1 Setup

Knowledge Graph. For our experiments, we chose DBpedia version 2016-10 as background knowledge. We chose this dataset because it is the reference dataset of a large number of fact validation benchmarks. We used the latest dumps[10] of `ontology`, `instance types`, `mapping-based objects` and `infobox properties`. We filtered out triples that (i) contain literals and datatypes or

[9] We used Virtuoso and Fuseki for our experiments and our runtime findings support [7].

[10] http://downloads.dbpedia.org/2016-10/.

(ii) link the entities in DBpedia to external sources. The final graph contains 44 million triples, which we stored using an instance of Openlink Virtuoso v7.2.5.1 hosted on VM with 16GB memory and 256GB disk space. To ensure the comparability of our results, we ran our evaluation using GERBIL [16]—a benchmarking platform that facilitates the evaluation of fact validation systems across different datasets.[11] We used the AUC-ROC as an evaluation metric and set $k = 2$ for the sake of comparability with previous works.

Competing Approaches. We compare our approach (COPAAL) to three state-of-the-art graph-based fact validation approaches: (i) Knowledge Stream (KS), (ii) its variant Relational Knowledge Linker (KL-REL) [18] and (iii) Discriminative Path Mining (PredPath) [17]. For all these approaches, we use the implementation provided by the authors [18].[12] We considered the configuration suggested in the original paper: (i) PredPath [17] uses the top-100 features while learning positive and negative facts. (ii) KS [18] and KL-REL [18] use the top-5 paths and single best path, respectively, for validating input triples.

6.2 Benchmarks

We evaluated all the approaches using two publicly available sets of benchmarks: (i) the *Real-World* and (ii) *Synthetic* datasets[13] made available by the authors of the literature [18]. In addition, we generated a new set of benchmarks dubbed *FactBench-DBpedia* from the *FactBench*[14] dataset. All the facts in *FactBench* are automatically extracted from DBpedia and Freebase for 10 different relations[15] and stored in the form of RDF models. In *FactBench*, the positive facts are generated by querying DBpedia and Freebase and selecting top 150 results returned for each relation. The negative facts are generated by modifying the positive facts while still following domain and range restrictions. The positive and negative facts are collected into 6 different benchmarks dubbed *Domain, Range, Domain-Range, Mix, Random, Property*. *FactBench-DBpedia* restricts the generation process of *FactBench* to DBpedia by extracting all facts belonging to DBpedia and facts from Freebase whose resources can be mapped to resources in DBpedia. Table 2 shows the stats for the different datasets.

7 Results

7.1 Comparison of Directed and Undirected Paths

We first aimed to determine the type of paths for which our approach performs best. We hence compared the AUC achieved by both variations of our approach

[11] All the datasets and result files can be found at https://hobbitdata.informatik.uni-leipzig.de/COPAAL/.

[12] https://github.com/shiralkarprashant/knowledgestream.

[13] https://github.com/shiralkarprashant/knowledgestream/tree/master/datasets.

[14] https://github.com/DeFacto/FactBench.

[15] *award, birthPlace, deathPlace, foundationPlace, leader, team, author, spouse, starring, subsidiary.*

Table 2. Summary of benchmark datasets

Dataset	*FactBench-DBpedia*						*Real-World*				*Synthetic*						
Subset	Domain	Domain-Range	Range	Mix	Property	Random	Birth-Place	Death-Place	Education	Nationality	US-CAP	NBA-Team	Oscars	CEO	US-WAR	US-VP	FLOTUS
Positive	1,124	1,124	1,124	1,124	1,124	1,124	273	126	466	50	50	41	78	201	126	47	16
Negative	1,119	1,006	1,123	1,014	1,153	511	819	378	1,395	150	250	123	4,602	1,007	584	227	240
Total	2,243	2,130	2,247	2,138	2,277	1,635	1,092	504	1,861	200	300	164	4,680	1,208	710	274	256

Table 3. Comparison of AUC-ROC achieved using directed and undirected paths

	Domain	Domain-Range	Range	Mix	Random	Property
Undirected paths	**0.9348**	**0.9389**	**0.8937**	**0.8561**	**0.9411**	**0.7307**
Directed paths	0.7741	0.7824	0.7416	0.5914	0.6411	0.4713

on FactBench-DBpedia (see Table 3). The results are clear: Using undirected paths (average AUC-ROC = 0.87) always outperforms using directed paths (avg. AUC-ROC = 0.66) and are 0.21 better on average w.r.t. the AUC-ROC they achieve. We studied the results achieved using the two types of paths. It became quickly evident that using undirected paths allows to detect significantly more corroborative evidence. Therewith, undirected paths achieve a better approximation of the probability of a triple being true (see Table 7 for examples). Consequently, we only consider our approach with undirected paths in the following.

7.2 Comparison with Other Approaches

Tables 4 and 5 show the AUC-ROC results of all the approaches on the benchmarks contained in the *Real-World* and *Synthetic* datasets, respectively. Our approach outperforms other approaches on most of these datasets. In the best case, we are roughly 4.5% (absolute value, Birth Place benchmark) better than PredPath and more than 20% (absolute value, Birth Place benchmark) better than KS on real data. A careful study of our results reveals that the *anchored predicate paths* used by PredPath for learning features are restricted by the types of subject and object irrespective of predicate of the input triple. Hence they

Table 4. AUC-ROC results of all approaches on *Real-World* datasets

	Birth place	Death place	Education	Nationality
COPAAL	**0.9441**	0.8997	**0.8731**	**0.9831**
PredPath	0.8997	0.8054	0.8644	0.9520
KL-REL	0.9254	**0.9095**	0.8547	0.9692
KS	0.7197	0.8002	0.8651	0.9789

Table 5. ROC-AUC results of all approaches on *Synthetic* datasets

	US-CAP	NBA-Team	Oscars	CEO	US-WAR	US-VP	FLOTUS
COPAAL	**1.000**	**0.999**	0.995	**0.912**	**0.999**	**0.953**	**1.000**
PredPath	0.996	0.923	**0.999**	0.897	0.995	0.944	**1.000**
KL-REL	**1.000**	0.999	0.976	0.898	0.873	0.891	0.983
KS	**1.000**	0.999	0.950	0.811	0.865	0.798	0.980

someetimes fail to generalize well. On the other hand, KL-REL uses single best paths, which sometimes limits its ability to validate facts if it is not able to rank the path which conveys the most evidence for the input triple to the first position. This is made evident by the examples shown in Table 7: We computed the union of the top-3 paths identified by our approach and all other approaches on the three datasets for which the difference in AUC values were the largest. We also computed the weights assigned by each of the approaches (i.e., $\widehat{\text{NPMI}}$ for our approach, average flow values of paths for KS and KL-REL [18] and weights learned by the classifier for PredPath [17]). While our approach finds all paths and allocated them weights, the other approach sometimes fail to detect relevant paths (marked by dashes in Table 7) and are hence not able to use them in their evidence computation. Having a large number of paths available however also means that our scores are (even if rarely) overoptimistic w.r.t. evidence for a triple, which explain the marginally lower scores we achieve on Death Place and Oscars.

The results on FactBench-DBpedia (see Table 6) confirm the insight we gained on the previous two datasets. Our approach outperforms the state of the art and achieve a better AUC-ROC on most datasets. We ran a Wilcoxon signed ranked test (significance = 99%) on all results we collected. The results state that our approach is significantly better than the state of the art.

One could assume that our approach is slower than the state of the art due to the larger amount of evidence it collects. Hence, we measured the average throughput of all the approaches including all phases of the processing. The average throughput of our approach was 21.02 triples/min. KS, which follows an approach similar to ours, achieves an average throughput of 10.05 triples/min while its counterpart KL-REL achieves 29.78 triples/min. PredPath's average throughput was 21.67 triples/min. Overall, our results show that our approach scales as well as the state of the art while achieving significantly better results.

Table 6. ROC-AUC results of all approaches on *FactBench-DBpedia* datasets

	Domain	DomainRange	Mix	Property	Random	Range
COPAAL	**0.9348**	0.9389	**0.8561**	**0.7307**	**0.9411**	0.8937
PredPath	0.9301	**0.9447**	0.8408	0.7154	0.9354	**0.8992**
KL-REL	0.8453	0.8619	0.7721	0.6154	0.8547	0.8219
KS	0.8019	0.8124	0.7215	0.6047	0.7911	0.8047

Table 7. Union of the top-3 paths identified by the different approaches and their weighting. The weights allocated by each of the approaches are given in the corresponding column. A dash (-) means that the approach was not able to find the said path.

Dataset	Path	COPAAL	KS/KL-REL	PredPath
BirthPlace	$\xrightarrow{\texttt{hometown}}$	0.65	0.28	–
	$\xrightarrow{\texttt{birthPlace}}\xleftarrow{\texttt{isPartOf}}$	0.65	0.23	26
	$\xrightarrow{\texttt{highSchool}}\xrightarrow{\texttt{city}}$	0.62	0.21	–
	$\xrightarrow{\texttt{parent}}\xrightarrow{\texttt{birthPlace}}$	0.63	0.08	29
	$\xrightarrow{\texttt{child}}\xrightarrow{\texttt{birthPlace}}$	0.60	0.04	21
CEO	$\xrightarrow{\texttt{foundedBy}}$	0.72	0.28	3
	$\xrightarrow{\texttt{owningCompany}}$	0.70	–	–
	$\xrightarrow{\texttt{owner}}$	0.70	–	–
	$\xleftarrow{\texttt{parentCompany}}\xrightarrow{\texttt{keyPerson}}$	0.70	0.08	7
	$\xrightarrow{\texttt{employer}}$	0.64	0.23	9
US-VP	$\xleftarrow{\texttt{successor}}$	0.62	0.19	5
	$\xrightarrow{\texttt{predecessor}}$	0.61	0.12	7
	$\xleftarrow{\texttt{vicePresident}}\xrightarrow{\texttt{president}}$	0.55	–	–
	$\xrightarrow{\texttt{associate}}\xrightarrow{\texttt{president}}$	0.49	–	2
	$\xrightarrow{\texttt{predecessor}}\xleftarrow{\texttt{successor}}$	0.48	0.02	13

8 Conclusion and Future Work

In this paper, we present a novel unsupervised approach for the validation of facts using an RDF knowledge graph $\mathcal{G}$ as background knowledge. Our approach uses domain, range and class subsumption information found in the schema of $\mathcal{G}$ to outperform both supervised and unsupervised fact validation approaches. We evaluated our results on 17 datasets against three state-of-the-art approaches. Our results show that our approach outperforms the state of the art significantly (Wilcoxon signed ranked test, $p < 0.01$). We studied the difference between the approaches and concluded that our approach performs better because it is able to score corroborative paths more accurately as it uses more information from the schema of $\mathcal{G}$. These results point to the importance of using the semantics of the data contained in RDF knowledge graphs when aiming to validate them. Another advantage of our approach is that it allows to verbalize the evidence found to support a given input triple.

The main limitation of our approach lies in its relying on the existence of type information. Well-defined ontologies are not always given in real world datasets and therefore our approach cannot be applied on them. Previous works have aimed at improving type information in noisy knowledge graphs [15]. We will evaluate whether combining our approach with such algorithms leads to better corroborative paths in future works. Additionally, the approaches evaluated herein are limited to evidence found in one RDF graph. In future work, we will consider performing fact validation at a larger scale. In particular, we will use the linked nature of Linked Data sets to detect paths across several knowledge graphs. We will focus on the scalability and the distributed execution of this novel solution. Moreover, we will consider relaxing the requirements to types used in the definition of $\Pi^k_{(t_x,t_y),\vec{q}}$ by using well-defined semantic similarities [10].

Acknowledgements. This work has been supported by the BMVI projects LIMBO (project no. 19F2029C) and OPAL (project no. 19F20284), the BMBF project SOLIDE (project no. 13N14456) and the EU project KnowGraphs (project no. 860801).

References

1. Athreya, R.G., Ngonga Ngomo, A.C., Usbeck, R.: Enhancing community interactions with data-driven chatbots-the DBpedia chatbot. In: Companion of the the Web Conference 2018 on The Web Conference, pp. 143–146 (2018). International World Wide Web Conferences Steering Committee (2018)
2. Auer, S., Bizer, C., Kobilarov, G., Lehmann, J., Cyganiak, R., Ives, Z.: DBpedia: a nucleus for a web of open data. In: Aberer, K., et al. (eds.) ASWC/ISWC -2007. LNCS, vol. 4825, pp. 722–735. Springer, Heidelberg (2007). https://doi.org/10.1007/978-3-540-76298-0_52
3. Bordes, A., Usunier, N., Garcia-Duran, A., Weston, J., Yakhnenko, O.: Translating embeddings for modeling multi-relational data. In: Advances in Neural Information Processing Systems, pp. 2787–2795 (2013)
4. Bouma, G.: Normalized (pointwise) mutual information in collocation extraction. In: Proceedings of GSCL, pp. 31–40 (2009)
5. Ciampaglia, G.L., Shiralkar, P., Rocha, L.M., Bollen, J., Menczer, F., Flammini, A.: Computational fact checking from knowledge networks. PloS One **10**(6), e0128193 (2015)
6. d'Amato, C., Fanizzi, N., Esposito, F.: Inductive learning for the semantic web: what does it buy? Semant. Web **1**(1, 2), 53–59 (2010)
7. Galárraga, L.A., Teflioudi, C., Hose, K., Suchanek, F.: Amie: association rule mining under incomplete evidence in ontological knowledge bases. In: Proceedings of the 22nd International Conference on World Wide Web, pp. 413–422. ACM (2013)
8. Gerber, D., et al.: DeFacto–temporal and multilingual deep fact validation. Web Semant. Sci. Serv. Agents World Wide Web **35**, 85–101 (2015)
9. Lao, N., Cohen, W.W.: Relational retrieval using a combination of path-constrained random walks. Mach. Learn. **81**(1), 53–67 (2010)
10. Lehmann, K., Turhan, A.-Y.: A framework for semantic-based similarity measures for $\mathcal{ELH}$-concepts. In: del Cerro, L.F., Herzig, A., Mengin, J. (eds.) JELIA 2012. LNCS (LNAI), vol. 7519, pp. 307–319. Springer, Heidelberg (2012). https://doi.org/10.1007/978-3-642-33353-8_24
11. Lin, P., Song, Q., Wu, Y.: Fact checking in knowledge graphs with ontological subgraph patterns. Data Sci. Eng. **3**(4), 341–358 (2018)
12. Lin, Y., Liu, Z., Sun, M., Liu, Y., Zhu, X.: Learning entity and relation embeddings for knowledge graph completion. In: Twenty-Ninth AAAI Conference on Artificial Intelligence (2015)

13. Malyshev, S., Krötzsch, M., González, L., Gonsior, J., Bielefeldt, A.: Getting the most out of wikidata: semantic technology usage in wikipedia's knowledge graph. In: Vrandečić, D., et al. (eds.) ISWC 2018. LNCS, vol. 11137, pp. 376–394. Springer, Cham (2018). https://doi.org/10.1007/978-3-030-00668-6_23
14. Nickel, M., Tresp, V., Kriegel, H.P.: Factorizing yago: scalable machine learning for linked data. In: Proceedings of the 21st International Conference on World Wide Web, pp. 271–280. ACM (2012)
15. Paulheim, H., Bizer, C.: Type Inference on noisy RDF data. In: Alani, H., et al. (eds.) ISWC 2013. LNCS, vol. 8218, pp. 510–525. Springer, Heidelberg (2013). https://doi.org/10.1007/978-3-642-41335-3_32
16. Röder, M., Usbeck, R., Ngonga Ngomo, A.: GERBIL - benchmarking named entity recognition and linking consistently. Semant. Web **9**(5), 605–625 (2018)
17. Shi, B., Weninger, T.: Discriminative predicate path mining for fact checking in knowledge graphs. Knowl.-Based Syst. **104**, 123–133 (2016)
18. Shiralkar, P., Flammini, A., Menczer, F., Ciampaglia, G.L.: Finding streams in knowledge graphs to support fact checking. In: 2017 IEEE International Conference on Data Mining (ICDM), pp. 859–864. IEEE (2017)
19. Socher, R., Chen, D., Manning, C.D., Ng, A.: Reasoning with neural tensor networks for knowledge base completion. In: Advances in Neural Information Processing Systems.,pp. 926–934 (2013)
20. Suchanek, F.M., Kasneci, G., Weikum, G.: Yago: a core of semantic knowledge. In: Proceedings of the 16th InternationalCconference on World Wide Web, pp. 697–706. ACM (2007)
21. Sun, Y., Han, J., Yan, X., Yu, P.S., Wu, T.: Pathsim: meta path-based top-k similarity search in heterogeneous information networks. Proc. VLDB Endow. **4**(11), 992–1003 (2011)
22. Syed, Z.H., Röder, M., Ngonga Ngomo, A.C.: Factcheck: Validating rdf triples using textual evidence. In: Proceedings of the 27th ACM International Conference on Information and Knowledge Management, pp. 1599–1602. ACM (2018)
23. Wang, Z., Zhang, J., Feng, J., Chen, Z.: Knowledge graph embedding by translating on hyperplanes. In: Twenty-Eighth AAAI Conference on Artificial Intelligence (2014)
24. Yin, X., Han, J., Philip, S.Y.: Truth discovery with multiple conflicting information providers on the web. IEEE Trans. Knowl. Data Eng. **20**(6), 796–808 (2008)
25. Zhao, M., Chow, T.W., Zhang, Z., Li, B.: Automatic image annotation via compact graph based semi-supervised learning. Knowl.-Based Syst. **76**, 148–165 (2015)

RDF Explorer: A Visual SPARQL Query Builder

Hernán Vargas[1,3], Carlos Buil-Aranda[1,3], Aidan Hogan[2,3(✉)], and Claudia López[1]

[1] Universidad Técnica Federico Santa María, Valparaíso, Chile
{hvargas,cbuil,claudia}@inf.utfsm.cl
[2] DCC, Universidad de Chile, Santiago, Chile
ahogan@dcc.uchile.cl
[3] Millenium Institute for Foundational Research on Data (IMFD), Santiago, Chile

Abstract. Despite the growing popularity of knowledge graphs for managing diverse data at large scale, users who wish to pose expressive queries against such graphs are often expected to know (i) how to formulate queries in a language such as SPARQL, and (ii) how entities of interest are described in the graph. In this paper we propose a language that relaxes these expectations; the language's operators are based on an interactive graph-based exploration that allows non-expert users to simultaneously navigate and query knowledge graphs; we compare the expressivity of this language with SPARQL. We then discuss an implementation of this language that we call RDF Explorer and discuss various desirable properties it has, such as avoiding interactions that lead to empty results. Through a user study over the Wikidata knowledge-graph, we show that users successfully complete more tasks with RDF Explorer than with the existing Wikidata Query Helper, while a usability questionnaire demonstrates that users generally prefer our tool and self-report lower levels of frustration and mental effort.

1 Introduction

Over the past decade, hundreds of datasets have been published using the Semantic Web standards covering a variety of domains [30]. These datasets are described using the RDF data model, which is based on graphs. Beyond the Semantic Web community, the idea of using graphs to model and manage diverse data at large-scale has also become increasingly popular, marked by the recent announcements of various *knowledge graphs* [12]. Some of these knowledge graphs are proprietary, maintained internally by companies such as Google, Microsoft, Apple, etc.; while others are open to the public via the Web, maintained by dedicated international communities, like DBpedia [22], Wikidata [36], etc.

A number of query languages have then been proposed specifically for graphs, including SPARQL for RDF graphs, Cypher for property graphs, etc. [3]. However, querying graphs using these languages can be challenging. First, users are

C. Ghidini et al. (Eds.): ISWC 2019, LNCS 11778, pp. 647–663, 2019.
https://doi.org/10.1007/978-3-030-30793-6_37

required to have technical knowledge of such query languages and the semantics of their operators. Second, graphs are often used to represent diverse data that may not correspond to a particular domain-specific schema, meaning that the users may not be easily able to conceptualize the data that they are querying, particularly for domain-agnostic knowledge graphs. Despite these limitations, query services for DBpedia and Wikidata are receiving in the order of millions of queries per day [23,28]; although many such queries are from "bots", tens of thousands are not [23], where such statistics indicate the value of being able to query graphs for many users and applications.

Several interfaces have been proposed to allow lay users to visualize, search, browse and query knowledge graphs, with varying goals, emphases and assumptions [15]. Some key approaches adopted by such interfaces (discussed further in Sect. 2) involve keyword search, faceted browsing, graph-based browsing, query building, graph summarization, visualization techniques, and combinations thereof. In general however, many proposed systems trade expressivity – the types of operators and interactions supported, and thus the types of queries that can ultimately be captured through the interface – for usability and efficiency. Few interfaces have been proposed, for example, that can handle graph-patterns with cycles, such as to find siblings who have directed movies together, drugs indicated and contraindicated for pairs of comorbid illnesses, pairs of binary stars of the same classification, and so forth. Interfaces that *can* capture such graph patterns often assume some technical expertise of the query language and/or knowledge of how data are modeled.

This work proposes a language and associated interface that enables lay users to build and execute graph-pattern queries on knowledge graphs, where the user navigates a visual representation of a sub-graph, and in so doing, incrementally builds a potentially complex (cyclical) graph pattern. More specifically, we first propose a set of operators, forming a language that allows users to build SPARQL graph patterns by interactively exploring an RDF graph; we further study the expressivity of this language. We then discuss the design of a user interface around this language, and the additional practical features it incorporates to improve usability, such as auto-completion, result previews, generalizing examples, etc.; we further describe how this interface can be implemented on top of an existing query service (SPARQL endpoint). Our claim is that the resulting interface allows lay users to express graph-pattern queries over knowledge graphs better than existing interfaces that support similar expressivity. To evaluate this claim, we present a task-based user study comparing the usability of our interface with the Wikidata Query Helper; the results indicate that users achieve a higher successful completion rate of tasks with our system.

2 Related Work

A wide variety of interfaces have been proposed in recent years to help lay users visualize and explore RDF graphs [11,15]. Amongst these works, we can first highlight search and browsing systems that allow users to find entities by keyword and potentially filter or modify results by selecting facets or following paths (e.g., *Tabulator* [9], *Explorator* [4], *VisiNav* [19], amongst others); these approaches are limited in terms of the types of queries that they can express, not allowing (for example) to express cycles. Other types of interfaces focus on providing visualisations to summarise data, be they domain-independent (e.g., *Sgvizler* [31], or domain-specific (e.g., *DBpedia Atlas* [35], *DBpedia Mobile* [8], *LinkedGeoData Browser* [34]) visualisations; such systems focus on providing overviews of data rather than exploring or querying for specific nodes/entities. Other systems combine browsing/exploration and visualisation, often following a graph-based navigation paradigm (e.g., *RDF Visualiser* [29], *Fenfire* [20], etc.); these systems allow to focus on a specific node and explore its neighborhood in the graph, but do not allow to generalize these explorations into queries.

To help users express more complex forms of queries over graphs, various *query editors and builders* have been proposed for languages such as SPARQL [16]. We provide an overview of such systems with publications in Table 1. For space reasons we focus on features that relate to the present contribution, omitting, for example, discussion of reasoning support in systems such as *QueryVOWL* [17] and *OptiqueVQS* [33], or the schema-based notation used by *SPARQLing* [7]. Such interfaces must deal with two antagonistic goals: supporting complex queries while assuming as little technical expertise on the part of the user as possible. Towards the more expressive end of the scale are query editing interfaces – such as *SPARQL Assist* [24], *YASGUI* [27], etc. – which offer users some helpful features when formulating SPARQL queries in a text field, but still assume knowledge of SPARQL. On the other hand, query builders aim to abstract away from SPARQL syntax, allowing to formulate queries in a more visual way, based on form fields or graphs. From Table 1, we conclude that the closest system to ours is *Smeagol* [14], which also supports key features such as autocompletion, example-based querying (where users explore a graph and then generalise some constants as variables), dynamic results (where query results are generated on the fly and used to guide query construction), and non-emptiness guarantees (to avoid users generating queries with zero results); furthermore, *Smeagol* offers a task-driven user evaluation against a baseline *Pubby* system with a substantial number of users and significance testing. Our proposal is distinguished from *Smeagol* in key aspects; most importantly, while *Smeagol* [14] focuses on supporting tree-shaped queries generated during user exploration, our proposal also has general support for graph patterns.

Research on usable interfaces for querying graphs can not only have impact beyond the Semantic Web community, it can also benefit from expertise in other communities. In particular, the area of Human Computer Interaction (HCI) can offer insights not only in terms of the challenges faced in such research, but also in the design of user studies to evaluate the claims made of such research. Along these lines, Bhowmick et al. [10] reflect on recent advances in what they refer to as the *visual graph querying paradigm* from the HCI perspective, characterizing the challenges in the area and the research directions that should be followed. The authors define the challenges as follows: (1) the development of graph queries

Table 1. Comparison of query interfaces for SPARQL, incidating the year of the associated publication, the mode of interaction, the features supported (AC = Autocomplete; EX = Example-based Querying; DY = Dynamic Results, NE = Non-Empty Results), details of user evaluation conducted, if any (B = Baseline, Q = Questionnaire, T = Tasks) and details of availability

System	Year	Mode	Features				User Eval.	Expressivity
			AC	EX	DY	NE		
NIGHTLIGHT [32]	2008	GRAPH	–	–	–	–	–	SPARQL 1.0$^-$
Konduit [2]	2010	FORM	✓	–	–	–	–	BGPs$^+$
RDF-GL [21]	2010	GRAPH	–	–	–	–	BQT (5 users)	SPARQL 1.0$^-$
Smeagol [14]	2011	GRAPH	✓	✓	✓	✓	BQT (43 users)	Trees
SPARQL Assist [24]	2012	TEXT	✓	–	–	–	–	BGPs$^+$
QUaTRO2 [6]	2013	FORM	✓	–	✓	✓	*no details*	Trees$^+$
QueryVOWL [17]	2015	GRAPH	✓	–	–	–	QT (6 users)	BGPs
YASGUI [27]	2017	TEXT	✓	–	–	–	–	SPARQL 1.1
OptiqueVQS [33]	2018	GRAPH	✓	–	–	–	T (10 users)	Trees
SPARQLing [7]	2018	GRAPH	–	–	–	–	–	Trees
ViziQuer [13]	2018	GRAPH	–	–	–	–	BT (14 users)	Trees$^+$
WQH [23]	2018	FORM	✓	–	✓	–	–	BGPs
RDF Explorer	2019	GRAPH	✓	✓	✓	✓	BQT (28 users)	BGPs$^-$

requires a considerable cognitive effort; (2) users need to be able to express their goal in a systematic and correct manner, which is antagonistic with the goal of catering to lay users; (3) it is more intuitive to "draw" graph queries than to write them, which implies the need for intuitive visual interfaces. Regarding the latter point, the authors claim that current visual querying tools suffer from poor aesthetics. They further indicate important primitives that such tools should support to cater to diverse users and support diverse queries: *edge creation, pattern creation* and *example-based querying*. Aside from this, they emphasize *action-aware query processing* in which the system is able to deliver partial information and immediate feedback while the user is developing the query, based on *dynamic result exploration and visualization*. They acknowledge, however, that these goals, when taken together, are challenging to address given large-scale graphs and complex queries.

In this paper, we propose (yet another) visual query builder for SPARQL. In so doing, we are particularly inspired by the discussion of Bhowmick et al. [10] in terms of the main interactions and features that are key to making such systems usable for non-experts, and by the "specific-to-general" paradigm adopted by *Smeagol* [14]; however, we adopt various extensions to improve usability and expressivity, key among which is support for graph patterns with cycles.

3 RDF Explorer

In this section, we propose our RDF Explorer system, whose goal is to enable lay users to query and explore RDF graphs. We first discuss the operators that form the basis of a visual query language in which users can express queries over graphs through simple interactions; we characterize the expressivity of the language in relation to SPARQL. Thereafter, we discuss how this query language is supported by the RDF Explorer interface, and how the overall system is implemented.

3.1 Visual Query Graph

The visual query language we propose is formulated with respect to a visual query graph. Let $\mathbf{I}$ denote the set of IRIs, $\mathbf{L}$ denote the set of literals and $\mathbf{V}$ denote the set of query variables. We define the visual query graph as follows.

Definition 1. *A visual query graph (VQG) is defined as a directed, edge-labelled graph* $\mathsf{G} = (\mathsf{N}, \mathsf{E})$*, with nodes* N *and edges* E*. The nodes of the VQG are a finite set of IRIs, literals and/or variables:* $\mathsf{N} \subset \mathbf{I} \cup \mathbf{L} \cup \mathbf{V}$*. The edges of the VQG are a finite set of triples, where each triple indicates a directed edge between two nodes with a label taken from the set of IRIs or variables:* $\mathsf{E} \subset \mathsf{N} \times (\mathbf{I} \cup \mathbf{V}) \times \mathsf{N}$.

We denote by $\mathrm{var}(\mathsf{G})$ the set of variables appearing in $\mathsf{G} = (\mathsf{N}, \mathsf{E})$, either as nodes or edge labels: $\mathrm{var}(\mathsf{G}) := \{v \in \mathbf{V} \mid v \in \mathsf{N} \text{ or } \exists\, n_1, n_2 : (n_1, v, n_2) \in \mathsf{E}\}$.

We say that the VQG is *constructed* through a *visual query language*, consisting of four algebraic operators that will correspond to atomic user interactions: adding a variable node, adding a constant node, adding an edge between two existing nodes with a variable label, and adding an edge between two existing nodes with an IRI label. More specifically, the VQG is initially empty: $\mathsf{G}_0 = (\emptyset, \emptyset)$. Thereafter, a VQG can be constructed through the visual query language (VQL), defined straightforwardly as follows.

Definition 2. *Letting* $\mathsf{G} = (\mathsf{N}, \mathsf{E})$ *denote the current VQG; the visual query language (VQL) is defined through the following four atomic operations:*

- *Initialize a new variable node:* $\eta(\mathsf{G}) := (\mathsf{N} \cup \{v\}, \mathsf{E})$ *where* $v \notin \mathrm{var}(\mathsf{G})$.
- *Add a new constant node:* $\eta(\mathsf{G}, x) := (\mathsf{N} \cup \{x\}, \mathsf{E})$ *where* $x \in (\mathbf{I} \cup \mathbf{L})$.
- *Initialize a new edge between two nodes with a variable edge-label:* $\varepsilon(\mathsf{G}, n_1, n_2) := (\mathsf{N}, \mathsf{E} \cup \{(n_1, v, n_2)\})$ *where* $\{n_1, n_2\} \subseteq \mathsf{N}$ *and* $v \notin \mathrm{var}(\mathsf{G})$.
- *Add a new edge between two nodes with an IRI edge-label:* $\varepsilon(\mathsf{G}, n_1, x, n_2) := (\mathsf{N}, \mathsf{E} \cup \{(n_1, x, n_2)\})$ *where* $\{n_1, n_2\} \subseteq \mathsf{N}$ *and* $x \in \mathbf{I}$.

Note that for the VQL operators $\eta(\mathsf{G})$ and $\varepsilon(\mathsf{G}, n_1, n_2)$, the variable is not specified, where rather an arbitrary fresh variable can be automatically generated. No matter what variables are chosen, since the variables added are always fresh, the resulting VQG will be unique modulo isomorphism; in practice, the system can thus take care of generating fresh names for each variable.

Though VQGs are a straightforward way to represent queries against graphs, since VQGs allow for representing cycles, they already go beyond the expressivity of many user interfaces for graphs (entity search, facets, etc.), and even many of the related visual query languages proposed in the literature, which are based on trees (see Table 1). On the other hand, we choose not to support query operators that go beyond simple graph patterns as covered by similar graph-based interfaces – such as NIGHTLIGHT [32] and RDF-GL [21], which support unions, optional, etc. – as we consider such systems to be aimed at users with some knowledge of query languages and do not know of an intuitive way to represent such operators in a manner that would be accessible to a lay user. On the other hand, VQGs will be converted to concrete SPARQL syntax, where a more expert user can modify the resulting query as required.

3.2 Translating VQGs to SPARQL

VQGs are designed as a visual metaphor for SPARQL basic graph patterns (BGPs), where the translation is thus *mostly* direct and natural; however there are BGPs that cannot be expressed as VQGs, and indeed, there are minor aspects of VQGs that cannot be translated to BGPs. Before we discuss such issues, we must first introduce some notation for RDF and SPARQL BGPs [26].

An *RDF triple* uses terms from the set of IRIs ($\mathbf{I}$), literals ($\mathbf{L}$) and blank nodes ($\mathbf{B}$); more specifically a triple $t = (s, p, o)$ is an RDF triple iff $s \in \mathbf{I} \cup \mathbf{B}$ (called the *subject*), $p \in \mathbf{I}$ (called the *predicate*) and $o \in \mathbf{I} \cup \mathbf{B} \cup \mathbf{L}$ (called the *object*). A finite set of RDF triples is called an *RDF graph*.

SPARQL *basic graph patterns* (BGPs) correspond to RDF graphs, but where variable terms ($\mathbf{V}$) can also be used. Along these lines, a triple $q = (s, p, o)$ is a SPARQL *triple pattern* iff $s \in \mathbf{I} \cup \mathbf{L} \cup \mathbf{V}$, $p \in \mathbf{I} \cup \mathbf{V}$ and $o \in \mathbf{I} \cup \mathbf{L} \cup \mathbf{V}$.[1] A SPARQL BGP is then a finite set of SPARQL triple patterns. The semantics of a BGP is defined in terms of its *evaluation* over an RDF graph, which returns a set of *mappings*. A mapping $\mu : \mathbf{V} \to (\mathbf{I} \cup \mathbf{B} \cup \mathbf{L})$ is a partial map from variables to RDF terms; the set of variables for which μ is defined is called the *domain* of μ, denoted $\mathrm{dom}(\mu)$. Given a query Q, we denote the set of variables it mentions by $\mathrm{var}(Q)$; furthermore, we denote by $\mu(Q)$ the image of Q under μ: the result of replacing every occurrence in Q of every variable $v \in \mathrm{var}(Q)$ by $\mu(v)$ (or v if $v \notin \mathrm{dom}(v)$). The *evaluation* of a BGP Q with respect to an RDF graph G, denoted $Q(G)$, is then defined as the set of mappings $\{\mu \mid \mathrm{dom}(\mu) = \mathrm{var}(Q) \text{ and } \mu(Q) \subseteq G\}$ (note that this is equivalent to – but more succinct than – defining the evaluation of a BGP as a join of the evaluation of its constituent triple patterns).

In terms of translating VQGs to BGPs, given a VQG $\mathsf{G} = (\mathsf{N}, \mathsf{E})$, we observe that by design, the set E is already a BGP, and we are done. However, first we must remark that this translation is agnostic to *orphan nodes* – nodes with no incident edges – in G; thus for example, G and $\eta(\mathsf{G})$ will give the same BGP. Second, while VQGs are BGPs have equivalent definitions, not all VQGs/BGPs

[1] We do not consider blank nodes in triple patterns, which can be modeled as unprojected (aka. non-distinguished) query variables.

can be constructed by the four operators in the visual query language described earlier. In particular, we cannot construct VQGs/BGPs where a join variable – a variable appearing in more than one edge/triple pattern – appears as an edge-label/predicate (since the $\varepsilon(\mathsf{N})$ operation is defined only for fresh variables, while $\varepsilon(\mathsf{G}, n_1, x, n_2)$ is defined only where x is constant); we do not consider this to be an important limitation in practice since analysis of real-world SPARQL query logs suggests that joins on the predicate position are rare [5].

The VQG can then be serialized in concrete SPARQL syntax: the corresponding basic graph pattern is written as the `WHERE` clause of a SPARQL query, where all variables are projected with `SELECT *`; at this point, a more expert user may wish to modify the query, e.g., adding query operators.

With respect to complexity, we remark that for the evaluation decision problem – which asks: given a mapping μ, a query Q and an RDF graph G, is $\mu \in Q(G)$? – the queries generated by a VQG are tractable for this problem as they do not feature projection (a trivial upper bound is given by $\mathrm{O}(|Q| \cdot |G|)$ [26]). However, in the interface we implement a number of features for usability, where one such feature is to suggest possible groundings of variables that will not lead to non-empty results. The corresponding decision problem for this autocompletion feature asks, given μ (where $\mathrm{dom}(\mu) \subseteq \mathrm{var}(Q)$), a query Q and an RDF graph G, is $\mu(Q)(G)$ non-empty? This problem is NP-complete in combined complexity (considering the size of G and Q in the input) since $\mu(Q)(G)$ can represent a graph, and one can reduce from the graph homomorphism problem; however, in data complexity (considering the query Q as fixed) the problem is tractable. In summary, the autocompletion task may become challenging as the VQG grows more complex; currently we rely on a SPARQL query to generate these suggestions, where we leave further optimizations for future work.

3.3 The RDF Explorer Interface

While the visual query graph offers a visual metaphor for basic graph patterns and the visual query language describes the interactions by which a visual query graph can be constructed incrementally by the user, these concepts leave many questions open regarding usability. One key issue, for example, is how the VQG should be visualized. Another practical issue we glossed over is that while $\eta(\mathsf{G})$ and $\varepsilon(\mathsf{G}, n_1, n_2)$ do not require any specific knowledge (in the latter, the user can select two nodes displayed in the visualization, for example), the operations $\eta(\mathsf{G}, x)$ and $\varepsilon(\mathsf{G}, n_1, n_2, x)$ require the user to give a specific (IRI or literal) term x, which assumes domain knowledge. Furthermore, we have yet to address the usability features discussed by Bhowmick et al. [10], such as *example-based querying*, *action-aware query processing*, or *dynamic result exploration and visualization*. Addressing such issues is key to achieving our goal of enabling lay users to formulate expressive queries over graphs. Along these lines, we now describe the RDF Explorer interface, which we propose to address these concerns.

The RDF Explorer interface is composed of six main components displayed in three panes. Figure 1 provides a screenshot of the interface for querying Wikidata, where we can see three components: a search panel (left pane), a visual

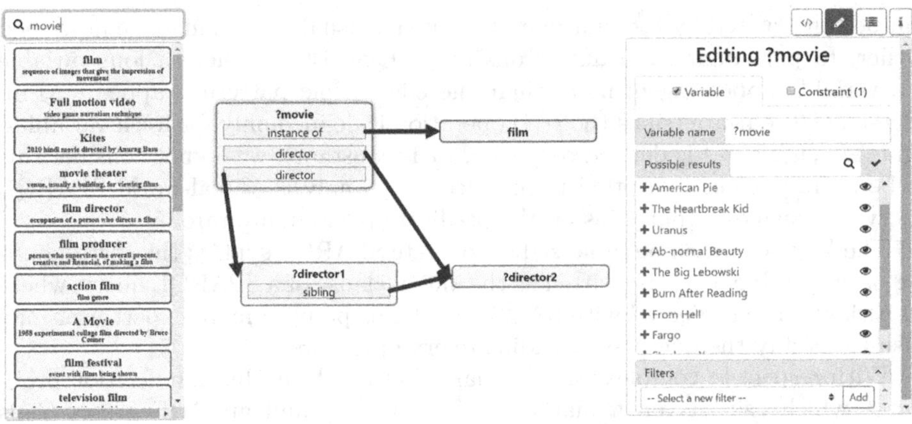

Fig. 1. Example visual query finding siblings who have directed movies together

query editor (center pane), and a node detail view (right pane); in the top right corner are buttons to switch the right pane to display one of the three other components: a node editor (allowing to add restrictions to a highlighted node), a SPARQL query editor (showing the current query), and a help panel.

The process starts with a blank visual query editor. The user must then start by adding a new node, be it a variable node ($\eta(\mathsf{G})$) or a constant node ($\eta(\mathsf{G}, x)$); for selecting x, the user can type a keyword phrase into the search pane on the left, which will generate autosuggestions, where any of the results shown can be dragged into the central query editor pane. The user may then proceed to add a second node by the same means. With two or more nodes available, the user can now click and drag between two nodes to generate an edge with a variable edge-label (shown as a box nested inside the source node); a list of potential IRIs will be suggested for replacing the variable, where only IRIs that generate non-empty results for the underlying query will be offered.

Figure 2 illustrates some further features of the interface. Following conventions used in the case of property graphs [3], we display datatype properties within a given node to avoid clutter; this can be seen for the number of children property in Fig. 2. At any point, the user may click on a node to view further details: if the node is variable (see Fig. 1), they will be shown a sample of current results for that variable (generated by mapping the current VQG to SPARQL and projecting that variable); if the node is constant (see Fig. 2), they will be shown the data available for that node, organized by datatype properties (which take a literal value) and object properties (which take an IRI value). In this way, per the discussion of Bhowmick et al. [10], the user can explore the graph and receive feedback on the results generated thus far, guiding next steps. Constant nodes can be converted to variables nodes, enabling the user to start with a specific example and then generalize the graph [14]. We claim that these features improve the usability of the system for lay users.

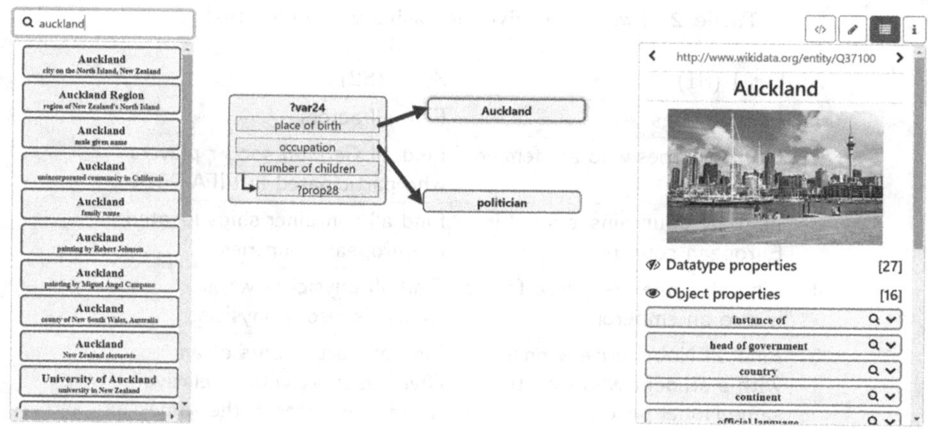

Fig. 2. Example visual query finding politicians born in Auckland

4 User Study

We now describe a user study that we conducted to evaluate our interface. We first make explicit our hypotheses and then describe the dataset, baseline system and user-study design that we selected to test these hypotheses. We then give details on the participants of the study and the metrics we collect.

Hypotheses. The goal of our work is to enable users without prior knowledge of the Semantic Web to explore an RDF database and correctly build SPARQL queries encoding a specific information need. Our hypotheses are as follows, where each hypothesis relates to user success at different levels of granularity:

H_1: *Non-expert users are able to correctly formulate more SPARQL queries with our visual query builder than a baseline system.* For a query to be considered correct, it must return the same results as the reference query for the task.

H_2: *Non-expert users are able to correctly formulate more triple patterns with our visual query builder than a baseline system.* For a triple pattern to be considered correct in the generated query, it must be contained in the reference query (modulo variable names).

H_3: *Non-expert users are able to generate more correct query graphs with our visual query builder than a baseline system.* For a query graph to be considered correct, its "shape" must be the same as that of the reference query graph, irrespective of edge labels or node types/values. More formally, given a visual query graph $\mathsf{G} = (\mathsf{N}, \mathsf{E})$, let shape($\mathsf{G}$) denote a directed graph $S = (V_S, E_S)$ such that $V_S = \mathsf{N}$ and $(x, y) \in S$ if and only if there exists an edge-label l such that $(x, l, y,) \in \mathsf{E}$; now given the reference query graph G', a user's query graph G'', and their corresponding shapes $S' =$ shape(G') and $S'' =$ shape(G''), the user's query graph G'' is considered correct if and only if there exists an isomorphism $h : V''_S \to V'_S$ such that $h(S'') = S'$.

Table 2. Two sets of five increasingly-complex tasks

№	Set 1 (S1)	Set 2 (S2)
1	Find all dogs	Find all actors
2	Find all popes who are female	Find all German soccer players who participated in FIFA 2014
3	Find all mountains located in European countries	Find all container ships located in European countries
4	Find all emperors whose father is also an emperor	Find all physicists whose spouse is also a physicist
5	Find all Nobel prize winners with a student who won the same Nobel prize	Find all participants of an Olympic sport with a relative who participates in the same sport

Dataset and Baseline. According to statistics recently published by Malyshev et al. [23], the *Wikidata Query Service* [2] receives millions of SPARQL queries per day, where tens of thousands of these queries are "*organic*" (written and posed by humans rather than bots). The Wikidata knowledge graph itself is a large, diverse graph, where at the time of writing it described 56,097,884 items and was being collaboratively edited by 21,049 active users; such a graph is unfeasible for any user to conceptualize in its entirety. We thus view Wikidata as a potentially challenging use-case for our visual query builder and adopt it for our study.

In fact, Wikidata already has a default query builder deployed to help users query the knowledge graph: the *Wikidata Query Helper* (WQH) [23]. The WQH visual interface accompanies a text field displaying the current SPARQL query; changes in WQH are reflected in the query and vice versa. WQH is based on two main functionalities: the ability to define a *filter* that allows to select a property p and an object o, and the ability to *show* more data than what is being filtered by fixing a property value and adding a variable to its associated o. To help users select a given value for p and/or o, a search field is provided that autocompletes a keyword query and provides ranked suggestions to the user.

Study Design. To test the hypotheses, we design a task-based user study to compare the subjects' ability to solve tasks on the proposed interface versus the baseline interface [25]. This comparison focuses on the users' ability to perform query-based tasks, including aspects such as the users' performance overall, their perceived cognitive load, and usability aspects. Given limitations to how many subjects we could recruit, we use a within-subject design where each participant completes five tasks using our query builder and five similar tasks with the baseline. Each task consists of answering a question (given in natural language) that requires formulating a query to retrieve answer(s) from the Wikidata graph.

[2] http://query.wikidata.org/.

Table 3. Basic graph patterns corresponding to tasks listed in Table 2

№	Set 1 (S1)	Set 2 (S2)
1	`?dog wdt:P31 wd:Q144 .`	`?actor wdt:P106 wd:Q33999.`
2	`?pope wdt:P21 wd:Q6581072 .` `?pope wdt:P39 wd:Q19546 .`	`?ppl wdt:P1344 wd:Q79859.` `?ppl wdt:P27 wd:Q298.`

3	`?mount wdt:P31 wd:Q8502 .`
	`?mount wdt:P17 ?country .`
	`?country wdt:P30 wd:Q18 .`
		`?ship wdt:P31 wd:Q17210 .`
		`?ship wdt:P17 ?country .`
		`?country wdt:P30 wd:Q46 .`

4	`?emp1 wdt:P39 wd:Q39018 .`
	`?emp2 wdt:P39 wd:Q39018 .`
	`?emp1 wdt:P22 ?emp2 .`
		`?phy1 wdt:P106 wd:Q169470 .`
		`?phy2 wdt:P106 wd:Q169470 .`
		`?phy1 wdt:P26 ?phy2 .`

5	`?winner wdt:P166 ?novel .`
	`?student wdt:P166 ?novel .`
	`?student wdt:P802 ?winner .`
	`?novel wdt:P31 wd:Q7191 .`
		`?ppl1 wdt:P641 ?sp .`
		`?ppl2 wdt:P641 ?sp .`
		`?ppl1 wdt:P1038 ?ppl2 .`
		`?sp wdt:P279 wd:Q212434 .`

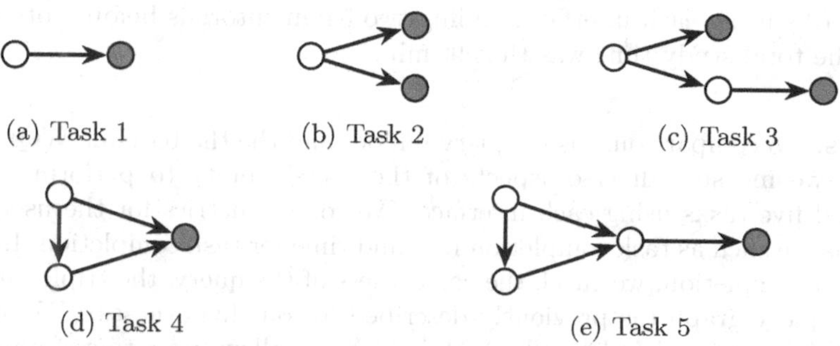

(a) Task 1 (b) Task 2 (c) Task 3

(d) Task 4 (e) Task 5

Fig. 3. Expected query shapes for each pair of tasks shown in Table 2 where constant (IRI or literal) nodes are shaded and variable nodes are unshaded

We divide the subjects into two groups. The first group is asked to build a set of five queries (S1) using the proposed interface; afterwards they are asked to build a different set of five queries (S2) using the baseline. Conversely, the second group is asked to build the first set of queries (S1) using the baseline and the second set (S2) with the proposed interface. This design controls for individual differences with participants using both interfaces. Counterbalancing the order of interfaces helps control for carry-over effects, such as learning or fatigue.

Table 2 list the tasks in sets S1 and S2. The queries in both sets are designed to be of increasingly difficulty to follow a learning curve and also to avoid users being discouraged early on. We further aim to keep the nth query of both sets of tasks comparable in terms of difficulty. Along these lines, as shown in Fig. 3, each pair of tasks corresponds to the same abstract visual query graph, and each successive pair incrementally adds more complexity. Table 3 lists the target SPARQL basic graph patterns corresponding to each task in Table 2.

Before presenting each set of five tasks, we provide some brief training for the participants on how to use the interface they are about to see. Our training involves a description of the system's main functionalities and formulating an example query using these functionalities. For example, we pose the task *"Find all Clint Eastwood movies in which any of his children participated"* and show how to build the query in the corresponding interface. A web page with other example queries for the interface is also provided to the participants.

Study Participants. The study was conducted with 28 students enrolled in the undergraduate course "User interface design". The students were in the fourth year of a Computer Science undergraduate program in a Spanish-speaking university. They have no previous knowledge of SPARQL nor the Semantic Web. Their native language was Spanish; the text of tasks was presented in Spanish and while both interfaces were offered in English, a tooltip was added that automatically translates an English word to Spanish when the user hovers the mouse over a word. Participants were given up to 40 min to solve each of the sets of five tasks using each interface; adding two 5 min tutorials before both sets of tasks, the total study time was thus 90 min.

Metrics. To compare our visual query builder and the the baseline WQH query builder, we measure diverse aspects of the users' ability to perform a set of requested five tasks using each interface. We collect metrics for the users' task performance such as task completion rate and time for task completion. In terms of level of completion, we check the correctness of the query, the triple patterns, and the query graph (as previously described for our hypotheses). We also use the NASA Task Load Index [18] (NASA-TLX) to allow users to self-report the level of workload perceived by the user in a scale from 0 to 100. We use Likert scales from 1 to 5 to ask for usability aspects. We also include open questions to describe the data structure that the users believe to be behind each interface. We ask users to answer such questions using simple natural language that avoids technical jargon where we restrict the words they can use to the 1,000 most common words in their native language; we also ask them to illustrate (draw) how they understand the data structure.

5 Results

We begin by presenting the ratio of correct responses broken down by three levels of granularity: queries, triple patterns and shapes. Next we evaluate our hypotheses with respect to these data. We then present analysis of the subjective impressions of the interfaces.

Ratio of Correct Responses. Figure 4 shows the mean ratios of correct responses for the proposed interface (RDF Explorer = RE) and the baseline interface (Wikidata Query Helper = WQH) at three different levels of granularity: queries, triple patterns, and shapes. Note that while queries and shapes are binary – either correct or not – in the case of triple patterns, we take the ratio of correct triple patterns versus total triple patterns provided in the response, where the presented results are then the mean of these ratios across all users.

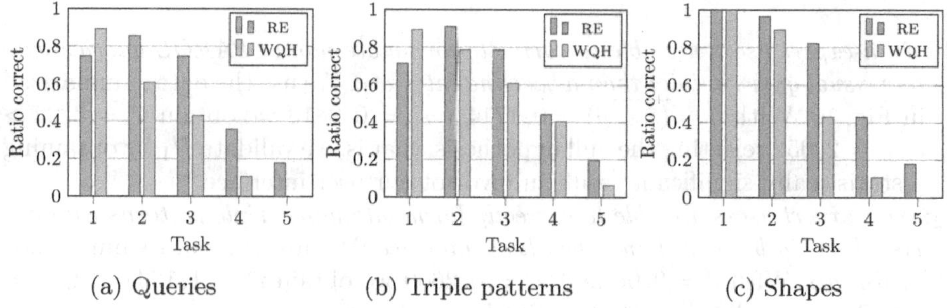

(a) Queries (b) Triple patterns (c) Shapes

Fig. 4. Mean ratios of correct results at three levels of granularity

Though we note a relatively high correctness ratio for earlier tasks, most users still struggled with later tasks; not only were earlier tasks easier, given the fixed time period for the study, some users did not reach the final task(s). Contrasting the two systems, in the first task, although all users of both systems got the query shape correct in both systems (which is trivially a single edge), they had more success correctly finding the terms of the triple pattern in WQH than RE; we believe that this is because WQH offers autocomplete forms that directly correspond to triple patterns whereas RE is more complex to use at first.[3] However, as tasks progress and queries become more "graph-like", users have more correct responses using the RE interface than the WQH interface; another possible interpretation is that users learn more about RE as the task progresses. Comparing the three levels of granularity, in the RE system, users generally have more success defining the correct query graph shape than identifying the terms (constants) in the query graph; the opposite trend is true for WQH, where users can more easily find the correct query terms, but not the correct query shape; we attribute this to two possible factors: the fact that WQH is form-based while RE is graph-based, and also based on the fact that RE blocks users from creating query shapes that give empty results while WQH does not.

Hypothesis Testing. To test our hypotheses, we assess the difference between completion rates of participants using both tools (whose mean values are depicted in Fig. 4). We use *paired-t* tests to assess differences in the users' ability

[3] Given that the first task results in a query with a single triple pattern, the results for queries and triple patterns are the same.

to perform the requested tasks; this test is appropriate because we are comparing the same participants using two different tools. We use $\alpha = 0.05$ to reject the null hypothesis and thus interpret that we have obtained a significant result when t^* is greater than $t_{crit} = 2.052$ ($t^* \geq t_{crit}$).[4] For our three hypotheses (see Sect. 4) the null hypotheses are that there is no difference between the tools or WQH performs better. The alternative hypothesis is that RE performs better. We denote the completion rates for RE as $\bar{x}$ and those for WQH as $\bar{y}$; the average distances we denote by $\bar{d} = \overline{(\bar{x} - \bar{y})}$, and the standard deviation by s_d. We can then test the three hypotheses:

H_1: *Non-expert users are able to correctly formulate more SPARQL queries with our visual query builder than a baseline interface.* We use the data summarized in Fig. 4a. With $\bar{d} = \overline{(\bar{x} - \bar{y})} = 0,1714$ y $s_d = 0,2813$ we obtain $t^* = 3,22 > t_{crit} = 2,052$ rejecting the null hypothesis; that is, we validate H_1 by obtaining a statistically significant result in favor of our user interface.[5]

H_2: *Non-expert users are able to correctly formulate more triple patterns with our visual query builder than a baseline interface.* We use the data summarized in Fig. 4b. With $\bar{d} = 0,06$ and $s_d = 0,2609$ we obtain $t^* = 1,1947 < t_{crit} = 2,052$: the results are not statistically significant.

H_3: *Non-expert users are able to generate more correct query graphs with our visual query builder than a baseline interface.* Here we use the data summarized in Fig. 4c. With $\bar{d} = 0,1928$ and $s_d = 0,2801$ we obtain $t^* = 3,6431 > t_{crit} = 2,052$ rejecting the null hypothesis; that is, we validate H_3 by obtaining a statistically significant result in favor of our user interface.

Our user study is thus conclusive regarding the claim that our proposed interface is better than the baseline at helping non-expert users formulate their queries as graphs, but is not conclusive regarding the claim of our interface being better at helping users to correctly generate triple patterns.

Time Results. For space reasons, we present the results regarding task completion time as online reference data [1]. In summary, the average time needed for completing all ten tasks was 65 min while the fastest participant needed 50 min to complete all tasks.

Subjective Results. Figure 5 shows the results of the NASA-TLX questionnaire, where lower scores are deemed better. We see that for both systems, users still expressed concerns about both systems, where they found WQH particularly frustrating and demanding of mental effort; on the other hand, they found the

[4] The value for t_{crit} is given by α and the number of participants ($n = 28$, giving $n-1 = 27$ degrees of freedom). See http://www.numeracy-bank.net/?q=t/stt/ptt/3.

[5] The data were found to be normally distributed and there were no clear outliers; hence use of the paired t-test is considered valid. We also conducted a non-parametric Wilcoxon test to compare the users' ability to perform the requested tasks using the different interfaces; the results indicate a p-value of $0.001647 < 0.05$.

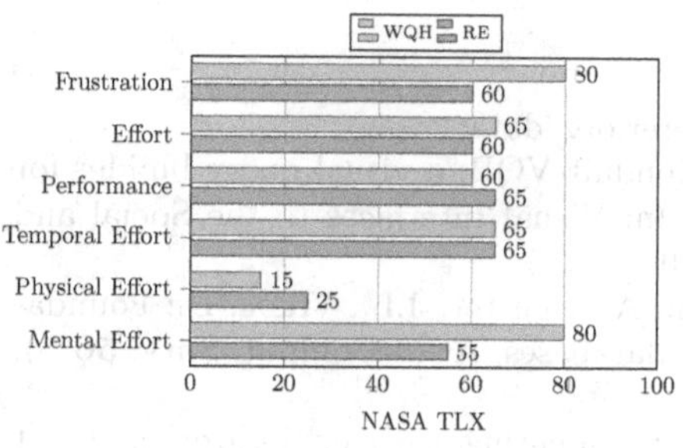

Fig. 5. NASA-TLX results

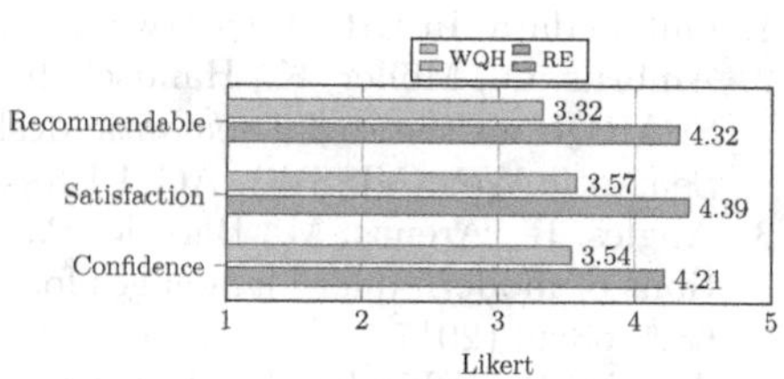

Fig. 6. Likert results

the physical effort required to use WQH to be lower (perhaps because RE requires more clicks, drags, etc.). Figure 6 shows the usability results, where higher scores are better; the users express a preference across all dimensions for RE when compared with WQH.

6 Conclusions

We present a language and its visual implementation (RE) to support non-expert users in generating graph queries. Our results indicate that our RE interface is more effective at supporting non-expert users in creating correct SPARQL queries than the baseline WQH system. The data suggest that this difference could be attributed to better support for generating the correct graph patterns rather than the correct triple patterns, as well as usability features such as non-empty suggestions. Even though these benefits come at the cost of higher physical effort, they require lower mental effort and generate less frustration.

Future work can be followed along several lines. First, additional user studies may reveal further insights into the RDF Explorer system, where it would be of interest to compare with other baseline systems (such as Smeagol), with other endpoints, with other types of questions, and with a more diverse set of users. More generally, we could explore the potential reasons behind these usability differences, including whether or not our graph-like visualization leads users to develop more productive mental representations of the data structures. Aside from evaluation, the system could be improved along a number of lines, most importantly in terms of approximations for non-empty suggestions to improve performance for more complex visual query graphs, and support for features such as optionals, unions, etc. (while maintaining the usability of the system) .

A demo of RDF Explorer is available at https://www.rdfexplorer.org/ operating over the Wikidata SPARQL Query Service.

Acknowledgements. Vargas and Buil-Aranda were supported by Fondecyt Iniciación Grant No. 11170714. Hogan was supported by Fondecyt Grant No. 1181896. Vargas, Buil-Aranda and Hogan were supported by the Millenium Institute for Foundational Research on Data (IMFD).

References

1. Online data. In URL http://www.rdfexplorer.org/data
2. Ambrus, O., Möller, K., Handschuh, S.: Konduit VQB: a visual query builder for SPARQL on the social semantic desktop. In: Visual Interfaces to the Social and Semantic Web (VISSW). ACM Press (2010)
3. Angles, R., Arenas, M., Barceló, P., Hogan, A., Reutter, J.L., Vrgoc, D.: Foundations of modern query languages for graph databases. ACM Comput. Surv. **50**(5), 68:1–68:40 (2017)
4. Araujo, S., Schwabe, D., Barbosa, S.: Experimenting with explorator: a direct manipulation generic RDF browser and querying tool. In: Visual Interfaces to the Social and the Semantic Web (VISSW 2009), Sanibel Island, Florida (2009)
5. Arias, M., Fernández, J.D., Martínez-Prieto, M.A., de la Fuente, P.: An empirical study of real-world SPARQL queries. In: Usage Analysis and the Web of Data (USEWOD) (2011)
6. Balis, B., Grabiec, T., Bubak, M.: Domain-driven visual query formulation over RDF data sets. In: Wyrzykowski, R., Dongarra, J., Karczewski, K., Waśniewski, J. (eds.) PPAM 2013. LNCS, vol. 8384, pp. 293–301. Springer, Heidelberg (2014). https://doi.org/10.1007/978-3-642-55224-3_28
7. Bartolomeo, S.D., Pepe, G., Savo, D.F., Santarelli, V.: Sparqling: painlessly drawing SPARQL queries over graphol ontologies. In: International Workshop on Visualization and Interaction for Ontologies and Linked Data (VOILA), pp. 64–69 (2018)
8. Becker, C., Bizer, C.: Exploring the geospatial semantic web with DBpedia mobile. Web Semant. Sci. Serv. Agents World Wide Web **7**(4), 278–286 (2009)
9. Berners-Lee, T., et al.: Tabulator: exploring and analyzing linked data on the semantic web. In: Proceedings of the 3rd International Semantic Web User Interaction Workshop, vol. 2006, p. 159. Citeseer (2006)
10. Bhowmick, S.S., Choi, B., Li, C.: Graph querying meets HCI: state of the art and future directions. In: ACM International Conference on Management of Data, pp. 1731–1736. ACM (2017)
11. Bikakis, N., Sellis, T.: Exploration and visualization in the web of big linked data: a survey of the state of the art. arXiv preprint arXiv:1601.08059 (2016)
12. Bonatti, P.A., Decker, S., Polleres, A., Presutti, V.: Knowledge graphs: new directions for knowledge representation on the semantic web. Dagstuhl Rep. **8**(9), 29–111 (2018)
13. Čerāns, K., et al.: ViziQuer: a web-based tool for visual diagrammatic queries over RDF data. In: Gangemi, A., et al. (eds.) ESWC 2018. LNCS, vol. 11155, pp. 158–163. Springer, Cham (2018). https://doi.org/10.1007/978-3-319-98192-5_30
14. Clemmer, A., Davies, S.: Smeagol: a "specific-to-general" semantic web query interface paradigm for novices. In: Hameurlain, A., Liddle, S.W., Schewe, K.-D., Zhou, X. (eds.) DEXA 2011. LNCS, vol. 6860, pp. 288–302. Springer, Heidelberg (2011). https://doi.org/10.1007/978-3-642-23088-2_21
15. Dadzie, A.-S., Rowe, M.: Approaches to visualising linked data: a survey. Semant. Web **2**(2), 89–124 (2011)
16. Grafkin, P., Mironov, M., Fellmann, M., Lantow, B., Sandkuhl, K., Smirnov, A.V.: Sparql query builders: overview and comparison. In: BIR Workshops (2016)
17. Haag, F., Lohmann, S., Siek, S., Ertl, T.: QueryVOWL: a visual query notation for linked data. In: Gandon, F., Guéret, C., Villata, S., Breslin, J., Faron-Zucker, C., Zimmermann, A. (eds.) ESWC 2015. LNCS, vol. 9341, pp. 387–402. Springer, Cham (2015). https://doi.org/10.1007/978-3-319-25639-9_51

18. Hart, S.G., Staveland, L.E.: Development of NASA-TLX (Task Load Index): results of empirical and theoretical research. In: Advances in psychology, vol. 52, pp. 139–183. Elsevier (1988)
19. Harth, A.: Visinav: a system for visual search and navigation on web data. Web Semant. Sci. Serv. Agents World Wide Web **8**(4), 348–354 (2010)
20. Hastrup, T., Cyganiak, R., Bojars, U.: Browsing linked data with Fenfire (2008)
21. Hogenboom, F., Milea, V., Frasincar, F., Kaymak, U.: RDF-GL: a SPARQL-based graphical query language for RDF. In: Emergent Web Intelligence: Advanced Information Retrieval, pp. 87–116 (2010). https://doi.org/10.1007/978-1-84996-074-8_4
22. Lehmann, J., et al.: Dbpedia - a large-scale, multilingual knowledge base extracted from wikipedia. Semant. Web **6**(2), 167–195 (2015)
23. Malyshev, S., Krötzsch, M., González, L., Gonsior, J., Bielefeldt, A.: Getting the most out of wikidata: semantic technology usage in wikipedia's knowledge graph. In: Vrandečić, D., et al. (eds.) ISWC 2018. LNCS, vol. 11137, pp. 376–394. Springer, Cham (2018). https://doi.org/10.1007/978-3-030-00668-6_23
24. McCarthy, E.L., Vandervalk, B.P., Wilkinson, M.: SPARQL assist language-neutral query composer. BMC Bioinf. **13**(S–1), S2 (2012)
25. Munzner, T.: Visualization Analysis and Design. AK Peters/CRC Press, Boca Raton (2014)
26. Pérez, J., Arenas, M., Gutiérrez, C.: Semantics and complexity of SPARQL. ACM Trans. Database Syst. **34**(3), 16:1–16:45 (2009)
27. Rietveld, L., Hoekstra, R.: The YASGUI family of SPARQL clients. Semant. Web **8**(3), 373–383 (2017)
28. Saleem, M., Ali, M.I., Hogan, A., Mehmood, Q., Ngomo, A.-C.N.: LSQ: the linked SPARQL queries dataset. In: Arenas, M., et al. (eds.) ISWC 2015. LNCS, vol. 9367, pp. 261–269. Springer, Cham (2015). https://doi.org/10.1007/978-3-319-25010-6_15
29. Sayers, C.: Node-centric rdf graph visualization. Mobile and Media Systems Laboratory, HP Labs (2004)
30. Schmachtenberg, M., Bizer, C., Paulheim, H.: Adoption of the linked data best practices in different topical domains. In: Mika, P., et al. (eds.) ISWC 2014. LNCS, vol. 8796, pp. 245–260. Springer, Cham (2014). https://doi.org/10.1007/978-3-319-11964-9_16
31. Skjæveland, M.G.: Sgvizler: a javascript wrapper for easy visualization of SPARQL result sets. In: Simperl, E., et al. (eds.) ESWC 2012. LNCS, vol. 7540, pp. 361–365. Springer, Heidelberg (2015). https://doi.org/10.1007/978-3-662-46641-4_27
32. Smart, P.R., Russell, A., Braines, D., Kalfoglou, Y., Bao, J., Shadbolt, N.R.: A visual approach to semantic query design using a web-based graphical query designer. In: Gangemi, A., Euzenat, J. (eds.) EKAW 2008. LNCS (LNAI), vol. 5268, pp. 275–291. Springer, Heidelberg (2008). https://doi.org/10.1007/978-3-540-87696-0_25
33. Soylu, A., et al.: OptiqueVQS: a visual query system over ontologies for industry. Semant. Web **9**(5), 627–660 (2018)
34. Stadler, C., Lehmann, J., Höffner, K., Auer, S.: Linkedgeodata: a core for a web of spatial open data. Semant. Web **3**(4), 333–354 (2012)
35. Valsecchi, F., Abrate, M., Bacciu, C., Tesconi, M., Marchetti, A.: DBpedia atlas: mapping the uncharted lands of linked data. In: LDOW@ WWW (2015)
36. Vrandečić, D., Krötzsch, M.: Wikidata: a free collaborative knowledge base. Commun. ACM **57**(10), 78–85 (2014)

Capturing Semantic and Syntactic Information for Link Prediction in Knowledge Graphs

Changjian Wang[1,2], Minghui Yan[1,2], Chuanrun Yi[1,2], and Ying Sha[1,2,3](✉)

[1] Institute of Information Engineering, Chinese Academy of Sciences, Beijing, China
{wangchangjian,yanminghui,yichuanrun,shaying}@iie.ac.cn

[2] School of Cyber Security, University of Chinese Academy of Sciences, Beijing, China

[3] College of Informatics, Huazhong Agricultural University, Wuhan, China

Abstract. Link prediction has recently been a major focus of knowledge graphs (KGs). It aims at predicting missing links between entities to complement KGs. Most previous works only consider the triples, but the triples provide less information than the paths. Although some works consider the semantic information (i.e. similar entities get similar representations) of the paths using the Word2Vec models, they ignore the syntactic information (i.e. the order of entities and relations) of the paths. In this paper, we propose RW-LMLM, a novel approach for link prediction. RW-LMLM consists of a random walk algorithm for KG (RW) and a language model-based link prediction model (LMLM). The paths generated by RW are viewed as pseudo-sentences for LMLM training. RW-LMLM can capture the semantic and syntactic information in KGs by considering entities, relations, and order information of the paths. Experimental results show that our method outperforms several state-of-the-art models on benchmark datasets. Further analysis shows that our model is highly parameter efficient.

Keywords: Knowledge graph embedding · Link prediction · Random walk · Language model

1 Introduction

Knowledge graphs (KGs) are databases that contain facts about the world. Each fact in KGs is represented as a triple $\langle head\ entity, relation, tail\ entity \rangle$ denoted as $\langle h, r, t \rangle$, e.g., $\langle Washington, capitalOf, USA \rangle$. Recent years, several KGs such as YAGO [35], Freebase [3], NELL [5], and DBpedia [16] have been constructed. These KGs are extremely useful resources for many real-world applications such as question answering, information extraction, recommendation, etc. However, KGs are usually far from complete, i.e., missing links between entities, which hinders their usefulness in the above applications. Therefore, *link prediction* or *knowledge base completion* is proposed to solve this problem.

C. Ghidini et al. (Eds.): ISWC 2019, LNCS 11778, pp. 664–679, 2019.
https://doi.org/10.1007/978-3-030-30793-6_38

Recently, many methods have been proposed for link prediction. The most successful models are embedding-based, such as TorusE [8], SimplE [14], and ConvE [6]. In these models, entities are represented as vectors while relations are represented as vectors or matrices. By using the scoring function which is defined on the representation of each triple, these models can measure the likelihood of each candidate triple being a fact. However, these models only consider the triples, so the information they can use is limited.

Compared with the triples, the paths that are connected by multiple triples provide more information. Similar to DeepWalk [27], some works [10,11,21] treat the paths as context information and use the Word2Vec [22] models to learn the latent representations of entities or relations on KGs. Since Word2Vec models discard the word order information, these methods discard the order information of the paths either. If we treat the paths as natural language sentences, these methods can capture the semantic information (similar entities get similar representations) but cannot capture the syntactic information (the order of entities and relations) of the paths.

However, the syntactic information is very useful, it can tell us what the next word is given previous words, which is exactly the goal of link prediction (predicting the next entity given previous entity and relation). For example, given a path $A \xrightarrow{sonOf} B \xrightarrow{wifeOf} C$, if we capture the semantic information (B and C have similar representations) and the syntactic information (B is the next entity of A and $sonOf$), there is a high probability that $\langle A, sonOf, C\rangle$ is a fact.

To capture the semantic information and the syntactic information simultaneously, we propose RW-LMLM, a novel approach for link prediction. Figure 1 shows the overview of our method. The first part of our method is a random walk algorithm for KG (RW) and the second part is a language model-based link prediction model (LMLM) which is constructed by the Transformer Decoder [20,40]. In order to obtain the paths more conveniently, the triples in KG are converted to a graph. RW generates a set of paths by performing random walks along the outgoing direction of entities on the graph. The paths generated by RW consist of entities and relations while maintaining their order. These paths will be viewed as pseudo-sentences to train LMLM like the standard language model. Benefitting from the masked self-attention mechanism and the positional encoding of LMLM, the previous entities, relations and their order are considered when predicting the next entity, which makes LMLM have the ability to capture both the semantic and syntactic information. We evaluate our method on four benchmark datasets: WN18 [4], FB15k [4], WN18RR [6], and FB15k-237 [38]. Experimental results show that our method outperforms several state-of-the-art models.

In summary, our contributions are as follows:

- We propose RW-LMLM— a novel approach for link prediction. RW-LMLM can capture the semantic and the syntactic information in KGs.
- We analyze the parameter sensitivity of RW and find that we do not need too many walk steps to get the best performance, for FB15k-237, 5 steps is

enough. This may guide some works to choose a more reasonable path length to improve their performance.
- LMLM that utilizes the path information is more parameter efficient than some methods that only use the triples information. Compared with two state-of-the-art models ConvE and DistMult, LMLM is 2x parameter efficient than ConvE and at least 4x than DistMult.

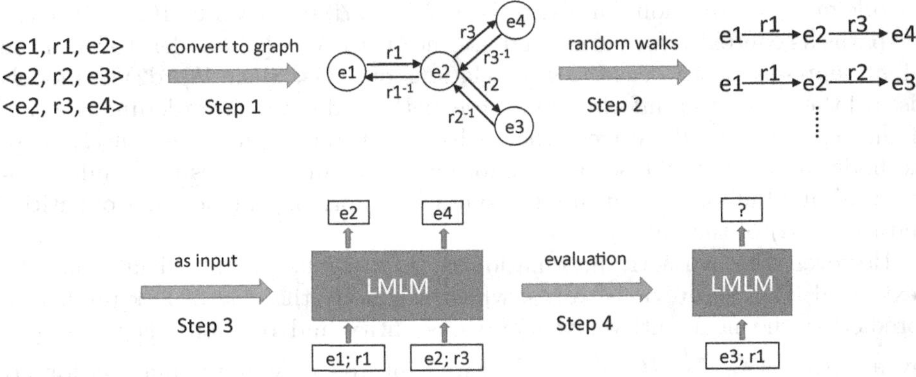

Fig. 1. Overview of our method. Step 1 converts triples to a graph; step 2 performs random walks on the graph to generate the paths; step 3 uses each path to train LMLM (taking $e1 \xrightarrow{r1} e2 \xrightarrow{r3} e4$ as an example); step 4 uses the trained LMLM to do link prediction task (taking $\langle e3, r1, ? \rangle$ as an example).

2 Related Work

Embedding models for link prediction have been quite popular in recent years. They usually use the triples to get the representations of entities and relations. We roughly divide them into three categories: translation-based, bilinear, and neural network-based. TransE [4] is the first translation-based model. It model the relation as a translational vector to correlate the head and tail entity embeddings. Many works extend TransE by projecting the head and tail embeddings into the relation vector space using projection vectors or matrices, such as TransH [42], and TransR [18]. Using the same principle as TransE, TorusE [8] embeds entities and relations on a torus. Unlike translation-based models, bilinear models represent the relation as a matrix. RESCAL [26] has no restrictions on the relation matrix. DistMult [43] restricts relations to diagonal matrices, and ComplEx [39] is DistMult's extension in complex space. SimplE [14] is a simple interpretable fully expressive bilinear model. The first two types of models are simple, efficient, and easy to expand, but they are less expressive than neural network-based models. NTN [33] has a neural network architecture, which allows mediated interaction of entity vectors via a tensor. MLP [7] is a simplified version of NTN where each relation is associated with one vector and then a standard multi layer perceptron is used to capture interaction terms. ConvE [6] is a highly parameter efficient model which uses 2D convolution over embeddings and multiple layers of non-linear features to model KGs.

The information provided by the triples is limited. Many works try to exploit richer context information. Some utilize neighbor information of entitie, such as GAKE [10], TransE-NMM [24], and R-GCN [32]. Relation paths between two entities are more deep information for link prediction. PRA [15] is an early work. Recent research usually combines the relation path into a new relation between two entities by addition, multiplication, or RNN, such as PTransE [17], TransE-COMP [12], and Bilinear-COMP [12]. Our method also uses the relation paths. Instead of treating them as new relations, we treat them as pseudo-sentences together with the entity paths, which can make full use of the intermediate information of the paths.

Our work is closely related to DeepWalk [27] which uses Skip-gram [22] on the information generated by random walks to get the latent representations of vertices on social graphs. Luo et al. [21], Goikoetxea et al. [11], and GAKE [10] use the similar idea on KGs. Our method differs from these in several aspects. (1) DeepWalk and Goikoetxea et al. only consider the entities, and they all do not consider the order information. Our method considers all three aspects of the path: entities, relations, and order information. (2) All these works use the Word2Vec models (CBOW or Skip-gram), but we use the multi-layer Transformer Decoder language model, which is more expressive, more suitable for ordered data, and better at capturing high-level information especially the syntactic information. (3) They are just embedding models which aim at obtaining the latent representations of entities or relations. Our model is not only an embedding model, but also a link prediction model which can be used directly for link prediction task.

3 Problem Definition

A KG is represented as a set of triples (facts) $\mathcal{O} = \{\langle h, r, t\rangle\} \subseteq \mathcal{E} \times \mathcal{R} \times \mathcal{E}$. Each triple $\langle h, r, t\rangle$ denotes a relation $r \in \mathcal{R}$ between head entity $h \in \mathcal{E}$ and tail entity $t \in \mathcal{E}$, where $\mathcal{E}$ and $\mathcal{R}$ are the sets of entities and relations respectively. We convert KG $\mathcal{O}$ to a directed graph $G = (V, E)$ where V is the set of vertices and E is the set of edges. We treat each entity e as a vertex, each relation r as a directed edge from h to t. We also add a directed edge from t to h to represent the inverse relation r^{-1}, which is widely used to make full use of the structural information of KG [10].

Link prediction usually refers to the task of predicting another entity for a given entity and relation, i.e., predicting t given h and r ($\langle h, r, ?\rangle$) or h given r and t ($\langle ?, r, t\rangle$). For example, $\langle Washington, capitalOf, ?\rangle$ means to predict which country's capital is Washington, and $\langle ?, capitalOf, USA\rangle$ means to predict which city is the capital of the USA. We unify the two tasks by converting the latter to the former, i.e., predicting head entity given tail entity and inverse relation ($\langle t, r^{-1}, ?\rangle$). Unlike other methods which learn the scoring function $f_r(h, t)$, we directly learn the conditional probability distribution of the target entity $P(T|I, R; \Theta)$ where I and R denote h and t or t and r^{-1}, and Θ denotes parameters which learned by LMLM.

4 Methodology

In this section, we will describe the two parts of our method (RW and LMLM) in detail. The purpose of RW is to obtain the paths in KGs. These paths will be viewed as pseudo-sentences to train LMLM. Just like the standard language model, the objective of LMLM is to maximize the probability of the entities in the paths.

4.1 RW: Random Walks on KG

We perform random walks on G to get a set of paths $\mathcal{P}_{\mathcal{ER}}$ for training. For the sake of convenience, we fix the length l of a path P_{ER}. Random walks are along the outgoing direction of entities, so the entities in the paths are in the form of head-to-tail and the relations are in the middle, such as $e_0 \xrightarrow{r_0} e_1 \xrightarrow{r_1} \cdots \xrightarrow{r_{l-1}} e_l$. A path P_{ER} in $\mathcal{P}_{\mathcal{ER}}$ contains $l + 1$ entities and l relations

Algorithm 1. Random Walks on KG

Input: graph $G = (V, E)$
  number of iterations t
  walk length l
Output: a set of paths $\mathcal{P}_{\mathcal{ER}}$

for $i = 1$ to t **do**
  $\mathcal{V} = Shuffle(V)$
  for each $v \in \mathcal{V}$ **do**
    add v to path P_{ER}
    for $j = 1$ to l **do**
      randomly choose an outgoing adjacent vertex e of v
      randomly choose an edge r between v and e
      add r and e to P_{ER}
      $v = e$
    end for
    add P_{ER} to $\mathcal{P}_{\mathcal{ER}}$
  end for
end for
return $\mathcal{P}_{\mathcal{ER}}$

Algorithm 1 shows our approach. We perform t iterations on V. At the start of each iteration, we generate a random ordering $\mathcal{V}$ of V. Random walks are performed staring from each vertex in $\mathcal{V}$. A random walk walks l steps along the outgoing direction of a start vertex to get a path P_{ER}. For each step, we randomly choose an outgoing adjacent vertex firstly, then choose the edge between the two vertices. If there are multiple edges between the two vertices, we will randomly choose one. Finally, we will get a set of paths $\mathcal{P}_{\mathcal{ER}}$.

This algorithm is similar to the algorithm proposed by [27]. The main difference is that our random walks are performed on directed graphs with relation information. Instead of randomly choosing an adjacent edge and the vertex on the edge, we first choose an adjacent vertex and then randomly choose an edge between the two vertices. Since there may be multiple edges (relations) between two vertices (entities), the former method may break the balance of the number of entities in the paths.

4.2 LMLM: Language Model-Based Link Prediction Model

Inspired by the ability of the standard language model to capture the semantic and syntactic information of natural language sentences as well as the ability to predict the next word given previous words, we construct the link prediction model LMLM based on the standard language model.

The standard language model usually defines a probability distribution over a sequence of tokens: $P(w_1, w_2, \ldots, w_n) = \prod_i P(w_i|w_1, \ldots, w_{i-1})$. The goal of language modeling is to maximize this probability. The conditional probabilities $P(w_i|w_1, \ldots, w_{i-1})$ can be learned by neural networks [2,23]. Recent years, the Transformer Decoder (TD) [20], the decoder part of Transformer [40], has been widely used for language modeling [20,30,31]. Our model is also constructed using the TD.

TD. Figure 2 shows the architecture of TD. The TD is mainly composed of two parts: masked Multi-Head Attention layer and Feed-Forward layer. The masked Multi-Head Attention consists of multiple scaled dot-product attention [40] which is a commonly used attention function [9,37,41]. The self-attention in this layer is masked to computes the hidden representation of each position by considering the representations of previous positions and itself. The Feed-Forward layer is a fully connected position-wise Feed-Forward Network (FFN) which consists of two linear transformations. It is applied to each position separately and identically. In addition, the TD uses residual connection [13] and layer normalization [1] between every two layers.

LMLM. We treat a path as a pseudo-sentence, and the set of paths is a corpus. We use the corpus to train our model. Formally, given a path $P_{ER} = e_0 \xrightarrow{r_0} e_1 \xrightarrow{r_1} \cdots \xrightarrow{r_{l-1}} e_l$ where $e_i \in \mathcal{E}$ and $r_i \in \mathcal{R}$, the input of our model is $((e_0, r_0), (e_1, r_1), \ldots, (e_{l-1}, r_{l-1}))$ and the target is $(e_1, e_2, \ldots, e_l)$. Similar to the standard language model, our objective is to maximize the following probability:

$$P(e_1, e_2, \ldots, e_l) = \prod_{i=1}^{l} P(e_i| (e_0, r_0), \ldots, (e_{i-1}, r_{i-1})). \quad (1)$$

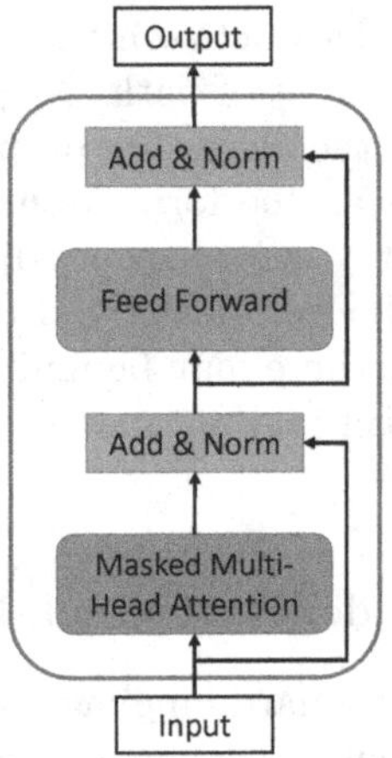

Fig. 2. TD architecture

We divide the input into two parts, the entities input $(e_0, e_2, \ldots, e_{l-1})$ and the relations input $(r_0, r_1, \ldots, r_{l-1})$. They are represented as the one-hot matrices $M_E \in \mathbb{R}^{l\times|\mathcal{E}|}$ and $M_R \in \mathbb{R}^{l\times|\mathcal{R}|}$ respectively. Each position of the input has a positional encoding, which is represented as a position embedding matrix $W_p \in \mathbb{R}^{l\times(d_E+d_R)}$ where d_E and d_R are the embedding dimension of entities and relations respectively. We use the fixed position embedding matrix proposed by [40]:

$$W_p(i,j) = \begin{cases} \sin\left(i/10000^{j/(d_E+d_R)}\right) & \text{if } j \bmod 2 = 0 \\ \cos\left(i/10000^{(j-1)/(d_E+d_R)}\right) & \text{if } j \bmod 2 = 1. \end{cases} \quad (2)$$

We use the TD to get the conditional probability distribution of the i-th target entity $y_i = \hat{P}\left(T|\left(e_0, r_0\right), \ldots, \left(e_{i-1}, r_{i-1}\right)\right)$:

$$h_0 = [M_E W_E; M_R W_R] + W_p, \quad (3)$$

$$h_k = TD(h_{k-1}), k \in [1, n], \quad (4)$$

$$y_i = softmax(h_n^i W_h W_E^T), i \in [1, l], \quad (5)$$

where $W_E \in \mathbb{R}^{|\mathcal{E}|\times|d_E|}$ and $W_R \in \mathbb{R}^{|\mathcal{R}|\times|d_R|}$ are the entity embedding matrix and the relation embedding matrix respectively; $[;]$ is a concatenation operator on row vector of two matrices; h_k^i is the i-th hidden representation of k-th TD layer; n is the number of layers of the TD; $W_h \in \mathbb{R}^{(d_E+d_R)\times d_E}$ is a linear transformation matrix.

Figure 3 shows the architecture of LMLM. Firstly, the model obtains the d_E-dimensional (d_R-dimensional) representations of entities (relations) by W_E (W_R). Then the model concatenates the representations of entities and relations. After adding the positional encoding, the representations are used as the initial input of the TD. After the multi-layer TD, the representations are projected

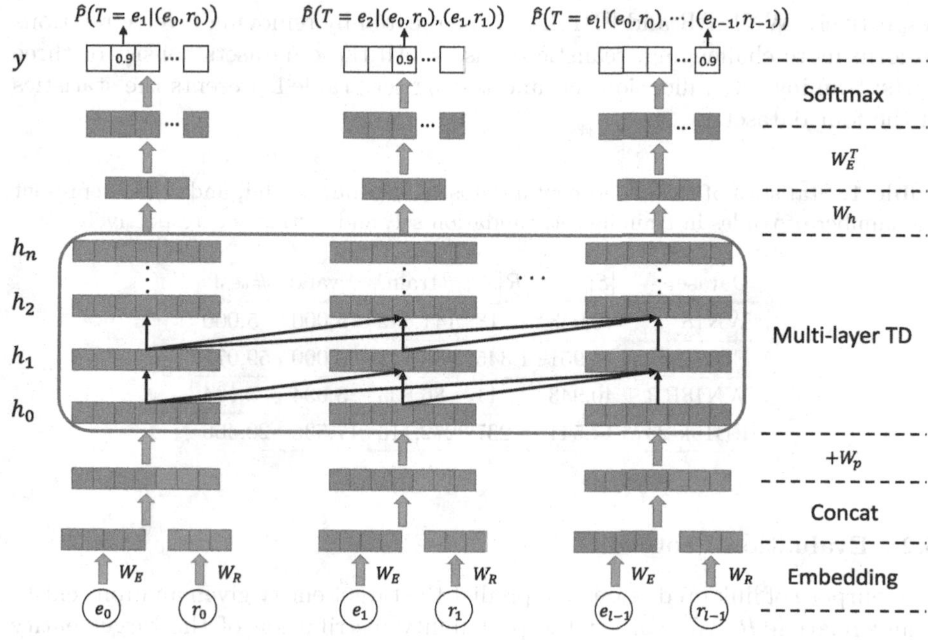

Fig. 3. LMLM architecture

to d_E-dimensional space using a linear transformation matrix W_h. The model then projects the representations to $|\mathcal{E}|$-dimensional space using W_E^T (i.e. output embedding [28]) and gets the probability distribution of the next entity using the softmax function. Since the positional encoding and the masked self-attention of TD, the previous i-1 entities, relations and their order are considered when predicting the i-th entity.

We train our model by minimizing the following loss function:

$$\mathcal{L} = -\sum_{i=1}^{l} \log \hat{P}\left(T = e_i | \left(e_0, r_0\right), \ldots, \left(e_{i-1}, r_{i-1}\right)\right). \quad (6)$$

We adopt stochastic gradient descent to train our model. To reduce overfitting, we regularise our model by using label smoothing [36] and dropout [34]. In particular, we use dropout on the embeddings and the FFN layers of TD.

5 Experiments

5.1 Datasets

We evaluate our method on four benchmark datasets: WN18 [4], FB15k [4], WN18RR [6], and FB15k-237 [38]. WN18 is a subset of Wordnet. FB15k is a subset of Freebase. WN18RR and FB15k-237 are subsets of WN18 and FB15k respectively. WN18RR and FB15k-237 are created by removing inverse relations to form more challenging, realistic datasets. All these datasets consist of three parts: training set, validation set, and testing set. Table 1 presents the statistics of the four datasets.

Table 1. Statistics of the experimental datasets. #train, #valid, and #test represent the number of triples in training set, validation set, and testing set, respectively.

Dataset	$\|\mathcal{E}\|$	$\|\mathcal{R}\|$	#train	#valid	#test
WN18	40,943	18	141,442	5,000	5,000
FB15k	14,951	1,345	483,142	50,000	59,071
WN18RR	40,943	11	86,835	3,034	3,134
FB15k-237	14,541	237	272,115	17,535	20,466

5.2 Evaluation Protocol

The purpose of link prediction is to predict the target entity given an input entity I and relation R. We can get the probability distribution of the target entity $P(T|I,R)$ by the trained LMLM. We rank the probability values in descending order. The top ranked entity is more likely to be the target entity which we want to predict.

Given an entity e_1 and a relation r_1, if the predicted entity e_2' ranks higher than the target entity e_2, but $\langle e_1, r_1, e_2' \rangle$ is a fact in KG, this is not wrong. In order to avoid this misleading behavior, we remove such type entities that exist in training, validation, or testing set before ranking. We call the original one *raw*, the filtered one *filt.* [4].

To measure the performance of different methods in link prediction, we employ several common evaluation metrics: Hits@N, Mean Rank (MR), and Mean Reciprocal Rank (MRR). Hits@N denotes the proportion of the target entities that are ranked within top N. MR is the mean of the target entities' rankings. MRR is the mean of multiplicative inverse of the target entities' rankings. Higher Hits@N, lower MR, and higher MRR indicate better performance.

5.3 Experimental Setup

We first utilize RW on the training sets to generate the paths for model training. For WN18 and WN18RR, the number of iterations is 50 and walk length is 10. For FB15k and FB15k-237, the number of iterations is 200 and walk length are 10 and 5 respectively.

We use grid search to select the hyperparameters of LMLM. The ranges of hyperparameters are as follows: entity embedding dimension d_E in {50, 100, 200}, relation embedding dimension d_R in {10, 30, 50}, FFN layer dimension d_f in {500, 800, 1000}, the number of TD layers n in {1, 2, 4, 5}, embedding dropout dp_e in {0.1, 0.2, 0.3}, batch size bs in {64, 128}. We fix some parameters: learning

Table 2. Link prediction results on WN18 and FB15k (*raw*)

Method	WN18			FB15k		
	MR	MRR	Hits@10	MR	MRR	Hits@10
TransE [4]	263	—	0.754	243	—	0.349
STransE [25]	217	0.469	0.809	219	0.252	0.516
GAKE [10]	—	—	—	228	—	0.445
ANALOGY [19]	—	0.657	—	—	0.253	—
R-GCN [32]	—	0.553	—	—	0.251	—
TransAt(asy,bern) [29]	**169**	—	0.814	**185**	—	0.529
TorusE [8]	—	0.619	—	—	0.256	—
RW-LMLM	318	**0.664**	**0.852**	211	**0.322**	**0.572**

rate is 0.01, label smoothing is 0.2, attention heads is 4, and FFN layer dropout is 0.1. We find the following hyperparameters work well on the four datasets: $d_E = 100$, $d_R = 10$, $d_f = 500$, $n = 2$, $dp_e = 0.1$, $bs = 128$ on WN18; $d_E = 100$, $d_R = 30$, $d_f = 500$, $n = 4$, $dp_e = 0.2$, $bs = 128$ on WN18RR; $d_E = 100$, $d_R = 30$, $d_f = 800$, $n = 2$, $dp_e = 0.1$, $bs = 128$ on FB15k; $d_E = 100$, $d_R = 30$, $d_f = 500$, $n = 4$, $dp_e = 0.3$, $bs = 64$ on FB15k-237. Best models are selected by using early stopping according to Hits@10 on the validation sets, with up to 30 epochs over the set of paths. Our code is available online[1].

5.4 Results

Table 2 shows the results of several methods on WN18 and FB15k under the *raw* setting. Our method achieves the best MRR and Hits@10 on the both datasets. Table 3 shows the results of several methods on the two datasets under the *filt.* setting. We evaluate methods on Hits@N in more detail, including Hits@1, Hits@3, and Hits@10. The results show that our method obtains the best MRR and all Hits@N. Compared with GAKE which is a work similar to ours but does not consider the order information (i.e. missing syntactic information), our method achieves the relative improvement of 7%/29% in MR/Hits@10 on FB15k (*raw*) and 37%/35% in MR/Hits@10 on FB15k (*filt.*)

It has been noted by [38] that many testing triples are inverse triples of training triples in WN18 and FB15k, which makes these triples easy to learn. Our method may benefit from it on the two datasets. To demonstrate the superiority of our method, we evaluate our method on more challenging datasets: WN18RR and FB15k-237 which remove inverse relations in WN18 and FB15k. Table 4 shows the results. We achieve the best MR and all Hits@N on WN18RR and the best MRR, Hits@3, and Hits@10 on FB15k-237. The results of MRR on WN18RR and Hits@1 on FB15k-237 are close to the best.

[1] https://github.com/chjianw/RW-LMLM.

Table 3. Link prediction results on WN18 and FB15k (*filt.*)

Method	WN18					FB15k				
	MR	MRR	Hits@N			MR	MRR	Hits@N		
			1	3	10			1	3	10
TransE [4]	**251**	—	—	—	0.892	125	—	—	—	0.471
ComplEx [39]	—	0.941	0.936	0.945	0.947	—	0.692	0.599	0.759	0.840
GAKE [10]	—	—	—	—	—	119	—	—	—	0.648
ANALOGY [19]	—	0.942	0.939	0.944	0.947	—	0.725	0.646	0.785	0.854
R-GCN [32]	—	0.814	0.686	0.928	0.955	—	0.651	0.541	0.736	0.825
SimplE [14]	—	0.942	0.939	0.944	0.947	—	0.727	0.660	0.773	0.838
ConvE [6]	504	0.942	0.935	0.947	0.955	**64**	0.745	0.670	0.801	0.873
RW-LMLM	308	**0.949**	**0.944**	**0.951**	**0.957**	75	**0.762**	**0.694**	**0.809**	**0.877**

Table 4. Link prediction results on WN18RR and FB15k-237 (*filt.*). Results marked * are taken from [6].

Method	WN18RR					FB15k-237				
	MR	MRR	Hits@N			MR	MRR	Hits@N		
			1	3	10			1	3	10
DistMult [43]*	5110	0.43	0.39	0.44	0.49	254	0.241	0.155	0.263	0.419
Node+LinkFeat [38]	—	—	—	—	—	—	0.226	—	—	0.347
Neural LP [44]	—	—	—	—	—	—	0.24	—	—	0.362
R-GCN [32]	—	—	—	—	—	—	0.248	0.153	0.258	0.414
ConvE [6]	5277	**0.46**	0.39	0.43	0.48	**246**	0.316	**0.239**	0.350	0.491
RW-LMLM	**4286**	0.45	**0.42**	**0.47**	**0.51**	358	**0.321**	0.231	**0.352**	**0.507**

We note that our method performs well on most metrics except MR. One explanation for this is that our method targets the most accurate entities given previous entities and relations, while MR reflects the average performance of methods, and a single bad ranking of target entity can greatly affect MR even the others perform well. Compared with MR, MRR is more reasonable and robust. It uses the mean of multiplicative inverse of the target entities' rankings, so the effect of bad triples is reduced, and the rankings of target entities can be distinguished, i.e., lower rankings will have higher scores. Our method achieves the best MRR on three of the four datasets and is on par with ConvE on WN18RR.

6 Analysis

We analyze our method on FB15k-237 in several aspects, including parameter sensitivity of RW, parameter efficiency of LMLM, and ablation studies. The experimental setup is the same as in Sect. 5.3 unless otherwise specified.

6.1 Parameter Sensitivity of RW

We investigate the effect of the two parameters (i.e. the number of iterations t and the walk length l) of RW on Hits@10. We experiment on the FB15k-237 dataset.

Figure 4 shows the results. We note that Hits@10 increases as t increases, and the trend slows down. This is intuitive. More iterations can get more information to help the improvement of performance. $l = 5$ has an improvement on Hits@10 compared to $l = 3$, but from $l = 5$ to $l = 10$ Hits@10 has almost no change. This means that we do not need too many walk steps to get the best performance on FB15k-237.

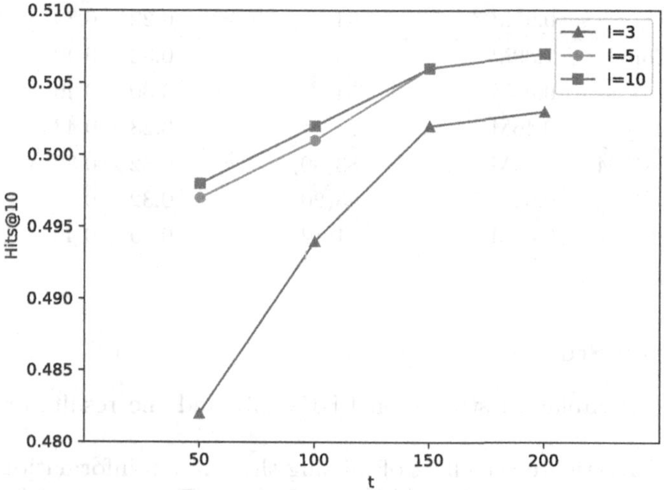

Fig. 4. Results of different parameters in RW. t is the number of iterations and l is the walk length.

6.2 Parameter Efficiency of LMLM

We compare the number of parameters with a bilinear model DistMult and a neural network-based model ConvE to demonstrate the parameter efficiency of LMLM.

Table 5 shows the results on FB15k-237. We can see that LMLM performs better than DistMult and ConvE with the same number of parameters. LMLM with 0.95M parameters performs better than ConvE with 1.89M parameters on Hits@10 and is the same on MRR. Similar results are also reported on LMLM with 0.46M parameters and ConvE with 0.95M parameters. LMLM with 0.46M parameters still performs better than DistMult with 1.89M parameters on both Hits@10 and MRR. Overall, LMLM is 2x parameter efficient than ConvE, at least 4x than DistMult.

LMLM is more parameter efficient than ConvE and DistMult, probably because LMLM utilizes the path information while the other two only utilize the triples, so even with fewer parameters, LMLM can still capture enough information.

Table 5. Parameter comparison on FB15k-237. Results of DistMult and ConvE are taken from [6].The embedding size refers to the entity embedding size and the numbers in brackets are the relation embedding sizes. For DistMult and ConvE, their relation embedding size and entity embedding size are the same.

Model	Parameter count	Embedding size	MRR	Hits@10
DistMult	1.89M	128	0.23	0.41
	0.95M	64	0.22	0.39
ConvE	1.89M	96	0.32	0.49
	0.95M	54	0.30	0.46
	0.46M	28	0.28	0.43
LMLM	1.89M	83(30)	0.32	0.50
	0.95M	43(20)	0.32	0.50
	0.46M	21(12)	0.29	0.46

6.3 Ablation Studies

We perform two ablation studies on FB15k-237 and the results are shown in Table 6.

First, we investigate the effect of missing the relation information on performance by removing relation embedding in LMLM. The model without relation information has a dramatic decline in performance compared to the full model. This is in line with expectations, since the relation information is one of the most important information in KGs and it is critical to performance. Second, we investigate the effect of missing the order information on performance by removing the position embedding and disordering the triples in LMLM. Compared with the full model, the performance of the model without the order information declines on all metrics, up to 8% relative decrease on Hits@1. The results demonstrate that the order information (i.e. the syntactic information) contributes to the performance improvement of link prediction.

Table 6. Ablation studies on FB15k-237

Model	MRR	Hits@1	His@3	Hits@10
Full model	0.321	0.231	0.352	0.507
w/o relation	0.035(↓ 0.286)	0.007(↓ 0.224)	0.017(↓ 0.335)	0.061(↓ 0.446)
w/o order	0.301(↓ 0.020)	0.212(↓ 0.019)	0.329(↓ 0.023)	0.484(↓ 0.023)

7 Conclusion and Future Work

This paper proposes a novel method RW-LMLM for link prediction in KGs. RW-LMLM consists of two parts, including RW—a random walk algorithm for KG, and LMLM—a language model-based link prediction model. The paths generated by RW are treated as pseudo-sentences and they are used to train LMLM like the standard language model. RW-LMLM has the ability to capture the semantic and syntactic information in KGs since it considers entities, relations, and order information of the paths. Experimental results on four datasets show that our method outperforms previous state-of-the-art models. Compared to some methods that only utilize the triples, our method that utilizes the path information is more parameter efficient. We also analyze the parameter sensitivity of RW and we find that more walk steps may not always necessary. This may help other works to choose a reasonable path length when they want to improve link prediction performance by the path information. Our work is an attempt to solve the problem in KGs using natural language processing method. Experimental results show the competitiveness of this way.

In the future, we plan to explore the following directions: (1) although the effect of the dimensions of entities and relations on performance is reflected in Sect. 6.2, more specific study is necessary. (2) We plan to study the relationship between the optimal path length and the number of entities or relations on more datasets.

Acknowledgements. This work is supported by the National Key Research and Development Program of China (2017YFB0803301).

References

1. Ba, J.L., Kiros, J.R., Hinton, G.E.: Layer normalization. arXiv preprint arXiv: 1607.06450(2016)
2. Bengio, Y., Ducharme, R., Vincent, P., Jauvin, C.: A neural probabilistic language model. J. Mach. Learn. Res. **3**(Feb), 1137–1155 (2003)
3. Bollacker, K., Evans, C., Paritosh, P., Sturge, T., Taylor, J.: Freebase: a collaboratively created graph database for structuring human knowledge. In: Proceedings of the 2008 ACM SIGMOD International Conference on Management of Data, pp. 1247–1250. ACM (2008)
4. Bordes, A., Usunier, N., Garcia-Duran, A., Weston, J., Yakhnenko, O.: Translating embeddings for modeling multi-relational data. In: Advances in Neural Information Processing Systems, pp. 2787–2795 (2013)
5. Carlson, A., Betteridge, J., Kisiel, B., Settles, B., Hruschka, E.R., Mitchell, T.M.: Toward an architecture for never-ending language learning. In: Twenty-Fourth AAAI Conference on Artificial Intelligence (2010)
6. Dettmers, T., Minervini, P., Stenetorp, P., Riedel, S.: Convolutional 2d knowledge graph embeddings. In: Thirty-Second AAAI Conference on Artificial Intelligence (2018)
7. Dong, X., et al.: Knowledge vault: A web-scale approach to probabilistic knowledge fusion. In: Proceedings of the 20th ACM SIGKDD International Conference on Knowledge Discovery and Data Mining, pp. 601–610. ACM (2014)

8. Ebisu, T., Ichise, R.: Toruse: Knowledge graph embedding on a lie group. In: Thirty-Second AAAI Conference on Artificial Intelligence (2018)
9. Fang, S., Xie, H., Zha, Z.J., Sun, N., Tan, J., Zhang, Y.: Attention and language ensemble for scene text recognition with convolutional sequence modeling. In: 2018 ACM Multimedia Conference on Multimedia Conference, pp. 248–256. ACM (2018)
10. Feng, J., Huang, M., Yang, Y., et al.: Gake: graph aware knowledge embedding. In: Proceedings of COLING 2016 the 26th International Conference on Computational Linguistics: Technical Papers, pp. 641–651 (2016)
11. Goikoetxea, J., Soroa, A., Agirre, E.: Random walks and neural network language models on knowledge bases. In: Proceedings of the 2015 Conference of the North American Chapter of the Association for Computational Linguistics: Human Language Technologies, pp. 1434–1439 (2015)
12. Guu, K., Miller, J.J., Liang, P.: Traversing knowledge graphs in vector space. In: Empirical Methods in Natural Language Processing, pp. 318–327 (2015)
13. He, K., Zhang, X., Ren, S., Sun, J.: Deep residual learning for image recognition. In: Proceedings of the IEEE Conference on Computer Vision and Pattern Recognition.,pp. 770–778 (2016)
14. Kazemi, S.M., Poole, D.: Simple embedding for link prediction in knowledge graphs. In: Advances in Neural Information Processing Systems, pp. 4284–4295 (2018)
15. Lao, N., Cohen, W.W.: Relational retrieval using a combination of path-constrained random walks. Mach. Learn. **81**(1), 53–67 (2010)
16. Lehmann, J., et al.: Dbpedia-a large-scale, multilingual knowledge base extracted from wikipedia. Semant. Web **6**(2), 167–195 (2015)
17. Lin, Y., Liu, Z., Luan, H., Sun, M., Rao, S., Liu, S.: Modeling relation paths for representation learning of knowledge bases. In: Empirical Methods in Natural Language Processing, pp. 705–714 (2015)
18. Lin, Y., Liu, Z., Sun, M., Liu, Y., Zhu, X.: Learning entity and relation embeddings for knowledge graph completion. In: Twenty-ninth AAAI Conference on Artificial Intelligence (2015)
19. Liu, H., Wu, Y., Yang, Y.: Analogical inference for multi-relational embeddings. In: Proceedings of the 34th International Conference on Machine Learning, volu. 70, pp. 2168–2178. JMLR. org (2017)
20. Liu, P.J., et al.: Generating wikipedia by summarizing long sequences. arXiv preprint arXiv:1801.10198 (2018)
21. Luo, Y., Wang, Q., Wang, B., Guo, L.: Context-dependent knowledge graph embedding. In: Proceedings of the 2015 Conference on Empirical Methods in Natural Language Processing, pp. 1656–1661 (2015)
22. Mikolov, T., Chen, K., Corrado, G.S., Dean, J.: Efficient estimation of word representations in vector space. arXiv: Computation and Language (2013)
23. Mikolov, T., Karafiát, M., Burget, L., Černockỳ, J., Khudanpur, S.: Recurrent neural network based language model. In: Eleventh Annual Conference of the International Speech Communication Association (2010)
24. Nguyen, D.Q., Sirts, K., Qu, L., Johnson, M.: Neighborhood mixture model for knowledge base completion. In: Conference on Computational Natural Language Learning, pp. 40–50 (2016)
25. Nguyen, D.Q., Sirts, K., Qu, L., Johnson, M.: Stranse: a novel embedding model of entities and relationships in knowledge bases. arXiv preprint arXiv:1606.08140 (2016)
26. Nickel, M., Tresp, V., Kriegel, H.P.: A three-way model for collective learning on multi-relational data. ICML **11**, 809–816 (2011)

27. Perozzi, B., Al-Rfou, R., Skiena, S.: Deepwalk: online learning of social representations. In: Proceedings of the 20th ACM SIGKDD International Conference on Knowledge Discovery and Data Mining, pp. 701–710. ACM (2014)
28. Press, O., Wolf, L.: Using the output embedding to improve language models. arXiv preprint arXiv:1608.05859 (2016)
29. Qian, W., Fu, C., Zhu, Y., Cai, D., He, X.: Translating embeddings for knowledge graph completion with relation attention mechanism. In: IJCAI, pp. 4286–4292 (2018)
30. Radford, A., Narasimhan, K., Salimans, T., Sutskever, I.: Improving language understanding by generative pre-training. URL https://s3-us-west-2.amazonaws.com/openai-assets/research-covers/languageunsupervised/languageunderstanding paper. pdf (2018)
31. Radford, A., Wu, J., Child, R., Luan, D., Amodei, D., Sutskever, I.: Language models are unsupervised multitask learners (2019)
32. Schlichtkrull, M., Kipf, T.N., Bloem, P., van den Berg, R., Titov, I., Welling, M.: Modeling relational data with graph convolutional networks. In: Gangemi, A., et al. (eds.) ESWC 2018. LNCS, vol. 10843, pp. 593–607. Springer, Cham (2018). https://doi.org/10.1007/978-3-319-93417-4_38
33. Socher, R., Chen, D., Manning, C.D., Ng, A.: Reasoning with neural tensor networks for knowledge base completion. In: Advances in Neural Information Processing Systems, pp. 926–934 (2013)
34. Srivastava, N., Hinton, G., Krizhevsky, A., Sutskever, I., Salakhutdinov, R.: Dropout: a simple way to prevent neural networks from overfitting. J. Mach. Learn. Res. **15**(1), 1929–1958 (2014)
35. Suchanek, F.M., Kasneci, G., Weikum, G.: Yago: a core of semantic knowledge. In: Proceedings of the 16th International Conference on World Wide Web, pp. 697–706. ACM (2007)
36. Szegedy, C., Vanhoucke, V., Ioffe, S., Shlens, J., Wojna, Z.: Rethinking the inception architecture for computer vision. In: Proceedings of the IEEE Conference on Computer Vision and Pattern Recognition, pp. 2818–2826 (2016)
37. Tan, Z., Wang, M., Xie, J., Chen, Y., Shi, X.: Deep semantic role labeling with self-attention. In: Thirty-Second AAAI Conference on Artificial Intelligence (2018)
38. Toutanova, K., Chen, D.: Observed versus latent features for knowledge base and text inference. In: Proceedings of the 3rd Workshop on Continuous Vector Space Models and their Compositionality, pp. 57–66 (2015)
39. Trouillon, T., Welbl, J., Riedel, S., Gaussier, É., Bouchard, G.: Complex embeddings for simple link prediction. In: International Conference on Machine Learning, pp. 2071–2080 (2016)
40. Vaswani, A., et al.: Attention is all you need. In: Advances in Neural Information Processing Systems, pp. 5998–6008 (2017)
41. Vemula, A., Muelling, K., Oh, J.: Social attention: modeling attention in human crowds. In: 2018 IEEE International Conference on Robotics and Automation (ICRA), pp. 1–7. IEEE (2018)
42. Wang, Z., Zhang, J., Feng, J., Chen, Z.: Knowledge graph embedding by translating on hyperplanes. In: Twenty-Eighth AAAI Conference on Artificial Intelligence (2014)
43. Yang, B., Yih, W.t., He, X., Gao, J., Deng, L.: Embedding entities and relations for learning and inference in knowledge bases. arXiv preprint arXiv:1412.6575 (2014)
44. Yang, F., Yang, Z., Cohen, W.W.: Differentiable learning of logical rules for knowledge base reasoning. In: Advances in Neural Information Processing Systems, pp. 2319–2328 (2017)

A Framework for Evaluating Snippet Generation for Dataset Search

Xiaxia Wang[1], Jinchi Chen[1], Shuxin Li[1], Gong Cheng[1(✉)], Jeff Z. Pan[2,3], Evgeny Kharlamov[4,5], and Yuzhong Qu[1]

[1] National Key Laboratory for Novel Software Technology, Nanjing University, Nanjing, China
xxwang1997@gmail.com, {jcchen,sxli}@smail.nju.edu.cn, {gcheng,yzqu}@nju.edu.cn

[2] Edinburgh Research Centre, Huawei, Edinburgh, UK

[3] Department of Computing Science, University of Aberdeen, Aberdeen, UK
jeff.z.pan@abdn.ac.uk

[4] Department of Informatics, University of Oslo, Oslo, Norway
evgeny.kharlamov@ifi.uio.no

[5] Bosch Center for Artificial Intelligence, Robert Bosch GmbH, Renningen, Germany
evgeny.kharlamov@de.bosch.com

Abstract. Reusing existing datasets is of considerable significance to researchers and developers. Dataset search engines help a user find relevant datasets for reuse. They can present a snippet for each retrieved dataset to explain its relevance to the user's data needs. This emerging problem of snippet generation for dataset search has not received much research attention. To provide a basis for future research, we introduce a framework for quantitatively evaluating the quality of a dataset snippet. The proposed metrics assess the extent to which a snippet matches the query intent and covers the main content of the dataset. To establish a baseline, we adapt four state-of-the-art methods from related fields to our problem, and perform an empirical evaluation based on real-world datasets and queries. We also conduct a user study to verify our findings. The results demonstrate the effectiveness of our evaluation framework, and suggest directions for future research.

Keywords: Snippet generation · Dataset search · Evaluation metric

1 Introduction

We are witnessing the rapid growth of open data on the Web, notably RDF, Linked Data and Knowledge Graphs [30]. Today, to develop a Web application, reusing existing datasets not only brings about productivity improvements and cost reductions, but also makes interoperability with other applications more achievable. However, there is a lack of tool support for conveniently finding datasets that match a developer's data needs. To address it, recent research efforts yielded *dataset search engines* like LODAtlas [32] and Google Dataset

C. Ghidini et al. (Eds.): ISWC 2019, LNCS 11778, pp. 680–697, 2019.
https://doi.org/10.1007/978-3-030-30793-6_39

Search [2]. They retrieve a list of datasets that are relevant to a keyword query by matching the query with the description in the metadata of each dataset.

These systems have made a promising start. Furthermore, a helpful dataset search engine should also explain why a retrieved dataset is relevant. A concise piece of information presented for each dataset in a search results page is broadly referred to as a *dataset summary*. It may help the user quickly identify a relevant dataset. Summaries presented in current dataset search engines, however, are mainly composed of some *metadata* about a dataset, such as provenance and license. Their utility in relevance judgment is limited, with users having to analyze each dataset in the search results to assess its relevance, which would be a time-consuming process.

To overcome the shortcoming of metadata, we study an emerging type of dataset summary called *dataset snippet*. For an RDF dataset retrieved by a keyword query, a dataset snippet is a size-constrained subset of RDF triples extracted from the dataset, being intended to exemplify the content of the dataset and to explain its relevance to the query. It differs from a *dataset profile* which represents a set of features describing attributes of the dataset [13]. It is also complementary to an *abstractive summary* which aggregates data into patterns and provides a high-level overview [4,8,38,39,45]. It is conceptually more similar to a snippet extracted from a webpage and presented in traditional Web search. However, little research attention has focused on this perspective.

As a preliminary effort along this way, we work towards establishing a framework for evaluating snippets generated for dataset search. That would provide a basis for future research, in terms of providing quantitative evaluation metrics and advising algorithm design. Existing evaluation metrics used in related fields such as snippet generation for ontologies [28] and documents [16] are mainly based on a human-created ground truth. However, an RDF dataset may contain millions of RDF triples, e.g., when it wrapped from a large database [18,19,23,33], or streaming data [24,25], or comes from a manufacturing environment [22,26,37] being much larger than an ontology schema or a document. It would be difficult, if not impossible, to manually identify the optimum snippet as the ground truth. Therefore, new evaluation metrics are needed.

To demonstrate the use of our evaluation framework, considering the lack of dedicated solutions to dataset snippets, we explore research efforts in related fields and adapt their methods to our problem. Using our framework, we analyze these methods and empirically evaluate them based on real-world datasets. We also carry out a user study to verify our findings and solicit comments to motivate future research.

To summarize, our contributions in this paper include

- a framework for evaluating snippets in dataset search, consisting of four metrics regarding how well a snippet covers a query and a dataset,
- an adaptation of four state-of-the-art methods selected from related fields to generate snippets for dataset search, as a baseline for future research, and

- an evaluation of the adapted methods using the proposed evaluation framework based on real-world datasets and queries, as well as a user study.

The remainder of the paper is organized as follows. Section 2 reviews related research. Section 3 describes our evaluation framework. Section 4 reports evaluation results. Section 5 presents a user study. Section 6 concludes the paper.

2 Related Work

Very little research attention has been given to the problem of snippet generation for dataset search. Therefore, in this section, we also review research efforts in related fields that can be adapted to the problem we study.

2.1 Snippets for RDF Datasets

In an early work [1], a snippet for an RDF document is generated to show how the document is relevant to a keyword query. Preference is given to RDF triples that describe central entities or contain query keywords. The proposed algorithm relies on manually defined ranking of predicates. In [12,36], an RDF dataset is compressed by keeping only a sample of triples in order to improve the performance of query processing while still serve query results as complete as possible. To this end, [36] samples triples that are central in the RDF graph and hence are likely to appear in the answers of typical SPARQL queries. By contrast, [12] iteratively expands the sample as needed to make it more precise. Completeness preserving summaries [15] help optimise distributed reasoning and querying.

In a recent work [7], an *illustrative snippet* is generated to exemplify the content of an RDF dataset. Snippet generation is formulated as a combinatorial optimization problem, aiming to find an optimum connected RDF subgraph such that it contains instantiation of the most frequently used classes and properties in the dataset and contains entities having the highest PageRank scores. An approximation algorithm is presented to solve this NP-hard problem. This kind of snippet can be used in dataset search, although it is not query-biased.

2.2 Snippets for Ontology Schemas

An *ontology snippet* distills the most important information from an ontology schema and forms an abridged version [42,43]. Existing methods often represent an ontology schema as a graph, and apply some centrality-based measures to identify the most important terms or axioms as an ontology snippet [34,35]. It is possible to adapt these methods to generate snippets for an RDF dataset because it can be viewed as an RDF graph to process.

We give particular attention to methods that are capable of generating *query-biased snippets for ontology search* [3,5,6,17,31]. An ontology schema is often represented as a graph where nodes represent terms and edges represent axioms associating terms [17,44]. In a state-of-the-art approach [17], such a graph is decomposed into a set of maximal radius-bounded connected subgraphs, which in turn are reduced to tree-structured sub-snippets. A greedy algorithm is performed to select and merge an optimum set of sub-snippets, in terms of compactness and query relevance.

2.3 Keyword Search on Graphs

Keyword search on a graph is to find an optimum connected subgraph that contains all the keywords in a query [9,41]. An optimum subgraph has the smallest total edge weight [11,21,29], or a variant of this property [27]. As each keyword can match a set of nodes in a graph, the problem is formulated as a *group Steiner tree (GST) problem*. This kind of subgraph can be used as a query-biased snippet for an RDF dataset viewed as an RDF graph. However, the problem is NP-hard and is difficult to solve. Many algorithms perform not well on large graphs [10].

A state-of-the-art algorithm for the GST problem is PrunedDP++ [29]. The algorithm progressively refines feasible solutions based on dynamic programming with an A*-search strategy. In dynamic programming, optimal-tree decomposition and conditional tree merging techniques are proposed to prune unpromising states. For A*-search, several lower-bounding techniques are used.

2.4 Snippets for Documents

A *document snippet* consists of salient sentences selected from the original document [16]. To adapt such a method to our problem, we could replace the three elements of an RDF triple with their textual forms. The triple becomes a pseudo sentence, and an RDF dataset is transformed into a set of sentences to process.

Among existing solutions, *unsupervised query-biased methods* [40] are closer to our problem setting because, at this stage, training data for dataset search is not available. The CES method [14] is among the state-of-the-art in this line of work. It formulates sentence selection as an optimization problem and solves it using the cross-entropy method. Preference is given to diversified long sentences that are relevant to a query.

3 Evaluation Framework

In this section, we firstly define some terms used in the paper, and then propose a framework for evaluating snippets generated for dataset search. Our framework, consisting of four metrics characterizing different aspects of a dataset snippet, will be used in later sections to evaluate selected methods reviewed in Sect. 2.

3.1 Preliminaries

Datasets vary in their formats. Search queries have various types. This paper is focused on keyword queries over RDF datasets because this combination is common. We will consider other data formats and query types in future work.

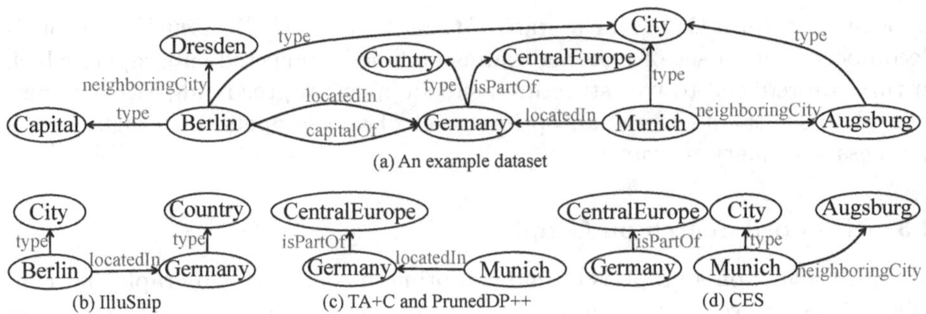

Fig. 1. (a) An example dataset and (b)(c)(d) three of its snippets generated by different methods w.r.t. the query *munich europe*.

Definition 1 (RDF Dataset). *An RDF dataset, or a dataset for short, is a set of n RDF triples denoted by $T = \{t_1, \ldots, t_n\}$. Each $t_i \in T$ is a subject-predicate-object triple denoted by $\langle t_i^s, t_i^p, t_i^o \rangle$.*

In RDF, t_i^{s}, t_i^{p}, and t_i^{o} can be IRIs, blank nodes, or literals, which are collectively known as RDF terms. An "RDF term" and the "resource" it denotes are used interchangeably in the paper.

Definition 2 (Keyword Query). *A keyword query, or a query for short, is a set of m keywords denoted by $Q = \{q_1, \ldots, q_m\}$.*

A snippet of a dataset is a size-constrained subset of triples extracted from the dataset. The extraction should consider the query.

Definition 3 (Dataset Snippet). *Given a positive integer k, a snippet of a dataset T is denoted by S subject to $S \subseteq T$ and $|S| \leq k$.*

An RDF dataset T can be viewed as an RDF graph denoted by $\mathtt{G}(T)$. Each triple $\langle t^{\mathrm{s}}, t^{\mathrm{p}}, t^{\mathrm{o}} \rangle \in T$ is represented as a directed edge labeled with t^{p} from node t^{s} to node t^{o} in $\mathtt{G}(T)$. Analogously, a snippet S is a subgraph denoted by $\mathtt{G}(S)$. In Fig. 1 we illustrate three snippets for an example dataset w.r.t. a query.

3.2 Evaluation Metrics

To assess the quality of a snippet w.r.t. a query, we propose four quantitative metrics: `coKyw`, `coCnx`, `coSkm`, and `coDat`. Recall that a snippet is generated to exemplify the content of a dataset and to explain its relevance to the query. So a good snippet should, on the one hand, match the query intent (`coKyw`, `coCnx`) and, on the other hand, cover the main content of the dataset (`coSkm`, `coDat`). Our metrics are open source[1].

[1] http://ws.nju.edu.cn/datasetsearch/evaluation-iswc2019/metrics.zip.

Coverage of Query Keywords (coKyw). Keywords in a query express a user's data needs. A good snippet should cover as many keywords as possible, to show how a dataset is plainly relevant to the query.

Specifically, let $\texttt{Text}(r)$ be a set of textual forms of a resource r. For r denoted by an IRI, $\texttt{Text}(r)$ include

- the lexical forms of r's *human-readable names* (if any), i.e., literal values of r's **rdfs:label** property, and
- r's *local name*, i.e., the fragment component of r's IRI (if its exists) or the last segment of the path component of the IRI.

For r denoted by a blank node, $\texttt{Text}(r)$ only include the lexical forms of r's human-readable names (if any). For r denoted by a literal, $\texttt{Text}(r)$ only include the lexical form of the literal.

A resource r *covers* a keyword q if any textual form in $\texttt{Text}(r)$ contains a *match* for q. Our implementation considers keyword matching, which can be extended to semantic matching in future work. A triple t *covers* a keyword q, denoted by $t \prec q$, if r covers q for any $r \in \{t^{\mathrm{s}}, t^{\mathrm{p}}, t^{\mathrm{o}}\}$. For a snippet S, its coverage of keywords in a query Q is the proportion of covered keywords:

$$\texttt{coKyw}(S) = \frac{1}{|Q|} \cdot |\{q \in Q : \exists t \in S,\ t \prec q\}| \,. \tag{1}$$

For example, Fig. 1(c) and (d) cover all the query keywords, so $\texttt{coKyw} = 1$. None of the keywords are covered by Fig. 1(b), so $\texttt{coKyw} = 0$.

Coverage of Connections between Query Keywords (coCnx). Keywords in a query are not independent but often refer to a set of related concepts which collectively represent a query intent. To show how a dataset is relevant to the query and its underlying intent, a good snippet should cover not only query keywords but also their connections captured by the dataset.

Specifically, for a snippet S, consider its RDF graph $\texttt{G}(S)$. Query keywords can be covered by nodes or edges of $\texttt{G}(S)$. For convenience, we obtain a *subdivision* of $\texttt{G}(S)$, by subdividing every edge labeled with t^{p} from node t^{s} to node t^{o} into two unlabeled undirected edges: one between t^{s} and t^{p}, and the other between t^{p} and t^{o}. The resulting graph is denoted by $\texttt{SD}(\texttt{G}(S))$. A snippet S *covers* the connection between two keywords $q_i, q_j \in Q$, denoted by $S \prec (q_i, q_j)$, if there is a path in $\texttt{SD}(\texttt{G}(S))$ that connects two nodes: one covering q_i and the other covering q_j. For S, its coverage of connections between keywords in Q is the proportion of covered connections between unordered pairs of keywords:

$$\texttt{coCnx}(S) = \begin{cases} \frac{1}{\binom{|Q|}{2}} \cdot |\{\{q_i, q_j\} \subseteq Q : q_i \neq q_j \text{ and } S \prec (q_i, q_j)\}| & \text{if } |Q| > 1\,, \\ \texttt{coKyw}(S) & \text{if } |Q| = 1\,. \end{cases} \tag{2}$$

When there is only one keyword, coCnx is meaningless and we set it to coKyw.

For example, Fig. 1(c) covers the connection between the two query keywords, so $\texttt{coCnx} = 1$. By contrast, although Fig. 1(d) covers all the keywords, it fails to cover their connections, so $\texttt{coCnx} = 0$.

Coverage of Data Schema ($\texttt{coSkm}$). Snippets are expected to not only interpret query relevance but also offer a representative preview of a dataset. In particular, the RDF schema of a dataset is important to users. A good snippet should cover as many classes and properties used in the dataset as possible, to exemplify which types of things and facts a user can obtain from the dataset.

Specifically, a snippet S *covers* a class or a property if S contains its instantiation. Let $\texttt{Cls}(S)$ and $\texttt{Prp}(S)$ be the set of classes and the set of properties instantiated in S, respectively:

$$\begin{aligned}\texttt{Cls}(S) &= \{c : \exists t \in S,\ t^{\mathrm{p}} = \texttt{rdf:type} \text{ and } t^{\mathrm{o}} = c\}\,,\\ \texttt{Prp}(S) &= \{p : \exists t \in S,\ t^{\mathrm{p}} = p\}\,.\end{aligned} \tag{3}$$

Classes and properties that are used more often in a dataset are more representative. The relative frequency of a class c observed in a dataset T is

$$\texttt{frqCls}(c) = \frac{|\{t \in T:\ t^{\mathrm{p}} = \texttt{rdf:type} \text{ and } t^{\mathrm{o}} = c\}|}{|\{t \in T:\ t^{\mathrm{p}} = \texttt{rdf:type}\}|}\,. \tag{4}$$

Analogously, the relative frequency of a property p observed in T is

$$\texttt{frqPrp}(p) = \frac{|\{t \in T:\ t^{\mathrm{p}} = p\}|}{|T|}\,. \tag{5}$$

For a snippet S, its coverage of the schema of T is related to: (a) the total relative frequency of the covered classes, and (b) the total relative frequency of the covered properties. We calculate the harmonic mean ($\texttt{hm}$) of the two:

$$\begin{aligned}\texttt{coSkm}(S) &= \texttt{hm}(\sum_{c \in \texttt{Cls}(S)} \texttt{frqCls}(c),\ \sum_{p \in \texttt{Prp}(S)} \texttt{frqPrp}(p))\,,\\ \texttt{hm}(x, y) &= \frac{2xy}{x + y}\,.\end{aligned} \tag{6}$$

For example, Fig. 1(b) covers a frequent class ($\texttt{City}$) and a frequent property ($\texttt{locatedIn}$) in the dataset, so its $\texttt{coSkm}$ score is higher than that of Fig. 1(c) which covers only properties but not classes.

Coverage of Data ($\texttt{coDat}$). Classes and properties high relative frequency are central elements in the schema used in a dataset. Complementary to them, a good snippet should also cover central elements at the data level (i.e., central entities), to show the key content of the dataset.

Specifically, let $\texttt{d}^+(r)$ and $\texttt{d}^-(r)$ be the out-degree and in-degree of a resource r in an RDF graph $\texttt{G}(T)$, respectively:

$$\begin{aligned}\texttt{d}^+(r) &= |\{t \in T : t^{\mathrm{s}} = r\}|\,,\\ \texttt{d}^-(r) &= |\{t \in T : t^{\mathrm{o}} = r\}|\,.\end{aligned} \tag{7}$$

Out-degree characterizes the richness of the description of a resource, and in-degree characterizes popularity. They suggest the centrality of a resource from

Table 1. Overview of selected methods and their alignment with evaluation metrics.

		coKyw	coCnx	coSkm	coDat
IlluSnip [7]	(illustrative dataset snippet)			✓	✓
TA+C [17]	(query-biased ontology snippet)	✓	✓		
PrunedDP++ [29]	(GST for keyword search)	✓	✓		
CES [14]	(query-biased document snippet)	✓		✓	✓

different aspects. For a snippet S, its coverage of a dataset T at the data level is related to: (a) the mean normalized out-degree of the constituent entities, and (b) the mean normalized in-degree of the constituent entities. We calculate the harmonic mean of the two:

$$\begin{aligned} \texttt{coDat}(S) = \texttt{hm}(&\frac{1}{|\texttt{Ent}(S)|} \cdot \sum_{e \in \texttt{Ent}(S)} \frac{\log(\texttt{d}^{+}(e)+1)}{\max_{e' \in \texttt{Ent}(T)} \log(\texttt{d}^{+}(e')+1)}, \\ &\frac{1}{|\texttt{Ent}(S)|} \cdot \sum_{e \in \texttt{Ent}(S)} \frac{\log(\texttt{d}^{-}(e)+1)}{\max_{e' \in \texttt{Ent}(T)} \log(\texttt{d}^{-}(e')+1)}), \end{aligned} \tag{8}$$

$$\texttt{Ent}(X) = \{r : \exists t \in X,\ r \in \{t^{\mathrm{s}}, t^{\mathrm{o}}\},\ r \notin \texttt{Cls}(T),\ \text{and } r \text{ is not a literal.}\},$$

where $\texttt{Cls}(T)$ is the set of all classes instantiated in T defined in Eq. (3), $\texttt{Ent}(S)$ is the set of all entities (i.e., non-literal resources at the data level) that appear in S, and $\texttt{Ent}(T)$ is the set of all entities that appear in T. Degree is normalized by the maximum value observed in the dataset. Considering that degree usually follows a highly skewed power-law distribution in practice, normalization is performed on a logarithmic scale.

For example, Fig. 1(b) is focused on `Germany`, which is a central entity in the dataset, so its `coDat` score is higher than that of Fig. 1(c) and (d) which contain more of subordinate entities.

4 Evaluation

In Sect. 2, each subsection reviews methods in a related research field that can be adapted to generate snippets for dataset search. The second paragraph of each subsection identifies a state-of-the-art method from each field that is suitable for our context: [7,17,29] and [14]. In this section, we evaluate these methods using the evaluation framework proposed in Sect. 3. We first analyze whether and how the components of these methods are aligned with each evaluation metric. Then we perform an extensive empirical evaluation based on real-world datasets.

4.1 Analysis of Selected Methods

Table 1 presents an overview of the selected methods and whether they have components that are conceptually similar to each evaluation metric. All the methods have been detailed in Sect. 2. In the following we focus on how their components are aligned with each evaluation metric.

Illustrative Dataset Snippet. Dataset snippets generated by existing methods reviewed in Sect. 2.1 can be used in dataset search without adaptation. The method we choose, IlluSnip [7], generates an illustrative snippet for an RDF dataset by extracting a connected subgraph to exemplify the content of the dataset. This intended use is very close to our problem.

IlluSnip explicitly considers a snippet's coverage of a dataset. Giving priority to the most frequent classes and properties, a snippet is likely to show a high coverage of data schema (`coSkm`). Besides, IlluSnip computes the centrality of an entity by PageRank, which positively correlates with in-degree. Therefore, a snippet containing such central entities may also have a reasonably high coverage of data (`coDat`), which is jointly measured by in-degree and out-degree.

However, IlluSnip is not query biased. A snippet it generates may not contain any keyword in a query, and hence its coverage of query keywords (`coKyw`) and the connections thereof (`coCnx`) can be very low.

For example, Fig. 1(b) illustrates a snippet generated by IlluSnip.

Query-Biased Ontology Snippet. Query-biased snippets for ontology search reviewed in Sect. 2.2 are useful for deciding the relevance of an ontology schema to a query. It is similar to our intent to support judging the relevance of a dataset. The method we choose, TA+C [17], extracts a query-biased subgraph from the RDF graph representation of an ontology schema. This method can be directly used to generate snippets for RDF datasets without adaptation.

TA+C explicitly considers a snippet's coverage of a query. It greedily adds query-biased sub-snippets into a snippet, giving preference to those containing more query keywords. A sub-snippet is a radius-bounded connected subgraph. Therefore, the resulting snippet has the potential to establish a high coverage of query keywords (`coKyw`) and their connections (`coCnx`), especially when keywords are closely located in the dataset.

On the other hand, coverage of dataset (`coSkm` and `coDat`) is not of concern to this query-centered method.

For example, Fig. 1(c) illustrates a snippet generated by TA+C.

GST for Keyword Search. Methods for keyword search on graphs reviewed in Sect. 2.3 find a GST, which is a connected subgraph where nodes contain all the query keywords. These methods can be straightforwardly applied to generate snippets for RDF datasets by computing a GST. The method we choose, PrunedDP++ [29], is one of the most efficient algorithms for the GST problem.

PrunedDP++ has two possible outputs. Either it finds a GST that covers all the query keywords (`coKyw`) and connections between all pairs of them (`coCnx`), or such a GST does not exist. In the latter case, PrunedDP++ returns empty results. So it is conceptually similar to TA+C but appears more "aggressive".

Coverage of dataset (`coSkm` and `coDat`) is not the focus of PrunedDP++. Nevertheless, these factors may be partially addressed by properly defining edge weights. Weighting is orthogonal to the design of PrunedDP++.

For example, Fig. 1(c) illustrates a snippet generated by PrunedDP++.

Query-Biased Document Snippet. Query-biased methods for generating document snippets reviewed in Sect. 2.4 can be adapted to generate snippets for RDF datasets, by replacing resources in a triple with their textual forms (e.g., labels of IRI-identified resources, lexical forms of literals) to obtain a pseudo sentence. The method we choose, CES [14], generates a query-biased snippet by selecting a subset of sentences (i.e., triples in our context). This unsupervised method fits current dataset search, for which training data is in shortage.

CES tends to select diversified triples that are relevant to a query, so it is likely to achieve a high coverage of query keywords (`coKyw`). CES also computes the cosine similarity between the term frequency—inverse document frequency (TF-IDF) vectors of the document (i.e., RDF dataset) and a snippet. This feature measures to what extent the snippet covers the main content of the dataset. It increases the possibility of including frequent classes, properties, and entities, and hence may improve a snippet's coverage of dataset (`coSkm` and `coDat`).

As a side effect of diversification, triples in a snippet are usually disparate. Connections between query keywords (`coCnx`) can hardly be observed.

For example, Fig. 1(d) illustrates a snippet generated by CES.

4.2 Empirical Evaluation

We used the proposed framework to evaluate the above selected methods. All the experiments were performed on an Intel Xeon E7-4820 (2.00 GHz) with 80GB memory for the JVM. Our implementation of these methods is open source[2].

Datasets and Queries. We retrieved the metadata of 11,462 datasets from DataHub[3] using CKAN's API. Among 1,262 RDF datasets that provided Turtle, RDF/XML, or N-Triples dump files, we downloaded and parsed 311 datasets using Apache Jena. The others were excluded due to download or parse errors.

We used two kinds of queries: real queries and artificial queries.

Real Queries. We used crowdsourced natural language queries[4] that were originally submitted to data.gov.uk for datasets [20]. They were transformed into keyword queries by removing stop words using Apache Lucene.

Artificial Queries. To have more queries, we leveraged the DMOZ open directory[5] to imitate possible data needs. For each $i = 1 \ldots 4$, we constructed a group of queries denoted by DMOZ-i. A query in DMOZ-i consisted of the names of

---

2 http://ws.nju.edu.cn/datasetsearch/evaluation-iswc2019/baselines.zip.
3 https://old.datahub.io/.
4 https://github.com/chabrowa/data-requests-query-dataset.
5 http://dmoz-odp.org/.

Table 2. Statistics about query-dataset (Q-D) pairs.

	#Q-D pairs	#keywords in Q		#triples in D		#classes in D		#properties in D	
		mean	max	mean	max	mean	max	mean	max
data.gov.uk	42	2.88	8	116,822	2,203,699	13	129	47	357
DMOZ-1	88	1.25	3	137,257	2,203,699	30	2,030	66	3,982
DMOZ-2	84	2.33	5	151,104	2,203,699	10	129	34	357
DMOZ-3	87	3.66	6	164,714	2,203,699	13	153	43	357
DMOZ-4	86	5.02	8	219,844	2,203,699	13	129	46	357

i random sub-categories of a random top-level category in DMOZ. Such closely related concepts had a reasonable chance to be fully covered by some dataset.

To conclude, we had five groups of queries: data.gov.uk, DMOZ-1, DMOZ-2, DMOZ-3, and DMOZ-4. For each group, we randomly retained 100 queries such that each query could be paired with a dataset that covered all the query keywords. These 500 query-dataset pairs were used in our evaluation. We required a dataset to cover all the query keywords in order to make sense of the experiment results. Otherwise, a low score of `coKyw` would be ambiguous: reflecting the poor quality of the snippet, and/or the irrelevance of the dataset.

Configuration of Methods. We detail their configuration in the following.

Size of Snippet. Following [7], we configured IlluSnip and CES to generate a snippet containing at most 20 RDF triples (i.e., $k = 20$). For TA+C, it would be inappropriate to bound the number of triples because the snippets it generated could contain isolated nodes. So we bounded it to output a snippet whose graph representation contained at most 20 nodes. For PrunedDP++, the size of its output was automatically determined but not configurable.

Weights and Parameters. For TA+C [17], edge weights were defined as in the original paper. For PrunedDP++ [29], its authors did not specify how to weight edges. Our weighting followed [11]—the predecessor of PrunedDP++. For CES [14], it had several parameters. Most of them were set to the values used in the original paper. However, due to the large size of RDF dataset, the sampling step in CES was performed 1,000 times (instead of 10,000 times in [14]) in consideration of memory use.

Preprocessing. We built inverted indexes for efficient keyword mapping in TA+C, PrunedDP++, and CES. For TA+C, following its original implementation [17], we precomputed and materialized all the maximal 1-radius subgraphs.

Timeout. After preprocessing, we set a timeout of one hour for each method to generate a snippet. The generating process would be terminated when reaching timeout. In that case, the runtime would be defined to be one hour. For IlluSnip and CES which iteratively found better snippets, the best snippet at timeout would be returned. For TA+C and PrunedDP++, timeout indicated failure.

Table 3. Average scores of evaluation metrics on all the query-dataset pairs.

	coKyw	coCnx	coSkm	coDat
IlluSnip	0.1000	0.0540	0.6820	0.3850
TA+C	0.9590	0.4703	0.0425	0.0915
PrunedDP++	1	1	0.0898	0.2133
CES	0.9006	0.3926	0.3668	0.2684

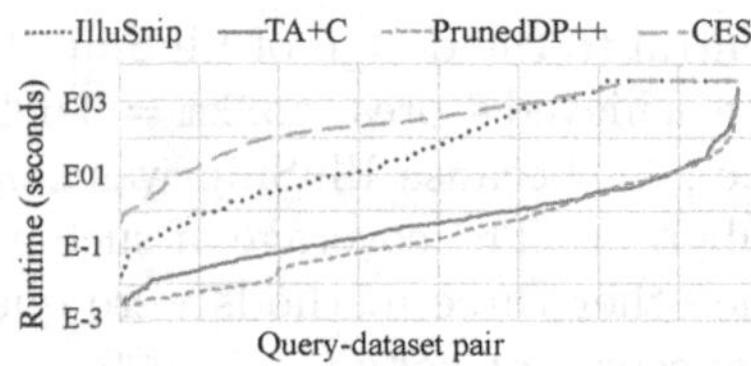

Fig. 2. Runtime on each query-data set pair, in ascending order.

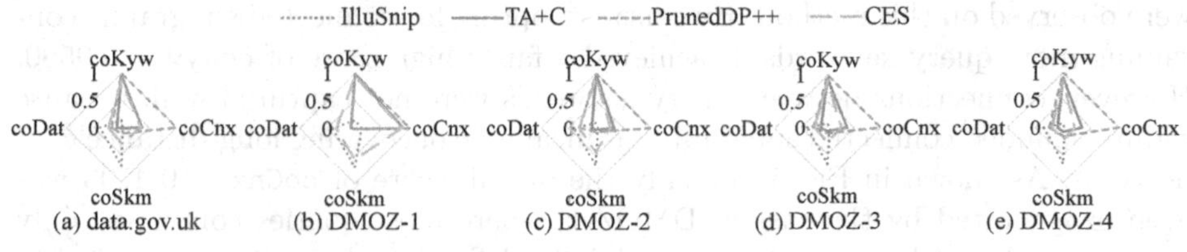

Fig. 3. Average scores of evaluation metrics on each group of query-dataset pairs.

Evaluation Results. Out of the 500 query-dataset pairs, 113 pairs were not included in our results for one of the following reasons.

- PrunedDP++ did not find any GST to connect all the query keywords, and hence generated an empty snippet.
- TA+C and PrunedDP++ were forced to terminate due to timeout.
- TA+C did not complete preprocessing after twelve hours.

We reported evaluation results on the remaining 387 pairs where every method successfully generated a non-empty snippet before timeout. Table 2 characterizes these queries and datasets. They are available online[6].

Note that IlluSnip and CES were configured to generate a snippet containing at most 20 triples, and they selected 19.68 and 19.89 triples on average, respectively. By comparison, for PrunedDP++ the size of its output was automatically determined, and the mean number of triples in the experiment was only 4.60. This may affect the evaluation results. Besides, TA+C and PrunedDP++ sometimes produced isolated nodes instead of triples. The query keywords covered by these nodes were considered in the computation of coKyw and coCnx.

Table 3 presents the average score of each evaluation metric achieved by each method on all the query-dataset pairs. Compared with Table 1, a higher score was generally observed when a metric was conceptually considered in the components of a method. We concluded that the results of our empirical evaluation were basically consistent with our analysis in Sect. 4.1. Figure 3 depicts the scores on each group of query-dataset pairs using radar charts.

IlluSnip achieved much higher scores of coSkm and coDat than other methods. It was not surprising because covering the schema and data of a dataset was

[6] http://ws.nju.edu.cn/datasetsearch/evaluation-iswc2019/query-dataset-pairs.zip.

central to the design of IlluSnip. However, there were still notable gaps between the achieved scores (`coSkm` = 0.6820 and `coDat` = 0.3850) and their upper bound (i.e., 1), because IlluSnip was constrained to output a size-bounded connected subgraph. The coverage of such a subgraph was limited. On the other hand, all the other three methods were query-biased, whereas IlluSnip was not. Its very low scores of `coKyw` = 0.1000 and `coCnx` = 0.0540 suggested that the snippets generated by IlluSnip usually failed to cover queries.

TA+C was opposite in scores to IlluSnip. Coverage of dataset was not the focus of its design. The lowest scores of `coSkm` = 0.0425 and `coDat` = 0.0915 were observed on this method. By contrast, opting for connected subgraphs containing more query keywords, it achieved a fairly high score of `coKyw` = 0.9590. However, connections between query keywords were not captured well, because radius-bounded connected subgraph was incapable of covering long-distance connections. As shown in Fig. 3, actually the overall score of `coCnx` = 0.4703 was even exaggerated by the case of DMOZ-1, where most queries comprised only one keyword and hence `coCnx` was trivially defined to be `coKyw` according to Eq. (2). In other cases, `coCnx` was not high.

PrunedDP++ could not find any GST to connect all the query keywords on 86 query-dataset pairs, which had been excluded from our results. On the remaining pairs, not surprisingly, its coverage of query keywords (`coKyw` = 1) and their connections (`coCnx` = 1) was perfect. In a GST, query keywords were often connected via paths that passed through hub nodes in a dataset. Involving such high-degree nodes, a GST's coverage of data (`coDat` = 0.2133) was considerably higher than that of TA+C (`coDat` = 0.0915). However, similar to TA+C, a GST's coverage of data schema was limited (`coSkm` = 0.0898).

CES appeared to be a more balanced method, as visualized in Fig. 3. Towards generating a query-biased and diversified snippet, its coverage of query keywords (`coKyw` = 0.9006) was close to TA+C and PrunedDP++, and its coverage of dataset (`coSkm` = 0.3668 and `coDat` = 0.2684) was notably better. However, similar to TA+C, its coverage of connections between query keywords was not satisfying because selecting diversified triples usually led to a fragmented snippet. The overall score of `coCnx` = 0.3926 was exaggerated by the case of DMOZ-1.

Runtime. We also evaluated the runtime of each method because fast generation of snippets is an expectation of search engine users. Figure 2 depicts, on a logarithmic scale, the runtime of each method used for generating a snippet for each of the 387 query-dataset pairs. Runtime was mainly related to the number of triples in a dataset.

PrunedDP++ was generally the fastest method, with a median runtime of 0.16 s. It rarely reached timeout, and it completed computation in less than one second in 68% of the cases. TA+C was also reasonably fast, with a median runtime of 0.43 s. These two methods showed promising performance for practical use. By contrast, IlluSnip and CES reached timeout in 22% and 18% of the cases, respectively. They often spent tens or hundreds of seconds generating a snippet.

Fortunately, IlluSnip was not query-biased, and hence could be used to generate snippets offline.

5 User Study

We recruited 20 students majoring in computer science to assess the quality of snippets generated by different methods. All the participants had the experience in working with RDF datasets. The results could be compared with the above evaluation results, to verify the effectiveness of our proposed evaluation metrics.

Design. From fifty random candidates, each participant chose 5 datasets with interest according to their metadata. For each dataset, the participant had access to a list of classes and properties used in the dataset to help understanding. The participant was required to describe some data needs that could be fulfilled by the dataset, and then repeatedly rephrase the needs as a keyword query until all of IlluSnip, TA+C, and PrunedDP++ could generate a non-empty snippet. For reasonable response time, CES was excluded from user study, and datasets containing more than one million triples were not used. Following [7,17], we visualized a snippet (which was an RDF graph) as a node-link diagram. The participant rated its usefulness in relevance judgment on a scale of 1–5, and commented its strengths and weaknesses.

Results. Table 4 summarizes the responses from participants about snippets for a total of $20 \cdot 5 = 100$ datasets. IlluSnip received a higher mean rating than TA+C and PrunedDP++. Repeated measures ANOVA (rANOVA) indicated that their differences were statistically significant ($p < 0.01$). LSD post-hoc tests ($p < 0.01$) suggested that IlluSnip was more helpful to users than TA+C and PrunedDP++, whereas the difference between TA+C and PrunedDP++ was not statistically significant.

Figure 4 shows the mean score of each evaluation metric, grouped by user ratings. For each evaluation metric we excluded the results of some methods when their scores were hardly distinguishable (all close to 1) because those methods had components that were conceptually similar to the metrics (cf. Table 1). The scores of all the four metrics generally increased as user ratings increased. The observed positive correlation demonstrated the effectiveness of our evaluation framework. Exceptions were the notable falls of `coSkm` and `coDat` at the end, where very few (<10) snippets were rated 5 so that the scores at this point might not be significant.

We analyzed participants' comments. For IlluSnip, 15 participants (75%) complimented the connectivity of its results which facilitated understanding, and 13 participants (65%) referred to the richness and diversity of the content, which accorded well with its high coverage of data schema. Not surprisingly, 16 participants (80%) criticized its weak relevance to the query. For TA+C, 15 participants (75%) appreciated its query relevance, but 19 participants (95%)

Table 4. Human-rated usefulness of snippets (1–5) in relevance judgment.

Mean ± standard deviation		
IlluSnip	TA+C	PrunedDP++
3.10 ± 1.28	2.36 ± 1.29	1.92 ± 1.19
rANOVA (p-value): 0.00264		
LSD post-hoc ($p < 0.01$): IlluSnip > TA+C, PrunedDP++		

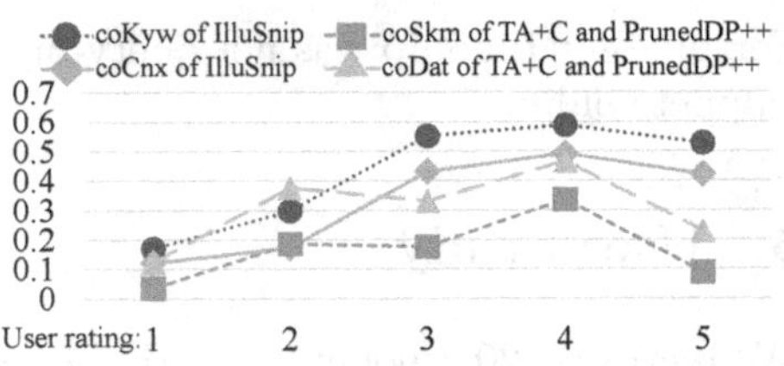

Fig. 4. Correlation between evaluation metrics and user ratings.

complained that its results sometimes contained many isolated nodes. It happened frequently when a query contained only one keyword. Although these nodes covered the query keyword, they were not associated with any further description, which dissatisfied 12 participants (60%). For PrunedDP++, similar feedback was received from 17 participants (85%) for some cases, but in other cases, 15 participants (75%) commented its high coverage of query keywords and the paths between them, which facilitated the comprehension of their connections. Besides, 8 participants (40%) favored the conciseness of its results.

Participants were invited to a post-experiment interview. Whereas they confirmed the usefulness of snippets, they generally believed that snippet could not replace but complement abstractive summary with statistics. Some participants suggested implementing interactive (e.g., hierarchical and zoomable) snippets for user exploration, which could be a future direction of research.

Discussion. Participants' ratings, comments, and the results of our proposed evaluation metrics were generally consistent with each other. The results justified the appropriateness of our framework to evaluating snippets in dataset search.

From the participants' comments, we concluded that a good dataset snippet should, on the one hand, cover query keywords and their connections to make sense of the underlying query intent. TA+C and PrunedDP++ were focused on this aspect. On the other hand, it should provide rich and diverse description about matched resources and triples to make sense of the dataset content. This was overlooked by TA+C and PrunedDP++, and it suggested a difference between snippet generation and keyword search. A trade-off between informativeness and compactness should be considered. IlluSnip showed promising results along this way. However, none of the three methods fulfilled these requirements completely, and hence their usefulness scores were far from perfection.

6 Conclusion

To promote research on the emerging problem of snippet generation for dataset search, we have proposed an evaluation framework for assessing the quality of dataset snippets. With our metrics, methods proposed in the future can be evaluated more easily. Our framework relies on neither ground-truth snippets which are difficult to create, nor human efforts in user study which are inefficient and expensive. Evaluation can be automated offline. This in turn will be beneficial to the rapid development and deployment of snippets for dataset search engines.

Our evaluation results reveal the shortcomings of state-of-the-art methods adapted from related fields, which are also verified by a user study. None of the evaluated methods address all the considered aspects. It inspires us to put forward new methods for generating dataset snippets with more comprehensive features. Efficiency and scalability of methods are also important factors. Storage will also be a concern because a dataset search engine may have to store and index each dataset for snippet generation.

Our work has the following limitations. First, our evaluation framework may not be comprehensive. It can partially assess the quality of a dataset snippet, but still is not ready to completely replace user study. There may be other useful metrics, such as distinctiveness, readability, and coherence, which we will study in future work. Second, our evaluation metrics are implemented specifically for RDF datasets. To extend the range of application of our framework, more generalized implementation for other data formats needs to be explored.

Acknowledgements. This work was supported in part by the National Key R&D Program of China under Grant 2018YFB1005100, in part by the NSFC under Grant 61572247, and in part by the SIRIUS Centre, Norwegian Research Council project number 237898. Cheng was funded by the Six Talent Peaks Program of Jiangsu Province under Grant RJFW-011.

References

1. Bai, X., Delbru, R., Tummarello, G.: RDF snippets for semantic web search engines. In: Meersman, R., Tari, Z. (eds.) OTM 2008. LNCS, vol. 5332, pp. 1304–1318. Springer, Heidelberg (2008). https://doi.org/10.1007/978-3-540-88873-4_27
2. Brickley, D., Burgess, M., Noy, N.F.: Google dataset search: building a search engine for datasets in an open web ecosystem. In: WWW, pp. 1365–1375 (2019)
3. Butt, A.S., Haller, A., Xie, L.: Dwrank: learning concept ranking for ontology search. Semant. Web **7**(4), 447–461 (2016)
4. Cebiric, S., Goasdoué, F., Manolescu, I.: Query-oriented summarization of RDF graphs. PVLDB **8**(12), 2012–2015 (2015)
5. Cheng, G., Ge, W., Qu, Y.: Generating summaries for ontology search. In: WWW (Companion Volume), pp. 27–28 (2011)
6. Cheng, G., Ji, F., Luo, S., Ge, W., Qu, Y.: Biprank: ranking and summarizing RDF vocabulary descriptions. In: JIST, pp. 226–241 (2011)
7. Cheng, G., Jin, C., Ding, W., Xu, D., Qu, Y.: Generating illustrative snippets for open data on the web. In: WSDM, pp. 151–159 (2017)
8. Cheng, G., Jin, C., Qu, Y.: HIEDS: a generic and efficient approach to hierarchical dataset summarization. In: IJCAI, pp. 3705–3711 (2016)
9. Cheng, G., Kharlamov, E.: Towards a semantic keyword search over industrial knowledge graphs (extended abstract). In: IEEE BigData, pp. 1698–1700 (2017)
10. Coffman, J., Weaver, A.C.: An empirical performance evaluation of relational keyword search techniques. IEEE Trans. Knowl. Data Eng. **26**(1), 30–42 (2014)

11. Ding, B., Yu, J.X., Wang, S., Qin, L., Zhang, X., Lin, X.: Finding top-k min-cost connected trees in databases. In: ICDE, pp. 836–845 (2007)
12. Dolby, J., et al.: Scalable semantic retrieval through summarization and refinement. In: AAAI, pp. 299–304 (2007)
13. Ellefi, M.B., et al.: RDF dataset profiling - a survey of features, methods, vocabularies and applications. Semant. Web **9**(5), 677–705 (2018)
14. Feigenblat, G., Roitman, H., Boni, O., Konopnicki, D.: Unsupervised query-focused multi-document summarization using the cross entropy method. In: SIGIR, pp. 961–964 (2017)
15. Fkoue, A., Meneguzzi, F., Sensoy, M., Pan, J.Z.: Querying linked ontological data through distributed summarization. In: AAAI (2012)
16. Gambhir, M., Gupta, V.: Recent automatic text summarization techniques: a survey. Artif. Intell. Rev. **47**(1), 1–66 (2017)
17. Ge, W., Cheng, G., Li, H., Qu, Y.: Incorporating compactness to generate term-association view snippets for ontology search. Inf. Process. Manag. **49**(2), 513–528 (2013)
18. Horrocks, I., Giese, M., Kharlamov, E., Waaler, A.: Using semantic technology to tame the data variety challenge. IEEE Internet Comput. **20**(6), 62–66 (2016)
19. Jiménez-Ruiz, E., et al.: BootOX: practical mapping of RDBs to OWL 2. In: Arenas, M., et al. (eds.) ISWC 2015. LNCS, vol. 9367, pp. 113–132. Springer, Cham (2015). https://doi.org/10.1007/978-3-319-25010-6_7
20. Kacprzak, E., Koesten, L., Ibáñez, L.D., Blount, T., Tennison, J., Simperl, E.: Characterising dataset search - an analysis of search logs and data requests. J. Web Semant. **55**, 37–55 (2019)
21. Kasneci, G., Ramanath, M., Sozio, M., Suchanek, F.M., Weikum, G.: STAR: steiner-tree approximation in relationship graphs. In: ICDE, pp. 868–879 (2009)
22. Kharlamov, E., et al.: Capturing industrial information models with ontologies and constraints. In: Groth, P., et al. (eds.) ISWC 2016. LNCS, vol. 9982, pp. 325–343. Springer, Cham (2016). https://doi.org/10.1007/978-3-319-46547-0_30
23. Kharlamov, E., et al.: Ontology Based Data Access in Statoil. J. Web Semant. **44**, 3–36 (2017)
24. Kharlamov, E., et al.: An ontology-mediated analytics-aware approach to support monitoring and diagnostics of static and streaming data. J. Web Semant. **56**, 30–55 (2019)
25. Kharlamov, E., et al.: Semantic access to streaming and static data at Siemens. J. Web Semant. **44**, 54–74 (2017)
26. Kharlamov, E., Mehdi, G., Savković, O., Xiao, G., Kalayci, E.G., Roshchin, M.: Semantically-enhanced rule-based diagnostics for industrial internet of things: the SDRL language and case study for siemens trains and turbines. J. Web Semant. **56**, 11–29 (2019)
27. Le, W., Li, F., Kementsietsidis, A., Duan, S.: Scalable keyword search on large RDF data. IEEE Trans. Knowl. Data Eng. **26**(11), 2774–2788 (2014)
28. Li, N., Motta, E., d'Aquin, M.: Ontology summarization: an analysis and an evaluation. In: IWEST (2010)
29. Li, R., Qin, L., Yu, J.X., Mao, R.: Efficient and progressive group steiner tree search. In: SIGMOD, pp. 91–106 (2016)
30. Pan, J., Vetere, G., Gomez-Perez, J., Wu, H. (eds.): Exploiting Linked Data and Knowledge Graphs for Large Organisations. Springer, Heidelberg (2016). https://doi.org/10.1007/978-3-319-45654-6
31. Penin, T., Wang, H., Tran, T., Yu, Y.: Snippet generation for semantic web search engines. In: ASWC, pp. 493–507 (2008)

32. Pietriga, E., et al.: Browsing linked data catalogs with LODAtlas. In: Vrandečić, D., et al. (eds.) ISWC 2018. LNCS, vol. 11137, pp. 137–153. Springer, Cham (2018). https://doi.org/10.1007/978-3-030-00668-6_9
33. Pinkel, C., et al.: RODI: benchmarking relational-to-ontology mapping generation quality. Semant. Web **9**(1), 25–52 (2018)
34. Pouriyeh, S., et al.: Graph-based methods for ontology summarization: A survey. In: AIKE, pp. 85–92 (2018)
35. Pouriyeh, S., et al.: Ontology summarization: graph-based methods and beyond. Int. J. Semant. Comput. **13**(2), 259–283 (2019)
36. Rietveld, L., Hoekstra, R., Schlobach, S., Guéret, C.: Structural properties as proxy for semantic relevance in RDF graph sampling. In: Mika, P., et al. (eds.) ISWC 2014. LNCS, vol. 8797, pp. 81–96. Springer, Cham (2014). https://doi.org/10.1007/978-3-319-11915-1_6
37. Ringsquandl, M., et al.: Event-enhanced learning for KG completion. In: ESWC, pp. 541–559 (2018)
38. Song, Q., Wu, Y., Lin, P., Dong, X., Sun, H.: Mining summaries for knowledge graph search. IEEE Trans. Knowl. Data Eng. **30**(10), 1887–1900 (2018)
39. Troullinou, G., Kondylakis, H., Stefanidis, K., Plexousakis, D.: Exploring RDFS KBs Using summaries. In: Vrandečić, D., et al. (eds.) ISWC 2018. LNCS, vol. 11136, pp. 268–284. Springer, Cham (2018). https://doi.org/10.1007/978-3-030-00671-6_16
40. Turpin, A., Tsegay, Y., Hawking, D., Williams, H.E.: Fast generation of result snippets in web search. In: SIGIR, pp. 127–134 (2007)
41. Wang, H., Aggarwal, C.C.: A survey of algorithms for keyword search on graph data. In: Managing and Mining Graph Data, pp. 249–273. Springer, Boston (2010). https://doi.org/10.1007/978-1-4419-6045-0_8
42. Zhang, X., Cheng, G., Ge, W., Qu, Y.: Summarizing vocabularies in the global semantic web. J. Comput. Sci. Technol. **24**(1), 165–174 (2009)
43. Zhang, X., Cheng, G., Qu, Y.: Ontology summarization based on rdf sentence graph. In: WWW, pp. 707–716 (2007)
44. Zhang, X., Li, H., Qu, Y.: Finding important vocabulary within ontology. In: ASWC, pp. 106–112 (2006)
45. Zneika, M., Vodislav, D., Kotzinos, D.: Quality metrics for RDF graph summarization. Semant. Web **10**(3), 555–584 (2019)

Summarizing News Articles Using Question-and-Answer Pairs via Learning

Xuezhi Wang(✉) and Cong Yu

Google Research, New York, USA
{xuezhiw,congyu}@google.com

Abstract. The launch of the new Google News in 2018 (https://www.blog.google/products/news/new-google-news-ai-meets-human-intelligence/.) introduced the *Frequently asked questions* feature to *structurally summarize* the news story in its full coverage page. While news summarization has been a research topic for decades, this new feature is poised to usher in a new line of news summarization techniques. There are two fundamental approaches: *mining the questions* from data associated with the news story and *learning the questions* from the content of the story directly. This paper provides the first study, to the best of our knowledge, of a *learning* based approach to generate a structured summary of news articles with question and answer pairs to capture salient and interesting aspects of the news story. Specifically, this learning-based approach reads a news article, predicts its attention map (i.e., important snippets in the article), and generates multiple natural language questions corresponding to each snippet. Furthermore, we describe a mining-based approach as the mechanism to generate weak supervision data for training the learning based approach. We evaluate our approach on the existing SQuAD dataset (https://rajpurkar.github.io/SQuAD-explorer/.) and a large dataset with 91K news articles we constructed. We show that our proposed system can achieve an AUC of 0.734 for document attention map prediction, a BLEU-4 score of 12.46 for natural question generation and a BLEU-4 score of 24.4 for question summarization, beating state-of-art baselines.

Keywords: Structured summarization · Question answering

1 Introduction

News summarization has been an important topic of natural language research for decades [20]. While there are many approaches, the end result has always been natural sentences that summarize the articles. The launch of the new Google News in 2018 [28] with its *Frequently asked questions* feature showed that *structured summaries* such as question-and-answer (Q/A) pairs can be beneficial to the news consumption experience[1]. Compared with natural language summaries,

[1] Private communication with Google's news team: FAQ is shown to improve users' understanding of the news stories in user studies, which is an important launch criteria.

C. Ghidini et al. (Eds.): ISWC 2019, LNCS 11778, pp. 698–715, 2019.
https://doi.org/10.1007/978-3-030-30793-6_40

Q/A pairs offer low cognitive overload because, being very short, questions are easy to digest and users can easily skip those they do not care and read the answer snippets for only those they are interested in. Furthermore, structured summary often does not try to capture an overview of the story, but rather highlights salient aspects that the users would like to know about, making them complementary to the conventional news summaries.

Question answering has been an important research topic for semantic web [11] and information retrieval [15], with the goal of answering users' questions based on the knowledge base or the documents in the corpus. Lately, major search engines have begun to leverage Q/A in more proactive ways. For example, Google search has been using an Q/A feature, *People also ask*, to proactively highlight the most salient aspects of the search results for the users. The success of Q/A features in search no doubt has played a role in the introduction of Q/A features into the various news consumption platforms such as Google News.

For a news article that has been published for a little while and queried by lots of users, many questions would have been asked about it. Thus, the intuitive first approach for generating Q/A pairs for a news article is to mine the query log for questions, cluster them into groups, identify a representative question for each group, and extract relevant answer snippets from the article for the representative questions. Indeed, this is the technique behind the *Frequently asked questions* feature of Google News full coverage[2]. The approach works well because the most salient aspects of a news article are reflected in commonly asked questions from the users (see Table 1):

Table 1. News stories and their top questions mined from anonymized query logs.

News story	Top asked questions
Starbucks closed for anti-bias training	- What time will starbucks close on may 29
	- Why are all starbucks closed
	- When are starbucks closing
Belgium beat England to secure third place at the 2018 FIFA world cup	- What time is the England game today
	- What channel is England vs Belgium
	- Who won 3rd place in world cup 2018
Audubon zoo closed after Jaguar escapes	- How did audubon zoo jaguar escape
	- Where is audubon zoo
	- What animals were killed at the audubon zoo

However, for the latest articles that have just been published or long-tail articles that have not been queried by many users, this mining-based approach does not work due to the lack of historical queries. To address this challenge,

[2] Private communication.

we propose a **learning-based approach** that first predicts important snippets from the article and then generates natural language questions with those snippets as answers. The resulting Q/A pairs can achieve the same summarization effect on latest and long-tail articles as those mined from the query logs for popular news articles. To make this learning-based approach work, it is crucial to be able to generate training examples at scale. In fact, we employ the mining-based approach to generate weak supervision data that we then leverage in the learning-based approach as training examples.

To the best of our knowledge, this is the first study to develop a learning-based approach to generate Q/A pairs as structured summaries for news articles. The rest of the paper is organized as follows. Section 2 discusses related works. Section 3 describes how we obtain Q/A pairs using a mining approach to generate large scale weak training examples. In Sect. 4, we tackle the core challenge of structured summarization in the absence of associated queries with two steps. First, we propose a deep learning model to predict the attention maps given a news article, Second, we propose a natural question generation model that generates questions given the snippets from the attended article. Together, this generates salient Q/A pairs for the given article. In Sect. 5, we compare our proposed learning approach with baselines on both an academic dataset, SQuAD [24], and a large-scale news article dataset we collected. Finally, Sect. 6 concludes our work.

2 Related Work

Document summarization is a major focus of NLP research and follows two main approaches: first, extractive or abstractive summarization of the article using a few natural language sentences [5,6,10,13,25], and second, extracting salient entities and relational triples from the article [1,7,21]. As discussed in Sect. 1, the first approach focuses on providing an overview of the article instead of capturing aspects of the story that is salient to the users and is thus complimentary to the structured summary approach we study here. The relationship extraction approach focuses on concrete attributes. For example, it will likely extract "date of closing" for the Starbucks anti-bias training story (Table 1), but it will not capture abstract notions such as "why is Starbucks closed", which is in fact central to the story. Our proposed structured summary approach aims to capture all salient aspects, both concrete and abstract. News event summarization is a line of document summarization work that is specialized to news events [9,13,16,22,27,29]. To the best of our knowledge, we are the first study to propose a mechanism for capturing salient aspects using abstractive Q/A pairs as summaries for news stories.

Open information extraction is another related area [1,7,21], where the goal is to extract relation tuples from plain text. Similarly, methods proposed here are more likely to extract "*is-CEO* (Kevin Johnson, Starbucks)", rather than the reason why Starbucks is closed for the whole day. The latter will be much more salient to the users for understanding the story.

Table 2. Question clusters and summaries for the story "Starbucks closed for anti-bias training"

Question cluster	Question summary
- When is starbucks closed for training	Starbucks training day closing time
- What day is starbucks closed for training	
- Why is starbucks closed today	Starbucks closed reason
- Why is starbucks closing	
- What is anti bias training	Anti bias training meaning

Answering questions based on a given corpus has been studied quite extensively. For example, [3] tackles open-domain question answering using Wikipedia as the unique knowledge source. It shows that open-domain Q/A is a very challenging problem and the performance of most state-of-the-art systems drops drastically when the passage that contains the answer is not already given. In [8], the authors propose to utilize question paraphrases from the WikiAnswers corpus to improve the performance of question answering. [26] proposes a bi-directional attention flow framework for question answering, by representing the context at different levels of granularity and generating query-aware context using attention. Our work took the opposite direction, namely we identify the important answer snippets first and attempt to phrase the questions afterwards.

Generating natural questions given a text passage only recently got some attention. [31] proposes a neural encoder-decoder model that reads a text passage and generates an answer-focused question, while [4] proposes to first identify question-worthy sentences in a input text passage, and then incorporates the prediction into an existing natural question generation system. The questions our work aims to generate is much more diverse and unpredictable (Sect. 5.2) than those works due to the nature of news domain.

3 Structured Summarization via Mining

Document queries [12] have long been used in various search tasks to improve quality. For news articles that have been published for a while (thus enough user-issued queries have been accumulated), mining the query log for salient questions for the article is an intuitive approach that works well.

While the idea is intuitive, there are two main challenges. First, identification of representative questions from the query log. For a single question intent, there are often many semantically identical but syntactically different queries the users may have issued. It is important to avoid semantically duplicate questions in the structured summary. Second, extraction of relevant answer snippets for the representative questions, which is akin to the traditional question-and-answering task, namely given a question and a document, identifying answers from the document. The difference for structured summary, however, is that

Table 3. Question summary and corresponding answer snippet for the news story "Starbucks closed for anti-bias training"

Question summary	Answer snippet
Starbucks training day closing time	Starbucks is closing more than 8,000 stores **Tuesday afternoon** for anti-bias training ...
Starbucks closed reason	... Tuesday afternoon **for anti-bias training**, a strategy some believe can keep racism at bay ...
Anti bias training meaning	... which offers training on **unconscious bias** and gave Starbucks input on its program

each representative question is backed by a group of similar queries, which can be leveraged collectively to identify the best answer snippet.

In this section, we describe how we leverage existing techniques to design a mining approach for structured summarization. Throughout the section, we will follow the examples in Tables 2 and 3, which illustrate the two main tasks for the mining approach, question summarization and answer snippet extraction, respectively.

3.1 Question Clustering and Summarization

There are many benefits of leveraging documents queries for structured summarization. For example, document queries can counter the bias inherent in the article content: while the article author often injects their bias into the article (especially when they have a strong opinion on the underlying news story), queries issued by a large number of users, in an aggregated fashion, are less prone to any individual's bias. However, document queries are also challenging to work with because of their inherent noise and the multiple ways for users to express the same semantic intent.

The first challenge is that most document queries are single entities or short phrases and only ~1% of any article's accumulated document queries are in question format. When they are present, however, those questions are more specific and thus more useful in capturing important aspects in a story. For example, for the story "Starbucks closed for anti-bias training" in Table 2, the top (single-entity) queries are "starbucks" and "anti-bias", which are useful for knowing what is being talked about but difficult for users to understand what exactly happened. On the other hand, the top *question queries* are "when is starbucks closed" and "why is starbucks closed", which represent the aspects that are most interesting to the users. We extract question queries from all queries associated with a news article using a simple pattern, i.e., any query starting with *what, when, how, why, who, where, which, etc.*

Table 4. Extracted question summary from queries for some example question clusters.

Question summary	Question cluster
Blockbuster last location	- Where is the last blockbuster store located
	- Where is the last open blockbuster
mlb trading deadline	- When is mlb trade deadline
	- When is trading deadline in mlb
Winner of pacquiao fight	- Who won the pacquiao fight last night
	- Who won pacquiao fight

The second challenge is that document queries contain many near duplicates since different users phrase the same question in different ways. We address this challenge by using hierarchical agglomerative clustering to cluster the question queries as shown, again, in Table 2. For the similarity measure between each pair of question queries $\text{sim}(q_i, q_j)$, we take a weighted average of the word embeddings to derive a single vector for each query q_i, q_j and the weights are the inverted word frequency. The similarity between two queries are computed using cosine similarity. The word embedding is a 300-dimension vector we borrow from fastText [19].

The third challenge is readability. Question clusters are great for identifying salient aspects that users collectively consider as important, but a list of questions are not easily consumable by the readers. To improve the readability, we further generate *question summary*. Intuitively, for each question-query cluster, we pick a non-question query that is most similar to all question queries within the cluster. Anecdotally, as shown in Table 2, most of the "when ..." questions are summarized using "... time/date", and the "why..." questions are summarized using "... reason." Note that we can also pick a representative query that is itself a question—we choose to have a non-question representative because the pool of non-question queries is bigger and a summary that is not a question can be used in more product features than a summary that is itself a question.

Specifically, for each question cluster C_q and question queries $q_1, q_2, \ldots, q_k \in C_q$, we find the closest non-question query q^* by: $q^* = \arg\max_{q \in C_{nq}} \sum_{i=1}^{k} \text{sim}(q, q_i)$, where C_{nq} is the set of non-question queries, and $\text{sim}(q, q_i)$ is the cosine similarity between the weighted average word embeddings of q, q_i as described in the clustering stage. In Table 4, we list examples of the question summary we automatically identified using this approach. In practice we found this approach can summarize the question clusters fairly well.

3.2 Answer Snippets Extraction

Identifying questions only partially fulfills the structured summary—it is also important to pair the questions with the correct answer snippets from the article so the users can grasp the whole story. We accomplish this in two stages. First,

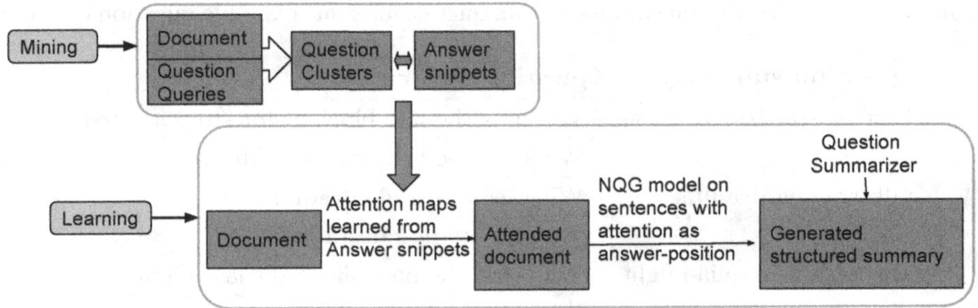

Fig. 1. Overview of the learning based structured summarization system.

for each question in the question cluster, we apply a state-of-the-art question-and-answering model, QANet [30], to extract the corresponding answer snippet from the article. While QANet achieved an 84.5% Exact Match score on SQuAD v1.1 dataset[3], it has a much lower accuracy in our open domain scenario: ~60% based on our evaluation over a random sample of 100 (question-query, news-article) pairs.

The main challenge we encounter, is that in some cases the questions are not directly answerable from the article content. This is expected because compared to datasets where the provided passage (or context) is known to contain the answer, our question queries have a weaker association with the document content: users might have clicked on a document without knowing whether their questions can be answered. Fortunately, we have many paraphrased questions for each question cluster. Instead of using QANet to identify answer snippets just for one representative question, we can apply QANet on all paraphrasing questions in the cluster and pick the answer snippet that have the highest aggregated confidence score for all question queries in the cluster. We found this extra step improves the answer snippet accuracy by a large margin for the mining approach (from 60% to 75%+), enabling us to leverage the data for learning.

3.3 Results from the Mining Approach as Weak Supervision Data

While the mining approach can be quite effective for articles with accumulated document queries, it does not address the challenge of producing structured summary for news articles in practice. The reason is that most news articles are consumed when they are just published and not enough document queries have been accumulated for the mining approach to be effective. Furthermore, long tail news articles, i.e., ones that do not have a large audience, also have very few accumulated document queries for the mining approach to be effective.

As a result, we do not consider our technical contributions on the mining approach as main contributions to the paper. Instead, we designed this mining approach with the main goal of using the results from this approach as weak

[3] https://rajpurkar.github.io/SQuAD-explorer/.

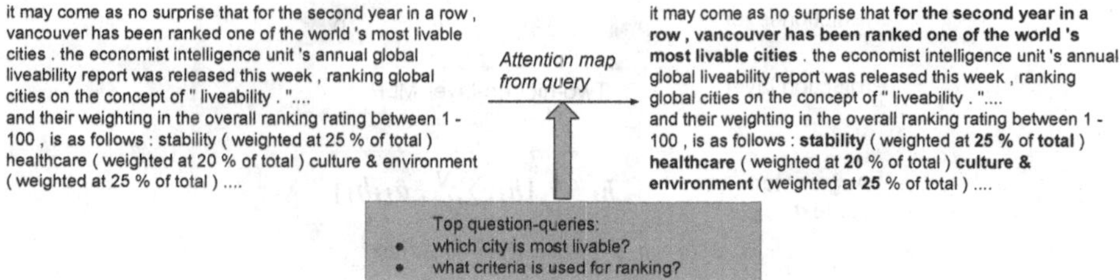

Fig. 2. Example document attention map built on a news article from its question-query clusters.

supervision data, which we can subsequently use for a learning based approach that requires a substantial amount of the training data. We describe this learning based approach next.

4 Structured Summarization via Learning

As motivated in Sect. 3.3, for structured summary to work in practice (i.e., on fresh and long tail news articles), a more general approach is to summarize the document from its content only, without using any document queries. In this section, we describe a weakly-supervised system that utilizes the training data generated in Sect. 3 to produce structured summary for documents without associated document queries.

Figure 1 shows an overview of the system. Given a news article, the system predicts the *document attention map* (i.e., important answer snippets) using a model trained from prior associations of popular news articles, their question-query clusters and corresponding answer snippets. Intuitively, this can be considered as the reverse process of answer snippet extraction as described in Sect. 3.2. The attention map specifies the attended positions (i.e., answer snippets), for which a *natural question generation* (NQG) model is then used to automatically generate questions to form the question-and-answer pairs. Finally, a *question summarizer*, which is trained using the question cluster data (Sect. 3.1), consolidates the questions and summarizes the resulting representative questions into readable format.

4.1 Document Attention Map Prediction

A document attention map model predicts which parts of a document the users are paying attention. The answer snippet extraction process (Sect. 3.2) we described earlier enables us to generate the training corpus of (document, attention map) pairs at scale. We further improve the attention map quality by being very selective on choosing the answer position—for the set of all answers A to each question cluster, an answer position p is chosen only if:

$$S(A, p) = \frac{\sum_{a_i \in A, p \in a_i} s(a_i)}{\sum_{a_j \in A} s(a_j)} > 0.5$$

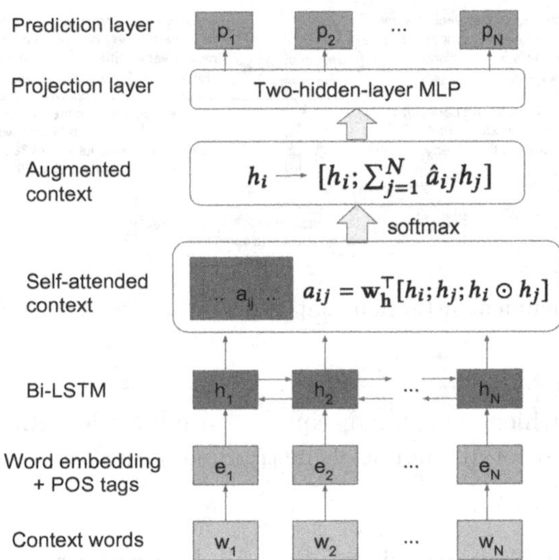

Fig. 3. Model architecture for predicting attention maps.

Intuitively, the aggregation score simulates majority voting, i.e., an answer position will be counted only if at least half of the paraphrased questions point to an answer that contains that position. Here $s(a_i)$ indicates the confidence score for answer a_i as computed by QANet [30]. Figure 2 illustrates an example document attention map.

Model. The overall architecture of the model is illustrated in Fig. 3. We take word embeddings from fastText [19] and Part-Of-Speech Tags[4] as input features to the model and use layers described below to obtain predictions for positive (attended places) and negative (unattended places) classes.

Context Layer. We place a bi-directional LSTM on top of the feature vectors, and concatenate the hidden states in both directions for each word i: $h_i = [\overrightarrow{h_i}, \overleftarrow{h_i}] \in \mathbb{R}^{2d}, i \in 1, ..., N$, where N is the total number of words in the context, and d is the dimension of the one-directional hidden state $\overrightarrow{h_i}$.

Self-attention Layer. To augment the weights of important words in a context, we use a self-attention layer to attend the context to itself. The attention weight a_{ij} between each pair of hidden state representations (h_i, h_j) is computed using: $a_{ij} = \mathbf{w}_\mathbf{h}^\top [h_i; h_j; h_i \odot h_j]$, where $h_i \odot h_j$ is the element-wise product between two vectors. $h_i, h_j, h_i \odot h_j$ are concatenated together, and $\mathbf{w}_\mathbf{h}$ is a trainable weight vector. The resulting attention matrix is denoted as $A \in \mathbb{R}^{N \times N}$. We mask the diagonal elements in A using a very large negative number (since the attention between a word and itself is not useful) and compute the softmax over the attention weights in each row, we denote the resulting matrix as $\hat{A}$. The attended-context is then given by: $\mathbf{H}_a = \hat{A}\mathbf{H}$, where $\mathbf{H} \in \mathbb{R}^{N \times 2d}$ is a matrix

[4] https://nlp.stanford.edu/software/tagger.html.

with row i being the hidden state representation h_i. We concatenate the context matrix $\mathbf{H}$ and the attended-context $\mathbf{H}_a$ as the augmented context representation $[\mathbf{H}; \mathbf{H}_a] \in \mathbb{R}^{N\times 4d}$, i.e., each hidden state representation h_i is augmented as $[h_i; \sum_{j=1}^{N} \hat{a}_{ij} h_j]$.

Output Layers. Finally, we place a two-hidden-layer feed-forward network with ReLU activations on top of the augmented context representation to get the logits $\hat{p}_i$, which is a two-dimension vector representing the prediction for negative and positive classes, respectively.

Weighted Cross-Entropy Loss. We apply a weighted cross-entropy loss function to balance positive and negative classes since attended places are usually a small fraction of the whole document context:

$$\text{loss} = -(1 - w_p) y \log(p) - w_p (1 - y) \log(1 - p),$$

where $p = \text{softmax}(\hat{p}_i)$, and w_p is automatically set based on the fraction of positive classes in the data.

4.2 Natural Question Generator

Given an answer position learned from the attention map model and the context surrounding it, we further train a sequence-to-sequence model to generate natural questions. As an example, for the answer "1724" in passage *The Old Truman Brewery, then known as the Black Eagle Brewery, was founded in* ***1724***, we can generate the following question: *When was the Black Eagle Brewery founded?* The answer position is crucial here, namely, if the answer is "The Old Truman Brewery", then the question should be *Which brewery was founded in 1724?*[5]

Training Data. We use the SQuAD [24] dataset as the training data. For each annotated passage, we generate the training pairs by first processing the passage using the PTBTokenizer[6] and obtaining the sentence segmentations. For each question-and-answer pair within the passage, we then generate (sentences, question) pairs by taking the sentence that contains the answer, the entire answer and answer_start position annotated in the dataset.

Model. The overall model architecture is described in Fig. 4. We take word embeddings, POS tags (categorical), and answer positions (binary indicator of 1 or 0) as input features to the model, for each word in the input sentences. We use the conventional encoder/decoder framework to generate the questions, where the **encoder** layer is a bi-directional LSTM similar to the context layer in the attention map model. We concatenate the hidden states in both directions as hidden-state representation $h_i^s \in \mathbb{R}^{d_s}$ for each source token i. The **decoder** layer is much more sophisticated and we describe that in details next.

[5] Note there can be multiple questions with the same answer snippet, for example, another question candidate could be: *Under which name is the Black Eagle Brewery also known?* Our learning based approach can learn those diverse questions provided that the training data captures the same diversity.

[6] https://nlp.stanford.edu/software/tokenizer.shtml.

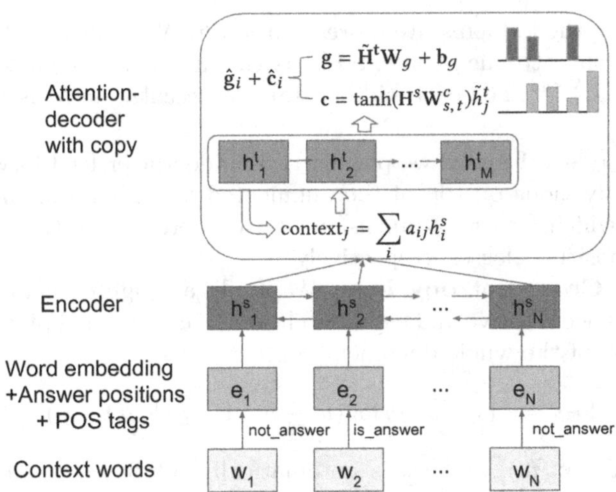

Fig. 4. Model architecture for natural question generation.

Decoder: We use an attention-based decoder [2,18] with the copy mechanism [10,25]. For a target state h^t_j, the attention weights over source hidden states h^s_i are computed by $a_{ij} = \text{softmax}(h^s_i \mathbf{W}_{s,t} h^t_j)$, where $\mathbf{W}_{s,t}$ is a trainable matrix placed between source hidden states and target hidden states. The attentional hidden state $\tilde{h}^t_j$, which is used for generating the current token given a sequence of previously generated tokens and inputs, is given by:

$$\tilde{h}^t_j = \tanh(\mathbf{W}_c[\texttt{context}_j; h^t_j]),$$

where $\mathbf{W_c}$ is a trainable matrix, and context$_j$ represents the current context for h^t_j, i.e., the attention-weighted source hidden states, $\texttt{context}_j = \sum_i a_{ij} h^s_i$.

We further project $\tilde{h}^t_j$ to a D-dimension vector $\mathbf{g}$ with D being the size of the generation vocabulary $\mathcal{G}$, the attention-decoder gives a probability distribution on the generation vocabulary:

$$\mathbf{g} = \tilde{\mathbf{H}}^\mathbf{t} \mathbf{W}_g + \mathbf{b}_g,$$

where $\tilde{\mathbf{H}}^\mathbf{t}$ is a matrix with each row being $\tilde{h}^t_j \in \mathbb{R}^{d_t}$, $\mathbf{W}_g \in \mathbb{R}^{d_t \times D}, \mathbf{b}_g \in \mathbb{R}^D$ are trainable weights in the projection layer, and d_t is the dimension of the attentional target hidden states from the decoder.

We augment the score by adding another probability distribution indicating whether a token in the target sequence should be copied from the tokens in the source sequence:

$$\mathbf{c} = \tanh(\mathbf{H}^s \mathbf{W}^c_{s,t}) \tilde{h}^t_j,$$

where $\mathbf{H}^s \in \mathbb{R}^{N \times d_s}$ is a matrix with row i being the hidden state representation h^s_i from the encoder. $\mathbf{W}^c_{s,t} \in \mathbb{R}^{d_s \times d_t}$ is again a trainable matrix as the weights for copying a source token to the current target state, and d_s, d_t are the dimension

Table 5. Dataset statistics for SQuAD and News

Dataset	# Articles	# QA pairs	# Question clusters
SQuAD	536	107,785	NA
News	91,675	3,096,289	458,375

of the hidden states from the encoder and decoder, respectively. The resulting vector $\mathbf{c} \in \mathbb{R}^N$ is a copy-score vector with each element c_i being the weight of copying source token i to the current target state $\tilde{h}^t_j$, $i \in 1,\ldots,N$ where N is the total number of words in the input context.

Finally, we extend the vocabulary to be $\mathcal{G} \cup \mathcal{C}$, where $\mathcal{C}$ denotes the copy vocabulary (i.e., all the tokens from the each input sentence). The augmented score for each token i is then given by $\hat{\mathbf{g}}_i + \hat{\mathbf{c}}_i$, where $\hat{\mathbf{g}}$ and $\hat{\mathbf{c}}$ are vectors produced by projecting $\mathbf{g}, \mathbf{c}$ to the extended vocabulary, i.e., $\hat{\mathbf{g}}_i = \mathbf{g}_i$ if token $i \in \mathcal{G}$ and $\hat{\mathbf{g}}_i = 0$ otherwise. Similarly, $\hat{\mathbf{c}}_i = \mathbf{c}_i$ if token $i \in \mathcal{C}$, and $\hat{\mathbf{c}}_i = 0$ otherwise. Note for some tokens the score will be augmented as $\mathbf{g}_i + \mathbf{c}_i$ if token i is in both vocabularies.

4.3 Question Summarizer

Intuitively, in document attention map prediction and natural question generation, the learning based approach is a reverse process to the mining based approach: instead of mapping existing questions to snippets in the articles as answers, we learn where the important answers are and generate the questions from the answers and the context they are in. The two approaches, however, share the same direction in question summarizer, both aim to consolidate the semantically equivalent questions and produce a readable summary of the questions. In the mining based approach, the summary comes from the non-question query q^* that is closest to all the question queries $\{q_1, q_2, \ldots, q_k\}$ in the question cluster C_q (Sect. 3.1). This is the process we leverage to generate training data for the learning based question summarizer at scale. Specifically, we construct each training pair as $\langle \{q_1, q_2, \ldots, q_k\}, q^* \rangle$, where $\{q_1, q_2, \ldots, q_k\}$ is the concatenation of all questions in cluster C_q, with an delimiter symbol $\langle s \rangle$.

The model architecture is similar to the sequence-to-sequence model we used for natural question generation as described in Fig. 4, where the input sequence is now multiple question queries concatenated via $\langle s \rangle$. Furthermore, augmentations that are specific to question generation are removed, e.g., answer positions. We skip the detailed model description due to lack of space. Section 5.3 will show examples of the question summarization.

5 Experiments

We conduct extensive experiments on all three components/models of the learning based approach, namely document attention map prediction, natural ques-

Table 6. Performance of document attention map prediction on the News data (test).

Method	Precision	Recall	AUC
Random	49.43	50.08	0.500
All-positive	50.00	100.00	0.500
MLP-only	57.44	67.17	0.590
+Bi-LSTM	68.94	**78.07**	0.731
+Self-attended context	**70.15**	74.22	**0.734**
Ablation experiments			
w/o pre-trained embedding	67.36	65.03	0.701
w/o POS tags	69.74	74.88	0.731

tion generation, and question summarization. Table 5 lists the characteristics of the two datasets.

SQuAD v1.1 [24]: The Stanford Question Answering Dataset is a reading comprehension dataset consisting of 107, 785 question-answer pairs posed by crowd workers on 536 Wikipedia articles. One limitation of this dataset is that the number of articles is relatively small and most of the questions posed by crowd workers are trivia questions and do not necessarily capture the important aspects presented in the article. As a result, this dataset can be used for learning natural question generation but is not very useful for learning document attention maps.

News. We collected a large set of news articles with their associated anonymized question queries from the Google search engine repository. We performed several filtering tasks: (1) removing articles that are too short (<50 words) or too long (>500 words, for efficiency consideration); (2) removing question queries that are too long (>20 words) or too infrequently issued by the users (<5 impressions); (3) for query clusters, only those have at least 3 valid question queries are considered; (4) removing articles with <5 valid query clusters. Eventually we collected 91, 675 news articles as the input to our system, paired with ~3M question-and-answer pairs and ~460K query clusters.

The two datasets vary greatly in the number of articles and average number of Q/A pairs per article. SQuAD is specifically designed for question-and-answering task and the number of pairs per article is large. As a result, the answer positions in the article are more "question-worthy" rather than *important* or *interesting* to the users. The News dataset, on the other hand, has a much smaller average number of question clusters per article (~5), most of which correspond to the most important aspects in the article since they are mined from actual user queries after proper anonymization.

5.1 Document Attention Map Prediction

We use the News dataset to evaluate the performance of our document attention map prediction model (Sect. 4.1). The evaluation data is generated as described in Sect. 4.1. In total we have 91,675 (news-article, attention-map) pairs and we split the entire dataset into 90% training (82,501), 5% development (4,587), and 5% test (4,587). The input texts are lower-cased and tokenized[7] for processing. The word embeddings are the 300-dimension vectors from fastText [19] and the vocabulary size is $134\,K$, which consists of the most frequent words in our corpus, plus an $\langle unk \rangle$ token for all unknown words. In the experiments we use a 2-layer bidirectional LSTMs with 512 hidden units, and a dropout probability of 0.2 is applied to all LSTM cells. The two hidden layers in the output layer are set to size 512, 512, respectively. A mini-batch size of 256 examples is used and during training we use the Adam optimizer [14] with a learning rate of 0.001. An exponential decay of 0.95 is also applied to the learning rate for each epoch. The hyper-parameters are chosen based on the best performance on the development set.

Results. The results on the test set are listed in Table 6. Since the class probability is imbalanced we use the *Area Under the ROC Curve* (AUC) to evaluate the proposed methods. Because the problem is really new, we design our own baseline methods. As naive baselines, Random (by randomly highlighting a word) and All-positive (by predicting positive for all positions) both achieve an AUC score around 0.5. The MLP-only method is a stronger baseline that lays a multi-layer perceptron output layer directly on top of the input feature vectors and it achieves an AUC of 0.590.

Our proposed model, with additional layers for bi-directional LSTM, self-attended context, and augmented contexts, achieves the best performance of 0.734 AUC, significantly higher than the baselines. Results from two ablation experiments demonstrate that the pre-trained embedding improves the performance substantially (AUC increases from 0.701 to 0.734) and the POS-tag feature improves the performance slightly (AUC increases from 0.731 to 0.734).

5.2 Natural Question Generation

We use the SQuAD dataset to demonstrate the performance of natural question generation (Sect. 4.2). The SQuAD dataset (which is randomly split into 90% for training, 5% for development, and 5% for test in our experimental setting)

Table 7. Performance comparison on the SQuAD dataset (test set).

Method	BLEU-4	ROUGE-L
Seq2seq with attention decoder [18]	6.87	30.42
Seq2seq + copy	8.31	32.92
Seq2seq + copy + ans_pos	11.79	38.96
Seq2seq + copy + ans_pos + POS_tags	**12.46**	**39.79**
Neural generation model from [4]	11.50	n/a

[7] https://nlp.stanford.edu/software/tokenizer.shtml.

Table 8. Example generated questions on the News dataset.

Input sentence	Generated question
PC James Dixon, **39**, who starred in Sky TV's road wars...	How old was James Dixon?
By tuesday, **it was downgraded to a post-tropical cyclone**	What happened to the cyclone?
Wilson is also a partner in a venture to bring the NBA back to Seattle	Who is a partner to bring the NBA back to Seattle?
Major tourists attractions, including the **Toronto Zoo, Ripley's aquarium of Canada, the CN Tower**...	What are some of the top attractions?

has the ground truth questions as well as the correct answer positions annotated for each passage. We employ n-gram matching score (BLEU-4 [23] and ROUGE-L [17]) as the metrics. We use beam search with beam width 10 for generating questions from the decoder. We use a generation vocabulary size of 30 K, and a copy vocabulary including all the source tokens. The combined vocabulary size is 80 K. We also experimented with different generation vocabulary sizes and the results were similar. The hidden unit sizes for the encoder and the decoder are set to 512 and 256, respectively. A dropout probability of 0.2 is applied to all LSTM cells. The training examples are sorted by input sequence length and divided into mini-batches of 128 examples each.

Results. Table 7 shows the results. The prior state-of-art model, which we adapt from the machine translation community to our problem as baseline, uses a sequence-to-sequence model with the attention decoder [18]. It achieves a BLEU-4 score of 6.83 and ROUGE-L score of 30.42. By incorporating the copy mechanism and answer positions into our model, the BLEU-4 and ROUGE-L scores can be improved significantly, reaching 11.79 and 38.96, respectively. The big improvements from adding the answer positions shows the importance of highlighting the right answers and demonstrates the value of our idea, namely using the mining-based approach to generate large scale training data for the learning-based approach. Finally, adding the POS tags leads to additional slight improvements, reaching BLEU-4 and ROUGE-L scores of 12.46 and 39.79, respectively. For completeness, we include the BLUE-4 result from [4] in the last row, even though it is focused on read comprehension, not news summary.

We do not have golden labels from the News dataset for this task. As anecdotal evidences of how well the natural question generation model works on news given predicted document attention maps, Table 8 shows some examples. In general, we observe that the topics on the News dataset are more diverse and the answer types are more open-ended. For example, there are a few "what happened" (2nd example) questions and answers with long-spans (2nd and 5th examples), compared to answers from the SQuAD dataset which are usually shorter and in most cases single entities.

5.3 Question Summarizer

We use the News dataset to evaluate the performance of question summarizer (Sect. 4.3). Similar to Sect. 5.1, we split the data into 90% training, 5% development and 5% test. As described in Sect. 4.3, the reference summaries used for evaluation come from the non-question queries that are closest to all the question queries in the question cluster.

Table 9. Performance of question summarizer on the News dataset (test set).

Method	BLEU-2	BLEU-3	BLEU-4	ROUGE-L
Seq2seq with attention decoder [18]	34.7	25.3	19.1	45.5
Seq2seq + copy + POS_tags	**41.8**	**31.5**	**24.4**	**52.3**

Results. Table 9 shows the performance of our model compared against the same state-of-art sequence-to-sequence with attention decoder model as we used in Sect. 5.2 but adapted for this task. Our proposed model improves the performance substantially through the copy mechanism, achieving BLEU-4 and ROUGE-L scores of 24.4 and 52.3, respectively. Note that for question summarizer, the output is usually much shorter than the output of natural question generator, thus both BLEU-4 and ROUGE-L scores are higher than the results in Table 7. For comparison we also attached the BLEU-2 and BLEU-3 scores in the table. Table 10 shows a few example generated summaries. By training from large amount of samples, the model is able to summarize question clusters in a more concise way, and is sometimes capable of correcting the reference summary (top non-question query), e.g., in the last example, "winner" is a better summary than "score".

Table 10. Example question summaries on the News dataset. The input to the model are all question queries in the same cluster, concatenated using the $\langle s\rangle$ symbol.

Input query cluster	Generated summary	Reference summary
How can i watch the golden knights game $\langle s\rangle$ where to watch golden knights $\langle s\rangle$ how to watch the golden knights game tonight $\langle s\rangle$	Watch golden knights game	Bars to watch golden knights
Which bishop offered to resign $\langle s\rangle$ bishops who resigned $\langle s\rangle$ bishops who resign $\langle s\rangle$ chile bishops who resigned $\langle s\rangle$	Bishops that resigned	Bishops that resigned
Who won stanley cup 2018 $\langle s\rangle$ who won the stanley cup 2018 $\langle s\rangle$	Winner of stanley cup 2018	Stanley cup 2018 score

6 Conclusion

In this paper, we propose to summarize news articles in a structured way by using question-and-answer pairs. We propose an unsupervised approach by clustering question queries of historical popular news articles, extracting answer snippets of each question query in the cluster, and consolidating the questions into readable summaries, to produce the structured summary. This mining based approach enables us to generate training corpus for a learning based approach that allows us to perform structured summarization for cases where document queries are not present or scarce (e.g., newly published or long-tail articles). We proposed three predictive models. First, a model to predict the document attention map given a news article. Second, a model to generate natural language questions given the attended positions as answer positions in the article. Finally, a question summarizer to provide readable and succinct query summary. We show that this learning based approach produces meaningful structured summaries to capture important aspects of news articles.

References

1. Angeli, G., Premkumar, M.J., Manning, C.D.: Leveraging linguistic structure for open domain information extraction. In: ACL (2015)
2. Bahdanau, D., Cho, K., Bengio, Y.: Neural machine translation by jointly learning to align and translate. In: ICLR (2015)
3. Chen, D., Fisch, A., Weston, J., Bordes, A.: Read wikipedia to answer open-domain questions. In: ACL (2017)
4. Du, X., Cardie, C.: Identifying where to focus in reading comprehension for neural question generation. In: EMNLP (2017)
5. Erkan, G., Radev, D.R.: Centroid-based summarization of multiple documents: sentence extraction, utility based evaluation, and user studies. In: NAACL-ANLP Workshop on Automatic Summarization (2000)
6. Erkan, G., Radev, D.R.: Lexrank: graph-based lexical centrality as salience in text summarization. In: JAIR (2004)
7. Fader, A., Soderland, S., Etzioni, O.: Identifying relations for open information extraction. In: EMNLP (2011)
8. Fader, A., Zettlemoyer, L., Etzioni, O.: Paraphrase-driven learning for open question answering. In: ACL (2013)
9. Feng, X., Huang, L., Tang, D., Qin, B., Ji, H., Liu, T.: A language-independent neural network for event detection. In: ACL (2016)
10. Gu, J., Lu, Z., Li, H., Li, V.O.: Incorporating copying mechanism in sequence-to-sequence learning. In: ACL (2016)
11. Höffner, K., Walter, S., Marx, E., Usbeck, R., Lehmann, J., Ngonga Ngomo, A.C.: Survey on challenges of question answering in the semantic web. Semant. Web **8**(6), 895–920 (2017)
12. Joachims, T.: Optimizing search engines using clickthrough data. In: KDD (2002)
13. Kedzie, C., Diaz, F., McKeown, K.: Real-time web scale event summarization using sequential decision making. In: IJCAI (2016)
14. Kingma, D.P., Ba, J.: Adam: a method for stochastic optimization. In: ICLR (2015)

15. Kolomiyets, O., Moens, M.F.: A survey on question answering technology from an information retrieval perspective. Inf. Sci. **181**(24), 5412–5434 (2011)
16. Koutra, D., Bennett, P.N., Horvitz, E.: Events and controversies: influences of a shocking news event on information seeking. In: WWW (2015)
17. Lin, C.Y.: Rouge: a package for automatic evaluation of summaries. In: ACL (July 2004). https://www.microsoft.com/en-us/research/publication/rouge-a-package-for-automatic-evaluation-of-summaries/
18. Luong, M.T., Pham, H., Manning, C.D.: Effective approaches to attention-based neural machine translation. In: EMNLP (2015)
19. Mikolov, T., Grave, E., Bojanowski, P., Puhrsch, C., Joulin, A.: Advances in pre-training distributed word representations. In: LREC (2018)
20. Nenkova, A., McKeown, K.: A survey of text summarization techniques. In: Mining Text Data, pp. 43–76. Springer, Boston (2012). https://doi.org/10.1007/978-1-4614-3223-4_3
21. Nguyen, D.B., Abujabal, A., Tran, K., Theobald, M., Weikum, G.: Query-driven on-the-fly knowledge base construction. In: VLDB (2017)
22. Nguyen, T.H., Cho, K., Grishman, R.: Joint event extraction via recurrent neural networks. In: NAACL (2016)
23. Papineni, K., Roukos, S., Ward, T., Zhu, W.J.: BLEU: a method for automatic evaluation of machine translation. In: ACL (2002)
24. Rajpurkar, P., Zhang, J., Lopyrev, K., Liang, P.: Squad: 100,000+ questions for machine comprehension of text. In: EMNLP (2016)
25. See, A., Liu, P., Manning, C.: Get to the point: summarization with pointer-generator networks. In: ACL (2017)
26. Seo, M., Kembhavi, A., Farhadi, A., Hajishirzi, H.: Bidirectional attention flow for machine comprehension. In: ICLR (2017)
27. Shen, C., Liu, F., Weng, F., Li, T.: A participant-based approach for event summarization using twitter streams. In: NAACL-HLT (2013)
28. Upstill, T.: The new Google news: AI meets human intelligence (2018). https://www.blog.google/products/news/new-google-news-ai-meets-human-intelligence/
29. Walker, C., Strassel, S., Medero, J., Maeda, K.: ACE 2005 multilingual training corpus (February 2006). https://catalog.ldc.upenn.edu/ldc2006t06
30. Yu, A.W., et al.: QANet: Combining local convolution with global self-attention for reading comprehension. In: ICLR (2018)
31. Zhou, Q., Yang, N., Wei, F., Tan, C., Bao, H., Zhou, M.: Neural question generation from text: a preliminary study. In: NLPCC (2017)

Product Classification Using Microdata Annotations

Ziqi Zhang[(✉)] and Monica Paramita

Information School, University of Sheffield, Sheffield, UK
{ziqi.zhang,monica.paramita}@sheffield.ac.uk

Abstract. Markup languages such as RDFa and Microdata have been widely used by e-shops to embed structured product data, as evidence has shown that they improve click-through rates for e-shops and potentially increases their sales. While e-shops often embed certain categorisation information in their product data in order to improve their products' visibility to product search and aggregator services, such site-specific product category labels are highly inconsistent and unusable across websites. This work studies the task of automatically classifying products into a universal categorisation taxonomy, using their markup data published on the Web. Using three new neural network models adapted based on previous work, we analyse the effect of different kinds of product markup data on this task, and show that: (1) despite the highly heterogeneous nature of the site-specific categories, they can be used as very effective features - even only by themselves - for the classification task; and (2) our best performing model can significantly improve state of the art on this task by up to 9.6% points in macro-average F1.

Keywords: Linked data · Product classification · Neural networks · CNN · LSTM · HAN · Machine learning

1 Introduction

Recent years have seen significant growth of semantically annotated data on the Web using markup languages such as RDFa and Microdata. Particularly in e-commerce, statistics from the WDC project[1] show that between 2017 and 2018, the number of URLs that use schema.org to embed structured product data has more than doubled; and the number of hosts has increased by over 40%.

Semantically annotated product data improve the visibility and accessibility of product information from e-shops. While different websites may sell the same products, the information about the products often differ significantly across different websites. Although product aggregator services such as Google Product Search[2] are created to integrate product information from disparate sources into a single representation, one of the first challenges they face is organising

[1] http://webdatacommons.org/structureddata/.
[2] https://www.google.com/shopping?hl=en.

C. Ghidini et al. (Eds.): ISWC 2019, LNCS 11778, pp. 716–732, 2019.
https://doi.org/10.1007/978-3-030-30793-6_41

all the products according to a universal product categorisation taxonomy. In practice, many e-shops embed category information as structured data within their web pages (to be called 'site-specific product labels'), it is known that the categorisation schemes vary dramatically across different e-shops, even if they sell the same products [11,16]

A large number of research has emerged over the years to study the very problem of product categorisation or classification on the Web [3,5,6,9,11,12,14, 19]. However, our work is different in two ways. *First*, a large number of previous work [1,3,4,7,9,11,12,14,19] looked at product classification within a single e-shop, that is assigning class labels defined by the e-shop to products listed on the same e-shop. In contrast, we explore the task in the context of product Microdata harvested from a wide range of e-shops. This is arguably more challenging as different e-shops may adopt different writing styles when publishing product information. While [16,17] also studied the task in the Microdata context, we propose new methods that obtain much better results.

Second, although it is widely recognised that site-specific product labels are hardly useful as universal categories beyond their source websites, little effort has been made to study how such heterogeneous information can assist in the task of product classification. While [16] used such information in an unsupervised approach, we carry out further studies to understand the impact of such highly heterogeneous information on supervised product classification.

Our contributions are three-fold. *First*, inspired by the deep artificial neural network (DNN) model 'DeepCN' used in product classification [7], we generalise and adapt it to three popular DNN architectures for a comparative analysis in this task: Convolutional Neural Networks (CNN), bidirectional Long-Short Term Memory (bi-LSTM), and Hierarchical Attention Network (HAN). We share our lessons of when different architectures work better than others in different settings. *Second*, we carry out in-depth analysis to understand the impact of the highly heteregenous site-specific product labels on the product classification task. This includes two methods of 'pre-processing' such labels in the hope to obtain better quality features for the task. *Third*, we empirically show a surprising insight that, despite the high level of heterogeneity in the site-specific product labels, they prove to be very useful features for the classification task, as they are more effective than traditional features widely used by previous research, as well as their 'pre-processed' versions. Compared to state of the art on the same dataset used for evaluation, our best peforming model obtains much better results with the highest improvement of 9.6% in macro-average F1.

The remainder of this paper is organised as follows. Section 2 discusses related work; Sect. 3 describes our methodology in details; Sect. 4 presents experiments, followed by a discussion of results in Sect. 5; finally Sect. 6 concludes this work.

2 Related Work

2.1 Text Classification

Text categorisation or classification aims to assign categories or classes to a given text according to its contents [2,18]. While early methods were largely based on manually crafted rules, current methods however, are predominantly based on statistical machine learning [18]. These methods involve a feature engineering process that represents each text by feature vectors (e.g., words, N-grams), followed by a training process where a machine learning algorithm is applied to instances labelled with appropriate classes to learn patterns for classification.

Many classic machine learning algorithms have been used in this task, such as Naive Bayes, Logistic Regression, Random Forest, and Support Vector Machines (SVM) [4,18]. Recent years have seen increasing interests in DNN models, due to their ability in automatic feature learning, which not only eliminates the feature engineering process, but also discovers very effective abstract features that traditional machine learning algorithms are unable to capture. Popular DNN models include, for example, CNN [8], LSTM [21], and HAN [20]. Using sentence-level classification for example, CNN scans a fixed-length consecutive sequences of words and transforms those into abstract features. It can be considered as a process of aggregating the meaning of the composing lexical sequences (e.g., phrases) in text reading. LSTM is a type of Recurrent Neural Network (RNN), and it captures long distance dependencies between words and simulates our reading of ordered words to incrementally develop a meaning for the sentence. HAN is based on the intuition that not all parts of a sentence are equally relevant for representing its meaning. Instead, certain sections (e.g., keywords) should be given more attention. Different adaptations of such models have been widely used in a range of text classification tasks, such as sentiment analysis [8,21], review classification [8,20], and question answering [8].

2.2 Product Classification

Product classification is typically treated as a text classification task, as the process involves assigning category labels (i.e., classes) to product instances based on their attributes - which we refer to as metadata - that are typically text-based (e.g., name, description, brands). Such labels usually reside in a categorisation taxonomy, therefore the task usually requires assigning multiple labels, one from each level of the taxonomy [14]. Below we summarise related work from different perspectives and highlight the similarity and difference in this research.

Metadata and Features. To classify products, features must be extracted from certain product metadata. Rich, structured metadata are often not available. Therefore, the majority of literature have only used product names, such as [1,4,9,11,19] and all of those participated in the 2018 Rakuten Data Challenge [14]. Several studies used both names and product descriptions [3,5,6,12,13], while a few also used other metadata such as model, brand, maker, etc., which need to be extracted from product web pages by an Information Extraction process [7,9,17]. In addition, [17] also used product images. The work by [16] used site-specific product labels found in product Microdata in an unsupervised approach based on the similarity between target class labels and other product metadata including site-specific product labels. While the authors argued that such heterogeneous labels may prove unusable for supervised learning, we specifically study the usage of such information in supervised setting and aim to understand if they need to be cleaned to support the classification task.

Generally speaking, for text-based metadata, there are three types of feature representation. The first is based on Bag-of-Words (BoW) or N-gram models, where texts are represented based on the presence of vocabulary in the dataset using either 1-hot encoding or some weighting scheme such as TF-IDF [1,3–5,7]. The second uses an aggregation of the word embeddings from the input text. For example, [11] averaged the embedding vectors of composing words from product titles, [12] summed them, while work in [8] joins word embedding vectors to create a 2D tensor to represent the text. The third applies a separate learning process to learn a continuous distributional representation of the text directly. This includes adaptation of the well-known Paragraph2Vec model such as in [6,12,17]. Our work represents input texts following the approach by [8].

Algorithms. The large majority of work has used supervised machine learning methods using popular algorithms mentioned before. These include those that use traditional machine learning algorithms [3–6,9,12,16,17], and those that apply DNN-based algorithms [7,14,19]. All DNN-based methods have used some adaptations of CNN or RNN. These include the majority of the participating systems in the 2018 Rakuten Data Challenge. Besides, [5,16] also explored unsupervised methods based on the similarity between the feature representations of a product and target classes. [1] studied product clustering, which does not label the resulting product groups. These represent unsupervised methods. Further, [13] also studied the problem as a machine translation task.

While the majority of literature either use a single type of metadata (typically product name) or concatenate several to merge into a single source of metadata, [7] argued to treat different types of metadata separately. The intuition can be that they may contribute different weights to the task. Thus they introduced the Deep Categorisation Network (DeepCN), which consists of i RNN models each taking text input from one of the i types of metadata. For example, using product name, description, brand and maker as product metadata, DeepCN combines 4 RNN models each applied to one of these input. Our work adapts DeepCN to generalise to three DNN structures including bi-LSTM, CNN and HAN, thus offers as a comparison of these popular DNN structures in this task.

Datasets. As mentioned before, the majority of methods are evaluated using datasets created within a single e-shop [3,5,6,9,11,12,14,19]. This typically involves classifying listed products on the e-shop using its own categorisation systems (i.e., their site-specific product labels). To the best of our knowledge, the work by [5,16,17] are the only ones that explored classification of products from multiple sources into a universal categorisation taxonomy, while [16,17] used the only dataset built on product Microdata. Furthermore, while the majority of datasets are proprietary, the only publicly available ones include that released in [14] and [16]. Among the two, [14] only contains product names (no site-specific product labels as the data were harvested from a single website), while [16] contains names, descriptions, and site-specific product labels. Our work uses the dataset by [16].

3 Methodology

We firstly describe the DNN models proposed for the task and the set of features to be used with them (Sect. 3.1). We then introduce two methods aimed at 'standardising' the heterogenous site-specific product labels. One uses clustering (Sect. 3.2), while the other is based on a set of heuristics (Sect. 3.3).

3.1 Models and Features

We propose to adapt the DNN architecture 'DeepCN' in [7]. DeepCN uses multiple RNNs each dedicated to a different type of product metadata for generating features. These then feed into fully connected layers that learn to integrate these features for the classification task. We generalise DeepCN (to be called 'GN-DeepCN') by replacing the RNNs with any kind of DNN structures. An adapted model is illustrated in Fig. 1.

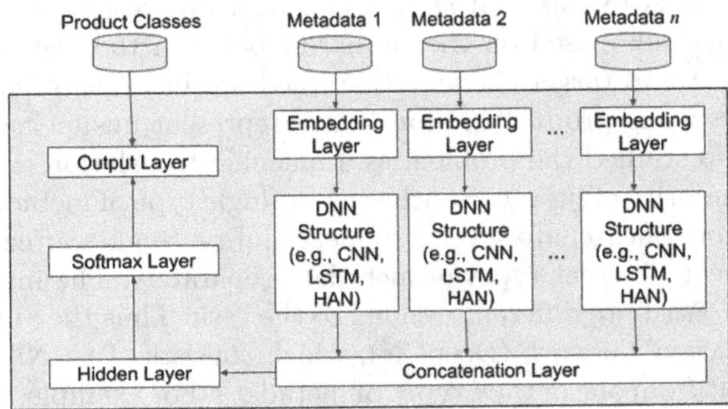

Fig. 1. Architecture of the proposed GN-DeepCN.

Adaptations. We introduce three adaptations to the original model. First, the authors used 1-hot encoding to represent each type of input metadata. We instead use the approach by [8] to use an embedding layer to represent input text as a 2D-tensor in the shape of $[words, dimensions]$, where *words* is the number of tokens expected in the input text and will depend on the type of metadata (see below in 'Features'); and *dimensions* is the dimension of the continuous vector representation of each word. In this work, we use the GloVe word embedding vectors pre-trained on the Common Crawl corpus[3] with 300 dimensions. Since we are dealing with content from e-commerce web pages, we consider GloVe vectors a better option than, e.g., Word2Vec that is trained on news corpora.

Second, for the internal DNN structure, the authors used a stack of two RNN layers to process each type of input metadata. We propose to compare three popular architecture in text classification, including bi-LSTM, CNN and HAN. We detail their parameter settings below.

Third, the original model consists of two hidden layers, one stacked on another. We use only one as the authors showed in their results that the contribution of an additional hidden layer to learning accuracy was rather insignificant. The hidden layer has 600 neurons, same as the best performing setting in [7].

DNN Structures. For the bi-LSTM structure, we use a single bi-directional LSTM layer with 100 neurons. For the CNN structure, we concatenate three convolutional layers each of which has 100 filters and uses a window size of 2, 3, and 4 respectively. Their concatenated output is then pooled by a max pooling layer with a pool size of 4. For the HAN architecture, we adapt the model by [20]. The original work has a two-level attention mechanism that simulates attention to particular sentences within a document, and then particular words within sentences. We simplify this structure to a one-level attention network that only encodes word-level attention. This is because product metadata are usually short-text. All other implementations remain the same as [20].

Features. We use three types of product metadata that are more available than the rest in the product Microdata, these include product name, description, and site-specific product labels. When product labels are not available, we use the breadcrumbs instead (if available). Breadcrumbs records the navigational path of the current web page, and in the context of e-shops, may indicate the site-specific category path. Texts of these metadata are then normalised by lowercasing, removal of non-alphanumeric characters, and lemmatisation. They are then passed into the internal DNN branches for feature extraction. We constrain product name or labels to a maximum of 20 words and product description to 100 words, truncating longer texts and pad shorter texts with zeros.

In order to study the impact of different metadata on the classification task, we evaluate different combinations of input metadata. Therefore, in some settings, the model may not take all three input metadata. In particular, we test each type of input metadata separately (i.e., using only name, description or site-specific product label). To the best of our knowledge, all previous work have used either name alone, or some combinations of name and other metadata. No work has studied how the highly heterogenous site-specific product labels alone can be used in the product classification task.

Also, for site-specific product labels, we test three different ways of using them in order to study the impact of the heterogeneity in the metadata. These include: (1) using the normalised labels as-is (to be referred to as the 'original' site-specific product labels); (2) clustering normalised labels and then using the cluster membership associated with a product's label as feature (Sect. 3.2, to

[3] http://nlp.stanford.edu/data/glove.840B.300d.zip.

be referred to as 'product label clusters'); and (3) 'standardised' labels by a 'cleaning' processs that aims to reduce the level of heterogeneity (Sect. 3.3, to be referred to as 'cleaned product labels').

Parameter Optimisation. We use the categorical cross entropy loss function and the Adam optimiser to train all models with an epoch of 20 using a batch size of 100. The categorical cross entropy loss function is empirically found to be more effective on classification tasks than other loss functions [15]. The Adam optimiser is designed to improve the classic stochastic gradient descent (SGD) optimiser and in theory combines the advantages of two other common extensions of SGD (AdaGrad and RMSProp) [10].

3.2 Clustering Site-Specific Product Labels

While different e-shops may categorise their products using different labels, we expect their labels to be semantically similar for products that belong to the same categories. For example, given '`USA Curling > USA Curling Sweatshirts & Fleece`' from an e-shop and '`Apparel & Accessories > Clothing > Shirts & Tops > T-Shirts`', from another, we can anticipate both products to belong to the category of 'clothing', or 'top clothing'. While this category may not match those in the gold standard per se, they may be useful features for classification.

To capture this information, we propose to apply clustering to split all unique site-specific product labels in a dataset into groups. Thus given a set of unique site-specific product labels, we firstly represent each product label as a fixed-length feature vector. To do so, we treat each label as a document and calculate the TF-IDF weights of its composing words. Next, given a product label, we find the pre-trained GloVe embedding vectors of its composing words. Then we represent each product label as the TF-IDF weighted sum of its composing word embedding vectors. A similar approach is used in [11] with product descriptions.

Finally, we apply agglomerative clustering to the feature vectors of product labels to split them into k groups (settings of k to be detailed in Sect. 4). Each product is then assigned a cluster number associated with its site-specific product label. This cluster number is used as a feature for product classification.

3.3 Cleaning Site-Specific Product Labels

As discussed before, site-specific product labels vary widely as e-shops adopt categorisation systems that use different vocabulary and granularity. For example, some items may be categorised based on their types (e.g., '`Audio & Video > Cables & Adapters`'), while others (e.g., clothing items) can be categorised based on the brands they represent (e.g., '`NFL > New Orleans Saints > New Orleans Saints Sweatshirts & Fleece`'), or by their prices (e.g., '`Dallas Mavericks > Dallas Mavericks Ladies > less than $10`'). Some of these labels are not informative of the types of products and we expect them to be unuseful in the product classification task. Therefore, we propose to clean site-specific product labels to reduce the level of heterogeneity.

Table 1. Different separators between category levels

<table>
<tr><th>Example of categories/breadcrumbs</th><th>Separators</th></tr>
<tr><td><code>Hardware > hardware accessories > cabinet hardware > ...</code></td><td><code>></code></td></tr>
<tr><td><code>Clothing, dresses, sale, the LBD, clothing, mini dress</code></td><td>,</td></tr>
<tr><td><code>Beeswax products|beeswax polish</code></td><td>|</td></tr>
<tr><td><code>Combination\|acne-prone\|sensitive\|normal\ |clinicians\|...</code></td><td>\|</td></tr>
<tr><td><code>Home hunting wildlife feed & feeders deer feeders ...</code></td><td><code>[multi-spaces]</code></td></tr>
<tr><td><code>Women/clothing/leggings</code></td><td>/</td></tr>
<tr><td><code>Home/gear/accessories/books/videos/stickers/ books</code></td><td><code>[space]/[space]</code></td></tr>
<tr><td><code>Toe rings >> double toe rings</code></td><td><code>>></code></td></tr>
<tr><td colspan="2">Note: This is not an exhaustive list of possible separators.</td></tr>
</table>

We firstly pre-process the site-specific product labels by normalising the different separators that are used in the category/breadcrumbs values across different sites (shown in Table 1) by replacing them with '`>`'[4]. We refer to each segment separated by '`>`' a product label at a different level. We also filter out meaningless category values by regular expression (e.g., blank nodes such as '`node35ea8dc879ed1d78...`' and URIs). Next, we follow the steps below to further clean the labels:

1. Divide the label values using the '`>`' to result in different levels.
2. If the top (parent) level label is written in all capital letters, remove it. This is because the top level labels written as uppercase are rare (about 4% in our experimental dataset) and are often generic (e.g., '`HOME`') or non-product related (e.g., '`NBA`', '`NFL`'). As an example: '~~`NFL`~~ `> Carolina Panthers > Carolina Panthers Shoes & Socks > Carolina Panthers Shoes & Socks Ladies > $20 to $40`'.
3. If the parent label exists as part of sub-level labels, remove the parent label from all these levels. E.g., '~~`Carolina Panthers`~~ `>` ~~`Carolina Panthers`~~ `Shoes & Socks >` ~~`Carolina Panthers`~~ `Shoes & Socks Ladies > $20 to $40`'.
4. Remove labels that include the word 'Sale', 'Deals' or contain prices, using regular expression. E.g., '`Shoes & Socks > Shoes & Socks Ladies >` ~~`$20 to $40`~~'.

[4] This separator is chosen as it is the most commonly used in the dataset (described in Sect. 4).

5. For the remaining labels at each level, compute their TF-IDF scores and keep only the one with the highest TF-IDF score (i.e., 'cleaned product labels'). The idea is to find the most specific label that's likely to be relevant. Specifically, we group the original, uncleaned labels by their source websites, then treat each label as a document. Next we calculate the TF-IDF scores of words from these 'documents' within the context of each website. The TF-IDF score of the remaining labels at each level is the average TF-IDF score of their composing words. E.g., as a result of this process, we may obtain '~~`Shoes & Socks`~~ `> Shoes & Socks Ladies`'.

4 Experiment

4.1 Dataset

Currently, the only publicly available product classification dataset containing site-specific product labels and based on Microdata is that created by [16]. The dataset[5] contains 8,361 product instances randomly sampled from 702 hosts. It is annotated using the GS1 Global Product Classification system[6]. Categories from the top three levels of the classification taxonomy are used to label each product instance. We refer to these annotations as level 1, 2, and 3 GS1 annotations. The number of target classes for level 1, 2, and 3 are 37, 76, and 289. The distribution of instances over these classes are largely imbalanced. For example, the largest class all three levels has over 3,000 instances; and in extreme cases, some small classes have only a handful of instances.

As mentioned before, we use three types of product metadata found in the dataset, including name (`sg`[7]`:Product/name`), description (`sg:Product/descri-ption`), and original site-specific product labels (`sg:Product/category`). When product labels are not available, we use the breadcrumbs instead (`sg:breadcrumb`). Overall, all instances have name, 8,072 instances have description, 7,181 instances have site-specific label, and 1,200 instances have breadcrumbs. When both site-specific product labels and breadcrumbs are considered, there are in total 4,111 (or 2,866 after lemmatisation, which is also used to standardise input text to all models) unique values distributed over all instances, indicating the extreme high level of heterogeneity in the categorisation systems used by different websites.

4.2 Model Variants

To compare the contribution of different product metadata on this task, particularly the impact of the highly heterogenous site-specific product labels, we create models that use different combination of product metadata as input.

[5] http://webdatacommons.org/structureddata/2014-12/products/data/goldstandard_eng_v1.csv.
[6] https://www.gs1.org/standards/gpc.
[7] sg: http://schema.org/.

Let ***n***, ***d***, ***c*** denote product name, description and original site-specific labels respectively, we firstly test our models using each of these input metadata only. We then use combined inputs of ***n+c***, ***n+d***, and ***n+d+c***[8]. Further, we replace the original site-specific labels with cleaned product labels (*c.clean*) and product label clusters (*c.cluster*) respectively, to create ***n+c.clean***, ***n+c.cluster***, ***n+d+c.clean*** and ***n+d+c.cluster***. We experiment with a range of cluster numbers including $k \in \{25, 50, 100, 200\}$.

Each type of the input metadata combination is then used on each of the three GN-DeepCN networks described before. As an example, we use $\mathbf{CNN_{n+c}}$ to denote the CNN version of our GN-DeepCN network using product names and original site-specific labels as input. All models are evaluated in a 10-fold cross validation experiment. We measure classification accuracy (Acc), precision (P), recall (R), and F1. For P, R, and F1, we compute micro-average, macro-average, as well as weighted macro-average. Our results are fully reproducible as our datasets and code (implemented in Python) are shared online[9].

4.3 Methods for Comparison

We compare our methods against those reported in [16] and [17], both of which used the same datasets. [16] used an unsupervised approach based on similarities between the target categories and product metadata. Their best performing model uses the combination of product name, description, site-specific product label and/or breadcrumbs, as well as distributional statistics computed using an external corpus. Results are reported in classification accuracy, macro-average precision and F1.

[17] evaluated a large number of different methods. In terms of machine learning algorithms, they used SVM, Naive Bayes (NB), Random Forest (RF) and K-Nearest Neighbour (KNN). Each of these models are then used with several different types of features. These include: (1) a TF-IDF weighted Bag-of-Words representation of the concatenated product names and description (*bow*); (2) product attribute-value pairs extracted from their name and descriptions using a separate Information Extraction process (*dict* as these can be consider a 'dictionary' of product attributes); (3) product embedding vectors trained using the Paragraph2Vec model applied to the concatenated product names and descriptions (*Par2Vec*); (4) two variants of product image vectors (*ImgEmb* and *ImageNet*); and (5) the concatenated vectors of Par2Vec and ImageNet. Results are reported in classification accuracy, macro-average precision, recall

[8] The literature has mostly used name + other features, which we also do in this work. Also, as we shall show in the results, among *n*, *d*, and *c* alone, *d* generally performs the worst. So we do not report results based on description + other features.

[9] https://github.com/ziqizhang/wop.

and F1[10]. For each GS1 level of annotation, we only compare against the best result obtained from all of their models.

5 Results and Discussion

We firstly present our results in Sect. 5.1 and show (1) surprisingly, the original site-specific product labels can be very effective for the classification task, while the 'processed' features based on cleaning or clustering are not; (2) when different GN-DeepCN architectures perform better depending on availability of metadata; (3) our proposed methods outperforms state of the art significantly. We then present our analyses to understand the product label clustering and cleaning quality and why they did not help the task (Sects. 5.2 and 5.3).

5.1 Detailed Results

Due to space limitations, in Tables 2 and 3 we only show our results in macro-average F1 and classification accuracy, as they are used in [16,17]. Further, for our experiments on product label clusters, we only include the best results obtained with $k = 50$. The full results however, can be found online[11]. We ran statistical significance test on every pair of configurations using the K-fold cross-validated paired t-test, and we are able to confirm that the results obtained by different configurations are statistically significant.

Table 2. Macro-average F1 of the proposed model variants. The best result on each level are highlighted in **bold**.

Input metadata	Lvl.1			Lvl.2			Lvl.3		
	bi-LSTM	CNN	HAN	bi-LSTM	CNN	HAN	bi-LSTM	CNN	HAN
n	53.3	54.3	53.2	41.9	40.7	40.9	28.1	27.2	28.5
c	57.6	59.3	56.6	42.4	43.0	43.2	27.1	27.9	28.5
d	52.4	51.0	51.5	39.6	38.4	38.4	25.3	23.3	24.7
n+c	65.7	66.3	64.9	50.8	52.3	51.2	34.8	35.1	34.8
n+d	61.8	61.1	59.5	48.9	48.0	45.2	30.8	29.2	31.1
n+d+c	**67.4**	67.3	65.4	**52.9**	51.2	51.4	35.2	33.5	**35.4**
n+c.clean	61.9	61.7	59.5	50.0	49.2	47.8	32.4	33.7	33.3
n+d+c.clean	66.4	64.4	64.3	53.7	50.2	50.7	34.4	31.9	34.5
n+c.cluster = 50	54.1	53.6	52.6	41.0	41.9	39.8	26.9	27.5	28.6
n+d+c.cluster = 50	61.7	60.7	59.8	46.7	46.4	46.7	30.8	29.0	32.2

[10] This is an assumption based on our observation, as we have been unable to confirm this with the authors despite our efforts. However, we assume this is the truth as our macro-average results are the closest, while our micro-and weighted macro-average results are significantly higher (in the range between 70 and 90).

[11] https://github.com/ziqizhang/wop/tree/master/iswc2019_results.

Table 3. Classification accuracy of the proposed model variants. The best results on each level are highlighted in **bold**.

Input metadata	Lvl.1			Lvl.2			Lvl.3		
	bi-LSTM	CNN	HAN	bi-LSTM	CNN	HAN	bi-LSTM	CNN	HAN
n	80.6	81.6	81.3	79.4	80.0	79.5	72.7	73.2	72.6
c	80.7	80.9	79.9	79.3	79.0	78.5	70.0	68.5	69.1
d	80.4	79.8	79.7	79.0	77.9	77.9	70.0	68.7	70.0
n+c	87.3	88.0	87.2	85.7	86.4	85.8	78.9	79.9	78.8
n+d	85.4	85.7	85.3	84.0	84.0	83.5	76.6	76.5	76.4
n+d+c	**89.0**	88.6	88.0	**86.8**	86.6	86.6	**80.3**	79.5	79.6
n+c.*clean*	85.6	86.2	85.5	84.8	84.7	84.1	77.1	78.1	77.8
n+d+c.*clean*	87.8	87.5	87.3	86.7	85.9	85.9	79.2	78.2	79.0
n+c.*cluster* = *50*	81.1	81.4	81.1	79.5	80.4	79.7	72.6	73.6	73.1
n+d+c.*cluster* = *50*	85.9	85.3	85.2	83.3	84.0	84.0	76.9	76.1	76.7

Effect of Different Product Metadata. Looking at each of three kinds of metadata lone, Table 2 upper section shows that we obtain the best F1 using the original site-specific product labels c, regardless of the DNN models or categorisation levels. In many cases, the difference from model variants that use only n or d is quite significant (e.g., CNN_c outperforms CNN_n by 5% points at Lvl. 1). It is also worth to note that product descriptions d appear to be the least useful metadata. This is rather surprising as no previous work has considered using site-specific product labels alone in this task, but has all exclusively focused on product names and descriptions. Yet we show c to be the most useful for this task, despite the high level of heterogeneity in the metadata.

Again inspecting the three kinds of metadata separately, Table 3 upper section shows that generally n contributes to the best classification accuracy. However, the difference from c or d alone is rather small.

For both F1 and accuracy, we can see that c can consistently improve performance when it is combined with any other metadata (e.g., $n + c$ against n), regardless of model variants or categorisation levels. The improvements are in many cases, quite significant. For example, HAN_{n+c} improves HAN_n by 10.3 points in F1 at Lvl. 2; CNN_{n+c} improves CNN_n by 7.4 points in accuracy at Lvl. 1. The majority of DNN models achieved their best results with $n + d + c$ (except CNN which works better more often with n+c instead), but also achieved comparable results with $n + c$ only. This is a useful finding, as n and c are much shorter than d and therefore, models using them as input can be more efficient.

Effect of Different GN-DeepCN Structures. Overall, the best F1 and accuracy scores are obtained by bi-LSTM in 5/6 cases, with the sixth case (i.e., F1 on $n + d + c$ at Lvl.3) being an extreme close-call. There is also a notable tendency for bi-LSTM to work better than CNN or HAN (in terms of either F1 or accuracy) when d is included in the input metadata. This could be because bi-LSTM captures more useful dependency information when long text input is used. Therefore, when product description is available, it may be beneficial to use recurrent network based models. Otherwise, CNN or HAN may suffice.

Effect of Pre-processing Site-Specific Product Labels. Neither product label clusters or cleaned labels help with the task, as shown in the lower sections of both Tables 2 and 3. In fact, when compared against the corresponding model variants using the original site-specific product labels (e.g. bi-LSTM$_{n+c.clean}$ v.s. bi-LSTM$_{n+c}$), the cleaned labels damage performance slightly, while the clusters harm performance quite signficantly. This may suggest that the original site-specific product labels could have provided useful contextual information which the supervised models have managed to capture. Either cleaning or clustering will cause this information to be lost instead. We carry out further analysis on this and discuss them in Sects. 5.2 and 5.3.

Comparison Against State of the Art. In Table 4 we compare our results obtained using the following input metadata against those reported in [16,17]: $n+c$ as this is more efficient than using d and led to very competitive results; $n+d$ which is used in [17]; and $n+d+c$ which is used in [16]. Overall, in terms of F1, our methods perform much better at Lvl.2 and Lvl.3, which are arguably more difficult because of the increasing sparsity in data. Using F1 as example, at Lvl.2, our best F1 is 9.6 points higher than the best state of the art result [17] when using $n+d+c$ with the bi-LSTM model (i.e., Lvl.2 in Table 4, 52.9 v.s. 43.3), or 5.6 points (i.e., 48.9 v.s. 43.3) higher when using the same $n+d$ input metadata as [17]. Correspondingly at Lvl.3, the highest F1 improvements are 8.5 and 4.2 (by HAN). Notice that the results cited from [17] at Lvl.2 and 3 are based on a model that uses both text and image inputs. Our models use only texts, but prove to be more effective. Our best F1 at Lvl.1 is comparable to that in [17], which however, requires a separate Information Extraction process to pre-process the data. Again it is worth to mention that our more efficient models variants using only $n+c$ have achieved very competitive results (better than our $n+d$ variants), which are much better than state of the art at Lvl.2 and 3, in both accuracy and F1.

Table 4. Comparison against results reported in the state of the art. The highest accuracy and macro-average F1 on each level are highlighted in **bold**. 1 - best results were obtained by their SVM model with *dict* features; 2 - best results were obtained by their KNN model with *Par2vec+ImageNet* features. Recall is not reported in [16]

	Lvl.1				Lvl.2				Lvl.3			
	Acc.	P	R	F1	Acc.	P	R	F1	Acc.	P	R	F1
bi-LSTM$_{n+c}$	87.3	67.0	64.8	65.7	85.7	52.5	49.8	50.8	78.9	36.2	34.7	34.8
CNN$_{n+c}$	88.0	69.4	64.1	66.3	86.4	54.7	51.1	52.3	79.9	36.8	34.9	35.1
HAN$_{n+c}$	87.2	67.8	63.0	64.9	85.8	52.2	50.9	51.2	78.8	36.3	34.6	34.8
bi-LSTM$_{n+d}$	85.4	64.2	60.3	61.8	84.0	51.1	48.1	48.9	76.6	32.1	30.8	30.8
CNN$_{n+d}$	85.7	65.8	58.5	61.1	84.0	53.0	46.1	48.0	76.5	30.6	29.1	29.2
HAN$_{n+d}$	85.3	60.5	58.7	59.5	83.5	47.3	44.7	45.2	76.4	32.7	31.0	31.1
bi-LSTM$_{n+d+c}$	**89.0**	70.4	65.8	67.4	**86.8**	54.4	52.3	**52.9**	**80.3**	36.5	35.2	35.2
CNN$_{n+d+c}$	88.6	70.4	65.1	67.3	86.6	54.8	49.6	51.2	79.5	35.8	33.0	33.5
HAN$_{n+d+c}$	88.0	66.2	64.9	65.4	86.6	53.1	50.3	51.4	79.6	36.4	35.7	**35.4**
[17], using n+d	88.3[1]	74.1	64.8	**69.1**	83.8[2]	43.9	42.8	43.3	77.8[2]	26.6	27.2	26.9
[16], using n+d+c	47.9	49.9	-	48.9	38.0	39.5	-	38.7	25.8	26.9	-	26.3

5.2 Analysis of Product Label Clusters

We undertake further analysis to investigate why clustering did not work. Essentially, we would like an ideal clustering algorithm to place as many instances belonging to the same category as possible within the same cluster, and not include instances of too many different categories. We refer to such an ideal cluster as a 'high purity cluster'. Thus using the 50 clusters created before as example, for each cluster, we map its instances to their category labels at each of the three levels in the gold standard, and count the number of unique labels within each cluster. Figure 2 ranks these clusters by the number of unique labels for the three levels. Apparently, clustering generated too many clusters (over 50%) of very low purity (over 10 different labels) at all levels. As a result, it does not create useful features for classification, but loses contextual information that can be otherwise useful to the classifiers.

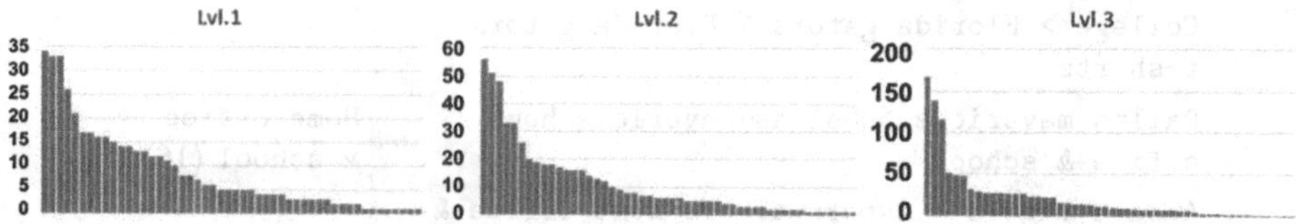

Fig. 2. Distribution of gold standard labels across each cluster (cluster number = 50) for the three classification levels. y-axis: number of unique gold standard labels. Each bar represents a separate cluster.

5.3 Analysis of Cleaned Product Labels

The cleaning process described before reduced the number of unique site-specific product labels from 4,111 to 2,394. Some examples of the different labels that were merged are shown in Table 5 (the number of different labels merged into the particular cleaned label is shown in the brackets). Although this process was shown to produce less heterogenous category labels, the cleaned labels were not shown to help with the product classification task. This might be due to a few reasons.

First, different websites may have used different names to refer to the same categories that our cleaning process failed to capture, e.g., `'Lawn & Garden'`, `'Lawn & Patio'` and `'Lawn Ornaments'`. Second, similar items (e.g., a ladies' jacket) may be assigned labels of different granularities across different sites (e.g., '`Ladies`', '`Jackets`' or '`Ladies Jackets and Coats`'). Since they do not necessarily contain lexical overlap, further method is therefore required to identify that these labels are related. Third, whilst a manual inspection seems to suggest that the cleaning process worked well with clothing items (e.g., in Table 5), in many other cases, this resulted in producing labels that are rather too specific, or less relevant. For example:

Table 5. Category cleaning results

Site-specific product labels	
Original	Cleaned
`NHL > New York rangers > New York rangers mens`	Mens (126)
`College > Boston college eagles > Boston college eagles mens`	
`San Jose sabercats > San Jose sabercats mens > sale items > $10 to $20`	
`Chicago bulls > Chicago bulls mens > $20 to $40`	
`ACC gear > ACC gear t-shirts`	`T-shirts` (114)
`Duke blue devils > duke blue devils t-shirts`	
`College > Florida gators > Florida gators t-shirts`	
`Dallas mavericks > Dallas mavericks home office & school`	`Home office & school` (16)
`Auburn tigers > Auburn tigers home office & school > $40 to $60`	
`NFL > Tampa bay buccaneers > Tampa bay buccaneers home office & school > NFL accessories`	

1. '`Hardware > Tools > Carving Tools > Chisels`' was cleaned into '`Chisels`'
2. '`Home > Ammunition > Pistol > Rifle Ammo > Shop Centerfire Ammo by Caliber > 5 mm - 7 mm > 6.5 X 55 SWEDISH`' was cleaned into '`6.5 X 55 SWEDISH`'
3. '`Electronics > Audio > Car` was cleaned into '`Car`'

These examples also confirmed our thoughts that the cleaning process might have caused useful contextual information from higher level labels to be lost (e.g., example 1 and 2). And it has been very challenging to identify the level of labels potentially most appropriate for classification. In certain cases, it may be beneficial to keep labels from more than one levels (e.g., example 1). We also found that 2,146 cleaned labels (89.64%) only contained one product each, which indicates that the cleaning process does not efficiently reduce the number of unique labels for most products in the dataset. One way to address this is to discard step 5 from the cleaning process, or revise it to allow multiple levels of labels to be selected (e.g., based on the ranked TF-IDF score). We will investigate this in the future.

To summarise, our current cleaning method might help with reducing the heterogeneity in the different categorisation systems used by some websites, but does not appear to be generalisable. Especially with websites that use very specific categorisation systems (which may be indicated by a larger number of levels of labels), it may produce labels too specific to be useful for classification. More work needs to be done to study if and how we can better clean the labels into an appropriate level of specificity. For example, can we use external knowledge resources (e.g., WordNet) to determine the relative level of specificity of labels at different levels? Could the target classification taxonomy be used to 'guide' the cleaning in an unsupervised way (e.g., by measuring similarity between elements in the taxonomy and labels at different levels)? If so, can and how can this information improve the cleaning process to be useful for product classification?

6 Conclusion and Future Work

This work studied product classification using product linked data on the Web. In particular, we investigated the effect of different kinds of product metadata on the classification performance. We showed that, although site-specific categorisation labels are highly inconsistent across different e-shops and therefore, cannot be directly used as product categories beyond the e-shops themselves, they can be very effective features when used for automated product classification tasks; even more so than other metadata widely used in the previous methods. By comparing three popular DNN architectures for classification tasks, we showed that when long product descriptions are available, RNN-based architectures work better; otherwise, CNN-or HAN-based architectures are more effective. Our new DNN architectures also significantly outperformed state of art on the same datasets. As future work, we will explore other strategies for cleaning the site-specific labels and their effect on the product classification task. In addition, we will also investigate two directions. First, site-specific product labels are not always available in the product linked data. Therefore, we will investigate if it is possible to generate 'fuzzy' labels based on product names or descriptions when they are absent. Second, we will look into research on mining product taxonomy from such highly heterogenous site-specific labels.

References

1. Akritidis, L., Fevgas, A., Bozanis, P.: Effective unsupervised matching of product titles with k-combinations and permutations. In: IEEE 30th International Conference on Tools with Artificial Intelligence, pp. 213–220 (2018)
2. Altınel, B., CanGaniz, M.: Semantic text classification: a survey of past and recent advances. Inf. Process. Manag. **54**(6), 1129–1153 (2018)
3. Cevahir, A., Murakami, K.: Large-scale multi-class and hierarchical product categorization for an e-commerce giant. In: Proceedings of the 26th International Conference on Computational Linguistics (COLING): Technical Papers, pp. 525–535. The COLING 2016 Organizing Committee (2016)
4. Chavaltada, C., Pasupa, K., Hardoon, D.R.: A comparative study of machine learning techniques for automatic product categorisation. In: Cong, F., Leung, A., Wei, Q. (eds.) ISNN 2017. LNCS, vol. 10261, pp. 10–17. Springer, Cham (2017). https://doi.org/10.1007/978-3-319-59072-1_2

5. Ding, Y., et al.: Automated classification of product data in e-commerce. In: Proceedings of the Business Information Systems Conference (2002)
6. Gupta, V., Karnick, H., Bansal, A., Jhala, P.: Product classification in e-commerce using distributional semantics. In: Proceedings of COLING 2016: Technical Papers, pp. 536–546. The COLING 2016 Organizing Committee (2016)
7. Ha, J.W., Pyo, H., Kim, J.: Large-scale item categorization in e-commerce using multiple recurrent neural networks. In: Proceedings of the International Conference on Knowledge Discovery and Data Mining (KDD), pp. 107–115. ACM (2016)
8. Kim, Y.: Convolutional neural networks for sentence classification. In: Proceedings of the Conference on Empirical Methods in Natural Language Processing (EMNLP), pp. 1746–1751. Association for Computational Linguistics (ACL) (2014)
9. Kim, Y., Lee, T., Chun, J., Lee, S.: Modified Naïve Bayes classifier for e-catalog classification. In: Lee, J., Shim, J., Lee, S., Bussler, C., Shim, S. (eds.) DEECS 2006. LNCS, vol. 4055, pp. 246–257. Springer, Heidelberg (2006). https://doi.org/10.1007/11780397_20
10. Kingma, D.P., Ba, J.: Adam: a method for stochastic optimization. In: Proceedings of the 3rd International Conference for Learning Representations (2015)
11. Kozareva, Z.: Everyone likes shopping! multi-class product categorization for e-commerce. In: Proceedings of the Conference of the North American Chapter of the Association for Computational Linguistics: Human Language Technologies (NAACL), pp. 1329–1333. ACL (2015)
12. Lee, H., Yoon, Y.: Engineering doc2vec for automatic classification of product descriptions on O2O applications. Electron. Commer. Res. **18**(3), 433–456 (2018)
13. Li, M.Y., Kok, S., Tan, L.: Don't classify, translate: multi-level e-commerce product categorization via machine translation. CoRR. http://arxiv.org/abs/1812.05774
14. Lin, Y.C., Das, P., Datta, A.: Overview of the SIGIR 2018 eCom Rakuten data challenge. In: eCom Data Challenge at SIGIR 2018. ACM (2018)
15. McCaffrey, J.D.: Why you should use cross-entropy error instead of classification error or mean squared error for neural network classifier training. https://jamesmccaffrey.wordpress.com. Accessed Jan 2018
16. Meusel, R., Primpeli, A., Meilicke, C., Paulheim, H., Bizer, C.: Exploiting microdata annotations to consistently categorize product offers at web scale. In: Stuckenschmidt, H., Jannach, D. (eds.) EC-Web 2015. LNBIP, vol. 239, pp. 83–99. Springer, Cham (2015). https://doi.org/10.1007/978-3-319-27729-5_7
17. Ristoski, P., Petrovski, P., Mika, P., Paulheim, H.: A machine learning approach for product matching and categorization. Seman. Web **9**(5), 707–728 (2018)
18. Sebastiani, F.: Machine learning in automated text categorization. ACM Comput. Surv. **34**(1), 1–47 (2002)
19. Xia, Y., Levine, A., Das, P., Di Fabbrizio, G., Shinzato, K., Datta, A.: Large-scale categorization of Japanese product titles using neural attention models. In: Proceedings of the 15th Conference of the European Chapter of the Association for Computational Linguistics (EACL), vol. 2, Short Papers, pp. 663–668. Association for Computational Linguistics (2017)
20. Yang, Z., Yang, D., Dyer, C., He, X., Smola, A., Hovy, E.: Hierarchical attention networks for document classification. In: Proceedings of NAACL 2016, pp. 1480–1489. Association for Computational Linguistics (2016)
21. Zhou, P., Qi, Z., Zheng, S., Xu, J., Bao, H., Xu, B.: Text classification improved by integrating bidirectional LSTM with two-dimensional max pooling. In: Proceedings of the 26th International Conference on Computational Linguistics: Technical Papers, pp. 3485–3495. The COLING 2016 Organizing Committee (2016)

Truthful Mechanisms for Multi Agent Self-interested Correspondence Selection

Nan Zhi[1], Terry R. Payne[1(✉)], Piotr Krysta[1], and Minming Li[2]

[1] The University of Liverpool, Liverpool, UK
{N.Zhi,T.R.Payne,P.Krysta}@liverpool.ac.uk
[2] City University of Hong Kong, Kowloon Tong, China
minming.li@cityu.edu.hk

Abstract. In the distributed ontology alignment construction problem, two agents agree upon a meaningful subset of correspondences that map between their respective ontologies. However, an agent may be tempted to manipulate the negotiation in favour of a preferred alignment by misrepresenting the weight or confidence of the exchanged correspondences. Therefore such an agreement can only be meaningful if the agents can be incentivised to be honest when revealing information. We examine this problem and model it as a novel mechanism design problem on an edge-weighted bipartite graph, where each side of the graph represents each agent's private entities, and where each agent maintains a private set of valuations associated with its candidate correspondences. The objective is to find a matching (i.e. injective or one-to-one correspondences) that maximises the agents' social welfare. We study implementations in dominant strategies, and show that they should be solved optimally if truthful mechanisms are required. A decentralised version of the greedy allocation algorithm is then studied with a first-price payment rule, proving tight bounds on the Price of Anarchy and Stability.

Keywords: Decentralised Ontology Alignment · Multi-agent systems

1 Introduction

Within open, distributed environments, agents may differ in the way they model a domain, and may assume different logical theories or *ontologies* [13]. This can result in the existence of numerous models that, despite modelling a similar domain, are themselves semantically heterogeneous, and thus not interoperable. These ontological models can be reconciled by computing an *alignment*: i.e. a set of *correspondences* (*mappings*) stating logical relationships between the entities in the different ontologies [10]. Two agents may be able to communicate and thus transact if their individual ontologies cover the same domains, and if a meaningful alignment can be found.

Various static (single-shot) and dynamic approaches [15,19] have explored how agents can propose, and exchange candidate correspondences with the goal

C. Ghidini et al. (Eds.): ISWC 2019, LNCS 11778, pp. 733–750, 2019.
https://doi.org/10.1007/978-3-030-30793-6_42

of aligning their respective ontologies. In many cases, agents acquire knowledge of different candidate correspondences from a variety of sources, or through negotiation with other agents. These candidate correspondences may have an associated *weight*, which may reflect the utility, significance, or simply the confidence that an agent has in the correspondence. Furthermore, in adversarial scenarios, the agents may not wish to disclose their private weights, and may lie when stating their preferences.

As the composition of different subsets of correspondences can result in different alignments, the challenge in negotiating a mutually acceptable alignment is that of selecting and proposing correspondences that result in a preferred alignment that satisfies the aims of both agents. Furthermore, some correspondences may map a single entity in one ontology to different entities in other ontologies (which can compromise the integrity of the resulting logical model), and therefore the outcome should ideally be injective (i.e. a matching).

In this paper, we take a mechanism design based approach to investigate and analyse theoretically the problem from a centralised perspective (*Dominant Strategies*), where the problem is characterised as a social welfare maximising matching setting with an additive valuation function. To model this from a mechanism design perspective, we use the term *"payment"* to refer to the agent's view of the correspondence's weight. We show that for a deterministic mechanism with payment, the only truthful mechanism is *maximal-in-range* (defined within Sect. 4), and any truthful mechanism which is not optimal can do no better than an approximation ratio of 2. Given our results on truthful centralised mechanisms, either the problem should be solved optimally (though costly) or strong lower bounds should be found for the approximation ratios of truthful mechanisms. We have also explored an implementation in Nash Equilibria [25] to efficiently approximate mechanisms for matching using the greedy allocation mechanism.

In Sect. 2, the challenges of selecting correspondences for injective alignments are discussed from a centralised and decentralised standpoint. In Sect. 3, the Ontology Alignment Selection problem is formalised, and examined from a decentralised (two agent) perspective. The problem is then analysed as a Mechanism Design game with payment in Sect. 4. A Greedy Algorithm is studied as a means of finding an approximate Nash Equilibria solution, and its properties are formally proved (Sect. 5). This is followed by a discussion and related work in Sect. 6, before concluding in Sect. 7.

2 Background

To date, the ontology alignment community has proposed many diverse approaches that *align* ontologies in order to find sets of correspondences between the ontology pairs.[1] However, most approaches rely on the ontologies being fully

[1] For a comprehensive overview of the different approaches, we refer the reader to the *Ontology Alignment Evaluation Initiative* - http://oaei.ontologymatching.org.

shared with some alignment algorithm [10,27] which attempts to find correspondences between entities. Alignment approaches usually initiate the process of identifying correspondences (mappings) by computing a *similarity matrix* (lexical, structural or a combination of these) between all the entities in the two ontologies that are being aligned [10,22]. This produces a number of different mappings involving the same entities from which an *injective* (one-to-one) alignment needs to be extracted (i.e. correspondences for which to each entity from the source ontology corresponds only one entity in the target ontology).

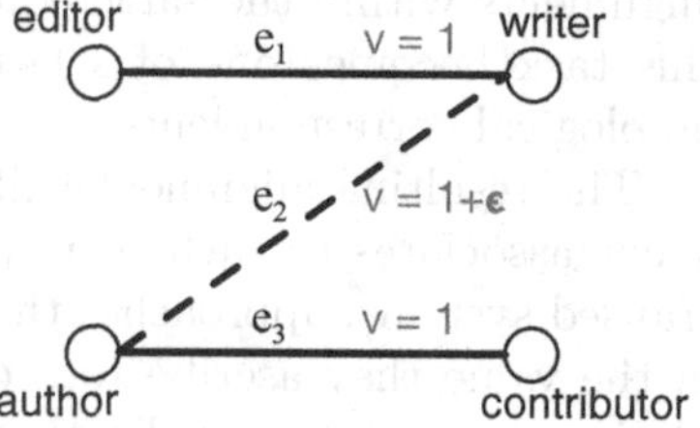

Fig. 1. Centralised example with two solutions: $\{e_1, e_3\}$ and $\{e_2\}$.

Typically, most alignment approaches model the alignment as a bipartite graph, and thus select an injective alignment alignment by finding a *matching* or independent edge set in the graph, such that the set of edges (i.e. correspondences) have no common vertices (i.e no entity in one ontology is mapped to more than one entity in the other ontology, and vice versa). This assumes that each edge (or correspondence) is weighted such that the weight represents the *quality* or *desirability* of the correspondence. The two most common methods used to select a *matching* are: (1) to find a global optimal solution (which is equivalent to the *Assignment Problem*) using algorithms such as the Hungarian method [18]; or to find a sub-optimal, but *stable* solution using algorithms such as Gale & Shapley's Stable Marriage algorithm [14]. Solutions to the assignment problem identify correspondences that maximise the sum of the weights (i.e. they assume some *objective function* that maximises *social welfare*), as opposed to the similarity of each pair of entities. This is illustrated in Fig. 1, where two correspondences are selected by maximising the weights; in this case the weights associated to the two correspondences $\{e_1, e_3\}$ are $1 + 1 = 2$. As ontologies can vary greatly in size, with several in the Bio-Medical domain possessing tens of thousands of entities [16], techniques such as the Hungarian method can become computationally costly ($O(n^3)$ for its most efficient implementation). Thus, sub-optimal approximate algorithms such as a greedy matching algorithm [22] or a variant from the family of Stable Marriage algorithms [14] are used that select a sub-optimal set of correspondences in those cases when a *stable* solution is sufficient. This can result in a different alignment that emphasises the weights of individual correspondences; given the example in Fig. 1, a greedy algorithm would generate an alignment with a single correspondence, e_2, as its weight is greater than either e_1 or e_3, resulting in a sub-optimal total weight of $1 + \epsilon$.

A similar problem arises in decentralised settings, where agents negotiate over a set of (partially observable) correspondences to agree upon a mutually acceptable alignment [3,6,9,15,19,26], often based on the aims or goals of the agents that may own or utilise them. As no single alignment approach can provide a panacea for all ontology pairs, agents are left with the problem of either: (1) *selecting* a suitable alignment approach from the plethora that exist; or (2) *assembling* alignments from a subset of relevant, candidate correspondences;

for example using an ensemble approach. This latter case occurs if agents have access to correspondences from shared repositories [19] or garnered from previous transactions with other agents. Furthermore, alignments with different constituent correspondences may be semantically equivalent with respect to one of the agent's ontologies and aims (due to the logical theory underlying each agent's ontology) but may have a different meaning to another.[2] As the agent may have preferences over the choice of correspondences used (e.g. due to privacy concerns [12,23]), agents can have a preference order over the resulting alignments within the same equivalence class. Hence, for *self-interested* agents, this task becomes one of selecting a mutually acceptable subset of preferred ontological correspondences.

The resulting alignment will typically be dependent on the *value* that each agent associates to each correspondence. Whilst this is uncontroversial in centralised systems, approaches that are decentralised (i.e. where agents may differ in the value they ascribe to a correspondence) are subject to strategic manipulation; i.e. agents may lie about the true value of a correspondence to ensure that the final alignment includes their preferred correspondences. The value that each agent assigns to each correspondence (i.e. its *private valuation*) relates to how useful this edge is in resolving a query or achieving a task, and in turn, the potential payoff the agent can obtain from performing a task. Note that this is not the same as the confidence the agent has in the edge (based, for example from some form of linguistic similarity metric over the concept labels). For example, an agent may know of two correspondences in the publishing domain $\{\texttt{writer}, \texttt{editor}\}$ and $\{\texttt{writer}, \texttt{author}\}$. Both are viable correspondences, depending on the task (e.g. for a conference proceedings and monograph respectively), but an agent may assign different valuations to each correspondence based on some preference; for example the agent can increase its payoff by resolving queries or performing tasks (by providing a service to its peers) pertaining to monographs. Conversely, it may have a low valuation for other correspondences for which it has little preference (e.g. $\{\texttt{writer}, \texttt{publisher}\}$). However, within a service landscape where several agents (providing services) may compete to perform a task for a requesting agent, they may not wish to disclose the true value of this payoff. This can potentially lead to agents strategically manipulating the combined value of sets of correspondences, in order to maximise their individual payoffs; potentially resulting in semantically compromised correspondences being selected, which may then prevent the query or task from successfully completing. Thus, in an ideal setting, the agents should be incentivised to adopt strategies that result in alignments that benefit both agents; i.e. find solutions that lie within a *Nash Equilibrium* [25].

3 The Decentralised Alignment Construction Problem

We consider the Alignment Construction Problem given the following setting in which there are two agents $i \in \{L, R\}$ (the *left* agent and *right* agent), where each

[2] A classic example of terminological difference exists with the term *"football"*, which has a different meaning depending on whether the reader is from the US or the UK.

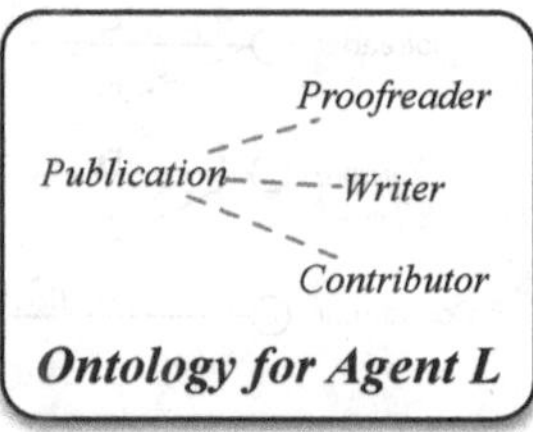

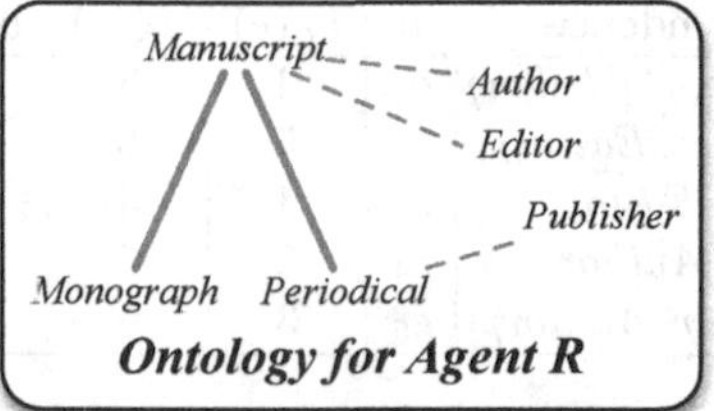

Fig. 2. Ontology fragments $\mathcal{O}_L$ (left) and $\mathcal{O}_R$ (right). The solid line denotes the *isa* class hierarchy relation, whereas the dashed line indicates property relations between classes (note that property names are not given).

agent i possesses a private ontology $\mathcal{O}_i$ that includes the *named concepts* (i.e. *entities*)[3] $\mathsf{N}_i^{\mathsf{C}} \in \mathcal{O}_i$ to be aligned. The alignment is modelled as an edge-weighted bipartite graph $G = (U \cup V, E)$, where the vertices of U and V correspond to the entities in the agents' individual ontologies $U = \mathsf{N}_L^{\mathsf{C}}$ and $V = \mathsf{N}_R^{\mathsf{C}}$ respectively, and the edges $e \in E$ correspond to the candidate correspondences. A matching M is a subset of E such that $e \cap e' = \varnothing$ for all $e, e' \in M$ with $e \neq e'$; i.e. no two edges have a common vertex. Each agent $i \in \{L, R\}$ has a non-negative valuation function for different matchings M, denoted $v_i(M)$, where $v_i : M(G) \to \mathbb{R}^+$, which is additive; i.e. $v(S) + v(T) = v(S \cup T)$ such that $S \cap T = \varnothing$ for all $S, T \subseteq M$, and $M(G)$ is the set of all matchings in a graph G. Each agent i also has a valuation function $v_i : E \to \mathbb{R}^+$ to represent the value $v_i(e)$ it privately ascribes to the edge e. The combined value for an edge e is therefore given as $v(e) = v_L(e) + v_R(e)$. Note that $v_i(M) = \sum_{e \in M} v_i(e)$ for every agent $i \in \{L, R\}$, and $v(M) = \sum_{i \in \{L,R\}} v_i(M)$ is the combined value for the matching M.

The goal is to establish an alignment which is equivalent to a matching M that maximises $\sum_{e \in M} v(e)$; i.e find a set of edges whose sum of weight is maximal. This problem, known as the *Assignment Problem*, is typically solved optimally using Kuhn's *Hungarian* Algorithm [18]. In a distributed negotiation setting, the valuation function v_i can be regarded as the agents' true valuation, or *type* that it attributes to each matching. Furthermore, we use v to represent the combined type profile for both agents, such that $v = \{v_L, v_R\}$, where v_i is the type profile for agent i, and similarly, b denotes the combined bid profile for both agents (see Sect. 3.1 below for details on bids), such that $b = \{b_L, b_R\}$, where b_i is the bid profile for agent i. We will also introduce the following useful notation: $b_i^e = b_i(e)$ and $v_i^e = v_i(e)$ for any $i \in \{L, R\}$ and $e \in E$.

Consider the Bookseller scenario illustrated in Fig. 2 for agents L and R, where each agent possesses a simple ontology fragment within the *publishing* domain. Agent L models the class entity *Publication* in $\mathcal{O}_L$ with three property relations (unnamed in this example) to three other entities: *Proofreader*, *Writer*

[3] We follow the standard practice of restricting ourselves to correspondences between named concepts within the respective ontologies [10], and omit the discussion of the property relations between entities within each ontology.

Correspondence	e	$v_L(e)$	$v_R(e)$	$v(e)$
⟨*Proofreader, Publisher*⟩	e_1	3	3	6
⟨*Proofreader, Editor*⟩	e_2	5	6	11
⟨*Writer, Editor*⟩	e_3	4	4	8
⟨*Writer, Author*⟩	e_4	5	5	10
⟨*Contributor, Author*⟩	e_5	3	6	9

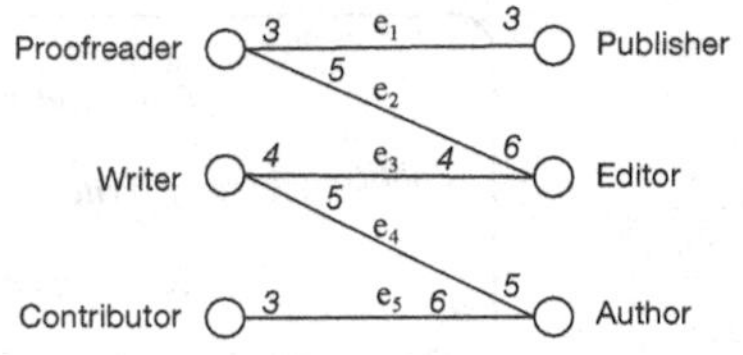

Fig. 3. The individual weights for different correspondences (left) that map entities from $\mathcal{O}_L$ to those in $\mathcal{O}_R$. The combined edges $v(e)$ appear in the final column. The resulting graph (right) has two possible matchings: an optimal matching $M_{opt} = \{e_1, e_3, e_5\}$ where $v(M_{opt}) = 23$, and a stable matching $M_{stable} = \{e_2, e_4\}$, where $v(M_{stable}) = 21$.

and *Contributor*. The other agent models the same domain but with entities from $\mathcal{O}_R$. The class *Manuscript* has two subclasses in particular: *Monographs* (i.e. a specialist work by a single or small number of authors) and *Periodicals* which are edited volumes containing numerous articles (written by different authors). Both subclasses have properties to the concepts *Author* and *Editor* (inherited from *Manuscript*), whereas *Periodical* also has a property to the concept *Publisher.* The table in Fig. 3 (left) lists candidate correspondences between entities in L's ontology, and those in the ontologies of agents R, complete with each agents private valuation function for each correspondence e, and a label e_i.

3.1 Alignment Construction with Payment

To model this problem from a mechanism design perspective (or a game, where two agents cooperate with each other to find a resulting alignment), we consider the notion of agents declaring a value for each correspondence. As this value could differ from their private value (because each agent may be behaving strategically to manipulate the outcome), we refer to the declarations as *bids.* For this reason, we consider a mechanism with *payments.* We define a direct revelation mechanism $\mathcal{M}(\mathcal{A}, \mathcal{P})$, which is composed of an allocation rule $\mathcal{A}$ to determine the outcome of the mechanism (i.e. this determines which of the correspondences are selected for the resulting alignment), and a payment scheme $\mathcal{P}$ which assigns a vector of payments to each declared valuation profile. The mechanism proceeds by eliciting a bid profile b_i from each agent i, and then applies the allocation and payment rules to the combined bid profiles to obtain an outcome and payment for each agent. As an agent may not want to reveal its type (i.e. its true value), we assume that b does not need to be equal to v.

The utility $u_i(b)$ for agent i given a bid profile $b = (b_L, b_R)$ and mechanism $\mathcal{M}$ is based on the allocation rule $\mathcal{A}$ and the payment scheme $\mathcal{P}$ over the outcome of $\mathcal{A}(v)$ (i.e. a matching or allocated set M), and can be written as $u_i(\mathcal{A}(b)) = v_i(\mathcal{A}(b)) - \mathcal{P}_i(b)$. For an implementation in Nash Equilibria (see Sect. 5), we assume a *first-price* payment rule, such that an agent is charged its declared bid $b_i(M)$ for any allocated set M. Our objective function maximises the social welfare SW given both agents' bids (generating either optimal or approximately optimal solutions); i.e. $SW(\mathcal{A}(b), v) = \sum_{e \in \mathcal{A}(b)} v(e)$. A (deterministic) mechanism $\mathcal{M}$ is called *truthful in dominant strategies* or *incentive compatible* if, for any agent $i \in \{L, R\}$, we have $u_i(\mathcal{A}(v_i, b_{-i})) \geq u_i(\mathcal{A}(b_i, b_{-i}))$ for any bid profile b_i of agent i and any bid profiles b_{-i} of the other agents.[4]

3.2 Nash Equilibria

Different types of Nash Equilibria may exist, depending on the strategy adopted by the agents. The bid profile b forms a *Pure Nash equilibrium* if, for both agents, there exists no other bid profile b'_i achieving a higher utility, i.e., $\forall b'_i, u_i(b_i, b_{-i}) \geq u_i(b'_i, b_{-i})$. As no agent can obtain a higher utility by deviating from b; they can do no better than to select alignments that result in a Nash Equilibrium [25].

We also permit a randomised strategy function which can result in a *Mixed Nash equilibrium*. Given the probability distribution $\omega_1, \cdots, \omega_n$ over the declarations, and any function f over the space of declaration profiles, we can state $\mathbb{E}_{b \sim \omega}[f(b)]$ for the expected value of f over declarations chosen according to the product distribution $\omega = \omega_1 \times \cdots \times \omega_n$. Thus, ω is a *Mixed Nash Equilibrium* if, for any agent and distribution ω'_i, we have: $\mathbb{E}_{b \sim \omega}[u_i(b)] \geq \mathbb{E}_{b \sim (\omega'_i, \omega_{-i})}[u_i(b)]$.

3.3 The Prices of Stability and Anarchy

As our aim is to maximise the social welfare, we state that the allocation algorithm $\mathcal{A}$ is a *c-approximation* algorithm if we have $SW(\mathcal{A}(v), v) \geq \frac{1}{c} SW_{opt}(v)$, where we denote $SW(\mathcal{A}(v), v)$ to represent the social welfare of the matching resulting from the allocation algorithm $\mathcal{A}$, and $SW_{opt}(v)$ for $\max_{M \in M(G)} SW(M, v)$ to represent the value of an optimal matching (and hence an optimal alignment) that maximises social welfare given the declaration vector v.

The trade-off between approximate (i.e. non-optimal) solutions and the optimal solution when identifying a matching is quantified as the *Price of Anarchy* [2]; i.e the ratio of the maximal possible social welfare and the social welfare emerging from an approximate solution. It is important to characterise this ratio as it provides a bound on how close an approximate algorithm can be to the optimal solution. The *Price of Anarchy* of the mechanism $\mathcal{M}(\mathcal{A}, \mathcal{P})$ in mixed (and pure, respectively) strategies can thus be defined as:

$$PoA_{mixed} = \sup_{v,\omega} \frac{SW_{opt}(v)}{\mathbb{E}_{b \sim \omega}[SW(\mathcal{A}(b), v)]}$$

$$PoA_{pure} = \sup_{v,b} \frac{SW_{opt}(v)}{SW(\mathcal{A}(b), v)}$$

where the supremum is over all valuations v and all mixed Nash Equilibria ω (likewise, all pure Nash Equilibria b) for v. Here, $\mathcal{A}(\omega)$ denotes a random matching with respect to ω.

[4] The notion of a bid profile across a set of agents that omits the bid of agent i, represented as b_{-i} originates from the definition of the *Vickrey Clarke Groves* (VCG) mechanism [25], used extensively in mechanism design.

The *Price of Stability* is the ratio of the best stable matching with respect to the optimal matching. A bipartite graph may generate a number of sub-optimal but stable solutions; for example the classic Stable Marriage algorithm [14] typically generated matchings where the initial solution was optimal for one agent and yet pessimal for the other. The Price of Stability is important from a Mechanism Design perspective, as a mechanism (such as that discussion in Sect. 5) may compute the best stable solution and suggest it to the agents, who would implement this solution since it is stable. Thus, the price of stability captures this notion of optimisation subject to the stability constraint [2]. The price of stability for pure strategy games defined by mechanism $\mathcal{M}(\mathcal{A}, \mathcal{P})$ is the ratio between the best objective function value of one of its equilibria and that of the optimum:

$$PoS_{pure} = \inf_{v,b} \frac{SW_{opt}(v)}{SW(\mathcal{A}(b), v)}$$

where the infimum is over all type valuations v, and all pure Nash equilibria b.

4 Analysis of Alignment Selection with Payment

In this setting, we model the scenario as if both agents have to pay money to establish a matching (or ontological alignment), where the total cost is based on the bids declared for each correspondence. An agent may be incentivised to falsely lower the value of a correspondence, although this could result in it being rejected. Conversely, it may artificially inflate the value of the correspondence in the hope of it being selected; this however could result in a weaker, or inaccurate alignment. The aim here is to devise a mechanism that incentivises agents to be truthful when proposing correspondences, and to understand its properties.

The first observation is that this problem can be solved optimally using the *Vickrey Clarke Groves* (VCG) mechanism with Clarke payment [25]; which has the property that bidders can do no better than to bid their true valuations. In this analysis, we show that it is *not possible to have a faster, non-optimal, approximate and truthful mechanism for our problem.* This can be proved using the following lemma from classic mechanism design theory [25]:

Lemma 1. *An allocation rule of mechanism $\mathcal{A}$ satisfies weak monotonicity if for all i and all v_{-i}, $\mathcal{A}(v_i, v_{-i}) = a \neq b = \mathcal{A}(v_i', v_{-i})$ implies that $v_i(a) - v_i(b) \geq v_i'(a) - v_i'(b)$. If a mechanism $\mathcal{M}(\mathcal{A}, \mathcal{P})$ is incentive compatible, then $\mathcal{A}$ satisfies weak monotonicity* [25].

The aim of Theorem 1 (below) is to determine if there is a mechanism that is not equivalent to VCG, yet is truthful, and to examine the quality of its solution. This theorem states that if any mechanism is not VCG, then: (1) it is not truthful; or (2) it is truthful but cannot achieve a solution whose approximation factor is smaller than 2.

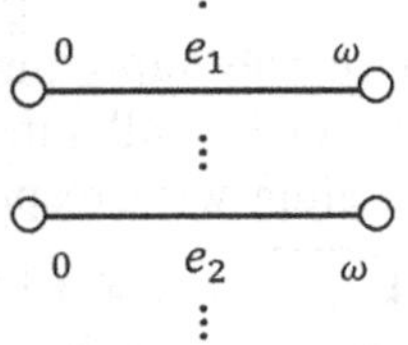

Fig. 4. Disjoint edges

Theorem 1. *For the alignment problem with payment, any mechanism which does not adopt an optimal solution when agents declare their true valuations is either non-truthful, or if truthful, the non-optimal solution has an approximation ratio of at least 2.*

Proof. Let $\mathcal{M}(\mathcal{A}, \mathcal{P})$ be a mechanism, and recall that $\mathcal{A}(v)$ denotes the outcome generated by $\mathcal{M}$, when the input is a bid v (which may not be the true valuation).

Consider a bipartite graph of arbitrary size, where for two positive integers ℓ, k, let the bipartite graph $G = (U \cup V, E)$ have ℓ nodes on the left side of bipartite graph ($|U| = \ell$) and k nodes on the right side ($|V| = k$). We assume the existence of two special edges $e_1, e_2 \in E$ that are disjoint (i.e $e_1 \cap e_2 = \varnothing$), such that their true valuations are $v_L(e_1) = v_L(e_2) = 0$ and $v_R(e_1) = v_R(e_2) = \omega$ (as illustrated in Fig. 4). As the valuations of all other edges in G are zero for both agents (and thus do not appear in the Figure), the optimal solution should contain both edges e_1 and e_2. As we only consider the problem from the perspective of the right agent in the discussion below, we omit the agent index when referring to valuations for simplicity.

Consider some mechanism $\mathcal{M}(\mathcal{A}, \mathcal{P})$ that generates a non-optimal solution which contains at most one of these edges. If neither e_1 and e_2 appear within the solution, the approximation ratio will be unbounded. Therefore, we assume that solution includes one of these two edges; w.l.o.g., assume that $\mathcal{M}$ will accept $e_1 \in \mathcal{A}(v)$ when the right agent declares its true valuation v. If the right agent deviates from its valuation v to some other valuation v', the mechanism has two options:

Case-1. The mechanism changes the current outcome to include both edges, such that original solution, $\mathcal{A}(v) \supseteq \{e_1\}$, is replaced with the solution, $\mathcal{A}(v') \supseteq \{e_1, e_2\}$. If we make the alternative valuation $v'(e_1) = v'(e_2) = 0$, this implies that $v'(\mathcal{A}(v')) \leq v'(\mathcal{A}(v))$. We also know that $v(\mathcal{A}(v)) < v(\mathcal{A}(v'))$. By adding the left and right hand sides of these two inequalities, we obtain:

$$v'(\mathcal{A}(v')) + v(\mathcal{A}(v)) < v'(\mathcal{A}(v)) + v(\mathcal{A}(v'))$$
$$v(\mathcal{A}(v)) - v(\mathcal{A}(v')) < v'(\mathcal{A}(v)) - v'(\mathcal{A}(v'))$$

As this violates the weak monotonicity condition in Lemma 1, it follows that $\mathcal{M}$ is not a truthful mechanism.

Case-2. The outcome is not changed, i.e., $\mathcal{A}(v') = \mathcal{A}(v)$ when the agent deviates its valuation to v'. The approximation ratio (i.e the ratio of the approximate optimal solution to the optimal one) is at least $\frac{v(e_1)+v(e_2)}{v(e_1)}$. Since we consider the worst case, the ratio is at least 2 (i.e. the optimal solution is guaranteed to be within a factor of 2 of the returned solution).

If the outcome changes from $e_1 \in \mathcal{A}(v)$ to $e_2 \in \mathcal{A}(v')$ and $e_1 \notin \mathcal{A}(v')$, then this case is symmetric to Case 2, and thus will also lead to a ratio of at least 2. Furthermore, if the right agent has only one non-zero value edge, and the valuation on the remaining edges is 0, then the approximation ratio is unbounded, and all such cases also lead to the lower bound on the approximation ratio. □

The motivation for the next theorem (Theorem 2) is that if a mechanism is not VCG but is truthful, then it must be *maximal-in-range* [8], defined below:

Definition 1. *A mechanism is called maximal in range (MIR) if there exists a fixed subset R of all allocations (the range of the mechanism), such that for every possible input v, the mechanism outputs the allocation that maximizes the social welfare in R with respect to v* [8].

If a mechanism selects an edge such that the resulting solution (or *allocation*) is not one that is maximal with respect to the bids, then an agent will be incentivised to declare a lower (untruthful) valuation for an edge that they want in the solution, as this dishonest strategy will result in a higher utility than one that relies on being honest for the same solution.

Theorem 2. *For the alignment problem with payment, any deterministic mechanism which does not adopt an optimal solution when agents declare their true valuation is either non-truthful, or is a maximal-in-range mechanism.*

Proof. Consider a bipartite graph $G = (U \cup V, E)$ which contains ℓ nodes on the left side ($|U| = \ell$), and a single node on the right ($|V| = 1$), and where there are ℓ edges, such that each node on the left is connected to the single node on the right. Thus, any solution will contain only a single edge. Furthermore, we assume that the optimal solution is $\{e_1\}$. If a deterministic mechanism $\mathcal{A}$ *does not* adopt the optimal solution; then the solution generated by $\mathcal{A}$ will be a single edge in $\{e_2, \cdots e_\ell\}$, where the optimal solution is e_2 (i.e. $v(e_1) > v(e_2)$). If the agents deviate from bidding their true value, the mechanism has three options:

Case-1. The solution adopted by mechanism $\mathcal{A}$ does not change as a result of the changed bid. Thus, if $\mathcal{A}$ is truthful then it is equivalent to a maximal-in-range mechanism, whose range is $R = \{e_2\}$.

Case-2. The solution adopted by mechanism $\mathcal{A}$ changes to $\{e_1\}$ (the optional solution for E) for some bid v': $\mathcal{A}(v') = \{e_1\}$. Therefore, given Lemma 1, the mechanism $\mathcal{A}$ cannot be truthful.
To show this, suppose w.l.o.g. that the mechanism adopts e_2 for the bid v: $\mathcal{A}(v) = \{e_2\}$, and that one agent deviates from its valuation v to v' such that $v'(e_1) < v'(e_2)$. Given that we have $v(e_1) > v(e_2)$; by adding the left and right hand sides of these two inequalities, we have:

$$v(e_2) - v(e_1) < v'(e_2) - v'(e_1)$$

As we have $\mathcal{A}(v) = \{e_2\}$ and $\mathcal{A}(v') = \{e_1\}$, this contradicts the monotonicity condition from Lemma 1, which states that: $v(e_2) - v(e_1) \geq v'(e_2) - v'(e_1)$.

Case-3. The solution adopted by mechanism $\mathcal{A}$ changes to a single edge from $\{e_3, \cdots, e_l\}$. In such a case, by Lemma 1, the same argument for Case-2 also applies for this case where the mechanism is not truthful as it violates the monotonicity condition. □

By combining the two Theorems 1 and 2, we have the following theorem:

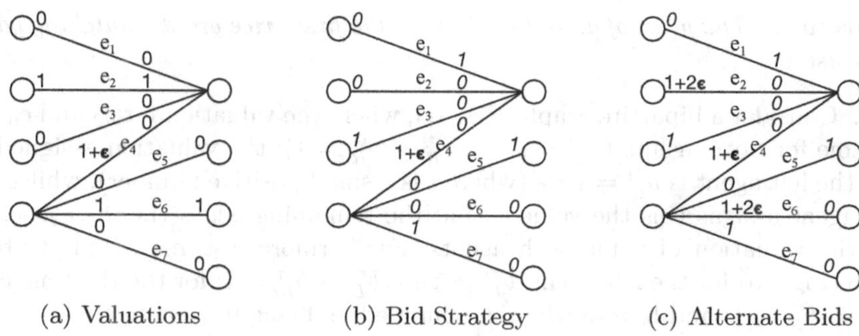

(a) Valuations (b) Bid Strategy (c) Alternate Bids

Fig. 5. Edge weights for the lower bound Price of Anarchy example

Theorem 3. *For the alignment problem with payment, the only truthful mechanisms are those that are maximal-in-range with an approximation ratio of at least* 2.

5 Nash Equilibria Implementation

Having analysed the Alignment Construction problem from a mechanism design perspective, we now explore the properties of a decentralised algorithm whereby two agents propose bids on candidate correspondences (not necessarily honestly) in order the determine a final alignment. In this section we explore a computationally efficient, yet sub-optimal setting using a *first price greedy matching* algorithm. This is a decentralised variant of the *NaiveDescending* algorithm given by Meilicke and Stuckenschmidt [22], and is presented in Algorithm 1. In this setting, the agents provide their declarations to the mechanism, which computes an outcome. The agents then measure their utility by subtracting their true valuation of this outcome by the payment. The payment scheme used models the notion that each agent would pay its own bid, i.e., $p_i = b_i(\mathcal{A}(b))$. The next two theorems provide a characterisation of the Price of Anarchy for a first-price greedy matching game. The proofs provide simple instances of the mechanism (from a game perspective) to give some intuition of pure Nash Equilibria.

Algorithm 1. Greedy algorithm

Require: Bipartite graph $G = (V \cup U, E)$, b_L, b_R are bids of the left & right agent.
Ensure: A matching M
  Let $M = \emptyset$
  if $E \neq \emptyset$ **then**
    Find the edge $e \in E$ that maximises $b_L^e + b_R^e$
    Let $M := M \cup \{e\}$
    Remove from E edge e and edges incident to edge e
  end if
  M is the outcome

Theorem 4. *The price of anarchy (PoA) of the first price greedy matching game is at least* 4.

Proof. Consider a bipartite graph (Fig. 5a), where the valuation for e_2 and e_6 are the same for both agents ($v_L^{e_2} = v_L^{e_6} = v_R^{e_2} = v_R^{e_6} = 1$); the valuation assigned to e_4 by the left agent is $v_L^{e_4} = 1+\epsilon$ (where ϵ is a small positive number), whilst the right agent assigns this the value 0, and the remaining edges (i.e. e_1, e_3, e_5, e_7) have the valuation of 0 for both agents. Furthermore, assume a bid strategy profile (Fig. 5b) for the left agent: $b_L^{e_4} = 1+\epsilon, b_L^{e_3} = b_L^{e_7} = 1$; for the right agent it is: $b_R^{e_1} = b_R^{e_5} = 1$; and bids on the remaining edges being 0. Denote this strategy profile for both agents as b.

The greedy algorithm's solution given this profile b is $\{e_4\}$ (the sum of bids for e_4 is $1+\epsilon$, whereas the sum for each of the other edges is either 0 or 1). The utility for the left agent given this solution is 0 (it would pay $1+\epsilon$ because of its successful bid, but it's valuation is $1+\epsilon$), whereas the utility for the right agent is 0, as it's bid and valuation for this edge are both 0.

The left agent could not unilaterally increase its utility; only one other solution $\{e_2, e_6\}$ has a positive utility, but to obtain this, new bids are necessary. If it chose two new bids (i.e. $\tilde{b}_L^{e_2}$ and $\tilde{b}_L^{e_6}$) on these edges such that $\tilde{b}_L^{e_2} > b_R^{e_1}$, which would result in the combined bids on e_2 being greater than that on e_1 (i.e. $v(e_2) > v(e_1)$) and $\tilde{b}_L^{e_6} > b_R^{e_5}$ (such that $v(e_6) > v(e_5)$), this solution would change to $\{e_2, e_6\}$ resulting in a negative utility for the left agent (Fig. 5c). This is because its combined bid would be $2+4\epsilon$, whereas its payoff would be 2. The left agent will also not decrease its bid on e_4, as the solution would be changed to another matching that is not $\{e_2, e_6\}$.

The right agent's behaviour is the same as the left, as this scenario is symmetric. It only has a positive valuation on e_2 and e_6. By changing its bids for either edge, a new bid (e.g. $\tilde{b}_R^{e_2} > 1+2\epsilon$) would be required, thus again reducing the utility. Therefore in this case we have a Nash equilibrium, as neither agent can do better than adopt the current strategy.

The optimal solution is $\{e_2, e_6\}$, due to the joint valuation of $1+1=2$ for e_2, and the same for e_6, resulting in a total valuation of 4 for that solution. As stated above, the greedy algorithm instead finds the solution $\{e_4\}$, resulting in a total valuation of $1+\epsilon$. Therefore, the Price of Anarchy is $\frac{4}{1+\epsilon}$, or at least 4. □

Theorem 4 provides a lower bound on the price of anarchy for our mechanism. For the upper bound (Theorem 5), we first need the following two lemmas:

Lemma 2. *Suppose that the current bid profile* (b_L, b_R) *produces outcome* M *using a greedy mechanism. The necessary condition for* (b_L, b_R) *to be a Nash equilibrium is that* $b_L^M \leq v_L^M$ *and* $b_R^M \leq v_R^M$.

Proof. Assume that for outcome M, some agent's bid satisfies $b_i^M > v_i^M$ (i.e. the bid is greater than the valuation). The utility would then be $u_i(b_L, b_R) = v_i^M - b_i^M < 0$; i.e. it would be negative. Therefore, agent i would change its bid to a new one which increases its utility to a value that is at least 0. □

Lemma 3. *Suppose that the current bid profile* (b_L, b_R) *produces an outcome* M *using a greedy mechanism, and* $b_L^M \leq v_L^M$, $b_R^M \leq v_R^M$. *There exists a bid for one agent, for example the left agent,* $\tilde{b}_L$, *that satisfies the condition* $\tilde{b}_L^{M'} < 2(v_R^M + v_L^M) + \epsilon$. *This would result in* $\tilde{b}_L$ *changing the outcome to* M'.

Proof. Let $\{e_1, \cdots, e_k\}$ be the set of edges in a matching M, indexed in decreasing order with respect to $b_L^e + b_R^e$. Denote e' as an edge in a different outcome M'. We assign each new bid $\tilde{b}_L^{e'}$ by the following procedure: $\forall j \in \{1, \dots, k\}$ (in this order), if the left side vertex of edge e_j has an adjacent edge e' in M', then let the sum of the new bid (left) and the corresponding original bid (right) for M' take a slightly higher value than the corresponding edge bids for e_j in the outcome M; i.e. $\tilde{b}_L^{e'} + b_R^{e'} > b_R^{e_j} + b_L^{e_j}$. Do the same for the right side vertex adjacent edge, i.e., for right side vertex adjacent edge $e' \in M'$ of e^j, let $\tilde{b}_L^{e'} + b_R^{e'}$ take a slightly higher value than $b_R^{e_j} + b_L^{e_j}$.

At any step of this procedure, if we need to reassign the bid $b_L^{e'}$ for some edge e', then the bid of the larger value is retained (in fact, the declaration will remain unchanged as this procedure is conducted in decreasing order with respect to $b_L^e + b_R^e$). This distribution of bids is valid, as it can be done such that $\tilde{b}_L^{M'} > 2(b_R^M + b_L^M)$, which always results in a change of outcome to M'. It can also be easily argued that $\tilde{b}_L^{M'} < 2(v_R^M + v_L^M) + \epsilon$. □

Theorem 5. *The price of anarchy (PoA) of a first price greedy matching game is at most* 4.

Proof. Let M be any matching whose total valuation is strictly smaller than a quarter of the optimum, i.e., $v_L^M + v_R^M < \frac{1}{4}Opt$. At least one of the following statements will hold on some other outcome M' given a different profile of valuations (either for the left or right agents respectively): $\exists M' v_L^{M'} \geq \frac{1}{2}Opt$ or $\exists M' v_R^{M'} \geq \frac{1}{2}Opt$. If M' is the optimal solution, then this will result in a contradiction. As they are symmetric, we assume the first statement is true. Assume $b = (b_L, b_R)$ is a fixed bid profile. If the outcome under b is M, then the agents will either have positive utilities; i.e. $b_L^M \leq v_L^M$ and $b_R^M \leq v_R^M$, or negative ones.

We want to show that the left agent would be incentivised to bid for the outcome M'. Let $\tilde{b}_L^{M'}$ be the bid that can achieve this change (i.e. from M to M'). Lemma 3 states that there exists some bid $\tilde{b}_L$ that will achieve this change to outcome M'. Thus, we want to show that the utility of M' for the left agent is greater than for M; i.e. $v_L^{M'} - \tilde{b}_L^{M'} > v_L^M - b_L^M$. By Lemma 3, since $\tilde{b}_L^{M'} < 2(v_R^M + b_L^M) + \epsilon$, we have:

$$v_L^{M'} - \tilde{b}_L^{M'} \geq v_L^{M'} - 2(v_R^M + b_L^M) - \epsilon$$

Since $v_L^{M'} \geq \frac{1}{2}Opt$ and $v_L^M + v_R^M < \frac{1}{4}Opt$, we can show that:

$$v_L^{M'} - 2(v_R^M + b_L^M) - \epsilon \geq v_L^{M'} - (v_R^M + v_L^M) - v_R^M - b_L^M$$
$$v_L^{M'} - (v_R^M + v_L^M) - v_R^M - b_L^M > v_L^M - b_L^M$$

As ϵ can be arbitrarily small, it can be removed. The last inequality shows that the left agent can change its bid from b_L to $\tilde{b}_L$ and get M' with a higher utility. This completes the argument as it shows that b cannot result in a Nash equilibrium. □

Theorem 6. *The price of anarchy (PoA) of the first price greedy matching game is precisely 4.*

This theorem is the logical consequence of the Theorems 4 and 5 that provide an upper and lower bound for the Price of Anarchy, so requires no further proof.

To conclude our analysis of the first-price greedy matching game, we investigate a lower bound for the Price of Stability through Theorem 7 (below).

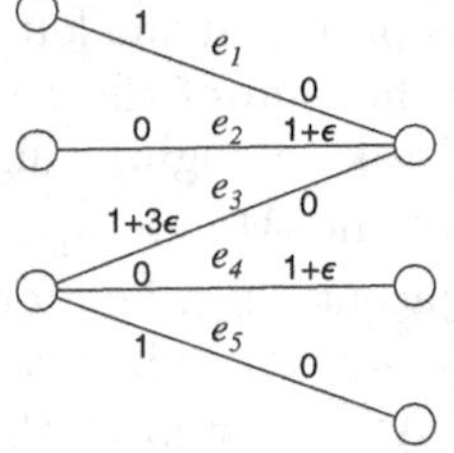

Fig. 6. Edge valuations for the PoS lower bound

Theorem 7. *The price of stability (PoS) of a first price greedy matching game is at least 2.*

Proof. Consider a bipartite graph (Fig. 6), where the valuation assignment for both agents are: $v_L^{e_1} = v_L^{e_5} = 1$, $v_R^{e_2} = v_R^{e_4} = 1 + \epsilon$, $v_L^{e_3} = 1 + 3\epsilon$. The valuations on the remaining edges are 0 for both agents. The mechanism has three options:

Case-1. Suppose the outcome of the mechanism is $\{e_1, e_5\}$. The current bid cannot result in a Nash equilibrium, as the right agent would improve its utility by changing the current outcome to $\{e_2, e_4\}$, when $\tilde{b}_R^{e_2} > b_L^{e_1}, \tilde{b}_R^{e_4} > b_L^{e_5}$.

Case-2. Suppose the current outcome is $\{e_2, e_4\}$. It also does not admit any Nash equilibrium. If $\max\{b_R^{e_2}, b_R^{e_4}\} < v_L^{e_3}$, then the left agent could improve its utility by changing to e_3, when $\tilde{b}_R^{e_3} > \max\{b_R^{e_2}, b_R^{e_4}\}$. If $\max\{b_R^{e_2}, b_R^{e_4}\} > v_L^{e_3}$, then let $b_R^{e_2}$ be a smaller bid, such that the left agent would then bid $\tilde{b}_L^{e_1} > b_R^{e_2}$ changing the outcome to $\{e_1, e_4\}$. This case is symmetric.

Case-3. Suppose the current outcome is $\{e_1, e_4\}$ (or $\{e_2, e_5\}$). The right agent would bid $\tilde{b}_R^{e_2} > b_L^{e_1}$ to improve its utility, and change the outcome to $\{e_2, e_4\}$.

To complete the proof, we provide a Nash equilibrium: $b_L^{e_1} = b_L^{e_5} = 1$, $b_R^{e_2} = b_R^{e_4} = 1 + \epsilon$, $b_L^{e_3} = 1 + 2\epsilon$. We can see in such a bid profile, the outcome would be e_3, and it is easy to check that no agent can increase its utility. □

It is usual in the literature to study the Price of Anarchy even if there might be instances without pure Nash equilibria [21]. Thus, Theorem 5 can be read as: *if there exists pure Nash equilibria, then their social welfare is at least* 25% *of the optimum*. We can also show that mixed Nash equilibria always exist, by transforming the problem into a new one in which each agent only has a finite number of strategies, where a strategy is for bids on edges. We define a small $\epsilon > 0$ as the minimum increment that any two bids can differ by. This leads to a finite number of strategies of any agent i as i will not bid more than $\sum_{e \in E} v_i(e)$. In particular, $b_i^e \in \{0, \epsilon, 2\epsilon, \cdots, \sum_{e \in E} v_i(e)\}$.

Corollary 1. *The mixed Nash equilibrium exists for all instances of the discretised first price greedy matching game.*

This corollary is deduced directly from Nash's theorem [25] which proves that if agents can use mixed strategies, then every game with a finite number of players in which each player can choose from finitely many pure strategies has at least one mixed Nash equilibrium.

Corollary 2. *The price of anarchy of the discretised first price greedy matching game for mixed strategy is 4.*

This proof can be found by extending that for Theorem 7.

6 Related Work

Approaches for resolving semantic heterogeneity have traditionally been centralised (i.e. with full access to the ontologies), resulting in the formation of a weighted bipartite graph representing the possible correspondences [22,27], and a matching (alignment) found by either maximising social welfare or utilising a greedy search. However, these approaches were generally task agnostic, and thus varied in the way they utilised the weights. The lack of strategy or means to restrict what was revealed (due to knowledge encoded within an ontology being confidential or commercially sensitive) [12,26] has resulted in an increased interest in decentralised, strategic approaches. Matchings have also been found through the use of *Argumentation*, based on private preferences over the correspondence properties (e.g., whether their construction was based on structural or linguistic similarities) [19], and public weights. More recently, dialogical approaches have been used to selectively exchange correspondences based on private weights for each agent [26]. Although polynomial approaches were used to determine the matching, the selection of revelations at each step was naive, and the resulting alignment failed represent the agents initial goals, whilst revealing the agents' private weights.

Several studies have explored the problem of finding matchings from a mechanism design perspective, and have studied deterministic and randomise approximate mechanisms for bipartite matching problems where agents have one-sided preferences [1,17]. Furthermore, there are a number of studies of truthful approximate mechanisms for combinatorial auctions, e.g., [5,8,20,24], and various mechanisms [7,11,21] have studied Bayesian Nash Equilibrium settings. In [7], the problem of selling m items to n selfish bidders with combinatorial preferences, in m independent second-price auctions was studied. The authors showed that given submodular valuation functions, every Bayesian Nash equilibrium of the resulting game provided a 2-approximation to the optimal social welfare. The efficiency of Bayesian Nash equilibrium outcomes of simultaneous first- and second-price auctions was also studied [11], where bidders had complement-free (a.k.a. subadditive) valuations. They showed that the expected social welfare of any Bayesian Nash Equilibrium was at least $\frac{1}{2}$ of the optimal social welfare in the case of first-price auctions, and at least $\frac{1}{4}$ in the case of second-price auctions. Lucier and Borodin [21] studied the general setting of combinatorial actions and proved that the Bayesian Price of Anarchy of the greedy algorithm is constant. A study of simultaneous second-price auctions [4] showed that the price of anarchy for pure Nash equilibrium was 2, and focused on Bayesian Nash equilibrium.

7 Conclusions

In this paper, we present, from a Mechanism Design perspective, the decentralised Ontology Alignment negotiation problem, whereby correspondences are selected for inclusion in an alignment (between two ontologies), and we provide a theoretical analysis of its properties. By demonstrating that different alignments can be generated depending on the selection process (e.g. by determining an optimal or sub-optimal solution), we characterise the problem analytically as a Mechanism Design problem, characterised as a Social Welfare maximising matching setting, where the valuation function is additive. We provide a complete picture of the complexity of this mechanism by showing that when coupled with a first-price payment scheme, it implements Nash equilibria which are very close (within a factor of 4) to the optimal matching. Furthermore, the *Price of Anarchy* of this mechanism is characterised completely and shown to be precisely 4 (this bound also holds for Mixed Nash equilibria), and when a pure Nash Equilibrium exists, we show that the *Price of Stability* is at least 2. Thus, decentralised agents can reach a Nash equilibrium, which produces a solution close to optimum within a factor of 4.

This analysis demonstrates that the type of alignment generated when selecting correspondences is sensitive to the algorithm used. However, by ensuring that the mechanism used is truth incentive, this ensures that agents will always do better by adopting strategies that accurately report the weights of their correspondences in decentralised settings.

References

1. Adamczyk, M., Sankowski, P., Zhang, Q.: Efficiency of truthful and symmetric mechanisms in one-sided matching. In: Lavi, R. (ed.) SAGT 2014. LNCS, vol. 8768, pp. 13–24. Springer, Heidelberg (2014). https://doi.org/10.1007/978-3-662-44803-8_2
2. Anshelevich, E., Das, S., Naamad, Y.: Anarchy, stability, and utopia: creating better matchings. Auton. Agent. Multi-Agent Syst. **26**(1), 120–140 (2013)
3. Atencia, M., Schorlemmer, W.M.: An interaction-based approach to semantic alignment. J. Web Semant. **12**, 131–147 (2012)
4. Bhawalkar, K., Roughgarden, T.: Welfare guarantees for combinatorial auctions with item bidding. In: Proceedings of the Twenty-Second Annual ACM-SIAM Symposium on Discrete Algorithms, pp. 700–709. SIAM (2011)
5. Briest, P., Krysta, P., Vöcking, B.: Approximation techniques for utilitarian mechanism design. In: STOC, pp. 39–48 (2005)

6. Chocron, P., Schorlemmer, M.: Vocabulary alignment in openly specified interactions. In: International Conference on Autonomous Agents and Multi-Agent Systems (AAMAS), pp. 1064–1072 (2017)
7. Christodoulou, G., Kovács, A., Schapira, M.: Bayesian combinatorial auctions. In: Aceto, L., Damgård, I., Goldberg, L.A., Halldórsson, M.M., Ingólfsdóttir, A., Walukiewicz, I. (eds.) ICALP 2008. LNCS, vol. 5125, pp. 820–832. Springer, Heidelberg (2008). https://doi.org/10.1007/978-3-540-70575-8_67
8. Dobzinski, S., Nisan, N., Schapira, M.: Approximation algorithms for combinatorial auctions with complement-free bidders. In: Proceedings of the Thirty-Seventh Annual ACM Symposium on Theory of Computing, pp. 610–618. ACM (2005)
9. Euzenat, J.: Interaction-based ontology alignment repair with expansion and relaxation. In: Proceedings of the Twenty-Sixth International Joint Conference on Artificial Intelligence, IJCAI 2017, pp. 185–191 (2017)
10. Euzenat, J., Shvaiko, P.: Ontology Matching, 2nd edn. Springer, Heidelberg (2013). https://doi.org/10.1007/978-3-642-38721-0
11. Feldman, M., Fu, H., Gravin, N., Lucier, B.: Simultaneous auctions are (almost) efficient. In: Proceedings of the Forty-Fifth Annual ACM Symposium on Theory of Computing, pp. 201–210. ACM (2013)
12. Grau, B.C., Motik, B.: Reasoning over ontologies with hidden content: the import-by-query approach. J. Artif. Intell. Res. **45**, 197–255 (2012)
13. Gruber, T.R.: A translation approach to portable ontology specifications. Knowl. Acquis. **5**(2), 199–220 (1993)
14. Gusfield, D., Irving, R.W.: The Stable Marriage Problem: Structure and Algorithms. MIT Press, Cambridge (1989)
15. Jiménez-Ruiz, E., Payne, T.R., Solimando, A., Tamma, V.: Limiting consistency and conservativity violations through negotiation. In: The 15th International Conference on Principles of Knowledge Representation and Reasoning (KR 2016), pp. 217–226 (2016)
16. Jiménez-Ruiz, E., Meilicke, C., Grau, B.C., Horrocks, I.: Evaluating mapping repair systems with large biomedical ontologies. In: 26th International Workshop on Description Logics, July 2013
17. Krysta, P., Manlove, D., Rastegari, B., Zhang, J.: Size versus truthfulness in the house allocation problem. In: Proceedings of the Fifteenth ACM Conference on Economics and Computation, pp. 453–470. ACM (2014)
18. Kuhn, H.W.: The Hungarian method for the assignment problem. Naval Res. logist. Q. **2**(1–2), 83–97 (1955)
19. Laera, L., Blacoe, I., Tamma, V., Payne, T., Euzenat, J., Bench-Capon, T.: Argumentation over ontology correspondences in MAS. In: International Conference on Autonomous Agents and Multi-Agent Systems (AAMAS), pp. 1285–1292 (2007)
20. Lehmann, D.J., O'Callaghan, L., Shoham, Y.: Truth revelation in approximately efficient combinatorial auctions. J. ACM **49**(5), 577–602 (2002)
21. Lucier, B., Borodin, A.: Price of anarchy for greedy auctions. In: Proceedings of the Twenty-First Annual ACM-SIAM Symposium on Discrete Algorithms, pp. 537–553. Society for Industrial and Applied Mathematics (2010)
22. Meilicke, C., Stuckenschmidt, H.: Analyzing mapping extraction approaches. In: Proceedings of the 2nd International Conference on Ontology Matching, pp. 25–36 (2007)
23. Mitra, P., Lin, P., Pan, C.: Privacy-preserving ontology matching. In: AAAI Workshop on Context and Ontologies, vol. WS-05-01, pp. 88–91 (2005)
24. Mu'alem, A., Nisan, N.: Truthful approximation mechanisms for restricted combinatorial auctions. Games Econ. Behav. **64**(2), 612–631 (2008)

25. Nisan, N., Roughgarden, T., Tardos, E., Vazirani, V.V.: Algorithmic Game Theory, vol. 1. Cambridge University Press, Cambridge (2007)
26. Payne, T.R., Tamma, V.: Negotiating over ontological correspondences with asymmetric and incomplete knowledge. In: International Conference on Autonomous Agents and Multi-Agent Systems (AAMAS), pp. 517–524 (2014)
27. Shvaiko, P., Euzenat, J.: Ontology matching: state of the art and future challenges. IEEE Trans. Knowl. Data Eng. **25**(1), 158–176 (2013)

Author Index

Printed in the United States
By Bookmasters

Printed in the United States
By Bookmasters